NIGEL HAMILTON

The author was born in 1944 and educated at Westminster School and Trinity College, Cambridge, where he studied history.

In 1966 he founded The Greenwich Bookshop, and two years later published his first book, ROYAL GREENWICH, which he wrote with his mother, Olive Hamilton. It was hailed as a 'landmark in topographical literature in this country' by *The Scotsman*.

Nigel Hamilton's much acclaimed biography of the German novelists Heinrich and Thomas Mann, THE BROTHERS MANN, was published in 1978. Mr Hamilton lives in Suffolk.

Volumes One and Three of MONTY: THE MAKING OF A GENERAL 1887–1942 and THE FIELD-MARSHAL 1944–1976, are also published in Sceptre.

MONTY: MASTER OF THE BATTLEFIELD
1942–1944

'One of the principal merits of Nigel Hamilton's second volume is that it clarifies Monty's concept of how to conduct campaigns and battles. It does so more clearly than Monty himself . . . A great deal of fascinating material about this period is revealed. It confirms Monty's high reputation as a soldier, while frankly admitting his faults as a human being'

Sunday Telegraph

'Above all, Nigel Hamilton brings out Monty's professionalism, his intense humanity and his vanity and feeling of omnipotence'

Daily Mail

'Mr Hamilton's industry and achievement are colossal . . . More than any other man on the British side except Churchill, Montgomery won the war for us. That is why he deserves a biographer so skilled in doing him justice'

Nigel Nicolson, Financial Times

'The general reader should find the book very satisfying; it is as easy to read as the average bestseller, and far more educative than most'

The Times Literary Supplement

'There is no doubt that Mr Hamilton has contributed a major landmark to the military literature of World War II'

Russell F. Weigley, The New York Times Book Review

'A book that will remain for many years to come an indispensable tool for students of the Second World War'

Lord Blake, The Illustrated London News

'Mr Hamilton's masterly presentation of the evidence deserves to hold the field for many years'

British Book News

'A deep and perceptive study showing Monty's triumphs and failures, his qualities and peccadillos . . . A wealth of fascinating detail covers all facets of Montgomery's spectacular career'

East Anglian Daily Times

'Nigel Hamilton conceals nothing of the oddities of character revealed in Montgomery's papers, and by extensive quotation paints the man and the events around him'

Oxford Times

'An absorbing picture of the great man, with full attention to quirks of character'

Liverpool Daily Post

'A splendid book. Mr Hamilton puts flesh on the bare bones of military and political events, shedding fresh light on Monty's remarkable career and personality . . . Monty's portrait emerges warts and all'

Birmingham Post

MONTY: THE MAKING OF A GENERAL
1887–1942

'A biography . . . as outstanding as the achievements of Montgomery himself. This is a splendid book: flawless in its scholarship, brilliant in its presentation and above all in its understanding of a difficult personality . . . magnificent'

A. J. P. Taylor, The Observer

'The definitive life of the most remarkable British soldier of World War II . . . written with extraordinary vivacity and colour'

Financial Times

'The most accurate, the most explicit, and by far the most illuminating of books about Monty'

The Times

'Mr Hamilton has written a most intelligent and careful book to explain the growth of the Monty legend . . . A remarkable book'

Nigel Nicolson, The Sunday Times

'Forthright and honest . . . every future historian of the Second World War will have to lean on Mr Hamilton's biography'

The Economist

'A personal though much younger friend of the Field-Marshal, he has not allowed himself to be partial or prejudiced. He has written quite simply the best biography of Montgomery yet to emerge and I wait with pleasurable anticipation for the second volume to appear'

Anthony Farrar-Hockley, New Statesman

MONTY: THE FIELD-MARSHAL 1944–1976

'THE FIELD-MARSHAL is the best of Hamilton's trilogy. No one need be put off by its size and length. Like a good wine, it is best sipped rather than gulped. Its short, self-contained, and lucidly written chapters make sipping easy and satisfying. It is vintage Montgomery, with the full bouquet of his brilliance as a commander of men in battle'

The Times

'There are grounds for nothing but praise at the totality of the author's achievement, both in this book and in the conception and execution of the whole work. It is an extraordinary man, painted as if by a literary Picasso from many points of view on the same canvas'

Daily Telegraph

'As a memorial to the Field-Marshal, a comprehensive and minutely detailed record, Nigel Hamilton's biography can never be surpassed – magisterial in its shape and scope, brilliantly woven, and a joy to read'

The Sunday Times

'Magnificent . . . utterly absorbing'

The Guardian

'The narrative is nearly always enthralling, sometimes amusing, and quite often horrifying . . . On the personal side Mr Hamilton is very strong . . . He brings out all the contradictory human qualities of this very strange man'

John Grigg, The Observer

'Every detail is significant. Every document and letter quoted adds to our understanding of the intricate difficulties of high command . . . Montgomery's personality emerges from these pages with quite brutal clarity'

The Listener

'This book, like the two earlier volumes of Mr Hamilton's massive and definitive biography of this most controversial of soldiers, helps to put the record straight . . . Excellent'

The Birmingham Post

'Remarkable . . . Mr Hamilton lends a fresh vigour and throws much new light on the Ardennes, for example'

Glasgow Herald

Nigel Hamilton

MONTY: MASTER OF THE BATTLEFIELD 1942–1944

Copyright © 1983 by Nigel Hamilton

First published in Great Britain in 1983 by Hamish Hamilton Ltd.

Coronet edition 1985

Sceptre edition 1987

Sceptre is an imprint of Hodder and Stoughton Paperbacks, a division of Hodder and Stoughton Ltd.

British Library C.I.P.

Hamilton, Nigel, *1944–*
  Monty: master of the battlefield, 1942–1944.
  1. Montgomery of Alamein, Bernard Law Montgomery, *Viscount* 2. Great Britain, *Army* – Biography 3. Marshals – Great Britain – Biography 4, World War, 1939–1945 – Campaigns
  I. Title
  355.3′31′0924   DA69.3.M56

  ISBN 0-340-40784-0

This book is sold subject to the condition that it shall not, by way of trade or otherwise, be lent, re-sold, hired out or otherwise circulated without the publisher's prior consent in any form of binding or cover other than that in which this is published and without a similar condition including this condition being imposed on the subsequent purchaser.

Printed and bound in Great Britain for Hodder and Stoughton Paperbacks, a division of Hodder and Stoughton Ltd., Mill Road, Dunton Green, Sevenoaks, Kent (Editorial Office: 47 Bedford Square, London, WC1B 3DP) by Richard Clay Ltd., Bungay, Suffolk. Photoset by Rowland Phototypesetting Ltd., Bury St Edmunds, Suffolk.

Contents

List of Maps   xv
Author's Note and Acknowledgements   xvii

PART ONE: *Desert General*
1 Alamein: the Decisive Battle   3
2 The Pursuit Begins   11
3 The Race to Fuka   16
4 A Change of Plan   29
5 Mersa Matruh – 'A Complete Nonsense'   38
6 The Lessons of Alamein   44
7 Rommel's Crisis at Benghazi   52
8 'The Real Way to Take Tripoli is from the West'   63
9 A Lull in the Battle   74
10 Agheila   85
11 'What is to Happen now Lies in God's Hands'   95
12 Tripoli: the Coping Stone   105
13 'My Experience in Fighting Rommel'   121

PART TWO: *The End in North Africa*
1 Churchill Visits Tripoli   131
2 'Wonderfully Conceited' – Monty's Study Week   141
3 'Rommel can go to Hell': The Battle of Medenine   152
4 Monty's Vanity: 'Eighth Army's Dynamo'   171
5 Mareth: The Bridgehead is Lost   182
6 El Hamma: The 'Blitz' Attack   194
7 Wadi Akarit – and the Flying Fortress Story   208
8 Tunis: Masterminding the Final Offensive   225

PART THREE: *Sicily*
1 Husky: Recasting the Invasion of Sicily   241
2 'I should run Husky'   259
3 Interlude in England   269
4 'The Stern Fight That Lies Ahead'   280
5 The Assault upon Sicily   292

  6 Monty's Gamble   304
  7 Patton Absconds to Palermo   314
  8 The End of the Flying Fortress   322
  9 'The Americans Have Done Splendidly'   330
10 The Axis Evacuation of Sicily   340
11 The End of the Honeymoon   350
12 Reflections on Teams   358

PART FOUR: *Italy*
1 'A Unique Incident in the History of War'   375
2 'Giant Two' and Salerno   388
3 Haphazard and Untidy   410
4 'Do You Want to Drive the Germans from Italy?'   422
5 The Sangro: a Sea of Mud   432
6 'Who will Command "Overlord"?'   445
7 Alexander: 'A Very Dear Person but . . .'   455
8 Leaving Eighth Army   464

PART FIVE: *Preparations for D-Day*
  1 The Take-over of 'Overlord'   475
  2 Preparing the Weapon   486
  3 Eisenhower: Buffeted by Winds from Every Side   497
  4 Cracking Along on the Revised Plan   516
  5 The 'Things that Really Matter'   528
  6 Exercise 'Thunderclap'   540
  7 The Problem of Manpower   558
  8 'I Send you a Salmon'   564
  9 The Final Presentation at St Paul's   570
10 Showdown with Churchill   579
11 Dinner with Monty   583
12 To Go or not to Go   594

PART SIX: *Normandy*
  1 Last-minute Interference   607
  2 The D-Day Landings   611
  3 A Chance to Checkmate the Enemy   618
  4 Serious Opposition   632
  5 A State of Crisis   641
  6 The Class is Dismissed   658
  7 'This Weather is the very Devil'   668
  8 Planning the Break-out   674
  9 The Fear of Stalemate   689
10 'What is Vital and What is Not'   699
11 The 'Plot' to Sack Monty   717
12 At the Bottom of the Celestial Ladder   727
13 Eisenhower Scents Victory   741

14 The Falaise Gap   756
15 A Fateful Week   776
16 A Lost Cause   792
17 Triumph, and Tragedy   805

    Sources and Bibliography   823
    List of Abbreviations   831
    Index   834

List of Maps

	Page
The North African Campaign, 1942–43	8 – 9
The Race to Fuka, 4–5 November 1942	17
The Failure to take Mersa Matruh, 6–8 November 1942	33
The Pursuit to Tobruk, Benghazi and Agheila, November 1942	59
The Battle of Agheila, 14–17 December 1942	88
The Battle of Tripoli, 14–23 January 1943	110
The Battle of Kasserine, 14–22 February 1943	147
The Battle of Medenine, 6 March 1943	157
The Battle of Mareth, 20–27 March 1943	188
The Battle of Wadi Akarit, 6 April 1943	217
The Final Offensive in Tunisia, April–May 1943	237
The Sicilian Campaign, July–August 1943	294
The Italian Campaign, September–December 1943	378
'Overlord' – Changing the COSSAC plan	483
Monty's Forecast of Operations from D-Day to 1 September 1944	574
The D-Day Landings and Monty's M501 map	639
Monty's second plan to take Caen by envelopment	666
30 June 1944: Monty's first plan for American break-out after the capture of Cherbourg (M505)	685
10 July 1944: Monty's plan for American breakout (M510)	711
14 July 1944: Monty's plans for Operations 'Goodwood' and 'Cobra' (M511)	715
21 July 1944: Monty's plan for Operation 'Cobra' and the American break-out to Alençon and Le Mans (M512)	732
24 and 27 July 1944: Monty's plans for American and British operations in conjunction with 'Cobra' (M514 and 515)	739
6 August 1944: Monty's plans for an Allied advance to the Seine after the success of 'Cobra' (M517)	764
11 August 1944: After the failure of the German counter-attack at Mortain, Monty's plans to surround the Falaise pocket (M518)	769
The Falaise pocket – and the climax of the battle of Normandy	779

Situation Map, 1 September 1944 – with Monty's and Patton's plans for a concentrated Allied thrust to the North-east 795

Author's Note

On 11 November 1942, one week after victory at El Alamein – the turning point of World War II – Lt-General B. L. Montgomery was knighted 'for distinguished service in the field', and promoted to the rank of full General. He had stepped into history.

For the great victory at Alamein 'made' Monty – he would later, as a peer, style himself by its name – and in the battles and campaigns that followed, a new lens must be fitted to the biographer's focus. No longer is this the little-known path of an unknown lieutenant-general. From 5 November 1942 Montgomery became a household name the world over. When he returned briefly to England in the spring of 1943, supposedly incognito, people fought to get sight of him, even to touch the hem of his garment – this military messiah who had, at last, shown that the spell of German predominance could be broken.

The Battle of Alamein forged Monty's reputation, but thereafter his performance must also be judged alongside those of other great players – Churchill, Brooke, Portal, Tedder, Cunningham, Eisenhower, Bradley, Patton, Clark, Slim, McArthur, Alexander. . . . Perhaps no general ever has so assiduously prepared himself for high command, or so dramatically imprinted his concepts upon an ailing army in the field; but once the ripples of his victory at Alamein had spread through the Allied world, once British and American forces had landed in North-west Africa on 8 November 1942, Bernard Montgomery became a member of an Allied team. The tide of war turned, and the glory of Alamein soon paled amidst the preoccupations of Allied strategy in the West. Within months Monty would be at loggerheads with colleagues and superiors over the future conduct of the land war, and the very virtues which gave his leadership its inspiring quality – absolute conviction, insistence on proper planning, ruthless professionalism – made him an infuriatingly opinionated and stubborn ally. Walter Bedell Smith's famous remark – 'you may be great to serve under, difficult to serve alongside, but you sure are hell to serve over!' – was uniquely apt, and it is certainly no business of a biographer to exonerate Montgomery from his grave failures as a soldier-statesman.

However, within that cussed, obstinate, cocksure vanity which sometimes so alienated Monty's colleagues there existed too a profoundly realistic and devoted warrior. That fame turned Monty's head and exaggerated aspects of a character already dangerously eccentric would seem undeniable; but the soldier who had snatched victory with such calculated assurance in the autumn of 1942 was no Nivelle, trumpeting triumph only to find further victory beyond his grasp. Alamein was indeed a triumph – but the general who drove his men to victory was no mere figurehead. After a lifetime's learning and rehearsal, his 'call' had come, and his country had entrusted him with command of an army in the field. That army he would rebuild into the most legendary army of the war; one which never failed him.

Latterly it has become fashionable to decry the reputation of Eighth Army, to point with disdain at its reputedly slow progress and failure to entrap spectacular bodies of enemy forces. Victory loses its lustre after a time, while the pain and disappointment of defeat are quickly exorcised from the mind. The disasters of British arms, from Norway and Dunkirk to Greece, Crete, Tobruk, Gazala and the flight to Alamein become subsumed in memory, while success seems in retrospect easy; indeed, given our latter-day knowledge of the forces available to the enemy, inevitable.

It was not so at the time. The men of First Army who bumped up against Axis forces in Tunisia in December 1942 soon received a rude shock – as did the innocent American forces at Kasserine. Salerno and Anzio would demonstrate that even overpowering naval and air superiority will not alone defeat a determined enemy. Many a fond illusion, fostered by America's active entry into the war in the West, would be paid for in blood; and Montgomery's generalship, as Commander of Eighth Army and later C-in-C Land Forces for the invasion of Normandy, warrants proper telling. Those persecuted peoples of Europe who suffered for their conscience, their creed and their race were not interested in bravado; their lives and the lives of their families, relatives and fellow-countrymen were at stake; they would be so until the day an Allied army liberated them. It was Bernard Montgomery's role to lead those offensive armies, from the turn of the tide at Alamein to the German surrender at Lüneburg – a feat unparalleled since the days of Wellington.

My aim is to chart intimately Bernard Montgomery's achievement as a general in the field: momentous years during which he miraculously restored the prestige of his country's army, and thus of Britain herself. Like Nelson he revived a sense of workmanlike pride in his service: the sense that there was nothing which, if properly prepared and ably commanded, his army could not do. Like Patton he would come very close to mania at times; but unlike Patton he was able to discipline himself to serve a higher cause. Likewise he would make mistakes, misjudge people, situations, plans. Often, as in Sicily and

Italy, his arrogance as an undefeated army commander caused resentment. There were occasions when – as in his insistence on the provision of a Flying Fortress, complete with American crew, as payment of a bet – he acted with complete disregard for advice or Allied embarrassment. Nor was his example – most closely imitated by Sir Oliver Leese and Lord Mountbatten – always good. High-handedness, total self-righteousness are poor tutors, and not even Monty's most intimate subordinates could condone these lesser virtues, since by tradition greatness is seen by Britons as the exercise of great talent with modesty. His ilk of autocratic rule had none of the aristocratic refinement of Wellington, something which often led to accusations that he was 'a little man on the make'.

But those who were permitted to visit the warrior in the field seldom went away unimpressed. Short in stature, with bony cheeks and long, sharp nose, steel-blue eyes and a precise, relentlessly logical mind, this captain of men imparted an aura of clarity and conviction which infused all who served under him. His mastery of detail, and his ability to seize and establish the essentials of any problem, were uncanny. He seemed to feel the pulse of the various formations and units of his army as no other Allied commander had ever done; he had a phenomenal memory for names, and together with all his vanity, a curiosity about others that was rare enough in ordinary men, let alone in exalted commanders. He conformed to no known mould and seemed an unlikely father-figure to gain the admiration of a whole army with his high-pitched voice, his seeming inattention to dress, his schoolboy rhetoric. Yet by his uncanny mastery of the various elements that comprise leadership in the field he seemed to vault the gulf between leader and led, exciting a following and faith unequalled, perhaps, by any other military commander in the war.

Between November 1942 and December 1943 General Sir Bernard Montgomery led Eighth Army in a march of victories comparable to the great military campaigns of Greece, Carthage and Rome – traversing some 2,000 miles of North Africa, commanding the British army assaulting Sicily, mounting the first Allied landings on the continent of Europe at Reggio, and throwing the German army in South-east Italy back to the river Sangro, beyond the latitude of Rome. It was hardly surprising that when an Allied army group commander had to be selected for the opening of the Allied Second Front in 1944, the general chosen was Sir Bernard Montgomery.

This seaborne and airborne invasion, the largest undertaking of its kind that will probably ever take place, was to prove as decisive as Alamein itself, as Montgomery's armies battled ashore in Normandy, established a bridgehead and forced the German military forces in France into a bitter contest, the outcome of which would decide the destiny of Europe.

By August 1944 the German cordon in Normandy was punctured, the German armies defeated – and within days the Allies were racing towards Germany itself. For this achievement Montgomery was promoted on 1 September 1944 to the rank of Field-Marshal.

Monty had been a full general only twenty-one months – months of generalship which deserve surely to be seen in separate focus from those of Montgomery the child, the youth, the subaltern, the rising officer, the gifted teacher, the visionary trainer – the general in the making. (It is unlikely now that any British general will ever command, for instance, a million Americans on the field of battle, not to mention Canadians, French, Poles, Czechs, New Zealanders, Indians and Nepalese.) With Montgomery's papers at hand and so much hitherto secret material open to historians, one can begin to chronicle in depth Montgomery's meteoric rise as a general in the field – from the battle of Alamein in 1942 to the victorious opening of the Second Front in the summer of 1944; an intimate view of generalship no longer in the making, but at work upon the field of battle; a story that reveals the true torment, frustration, misunderstanding and dissatisfaction that are the hand-maidens of those who make history.

Inevitably, in seeking to describe intimately Montgomery's two years as a general in the field, this volume is more historical than its predecessor. Fame and military success may have affected Monty's ego, but Monty the man was already made. My object therefore has been to help the reader towards a better understanding of Monty's often controversial role at the centre of great military and historical events, using the mass of his unpublished papers.

Many of Monty's views concerning his fellow soldiers, from General Eisenhower to General Alexander, from General Anderson to Admiral Mountbatten, during these two years of battle, were unkind and did not do justice to colleagues of great stature. Too often, however, historians have been offended by Monty's summary denunciations of others, and have declined to see them in the context of battle. From the time he was appointed to take over Eighth Army in August 1942 Monty was in constant command of armies either in battle or preparing for specific battle. If he criticised colleagues and superiors, particularly his two immediate C-in-Cs, Alexander and Eisenhower, it was not to belittle their overall contribution to the war; they were leaders who rightly aroused the highest respect not only in the ranks of their own national contingents but all nationalities. Rather, his exasperation was that of a uniquely talented and highly professional battle-soldier. How difficult *he* would find the government of allies and men beyond the immediate battlefield will be shown in *Monty: The Field-Marshal, 1944–76*.

In chronicling this story of Mongtgomery's years as a full general I have been privileged, as I was in the writing of *Monty: The Making of a*

General, 1887–1942, to receive the encouragement and help of many individuals as well as institutions. Since I am not by profession a military historian, the debt I owe them is incalculable.

First, my dear father Sir Denis Hamilton, who fell ill during the writing of the book, remains my sponsor and closest *Mitarbeiter*. Without his vision and patient, caring assistance this biography could not have been undertaken. He has spent a lifetime editing newspapers and commissioning works. His integrity is well known, and was the reason why Montgomery chose to entrust to him the safekeeping and eventual publication of his controversial private papers and diaries. I hope I have justified the faith he put in me, in asking me to write this work – for he has never sought to influence my judgment, only to provide help and encouragement in the long labour of biographical excavation.

Likewise Lord Montgomery of Alamein has been a tower of strength. As the son of Field-Marshal Montgomery he might well have felt offended by some of my interpretations of events – but he has maintained a scrupulous impartiality and anxiousness to assist: a friendship I prize.

Members of the Mongtgomery family, friends and military colleagues of the Field-Marshal in Britain and the United States have all been unstinting in their help, and I extend my sincerest thanks to: the late Major-General R. F. K. Belchem, Brigadier R. H. S. Bidwell, Air Chief Marshal Sir Harry Broadhurst, Ian Calvocoressi, Lt-Colonel John Carver, Mrs Jocelyn Carver, Colonel R. O. H. Carver, Field-Marshal Lord Carver, Eric Casswell, Warwick Charlton, General Mark Clark, General J. Lawton Collins, Jnr., Sir John Colville, Lt-Colonel C. P. Dawnay, the late Major-General Sir Francis de Guingand, Mrs Frances Denby, Lt-Colonel Carlo D'Este, General James M. Gavin, the late General Alfred Gruenther, Field-Marshal Lord Harding of Petherton, J. R. Henderson, Lt-General Sir Otway Herbert, J. E. B. Hill, Major-General Patrick Hobart, Lt-General Sir Brian Horrocks, Lt-General Sir Ian Jacob, the late Geoffrey Keating, the late General Sir Sidney Kirkman, Ronald Lewin, Sir William Mather, Lt-Colonel Brian Montgomery, Nigel Nicolson, Paul Odgers, Major-General M. St J. Oswald, Forrest C. Pogue, Robert Priestley, the late Major Tom Reynolds, General Sir Charles Richardson, General Matt Ridgway, Major-General G. P. B. Roberts, Major-General Richard Rohmer, Wing Commander R. W. F. Sampson, Norman Scarfe, Group Captain F. H. L. Searl, General Sir Frank Simpson, Ed Stevens, General Maxwell Taylor, Brigadier H. R. W. Vernon, Lt-Colonel Trumbull Warren, the late Eugene R. Wason, Brigadier Sir Edgar Williams, Lt-General Sir James Wilson, Major-General Douglas Wimberley, Philip Ziegler.

Once again, in order to observe as strict a rule of accuracy and fairness as possible, I asked a number of veterans to read appropriate sections of the typescript: Lt-Colonel J. Carver, Lt-Colonel C. P. Dawnay, Major J. R. Henderson, Major P. R. Odgers, Major-General M. St J. Oswald, General Sir Charles Richardson, General Sir Frank Simpson, Brigadier Sir Edgar Williams, and Major-General Douglas Wimberley. I am most grateful for their corrections and suggestions.

To the staffs of the following institutions I owe especial gratitude: Dr Noble Frankland, former Director, and Dr Alan Borg, Director, Mr Robert Crawford, Deputy Director, Mr Roderick Suddaby, Mr Jim Lucas, Miss Rose Gerrard and the unfailingly helpful staff of the Imperial War Museum, Lambeth; Marshal of the Royal Air Force Lord Cameron, Principal, King's College, Miss Patricia Methven and the staff of the Liddell Hart Centre for Military Archives, King's College, London; Dr Nicolas Cox and the staff of the Public Record Office, Kew; the staff of the London Library; Mrs E. M. Denton, Archivist, St Paul's School; Mr Roy Lilley, Editor of the *Belfast Telegraph*; William Brown, Managing Director, Scottish Television; H. A. Faircloth, Editor, *The News*, Portsmouth; the staff of the National Archives, Washington; Lt-Commander Collett and the Archives staff of the Citadel, Charleston, South Carolina; Dr John E. Wickman and the staff of the Eisenhower Library, Abilene, Kansas; Colonel Donald P. Shaw, Director, Mr John Slonaker and Dr Richard Sommers and the staff of the Military History Institute, Carlisle, Pennsylvania (and their generosity in awarding me a Research Grant); General James L. Collins, Chief of Military History, Washington, D.C.; Glen Renfrew, Managing Director, Reuters and Mr Bruce Russell, Head of Reuters Bureau, Washington, D.C.; Dr Ralph Shrader of West Point Military Academy, New York; and Mr J. R. Wiggins, formerly Editor of the *Washington Post* and U.S. Ambassador to the United Nations.

No project of this magnitude could be undertaken without unstinting editorial and clerical assistance. I am deeply grateful to Christopher Sinclair-Stevenson and Julian Evans of Hamish Hamilton; Gladys Carr of McGraw-Hill; Bruce Hunter and Claire Smith, my agents; Miss Winifred Marshall and Mrs Roslyn Kloegman, my typists; Miss Joan Crockford, my father's secretary; Robin Dodd, who was responsible for the maps and the layout of the illustrations; Ken White, who compiled the index; and my devoted wife Outi who, once again, held the domestic fort.

Finally, I would like to thank the many readers who wrote to me after publication of *Monty: The Making of a General*. Apart from providing much valuable information and countless recollections, these letters served to remind me of the place 'Monty' still holds in the hearts of those who campaigned with him, and I am most grateful for them. I would have liked to record more anecdotes, and to picture Monty's domestic life in the field more fully – his habits, his sense of humour, the strange aura of discipline and yet at the same time of freshness and fun that surrounded him. But as Monty would undoubtedly have said, it is unwise to attempt to do everything. In concentrating in this book on Monty's generalship in the field during the two most crucial years of World War II, culminating in his greatest achievement – the Allied victory in Normandy – I hope I have done a measure of justice to a great commander; and a devoted friend. I treasure, in particular, a letter which he wrote to me in 1970:

Nigel my dear
I got this morning your letter dated 23 October. I was at the Alamein Reunion in London that night. Apart from that I live a quiet life in my home and seldom go anywhere; I have to face the fact that I am getting old – 83 on Nov. 17. But I enjoy old age, and keep well, and do a great deal of thinking. . . .
You and I have been through a great deal together, and during those years I developed a great affection for you – which has never died. . . . You can unburden your soul to me, and I will listen with love, and ask no awkward questions. . . .
    With all my love,
        Montgomery of Alamein

In fact he *did* ask awkward questions – and even counselled me to give up writing – 'nobody wants anything you write anyhow'! But that was Monty: a strange mix between considerateness and uncompromising frankness. I hope, at any rate, that my personal knowledge of the man has helped me to depict Monty's extraordinary career with understanding and honesty.

NIGEL HAMILTON
Suffolk 1983

PART ONE

Desert General

CHAPTER ONE

Alamein: the Decisive Battle

'AXIS FORCES IN FULL RETREAT: OFFICIAL' ran the headline in the *Daily Telegraph* on 5 November 1942. 'Rommel's disordered columns attacked relentlessly. 9,000 prisoners: 260 tanks destroyed.'

'GREAT NEWS FROM EGYPT' announced the *Daily Express*; 'the enemy is beaten – and our advance continues'. Even the BBC announcer abandoned for the first time his Reithian delivery, and declared with undisguised excitement:

I'm going to read you the News and there's some cracking good news coming in. . . .

Given the 'dramatic night communiqué' from Cairo, it was understandable that editors at home were momentarily confused about whom to eulogise. 'General Alexander has won a great victory in the Egyptian desert – there is no other way to describe his matter-of-fact announcement of the destruction done to the Axis army,' commented Morley Richards in the *Daily Express* at midnight on 5 November. The *Daily Telegraph* went even further. 'A Military Correspondent recently returned from Egypt reported: "I am now in a position to state that Gen. Alexander, who succeeded Gen. Auchinleck as C-in-C, Middle East, in August, is in the field with the Eighth Army. With Gen. Montgomery as his right-hand man, he personally planned and directed the British offensive." ' Even *The Times*, devoting its first leader to the 'Victory in Egypt', scarcely mentioned Montgomery. 'No doubt remains that the victory in North Africa for which the country has waited so many weary months has been achieved at last. . . . From the start of General Alexander's great offensive there has been confidence about his operations, a sense of completeness in the planning' – and the battle itself was extolled as a 'classic operation' which reflected 'the highest credit on the Commander-in-Chief. . . . Already we are launched upon a more powerful tide of victory than we have yet known, and for that General Alexander, with the officers and men of the three services who have shared in his great triumph, have abundantly earned the gratitude of their country and all the United Nations.'

For the German broadcasters there seems to have been no such confusion. General Alexander's name had scarcely appeared in broadcasts since the opening of the battle; as British correspondents had once characterised the German-Italian Panzer Army as 'Rommel', so now the German press reports referred simply to Montgomery. At 4.56 p.m. on 3 November 1942 the German News Agency announced: 'General Montgomery has thrown in some 500 tanks in the greatest tank battle of the whole African campaign,' and at 11.15 p.m. Berlin Radio had predicted 'a decision one way or another in the Battle of Egypt soon'. The following afternoon, on 4 November, the German News Agency announced: 'In today's early hours the Commander of the Eighth Army renewed the expected assault on the north flank of the Alamein front with the concentration of all the forces still remaining to him. . . . While this report is being written, at 4.30 p.m., the battle, which in the meantime has flared up with great ferocity, continues.' Twenty-four hours later the truth could no longer be suppressed. Rome Radio confessed: 'The Axis forces in Egypt are steadily retreating to new positions. The battle is still raging furiously.'

In America there was one man at least who was quite clear about the Alamein victory. 'It is a thrilling and far-reaching accomplishment. When I visited General Montgomery some two months ago,' Wendell Willkie told newsmen, 'I was convinced the present results would follow in a short time. Montgomery told me he would eliminate Rommel. He is apparently well on the way.'

C. V. R. Thompson reported from New York: 'Americans have forgotten their criticisms of Britain, and full credit to the British is given in the American Press and by the American people for the desert victory. . . . The International News Service, which goes to 700 American newspapers, had this to say: "The question, can the British soldiers really fight? need never again be asked. The Germans themselves are the best judges of their fighting spirit." ' Thompson recorded in his *Daily Express* 'U.S. Newsfront' column: 'Another important change has come over America in the past 48 hours – a change in her attitude towards Britain. Singapore, then Tobruk, did Britain damage with the people. Even some of our friends began to question the ability of our High Command, even the fighting of our troops. Because of that questioning, other anti-British talk gained some credence in this country. Overnight that talk has been swept away by the great victory in Egypt. What is also significant is that there is little talk about America's elections today; it is all about the defeat of Rommel. Montgomery has driven the election off America's front page.'

President Roosevelt had thus much to thank Montgomery for; so had Churchill. Some post-war writers, resenting the political ramifications of the victory, have attempted to diminish its import-

4

ance by derogating it as a 'First World War-style' battle, even suggesting that it was unnecessary – that a further few months of 'sitting tight' at Alamein would have seen Rommel withdraw anyway. Not only was it vital, however, to reach the Martuba airfields if Malta was to be re-supplied by protected convoy, but the success of the 'Torch' landings in Morocco, Algeria and Tunisia depended on evidence that the Allies were both intent on, and capable of, ousting the Germans from North Africa. The victory at El Alamein was proof to the French in North Africa, and one has only to examine the newspapers and broadcasts of the time to see how much Montgomery's Eighth Army triumph altered the political complexion of the war. Churchill's phrase: 'Before Alamein we never had a victory; after Alamein we never had a defeat,' might have been exaggerated – but its essence was true. If the battle of Alamein was considered by so many millions of people to be the turning-point of the war, it was not simply because it was a welcome victory, but because it marked a significant change in the prosecution of the war in the West: a change from German to Allied initiative. It was moreover an initiative which, once grasped, the Allies never surrendered. No longer were Britain – the last major stronghold of freedom in the West – or her forces under threat. The balance, so precariously poised in the summer, had begun to swing in favour of the Allies. Again, as Churchill put it, it was not the beginning of the end; but certainly it was the end of the beginning.

Nor was this a fortuitous advantage enjoyed by the new Commander of Eighth Army. On the contrary, it was Montgomery himself who had deemed it so. He had formed the conviction in Home Forces in England, after two years of strenuous but limited exercises, that a decisive battle, lasting at least eleven days, *must* be fought – and Exercise 'Tiger'[1] had been his rehearsal for it. In the desert, commanding Eighth Army, he had parried Rommel's final assault on the Nile delta at Alam Halfa, thus giving Eighth Army time to re-equip with the new Sherman tank, the 6-pdr version of the Crusader tank, 6-pdr anti-tank weapons, and new artillery. He had insisted that Eighth Army be given sufficient time also to prepare plans and train for a decisive battle, deliberately playing down the success of Alam Halfa in order to retain Rommel's forces at the end of vulnerable lines of communication and as far as possible from the 'Torch' landings – of which, for twenty-four hours in August, Montgomery had himself been appointed senior British commander.

The resulting battle of El Alamein had been considerably more difficult to pull off than even Montgomery had anticipated, and there can be little doubt that Montgomery was, at that stage in the war, the sole Allied commander capable of winning it. General 'Strafer' Gott,

[1] See *Monty: The Making of a General, 1887–1942*, London 1981.

5

Churchill's appointed nominee for Eighth Army, was not only too exhausted to command such a protracted and savage engagement, but was also profoundly opposed to it in principle.

Gott was a 'very tired man at Alamein', a veteran – later Field-Marshal Lord Carver – recalled after the war.

> For so long he [Gott] had borne the burden not only of command in the field, but more of being the figure to whom all, high and low, turned for advice, sympathy, help and encouragement in difficulty. He continued to give it, but it exhausted him; and the prospect of the heavy responsibility before him must have been a heavy addition to the weight he carried, particularly as the only way to carry it out appeared to be a reversion to 1914–1918 warfare with its heavy casualties, which he detested. He hated to see men killed and was determined to avoid the vast casualties for minor tactical gains which that type of battle involved. We discussed this a few days before his death – it may have been the very day. He was determined to see if he could not organise a vast left-hook through Siwa rather than face a dog-fight on the Alamein line.

Carver, the GSO 2 (Operations) on the staff of 30 Corps, assured Gott it was unfeasible; that only a direct assault was possible.

> He had not the ruthless determination, one might almost say the callousness, which enabled Monty to face the colossal casualties in the first week of Alamein with equanimity. . . . Strafer imagined all too keenly what casualties meant in terms of human suffering. Perhaps he was too great a man to be a really great soldier. . . .[1]

Montgomery's ruthlessness was certainly different from Gott's, but it was not simply callousness with men's lives. Rather it was born of the recognition that the morale of an army cannot be created by hesitant or over-humane commanders. Etched on Montgomery's mind was the débâcle of the BEF, the indignity of retreat and defeat. As von Moltke once remarked, only when a commander has faced and proven himself in retreat can he be said to have earned one of the essential laurels of greatness as a military commander. Like Gott, Montgomery had faced retreat and defeat: but in contradistinction to Gott, this bred in him the conviction that, in order to rebuild morale, offensive thinking and offensive victory were vital. This victory could not be achieved by minor engagements. The enemy *must* be brought to battle, and fought to the bitter, decisive end. Such a victory would achieve far more than the gain of ground: it would be

[1] Letter of 14.6.50 to J. A. I. Agar Hamilton (South African Official Historian), communicated to author, 17.1.81.

the basis of the professional self-confidence of the entire army in future – while at the same time shattering the pride and morale of the enemy. This conviction, born in England in the summer of 1940 after Dunkirk, had been the foundation of Montgomery's dedicated command thereafter. He had been mocked by many, considered mad by some: but the record of his self-preparation and the training of the officers and men beneath him probably has no parallel in the history of British arms since the days of Wellington and Nelson.

At Alamein, Montgomery's conviction was at last put to the test – and justified. The battle was decisive in a more profound respect than any other Allied engagement in the West during the war, save perhaps D-Day and the Battle of Normandy. Not only did it herald a new era in Allied offensive operations in the West, but it rocked Axis morale to an incalculable extent. The legendary Rommel had been beaten, and a demonstration of the relentless Allied intention to prosecute the war until final victory had at last been given. The ruthless professionalism of the German armies which had overrun Poland, France, Norway, Greece, Crete and North Africa was now being matched and surpassed – a fact which many journalists noted at the time, if perhaps a trifle vindictively: 'Survivors of the French débâcle or of the retreat through the defiles of Greece know its significance,' *The Times* leader-writer remarked of Rommel's helter-skelter retreat, blitzed by the RAF and given no time to form a new defensive line. 'Now for the first time a German army has to pass through the same experience.' Even Churchill gloated over the prospect of immobilised Germans and Italians at Alamein being 'cut out' like limpets from a rock. 'And what happens to a limpet when it loses its rock? It dies a miserable death. Thirst comes to it – aching, inescapable thirst. I should not like our armies to be suffering what the Afrika Korps will suffer in these days.'[1]

There was, however, no vindictiveness in Bernard Montgomery's conduct as Eighth Army Commander. Not only did he invite the captured Commander of the Afrika Korps, General von Thoma, to dine with him at his headquarters at El Alamein, but to stay the night there. The next morning, 5 November 1942, the two generals breakfasted together. Then Montgomery addressed the assembled Allied war correspondents.

Standing by the seashore after despatching his captured adversary, General von Thoma, back to detention in the Delta, General Bernard L. Montgomery this morning announced complete and absolute victory in the battle of Alamein,

[1] Harold Nicolson, *Diaries* Vol. II, 1939–1945, London 1967.

reported Alaric Jacob of the *Daily Express*. Christopher Buckley of the *Daily Telegraph* described the Eighth Army Commander as 'wearing a tank beret and a grey pullover':

'It has been a fine battle. There is no doubt of the result. Two nights ago I drove two armoured wedges into the enemy and I passed three armoured divisions through those places. They are now operating in enemy's rear.
'Those portions of the enemy's armour which can get away are in full retreat. Those portions which are still facing our troops down in the south will be put "in the bag". It is complete finish.
'I did not hope for such a complete victory; or rather I hoped for it but I did not expect it.
'After 12 days of very hard fighting, the Eighth Army and the Allied air forces have gained a complete victory over the German and Italian forces. The enemy is completely smashed.
'For the last two nights the road behind the enemy lines has been blocked with stuff four deep trying to get away. They have been bombed day and night.
'But we must not think that the party is over. We have no intention

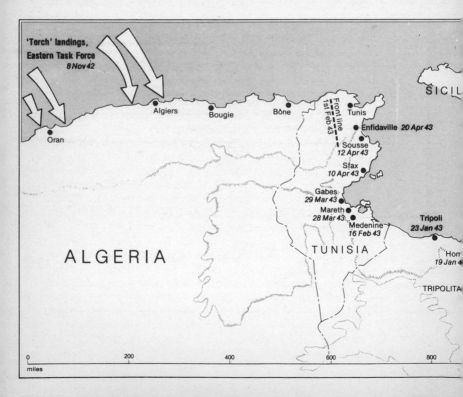

of letting the enemy recover. We must keep up the pressure. We intend to hit this chap for six out of North Africa.'

Montgomery went on to describe von Thoma's capture, and their discussion over dinner. Von Thoma had at Dunkirk captured British Intelligence papers containing a British character sketch of himself, so Montgomery had asked if the Germans had a character sketch of the Commander of Eighth Army.

'He replied that they had. I asked him to tell me what it contained. He appeared embarrassed and excused himself from telling me over the dinner table.

'But this morning he told me. It said I was a hard man – I do not think I am – quite ruthless in carrying out anything I had determined to do.

'Thoma said: "We expected a new form of tactics when we heard of your appointment. We got them and we couldn't deal with them."'

Gen. Montgomery then paid tribute to the soldiers. 'They've been magnificent,' he said, 'quite magnificent.'

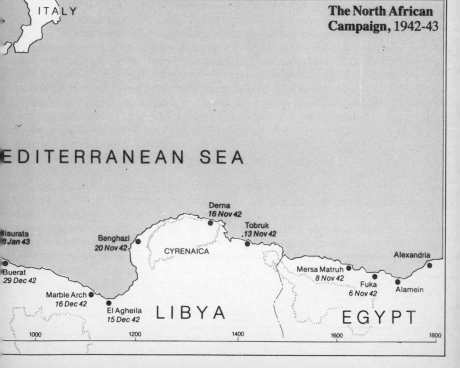

The North African Campaign, 1942-43

A very great part, he said, had been played by the gunners of the Royal Artillery. They had put down a concentration of fire never known before, in this war at any rate. It was too much for the enemy. The sappers also had done wonders, for the battle had been fought in one enormous minefield.

The infantry had got their own back. Some people thought the day of the infantry was done. There had been a time when the people thought the infantry was no more use in modern warfare.

But in a situation like this, faced with a front which had no flanks, the infantry had got a break-through.

They had shown that they mattered more than anyone. It was the armour's turn now that the break-through had been achieved.

It was indeed. The speed of Rommel's subsequent flight took the world by surprise – particularly Mussolini, who helplessly listened to enemy reports recording the capture of entire Italian unmotorised divisions, together with their commanders. Some commentators wondered whether Mussolini might even sue for a separate armistice – for within days the war in the Mediterranean, from having been subsidiary to the Russian campaign, flared up to become its counterpart. Overnight the strategy, tactics and morale of the war in the West overturned. In Allied eyes, the future suddenly seemed miraculously hopeful. With the first reports of Allied landings in North-west Africa – near Casablanca, Oran and Algiers – on 8 November it was evident that the Allies were now seizing the initiative – despite Hitler's claim to have finally captured Stalingrad.

Within three weeks, Rommel had retreated over one thousand kilometres to El Agheila. In fact the question in many minds was whether Rommel could flee fast enough to avoid being cut off altogether by Anglo-American forces racing across Tunisia and severing his lines of communication west of Tripoli:

As American troops pressed on in North Africa, President Roosevelt made it clear tonight that General Eisenhower's forces are to go through Tunisia, separating Algeria from Libya, in order to link up with the advancing Eighth Army,

the *Daily Express* reported.[1]

The unthinkable had, in a matter of weeks, become the taken-for-granted. To those surveying newspaper diagrams, Eisenhower's route across the mountains of southern Tunisia and then southwards to Tripoli looked deceptively straightforward, while the possibility of the Eighth Army encircling Rommel's remnant Axis African Army in Libya – as General O'Connor had done against Graziani's Italian army in 1940/1 – appeared equally enticing.

[1] *Daily Express*, 10.11.42.

CHAPTER TWO

The Pursuit Begins

Some time before the battle of Alamein, Monty had given instructions that a small Tactical Headquarters be set up for his use. Small, mobile, and with good communications, this headquarters would enable him to control Eighth Army well forward, while his Chief-of-staff, Brigadier de Guingand, conducted the detailed administration at Main Headquarters. Thus, a few days before the opening of the Alamein offensive, Tac Eighth Army had established itself alongside the leading Corps headquarters, about fifty yards from the sea, at El Alamein.

I can remember that,

recalled the senior Tac Army officer some forty years later,

> because the officers' latrine was on the beach. I think it had a screen around it, but certainly it didn't screen the chap enthroned from the sea, because one aircraft, I think a German one, flying very low went slap past this chap, followed by a Spitfire with everything blasting – one behind the other -- and enthroned here, incapable of movement, was this chap who was twenty yards from the tide! So that was how close we were – within fifty yards of the sea.
> And Main 30 Corps HQ was, oh, in easy walking distance away, a couple of hundred yards away. And Tac 10 Corps was somewhere equivalent in that sort of direction – quite a galaxy of bombable targets!
> Monty had said where he wanted it to be, decided the place. It was pretty crowded at that time, the Alamein position. And he'd made clear, and so had de Guingand, that the object of there being a Tac was so that Monty could be up with whichever Corps was mainly engaged, so that he was within easy discussion distance of the Corps Commander – as he was at Alamein, where he'd got two of his three Corps Commanders literally on the spot for the course of the battle.[1]

[1] Maj-General M. St J. Oswald, interview of 1.2.83.

Tac Army was in fact within Eighth Army's gun lines – 'I mean, when that terrific barrage broke out, it wasn't a question of going forward to look at the guns – the guns were some behind you and some in front of you and you could see it all.' To protect Monty's headquarters there was a troop of Derbyshire Yeomanry; otherwise the Tactical Headquarters was

a fairly modest affair consisting of between thirty and forty vehicles. The composition was myself, the GSO 2. I had two GSO 3s and a signal officer. And Monty had his two ADCs. I presume I was picked because I'd done quite a lot of this sort of thing before – I'd commanded a 'Jock' column and that sort of thing, and I knew about movement by day and by night, and also how to move dispersed, that sort of thing. And we did quite a bit of practising in odd bits of the desert that didn't belong to anybody, without getting in their way – how they should move, what order they should move in, and how, if you had to move at night, how they'd have to close within visible distance, and how the signals communications would work. . . .[1]

Apart from Monty's three caravans, the 'hub' of the headquarters was the Armoured Command Vehicle which housed the small operations staff with radio operators and their sets and from which it was possible to keep communications open with Main HQ and to all Corps HQs. Powered by a London bus engine, the ACV would enable Monty to remain in touch with both de Guingand and subordinate commanders after the break-out – though de Guingand had reservations about the Army Commander being so far forward.

Of course de Guingand and his senior staff officers like Kirkman, they loathed Tac Headquarters, for it often meant a hell of a journey to go and get hold of Monty. They liked to have Monty available so that they could go and consult him. Even more so Monty's logistics people from Rear Headquarters, they thought it's a bit of a trek to Main, but at least we can get him when we get there. But once he's off in his Tac Headquarters – he's away.[2]

In General Oswald's later view, this was indeed one of Monty's purposes in establishing a Tac Headquarters: to disentangle himself from the detailed running of the Army, and to impose his personality on the commanders and men at the front. Alamein was to be the decisive battle of the Second World War so far: it was vital that Monty ensure the ruthless prosecution of the offensive by his personal presence at the front, even before commencement of the battle.

[1] Ibid.
[2] Ibid.

We were in position a bit before the battle because he had a Final Conference of his most senior officers – Corps Commanders and maybe divisional commanders, actually sitting on the sand at Tac.

And I well remember it because there were quite a lot of duck flying up and down the coastline and when he wasn't there we'd been in the habit of getting the armoured car chaps [Derbyshire Yeomanry] to see whether they could shoot a duck with a machine gun, and then someone would swim out and get it. . . .

Well as Monty was sitting there talking to Leese and everybody, and explaining on a map, out in the open, off went a machine gun. It went da-da-da-da, and everyone started to move, cowering. And Monty was frightfully angry, for down from the sky came spiralling a duck, which landed not actually at his feet, but damned nearly. And he had it for dinner that night. And certainly there was this sheepish lot of chaps who hurried off looking at the sky, having realized that it wasn't a Messerschmitt, it was a duck![1]

It was from this Tac Headquarters that Monty had conducted the battle of Alamein; and it was there, having breakfasted with General von Thoma, and having addressed the Allied war correspondents on 5 November 1942, that Monty had to make crucial decisions about both the pursuit of Rommel's retreating forces and the rounding-up of those unmotorised elements which Rommel had abandoned. From violent but static warfare on a fixed front, operations now became mobile in the extreme – and Montgomery had always taught that in these circumstances commanders must decentralise: 'the more fluid the fighting, the greater should be the degree of decentralisation, the aim being to have *available immediately* those weapons which are necessary for cracking the nut involved at the moment.'[2]

Though there was decentralisation in the extreme, the nut proved more difficult to crack than most anticipated. Indeed the aftermath of Alamein may be said to have proved as frustrating and frequently disappointing as the battle itself. The enemy had been decisively beaten in a fortnight's battle with more than half his front line forces killed, wounded or captured; but the protracted nature of the battle upset plans for what would happen in an eventual break-out.

Because Rommel's mobile remnants of the German-Italian Panzer Army were not in fact encircled in the aftermath of the battle of Alamein, a belief has arisen that this was primarily due to the excessive caution displayed by the Eighth Army Commander. This, however, is to telescope events; and the evidence, both of those closest to Montgomery at the time and of surviving documents, shows that, to start with at least, Montgomery intended to go all out

[1] Ibid.
[2] Address to 5 Corps, after Exercise No. 3, 17.2.41. See *Monty: The Making of a General, 1887–1942*, op. cit.

for a *coup de grâce* that would cut off Rommel's retreating forces as well as rounding up all unmotorised enemy troops:

By 5 November, SUPERCHARGE operation was finished, and a brilliant victory had been won,

the GSO 3 (Operations), Captain 'Dick' Vernon, recorded in his diary at Eighth Army Tac HQ.

The enemy was in full retreat and, through lack of transport, he was forced to leave a large portion of his force behind.
The battle was over, the pursuit began.
It must be realized, though, that the enemy, although defeated, was not destroyed. The power of recuperation of the Germans must not be underestimated. Two alternatives presented themselves:
a) With a small fast force, to cut him off and delay and perhaps destroy the disorganised remnants – at the same time attacking them from the air, and from the flank and rear with light forces;
b) To advance, as administrative limitations will allow, a large force, so large that he cannot possibly defeat it with one of his counterattacks, at the same time keeping contact with armoured cars.
At first, the first alternative was the one which the Army Comd [Commander] decided on.

Two plans for 'cutting off' forces had been laid before the battle. The first was a proposal to slip 4th Light Armoured Brigade to Daba through 13 Corps' front, if a break-through was made in the south; the second, Operation 'Grapeshot', was entered in Vernon's pre-battle diary as an all-out outflanking thrust by a force of almost a hundred tanks, directed as far as Tobruk:

b) A plan has been made and carefully studied for a force to move direct to TOBRUCH, should the Army Commander wish, at any time.
The force, probably commanded by Gen Gairdner (8 Armd Div) is based on 96 heavy tanks (3 Regts less their Light Sqns) on Diamond T transporters, each transporter carrying 5 tons am[munitio]n & petrol. 2 Bns Inf[antry], 16 × 25-prs, 45 Armd Cars, 3 Btys Lt AA with the bare minimum of transport. The force would be self-contained for 7 days after arrival at Tobruch. It can move to the frontier, if required. The ground staff for a Fighter Wing & NLO [Naval Liaison Officer] for Naval supply were incorporated in the force.[1]

[1] Brigadier H. R. W. Vernon, unpublished El Alamein diary, communicated to author.

Amidst the speculation that arose when Rommel's forces were *not* cut off, there were those who felt Operation 'Grapeshot' ought to have been put into effect, and might well have bottled up the remains of the German-Italian Army. Major-General de Guingand still felt so up to his death in 1979:

> I thought he ought to have rounded up the enemy. . . . During the battle of Alamein, taking bits and pieces from various Corps, I built up a reserve – tanks, armour, guns, troops, etcetera, and had them all formed up and ready; I used to see the commander General Gairdner every day. . . . But every day Monty would say he wanted some more troops and he'd pinch them from my 'Grapeshot' reserve and so when the great moment came – the breakthrough – it wasn't available. He just used Freyberg's forces to push on, instead of using fresh troops and armour.[1]

Liddell Hart, writing on the eve of his own death, blamed 'caution, hesitation, slow motion, and narrow manoeuvre' for missing the 'magnificent opportunity of cutting off and destroying Rommel's entire army'.[2]

Monty himself spurned such criticism, but forebore blaming anyone but the weather – which only broke some days after the pursuit had begun. To those who criticised the pace of the pursuit he pointed to its remarkable speed, '560 miles in 13 days', he recalled in his *Memoirs*; but as for 'missed opportunities' he refused to fret over them. He had been disappointed so many times during the battle of Alamein – particularly during 'Supercharge' when he hoped to put the Afrika Korps 'in the bag' – that it was futile, he felt, to concern himself over 'might have beens'. In his own mind he knew he had done everything possible to act boldly at the climax of the battle, and to try if possible to cut off those mobile Axis forces which succeeded in getting away from the battlefield. He had not succeeded because, despite the years spent fighting in the Middle East, Eighth Army was still not sufficiently trained in bold operations of manoeuvre – particularly at night. The *Corps de Chasse* he had created over the past nine weeks, and which had put up such a disappointing performance during the battle of Alamein, proved now equally disappointing in its mobile role.

---

[1] Interview of 7.5.78.
[2] B. Liddell Hart, *The Second World War*, London 1970.

CHAPTER THREE

The Race to Fuka

All through the battle of Alamein, de Guingand and his GSO 1 (Plans), Colonel Richardson, had attempted to have ready the Tobruk force envisaged by Montgomery before the battle. The original plan for ninety-six tanks to be carried on Diamond-T transporters, however, had to be dropped. There was no sign that Rommel would surrender his line of retreat along the coast road, and on investigation it was found that Diamond-T transporters would not be able to cope with the soft sand in a trans-desert operation; they could not therefore be launched before Eighth Army secured the harder going beyond Mersa Matruh – eighty miles from Alamein.

The plan 'was changed to Valentines on ordinary transporters,' Captain Vernon recorded in his diary. Major-General Gairdner[1] was to command the operation, 'making use of HQ 8 Armoured Div. Valentine tanks will be allotted to this Force. Assembly area south of Ghazal Station,' Brigadier de Guingand confirmed in orders on 3 November;[2] however, the fierce resistance put up by Rommel's mobile units made it less and less likely that a force of ill-armed Valentines, beyond air cover or administrative support, would achieve its object – and the proof of this is to be found in Major-General Gairdner's report, issued even before 'Supercharge' (Eighth Army's tank break-out) began. The whole concept of transporters and Valentines was mistaken, he felt now. 'The quickest method would appear to be with Sherman tanks across the desert,' he concluded.[3] It therefore came as little surprise when the operation was cancelled on 5 November.

Instead Montgomery concentrated on the Sherman and Grant tanks poised to encircle Rommel following the success of 'Super-

---

[1] Maj-General [later General Sir] Charles Gairdner held command of the skeleton 8th Armoured Division – a headquarters staff without troops or tanks. He later became Chief of Staff to Alexander during the planning stage of 'Husky', the invasion of Sicily, but was eventually relieved of this post. In 1944 he succeeded General Lumsden as Churchill's personal emissary to General Mac-Arthur in the Far East, and later became Governor of the State of W. Australia.

[2] Operation 'Grapeshot' (WO 169/647), PRO.

[3] Ibid.

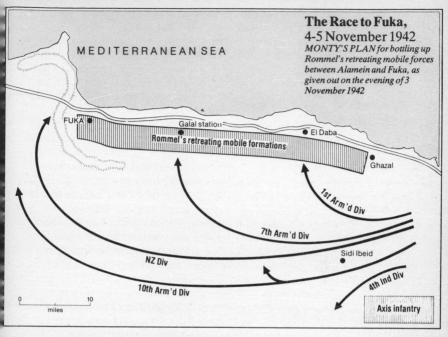

The Race to Fuka, 4-5 November 1942

MONTY'S PLAN for bottling up Rommel's retreating mobile forces between Alamein and Fuka, as given out on the evening of 3 November 1942

MEDITERRANEAN SEA

FUKA

Galal station

El Daba

Rommel's retreating mobile formations

Ghazal

1st Arm'd Div

7th Arm'd Div

NZ Div

Sidi Ibeid

10th Arm'd Div

4th Ind Div

0   10
miles

Axis infantry

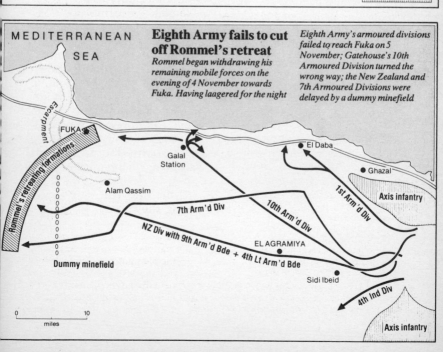

Eighth Army fails to cut off Rommel's retreat

Rommel began withdrawing his remaining mobile forces on the evening of 4 November towards Fuka. Having laagered for the night

Eighth Army's armoured divisions failed to reach Fuka on 5 November; Gatehouse's 10th Armoured Division turned the wrong way; the New Zealand and 7th Armoured Divisions were delayed by a dummy minefield

MEDITERRANEAN SEA

Escarpment

FUKA

Galal Station

El Daba

Ghazal

Rommel's retreating formations

Alam Qassim

Axis infantry

1st Arm'd Div

7th Arm'd Div

10th Arm'd Div

NZ Div with 9th Arm'd Bde + 4th Lt Arm'd Bde

EL AGRAMIYA

Dummy minefield

Sidi Ibeid

4th Ind Div

0   10
miles

Axis infantry

charge'. His orders were laid on the evening of 3 November, in the light of latest Y and Ultra intelligence about Rommel's plight. This plan was for the New Zealand Division to take 4th Light Armoured Brigade under command, by-pass Rommel's rear-guard, and make straight along the 'Barrel-Track' to Fuka where General Freyberg, the Commander of the force and 'hero' of the Alamein battle,[1] was to cut the coast road.[2] Meanwhile Herbert Lumsden, commanding 10 Corps, was to use his three armoured divisions to smash Rommel's remaining armoured and motorised units up against the sea – 'main task to operate Northwards and deal with cleaning up the coastal belt.' Oliver Leese, commanding 30 Corps, would press relentlessly westwards with his infantry into the northern sector while retaining command of Freyberg's outflanking force. Thus, in effect, 30 Corps would stopper both ends of Rommel's bottle, while 10 Corps would compress it like a steel corset against the sea.

Ultra decrypts on 4 November confirmed that Rommel did indeed intend to hold out around Daba, on the coast road short of Fuka[3] – and it was with some confidence that, on the white tablecloth in his mess-tent, Montgomery revealed to von Thoma the critical situation faced by Rommel on the evening of 4 November.

Though there were chances later of exploitation, this was in the eyes of most participants the only serious opportunity of surrounding with heavy armour the bulk of Rommel's motorised forces: a moment when the enemy was acknowledging defeat, when Axis communications were breaking down, and Hitler's 'stand or die' order had forced Rommel to risk staying to the bitter end.

Unfortunately, confusion on the British side was even greater than on the Axis side. The very concentration of so much armour and so many units in the narrow 'Supercharge' salient entailed enormous difficulties of organisation: and those theorists who later felt Montgomery should have done things differently had little idea of the complications. A great set-piece battle 'in one enormous minefield' was undergoing its metamorphosis into a race westwards – and the transformation involved a change in administration, tactics and psychology. Freyberg was the only divisional commander to have shown the leadership and toughness Montgomery looked for in his

[1] 'Freyberg is superb and is the best fighting Div Comd I have ever known . . . he *leads* his Division into battle, going himself in front in a Honey tank' – letter of 1.11.42 from Montgomery to Sir Alan Brooke, quoted in *Monty: The Making of a General, 1887–1942*, op. cit.

[2] 'NZ Div with 4 Lt Armd Bde and portion of 9 Armd Bde to break out and make for SIDI IBEID, and be prepared to move immediately to Fuka in order to block the enemy's withdrawal to the West' – confirmation of decisions made by Army Commander and communicated verbally to Corps Commanders concerned, 2030 hrs, 3.11.42, in Eighth Army Tac HQ Logs, Oct–Dec 1942 (WO 169/3911), PRO.

[3] Cf. F. H. Hinsley, *British Intelligence in the Second World War* Vol. I, London 1981.

armoured commanders in the North. Freyberg had been made responsible for the overall 'Supercharge' break-in, and it was entirely understandable that the Army Commander should wish to entrust him with the vital outflanking operation that would now take place, directed on Fuka. Nevertheless Freyberg was essentially an infantry commander; his elevation to command the counterpart of Rommel's mobile 90th Light Division only dated back a few weeks, and Montgomery was, therefore, entrusting the operation to a commander still relatively inexperienced in the handling of armour. As the senior officer in charge of Eighth Army Tactical Headquarters wrote, in annotating Vernon's diary: 'Surely wrong to place 4 LAB [Light Armoured Brigade] under NZ Div (putting a race horse in shafts)[1] – for, having delayed many hours while 4th Light Armoured Brigade joined him from Alamein station on 4 November, Freyberg faltered that evening and instead of continuing all night to Fuka as ordered, he cautiously signalled to all his echelons to close up and laager till morning.

In retrospect it might have been more sensible to have given the cutting-off role to Major-General John Harding's 7th Armoured Division – the 'Desert Rats'. Harding certainly felt so:

Once Supercharge had been launched and had secured a break-through I was ordered into pursuit to follow up the German forces. My first feeling was one of complete confusion when we started the breakout. We passed through the remains of 2nd Armoured Brigade, with a lot of burned-out tanks and that sort of thing: tremendous smoke and dust and you couldn't see or understand what was happening – it was an impression of unutterable confusion until we got clear of the battle fighting area. Once we were out in the open, then it was a feeling of tremendous exhilaration, that we'd got through and were heading in the right direction and were chasing the enemy. And then we came up against a rearguard position held by one of the Italian armoured divisions – Ariete, I think it was – and we fought them for the rest of the afternoon, and then we went on again. But to start with, getting out of the Alamein position into the open, my impression was only of terrible confusion and uncertainty. Mainly we kept together because Pip Roberts was commanding the armoured brigade and he kept very tight control of them.

My feeling is that after the initial exhilaration of getting out into the open and being on the move, and of disposing of the Italian armoured division that got in our way, was then one of frustration because the rain came down, also we couldn't get our petrol

[1] Maj-General M. St J. Oswald, annotations in diary of H. R. W. Vernon, loc. cit.

supplies, and of a feeling that Monty was being over-cautious, carrying out the pursuit on too broad a front. We had two armoured divisions and the New Zealand Divisions all competing for petrol and supplies and at that stage I felt frustrated. I reckoned I could have gone on my own.[1]

This was said with hindsight, knowing that the New Zealanders had taken three days to get round Fuka. Moreover it telescoped events – for to start with, it was not so much caution as control. Certainly the handling of the three armoured divisions of 10 Corps left much to be desired, and there is evidence that Montgomery's policy of decentralisation in fluid operations proved counter-productive in view of the lack of armoured leadership shown during the battle of Alamein. If Monty hoped that the reluctance which had characterised so much of the armour's performance at Alamein would turn to eager co-operation once the break-out had been achieved, he was to be disappointed – as well as maddened by General Lumsden's failure to maintain communications necessary for the Army Commander to control the pursuit. Determined to ensure a direct link with Lumsden, Montgomery detailed one of his headquarters staff, Major Mather, to act as Liaison Officer, attached personally to General Lumsden, and equipped with a special radio transmitter:

What happened: I was posted to 10 Corps Headquarters as a GSO 2 (Ops), but I was GSO 2 (Liaison) actually. My instruction was that I'd always got to be in a position to send back immediate information on what was happening at 10 Corps Headquarters. I had a jeep, a thing with a sort of aerial, which was two poles you stuck in the ground and you rigged the thing in between and sent back information on these two-pole Number Nine sets. This was when Herbert [Lumsden] was leading the break-out.

Now Herbert was a cavalry officer and wanted to get away from Monty, to be out of touch with him, and every time we stopped I tried to stick up my aerial, but before I had a chance to transmit the message we'd be off again. You see, I was complaining, saying we've got to get this back, Monty'll be furious. And he'd say, 'I was taught by Monty at the Staff College that it was the duty of the senior officer to come up to the junior officer when there's a battle on. It's not for me to go back to him.' And I said, 'But you've got to keep in touch with him, send a message back, he must know what's happening' – and Herbert got very stubborn. He said, 'It's his job to keep in touch with me, not me with him.' I said, 'Well,

[1] Field-Marshal Lord Harding of Petherton, interview of 9.4.81.

look, that's what I'm supposed to be doing, you must let me do it.'
But he wouldn't.

It was Herbert's fault. I was the person responsible for sending
that information back, and the moment I was ready to send it back,
off we went. I think he definitely intended to be out of touch with
Monty. He had his own plan for what he'd do. I think his main idea
was to advance as quickly as possible – we had them on the run,
his idea was to keep them on the run – and demolish them.[1]

For this outrageous obstructionism Monty eventually summoned
Lumsden back to army headquarters for a 'ticking off' – a summons
which the staff officers present well remembered. Lumsden was
furious at being recalled, and went into Montgomery's caravan an
angry man, evidently unaware that his own lack of professionalism
was about to cost him his job:

You've probably heard, we had a barometer in the ops room –
which was four ACVs [Armoured Command Vehicles] in a square
and over the whole thing a huge camouflage net. We had all these
big maps up, how the operations were going. Now on one map
wall we merely had a great barometer of all the leading figures and
commanders in the Eighth Army, all plotted up on a sort of graph,
like a stock exchange, showing how they were doing – which
general was on the way up, which general on the way down,
which brigadier on the way up, which down – all plotted on the
chart. . . .

I came back with Herbert Lumsden and he went in to see Monty.
Bill Williams [GSO 2, Intelligence] listened outside, and came back
and marked Herbert Lumsden's stock right down to bottom. And
Herbert came into the operations room afterwards, drew the
covering aside and looked, and never said a word, and went. A
very dramatic moment. . . .

He was very chastened, I must say. Later he was fired, but I
mean it was certainly decided in Monty's mind at that time when
he came back.[2]

Major (later Major-General) Oswald also remembered the occasion
vividly:

'Dick' Vernon, the GSO 3, and I were both there when Lumsden
came back and had a shouting match, and everybody said: 'Sell
Lumsden's!'
That was a hell of a slanging match. Our Tac and Main [head-

---

[1] Sir William Mather, interview of 23.1.80.
[2] Ibid.

quarters] must have been in the same place, the other side of Mersa Matruh, because Lumsden was saying loud and clear for everybody to hear: 'It's quite wrong that you've brought me all the way back here, when you taught me at the Staff College – you always said that the senior commander should come up and see the junior one – and here am I, I've come back miles and miles. . . .'[1]

Though Lumsden was upset at being thus reprimanded, there can be no doubt that his behaviour, as Commander of the *Corps de Chasse*, was an important factor in Eighth Army's missing the best chance it would ever have of surrounding Rommel's main mobile forces in a ring of armour. Whether Lumsden was entirely to blame is debatable. The orders given out by the Army Commander on the evening of 3 November were logical enough: 10 Corps would crush Rommel's armour against the Daba coast while 30 Corps would hold each end of the coastal bottleneck, at Fuka and Alamein. But in the very different circumstances of 4/5 November, with Army intelligence accurately monitoring Rommel's night retreat-march, Montgomery found himself powerless to alter either his plans or his command grouping. Vainly he attempted to signal to Lumsden, telling him to ignore the coast, concentrate all his forces on taking Fuka now, together with the Sidi Haneish landing grounds and, if he could, to push a force forward to 'Charing Cross', the exit road from Mersa Matruh, which was vitally needed as a port to bring up petrol and supplies.

Would Montgomery's change of policy on 5 November have succeeded in cutting off 90th Light Division and the remnants of the Afrika Korps if he had been able to contact Lumsden, and if Lumsden had ensured the Army Commander's new policy was obeyed? There is certainly no evidence that Montgomery was at this stage hindered by over-cautiousness or anxiety; on the contrary the evidence suggests he was vastly over-optimistic in assuming that he could effectively control the immediate aftermath of a twelve-day battle fought in relatively fixed positions. His decision initially to put Freyberg in charge of the cutting-off operation, and to retain Freyberg under Leese's operational command in 30 Corps, turned out to be his gravest error since taking command of Eighth Army in August – for even if Freyberg *had* shown the drive required to reach Fuka during the night of 4 November, it was impractical to expect Leese, with his main 30 Corps headquarters still in the north of Alamein, to control Freyberg out beyond another Corps, with appalling difficulties of communication by wireless or by land. Yet if Freyberg failed to stopper Rommel's retreat at Fuka by the morning of 5 November, then the whole rationale of Lumsden swinging his three armoured

[1] Loc. cit.

22

divisions up against the coast between Daba and Fuka was redundant. Message after message had been sent during the evening and night of 4 November, urging Freyberg to race for Fuka; at 6.30 p.m. on 4 November Leese had signalled 'by special cipher' that the South African Armoured Car Regiment claimed already to be in possession of the Fuka escarpment: '2 NZ Div to join them as soon as possible.' A little later Eighth Army's intelligence sent word that the Afrika Korps was 'preparing to withdraw', and at 10.40 p.m. the GSO 1 (Intelligence) telephoned Montgomery to say that 15th Panzer Division at least was 'directed on FUKA. If NZ Div go flat out they should just arrive first'. This information was passed by radio straight to Lumsden's and Leese's headquarters,[1] together with Montgomery's instruction that Lumsden's reserve armoured division (10th Armoured Division under Major-General Gatehouse), which earlier that evening had been ordered to move 'all night' on Daba, should now be re-routed to reinforce Freyberg at Fuka, as per Montgomery's contingency plan of 3 November.[2] At 3 a.m. on the morning of 5 November Monty's headquarters became alarmed lest Lumsden miss his chance, and another call was made to Lumsden's main headquarters: 'Army state RAF report solid mass of MET on road between FUKA and DABA and suggest 10 Corps press on.' This message was passed to Lumsden's Tactical Headquarters three-quarters of an hour later, and at 5.35 a.m. Lumsden sent out new orders: 10th Armoured Division, currently held up south of Ghazal station, only a few miles beyond Alamein, was now directed on Fuka 'and should press on as quickly as possible'.[3] Unfortunately Lumsden omitted to say exactly *how* or why Gatehouse should get to Fuka: and Gatehouse went the wrong way. Instead of taking the 'wider sweep directed on Fuka' as 10 Corps assumed at 6 a.m. when informing 30 Corps of its intentions, Gatehouse carried out a short hook to the coast to Galal station, fifteen miles *short* of Fuka – and then, in response to mistaken orders, he turned back towards Alamein instead of Fuka. Only 'at dusk' on 5 November did Gatehouse finally give orders for armoured regiments to move westwards again – *twelve hours* too late. Moreover, instead of holding his 7th

[1] 'There are indications that 15 Panzer Div is making for Fuka and should arrive approximately the same time as 2 NZ Div. 2 NZ Div was informed by 30 Corps and was instructed to get to Fuka as fast as possible' – Eighth Army HQ logs, 2300 hrs, 4 November; copy in consolidated formation and unit War Diaries drawn up by the office of the British Official Historian (CAB 106/792 *et seq.*), PRO.

[2] 'On reaching Fuka if the situation demands it, [Freyberg's force] to be prepared to send detachments to MATRUH. In this case 10 Corps may be ordered to move an armoured division to FUKA' – ibid.

[3] 10 Corps War Diary, ibid. At 6 a.m. on 5 November 10 Corps HQ had confirmed Lumsden's receipt of the Army Commander's instructions, and stated that '8 Armoured Brigade [the armoured brigade of 10th Armoured Division] is to take a wider sweep and is directed on Fuka' – ibid.

and 1st Armoured Divisions ready to push on *beyond* Fuka if necessary, Lumsden continued to direct them in onto the coast (between Galal and Daba) during the morning of 5 November – as per Montgomery's original directive thirty-six hours before. Harding was so disgusted with Lumsden that he now kept radio silence and tried to push westwards without Lumsden knowing:

> My idea was to go as hard and fast as I could across the desert and not to turn – I was under pressure to turn in to the road, which I resisted. That pressure was coming from the Corps, from Lumsden, or Lumsden's staff. I refused to turn in.[1]

By mid-day on 5 November, when he sent Alexander his latest 'Sitrep', Montgomery still had no idea that both Freyberg and Gatehouse had muffed their instructions: 'Progress of armoured divisions continued all night,' he declared, although none had moved. 'Results difficult to obtain owing to lengthening communications. 10 Armoured Div directed last night [4/5 November] on FUKA. Progress not at present known. . . .'[2]

Progress was, in fact, non-existent. Intercepts had warned Eighth Army Intelligence that the remnants of the Afrika Korps would be withdrawing during the night, but with Freyberg and all the British armoured divisions laagering like biblical caravans for the night where they were, there was little chance now of outflanking Rommel's German rearguard, let alone crushing it – and the waste of 5 November proved fatal to any prospect of atoning for the mistake. Already by 8.45 a.m. on 5 November Lumsden's headquarters knew that Gatehouse, 'who had been moving slowly' and had been 'requested to push on energetically and to act as long stop' at Fuka, was nowhere near Fuka – but still it failed to draw the correct conclusion and simply reported obtusely at 12.30 p.m. that 10th Armoured Division had only reached Galal 'having had small tank battle'. In fact Gatehouse was claiming to have knocked out twenty-eight Italian M13 tanks, four German Mk 3s and one German Mk 2 – a respectable 'bag' which virtually destroyed the surviving Italian 20 Mobile Corps, but fatal to Eighth Army's hopes of cutting off Rommel's German rearguard. Worse still, Gatehouse had been 'particularly anxious that air does not attack' his '8th armoured brigade'.[3] So from eight till ten in the morning he had insisted on full fighter cover 'when he expects to be in the Daba area'.[4] This meant that the RAF, nervous of German Air Force intentions west of Alamein, failed to bomb the retreating Axis forces and merely

---

[1] Interview of 23.5.79
[2] Eighth Army Sitrep, 1200 hrs, 5 November (CAB 106/794), PRO.
[3] 10 Corps War Diary extract (CAB 106/794), PRO.
[4] Ibid.

sheltered behind Gatehouse's – and Freyberg's – appeal for fighter cover.

Montgomery's wrath was rising. He had intended Lumsden to 'push on' all night on 4 November to Fuka, where the New Zealand Division ought to have been attacking the escarpment that commanded the sole coastal road. Instead Lumsden was dithering near Daba; the New Zealanders – after stopping for the night – got held up by a dummy minefield and failed to reach Fuka even by the following nightfall; and Coningham, instead of relentlessly punishing Rommel's only escape road westwards with his Desert Air Force, merely gave fighter cover to Gatehouse and Freyberg, while sending a message to Montgomery, via de Guingand, asking the New Zealanders to send detachments forward to take the German landing grounds twenty miles *beyond* Fuka, in order to stop the Luftwaffe from interfering with British air force operations!

De Guingand, at midday on 5 November, had sent a desperate message from Eighth Army Main Headquarters warning the Army Commander that Rommel was getting away: 'Enemy transport now extends 4 miles west of Fuka to Matruh. Time of report 1000 hrs. Our party moving up will be too late.'[1] De Guingand suggested that Lumsden take command of the New Zealanders immediately and send 4th Light Armoured Brigade across the desert to take the 'Charing Cross' cross-roads west of Mersa Matruh 'which I mentioned this morning'. He also begged that Coningham be asked to 'reduce protection' of Eighth Army's units and 'act offensively against transport'.[2] His message was received by Montgomery's Tactical Headquarters, but Montgomery was out. An hour later, though, Montgomery confirmed that 'RAF fighter cover can be dispensed with and all fighters used against the enemy'. He had, he also stated, now spoken to Lumsden and 'discussed role of 4th Light Armoured Brigade and armoured cars' – the brigade being ordered on 'Charing Cross' forthwith.[3] In order to spur Lumsden on, moreover, Montgomery regrouped the army, putting Freyberg under Lumsden forthwith, and relegating the dilatory Gatehouse to Leese's 30 Corps.

Lumsden had intended that Gatehouse's 10th Armoured Division should act as 'longstop' in the original 'crushing' operation after Alamein; after his new 'discussion' with Montgomery it was decided that only an all-out, all-night outflanking march by the 1st and 7th Armoured Divisions might still cut Rommel off. It looked as though Rommel was intending to hold Fuka with his remaining German infantry; by racing Eighth Army armour deep across the desert, and

[1] Eighth Army HQ Logs extract (CAB 106/794), PRO.
[2] Ibid.
[3] Ibid.

25

bringing 7th Armoured Division in behind Fuka, while 4th Light Armoured Brigade and 1st Armoured Division closed off the 'Charing Cross' exit from the Mersa Matruh, Rommel's fate might yet be sealed. Gatehouse's 10th Armoured Division would be passed back to Leese's 30 Corps, and 'Grapeshot', the Valentine-tank sortie aimed at Tobruk, cancelled completely.[1]

Eighth Army had bungled its first chance of destroying the fleeing enemy in an unfortunate display of confusion, lack of communications, and incoherent command – something which Bernard Montgomery's supremely logical, clear-cut mind was loath to acknowledge. In his diary and in his later accounts, Monty simply excised all mention of the confusion that had reigned on 5 November. In his diary he recorded the break-out as though it was a copy-book exercise:

During the night 4/5 November the enemy withdrew from his delaying position South of GHAZAL Station and the pursuit then began in earnest. I regrouped the Army.

10 Corps [Lt-General Lumsden]
    1 Arm'd Div   [Maj-General Briggs]
    7 Arm'd Div   [Maj-General Harding]
    2 NZ Div   [Lt-General Freyberg]

30 Corps [Lt-General Leese]
    10 Arm'd Div   [Maj-General Gatehouse]
    51 Highland Div   [Maj-General Wimberley]
    9 Aust Div   [Maj-General Morshead]

13 Corps [Lt-General Horrocks]
    SA Div   [Maj-General Pienaar]
    44 Div   (132 Bde, 1 FF Bde)   [Maj-General Hughes]
    50 Div (69 Bde, 2 FF Bde, 1 Greek Bde)   [Maj-General Nichols]

10 Corps to lead the advance.
Obectives
1. FUKA
2. MATRUH
3. BARRANI–KHAMZA
4. SOLLUM–HALFAYA–AZIZ–BARDIA
5. TOBRUK–EL ADEM
6. DERNA–MECHELI [Martuba airfield area]

Immediately we broke through on morning 4 November, I had ordered the SA Armd Car Regt to secure the bottle-neck at FUKA. These cars reached FUKA on late afternoon 4 November.

The NZ Div followed up on 4 November, but met a large enemy

---

[1] It was cancelled at 1745 hrs on 5 November. Order from Main Eighth Army, in Operation 'Grapeshot' (WO 169/647), PRO.

column [sic] and became engaged with it. The Div pressed on towards FUKA on 5 November.

30 Corps to remain in the area GALAL Station to ALAMEIN.

13 Corps to remain in the original ALAMEIN position and get the area cleaned up.

However the pursuit itself on 5 November was anything but copy-book, and there can be little doubt that its failure – though suppressed by Montgomery – reinforced his already growing conviction about the inherent inability of British armoured formations to function with the aplomb of their German counterparts. It is easy to say, in retrospect, that he ought to have launched one of his armoured divisions deep into the desert to secure 'Charing Cross' and Mersa Matruh – fifty miles beyond Fuka – the moment the break-out occurred on 4 November, lest his plan for crushing Rommel's remnants against the sea between Alamein and Fuka failed. But this is said with hindsight. In the euphoric atmosphere at the end of the twelve-day battle, knowing that an historic victory had been achieved, with tens of thousands of prisoners being taken – including the Commander of the Afrika Korps himself – no one could have predicted Rommel's escape. And if Freyberg's force could not even reach Fuka before Rommel, could any Eighth Army formation have achieved the deeper and longer outflanking march to 'Charing Cross'?

Even on the evening of 5 November there was no slackening in the euphoria, however. Like a tidal wave the whole of Eighth Army was poised to rush forward in the aftermath of victory, and it was necessary for the Army Commander to be quite firm in grounding the two infantry Corps commanded by Generals Leese and Horrocks.

The pursuit would be a strictly mobile operation, he declared – even to the point of taking away the third armoured division in Lumsden's Corps (Gatehouse's 10th Armoured Division) and assigning it to Leese. Lumsden's failure on 5 November was to be regretted, but it was by no means catastrophic: the New Zealand, 1st Armoured and 7th Armoured Divisions were all fully-equipped, well-armed bodies of fighting men who, with luck, could still outflank Rommel's remnant flight along the coast road.

There were now conflicting objectives, though. It was imperative to reach the Cyrenaican airfields around Derna – still four hundred miles away – within eleven days if Malta was to be saved; more forward landing grounds were required if the forward movement of 10 Corps was to be given full air support; and there was the military priority of bringing Rommel's remaining forces to battle – preferably between Fuka and Mersa Matruh – in order to complete the victory of Alamein.

The first two objectives Montgomery would achieve. But the third would come lamentably to grief in a morass of rain-bogged vehicles and petrol-starved tanks.

CHAPTER FOUR

A Change of Plan

To change the whole accent of Eighth Army's operations from armoured *coup de grâce* to one of deep-desert manoeuvre more than a hundred miles beyond the battlefield of Alamein was to acknowledge that Montgomery's first plan had failed. Yet to effect such a change of plan beyond the field of battle when operations are fluid and communications difficult was perhaps too much to expect of an army that, despite its proud cavalry traditions, was still no match for Rommel's Afrika Korps in dexterity and speed of deployment. In fact there would be evidence that Monty was living almost in a different world, a state of post-battle optimism in which he could not immediately credit the slowness and failures of command of his own army – an army which knew more accurately the dispositions of Rommel's echelon headquarters than it did its own, so that, for instance, on the morning of 5 November Leese had no idea where Freyberg's headquarters were, nor that Freyberg had laagered for the night fifty kilometres short of his object; and Lumsden's headquarters, similarly, was at 6 a.m. still unaware where two of its armoured divisions – 1st and 7th – might be: 'cannot get their exact location,' as it reported to Army headquarters dolefully.[1]

Monty's fatal mistake had been to imagine he could effectively seal Rommel's escape route by sending Freyberg in a night march around the enemy's armoured flank to cut in 'behind his back'. It was a bold gamble which committed his entire *Corps de Chasse* to an armoured battle on the coast between Ghazal, Daba, Galal and Fuka – but one which would work only if Freyberg was successful in outflanking Rommel – which he was not. Gatehouse had, as reserve armoured divisional commander, either never personally received the order to reinforce Freyberg's thrust or had ignored it; and when the two other armoured divisions *did* thrust up against the coast on the morning of 5 November the cupboard had been bare – for Rommel had shunted his rearguard into a semi-circle around Fuka: a screen with which the unfortunate Freyberg had then collided.

Ironically it was Montgomery's desire to destroy the enemy's remaining forces which had been his undoing – a far cry from the

---

[1] Eighth Army HQ Logs extract (CAB 106/794), PRO.

'cautiousness' which critics have ascribed to him after Alamein.

But how to recover from the errors that had been made? Tremendous pressures were now being brought to bear. Nervous of committing his air forces over enemy territory, Air Marshal Coningham, the Desert Air Force Commander, had failed to take advantage of the 'sitting-duck' targets afforded by the fleeing Axis transport columns. Instead he had concentrated on the 'safer' tasks of giving close air support to Eighth Army's pursuit forces – and declaring that until these forces flushed the enemy landing grounds beyond Fuka, at Sidi Haneish, they could not undertake more. This was a tragedy – as the almost 'empty' escape road would later bear witness. Yet simultaneously Ultra intelligence was suggesting that Rommel's intention *was* to stand and 'fight it out' on the coast around Fuka – and as late as 2 p.m. on 5 November Major Williams was signalling to Monty: 'Reliable information points to enemy attempt to make stand at Fuka. Disorganisation considerable. Should create good opportunity.'[1]

Monty's new plan, for a wide outflanking march across the desert, this time using his armoured divisions rather than Freyberg's New Zealanders, thus looked appropriate on paper. Freyberg would now attack and pin Rommel down at Fuka, while Generals Harding and Briggs followed 4th Light Armoured Brigade with their 7th and 1st Armoured Divisions across the desert and then cut in behind the enemy at Mersa Matruh – where armoured cars of Eighth Army were already operating.

Freyberg, however, either never received Lumsden's new order to release 4th Light Armoured Brigade, or found it too heavily engaged towards the evening of 5 November at Fuka to detach it – so that, once again, the 'plugging of the bath', this time at Mersa Matruh, never took place. It was then left to the two armoured divisions to perform the manoeuvre without the fast reconnaissance brigade on which de Guingand and Montgomery had both reckoned.

Harding, at least, was well-placed for the change in plan for, as has been seen, he refused to turn his 'Desert Rats' in towards Daba on the morning of 5 November, sensing that the bird had flown. Lumsden's new orders reached him shortly after mid-day, instructing him now to outflank Fuka entirely by moving westwards across the desert. However he too hit the dummy minefield encountered by the New Zealanders, and it was only in failing light on 5 November that his division managed to push through – close laagering for the night at 5 p.m. while waiting for 'replenishment' echelons to bring up petrol and ammunition for the next day's leap forward.

General Briggs, commanding 1st Armoured Division, only received the new orders at 2 p.m. on 5 November when surveying the

[1] Ibid.

empty net at Daba, but 'was carrying out replenishments' and couldn't move. At 4 p.m. Briggs made a plan 'to contain the enemy in Matruh by making a quick night march and cutting up North via Bir Khalda',[1] and soon after 5 p.m. on 5 November the first elements moved off into the dusk. Despite running into an enemy laager in pitch dark shortly before midnight the division managed admirably, and by dawn on 6 November was almost at Bir Khalda, well behind the enemy, ready to make north for 'Charing Cross'.

Brigg's night march was exemplary, but in the two nights since the final break-through at Alamein it was the only major formation to have moved by night, at a time when Rommel's rearguard was moving by night and fighting by day. Whether Monty yet realised that no Eighth Army formation had in fact moved during the night of 4 November is unclear; but he was certainly adamant that on the night of 5 November the opportunity be seized, and Mersa Matruh be taken from the rear. At 7.30 p.m. on 5 November he sent a 'Most Immediate' signal both to Lumsden personally and to Lumsden's Main Headquarters: 'Following from Army Commander for General Lumsden: Important you secure Matruh as early as possible as enemy is using that place to evacuate personnel and stores on lighters. Enemy may land petrol for use of his MT east of that place. Press on with all speed to Charing Cross and Matruh and thus prevent petrol from coming forward. Also drive enemy off airfields 13 and 101 South of Sidi Haneish which are now his chief air bases.'[2]

Rommel had meanwhile hoped that by making a stand at Fuka he could hold off Montgomery 'long enough for the Italian and German infantry to catch up', as he recorded in his papers;[3] but was soon alarmed by the prospect of his remnant forces being outflanked. His 15th Panzer Division recorded in its War Diary that already by the evening of 4 November it had been reduced to six tanks, and at 1.45 p.m. on 5 November it noted that 'the enemy was trying to outflank the division'. By 5 p.m. the Acting Afrika Korps Commander had ordered the division 'to withdraw that night to the Mersa Matruh area to avoid being encircled by vastly superior enemy forces which were in pursuit'. However, for this withdrawal the division urgently needed more petrol which did not arrive till late in the evening. Only at 11 p.m. on 5 November did the division move off again, 'having been directed to the area 30 Km South-East of Mersa Matruh'[4] – 'Charing Cross'. But 21st Panzer Division, although ordered to do the same, ran out of petrol half-way there, right by the

[1] 1st Armoured Division War Diary extract (CAB 106/794), PRO.
[2] Eighth Army HQ Logs extract (CAB 106/794), PRO.
[3] Rommel's decision to delay at Fuka was confirmed by Eighth Army Intelligence identifications of the two remnant Panzer divisions near Fuka at 3 p.m., 6 p.m. and 6.35 p.m.
[4] 15th Panzer Division War Diary (GDMS 24902), IWM.

Sidi Haneish landing grounds so urgently needed by the RAF. 'It was a wild helter-skelter drive through another pitch black night,' Rommel recalled.[1]

Here then was the making of a second great opportunity for Eighth Army to close a trap, but when Monty awoke on the morning of 6 November in bouncing form he was unaware that, once again, his Army had slept while the enemy withdrew 'to avoid encirclement'. 7th Armoured Division was still south of Fuka, and the New Zealanders, instead of relentlessly *attacking* the Afrika Korps in the afternoon to pin Rommel down, merely positioned itself, as was recorded in its War Diary, 'ready to prevent the enemy breaking out from the Fuka escarpment to the South'.[2]

Quite why Rommel should have wished to move *south* into open desert when he was protecting his baggage train fleeing westwards is unclear – for the War Diarist was well aware of the enemy's real intention:

It was considered quite likely that the enemy would withdraw along the main road during the night as he was obviously merely covering the withdrawal of his last retreating force.[3]

Instead of forcing the enemy to stand and fight as Monty wished, Freyberg – who had 'rations and water for 8 days' and 'petrol for 200 miles' – had clearly decided to avoid battle, reserving his force for future mobile manoeuvre.

This was fiddling while Rome burned, as Lumsden made bitterly clear to Freyberg some days later when the fiasco was over. Of course Lumsden, as Corps Commander, should have been on the spot to ensure Freyberg played his part in the trap, instead of which, at 5.09 p.m. on 5 November, Lumsden merely sent a signal to 10 Corps formations laying down the future policy – a policy in which the New Zealanders were, the next day, simply to move west and take over the Sidi Haneish/Quasaba landing grounds. 'Accordingly the 5th [New Zealand Infantry] Brigade were ordered not to get heavily involved [at Fuka],' the New Zealand Divisional War Diarist explained, 'as a fast move to Baggush to secure the landing grounds might be necessary on the following day.'[4]

Finally, 10th Armoured Division which, on the afternoon of 5 November, Lumsden had ordered to attack Fuka along the coast, only began to move towards the escarpment at dusk – and *also* closed down for the night. This tragedy cannot have escaped Lumsden's attention, for Lumsden stayed the night at Gatehouse's 10th

[1] Ibid.
[2] NZ Division War Diary extract (CAB 106/794), PRO.
[3] Ibid.
[4] Ibid.

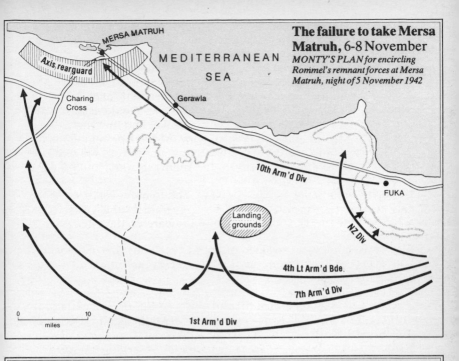

The failure to take Mersa Matruh, 6-8 November

MONTY'S PLAN for encircling Rommel's remnant forces at Mersa Matruh, night of 5 November 1942

MERSA MATRUH

MEDITERRANEAN SEA

Axis rearguard

Charing Cross

Gerawla

FUKA

10th Arm'd Div

NZ Div

Landing grounds

4th Lt Arm'd Bde.

7th Arm'd Div

1st Arm'd Div

0   10
miles

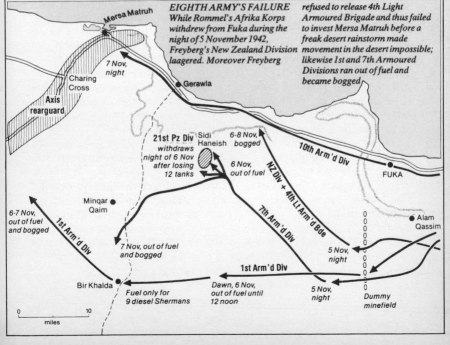

EIGHT ARMY'S FAILURE
While Rommel's Afrika Korps withdrew from Fuka during the night of 5 November 1942, Freyberg's New Zealand Division laagered. Moreover Freyberg refused to release 4th Light Armoured Brigade and thus failed to invest Mersa Matruh before a freak desert rainstorm made movement in the desert impossible; likewise 1st and 7th Armoured Divisions ran out of fuel and became bogged

Mersa Matruh

7 Nov, night

Charing Cross

Axis rearguard

Gerawla

21st Pz Div withdraws night of 6 Nov after losing 12 tanks

Sidi Haneish

6-8 Nov, bogged

10th Arm'd Div

FUKA

6 Nov, out of fuel

NZ Div + 4th Lt Arm'd Bde

Minqar Qaim

6-7 Nov, out of fuel and bogged

1st Arm'd Div

7 Nov, out of fuel and bogged

7th Arm'd Div

5 Nov, night

Alam Qassim

Bir Khalda

Fuel only for 9 diesel Shermans

1st Arm'd Div

Dawn, 6 Nov, out of fuel until 12 noon

5 Nov, night

Dummy minefield

0   10
miles

Armoured Division headquarters, a division at the tail end of his pursuit Corps, and which Monty had ordered to be assigned to Leese's follow-up Corps at first light on 6 November.

Only gradually on that morning did it become clear to Monty that Lumsden had yet again failed to carry out his orders. 4th Light Armoured Brigade had never been detached and sent ahead to 'Charing Cross'; 7th Armoured Division had closed down for the night near Fuka; 10th Armoured Division had closed down for the night near Daba – and only 1st Armoured Division was following the South African and British armoured cars through the night to reach Mersa Matruh. That Monty was plainly not amused was reflected by a signal that went out to 10 Corps Headquarters from de Guingand:

My 9 wishes to see your 9 at my new home tonight.[1]

Lumsden, however, remained out of touch all day on 6 November, and at 2 p.m. a further signal was despatched to *all* 10 Corps formations:

Army Commander stated that he must see Commander 10 Corps today. . . . If he fails to meet Cmdr 10 Corps during the afternoon, Cmdr 10 Corps must meet the Army Cmdr at 835321 late afternoon.[2]

All that day Eighth Army Intelligence charted the positions, panic and petrol crises of the German Panzer divisions as they dug in or – in the case of 21st Panzer Division – attempted to reach the minefields outside Mersa Matruh. Moreover at 8.30 a.m. Eighth Army's South African armoured car regiment had appealed for support in the 'Charing Cross' area: '4/6 SAAC report two squadrons now operating in area CHARING CROSS have taken large number PW's, probably about 1800. Asked 10 Corps to take action regarding them.'[3]

To Monty, the failure of the tank units of 10 Corps to move through the night and reinforce the valiant armoured car squadrons was galling, as it was to others at Eighth Army headquarters. Brigadier Sidney Kirkman, Eighth Army's Chief Gunner, shook his head sadly when, almost forty years later, he reflected on the 'lack of an effective pursuit':

But again, this is war. It is a terrible thing, but when you have got on well, had a victory, there's a tendency for everyone to sit down

[1] Eighth Army HQ Logs extract (CAB 106/794), PRO.
[2] Ibid.
[3] Ibid.

and do nothing. And we're particularly bad at this aspect of war – we were in the war anyway. But you can't blame it all on Monty. He didn't plan the pursuit well in my view, but who got through? Armoured cars! What a nonsense! Armoured cars are one of the most vulnerable . . . to think that the armoured cars had the guts, if you like, to break through as they did, and the tanks hadn't done it, is a terrible reflection on the tanks.

It was the armoured car regiments, who had been kept out of all these casualties [at Alamein], kept in the rear, fresh, full of enthusiasm, who broke through. And Monty should have kept some tanks out for that purpose, in my view.

In Kirkman's opinion one fresh division – one fresh brigade – could have ended Rommel's flight, as a cheetah leaps upon a fleeing prey and, clinging to its neck, chokes it to death. Kirkman insisted that

> you didn't want a whole lot of troops. You wanted at most a division – I'd almost say a brigade – it was all that was required. The place was cluttered up with too many people trying to get through. All that was wanted was one division under a determined commander – that's essential – that's all you wanted. You didn't want a whole *Corps de Chasse*.

> It didn't need to be an armoured division either, merely mobile. Might have been Tuker [Commander 4th Indian Division], might have been Bernard Freyberg, might have been John Harding himself. . . .[1]

Freyberg's desultory performance at Fuka, and even Harding's failure to get beyond Fuka by first light on 6 November, scarcely bear out this proposition: but the fact is undeniable that Eighth Army's attempt to wrap up the remaining Axis mobile forces came ultimately to grief in a mixture of lethargy, confusion, caution, lack of communication and administrative chaos; and it certainly explains why Kirkman, Harding, Tuker and many other distinguished commanders later rued Monty's decision to employ Lumsden and his unwieldy, often plainly disobedient *Corps de Chasse*.

Events on 6 November, however, were to bring Eighth Army's failings to a head. Freyberg, who had slept behind the dummy minefield all night, announced obtusely at 8 a.m. on that day that 'might have to do a set-piece this morning'[2] – in spite of the fact that the enemy in front of him at Fuka had vanished overnight. Worse, he *still* refused to part with 4th Light Armoured Brigade, which should

[1] General Sir Sidney Kirkman, interview of 16.4.80.
[2] Message from 10 Corps, in Eighth Army HQ Logs extract (CAB 106/794), PRO.

have been securing 'Charing Cross' the previous night. On the coast road, Gatehouse's armoured division only reached Fuka at *midday* on 6 November, so that, in effect, no attempt had been made to pin Rommel's rearguard down at Fuka while the armoured divisions raced across the desert to outflank Rommel.

These two armoured divisions did at least try to reach their objectives. Major-General Briggs's 1st Armoured Division, having moved all through the night of 5 November, found at dawn on 6 November that its new Sherman tanks were completely out of fuel – having consumed an average of one gallon every three miles. 'At dawn 2 Armoured Brigade deployed 16 miles short of Khalda and there waited until noon for petrol to arrive with B1 echelon,' the War Diary recorded. 'A plan was made for 10th Hussars to cut the main road west of Charing Cross' with another tank regiment on the Siwa track, and the third tank regiment 'half-way between, in a position to support either regiment'.[1] After six hours of waiting a petrol convoy arrived, but tragically with only enough fuel for nine diesel Shermans to continue. Both Briggs and the Brigadier went with this group – but at 5.30 p.m. on 6 November it too came to a halt 'for want of petrol'. 'There was no petrol in the brigade and the 9th Lancers laagered for the night at that point' – a bare ten miles short of 'Charing Cross', and within sight, by recce elements, of 'a column of 1,000 MT and guns. 2 Armoured Brigade unable to cut off this column owing to lack of petrol.'[2]

Meanwhile 7th Armoured Division, which was ordered to seize the Sidi Haneish landing grounds and then encircle the enemy at Matruh, *also* ran out of fuel on 6 November, ironically at the same spot where 21st Panzer Division was immobilised for the same reason. The two divisions joined battle, and in the ensuing skirmish 21st Panzer Division left twelve of its remaining tanks knocked out or demolished. To its chagrin 7th Armoured Division had to watch while the surviving Germans, receiving fresh fuel, retreated into the night, leaving their British opponents in possession of the battlefield but paralysed without petrol.

But the want of fuel was not all. By midday on 6 November rain began to fall, and instead of the light 'showers'[3] that had been forecast the lowering sky turned black, lightning struck and torrential rain descended on the desert, turning it rapidly into a morass. The extra supply vehicles ordered up failed to arrive as the lorries sank axle-deep into the sandy bog; radio communication became impossible and any hope that Eighth Army might, at its second

[1] Ibid.
[2] Ibid.
[3] 'Weather report for the next 3 days: Belt of cloud 15,000–20,000 ft . . . moving slowly eastwards. Cloud will probably produce local showers. Remainder of area: outlook fair to fine.' Eighth Army HQ Logs extract (CAB 106/794), PRO.

attempt, cut off the enemy retreat was washed away. 'All ranks soaking wet and no question of sleep,' the War Diary of 22nd Armoured Brigade recorded dolefully that night.[1]

Lumsden, ordered to appear before the Army Commander that evening, duly received his 'rocket' – but even as Monty spoke, Eighth Army's chance of encirclement was being wrecked by the rain. The Desert Air Force had to suspend use of its forward landing grounds, and Rommel, who thought his last hour had come, was saved.

'Move by night – fight by day' had been the motto of Major-General Montgomery when training his 3rd 'Iron' Division in the months preceding Dunkirk. It was a maxim which the survivors of the Afrika Korps had carried out as brilliantly as had the 3rd Division in 1940, whereas with the exception of Briggs's 1st Armoured Division on the night of 5 November, no British armoured formation moved by night after Alamein.

Every participant had his own explanation of the failure – and his own scapegoat. But in the final analysis Montgomery must bear the blame. He had not himself assumed direct command of the pursuit, but had entrusted the encirclement of Rommel's rearguard to a Corps Commander who proved unable to control or administer his forces in a battle of manoeuvre.

The lesson would not be lost on Montgomery. In the prolonged and bloody battle of Alamein he had had repeatedly to overrule Lumsden and to keep the tightest personal control over the progress of the battle. In doing so he had hoped the *Corps de Chasse* would perform better, once out of the confines of the 'enormous minefield' of Alamein. But it had not: it had slept while the defeated enemy fled. Heads would have to roll, and as Army Commander he would have to re-think both his own role as Army Commander and his expectations of what was still a very amateur army. The great achievement of Alamein must not be squandered by undertaking ambitious operations that were beyond the capabilities of Eighth Army's formations.

If the battles of Alam Halfa and then Alamein had formed the foundation-stones of the reborn Eighth Army, it was the two chaotic failures *after* Alamein, at Fuka and Mersa Matruh, that provided the catalyst in creating a legendary desert army that would make its way across the North African continent thereafter.

[1] Ibid.

CHAPTER FIVE

Mersa Matruh – 'A Complete Nonsense'

Eighth Army had undoubtedly let the remaining enemy escape. Nevertheless it was a defeated enemy, which had left almost a third of its forces to be captured, had suffered grievous casualties, and lost all but a skeleton of its equipment. 'Thousands of the troops do not even have rifles,' Rommel complained to Hitler some weeks later. 'Because they threw them away,' was Hitler's acid reply. In the account he wrote after the fall of Africa, Rommel confessed: 'The only forces which retained any fighting strength were the remnants of the 90th Light Division, the Afrika Korps' two divisions – now reduced to the strength of small combat groups – the Panzer Grenadier Regiment Afrika and a few quickly scratched together German units, the remains of 164th Light Division. Tanks, heavy AA guns, heavy and light artillery, all had sustained such frightful losses at Alamein that there was nothing but a few remnants left.'[1]

On the afternoon of 6 November an emissary from Marshal Cavallero of the Comando Supremo arrived to hear the latest news from Rommel, and was 'visibly shaken' when Rommel told him the Axis army was shattered, the unmotorised Italian infantry lost, the 20th Italian Motorised Corps 'practically wiped out' – and that there was no chance of holding on to Egypt. 'Speed was the one thing that mattered,' Rommel declared – speed of retreat. His intention was to 'hold on to Mersa Matruh for a few more days and thus gain time for some defences to be constructed at Sollum' on the Libyan-Egyptian

[1] *The Rommel Papers*, London 1953. Only 12,900 Germans and 17,456 Italian casualties were admitted by German sources, but as 31,802 prisoners were counted in British POW cages alone, after the battle, the British Official Historian revised the estimated total of Axis casualties – killed, wounded and missing (mostly prisoners) to 39,000 (CAB 106/770, PRO). In his C-in-C's Despatch, Alexander claimed that 'rather less than one third of Rommel's original force' escaped death, wounding or capture. His staff calculated that '10,000 of the enemy are believed to have been killed and 15,000 wounded'. This together with the prisoners who were actually counted, would make a total Axis figure of almost 57,000 casualties (extract CAB 106/794, PRO).

Of the 600 Axis tanks '450 were left on the battlefield of Alamein. Over 1,000 pieces of artillery were destroyed or captured, and large quantities of ammunition, stores. . . .' – ibid.

frontier; for the 'torrential rain', though it forced the Axis retreat to keep to the single coastal road, promised at least to paralyse any British outflanking moves through the bogged desert.[1]

Meanwhile, despite the 'dressing down' he had given Lumsden on the evening of 6 November, Monty was still full of optimism. He had already grounded both 30 and 13 Corps at Alamein the previous day, and like Rommel his eyes were now on Sollum and the Halfaya Pass, on the Egyptian frontier. Once he had taken this, he planned a 'four days pause' before moving on Tobruk on 14 November, thus ensuring capture of the Martuba airfields in time to cover the Malta re-supply convoy. He wanted Lumsden to take Matruh 'on the evening 6 November', Sidi Barrani on 7 November, and the whole Sollum-Halfaya-Aziz frontier position by 9 November; and in anticipation he therefore ordered Main Eighth Army Headquarters forward from Burg-el-Arab to Daba on the morning of 6 November, and gave instructions that it should set up shop in Mersa Matruh on the 7th.

'The method of advance to the frontier,' General Alexander's Liaison Officer to Eighth Army Headquarters reported to Cairo on the morning of 7 November, 'will be NZ Div along the coast road, 7 Armoured Div South of the escarpment. 4/6 SAAC will patrol to the frontier and if they encounter no opposition will recce as far as Tobruk. If Tobruk is strongly held and an attack in force is needed to capture it there will be a pause for maintenance preparatory to the attack. If it is not held the pursuit will continue.'[2]

However, it was not Tobruk which was held, it was Matruh. Montgomery was taken completely unawares by Rommel's stand, for it seemed to him inconceivable and unsoldierly for Rommel to allow his whole rearguard to become bottled up in a peninsular town that could so easily be outflanked. Thus when unconfirmed reports came in on the morning of 7 November that Matruh had fallen, Monty eagerly believed them, as did his Main Headquarters staff. Taking Monty's stepson Dick Carver with him, Hugh Mainwaring, the Chief of Eighth Army's Operations staff set off that morning to find a new site for Main Eighth Army Headquarters in Mersa Matruh – and was straight away captured.

The euphoria which, like a tidal wave, had swept the pursuit formations and their headquarters forward from Alamein now at last began to dissipate. Once again Monty felt let down by Lumsden, who had failed to give 'even approximate location of Corps, Divisions etc.' since the previous evening. Far from having captured Mersa Matruh the previous night, 1st Armoured Division was stuck in the desert south of the 'Charing Cross' minefields without petrol,

[1] *The Rommel Papers*, op. cit.
[2] LO Reports from Eighth Army (WO 169/3802), PRO.

as were 7th Armoured Division at Quasaba, and the New Zealand Division at Sidi Haneish. The *Corps de Chasse* was at a standstill, and all eyes turned now to Gatehouse's 10th Armoured Division, working its way westwards along the asphalt highway of the coastal axis, relatively unaffected by the rain and with ample petrol.

The unfortunate Gatehouse, dismissed from the *Corps de Chasse* after his failure to take Fuka as ordered on the night of 4 November, may justifiably have felt at sixes and sevens when, on the morning of 7 November, he suddenly found himself leading Eighth Army's pursuit – 10 Corps being bogged in the desert. However, instead of seizing this golden opportunity, he gave the same display of poor leadership as he had in the opening stages of the battle of Alamein – recalled by Sir Sidney Kirkman many years later. Following in the wake of Eighth Army's headquarters staff, Kirkman found himself 'eventually alongside some tanks and I saw ahead of me an empty road'.

Now I thought: in the First World War an empty road always worried me – because you always worried who was in possession: sometimes they were your property or the Boches'. I was always cautious about empty roads. I didn't go motoring on, I remained with those tanks, and eventually I found out they were the leading tanks of Eighth Army.

So I said to myself, it may well be that our Headquarters is going to be established in Mersa Matruh – but I'm not going on beyond our leading tanks. And eventually I went up a hill and a German anti-tank shell came over the top of my car – and we got off the road at once, turned off left just behind a hill. That was that. I then went, saw ahead of me a group of officers on the hill and I went up there on my feet and I found Gatehouse, his CRA [Commander, Royal Artillery] and various other people. And one was able to see down to Mersa Matruh. And on the left, which was lower ground one overlooked in the desert, were a whole mass of tanks, all with their engines running, all stationary. And nothing was happening.

Someone said to Gatehouse: 'What are you going to do?' And Gatehouse's reply was: 'This is Custance's battle and I'm not going to interfere.' Custance was the Brigadier [of 8th Armoured Brigade]. So I stayed there a short time. It was quite obvious to my mind that this was a complete nonsense. Here were these tanks held up by perhaps one anti-tank gun in Mersa Matruh. Here were thirty to forty tanks in the desert, stationary with their engines running and the divisional commander was taking no control and nothing was being done.

Someone told me Monty was behind. So I motored back, found Monty and I said: 'There's a complete nonsense going on up there, you'd better go and look at it, I'll tell you as we go, they are just doing nothing. They might attack with infantry, they might attack with tanks, but they're just sitting there.' And I took Monty up, got off the road in good time so we shouldn't be shelled, ushered him up towards the people – and then I thought I'd better retire! . . . It was a nonsense. There was no *desire* to go on among Gatehouse and his staff.

Well it was quite clear that these tanks out with us should have bolted straight on past Mersa Matruh and seized the high ground beyond. But the lack of desire to do anything of that sort – it was completely missing. They'd had a bad time [at Alamein] of course and they were over-cautious and had lost the thrust which the armour should have.

Now here was a case where, whatever Monty wanted, his battle was being ruined by Gatehouse sitting on a hill saying: 'This is Custance's battle. . . .'

Army headquarters thought that Mersa Matruh had been captured. It hadn't been – and Carver [GSO 2 (Ops)] and Mainwaring [GSO 1 (Ops)] just walked straight into the Boche. . . .

Gatehouse . . . should have been up at a place called 'Charing Cross', beyond Mersa Matruh, that night. The whole thing was to my mind a complete mishandling of the business. It shows how, however good an Army Commander's plan is, he can be let down, certainly by a divisional commander, but he can also be let down by a much more junior officer as well. It's just one of those facts of life in war.[1]

Ironically it would be Gatehouse who, having been sacked, spread the post-war doctrine that Monty had been too cautious after Alamein – and that he, Gatehouse, had begged for permission to take his division through the desert to Sollum – and been turned down![2]

At Monty's insistence an attack was put in with infantry at dusk. But with mines, wire, and 90th Light Division having settled down to form a defence, it came to grief, a further salutary example of the failure of the British armoured commanders to train their formations in quickly co-ordinated infantry/artillery/armoured co-operation.

Rommel was surprised nevertheless by the speed with which the British had acted. He had hoped to hold the 'Charing Cross'–Mersa Matruh line for several more days, but the sight of British armoured cars working their way south of 'Charing Cross' on the afternoon of 7 November, as the desert began to dry, convinced him he must expedite his rearguard's withdrawal. At 9 p.m., again in pitch dark, 15th Panzer Division began withdrawing towards Sidi-Barrani, some seventy-five miles further west.

[1] Loc. cit.
[2] R. W. Thompson, *The Montgomery Legend*, London 1967, *inter alia*.

As the Afrika Korps withdrew, Monty set up a temporary Army and Tactical Headquarters just east of Mersa Matruh, ahead of Lumsden's Corps headquarters, and even of Gatehouse's divisional HQ. 'Army H.Q. opened just East of the town and was now the leading H.Q. in Eighth Army,' Monty recorded with some irony in his diary. 'The advance was becoming lethargic. . . . The port was badly wanted as supply and maintenance were now going to be our great problem. When the advance becomes sticky it is obviously a good thing to move Army H.Q. up in front of the H.Q. of the leading Corps!! The reaction was immediate.'

But was it? Lumsden was told in new Army orders that night to 'drive hard' for Halfaya, Rommel's next delaying position, clearing the landing grounds at Misheifa and Sidi Azeiz as he went – but once again he made a nonsense of his task. Instead of checking the latest situation at 1st Armoured Division, Lumsden told 7th Armoured Division to continue the pursuit to Halfaya, while the New Zealand Division would follow with 4th Light Armoured Brigade and 9th Armoured Brigade after first taking Mersa Matruh from the south and west. To his consternation, therefore, Lumsden was just detailing Freyberg's tasks at 8.30 a.m. on 8 November when he received a signal to say that 1st Armoured Division had de-bogged itself, had assaulted Mersa Matruh from the rear – and found it empty.[1]

Once again Rommel had pulled out before the dawdling formations of Eighth Army could spring their trap. Instead of moving ahead with his most forward troops, Lumsden had hung back east of Mersa Matruh, possibly stung by both his failure to take the town as ordered by Monty on the evening of 5 November, and his failure to keep in good touch with the Army Commander. Despite Lumsden's personal presence, however, Freyberg's force took a further *entire day* to drive past the empty town – and only set off for Sidi Barrani on 9 November.

This monument to the ineffectiveness of the *Corps de Chasse* was the final nail in its coffin. Conceived of on Montgomery's flight out from England in August, the Corps had put up a dismal performance during the 'sticky' fighting of the battle of Alamein, and had now failed utterly to emulate its great adversary, the shattered, skeleton remnants of the Afrika Korps. Across the empty sands of Egypt the 7th Armoured Division now raced in a three-day dash to the wire fence that separated Libya from Egypt. But as Rommel noted in his desert papers, 'There is never any point in attempting an outflanking movement round an enemy force unless it has first been tied down frontally'[2] – and this, thanks to the cumbersome progress of

[1] Ronald Walker, *Alam Halfa and Alamein (Official History of New Zealand in the Second World War, 1939–45)*, Wellington, N.Z. 1967.
[2] *The Rommel Papers*, op. cit.

Freyberg's force around Mersa Matruh and then along the coast, was not achieved. By the time the 7th Armoured Division turned north along the 50° line of longitude, the Afrika Korps was through the Halfaya bottleneck, and Egypt had been evacuated. Kippenberger's 5th New Zealand Brigade managed to storm the Halfaya Pass in a model night attack on 10 November, netting the entire Italian force of defenders; but Freyberg, having finally released 4th Light Armoured Brigade nearly a week after his first order, then refused to go on to Tobruk without more infantry and tanks.[1]

Lumsden was furious with Freyberg over his dilatory advance – and must have bitterly regretted the decision to use Freyberg rather than simply replenishing the tanks and transport of 1st Armoured Division and driving them from Matruh along the coast. In Lumsden's view, the Germans had 'withdrawn in orderly fashion and are not unduly perturbed at reverse',[2] and he was now certain they would stand at Tobruk, necessitating a pause while 10 Corps brought up sufficient forces to invest the town. Without access to Ultra, however, and with a poor operations staff,[3] Lumsden misread the situation – for on the night of 7 November a vast Allied armada had approached the coasts of North West Africa – the 'more jam' which Churchill had mysteriously promised after Alamein.[4] Rommel's morale, shattered by his decisive defeat at Alamein, was now doubly assailed. Mussolini and Cavallero might send urgent signals ordering him to make a stand at Halfa, to reorganise and counter-attack the enemy; but they were signals to a broken man, whose instinct was now to evacuate North Africa entirely.

[1] Ronald Walker, op. cit.
[2] Ibid.
[3] On 18 December 1943 Monty recorded Horrocks as saying: 'The G staff in 10 Corps was quite frightful; no proper system; no organization; most of the G[SO]2s complete duds' – quoted in F. W. de Guingand, *Generals at War*, London 1964.
[4] Harold Nicolson, *Diaries*, op. cit.

CHAPTER SIX

The Lessons of Alamein

With the capture of the Halfaya Pass and 7th Armoured Division's thrust from the frontier towards El Adem, the Battle of Egypt was over. In six days Eighth Army had driven back the remnants of Rommel's once proud African Panzer Army some 270 miles, an average of forty-five miles a day. 'We received signal after signal calling on us to gain as much time in our retreat as possible. But the speed of the retreat was now dictated solely by the enemy and our petrol situation,' Rommel recorded later. To his wife he wrote on 10 November: 'I've had no time to write since the enemy break-through at Alamein. . . . Things go badly with an army which has been broken through. It has to fight its way out and lose what's left of its fighting power in the process. We can't go on like that for long, for we have a superior enemy after us. . . .'[1]

It was Rommel's turn to feel the bitter taste of defeat and retreat while his adversary, remembering the disastrous days of May 1940 when he had retreated from Louvain to Dunkirk, penned a long letter to his erstwhile Corps Commander, now the CIGS, General Sir Alan Brooke: 'The battle is over, in that Rommel's army has been smashed up and we are now in pursuit. . . . It has been a great party and I have enjoyed it immensely.' To his son David's guardian, however, Monty confessed his concern over the capture of his stepson Dick:

> I regret to say my stepson Dick Carver was captured by the Germans at Matruh on 7 Nov; he was on a forward reconnaissance in the early morning. I am very sad about it as I was devoted to him and he to me.
>
> Would you make enquiries through the Red Cross as to where he is. When we know where he is we must arrange for a proper and regular despatch of parcels; but it is too early to do that yet; we must first locate his Prison Camp.

Already he was himself being pursued – 'the photographers and cinema people never leave me alone' – and like Rommel he looked

[1] *The Rommel Papers,* op. cit.

44

forward to the time when the war in Africa would be over and he could take some leave: 'When we have cleaned up N. Africa I shall try and get home for a few days' holiday to see you all. I really think I deserve it.'

Now that the Battle of Egypt was over, however, Monty was determined that its lessons should not be forgotten or wasted. The two battles of defence and offence, at Alam Halfa and Alamein, provided 'much to be learnt' as he informed Brooke, 'and together I think they provide the material for a very short and quite small pamphlet on "The Conduct of Battle". This might be given to all Generals, and perhaps Brigadiers, and would be good doctrine for the whole Army,' he continued without undue modesty. 'The two battles were fought on very definite lines. This last one was planned to take the form it did take, and there is no doubt it was too much for Rommel. But I have not time to write it out just yet. I believe that unless the Army in England can be given some very clear doctrine, in which the basic fundamentals stand out like beacons, we shall have many failures. . . .

'Lumsden is out of his depth with a Corps; he is not fit for high command in the field; he is excitable and he loses his nerve at critical moments. He is a good trainer and would do for a Corps District in England, but nothing more.

'Oliver Leese is 1st class. Horrocks is very good. Lumsden is poor; I would not take him into another battle as a Corps Commander.'

In a postscript Monty remarked: 'The real trouble with Lumsden is that he lacks that steadfast character which is your stand-by when things are not going too well. There were several moments in the battle when his heart failed him and he advised we should stop, as we could not break through. He is very excitable and highly strung and I had to calm him down on many occasions. He was a 1st class unit commander; a very good Brigadier; a good Divisional Comd. He is a good trainer. He is young and may come along later. At present he is quite unfit for a Corps Command, and I have had many anxious moments with him. He is not really a high class professional soldier & knows very little about the co-operation of all arms on the battle-field.'

This personal condemnation of Lumsden is quoted in full, not to cast further mud upon a man who was to many of his subordinates the epitome of Polish and English cavalry tradition, but to point up Monty's concern about professionalism. 'They were wonderful chaps,' one artillery officer in 1st Armoured Division later described his fellow officers in the armoured units of the division, 'but they were really only *playing* at war. Their jargon was that of the hunt. At heart it was all a game to them.'[1] How poorly some of these units

[1] Mark Wathen to author, December 1981.

45

would fare in close fighting with strictly German opponents would later be shown in Normandy; for the moment Monty found himself after twelve weeks in the desert in command of an army which, though it had won an historic victory at Alamein, had in reality only scraped through the test – and bungled the aftermath.

As the years went by, there would be many voices raised in protest at Monty's over-inflated reputation as a commander; indeed it has become fashionable to decry his performance in the desert after Alamein – his over-insurance against enemy riposte, his concern about minimising casualties, and his set-piece attitude to war. Certainly it would be idle to compare him as a commander with Rommel, who was a master of opportunism, disruption and surprise. Yet even Rommel appears amateurish when considered alongside the professionalism with which Monty reformed a defeated, largely citizen army and made it into a legend. For, having recognised the weakness of his armour in a war of manoeuvre, Monty now decided – as at Alamein – to adopt a less ambitious approach, building upon the inherent strengths of a democratic army. Thus he would later be labelled as a ponderously slow and rigid commander who passed up numerous opportunities of spectacular success in or after battle. But to the men of Eighth Army and those serving in various units in the Mediterranean he was the general who, at last, restored reason and meaning to the British battlefield. Very few soldiers would emerge from his command without feeling they had learned a great and lasting lesson – he set an example of professionalism in command that rippled back through every echelon, fighting or administrative, even into other services. He simplified war – and nowhere is this more clear than in the transition of Eighth Army after Alamein: a transition from incompetent armoured manoeuvre to the relentless march of a great army. Historians and cryptographers might later brand it 'weary' – but in the eyes of Eighth Army and those who watched its epic campaign across North Africa there was nothing wearisome about it. Every mile travelled was a mile nearer home; every battle won a further notch in the burgeoning professional pride of Eighth Army, a pride and a morale fostered by an Army Commander determined to bring clarity and logic to the battlefield.

One of the most interesting points to my mind about all this business of making war

Monty noted in his letter to Brooke,

is the way that people try and shake your confidence in what you are doing, and suggest that your plan is not good, and that you ought to do this, or that. If I had done all that was suggested I would still be back in the Alamein area! One of the things that smashed the Germans was our use of artillery. I suppose I must have fired 1000 rounds a gun in the 12 days battle. The CCRA [Corps Commander, Royal Artillery] of the Corps commanded all the artillery in the Corps, and that enabled me to develop new thrusts *very quickly* and to support these thrusts with such artillery fire that nothing could stop them.

His discussion of the battle with von Thoma had borne this out – as he recorded in another letter to Brooke a few weeks later:

Von THOMA told me that Rommel began to get rattled as the battle proceeded and I kept switching the thrust lines; that was probably the root cause of his undoing.[1]

The problem, however, was one of training. None of the artillery colonels in Eighth Army was fit to command the whole artillery of a Corps, and only about '50 per cent' of the divisional artillery chiefs were 'fit to hold that appointment. Many of the Lt-Colonels were out of their depth; they always had their batteries away in battalion columns. No C.C.R.A or C.R.A. [Commander, Royal Artillery] here ever taught his subordinates, or held artillery exercises. Luckily we had in Mead Dennis a really 1st class C.C.R.A of 30 Corps; he was magnificent and is a high class gunner.'

It was vital, in Monty's view, that the experience and lessons of Alamein be made use of at home in England in the training of the troops there, and his letters to Brooke became, increasingly, the notes of a missionary bishop to the Church at home, unconsciously paralleling the work of his father when missionary Bishop of Tasmania. To Brooke Monty sent even a copy of his nightly notes, written during the battle of Alamein, adding, 'I have summarised the main lessons at the end.'

These lessons, which were to form part of Monty's first pamphlet for senior officers in December 1942, are surely historic, for they illustrate the pedagogic quality that had inspired his slow rise to high command – and which was not in any way forgotten in the moment of triumph. Rommel too sought to draw the tactical and strategic lessons of his campaigns – but only long after he was finally relieved of his North African command. That Monty should have sought to articulate the lessons of Alamein a bare six days after the breakout, as his troops raced to the Egyptian frontier, was symptomatic of his strange genius – his determination both to learn and to teach. 'It will take time to extract all the tactical lessons of the battle,' he began. 'A mass of detailed lessons will emerge. But we are very apt in the British Army to become immersed in details without *first* being clear

[1] Letter of 13.12.42, Montgomery Papers.

as to the main fundamentals on which all the details hang; it is the broad fundamentals which governed the whole battle and formed the basis of the victory. We must therefore be clear about *them* before we pass on to more detailed lessons:

Main Lessons of the Battle

1. Careful planning of the initial break in battle. You must be so positioned at the close of this phase that you have the tactical advantage. This was achieved.
2. Careful selection of the axis of operations following the break in battle, and *rapid switching* of the thrust line as opposition grows too stiff on any one axis.
3. The various axes of operations must be so thought out that the enemy is led gradually to believe that your main subsequent effort is going to be in one definite area. Having thus deceived him, you put in a really hard blow at *some other* point which is so selected that he will be thrown off his balance.
4. The quick re-grouping of an Army after the break-in battle, so as to have reserves available for developing new axes of operations.

   As reserves are used, fresh ones must be collected so that new axes of operations can be developed quickly.

   It is not possible to develop a new thrust quickly unless reserves are available.
5. The initiative having been gained in the break-in battle, it must not be lost. This will necessitate thinking ahead, always having small reserves available, rapid development of fresh thrusts, and centralised control of artillery; if these things are done then the enemy can be made to dance to your tune all the time.
6. The concentrated fire of artillery is a battle-winning factor of the first importance.

   The CCRA of a Corps must understand how to take command of the artillery of the Corps, centralised under his own control. A concentration of 400 guns can then be brought to bear quickly to support a new thrust, and nothing will be able to stand against it.
7. Strategical surprise is difficult to obtain. But tactical surprise is quite possible, even when two Armies are in close contact and open flanks do not exist.

   Complete tactical surprise was obtained in the break-in battle; the enemy considered the attack would be in the South, and it was delivered in the North.

   Tactical surprise was again obtained for the final thrust, before the break; the enemy expected this blow to be in the extreme North and he concentrated his German troops to meet it; the blow was then delivered against the Italians, at a point about 2 miles South of the purely German flank.

8. A Commander must so plan and conduct his battle that his operations will be in keeping with the standard of training of his troops.

I had an untrained Army, due to Auchinleck and his regime, and I had to be very careful what I did with it.

Commanders especially did not know how to fight a good enemy in a real dog-fight; they had been used to dispersion, and to battle-groups and tip and run tactics.

The training of Commanders by their superiors was unknown; there had been no firm doctrine of war on which to base training.

9. Determined leadership is vital, and nowhere is this more important than in the higher ranks. Other things being equal the battle will be a contest between opposing wills.

Generals who become depressed when things are not going well, and who lack the drive to get things done, and the moral courage and resolution to see their plan through to the end, are useless in battle. They are, in fact, worse than useless – they are a menace – since any lack of moral courage, or any sign of wavering or hesitation, has very quick repercussions down below.

10. To win battles you require good Commanders in the senior ranks, and good senior staff officers; all of these must know their stuff.

You also require an Army in which the morale of the troops is right on the top line. The troops must have confidence in their Commanders and must have the light of battle in their eyes; if this is not so you can achieve nothing.

10 Nov 42   B. L. Montgomery
                                                      Lt. Gen.
                                                   G.O.C.-in-C.
                                                   Eighth Army.

It was the last document Monty would sign as a Lieutenant-General, for next day came news that the King had knighted him 'for distinguished service in the field', and that he had been promoted to the rank of General.

To his son David's guardian he wrote, 'Great things seem to have happened during the last few days. I have jumped over the heads of all the Lieut. Generals. David will be pleased; for myself I regard it as a recognition of the fine work done by my soldiers. I enclose a message I have sent out to my troops.'[1]

[1] Letter of 14.11.42, Montgomery Papers.

The message, the first he would sign as a full general, was the counterpart to his historic declaration on the eve of Alamein – 'the turning point of the war':

EIGHTH ARMY

PERSONAL MESSAGE FROM THE ARMY COMMANDER

To be Read Out to All Troops

1. When we began the Battle of Egypt on 23 October I said that together we would hit the Germans and Italians for six right out of North Africa.

   We have made a very good start and to-day, 12 Nov., there are no German and Italian soldiers on Egyptian territory except prisoners.

   In three weeks we have completely smashed the German and Italian Army, and pushed the fleeing remnants out of Egypt, having advanced ourselves nearly 300 miles up to and beyond the frontier.

2. The following enemy formations have ceased to exist as effective fighting formations:

Panzer Army.	15 Panzer Div.
	21 Panzer Div.
	90 Light Div.
	164 Light Div.
10 Italian Corps.	Brescia Div.
	Pavid Div.
	Folgore Div.
20 Italian Corps.	Ariete Armd. Div.
	Littorio Armd. Div.
	Trieste Div.
21 Italian Corps.	Trento Div.
	Bologna Div.

   The prisoners captured number 30,000, including nine Generals.

   The amount of tanks, artillery, anti-tank guns, transport, air-craft, etc., destroyed or captured is so great that the enemy is completely crippled.

3. This is a very fine performance and I want, first, to thank you all for the way you responded to my call and rallied to the task. I feel that our great victory was brought about by the good fighting qualities of the soldiers of the Empire rather than by anything I may have been able to do myself.

4. Secondly, I know you will all realise how greatly we were helped in our task by the R.A.F. We could not have done it without their splendid help and co-operation. I have thanked the R.A.F. warmly on your behalf.

5. Our task is not finished yet; the Germans are out of Egypt but

there are still some left in North Africa. There is some good hunting to be had further to the West, in Libya; and our leading troops are now in Libya ready to begin. And this time, having reached Bengasi [*sic*] and beyond we shall not come back.

6. On with the task, and good hunting to you all. As in all pursuits some have to remain behind to start with; but we shall all be in it before the finish.

12.11.42   B. L. Montgomery
                                               General,
                                    G.O.C.-in-C, Eighth Army.

CHAPTER SEVEN

Rommel's Crisis at Benghazi

Though Mussolini had decreed that Rommel must make a stand at Sollum, Rommel paid little heed. The defeat at Alamein had been decisive, and in his heart he knew that resistance was impossible. The failures in British command and operational technique he could not know; what he saw was a vast enemy army surging after his forces and constantly threatening him with encirclement.

Simultaneously, in his war diary Monty put aside the floundering of his *Corps de Chasse*. His strict, logical mind refused to give disappointment its head; instead he chose to regard the pursuit from Rommel's point of view.

> It was clear that the enemy would have great difficulty in holding us off, as his army was completely crippled, whereas I was launching after him a Corps of two armoured divisions, and one infantry division containing an armoured brigade.

Undoubtedly there were officers and men in Eighth Army who, as we have seen, believed that Rommel was so completely crippled after Alamein that Montgomery was wrong to send an entire Corps in pursuit. Certainly this was felt by the commander of 7th Armoured Division, Major-General (later Field-Marshal Lord) Harding who reckoned he 'could have gone in on my own'.

The commander of 22nd Armoured Brigade agreed with Harding:

> I could never understand why he [Monty] ordered them all up. We, with the oldest tanks of the whole lot, thought we would be relegated to the rear. It was extraordinary. . . . It was there I think that Monty failed – if he failed at all in the war. I don't understand why he didn't go on with his [pre-battle] plan of only having one Corps, of perhaps only two divisions. They'd have been quite enough to cut the enemy off. But they *all* moved up.[1]

Even with its older tanks, though, Roberts felt 7th Armoured Division could have done the job on its own, if so ordered:

[1] Maj-General G. P. B. Roberts, interview of 15.1.80.

52

Oh, it could have, on its own, without a doubt. Absolutely. I agree with him [Lord Harding] – any one [division] could have done it, but providing only one went on. It was an administrative problem . . . we were disappointed when we were out of petrol and saw the Germans streaming back in front of us and couldn't do anything about it. Oh yes, it was quite distinct from the rainstorm, quite different.[1]

Doubtless this was so – but it was said with hindsight, when the failure of the Sherman tank to travel more than three miles per gallon had been discovered, and the impossibility of administering a whole armoured corps in pursuit beyond a congested, mined and confused battlefield had been made manifest. Equally, Freyberg's painfully slow progress, and the failure of Harding, Briggs and Gatehouse to move as the Germans did by night must cause the careful historian to wonder whether this euphoric feeling after the battle – when the enemy seemed utterly vanquished and complete encirclement possible by even a small but determined British force – was not deceptive. Certainly Monty shared it – as was witnessed by his approving the move of his Main Headquarters to Matruh without questioning reports of the town's capture. Yet, despite the British failure to entrap Rommel's rearguard, there is ample evidence that it was the sheer size of the Eighth Army pursuit force which frightened Rommel into his precipitate evacuation not only of Egypt, but also the whole of Cyrenaica almost to the Tripolitanian border. In his diary Monty noted: 'I was advancing strong in front, with armoured divisions making wide outflanking movements on the Southern flank. The pace was hot and we were too quick for him: before he could organise any proper defence, we were on top of him.' Though this might sound boastful, and though it conveniently overlooked the failures that had led to the escape of Rommel's remnant forces, which Monty simply attributed to the rain at Mersa Matruh, it was otherwise a fair, indeed psychologically perceptive account. The German War Diaries testify to the shock experienced by their units when the sheer size of Eighth Army's pursuit force became apparent. Enemy tanks like vultures were reported not in tens but in 'hundreds' preceded by the swarming of Eighth Army's wasps – the ubiquitous armoured cars. Again and again delaying positions were abandoned prematurely as the sheer magnitude of Eighth Army cast fear and even panic through the remnants of the African Panzer Army. 15th Panzer Division for instance estimated that it was being attacked by no less than '200 tanks' and '200 carriers'. Again at Mersa Matruh, even during the afternoon of 7 November, the appearance of enemy 'armoured recce vehicles' was considered proof 'that the

[1] Ibid.

English were beginning to outflank the Mersa Matruh fortress. The danger of encirclement would be increased if the division did not move West or if the coast road was not kept open.' The War Diarist was surprised that the retreat through the Halfaya Pass was not blocked – 'the division had thus passed another danger point in safety. Here again the English had not dared to make a bold thrust to take and block this very vulnerable defile. They might have cut off the whole division had they done so,' the diarist opined – unaware of Harding's complete armoured division racing round their southern flank at that very moment. On 10 November 15th Panzer Division thus innocently began to draw up 'plans to defend the area South-West of Capuzzo' until mid-afternoon, when some '20 enemy tanks and 15 armoured cars were seen moving North . . . 40 kilometres *West* of the division. In view of this Afrika Korps decided to move earlier than anticipated' to the Sidi Rezegh area, the War Diarist chronicled. Here Bayerlein, the Chief of Staff of the Afrika Korps, 'planned to hold the enemy up for a time in the easily defensible Belhamed area, with the main aim of doing as much damage to him as possible with our artillery. The Tobruk area,' the diarist made clear, 'which had cost us so much effort to take, was not going to fall into his hands without a struggle.' But the next day the division was again in retreat: '*Erneut besteht die Gefahr des Abgeschnittenswerdens*' ('once again we are in danger of encirclement').[1]

Rommel, in his memoirs, was equally depressed by Eighth Army's vulture-like pursuit, and not even the air transporting of a thousand infantrymen to Tobruk could persuade him to accept battle there on 11 November. Many of his columns 'were still in a bad state of disorganisation' after their helter-skelter flight from Alamein conveying 'unmotorised troops, the sick and the wounded'; indeed Rommel had simply let them panic, for he felt it was 'a great mistake in circumstances like these to attempt to get order into supply troops which have panicked and lost their organisational structure, until it can be done in peace and quiet. One should simply allow them to run and try to channel their flight gradually into ordered routes.' The British threat to encircle Tobruk from the south on 11/12 November forced Rommel prematurely to evacuate the fortress which 'now possessed only symbolic value. . . . Thus the enemy was able to occupy it, virtually without fighting, on the night of the 12th, after its evacuation by the 90th Light Division.' By the following day, after a Luftwaffe report of 'over 1,000 vehicles moving West' in 'another attempt to outflank us by a thrust in considerable strength', Rommel was pessimistic in the extreme: 'The end will not be long for we're being simply crushed by the enemy superiority.'[2]

[1] 15th Panzer Division War Diary (GMDS 24902), IWM.
[2] *The Rommel Papers*, op. cit.

That day, as advanced units of Eighth Army took over Tobruk, the first units of the Panzer Army reached Mersa Brega or the Agheila line as it was known to the British – 150 miles beyond Benghazi on the Gulf of Sirte. 'The army is in no way to blame. It has fought magnificently,' Rommel informed his wife[1] – even though, when Freyberg's New Zealand Division halted at Halfaya on 11 November, Rommel's fleeing Panzer Army was being pursued by no more than a single British armoured division with worn-out tanks, together with a light armoured brigade composed mostly of armoured cars.

Eighth Army had certainly failed to cut off Rommel's retreat or rearguard, but the speed and size of the pursuit force had at least succeeded in bluffing Rommel into premature flight from Egypt and, increasingly, Cyrenaica. For this Montgomery deserves more credit than some revisionist historians seem willing to give, particularly in view of the failure of the Desert Air Force to impede Rommel's retreat along a single coastal road. The RAF squadron leaders had not trained their pilots in modern strafing techniques, had used the wrong sort of bombs, had failed to use up-to-date methods of ground-to-air control; and were wary of flak. General Kirkman later recalled:

> At that stage [the break-out after Alamein] the Air really failed. The Air claimed they could destroy a retreating army. Well they didn't – I mean, I motored along these roads afterwards, there wasn't a mass of German burned-out vehicles. The fact is, our bombing was a bit inaccurate in those days, and a retreating army isn't quite as vulnerable as the Air likes to think. . . .[2]

Not until 'Maori' or 'Mary' Coningham left and was succeeded by Air Vice-Marshal Broadhurst did RAF techniques improve, but Tedder's policy of applying the heavy bombing effort to the enemy's rear installations and supply lines was brilliantly successful, as Rommel's nightmare at Benghazi was soon to show. 'I punched him on the nose,' Monty afterwards pithily acknowledged; 'Tedder bit his tail.'

Yet if the drubbing at Alamein and the vulture-like pursuit had shattered Rommel's nerve and forced him into premature evacuation of Egypt, Monty now made an important strategic error. With only a single armoured division across the frontier, and driving the oldest Grant tanks in Eighth Army ('Egypt's Last Hope' of Alam Halfa times), Monty was frankly dubious about whether he could catch Rommel. Having evacuated Tobruk without a fight, Rommel was unlikely to accept battle east of Mersa Brega/El Agheila – where

[1] Letter of 13.11.42, *The Rommel Papers*, op. cit.
[2] Loc. cit.

Hitler was insisting he reorganise, re-equip and mount, in time, a counter-offensive. In the circumstances Monty considered it would be enough to bluff Rommel out of Cyrenaica (including the Martuba airfield area and the port of Benghazi), while building up stocks at Matruh, Tobruk and then Benghazi ports. When this was done he could administer a powerful Eighth Army thrust *and* maintain the vital RAF squadrons at Martuba which alone could guarantee the re-supply of Malta. Rommel, he knew from Ultra, would fall back on ample petrol stocks and ammunition at Benghazi, as well as up to twenty newly unloaded Panzer tanks. Monty therefore concentrated on bluff, beginning as early as 9 November to consider a fast outflanking force of armoured cars. These were to be guided by the Long Range Desert Group inland across the desert, by passing the hilly Jebel country altogether, and threatening to cut the road between Mersa Brega and Benghazi at Agedabia.

Futures: In case the enemy decides to withdraw altogether to El Agheila

the C-in-C's Liaison Officer reported back to Cairo on 10 November,

a force of armoured cars is being organized to pursue, supplied by air.
8 Army would like to know what the LRDG are doing. They would like a set of details that are necessary to coordinate their action with those of the armoured cars. . . .[1]

Thus Monty's intention, verified by the C-in-C's LO and his own diary, was to give first priority to the securing of the Martuba airfields for the RAF near Derna, while sending only 'a small force across the desert towards El Agheila to act as a threat and hasten the enemy out of Benghazi'.

The administrative situation was now causing me anxiety. We had come so far and so fast that we could go no further without a pause, until we could get TOBRUK port working,

Monty recorded in his 'Pursuit' diary.

One of my chief objects during the pursuit was to establish the RAF on the forward aerodromes, and to use the air arm as my long range hitting weapon in conjunction with armoured cars. . . .
My final objective was to establish the RAF in the triangle DERNA–TMIMI–MECHILI, and especially on the Martuba group

[1] LO Reports from Eighth Army (WO 169/3802), PRO.

of aerodromes. From this area the RAF could dominate the MEDITERRANEAN, and could see the Malta convoys safely on their way.

So I 'drove' the Eighth Army *hard* to get this area and we did in fact secure the MARTUBA aerodromes on 15 November, just in time to be able to operate from there in support of a MALTA convoy leaving ALEXANDRIA on 16 November.

This was all very fine, but it overlooked the fact that, in concentrating upon the airfields at Martuba, Monty missed what was to be a unique – because entirely unexpected – opportunity to send a stronger force across the desert to Agedabia and cut off the retreat of the Panzer Army rearguard at Benghazi.

This missed opportunity was the first evidence of excessive caution by the Eighth Army commander after Alamein. With the first motorised Axis infantry units already streaming back to El Agheila on 13 November, there seemed little chance of Eighth Army's being able to do more than bluff Rommel into premature evacuation of Benghazi. Given that 10 Corps was stretched out over 300 miles of Egypt and Cyrenaica, and that almost all its divisions were split up because of administrative difficulties (part of the New Zealanders in Bardia, part in Matruh; part of 7th Armoured Division at El Adem, part in Tobruk; part of 9th Armoured Brigade at Sollum, part at Matruh still), it seemed imperative to Monty to harass Rommel *as though* threatening to outflank him, while in fact using the time to reorganise 10 Corps into a coherent, powerful formation again. With water so scarce that only 'essential' units of Eighth Army were allowed forward of the Alamein–Daba area, and no air transport system such as that operated by the Luftwaffe, Eighth Army was dependent for its entire logistical supply on the 450-mile road from Alamein to Tobruk, with only Matruh port in working order by 11 November. In his diary Monty was quite emphatic:

> But having reached it [Martuba aerodrome group] I could proceed no further; the administrative situation dictated a pause to get supplies, petrol, water, etc. forward.

It was now that the 'desert sweats' began to chafe at the bit. O'Connor had cut across the desert in the winter of 1940/1 with spectacular results against Graziani's forces – but had soon been driven to retreat and captivity in the spring of 1941. Auchinleck had then attempted to repeat the manoeuvre in December 1941 – but had lost no less than sixty British tanks in a futile attempt to stop Rommel gaining Agheila – and then been forced to surrender all his 'gains' when Rommel launched his next offensive in the spring of 1942.

Monty refused therefore to countenance a major move forward yet by 10 Corps, and was furious when Tedder sent a signal urging that the moment was 'ripe for exploitation'.[1] It was essential, Monty maintained, to recognise priorities and not dissipate one's forces in trying to do too many things at once. Without administrative back-up and without training in night movement, Eighth Army had botched-up the aftermath of Alamein. From now on, Monty felt, he must himself exert tight control and only undertake operations within the capacity both of the troops and of Eighth Army's supply administration. He had, forward of Sollum, a single armoured division with worn-out tanks, which secured Tobruk on 13 November, and only 4th Light Armoured Brigade following up the enemy towards Derna and the Martuba airfields. Even his orders that the New Zealand Division move up to Tobruk from Bardia on 13 November could not be acted upon, owing to administrative problems. If Rommel discovered he was only being pursued by armoured cars and light Crusader tanks he might well dispute possession of the Martuba airfields. It was vital, therefore, that while Monty threatened to outflank Rommel with armoured cars, he should waste no time in bringing 1st Armoured Division, with its fresher tanks, forward from the Sollum bottleneck to reinforce the worn-out tanks of 7th Armoured Division and ensure that Rommel did not have time to reorganise and even mount a counter-attack while Eighth Army was so weak in front.

With hindsight this was an inversion of the strategy Monty should have employed, for Rommel was in no frame of mind, despite Mussolini's and Cavallero's orders, to accept battle east of Agheila. Thus, on the afternoon of 15 November, when the reconnaissance elements of 4th Light Armoured Brigade reached Martuba, they found the aerodromes bare. 'An Arab reports Germans evacuated Martuba yesterday afternoon. Very few vehicles, and these seemed to take desert route to Agheila,' was the 0930 report logged at Lumsden's headquarters.[2]

Rommel was beating a hasty retreat – 'we have to be grateful for every day that the enemy does not close in on us,' he had written on 14 November[3] – having wished 'I were just a newspaper vendor in Berlin,' as he told his ADC the previous day.[4] He was on the watch for a British outflanking move, and hoped his look-outs could give him enough time to despatch motorised forces to 'intercept' the columns – but everything depended on petrol supply which, after the lorried passage of the Axis infantry and 'baggage train', and the premature Italian demolition of the railway line east of Benghazi, was utterly dependent on German air transport.

[1] Cf. F. W. de Guingand, *From Brass Hat to Bowler Hat*, London 1979.
[2] 10 Corps War Diary extract (WO 169/3990), PRO.
[3] *The Rommel Papers*, op. cit.
[4] David Irving, *The Trail of the Fox*, London 1977.

Lumsden's first outflanking columns left Tobruk on 15 November, two days after its capture, with a second column on 16 November – each column consisting simply of an armoured car regiment, an infantry company, some light artillery, an anti-tank gun troop, two troops of anti-aircraft batteries, a Field Squadron and ambulances. But in the meantime Rommel's petrol crisis began to take 'an even more acute turn', and in a signal to Hitler early on 16 November Rommel referred to his fuel situation as 'catastrophic'. Moreover Rommel declared that, in view of the fact that the British coastal thrust was dying down beyond Martuba, he now planned to relinquish Benghazi port only on 19 November.[1]

When Major Williams reported this decrypted message late on 16 November to Monty, the latter realised he had made a mistake. Williams was instantly told, as he later recalled, to go personally to see Lumsden that night:

I remember we got a sort of Ultra thing . . . and it looked as though if [Lumsden] got a sprint on he could do the same sort of Beda Fomm as we'd done against the Italians. I was sent out into the night and I remember we drove through Tobruk – which was fascinating to be able to do because I'd been locked up there years before. It was an extraordinary sensation when you are driving

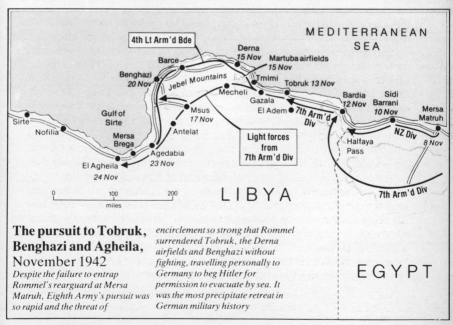

The pursuit to Tobruk, Benghazi and Agheila, November 1942
Despite the failure to entrap Rommel's rearguard at Mersa Matruh, Eighth Army's pursuit was so rapid and the threat of encirclement so strong that Rommel surrendered Tobruk, the Derna airfields and Benghazi without fighting, travelling personally to Germany to beg Hitler for permission to evacuate by sea. It was the most precipitate retreat in German military history

[1] F. H. Hinsley, op. cit.

through a place which has previously been besieged. I was to report to [Lumsden] immediately.

And of course he was asleep and they refused to wake him up! I was kept waiting, I'm sure I was kept waiting because I was a messenger from Monty – and of course I couldn't explain to them it was Ultra because he didn't know that stuff. So one had to say, well we know, we've got this thing. And Brian Robertson had said to me just as I was leaving: 'And do tell him he can have, you know, petrol if he needs it,' because this had always been a problem. . . .[1]

Eventually Lumsden was woken, and after giving an 'Imperial rocket', listened to Williams's new Intelligence. 'It was all very amiable,' Williams recalled, once Lumsden had seen the King's Dragoon Guards badge on Williams' cap, 'but I don't think he really *did* decide to get the whips out and go across as he might have done.'

Monty himself went up to Lumsden's headquarters the next morning. He had sent a signal the previous night wishing 'to be informed whether or not 22 Armoured Brigade [of 7th Armoured Division] would be fit to fight in Western Cyrenaica in view of the present state of their tanks' – but at 6 p.m. that same evening Roberts had already given Lumsden a report on the brigade's latest tank situation. Only four Grants, one Sherman and one Crusader tank were considered capable of travelling a further three hundred miles – even less if traversing desert. The only way of inflating the outflanking force with tanks therefore was to have Shermans rushed forward on transporters from 1st Armoured Division near Sollum, and this was done the next day, on 17 November, as 10 Corps War Diary records: '2235 hours: 2 Armoured Bde less 10 Hussars arrive area P7302, 28 tanks being handed over to 22 Armoured Brigade.'[2] However, despite Monty's personal presence at 10 Corps Headquarters and his orders that 'maximum supply transport be held in readiness to supply MSUS' (on the trans-desert route) by ground and air, there was really little prospect that it would beat Rommel to Agedabia. To do so, Monty would need to have planned the move much earlier, giving special priority to the move of 1st Armoured Division's tank transporters. As it was, it took twenty-four hours for the tanks to be unloaded and the new armoured column to be assembled – and thirty-six hours before it finally left.

Such delay may seem incomprehensible to the later observer, but no responsible divisional commander will send his men across three hundred miles of desert without reasonable preparation. Tobruk port was still not working, and the latest Eighth Army Intelligence

[1] Sir Edgar Williams, interview of 20.12.79.
[2] 10 Corps War Diary, loc. cit.

report on the morning of 17 November revealed an estimate of '11,000 fighting men and between thirty and forty tanks of Panzer Army' forming Rommel's rearguard. 'Of these tanks some are believed to have been landed recently,' the assessment continued, and credited Rommel with 'approx. 20,000 Italians, the remnants of 20 Corps' – most of whom were now behind the Mersa Brega defences.[1]

Unless Rommel's petrol situation precluded him from fighting at all, then, there was little chance that even a reinforced column, with twenty-three Shermans and Grants, could defeat Rommel's 11,000 rearguards. Nevertheless on 19 November Lumsden issued orders that while the new British tank force seized and blocked the Benghazi–Agheila road west of Antelat, the earlier column of armoured cars that had moved off on 16 November should turn south and follow the enemy, if possible, passing through AGHEILA and forming a bridgehead in the area WADI EL HATEMA'.[2]

Whether Lumsden really believed it was possible for a regimental column of armoured cars to push through the Agheila defences except in pursuit, is doubtful however, for at a BGS Conference on the morning of 18 November de Guingand referred to the reinforced column or 'regimental group', giving its object as the straddling of the road south-west of Agedabia, but remarking: 'if enemy opposition is too much for it, it is to give ground and not get mopped up.'[3]

Rommel had in fact been crying 'wolf' in order to ensure increased petrol supplies. Rain and sandstorms swept the desert from 16 November, and a mere reconnaissance unit of Germans was able to hold off the entire British armoured car columns attempting to push west of Msus. By the time the British tank column set off on the morning of 19 November, Rommel was already moving out the last of his troops by road from Benghazi, and by nightfall all German forces had reached Agedabia. By 23 November Rommel's remnant army was inside the Mersa Brega line, having retreated eight hundred miles in less than three weeks – the longest and most precipitate retreat in German military history.

To push the enemy back such an immense distance, without ports or more than a single line of communication, was a tribute to the victors of Alamein, as well as a tonic to the morale of the free world. But with the passage of time Eighth Army's feat has tended to be downgraded; indeed some British writers have even questioned why Lumsden's regimental group which clashed with Rommel's rearguard at Agedabia on 21 November did not then 'gate-crash' the

[1] LO Report from Eighth Army of 16/17.11.42 (WO 169/3802), PRO.
[2] 10 Corps War Diary, loc. cit.
[3] LO Report from Eighth Army, 18.11.42 (WO 169/3802), PRO.

Agheila defences, manned by up to 50,000 Axis troops, artillery and some thirty-five German tanks.[1]

While every credit must go to Rommel for evading Eighth Army's attempts at encirclement after Alamein, it would be idle to imagine that his 800-mile flight had been anything but the disastrous consequence of his defeat. Though ordered to stand and fight at Sollum, Tobruk and Gazala, the pace of Eighth Army's pursuit and the disorganisation of his own fleeing columns made it impossible for Rommel to contemplate accepting battle. He was himself under no illusions. 'The great retreat,' he wrote later, 'had been the result of our defeat at El Alamein.'[2] He was subject to fainting fits, and, ever since news of the Allied landings in North-west Africa, given to despair.[3]

---

[1] D. Irving, op. cit.

[2] *The Rommel Papers*, op. cit.

[3] Axis casualties from El Alamein to the loss of Benghazi were calculated at the time to be 61,000 men (killed, wounded, missing and captured); losses of tanks and guns were calculated to be 720 anti-tank guns, 380 guns, 50 88 mm guns, and 536 tanks – from desert diary of Maj-General M. St J. Oswald, communicated to author.

CHAPTER EIGHT

'The Real Way to Take Tripoli is from the West'

If Rommel's morale had touched rock-bottom – so much so that he would fly personally and without permission to Hitler's Rastenburg headquarters to sue for complete evacuation of North Africa – a very different mood prevailed in his opponent's camp. Nevertheless, for the first time since the critical days during the Alamein battle, Monty was becoming concerned about the way things were going, and the future. In this respect there was a curious parallel between his own and Rommel's thinking which has never been revealed before. While Rommel first sent an emissary, General Stefanis, asking to be spared a further gruelling retreat to Buerat and Tripoli on 20 November, then repeated his request for evacuation to Kesselring, Cavallero and Bastico on 24 November, and finally left to make a personal appeal to Hitler in East Prussia on 28 November, Monty was writing to Alexander (his C-in-C), to Brigadier Simpson (Deputy Director, Military Operations in the War Office) and even to Brooke himself (the CIGS) in a vain attempt to be spared the same march westwards. 'My dear Alex,' he wrote to the C-in-C in Cairo on 18 November, while Rommel was still at Benghazi, 'I think the time has come to take stock of the situation.' Eighth Army's planning ought, he felt, to be 'linked with the efforts of the Allied forces now in Tunisia'. As Monty saw it, Tripoli was the key. 'If the enemy wants to remain in N. Africa he requires the use of Tripoli. Our object is to remove the Axis forces from N. Africa; therefore an essential step in this direction must be the capture, or complete neutralisation, of Tripoli.' But who should be asked to capture the port – still almost eight hundred miles beyond Benghazi? 'It is obvious, from the communication point of view alone, that the capture of Tripoli should be undertaken from the West' – i.e. by Eisenhower's forces attacking through Tunisia.[1]

The assumption by historians and even veterans of Eighth Army that Montgomery always intended, in launching his offensive at Alamein, to continue to Tripoli and Tunisia, is therefore mistaken. At

[1] In Alexander Papers (WO 214/18), PRO.

the time of Alamein, while plans for the 'Torch' landings were still secret, Tripoli might well be given as Eighth Army's goal; but in reality Monty felt that Eisenhower's Allied forces, who had faced no opposition save the questionable reaction of the Vichy French, were much better poised to sever Rommel's lines of communication from Tunisia.

They have a short sea route to the ports of N. Africa; and they have a good railway and road system which stretches nearly to the Tripolitanian border.
We have the long sea route via the Cape to Egypt, the small railway terminating at Tobruk, the indifferent port at Benghazi, and the 760 miles of road from Benghazi to Tripoli which would have to be our main channel of maintenance.

The enormous administrative waste in maintaining an entire army between Cairo and Tripoli – a coastline longer than that of Atlantic France – quite apart from the problem of capturing the area from an enemy that had been in occupation for several years – seemed senseless to Monty, if Eisenhower's forces were virtually unopposed and could be built up much more rapidly. Ever since Alamein, Monty had been trying to obtain accurate information about Eisenhower's progress and intentions – to no avail. In his letter to Brooke on 10 November, Monty had remarked, ' "Torch" seems to be going very well. We have very few details so far, but I expect some will come along soon.' None did, however, and the next day de Guingand asked Alexander's LO for 'a précis of the happenings on the Western N. African coast'. When, a week later, Monty *still* had no news about Eisenhower's progress, he insisted in a letter to Alexander that it was 'essential we should be supplied immediately with the following information from UK.

a) Details as to the <u>real</u> progress of events in N. Africa in general, and in Tunisia in particular.
b) The immediate, and distant, objectives of the 'Western Army'.
c) The date by which Malta, and air forces based in Algiers –Tunisia, will be in a position to begin large scale neutralisation of the enemy shipping to N. Africa, and the port of Tripoli itself.
8. It is most important that the Chiefs of Staff should be left in no doubt as to the problem facing Eighth Army in an advance to Tripolitania. The real way to take Tripoli is from the West. If however, the Western Army is likely to be "seen off" by the Germans, then we should have to do something about it; but it would take time, owing to the need for building up stocks. Benghazi as a port is not good, and the maintenance of a Corps, even in Cyrenaica, is difficult; in Tripolitania it would be colossal.'

Monty's postulation that the 'Western Army' might be 'seen off' by the Germans was, however, prophetic, and in a further paragraph he emphasised the point:

9. It is so important to find out what the real situation of the 'Western Army', what it is doing, what it hopes to do, its condition, and its resources, etc. etc., that I suggest someone should fly over and see them.

You could fly there in one night from Cairo in a Liberator.

If this were done we could find out the whole situation for ourselves.

10. To sum up:

a) We must begin the heavy neutralisation of Tripoli *at once*. This is the surest way to shorten the time required to secure the Agheila position. . . .

b) We must find out what is going on in the West. . . .

Yours ever

Monty[1]

Alexander reacted immediately by sending his GSO 2 (Intelligence) to Eisenhower's headquarters for a 'personal reconnaissance' of the 'Western Army'. 'What you suggest is being done,' he signalled back to Montgomery – though he was doubtful about the chances of Eisenhower taking Tripoli, feeling that Eisenhower might wish to use his Anglo-American forces in further amphibious operations, such as a landing in Spain, if Hitler moved into the Iberian peninsula.

There is a tendency that the West want to leave Tripoli to us. I have already sent a strong wire to Prime Minister and CIGS stressing our difficulties and urging paramount importance of first of all clearing whole North African coast before embarking on other ventures. This was followed yesterday by C-in-C's telegram to COS reinforcing this view and pressing Eisenhower to operate against Tripoli by sea, land and air at earliest possible. So far his communiques have been very meagre. Home have been left in NO doubt as to tremendous difficulties facing us.[2]

Churchill, beset by the political problems of French co-operation in Algeria and Tunisia, stalled for the moment, and in typical fashion replied by asking what steps Montgomery was taking to cut off Rommel's forces still at Benghazi – about which Montgomery had to dictate a long letter on 19 November, pointing out that he had 'advanced nearly 600 miles in 15 days and am administratively

[1] Letter of 18.11.42 in Alexander Papers (WO 214/18), PRO.

[2] Ibid.

stretched out', and explaining that not only would he require time to build up supplies for a successful attack on the Agheila defences, but time thereafter if he was to be able to maintain a pursuit force all the way to Tripoli. Meanwhile, unaware of the administrative realities of conducting a full-scale campaign in North-west Africa, Churchill complained that he 'never meant the Anglo-American Army to be stuck in North Africa. It is a springboard and not a sofa. . . .'[1]

In fact Churchill was as perturbed as Montgomery by the paucity of military information coming from Algeria and Tunisia, and Field-Marshal Smuts was despatched to Algiers on his way back to South Africa. On 20 November Smuts reported that he had 'had a long talk with Eisenhower and Cunningham [Naval C-in-C]. . . . As regards coming operation next Sunday or Monday, it is doubtful whether Anderson is strong enough to take Bizerta, but Tunis appears more hopeful. . . . Farther South attempt will be made to clean up small pockets of enemy at Sfax and elsewhere, but no large forces will be employed in the Tripoli direction at present.'[2] Five days later Churchill was still unsure whether Tripoli was to be taken from east or west, as his 'Note by the Minister of Defence' of 25 November showed:

> As soon as we are sure of ourselves, and consolidated, in French North Africa, including specially Tunis, two successive operations present themselves. The first is the advance to Tripoli. It is possible that General Alexander may be able to take this important prize from the East, and I have asked him how he feels about it, and how long he thinks it would require; but we must also be prepared for a rapid advance from the West. Would General Anderson's two British divisions be sufficient assuming that Tunis itself can be held by American and French Allied troops? . . . The second immediate objective is obviously Sardinia or Sicily. . . .[3]

To Monty such optimism was quite unrealistic, and ruefully he resigned himself to the business of planning an Eighth Army advance on Tripoli, for without reinforcement and with relatively 'green' divisions he doubted whether Anderson could even take the Tunis peninsula if Hitler chose to reinforce the Axis bridgehead there – which he did. By 28 November Anderson was only twelve miles from Tunis: but there, before Djeida, Anderson's progress came to an end, as did any hope that the Allies might take Tripoli from Tunisia.

The lack of understanding displayed not only by Churchill but

[1] Michael Howard, *Grand Strategy* Vol. IV, London 1972.
[2] In Smuts file, Personal Correspondence of Dwight D. Eisenhower, 1652 series, Eisenhower Library, Abilene, Kansas.
[3] W. S. Churchill, *The Hinge of Fate*, London 1951.

various people in Cairo evidently annoyed Montgomery, however, for on 19 November he wrote a very personal letter to his erstwhile Chief-of-Staff, Brigadier Simpson, at the War Office:

> We have been to Benghazi several times before and have then always had a disaster which has negatived all the success gained. I can seen now why these things have happened.
>
> If I accepted all the advice I have received we would not be where we are now.
>
> If I accepted all the advice I am now being given we might well have a disaster even now.
>
> There are in Cairo a complete lot of lunatics, who sit in War Rooms completely out of touch with realities, and who try and plan what I ought to do. A good many of these are of the RAF.
>
> One of the big lessons I have learnt from this business is to decide what you want to do, and then *do* it; never be drawn off the job in hand by gratuitous advice from people who know nothing about it.
>
> I am determined that this time there will be NO setbacks, but it is hard work.
>
> Alex is my great supporter; he never bothers me; never suggests what I ought to do; keeps people away from bothering me; gives me at once everything I ask for. We have so far advanced 600 miles in 15 days and I have firmly established the RAF in Cyrenaica; that is not bad.
>
> I have now got to pause, to collect my scattered forces, and get my administration on a firm basis − it is stretched almost to breaking point at the moment. Then I shall face up to the Agheila position.

One of the reasons why Montgomery was angered by presumptuous messages about 'exploitation' from the Air C-in-C in the Mediterranean, Air Marshal Sir Arthur Tedder, was that Tedder evidently did not understand the extent to which supplies to his own long-range RAF bomber squadrons would affect what Eighth Army could meanwhile do, on the ground. As Monty noted in his diary: 'The question of RAF maintenance was now becoming a great problem: it was closely linked with Army maintenance. Only a certain definite tonnage could be delivered in CYRENAICA.' He went on:

> My main objects right through this battle had been two:
>   a) To smash Rommel's army
>   b) To establish the RAF firmly in CYRENAICA.
> Both these objects had been achieved. But we would not get full value from having put the RAF into CYRENAICA unless they

could operate at full blast against Tripoli, enemy shipping, Sicily, Italy, the supply lines of the Panzer Army in the AGHEILA position and so on.

The RAF requirements were as follows:

By 28 Nov.	400 tons per day
By 2 Dec.	800 tons per day
By 9 Dec.	1050 tons per day
By 16 Dec.	1400 tons per day (1000 at TOBRUK and 400 at BENGHAZI)

If the enemy intended to stand firm on the AGHEILA position and fight seriously, I would have to build up resources of supplies, petrol, ammunition before I could attack the position.

The enormous totals required by the RAF would make it difficult to build up these resources quickly.

In fact the proof of Montgomery's stretched administrative position was the way in which his foremost units – of 7th Armoured Division – were severely bombed and strafed by the Luftwaffe once they had hustled Rommel's rearguard out of Agedabia, on the approach road to Agheila. There were a number of casualties, but until the last week in November the RAF was powerless to help, for only on 26 November did it manage to get two fighter wings operational at Msus.

Already on 12 November, a week after Alamein, Montgomery had told Leese that Lumsden would be sent home once Eighth Army reached Benghazi, and that Leese would conduct the battle for Agheila. Thus on 24 November Leese's 30 Corps Headquarters took responsibility for the front; Lumsden was dismissed[1] and General Horrocks took command of 10 Corps, charged with the retraining and organisation of Eighth Army reserve formations, in preparation for mobile operations beyond Agheila. Harding's 7th Armoured Division was meanwhile ordered to reconnoitre the Agheila defences while Leese brought up enough infantry to conduct an attack – 51st Highland Division and Freyberg's New Zealanders. Simultaneously, one hundred miles away at Arco dei Fileni or 'Marble Arch', Rommel, Kesselring, Cavallero and Bastico were holding a council of war in which Rommel, depressed and anxious, pretended he was unaware of Montgomery's real administrative situation. He credited Montgomery with possessing 420 tanks and 300 armoured cars and asked what would happen 'if the enemy

---

[1] Back in England Lumsden was again given an armoured corps, knighted, and sent early in 1944 to the Far East as Churchill's personal Liaison Officer to General MacArthur. He was killed by a kamikaze plane while aboard the battleship USS *New Mexico* on 6 January 1945.

launches into my army in the next day or two and then outflanks me with strong forces'?[1]

In fact Montgomery had no intention of risking his meagre forward units in a premature attack on prepared defences, without even proper air support. In artillery and men Eighth Army was vastly outnumbered in the Gulf of Sirte,[2] and it was imperative, he felt, not to surrender the tactical initiative, but to keep Rommel guessing, not knowing when Eighth Army would strike. For the moment he was thus content to let 7th Armoured Division skirmish before Agheila, while supplies were built up overland from Tobruk, 30 Corps built up its strength, and the desert tracks inland were reconnoitred for possible outflanking moves. While this was being done Monty set down his 'Notes on the conduct of Battle for senior officers' based on the battle of Alamein, and considered what would happen once he was out beyond Agheila. Reluctantly he now accepted that Eighth Army would have to go on to Tripoli, almost 750 miles from Benghazi – but what then?

> I have been thinking a good deal about our next moves when we have cleaned up N. Africa,

he wrote on 27 November to the CIGS, General Brooke.

> It is curious how very difficult it is to get any reliable news about what is happening over Tunis way, and as to what progress our force is making there. I am making plans to move on towards Tripoli after I have dealt with the Agheila position; but maintenance and supply will be the very devil; it is 750 miles from Benghazi, a very indifferent port, and there is only one road. . . .
> After that I am not so sure,

he remarked. Opinion in most desert and Middle East circles was that the Allies would then proceed to knock Italy out of the war by invading Sicily and the Italian mainland; but Monty frankly wondered whether it would be worth the enormous cost, given German superiority in the Northern Mediterranean:

> If the Bosche collects a really strong air force in Sicily and Italy I foresee great difficulties in any invasion of those parts. It may well be that our offensive on land against the Germans would be best

---

[1] *The Rommel Papers*, op. cit.
[2] 'The defence, with an adequate supply base behind it in the West, can fall on and destroy the enemy's vanguard before other formations can arrive. The British dispositions were excellently suited for such an operation,' Rommel acknowledged in his *Papers*.

developed from England across the Channel; this obviates all difficulties of shipping, air support, and so on; we should be developing the offensive from a firm base. It would be costly

he acknowledged.

But it would bring off a fight with the Germans. I am quite certain that the way to deal with the German is to face up to him in battle; it is the only way to deal with him, because then you kill him. The trouble with our British lads is that they are not killers by nature; they have got to be so inspired that they will want to kill, and that is what I tried to do with this Army of mine.

Given a large number of Americans I believe the invasion of Western Europe could be brought off successfully next summer, about June when the weather is good. But the Army in England would have to be tuned up, and made battle worthy in no uncertain manner.

Brooke's reply, when he received this letter two weeks later, was immediate. By secret cipher he cabled back:

Your ideas about future moves are NOT quote related to existing fact. In any case imperative to finish clearing Germans out of North Africa first of all. Let me know your views concerning admin problems connected with advance to TRIPOLI.[1]

Thus both Rommel and Montgomery were slapped down for considering any future moves other than the desert campaign in hand. Had Hitler surrendered North Africa in 1942 as Rommel hoped, he would almost certainly have had to face a Second Front in Western Europe in 1943 – with incalculable effects on the war in Russia. Meanwhile Brooke's calculations and Intelligence suggested that unless North Africa fell to the Allies before Christmas, a cross-Channel Second Front in 1943 was unlikely to succeed. Brooke had taken a Corps to France in 1939, and been Commander-in-Chief of the ill-fated British forces left below the Somme in July 1940. He had reluctantly allowed Mountbatten at the Chiefs of Staff meetings early in 1942 to argue the case for a landing at Dieppe – and the casualties had been unacceptably high. Unless the Russians broke through in the East, or the Americans and British immediately furnished the necessary forces for an all-out commitment in France, Brooke felt it was better to build step-by-step on Allied success in the Mediterranean; to force Hitler and Mussolini on the defensive in Southern France, Italy, Greece, Corsica, Sardinia, Sicily, Crete, and the Dode-

[1] In Montgomery Papers.

canese. Logistically this would do more to draw off German forces from the Russian front than would a weak cross-Channel assault, and would meanwhile preserve the Allied initiative for a cross-Channel landing in 1944 while a large proportion of Hitler's forces was engaged in Southern Europe. Above all, though, it was futile to talk of 1943 cross-Channel landings when the campaigns in North Africa were far from over, and in this respect events were to prove Brooke wiser than his Minister of Defence, the Prime Minister.

Meanwhile, preoccupied with political considerations and insufficiently versed in military realities, Eisenhower had, in the words of his military biographer, given 'only cursory glances at the battle situation' after the 'Torch' landings.[1] He only moved his headquarters to North Africa some sixteen days after the landings, and only on 27 November did he actually visit the front for the first time. By then Hitler's orders that a powerful German bridgehead be formed in Tunisia had become reality, and Churchill's hope that the campaign might be over by Christmas was doomed. Far from eliminating the German presence in Tunisia, Eisenhower would be forced to wait until Montgomery's Eighth Army had traversed the entire North African coastline to the Cape Bon peninsula before Tunis could be taken.

Montgomery, however, did not take Brooke's stricture any more quietly than did Rommel the Führer's insistence on holding out in Africa to the last moment. Though Montgomery did not fly back to England to argue his case, he answered Brooke's cable with a letter which, in the light of subsequent events, must be considered historic. In it Montgomery argued once again for a cross-Channel assault in 1943, this time making clear that his views were not based on strategic opportunism, but on a logistical conviction, born of his experience in the Middle East since August that year:

About future plans,

Montgomery wrote back:

perhaps I was not clear. It is essential to clear the Germans out of North Africa before we weaken our forces there, and before we begin other ventures,

he acknowledged;

I suppose everyone is agreed about that.

But after we have done that it is not so easy to plan the next move from North Africa. An invasion of SICILY, or SARDINIA, or

---

[1] Stephen E. Ambrose, *The Supreme Commander*, New York 1970.

ITALY, or all of them, is going to be a very difficult job so long as the enemy maintains strong air forces in SICILY; the distance for our fighters would be very great.

It seems to me that any *large scale* operations against ITALY from North Africa have four major troubles to contend with:

a) The long sea journey to African ports; this is all mixed up with shipping problems, submarine attack, and so on.

b) The great difficulty of giving adequate air support to the operations.

c) The fact that you are not operating from a well established base, with workshops, repair facilities, depots, etc., all well organised and equipped.

d) The great difficulty of keeping the field army up to strength with reinforcements, equipment, supplies, petrol, and so on.

All these troubles disappear if you launch the main operations from England. At once you get:

a) Short sea passage.

b) No difficulty about air support.

c) A well established base behind you.

d) No difficulty about getting reinforcements of men and material to the field army.

You have of course other troubles, but these four are fundamentals.

I therefore feel that our operations against ITALY from North Africa should take the form of the most terrific bombing; this must be a prolonged and sustained effort.

This air effort could be accompanied by small scale operations, such as are within the capacity of our forces.

This capacity was the crux of Monty's argument. Ever since the break-out at Alamein, Monty had relied heavily on the advice of his BGS A&Q, Brigadier Sir Brian Robertson – in Monty's subsequent view the best chief of administration in the British Army.

Actually we have not got the reserves of manpower and equipment out here to undertake *prolonged large-scale* operations; such operations cannot be undertaken without certain casualties to personnel and equipment. In all my operations now I have to be very careful about losses, as there are not the officers or men in the depots in Egypt to replace them.

It is quite useless to initiate large-scale operations against ITALY from North Africa unless you are prepared to see them through. Are we so prepared as regards reserves of men and equipment actually ready to hand? I think the answer is 'No'.

It is quite obvious that the Bosche is beginning to get stretched. I don't believe he has any intention of going over the CAUCASUS and down to ABADAN; he could not do it. The Russians will keep him fully occupied on the Eastern Front.

From North Africa we should keep him looking towards the Mediterranean, very anxious about an invasion of SICILY, ITALY, and so on; and we bomb ITALY day and night so that she screams for help, and possibly may want to chuck it. And possibly we land forces in SICILY.

But the real thing is elsewhere, and suddenly about June 1943 we nip across the Channel. And the big thing is going to be sustained, therefore we must be on a good wicket as regards the four fundamentals referred to in para 3, i.e.

Secure sea journey.

Proper air support.

A firm and well stocked base.

Reserves of personnel and material within easy reach.[1]

Like Rommel, Monty could make no headway, although, ironically, both commanders would ultimately be selected to command their countries' forces in the battle of Normandy. In the meantime Rommel was sent back to Africa by an angry Hitler, while Monty was told he would have to fight on at least as far as Tripoli – if not further.

[1] Letter of 13.12.42, Montgomery Papers.

CHAPTER NINE

A Lull in the Battle

On 26 November 1942 Marshal Bastico signalled to Rommel that Mussolini expected him to launch counter-attacks against Eighth Army. Given the over-extended lines of communication and administrative problems confronting Eighth Army, this was not a fanciful suggestion, as was all too clear to Montgomery, whose forward troops were now more than eight hundred miles from their administrative depots at Alexandria.

Rommel's confidence had, however, been shattered by his defeat at Alamein. The previous evening he had seen a newsreel of his last visit to Berlin, receiving his Field-Marshal's baton, and boasting of his imminent capture of Cairo and Alexandria. Sick at heart he had given temporary command of the Panzer Army to von Thoma's successor, General Fehn, and had flown to East Prussia to argue his case for total evacuation of North Africa before Hitler. Hitler had refused point-blank to countenance such a plan, and Rommel was merely sent back via Italy with promises of more weapons. On the way Rommel nevertheless persuaded Goering that, instead of counter-attacking Montgomery, he should withdraw his Axis Army to Tunis and counter-attack Eisenhower's virgin forces there.

Kesselring immediately put a stop to such ideas, but in the ensuing days Rommel was able to convince even Kesselring – the C-in-C South – that a phased withdrawal to Buerat, two hundred miles east of Tripoli, was advisable, as the 100-mile-wide front at Agheila was untenable.

It is now clear both from Rommel's diary and Montgomery's that Rommel seriously miscalculated the threat posed by Eighth Army at Agheila in November 1942. With at least 'sixty to seventy thousand' troops[1] confronting the meagre forces Eighth Army could maintain beyond Tobruk, Rommel was in no immediate danger. Indeed such was the stretched administrative situation that Monty decided to fly back to Cairo for urgent talks with Alexander and the senior staff officers at GHQ, for, as Monty noted in his diary, it would now be

[1] Rommel's own estimate, given to Hitler on 28.11.42. Quoted in David Irving, op. cit.

impossible for him to 'begin the operations against the AGHEILA position till about the middle of December'. He had given priority of administrative build-up to the RAF, and had so few troops forward that he could not risk 'another battle which involved heavy casualties'. The veteran 9th Australian Division had been ordered to return to Australia, and even the New Zealand Division was in danger of being recalled. Somehow Montgomery had to convince Rommel that the threat was greater than in fact it was – 'I must use metal, artillery fire and air bombing, and have a minimum of casualties,' he reflected in his diary. Moreover it was quite clear to Monty that the Agheila position was the key to both Buerat *and* Tripoli. 'The next position was known as the BUERAT position. Success at AGHEILA would make it very difficult for the enemy to hold the BUERAT position, or any other position, at all adequately. . . . My problem was how to get the enemy out of the AGHEILA position quickly. It was a very difficult position to attack; if I could use bluff and manoeuvre, and frighten him to such an extent that it would appear that, if he stood to fight, he would probably lose his whole force, then he would probably withdraw. This would suit me, as I could then attack him in the easier country to the West of AGHEILA.'[1]

Monty's bluff succeeded beyond all expectation. Using the long-range RAF weapon to the full, as well as judicious publicity concerning his build-up, he deceived Rommel and finally Rommel's Italian and German superiors into withdrawing virtually all the Italian holding infantry, beginning around 6 December. He had thus persuaded Rommel to split his army and to defend Agheila with only a mobile rearguard, thus affording Eighth Army the chance to outflank and cut this off – if the rearguard could be induced to stay long enough. The prospect was encouraging, as he wrote from Cairo to Brigadier 'Bobby' Erskine, his acting BGS at Eighth Army headquarters on 6 December. He was 'very doubtful if the enemy will be able to withdraw all his stuff from the Agheila position *quickly*. He is very short of petrol, and two more petrol ships were sunk off Tripoli.' Administrative officers in Cairo were meanwhile saying that it was impossible to build up sufficient stocks of ammunition, men and supplies by the single 800-mile long road from Alexandria for a British attack before the end of December. After giving priority in supplies to the RAF in Cyrenaica, Benghazi was only bringing in a trickle for Eighth Army; a railhead was pushed through to Tobruk at last on 1 December, but it was only capable of taking four trains a day along a single track. What was desperately needed was 'a really high class expert in port development' who would develop Benghazi 'into a sort of minor Southampton', as Monty remarked; but Eighth Army was not to be deterred or to sit back, he insisted:

[1] The Mersa Brega–Agheila battle, Diary: The Desert campaign, Montgomery Papers.

It is therefore very important that we should carry on with all preparations for the battle we are planning to begin on 14 Dec; *there must be no change from this*; I fancy we shall probably find a good deal still there by 16 Dec.

It was vital to 'make great efforts by air observation, by day *and* night, to discover any signs of withdrawal or big movements on roads'; moreover he had assembled all the senior administrative staff officers in Cairo, including naval liaison officers, to impress upon them the 'importance of stepping up the supply of petrol'. By 7 December he was writing even more hopefully: 'I do not think Rommel can get his chaps away and we may do them in on 16 Dec.'

Montgomery now journeyed to his invalid Chief of Staff, a hospital visit which de Guingand later clearly recalled. De Guingand had been flown back from Benghazi suffering from a gallstone and his doctors had recommended three months' sick leave. Remembering his own sudden hospitalisation in 1939, Montgomery asked de Guingand when he thought he would be fit to rejoin Eighth Army. De Guingand replied, in two or three weeks – whereupon Montgomery squared the doctors. 'I had not at that time appreciated fully the amazing determination or the character of my Chief,' de Guingand wrote later – for he had been certain that his hospitalisation had marked the end of his active career in the war. Instead, 'on the condition that I "worked gently" to start with,' Monty got the doctors to agree to a three-week convalescence, instead of three months.[1]

In fact Monty was on the top of his form, and felt that if Rommel could not succeed against him, then certainly the doctors of the Scottish Hospital in Cairo had little chance.

I am spending a day or two in great luxury

he informed his son's guardians, the Reynolds, with amusement,

and I must say it is rather pleasant to live in a nice house again. And also to have a good bath and a proper hair-cut by a good barber!!

General Alexander had just had his portrait painted by the South African artist Neville Lewis; when Lewis had finished it he had asked if he might also do one of Monty, as Official War Artist working for the South African Government. 'That will be very easy to arrange,' Alexander had said, and thus Monty followed Alexander onto the sitting-dais (comprising two cut-down table tops and a wicker chair) in the Hotel Continental in Cairo:

[1] F. W. de Guingand, *Generals at War*, op. cit.

I had a room with a good light in the Continental Hotel, and at the exact time arranged General Montgomery, accompanied by a young A.D.C., came in. He asked how long I wanted him to sit and I told him I would like two hours if he could spare the time. The A.D.C. was told he could go, and to call back at the end of two hours. The General seemed a little nervy: I don't think he had sat for a portrait before.[1]

Monty had certainly not sat for a portrait during the war, nor in fact since the days of his marriage to Betty. When Lewis, during a break, showed photographs of a previous sitter, Field-Marshal Smuts, with the painting on the easel and Lewis working on it, Monty would not be outdone. Immediately a signal went to Eighth Army headquarters summoning Captain Geoffrey Keating, the officer responsible for the Army Film and Photographic Unit in the desert, to Cairo – 'and the next morning when he came for a sitting he had with him his official photographer to do a similar one,' Lewis recorded with astonishment. Within hours the photograph had been sent to the United States by wireless and published 'as far as I can remember . . . something like this: "Desert rat takes time off from chasing desert fox to sit for his portrait by South African war artist, Captain Neville Lewis, in Cairo." '

Monty's actions were now 'news' the world over, as he was becoming aware from the growing mailbag of letters that arrived in the desert. Whether Monty was, as some thought, determined to take personal advantage of the chance of widespread publicity is debatable. He had spent a lifetime preparing and rehearsing for high command in battle, and it had taken four years of British failure and defeat before he had finally been given command of an army in the field. If the victory of Alamein had gone to his head, it was perhaps understandable in a man not given to quiet and self-effacing modesty. Yet it cannot have been mere self-advertisement that prompted Monty, for as his Canadian ADC in England in 1942 later recalled, Monty was surprisingly innocent about the power of the press, having been entirely concerned until then with the task of putting himself over in person to his men.[2] His quick mind had, however, soon seized on the usefulness of publicity in rebuilding the morale and self-confidence of Eighth Army, and in competing with the highly effective German propaganda machine which had underscored Rommel's previous achievements in the desert.

Perhaps no one at Eighth Army HQ was as aware of the importance of morale as the editor of Eighth Army's two newspapers – the daily *Eighth Army News* and the weekly *Crusader* – Captain Warwick

[1] N. Lewis, *Studio Encounters*, Cape Town 1963.
[2] Lt-Colonel Trumbull Warren, interview of 9.11.81.

Charlton. Charlton had served in this capacity since the formation of Eighth Army in 1941.

I'm aware of the faults he [Monty] had, but the army he took over had no morale – there was very little left. It didn't trust its generals – the most popular general in the Eighth Army was probably Rommel!

There had been occasions before Monty came of guns failing to fire – that happened. The British soldiers respected the Germans – and Rommel played up to that: you know, when he said: 'You fought like lions and were led by goats' – all that sort of stuff.

The British soldiers admired the Russians and they admired Rommel.

Until Monty came. There was this extraordinary little man whom nobody knew anything about, really. And what he did was a sort of Wesleyan thing – in my view. It was a revival thing – to revive their spirits, revive their minds. . . .

What he did – he did something that doesn't appear in the military books. You know, when you think about it, war isn't about battles, it is to do with men's minds – more than ever.

Monty inherited some highly intelligent people – but intellectually, if they were honest, they could see no future: it was up and down the desert. Until this man came and got through to their minds.

The first thing he did was to preach a sermon, about victory and success. And with this trick of repetition – he had quite a small vocabulary really. But nevertheless he knew where he was going and what he wanted to do. And he preached at us; and people felt impelled to go out and carry this message, you know.

All the great revolutionary leaders of history had understood the importance of the word, the gospel, Charlton felt: and it was in this sense that Monty was a 'revolutionary' general.

This was what was new. It's all very well people talking afterwards about the guns and the ammunition – but what Monty created was a revolutionary army.[1]

To counter the morale of Rommel's army, Monty preached an Eighth Army gospel based on simple virtues, understandable by all: the infectious pride of belonging to a great and professional team, fighting for time-honoured principles, paramount among which were freedom and respect for the individual. There was no element of coercion: of a ruthless general imposing harsh discipline upon an

[1] Warwick Charlton, interview of 31.3.83.

ailing army. Although Monty had brought with him from England a great vision of modern battlefield 'stage-management', it was the manner in which Monty adapted himself and his vision to desert conditions which in retrospect so impressed Charlton and others. Monty's Australian hat, for example, though glinting with the badges of Eighth Army's multifarious regiments, neither suited his head nor conveyed the right connotation in an army in which the Australians were admired but not always well-liked. Monty's veteran ADC, John Poston, and Geoffrey Keating, the head of the Army Film and Photographic Unit, thus conspired to get Monty to adopt the tank beret – as Charlton remembered.

At the climax of the battle of Alamein, Geoffrey Keating called me to come out with him one morning. And it was to take Monty out, with John Poston, to photograph him for the first time in the beret and see whether it was really suitable. Geoffrey said it would be better if they could go where there was a bit of something happening, to 'liven it up'.

So they went where there was some counter-battery artillery action, guns firing at each other. We all went up. And then the most extraordinary scene took place with Geoffrey and Monty. Some shells landed not too far away – and people started taking cover!

And Geoffrey said: 'I might get one [shell] in focus, that would look really good!'

And they stood there, the two of them, neither was going to give way. Monty of course wouldn't think of it.

But it was an absurdity – we could have lost him.

There's a picture of Monty – a famous picture of him looking out of a tank, wearing his beret – that was one of the pictures taken then. It went all over the world.[1]

It is important to remember that Monty did not import either John Poston, Geoffrey Keating or Warwick Charlton into Eighth Army. All were veterans of the desert, and all had served under Generals Cunningham, Ritchie, and Auchinleck before Monty arrived. Conscientiously Keating and Charlton had tried to 'publicise' Monty's predecessors, on film, in photographs and by the printed word. If their response towards Monty was different, it was because the new Eighth Army commander was different. Monty arrived with no preconceived ideas about publicity; what he possessed was a probing mind, intent upon learning each man's 'trade' in Eighth Army, and 'sizing him up'. This process had begun the moment he interviewed John Poston as potential ADC in Cairo on arrival in August;

[1] Ibid.

the moment he had met Brigadier de Guingand at the crossroads leading to El Alamein the next morning; and every day thereafter he had made it his business to inspect the men who comprised his army: the soldiers, the NCOs, the officers, the headquarters staffs:

Within two or three weeks of taking over I was introduced to him,

Charlton recalled.

He would ask people in to explain their jobs.
And I said, 'Sir, well what I've got is a printing press, a captured printing press we've mounted on wheels, it's not very efficient, but it's the best we have until we get to where there are better presses. That is – other than in Cairo! – in Benghazi or in Tripoli.'
Now this was *before* Alamein.
And he gave me a chit, saying I could take over – there was a military word for taking over – 'Warwick Charlton has the personal authority of the Army Commander to take-over any presses between Alamein and Tripoli.'
And that was pretty good. It's a thousand bloody miles.[1]

From then on, Monty was to show absolute and inviolate trust in the twenty-four-year-old journalist, permitting him to print exactly what he wished and defying any attempts by jealous or anxious Public Relations officers in Cairo or in London to interfere in Charlton's free exercise of his rights as an editor in Eighth Army. From being a 'record of letters and battles', something which 'wouldn't have disturbed the sleep of anyone', Charlton's newspapers became contentious, political – and a powerful new weapon in the arsenal of Eighth Army's mounting morale:

The other thing he did,

reflected Charlton,

he made everybody, no matter what their job, into soldiers. People who were doing specialist jobs – it might have been filming, it might have been baking – but Monty made this clear: that you were, first and foremost you were soldiers – it didn't matter whether you were cartographers, or this or that, or painting camouflage: but you were *soldiers*, of Eighth Army.
And the thing was, instead of feeling, 'Sod that!', we felt, 'This is marvellous: that's what we are – not bloody well Royal Service Corps or this, that or the other – but soldiers!'[2]

[1] Ibid.
[2] Ibid.

The unprecedented publicity now being given to Monty and to the exploits of Eighth Army was nevertheless disturbing to those traditional, aristocratic minds who equated publicity with vulgarity and believed gentlemen should only back into the limelight. Monty's cocksure and combative spirit was anathema to them, and within weeks of Alamein there was a move to get rid of Keating, Charlton and other officers who were encouraging this popular acclaim for a mere soldier in the field. Keating was removed from his post, and Charlton arrested and imprisoned in Tobruk, for attempting to expose the 'plot'. His court-martial – which became a test case – resulted in acquittal; Keating was recalled and given a written order by Monty forbidding him to be posted elsewhere save with the written authority of the Eighth Army Commander – an *imprimatur* which Charlton also thereafter enjoyed. Thus, day by day, Eighth Army became Montgomery's personal army – an army where men got on with their jobs, secure in the knowledge that Monty trusted them to do their best, and would tolerate no bureaucratic interference from outside. Wounded men began to refuse to go into holding units on leaving hospital, but would instead disobey the regulations and rejoin their regiments in the field – for to fight with Eighth Army was now a matter of personal honour. As Charlton explained, it was not simply a desire to campaign but, increasingly, a sense of being one of the elect, like Nelson's tars or Napoleon's immortals:

It was a tremendous time because people could see – after Alamein of course people could see the light!

No longer were democracy and freedom the poor relations of teutonic supermen: they were ideals that would triumph.

People could see what war was really about: one set of ideas trying to prevail against another. The battles were almost incidental.
And suddenly people could see not just going up and down the desert and firing and being wounded or not wounded, or getting into a city and having a marvellous loot or whatever, but really that they were going to be the chosen people – that this was going to make possible a renewing, a changing for the better: a new Jerusalem. And that was heady stuff – a pretty powerful medicine!
And this man Montgomery, seeing, ensuring it happened.[1]

It was not surprising to Charlton that the establishment jibbed at such an army of crusaders – an army of increasing moral and political dimension, under the leadership of a revolutionary figure who would brook no outside tampering with his army and exacted the

[1] Ibid.

strangest depth of loyalty from all manner, rank and creed of men. Moreover, just as his army had undergone its 'baptism of fire' at Alamein, so in his personal relationships Monty seemed to test the mettle of his subordinates and staff – a test that was the basis of lifelong loyalty and friendship. Keating's courage under fire impressed Monty, to the extent that Keating thereafter had the *entrée* to Monty's personal mess at Tactical Headquarters.

Another man tested was Captain Henderson; his baptism was rather different. Prior to the battle of Alamein Monty had cast around certain Eighth Army regiments for another ADC more versed in the ways of the desert than the one he had brought with him from England. After quietly meeting a number, he had chosen a 22-year-old captain from a cavalry regiment: Johnny Henderson. Henderson had joined Monty and his Tactical Headquarters just after the breakout at Alamein:

When I went to him, I was told that it was for a fortnight; if I didn't like it I could come back, and if he didn't like me . . .

Henderson was still in two minds about the appointment when he flew back to Cairo with Montgomery, where an episode at the zoo decided the issue.

Yes, a funny thing happened then [in Cairo]. I went to the zoo with this friend of mine, having been told to have the afternoon off, and to meet him at 7.30 a.m. the next day at the aerodrome to go back to the desert.

Well I went off with this chum of mine, we had lunch, went off in the afternoon to the zoo there, and we were walking round the elephant house. They were rather sleepy old elephants and for some unknown reason this fellow took my hat off and offered it to this elephant – who ate it! It was in the afternoon, no shops open – so when I got in the morning to the airport I thought I'd better wait by the aeroplane because I couldn't appear at the guard of honour.

So when Monty got to the aircraft he said, 'Johnny, why weren't you at the Guard of Honour as I told you?'

So I said, 'I'm very sorry, sir, I couldn't as I haven't got a hat. It was eaten by an elephant yesterday afternoon.'

He said, 'If you feel as bad as that, you'd better get inside and lie down'!

Henderson was relieved. 'I thought it hadn't gone too badly. Well, when we got back, after the flight, I always drove him. And as he got out he said: "Are you capable of driving?" I said, "Certainly, why not?" He said, "Oh, that extraordinary story you told me!" '

At dinner that night Henderson related the whole story, and Monty at last chose to believe him.

It broke down a sort of barrier between us,

Henderson recalled,

having survived that. And I stayed there – from then on after.[1]

Certainly, once Monty's trust and friendship were won, it was for life. Henderson remained with Monty as his ADC throughout the war, and although he then returned to a civil career, Monty kept in touch with him right up to his death. With the sparring, competitive side to his character, Monty wanted a personal staff with spirit and a sense of humour – young men with energy who would speak up for themselves. 'You had to say at all times what you thought,' Henderson recalled. 'It was no good dissimulating. . . . He did like the people around him to stand up to him – perhaps that's why in the end he didn't have regular soldiers on his personal staff.'[2]

Monty's manner, his forthright character and his schoolboyish sense of fun did not endear him to everybody. His competitive streak was undoubtedly best served in war, when he had to pit his wits, his will and the men under his command against a challenging opponent. But it was a competitiveness not confined to the fight against the enemy; it permeated Monty's whole life and was at the heart of most 'conundrums' concerning Monty's sometimes outrageous remarks and behaviour. Lewis must have worked extremely hard at the oil portrait, for it was ready before Monty left Cairo on 9 December 1942.

The portrait of General Alexander was still in my studio, and when Monty's was finished he [Monty] said, 'Put the two of them side by side; I want to compare them.'

I did this, and he spent a few minutes looking at them, and then turned to me and said, 'Mine is far better, much better, no doubt about it, no doubt about it at all. We have knocked him [Alexander] for six, we have knocked him for six right out of the ground.' I was amused at the 'we',

Lewis – who had been deeply impressed by Alexander's charm and modesty – recorded.[3]

Before leaving Cairo Monty sent a quick message of encourage-

[1] J. R. Henderson, interview of 13.8.81.
[2] Ibid.
[3] N. Lewis, op. cit.

ment to de Guingand in hospital, ascertained that his pamphlet on 'how to fight battles'[1] had been properly printed, and arranged for Neville Lewis to fly out to the desert some weeks later to do a second portrait 'in the field of battle'.

[1] F. W. de Guingand, *Generals at War*, op. cit.

CHAPTER TEN

Agheila

Monty's plan for the battle of Agheila (or Mersa Brega as it was called by the Germans) was to attack frontally with the infantry of 51st Highland Division on his right, seaward flank; to hold his heavy armour of 7th Armoured Division in the centre; and to send the New Zealand motorised division with 4th Light Armoured Brigade round the enemy's southern flank. The latter would move two days before the infantry attack, cutting off whatever enemy it could at 'Marble Arch'. It was a long, tortuous outflanking march, and Monty was in no doubt that Rommel could, if he wished, negate it simply by withdrawing his mobile rearguard along the coast road: 'If the move round the Southern flank could be concealed from the enemy, then success was certain. If the enemy detected the move, he would probably pull out before it was too late,' Monty noted straightfor-wardly in his diary.

Reconnaissance reports of the build-up of Eighth Army's forces had meanwhile enabled the nervous Rommel to convince his super-iors he must pull out without accepting battle at Agheila.[1] What Rommel did not seem to realise was that Montgomery did not possess sufficient heavy tanks or fuel to conduct both an armoured outflanking move *and* attack the main Mersa Brega position with armour. Rommel had only to sit tight at Mersa Brega/Agheila, parry the frontal attack of 51st Highland Division with infantry and, with his fifty-seven heavy tanks, destroy the New Zealanders' outflank-ing party as and when it emerged from the desert to the south.

What tipped the scales, however, was the memory of Alamein: that relentless assault by the infantry and armour of Montgomery's army, supported by aircraft and massive artillery bombardment – and the subsequent loss of almost all unmotorised Axis infantry. Given his shortage of fuel – which had to a large extent been used to ferry his unmotorised units to Buerat – Rommel was in a dilemma. He no longer had the requisite infantry to hold off a powerful frontal thrust while allowing his Panzer divisions to deal with an Eighth

---

[1] German photographic reconnaissance was, in the words of one Specialist Intelligence Officer in Cairo, 'laughably amateur' throughout the desert cam-paign – Dr Richard Hey, interview of 10.3.81.

Army outflanking move; all he could do was maintain a posture of defiance at Agheila, and be prepared to run as soon as Eighth Army showed signs of attacking.

Both commanders were therefore trying to bluff each other rather than risk heavy casualties. Ultra Intelligence, however, began to indicate that Rommel might not now wait until 16 December before withdrawing his rearguard, so nervous had he become about Eighth Army's strength and so anxious about his fuel situation. On 11 December Montgomery therefore advanced the Agheila assault by two days, beginning a 'very active raiding policy at once'.

This certainly precipitated Rommel into thinking that the battle had begun, for late that night Rommel gave the code-word for the evacuation of Agheila – before Montgomery's main offensive had even started. Contrary to the forecast of all the administrative 'experts', Monty's bluff had succeeded. Yet there now began one of the most tantalising episodes of the entire desert campaign.

The New Zealand outflanking march, involving a march of nearly two hundred miles, had already begun on the night of 11 December. Did it have any chance of cutting off Rommel's rearguard? And if it did, were its twenty-one heavy tanks sufficient in an armoured battle with Rommel's fifty-seven? Monty had agreed to give Freyberg another nine from 7th Armoured Division – but he would not commit himself to giving more lest 51st Highland Division got held up in the heavily mined and easily defended Agheila defences. The Highlanders suffered punishing casualties from anti-personnel mines; then when on the night of 13 December they attempted to send in infantry behind an artillery barrage, they were heavily machine-gunned and shelled, and were only partially successful.

'It was a frustrating moment,' the Corps Commander, Oliver Leese, recalled.

All indications pointed to an enemy withdrawal. Yet they appeared to be still firmly in position. The Highland Division had suffered severely in their patrols and they needed time to absorb the large number of reinforcements which they had received after Alamein. I hoped against hope that I might not have to put them into a dog-fight battle at this stage.[1]

Major-General Wimberley's own desert narrative bears out his reluctance to make his Highlanders face another Alamein:

The 14th December is a day I will never forget. . . . As I motored forward I saw every 100 yards or so wounded men, mostly sappers

[1] General Sir Oliver Leese, unpublished memoirs, communicated to author by Ian Calvocoressi.

who had become casualties on the mines. The black Macadam road wound through the soft sand of the desert, pitch black in the brilliant sunshine. At intervals all down the road, mile after mile, the enemy had spread shovel-fulls of sand, and under every sixth heap or so, a mine had been buried, a hole having been drilled in the Tarmac for it. . . . On the verge of the road a mixture of Teller Mines and anti-personnel mines had been thickly strewn. At any place where a vehicle could get off the road on to hard sand, the side tracks leading towards it were all mined. About every quarter of a mile along the road derelict vehicles had been pulled across it, to block it, and each vehicle was a mass of trip wires and booby traps. . . . I was told the very corpses of our poor dead, which we lost out on patrol, were all booby trapped, when later the burial parties went out to clear the battlefield and bury them. . . . Never again, while I commanded the Highland Division, did we ever meet such a heavily mined area.[1]

It was not until the evening of 14 December that the division managed to thread a reasonably safe route through the mined and booby-trapped main defences at Mersa Brega/Agheila – and it was thus left to 153rd Highland Brigade and 7th Armoured Division to smash a passage through the southerly minefields in pursuit of Rommel's withdrawing echelons. Even with the heavy armour of 8th Armoured Brigade this was not easy, and Harding was forced to leap-frog his infantry and armour to keep up momentum against the Ariete Division's stiff opposition.

For a while the issue of the 'battle' had hung in the balance: the Highlanders could not reasonably be expected to sacrifice large numbers of men on booby traps and mines. Harding's armour was still fighting a strongly contested passage through the southern Agheila minefields and defensive system, and Freyberg's New Zealanders, having found the desert route much softer going and heavier on petrol than the LRDG reported, were alarmingly isolated from the rest of the Eighth Army. Meanwhile Rommel, alerted by air reconnaissance patrols to the existence of the New Zealand group at Maaten Giofer on 14 December, was urged to attack it – and for a brief while he toyed with the possibility. He had more than enough tanks – but what if he was unable to effect a quick attack or it was held? Would the Ariete Division be able meanwhile to hold the enemy's armoured attack in the southern minefields at Agheila on its own? If he used up too much fuel in an abortive counter-attack, would he then have enough to conduct his retreat to Buerat?

As 7th Armoured Division squeezed westwards behind Agheila,

[1] Maj-General D. N. Wimberley, 'Scottish Soldier', unpublished autobiography, communicated to author.

Rommel's calculated withdrawal broke down. The fuel crisis which occurred now put Eighth Army in a position to annihilate or capture Rommel's entire mobile rearguard – for Freyberg's force had on the evening of 15 December reached sight of the Mediterranean more than thirty miles west of 'Marble Arch', and had thus effectively cut Rommel's line of retreat. There followed, during the next twenty-four hours, the climax to the battle, as Monty recorded in his diary:

> The German units were in a desperate situation as behind them was 7 Armd Div advancing strongly and in front was the NZ Div. The Germans broke up into small scattered groups and burst their way through gaps in the NZ positions. Fighting was intense and confused all day on 16 December and prisoners were captured and recaptured on both sides.

In fact there was a six-mile gap between the New Zealand 5th and 6th Brigades – and the latter had not in fact reached the coast road, but was still two miles from it, Leese later lamented.

> It was the first time that we, in 30 Corps, had an opportunity to destroy and cripple the Panzer Corps. Could we have done so? This is bound to be a theoretical question and I think the theoretical

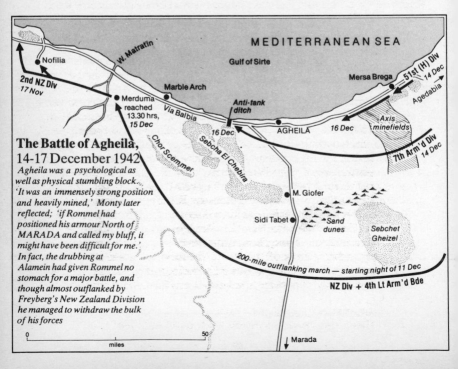

The Battle of Agheila,
14-17 December 1942
Agheila was a psychological as well as physical stumbling block. 'It was an immensely strong position and heavily mined,' Monty later reflected; 'if Rommel had positioned his armour North of MARADA and called my bluff, it might have been difficult for me.' In fact, the drubbing at Alamein had given Rommel no stomach for a major battle, and though almost outflanked by Freyberg's New Zealand Division he managed to withdraw the bulk of his forces

answer is, 'Yes, we might have done so if we could have given General Freyberg all our available tanks and anti-tank guns.'[1]

To Leese 'the situation map on the night in question made it look as if the Germans were in the bag', but by the night of 16 December it was evident the New Zealanders had failed.

Lamentable as it might appear, there had never been any chance of reinforcing Freyberg with more armour and guns than he was given. No further tanks or anti-tank guns could have been taken from Harding's south-frontal thrust, and even if further forces had miraculously been brought up from the east to reinforce Freyberg, they could not have been administratively maintained at that time over the long desert outflanking route. Indeed the delays and frustrations experienced by Freyberg's relatively minor outflanking force make it inconceivable that a larger force could have achieved even as much as Freyberg.[2]

Yet the feeling that 30 Corps had come within an ace of 'bottling up' the Afrika Korps rankled in Leese's mind – the more so since Agheila was the end, temporarily, of 30 Corps' responsibility for the pursuit, which could only take place now after an administrative pause and which would be conducted by 10 Corps. 'Could we at that time have taken an all out risk to destroy the Panzer Corps? If we had sent all our tanks round with General Freyberg would it have been possible for Rommel to counter-attack us at Mersa Brega and give us a bloody nose? Who knows?' Leese pondered after the war.

The Eighth Army has often been criticised for being slow and not taking risks and I expect we often shall be criticised again. In almost every action after Alamein, we had the same problem – to balance speed and the taking of a risk against the state of our administration and the need for ultimate victory. It was surely no good to put troops into a battle with insufficient petrol or ammunition for the particular job in hand; and as a matter of fact I never remember the Army Commander waiting till he had sufficient of both commodities. We either went into battle with sufficient ammunition for a battle or sufficient petrol for a pursuit. In this case it was sad to see Rommel get away, but in my opinion it was firstly too big a risk to forfeit our firm base at Agedabia, by sending all our tanks on with the New Zealanders and secondly I don't think we could have brought up sufficient ammunition and petrol to supply a large force of tanks by the time Rommel started to withdraw. Finally I am very doubtful whether even a larger force of tanks at General Freyberg's disposal could have stopped the

---

[1] General Sir Oliver Leese, loc. cit.
[2] Cf. W. G. Stevens, *Bardia to Enfidaville*, Wellington, N.Z. 1962.

Panzer Corps breaking out by night on the open desert ground in the area in question.[1]

Montgomery himself spent no time lamenting Rommel's 'escape'. The more he saw of the Mersa Brega/Agheila defences, the more satisfied he felt that Rommel had been forced to surrender them so easily. Even after Scorpion tanks had cleared lanes through the minefields one of Leese's two jeeps was blown up. 'It was an immensely strong position,' Monty noted in his diary, 'and the enemy came to rest in it after 1000 miles of retreat; his troops must have felt that here at any rate they would be secure. But far from it. When our offensive intentions became clear he decided he must pull out and go.' Moreover, despite the straightforward coastal route along which Rommel's forces were to withdraw, they had been outflanked and temporarily cut off, losing twenty tanks, five hundred prisoners, thirty guns and many hundreds of vehicles. 'So I am quite pleased with the results of the Agheila affair,' Monty wrote to the CIGS on 18 December. 'We turned the enemy out of a very strong position by aggressive tactics; he was not quick enough and before he could get clear he got a very severe mauling.'

Freyberg pursued the Panzer rearguard to Nofilia, but there Montgomery halted him. It was imperative, Monty felt, to retain the initiative – and not to become drawn into the day-to-day vagaries of a close pursuit in which the enemy, retreating back along his own lines of communication, could call the tune.

Since 23 October, when we began the Battle of Egypt,

he reflected in his diary.

I have held the initiative and have never once lost it; the enemy has been on the defensive and has never once been allowed to call the tune. He has been pushed back more than 1000 miles; his troops must be defensively minded by now, and also dispirited.

This fact is of great importance. The enemy is becoming used to being turned out of his positions, to be hustled in his retreats, to being shot up from the air. All this must have had a very considerable adverse effect on the morale of the enemy commanders and troops.

[1] General Sir Oliver Leese, loc. cit. It is evident from the German War Diaries that Freyberg's outflanking threat was discounted because of the paucity of armour, hence the German surprise when enemy infantry units reached the Via Balbia. Had Freyberg possessed more armour, Rommel would have been forced to withdraw faster, but there was little likelihood of being 'put in the bag'.

This was no exaggeration as Rommel's diary and letters home reveal. In his memoirs Rommel candidly admitted having favoured immediate retreat to Gabes without accepting any further major defensive engagement. 'If it had been left to me and I had had more petrol,' he would not have sought to counter-attack Eighth Army but 'would probably have moved across into Tunisia far earlier than I actually did', he confessed. Inevitably he was tarred a defeatist, particularly by Kesselring, who afterwards maintained: 'One thing was certainly a mistake, which was to leave Rommel in command at all.'[1] Kesselring accepted the ultimate inevitability of surrendering Cyrenaica and Tripolitania, but felt with Cavallero that 'opportunities for counter-attacks with modest objectives must be exploited to the full' – a policy that was to work brilliantly in Tunisia against Eisenhower's forces. With all its training and experience, he felt, the African Panzer Army ought to have been able to do far more in mauling Montgomery's over-extended pursuit forces. 'The fighting spirit was there,' he remarked. 'Given leadership even our lamentably small trickle of supplies would have been ample for this limited task' – and recalled that the year before Rommel had been eminently capable of such counter-attacks.[2]

Given Rommel's failure of nerve, ought Montgomery to have done more to discomfit Rommel in his retreat, and been bolder in his attempts to outflank him?

It is tempting to think so in hindsight; but the circumstances of the time must not be forgotten. However much insight Ultra Intelligence might give into Rommel's supply situation there was no doubt from the orders sent by Hitler, OKW, Mussolini and the Italian High Command that Rommel was constantly being urged to make more of an effort to halt or counter-attack Eighth Army – as Brigadier Sir Edgar Williams later recalled:

Rommel of course had to suggest [in his signals, decrypted by Ultra] that he was going to hang on to the last moment because of Hitler; one therefore had to inform Monty that Rommel's intention – expressed intention – was to stay put here.

The trouble was that while we were helped enormously by Ultra – because Ultra expressed Rommel's intentions to the All-Highest [Hitler] – we were sometimes hindered by Ultra, because Rommel was too good a soldier to carry the intentions out. . . . I think we probably asked Monty to lay on too many preparations – which was in any case his natural inclination – because we could see Rommel was told to stay put: 'Here it is in Ultra'. . . .

The source material was too good. If one had just done one's

[1] Kesselring, *The Memoirs of Field-Marshal Kesselring*, London 1953.
[2] Ibid.

thinking and intelligence without the [Ultra] signals intelligence, one would have said: Well, Rommel will get us as far as this – and then he'll be off. And we'll be left sort of dangling once again. . . .

I think that all that time during that campaign you have two elements about the withdrawal: the 'hold to the last ditch' Hitler stuff, and Rommel's very astute generalship, so that you could bet your bottom dollar – although you couldn't bet your bottom dollar, because that's exactly what you *couldn't* do with Rommel – you could take a sly bet that if Rommel was telling Hitler that he was holding to the last drop of blood, that he was in the process of doing a very calculated false front to us.[1]

Moreover, there was the matter of British morale, as Williams also recalled; no British general had successfully held the position beyond Agheila – not even General Richard O'Connor after his magnificent victory over the Italians at Beda Fomm. Agheila was to the 'desert sweats' a considerable stumbling block in psychological terms therefore:

It was very interesting because in a way, looking back, one realizes all sorts of ways in which without in the least seeking to influence him [Monty], one *did* influence him by suggesting the odd thing. I was thinking of the Agheila complex particularly, you see, because I'd been in the first Agheila myself, so I knew that little area quite well. . . .

Monty, Williams recalled,

was determined not to have a set-back which would affect the morale of his soldiers. There was in his nature this business of being always carefully prepared so that you were always in balance, but there was also a tremendous awareness of this Agheila complex – which I think he very much picked up, alas, from me: that you must get round Agheila and on, because Agheila had become a sort of bogey – because you got as far as Agheila and then back again.

Monty had thus refused to attack prematurely. 'I think he was studying the inherited legend that he didn't want to find repeated – and knew that a lot of his command depended on the careful nurturing of Eighth Army's morale.' To Williams it 'wasn't a matter of over-estimating or under-estimating', but of convincing his soldiers that they were unbeatable, and Williams recalled with a mixture of amazement and fascination – as an Oxford don in civil

[1] Loc. cit.

life – the moment during the battle when Monty released premature news of Eighth Army's victory:

> When we went round Agheila – the New Zealanders' left-hook – Monty wrote a Sitrep himself, a press release about this, which I'm sure he did because he wanted to make this impression about Agheila at last being taken – not for England, but for his own chaps, so to speak. It was premature because when he'd released the thing we were still doing it! He hadn't captured it! . . . I can remember being very, very genuinely shocked by this business of announcing that we'd done it, before we had.[1]

Rommel was equally surprised when he heard both the BBC and Cairo Radio broadcast that the Axis forces were bottled up at Nofilia and Montgomery was 'hammering home the cork', but seemed to have no understanding that, as Williams realised, Montgomery was 'doing this for local morale consumption rather than stunting in England. I remember thinking: I suppose it'll be all right, because by tomorrow or the next day, it'll come true, but. . . . This particular instance stays in my mind,' he summarised, 'because of the "Agheila complex" and the premature issue of the victory signal, in the sense of the successful outflanking of the Agheila position, when he was really telling his chaps that it was done and it was all right.'[2]

What was ironical, in Williams's sometimes sardonic mind, was the fact that both Rommel and Montgomery were capable of using their signals home to further their local ends. While Monty judiciously used his press releases to bolster the morale of his men at Agheila, Rommel 'cried wolf' to Hitler in order to wrest permission for further withdrawal: pretending he had valiantly hung on to the almost bitter end when in fact he was withdrawing according to agreed and well-rehearsed plans – a withdrawal which was 'extremely skilfully done, because he was a frightfully good soldier', Williams recalled, 'but of course you don't tell Hitler that you've done a skilful withdrawal – because you've not been told to withdraw.'[3]

Monty was thus genuinely well pleased to have forced Rommel's withdrawal from Agheila with so few casualties, as he wrote to de Guingand on 18 December:

> I have had a look at the famous Agheila position. It is immensely strong and we have been saved considerable casualties by not having to attack it seriously, it was a complete mass of mines,

[1] Ibid. Williams had been a troop leader in a King's Dragoon Guards armoured car when, on 20 February 1941, he first 'bumped into the Germans on the ground' at Agheila.

[2] Ibid.

[3] Ibid.

especially on the approaches and we have had a good many charges blown up. We had to concentrate most of the R.E. in the Army to clear the mines and get safe roads through.[1]

The next stop, when Eighth Army was ready, would be the city Eisenhower had not been able to take from the west: Tripoli.

[1] Letter of 18.12.42 in F. W. de Guingand, *Generals at War*, op. cit.

CHAPTER ELEVEN

What is to Happen now Lies in God's Hands

Monty's appreciation, after Alamein, that the key to Rommel's retreat would be neutralisation of Tripoli by naval and air attacks proved salutary. Not only was the Axis advantage of being able to fall back on existing lines of communication thereby reduced, but, as Rommel withdrew towards Tripoli, the value of holding the port at all became questionable.

Rommel now felt that it was time the two North African campaigns – in Tunisia and Tripolitania – should be married by unified command. Monty felt so too – and in his diary, on Christmas Eve, one week after the capture of Agheila, set down the conflict of priorities and strategies which had now begun to complicate the war in North Africa. If fuel was a problem for Rommel, so too was it for Eighth Army.

> The problem is petrol. I require 1200 tons of petrol delivered daily by sea into BENGHAZI. At present this is not being done and I am having to move 800 tons daily by road from TOBRUK. This is a great strain on my transport, and I require this transport for dumping South of BENGHAZI for the BUERAT battle, and for maintenance up towards TRIPOLI. Unless BENGHAZI port can be developed to handle a greater daily tonnage, and unless substantially more petrol can be put into BENGHAZI by sea than is being done at present, we shall have great difficulty in getting to TRIPOLI.

Moreover, petrol, transport and labour were required for construction of all-weather airfields at Benghazi for the RAF's strategic bombers.

> This means that transport and labour have to be produced by Eighth Army for the purpose. It also requires bitumen and all bitumen and labour is wanted for the roads, which are getting badly broken up. . . .
> So the problem of getting to TRIPOLI has now become very difficult, and there are many vested interests involved.

My own view is that the surest way of getting to TRIPOLI quickly is for Eighth Army, with its accompanying Air Force, to 'drive' forward and that everything should be done to make this possible.

But it is a matter of priorities and these can be settled only at GHQ. It is a nice point as to who to put your money on. . . .

The war is not so clear cut as it was in October and November; we are away in TRIPOLITANIA, and are 1200 miles from where we started.

Our war, and the TUNISIA war, are now getting close to each other and require co-ordination.

Vested interests are beginning to creep in. We want some very clear thinking; the object must be kept very clear and pursued ruthlessly; we must not be led away on ventures that do not help in achieving the object.

We really want unified command; you cannot conduct operations in a theatre of war with a committee.

Not for another two and a half months would there be a commander-in-chief of both Tunisian and Eighth Army campaigns; in the meantime Montgomery successfully pushed Rommel out of Sirte with a single armoured brigade on Christmas Day, thus concealing Eighth Army's administrative problems. 'Mentally, and from the point of view of morale, I think we are on top of the Bosche,' Monty declared with satisfaction in a Christmas Day letter to Brooke. To Phyllis Reynolds he also wrote confidently, thanking her for 'the lovely soft leather waistcoat you sent me', and for visiting his son David at Winchester, and describing the arrangements made in the mess for Christmas.

I sent an ADC to Cairo to get supplies for the mess and as a result we have half a pig, six turkeys, six chickens, and various fruits and fresh vegetables. All this is very welcome as for the last month or so we have lived on biscuits and bully beef.

In fact Monty was himself quite uninterested in food, as the officer in charge of Tactical Headquarters recalled. Dinner in the evening was the only meal over which he took time.

He liked to discuss things, anything – liked to enjoy the company of his two ADCs and if anybody was there it went on for quite a long time, over coffee. And at half past nine he'd say: 'I'm off to bed' – and off he'd go. I don't think, apart from that time at Alamein – I can't remember him being woken up.

This aura of professional calm and confidence was, to Major Oswald, almost uncanny. One day Oswald asked Monty if he would care to see exactly how his Tactical Headquarters functioned:

I remember after the pursuit had been going on for some time I asked him, 'Would you like to come round and just see what Tac Headquarters does?'

So he said, 'Yes, yes, I'll come round at eleven o'clock and meet your chaps.' So he came round.

There wasn't very much to show him – I showed him the Armoured Command Vehicle and I showed him: 'This radio's on to 30 Corps, and that's on to Main; and now we've been stationary for a couple of days, we've got telephone lines as well. When we do operate on the move we've got radio communication to Corps Headquarters and to Main and at a pinch we could get on to another Corps as well. And here's our map: I bring information over and mark up your map, or one of your ADCs does it.' (In the ACV I had a map either on the wall or a mobile one in a map case, marked with chinagraph. Either I took it over and marked up the progress on his map or if he wanted it particularly in a hurry or anything he sent one of his ADCs over.)

I said, 'This is Captain So-and-so, and there's the Signals Officer and so on, and Sergeant-Major –'. And he said, 'Oh, yes, nice to see you' – and said [to me], 'Well that was very interesting. Yes, I enjoyed that.'

He never bothered again. He never – he just rang me up and said quietly, 'Oswald, I want you to find out what's happening to so-and-so, give me a ring back, or come over and tell me, or mark up my map. . . .'

So he was never breathing down one's neck at any time, demanding, 'What's happened to so-and-so?' – which some commanders would do.[1]

This ability to set an example of unfussed, tidy professionalism and of delegating responsibility to young staff officers (Oswald was thirty-one) created an atmosphere that was unique to Eighth Army. The strain of continuous campaigning was, as the GSO 1 (Ops) at Main Headquarters recalled, surprisingly small:

If you were fit and mentally alert, I would say minimal. . . . You had to be on your toes, you had to anticipate, get moving quickly – no belly-aching. You had to accept responsibility well beyond your age and sometimes beyond your rank. You had to be good on the wireless, your staff duties had to be good. There was very little

[1] Loc. cit.

paper. You had to be able to navigate in the desert. We lived hard. We lived on bully beef and biscuits really practically the whole way from Alexandria to Tunis with a little bit of whisky now and again. . . .

You lived at night in a slit trench with a 40-lb tent over you – occasionally a scorpion for company. You had a shovel for your morning business. You were occasionally shot up by Messerschmitt 109s. You had to keep your team happy and make certain they were all kept very well in the picture. If you were tired after a 20-hour stretch you had to ignore it, which was quite easy really, because you were buoyed up by this terrific exhilaration, the inspiration which came from 'on top', by the success of operations.[1]

Apart from cap and battle-blouse, there was no uniform – for until late 1941 none had been issued to combat the intense cold of desert nights, thus leading to a tradition of corduroy trousers, woolly jumpers, and thick scarves: a tradition Monty, with customary realism, was not slow to adopt. In fact it was wearing his Australian bush-hat, with its myriad unit badges, that Monty now had his portrait painted in the field – the first unmistakable mark of his vanity since winning the battle of Alamein. Neville Lewis's first portrait of him in Cairo had pleased him greatly.

It is good and I have sent David a photograph of the picture. It is the property of the S. African Government and I cannot have it,

Monty explained to Phyllis Reynolds.

But I asked him to come and stay with me in my camp and paint my picture on commission; I would pay for it and it would belong to me.

Monty was simplifying. When Monty had asked Neville Lewis how pleased he was with the first portrait he had painted in Cairo, Lewis had replied, 'I might do better if I did another.' At once Monty said 'that if I would like to do another he was willing to sit, but he could not spare the time to sit in Cairo. He said he would like to have one done in his Australian hat with all its badges, and said, "Come to my Headquarters and stay with me for a while and get it done in the desert. . . ." So it was arranged that he would sent his aeroplane for me,' Neville Lewis later recorded, 'and fly me to his Headquarters.' This second portrait was also painted as a war picture, on behalf of

[1] General Sir Charles Richardson, 'Montgomery and his Staff': MOD filmscript, communicated to author.

the South African Government. Monty's hospitality in the field came as a surprise to the artist, who expected to sleep on the ground:

I had had quite a bit of experience of sleeping in the desert. . . .
While I was looking around Monty arrived. He asked if I had had a good flight, if I had had a drink and whether I had been shown where I was to sleep. To the first two questions I answered that I had had a good flight and I had just had a drink, but I was having a look around to decide on a good place to put down my mattress. He then said: 'You won't need that, you will have my guest caravan. . . .'
Headquarters consisted of three large caravans parked close together and covered with a net and bits of coloured rags for camouflage and a few small tents camouflaged in the same way.

Of the three caravans 'one Monty slept in, one was his map room and office, and one was for guests. I certainly did not expect such treatment. The caravan had belonged to an Italian general before it was captured and was as comfortable as any ship's cabin, a built-in bunk with a reading lamp at the head, drawers under the bunk, a table with a light, a small hanging cupboard, an electric fan and an electric heater and, what is much more important, a basin with running water. The troops in the desert were rationed to a small amount of water daily, but the water tank on the roof of the caravan was kept filled. I could shave and wash myself and my paint-brushes without any worry. . . .'
The portrait was painted

in a small tent, and he wore the New Zealand jersey, which he often did in the desert, a plain jersey and no badges of rank. There was no risk of his not being recognised as the Army Commander. His hat could be seen a long way off, and was familiar to everyone.
As this hat was so important, I had to take quite a bit of trouble over it, and it took time painting so many badges so that each one could be recognised. I suggested to one of his A.D.C.s, a young man called John Poston, that he should sit in the hat to save Monty some time. He was quite indignant and said: 'You won't catch me wearing that bloody thing'. . . . I must say I agreed it was a silly-looking hat, and Monty looked much better in his tank corps beret, which was what he wore for the first portrait which I had done in Cairo. . . .
When the portrait in the hat was finished Monty said, 'I want to give you a commission. I want you to paint another portrait of me in my beret. I want to send it to my son. . . .' He was determined to have the portrait done and so I painted a third one of him. . . .
I stayed with Monty about two weeks, and of course it was a

most interesting experience. . . . As I must confess, I like drinking and was embarrassed to think that Monty would have to pay for all that I drank. I managed to persuade the mess corporal to let me have a bottle of whisky from time to time in my caravan, for which I paid him in cash. I was thus able to have a quiet drink by myself and to ask some of the staff to come and join me. . . .

Soon after dinner Monty used to go to bed. . . . Every night before he left us he would say: 'The night is meant for sleep and so I shall leave you. Of course I know what you will do as soon as I have gone. You will all start drinking and smoking – very bad for your health.'

I think the words were exactly the same each night.

The night before I left he asked me to come with him to his caravan after dinner. I was to leave by air early in the morning back to Cairo. I was invited to sit down and we chatted for a while, and then he came to the point. He wanted to know what my fee was for the portrait he was going to send to his son.

I said I would not accept a fee and would be glad if he would take it as a present. He then said he would take it as a present, but as Christmas was not far off, only about a week ahead, he was going to give me a present. He wrote out a cheque and, folding it up, handed it to me.

After we had said goodbye to one another and back in the mess I looked at it. It was for a hundred pounds. . . . I thought it was very generous of him and must say that all the time I stayed at his Headquarters he treated me extremely well.

A month or so after my visit to the Eighth Army Headquarters I was having a drink in the Continental Hotel in Cairo, when John Poston walked in. I asked him to join me in a drink, and with much laughter he said, 'You should have seen Monty's expression when he got his mess bill after your visit. He nearly passed out.'

It was just as well that I had taken the precaution of having a few bottles of whisky in the caravan.[1]

If Monty was agog at the size of Lewis's drinks bill, the reaction did not last long. The portrait was first-class 'and the picture is now in Cairo packed up and ready to be sent back to England,' Monty informed Phyllis Reynolds. 'It will be a very good addition to the family heirlooms. Actually we have none, as everything I possess was destroyed by bombing in Portsmouth. The picture he did for me is much better than the first one, done for South Africa,' Monty boasted – and added without the least diffidence, 'It will be nice for David to have it in the house, and to show his friends.'

This singular, somehow schoolboy vanity would in time cause

[1] Neville Lewis, op. cit.

consternation among those who did not know Monty well, even among those who did. Equally, it would have been surprising had Monty not been influenced by the rippling effect of his command and his victories in battle. The pride and professionalism he had inculcated in Eighth Army soon spread throughout the Middle East theatre. As one photo-reconnaissance analyst at Cairo later recalled:

> It wasn't that the staff was different or that we didn't work hard before Monty came. We put in a full day's work, and in the evening we relaxed in the clubs of Cairo. . . .
>
> But once Monty came, the whole atmosphere changed. Suddenly it was really war. Everything was tighter – security for instance had been terribly lax. Somehow there had been no driving force, no sense of an important object behind all our work until Montgomery arrived. Anyone who had anything to do with Monty or Eighth Army in the Middle East would agree. . . . One couldn't help feeling tremendously impressed, awed by the professional spirit he exuded. . . .[1]

Nor did such effects stop in the Middle East. In England Churchill had ordered the bells of every church in Britain rung to celebrate the victory of Alamein on 15 November. The RAF war poet John Pudney cast the moment into verse, and wives, mothers and relatives of Eighth Army soldiers from all over the world wrote personally to General Montgomery, and were answered in the Army Commander's own hand. Yet in Parliament Montgomery's personality rightly became an anxiety to those – like Harold Nicolson – who believed that even successful soldiers should remain silent servants of the crown.

Perhaps the greatest paradox, in retrospect, was the growing personal vanity of the Eighth Army Commander on the one hand, and his real concern to identify and promote the talent and welfare of his men on the other. Though he might hold court at Tactical Headquarters like a Shakespearean king, encouraging wits and sometimes even fools to amuse him, beckoning painters to portray him, corresponding at once with the CIGS, the guardian of his son, and a Yorkshire mother of one of his soldiers, he was by no means as self-obsessed as is often implied. His concern for the professional fate of his Chief of Staff, Brigadier de Guingand, did not diminish after Monty visited him in hospital in Cairo. 'I would certainly get married and have a quiet honeymoon in Jerusalem,' Monty had written to him on 18 December, remembering his happier days with his wife Betty in 1931; 'but you must *be* quiet and not rush to parties, etc.'

[1] Dr Richard Hey, loc. cit.

Ten days later Monty temporarily abandoned the idea of bringing de Guingand back to Eighth Army, and in a letter to the CIGS, offered to send him home to England to a less physically demanding appointment. This letter reveals how unselfish Monty could be in professional matters, and how his diary entry on the eve of Alamein – 'the real point is that we have an active front and we make no use of it in order to fit our *Army as a whole* for battle' – was not merely pious thinking.

Some weeks ago I offered my GSO 1 (Intelligence) to go to England and lecture the Field Army on practical intelligence work in the field,

Monty reminded Brooke.

He is 1st class and what he does not know about intelligence in the field is not worth knowing; he has been through all my battles with me.
    His name is Lt-Col Murphy. He is Indian Army. When you have got what you want from him, I suggest you put him into MI as a GSO 1 in the Middle East Section or in the MO Directorate.[1]

For de Guingand, Monty had however even higher ambitions. Not only did he recommend that de Guingand have the chance of returning to England for health reasons ('he has been out here a very long time. [He] really ought to go home'), but recommended him for the top Intelligence post in the British Army: 'I do not know what I should do without him as he is quite 1st class. He was DMI at GHQ before he came to Eighth Army. He would be a high class DMI for you at the War Office, to succeed Davidson.'

There were others, too, whom Monty wished to send home – the Chief Engineer of 13 Corps, and the Chief Signals Officer of 10 Corps: 'I suggest that they should in the first instance be used at the SME and School of Signals respectively to take part in discussions attended by all senior sappers and signal officers. They are both in the top class, and are both fit to be at an Army HQ as CE and CSO respectively.'

Promotion, chance of responsibility, the value of imparting knowledge from the field of battle to the army at home: whatever Monty's growing reputation for egoism in some circles, it is quite clear that his passion for education of the army – even armies – in the 'art of war' went deeper and was more professional than any other British commander's at this time. 'I am also sending home ROBERTS, who

---

[1] Murphy was posted back to England, where he eventually became GSO 1 (Int), British Second Army, for the campaign in North-west Europe.

commands 22 Armd Bde,' Monty added. 'He has won out here the MC and two DSO's. He is easily the best commander of an Armd Bde in the Field Army, and the Division that gets him will be very lucky. He is a bit young yet for a Division being only 36, but he will command a Division very soon. Send for him and have a chat to him; you will take to him at once.'

Moreover, whatever others might say or feel about taking more advantage of Rommel's difficulties, Monty was quite clear after the New Zealand failure to 'bottle up' Rommel's Panzer rearguard that there was almost no way in which a skilful, professional enemy could be held if he wished to retreat. Better therefore to retain the tactical initiative by operating as an army rather than a pursuit force: by watching the enemy with long range desert patrols, harrying him with a lightly armed vanguard, and yet relentlessly building up the concentrated troops and material which threatened the one thing neither Rommel nor Kesselring, Cavallero nor Bastico, Hitler nor Mussolini would, in the last resort, permit: a repetition of the battle of Alamein.

It is for this reason that the victory of Alamein was always looked upon, both by Axis and British combatants, as the seminal battle of North Africa. Its shadow hung over the Axis army for the rest of the North African campaign, haunting Rommel and his troops, giving heart and heady confidence to the soldiers of Eighth Army. Time and again Rommel made as if to defend a given position – but as Eighth Army brought up its heavy tanks, guns, bombers and bagpipes, abandoned it. As Monty thankfully remarked of Agheila: 'we have been saved considerable casualties by not having to attack it seriously'; and the reason, as would be repeated each time Rommel halted, was always the Damocletian sword of Alamein.

For the first time in the Second World War the western Allies had produced a field commander with the professional ability to wield superior Allied numbers to a ruthless and unfolding offensive purpose. As Eisenhower's campaign in Tunisia faltered and ground to a halt through over-dispersion, lack of energetic command, disastrously poor air force support, and fundamental lack of tactical expertise, General Sir Bernard Montgomery made certain that in Tripolitania the Eighth Army should conduct a model campaign, retaining the strategic and tactical initiative by refusing to play Rommel's game of opportunistic exploitation. Instead, Eighth Army applied a stinging whip around the retreating enemy's ears, while relentlessly threatening another Alamein each time the Axis Panzer Army fell back to a defensible position.

Three days after Christmas Monty explained in a letter to Brooke the latest situation:

I am getting on with my preparations and am making forward dumps of petrol, supplies and so on. I shall have completed these by 14 January.

Case 1: If the enemy has withdrawn by then and left only light forces to delay me, so that no staged attack is necessary, I shall move forward on 14th January and 'drive' straight for Tripoli. In this case I would hope to reach Tripoli by 21st January.

Case 2: If the enemy has not withdrawn, and a staged attack is necessary, then I can put in this attack on night 19/20 Jan – not before. In this case I would hope to destroy the enemy in front of me and reach Tripoli by 1st February.

I am building up my tank strength and will have over 400 tanks for the party. So I would prefer it to be Case 2. If I can destroy the enemy in front of me, or can maul him so badly that he is incapable of further operations for a very long time, then I feel that the war in N. Africa will not last much longer.

Once I get to Tripoli I will not be able to operate west of that place and towards Tunisia until the port of Tripoli is working well and able to maintain two Corps. When this will be will depend on the degree of damage done to the port by the enemy; at the best it will not be for 7 to 10 days after I have secured the port.

I cannot operate west of Tripoli with my base 800 miles away at Benghazi, and only one road!!

Yours ever
Monty

Meanwhile, Rommel's chance of successfully counter-attacking Eighth Army was passing: and the inexorable build-up of Montgomery's two corps at Agheila was observed by the Commander of the newly re-named German-Italian Panzer Army with increasing forboding. 'It would need a miracle for us to hold on much longer,' Rommel wrote to his wife on the same day as Monty's letter to Brooke. 'What is to happen now lies in God's hands.'[1]

[1] *The Rommel Papers*, op. cit.

CHAPTER TWELVE

Tripoli: the Coping Stone

On 30 December Rommel mistakenly interpreted a patrolling raid by Montgomery's only forward brigade at Buerat as the start of Eighth Army's assault: 'The battle has now been joined. I haven't the slightest doubt about the outcome, the forces are too unequal,' he confided to Frau Rommel;[1] and when the next day Kesselring, Marshal Bastico and Rommel met for a planning conference, Rommel retorted, to Bastico's insistence on a two-month stand, 'that the length of our stay in Tripolitania would be decided by Montgomery and not by the Comando Supremo'.[2]

In his memoirs, Rommel expressed his 'surprise' that Montgomery halted at Buerat, and did not try to force the German defenders from it. Some Intelligence officers and cryptographers were later duped by this surprise and propagated a legend that, with the forces available to him and Ultra Intelligence to guide him, Montgomery could have acted much sooner to take Tripoli. Sir David Hunt, GSO 2 (Intelligence) at Alexander's Cairo headquarters at this time, later likened Eighth Army's progress to that of a 'pachyderm'.[3] The British Official Historian of Intelligence, Professor Hinsley, referred to the 'long and onerous pursuit' by Eighth Army and echoed, with discernible malevolence, one official Air Force account of the desert campaign that considered Montgomery's 'plans for the assault' of Tripoli as 'most ponderous'.[4]

However there is a strong case for attending closely to Monty's handling of the battle for Tripoli – undoubtedly, apart from Medenine, Rommel's most ill-judged performance of the desert war. By laying 'every mine we had' at Buerat and not properly preparing for a stalwart defence of the Tarhuna–Homs line (two hundred miles west of Buerat), Rommel was to surrender the best natural defensive position between Alamein and Gabes in a matter of hours, a position which even Rommel later confessed would, with 'a somewhat better

---

[1] *The Rommel Papers*, op. cit.
[2] Ibid.
[3] D. Hunt, *A Don at War*, London 1966.
[4] F. H. Hinsley, op. cit.

stock of supplies', have enabled him to have 'kept the enemy at bay here for a very considerable time'.[1]

Monty refused to be drawn into premature attack. His plan (issued before the January 1943 gales which necessitated the grounding of 10 Corps) was given out on 28 December 1942. Entitled 'Fire-eater', it was a model of clarity, foresight and tactical perception. He made it quite clear that Rommel was 'nervous about outflanking movements and could easily be manoeuvred out of the BUERAT position'. But was this what was wanted? 'If this were done we should lose the chance of destroying him, as our administrative situation precludes any advance at present.' It was far better, Monty declared, that the enemy 'be induced to stay in the BUERAT position', where Eighth Army would have a chance of destroying him *in situ*. If, once attacked, the enemy decided to withdraw to the Tarhuna–Homs line, Eighth Army would then be in a position to bounce him out of it on the run: 'the whole operation will be so organised that the momentum of the advance, or attack, will carry on right through to TRIPOLI. This necessitates a pause now for dumping petrol, supplies, ammunition etc. well forward; and it is for this reason that any forward movement before 14 January is not possible.' The administrative side, Monty emphasised, was 'of vital importance. If we are to build up adequate resources to allow of an advance to TRIPOLI, and of maintenance in that area for 7 to 10 days, then the port of BENGHAZI must operate at full pressure from now till the end of January.' Intelligence estimates gave the strength of Rommel's army as 55,000 men (30,000 of them Germans), and 150 tanks. If Rommel remained at Buerat and Benghazi port off-loaded at full capacity, then Eighth Army could field over four hundred tanks by 20 January. 'If the enemy stands to fight at BUERAT we shall be very well placed; our force is so strong in tanks and in air power that he must be destroyed. This would probably end the war in North Africa since we could then advance Westwards at our own pace and join up with First Army.' This, he conceded, was unlikely – 'it is quite possible that the enemy will withdraw his immobile forces before 14 January, leaving only light forces to delay us.' Eighth Army would nevertheless remain at Buerat until 14 January 'when it should have sufficient supplies to "drive" right through to TRIPOLI, taking the BUERAT position in our stride. We cannot allow,' he warned, 'the enemy to delay us so that we get more and more strung out from our present base at BENGHAZI. We will call the tune and force the pace, and jump right on to TRIPOLI – our next base.'[2]

The storms at Benghazi and the dilatory performance by the Royal

[1] *The Rommel Papers*, op. cit.
[2] 'Operation Fire-Eater', Appendix to Desert Campaign diary, Montgomery Papers.

Navy in getting Benghazi harbour fully operational (for which Admiral Harwood was sacked) threatened to upset the whole 'Fire-eater' plan, which was built upon all-out administrative perform-ance. Monty, however, was determined not to let Rommel become aware of Eighth Army's misfortune. Ultra decrypts on 31 December gave clear evidence that Rommel's desire to withdraw directly to Tunisia had been overruled; maintaining mobile rearguards at Buerat he would be permitted to withdraw only his infantry to the easily-defensible Tarhuna–Homs line which, as the Comando Supremo officially ordered on 2 January, was to be held for some six weeks. If Eighth Army was to 'bounce' Rommel out of the Tarhuna–Homs line, on the run two hundred miles beyond Buerat, Rommel *must* be made to believe that Eighth Army's strength and resources were greater than they were. By grounding 10 Corps and using its transport in a mammoth Carter-Paterson ferrying operation from Tobruk – 850 miles away – Monty was able to keep to his 15 January target-date for the assault, though it would now only be mounted by a single Corps, 30 Corps under Oliver Leese.

On 10 January Monty addressed a gathering of all commanding officers, down to Lt-Colonel level, at Leese's headquarters, explaining the plan of 'Fire-Eater', and stressing the importance of breaking through to Tripoli in one bound. As Horrocks's 10 Corps transport drivers drove day and night to bring up stocks of petrol and ammunition, Leese's engineers cleared the road to Buerat of mines, ready for the attack.

It was one of the most trying operations that I have ever carried out. It was never-ending,

Leese recalled after the war.

We staggered the Field Companies along the road, each Company working on a given section. Every day there were casualties somewhere along the road and it was most nerve racking. It was such a cold-blooded business. You could only keep a Field Company on the job for a limited time. The road was long and the number of Field Companies available was limited. That the job was finally accomplished in good time is to the everlasting credit of the gallant men of all nations who formed those Field Companies. I have seen the Royal Engineers do many magnificent jobs, but seldom a finer one than this. Never once in my many hours up and down the road did I find the men anything but cheerful, confident and efficient. It was very inspiring.[1]

[1] General Sir Oliver Leese, loc. cit.

With Horrocks's 10 Corps assigned to its transport role, Monty decided not only to conduct the battle as Army Commander, but also to take operational charge himself of the centre and right wing of the attack, while Leese moved with forces of the left wing, directed on Sedada, Ben Ulid, Tarhuna, Garian and Azizia – a 250-mile outflanking move requiring the utmost skill and co-ordination. Those at Main Eighth Army Headquarters might become anxious lest Monty, in moving forward with the right wing of the attack, lose contact with Main Headquarters, but Monty was determined that, once the Buerat line was breached, the break-out should not be bungled as it had after Alamein, when he had decentralised command, allowed Lumsden to race forward, out of communication, and though motoring forward himself by day to visit commanders, had not established his Tac Headquarters alongside Lumsden.

> During Alamein itself I suppose we were within walking distance of their [10 Corps] Tac; but then when the thing started to loosen up,

Major-General Oswald recalled,

> and we moved forward, we never got anywhere near Tac, never got alongside 10 Corps headquarters, that I can recall. We were in wireless communication, but that's not nearly the same thing – it's got to be coded and so on – and then you find the Corps Commander is out. . . .[1]

Given Lumsden's inefficient headquarters, Oswald considered Monty had been wrong not to 'make proper use of his Tac headquarters during that period of the breakout' after Alamein – 'in fact he made no use of it at all except as somewhere to lay his head. . . . We certainly weren't made the use of that I had visualised in that early stage and really, I didn't feel we were fulfilling any particular useful purpose.'[2]

Now, as Eighth Army prepared for its assault on Tripoli, Oswald felt that at last Tac HQ was about to come into its own.

On 14 January, nervous about an Allied move from Tunisia to Gabes, Rommel was authorised to transfer the personnel of 21st Panzer Division, without their artillery or tanks, to the Tunisian theatre. The next morning Eighth Army began its assault aimed at Tripoli. Monty was well aware, from Intelligence sources, that Rommel was unlikely now to stand and fight in the Buerat line if Eighth Army threatened to outflank the coastal sector; he had

[1] Loc. cit.
[2] Ibid.

therefore 'ordered that, on the first day of the movement, caution was to be exercised so as not to have heavy casualties from anti-tank guns; a *tank to tank* fight would be welcomed. The advance therefore proceeded quietly and by the evening we had secured FASCHIA and reached the lines of the WADI ZEM ZEM,' Monty recorded in his diary.

Monty's aim was to force Rommel to withdraw his holding troops in the coastal sector *before* launching 51st Highland Division, which was so short of infantry officers that he had cabled GHQ Cairo on 12 December, 'it would be a great help if you could fly up even 20.'[1] Thankfully he noted in his diary: 'As the afternoon [15 January] wore on it was clear that the enemy was beginning to withdraw, and after dark this was confirmed. He could not stand up to the weight of the movement round his right or Southern flank. . . . 51 Division attacked South of the main road at 2230 hours and encountered little opposition.'

The enemy had surrendered the Buerat line with almost no resistance. The important thing now was to follow up his withdrawal so fast and powerfully that he would be unable to dig in on the Tarhuna–Homs line:

At dawn [on 16 January] it was clear that on the left we were through the main enemy resistance on his Southern flank and were across the WADI ZEM ZEM; and on the right we were through the minefields of his main position and well set for an advance on GHEDDAHIA and thence Northwards astride the main road.

By our operations we had turned the enemy out of the BUERAT position; we had got through it and out into the open. I at once ordered the advance to be conducted now with great resolution and determination; the caution ordered for the 15 January was cancelled.

The main thrust of 30 Corps on the left was to 'drive' hard for SEDADA, and be conducted with great determination.

On the right 51 Div was to 'drive' hard up the axis of the coast road.

22 Armd Bde (in Army Reserve) was to move forward between these two thrusts. . . .

What now took place was – as is clear from the formation and unit War Diaries, as well as both Leese's and Montgomery's personal diaries – almost unbelievable to the Eighth Army participants.

Unaware that 21st Panzer Division personnel had departed on 14 January, Leese was understandably anxious lest Rommel attempt a

[1] In Alexander Papers, loc. cit.

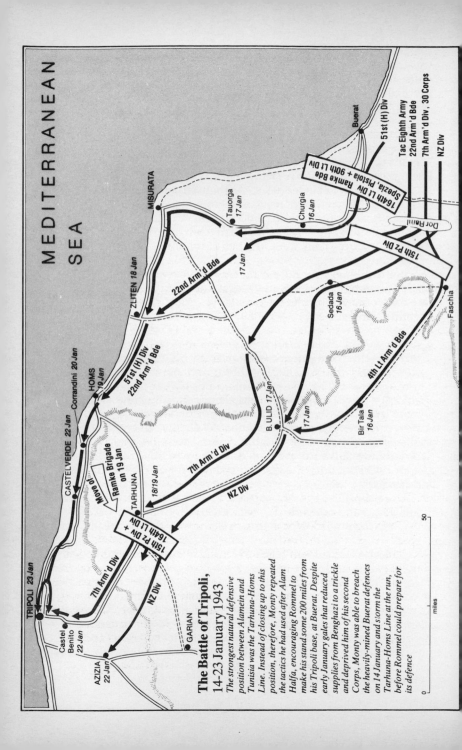

MEDITERRANEAN SEA

TRIPOLI 23 Jan

Castel Benito 22 Jan

CASTEL VERDE 22 Jan

Corradini 20 Jan

HOMS 19 Jan

AZIZIA 22 Jan

GARIAN

7th Arm'd Div

NZ Div

15th Pz Div + 164th Lt Div

Ramke Brigade on 19 Jan

Move of

TARHUNA

51st (H) Div 22nd Arm'd Bde

18/19 Jan

ZLITEN 18 Jan

22nd Arm'd Bde

7th Arm'd Div

NZ Div

17 Jan

B. ULID 17 Jan

17 Jan

Bir Tala 16 Jan

Sedada 16 Jan

4th Lt Arm'd Bde

Faschia

15th Pz Div

Dor Raui

16th Lt Div Spezia, Pistoia + 90th Lt Div

Tauorga 17 Jan

Churgia 16 Jan

MISURATA

17 Jan

22nd Arm'd Bde

Buerat

51st (H) Div

Tac Eighth Army
22nd Arm'd Bde
7th Arm'd Div, 30 Corps
NZ Div

The Battle of Tripoli, 14–23 January 1943

The strongest natural defensive position between Alamein and Tunisia was the Tarhuna–Homs Line. Instead of closing up to this position, therefore, Monty repeated the tactics he had used after Alam Halfa, encouraging Rommel to make his stand some 200 miles from his Tripoli base, at Buerat. Despite early January gales that reduced supplies from Benghazi to a trickle and deprived him of his second Corps, Monty was able to breach the heavily-mined Buerat defences on 14 January and storm the Tarhuna–Homs Line at the run, before Rommel could prepare for its defence

0   miles   50

counter-attack with two Panzer Divisions against his own single armoured division and the New Zealand motorised division on the southern flank. To his surprise 7th Armoured Division was permitted to smash its way forward, taking a steady toll of Axis anti-tank guns by day, and finding the enemy defensive positions evacuated each night. Only south of Tarhuna did the Axis forces maintain a defensive line – and when, on 19 and 20 January, 7th Armoured Division established a screen there while passing its armoured car brigade westwards to outflank it, the enemy withdrew. There was a struggle on 21 January to get tanks down the Tarhuna defile, but again the enemy rearguard withdrew in the night – and on 22 January 7th Armoured Division was into the plain. Meanwhile both armoured cars and the New Zealand Division were through into the plain west of Tarhuna Gorge – within striking distance of Tripoli. 'By now there were signs that the enemy was on the run, and it was rapidly becoming a race between the coastal and inland columns as to who would be first into Tripoli,' as Lt-Colonel Oswald noted in his Tac HQ diary[1] – for, driving 51st Division and 22nd Armoured Brigade in tandem, Monty had ensured that the coastal thrust also was through the Homs position by 22 January.

All were amazed at the enemy's failure to put up effective resistance, and none more than Monty. He had intended, as he noted on 17 January, that Leese's operations 'were to be developed in such a way as to keep feeling all the time round the enemy right or West flank, as if we intended to secure GARIAN and then move on TRIPOLI from the South; the enemy would be very sensitive to such a threat and would tend to be drawn away to the West, and possibly to weaken the Homs front thereby'. Against this Homs front Monty had in line the unmotorised 51st Highland Division; he also had 22nd Armoured Brigade ready to loose into the Tripoli plain the moment the infantry breached the Homs defences. That this was possible already by 22 January was incredible – the more so once he saw the configuration of the ground. 'The country between Homs and COR-RANDINI resembled the NW frontier of India,' Monty noted in his diary. Why, then, had Rommel given in so easily?'

In his diary Monty had noted on 19 January the move of the 'Ramcke Bde across from Homs to TARHUNA', which proved how 'nervous' Rommel must be 'about our possible penetration on this [inland] flank'. From Rommel's memoirs it is clear that this was an understatement: that Rommel in fact panicked. Overestimating the number of tanks involved in Leese's thrust – he reckoned there were two hundred – he also misconstrued the 4th Light Armoured Brigade's threatened attack towards Garian, ignoring Tripoli and mov-

[1] Maj-General M. St J. Oswald, unpublished desert diary, communicated to author.

ing westwards as if to outflank it, as 'a thrust on Garian with a whole armoured division'. How Rommel had failed to prepare for such a move, and how he allowed himself to be thrown off guard in this way, is not explicable in military terms. 'This was a particularly threatening move,' he recalled in his memoirs, 'and I threw in the whole of our artillery to meet it. Immediate regrouping became necessary. The 164th Division, units of the [Ramcke] Parachute Brigade and the Reconnaissance Group were deployed in a screen to the west to prevent a British attack on the Tarhuna–Castel Benito road. Soon the enemy brought his artillery up and poured shells into our positions near Tarhuna. The British commander was now conducting his operation far more energetically than he had done in the past.'[1]

Ironically the British Commander was not Montgomery, who was away on the right wing with 51st Highland Division and 22nd Armoured Brigade, where the Highlanders were attacking Homs. Leese was responsible for the energetic performance on the left wing, and his star performer was the young Major-General whom Montgomery had appointed, after Alam Halfa, to command 7th Armoured Division: John Harding. It was while directing the 'pouring of shells' into Rommel's defences south of Tarhuna that Harding was hit by an exploding German shell on 19 January – and the whole vigour of Leese's operations slowed almost to a halt.

Monty's reaction was immediate: he sent the 36-year-old Brigadier of 22nd Armoured Brigade, 'Pip' Roberts, to take temporary command; and within twenty-four hours 7th Armoured Division was once again on the loose.

Harding's flair for front-line leadership, Leese's aptitude for organisation and 'getting on with the job', and Monty's grasp of tactical strategy – taking the risk, which he had been unable to do at Agheila, of sending a powerful, tank-armoured left hook through unreconnoitred mountainous country – were responsible for the speed and success of Operation 'Fire-eater'. Not that Monty was taking undue chances; even if Leese's left wing were stopped in the difficult Tarhuna country, it would be enough that it drew away Rommel's main German troops holding the coast road – and for this reason Monty was almost unmercifully hard on the unfortunate General Wimberley, Commander of the 51st Highland Division. It was essential, Monty felt, that the infantry press on and pierce a hole through the Homs line, as he noted in his diary for 17 January: 'If the left thrust at TARHUNA met with serious resistance, and the enemy weakened the Homs front in order to secure his right, then I would drive in hard on the right with 51 Div and loose the 22 Armd Bde into the plain of TRIPOLI. The 22 Armd Bde was at full strength in

[1] *The Rommel Papers*, op. cit.

112

tanks,[1] and if once I could launch it through the Homs front into open country the whole party would be about over, and TRIPOLI must fall to me.'

He was very pleased – he had the light of battle in his eye,

Major-General Oswald later recalled. In Oswald's view this was the first time Monty had really used his Tactical Headquarters to full advantage:

I'll tell you when he *did* begin to use it: on the advance on Tripoli, when he made himself really a Corps Commander, Monty really got the feel of things then, and of course he made Wimberley's life hell because there was no intervening Corps Commander to take the sting out of it! He liked having the 22nd Armoured Brigade, and 51st Highland Division and the 12th Lancers all to himself. And issuing direct orders, or telling me what to tell them, where to go! . . .

Anyway Monty enjoyed it. He really felt he was getting on with the battle. And it's only supposition on my part but it may have dawned on him then that this was really – if you are going to take part in a pursuit, this was where the Army Commander should be, here or hereabouts – because after that Tac HQ was always pretty near the front. . . . As far as Monty was concerned it gave him a great feeling of 'getting on with the job'.[2]

Charles Richardson, the GSO 1 (Operations) at Main Headquarters, also recalled the occasion:

I remember: Monty set off like a forward troop of armour. I mean he had his tanks with him, under his personal command, and they were operating in territory which certainly hadn't been cleared of enemy.

It alarmed Freddie [de Guingand] considerably. But I think Monty rather enjoyed it. He was utterly fearless of course – I think he had sterilised that aspect of war completely in his mind. . . .[3]

By taking 22nd Armoured Brigade across country, Monty actually reached Zliten (twenty miles east of Homs, on the coast) before 51st Highland Division on the evening of 18 January.

---

[1] Although only obsolete Valentines, armed with 2-pdr guns.
[2] Interview of 1.2.83.
[3] General Sir Charles Richardson, interview of 27.1.83. Sir Alan Brooke summed up Monty's attitude when he said to General Franklyn (GOC in Northern Ireland) in July 1942: 'Do you enjoy fighting battles, Franklyn? I don't. I think Monty does' – D. Fraser, *Alanbrooke*, London 1982.

Tac Army was now the leading formation HQ of Eighth Army

Monty noted.

> The 51 Div in the coastal sector were very slow and the movement was sticky; by dark the leading Bde had not reached ZLITEN; by this time the enemy was back at HOMS.

The next evening, 19 January, he was happier:

> . . . the advance of 51 Div had been very slow on 18 Jan; but I applied the whip and today the Division spurted forward and by dark its leading troops were in HOMS, the enemy having evacuated that place.

Intelligence reports regarding Rommel's anxiety over the inland threat, and the movement of German troops from Homs to Tarhuna, made it clear to Monty that he must take immediate advantage of this weakening on the coastal axis. Noting the natural slowdown of Leese's operations after Harding was wounded, Monty recorded his continued dissatisfaction with the performance of the Highlanders on the coast: 'On this side there were plenty of infantry and progress should have been more rapid. 51 Div seemed to be getting weary and generally displayed a great lack of initiative and ginger. So I issued an imperial "rocket" to the Div Comd; this had an immediate effect and the Division moved on.'

In his own unpublished memoirs, Wimberley refuted this allegation. In the planning stages for the battle of Buerat he was 'very definitely told by Monty there was to be no hurry about our advance as we were not expected to be the first division to reach Tripoli. We were to breach the enemy's defences at Buerat by a frontal attack, and then advance along the main coastal road, clearing this as we advanced, as it would be the axis for supplies getting forward to Tripoli, once captured.'[1] Short of shells, transport and petrol for the 230-mile attack-and-advance to Tripoli, Wimberley first became aware how critical it was to break through the enemy defences with his infantry when giving his final orders at a Divisional Conference on 15 January – for Leese sent a message that if the enemy stood firm he was to attack again and again for three consecutive nights.

After the casualties at Alamein and those incurred from mines during the pursuit, Wimberley was not sanguine: 'For me, this was not a pleasant prospect, as I knew that if we failed the first night, there would be a grave shortage of shells for any further attack. I now felt sure that, for the first time since Monty took command of the

[1] Loc. cit.

114

Eighth Army, he was getting a little anxious over his supply situation. He knew that if Tripoli was not captured quickly to open that port for supplies, the whole Eighth Army would again have to retreat.'[1] Years later, in his *Memoirs*, Monty confirmed Wimberley's appreciation: 'I well know that if we did not reach Tripoli in 10 days I might have to withdraw – for lack of supplies.' More gales had struck between 13 and 16 January, only four hundred tons per day were being off-loaded at Benghazi instead of three thousand, 50th Division's part in the coastal attack had had to be cancelled entirely, and all 10 Corps transport was being used to ferry supplies from Tobruk and Benghazi – a six-hundred-mile journey from Benghazi to Buerat alone.

Wimberley's first concern, then, was to ensure a definite breach in the Buerat defences on the night of 15 January, and to make a steady, co-ordinated advance thereafter, clearing the road for future traffic. Early on 17 January Leese came over from the left wing and Wimberley 'got the impression that the Eighth Army plan was changing, and that we in H.D. on the coastal road were expected to get a move on! Accordingly I ordered my leading Brigade, the 152, to carry on the forward movement all through the night, as well as through the day.'[2] However, later that evening Wimberley was sent for personally by Montgomery. Arriving at about 1 a.m. on 18 January, Wimberley recorded, 'I went straight to Monty's caravan. Monty was fast asleep in bed with his light off. He woke up at once, seemed pleased to see me, and explained the situation on his big wall map.' The anxiety over supplies which Wimberley had detected on the first day of the attack was now even more in evidence. 'The reason for my summons was to impress on me, in person, the need for speed now on the coastal route. Apparently Oliver Leese's column had not been able to get on as expected, and it might now be that the coastal and 22 Armoured Brigade column might reach Tripoli first. He said that if the Eighth Army did not get to Tripoli by the tenth day of the advance he might well have to order a retreat on the grounds of lack of supplies. Our talk must have lasted about half an hour, and as I left, out went his light, and he settled down to sleep again!' Wimberley recalled with admiration.[3]

The next night, at Zliten, the summons was repeated – 'I could sense that he was an anxious man, as well he might be, at how the days and nights were passing,' Wimberley remembered.[4] Four days had passed, and the most difficult territory – the Tarhuna–Homs line – still remained ahead.

All day on 19 January Wimberley personally drove on his leading

[1] Ibid.
[2] Ibid.
[3] Ibid.
[4] Ibid.

brigade and leading battalion, and in the evening they came up at last against the main Homs defence line.

We attacked at dawn the next morning [20 January], but made little progress, so at about mid-day I ordered a conference at the H.Q.'s of the 7th Black Watch of all the forward commanders that I could collect, and ordered them to make a long flank march by the seashore to get behind the Homs position. This made the troops of the German 90th Light Division evacuate Homs in the late afternoon, and take up another rearguard position at a place Corrandini, about twelve miles nearer Tripoli. We made contact with the position in the dark, and I at once ordered a hasty attack on it, in the moonlight, using the Seaforth battalion, now in the lead. This was now the evening of the 20th, and I was talking with Brigadier Murray commanding the 152 Bde, when a Despatch Rider from Monty arrived with a letter. This was to give me a 'rocket' for now being slow. I felt very angry, as with the difficult terrain, the enemy's mines and craters on the road, and my shortage of M.T. and of petrol, being supplied me by rear Eighth Army's H.Q.'s now hundreds of miles behind me, I considered that my division had done well. I showed the message to Brigadier Murray, and then tore it into little bits.[1]

Wimberley may well have been right to express disgust at his Army Commander's ingratitude, for Rommel only positioned his 90th Light Division in the Homs defences on the night of 19 January, and to have 'bounced' them out within a dozen hours was no mean feat by the almost transportless Highlanders. Monty's Intelligence reports and his every instinct, however, told him that the critical hour of the battle had come: that while Rommel's attention was focused on Leese's thrust, Eighth Army *must* threaten Tripoli from the coast, whatever the cost in casualties: and in this Monty was proved absolutely correct. Early that morning Marshal Cavallero signalled to Rommel, on behalf of Mussolini – an angry signal 'in which the latter stated that my decision to withdraw our forces from the Tarhuna–Homs line and position them to meet the expected major attack in Azizia-Sorman area was contrary to his instructions to hold the Tarhuna–Homs line for at least three weeks. The situation was not serious enough to justify my action, which had been over hasty. A stand simply must be made. . . . Cavallero referred me expressly to the Duce's directives and demanded my compliance. We gasped when we received this signal.'[2]

Whatever the failure of the Italians in other directions, the Duce

[1] Ibid.
[2] *The Rommel Papers*, op. cit.

was in this case well informed: Rommel had made perhaps the most blatant error of his career – and the last (for the moment) against Montgomery, for a few days later he was dismissed as C-in-C of the German-Italian Panzer Army of Africa. He had misjudged Montgomery's dispositions at Alam Halfa, had employed the wrong tactical principles in the defence of Alamein, had failed to mount a single counter-attack of the merest magnitude against Montgomery's administratively overstretched forces in a retreat of more than a thousand miles, and had now blundered by abandoning the best natural defensive line between Alamein and Tunisia to counter a daring but comparatively weak threat by the New Zealand Division to his flank.

By the time Cavallero's telegram had arrived, however, it was too late. Stung by Monty's accusations of dilatoriness, Wimberley was through the Homs position by midday, and attempting to smash his way through Corrandini by nightfall. Behind the Highlanders, in addition, was a complete Armoured Brigade, being held under Monty's personal command at Zliten and waiting for the Army Commander's order to leap-frog through 51st Division and thunder into Tripoli.

Rommel had completely over-estimated the strength of Leese's column. The New Zealanders possessed only fourteen tanks by the time of their thrust on Azizia, and 4th Light Armoured Brigade no heavy tanks at all.[1] Even 7th Armoured Division could only muster, by 20 January, some thirty heavy tanks[2] – in country ideal for defence, with off-road movement virtually impossible and the roads themselves easily mined and covered by anti-tank guns and artillery.

Montgomery's plan, laid down on 28 December 1942, had been spectacularly vindicated. While Rommel gasped at Mussolini's criticism, the forward troops of Eighth Army were equally amazed at the way the Axis forces surrendered such easily defensible territory – terrain far more difficult to penetrate than had ever been anticipated by Eighth Army's planning staffs.

The note of excitement in the surviving records of Eighth Army headquarters signals is visible to this day. The Army Commander and Lt-General Leese might indeed feel awed once they saw with their own eyes the country through which they had been expecting to force a passage, but the officers and men who had fought their way from Alamein were thrilled at the speed of the advance and concerned with only one matter: proximity of their long-awaited goal, Tripoli. By 21 January Tac/R air patrols reported 'non-stop withdrawal of enemy from Tripoli', as the 7th Armoured Division War Diarist recorded, and soon the sound of gigantic demolitions could be

[1] W. G. Stevens, op. cit.
[2] 7th Armoured Division War Diary (WO 169/8738), PRO.

heard. On 23 January, the day on which Tripoli was captured, the diarist wrote with some emotion:

> The enemy evacuated Castel Benito area after last light and after a night march the 11 Hussars and Divisional Tac HQ entered Tripoli at 0530; an hour ahead of the 51 Highland Division who were approaching along the coast road. Since the entry of Italy into the war the 7th Armoured Division has been fighting in the Western Desert and always Tripoli has been our goal: to be first there was the only reward we wanted.[1]

Not even O'Connor's great action against the Italians in the winter of 1940/41 had reached Tripoli. It was indeed a proud moment for the 'Desert Rats' to capture the town after two long years of desert struggle.

In fact Tripoli was the prize won by the battle of Alamein. At Alamein, save for the few concrete buildings around the station, the only visible gain for so much loss of life had been the endless grains of sand and rock beyond the Rahman Track. Now, in the early morning Mediterranean sunshine of 23 January 1943, three months after the commencement of the battle of Alamein, the 'Desert Rats' drove through the deserted streets of the capital of Tripolitania, the legendary city of Carthaginian times, with its triumphal arch of Marcus Aurelius testifying to the centuries of Roman rule. Captured briefly by Montgomery's Norman ancestors in 1146, lost in 1551 by the Knights of St John to the Ottoman Turks, it had been occupied by the Italians in 1911 during the Italo-Turkish war and had remained ever since under Italian rule.

TRIPOLI HAS FALLEN. CAIRO RADIO FLASHED THE GREAT
NEWS TO THE WORLD TONIGHT

declared the front page of the *News Chronicle* on 23 January 1943. The same day Christopher Buckley, correspondent of the *Daily Telegraph*, cabled: 'It is hardly possible to realise that Tripoli has been reached only eight days after the launching of the attack.'

The impending entry of Eighth Army into the city was described with some emotion in the *News Chronicle*:

> It is a matter of hours now before the advance guard of the Eighth Army, weary but triumphant, ground arms before the ancient arch of Marcus Aurelius in the centre of Tripoli. . . . It is believed that the greater part of Tripoli's 100,000 inhabitants remain in the town. They will witness the triumph of an army they believed was broken for good eight months ago.

[1] Ibid.

Over the week-end – 'Berlin's blackest week-end of the war', as the *Daily Telegraph* called it – Goebbels recalled all German war reporters for 'fresh instructions'. On Sunday 26 January 1943 Christopher Buckley cabled from Tripoli: 'Gen. Montgomery has won the final trick giving him game and rubber in this long-drawn-out desert war which has seen such dramatic changes of fortune. . . . Best of all, he has fairly and squarely beaten a powerful Axis army, led by a reputedly invincible commander, so thoroughly that it has never once seriously given battle since its initial defeat at the beginning of November.' William Munday, *News Chronicle* War Correspondent, described the capture of Tripoli itself:

> British troops entered Tripoli from the North before dawn today and linked up in the Piazza Italia, in the centre of the city, with armoured cars of the Hussars unit belonging to the other column of the Eighth Army which had been moving in from the South. . . . Italian police, stiff in musical comedy uniforms, were still on duty. The capture of Tripoli exactly three months after the Alamein offensive had completed the taking from Mussolini of the last of the Italian overseas possessions.
>
> It was the first major enemy town occupied by the Allies since the war began.

In the pre-dawn darkness Gordon Highlanders, riding on the Valentine tanks of their support brigade, had been the first infantry into the city. By the time the sun rose, the bagpipes were playing 'Cock o' the North', the Gordons' regimental air. A concentration camp containing over 2,500 Jews was liberated, and 'in the city itself Italian civilians crowded to watch the procession of tanks and battle stained Highlanders stream through the streets. . . . "Coming into town was the biggest thrill I've ever had," Corporal William Resach from Aberdeen, who rode on the first tank, told me. "What do we want to do now? Why kick the blighters right out of Africa; then go home." '

Even *The Times*, in its leader column, congratulated Montgomery, while the *Telegraph*'s 'Student of War' remarked: 'Tripoli sets the coping stone on the triumph of the Eighth Army at Alamein. It demonstrates, as little else could, the decisive character of that earlier battle. If this new success stood alone, the United Nations would be entitled to congratulate themselves on an achievement that is without parallel' – for in three months to the day since the opening of the battle of Alamein, the Eighth Army had defeated Rommel's German-Italian Army in position and run its retreating remnants back across 1,400 miles of desert and Jebel. 'If one excepts the entrance of the Germans into Paris, of the Japanese into Singapore and the return of the Russians to Stalingrad, there can have been no moment in the war to equal this one,' the experienced reporter Alan Moorehead later remarked. 'In the swaying battle of the desert, Tripoli had for two and a half years appeared as a mirage that grew strong and now faded away again, and was for ever just beyond the Eighth Army's reach. So many had died or been withdrawn through wounds at a time when the struggle looked futile and endless. So many had recovered hope only to lose it again.'[1]

Now Tripoli had fallen to the Eighth Army, with its tens of thousands of inhabitants, its almost unscarred buildings, playing fountains, and its great and ancient harbour.

The operations staged on the right and left flanks were both successful, and both thrusts entered TRIPOLI at about 0400 hours on 23 January

Monty recorded with relief in his diary three days later.

The troops had a good reception from the population. The city was quiet and there was no panic.

I myself arrived outside the city at 0900 hours, met Comd 30 Corps, and gave orders as to the continuance of the operations, procedure in the city and so on.

I sent for the leading Italian officials to come and report to me outside the town;[2] this they did and I gave them my orders about the city and requested their co-operation in ensuring the well-being of the population. I then drove into the town and had my sandwich lunch on the sea front.

---

[1] Alan Moorehead, *The Desert War*, London 1965.
[2] Ed Stevens, the War Correspondent, witnessed the occasion. 'So there, in the suburbs of Tripoli, on the outskirts, two gorgeously dressed Italians – one the General commanding the forces, the other the Military Governor of Tripoli – appeared, beautifully turned out. Now Monty arrives, I forget who was with him, in his dusty old beret and a battledress with a fringe of sweater hanging out. . . . He takes the surrender. There was quite a long speech one of these fellows made. Monty whispered to me – I had Italian – "Who the hell is this bugger?"! And everything went off quite happily!' – interview of 29.12.79.

CHAPTER THIRTEEN

'My Experience in Fighting Rommel'

To those who watched it must have seemed a strange sight: the victorious commander of Eighth Army, in the metaphorical shoes of the great Roman army commanders, seated on stone steps beneath an Italian statue, quietly eating sandwiches from a hamper, like a humble English tourist on an outing to the sea. Lt-General Leese sat beside Monty and they argued about which unit had been first into the city. 'Our ADCs and police escort sat not far away, also having their lunch,' Monty recollected in his *Memoirs*. Having discussed 'the past and the future' with him, Monty asked Leese 'what he thought the ADCs were talking about' after many months of monastic life in the desert; Leese reckoned 'they were speculating on whether there were any suitable ladies in the city. I had no doubt that he was right,' Monty wrote candidly – and decided to 'get the Army away from Tripoli as early as possible'.

Perhaps Monty's military asceticism is crystallised in that moment, at lunchtime beneath an Italian statue in Tripoli. Churchill, historian as well as politician, had already noticed his new Army Commander's penchant for sandwiches and simplicity before the battle of Alam Halfa. Now, four months later, Churchill wished once more to see his Eighth Army in the field; he was at Casablanca with Roosevelt when news of the capture of Tripoli came through – erasing the terrible scar of June 1942 when, in Washington with Roosevelt, he heard news of the fall of Tobruk. He therefore proposed that, on his return flight from a meeting with the Turkish President at Adana, he should stop over in Tripoli.

In the meantime the victorious Eighth Army Commander gave his orders for the New Zealanders to keep Rommel 'on the run until he was back at ZUARA near the TUNISIAN border, i.e. about 70 miles west of TRIPOLI', issued a personal message thanking his troops, and in the peace of his headquarters encampment four miles outside Tripoli (having rejected a suggestion that he occupy the Governor's Palace) he penned his own secret confession of amazement that Rommel, falling back on his well-established lines of communication, often with superior forces and in ideal defensive positions, had failed to counter Eighth Army's bluff.

121

It is interesting to reflect on certain points,

Monty began.

a) Why, during all the fighting that has taken place in NORTH
   AFRICA, has this not happened before?
   There has undoubtedly been a great deal of bad generalship.
   But I think a main reason is that no previous General ever
   defeated ROMMEL decisively *at the beginning*; having defeated
   him decisively at ALAMEIN, the rest was easy.

In Monty's view, then, the victory of Alamein had thus been the
key to all subsequent success. Nevertheless he was puzzled why
Rommel had failed ever to stand and fight.

b) The first place where ROMMEL could stand and fight, with any
   chance of success, was at MERSA BREGA. Why did he not do
   so? It was an immensely strong position and heavily mined; if
   he had positioned his armour North of MARADA, and called
   my bluff, it might have been difficult for me; I was weak in
   strength, and administratively I was very stretched.
   I think the reason was that he was also very stretched
   administratively, and he could not supply his forces over the
   very long L of C from TRIPOLI.

If Rommel's failure to make a stiffer stand at Mersa Brega was a
puzzle to Monty, Rommel's recent surrender of the natural defensive
line between Homs and Tarhuna was even more mystifying:

c) Why, having given up MERSA BREGA, did he stand at
   BUERAT?
   This position could be outflanked, and was.
   Behind was the TARHUNA–HOMS line. This could have
   been made very strong indeed; the position favoured the
   defence; if the work put into the BUERAT position had been
   put, instead, into the TARHUNA–HOMS line then I consider
   we would not have been in TRIPOLI on 23 Jan

Monty confessed quite candidly.

The answer to this question is beyond me. I consider ROMMEL
made a mistake.

Others, from Mussolini to Kesselring, Cavallero to Bastico,
thought so too, and three days after Montgomery formally accepted
the surrender of Tripoli, Field -Marshal Rommel was removed from

his post as Commander of the German-Italian Panzer Army. General Montgomery had outclassed him, and Rommel's headaches and 'fits of depression . . . in which nothing seemed as it really is'[1] were undoubtedly a reflection of his failure. He had managed, at a local level, a skilful retreat over some 1,400 miles; but in a larger sense he had made error after error since his previous August. His bid for Cairo and Alexandria had been easily parried at Alam Halfa and his decision to stand at Alamein had been strategically and tactically mistaken. Thereafter his once famed Afrika Korps had been but a ghost of its former self, and the African Panzer Army Commander a haunted man. Both at Agheila and Buerat his Intelligence had vastly overestimated the forces Eighth Army could actually bring to bear in battle, and on 19 January 1943 he had undoubtedly panicked. The general once celebrated for his ability to do the unorthodox, for counter-attacking and miraculously wresting the initiative from his foe, had failed to discomfit his opponent on even one occasion since Alamein – and had surrendered 1,400 miles of territory in one of the longest and most precipitate retreats in military history.

On the same day that Field-Marshal Rommel was relieved of his command, his opponent, General Sir Bernard Montgomery, listed his own ingredients for victory:

> As a result of my experience in fighting ROMMEL, not unsuccessfully, I issued to my Army a small pamphlet on the 'Conduct of Battle'. This is meant for senior officers only; it deals with the basic fundamentals, it goes into no details.
>
> I am quite convinced myself that in battle it is 'the man' that counts,

he declared, refuting the common notion both in Britain and among the Allies that it was equipment that guaranteed success.

> You cannot make war successfully, and win battles, with bad commanders. Down to the Brigadier level inclusive you require Commanders of character, energy, and 'drive'; and these must know their stuff. Without such Commanders you will gain few successes.
>
> The higher commander must ensure that dispositions are always 'balanced', and that operations are conducted from firm bases; he must then 'grip' the battle firmly himself and *ensure that it goes as he has planned*.

It was this last principle which offended some contemporaries, such as Patton, and many later historians: especially those irked by

[1] David Irving, op. cit.

the dogmatic tone of Montgomery's *Memoirs*. However it is quite clear from such reflections in Montgomery's diary that these dogmas were the contemporary thoughts of a successful soldier, penned only a few days after the culmination of five months' campaigning in North Africa. Moreover what Monty intended to make clear in the remark was not that a Commander must stick to his plan to the bitter end, as had happened in the futile battles on the Western Front in World War One. Within the next eight weeks, at Mareth, Monty would show his instinctive unwillingness to persevere in the face of heavy casualties if he felt the thrust in question had no reasonable chance of success. What Monty meant was that operations must conform to an overall strategy. The battle of Alamein had demonstrated the need for this when there was determined opposition; but flexibility within an overall plan had proved equally necessary in the battle for Tripoli when Monty perceived Rommel's fatal mistake, and swiftly exploited it on the right wing before Rommel could rectify his error. That Monty had been able to do this was not simply a matter of opportunism, still less of 'following' the fruits of Ultra (however helpful), but of fighting according to a tactical strategy that would place the Commander in a good position to seize the final advantage ruthlessly and decisively once offered.

He has got to understand thoroughly the whole technique of the employment of air striking forces in support of the land operations,

Monty added – for indeed it was the amazing ability of the Desert Air Force to move with the forward units of Eighth Army which had made it so difficult for Rommel to countenance counter-attack or even gather clear photographic or Tac/R Intelligence.

These air forces cannot operate without landing grounds, and the securing of proper and adequate landing grounds as the battle proceeds must play a large part in the planning.

Often the needs of the Desert Air Force as well as the strategic air force behind it had determined the scale and even direction of Eighth Army's effort – for instance in the pursuit directly after Alamein, when the need for advanced landing grounds had been given priority over the possible outflanking of enemy rearguards. Similarly the need to possess the Martuba airfields in time to protect the vital November convoy to Malta had taken priority over operations to cut off remaining Axis forces in the Cyrenaican 'bulge'. As Monty noted in his diary at the time, such precedence was not simply a matter of army deferring to air: the long-term rewards of air superiority would be felt far beyond forward troop support – namely in the long-range bombing of Rommel's lines of communication, and especially in the neutralising of Tripoli itself. In fact it was the evident vulnerability of Tripoli harbour to RAF attack which had helped convince Rommel he could not hold out in the Tripoli area as Mussolini ordered.

If Monty felt any disappointment at his own failure to cut off Rommel's forces during the pursuit from Alamein, he did not show it, either at this time or later. A beaten enemy that does not stand to fight and withdraws further and faster than any army in history is not an easy one to 'put in the bag'.[1] More importantly, Monty had caused Rommel to adopt such a rapid withdrawal by a mixture of initial ruthlessness in battle at close quarters followed by dexterity and bluff. With only the minimum of forward troops he had forced Rommel not only to surrender almost one and a half thousand miles of territory, but to give up two excellent defensive positions in which he could have checked Eighth Army sharply, causing a blow to its morale and, as in Tunisia, perhaps months of dislocation while building up forces to remount its attack, not to speak of casualties.

'Looking back over the last three months,' Monty concluded this phase of his diary on 26 January 1943,

I cannot help being thankful for the great variety and types of battles I have had to fight, and for the truly enormous experience in these matters that it has been my good fortune to gather in.

There was the set-piece battle of ALAMEIN, which began the whole affair.

There was the break-through battle.

There was the pursuit battle, which introduced mobile operations of the highest type.

There were the battles where the enemy stood to fight, and which involved on my part the approach, the gaining of contact, the holding back of main bodies, while the battle was built up, and then flinging my troops on the enemy with a sudden 'drive'; in this type were the battles at MERSA BREGA and BUERAT; and I enjoyed them greatly.

There was the final 'drive' towards TRIPOLI, conducted through country totally different from the wide and open desert plains, country in which operations were canalised to certain definite avenues of approach.

The only type of battle in which I have gained no experience

he reflected on his period as Commander, Eighth Army,

---

[1] For example, despite routing Eighth Army at Gazala in May 1942, Rommel had failed to cut off any sizeable portion of the British retreating forces, save those that accepted investment at Tobruk.

is the withdrawal battle; I learnt a great deal about that type of fighting in the B.E.F. in BELGIUM in 1940, and see no reason for repeating those experiences.

If this was boastful, it was forgivable. Few Army Commanders in history had experienced in their first few months of command in the field such a variety of challenges, or seen such a march of victories. The revolution Monty had initiated in the professionalism with which the Eighth Army conducted its operations was even acknowledged by the German Commander after Alamein – who accused Eighth Army of adopting 'German' methods of fighting. Step by step Monty had since August 1942 first wrested the initiative from Rommel, then retained it in the battle of will between himself and the Panzer Army Commander – and the straightforward clarity of his diary, his plans for the battles, together with summaries and lessons, testify to his achievement in bringing purpose and lucidity to the traditionally incoherent operations of Eighth Army. Moreover Monty's reference to Dunkirk was not rhetorical. It was the shame of Dunkirk, without doubt, which gave to Monty's existing professionalism a deeper and more urgent quality. Throughout his period of command in Home Forces Monty had 'driven' himself to examine and rehearse the techniques of offensive warfare against a professional and determined enemy. Despite the advantages of its multinational formations, the distrust between the various arms, the lack of effective co-operation between army and air, and the reduction in ruthless zeal among senior officers after the wearying previous campaigns, Monty had, almost overnight, restored hope and given a new sense of professional purpose to Eighth Army. The operations conducted thereafter had still left much to be desired and were by no means perfectly executed, as we have seen. The average Briton was not a killer, as Monty acknowledged in his letter to Brooke of 27 November 1942. But after three years of almost unremitting defeat Monty had shown that victory *was* possible; not only an occasional victory, but a carefully orchestrated programme of victories, beginning at Alam Halfa and culminating, after 1,400 miles of advance, in the capture of Tripoli. Even the Germans were amazed at the professionalism and determination of men who, when captured, revealed no expected indoctrination other than that General Montgomery had, before Alamein, assured them they were fighting for their families and the eventual opportunity of returning home.

The storming of the Tarhuna–Homs line and the taking of Tripoli was thus the crowning achievement of a transformed Eighth Army, as well as the successful enactment of Churchill's original directive to clear Axis forces from Egypt and Libya.

'The outlook for the future is bright. But I have serious misgivings,' Monty warned, when I think of the large Army in England, commanded by Generals who do not know the practical technique of modern battle fighting, many of whom have not seen a shot fired in this war, who do not know the 'feel of the battle', who have no practical experience of the stresses and strains of the battle, and who have mostly got a wrong sense of values.

The tendency of most Commanders in England is to become involved in details which have nothing to do with the practical realities of the battlefield.

If all this is not put right, and that quickly, then we can look forward to some very unpleasant shocks when that Army goes overseas to fight.

Three weeks later, at the battle of Kasserine, the 10,000 Allied casualties would fulfil Monty's prophecy.

In the meantime, in Tripoli, Monty now staged perhaps the most remarkable 'teach-in' of the entire war. While Rommel raced back to the Mareth line inside Tunisia, Monty decided to use to advantage the period while the port of Tripoli was got working once more. He therefore gave orders that an Eighth Army 'study week' be organised to which senior officers from other theatres of war, British, American and French, were invited, as well as from Home Forces in Britain. As no other Field Commander before or after him, General Sir Bernard Montgomery was determined that the problems of current hostilities should be identified, presented and discussed. Egocentric or eccentric, the man whose life had been committed to the study and practice of the art of war was adamant that the operational lessons of his desert campaign should not be squandered when men's lives were still at stake.

PART TWO

The End in North Africa

CHAPTER ONE

Churchill Visits Tripoli

Churchill's visit to Eighth Army took place on the third and fourth of February 1943. The Prime Minister was met by Monty at Castel Benito aerodrome, near Tripoli, and driven straight to Montgomery's camp, where he was installed – as on his visit to Eighth Army on the eve of the battle of Alam Halfa – in Monty's personal caravan.

Churchill's doctor was disappointed that he and Churchill should be given accommodation in military caravans when there were palaces to be had in Tripoli – even ascribing the caravan-complex to a 'modern, thought-out approach to democracy, of which Monty is a master and the others eager disciples'.[1]

This was silly – as Monty's contempt for Auchinleck's 'Meat-Safe' on the Ruweisat Ridge the previous August had demonstrated. Indeed in Normandy, as will be seen, Bradley's aides considered that in comparison with their frill-less Army Commander, Monty lived a life of great luxury in his caravan. Caravans had less to do with self-conscious democracy and more to do with professionalism. 'Much fighting lies ahead and I cannot have my army getting "soft" and deteriorating in any way,' he had noted in his diary on 26 January, three days after his entry into Tripoli. 'I have forbidden the use of houses, buildings, etc. for headquarters and troops. The Army will live in the fields and in the desert, and will retain its hardness and efficiency.'

Far better than Dr Sir Charles Wilson, Monty understood the psychology of his Prime Minister. Just as Monty had invoked Gort's anger by parading his 3rd Division in France before Neville Chamberlain in 1939, so now he reasoned that Churchill – always so impatient for the offensive, so sweeping in his generalisations and in his military strategy – should be brought down to soldierly earth by incarcerating him under his control at Eighth Army headquarters, rather than allowing him to stay in splendour in Tripoli. No sooner had Churchill and his entourage arrived at Monty's headquarters than Monty 'gave the P.M. and me a long talk on his situation', Brooke noted in his diary that night. 'He then paraded the whole of

---

[1] Moran, *Churchill: The Struggle for Survival*, London 1966.

his H.Q., which was addressed by the P.M. on a loud-speaker. Then we had further talks with Monty and dined in his Mess – the same tent we had dined in with him before the battle of El Alamein. Now I have retired to my caravan. It is infernally cold, so I shall get into bed quickly so as to get warm.'[1]

As in war, so in personal relations Monty was determined to gain and retain the initiative. Churchill might well have wanted a palatial bedroom in an Italianate Tripolitanian building, but the Eighth Army Commander's carefully conceived programme – deferential, honouring, while subtly and militaristically domineering – was too flattering and too fundamentally well-intended for Churchill to take it amiss. Churchill certainly rose to the occasion and his speech to Monty's staff – in which he quoted from Hymns Ancient and Modern 'You have nightly pitched your moving tent a day's march nearer home' – struck a deep chord amongst the gathered officers. It was a theme which touched every man in Eighth Army, many of whom had been in the desert since 1940. Ten years later, almost to the day, Wilson – elevated to the peerage as Lord Moran – found him singing the hymn 'A day's march nearer home': 'Do you remember when Monty gathered his staff officers round him in the desert after El Alamein, I gave them this hymn?' Churchill asked Moran, his eyes sparkling with indelible pride.[2]

The next day, after a safe night's sleep in the spartan but professional atmosphere of a victorious army in the field, the Prime Minister was treated to his first victory parade of the Second World War: a triumphal drive into Tripoli, his entry flanked by the long rows of tanks and anti-tank guns of Eighth Army's armoured brigades; then a march-past of the 51st Highland Division, complete with bagpipes, in the city square of Tripoli; a visit to 30 Corps Artillery and Engineers in the field followed by lunch with the Corps Commander, General Leese; a review of General Freyberg's 2nd New Zealand Division; inspection of the Desert Air Force at Castel Benito aerodrome; and finally a tour of Tripoli harbour – which had just admitted its first 3,000-ton ship, despite the breaching of the mole and extensive German demolitions.

Churchill left Tripoli delighted by all he had witnessed. Moreover his visit – though ordered to be kept secret at the time – was an undoubted tonic to the officers and men of Eighth Army after their 1,400-mile march from Alamein.

The P.M. spent a whole day with me and I made him review troops,

[1] Arthur Bryant, *The Turn of the Tide*, London 1957.
[2] Moran, op. cit.

Monty wrote on 6 February 1943 to Brigadier Simpson at the War Office.

> I showed him soldiers that I do not believe you would see in any other Army in the world; magnificent fighting men from all over the world; the parade and march past in the main square of Tripoli was a wonderful sight; the P.M. was deeply moved and could hardly trust himself to speak.
>
> I do not believe you would see such a display of fighting men in any Army in the world except in the Eighth Army.
>
> The morale is right up on the top line and the sick rate is 1 man per 1000 per day; you cannot want anything better than this.

But behind the pride shown by Eighth Army there was nagging uncertainty and anxiety over the Tunisian campaign.

> I had long talks with the P.M. and Brookie over the Tunis situation,

Monty informed Simpson privately.

> I doubt myself if Anderson is the chap to handle that party; it seems to me the whole show wants some inspiration and uplift; unless morale is high, and you have the initiative, you can do nothing in war.

More and more Monty worried lest the real lessons of fighting an enemy as indoctrinated and professional as the Germans, be ignored or misunderstood, and the news from Simpson that Lord Gort had been elevated to the rank of Field-Marshal struck Monty as outrageous.

> I feel that to make Gort a Field-Marshal was quite dreadful, and I told Brookie so; apparently the P.M. was sorry for him!!

In the only surviving letter of the war to his mother, Monty also narrated the capture of Tripoli, recounting with pride how Neville Lewis had painted his portrait not only 'for the Nation', but another for Monty personally, which was 'better than the one he did for the Nation', of which Churchill had offered to take back to England with him to hand over to David:

> It will be a very proud day for David when he is sent for by the Prime Minister of England, and is given my portrait. . . . It will be kept at Amesbury School, Hindhead, which is David's home.

To Amesbury Monty also wrote with news of the portrait's imminent home-coming, but his anxiety about its resting place began to reveal the same defensive streak that had marked his private letter to Tom Reynolds on the eve of his departure from England in August 1942:

> The picture when framed is to be kept at Amesbury School, and nowhere else,

he wrote on 15 February.

> You may be approached by my family to let them have it; my Mother may say she ought to have it. *Be very firm and refuse.*
> They can all come and see it, but it is to be kept by you. Tell them that those are my orders.

Nor was the Lewis portrait the only item threatened. 'I think my Mother will be over in England in the spring,' Monty continued.

> She may ask David to go over to Ireland for his holidays. *On no account is he to go*; my Mother is a very old lady and is quite hopeless with children and boys.

This concern to keep away his ageing mother, who had written excitedly from Ireland to tell how she had been asked to broadcast and give interviews now that her son was achieving fame, might in itself have been comprehensible, however exaggerated. But other letters concerning David's welfare and the Montgomery family leave little doubt that Monty was becoming not only overwrought – as well he might be by such a critical campaign – but, like Rommel, 'imagined that everything has a different cause from the real one,' as Rommel's ADC noted. In Monty's case this was reflected in his amazing campaign to separate David from the last remaining Montgomery relative – the wife of his stepson John Carver. Though, as has been seen, Jocelyn had looked after David Montgomery in Burnham-on-Sea and sat by Betty Montgomery's bedside as her life ebbed away in the autumn of 1937, Mrs Jocelyn Carver was now to be struck off the list of those permitted to look after David – for (according to Phyllis Reynolds) she had denied David the farmer's milk he needed for her own two small children over the Christmas holiday, and permitted him to return to Amesbury looking ill (he was in fact on the verge of 'flu).

> I gathered from Phyllis that Jocelyn Carver was somewhat annoyed that David did not go there any more,

Monty wrote to Tom Reynolds on 30 January, after receiving a disturbing letter from Phyllis.

But it is no good him going there if he does not get enough to eat. You and Phyllis are in complete and absolute charge of David; you do exactly what you think right; you can tell the whole of my family to go to the devil.

Several days later Monty addressed himself directly to Phyllis:

I am horrified to hear of David's condition when he arrived from Jocelyn.
  She has no idea how to look after a growing boy; and the food problem in that small cottage[1] must obviously be very difficult. . . . I do not think he should stay with Jocelyn in the holidays; she cannot look after him, or feed him properly. However, you do whatever you think right. You are in complete charge, and see her 'right off' if she gets upset.

In the ensuing weeks this concern about David amounted to an absolute obsession, particularly when Churchill cabled on 10 February to say that David's visit to the Prime Minister was being put off because 'your son is laid up with flu at the moment'. By the time Phyllis Reynolds' letter arrived giving details of David's illness, Monty was beside himself.
  'I gather he got flu and a touch of bronchitis,' Monty wrote on 10 March.

I have a feeling the seeds were sown when he was with Jocelyn. *I would sooner he did not go there any more in the holidays.*

When he heard the latest gossip about David – that he had been allowed a glass of sherry at midday on Christmas Eve at Jocelyn's and had become tipsy, Monty exploded – Phyllis was always 'to do exactly what you think best; *never wait for an answer, or for approval from me; do whatever you like,* and I will always agree; I have complete trust in you,' Monty wrote on 16 March.

There is only one point I am anxious about, and it is that David should NOT go to Jocelyn any more in the holidays. It is quite obvious she has no idea of how to handle a growing boy; late hours, and drink, are quite dreadful for him.

As if this were not enough, Monty wrote again only three days later:

---

[1] In fact Jocelyn Carver's 'cottage' contained five bedrooms and two bathrooms.

Just got your letter of 8th March.

David is NOT to go to Jocelyn in the holidays.

Tell him this from me.

And you can put the blame on me when you tell Jocelyn; tell her that it is my direct order.

She does not understand how to handle a growing boy and I am not going to run risks merely for sentimental reasons. If Jocelyn protests, let me know and I will tell her exactly where she gets off.

This letter was dated 19 March 1943. The following day Monty repeated his now paranoid order:

He is quite definitely NOT to go there; tell him this from me; it is an order, and he has got to accept it. . . . If Jocelyn makes a fuss you can tell her that it is not in any way your doing; it is entirely _my_ doing.

Nor was this the end of the matter. Monty's obsession about Jocelyn continued into April, and transformed itself into renewed distrust and suspicion of his family, and his mother, as will be seen.

Was all this a defensive matrix to his growing *folie de grandeur*? The mark of exhaustion? Or an extension of that same 'madness' that had progressively characterised Monty's behaviour after Dunkirk?

It is easy to understand how Monty's reputation as a vain, boastful, egocentric, even megalomaniac personality began to spread like an insidious undercurrent to his growing fame as a victorious general. His obsession about his portrait, about which he boasted in letters to all and sundry; his insubordinate, almost insulting manner towards his Commander-in-Chief, Sir Harold Alexander; his almost paranoid fears for the welfare of David and his rejection of his family: these were not the marks of personal greatness or nobility of spirit. They caused hurt to the members of Monty's family, and they are distressing for his biographer to have to record.

It should however be remembered that Monty's opponent, after almost two years of desert campaigning, had been relieved of his command following the surrender of Tripoli. 'I'm so depressed that I can hardly work,' Rommel confessed in a letter to his wife.[1] Professor Horster however could find nothing physically wrong with the Field-Marshal and his virtual break-down was considered a psychological one. Similarly, not many months later, George S. Patton would also be relieved of his command after an outburst considered by some to be mad – the striking of hospitalised soldiers for 'cowardice'.

[1] Letter of 23.1.43, *The Rommel Papers*, London 1953.

The truth is, command in the field of battle is taxing in a manner that few save veterans can fully grasp. The Mediterranean theatre proved a veritable mortuary of senior commanders and their reputations – both Axis and Allied. When Lt-General Montgomery arrived in the desert Freyberg remarked: 'Africa is the graveyard of generals. How long do you think you will last?' Wavell, Auchinleck, O'Connor, Gott, Ritchie, Norrie, Godwin-Austen, Ramsden, Dorman-Smith – all had come to grief in North Africa, and Gott's unwillingness to countenance the inevitable casualties of a head-on battle at Alamein well illustrates the dilemma of the great human being as against the ruthlessly great soldier. Lumsden, Gatehouse, and Renton had failed under Montgomery's command; even Monty's brilliant Chief-of-Staff, Freddie de Guingand, had suffered a physical breakdown in December 1942 and been hospitalised. The conduct of battle – and the constant proximity to death – is a test few mortals can stand over a prolonged period without showing the strain. That Monty gave rein to it in a distressingly mean and vindictive way in his relations with his family is incontrovertible. The question remains: did it show also in his conduct of battle and his behaviour as a Commander – as had been the case with Rommel and Patton?

The question is not easy to answer. Within ten weeks of the capture of Tripoli Monty would certainly create a storm in inter-Allied relations by his insistence on being given a £100,000 Flying Fortress, together with American crew, for his personal use – as payment of a bet. During the battle of Mareth there would be indications of obsessive assumptions in planning which mystified even Monty's own planning staff; in the race towards Enfidaville there would be signs of contemptuous distrust of other formations than those under his own command – as would again be evidenced in the planning for the invasion of Sicily. Even Rommel, in his memoirs, referred to Montgomery's 'absolute mania for always bringing up adequate reserves . . . and risking as little as possible'.[1] British officers too felt that the Eighth Army Commander carried caution and build-up of administrative resources to manic excess.

Such criticism is entirely understandable. Age, war and battle did combine after Dunkirk to intensify those areas of Bernard Montgomery's character that tended towards excessive rigidity, distrust of others, even paranoid fears. What is perhaps remarkable is that this flawed, profoundly limited individual, widowed and without close friends of his own age or experience, actually managed to achieve all that he did achieve: for whatever jealous minds might then or later make of Montgomery's performance ('there wasn't room for *two* shits in the desert,' the sacked General Lumsden was heard to say at his club in London), there was no gainsaying the magnitude of his

[1] Ibid.

137

achievement. As Brigadier Ian Jacob, accompanying Churchill to Tripoli, recalled in his diary, the tears were real:

> All around were the veterans of the 8th Army, standing in the last city of Mussolini's Empire. No wonder the tears rolled down the Prime Minister's cheeks as he took the salute of one of our finest Divisions, with General Alexander and General Montgomery standing beside him. It was an occasion that made all the anxiety, the disappointments, the hardships and the setbacks of the Middle East campaign seem to be robbed of their sting. The bitter moment in the White House when Tobruk fell was swallowed up in the joy of the morning in Tripoli.[1]

Brooke later expressed the same exultant joy:

> The depth of these feelings can only be gauged in relation to the utter darkness of those early days of calamities, when no single ray of hope could pierce the depths of gloom. . . . I felt no shame that tears should have betrayed my feelings, only a deep relief.[2]

To those in Eighth Army the miracle was the way the men marched, as Warwick Charlton recalled:

> The square – it looked like a set for Moorish pirates. And there was Churchill with Monty. And Monty had produced this victory for him at the right time. And for the first time in their bloody lives this army had to march! Probably they had it in them somewhere – but they had discovered seemingly out of thin air the way to march in unison, swinging their arms properly, even to dress decently! – for this one occasion.
>
> I saw Monty looking down, so pleased. And Churchill just cried.[3]

Moreover in General Sir Ian Jacob's later recollection, there was little doubt that the desert campaign was Montgomery's triumph, and that he was in no way robbing others of the glory. Indeed so utterly did Monty now seem to be in charge of the conduct of the campaign that the astute Jacob began to wonder what exactly Alexander's role might be. 'It's a funny thing,' he recalled almost forty years later,

---

[1] Operation 'Symbol', unpublished diary of Brigadier E. I. C. Jacob, January–February 1943, communicated to author.

[2] Arthur Bryant, op. cit.

[3] Warwick Charlton, interview of 31.3.83.

but I believe that we all at that time felt that they [Alexander and Montgomery] were doing a very good double act – I mean, that Alex was doing his stuff as C-in-C, and Monty was fighting the battle very well.

But I had begun to wonder what Alex was really doing. And I asked a whole lot of people – Cornwall-Jones, for example, who was in Cairo – he was the Secretary to the Commanders-in-Chief, and who therefore saw Alex regularly. I asked him about it, on the way to Tripoli [from Turkey]. He said: 'Well, Alex did nothing. He used to go up from time to time to see Monty, with a notebook. He'd come back and say, General Montgomery wants this or that – see that he gets it. And as far as we could see, he didn't do anything. When Alamein took place, he was driving an engine on the Egyptian Railway!'[1]

Certainly Alexander appeared to Jacob to have very little grip on field operations or, at this stage, any great concern for them. Alexander was present at Casablanca for the Churchill-Roosevelt summit conference in December 1942; he was in Cairo to greet Churchill when the latter landed on 26 January 1943; he was part of Churchill's entourage in Adana for Churchill's negotiations with the Turkish President; and though present again at Tripoli when Churchill visited Eighth Army, there was no business conducted in the C-in-C's camp, as far as Jacob could recall. 'As far as I remember we didn't do any business at all. Any business that was done was done by Monty in his caravan with the PM. There was no formal sitting down sort of business at all.'

Moreover all except Montgomery seemed to view the Tunisian campaign as progressing slowly but satisfactorily – certainly giving no cause for anxiety. 'During Casablanca,' Jacob remembered,

there was a general feeling that Eisenhower was totally inexperienced – didn't know what to do – was far too far back – ought to have had an Advanced Headquarters. Anderson was fair, but with the three nationalities all competing for the same roads and this mountainous terrain – it was pretty difficult. And then eyes were more looking forward to the time when the Eighth Army would be on the flank too, and it would therefore be a question of co-ordinating the two.[2]

Churchill thus foresaw no problems, and was disinclined to take Montgomery's warnings seriously. 'It wouldn't be a bad moment to leave,' he remarked a few days later at Algiers when considering the

[1] Interview of 7.4.81.
[2] Ibid.

possibility of an air crash on the return flight to England. 'It is a straight run in now, and even the Cabinet could manage it.'[1] He had arranged with Roosevelt that, when Eighth Army reached Tunisia proper, General Alexander was to become Eisenhower's deputy, and co-ordinator of the two Allied armies for the final phase of operations. 'It didn't appear very difficult,' Jacob recalled. 'Alex was after all the C-in-C, Middle East, and he'd got nothing whatever to do there. So here's a man you call in to co-ordinate the two armies. . . . The PM had a great opinion of Alex. Alan Brooke didn't – but the PM did.

'I don't believe that there was any serious feeling that things were actually going wrong. Kasserine came as quite a shock!' Jacob vividly remembered.[2]

Whatever Monty's overwrought mental condition, he had and would always possess a knack for sniffing out inefficiency, for sensing weakness, for locating potential trouble before it arose. In part this was the result of his extraordinary and relentless curiosity – that trait which Betty Montgomery had so well captured when she remarked that 'Monty's conversation consists in asking questions'. It was a characteristic some found tiresome, but it paid dividends – as events were now to show. For Rommel's forces had now reached the Tunisian border, beyond which was an Axis bridgehead in good, defensive country and amply reinforced. Monty was convinced that fireworks must soon be expected – the more so since, from all he could gather, the First Army, Free French and American fronts were ill-co-ordinated and, by Eighth Army standards, amateur in command, intelligence, and air co-operation. He warned Brooke and Churchill, and he refused to extend his own forces too far beyond Tripoli until the port was in working order and capable of sustaining forward operations. In the meantime he decided to mount an Army Study Week on the same lines as he had done in Home Forces, extending invitations to senior officers from Britain, First Army and American forces in North-west Africa. A good contingent flew in from England; but from Anderson's First Army scarcely any came, and from the Americans only one senior commander: General George S. Patton.

[1] Operation 'Symbol', loc. cit.
[2] Loc. cit.

CHAPTER TWO

'Wonderfully Conceited' – Monty's Study Week

Monty's insistence on stringent training and rehearsal of operations had not lapsed after Alamein. All units and formations not currently in line were required to undertake training schemes, and the attacks on El Agheila and Buerat were first rehearsed in tactical exercises without troops and then by constituent brigades behind the front line.

Monty's Tripoli study week was therefore by no means the self-glorying rally that some suspicious minds took it to be. Its genesis lay undoubtedly in the deeply professional training programme undertaken by Sir Herbert Plumer's Second Army in 1917, and the gradual development of training concepts which Monty had personally evolved in the ensuing years.

'Between 14 and 17 February a meeting was held in TRIPOLI,' Lt-Colonel Oswald recorded in his diary,

which was attended by C in C HOME FORCES, Army and Corps Commanders from ENGLAND, and Senior Officers, including those from the US Forces in TUNISIA.

The arrangements of their visit included lectures by the Army Commander on the Battle of EGYPT and the advance to TRIPOLI, by General FREYBERG on the handling of a Motor Division, by General Wimberley on the attack against the enemy rearguard position, and a demonstration by 8 Armd Bde of an Armoured battle. In addition a demonstration was given of the working of the combined Army and Air HQ and another of the method used in clearing gaps through a minefield.[1]

Even the study week itself was rehearsed beforehand so that it should be, as far as possible, a challenge both to the presenters, who faced a critical barrage during their rehearsals, and the eventual audience. Leese recalled in his memoirs that the Army Commander's

[1] Maj-General M. St J. Oswald, unpublished desert diary, communicated to author.

141

opening address, which lasted some two hours, 'was one of the best addresses I have ever heard and that is saying a lot'.[1] Monty chose to begin the address in his now traditional manner, announcing that there was to be no coughing and no smoking. Whether it was this edict, or the transparent confidence with which General Montgomery spoke on the subject of modern warfare, the chain-smoking Patton was incensed. 'I may be old, I may be slow, I may be stoopid, and I know I'm deaf, but it just don't mean a thing to me,' Patton is said to have remarked very loudly as the audience left their seats.[2] Yet even this was spoken for show, for in the privacy of his diary Patton noted of Montgomery: 'very alert, wonderfully conceited, and the best soldier – or so it seems – I have met in this war.'[3]

'The Army Commander was in his element,' the Commander of the 4th Indian Division later recalled – for General Tuker had been a student under Montgomery at the Staff College in 1926 and likened the study week to 'a short staff course'.[4] To have mounted such a 'staff course' in the midst of a campaign was certainly a unique achievement in the annals of military history. Yet the British Official Historian did not mention the study week in his narrative of the campaign[5] – perhaps thereby reflecting the blinkered attitude to the art of war which Monty so consistently sought to break down. For it had been Monty's conviction since the eve of the battle of Alamein that the lessons of the Mediterranean campaign must be articulated and disseminated if the Allies were to avoid future failures; moreover the disastrous BEF campaign in 1939/40 had intensified Monty's determination that if one day he was given command of an army, he would run it on very different lines from those of Lord Gort. An Army Commander must not simply be a figurehead: he must constantly initiate, and be one step ahead of others. The Tripoli study week was a *tour de force*: a 'senior management conference' which would become common doctrine in both civil and military life in the years to come, but which at the time was viewed with much suspicion in many quarters. In his diary Monty recorded that he was well satisfied:

I must here mention the tactical discussions that took place in TRIPOLI on 15, 16 and 17 Feb. The object of our discussions was to check up on our battle technique, and to put our house in order for the future. I invited general officers to attend from England, from TUNISIA, from SYRIA, from IRAK; and they all came.

[1] General Sir Oliver Leese, unpublished memoirs, communicated to author by Ian Calvocoressi.
[2] Major-General M. St J. Oswald, interview of 22.4.80, *inter alia*.
[3] *The Patton Papers*, ed. Martin Blumenson, Vol. II, Boston 1972.
[4] Francis Tuker, *Approach to Battle*, London 1963.
[5] I. S. O. Playfair and C. J. C. Molony, *The Mediterranean and the Middle East* Vol. IV, London 1966.

It was a very representative gathering and a great success.

However in his private letters home to England, Monty told a different story. The invitees did not 'all' come, and those who did were a disappointment to him. On the first day of the conference – 15 February 1943 – he wrote to Brooke:

> The whole party has now arrived for my discussions. The party from Tunisia is very disappointing. Not one British general has come; no Inf. Bde. Comds. have come; only one American General has come (the Comd. of an Armoured Corps; an old man of about 60). I had hoped to get over here Anderson, Allfrey, the British Div Comds, and some American Div. Comds. The party is all staff officers of the Lt.-Col. level, and mostly A/Q staff. What a great pity.

The 'old man of about 60' was Patton – a general about whom Monty would very soon have to revise his opinion; and the weak Tunisian contingent was possibly the result of the military situation there. For with Eighth Army temporarily stalled until Tripoli harbour could be got working, Rommel was given temporary command in Tunisia, with a view to counter-attacking Eisenhower's badly unbalanced 'broad front'. Ultra-based Intelligence predicted an Axis attack, so that there could be no question of releasing senior field commanders from First Army – and the German attack duly began on 14 February 1943.

Monty himself had already felt increasing misgivings about the First Army sector, which neither Churchill nor Brooke would take seriously. Eisenhower had been asked to accept Alexander as virtual Land Forces Commander at the Casablanca Conference, but the timing of the appointment was left to Eisenhower – who only issued the official directive on 20 February, when Rommel's thrust at Kasserine had brought panic and confusion to the Allied Headquarters in Algiers. By then Alexander had already assumed command in the field two days early.[1] His accession, modelled on Montgomery's take-over at Eighth Army, aroused no subsequent historians' cavilling, for Alexander was never a controversial figure.

> A very great personal friend of mine has come over with the Tunis party for my discussions

Monty meanwhile related to Brooke on 15 February.

---

[1] Cf. Harold Alexander file, Papers of Dwight D. Eisenhower, 1652 series, Eisenhower Library, Abilene, Kansas.

He is on First Army staff. In a heart-to-heart talk he told me that First Army H.Q. was not a happy party; there is no pep or uplift; the show does not run smoothly. Anderson insists on going himself personally into every detail and no one is left to run his own show. McNab [Anderson's BGS] is not popular. They will never run a good show with an Army H.Q. like that. I will pass this on to Alex and I expect he will investigate.

Alexander did – and confirmed Monty's impression, as will be seen. Monty's views on the organisation and staff both at Algiers and First Army were doubtless exaggerated by distance and tinged with competitive jealousy, but the chronology of their expression is certainly remarkable. Already four weeks previously Monty had added a postscript to his letter to Brooke:

An officer over here from the Tunis side tells me that the Allied Force H.Q. consists of 2000 American officers and 800 British officers. What a dreadful party!

Now, on 15 February Monty made some searching remarks about individuals in Algiers, 'now that my war, and the Tunis war, are merging into one'.

Whiteley is no good; he proved a failure here.
Mockler-Ferryman is also not the chap; he is a pure theorist and has no practical experience.
It seems to me that what Eisenhower ought to have is some 1st class *practical* chaps, who know exactly what is wanted and how to get it.
I suppose the truth is that there are not enough 1st class chaps to go round.

Given Monty's insistent attempts to exchange experienced officers with Home Forces and his study week being mounted at Tripoli for contingents from Tunisia, the charge of bigotry often levelled at him is exaggerated. In fact Eisenhower would shortly be forced to relieve Mockler-Ferryman of his post after the disaster at Kasserine, for as Eisenhower's Chief of Intelligence he had relied too heavily on Ultra, misinterpreting both the strength and direction of the German offensive, at a time when neither the American forces in the field nor the French had access to Ultra at all.

The American disaster at Kasserine came as a rude shock to those who felt Montgomery was being over-cautious in his pursuit of Rommel. Overnight Rommel split open the Allied line in Tunisia and demonstrated that even the best equipment in the world will not of itself win battles: it was the spirit of the soldiers who manned it and their training which were critical. Patton's comment on General Montgomery's opening address at Tripoli suddenly seemed very complacent. American soldiers were literally running away from the enemy, abandoning weapons and pride, while over four thousand surrendered; Allied communications broke down utterly, and there were days and nights of panic and pandemonium before a semblance of discipline and order could be restored. This wilful squandering of men, equipment, stores and defensive positions was anathema to Monty, for it was wholly unnecessary. In the end, he felt, it all came down to leadership; and leadership entailed the willingness to train *oneself* before one presumed to command the fate of others.

The Tripoli conference thus took place against the background of a German come-back of alarming vigour, the more so since Monty and the C-in-C 18th Army Group-elect had privately discussed future policy 'to finish off the North African campaign' on 16 February – a policy based on the Allies retaining the initiative.

Alex came over here today

Monty had written that night to Brooke,

and we have had long talks. There is no doubt he has a very difficult task in front of him; the party in Tunisia is a complete dog's breakfast and there is an absence of good chaps there. But he and I are tremendous friends and he knows that I am 100% at his disposal and stand firm behind him in everything he does. We have fixed up a plan of campaign to finish off the N. African War; it is quite simple and everything is really based on getting Eighth Army north of the GABES gap and out into the open; I will then roll the whole show up from the south, moving north with my right on the sea. If we play our cards properly we cannot fail. I look forward to a 1st class Dunkirk on the beaches of Tunis. I have a few old scores to pay off myself in respect of that other Dunkirk!!

In fact Alexander and Montgomery were casting their thoughts ahead to the invasion of Sicily:

Alex wants me to come in on HUSKY, and of course I am delighted,

Monty continued.

I have told him that the British part should be called Eighth Army and that full use must be made of the Eighth Army name and morale. I can use such portions of the Army as I want initially,

145

ensure a good battle experience in all levels, and cast the Eighth Army mantle and morale over Dempsey's Corps at once.[1]

Only envious tongues could construe in this the self-glorification of an egotist, for Monty had recognised the importance – particularly against the background of First Army's poor showing – of ceasing to send abroad War Office contingents but instead sending Armies – Armies with a pride and a reputation, in which men were anxious to serve, and if necessary die.

This morale factor is terribly important

Monty stressed.

I have built up a really good fighting team here in my H.Q., and indeed all through the Army. We must use all that experience, and battle experience, and *this* will ensure success.

It will take the rest of this year to finish the show in N. Africa, and to give Italy a proper bang,

he prophesied.

Then next year, 1944, we had better land in Western Europe and I would like to come home and take part in that.

I look forward to leading the Eighth Army into Rome. By Jove, what a party!

Yours ever
Monty

In fact not Monty but an American general, Mark Clark, would lead the first Allied army into Rome; and that would take place not in 1943 but 1944. Evidently though, Brooke's testy reaction to Monty's letter in December 1942 suggesting a cross-channel assault in 1943 had been effective, and Monty was, for the moment at least, won over to Brooke's Mediterranean strategy. As a postscript Monty added:

First Army should never have withdrawn from GAFSA. I do not hold with any withdrawals, anywhere.

They will have to recapture it. When I get through the GABES

---

[1] Lt-General Miles Dempsey had been a student under Monty at the Staff College, Camberley, in the 1920s; he had commanded 13th Infantry Brigade in the vital defence of the Ypres–Comines canal area during the evacuation of the BEF at Dunkirk. At Montgomery's request he had been flown out to the Middle East and had taken command of 13 Corps when Lt-General Horrocks replaced Lumsden in command of 10 Corps.

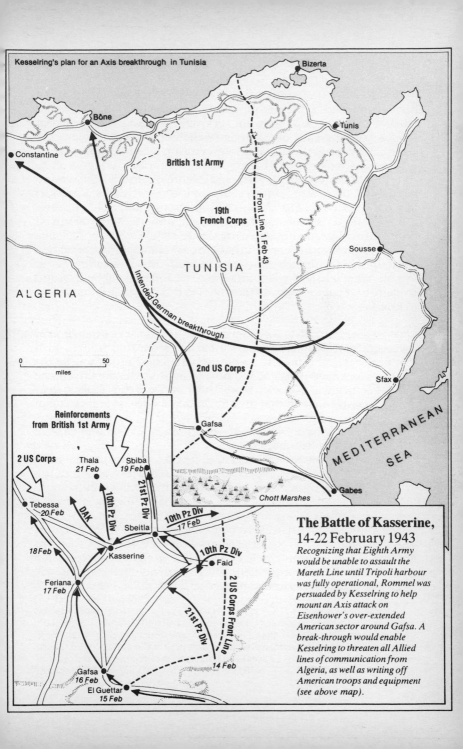

Kesselring's plan for an Axis breakthrough in Tunisia

Bizerta

Bône

Tunis

Constantine

British 1st Army

19th
French Corps

Front Line, 1 Feb 43

Sousse

TUNISIA

ALGERIA

Intended German breakthrough

2nd US Corps

Sfax

0   50
miles

Gafsa

MEDITERRANEAN

SEA

Gabes

Chott Marshes

Reinforcements
from British 1st Army

2 US Corps

Thala
21 Feb

Sbiba
19 Feb

Tebessa
20 Feb

DAK

10th Pz Div

21st Pz Div

10th Pz Div
17 Feb

18 Feb

Sbeitla

10th Pz Div

Kasserine

Faid

Feriana
17 Feb

21st Pz Div

2 US Corps Front Line

14 Feb

Gafsa
16 Feb

El Guettar
15 Feb

The Battle of Kasserine,
14-22 February 1943
*Recognizing that Eighth Army
would be unable to assault the
Mareth Line until Tripoli harbour
was fully operational, Rommel was
persuaded by Kesselring to help
mount an Axis attack on
Eisenhower's over-extended
American sector around Gafsa. A
break-through would enable
Kesselring to threaten all Allied
lines of communication from
Algeria, as well as writing off
American troops and equipment
(see above map).*

gap I want to draw petrol from GAFSA, and save a long lift from Tripoli.

Hundreds of thousands of tons of petrol and ammunition had been abandoned by the Americans at Gafsa the previous day, and it is easy to see in Eisenhower's February débâcle the origins of Monty's controversial views on the leadership of the Allied forces in Tunisia – particularly the value of green Americans in battle. What is strange is that there was no attempt by Eisenhower to co-ordinate the actions of First and Eighth Armies at this critical moment in the North African campaign. Monty thus remained an amazed spectator of Eisenhower's Tunisian reverses from 14 February when the Axis offensive was launched, until Alexander assumed premature command of 18th Army Group on 18 February, and even then it was only on 21 February that Alexander cabled his famous 'cry for help'. Yet Eisenhower's Chief-of-Staff, Bedell Smith, was in Tripoli, attending Monty's conference: and still no combined tactical strategy was put forward, so that by 23 February Monty was writing to Brooke:

There seems to be a real good party going on up in Central Tunisia! We get odd people passing to and fro from that front, and it appears that the Bosche does just whatever he likes with the Americans; they do not know how to fight the battle; the Bosche has got a great many of their tanks and a great deal of their equipment. I am told that they haven't got a decent anti-tank gun with the infantry.

I received a cry for help yesterday.[1] My trouble is that half my Army is back at Benghazi.

My admin. situation is not good; it will remain so till about 15 March.

My tank strength is low at the moment; it will be good by 15 March.

The German offensive had been excellently timed; with Tripoli only just beginning to receive large consignments of stores, weapons and ammunition, Montgomery's overland lines of communication from Benghazi made a premature Eighth Army attack against the almost impregnable Mareth defences impracticable. Although Mon-

[1] Signal despatched on 21 February, received 22nd. Thanking Monty for his immediate response, Alexander then cabled on 22 February: 'Well done, I am greatly relieved. I have seen enough in the short time available to be very shocked. There has been no policy and no plan. The battle area is all mixed up with British, French and American units. I have issued the necessary directives but need time to make them effective. Present battle situation extremely critical' – in Alexander Papers (WO 214/18), PRO.

ty assured Alexander he would 'do everything I can and as soon as I can', there was in fact little he could do, save demonstrate. In the past few days he had independently pushed forward troops 'right on to the main MARETH line'; he therefore promised merely to 'begin thrust in a small way now and it should have become a strong threat to enemy by 25 February'; but to Brooke he wrote the next day explaining his dislike of such amateur pugilism, dancing to the enemy's tune:

> The worse the situation becomes up in Central Tunisia, the more necessary it is that my Army should not be used piecemeal but should appear about 15 March as a really strong and powerful threat which nothing can stop.

As in the campaign from Alamein to Tripoli, Monty's intention was to resist opportunism and to defeat the enemy by retaining the initiative – building up his forces, and then 'driving' so hard that he could maintain sufficient momentum to reach his considered objective in one operation. Tripoli had fallen in this way; and Monty, wary of the easily defensible 'Gabes gap' fifty miles beyond Mareth, was determined not to squander the few forces he could administer in a precipitate attempt to 'rush' the Mareth defences. Not only did he risk Eighth Army failing, in the wake of the Kasserine débâcle – which would be a tremendous blow to Allied morale – but even if by some miracle he forced the estimated 200,000 Axis troops defending Mareth to withdraw, he would have insufficient troops and supplies to penetrate the Gabes gap – which Rommel considered the best defensive position between Cairo and Tunis. 'I must try and draw attention my way, and relieve pressure on the First Army,' he acknowledged to Brooke; but he doubted whether it would be more than bluff.

The failure of the Americans was thus not simply an opportunity for Monty to express bigoted contempt, but an irritating distraction from his preferred strategy.

> The whole business is quite dreadful

he told Brooke.

> If only the Americans had come over here earlier and asked about how you fight the Germans, these troubles might have been avoided. The rules of the game are quite simple:
>> You must fight your Divisions *as* Divisions and not split them into groups.
>> You must have firm bases from which you operate.
>> You must knit the army and air closely together. If the great

power of the air, and the great power of the army, are welded together into one great entity, the resulting military effort is terrific; nothing can stand against it.

You must train. The more you fight the more necessary it is to train. The Americans could not understand my having tactical discussion round the model in war time,

he remarked with feeling. Moreover it was no good just relying on armour:

You must have your Army balanced, with the right types of Divisions. At least 50% of your Army, and usually more, must be infantry Divisions of three Inf. Bdes; and Rifle Bns must have 4 comps. You can then sustain a thrust night after night, or switch your thrust about, and finally the Bosche cracks.

You must understand how to handle a mass of artillery. The CCRA of a Corps must be a 1st class chap.

You must keep armoured resources fluid. They must be controlled and positioned by the Army Commander, so as to maintain balance throughout the area.

It is clear from this letter that Monty's erstwhile notion of an Armoured Corps, or *Corps de Chasse*, trained out of the line and modelled on the Afrika Korps, was redundant, save for special occasions. This was the lesson of Alamein, and Monty was adamant it should be made known throughout the British – and American – armies before the 'Liddell Hart' theoreticians wrecked the chances of exploiting Eighth Army's campaign of victory. 'I do not agree with the policy of keeping Armd. Divs. in separate Corps. Harry Crerar [the Canadian Corps Commander] told me he had never handled an Armoured Division; it is probably one of the first things he will have to do in battle; he should learn how to handle armour in peace training. I never decide on the grouping of Divisions, and of the armour, till the problem has emerged; then my Corps Commanders have to be able to handle any types of formations. I tried to make Bernard Paget [C-in-C, Home Forces] see this, but I think I failed.'

The bitter fighting in Sicily, Italy, and North-west Europe would prove Monty's contention. He refused to accept that the 'desert' was somehow 'peculiar': 'When one talks to these chaps from Home Forces they always retaliate by saying that conditions here are peculiar, that it will be quite different in Europe, and so on.' To Monty this was nonsense – for the reason was very simple:

The answer is that the German is the German, wherever you meet him. The basic principles of how to fight him remain the same; you merely adjust your methods to suit the conditions.

One thing stands out crystal clear –

he emphasised –

it is this. When you meet the German, and he means to fight, it will be a rough house; to beat him you must be able to last the course; you will never do this unless you have Infantry Divisions of three Inf. Bdes. and plenty of artillery.

This letter was written on 23 February 1943. During a discussion with Bedell Smith at Tripoli, Monty had boasted that the Eighth Army would 'finish it [the North African war] for them'. Asked what Eisenhower would give if Eighth Army breached both the Mareth defences and Gabes gap to reach Sfax – still some four hundred miles from Tripoli – within the next six weeks, Bedell Smith unwisely offered to 'give me anything I liked', as Monty later recounted to Brooke.

Monty immediately replied that he would like 'a Flying Fortress, complete with American crew to remain on their pay roll; the whole to be my personal property till the war ended. He agreed and said I should have it'.[1]

In the context of the American débâcle at Kasserine, Monty's boast seemed difficult, if not impossible to fulfil, and a Flying Fortress small reward if he did so. In fact, as the Germans prematurely closed down their limited offensive at Kasserine, it looked increasingly likely that they would switch fronts and attempt an attack on forward units of Eighth Army, now dangerously over-extended east of Mareth, in the attempt to answer Alexander's 'cry for help'.

---

[1] Letter of 12.4.43, Montgomery Papers.

CHAPTER THREE

'Rommel can go to Hell': The Battle of Medenine

If lack of co-operation between First and Eighth Armies had seriously jeopardised hopes of a rapid conclusion of the war in North Africa, co-operation between the German armies in Tunisia was even worse. It was intended that Rommel return to Germany on 20 February 1943, but his replacement as C-in-C German-Italian Panzer Army, General Giovanni Messe, had not pressed him to go, and Kesselring, elated by the initial success of the German offensive in Tunisia, reversed his earlier decision and made Rommel, not von Arnim, temporary Army Group C-in-C for North Africa.

This elevation was simply to paper over the desperate breakdown of communication and goodwill between von Arnim and Rommel. Moreover instead of pursuing success against the Americans and First Army, Rommel seemed obsessed now with striking back at Montgomery – as though victory against the Americans merely sharpened his shame at having been run back by the British to Tripoli – his erstwhile starting point in North Africa.

In his memoirs Rommel later gave a contradictory account of the genesis of Operation 'Capri' – the battle of Medenine. Originally, it would appear, this 'spoiling' attack against Eighth Army was conceived as Part Two of a scheme to destroy the Allies' two main assembly areas. By first attacking the Americans in the Western Dorsale (at Kasserine), the Allied threat to the two Axis armies from Gafsa was effectively scotched; by then attacking Montgomery at Medenine, Eighth Army's preparations for the assault on Mareth would be considerably delayed.

Rommel's initial plan was, at the last moment, to surrender the Medenine area in front of Mareth, and then to strike back hard with armoured forces before Eighth Army could meet them in prepared defences.

In fact Monty took the Medenine area – with its four vital airfields – on 17 February, using 7th Armoured Division backed by 22nd Armoured Brigade, and with infantry units of 51st Highland Division – 'rather earlier than we had bargained for,' as Rommel acknowledged, and five days *before* Alexander's 'cry for help'. Nevertheless by now putting a full infantry division, with only limited transport, into the most forward line, Monty had definitely unbalanced himself. Although on 23 February Monty signalled to Alexander that First Army should 'be very offensive' in following up 'any withdrawal on [enemy's] part at Kasserine', and even remarked that it would be 'great fun if we can get him running about like a wet hen between you and me', Monty was none the less alarmed when, two days later, he received an Ultra decrypt, indicating that Rommel *was* breaking off his Kasserine offensive in order to attack Eighth Army at Medenine. Rommel could in fact put three German Panzer Divisions into battle – scarcely a 'wet hen'. Ought Eighth Army then to withdraw? Yet Monty had only just written to Brooke claiming that he did not 'hold with any withdrawals, anywhere'. Moreover, if he was going to withdraw, how far should the withdrawal be – for there was no natural defensive position before the Tarhuna–Homs line – beyond Tripoli! There was thus no alternative: the forward units must be dug in, and as many reinforcements brought forward as possible in the time available.

Some writers have been inclined to underrate the subsequent battle of Medenine as merely the fruit of Ultra – forgetting the fiasco at Kasserine when Eisenhower and his Intelligence staff placed too much credence in Ultra, and ignored the basic tactical military opportunities open to the Germans. Photo-reconnaissance reports of German withdrawal on the Kasserine front, moreover, all pointed towards the same conclusion – but, as at Kasserine, the exact direction of the German thrust was not revealed – was not in fact decided upon by Rommel until the very last moment, in a conference with Messe and Buelowius, his Chief Engineer, on 28 February, four days before the intended attack. Even then there was such disagreement at this planning conference that no final decision was taken, and Messe was permitted to devise his own plan, which was not given out to the constituent formations until 3 March, far too late for Ultra to play an effective part. David Irving, in his biography of Rommel, suggested that Montgomery had moved 'guns and men from the coast to the southern sector' as the direct result of 'advance notice by the Ultra code-breakers of both the direction and precise timing of the attack'[1] – but this was scarcely the case, as the British Official History of Intelligence, Eighth Army War Diaries and the testimony of all survivors agree. Not until the Axis formations emerged from the mist on 6 March 1943 did Montgomery know for certain the line of the enemy attack – and if he was bullishly confident that he could meet the armoured offensive, it was because he had taken immediate advantage of the warning of a possible attack to bring up and dispose

---

[1] David Irving, *The Trail of the Fox*, London 1977.

adequate reinforcements, not because of 'inside' knowledge about the enemy's actual plans.

The week of preparation for Rommel's possible attack was certainly hectic, and a triumph of administration and operational teamwork. In his hospital bed in Tripoli, Eighth Army's head of Intelligence had been certain Rommel would not stray for long from Mareth:

I can remember this so well because one got the Medenine battle in one's head just knowing how Rommel would behave, so to speak. I was so determined about it that I went back [to Army Headquarters] by expelling myself as it were from hospital. I wrote a charming letter to Matron saying, 'I've just been telling the Army Commander what a superb hospital you are running, please send me my discharge papers, and . . .!' But you didn't need Ultra to know that this was going to happen. . . .

I'd got no evidence in terms of the facts reaching me, but it was quite clear to me that Rommel was going to counter-attack. I flew back to the Eighth Army Headquarters and was met by Joe Ewart who was my counterpart and I said, 'Is Rommel or the Germans going to counter-attack?' And he said, 'Yes – we've got it absolutely cold on' – they didn't call it Ultra in those days – 'BBR.'[1]

Rommel's message to Hitler, announcing that he was breaking off the Kasserine offensive and returning to face Eighth Army, was decrypted on 25 February 1943.[2] The following day, in issuing his 'Masterplan' for the forthcoming Eighth Army offensive at Mareth [Operation 'Pugilist'] Monty began by predicting a possible 'spoiling' attack by Rommel:

As he [the enemy] has broken off the fight in Central TUNISIA it is quite possible that he will transfer troops quickly to the MARETH front, in order to strengthen that front. He might even consider the possibility of an offensive himself against us, in order to inflict casualties and force us to postpone our own attack – which he must realise is bound to come sooner or later.

From our point of view, such an offensive by him in the near future would be exactly what we would like; it would give us a great opportunity to take heavy toll of the enemy as a first step, and then put in our own *heavy attack* when he was disorganised as a result of his abortive offensive.

Monty had therefore ordered 30 Corps 'to organise the 30 Corps

[1] Sir Edgar Williams, interview of 20.12.79 (BBR stood for: Burn Before Reading).
[2] F. H. Hinsley, op. cit.

area for defence, so that any attack by the enemy to interfere with our own preparations for "PUGILIST" will have no possible chance of success'.

To Alexander Monty wrote confidently:

I am getting myself well poised in case Rommel tries to lash out my way. By 6 March I shall have over 300 tanks in action up here, and it would be a 1st class party if only he would try it on!! I fear he will NOT!

Leese, as Commander of 30 Corps, was less sanguine. In obedience to the Army Commander's orders he had ordered the whole of 51st Division to close up to the Mareth defences after Alexander's 'cry for help', but his military instinct was much against such an advance.

'We reached the Wadi Zessar on 22nd February and the Wadi Zeuss on 25th February,' he recalled after the war.

It was one of the weirdest advances that I carried out during the war. There was very little opposition – just a few patrols covering the strong defences known to be in the Mareth Line; yet no one had any confidence in the manoeuvre and many of us got a stiff neck through looking nervously at the mountains over our left shoulder. For the mountains stood up clearly across the plain . . . our left flank was completely exposed to the German threat from the mountains.[1]

Rommel's own predilection was for a pincer attack, with an infantry and Panzer attack via the mountains, but the main attack being mounted by two Panzer divisions striking frontally from the Wadi Zigzaou, along the road from Mareth to Medenine. Here the British would be most extended and most defenceless in a geographical sense. It was certainly what Leese feared.

I was not at all happy about this [prospect of a frontal attack by the enemy], as the Highland Division were holding the line here on a wide front and they had insufficient anti-tank guns to ensure adequate defence in depth. This was a serious matter in desert country, as infantry, even if they are in strong detached posts, can only withstand a powerful tank attack if their anti-tank gun and machine gun defences are in depth and are supported by the availability at call of heavy artillery concentrations on any part of their front.[2]

[1] Loc. cit.
[2] Ibid.

Monty too was convinced, almost to the last moment, that Rommel would attack from the North, astride the main road.

It is remarkable, then, how accurately Monty had read Rommel's original intention – one which Buelowius had countered on the ground that, owing to the booby-trapped Axis minefields which would first have to be cleared, it could never achieve surprise. A right hook had thus been adopted, through the flanking hills, by all three German Panzer divisions, together with combat groups of 164th Light Division, while 90th Light Division merely feinted frontally, along the coast, in order to get the British looking that way. However, even this variation was doomed, for as at Alam Halfa Rommel delayed too long while setting up the attack and, as at Alam Halfa, he did not dare by-pass the Tadjera Khir/Medenine position to strike Montgomery deep in the rear.

Nevertheless, although Ultra had – as before Kasserine – given fair strategic warning that a German counter-attack might be attempted, Rommel *did* achieve tactical surprise. Ultra had afforded no hint of Rommel's battle plan, and to the very moment when the assault began, Eighth Army incorrectly deduced that Rommel was mounting a pincer attack with Panzer divisions striking both frontally and in the flank. 'The enemy made numerous efforts to conceal the direction of his thrust and succeeded in causing some doubt as to his main axis of advance,' the officer in charge of Montgomery's Tactical Headquarters noted in his diary.[1] RAF reconnaissance aircraft reported movement in the Toujane–Hallouf hills on the afternoon of 4 March, and Oswald recorded his own personal view that the 'main attack would come from this direction, either on the afternoon of 5 March with the sun behind him, or at dawn on 6 March'.[2]

Monty, however, was not convinced. A preliminary German attack had been launched frontally on 3 March, pushing back 51st Highland Division's outposts near Mareth, and Monty noted in his own diary on 4 March that 'it began to look as if the enemy had split his forces, and his armour; if he does this he will do no good'. By the following day he was sure that Rommel was trying to bluff him by moving one Panzer Division by daylight through the mountains, while all the time preparing a main frontal assault: 'I came to the conclusion that the enemy move through the mountains was a Panzer Div, and had been done by day so as to ensure I would see it,' he recorded on 5 March after receiving 'no new features' from Tac R; 'it was obviously meant to get me looking that way, i.e. to the West, and this it did. But it was too obvious. I decided that the main enemy thrust was more likely to come on the axis of the main road MARETH –MEDENIN. . . .'

[1] Maj-General M. St J. Oswald, loc. cit.
[2] Ibid.

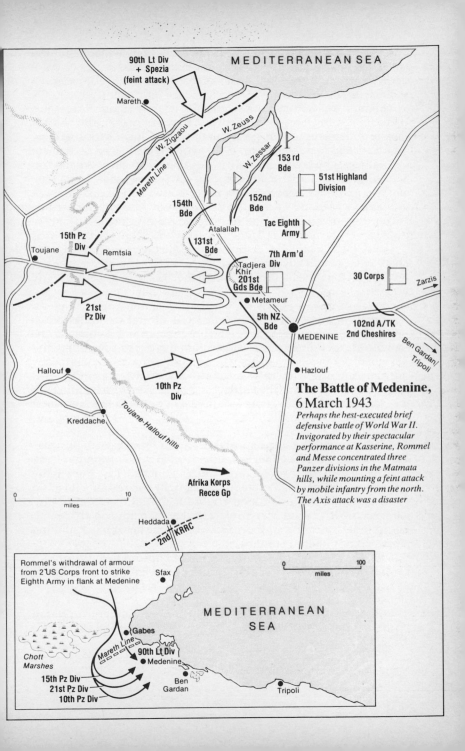

90th Lt Div
+ Spezia
(feint attack)

MEDITERRANEAN SEA

Mareth

W. Zeuss

W. Zigzaou

W. Zessar

153rd Bde

Mareth Line

152nd Bde

51st Highland Division

154th Bde

Atalallah

131st Bde

Tac Eighth Army

15th Pz Div

Remtsia

Toujane

7th Arm'd Div

Tadjera Khir 201st Gds Bde

30 Corps

Zarzis

21st Pz Div

Metameur

5th NZ Bde

MEDENINE

102nd A/TK 2nd Cheshires

Ben Gardan/ Tripoli

Halllouf

10th Pz Div

Hazlouf

The Battle of Medenine,
6 March 1943

*Perhaps the best-executed brief
defensive battle of World War II.
Invigorated by their spectacular
performance at Kasserine, Rommel
and Messe concentrated three
Panzer divisions in the Matmata
hills, while mounting a feint attack
by mobile infantry from the north.
The Axis attack was a disaster*

Kreddache

Toujane-Halllouf hills

Afrika Korps Recce Gp

0   10
miles

Heddada

2nd KRRC

Rommel's withdrawal of armour
from 2 US Corps front to strike
Eighth Army in flank at Medenine

Sfax

0   100
miles

MEDITERRANEAN
SEA

Chott
Marshes

Mareth Line

Gabes

90th Lt Div

Medenine

15th Pz Div

21st Pz Div

10th Pz Div

Ben
Gardan

Tripoli

Monty was quite mistaken – and Rommel's double-bluff therefore succeeded beyond all expectation. The battle of Medenine became a classic encounter between the victors of Kasserine and the victors of Alam Halfa and Alamein.

Medenine was Rommel's first offensive against Eighth Army since Alam Halfa – and it repeated the worst mistakes of the earlier battle. Despite uninterrupted air reconnaissance by Focke-Wolf fighters, Rommel failed to note the forces Montgomery had raced up to meet him – forces which were already in position by 3 March. As at Alam Halfa Rommel did not trust his fuel supply to dare strike deep in the enemy's rear with his whole Panzer force while leaving the high ground near Medenine occupied by the enemy – so two of the three Panzer divisions, together with infantry, were ordered first to take the 'Alam Halfa' feature of Medenine, known as Tadjera Khir. But as at Alam Halfa, it was the importance of this feature that had also struck Monty, with what de Guingand termed his *coup d'œil militaire*, from the moment he first reconnoitred the ground – as Leese clearly recalled:

> General Montgomery and I carried out several reconnaissances from the top of Tadjera Khir, which was steep and dominated the whole surrounding countryside. From it we could see the entire extent of our position and also the westerly approach routes to it by the enemy. It was too to be a wonderful Corps Artillery Observation Post on the day of the battle. . . . The Tadjera Khir feature with its magnificent observation was the pivot of the defence which it was vital to retain at all costs.[1]

Eighth Army was thus disposed in such a way that, pivoting on Tadjera Khir, a thrust either from the coastal axis *or* from the flank could be met. 'The Army Commander estimated that the enemy could attack on the 3rd March but he thought that [Rommel] would find it difficult to put in a properly co-ordinated effort before the 4th,' Leese recalled. 'On 3rd March we were barely ready; on 4th March the position was fairly well organised. To our amazement nothing happened on either of these days.'[2]

To his erstwhile Chief of Staff, Brigadier Simpson, Monty wrote on the eve of the battle – 5 March – outlining recent events and forecasting what was to come)

> On 20 Feb [sic] I received a cry for help from Alexander who was in Tunisia. The Americans were being pushed back; in his wire Alex

[1] Loc. cit. Monty's ADC, Johnny Henderson, also vividly remembered one such trip, with German shells actually falling behind them as the Tadjera Khir feature was so far forward – interview of 5.5.83.

[2] Ibid.

said the situation was very critical and that a major disaster was possible.

At that time I was pressing on slowly and making good progress, being careful not to get unbalanced.

But on receiving the cry for help I at once took out the whip; I 'drove' forward hard; I took every sort of risk; and by 25 Feb I had got right forward to within a few miles of the MARETH position proper.

I think there is no doubt that this pressure exerted by me did definitely make Rommel draw off in central Tunisia. But I was now definitely 'unbalanced', for the first time since I have been out here. My tank strength was low; and I had only two Divisions up forward [7th Armoured and 51st Highland Divisions].

The N.Z. Div were at Tripoli, 200 miles away. The whole of 10 Corps was at Benghazi, 1000 miles away. On 27 Feb it was clear to me that Rommel was pulling out in central Tunisia, and was transferring armoured Divisions down to my front.

My position was not good.

Whether it was Monty's bluff in exposing Eighth Army's weak forward forces at Medenine, or whether Rommel was – as his English biographer argued – obsessed with getting even with Montgomery, 'the only enemy general to have got the better of him',[1] is debatable. Kesselring considered that Rommel's 'heart was not in his task' of defeating Eisenhower's green forces – even when, on 22 February, he had captured over 4,000 'doughboys' and inflicted 6,000 casualties on the enemy. 'I was particularly struck by his ill-concealed impatience to get back as quickly as possible to the southern defence line,' Kesselring recalled after the war.[2]

Eighth Army's forces at Medenine were certainly vulnerable to a concentrated Panzer attack, as Leese was aware. Kesselring felt that the axis of the assault was immaterial 'if executed effectively and with the element of surprise'.[3] Quite how he imagined that Rommel could transfer three Panzer divisions from Tunisia to Tripolitania without Eighth Army becoming aware of the move is difficult to understand, save in terms of the exhilarating success at Kasserine. But the swiftness with which Eighth Army prepared for battle at Medenine, and the positions they took up, were exemplary. On 27 February, Eighth Army had barely 120 tanks of all classes at Medenine, as Monty explained on 5 March to Simpson:

---

[1] David Irving, op. cit.
[2] Kesselring, *The Memoirs of Field-Marshal Kesselring*, London 1953.
[3] Ibid.

My tank state on 17 Feb was:
        22 Armd Bde 120
        8 Armd Bde NIL
8 Armed Bde had fought itself to a standstill, having been in the van all the time from 15 Jan when my advance on Tripoli began.

Reinforcements were only due at the end of the month – and then only at Tripoli, two hundred miles away.

The tanks of 1st Armd Div (10 Corps) were due to arrive in Tripoli by road on transporters on 28 Feb and 2 March. They headed the movement of 10 Corps forward from Benghazi.

If the failure to exchange 8th Armoured Brigade's fit tanks for the worn-out Grants at Tobruk in November 1942 had cost Montgomery an unexpected chance of bottling up Rommel at Benghazi, the threat of Rommel's first riposte since Alamein now stirred Monty to decisive action. Once again 10 Corps was grounded to provide emergency transport – but this time it was racing up not only fuel, ammunition and guns but the fit tanks of 1st Armoured Division.

I immediately had all these tanks rushed forward by night with headlights from Tripoli to Ben Gardan, where 8 Armd Bde was resting, with no tanks.
All these tanks were immediately taken over by 8 Armd Bde. I had by then managed to get about 40 tanks out of shops, and also some Valentines for 23 Armd Bde.
I rushed 23 Armd Bde forward.
I then cleared the road, and moved 2 NZ Div up from Tripoli to Medenine in 36 hours, day and night, using headlights.
By morning 4 March I had with me in the Medenine area:
        7 Armd Div
       51 (Highland) Div
        2 NZ Div
        All Corps Artillery of 30 Corps.

The two tank brigades possessed three hundred tanks, plus eighty Valentines in 23rd Armoured Brigade. Further anti-tank guns, machine guns and 18-pdrs came up on 5 March.

So my position today is that I have with me up forward:
        Three veteran Divisions
        A great mass of artillery
        Nearly 400 tanks
        About 500 six-pdr A. Tk guns.
I am in fact sitting 'very pretty', and Rommel can go to hell. If he

attacks me tomorrow (as he looks like doing) he will get an extremely bloody nose; in fact it is exactly what I would like him to do.

The situation has great possibilities and I may possibly be able to write off a good bit of Rommel's army.

We shall see.

The point is, you need not worry and no one need bellyache.

Monty was in his element. It was a repetition of Alam Halfa – and just as he had then astonished his staff by planning the offensive battle of Alamein while Eighth Army prepared itself for a defensive battle at Alam Halfa, so now he gave Simpson details of his forthcoming offensive at Mareth.

I am launching Operation 'PUGILIST' on night 20/21 March.
The object is:
   a) To break through the Mareth position
   b) To capture GABES and burst through the gap
   c) To advance on SFAX and capture that place
I shall aim at presenting you with SFAX early in April.

The secret, as he had learned in the aftermath of Alamein and demonstrated in the battle for Tripoli, was not simply to follow up the enemy, but to prepare men, material and supplies so that, having once broken through the crust of opposition, Eighth Army had sufficient momentum to smash its way through to its further objectives. In a letter of 2 January 1943 Monty had explained his tactical strategy to the CIGS, Sir Alan Brooke:

My present situation is that the further I get from BENGHAZI, the more difficult my administration becomes. I have now got to the point where I cannot let the enemy go on drawing me forward slowly. My solution is to stand where I am, to spend up to 14 Jan in building up resources of petrol, supplies, ammunition, etc. and then to smash my way through to TRIPOLI *in one big bound*.

This tactical strategy, so mocked later by romantic historians enamoured of the pragmatic cut-and-thrust type of military manoeuvre, was Monty's greatest contribution to the war in North Africa. The Allies under Eisenhower had attempted to exploit the success and surprise of their 'Torch' landings by piecemeal advance into Tunisia. Within a month Anderson was confessing to Eisenhower he had reached a 'point of "diminishing power" being at the end of a long and tortuous line of supply. Axis dive bombers, strafers, tanks, and sabotage have virtually stopped the advance within 25 miles of Tunis and Bizerta. Our air forces have worked themselves into a state of exhaustion,' Lt-Commander Butcher, naval aide to the Allied C-in-C, noted in the diary he kept for Eisenhower. 'Overnight it looked to Ike like we would be stalemated and would have to begin the slow process of methodically building up, just as Generals Alexander and Montgomery did at El Alamein.'[1] But this Eisenhower could not then do – for having urged it far beyond its supply capability and within easy domination of the German air force, First Army was rocked by enemy counter-attacks before it could think of mounting a final offensive to take Tunis. By 6 December 1942 Eisenhower was openly saying 'that we may have to retreat in Tunisia' – which, in the circumstances, might have been a wiser option than the 'broad front' which Eisenhower adopted – thus dooming his Allied forces to a six-month campaign of attrition which, without the assistance of Eighth Army, it was unable to win. Far from being able 'to keep on to Tripoli after Tunis was taken' as Anderson hoped even in late December 1942,[2] First Army found itself stalled in the mountains west of Tunis under the overall command of an American general who had unfortunately never commanded troops in battle in his life. By early January Eisenhower – who was beset also by political problems with the French – was considering resignation, as Butcher noted in the C-in-C's diary:

> The succession of political difficulties, the set-back in Tunis, the bombing of Bone . . . the apparent ability of German air to hit us effectively and our air's fumbling and apparent inability to hit commensurately hard with its proportionately larger forces

had contributed to a 'foul frame of mind' in which Eisenhower would, if the French did not join in the fighting, cause him 'to ask to be relieved, which would no doubt mean reversion to the rank of Lieutenant Colonel, and retirement'.[3]

Monty, by contrast, was well served by his C-in-C, Alexander, and after his great victory at Alamein the star Allied performer. His contempt for the French troops was in marked contrast to Eisenhower. To Brooke Monty confided:

> There is great pressure to employ the French troops in the fighting here. But perhaps it is not realised that they are no good; I have had them once in battle and never want them again. I use them to guard aerodromes; they have no other value. Alex is very good about it and keeps them away from me. I am arranging for a small Flying Column to be employed, as this is a mobile unit and can be

[1] Diary of Harry C. Butcher, entry of 3.12.42, in Papers of Dwight D. Eisenhower, loc. cit.

[2] Diary of Harry C. Butcher, entry of 24.12.42, loc. cit.

[3] Diary of Harry C. Butcher, entry of 4.1.43, loc. cit.

used on a flank. The infantry brigades are of no value and merely let you down. A very essential part of my doctrine is that there shall be no failures; if I tackle a thing it must succeed; I train the troops in the technique I am going to use in the next battle, and I do not crack off until I am ready. My troops all understand this and have confidence. If I use the French they will let me down; they did so once, on 23 Oct [1942], and therefore I am not risking it again; they do not understand how to train for battle and how to employ a special technique to fit a special problem. They are in fact quite useless, except to guard aerodromes.[1]

With only a few exceptions in the case of special units, this view of French troops would not be revised by Monty. As he had noted in his diary on the eve of Alamein, it was not the quantity of troops that counted, but the quality. The self-sacrificing guts of the Australians, the Highlanders and the New Zealanders at Alamein had given a spur to Eighth Army – and though later historians might mock it for its 'onerous' progress, all contemporary evidence shows that Eisenhower's headquarters was amazed at the rapidity with which Eighth Army overcame its supply problems and the vast distances of its lines of communication. Not only did Eighth Army assume First Army's responsibility – as dictated by the Combined Chiefs of Staff directive of 14 August 1942, and still envisaged in late December 1942 – for the capture of Tripoli, but it even removed the need for Eisenhower's planned assault on Rommel's supply line at Sfax – as Butcher noted on 18 January 1943:

> The essence of the meeting was that the plan to cut Rommel's supply line, which had been 'laid on' for the II Corps under Major-General Fredendall, was called off because General Alexander's Eighth Army had made such rapid progress.[2]

On 20 January Butcher recorded: 'Rommel was being driven our way much faster than even the Combined Chiefs had expected.'[3]

By contrast Eisenhower's own forces were causing him ever greater depression. On 19 January 1943 he noted: 'The French began showing signs of complete collapse along the front as early as the 17th [Jan]. We will be pushed to make a decent front covering Tunisia';[4] and a month later, chronicling the campaign to date, he chided himself for his erstwhile faith in the French. The German attack had 'resulted in complete demonstration of the inability of

---

[1] Letter of 2.1.43, Montgomery Papers.
[2] Loc. cit.
[3] Ibid.
[4] *The Eisenhower Diaries*, ed. Robert H. Ferrell, New York 1981.

French troops to hold the mountainous Dorsale region'. He had hoped that with 'the employment of French infantry through the hilly regions, that area would be safe from assault. We made a bad error in this conclusion.'[1]

But the failure of the French was, however disappointing, nothing like as dramatic as the failure of the Americans at Kasserine. On 10 February Butcher recorded in his diary Eisenhower's appreciation that 'the Axis is massing for an attack at Pichon. I asked him if we had enough there to hold. He said we had "bits and pieces". Seems to me we have stretched out so far, and von Arnim and Rommel's forces have begun to consolidate so much that they are pressing out of the ring, or trying to, and our ring is all too thin.'[2]

In fact, as Eisenhower later acknowledged, Intelligence intercepts had pointed to an Axis offensive since late January.[3] But, as at Medenine, the timing and direction of the attack were not revealed by the code-breakers. On Thursday 11 February Eisenhower was promoted full General; but by the following Monday it looked very much as though his four stars would be removed. In his despatch to the Combined Chiefs of Staff from his advanced command post Eisenhower was quite frank about the gathering American defeat: 'our present tactical difficulties result from my attempt to do possibly too much, coupled with the deterioration of the French resistance in the central mountainous area, which began about January 17th.'[4] To Marshall he was more sanguine: 'I really believe that the fighting of today will show that our troops are giving a very fine account of themselves,' he remarked blithely. He was 'placing a lot of confidence' in Fredendall, the American 2 Corps Commander, and was 'impressed by his thorough knowledge of his battlefront and of all his troop dispositions'; moreover Eisenhower felt the senior American officers in the field 'make up a good representative class of American officers and that the difficult operations they are now conducting are in good hands.'[5]

That night, as the true dimensions of the American rout became apparent, Eisenhower was 'somewhat blue'. By 17 February, as Montgomery wound up his Tripoli study week, Butcher was noting: 'We have taken a severe licking in the battle for Sidi Bou Zid in Central Tunisia. Ike fears we may have lost as many as four to five thousand men and considerable equipment, including tanks, self-propelled artillery, numerous trucks, half-trucks and guns. It's the worst walloping we have taken in this fight, and perhaps the stiffest

[1] *The Eisenhower Diaries*, op. cit., entry of 25.2.43.
[2] Loc. cit.
[3] *The Eisenhower Diaries*, op. cit., entry of 25.2.43.
[4] Cable of 15.2.43, in *The Papers of Dwight David Eisenhower*, ed. Alfred D. Chandler, *The War Years* Vol. II, Baltimore 1970.
[5] Ibid.

set-back of our ground forces in the war.'[1] First Army acknowledged, in its Sitrep that day, that some eighty-six American medium tanks had been lost, together with 'most' of the infantry transport at Sbeitla. To Churchill Eisenhower now cabled that a June invasion of Sicily was 'off', given the current 'reverses we have suffered in the southern sector' of Tunisia, and he doubted whether 'we can count upon the final destruction of the Axis forces before the end of April'.[2]

Later that evening Alexander arrived at Algiers, to Eisenhower's immense relief. He was 'for Christ's sake to let him know what the hell was needed at the front in men, supplies or whatever, and the C-in-C would do his damnest to get it from the rear, from the UK or from the USA.'[3] Not only were the French blamed for causing the weak Allied front, but now Ultra too. 'Ike told [Alexander] General Anderson had been influenced *not* to send reserves to Fredendall because the "ultra" had disclosed that this was to be merely a diversionary move, that the real one was coming farther North. So the ultra proved to be wrong, and makes me wonder if we have been listening to something the Germans have purposely been using to build us up for a grand let-down at deception.'[4]

But the problem was not simply the French, nor Ultra, as Alexander quietly tried to make clear. Monty's somewhat insubordinate pedagogic attitude had not blinded Alexander, as it did many of his staff, to Monty's profound professionalism, and Alexander arrived in Algiers determined to take a 'Monty' approach to the situation. Though his new role as Deputy C-in-C would only be dated from 20 February, he assumed command of the entire Tunisian sector already on 18 February, the day he set out from Algiers, and as Montgomery had done at Alamein in August 1942. Most official accounts of the campaign are protective of the reputations of Eisenhower and Anderson, but to Monty Alexander confided the true situation he inherited on 18 February a fortnight later, without dissimulation, on the eve of Rommel's attack at Medenine:

My dear Monty,
    I won't bother you with my troubles here, but they are and have been immense. As you know, I found a complete state of stagnation, except that we were being attacked in the south and everything looked like sliding there.
    No policy, no plan, no Training *anywhere*. No building up for the future. So called Reinforcement camps in a disgraceful state, etc. etc. You know as well as I do how long it takes to get all this ship shape. . . . The Americans need a great deal of teaching – they are

[1] Loc. cit.
[2] Cable of 17.2.43, in *The Papers of Dwight David Eisenhower*, op. cit.
[3] Diary of Harry C. Butcher, loc. cit.
[4] Ibid.

only in the 'territorial' stage – the French are quite good, but have practically no modern arms. The British strangely enough are in very good heart, but are still learning from battle experience.[1]

American quartermasters were already counting the number of wristwatches lost at Kasserine by 20 February, and the work of creating soldiers out of the green doughboys was not to be achieved overnight: 'the poor body has a great weakness from its illness', as Alexander observed.[2] We sent out some 112 tanks,' Butcher noted sourly but honestly in his diary on 23 Feburary, 'and 112 didn't come back. That doesn't sound like the famous fighting American spirit.'[3] In fact Eisenhower – belatedly recognising the failure to send combat commanders to Montgomery's study week – was now asking for 'a number of [Eighth Army's] experienced officers who had been fighting Rommel across the desert. This was agreed.'[4]

Small wonder then that Eisenhower's forces looked with foreboding, then with astonishment as Rommel withdrew from Kasserine and prepared to spoil Eighth Army's preparations for its offensive at Mareth – for Montgomery showed not the faintest sign of trepidation. On the evening of 5 March he issued a 'Personal Message from the Army Commander, to be read out to all troops'. To Tom Reynolds Monty had written on 28 February that 'the Bosche is hemmed in all round and will do his best to lash out, and to hit each Army a hard blow in turn; he is on interior lines and can switch his forces about more easily than we can. His most formidable opponent is without doubt the Eighth Army, and it will be interesting to see if he lashes out at me – before I set about him.' To his troops Monty meanwhile set out the position in his characteristically concise, clear and vibrantly personal way. It began:

The enemy is now advancing to attack us. This is because he is caught like a rat in a trap and he is hitting out in every direction trying to stave off the day of final defeat in North Africa.

This is the very opportunity we want. Not only are we well equipped with everything we need, but in addition the soldiers of the Eighth Army have a fighting spirit and a morale which is right on the top line.

We will stand and fight the enemy in our present positions.

There must be NO WITHDRAWAL anywhere, and of course NO SURRENDER.

The enemy has never yet succeeded in any attack against a co-ordinated defensive layout, and he will not do so now.

[1] Montgomery Papers.
[2] Letter of 18.2.43, ibid.
[3] Loc. cit.
[4] Ibid.

We have plenty of tanks, and provided the defended localities hold firm then we will smash the enemy attack and cause him such casualties that it will cripple him; we will in fact give him a very 'bloody nose'.

IT WILL THEN BE OUR TURN TO ATTACK HIM. And having been crippled himself, he will be unable to stand up to our attack and we will smash right through him.

This attack of the enemy therefore really helps us, and is one more step towards the end of the war in North Africa.

I did not expect for one moment that the enemy would attack us; it seemed absurd.

But he has done it, and we must show our gratitude in no uncertain way.

Let us show him what the famous Eighth Army can do.

Good luck to each one of you, and good hunting.

B. L. Montgomery
General, GOC-in-C, Eighth Army

Rommel, too, had issued his own message. The battle for Medenine would, he declared, be of 'decisive importance for the defence of the whole Tunisian bridgehead'; in fact upon it depended the very future of an Axis presence in Africa. 'I therefore expect *the utmost commitment from every soldier participating in the attack,*' Rommel declared.[1]

The German attack itself was to overwhelm the Eighth Army defenders by 'the *speed* and fierceness' of the assault. Success must be achieved on the first day – an extended battle could not be undertaken in view of the 'general picture' in Tunisia.[2]

The forces involved in the attack – Operation 'Capri' – exceeded those of any tank assault mounted by the Germans in Africa. While 90th Light Division launched its infantry feint along the coast road, three Panzer Divisions would emerge from the hills to the south of Medenine; two would attack the British flank between Tadjera Khir and Medenine, while the third (10th Panzer) division would, with infantry of 164th Division, strike across the rear of Eighth Army's position, running a cordon up to the sea and thus cutting off the enemy forces at Medenine from reinforcement via Tripoli. German Intelligence reckoned there were '2–3 divisions' at Medenine on 4 March – '51 Highland Division, 44 Division, and elements of 7th Armoured.'[3]

Rommel was thus utterly baffled when, on the morning of 6 March 1943, his army of Panzers debouched from the mist-decked hills – and failed to achieve the merest penetration of Eighth Army's flank.

[1] HQ 90th Light Division War Diary (AL 880/2), IWM.
[2] Ibid.
[3] Ibid.

Montgomery, Leese, Wimberley (Commander of 51st Highland Division) and even Brigadier Whistler, Commander of 7th Armoured Division's motorised infantry brigade, had all expected the main German assault to come from the coastal axis – but the attack 'from a different angle' and 'much more severe' than Whistler had expected,[1] did Rommel no good, for Monty had ensured that Eighth Army could withstand an attack from *any* direction. Kesselring, Rommel, Westphal and Bayerlein would all put down the German defeat to betrayal of the Axis plans by traitor – but the simple truth was that the moment Monty learned that Rommel was breaking off his Kasserine offensive, he had pulled out every stop to ensure that Eighth Army was ready for an Axis attack, from whatever angle and in whatever strength. General Wimberley later recalled how, on 4 March, Monty visited the Highlanders' headquarters 'and asked me, in his usual phraseology, if I was "happy in my dispositions", and ready to meet a really heavy armoured attack on the Wadi Zessar. I told him I felt confident that my three Brigade "keeps" would hold out till "Kingdom Come", but that, with the very wide Front I was responsible for, I felt a heavy attack would soon get established east and across the Zessar between them, as I was too short of anti-tank guns to be able to hold all the possible tank crossing places. He did not say much, but within 24 hours of his leaving me, another whole gunner battery of anti-tank guns was unexpectedly placed under my orders, from the Corps troops. I felt grateful, and thought, again, what a wonderful little Commander I was serving under, in Monty.'[2]

'Monty a grand commander and we all trust him to win,' Brigadier Whistler had noted in his diary[3] – but even Lt-General Leese was amazed when he went over to Monty's adjacent headquarters on the morning of 6 March.

I told him that things had started well and that Rommel seemed to be attacking piece-meal and that so far we had knocked out 20 tanks, with no tank losses to ourselves. He thought for a moment and then said, 'The Marshal', as he now always called Rommel after his promotion, 'has made a balls of it. I shall write letters.' And he did so all day. I rang him up at intervals but he didn't show much concern till the evening when we discussed the day's fighting very fully.[4]

Perhaps no other image conjures so vividly Monty's professionalism and self-confidence than this recollection by Leese. The Army

[1] John Smyth, *Bolo Whistler*, London 1967.
[2] Maj-General D. N. Wimberley, 'Scottish Soldier', unpublished autobiography, communicated to author.
[3] John Smyth, op. cit.
[4] Loc. cit.

Commander had disposed his veteran army for a defensive battle, had sent out his message to the troops, and was so certain of victory that he simply remained in his caravan all day, attending to his correspondence.

Several of these letters have survived. One was to Phyllis Reynolds – enclosing two photographs of himself. 'They are both rather good I think,' he commented immodestly, and he planned to send copies to his son David too. His stepson John Carver had arrived 'out in Egypt and has communicated with me', he related; and only at the end of the letter did he mention the battle at that moment in progress:

> Rommel flung himself on me at dawn this morning; it was very foolish of him and he is being seen right off.

To Sir Alan Brooke he was equally contemptuous of Rommel's first counter-attack since August the previous year:

> Rommel attacked me at dawn this morning. It was very foolish of him. There is only one way in which he could break into my positions and that is by infantry attacks by night, supported by a great weight of artillery; and the thrusts would have to be sustained night after night. But he has no infantry with which to do this; his positional infantry are all Italians. He is trying to attack me in daylight with tanks, followed by lorried infantry. I have 600 6-pdr A/Tk guns dug in on the ground; I have 400 tanks; and I have a good infantry, holding strong pivots; and a great weight of artillery. It is an absolute gift, and the man must be absolutely mad.

In fact Eighth Army had no need of its tanks, for the infantry and gunners were now imbued with a will to win without the help of armour. Great acts of heroism were recorded – as for instance the anti-tank gunners defending the Tadjera Khir feature whom Leese visited the following day. 'The Colonel took me to see one particular gun team,' Leese later recalled. 'As we approached the position, I noticed that there were only 3 men. I then looked ahead of the position and I saw several brewed-up German tanks at the end of a wadi a few hundred yards in front. I asked what had happened, and one of the men started to tell me the story. A tank had come round the corner of the wadi bed. The gun had fired and knocked it out. Two other tanks followed it up quickly. The gun hit one and missed the other, which in its turn hit the gun. It knocked the gun over and the tripod fell on the chest of the No 1. At the same time the layer was wounded in the right eye. The No 1 shouted to the gun team to carry on firing. "Don't mind about me," he cried, "keep the gun going." The layer laid with his left eye and then knocked out two more tanks.

'It was a magnificent story, but it was, I am proud to say, just one example of the many feats of gallantry shown by our soldiers that day all over the battlefield,' Leese remarked – adding that he told the story 'to indicate the terrific morale and will to win that was so evident everywhere in the Eighth Army.'[1]

At 11 p.m. Rommel, in pitch dark and pouring rain, sent out orders for his crippled forces to start withdrawing from the battlefield. The battle of Medenine had been a fiasco, and it marked Rommel's final downfall as Temporary Army Group C-in-C North Africa. Three days later he left Sfax aerodrome for Austria, never to return. Eighth Army had destroyed over one-third of his tanks (some 52), and damaged many of the remainder; casualties had been heavy. 'I lost NO tanks and my casualties in killed and wounded were only 130,' Monty cabled Sir Alan Brooke on the night of 6 March.

'We have some prisoners from 21 Panzer Div,' Monty had mentioned in his letter to Brooke, 'and they were asked if they had been told there would be much opposition. They said they had been told it would be the same sort of party they had had up on the American front – quite an easy affair. They have had a severe disillusionment!!' In fact 'hundreds of packets of American cigarettes and chocolate which the Germans had recently taken from the Americans at Kasserine' were found in the vacated Axis positions.[2]

Within a matter of days the victors of Kasserine had been subjected to the most humiliating defeat by Eighth Army – and Hitler's policy of repeated 'spoiling-attacks', laid down on 4 March, was sundered. Eisenhower, whose defeat at Kasserine had put his position as a four-star general and Allied C-in-C in doubt, was understandably relieved. 'Will you please convey to General Montgomery and the forces under his command my sincere congratulations on their magnificent performance of March sixth,' he cabled to his Deputy, General Alexander.[3]

Montgomery had saved the Allies from further military embarrassment, as well as giving a great uplift in morale. To Eisenhower he cabled back: 'Thank you for your message which I have communicated to my troops and has been greatly appreciated by them. We all look forward to joining up with the USA forces very shortly and after that we will finish off the business very quickly between us.'[4]

But privately Monty felt now even greater contempt for the 'doughboys' – and his own vanity began to inflate alarmingly in the wake of his classic defensive victory at Medenine.

[1] Ibid.
[2] H. P. Samwell, *An Infantry Officer with the 8th Army*, Edinburgh 1945.
[3] Harold Alexander file, in Papers of Dwight D. Eisenhower, loc. cit.
[4] Montgomery file, in Papers of Dwight D. Eisenhower, loc. cit.

CHAPTER FOUR

Monty's Vanity: 'Eighth Army's Dynamo'

The battle of Medenine was probably the most immaculate brief defensive battle fought in World War II, the crowning laurel upon the head of Eighth Army – an army which, since August 1942, Bernard Montgomery had sought to mould into a professional instrument of war. But it was from the time of Medenine, too, that Monty's egoism, his doctrine of quasi-Papal infallibility, began to mushroom, and the final vestiges of modesty were cast overboard. The black tank beret, with its two badges, suited him. Fame did not.

On the eve of Medenine Monty had written to 'Simbo' Simpson:

I did not know I was becoming a celebrity, and a household word, in England. One is so busy fighting Rommel that one does not know what is going on anywhere else.

Intimations of his fame were, however, beginning to filter through. In South Africa Monty's brother Harold had auctioned an envelope signed by Monty for £25, and to Simpson Monty boasted: 'Apparently I am rather popular down there, I get an enormous fan mail, and have now had 3 proposals of marriage!!!' The film *Desert Victory* (the story of the Battle of Egypt, as filmed by Eighth Army's Film unit) had just been edited in London, as Britain's answer to Stalin's film of the battle for Stalingrad. Roosevelt considered *Desert Victory* 'about the best thing that has been done about the war on either side'[1] and arranged special showings for government employees even before it went on general release. Some days later Stalin also wrote to Churchill:

Yesterday, together with my colleagues, I have seen the film *Desert Victory*, which you have sent me. It makes a very strong impression. The film depicts magnificently how Britain is fighting, and stigmatises those scoundrels (there are such people also in our country) who are asserting that Britain is not fighting at all, but is merely an onlooker. . . . The Film *Desert Victory* will be widely

[1] W. S. Churchill, *The Hinge of Fate*, London 1951.

shown in all our armies at the front and among the widest masses of our population.[1]

Monty himself heard news of the film soon after Medenine. 'I believe the film *Desert Victory* is quite 1st Class,' he wrote to Phyllis Reynolds on 10 March – after dictating that David be forbidden to stay with Jocelyn Carver any more. 'I understand I figure in it a good deal myself!!' he swanked. By 20 March he had inflated the auction value of one of his signed messages to the troops to £50 – 'you ought to have got more than £6 odd for my Tripoli message,' he chided Mrs Reynolds; 'in South Africa it would certainly have fetched £50.' In fact he now directed her not to sell 'any more of these messages' for Red Cross funds. 'They will be very historic in years to come and they should be kept; they will increase in value.' He wondered where the Reynolds would choose to hang his portrait at Amesbury School, and plied them with more and more signed photographs of himself.

Such manifestations of vanity, or lack of modesty, were certainly worrying symptoms, as were the endlessly repeated 'orders' to Mrs Reynolds about keeping David 'away from' Jocelyn Carver. This side to Monty was reflected, too, in the increasingly damning way in which he spoke of his fellow soldiers and his Allies. At the time of his Tripoli study week he was delighted to welcome, from First Army, his young protégé from 3rd Division days, Kit Dawnay, who was Anderson's Chief Intelligence officer. Dawnay was immediately asked to dine in Monty's Tac HQ mess, where, 'knowing perfectly well with whom I was working,' as Dawnay later recalled, 'he said: "Kit – what did you say you're doing now? Who are you with?" "I'm with General Anderson, sir." "Ah, yes – good plain cook." It was deliberately intentioned,' Dawnay remembered. 'He knew perfectly well I was with General Anderson, that I'd come over for the conference and all the rest of it. He did it very publicly – it was very naughty of him!'[2]

Verdicts such as this swept the armies like wildfire: 'You see, Monty's vanity was Eighth Army's dynamo,' Sir Edgar Williams later recalled. 'And he made these abominably quotable remarks – and of course they sped round the army in five minutes.'[3]

Monty had always inclined to such off-the-cuff disparagements, but they now grew in intensity and – given his rising rank – indiscretion. 'I was horrified at the low standard of knowledge of battle fighting displayed by the Generals who came out from U.K. to my discussions at Tripoli,' he wrote to Simpson. 'From Paget downwards they knew *nothing whatever* about it; they were just full of theory and their knowledge of practical battle stuff was NIL. I wrote

[1] Ibid.
[2] Lt-Colonel C. P. Dawnay, interview of 24.8.78.
[3] Sir Edgar Williams, loc. cit.

and told Brookie this, but I do not know if he has got my letter yet.' The disaster at Kasserine had proved his point that 'unless you do something of this sort [sending out senior staff officers to "learn the stuff" in Eighth Army] you will have the most appalling disasters when the Army in England goes overseas.

Look what happened in Tunisia.
Alex tells me that the show there was just too shocking for words.
Even Paget himself, the C-in-C, was completely ignorant of practical battle knowledge.
We are an Army!!!

Sir John Dill had cautioned Monty after Dunkirk not to speak openly in criticism of his superiors – but there was no way, after the battles of Alam Halfa, El Alamein, Agheila, Tripoli and now Medenine, in which Montgomery's condemnatory tongue could be stifled: he was becoming a law unto himself. 'I think he was frightfully disappointed,' recalled Dawnay of the absence of senior fighting commanders at Monty's Tripoli study week. 'I mean he did feel he had got a message to give and he felt that everybody who hadn't got battle experience should come and listen to it. But at that time senior officers in England were loath to be taught by Monty!' To Dawnay it was simply a personality problem. 'He was rather aggressively a teacher. And a lot of people felt they knew their stuff and why should they go back to school and be taught by Monty.'[1]

What made Monty's 'showmanship' and his arrogance less tolerable was that, to a large extent, he was right, as the battle of Medenine demonstrated. Swank he might, but he did have something about which to boast. He had raised the reputation of the British Army to heights unknown so far in 'Hitler's war'; and his vanity and conceit were paralleled by a genuine concern for the lives and welfare of his men. Casualties in the 1,650-mile march from Alamein had been nominal, the sick rate reflected the highest morale on any active front since the beginning of the war, and Monty's paternalistic care was clear to all. The sophisticated might mock the schoolboy tone of Monty's messages; but his heart, they knew, was in the right place. Almost the first thing he had done on assuming command of Eighth Army was to sack the chief chaplain and appoint a new one. He even had the temerity to ask the Reverend F. W. Hughes what was the most important thing he must, as prospective senior chaplain of Eighth Army, remember.

Come in Padre. Everybody ought to know at all levels what is the thing in his job which matters most. . . . Now Padre, in your job and at your level, what is the thing that matters most?

[1] Loc. cit.

Hughes, astonished, thought for a moment, then answered: 'Spiritual power.' To which Monty responded:

Now Padre, it will be your business as the big shot, never to take your eye off that. . . . If you do take your eye off it, even for half a second, you will make your big mistake. And you will never get a chance to make another – not in this Army![1]

Such concern that the men of Eighth Army should not be let down by their religious leaders was mirrored by his concern with the medical services in Eighth Army. He might be strict to the point of tyranny about women in Eighth Army's area, as when he wrote to Eisenhower's chief of staff saying he had heard 'rumours that Allied Force H.Q. have authorised a lady newspaper correspondent to come to Tripoli and visit my Army area. Will you please note that I allow no women in my Army area,' he admonished, 'except nursing sisters.'[2] This exception was, however, typical – for the wounded and sick must have nothing but the best. As he wrote in a letter to Brooke on 2 January 1943: 'In operations it is essential to have very good medical arrangements well forward, and to have plenty of ambulance cars working well forward so that the troops see them, and to have red cross aircraft so that bad cases can be flown away to good hospitals. As long as you do this the troops do not mind the risk of being wounded, they know they will be well looked after *at once*. If you do *not* see to this, then the troops get anxious, and then morale suffers, and then other troubles creep in.

Even when still in England in Home Forces, Monty had declared at a big briefing conference:

The most important people in the Army are the Nursing Sisters and the Padres – the Sisters because they tell the men they matter to us – and the Padres because they tell the men they matter to God. And it is the men who matter.[3]

It was a sincerely-held belief, as his letter from the desert to the CIGS proved – a letter designed not only to alert Brooke to Eighth Army doctrine, but set out in the hope that 'you may think it worth passing on to Home Forces'. Similarly, the advent of the 'mine and the booby-trap' was a 'definite feature of all operations' and so Monty had set up both Corps schools and an Army instructors' school to teach men 'how to recognise the various types of enemy mines, how to handle them, how to disarm them, how to recognise

[1] John Smyth, *In This Sign We Conquer*, London 1968.
[2] Montgomery file, in Papers of Walter Bedell Smith, Eisenhower Library, loc. cit.
[3] John Smyth, op. cit.

and deal with the booby-trap, types of booby-traps used by the enemy, and so on' – for when troops 'work day after day in the middle of mines and booby-traps, they are apt to get a bit nervy unless you are careful. . . . Casualties occur even when there is no enemy about and no man knows when he may be unlucky and lose his life.' The answer was simple.

> *First* Make everyone familiar with the problem. Hence the schools.
> *Second* Sapper units, who of necessity bear the biggest burden, must not be kept too long on the job, especially if they are suffering casualties. Constant relief of Field Sqns and Fd Corps is necessary so that each can have a rest in turn.

If neglected these matters 'will definitely have repercussions on morale,' he declared. Even Winston Churchill was astonished when, upon asking Monty at Tripoli whether there was anything which as Prime Minister he could do for him, Monty instantly replied by saying that the troops, many of whom had not seen their families since 1939 or 1940, would like a faster mail service to Britain. Churchill agreed to look into this, and by 6 March 1943 Monty was writing to the Reynolds that 'the quickest way to write ordinary stuff is now by Air Letter Card. I arranged with the Prime Minister for a special Air Mail Service direct from London to Tripoli, so that the soldiers could gain some real benefit to themselves for having got so far as Tripoli. He agreed and promised he would do it; I think it is working now, and goes twice a week each way.'

Was this simply the egotistical morale-raising of a 'crooner'? One British historian lamented that Montgomery was not more like Marlborough and Wellington in abjuring any 'personal appeal to the army', and extolled Rommel as a modern equivalent of Nelson in the loyalty he inspired.[1] Yet was it not Monty's Nelsonian ego, along with his professionalism and ability to identify with the every-day life and concerns of his men, that made him unique among Allied generals of World War II? General Patton, ordered to take over the American 2 Corps that had been defeated at Kasserine, began by a calculated policy of harsh discipline ('The uniform regulations were unknown here . . . just socked two officers $25 each for not wearing tin hats as we have ordered,' he reported to Eisenhower on 13 March);[2] whereas Monty's contempt for army regulations was epitomised by his adoption first of an Australian hat, then of a tank beret with two badges, and his refusal even to wear battle dress. He cared nothing for uniform regulations, but was only concerned that the men should be keen to fight. As he put it in a letter to 'Simbo' Simpson at the War Office:

[1] Correlli Barnett, *The Desert Generals*, London 1960, rev. edn. 1983.
[2] George S. Patton file, Papers of Dwight D. Eisenhower, loc. cit.

The real trouble with the Americans is that the soldiers won't fight; they haven't got the light of battle in their eyes.

To Monty this aggressive morale could not simply be created by orders, exhortations or penalties.

The reason they won't fight is that they have no confidence in their Generals. If they had confidence that their Generals would put them into battle properly, then they would fight.
I have told Eisenhower and Alexander that the proper way to get the American Army ready for battle is to teach *the Generals*. It is no good having Battle Schools

he maintained, referring to Alexander's pet interest,[1]

for the young officers and NCOs. In the Eighth Army I concentrate on the Generals. If they know their stuff, they will teach the soldiers. To my mind they are going the wrong way about it,

Monty claimed – and his damning references to Anderson, Eisenhower, Paget, Crerar and so many of his fellow Allied commanders must, beyond the indiscreet and often offensive manner in which he made them, be seen at heart as a moving and respectable concern that Allied troops be properly led in modern battle. Again and again in his letters, diaries and published training notes he stressed that the responsibility for success in battle rested first and foremost with commanders, from generals down. 'I am really very fond of him,' he remarked of General Crerar, the Canadian Corps Commander who had attended his Tripoli study week; but added, 'I don't think he has any idea how to handle a Corps in battle.' Yet a Corps Commander who could not handle his constituent divisions not only failed the expectations of his Army Commander, he failed the troops he commanded; and this, to Monty, was the greater crime. Troops who risked their lives in battle operations had a right to good leadership, and Monty was determined that, however exalted his own command, he would be the soldier's champion. From August 1942 his letters to the CIGS, Sir Alan Brooke, bristled with views, ideas, lessons learned which might be put to use in the army at home; but his chief consideration, beyond the muzzle-velocity of Sherman tanks, composition of independent armoured brigades, infantry organisation and artillery control, was always the Eighth Army

[1] 'The C-in-C is awfully keen to start his Battle School here which is to take American as well as British troops by 15 March, so he hopes you will be able to find the three good infantry officers as Instructors for whom he has asked' – Maj-General McCreery, Alexander's Chief of Staff, to General Montgomery, 4.3.43, in Alexander Papers (WO 214/18), PRO.

soldier. In a letter of 12 March 1943, six days after Medenine, Monty set down 'one point which I suggest should receive your very earnest consideration.

There are in the Eighth Army a great many men who have been out here a very long time; there are still some who have been out here for 7 years, some for 6 years, many for 5 years, many more for 4 years. As long as there was a job to be done, and it was a matter of turning the Bosche out of Africa, the men were happy and were determined to do that job. They realised that they could not be sent home. But when that job *has been done* I think you must get these men home. If you do NOT, and they have to sit down in N. Africa, and train, and wait for the next show, they will all become fed up. These men will have won N. Africa for us; they must get home, cost what it may. When a man hasn't seen his wife and family for 6 years, he has some grounds for a grievance.

It was this kind of forethought, months before the African campaign was over, that comprised the reverse side of Monty's somewhat distastefully boastful ego. His critics would ignore it, but the men of Eighth Army responded very much as the 'British tars' to Nelson: with a professional pride that caused Churchill to remark on 22 February to the King: 'I suppose Your Majesty realises that these two Corps of the Eighth Army, comprising together about 160,000 men, are perhaps the best troops in the world;'[1] and in the House of Commons to declare: 'I have never in my life, which from youth up has been concerned with military matters, seen troops march with the style or air of the Desert Army.'[2]

Entertainment was another important factor in morale, Monty felt. Formations were encouraged, as in peacetime, to mount their own 'shows' whenever resting, and pressure was put on Cairo to send up the best possible entertainers. At one such gathering in Tripoli, General Horrocks later recalled, the troops' enthusiasm for their Army Commander outweighed even their appreciation of the concert performers, headed by Leslie Henson. 'We want Monty, we want Monty,' the men chanted at the end, turning their backs upon the stage and cheering Monty as he left his box. 'The British soldier is not as a rule very demonstrative,' Horrocks reflected, 'and his attitude to brass . . . is normally far from complimentary. So this spontaneous outburst from a British audience was all the more remarkable.'[3]

Similarly, although Monty's attitude towards the press was later

[1] W. S. Churchill, op. cit.
[2] Ibid.
[3] Brian Horrocks, *A Full Life*, London 1960.

styled 'contrived lionizing'[1] by jealous critics, there was considerably more to it than that. As will be seen, Monty was anxious that the exploits of Eighth Army be fully reported at home to the families of the men, but was himself wary of the correspondents' true loyalties[2] – whereas, in his eyes, the men who produced Eighth Army's own newspaper could do no wrong and were, as Geoffrey Keating later remembered, a 'protected species':

I found myself in effect Monty's PRO, often with him at Tac HQ but going away for battles. . . . Monty gave my activities top priority. He felt that any publicity – the media's interpretation of him – affected the morale of the troops. And he saw in me an instrument of giving effect to that, right from the beginning, from his arrival.[3]

Keating not only ran the Film and Photographic unit in the field, but was responsible for the war correspondents and Eighth Army journalists such as Warwick Charlton, who edited Eighth Army's newspaper 'Crusader'. Top priority was given to the transmission to Cairo of press despatches, as well as the transport of war films – fighter pilots even being detailed on occasion for the task. This awareness of their importance to the morale of Eighth Army caused the journalists to work as hard or harder than the soldiers, and Keating laughed at the memory of Warwick Charlton's entry into Tripoli:

We went in the Grand Hotel – I showed you the Hotel Register – and then Charlton, he wanted to get a printing press going, and his only piece of army equipment was a block of Monty. He had it ready – he had a 'Tripoli Times' out next morning, which he produced at pistol point. They had some recalcitrant fascists to print it.
  Monty thought a lot of him [Charlton]. . . . After we captured Tripoli Charlton had to stay behind publishing his 'Tripoli Times', and he and Edward Ardizzone, the artist, they both set up house, with a couple of demi-mondaines, in a place called Garran, just outside Tripoli. And this was scandalous. By this time the army had gone way ahead, and Brian Robertson had come up and become GOC Tripoli – he got the port going and one thing and another. But Brian Robertson knew all about Charlton. He was a

---

[1] Correlli Barnett, op. cit.
[2] 'I am quite sick of the Press; I have not spoken to any of them since 5 November and shall not do so again. . . . They misinterpret everything you say; in many cases they say what is quite untrue; they play for sensation' – letter to Sir Alan Brooke of 13.12.42, Montgomery Papers.
[3] Geoffrey Keating, interview of 30.11.79.

man of very puritanical stock – and he absolutely picked the 'Tripoli Times' with his fingers as though it were filth, because of the odious way in which it was produced.

Well, Robertson decided he was going to send back, to get rid of Charlton altogether. This couldn't go on, it was an offence against all morality and everything like that – and of course Charlton's material in the paper *was* sometimes very provocative. So I remember, when Eighth Army's Tac Headquarters was away up somewhere near Sousse or Sfax, Brian Robertson had come up for a conference about supplies. And Freddie de Guingand told me, 'Oh God, Geoffrey, you would have laughed!' Because Brian had his meeting with Monty and they came out of the caravan, Monty, Freddie and Brian, and they were standing there, Brian was taking his leave of him, and just as a throwaway remark he said:

'By the way, sir, I hope I have your approval. I've decided to get rid of Charlton.'

And Monty said: 'What?'

'I've decided to get rid of Charlton, the Editor of the "Tripoli Times".'

'Why do you want to do that?'

'Well, sir, he is a bad man.'

There was a silence. And Monty said: 'I don't think he's a bad man. I think he's a funny man.'

It's etched in my memory. So Brian Robertson went back totally defeated – and Warwick Charlton went on producing these newspapers in the field, with his captured printing press.[1]

The cynical might remark that such softness towards journalists was merely a feathering of Monty's own image-nest – but as Horrocks witnessed, the effect was extraordinary in terms of morale. General Oswald, in charge of Tactical Headquarters, felt the same:

It was a tremendous boost to morale. I mean the ordinary soldier. He knows his CO. He probably knows his brigade commander by sight. His divisional commander – particularly in a place like the desert – he'd only see at rare intervals. But they did know Monty, because Monty got the limelight in the press at home in England. There'd be a cutting that Mum and Dad, or even a picture . . . so that the limelight was on Monty. And if the soldiery were around being addressed by Monty, they wrote in their letters home, and their parents would probably have seen a picture of Monty talking to their son, or handing out cigarettes, that sort of thing. And the result of this was, when it was obviously clear that another battle was imminent, the sick rate dropped. The people reporting sick

[1] Ibid.

tended to say, No! we'd like to be in on this! No soldier actually wants to get himself killed, but on the other hand they didn't want to miss anything.[1]

After the 'model defensive battle' of Medenine the soldiery was certainly keyed up for the offensive battle that would take them, after 1,650 miles, into Tunisia. The sick rate dropped, and the tension rose. For the first time since Alamein there was sufficient administrative back-up to put two corps into line. 'My maintenance situation is very good,' Monty informed Simpson. 'I can maintain my whole Army of six divisions for the recapture of Tunisia without difficulty,' he declared. 'I shall go all out on "PUGILIST", and once I have opened the battle on night 20/21 March I will keep it up till he cracks. I have a feeling that this may well be the beginning of the end of the North African party,' he wrote to Brooke on 11 March.

Despite pressure from Churchill, Monty had refused to assault the Mareth line until he had built up sufficient supplies to carry Eighth Army through the Mareth line *and* the Gabes gap – the narrow marshes which Rommel considered the best defensive line between Alamein and Tunis. It was to be a repetition, therefore, of Eighth Army's capture of Tripoli: building up sufficient men and supplies to capture not just the immediate enemy defence line, but the one behind it too – 'in one bound,' Monty had explained in January to Brooke. 'I shall use the period of the March moon to smash my way forward to SFAX,' Monty now assured Simpson. To Brooke he wrote, 'Once I loose my Army on night 20/21 March I am going right through with the business, and I shall go on fighting and pushing northwards till I get right up towards SOUSSE and Tunis. I am sure it is the right thing to do. Having turned him out of the Mareth position, we must attack him and harry him relentlessly on the ground and in the air; we must not give him time to settle down anywhere, or to organize new positions. My soldiers are full of beans, and we will take a lot of stopping. I enclose a copy of a Personal Message I am sending them.'

This message made quite clear to every soldier that the battle that was about to begin was not simply to capture Mareth, but to drive through thereafter:

In the battle that is now to start, the Eighth Army
a) will destroy the enemy now facing us in the MARETH position,
b) will burst through the GABES GAP,
c) will then drive Northwards on SFAX, SOUSSE, and finally TUNIS.
We will not stop, or let up, till TUNIS has been captured, and the

[1] Loc. cit.

enemy has either given up the struggle or been pushed into the sea.

Those who later criticised Montgomery for being the master only of the 'set-piece' battle, in the mould of World War I, simply ignored this feature of Montgomery's generalship: one in which he had no peer among the Allies. After Alam Halfa he had muzzled public acclamation of the victory, lest Rommel shorten his lines of communication. Thus, having once breached the Axis line at Alamein, Eighth Army had been able to clear Egypt and Libya in one bound, despite all the failures of its armour, right up to the Agheila defences, in three weeks. At Buerat he had done the same, holding Rommel forward until Eighth Army was ready to attack – and then penetrating the much stronger Tarhuna–Homs line behind it as Eighth Army stormed forward. How well this was understood by General von Thoma, when he declared after the war: 'in modern mobile warfare the tactics are not the main thing. The decisive factor is the organization of one's resources – *to maintain the momentum*.'[1]

Montgomery's plan for Mareth, then, was to be his third great 'spring' or bound since Alamein. Eighth Army would indeed capture the Mareth position, breach the Gabes Gap, take Sfax and Sousse, and square up to the Enfidaville line in a bare three weeks of almost continuous fighting from 20 March 1943 – a magnificent achievement given that Mareth and the Gabes Gap were considered by most observers to be the best defensive lines between Alamein and Enfidaville. But like Alamein and its aftermath, this final campaign did not go quite according to plan, leading to some considerable dramas, as well as a total recasting of the 'Dunkerking' operation Monty had intended.

---

[1] B. H. Liddell Hart, *The Other Side of the Hill*, London 1948 and rev. edn. 1962.

Mareth: The Bridgehead is Lost

Was Monty too sure of himself at Mareth? There can be no doubt that the defeat of his 'break-in' attack came as a very rude shock, and in the later recollection of his Chief-of-Staff it was one of only two occasions in the entire war when Monty showed himself to be taken by surprise.

Monty had, after all, defeated Rommel in a brilliant one-day battle at Medenine, and had mocked the American performance at Kasserine. He was riding on the crest of success, and had every faith in the outcome of the Mareth offensive. On 10 March, the enemy launched a sudden attack on the section of Eighth Army's front held by General Leclerc – who had made an epic march from Chad to join Montgomery's army at Tripoli on 1 February. Leclerc 'stood firm and drove off the enemy attack, inflicting casualties to the tune of twelve armoured cars, twelve guns and forty vehicles.

'This was a fine performance and I sent my congratulations to General Le Clerc,' Monty recorded with satisfaction in his diary. It had been a salutary little action in that it showed the French *would* fight, given good leaders and a professional army alongside them.

Leclerc was magnificent,

Sir Charles Richardson later recalled.

He was very savagely attacked by the Luftwaffe. I had a wireless set on his command net throughout that battle – there was nothing I could do to help them really. He was a very phlegmatic Frenchman, reporting his casualties, saying he was sure he could maintain his position there.

I had a great admiration for Leclerc – particularly when he appeared in a pair of 'Huntsman' [famous tailor in London] breeches – he came up from Chad in a pair of Huntsman breeches!

He touched his hat to Monty, virtually swore his allegiance or some such thing, and then Freddie [de Guingand] had a few words and handed him over to me to find out what he wanted to continue the war, you see. And knowing my French was a bit rudimentary

. . . anyway I expected him to open his mouth enormously wide, and say a lot of things we hadn't got.

And he produced the tiniest piece of paper, notepaper, I've ever seen, about that size [indicating the size of a thumb] – the only bit he'd been able to keep for 2,000 miles or whatever!

He looked at this and he said, '*Deux camions.*'

I said, '*Oui, mon Général, c'est possible.*'

'*Cinq mitrailleuses*' – he looked at me as if I were going to turn it down!

And so it went on – very modest indeed and we were able to produce these items of equipment.

It was very heartening really. It was the first time on our front. He was a very English Frenchman really, Leclerc![1]

However, the euphoria induced by Medenine and Leclerc's minor engagement began to wear thin as the date of Operation 'Pugilist' drew near. On the night of 16 March Eighth Army was to close right up along the length of the Mareth defences, and 'mislead the enemy as to where the blow would fall', Monty noted in his diary.

Eighth Army, however, was equally at a loss as to where the blow was to fall – as the GSO 1 (Ops) clearly remembered almost forty years later:

It was one of the few occasions where it was not clear where he was putting his money. And Freddie [de Guingand] wasn't clear either.[2]

There were three possible axes of attack: a frontal attack on the right-hand coastal axis; an assault in the centre through the hills where Rommel's three Panzers had debouched; and a left hook involving a circuitous 250-mile journey inland and around the enemy's rear. Monty's first plan was to feint in the middle, attack on both right and left flanks, and for the first time since he arrived in the desert, to hold back a reserve corps which could reinforce whichever flank seemed most to prosper – thereafter driving straight on to Sfax or Sousse, breaching the Gabes Gap as it went.

The problem here was that General Messe, who had taken full command of the German-Italian army at Mareth after Rommel's secret departure on 9 March, could do the same as Montgomery. The French-built fortifications at Mareth were for many years considered impregnable, and with good reason, particularly after the introduction of minefields. Messe could therefore hold both the fortified

[1] General Sir Charles Richardson, interview of 27.1.83.
[2] General Sir Charles Richardson, interview of 20.11.79. Richardson had succeeded Colonel Mainwaring after the latter's capture at Mersa Matruh.

position at Mareth and the hills in the centre with infantry, while keeping his Panzer Divisions in reserve, to be engaged only when the direction of the British thrust was clear, and with all the weight of concentrated German armoured divisions – something which, given the extent of the front, Rommel had considered too risky at Alamein.

The first intimation of British failure came on the night of 16 March when Leese drove forward his 30 Corps both in the centre and the right. Leese afterwards maintained that the 'original Army plan was to tackle this position on a two Corps front with at least two more infantry divisions,' but that the break-down of the harbour at Benghazi in January, and the need to push on 'to help Gen. Eisenhower' had meant that Eighth Army could only administer a single Corps infantry attack.[1] This was certainly so, in a purist sense,[2] but the fact remains that Leese was able to employ, in addition to 51st Highland Division, two new veteran divisions that he had not had at Medenine: Tuker's 4th Indian Division and 'Crasher' Nichols' 50th Northumbrian Division. Although the New Zealanders – as at Agheila – were detailed for the left hook, Leese also had 201st Guards Brigade which had fought well at Medenine. By asking Horrocks's reserve Corps to take responsibility for all ground south of 'Horseshoe Hill' Leese was thus able to dispose some three infantry divisions, a Guards infantry brigade, full Corps artillery, and an armoured support brigade: forces similar to that of 30 Corps at Alamein.

What then went wrong? Those writers who later declared that after Alamein, Eighth Army could with impunity have rushed its fences – at Agheila, Buerat, or beyond Tripoli – might have done better to study the battle of Mareth: for it was very soon evident that even Montgomery and Leese had miscalculated. Not only was the Mareth position like a Norman castle protected by a deep moat – the Wadi Zigzaou – but the defences were manned by two refurbished German infantry divisions (90th Light and 164th Division), as well as four Italian infantry divisions, behind which were both 15th and 21st Panzer Divisions.

When Leese thus attempted to improve his positions by taking the high ground overlooking the main Mareth road on the night of 16 March with his Guards brigade, he received his first warning: the battle for Horseshoe Hill.

This Brigade struck considerably stronger opposition than had been expected,

Leese recalled with great frankness,

[1] General Sir Oliver Leese, loc. cit.
[2] Formations too were deliberately held back for 'Husky', the invasion of Sicily.

including a vast uncharted mined area. A very gallant advance was carried out, by the Grenadiers and the Coldstream, and the objectives were reached; but the battalions suffered such heavy casualties in the minefields that it was impossible to get any transport through to them and they had to be withdrawn at dawn.[1]

Not even the veteran Highland Division's commander had expected such deep and vicious minefields, though by dint of a different assault technique both Wimberley and Nichols were able to close up to the Wadi Zigzaou without heavy casualties, beginning that same night. Nevertheless Wimberley at least, who loved his Highlanders like a father, was thankful that the main offensive task had been given to 50th Division, with 4th Indian Division in reserve, ready to leapfrog through the bridgehead, once established. 'I was not sorry we were to be called upon to play a more subsidiary role,' Wimberley recorded privately after the war – for within several days even this subsidiary role was to give him 'one of the most anxious nights and days of the whole of the Eighth Army's campaigns in Africa and Sicily'.[2]

Monty had given out his plans for the battle of Mareth at a conference of commanders already on 9 March, three days after Medenine. By sending Freyberg with two hundred tanks and 27,000 men in a wide outflanking march across the desert, Monty felt assured of victory, for the Panzer divisions had lost so heavily at Medenine that it seemed impossible that they could hold off attacks on both flanks at the same time, as he noted in his diary on the eve of the attack.

The enemy would find himself attacked in very great strength on *both* his flanks simultaneously; he was not strong enough to hold off both attacks at the same time; if he concentrated against one attack, then the other would make progress.

This would indeed be the case, but it was to be small consolation to the thousands of men in Leese's Corps who lost their lives or were wounded when their coastal flank attack came to grief.

There were many reasons for Leese's failure, but like Rommel at Tobruk in 1941, the real failure was Monty's own miscalculation of the difficult task faced by Leese's men. Fame, adulation and a growing feeling of infallibility after Medenine all contributed to a dangerous over-confidence in his own tactical genius. Instead of concerning himself with the detailed plans for Leese's assault – especially after the failure of the Guards Brigade on 16 March –

[1] Loc. cit.
[2] Loc. cit.

Monty ignored his responsibility to ensure the coastal thrust was mounted 'in great strength', and seems to have concentrated instead on guiding the tactical strategy of the operation. To Alexander he outlined on 11 March his outflanking march by the New Zealanders, the feint in the centre around Haluf, and 'then on night 20/21 March', when these moves had 'drawn attention away to the S.W. and West, I shall put in a terrific blow at the north end of the MARETH position i.e. the sea end – break in to the position on a narrow front – turn left, and roll up the defences from the north. This may involve a dog-fight battle for 3 or 4 days; if it does, so much the better as we will kill the enemy *there*. . . . So there are very great possibilities. I am building up my strength, and my maintenance, to be able to continue the battle until the Bosche cracks. If he likes to have a "show down" and fight it out, I can go on as long as I like.'[1]

Thus on 19 March, when he learned from Ultra that the enemy had discovered Freyberg's desert force at Wilder's Gap, Monty scrapped his plan for the New Zealanders to lie concealed all the following day, and ordered them instead 'to move by day and night and press on relentlessly round the enemy western flank'. Although he had lost all chance of surprise in his outflanking move, he hoped by converse logic that this would now give greater surprise to his infantry attack, due to be mounted the following night, 20 March.

> The daylight move of N.Z. Corps all day on 20 March would direct all eyes to the West; meanwhile I would keep very quiet on the East, and the strong attack which was to go in by 30 Corps at 2230 hours on the enemy Eastern flank near the sea would have all the more chance of success,

he recorded in his dairy.

Once again he issued a message to the troops, a copy of which he sent on the evening of 20 March 1943 to the Reynolds: 'Tonight I launch my big attack against the Mareth position, and this message was read to all my soldiers today,' he wrote; but seven days later, when he next wrote to repeat his endless order forbidding David to go to stay with Jocelyn Carver, there was no bragging. Exhausted by the set-back to his great Mareth offensive, his conviction about the danger to David's health had grown to fever pitch, and Jocelyn was undoubtedly made the scapegoat of his failure in the field. 'She does not know how to look after a growing boy and I am not running any risks,' he declared. David was 'definitely NOT to go. Tell him this from me; it is an order and must be obeyed. . . . If Jocelyn makes a fuss you can tell her that it is no way your doing, it is entirely my doing. I should never be happy if I knew he was there, and I would

---

[1] Alexander Papers, loc. cit.

be worried about him. I do not want to have to worry, as I am far too busy fighting Rommel. Therefore he must NOT go.'

Jocelyn afterwards found it in her heart to forgive such monstrously ungrateful and ungracious dealings; she knew the pressure Monty was under, in the field; was indeed one of those 'millions of people [who] still listen to the wireless every day' – as Monty had written in his message to his troops – 'hoping for good news. We must not let them be anxious. Let us see that they get good news, and plenty of it, every day. If each one of us does his duty, and pulls his full weight, then nothing can stop the Eighth Army. And nothing will stop it. With faith in God, and in the justice of our cause, let us go forward to victory. Forward to Tunis! Drive the enemy into the sea!'

At 2230 hours that night the guns of Eighth Army opened fire in the biggest barrage since Alamein. In an ominous repetition of Alamein, however, Monty was very soon faced by failure, for the attack by 30 Corps was delivered on far too small a frontage and by a single brigade of 50th Division: 151st Brigade, commanded by Brigadier Beak, VC. Though the 'Tyne and Tees' troops fought with exemplary courage in the fiercest struggle since the previous October, the bridgehead they created was far from secure. Like the Guards Brigade at Horseshoe Hill, the Geordies got across the Wadi Zigzaou – in places some two hundred yards wide, with steep banks and a muddy bottom, all overlooked by the enemy – but found it impossible to get wheeled or even tracked vehicles across, and the divisional commander then decided not to penetrate to his second line of objectives until proper crossings were secured across the wadi.

So far Monty had no cause for alarm. Freyberg reported that he had reached a point only fifteen miles south-west of Hamma, known as the Plum. Although more extensively mined than expected, Monty gave orders at 10 a.m. that when Freyberg 'had dealt with that situation he was to push on to El Hamma and Gabes, and then be prepared to operate with armoured and mobile forces from Gabes towards Mareth so as to threaten the rear of the enemy in the Mareth position itself'. Meanwhile 30 Corps was to ensure that 'the bridgehead in the Mareth position was to be widened and extended on night 21/22 March, and that exploitation was to be conducted with great energy. Two good crossings over the Wadi Zigzaou were to be made.'[1] All Intelligence pointed to the fact that 'the enemy was going to stand and fight it out. In this case the presence of the N.Z. Corps at Gabes might well have a decisive influence on the battle,' he noted – adding that Italian prisoners who had begun to surrender in sizeable numbers 'all said they could not stand the artillery fire. The enemy cannot stand and fight if all his Italian troops surrender.'[2]

[1] Desert diary, 21.3.43, Montgomery Papers.
[2] Ibid.

However, it was now that the battle of Alamein began to assume, in retrospect, a classical quality. At Alamein Monty had insisted in driving a wedge more than three divisions wide into Rommel's defence line, backed by two armoured divisions of the *Corps de Chasse*. The sheer extent of the break-in frontage made it impossible for the Axis artillery to isolate the bridgehead by shelling the approaches; moreover with so much armour and so many guns operating in the British front line the Axis forces had been forced to fight for their lives in penny packets to prevent a breakthrough; and when the Eighth Army break-in reached stalemate on the left-hand side of the bridgehead, Monty had been able to keep the initiative by switching his thrust to the right-hand (Australian) side of the salient.

At Mareth, owing to the narrowness of the break-in front, none of

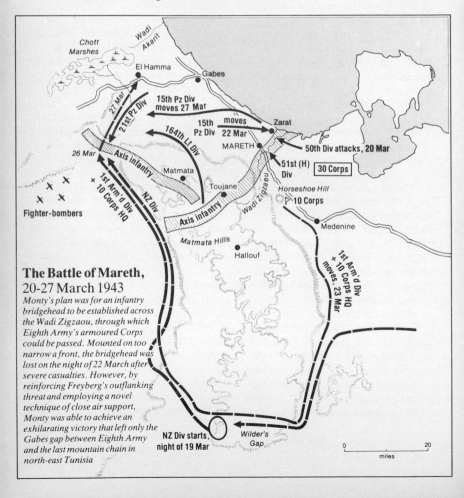

The Battle of Mareth,
20-27 March 1943
Monty's plan was for an infantry bridgehead to be established across the Wadi Zigzaou, through which Eighth Army's armoured Corps could be passed. Mounted on too narrow a front, the bridgehead was lost on the night of 22 March after severe casualties. However, by reinforcing Freyberg's outflanking threat and employing a novel technique of close air support, Monty was able to achieve an exhilarating victory that left only the Gabes gap between Eighth Army and the last mountain chain in north-east Tunisia

this was possible, and Monty's decision to keep back his heavy armour gave his wretched infantry no security in the hand-to-hand fighting in the front line. Lumsden's armoured commanders may have lacked zeal at Alamein, but by ordering them straight into the bridgehead on the first night – however impossible a task to fulfil – Monty had left no one in any doubt that he meant business, and would tolerate no 'bellyaching'. At Mareth, with the enemy shelling and machine-gunning the single crossing across the Wadi Zigzaou, and only two battalions of infantry and a handful of tanks across the obstacle, there was no comparable decisiveness of intent. Messe could not fail to be aware of the axis of Eighth Army's attack now,[1] and he wisely began to sidestep units of 90th Light Division and Panzer Grenadiers onto the bridgehead front at Zarat.

The Geordies of 151st Brigade had been given a single tank regiment of obsolete Valentines in support, most of them still armed with 2-pdr guns. Recognising his mistake, Monty now ordered the armoured brigade of 7th Armoured Division – armed with Shermans – to be passed 'through the bridgehead as soon as crossings were ready over the Wadi Zigzaou. . . . Once this Armoured Bde could be got through into enemy rear areas resistance would begin to loosen, as the only formation to oppose it was 15 Panzer Div with only 38 tanks,' he noted optimistically on the afternoon of 21 March. That evening he received Intelligence reports confirming that the enemy was splitting the Afrika Korps, for 21st Panzer Division was known to be 'moving to oppose the advance of N.Z. Corps; this Division had 74 tanks'. If Freyberg could tie down 21st Panzer Division and threaten the rear of Mareth, then Monty had only to pass out his heavy armour through Leese's bridgehead to wrap up the battle, and he hoped, annihilate the Axis infantry *in situ*, as at Alamein.

Thus when dawn broke on the second morning of the battle – 22 March 1943 – Monty was still confident of success, as his diary demonstrates:

> By dawn on 22 March the bridgehead had been widened, one crossing had been made across the Wadi Zigzaou, and one Regt of Valentine tanks had been got over.
> This was good.
> So far only one Inf Bde of 50 Div has been used.
> We had got a bridgehead which included all the main minefields, and all the prepared defended localities. If this bridgehead were now widened and extended, we would be out into better country and I would be able to bring the armour forward.

[1] German field Intelligence had in fact obtained advance information about Eighth Army plans for Mareth 'in what it considered to be its most important achievement' – F. H. Hinsley, op. cit.

This may have looked a splendid achievement on paper, making the Alamein break-in appear by contrast vastly overweight and expensive in terms of casualties; but in reality it was not as simple, and Monty was too good a soldier not to see the pitfall.

The crossings over the wadi were now the great problem

he confided in his diary.

Until they could be made good we could not get wheeled vehicles across. Counter-attack before we were ready was what we did NOT want, and I issued orders that 6-pdr guns and machine guns must be manhandled across the wadi at once.

He was too late however; as at Fuka the battle would now pass from his control into the hands of the divisional commander, and the brigadier in the front line, irrespective of any orders Monty might formulate. It was the clarity and realism of Monty's planning which had hitherto enabled Eighth Army to overcome its legacy of amateur warfare – its anachronistic cavalry tradition, its failure to see in success the need for training and for co-operation between all arms – so that Monty's mantle, as it were, helped to conceal the multitudinous errors in its polyglot, largely citizen army. But this time Monty's *own* planning had been at fault, and no amount of paper orders could rectify the mistake. Already the previous day Wimberley's Highlanders had been sucked in, not to give strength to the break-in thrust, but to help neutralise the growing threat to the Wadi Zigzaou crossing posed by the Axis positions on its flank. As Wimberley recalled of 21 March: 'I found it very difficult, all that day, to discover what was really happening. I saw the capable GSO 1 of the 50th [Division], but he seemed out of touch with his General, who was apparently permanently up in the forward area, and certainly at Divisional HQ the fog of war was thick!'[1]

General Nichols, instead of ensuring the overall success of his operation from his headquarters, was making a gallant but mis-guided attempt to hearten and 'ginger' his Geordies in the front line, across the wadi. Thus while Monty planned on 22 March to leapfrog his armour the following day under the aegis of 30 Corps, and considered that 'we would be quite all right and very well placed to get on with the battle', 50th Division was undergoing its most painful trial by battle of the war. Although 'strings of prisoners' (Monty recorded 1,700 by evening) were seen by Wimberley's men coming in across the wadi on 22 March, the situation had begun to deteriorate

[1] Loc. cit.

already at midday, Wimberley recalled.[1] The 5th Seaforth Highlanders began to report 'that troops of 50th Div were now withdrawing away to their right. All this time it was very difficult to get any sort of picture of what was really happening. . . . By the afternoon 30 Corps seemed to be getting worried, and it became a matter of orders and counter-orders because, if we did not know the real situation, presumably Corps did not either!'[2]

Small wonder then that Monty's orders for a renewed assault on the evening of 22 March, to strengthen the bridgehead and extend crossings across the wadi, were too late. Far from mounting a renewed attack, Beak's 151st Brigade was now attacked itself by a whole German Panzer Division, working hand-in-glove with infantry units of 90th Light Division, Panzer Grenadiers and the Ramcke Brigade. The German counter-attack was both brilliant and merciless: one by one they picked on the Mareth strong-points captured by the Geordies and annihilated the defenders. Casualties mounted; the wadi and trench systems became a devil's cauldron and though Monty blamed the divisional commander for tactical failure to move up machine guns and anti-tank guns for defence of the bridgehead, the true fault lay, as it would eighteen months later, in an operation improperly conceived: an operation in which the weight of assault was too weak and the single channel of reinforcement subject to interdiction by the enemy.

Thus while Monty slept in his caravan at Eighth Army's Tactical Headquarters on the night of 22 March, Eighth Army was facing its first withdrawal since the days of Auchinleck. Poor Nichols attempted to mount the attack Monty had ordered at 1 a.m. on 23 March; but already at midnight the Germans had launched their own assault. The 30 Corps artillery programme, timed to support Nichols' attack, ran into difficulties and was postponed for an hour, but 'some of the infantry did not receive this warning and started to attack without artillery support,' the officer-in-charge of Monty's Tactical Headquarters noted balefully. 'The artillery fire plan then had to be cancelled for fear of hitting our own infantry.'[3]

Leese watched with growing alarm as the battle disintegrated and his troops were slaughtered. He still had the Sherman tanks of 7th Armoured Division to throw in, but the poor going of the wadi as well as its vulnerability to enemy fire did not inspire hope. He had a fresh infantry division, Tuker's 4th Indian, in reserve, 'but the enemy were now so strong along the Wadi Zigzaou that I felt doubtful of success,' he related in his unpublished memoirs.[4]

There was no alternative therefore but to wake the Army Com-

[1] Ibid.
[2] Ibid.
[3] Maj-General M. St J. Oswald, desert diary, loc. cit.
[4] Loc. cit.

mander. There were still two battalions of Beak's brigade across the wadi, together with the original squadron of Valentine tanks, but not even Leese knew how many had survived the German counter-attack.

At 2 a.m. Leese was led into Monty's map lorry, where the Army Commander was waiting. Without dissimulating, the burly Guardsman confessed that Eighth Army had 'lost its bridgehead'. In Leese's recollection Monty was 'quite calm and sent me away to come back in a few hours' time'.[1] But de Guingand's memory was rather more searching. It was one of the only two occasions when de Guingand, who had arrived soon after Leese, saw Montgomery lose the otherwise iron composure that characterised his generalship throughout the Second World War. 'What am I to do, Freddie?' Monty is said to have asked, momentarily stunned by the news[2] – although he had sent his ADC, Johnny Henderson, to General Nichols' headquarters the previous day for a personal assessment, and was thus aware that matters were deteriorating.[3]

Once before Monty had been woken in the night – at Alamein – and had insisted that Eighth Army keep up its attack, whatever the casualties. This time, however, the position was very different. Deprived even of artillery support, men were dying in hand-to-hand fighting across the Wadi Zigzaou – fighting that was reminiscent of the First World War in its intensity. At the Somme Haig had thrown in his reserves, reinforcing failure after failure in suicidal assaults that bled his armies to the brink of collapse. Monty had himself been sucked in on 20 July 1916, and within days his brigade had suffered almost a thousand casualties.

In his diary during the first days of the battle of Mareth Monty had written: 'It was clear that the fighting was very similar to that of the ALAMEIN battle in October last; we had broken in to the enemy position, and had now to conduct a real dog-fight battle till he cracked.' To Brooke he had written only a few weeks before that he did not agree with 'withdrawals anywhere' – nor had he done so when threatened at Medenine. Yet to persist with an Alamein-type crumbling operation at Zarat 'would be very costly', as he acknowledged in his diary. De Guingand had never liked the coastal axis of attack – 'terrible country, great big wadis, frightfully difficult'[4] – and he argued strongly against continuation there. Leese too gave it as his opinion that the coastal thrust would prove prohibitively expensive if re-launched – and might still fail.

But where else could Eighth Army strike? Freyberg's column was

[1] Ibid.
[2] Interview of 22.4.78. Also referred to in letter from General Eisenhower to de Guingand, 13.1.49, Montgomery Papers.
[3] J. R. Henderson, interview of 5.5.83.
[4] General Sir Francis de Guingand, loc. cit.

some *two hundred* miles away; it had, moreover, run up against 21st Panzer Division, in a heavily mined area which greatly favoured the defence, and Freyberg was signalling that it might take a further week to bring up sufficient artillery to blast his way through to El Hamma – a week in which the enemy could easily reinforce this flank.

The picture was grim. Eighth Army's much-vaunted offensive, designed to smash a passage not only through the Mareth defences, but the Gabes Gap to Sfax, Sousse, and even Tunis, had failed. Leese was ordered for the moment to hold on to his bridgehead as best he could; de Guingand was told to return to Main Headquarters and to investigate what could be done to reinforce Freyberg's left hook; General Horrocks was asked to appear at 9 a.m., together with Leese, for a conference of the two Corps Commanders.

Quietly Monty returned to his sleeping-caravan. The night was alive with the pounding of guns, and the earth shook with the concussion of German shells. It was a night no one in Eighth Army headquarters or in 30 Corps would forget – 'a whole night being shelled like hell,' as de Guingand recalled.

'At 0200 hrs 23 March I had lost nearly all my gains on my right flank,' Monty recorded a week later in a letter to Brooke. 'This is not pleasant at any time; but it is particularly unpleasant at 0200 hrs in the early morning!!!' he remarked jovially,[1] the battle having by then been won and almost 10,000 prisoners taken. But as Monty climbed the wooden steps to his caravan door in the early hours of 23 March, the situation was far from jovial. Somehow he would have to remount his offensive: to snatch victory from the jaws of defeat. He had not brought his army almost two thousand miles across North Africa only to be drubbed at Mareth. His reputation, as well as that of Eighth Army, was at stake. Failure at Mareth might put back not only the whole Allied time-table for the reduction of the Axis stronghold in Tunisia, but the subsequent invasion of Sicily – for which Monty had been nominated British Task Force Commander.

The shadow of defeat seems to have kindled Monty's most pungent professionalism. When he reawoke at dawn on 23 March he radiated confidence, determination and clarity. The tactical indecision which had jeopardised his strategy for the battle of Mareth was over. He would close down his frontal attack entirely, and switch his main thrust to Freyberg's outflanking column.

It was as though, in the midst of defeat, Monty had had a dream of victory; and all were suddenly infected.

[1] Letter of 4.4.43, Montgomery Papers.

CHAPTER SIX

El Hamma: The 'Blitz' Attack

Well of course he *pretended* not to be rattled, naturally, because this was part of the business; but it seemed to me that when he saw that the frontal attack was foundering, he cut it off right away. And it seemed to me the best piece of generalship he'd shown for some time was when he pushed away to the left, absolutely straight away, closed that [frontal] one down and went *like that* –

Brigadier Sir Edgar Williams recalled nearly four decades afterwards, snapping his fingers.[1]

A good commander must know when to persevere – and when to pull back. Those who later accused Montgomery of inflexibility and of First World War blinkers deliberately overlooked the fundamental streak of realism that ran through his life. To Churchill Monty had promised a 'dog-fight' lasting three or four days, while Eighth Army would relentlessly assault the seaward end of the Mareth defences; but pride could not come before common sense. He had made a grave error in attempting to assault on such a narrow front over such difficult terrain – and though in a letter to Alexander on 23 March he blamed Brigadier Beak ('I think there is no doubt that Beak [151 Bde] let the party down by not having his front ready to receive a counter attack, with 6-pdr guns ready, and so on – in spite of repeated enquiries from above whether this was being done'),[2] he must have recognised, privately, his own guilt, for when Beak's brigade was withdrawn that night, he insisted that Beak should stay as his guest at Tac Headquarters.[3] 'During the night 23/24 March the 50 Div was relieved in front of ZARAT and brought into reserve. One Inf Bde, 151 Bde, had suffered severely and had lost about 600 casualties; this Bde had borne the brunt of all the fighting; it had fought splendidly,' Monty recorded in his diary.

The mood at Eighth Army Headquarters was certainly one in which strong leadership was required. 'My feeling was that it was a

---

[1] Sir Edgar Williams, interview of 20.12.79.
[2] Alexander Papers, loc. cit.
[3] General Sir Charles Richardson, loc. cit.

very, very serious setback, undoubtedly,' Sir Charles Richardson later recalled. 'We weren't used to this sort of failure – so it was a considerable shock.' Moreover 'as GSO 1 (Operations) the whole of the left flank looked rather vague to me,' Richardson confessed, 'frightfully vague.'[1] Far from threatening to come in on the rear of the Mareth defenders, Freyberg was making painfully slow progress, and was still held up before the 'Plum' gap.

At his 9 a.m. Corps Commanders' conference on 23 March, therefore, Monty was determined to be positive. Leese's 30 Corps attack was ordered to be closed down. Instead General Horrocks was immediately to take command of the left hook towards El Hamma, using his 10 Corps headquarters and 1st Armoured Division. As Horrocks later recalled, Leese was abashed but not without grace. 'As we left the conference Oliver Leese turned to me with a smile and said: "Off you go, Jorrocks, and win the battle" – a very generous gesture from a commander whose attack had failed.'[2]

Winning the battle, however, was no straightforward matter. Twenty-four hours after the conference, the tail of 1st Armoured Division was still at Medenine. When Horrocks reached Freyberg, the latter was pessimistic. A 'step by step attack' to clear a path through the Plum position would take between five and seven days, he radioed on 24 March. Alternatively the force could be split: Freyberg 'containing the enemy at Plum, while Horrocks searched for a way inland around the Djebel Tebega, to attack El Hamma from the rear. The third possibility was a 'blitz attack supported by artillery and air force. This might prove costly' was the way the Lt-Colonel in charge of Monty's Tactical Headquarters recorded the message.[3]

Monty was in the Mess. I said, 'That was General Horrocks, he wants to put a proposition to you.'

'Tell me what it is,' he replied.

So I gave him these three alternatives – including the one to split his forces – Freyberg to go on up the Hamma gap, and Horrocks to take the 1st Armoured Division round the other side. You see, Horrocks was a bit frightened of Freyberg. Freyberg was a well-known character, he was a Commander in his own right, and no man, even Monty couldn't have sacked Freyberg, he'd have had to go through the New Zealand Government to do it. And Freyberg wasn't a bit slow in throwing his weight about. If he didn't like an order from somebody or other, he'd say, 'Well, I'll just have to let my government know about that one' – which generally put the

[1] Ibid.
[2] Brian Horrocks, op. cit.
[3] Maj-General M. St J. Oswald, desert diary, loc. cit.

stopper on a Corps Commander.

Anyway Horrocks was rather taking over from Freyberg there, and it wasn't easy. So he put forward these alternatives, and Monty quite firmly said: 'Tell that boy Horrocks, tell him to get on with it, the way I told him to do it! Get on with it and stop bellyaching!' That sort of attitude.[1]

Monty's firmness and de Guingand's hurried consultations with the new Desert Air Force Commander put a new complexion on the battle. There was no time to send further artillery and ammunition along the 200-mile detour to Freyberg; instead, the Desert Air Force would become the added artillery weapon. Alexander would be asked to ensure that the Allied Air Forces in Tunisia take over responsibility for securing air superiority over the El Hamma region, while Air Vice-Marshal Broadhurst devoted his entire Desert Air Force to support of Eighth Army's attack. If 2 US Corps (under Patton) could pin down 10th Panzer Division, as Monty had begged Alexander since early March, then Monty was certain he could break through in a blitz attack towards El Hamma. For by staging such an attack immediately he hoped to take advantage of the way the German armour in Tunisia was now divided into three, as he wrote to Alexander:

I think we have got the enemy pretty well stretched between us. The whole of his armour, and mobile forces, is now between MACKNASSY and MARETH, and his armour is split in three packets, and each packet is quite weak.

There can be very few enemy tanks up in Northern Tunisia.

I think if we keep up heavy and steady pressure on all fronts from Northern to Southern Tunisia, that the enemy will not be able to stand it.

In fact the 'blitz attack' by Eighth Army could not be mounted on 25 March, as Monty had hoped, and this gave Messe time to start transferring 15th Panzer to the El Hamma position. Nevertheless the kind of attack envisaged, employing no less than sixteen Kittyhawk fighter-bomber squadrons, a Spitfire wing, two light bomber wings and a tank-buster squadron, promised to make up for the delay:

I am putting in a very heavy attack tomorrow afternoon, 26 March, with my left thrust against EL HAMMA

---

[1] Maj-General M. St J. Oswald, interview of 1.2.83.

Monty informed Alexander.

It is being supported by a great weight of air, and the attack will go in with the sun behind it in the late afternoon.

Meanwhile de Guingand was writing to his opposite number, Major-General McCreery, at Alexander's headquarters:

N.Z. Corps are going hammer and tongs, and their main problem is to get through the narrow bottleneck overlooked by the TEBEGA and MATMATA hills. We felt the best way to get them through was to stage a real blitz attack, using all possible air support, and thrust our way through. We had hoped to stage this attack today, but Generals FREYBERG and JORROCKS say the 26th is the earliest. My own view is that today might prove easier than tomorrow in view of the fact that the enemy is reinforcing with 15 Panzer Div, and also we must sooner or later expect more attention by enemy air on our front. We are now going all out to deal with the air support for tomorrow; the air are co-operating in the most whole-hearted way and are prepared to run considerable risks to give the very closest type of support. We have never tried out this blitz method before, of trying to demoralise and disorganise the enemy's defences by very strong straffing attacks. I have great hopes that success will result provided the main drive by the tanks is pressed resolutely.

As to the delay of a day, I do remember that the SUPERCHARGE operation at ALAMEIN had to be delayed a day which at the time we felt was a mistake, but events showed it was right. We have, incidentally, christened this operation SUPERCHARGE.

I hope General ALEXANDER is not too disappointed that we have not produced quick results; I never felt we could. The Army Commander is full of fight and I know he signals daily to the C. in C.[1]

Monty's signal to Alexander about the part to be played by the RAF paradoxically produced an uproar in Algiers, where Air Marshal Sir Arthur Coningham had been appointed Air-Officer-Commanding the Allied Tactical Air Forces, Coningham's childish envy of Montgomery, his prima donna ego and 1940-tactical obsession caused him to revolt at what he believed to be the 'misuse' of the air arm in Eighth Army by his successor in command of the Desert Air Force, the thirty-six-year-old ex-Battle of Britain fighter ace, Air Vice-Marshal

[1] Alexander Papers, loc. cit.

Broadhurst.[1] As Chief of Staff to Coningham since Alamein, Broadhurst had been forced to watch impotently while Coningham perpetuated a tactical policy of fighter protection for bombers that went back to the earliest days of German air superiority. Unable to accept that he had almost complete Allied air superiority after Alamein, Coningham had persisted in the belief that bombers must maintain an altitude of 15,000 feet, and fighters be used primarily to protect the bombers.

With the departure of Coningham from the Desert Air Force, Broadhurst had decided to review the entire tactical air force operational practice in line with Monty's Army study week at Tripoli in February 1943. He asked Monty to 'furnish the typical outfit of enemy vehicles – captured vehicles, tanks, lorries, wireless vehicles. We put them out in the desert and we had a great exercise,' Broadhurst later recalled. The Wing Commanders were told to attack the stationary vehicles and 'knock them out'.

> Well! They didn't hit very much. They then realised that of course they'd never practised this sort of thing. And even with the vehicles standing still it wasn't all that easy to hit them – never mind going along with flak shooting back!'[2]

The pause at Tripoli thus enabled Broadhurst's new Desert Air Force to pull up its socks, and to practise the technique of close ground-to-air co-operation. 'Thereafter there were never any complaints from the army!' Broadhurst laughed.

From Algiers, however, there was consternation, so much so that Coningham now sent his Chief of Staff, Air Commodore Beamish, to tell Broadhurst that the operation was unsound, that Broadhurst 'could lose the whole of your Air Force doing this' – and reminding him that his permanent rank was only that of Squadron Leader. 'One kick up the arse and you've had it!' Beamish warned.[3]

Though Coningham would do everything in his power to discredit Broadhurst, even suppressing the Desert Air Force despatches on the campaign, there can be no doubt that the triumphant breakthrough in the battle of Mareth was in large part due to the ex-Battle of Britain pilot, and a concept of air support which was to colour Allied Army operations for the rest of the war.

Broadhurst himself was called 'Murderer!' when he attempted

---

[1] Coningham, a New Zealander, was soon in trouble with Patton, whose 2 US Corps troops he accused of being unbattleworthy on 2 April, when Patton's head of operations complained about the 'total lack of air cover for our units'. Coningham's accusation, widely distributed (and subsequently rescinded), epitomised his prickly vanity and his reluctance to co-operate in army operations.

[2] Air Chief Marshal Sir Harry Broadhurst, interview of 21.12.79.

[3] Ibid.

personally to brief the fighter-bomber pilots for Operation 'Supercharge' on 25 March; but at 10 p.m. the following evening a proud Monty was able to signal to Alexander:

> My attack on the left flank went in at 1600 hours today with the sun behind the attacking troops. Attack preceded by heavy air bombing and supported by some twenty squadrons of Spitfires, Kitty bombers and Tank busters. Attack was a complete success and broke through enemy defences. First Armoured Division passed through and is now in good position to exploit success in moonlight tonight and at dawn tomorrow toward El-Hamma and Gabes and this thrust will be pressed all day tomorrow. Enemy certain to resist desperately and he will be fought relentlessly. Enemy about Mareth and Zarat will soon I hope be in a very awkward situation.

In fact a great desert sandstorm had blown up at midday on 26 March – 'and this had the most ghastly effect on the Desert Air Force,' the GSO 1 (Ops) recalled. 'It was a test of Harry Broadhurst's remarkable competence and courageous command that in much reduced scale he got them into the air. At midday the duststorm started. I was watching this minute-by-minute, as you can imagine, sitting in our combined RAF/Army vehicle. And then one o'clock, reports coming in from the air strips: visibility ten yards, impossibility of taking off, and so on. And then Harry Broadhurst started moving them around – from airstrips where visibility was impossible to ones where it was better – right up to the very last moment. But even so, the scale of the attack was cut considerably. I couldn't help wondering if we wouldn't have to call the whole thing off – because I knew the RAF contribution was absolutely vital, not only in terms of effect, but because of the store which Freyberg put on them. It was a marvellous feat by the Desert Air Force under terribly difficult circumstances.'[1]

At Alamein Eighth Army had carried out a brilliant night assault by infantry, following closely behind a 'creeping' artillery barrage. This time the New Zealand infantry also advanced behind a creeping artillery barrage – in broad daylight. What made the battle historic, from a military point of view, was that the creeping barrage now enabled Broadhurst's brave pilots to intensify the stunning effect of the artillery shelling by bombing and strafing everything beyond it as it moved forward, guided both by the 'moving' bomb line of the barrage as well as the RAF ground-to-air links below. Moreover, in contrast to Alamein, Horrocks was determined to push the tanks of 1st Armoured Division through the Axis gun line while it was thus

[1] General Sir Charles Richardson, loc. cit.

stunned,[1] and within several hours German and Italian Medium gunners were surrendering some 20,000 yards behind their supposed front line.

Monty's pride in Eighth Army's achievement knew no bounds. At 11.20 a.m. on 27 March he signalled again to Alexander:

> Leading troops of 1 Armd Div now within 3 miles of EL HAMMA . . . Great point is that by means of blitz attack 1 Armd Div got through and is now attacking EL HAMMA. No doubt repeat no doubt whatever that agreed policy by which your air dealt with enemy air and enemy aerodromes whilst my air attacked enemy army and directly supported my land battle has been a complete success. . . . Action of my air in support of land battle has been quite magnificent throughout. We must continue this very successful policy, and if we do, the outcome is certain.

Once again Monty was concerned with the future, and the lessons being learned from battle experience. The British Official Historians would later pretend that no 'new technique had been used. In fact the technique had long been worked out by the Desert Air Force,' but this is belied by Montgomery's version, by de Guingand's testimony, and that of General Sir Charles Richardson, who as GSO 1 (Operations) worked hand-in-glove with his Air Force opposite number.

> When Harry Broadhurst took over from Coningham in North Africa the whole scene changed. I mean 'Mary' Coningham up to that moment, he had to be handled with kid gloves. And Monty was very successful, because he said: 'We've got to get these chaps to play', and of course Freddie [de Guingand] was very tactful and so on. And so 'Mary' Coningham, who had been very bloody-minded under the previous regime [Auchinleck] was encouraged to play. But we all knew – I knew because I was in the middle of this – we had to be frightfully careful not to have one of these frightful outbursts of prima donna-ish behaviour.[2]

Broadhurst's promotion to command of the Desert Air Force was vividly recalled by his senior officer at Advanced Air HQ, Group Captain F. H. L. Searl:

> Monty's suggestion that we hang bombs onto fighters was not welcomed by the Hurricane and Spitfire wings. . . . Much of the

---

[1] 'I remember Freyberg turning to me and saying, "If we punch the hole will the tanks really go through?" (shades of Alamein!) I said: "Yes, they will, and I am going through with them myself"' – Sir Brian Horrocks, op. cit.
[2] Loc. cit.

Battle of Britain élite had been posted to the Desert Air Force and in general did not respond to Monty's ideas. Until one day 'Mary' Coningham was posted to the newly-formed 1st Tactical Air Force based in Algiers; Desert Air Force passed into the command of Group Captain Harry Broadhurst, who had been posted to it as Senior Air Staff Officer in the acting rank of Commodore. He had barely got his broad stripe sewn on before he was told to add another one in the acting rank of Air Vice-Marshal. . . . His position with the fighter boys was unique, for he had been one of them as a most active and gallant wing leader. . . . He was one of the very few senior officers who had experience in battle. He very soon altered the attitudes of those who held that a Spitfire wasn't meant to be a fighter-bomber, and sacked anyone who didn't hold with the new role.

With the army we worked out a new technique; we would put into the air perhaps three pairs of fighter-bombers. . . . If the army came up with targets, they would be briefed in the air in plain language, no codes at all, by an airman whom they knew and trusted not to fly them into a lot of flak. We first used this at the Hamma gap battle, operating from a converted Sherman. . . . It worked like a dream, and thereafter was referred to as the cab-rank system.[1]

For Kesselring, the attack by Eighth Army beginning on 20 March 'sealed the fate of the Axis forces in Tunisia . . . on 27 March the intensifying pressure of the Eighth Army against El Hanna [sic], in front of which our hastily concentrated flak [88-mm guns] had erected a pretty tough barrier, and the increasingly worrying developments north necessitated abandonment of the Mareth line.'[2]

It is important to remember these 'worrying developments further north', for the battle of Mareth was the first occasion on which the Allies in North Africa began to concert their operations, not only in the brilliant air blitz at El Hamma, but on the ground too. Though despised by most of his staff at 2 US Corps, Patton had begun to remould the victims of Kasserine into a fighting force to be reckoned with – and the effort of 2 US Corps at Gafsa and beyond was considered by Monty to be a key rivet in his masterplan for Mareth – though his faith in the Americans was still far from pronounced:

'My plan was very simple,' Monty had written in his diary on the afternoon of 20 March before the battle of Mareth began,

and I was prepared to go through with it.
    My plan was in outline:

[1] Letter to author, 16.6.81.
[2] Kesselring, op. cit.

a) A very heavy attack on my right which could be sustained and exploited indefinitely
b) A very powerful outflanking movement or 'left-hook' (round the enemy's right flank)
c) My 'vitals' in the middle, i.e. all my dumps of petrol, etc. and the vital ground, were held and covered by two armoured Divisions. These two Divisions were ready to exploit success when the enemy cracked
d) I had very powerful air support and was assured of local air superiority. . . .

If only the American 2nd Corps at GAFSA could operate energetically towards the East, then come in behind ROMMEL at GABES, the whole thing would be over.

But I was quite clear that I could expect no real help from that quarter; I had seen enough at the TRIPOLI exercise in February to realise that the Americans were complete amateurs at fighting.

I knew I would have to do the whole thing myself and I was determined to do it somehow.

If this was condescending, the fact remains that Eighth Army had fought its way almost two thousand miles across North Africa, often with a single supply road, in the time it had taken the 88,000 troops of 2 US Corps to establish its presence in the virtually undefended southern sector of the Eastern Dorsale and then be driven back to the Western Dorsale. With Eighth Army drawing upon itself all three Panzer Divisions at the battle of Medenine, and then forcing Messe to keep two of them behind the front at Mareth, Monty felt that a true fighting Corps could, by an energetic offensive, recapture Gafsa and threaten at least the supply routes to Mareth from Tunisia. Predicting the Axis strategy three days after Medenine, Monty had written to Alexander:

The enemy reactions to his defeat down here will be interesting.

He has discovered that I am pretty strong; far stronger than he thought. He must know, or can deduce, that I have offensive intentions against him. He may therefore decide to keep all three Divisions down here, or at any rate two of them.

This makes the offensive of 2 US Corps in the GAFSA area on 15 March very important. Having captured GAFSA they need do only enough to keep 10 and 21 Panzer Divs (both now weak in tanks [after Medenine]) up that way.

The first priority, Monty felt, was to secure the Gafsa–Gabes road, so that Eighth Army's break-through, after Mareth, could be sustained with sufficient fuel to take it the two hundred miles to Sousse in one bound. The second priority, 'if they can manage it, could be towards

MACKNASSY' – thus threatening the Axis road and railway supply route to Mareth. Two days later Monty repeated the suggestion in a further letter to his ex-pupil of Staff College days:

> The operation of 2 US Corps at GAFSA. GAFSA must be secured, AND HELD FIRMLY. . . . Having done this a strong thrust from GAFSA towards GABES would help me enormously [in drawing petrol stocks]. . . .
>
> If, *having made certain of the above two points*, 2 US Corps can also develop a thrust towards MACKNASSY – then that would also be of the greatest value.
>
> Above wants to be got going on 15 March, so that by 17 or 18 March the enemy is seriously worried by it.

On 14 March Alexander confirmed that 2 US Corps would operate in this way, and agreed to all Monty's stipulations about keeping the Americans off the Gabes–Sfax road once Eighth Army had breached the Mareth and Chott defences.[1]

On 17 March Monty wrote yet again: 'The situation on 21 March, and more so on 22 March,' he prophesied, 'will be very interesting.'

> I hope that the GAFSA operation, and the thrust from that place towards GABES and MACKNASSY, will by then have caused the Bosche to re-act seriously.

On the evening of 19 March, on the eve of 'Pugilist' Monty signalled:

> Everything going well here. What can we expect regarding American thrust East of GAFSA to draw off enemy mobile reserves?

To which Alexander signalled back the following morning:

> Ref your U 3226 of 19 Mar. Firmly established in GAFSA. EL GUETTAR held. Attacking SENED [north-east of El Guettar, on the route to Maknassy]. Further thrust then towards MAKNASSY.[2]

However, by the time Monty realised on 21 March that he was in for a very expensive fight for the Mareth line, he began to regret his condescending caution about the tasks Alexander should allot 2 US Corps.

[1] Letter of 14.3.43, Alexander Papers (WO 214/18), PRO.
[2] Alexander Papers, loc. cit.

Enemy obviously intends to stand and fight and I am preparing dogfight battle in Mareth area which may last several days,

he signalled that morning.

Strong Eastward thrust of USA Armd Div through Maknassy to cut Sfax–Gabes road would have very good results.

This was a much bolder role for the Americans – and in direct contrast to his almost despondent diary entry the day before about 'no real help' to be expected from 'complete amateurs' such as the Americans.

Patton had in fact ignored Alexander's orders of 19 March to stop at Maknassy and had already instructed the commander of his 1st US Armoured Division to prepare for just such an operation as, two days later, Monty suggested,[1] but it took the division until 22 March to secure Maknassy, and there it bumped up against its first German opposition since Kasserine. Although Monty begged Alexander to start co-ordinating the operations of the two armies ('Enemy is closely engaged with me in area MARETH–ZARAT and also SW of EL HAMMA. If 2 US Corps could move SE and sit tight in gap about 15 miles NW of GABES none repeat none of the enemy army facing me could get out of the net. It is worth making a great effort to achieve this desirable end. No repeat no enemy could possibly escape. What can you do about this?'),[2] it was too late.

The role you suggest for 2 US Corps is too ambitious at the moment

Alexander signalled back that night.

It is not sufficiently trained and maintenance so close to GABES would be difficult because 10 Pz Div believed now on the move might attack their rear.[3]

Alexander was right. At 6 a.m. the next day Patton's forces at Maknassy were violently assaulted by 10th Panzer Division, which advanced to within two miles of the divisional command post. The American division did well to stand its ground, and Monty, in writing to Alex during the day, now modified his request:

10 Panzer Div is going for GAFSA, and if you can keep that Division away from my area I think I can reach GABES with my left

[1] Ladislas Farago, *Patton's Ordeal and Triumph*, New York 1964.
[2] Signal of 1600 hrs, Alexander Papers, loc. cit.
[3] Signal of 2200 hrs, ibid.

thrust: *this would produce decisive results*. This is the really important thing i.e. *to keep 10 Panzer Div away from my front*.

Although Alexander later signalled that '2 Corps was very slow seizing MAKNASSY defile', he went to see Patton on 25 March and worked out a plan whereby Patton was to use the full strength of his three divisions as Monty wished, and by 27 March he hoped to 'pass 1 US Armd Div through for a strong thrust to Djebel TBEGA', in the rear of the Gabes gap, or Chott, position. 'Three divs of 2 Corps will therefore be I hope helping your operations.'[1]

This Patton failed to do, 'making only negligible progress' in the attack beginning on 28 March, as his biographer Ladislas Farago chronicled, leading to 'irritation and confusion' – a week of fighting that resulted only in 'stalemate'.[2]

Whatever the failure of the Americans, Patton's threat at Maknassy *did* bear fruit, for although Kesselring was seized by optimism at 15th Panzer's success at Mareth and the initial failure of the New Zealanders to force a passage through the Plum gap, the new Axis Army Group C-in-C, General von Arnim, panicked. Despite 10th Panzer Division's neutralisation of Patton's thrust at Maknassy, von Arnim now became as gloomy as Rommel had been. Even before Eighth Army put in its 'blitz' attack towards El Hamma, von Arnim gave orders – on 24 March – that the Mareth line was to be gradually given up. The following day both Kesselring and Messe, still flushed with success, recommended Axis counter-attacks and postponement of von Arnim's order, but von Arnim would not listen, arguing that if the Americans cut into Gabes (as Montgomery was urging), the whole of Messe's army would be lost. The withdrawal, he insisted, should begin on 25 March and take three days.

The success of Eighth Army's El Hamma operation meant that the threat to Messe's army was now from the flank, and not the rear. Eighth Army's blitz attack, by a single infantry division and an armoured division, swept away the defences of 21st Panzer Division, 164th Infantry Division, and those elements of 15th Panzer Division which tried to stem the onslaught. For a moment on the night of 26 March, it looked as though Horrocks had checkmated the enemy, but 21st Panzer Division won the race back to El Hamma in the early hours of 27 March, and Monty was too far away effectively to control the climax of the battle.[3] An anti-tank gun screen was strung across the El Hamma pass, and when Briggs's 1st Armoured Division failed to pierce it, Freyberg was too slow to follow and the chance of

[1] Signal to Montgomery, 1735 hrs, 25.3.43, Alexander Papers, loc. cit.

[2] Ladislas Farago, op. cit.

[3] 'Once the battle was launched, Monty couldn't of course exercise any detailed control in terms of tactics, it was impossible at such a distance' – General Sir Charles Richardson, loc. cit.

repeating the 'Supercharge' operation and cutting off the Italian infantry as it withdrew with 90th Light Division from Mareth was lost. Though Monty signalled to Alexander that evening that he understood Patton was attacking 'with three divisions tomorrow' and gave as his belief that 'a vigorous and determined thrust by his Corps down to Gabes would enable me to round up all this party,'[1] the threat of annihilation to Messe's army was averted. Patton made no headway, and the Horrocks-Freyberg combination found itself following up another helter-skelter Axis retreat, as Messe sought the protection of the Wadi Akarit line in the Gabes gap. Alexander signalled back to Monty on 29 March:

Well done. Your attack on afternoon 26 Mar with that magnificent air support was a decisive success,

but he was less than hopeful about Patton breaking through into the enemy rear:

The present great opportunity has been stressed but I do NOT think the armour will get through before 30 Mar at earliest.[2]

Nevertheless Eighth Army was at last in possession – on 28 March – of the Mareth defences. 'After seven days of continuous and heavy fighting have inflicted severe defeat on enemy,' Monty announced[3] – and in his diary he noted:

By dawn it was clear that the enemy had pulled out from the MARETH position. . . . By 0900 hours the whole of the famous MARETH position was in my hands and Divisions of 30 Corps were pushing ahead towards GABES.

The 'blitz' towards El Hamma had netted 2,500 prisoners; and by 28 March this had risen to 7,000.

Reflecting some days later, on 31 March 1943, Monty acknowledged in his diary that the battle had been 'the toughest I have had since ALAMEIN in October last. The position was very, very strong; when I walked over it after the battle, and examined it, one saw that to have turned the enemy out of the position in a space of one week was a truly amazing performance. The Germans had taken the original position made by the French, and had improved and strengthened it in many ways; in particular a forward or outpost line had been created which made contact with the main position in rear very difficult. I think the real reason for the victory was that we never lost

[1] Signal of 1700 hrs, Alexander Papers, loc. cit.
[2] Alexander Papers, loc. cit.
[3] Ibid.

the initiative, and we made the enemy dance to our tune the whole time.'

Monty next proceeded to spell out the reasons for the victory – in particular the 'outstanding feature' of the 'blitz' attack, with 'brilliant and brave use of air superiority'. He acknowledged that the battle had produced 'some unpleasant moments' and that the issue had 'hung in the balance for several days', but 'we never once lost the initiative, even when the situation appeared very bad, and the enemy danced to our tune the whole time. By sticking to it, we won through.'

What Monty did not do was set down the reasons for Eighth Army's initial failure. Whether his vanity, inflamed by further victory, was the reason; whether it stemmed from a desire to stress the positive factors rather than dwell on the negative; or whether his mind drew a veil across humiliation, forbidding him to examine it, one cannot say, but it was left to the commander of his Tac Headquarters, the thoughtful Lt-Colonel Oswald, to draw the lessons of the break-in battle:

'There is no doubt,' Oswald reflected in his diary,

> that a defended line such as at MARETH is a very serious obstacle when reinforced by minefields, when outposts are held in advance of the main obstacle, and when an armoured reserve is kept ready for counter-attack. It seems certain that in order to secure sufficient crossing places which are free from observed fire, that the attack must be made on a wider front than that of one brigade.[1]

But if Monty declined to examine his failure in his diary, he cannot have forgotten it. His hope of breaching the Wadi Akarit position in one continuous bound, as in the thrust to Tripoli, had been completely upset by the strange development of his own Mareth battle as well as Patton's failure to break out of the Eastern Dorsale. By 30 March 'it became clear in the morning that the enemy intended to delay us on the line of the WADI AKARIT in the GABES Gap, the narrow gap between the sea and the CHOTT lakes North of EL HAMMA'; and though both the New Zealand Division and 1st Armoured Division had butted up against the line by midday, it was soon clear that to force an immediate passage would 'involve considerable casualties' unless Leese's infantry was brought up and a set-piece battle mounted.

This time, however, the attack would not be launched on the front of a single brigade. Mareth *had* taught Monty a lesson, and he reverted to the tactical strategy which had brought victory in the battle of Alamein: the full 'punch' of three infantry divisions attacking together in a single night.

[1] Loc. cit.

CHAPTER SEVEN

Wadi Akarit – and the Flying Fortress Story

On 29 March as Eighth Army squared up to the Wadi Akarit position, General Montgomery received a visit from the Supreme Commander, General Eisenhower.

> The Eighth Army is tops. A grand bunch of soldiers imbued with the spirit to win, led by officers, young but capable, and aching to remove the last traces of the humiliating retreats of '41 and '42, and what a pasting they have been giving Schickelgruber's boys,

ran the entry in Eisenhower's ADC's diary.[1]

Although Patton's failure to break out of the Eastern Dorsale mountains had delayed the meeting between British and American forces, it could now only be a matter of days before the two Armies joined hands. It was therefore appropriate that Eisenhower – who had now delegated all field command decisions to Alexander – should pay a visit to the man who had brought Eighth Army from Alamein to Tunisia. Eisenhower recorded the visit in a hitherto unpublished letter of 5 April 1943, addressed to General Marshall, Chief of Staff of the American Army, in Washington:

> In the very early part of the week I made a trip to Montgomery's Headquarters and had a most interesting time. I was particularly fortunate in getting to traverse critical portions of the Mareth position (by jeep airplane) before the debris of battle had been cleared away. Many lessons were plain right on the ground. Montgomery is of different caliber from some of the outstanding British leaders you have met. He is unquestionably able, but very conceited. For your most secret and confidential information, I will give you my opinion which is that he is so proud of his successes to date that he will never willingly make a single move until he is absolutely certain of success – in other words, until he has concentrated enough resources so that anybody could practically guaran-

[1] Diary of Harry C. Butcher, entry by Major Lee, loc. cit.

tee the outcome. This may be somewhat unfair to him, but it is the definite impression I received.[1]

Here indeed were the seeds of future discord and misunderstanding, though Eisenhower was too shrewd to leave Marshall with the impression of sour grapes, after the American disaster at Kasserine and Patton's failure, despite overwhelming superiority, in the Eastern Dorsale at Maknassy and El Guettar:

Unquestionably he [Montgomery] is an able tactician and organ-
... iser and, provided only that Alexander will never let him forget for one second who is the boss, he should deliver in good style. The elan, esprit and efficiency of the 8th Army and Desert Air Force are obvious to anyone. They have operated a long time with almost complete supremacy in their sector and with the advantage of concentrating all their power at a particular point,[2]

he remarked a trifle enviously, thinking of the extended First Army front, but overlooking that it was his own 'broad-front' strategy in Tunisia, coupled with the pre-Alamein style of piecemeal penny-packet attack, which had doomed Eisenhower and Anderson's forces to a long and arduous winter stalemate.

Monty's arrogance must indeed have appeared overpowering to Eisenhower who, stating that he knew Monty's habit of early retirement at night, excused himself after dinner and 'hit the sack' before the Eighth Army Commander. Monty's searching questions and his evident contempt for what he knew was at fault on the First Army side of Tunisia must have been painful to the Supreme Commander – who still had no idea of the true relationship between Alexander and Montgomery. On the same day that Eisenhower was visiting Monty, Alexander was writing:

My dear Monty,
    First of all let me congratulate you on your magnificent exploits about Mareth. It is very fine indeed. The Americans, I'm sorry to say, are proving to be most disappointing. Of course they started off with a set-back about Tebessa when they lost so much armour. But since then I have taken infinite trouble with them – and mind you one has to deal very carefully with them because they are not one of us. I had to start off by gaining their trust and confidence and to a certain extent their liking for me. I think I have succeeded in doing that – I then had to put accross [sic] advice and to deal firmly on certain matters. They willingly accept my plans and my

[1] Diary of Harry C. Butcher, appendix, loc. cit.
[2] Ibid.

209

suggestions for carrying them out and all that part of the programme is O.K. But I have not been able to influence the soldiers
on the field of battle – the men who ultimately decide the issue
between victory and defeat. And I have grave doubts that those
soldiers are really doing their duty as we understand it.[1]

Alexander was saying no more than American journalists themselves were saying – as Monty was writing to Alexander, simultaneously, on 29 March:

A rather curious American Newspaper man accosted me yesterday – [Hanson] BALDWIN, of the New York Times. He suggested
that he didn't think the American soldiers had their heart in this
war, & and were not fighting properly. I told him I had not seen the
American soldiers but that I could not believe him; I then changed
the subject & got rid of him. He struck me as a dangerous chap.

Alexander's letter, meanwhile, maintained that 'Patton is alive to
this – he is a good man although not a highly trained Commander. I
went down to his front yesterday and spent a long time with him and
his Divisional Commanders – their plans are good. I showed them
your wire about the necessity for a strong thrust on Gabes *now* – they
agreed. I urged them to accept loss and risks to gain a great victory –
they agreed. I have sent them an urgent call this evening for a big and
final push, otherwise it will be too late.'[2]
But not all Alexander's and Montgomery's urging could shift
Patton's paralysed divisions – and the Americans never did break
through the Eastern Dorsale.

The trouble as I have said is with the troops on the ground who are
mentally and physically rather soft and very green. It's the old
story again – lack of proper training allied to no experience of
war – and too high a standard of living,

Alexander reflected.

It worries me a lot but I know it can be put right, unfortunately it
will take time.[3]

[1] Montgomery Papers.
[2] Ibid.
[3] Ibid. Later, of course, both Alexander and Montgomery came to see that the
American performance in Tunisia represented an astonishingly quick assimila-
tion of battle experience compared with the years it had taken Britain to learn,
from 1940 to the summer of 1942.

Had Eisenhower known what was passing between his British commanders he would have been less facile about Eighth Army 'superiority'. What he would have thought had he known the impression he himself had made on Monty can only be surmised. No sooner had Eisenhower left Eighth Army Tactical Headquarters than the French C-in-C, General Giraud, arrived. Some days later Monty wrote to Alexander:

Giraud has just left. He is a nice chap and I enjoyed his visit, but we are so busy fighting that I find these visitors a considerable trial. He brought 4 staff officers with him, and none of the party had any bedding!! I suppose they think we live in hotels. Eisenhower also brought no bedding!!

I liked Eisenhower. But I could not stand him about the place for long; his high-pitched accent, and loud talking, would drive me mad. I should say he was good probably on the political line; but he obviously knows nothing whatever about fighting.

This would be Monty's verdict on Eisenhower for the rest of the latter's life. In his diary on 30 March Monty logged simply:

General EISENHOWER stayed the night with me. He knows practically nothing about how to make war, and definitely nothing about how to fight battles. He is probably quite good at the political stuff.

To Brooke, too, Monty wrote about the visit – a correspondence which exactly mirrored that between Eisenhower and his mentor Marshall. 'The American contribution to the party up to date has been very disappointing. Eisenhower came and stayed with me on 31 March. He is a very nice chap. I should say he is probably quite good on the political side. But I can say, quite definitely, that he knows nothing whatever about how to make war or to fight battles; he should be kept right away from all that business if we want to win this war.'[1]

Both Eisenhower and Montgomery were being unfair to one another, for Eisenhower was very swiftly learning the lessons of coalition warfare that would enable him to attain remarkable harmony in the Allied military effort in the West. Though he had none of MacArthur's military genius, he possessed quite remarkable conciliatory talents, and was no fool – as his copious contemporary correspondence proves. Like Alexander he needed an astute and practical Chief of Staff in order to complement his diplomatic virtues – and this he had in Major-General Walter Bedell Smith.

[1] Letter of 4.4.43, Montgomery Papers.

Yet Monty's low opinion of Eisenhower's military ability was not simply British bigotry. Monty's sharp eye registered immediately Eisenhower's ignorance of tactics, but it was not a criticism reserved for Americans. One by one since his take-over of Eighth Army, Monty had weeded out the inefficient, the weary, and the accident-prone. Though he might ask Brigadier Beak to stay the night at his caravan after the failure of the frontal attack at Mareth, Beak was soon on his way home – as was the divisional commander, 'Crasher' Nichols. 'The Comd 50 Div did not show up very well; he had no grip on the situation,' Monty noted in his diary for 22/23 March, and on 27 March he explained to Alexander: 'Oliver [Leese] is not at all happy about Crasher Nicholls [sic] (50 Div). It was quite clear in this battle that Nicholls does not know how to handle a Division; he made a complete mess of it and it was really his fault that we lost the initial gains on the right flank. He has no brains, and is really stupid. The division does not pull together as a fighting machine. I may have to change him. I am going into the matter carefully with Oliver, & will decide definitely tomorrow. The point is, have you got in First Army a really high class Brigadier who could command a Division; he must be high class, and he must understand how to fight the Bosche; we are in the middle of a battle and have no time to teach him. I do not know what Brigadiers you have got your side. Would you let me know who you have in the market.' In his letter of 29 March Alexander offered his deputy Chief of Staff, General Steele, but Monty had by then made up his mind. As part of his policy of helping First Army by transferring experienced Eighth Army commanders and officers to Anderson's front, Monty had sent both 'Pip' Roberts, his best armoured formation Brigadier, and Brigadier Kirkman, his artillery chief. He now requested that Kirkman return and take command of 50th Division, as Kirkman later recalled:

I was summoned back to command 50 Div, much to my surprise I may say. I reported to Monty – who was terribly nice. I want to tell you about this.

He was very complimentary about our past together and he said, 'Well, now you're going to command a division you must be properly dressed. Come along now, I'll give you a proper rank.' And he went and fumbled in his drawers [in his caravan] and produced a general's badge – a hat badge, and things to clip on the shoulders. And said, 'Don't forget the sword has got to be pointing to the front, not the back' – which I didn't know. He was nice, terribly nice – couldn't have been more charming. I thought I'd mention it because it shows how kind and thoughtful he could be, couldn't have done anything more to make my arrival satisfactory. He didn't give me any instructions about why I'd been sent for or why he'd sacked my predecessor. . . . Anyway I wanted to make the point, he couldn't have been more thoughtful about me personally.[1]

This quiet attention to small, almost psychological detail in the elevation of one of his protégés to the rank of general must not be forgotten when considering the grosser acts of insubordination, conceit and bossiness which came more and more to mar Monty's own generalship. If he had no qualms about criticising the Allied Commander-in-Chief to Alexander, this was because he had no qualms about criticising anybody who, in his eyes, failed to match up to his exacting professional expectations. Eisenhower he acknowledged at least to be 'politically' talented; Anderson he considered, as he heard more and more reports of ineptitude in the command of First Army, to be not simply a plain cook but, by mid-March 1943, a bad chef. When Alexander cabled to ask if he could instal Leese as Commander of First Army and sack Anderson, Monty responded with blanket condemnation of Anderson:

Eighth Army
17.3.43

My dear Alex,
Your wire re Oliver Leese. He has been through a very thorough training here and has learned his stuff well. I think he is quite fit to take command of First Army. From all I have heard from you, and from many others it is obvious that Anderson is completely unfit to command an Army; he must be far above his ceiling and I should say that a Divisional Command is probably his level. You must have had an awful time trying to restore order out of chaos and I really am very sorry for you.

The transfer of Leese, however, would necessitate an almost musical-chairs shift in commanders. If Leese moved to First Army after Mareth, Monty proposed that Freyberg take over 30 Corps, both for the end in Tunisia and for the invasion of Sicily; but this was not all.

I consider that when we have cleaned up the war in N. Africa we ought to send an experienced Corps Commander home to UK to command a Corps in the expeditionary force being got ready there.
HORROCKS is the man.
I understand that LUMSDEN has been given command of a Corps of two armoured Divisions which is to go overseas to fight in Europe. He must NOT be allowed to command a Corps in battle on the continent; he will merely let the show down. We have made

[1] General Sir Sidney Kirkman, interview of 16.4.80.

213

many mistakes in our senior commanders; do not let us go on
doing it – especially when we have seen the red light once.
   HORROCKS should go home and take LUMSDEN'S Corps.
   Dick McCreery could succeed Horrocks in 10 Corps.

Alexander, having determined to sack Anderson, baulked however at actually doing so. Monty wrote on 29 March that he could 'let
you have Oliver for First Army' now that he had 'dealt with the
Mareth position' – but warning that Leese would not put up with
Anderson's Chief of Staff MacNab 'for a moment; but Cam Nicholson would do the job well.'
   Alexander was embarrassed:

As regards Anderson. I have told him to get rid of his B.G.S. and
take Nicholson – of course if he refuses I shall call on you for
Oliver – but now he has been given a clear directive from me how
to organize his front and what operations to carry out, he is doing
satisfactorily. I have considered the whole situation very carefully – I don't want to upset things at this stage – they are going well.
He knows the French and gets on extremely well with them. He
knows a very intricate front and all his people. All things considered I feel it best to leave alone. But if things get held up and we
have to start to rearrange the whole of our Forces, then I should
take that opportunity of making a change.[1]

Things would indeed get held up, and in due course Horrocks
would have to be sent over to save Alexander's stalled offensive. In
his letter of 29 March Alexander had enclosed 'a diagrammatic plan
for the conquest of Tunisia. . . . We now have the initiative and I
intend to keep it by punches here and there designed to improve our
positions for the final offensive marked in green.'[2]
   The trouble with Alexander's plan was that it relied on a series of
ill-coordinated attacks which so exhausted First Army that it then
had no strength to break through – 'a partridge drive' as Monty was
to call it contemptuously. The policy of bringing overwhelming
concentration to bear on one chosen position seems to have escaped
Alexander as it had escaped Anderson – and like Patton before him,
Alexander would completely fail to break through the Eastern Dorsale to sever Messe's vulnerable line of communication. Eighth
Army, still being supplied along a single road from Tripoli, was thus
left to fight its own way forward without material help from Alexander's forces on the enemy's rear flank. 'Contribution of 2 US Corps
has been very poor so far,' Monty signalled on 1 April 1943 to

[1] Letter of 29.3.43, Montgomery Papers.
[2] Ibid.

Alexander. 'If that corps could come forward even a few miles it would make my task very simple.' But Patton was stuck, and Eighth Army thus prepared itself for what was to be its last great battle in North Africa. 'My big attack to burst through the GABES gap will be night 5/6 April, working up to a crescendo at dawn on 6 April,' Monty informed Alexander two days later. Monty's original plan for the battle of Wadi Akarit had called for a two-divisional infantry assault by 30 Corps, but neither General Tuker (commanding 4th Indian Division) nor General Wimberley liked the idea when they reconnoitred the ground. With Patton stalled at Maknassy, Monty had therefore permitted Leese to use also 50th Division, lest there be any repetition of the setback at Mareth:

I am attacking with three infantry Divisions
    51 Div
    50 Div
    4 Indian Div
and will pass NZ Div and 1 Armd Div through the hole thus made.
    I will keep 7 Armd Div in reserve.

The following day – 4 April – he signalled: 'As my attack goes in at 0415 hours 6 April obviously most desirable that 2 US Corps should exert maximum pressure at same time.'

Alexander tried, and in fact Patton was ordered to take the all important Hill 369 'regardless of losses',[1] but it was to no avail. Patton's troops had taken considerable casualties – over a thousand men in each infantry division – and only when the Germans retreated after Eighth Army's tremendous victory at Wadi Akarit did Patton reach the plain.

Rommel had successfully argued with Hitler, on his recall, that the Wadi Akarit position was virtually impregnable, and only Messe's and Kesselring's faith in the Mareth line had caused Hitler to rescind his order to start the withdrawal of Messe's army to Wadi Akarit on 16 March. Indeed the Akarit position was deemed so naturally strong by the Axis forces that it was considered impossible for Eighth Army to attack except at night, and not therefore before full moon in the middle of April.

Eighth Army's assault in the first week in April, beginning in complete darkness, took both Germans and Italians by surprise. 'Large numbers of prisoners were taken with their boots off,' Leese later recalled. 'So complete was our surprise that the 21st and 10th Panzer Divisions, which were operating against the Americans in the Guettar area, were not able to return in time to intervene in the battle.'[2]

[1] Ladislas Farago, op. cit.
[2] Loc. cit.

The lesson of Mareth had truly been taken, and the assault on Wadi Akarit was a triumph for the infantry of 51st Highland Division and General Tuker's 4th Indian Division, who were fighting in their first major battle since Alamein. Some six hundred men lost their lives in as many minutes, with almost two thousand men wounded: but though the Germans counter-attacked all day the British and Indian infantry held tight to the hump- and razor-backed hills they had captured, and the great Tunisian plain as far as Enfidaville was at last penetrated. 'Bitter fighting went on all day,' Monty recorded in his diary; 'we had on this day the heaviest and most savage fighting we have had since I have commanded the Eighth Army. Certain localities and points changed hands several times. My troops fought magnificently, especially the 51 (Highland) Division and the 4 Indian Division.'

At 9.30 a.m. on 6 April the 10th and 21st Panzer Divisions confronting Patton were ordered across to the Akarit battle, and though military historians have thrashed the vexing question of whether Horrocks failed to ram his armour immediately through the two passages created by 4th Indian and 51st Highland Divisions, the real failure was an inter-army one. Patton, humiliated by the initial role of tying down enemy reserves, then humbled by his own failure to break through into the enemy's rear, had no idea what to make of the situation. Thus when von Arnim switched away the Afrika Korps divisions from Patton's front to try and contain Eighth Army's successful break-in at Wadi Akarit, Patton was in no mood or position to exploit the sudden weakening on his front. Alexander urged again and again, but despite the 88,000 troops under his command, Patton would not take the risk of further infantry casualties.[1] 'Had this Corps been able to get on, the whole of the AKARIT posn would have been taken in the rear,' Lt-Colonel Oswald noted with feeling in his diary.[2]

Nevertheless a great British victory was won that day, and by evening it was obvious to von Arnim and to Messe that only retreat could save the Axis army. By dawn on 7 April the entire Wadi Akarit position had been vacated, refuting Rommel's insistent claims since Alamein that it was the best lay-back position in North Africa. Eighth Army now swept forward to Sfax, which was captured on 10 April. Once again, as the Axis army retreated before Eighth Army, Alexander was given an opportunity to strike into the flank of its rear, this time from Fondouk. The 34th US Infantry Division however failed to take the necessary covering heights, and Alexander's orders that the armour of 9 Corps should attack without cover proved suicidal and abortive. 'Owing to the inability of 34 US Inf Div to capture the high

[1] George F. Howe, *Northwest Africa: Seizing the Initiative in the West*, Washington 1957.
[2] Loc. cit.

The Battle of Wadi Akarit, 6 April 1943

In mounting Eighth Army's offensive on 20 March Monty had intended to repeat his Tripoli manoeuvre, forcing the German-Italian Panzer Army to defend positions as far as possible from its base, and then storming the better natural defensive line of the Gabes gap at the run. However, the failure of Eighth Army's frontal assault at Mareth forced Monty to pause for a week at the Wadi Akarit until he could bring up sufficient infantry to mount a major attack. Launched before dawn on 6 April it achieved complete tactical surprise (see inset).

'Large numbers of prisoners were taken with their boots off,' General Leese, commanding 30 Corps, later recalled. The best natural defensive position in North Africa was thus surrendered by the German-Italian Panzer Army in a matter of hours. Within three days Eighth Army was in Sfax — though Patton's 2 US Corps failed to cut into the Axis retreat, to Roosevelt's chagrin

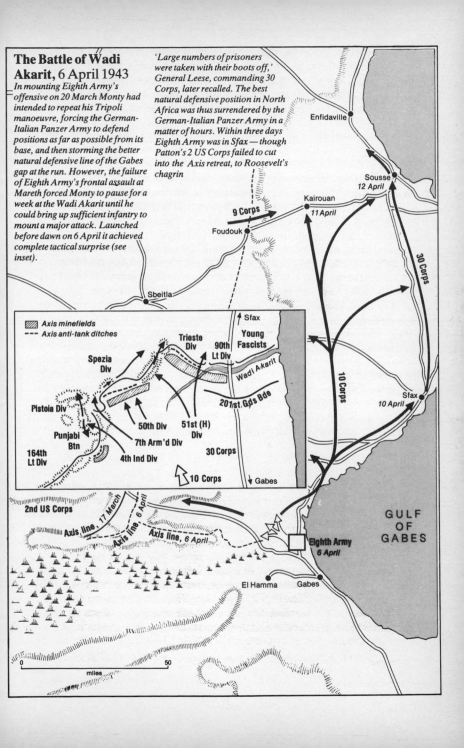

Enfidaville

Sousse
12 April

Kairouan
11 April

9 Corps

30 Corps

Foudouk

Sbeitla

Sfax

10 April

10 Corps

Inset:

▨ Axis minefields
--- Axis anti-tank ditches

↑ Sfax

Trieste Div

Young Fascists

90th Lt Div

Spezia Div

Wadi Akarit

Pistoia Div

201/st Gds Bde

Punjabi Btn

50th Div

51st (H) Div

164th Lt Div

7th Arm'd Div

4th Ind Div

30 Corps

⇧ 10 Corps

↓ Gabes

2nd US Corps

Axis line, 17 March

Axis line, 6 April

Axis line, 6 April

Eighth Army
6 April

El Hamma

Gabes

GULF OF GABES

0 ____ miles ____ 50

ground overlooking the FONDOUK Pass, British 6 Armd Div was delayed in its thrust to KAIROUAN and was finally forced to break out unaided. In the ensuing battle both 6 Armd Div and 10 Pz Div lost a considerable number of tanks, but 9 Corps attack was delayed sufficiently long to enable the enemy to reach the security of the hills about ENFIDAVILLE. If this attack had been launched earlier, and in sufficient strength, it seems improbable that any of the enemy could have escaped,' Lt-Colonel Oswald bemoaned.[1]

Paradoxically the speed, violence and determination of Eighth Army's operations since the commencement of the battle of Mareth on 20 March had taken Alexander's Anglo-American forces by surprise, so that even Alexander's personal orders on the battlefield to advance 'without regard to casualties' was counter-productive. Neither 2 US nor 9 British Corps possessed the morale or the leadership to mount the sort of operations which the veteran Eighth Army was performing, and they could only look with bemused envy and admiration as the two armies now at last made contact beneath the lowering hills of the Eastern Dorsale. Since 20 March Eighth Army had taken some 20,000 prisoners, and for the past two battles the sick rate had fallen to a phenomenally low 0.6 per thousand. 'Since the advance began Eighth Army must have been the healthiest in the history of warfare,' Lt-Colonel Oswald recorded piously;[2] but when the British and American troops saw the incredible informality of dress adopted by their Eighth Army counterparts, plus the motley collection of vehicles they had driven the two thousand miles from Alamein, they often did not know whether to laugh or gape.

Yes, I think we were rather hard on First Army,

Sir Edgar Williams reflected much later.

I'm sure we were. We'd forgotten what we'd been like when we were green troops. And by then our tails were up, you see, we were a frightfully arrogant lot really. We'd had these successes and – 'there were these silly chaps making a balls of it' sort of attitude.[3]

Even the Russian War Correspondent, Lt-Colonel Solodovnik, became infected by the atmosphere in Eighth Army, as Geoffrey Keating remembered with a chuckle. 'Here everything different!' Solodovnik remarked when posted to Eisenhower's headquarters for the end of the campaign.

[1] Ibid.
[2] Ibid.
[3] Loc. cit.

He identified himself with Monty and the Eighth Army. He was really comparing a really professional fighting machine with the amateurism of the people in Algeria–Tunisia – 'Here everything different!'[1]

This was indeed Eighth Army's heyday, with Americans even paying to buy the grains of historic Alamein sand contained (so the owners claimed) in the sandbags protecting jeeps and other Eighth Army vehicles against mines; and Monty's ego reflected the ego of a whole army.

To his army Monty had been a tonic, an elixir, a constant source of encouragement, and of professional pride. His vanity was, as Sir Edgar Williams put it, 'Eighth Army's dynamo'. Warwick Charlton felt this too:

Looking back of course it was naïve – you see Monty wasn't the only one that had this vanity: the whole army did! Every man did, every man behind a gun, everybody that was carrying a rifle or manning a tank. Everybody felt, more and more, disproportionately perhaps, this tremendous upsurge, that you were the 'chosen', you were the élite, that you were with this guy and he was with you.[2]

Thus when Eighth Army entered Sfax early on the morning of 10 April 1943 Monty had no hesitation in calling over Lt-Colonel Oswald, in charge of Tactical Headquarters:

He summoned me over, and he said, 'Now send this off:
MOST IMMEDIATE. Personal from Montgomery to Eisenhower. Have arrived Sfax 10 April. Recall our bet. Despatch Flying Fortress such and such an airfield.'
That was after breakfast. And about the middle of the morning he rang up and said, 'Any answer yet, any reply?' I said no, no, nothing. And after lunch he sent another one: MOST IMMEDIATE, Copy to . . . – and you know, demanding like a child who's been deprived of a toy or a prize. And he went on and on and on about this Flying Fortress, and I gather put Eisenhower to quite a lot of embarrassment. He got it in the end of course.[3]

Perhaps no other act would so typify Monty's monstrous insensibility to the problems of coalition warfare than this insistence on the payment of an unwritten bet, agreed to originally not by Eisenhower but by his Chief of Staff Bedell Smith, involving an aircraft which

[1] Loc. cit.
[2] Loc. cit.
[3] Maj-General M. St J. Oswald, interview of 22.4.80.

Eisenhower would have to procure from his senior Air Commander, and which, since the bet entailed the provision of a permanent American crew on the American payroll, would inevitably have to be 'explained' to the US War Department. Worse still, it was an insistence that rubbed salt in Eisenhower's undoubted wounds, for his ADC, Commander Butcher, had returned from Washington bearing the President's disappointment that Patton's Corps had failed to break out of the Eastern Dorsale or even reach a position where they could shell the Axis retreat. Soon Marshall would be complaining that American newspaper reporters were voicing open criticism of American failure in Tunisia, as Eisenhower warned Bradley:

I have just received from General Marshall a lengthy telegram that is quite disturbing. Faulty censorship at this Headquarters allowed stories to go out that attributed specifically and apparently almost exclusively to American units the blame for not securing a more decisive victory over Rommel in the south and cutting him off during his retreat. This has had a most disheartening effect at home and apparently morale is suffering badly.[1]

He also pointed out that US formations had to be prepared to accept casualties: 'A General Officer reported to me this morning that a battalion of infantry, working under him, requested permission to withdraw and reorganize because it had a total of *ten killed* during an attack. We have reached the point where troops *must* secure objectives assigned by Commanders.'[2]

It was in this atmosphere that Monty's telegrams began to arrive at Allied Force Headquarters in Algiers. But if Monty's signal caused consternation, there was little Eisenhower could do without appearing churlish to the man who had, in effect, saved his skin. General Marshall had told Eisenhower's ADC when in Washington that 'Ike's rise or fall depended on the outcome of the Tunisian battle'[3] – and without Eighth Army's magnificent march across Africa from Alamein, Eisenhower might have been relieved of his command. 'Monty' was already a household name in America, and the exploits of his Eighth Army had not only distracted American attention from the feeble performance of Eisenhower's forces over the past half year, but preserved American faith in Roosevelt's strategy – that of giving priority to the war against Germany rather than the Pacific. As Eisenhower warned Alexander: 'Ike explained to Alexander the home front in America. Ike emphasised the danger to Britain and America if Americans were given to feel that they had not taken an effective part in the Tunisian campaign. . . . If the Americans feel we

[1] Diary of Harry C. Butcher, letter appended of 16.4.43, loc. cit.
[2] Ibid.
[3] Diary of Harry C. Butcher, entry of 8.4.43, loc. cit.

have not played a substantial part they will be even more intent upon prosecution of the war against the Japs.'[1]

Eisenhower thus acceded to Monty's demand, and on 11 April Monty noted in his diary:

I received a message from general SPAATZ, Comd of the N.W. African Air Force under General EISENHOWER, saying that a B.17 (Fortress) with crew would be sent to me and asking where it was to be delivered. I replied it should be sent to GABES. It will be a great thing to have my own aeroplane!

Whether or not Monty was right to insist on such an embarrassing demand, the question remains. Why did he want a Flying Fortress?

'I mean, this is evidence of Monty's forward planning,' recalled Geoffrey Keating, who remembered the occasion when the bet was struck.

Montgomery was saying – we were discussing how the various armies were going to meet up and where – and Monty was saying 'Well I think I will have the Eighth Army by the' – there was a date given [15 April] – so preposterous that Beedle Smith said, 'Oh, General, come come' – and Monty lured him into making that bet about the Flying Fortress.

I mean this is absolute evidence of Monty's forward planning, because he wanted to go to England as the victor, he wanted to go to England in a safe way and the only safe way he could go was in a Flying Fortress.

That was the bet – made in precise terms.[2]

Did Monty want the aeroplane, then, so that he could return to England 'as the victor'? 'They have played up well, and I have my Fortress – my own personal property!! I shall come home in it!' Monty boasted to Brooke in a letter the next day, 12 April – explaining:

The Chief of Staff (Bedell Smith) came to my Tripoli exercise and we were talking about the war. I said Eighth Army would come along and finish it for them, and asked what he would give me if I got to SFAX early in April. He said they would give me anything I liked. It was then the end [sic] of February. So I said I would like a Flying Fortress, complete with American crew to remain on their pay roll; the whole to be my personal property till the war ended. He agreed and said I should have it. I captured SFAX on 10 April. I at once sent a wire to Eisenhower and said, 'Have captured SFAX. Send Fortress.'[3]

[1] Diary of Harry C. Butcher, entry of 17.4.43, loc. cit.
[2] Loc. cit.
[3] Montgomery Papers.

Brooke was not amused, especially when he discovered how much ill-feeling had been caused at Algiers by the matter. Some months later, having been chided by Brooke for having disturbed Allied relations by the incident, Monty set out what he later annotated as 'the true story of the Flying Fortress which I got from Eisenhower. Alanbrooke says in his diary that Eisenhower was very upset about it when I demanded the B 17 in return for handing him SFAX by 10 April 1943 – five days earlier than he expected. He never displayed any anger to him. He paid up willingly.'[1] The original document, signed 'B. L. Montgomery, General, Eighth Army', must have been written before the aeroplane crashed in July 1943. It runs as follows:

The Fortress aircraft was given to me by General Eisenhower in April 1943, after I had captured SFAX. He came to visit me at my Army H.Q. shortly after the battle of MARETH; it was the 2nd April and I was busy preparing to attack the AKARIT position, and then to burst through the GABES Gap and out into the plain of central Tunisia.

I told General Eisenhower that when I had captured SFAX there would be need for considerable co-ordination between the action of the Allied armies in Tunisia, and this might mean a good deal of travelling about for me. I asked him if he would give me a Fortress (B 17); the splendid armament of these aircraft makes an escort quite unnecessary, and I would be able to travel at will and to deal easily with any enemy opposition. I said I would make him a present of SFAX by the middle of April, and if he would then give me a Fortress it would be magnificent. He agreed. I captured SFAX on 10 April and the Fortress was sent over to me a few days later.

I have travelled many miles in it and it has saved me much fatigue. I have no hesitation in saying that having my own Fortress aircraft, so that I can travel about at will, has definitely contributed to the successful operations of the Eighth Army. I cannot express adequately my gratitude to General Eisenhower for giving it to me; he is a splendid man to serve under, and it is a pleasure and an honour to be under his command.[2]

In his attempted character-assassination *The Montgomery Legend*, R. W. Thompson claimed that 'the incident was not mentioned to Eisenhower, nor was it referred to by Montgomery at Gabes. . . . According to Eisenhower and his Chief of Staff, Montgomery had signalled his demand to Bedell Smith, and not to Eisenhower.'[3] This is in direct contradiction to Monty's contemporary document;

[1] Montgomery Papers.

[2] This account was later corroborated by Monty's ADC who was present – J. R. Henderson, interview of 5.5.83.

[3] R. W. Thompson, *The Montgomery Legend*, London 1967.

moreover it does not tally with the documents Eisenhower kept, for Eisenhower most certainly received the signal about the Flying Fortress direct from Montgomery on 10 April 1943, addressed to him personally, and kept it in his C-in-C's file marked 'Montgomery', initialled DE in the right-hand corner:

INCOMING MESSAGE Ref U 3567 10 Apr 43
TO: Eisenhower, Personal
FROM: Montgomery

Captured SFAX early this morning. Please send Fortress to report for duty to Western Desert Air Force and the Captain to report personally to me.[1]

The following day, as Monty recorded in his diary, the message arrived from General Spaatz, requesting delivery destination.

Certainly neither Eisenhower's nor Bedell Smith's papers reveal any umbrage taken. On 12 April Monty sent a message announcing the capture of Sousse, and Eisenhower immediately signalled back his 'sincere congratulations'[2] – Bedell Smith adding, humorously: 'However your Fortress will operate much better from landing fields at Tunis' – which was still four weeks of hard fighting away.

Monty was cock-a-hoop about the aeroplane, as his letter of 12 April to Brooke demonstrates, and had no notion that he had caused any ill-will. Moreover, the reason he gave for choosing such a prize was also founded in fact. No sooner had he received the machine than he signalled to Eisenhower:

Thank you for Fortress. Can I elect to come to Algiers Monday 19th April and pay my respects? Will arrive about 1100 hrs. and will have to leave about 1430 hrs to return here.[3]

Given Monty's later propensity for isolating himself in a forward headquarters near the front, Eisenhower must have been grateful, in retrospect, that the Fortress made Monty so willing to travel, and to hammer out the vital questions of 'Husky', the forthcoming invasion of Sicily. After all, Patton was relieved of command of 2 US Corps on 16 April – the day when Monty's Fortress was delivered – in order that Patton might concentrate *solely* on the planning for Husky, whereas Monty, as the other Task Force Commander for Sicily, was nevertheless expected to go on leading Eighth Army into battle until the end of the campaign in Tunisia, while simultaneously preparing for the invasion of Sicily. The Flying Fortress permitted him to do

---

[1] Papers of Dwight D. Eisenhower, loc. cit.
[2] Ibid.
[3] Ibid.

both, whatever personal embarrassment it may have caused. Moreover Eisenhower, who had deliberately delegated field command in Tunisia, as well as all planning responsibility for 'Husky', to Alexander and the Task Force Commanders, had a Flying Fortress not only at his constant personal disposal, but also for the use of his staff.[1]

What rankled in Eisenhower's mind was not so much Monty's insistence on an aeroplane, but his insistence upon a proper plan for the invasion of Sicily. An aeroplane could be found without difficulty; an acceptable plan could not.

[1] Cf. diary of Harry C. Butcher, loc. cit.

CHAPTER EIGHT

Tunis: Masterminding the Final Offensive

Even before Eighth Army captured Sfax and Sousse, Monty had become anxious about current Allied planning for Sicily – Operation 'Husky'. Here was an operation determined upon by Roosevelt, Churchill and their military Chiefs of Staff against the advice of the Anglo-American Planning Committee – which preferred Sardinia to Sicily[1] – at Casablanca in January 1943; since when the operation had been planned by further committees of staff officers who for the most part had no experience of field command or the realities of battle fighting against Axis troops.

Monty's first reference to the 'Husky' operation had been in his letter to Sir Alan Brooke on 16 February 1943, in which he had expressed his delight when informed by Alexander that he was to command the British Task Force, and his intention of preserving the title 'Eighth Army' in order to cast the Eighth Army mantle and morale over Dempsey's Corps at once.

'This morale factor is terribly important,' he had continued.

I have built up a really good fighting team here in my H.Q. and indeed all through the Army. We must use all that experience, and battle experience, and *this* will ensure success.

It will take the rest of this year to finish the show in N. Africa, and to give Italy a proper bang,

he had predicted with uncanny accuracy.

A month later, he had written (on 17 March 1943):

I am NOT happy about the present plan for HUSKY. In my opinion it breaks every common sense rule of practical battle fighting, and the present plan would have no hope of success. I have given my views to Alex as to how it ought to be recast. I have not heard from him so do not know if he agrees. I am very sorry for Alex, for there is no doubt he found a real 'dog's breakfast' over the First Army and has had a dreadful time. The real trouble is that neither Alex nor myself have time to bother about HUSKY at the moment.

[1] Michael Howard, *Grand Strategy* Vol. IV, London 1972.

In his letter giving his 'views' to Alexander Monty had stressed that he must use at least some 'experienced fighting Divisions; if we do it at all, let us make a certainty of it'. His proposal was to have two Corps headquarters, with Leese commanding 51st Highland Division and the New Zealand Division, while Dempsey took command of 5th and 56th Divisions. 'A Corps Commander who had not fought in battle in this war would be quite useless to me,' he remarked, suggesting that Freyberg take 30 Corps if Leese replaced Anderson at First Army.

Monty's view was that the plan for the invasion of Sicily resembled a flock of birds alighting on the island, nowhere in strength, and – given the speed with which the Axis forces (currently estimated to total some 208,000 troops[1]) could be reinforced across the narrow Straights of Reggio – doomed to failure. It was the widely-separated Torch landings in North-west Africa all over again. By 25 March Alexander had agreed that the invasion plan must be recast, and had persuaded Eisenhower of the same. To his credit Eisenhower immediately accepted the need for concentration, though his subsequent statements would reveal that, like Alexander, he tended to bend whichever way the wind was blowing strongest.

Thus Eisenhower's 'revised' plan for Operation 'Husky', incorporating the Monty-Alex recipe, which was to postpone the Western Task Force landings and concentrate on a really powerful landing in the south-east of the island, was submitted by Eisenhower to the Joint Chiefs of Staff already on 20 March, and rejected a week later at their meeting of 26 March.

Eisenhower, embarrassed, excused himself on 29 March to General Marshall, saying:

I reported to the Combined Chiefs of Staff the changes I had to make in the plan in order to satisfy Alexander and Montgomery that they had a chance of taking the south east sector, which is of course vital to us. I didn't like it, but it seemed to me there was no other recourse.[2]

Yet a month later he was writing the opposite. 'As a result [of Montgomery's insistence on priority being given to the invasion of south-eastern Sicily] all commanders concerned desire to throw our whole weight to the east and south, which plan was the first outline that I drew up and personally wanted to adopt'.[3]

Such disingenuousness and ability to plant his feet in opposing camps made Eisenhower a superlative politician, but an infuriating

---

[1] 'AFHQ G2 Estimate of the Garrison of Sicily and its likely Tactical Employment, 15.5.43,' ABC Husky File, National Archives, Washington.

[2] *The Papers of Dwight David Eisenhower*, op. cit.

[3] *The Papers of Dwight David Eisenhower*, letter of 4.5.43, op. cit.

Supreme Commander. However little Monty managed to master the art of dissimulation, one must at any rate admire the consistency with which he fought for what he considered was *militarily* right, on behalf of the men whose lives were at stake in such planning. On 3 April, two nights before the great assault at Wadi Akarit, he wrote to Alexander:

> Re HUSKY. There is some pretty woolly thinking going on – tactically and administratively. I do not really know who the head planner is, but I do suggest he comes to see me very soon, and before the thing gets too far. I have no intention of doing some of the things they suggest.
>
> We must get the initial stage-management right before we go on to details. . . . Perhaps Charles Gairdner could come & see me before they make a complete mess of the whole show.

He was adamant that the operation was being mounted upside down – with the Force Commanders being assigned roles by planners instead of vice-versa.

> It is very difficult to fight one campaign and at the same time to plan another in detail,

he wrote to Alexander the following day.

> But if we can get the general layout of HUSKY right, other people can get on with the detail.

This cardinal principle is important, for there can be little doubt that the problem of the invasion of Sicily was, for Montgomery, an essential rehearsal for the invasion of France, as he had written to Brooke. The lessons of Husky, however fraught with inter-service and inter-Allied rivalry and ill-feeling they might be, were the seedbed of 'Overlord', the invasion of France, whose planning was being misconducted in precisely the same way as 'Husky' at that very time.

In a sense, then, Monty saw himself in the guise of Alexander the Great at Gordium, and his insistence that the Commander must dictate the plan, not vice-versa, was his own way of cutting the Gordian knot which so bedevilled the Allies in a coalition war. By the time he reached Sfax he was signalling to Alexander: 'In my opinion the operation planned in LONDON breaks every common sense rule of practical battle fighting and is completely theoretical. It has no hope of success and should be completely recast. Have given DEMPSEY letter for you stating my views as to lines on which planning should proceed.' London had naturally planned that units from England should perform the westernmost landings, while Eighth Army units mounted those on the eastern side of Sicily. But as Monty pointed out, this would mean that 30 Corps (51st and NZ Divisions) 'would have to be back in Egypt early in May. That is not possible' – for there was obviously much fighting to be done before the Axis forces would be induced to surrender their Tunisian bridgehead. Eighth Army was already maintaining itself over a single road three hundred miles from Tripoli, and was fast outrunning essential stocks of ammunition, spares and petrol. If one of its two constituent Corps was required to start preparing for the invasion of Sicily, then Alexander would have to re-think his strategy for the final reduction of the Axis bridgehead. 'I suggest a decision is required as to who is to play the major part in the final assaults on the enemy positions,' Monty therefore wrote in his letter of 10 April.

There seem to be two alternatives:
A. *Eighth Army does it*
   In this case I must move forward all my Divisions and face up to a real battle on the ENFIDAVILLE position.
   In this case I would have to draw *very heavily* on Charles Miller [Major-General in charge of supplies, 18th Army Group], and have at my disposal all the resources in Northern Tunisia.
   Presumably this could be done, since First Army would merely sit tight and exert pressure.

B. *First Army does it*
   In this case I would sit tight, and merely exert pressure.
   I could do this on my own resources as far as maintenance goes.

As in his attitude towards the invasion of Sicily, Monty was determined that the climax to the North African offensive campaign, which he had initiated at the battle of Alamein, should not be squandered by dispersion of effort.

I suggest to you that whoever is to do the business must be able to *keep up a heavy and sustained effort*. A very great quantity of artillery ammunition would be required. On no account must we split our effort and launch two or more thrusts none of which can be sustained.

The great issues of Normandy and the Allied break-out in September 1944 were thus being rehearsed in the spring of 1943:

Whoever does the business must have the resources in Divisions, men, artillery, and ammunition, to be able to carry on day after day, and night after night.

Only in this way can you beat the German. You blast him with artillery and with bombs from the air, and you attack him daily.

Presumably you will decide if it is to be A or B.

Monty's view was in direct contradiction to Alexander's 'final offensive' as Alexander had stated it in his letter of 29 March to Monty. Nevertheless Alexander was not slow to recognise Monty's logic. He therefore signalled back the following day:

Main effort in next phase operations will be by First Army. Preparations already well advanced for attack earliest date 22 Apr. Most suitable area for employment of armour is the plain West of Tunis so require one armd div and one Armd C regt to join 9 Corps from you as early as can be arranged. Hope you can develop maximum pressure possible against ENFIDAVILLE position to fit in with First Army attack.[1]

Alexander's signal crossed with one from Montgomery in which, not having received a reply from Alexander about the 'two alternatives', Monty proposed to 'try and gate crash' the Enfidaville position during the April full moon period, for which he would require First Army's 6th Armoured Division, already at Kairouan, thus enabling him to leave 1st Armoured Division at Sfax. Alexander's decision rendered this 'gate-crashing' operation redundant, though the need for Eighth Army to 'maintain maximum pressure' at Enfidaville meant that Eighth Army could not close down its front.

'My dear Alex,' Monty replied on 12 April,

I note that the main effort will be by First Army.

I will face up now to the Enfidaville position and will make things very unpleasant there for the Bosche about 21 April; that will get him looking my way before First Army go in on 22 April.

I will send you 1st Armd Div (Briggs) and the K.D.G.'s [Armoured Car Regiment]. They are concentrated now on the Faid-Sbeitla road and can go off that way. They can move on 14 April, or any day after that. K.D.G.'s a day or two later.

Perhaps no other document better illustrates Monty's essential loyalty and willingness to co-operate when assured of firm direction and sound operational objectives. His intransigence over 'Husky' would soon earn him the opprobrium of American and even British

[1] Alexander Papers.

staff officers, many Americans preferring to believe that Monty was simply in all-out pursuit of personal glory and British honours, but this view is certainly belied by Monty's behaviour over the 'finale' in Tunisia. Eighth Army's offensive action at Enfidaville now became primarily a feint. Indeed in his letter of acceptance of 12 April, Monty informed Alexander that he was already leaving 51st Highland Division behind at Sfax, and wanted urgently 'to get NZ Div back to Egypt as soon as possible' to train, equip and embark for the Sicily operation; and by 17 April he was insisting that Eighth Army headquarters must also be 'freed from present battle operations and sent back to get down to Husky' or 'the success of that operation will be in grave danger'.

Alexander was clearly rattled by this. 'I should look upon it as a disaster if you were released prematurely,' he signalled back on 18 April.

In his diary Monty chronicled the situation.

12 April

I had written to ALEXANDER on 10 April saying that a decision was now required as to which Army was to make the main effort for the final phase.

I received his answer today saying that First Army would do so, and that my Army would exert pressure and so on. He said that the plain West of TUNIS was the most suitable ground for armour and asked me to send one Armd Div and one Armd Car Regt to join First Army. I decided to hold 1 Armd Div and the K.D.G.'s ready to join First Army.

Alexander's decision suited me very well. There was a great deal to do in preparation for 'HUSKY'.

Also, I was very anxious to get the N.Z. Div back to EGYPT early, to get it ready for 'HUSKY'.

Also, my Commanders, staffs, and troops, wanted an easy time; the pace has been very hot since August, 1942.

I am not happy about the final outcome, all the same.

ANDERSON (First Army) is not fit to command an Army in the field; everyone knows it, including his own Army.

ALEXANDER has had to supervise him very carefully, and to lay down exactly what he is to do.

There is no one at H.Q. 18 Army Group who has got practical experience of facing up to the Germans in battle. ALEXANDER has to do everything himself and thus no one is thinking out the larger issues.

McCREERY is quite out of touch with the practical side of battle fighting.

It would be all right if ANDERSON was any good, as he would do it all. But he is no good.

So ALEXANDER will have to do it, and he does not really know; he has a great deal of common sense, and is quite charming; but he has no great brain for the larger issues. He is good at minor tactics, battle schools and so on.

It would be dreadful if we made a mess of the final phase.

It is very necessary to finish this party early so that we can get on with 'HUSKY'. It is my opinion that the party might have been best part over if 18 Army Group had taken a grip and co-ordinated the whole show; ROMMEL's army should never have got away from the AKARIT position back to the TUNIS bridgehead,

Monty declared, blaming Alexander. Moreover

we can get no clear direction about the 'HUSKY' operation.

18 Army Group is too busy commanding First Army,

he added caustically.

You cannot in war do your own job and someone else's; if you try to, then the whole show suffers.

ALEXANDER is trying to 'bolster up' ANDERSON. The whole show is suffering in consequence because 18 Army Group is not doing its proper job.

The proper thing to do is to remove ANDERSON.

I have given my views about it to ALEXANDER in no uncertain voice.

Whatever his reservations, Monty certainly did his best to ensure that his feint attack or demonstration, now brought forward to the night of 19 April, would force the enemy to look towards Eighth Army. He put Horrocks' 10 Corps Headquarters in to command the assault and thus allow Leese and the Highlanders to be 'clear of the battle so that they could get on with preparations for HUSKY'. Horrocks was given four divisions for his Corps, and the attack, in the centre, was to be conducted by the New Zealanders[1] and 4th Indian Division. The hope was that if 10 Corps could obtain a foothold in the Enfidaville mountains, it would force von Arnim to switch German troops to that front; then if Alexander's 'final offensive', beginning on 22 April, was successful on First Army's front, 10 Corps would be well placed to exploit any consequent breakdown of resistance; in particular to stop the enemy opposite First Army from retreating into the Cape Bon peninsula.

Eighth Army's attack certainly caused von Arnim to leaven Mes-

[1] No agreement could be wrested from the New Zealand Government as to the employment of Freyberg's 2nd NZ Division in European operations, so that the division was eventually ruled out for inclusion in 'Husky'.

se's Italian troops with two German light armoured divisions (90th Light and 164th Division) and to back them by 15th Panzer Division; moreover when the two 10 Corps divisions succeeded in storming the enemy heights at Garci and Takrouna, the Germans were ordered to counter-attack in strength and at the cost of heavy casualties on 20 and 21 April, the eve of First Army's much vaunted 'Vulcan' offensive. Eighth Army was thus well placed to race up the coastal corridor with armoured forces to Bou Ficha and Hammamet the moment news came of First Army's breakthrough: 'I am concentrating three Divisions in the coastal plain and will "drive" along hard on the Axis ENFIDAVILLE-BOU FICHA . . . on 25 April,' Monty informed Alexander on 21 April. 'I shall now re-group, mass artillery and blast my way forward,' he explained. 'It suits me just as well to kill Germans down in this area, instead of nearer to Tunis. And it keeps them occupied here while you are doing your attack astride Mejdez-el-Bab.' However he warned Alexander not to expect enemy resistance to crumble: 'There is no doubt that the enemy is desperate; any idea that he is going to pull out is completely wrong as far as my experience here goes. We had yesterday, and on night 19/20 April, really heavy and savage fighting. The Gurkhas ran out of ammunition and drew their kukris, and went in with the knife. He counter-attacked again and again; *that* is exactly what we want; he was seen off every time with heavy casualties to himself. 4 (Ind) Div alone reckon he had 1000 casualties on their front, killed and wounded.'

It was now up to First Army; Monty was going to fly to Cairo for three days, and hoped to be back on 26 April – 'I will be back on 26 April, ready to handle the show if the [enemy resistance] begins to crack.' On 22 April he signalled: 'My gains are firmly held and his counter-attacks are all defeated. Am regrouping so as to be able to continue strongly on coast axis towards Bou Ficha and to be in a good position to burst through should a break occur on your front.'

But the break did not occur. First Army attacked on all sector fronts and Alexander's 'Vulcan' offensive, or 'partridge drive', quickly foundered. Thus when Monty returned from Cairo on 26 April he found a 'dog's breakfast' in Tunisia, as he had privately predicted would happen in a letter to Brooke already a fortnight before, on 15 April:

My dear General,
    Events here are slowly taking shape. My own view is that the Bosche intends to stand and fight it out, and there will be a good deal of dirty work before it is over. . . .
    I am not happy about the final end of this show. It is *terribly important* to get it finished soon. I have an unpleasant feeling in the pit of the stomach that we may make a mess of it. The attack plan

for the major effort, on First Army front, is NOT the way that I fight the Germans. My experience is that the way to beat him is to concentrate all your strength and hit him *an almighty crack*; then through that place, while the enemy is reeling under the blow, you burst through with armoured and mobile forces; these armoured forces have got to be prepared to fight their way out, dealing with any jagged edges that remain. The weight of your effort is such that in the end the enemy cracks, and through you go. But the plan for the big blow up north, on First Army front, does not do this. 5 Corps with three Divisions attacks in one place. 9 Corps with two armoured and one infantry Division attacks *somewhere else*. It may come off; I hope to goodness it does, but I have an awful feeling that both attacks will be held, neither being strong enough alone. I shall do my utmost on the coast axis to be very unpleasant, and draw enemy strength down to me and away from the main attack – and this may turn the scale.

I really believe I would burst into tears if, having come 2,000 miles and got the enemy cold, we mess it up in the end. It would be too frightful. The present plan has all the seeds for failure. However, perhaps I am being too pessimistic and it will do the trick. I do hope so. But it is quite contrary to all *my* ideas on how to win battles, and so I am not happy. I shall have to crack about like anything on my front, and try and draw the *Bosche on to me*.

In a postscript to the letter Monty warned:

The ENFIDAVILLE position is very strong naturally, and has been strengthened artificially. We may have some tough fighting.

After the failure of Alexander's 'Vulcan' offensive, Monty's worst fears were now fulfilled, and soon after his return to Eighth Army from Cairo he wrote again to Brooke:

My dear General,
You will remember I wrote you some time ago – I cannot remember the date – and said I had a horrible and unpleasant feeling that we might make a mess of the final phase. I fear we have made a good start in that direction.

In my opinion the plan of First Army had no hope of a quick success. 5 Corps attacked with all three Divisions forward, each Division being on a front of 6 miles with all three Bdes up. There was no depth and no 'punch'. The armour (9 Corps) tried to break through somewhere else.

Away on the right flank in my Army I am struggling to gain ground in country which is like the N.W. Frontier of India. I have 200 tanks which I cannot possibly use.

233

I foresaw what the problem was going to be, and on 10 April (when we were on the SFAX line) I suggested to Alex that he should decide where to put in the big blow for Tunis, should re-group and should concentrate *every possible resource* for that blow so as to knock the Bosche right off his perch before he had time to collect himself.

I fear it was never done . . .

I could almost burst into tears at the tragedy of the whole thing. I have no doubt we shall put it right in the end, but we have lost a great opportunity, and we have lost a lot of good chaps.

For a moment Monty considered whether, despite the formations he wished to keep out of the battle in order to prepare for 'Husky', Eighth Army could break the deadlock by mounting a 'blitz' attack along the coastal corridor, leaving the Germans and Italians in possession of the mountains. No one in Eighth Army liked the plan, however, which still depended on Alexander being successful on First Army's front. To improve Eighth Army's positions preparatory to such an attack, the newly arrived 56th Division was put into battle on 29 April. 'I am glad I said 56 Div must come up and join me [after Mareth],' Monty had previously remarked to Brooke. 'I do NOT want to use that Division on HUSKY as it has never fired a shot in this war, but it will be wanted up here when the HUSKY Divisions have to pull out – which will be very soon.'

When, however, 56th Division's attack failed on 29 April, Monty's patience snapped. It was obvious that Eighth Army would be unable to make up for the failure of 'Vulcan' without using the divisions earmarked for 'Husky'. If casualties were heavy, then 'Husky' itself would be prejudiced. As he noted in his diary:

Plans were made to break through the narrow gap between the mountains and the sea, by a blitz attack. This would take place about 2 May. But the more I examined the problem the more it became clear that the operation was very difficult with the re-sources available. . . . It was ideal defensive country. The operation had only a 50/50 chance of success; it might very easily fail; in any case, success or failure, casualties would be very severe. After much thought I came to the conclusion that we were not running the war in TUNISIA at all well. . . . What was required before we approached this very difficult country was a re-grouping of the Armies designed to enable a terrific blow to be delivered on the front of the selected Army, quickly. This was not done. . . . So I wired to ALEXANDER on 29 April.

The cable was historic. Sent at 6 p.m. on 29 April 1943, it marked the true beginning of the end of the war in North Africa:

56 REPEAT 56 DIVISION GAVE VERY BAD SHOWING TODAY UNDER HEAVY SHELL FIRE AND I MUST ACCEPT FACT THAT THE DIVISION HAS LITTLE FIGHTING VALUE AT PRESENT AND WILL TAKE TIME TO LEARN. HAVE TO CANCEL RE-PEAT CANCEL ATTACK BY 4 INDIAN DIVISION TONIGHT. AM NOT REPEAT NOT HAPPY ABOUT PRESENT PLAN FOR FINISHING OFF THIS BUSINESS. CAN YOU POSSIBLY COME AND SEE ME TOMORROW OR IF NOT REPEAT NOT SEND MGS.

To his credit Alexander came in person, with his Chief of Staff, early the next day. In a letter to Brooke Monty recorded what transpired:

Today I told Alex it was just madness to go on as we are doing; and that he *must re-group*. My front should be a holding one; the real blow should go in on First Army front. In fact, that which should have been done some weeks ago, *must* be done now. He agreed and I have today sent across two Divisions, some artillery, Gds Bde, etc. ammunition, hospitals, labour Coys, and so on.

In his diary he recorded the same: 'I wired to ALEXANDER on 29 April and asked him to come over and see me, as I was not happy about the business. He came on 30 April. I explained the problem and said he really must re-group, so that the operations could be continued with the maximum weight in the most suitable area. He agreed, as he always does when I suggest things to him.'

The proposal that Eighth Army should transfer its weight to First Army for the 'terrific blow' was thus entirely Monty's. He not only sent over 7th Armoured Division (the 'Desert Rats'), Tuker's 4th Indian Division and 201st Guards Brigade, but turned down Alexander's request that Freyberg take command of 9 Corps in First Army, in place of General Crocker, who had been wounded during the abortive 'Vulcan' offensive.

If I could mention one incident that has never been recorded that I know of,

recalled Air Chief Marshal Sir Harry Broadhurst many years later,

when we got to Enfidaville I got a message to pick up Alexander and bring him over for breakfast. I took my Storch to Monaster and picked Alex up and flew him to Monty's.

Monty was in his caravan, forward. There were just the three of us – I don't think Freddie was there.[1] We had breakfast and then we went into the map caravan. Alex said he would like Bernard Freyberg to command the final thrust on Tunis – the British part. . . . And Monty said, 'You'd be silly to have Freyberg. He's a nice old boy, but he's a bit stupid. You'd better have Jorrocks. Jorrocks – he's the chap. Now what's your plan?'

So Alex told him broadly the plan – which was to attack the whole front.

'Oh,' Monty said, 'you don't want to attack on the whole front – that suits the Germans fine! They've got no transport, no petrol. . . . The thing is to pick the best place and then overwhelm it. And the Air Force'll see they [the Germans] don't move anything – they haven't the petrol to move anything. Then just punch home – you'll be through in 48 hours. Jorrocks'll do it for you.'

So we got back in the aeroplane and I flew Alex back.

Next thing I knew, Jorrocks was calling in at my headquarters. 'Got this job. Now what can I do with the Air Force? Can they do what they did at El Hamma?'

I said: 'Look it's not my Air Force any more [in First Army]! But I'll ring up a chum of mine, first-class chap called Cross, he'll look after you all right.'

So they were through in forty-eight hours.

And Monty – to me it made absolute, simple common sense. Of course, it wasn't an easy thing – these things never are. . . . But that's the way it happened: I was there when it was said. And it went absolutely according to plan – and Jorrocks went through like a dose of salts.[2]

Horrocks remembered his new assignment vividly: 'On 30 April I was once again ordered by wireless to report forthwith to 8th Army headquarters. . . . Inside the caravan were Generals Alexander and Montgomery standing in front of a map. Monty turned to me and said: "The whole weight of the final attack is being shifted from here round to the 1st Army front, from where the *coup de grâce* will be administered. You will go off today, taking with you the 4th Indian Division, 7th Armoured Division, and 201st Guards Brigade, and you will assume command of the 9 Corps in General Anderson's

---

[1] De Guingand was in Cairo, concussed after a flying accident. McCreery accompanied Alexander. His diary entry for 30 April 1943 confirms Montgomery's and Broadhurst's accounts: 'Left 0630 for 8th Army. Alex had long conference with Monty. Decided to abandon major operations of 8th Army due to great difficulties of ground and 7th Armoured Division and 4th Indian Division, 201 Guards Bde all to come to join 1st Army' – General Sir Richard McCreery, diary communicated to author by Nigel Nicolson.

[2] Air Chief Marshal Sir Harry Broadhurst, loc. cit.

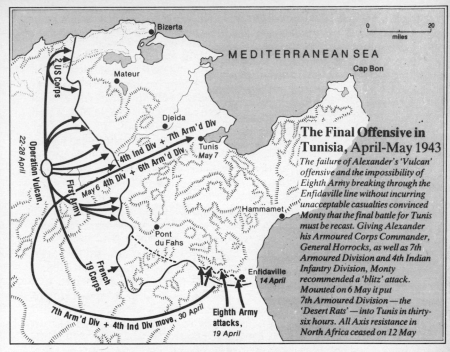

The Final Offensive in Tunisia, April–May 1943

The failure of Alexander's 'Vulcan' offensive and the impossibility of Eighth Army breaking through the Enfidaville line without incurring unacceptable casualties convinced Monty that the final battle for Tunis must be recast. Giving Alexander his Armoured Corps Commander, General Horrocks, as well as 7th Armoured Division and 4th Indian Infantry Division, Monty recommended a 'blitz' attack. Mounted on 6 May it put 7th Armoured Division — the 'Desert Rats' — into Tunis in thirty-six hours. All Axis resistance in North Africa ceased on 12 May

army. You will then smash through to Tunis and finish the war in North Africa. . . .'' My heart leapt. This was the art of generalship – a quick switch, then a knock-out blow.'[1]

If the plan for 'finishing the war in North Africa' was thus Monty's, Alexander nevertheless deserves full credit for the fact that, without reference to Eisenhower, he responded so swiftly. By 3.15 p.m. Horrocks was on his way, and General Anderson was evidently told to give Horrocks his head. By working hand-in-glove with Lt-General Allfrey, commanding 5 Corps, Horrocks devised an assault which pierced the German line at Medjez el Bab and captured Tunis in even less than the forty-eight hours Monty had predicted. Launched at 3 a.m. on 6 May, Operation 'Strike' 'went like clockwork,' Horrocks recorded. 'The two infantry divisions punched the initial breach, and at 7.30 a.m. I was able to order the two armoured divisions forward. By midday they were through the crust and the tanks were grinding their way forward down the valley towards Tunis.'[2] The city which had eluded capture by Anderson's First Army for twenty-four long weeks now fell in almost as many hours – and Alexander had earned his title. 'He has had a rotten time

[1] Brian Horrocks, op. cit.
[2] Ibid.

since he went across to Northern TUNISIA in February,' Monty noted a trifle condescendingly in his diary; 'he found a dreadful "mess" there and has had to do everything himself.'

There can be little doubt that Monty would have made considerably shorter work of the Tunisian campaign than Anderson and Alexander took over it. But with his gift for inspiring admiration and liking, Alexander had at least kept the British, American and French forces harnessed together, and the overall victory in Tunisia must rightly be credited to him, a credit which Monty himself never attempted to take, confining his true feelings to his private letters and to his diary, which was seen only by a handful of people. As he wrote on 18 July 1943 on the eve of 'Husky': 'I do not suppose there are many people who know that the plan for the final phase of the Tunisian war was given out by me in my caravan at Army H.Q. on Friday 30 April, ALEXANDER and McCREERY having come to see me at my urgent request because I saw failure unless the battle was handled better.' More and more Monty had tended to look upon Alexander as his lieutenant – his erstwhile student at the Staff College, Camberley in the 1920s and now again in the desert campaign. That this student should have learned from the experience of Eighth Army, should have imposed a better grip on operations in Tunisia after taking over from Eisenhower on 18 February 1943, and ultimately brought the campaign to a victorious conclusion in Eighth Army style was a matter of pride to Monty. 'It was done on Eighth Army lines and was a complete success,' he remarked of Horrocks' break-through to Tunis in his diary – attaching a moving letter written by Major-General Erskine, commander of 7th Armoured Division, the day after Tunis fell, which ended: 'We are all very proud to have been your representative here to finish the job.' In a postscript, Erskine added, tongue-in-cheek, 'the prisoners say they knew a week ago that the 7th Armd Div was coming round to the First Army front and they therefore regarded the situation as hopeless!'

Organised resistance would only cease on 12 May; meanwhile Monty's primary concern, having persuaded Alexander to mount Operation 'Strike', was not Tunisia but Sicily. 'The battles I am having now with the planning staffs are far more exhausting than my battles against the Germans,' he confided to Brooke the next day. 'I think when we see daylight a bit more here, and HUSKY is on a firm basis, I must get home for a short rest. There is a great deal I would like to talk to you about; but,' he added ominously, 'it would have to be *alone* and *in private*.'

PART THREE

Sicily

CHAPTER ONE

Husky: Recasting the Invasion of Sicily

Sicily, like Malta, was one of the keys to the Mediterranean. Once the Allies succeeded in taking the island they would possess a stepping stone to Italy, which might even withdraw from the Axis alliance if Sicily fell.

The island was therefore a considerable strategic prize. But its capture was no foregone conclusion. The 'Torch' landings had been opposed only by the Vichy French; even so, they had demonstrated how difficult it was to maintain momentum when once ashore. The Allies had been outdone by the speed of German reinforcements and therefore been condemned to six months of winter stalemate in Tunisia.

Doubtless this was already clear to the Allied planners when, in January 1943, they began to draw up proposals for 'Husky'. Eisenhower later claimed, in a memorandum on 1 July 1943, that his own initial tactical plan provided for a 'single concentrated assault on the eastern and southern portions of the island', but was overruled by 'the logistic people', who claimed that 'this was absolutely impossible to maintain'.[1] The planners had thereupon altered their plan of invasion: small forces would be put ashore in many dispersed landings on east, south and north coasts in the hope that if some failed, others would prosper and could be reinforced. Alexander and Montgomery had refused to have anything to do with such a ridiculous plan, Monty signalling to Alexander on the afternoon of 13 March 1943, a week before the battle of Mareth:

DEMPSEY and RAMSAY visited me today on way to ALGIERS and before they came I studied HUSKY. In my opinion the operation planned in LONDON breaks every common sense rule of practical battle fighting and is completely theoretical. It has no hope of success and should be completely recast. Have given DEMPSEY letter for you stating my views as to lines on which planning should proceed.

[1] *The Papers of Dwight David Eisenhower*, ed. Alfred D. Chandler, *The War Years* Vol. II, Baltimore 1970.

Alexander's resultant view was that the landings on the west side of Sicily should be dropped in order to provide more forces for Montgomery's eastern landings. Eisenhower agreed on 20 March, but in such a way that, if the extra forces for Montgomery could be found in the Middle East, then planning at least for a three-pronged invasion could resume. In due course the extra forces *were* found, and after a further month of time-wasting, the 'Husky' plan reverted to a multi-pronged composition.

Monty was agog at this see-saw story. 'Re HUSKY,' he wrote to Alexander on 3 April. 'There is some pretty woolly thinking going on – tactically and administratively. I do not know who the head planner is, but I do suggest he comes to see me very soon, and before the thing gets too far. I have no intention of doing some of the things they suggest.

'We must get the initial stage-management right before we go on to details,' he remarked, and insisted that, whereas the operation was seen by the planners as an independent 'show', mounted by the anonymous Forces 141, 343 and 545, there was no question of Eighth Army being broken up merely at the whim of planners in London, Algiers or Cairo. Ever since Alexander had nominated him for the British part of 'Husky', Monty had insisted on casting the Eighth Army mantle over the British contribution, as he wrote on 16 February 1943 to Brooke, and he refused to go back on this. 'We must use the whole Eighth Army team, as we do now,' he wrote to Alexander – and informed his superiors that, when the fighting was over, he would take his Eighth Army HQ to Tripoli, midway between the two Corps selected for 'Husky': 30 Corps at Sfax/Sousse, 13 Corps in Egypt.[1]

To Monty this seemed the obvious way to approach the invasion of Sicily, as a sort of roll-over or next bound in Eighth Army's now legendary advance from Alamein. 'Perhaps Charles Gairdner could come and see me before they make a complete mess of the thing,' he suggested to Alexander.[2] Alexander replied by inviting him to come to 18th Army Group to discuss the plans, but, on the eve of the Wadi Akarit battle, Monty felt it was 'quite impossible to leave here'[3] – and suggested Alexander fly over on 5 April – which Alexander did. It was agreed that, an extra division having been found from the Middle East for Montgomery's Eastern Task Force landing, this would employ the landing craft hitherto assigned to the American landings at Marinella and Sciacca which would be scrapped, and the American Palermo operation postponed until D + 5 at the earliest.

[1] Alexander Papers (WO 214/18), PRO.
[2] Ibid.
[3] Ibid., signal of 4.4.43.

On the previous day Monty had opined: 'It is very difficult to fight one campaign and at the same time to plan another in detail!!! But if we can get the general layout of HUSKY right other people can get on with the detail.'[1] After Alexander's visit he felt they had got the layout right: two experienced Eighth Army Divisions would land and capture the airfields Tedder demanded at Gela and Comiso on the south coast; meanwhile two further divisions would land south of Syracuse on the east coast, plus a brigade from Malta to capture the Pachino airfield on the south-eastern peninsula. Alexander had been ordered to submit a final outline plan 'by 9 April latest' to Eisenhower and the Combined Chiefs of Staff; thus Alexander's chief planner, General Gairdner, rushed off with the new plan to London to get Whitehall approval. But meanwhile Monty was already having doubts:

> Have further considered set-up for HUSKY and am convinced must use experienced troops to utmost extent,

he signalled to Alexander on 7 April, suggesting that, instead of using his two experienced Eighth Army divisions in securing mere airfields, he switch them to the vital eastern coast landings – to capture Syracuse, Augusta and, in time, Catania. In fact, instead of being a two-Corps affair, he now believed the Eastern Task Force should comprise *three* Corps, with General Horrocks using 10 Corps Headquarters to take the airfields for Tedder with an armoured division plus an enlarged infantry division with tanks, while Dempsey would take charge of all reserves, including 50th Division, ready to feed into the island 'as necessary'. 'If you agree signal me by return so I can get on with it.'[2]

Alexander did not signal, for he had no idea what to say; nor did he have time to spend pondering the matter, given his forthcoming 'Vulcan' offensive in Tunisia. In Gairdner's absence the Brigadier in charge at Force 141 replied that 'change even if practicable is not welcome', and used a trump card: Monty's new proposal would 'delay the mounting of the operation by at least one month beyond the date . . . to which you have already agreed.'[3] Monty was reluctantly forced to rescind his suggestion, which he did on 9 April. 'It seems clear that if HUSKY is to be in July repeat July, the divisions must be in the Middle East [for training and embarkation] first week in May, repeat May. This rules out my latest suggestion. . . . Presume any postponement HUSKY is not repeat not possible. Therefore only possible set-up is outline plan agreed between us when you

[1] Ibid.
[2] Alexander Papers (WO 214/20), PRO.
[3] Ibid.

came here on 5 April.'[1] To Brooke he wrote on the same day, trying to put on a brave face, despite his reservations: 'I have now managed to get the HUSKY affair put on a proper basis, and a good layout agreed to,' for he had, he believed, at least squashed all existing plans for piecemeal landings by mutually unsupporting brigade groups. 'Detailed planning can now proceed on a firm framework,' he declared, adding 'if the American troops were any good we could finish off this [Tunisian] party by 1st May.'[2]

The following day Eisenhower approved and 'issued' the new plan, and Monty began to give out his guidelines for the invasion, although switching the component landing forces so that divisions fighting in Tunisia could embark at Sfax rather than returning 2,000 miles to Alexandria, and deciding to use de Guingand as his personal representative in Cairo where the Force 545 planning was being done – planning which, according to rumour, was so subject to inter-service dissension that two days later Monty was insisting that de Guingand 'be made a Major-Gen so that he can carry weight'. Yet the main problem was that Alexander's headquarters was too busy trying to run operations on the First Army front, and could give no clear leadership over the very 'Husky' planning which Eisenhower had delegated to Alexander:

18 Army Group ought to be sitting back and controlling the battle in its bigger aspect; they ought to be giving very clear and definite directions about HUSKY. But they don't do so; they have to exercise operational command of a part of the front; but what is far worse is that they are busy commanding First Army and trying to unravel the awful mess there. In war a commander cannot do someone else's job as well as his own. It merely means he neglects his own job and the show suffers. That is what is happening here now. There is a lack of 'grip'. The HUSKY planning is in a hopeless mess.

We have made such a mess of it so many times in this war that it makes me quite angry to see us drifting the same way now. I should have thought we had learnt our lesson – after nearly 4 years of war. But apparently not. To my mind there is only one answer. Anderson has been found to be no good and not up to it; remove him at once and put in a proper chap; that will relieve 18 Army Group of having to command First Army; and that will mean that it will *at last* be able to do its proper job. It hasn't done it yet; and if it doesn't start doing it soon we shall be in for trouble.

This was written to Brooke on 12 April. Three days later his tone was becoming slightly hysterical, for it was now high time that the

[1] Ibid.
[2] Montgomery Papers.

divisions selected for 'Husky' should begin pulling out of Tunisia, the New Zealanders to Egypt and 50th Division to Tripoli:

> But there does not seem to be any senior commander who is handling HUSKY. I can't get anyone to give decisions on big matters. I have given a number myself and upset a good many people by so doing!!
> If you want to have a successful overseas expedition, you must take the commander of it and let him do that *and nothing else*.
> Alex is, I suppose, in charge of it. But he hasn't time to bother about it. And his C.G.S. (McCreery) is not in on it, and knows nothing of it!! We are an amazing race, and it is quite wonderful how we ever win wars!! Alex is commanding First Army and has not time for other matters.
> More, and more, and more do I say that the higher commander must sit back and attend to his own job, and have plenty of time for quiet thought and reflection. Only in this way can you win wars. If he does not do so, then the whole show suffers – as we are suffering now.

There can be little doubt that Monty was voicing the simple truth. Eisenhower had 'passed the buck' in assigning to Alexander the planning of 'Husky', but had then saddled Alexander with his own mess in Tunisia. And Alexander, as Sir Edgar Williams once later remarked, was not by inspiration a higher commander, though his natural charm and integrity were important qualities in such a role during coalition warfare. By temperament Alexander was, like Lord Gort, a fighting man. He enjoyed, as an antidote to his natural indolence, being near the front, and his unwillingness to find a First Army commander capable of completing the Tunisian campaign was very probably a mark of his own delight at being able, once again, to play soldier rather than administrator.

There was thus a seeming conspiracy among the Allies to ruin the 'Husky' operation by sheer lack of leadership. Even Sir Alan Brooke, to whom Monty so bitterly poured out his heart, would do nothing to rectify the situation, a situation which Monty was not alone in deploring. General Wilson, the C-in-C in Cairo after the departure of Alexander, added his own personal plea to Monty's. On 1 April 1943 he had signalled to Brooke: 'It would appear planning in Algiers is suffering from lack of a full time Commander on the spot, and instead is relying on snap decisions from those who are fully engaged with Vulcan, and you may wish to send someone out there to sort things out.'[1]

[1] C. J. C. Molony, *History of the Second World War: The Mediterranean and Middle East* Vol. 5, London 1973.

But whom could Brooke send? Wilson and Montgomery were incontrovertibly correct, but at this stage of the war, with the campaign in the Far East still showing no sign of turning an equivalent tide to that in North Africa, there was really no one with the authority and practical battle experience to take over the reins of 'Husky'. General Paget, commanding Home Forces, had no experience of the larger battlefield, and Montgomery had voiced grave doubts about his comprehension of modern battlefield command and techniques. Auchinleck was experienced but discredited by his failure in the desert, Anderson was proving a broken reed. Indeed there *was* only one solution, and that was Monty's: to replace Anderson by Leese and let Alexander concentrate more on mounting 'Husky'. Yet even this, at a time when First and Eighth Armies were converging upon the Axis bridgehead in Tunisia, might not have worked, for an Army Group Commander was essential to the effective completion of the campaign. Thus Brooke did nothing. Monty was left to sort out the 'mess' alone, and to take the opprobrium heaped upon him by all those who, like Tedder and Admiral Cunningham, felt Monty was too 'junior' in the 'Husky' hierarchy to be dictating planning policy.

On 17 April, therefore, Monty insisted he must pull out of the Tunisian campaign, along with his headquarters and constituent divisions for 'Husky' – as Patton had already done: 'Crux of the matter is that unless Eighth Army is freed from present battle operations and sent back to get down to Husky the success of that operation will be in grave danger.[1] Alexander, anxious lest his Vulcan offensive come to grief, wired back that he would 'look upon it as a disaster if you were released prematurely' and considered Eighth Army's presence essential 'until final battle is won'.[2] The two men met the next day at Algiers, together with Eisenhower. Shortly before the meeting, to which he flew in his new Flying Fortress, Monty wrote to Brooke, insisting that if Husky were to be mounted in July 1943, the constituent divisions from Eighth Army *must* be released. This led to the question of whether First Army could finish off the Tunisian campaign without them.

If my H.Q. and my best fighting troops go away, can you be sure of finishing off the war in N. Africa? If you don't finish it off, there can be no HUSKY. It is therefore a big risk to take my experienced H.Q. away from the battle just yet.

So you see the problem. What you do not see, because you are not here, is that NO ONE is tackling it. There is no shadow of doubt about one thing i.e. unless some one will face up to this

[1] Alexander Papers (WO 214/18), PRO.
[2] Ibid.

problem and give a decision, there will be a 1st Class disaster.

I am going today in my Fortress to lunch with Eisenhower and thank him for giving it to me. I have told Alex it is vital he should meet me there. I shall put the facts of the case quite clearly to them, and make it clear that we cannot go on 'drifting' in this way. If we do HUSKY, it must succeed. But as things are being handled now it looks like being quite a good failure. . . . Even some compromise decision would be better than no decision.

I am fighting to get some sanity into the planning. It is hard work; and I am also fighting the Germans – which is much easier. If there was some proper commander for HUSKY, who would do that and nothing else, we would get on all right. . . . I shall speak very plainly at Algiers today and possibly may get some decision.

At lunch with Eisenhower and Alexander, Monty put forward his 'compromise', which was that the Eighth Army continue the fight in Tunisia, but that a proportion of its staff move to Cairo, headed by de Guingand who would be promoted to the rank of Major-General and take over the planning of 'Husky'. Monty himself would commute between Tunisia and Cairo to ensure that both operations functioned smoothly. 'Above notes read out by me to General EISENHOWER and General ALEXANDER at ALGIERS on Monday 19 April, and were agreed to in all respects,' Monty remarked on his typescript. To Brooke he wrote the next day:

My dear General
I had a very satisfactory conference at Algiers yesterday. The whole thing is very far from satisfactory *really*; but my suggestions as to the only possible compromise were agreed to. . . .

In theory, Alex should be doing it. In practice, Alex is hopelessly involved in keeping First Army on the rails. In fact the whole underlying cause of the mess we are now in is that we chose a man to command First Army who was not fit for the job; then having discovered he was not fit for the job, we still keep him on. But do not worry. I will do it somehow; but it will be the devil of a job. Both Eisenhower and Alex were very good. I did suggest that I might leave the Tunisian front and get down to HUSKY; but they would not hear of it. So I shall remain, and will somehow do both jobs.

Monty now clearly imagined that Eisenhower and Alexander had given him authority to take over the planning of 'Husky' – at any rate the invasion of the south-eastern corner of the island – and direct it through his Cairo *alter ego*, de Guingand. But this was very far from being the case, as now became clear when Monty attempted to throw his weight around. For on 23 April 1943 Monty left his

Eighth Army headquarters and flew to Cairo – he had not been back since December 1942. There 'for the first time I learnt what the planning staffs suggested I should do. . . . They want me to operate in little Bde Gps [brigade groups] all over the place. I refuse. They say there will only be slight resistance. I say that here in Tunisia the Italian is fighting desperately; he has never done so before; but he is doing so now. To operate dispersed, means disaster. We cannot go on in this way. Unless we get a good and firm plan *at once*, on which we can all work, *there will be no HUSKY in July*. I hope that this is realised your end,' Monty wrote to Brooke.

Monty's refusal to carry out the plan to which he himself had agreed on 5 April was not simply the mark of a 'cautious and inflexible General Montgomery' in comparison with the restless and attacking Patton. As Bradley was to note, Patton did not interest himself in the details of 'Husky' planning and was eminently prepared to follow the fantasies of London or Washington staff officers as long as they got him ashore and into combat. 'Patton was not at all familiar with planning details of Sicilian invasion,' Bradley later recounted to his ADC. 'Patton never concerned himself with planning details. As a result plans were never second-guessed [checked]. Did not go into logistics as much as I thought necessary. Did not go into enemy situations as thoroughly as I would have done. . . . George is spectacular. Does not like drudgery. And that is drudging work. No glamour in that.'[1]

Though Monty might incense jealous officers and Allies by his own theatrical behaviour, such as his ostentatious reading of the lesson in Cairo cathedral on Easter Sunday 1943 as well as a talk to the press at an Embassy function, his 'secret' mission was in deadly earnest. Together with Ramsay, Leese, de Guingand, and equipment, logistics, administrative and intelligence representatives, he personally 'second-guessed' the plan to which he had, three weeks previously, given a somewhat reluctant blessing, and which he now found wanting. Both Leese and de Guingand felt that the great strength of the Eighth Army was being dissipated by two separated British landings with separate strategic aims. There were not sufficient troops both to capture the vital ports on the eastern coast *and* take the airfields further west which Tedder wanted. By dividing his forces Monty opened himself to defeat in detail; worse still, he forfeited the chance of using Eighth Army's concentrated strength to seize the seaports and smash northwards towards Catania and

[1] 'Bradley Commentaries, World War II' (based on interviews carried out in 1947), Chester B. Hansen Collection, Military History Institute, Carlisle, Pennsylvania. Bradley's supposed autobiography, published in 1983 as *A General's Life* (New York) is not to be trusted, as the chapters relating to World War II, written by Bradley's co-author Clay Blair, were never seen or authorised by General Bradley, who died in 1981.

thence to Messina – the enemy's only channel of supply and reinforcement.

Monty's decision to back now the views of his staff and his most
experienced Corps Commander was not an easy one. Within twenty-
four hours of his arrival in Cairo he was cabling Alexander: 'We have
now reached the stage when we can say quite definitely that we
require two more divisions, assault loaded and to be landed on
D-Day in the Gulf of Gela if the invasion of Sicily is to be a success.'[1]
By switching his erstwhile Gela divisions to the eastern coast beaches
he was thus able to ensure that Eighth Army had the concentrated
punch it needed, against opposition which, though difficult to
predict in quality, already looked ominous in numbers: no fewer
than 153,000 Italian troops estimated to be defending the island on 20
April together with 20,000 Germans, and a further German division
likely to be transferred from Italy the moment the invasion started.[2]
As Monty explained a few days later to Brooke:

> The proper answer is to bring two USA Divisions in to land at
> CENT [Scoglitti] and DIME [Gela], on the south coast, and get the
> aerodromes. And chuck the Palermo landing for the present. If this
> was agreed to, then we could all go ahead. The operation would
> then have every prospect of being a really first class show. The
> effort at present is too dispersed. If we work on the present plan
> there is likely to be a 1st Class disaster. . . . We have got ourselves
> into a real high class mess and I feel the judgement of history will
> be that we have only ourselves to blame. No one is sitting right
> back, and thinking out quietly the various moves in the game –
> and doing the high level stuff – for the Tunisian war or for
> HUSKY.[3]

Had the Sicily landings proved – as Salerno and Anzio would
prove – near-disasters, then history might well have cast Eisenhower and Alexander in the same noble but failed mould as their
predecessors in the Middle East, Auchinleck and Wavell. It is for this
reason surely that General Dempsey, on his deathbed, referred to
Sicily as Monty's 'finest hour'[4] – for Monty alone among the senior
Allied military commanders had the courage to refuse to carry out an
ill-conceived plan, and to insist that, if tackled, the invasion be
mounted properly. Though he would be pilloried by the ignorant or
envious, and his motives made out to be megalomaniacal rather than
military, the accusations tell us more about his accusers than about

[1] Montgomery Papers.
[2] See Koch Papers: Intelligence Appreciation by G2, 7th Army in Koch Papers,
MHI, Carlisle, Pennsylvania.
[3] Letter of 30.4.43, Montgomery Papers.
[4] R. Lewin, *Montgomery as Military Commander*, London 1971.

Monty. As one British colonel – not friendly towards Monty – would later remark: 'I find those who criticise Monty loudest are so uniformly second-rate that I prefer not to make my own views known!' However tactless he might be in advancing his cause, Monty was certainly acting out of responsibility towards Allied success in the Mediterranean and above all towards the lives of his men. As he wrote in his letter to Brooke on 15 April: 'The high morale of my soldiers is almost unbelievable. I sometimes wonder if it is not a bit too much, and possibly dangerous; they believe that this Army is invincible and can do nothing wrong. I hope they are right. I realise what a great responsibility rests on me to ensure that we fight our battles properly, and have no failures.' In recasting the invasion of Sicily, therefore, Monty was determined to see that his troops had the very best chance of success, and events would show that, despite tragic failures in the parachute drop, the plan Monty insisted upon was sufficiently powerful to ensure that the momentum of beach-head assault was not seriously impaired, something which could not be said either of Salerno or Anzio. Similarly, although Eighth Army proved much less effective in Sicily after its legendary desert campaign than most had expected, the plan of invasion was such that, unlike First Army in Tunisia, the Germans never really stood a chance of containing it, despite having only a two-mile crossing to the island, compared with the Allies' ninety miles from North Africa.

In this sense, Monty's intransigent recasting of the invasion of Sicily was indeed his 'finest hour', comparable to his premature assumption of command of Eighth Army the year before and his complete recasting of the plans for the battle of Alam Halfa. As at Eighth Army headquarters on the Ruweisat Ridge on 13 August 1942, Monty had now arrived in Cairo in his Flying Fortress determined to see that, after three months of Allied muddle, indecision, revision and confusion, he would dictate a simple plan in which the soldiers would have confidence. After his conference with Eisenhower and Alexander on 19 April he believed he had *carte blanche* to act in lieu of Alexander as the real commander of 'Husky', at least as far as the east-coast landings were concerned. He therefore dismissed the existing plans, drawn up by Major-General Gairdner and approved by Alexander, for landings at Pozallo, Pachino, Cassibile and Catania as well as Gela, and plumped instead for two British landings: on the Pachino peninsula ('Bark') and at Avola ('Acid'). On 24 April he therefore cabled Alexander not even to ask approval let alone an opinion, but to state categorically what he had done, unilaterally and in spite of possible air and naval objections. He was, he signalled, certain that 'a prolonged dogfight battle will follow the initial assault', since the Sicilian mountains made it ideal defensive country. 'In view of above considerations,' he informed Alexander, 'my Army must operate concentrated with Corps and Divisions in supporting distance of each other. CENT and DIME landings [American assaults in Gulf of Gela to secure landing grounds] must be given up and the whole effort be made in the areas of ACID and BARK. Subsequent operations will be developed so as to secure airfields and ports and so on. The first thing to do is to secure a lodgement in a suitable area and then operate from a firm base. Time is pressing and if we delay while above is argued in LONDON and WASHINGTON the operation will never be launched in July. Whole planning and work in CAIRO is suffering because everyone is trying to make something of a plan which he knows can never succeed.' He had therefore 'given orders that as far as the Army is concerned all planning and work as regards ETF [Eastern Task Force] is now to go ahead on lines indicated in para. 5'.[1]

This unilateral decision to scrap the existing Allied plan and to proceed immediately upon a new Montgomery plan in Cairo came as a bombshell to Alexander and Eisenhower, to whom a copy of the cable was also sent. At the end of the cable Monty had written: 'I am not able to judge the repercussions of this solution on the operation as a whole' – and had declared that 'Admiral Ramsay is in complete agreement with me and together we are prepared to launch the operation and see it through and win'.

Ramsay had in fact been hesitant about being quoted in this way, though he was entirely won over by Monty's logic on the military side, as de Guigand remembered with amusement shortly before he died:

Monty came to Cairo and we gave him a demonstration of the plan and our comments on it. And then we had dinner at the Ambassador's house with Dempsey and Ramsay, the Admiral, and after dinner we went into a room to discuss the plan and Monty said he had to change it, he wanted some more troops, needed to widen the frontages of attack and he asked me to draft a signal to Alex, which I did. And then there was that funny little thing when he said to Ramsay, 'Do you agree with that?' And Ramsay said, 'Yes, I agree with it.' And so Monty said to me, 'Well, just add a little excerpt: Admiral Ramsay agrees.'

And then Bertie [Ramsay] said, 'Hey, hey, I think you'd better leave that out.' I think he was rather frightened about making a decision about a plan without his naval commanders. And Monty said, 'But you said you agreed!'

So in the end Ramsay said, 'All right – send it off.'[2]

Ramsay had good reason to be chary, for when Alexander showed the cable to Cunningham and Tedder in Algiers, Tedder exploded,

[1] Montgomery Papers.
[2] Maj-General Sir Francis de Guingand, interview of 7.5.78.

saying that without the immediate capture of the big Axis aerodromes at Gela and Comiso he could not guarantee air cover to the navy, at which Admiral Cunningham announced he would not commit the navy to an assault operation without guaranteed air cover.

A veritable pantomime now followed. Not only had Monty enlisted the support of Ramsay, which irritated the Commander-in-Chief, Mediterranean, Admiral Cunningham, but he had insisted that his protégé, the young Air Vice-Marshal Broadhurst, should command the whole air support operation, instead of the more senior Air Marshal at Malta: 'We cannot consider seniority and sentiment,' Monty had declared at Algiers on 19 April, 'We have so little time available that we must go for SIMPLICITY.'

Tedder and Cunningham now did everything possible to squash Monty's new plan, and the day after informing Alexander of his unilateral decision to recast his assault, Monty signalled again to Alexander:

> I understand that Cunningham and Tedder have expressed to you their complete disagreement of my proposed plan. . . . I can NOT repeat NOT emphasise too strongly that if we carry out the existing plan it will fail. I am prepared to state on whatever reputation I may possess as a fighting man that the plan put forward by me will succeed. I have reached these conclusions after examining the whole problem with Admiral Ramsay. Would you like me and Ramsay to come over and explain our plans. Meanwhile work is continuing on my plan as time is short.

The Allies were now working on two different plans, Algiers on one and Monty's staff in Cairo on another. Cunningham signalled to the First Sea Lord: 'I am afraid Montgomery is a bit of a nuisance; he seems to think that all he has to do is to say what is to be done and everyone will dance to the tune of his piping. Alexander appears quite unable to keep him in order. Tedder is also absolutely opposed to this new plan.'[1]

Monty, Cunningham and Tedder were thus all complaining at Alexander's lack of clear leadership. Poor Alexander convened a conference on 29 April in Algiers, but Monty fell ill with tonsilitis, de Guingand's aeroplane crashed en route for Algiers, concussing him, and the Commander of 30 Corps, Lt-General Leese, found it impossible to make headway against the most senior Allied Naval and Air Commanders in the Mediterranean. No one met Leese at the aerodrome in Algiers and he had to thumb a lift in a lorry to Allied Forces headquarters. 'I went into the Conference Room to find a table

---

[1] Quoted in Tedder, *With Prejudice*, London 1966.

surrounded with the flags of the Allied Nations and a group of senior officers, all very well and correctly dressed. I had on my usual shirt and shorts and no medal ribbons,' Leese recalled. 'Everyone listened politely. General Alexander was splendid and stood up for me from the start. But the rest of the American and British Officers would have nothing of it until they had heard it from General Montgomery himself. Some would not even believe me when I said that he was ill. . . . That evening I flew back to the Army Commander who did not give me at all a good reception, telling me that I failed in my mission and was no good as a negotiator.'[1]

Ought Monty to have acquiesced? As has been seen, Monty was not originally in favour of landings in Sicily or Italy, feeling that the German forces could be kept tied down in the area by the mere threat of invasion, which should in fact come from Britain across the English Channel. Moreover Monty cannot have been unaware that his staff and senior commanders did not favour an extension of the war into southern Europe either, after the long and taxing march across North Africa. As his GSO 1 (Operations) later explained:

Of course we were amazed that we were invited to invade Sicily. We didn't see any point in doing it. That was our initial reaction – Italy as well – we thought it would take us nowhere: which of course was correct.

I remember great surprise in my mind – I hadn't thought as far ahead as that. . . . And I remember talking, probably to Freddie [de Guingand], saying, 'What on earth, what's the point of this? You get to the Alps, where the hell d'you go from there?'[2]

In General Richardson's later view, 'neither Eisenhower nor Alex had any grip' on the 'Husky' operation, and he recollected that de Guingand, in answer to the question, 'Why the hell are we going there?' had replied with a great combination of frankness and loyalty, 'Well, Master's not very happy about it either, but let's stop bellyaching and get on with it.'[3]

It is clear from his private letters to Brooke, 'Simbo' Simpson and the Reynolds, that Monty was, by the closing stages of the Tunisian campaign, quite exhausted and longing to come home to England for a few days. Even this wish would be misconstrued both by Americans at Algiers and the War Office in London as a desire to 'cash in on' his mushrooming fame at home.[4] Yet from the moment the battle of Alamein was won, Monty had expressed to the Reynolds his

---

[1] General Sir Oliver Leese, unpublished memoirs, communicated to author by Ian Calvocoressi.
[2] General Sir Charles Richardson, interview of 7.11.79.
[3] Ibid.
[4] Cf. diary of Harry C. Butcher, Eisenhower Library, Abilene, Kansas.

desire to take a week's leave in England, and the hope that this would soon be possible he expressed again and again in the succeeding months: 'When the situation here allows,' he wrote on 26 April, 'I shall fly home for a 10 day rest. I sometimes feel I am getting rather exhausted,' he confessed. 'I have been going hard without a break ever since I came here and that was last August; and a great deal has happened in that time. But we have got to get this show properly cleaned up first.'

Others would also feel the strain of unremitting operations in the field without necessarily imagining they would have a week's leave in England. But Monty had not simply played a part in Eighth Army; he had personally re-created it, run on lines of decisiveness and professional efficiency unknown in any other Allied army at that time. Rommel had departed from the North African theatre a broken man; even Monty's Chief of Staff, de Guingand, had suffered under the strain. To give the kind of leadership and inspiration in the field which Montgomery had evinced since his arrival in August 1942 was an unparalleled feat – and if, at the end of the great march across North Africa, he no longer had the resources of tact and discretion to couch his feelings concerning the 'Husky' operation in diplomatic terms, can one blame him? Leese, even though he was directly responsible for the assault landings in the revised southern peninsula area, was unable to make his views prevail at Algiers, and, in Tedder's account, was despatched 'after our conference [to] explain our views to Montgomery.'[1]

Despite exhaustion and rebuff, therefore, Monty refused to recant. He was determined that his faithful veteran troops should make a landing so powerful that not even Hitler would countenance repelling or containing it by the transfer of German troops from the mainland. Thus when Alexander came the next day (30 April) to Monty's Tactical Headquarters Monty not only insisted he recast his plans for the ending of the Tunisian campaign, but concocted a new telegram to be sent to Eisenhower under Alexander's name, recommending the abandonment of Patton's Western Task Force landings in favour of a single thrust in the east.

Whether Monty realised that Tedder and Cunningham now regarded the matter as one of personal prestige is unclear. Tedder had cabled the Chief of the Air Staff, Sir Charles Portal, that he considered 'no compromise is possible on this issue'.[2] Moreover he claimed that 'Eisenhower and Bedell-Smith take a poor view of this affair. . . . Unofficially (since they have not yet been officially involved) they support me and the Admiral.' He also told the C-in-C Air Forces in Cairo that under no circumstances would he accept Broadhurst's

---

[1] Tedder, op. cit.
[2] Ibid.

elevation to command the air side of the invasion, despite Sholto Douglas's agreement with Montgomery that this was sensible. Although he assured Portal that he would 'do all possible to avoid deadlock', Tedder declared that 'if Montgomery proves to be obstinate, a dangerous deadlock is inevitable'.[1]

Monty cannot have seen these cables, but the wise Admiral Ramsay recognised that a telegram emanating from Alexander at Montgomery's field headquarters would look too conspiratorial. Thus shortly after Alexander's departure on 30 April, Monty signalled to him:

> On advice of RAMSAY did not send your wire to EISENHOWER. He considered it might make other people suspicious. Much best to have everything in open court. I suggest full scale conference ALGIERS Sunday 2 May. I can arrive MAISON BLANCHE 1030 hrs. Reply if conference is on.[2]

'Other people' meant Tedder and Cunningham. That evening, after receiving confirmation that the conference was 'on', Monty wrote his letter to Brooke, enclosing a memorandum of the points he would make at Algiers. In this he argued that if the RAF were adamant about securing the Gulf of Gela aerodromes, then: 'The proper answer is to bring two USA Divisions in to land at CENT and DIME, on the south coast, and get the aerodromes. And chuck the Palermo landings for the present. If this were agreed to, then we could all go ahead. The operation would then have every prospect of being a first class show. The effort at present is too dispersed. If we work on the present plan there is likely to be a 1st Class disaster.'

Thus, rather than Alexander having to put pressure privately on Eisenhower, as Tedder and Cunningham were doing, Monty felt that a full-scale showdown 'in the open' was the only way in which the matter could be resolved quickly, and 'unless we get a good and firm plan *at once*, on which we can all work,' he warned Brooke, '*there will be no HUSKY in July*.'

The stage was thus set for the first major breakdown in Allied combined planning since the entry of America into the war – and on 2 May it took place. Monty arrived at Algiers in his Flying Fortress and was driven to Allied Force HQ, 'to find that Alexander could not fly over that day, owing to mist and low cloud,' Monty recorded in his diary. 'Tedder and Cunningham refused to sit in conference unless Alexander was present.'

To Monty this was galling, for on the flight to Algiers he had

[1] Ibid.
[2] Montgomery Papers.

written out the points he would make at the conference, as Charles Richardson, who accompanied him as BGS, later recalled.

> I was sitting next to him and he started to write on his mill-board with his HB pencil and his india rubber close at hand to clear his own mind about how he was going to put forward his plea, or should I say his demand. And he wrote this out, and he then passed it to me and said, 'Charles, Charles, read that, is it clear?' So I read it through and it seemed to me admirably clear. . . . 'Anything you want to add – anything to add?' and I said, 'No, nothing to add, sir.'
> And he said, 'Y'know I've got to say it, got to say it.'

To Richardson this was the mark of great generalship, and 'a great example of the way he did this high level thinking entirely on his own. He used to frequently write it out, I think really to ensure that subsequently he wasn't kicked off it by either different propositions that were put forward, or by the "fog of war".'[1]

Monty's conference address was published subsequently in his *Memoirs*, in 1958. It was indeed a model of clarity – and some cunning. For at the risk of seeming devious, Monty had decided already in Cairo that he would not initially involve Patton's Western Task Force in the dispute, lest it become a British versus American row: 'I had my own ideas about the American landings but did not think the moment was yet opportune to put them forward.' On Ramsay's advice he had even decided not to send the signal he and Alexander had concocted at Eighth Army HQ – for what Monty had in mind was a technique he was to employ more and more in the course of the war: a technique whereby he would paint a picture of deadlock or failure, only to produce, *deux ex machina*, a practicable solution – if all was left up to him.

Tedder and Cunningham's refusal to sit in conference without Alexander appeared to 'put the kaibosh' on Monty's carefully laid plan. Luck, however, now came to Monty's assistance – as he recorded in his diary a few days later.

> Shortly after my arrival at Allied Force H.Q., I met by chance the Chief of Staff to General Eisenhower – in the lavatory. He was Maj-Gen Bedel-Smith, and a very good man.
> He was much upset about the whole thing and we discussed it in the lavatory!! He said that for *political reasons* it was absolutely essential to reach a firm decision, and to get on with it.

[1] Loc. cit.

Bedell Smith, knowing of both Marshall's and Churchill's pressure on Eisenhower to undertake an invasion of Sicily in June, which had been shown to be administratively impossible, was undoubtedly frightened by the political repercussions if the invasion could not even be undertaken in July. Monty thus seized his chance:

I said it was far more important to do so for *military reasons*, and that I would give him the answer to the whole problem at once.

He implored me to give him the answer. I said that the American landings at PALMERMO should be cancelled, and the whole American effort should be put in on the South coast and West of the PACHINO peninsula, with the object of securing the vital airfields in question.[1]

Bedell Smith capitulated. As he later explained, the original plan whereby Patton's Task Force was directed upon Palermo, which had no strategic value other than its port facilities, 'did not please us. So the changes desired by Monty were readily conceded despite the inherent supply problem if Palermo was left for later capture.'[2]

Monty's new plan at least promised to involve the American forces in the main invasion. Eisenhower was consulted, and though he refused to make a formal decision without Alexander being present, he permitted an immediate planning conference to take place at which senior staff officers to Tedder and Cunningham would be present. The Navy protested that they would not be able to supply Patton's force across the Gela beaches indefinitely, but Monty countered this by offering to unload American supplies through Eighth Army's ports of Syracuse and Augusta, once captured. That night, at Eighth Army Tactical Headquarters, Monty signalled to Alexander:

At ALGIERS today I proved that if RAF must have the [Gela] aerodromes in initial bridgehead we could not do our part of HUSKY. I said only sound plan was to put whole US effort in at CENT and DIME [Gulf of Gela] and abandon NW project [Palermo]. EISENHOWER will accept this plan if you agree and recommend it. Only possible snag may be administration and this is being worked out and will be ready for you tomorrow. Suggest you go all out for this plan. EISENHOWER and BEDEL-SMITH completely in favour.[3]

After so much vacillation and argument this did, indeed, seem a miraculous break-through. But Monty, exhausted by battles both

[1] Montgomery Papers, diary entry 6.5.43.
[2] Sidney Matthews, OCMH interview, Military History Institute, Carlisle, Pennsylvania.
[3] Montgomery Papers.

with Germans and with Allied planners, now gave way to that part of his military vanity which seemed completely oblivious to the feelings of Britain's allies. In this very moment of triumph he could not resist inflicting a sore that would fester throughout the war.

CHAPTER TWO

'I should run Husky'

For Monty, the addition of two American divisions to his assault landings in south-eastern Sicily meant that he would in fact have three Corps under his command instead of two, as he had once hoped. 'Add on to message (Most Immediate) to 18th Army Group,' he therefore ordered his signals officer at 8.50 p.m. on 2 May 1943:

> Consider proper answer would be to put US Corps under me and let my Army HQ handle the whole operation of the land battle.[1]

This message marks, after the prelude of the Flying Fortress, undoubtedly the first chapter in the doleful tale of Monty's wartime relations with his American counterparts: a sad tale because Monty was so often correct in his thinking from a purely military standpoint, but so rarely from that of coalition war. Some observers have put this down to a fundamental insensitivity on Monty's behalf; but this does not adequately explain the flaw, for there can be no doubt that in regard to his own men Monty possessed an uncanny sensitivity to the psychology of the British or Commonwealth soldier. Though he might liken his Eighth Army to a great machine of war, its engine perfectly maintained and capable of delivering immense power over prolonged periods, he never sought to liken his soldiers to mechanical objects. If, as Sir Edgar Williams put it, 'Monty was Eighth Army's dynamo', then it was a dynamo that fed on electricity coming from his troops. As Sir Harry Broadhurst later described:

> You see, he made himself unpopular [with other commanders and services] quite unnecessarily. And yet with the troops – oh he was splendid! He used to take me round the front-line after Tripoli – I hated it, didn't like bullets being fired at me unnecessarily getting in and out of bloody jeeps – and then he'd pick on a few people, some corporal lying in a dug-out bit of sand and say: 'Corporal . . .' – and find out all about him. And then the ADC would get the address of his parents and Monty'd go back to his caravan

[1] Montgomery Papers.

after supper in the evening and he'd sit down: 'Dear Mrs Snooks, I met your Charlie today, he's doing very well, could be a sergeant quite soon . . .' – all this sort of thing. And this would go home Air Mail uncensored – you can imagine the impact! And he did it all in his own handwriting, no question of telling his ADC to dictate a letter as most people would, and of course this signature: B. L. Montgomery, General – it made in effect the rounds of the East End of London. And then the letters back [from England] to the front line. . . .

I don't think he did it as a PR exercise. I think he had enormous sympathy for, feeling for the soldiers, and hated casualties, loathed them. . . .[1]

One such soldier was Private Geoffrey Glaister, who later recalled that 'while his [Monty's] showmanship had its detractors among the officers it was a tonic to other ranks', and quoted a letter Monty had written to him in his own hand in the desert on 30 December 1942:

Dear Glaister,
    Thank you for your letter of the 23 Dec.[2] I am glad you wrote to me. A general needs encouragement and inspiration just as much as do his troops, and your letter supplies it. It encourages me to know that you and other soldiers have confidence in me, and are prepared to follow me to victory. And it will be 'Victory'; there is no place for the enemy in N. Africa, and together we will see that he leaves it.
    Good luck to you in 1943.
                        Yours sincerely
                        B. L. Montgomery
                        General

'Monty's secret,' Glaister considered in retrospect, 'was not only that he thought other ranks mattered, but actually showed them that they did, hence their response.'[3] Similarly Sir Edgar Williams later came to feel that Monty 'was able to be a very good commander of soldiers because he had a kind of nous about their reactions. Because on the whole they weren't awfully dissimilar from his own. His was a complex nature, but it was a streamlined nature too. A lot of his ordinary gut-reactions were very much those of the sergeants' mess. . . . Of course he was an astonishingly ill-educated man. I think he rather gloried in being the snook-cocker from Tasmania – he'd been treated at St Paul's as a "colonial", a word of disapprobation in those days. . . . His sense of humour was schoolboyish – the banana-skin

[1]   Air Chief Marshal Sir Harry Broadhurst, interview of 21.12.79.
[2]   Letter quoted in B. L. Montgomery, *Memoirs*, London 1958.
[3]   Letter to author.

joke style. It was astonishing. It was also a little unkind humour too, he did think other people's misfortunes were very funny. Very often they are of course. . . . He did behave in a rather mountebank way, and added fuel to the prejudices against him.'[1]

Much of this prejudice came, as Williams recollected, from a sense of betrayal among the upper and middle classes in England – something Williams discovered when posted back to the United Kingdom later:

> You were always asked, anyone you met, they'd say: Is it true the men all like Montgomery, but the officers all hate him, don't they?
>
> There was a good deal of class about it – this was the young Guardsman on the Staff, or the Cavalry Club gossip deriving from Herbert Lumsden's return and that sort of thing. Montgomery was a chap who 'played up to the proletariat', you see, so the officers couldn't possibly like him – that sort of argument.[2]

Williams, who knew what loyalty and professional admiration Monty inspired among the officers in Eighth Army, was amused by this 'gentlemen versus the players' snobbism, but, while he considered Eighth Army's advance from Alamein to Tunis to have been a 'triumphant' campaign, he would be far from complimentary about the campaign in Sicily, a feeling common to a large number of Eighth Army's desert veterans.

Monty's additional signal to Alexander was indeed the forerunner of many such signals that would bedevil Monty's career now as an Allied and no longer simply British commander. Had Brooke himself accepted Churchill's offer of overall command in the Middle East in August 1942 and thus become Monty's senior officer in the field, matters might have turned out very differently, for Alexander's response to Monty's arrogant and ill-considered suggestion was as evasive as ever. Alexander reached Algiers on 3 May and recommended acceptance of Monty's new 'Husky' plan, signalling to Eighth Army Tactical Headquarters that night: 'Your plan has been approved by C-in-C. Essential for DE GUINGAND or an accredited representative to come here at once to work out details and to ensure co-ordination of both task-forces.'[3]

This signal completely side-stepped the issue of unified command for both planning and assault under the new plan. Had Alexander stamped firmly on the suggestion that Monty take over the reins, a tragic development in Monty's blinkered approach to coalition command might have been stopped at the outset. Brooke would try some

---

[1] Sir Edgar Williams, interview of 20.12.79.
[2] Ibid.
[3] Montgomery Papers.

eight weeks later, but by then the seed was well sown, and Brooke's role too peripheral. Forty-five minutes after receiving Alexander's signal, Monty cabled to Cairo to his administrative representative Colonel Graham: 'My plan has been approved by EISENHOWER. Inform RAMSAY LEESE and FREDDIE. I recommended American Corps should be placed under me and that Eighth Army should run whole operation. Essential for BELCHEM and any others you think necessary to visit ALGIERS at once to work out details and to ensure coordination of both task forces;' and the following morning he offered his BGS, Brigadier Richardson, to help 'ensure coordination'. Although he told Alexander he was 'most anxious to do anything I can to make Husky a success and will do everything in my power to help see this joint operation through and to assist 2 US Corps in dealing with its problems', Monty still considered Patton's Corps should come under Eighth Army's wing, with which Alexander concurred, as Alexander's message to Eisenhower that night (4 May) demonstrates:

> As a result of acceptance by all concerned of present plan, land operations by British and American Task Forces really become one operation. Each will be dependent on the other for direct support in the battle and their administrative needs. As time is pressing, I am convinced that the co-ordination direction and control both tactically and administratively, must be undertaken by one commander and a joint staff. . . . You will see from Montgomery's telegram that he is only too anxious to help in overcoming the problems facing the American Task Force.[1]

Perhaps by not initially mentioning Montgomery as the 'one commander', Alexander hoped to convince Eisenhower first of the logic, then of the commander himself. Meanwhile Monty, who had received a copy of Alexander's signal to Eisenhower, fretted at the waste of time and attempted to ginger Alexander with yet more messages. On 5 May he wrote an extended letter to Alexander, ending with his views on the command structure for Husky:

Organisation for Command
Only one commander can run the battle in HORRIFIED in the new plan. It seems clear that Eighth Army HQ should command and control the whole operation, with 2 US Corps included in Eighth Army.

This was not all. The Army HQ should be situated in Malta, Monty laid down, and 'at all costs Allied Force HQ should be prevented

[1] Ibid.

from going there too. I must have there the Main HQ of all three Corps. There will be no room for anyone else.'

However militarily sensible such a proposition, the reference to Allied Force HQ must have seemed a considerable insult to Alexander – an insult which Monty attempted to conceal by his insistence on great urgency now: 'It is impossible to overstress the vital need for decisions. . . . Every day matters. We cannot have more delay. If [this] is agreed, I suggest I then deal direct with Bedel-Smith. You will be fully occupied with the battle in Tunisia, and will not have time to bother about it.'[1] Lest this letter take too long by courier, Monty that afternoon sent a signal:

Essential I go ALGIERS on Friday 7 May and get decisions and an agreed set-up. Every day now is vital. Please tell BEDEL-SMITH of my visit and ask him to help me to get things sorted out. Will arrive Maison Blanche 1000 hrs 7 May.[2]

From Monty's point of view, he had leaned over backwards as Eighth Army Commander to ensure a successful conclusion to the Tunisian campaign, insisting on Alexander regrouping, and mounting Operation 'Strike' using Eighth Army formations. In return he now expected Alexander to hand over to him the running of the Sicily operation, as he clearly set down in his diary on the eve of his trip to Algiers.

I am going to ALGIERS tomorrow, 7 May, to have the whole matter out with the Chief of Staff to Eisenhower, and to try and get something settled. He is a firm ally of mine and I hope to get a move on. I very much doubt if Eisenhower will allow 2 U.S. Corps to be in Eighth Army; he will want it to be an American expedition of its own, and under Force 141 [Alexander's 'Husky' staff].

But Force 141 is not capable of exercising command; it is a very theoretical planning staff, which up-to-date has shown itself to be of little value. There is no doubt that Allies are very difficult people to fight with, especially when political considerations are allowed to over-ride all sound military common sense.

I shall see tomorrow what the answer is. But *some* answer we must have.

To the CIGS, Sir Alan Brooke, Monty wrote in the same vein on 6 May 1943:

I am going to Algiers tomorrow to suggest that I get my decisions straight from Allied Force HQ . . . If they will NOT agree to this,

[1] Ibid.
[2] Ibid.

then I think we shall be sunk as we have no more time left. We must either get on with it, or chuck it. I imagine I can get them to agree. But I feel we shall have a very complicated set-up for organisation and command, because for political reasons I don't think they will agree to 2 U.S. Corps being in my army; they will insist on a separate American Task Force. So we will have to make the best of that.

Bedell Smith *was* an ally, certainly. Lt-Commander Butcher, Eisenhower's ADC, recorded in his diary on 5 May: 'The command set-up is developing more levels than a battleship. . . . Eisenhower, to Alexander to Montgomery and to Patton, for the Husky job. Too many headquarters, Beetle says, and maybe so;'[1] and Patton, after attending the 7 May conference in Algiers, noted in his diary that 'Smith talked a lot and made nasty remarks'.[2] But not even Bedell Smith could fail to be aware of the blow to American morale, both in the field and at home, if after six whole months in North Africa and the Mediterranean the United States was still fielding only a single Corps in battle, and one that was to be placed under the famous British Eighth Army umbrella. Bedell Smith thus ruled, on behalf of Eisenhower, that 'the American contingent had to be a separate expedition, and that meant Force 141 coming into it,' as Monty recorded in his diary. 'It was something to get that clear, as the organisation for command and control could now be worked out.'

Monty thus accepted that Alexander would command 'Husky' – to his private chagrin. 'Political reasons necessitated a very clumsy and complicated set-up, and one opposed to all sound military commonsense. The task of running the battle in SICILY was really one for a single Army HQ,' he remarked sourly of the decision. He was becoming irritated by Alexander's ineffectiveness. In his diary Patton also referred to the 'lack of force on the part of Alexander, who cut a sorry figure at all times. He is a fence walker,' and he called Alexander's Force 141 Headquarters 'a mess';[3] meanwhile Monty, in *his* diary, referred to Force 141's planning as 'unreal and unsound. Every plan put up by the Planning Staff had been agreed to by Alexander, and I do not think he ever had the full operational repercussions put before him by anyone qualified to do so. But he agreed with all the plans. And then when I sent in and disagreed and said the plan would result in a military disaster, and submitted an alternative plan – *he agreed with me also.*' In Monty's eyes Force 141 was 'a theoretical planning staff. The head of it, Major-Gen Charles Gairdiner [sic] is not up to it; he does not know the battle repercussions; he is a bundle of nerves; he inspires no confidence. The whole

[1] Loc. cit.
[2] *The Patton Papers, 1940–1945*, ed. Martin Blumenson, Boston 1974.
[3] Ibid.

Monty and his three Corps commanders: from left, Lt-Generals Leese, Lumsden and Horrocks. (*Imperial War Museum*)

General von Thoma, Commander of the famed Afrika Korps, surrenders to Lt-General Montgomery at Eighth Army Tactical Headquarters on the afternoon of 4 November 1942. (*Collection of J. R. Henderson*)

Above the famous Halfaya Pass Monty pauses for lunch from a hamper. Behind him stands his ADC, Captain John Poston. (*Imperial War Museum*)

Monty looks at coastal guns against the background of smoking ships in Benghazi harbour. (*Imperial War Museum*)

'Desert rat takes time off from chasing desert fox to sit for his portrait by South African war artist, Captain Neville Lewis, in Cairo.' In fact Monty's return to Cairo on 6 December 1942 was made to ensure full logistical support in the forthcoming offensive to capture Tripoli from the east. (*Imperial War Museum*)

The Battle of Tripoli. Monty himself controlled the right flank of the advance, while Leese's 30 Corps attacked inland via Azizia (*Imperial War Museum*)

Monty receives the surrender of Tripoli by the immaculate Italian Military Governor of Libya at the city gates, 28 January 1943. (*Imperial War Museum*)

Lt-Colonel 'Bill' Williams, an Oxford don, rapidly became Monty's senior Intelligence officer. (*Imperial War Museum*)

Brig. Sir Brian Robertson was Chief Admin Officer. (*Imperial War Museum*)

Brig. Kisch, the Chief Engineer. (*Imperial War Museum*)

Chief of Staff, Brig. 'Freddie' de Guingand, acknowledged to be one of the cleverest and most affection-inspiring staff officers in the British army. (*Imperial War Museum*)

Brig. Kirkman, the Chief Gunner (*Imperial War Museum*)

Lt-Col. Richardson, the Chief of Operations, Eighth Army. (*Imperial War Museum*)

Tripoli was the first Axis city to fall to the Allies in World War II, exactly three months after the Battle of Alamein. After Eighth Army's epic 1,450-mile march, Monty arranged a parade in the city, but otherwise declared it out of bounds lest the army become 'soft'. He himself set up his headquarters some miles outside the city. (*Imperial War Museum*)

At Tripoli there was a pause until the harbour was cleared and supplies were brought up. Monty was soon joined by the intrepid French general Leclerc, who had made a 2,000-mile march to fight with the Eighth Army. (*Imperial War Museum*)

During the four-week pause at Tripoli, Monty arranged perhaps the most remarkable 'teach-in' of WWII: an in-depth discussion of modern battle techniques. He invited senior officers from all over the world. General Patton, attending, from Morocco, was heard to say: 'I may be old, I may be deaf, and I may be stoopid, but it just don't mean a thing to me.' (*Imperial War Musuem*)

Rommel's attack at Kasserine was a severe blow to Eisenhower and the inexperienced 2 US Corps. On 6 March Rommel launched a similar spoiling attack on Eighth Army but met a very different reception. One of the 52 tanks the Germans left on the battlefield when they retreated. (*Imperial War Museum*)

AVM Harry Broadhurst, legendary commander of the Desert Air Force and pioneer of 'blitz' close-air support, talking to Eisenhower. De Guingand, Monty and General Horrocks listen. (*Imperial War Museum*)

Monty receives the surrender of Field-Marshal Messe, Rommel's successor as commander of the German–Italian Panzer Army. (*Imperial War Museum*)

General Alexander walking with Lt-General Anderson, commander of the Br. First Army. Alexander had intended to sack Anderson in February, but was too weak-willed. (*Imperial War Museum*)

On 17 May 1943, five days after the Axis surrender in N. Africa, Monty flew back to England in his Flying Fortress. At Northolt aerodrome he was 'mobbed' — the first actual indication of the national hero he had become. (*Imperial War Museum*)

In the street the crowds fight literally to touch the hem of Monty's garments — the man who brought victory to Britain's army after four years of war and defeat. (*Fox Photos*)

Monty relaxes in the country with the guardians of his son David: Major Tom Reynolds and his wife Phyllis, to whom Monty would write every two or three days of the war. (*Fox Photos*)

atmosphere is far removed from war, and the work they produce has no relation to the practical realities of battle.' The problem was, as he had written to Brooke, that Alexander was too 'deeply involved in ensuring all is well in First Army, since Anderson is no good. . . . We get back always to the same point – Alexander ought to be sitting back and thinking, and instead he is trying to bolster up Anderson (First Army). If he had removed Anderson at once, in March, we would not be in the mess we are in now.' However Eisenhower's and Alexander's acceptance of this new plan at least augured well – if he, Monty, could conduct the Sicilian enterprise. 'The proper answer is to let Alexander finish off the TUNISIAN war, and to cut him right out of HUSKY. I should run HUSKY. With the new plan it is a nice tidy command for one Army H.Q., and Eighth Army should run the whole thing. I would then deal direct with Allied Force H.Q. [Eisenhower]. . . . I have done my part in the Tunisian war coming 2,000 miles from EGYPT. I should now pull out, and should run HUSKY,' he entered on 6 May.

It is easy to see, therefore, how men like Tedder began to spread word that Monty 'thinks of himself as Napoleon', as Tedder remarked over a private lunch with Patton;[1] yet the fact remains that once Patton had got over the crisis in 'Husky' planning induced by Monty's new plan, he very quickly came to see that Monty's solution was, militarily, the simplest, neatest and in fact easiest to perform. On 7 May he noted in his diary that 'the new set up is better in many ways than the old', and he jotted down that 'Monty is a forceful, selfish man, but still a man. I think he is a far better leader than Alexander. . . . I begin to think that the new operation, from every standpoint except supply, is easier than the old [plan].' By 9 May he was noting that he did not 'wholly trust' Tedder, who 'seems to me more interested in producing an independent air force . . . than in winning the war', and was completely reconciled to Monty's plan.[2]

Monty's concern with the arrangements for command, however megalomaniacal it might appear to rivals like Tedder, and however innocent of political ramifications, struck at the very heart of the problem now, a problem that would pervade the conduct of the rest of the war in the West. It is for this reason that one needs to consider the planning stage of 'Husky' in such detail, a development largely ignored by historians; for in many fundamental respects the problems of the later Allied campaigns in Italy as well as North-west Europe were prefigured in the problems over 'Husky'. Among these, the question of command, of the proper organisation of the invading forces and their commander, was probably the most crucial: for on 17 May, in response to a suggestion received the previous day from

[1] *The Patton Papers*, op. cit.
[2] Ibid.

General Marshall, Eisenhower telephoned Patton 'to say we will probably do Husky as an Army'. Although he had never asked him to do this, Patton was 'glad he is going to', as Patton noted.[1]

This decision, on top of Bedell Smith's rejection of Monty's proposition on 7 May that Eighth Army should 'run Husky', with 2 US Corps under command, finally opened the doors to coalition battle of a kind not seen since the fateful days of spring 1940, when British, Belgian and French Armies each went their separate ways to destruction. For the creation of *two* Allied Armies for Sicily, instead of Monty's preferred single Army, now ushered into Allied operations a political principle that committed the Allies to failure upon failure, since no overall commander could be found with both the tact to combine the separate national wills of their forces *and* the military genius to command them in the field.

Sicily, then, was the forerunner of this development, and though the historian may be right to decry Monty's insensibility to the likely political repercussions of his views and behaviour, he must nevertheless acknowledge the military logic which inspired such attitudes.

Shortly after his return from leave in England, Monty set down his private views on the way the 'Husky' operation had been mounted. Like the disastrous BEF campaign before Dunkirk, it was Monty's clear-cut appreciation of how *not* to command and mount an expedition that would be the key to his own efforts when entrusted, himself, with command of such a force. Just as Gort's ineffectual display in Flanders and France became the motor behind Monty's great training exercises in England and his take-over of command of Eighth Army from Auchinleck in August 1942, so the lessons of Eisenhower's and Alexander's vacillations and weakness in 1943 would not be lost on Montgomery when, at the end of the year, he was at least entrusted with command of the Allied armies for the long-awaited cross-Channel assault.

Sicily, then, was to Monty an object-lesson in how *not* to plan and command an invasion. On the eve of embarkation he set down the salient feature of the lesson, which would stand him in such good stead the following year. 'Fighting the Germans is quite easy,' he began;

> the tiring thing is the way one has to fight to keep one's own show from going off the rails.
>
> Allied Force H.Q. at Algiers is a most curious place. The atmosphere there is international, cum War Office, cum Washington, cum Downing Street. The great thing is to reach an agreement, or find a formula, and little or no attention is paid to the fact that the

[1] Ibid.

agreement or formula is NOT one that will win the battle. There is little knowledge there as to what is wanted to win battles.

Obviously some such H.Q. is necessary. But it must keep itself well clear of operational planning and such like things.

The cardinal error behind the current Allied approach to strategic operations was to Monty quite straightforward:

There is an idea current in our army that a planning staff is all that is necessary to plan an operation; this staff is then collected from such officers as are available, and generally very few of them know much about battle fighting.

No commander is appointed.

It is like an orchestra trying to play without a conductor.

The staff make a plan and work out the details; no experienced fighting commander handles the party.

This was plainly nonsensical.

The plan for all battle ventures or operations of war must be made by the Commander who is to carry it out,

Monty insisted;

he must make the original outline plan on which detailed planning will begin. Nothing else is any good.

The broad strategic conception is decided by the Chiefs of Staff and the Statesmen. Once that is decided the operational commander must take charge and make his outline plan; then the planning staff get down to details.

To attempt any other method, or to think that a planning staff can work out a plan without a commander, is merely to ask for trouble. But this is what we did in HUSKY; and it is being done now in England over the cross-channel venture.

This alarming truth had become clear when, having got the outline plan for 'Husky' settled and the detailed planning properly set up, Monty had flown in mid-May to London. There he had found the whole Allied Second Front venture being planned by an artillery staff officer who had never commanded more than a battery – a man whose only experience of modern war was when, as a Brigadier, he had taken an ill-fated unarmoured artillery support group in search of 1st Armoured Division south of the Seine in June 1940: Lt-General Frederick Morgan, Chief of Staff to an as yet unappointed Supreme Allied Commander (COSSAC).

The result of such unrealistic planning, in Monty's eyes, could only be that the weak and charming prospered, while those with direct responsibility for soldiers' lives had to speak up at the cost of becoming highly unpopular.

The whole story of Husky is that of one long continuous fight to get what we wanted. The moment the planning became operational it at once became clear that there was no one at Allied Force H.Q. or at Force 141 (ALEXANDER'S H.Q.) who knew what was necessary, or how to build up an operation, or the operational repercussions of decisions given.

No one, from EISENHOWER and ALEXANDER downwards, really knew the business. But the senior staff officers *thought they knew*, so our troubles then began and it became one long fight to get what we wanted.

Force 141 should have fought our battles for us. But ALEXANDER liked to do things by agreement and compromise; this is very pleasant, and everyone says what a nice person you are, and how easy you are to work with. But you don't get what you ought to get. . . .

The whole thing has been most exhausting, and one has felt at times that one just could not go on with it.

But of course one had to go on with it. Some people would take the line of least resistance and always agree with everything. Personally I will always fight for what I know is right, and which means men's lives if you don't get it.

CHAPTER THREE

Interlude in England

By the time Monty had wrested approval of the new 'Husky' plan from Algiers and cleared up outstanding questions at Force 545 headquarters in Cairo, he was a weary man. Though his Army was still fighting at Enfidaville, he flew to Algiers to get a decision on unified command for 'Husky' on 7 May; on 9 May he flew once more to see Alexander at Constantine, and on 10 May he journeyed to Cairo for three days 'and saw my staff there, and had conferences with them'. He was thus in Cairo when the news was announced that military resistance in North Africa had ended – 'a major disaster for the Germans,' as Monty wrote several days later. 'All his troops, stores, dumps, heavy weapons and equipment, were captured. Very few personnel got away'. Together with the surrender of Paulus's 6th Army in February, the capitulation of the Axis forces in North Africa marked the beginning of Hitler's downfall. At Stalingrad some 94,000 Axis troops surrendered with General Paulus; in North Africa some 275,000 prisoners were taken – losses of men, equipment and morale which could never be restored. 'From a purely military point of view the holding on in North Africa once the MARETH line and GABES Gap had been broken through, could never be justified,' Monty noted in his diary. 'Politically it may have been necessary. . . . The lesson surely is that it is very dangerous to undertake things which are militarily quite unsound, just for political reasons. It may sometimes be necessary; but it will generally end in disaster. The contribution of the Eighth Army to the final victory in Tunisia has been immense. It drove Rommel and his Army out of Egypt, out of Cyrenaica, out of Tripolitania, and then helped the First Army and the Americans to finish him off in Tunisia. Only first-class troops could have done it, and it has been a great honour to command such a magnificent Army.' Simultaneously he issued his last desert message to the troops, congratulating them:

As our Prime Minister said at Tripoli in February last, it will be a great honour to be able to say in years to come:
  'I MARCHED AND FOUGHT WITH THE EIGHTH ARMY.'

However he warned too that the war was not over:

And what of the future? Many of us are probably thinking of our families in the home country, and wondering when we shall be able to see them.

But I would say to you that we can have today only one thought, and that is to see this thing to the end; and then we will be able to return to our families, honourable men. . . .

Unlike any of the other speechifying and self-congratulation that went on in Tunisia at the end of the campaign, Monty had gone to the heart of the simple soldier's psychology, which, as Sir Edgar Williams reflected, was not so different from Monty's own. On 13 May Monty returned from Cairo to Eighth Army headquarters near Sousse and received Field-Marshal Messe, who had surrendered earlier in the day to General Freyberg, Acting Commander of 10 Corps. 'He dined with me at Main Army H.Q. on 13 May and we discussed various aspects of the battles we had fought against each other,' Monty recorded in his diary. What he did not record was that in surrendering to Freyberg, Messe had said he wished General Freyberg to have his special caravan – 'which was rumoured to have a special marble bath and great internal luxuries,' as Major-General Oswald later recalled.

However Messe could not give it to Freyberg as it had disappeared. Freyberg immediately sent out a signal to all units of Eighth Army asking for the whereabouts of Field-Marshal Messe's caravan, and asking that it be returned to 2 NZ Div. HQ. Unfortunately a copy of the signal went to Monty's Tac HQ.

'What's all this about?' queried Monty, seeing the signal. On being told about the luxury caravan he said, 'Send a signal to NZ Div HQ: "Caravan to be brought to my Tac HQ straight away"!'[1]

Messe had handled his army with more aplomb than Allied historians have usually given him credit for – certainly as well as Rommel, after the latter's disastrous Medenine offensive. 'He wasn't a fool,' Sir Edgar Williams later remarked, 'he was quite a shrewd old codger, much as I imagine that Joffre was.'[2]

Monty, having taken possession of his opponent's caravan, complete with its marble bath, remained at Eighth Army headquarters for a few more days, making final arrangements for those divisions which would be leaving Eighth Army, such as the New Zealanders, as well as those earmarked for 'Husky'. Then with some relief he

[1] Maj-General M. St J. Oswald, interview of 22.4.80.
[2] Loc. cit.

boarded his Flying Fortress, setting a course for London. 'It is a great thing to have your own aeroplane, to start *when* you like and go *where* you like,' he had written to the Reynolds ten days after the delivery of the Fortress. 'A part of it has been fitted up as a very comfortable little study for me, with two armchairs and a table for writing, etc. You can fly at 200 miles an hour for eleven hours, without a stop. When the situation here allows I shall fly home for a 10 day rest.' Now the moment had come – and with it emerged again that strenuous concern to keep his 'family' at arm's length. 'My sister (Mrs Holderness) wrote and told me how well he [David] was looking when she visited you to see the portrait,' he wrote on 7 May. 'I find the various members of my family are apt to be very trying, and particularly my mother – who is on the 80 mark. They are all now writing and saying they must see me if I should come home. It will be my one desire to see *none* of them; they would drive me mad between them. So you must always display complete ignorance of my movements, and tell them you have no idea where I am – even if I should be at Amesbury [School, the home of the Reynolds].

'I must say I long to be able to get home and have a quiet rest at Amesbury. It may be possible before long. But not a word to anyone, and especially not to my family.'

There can be little doubt about the emotional intensity of Monty's feelings, for this letter followed another, even more negative, letter of 2 May, the day on which Monty went to Algiers to present his case for a revised 'Husky':

One of my sisters wrote & said they had heard from you or Tom that I might be home soon on leave.

It is most important *NEVER* to mention *anything* about me or my movements to ANY of my family at ANY time.

If and when I come to England it will be kept a very close secret, and the world in general will not think I have left Africa.

Yet if this strange family-phobia, like the sudden rejection of his step-daughter-in-law, must cause us to question Monty's equilibrium, it must also be set beside a concern for the welfare of others. From the British Embassy in Cairo on 12 May he had written to his again recuperating Chief of Staff, Freddie de Guingand:

My dear Freddie,

I am in Cairo checking up on HUSKY. Before coming here I visited Algiers and got various things agreed as a result of the acceptance of my plan.

I then visited Alexander and got everything I wanted agreed to. There is now no need for worry on any matter. I have had conferences here and have explained the whole business to everyone; the foundations and framework of the whole project are now firm.

I am quite happy about the Air matters.

In fact everything is going along so well that I am myself going off to England on Sunday next, 16 May; Army H.Q. pulls out of the battle that day and goes back to the Tripoli area. Oliver [Leese] will be in charge while I am away; Belchem[1] is running everything quite excellently. Charles Richardson will be at Algiers as my representative at Force 141. I have persuaded Alex to remove Charles Gairdner; he is useless.

Now about yourself.

It is absolutely vital that you should get quite fit *before* you come back.

You are not to worry about the business, or even to think about it. It is quite unnecessary for anyone to go up and see you, and keep you in touch.

There is nothing to worry about; everything is now splendid.

You must stay where you are; amuse yourself; have a thorough good rest; and be back here on 1st June *and not before*. I will be back myself by 5 June at Tripoli (Main Army).

I shall come to Cairo about 8 June, & go off with Ramsay to the rehearsals about 11 or 12 June.

Show these orders to your wife and tell her I rely on her to see them carried out. You are far too valuable to be wasted, and I should be 'in the soup' if you came back too soon and cracked up again later.

So stay where you are and be back here by 1st June.

Good luck to you.

Yours ever
B. L. Montgomery

It was hard for a senior staff officer not to feel loyalty and gratitude for an Army Commander who showed such consideration; indeed for his staff he was a commander whose ilk would not be seen again. By leaving all the detail to them, Monty was 'free for the really important issues,' recalled Sir Charles Richardson, 'and it was quite clear to all of us that it was his brain and his decisions that were dominating the scene the whole time'[2] – something which certainly could not be said of Alexander, nor of Anderson; moreover 'decisions once made were very very rarely changed and so the staff were able to get going, in a very informal atmosphere to do all their

---

[1] R. F. K. (David) Belchem became Eighth Army GSO1 (Operations) when Charles Richardson was sent to Algiers.

[2] Interview of 20.11.79.

business without having chopping and changing brought in – getting on with the detail'.[1]

As the staff got on with the detail – the planners now finding 'a new sense of direction' as even the British Official Historian acknowledged[2] – Monty flew to England, arriving on 17 May. Allied Force HQ in Algiers, according to Commander Butcher's diary, was particularly concerned that, if Monty gave press conferences in Britain, he might hog the limelight which, after victory in North Africa, Eisenhower's headquarters naturally considered due to Algiers.[3] Even Horrocks's final offensive which took Tunis and the Cape Bon peninsula had been light-heartedly described by the BBC as a 'left hook by Eighth Army', to the righteous indignation of General Anderson. Both Alexander and Eisenhower had formally complained to the War Office. On behalf of Brooke, the Vice-CIGS, Lt-General Nye 'sent Ike a story from a London newspaper giving credit to Alexander and Anderson and sort of by-passing Montgomery. It is apparent the British have a way of dealing with glory-grabbing generals,' Butcher noted with satisfaction.[4]

This concern about Montgomery's popularity was unfortunate, for it often made Monty's obstinate insistence on sound military decisions appear to be the product of vanity rather than logic or battlefield experience. Yet it was understandable enough in a largely American headquarters almost a thousand miles from the front and abounding with staff officers who were all too similar to those in rear-line HQs during the First World War. Monty's insistence on the Flying Fortress might cause bitter resentment, yet not only Eisenhower flew everywhere in Tunisia, Algeria and Morocco in his own Flying Fortress, but so did his Chief of Staff, Major-General Bedell Smith and even the senior administrative commanders.[5] Equally there was great resentment when Bedell Smith returned from a trip to Washington and announced that Montgomery was now a national hero in America, whereas Eisenhower was still comparatively unknown. When 'Vulcan', Alexander's first attempt at a 'final' offensive, failed, Butcher noted in his diary that Eisenhower's days as Commander-in-Chief were numbered unless something happened quickly: '[Ike] is shooting "the wad". If they can't break through then he may be on his way home, defeated,' Butcher recorded on 25 April 1943.[6] The necessity for transferring more Eighth Army units to Anderson's front for the eventual break-out

[1] Sir Charles Richardson, MOD filmscript 'Montgomery and his Staff'.
[2] C. J. C. Molony, op. cit.
[3] In Butcher diary, loc. cit.
[4] Ibid.
[5] Ibid.
[6] Ibid.

only increased the feeling of aggravation, which reached its apogee when Monty forced Allied Headquarters to alter the Husky plan on 2 May. Butcher's diary for 2 May is missing, but his account of the 'preliminaries' at the end of April demonstrate the extent of Allied Force HQ's suspicions of Monty's motives. 'Essence of his [Monty's] objections was that his part in Husky had to be so strong his risk of defeat would be nil. . . . Ike sides with Air and Navy viewpoints and may have to referee the inter-service British scrap. Then "Monty" could appeal to his home government, worse still, says he won't attack if it isn't done his way! "Monty" is riding a wave of popular acclaim and seems to think he can't be wrong,' Butcher recorded for 29 April.[1]

Butcher, whose main responsibility was the PR side of Eisenhower's headquarters, reflected the public relations man's concern with 'acclaim' and laurels, a concern which has characterised so much writing about Eisenhower as a military commander ever since. Yet there can be no doubt that men such as Butcher, who was as ignorant about military matters as he was about naval matters (he confessed in his diary to not knowing the difference between longitude and latitude), only contributed further to the unreal atmosphere that pervaded Eisenhower's headquarters: a headquarters which, as the Tunisian campaign came to its belated close, became a hot-bed of jockeying for position. Eisenhower, dealing directly with Marshall, held ultimate power over the fortunes and careers of many thousands of officers, British as well as American, and a shameful air of obsequiousness began to fill the endless offices of AFHQ Algiers once victory was assured.[2] Patton, dependent on Eisenhower's 'favour', was even cajoled into writing a hymn of praise about Ike's merits to Marshall. 'He walked the floor for some time, orating, and then asked me to mention how hard he had worked – what great risks he had taken – and how well he had handled the British, in my next letter to General Marshall. I wrote a letter which largely overstated his merits, but I felt that I owe him a lot and must stay in with him. I lied in a good cause.'[3]

In fact Eisenhower *had* performed miracles of diplomatic and political skill in harmonising the Allied effort in North-west Africa, but this only served to overshadow and conceal his failings as a military commander – failings which, like Alexander's, Monty felt he must make up for on behalf of the troops. Aware that he was regarded in Algiers as a very tiresome person, he was therefore the more glad to get far away from that imbroglio to England. His plane, carrying his Chief of Intelligence, Colonel Willliams, his 'official

[1] Ibid.
[2] Ibid.
[3] *The Patton Papers*, op. cit.

photographer' Geoffrey Keating, his two ADCs and an assortment of passengers from North Africa, landed first at Prestwich, then at Northolt on 17 May, escorted by two squadrons of Polish Spitfires stationed at the aerodrome:

> When he stepped out of the aeroplane he chatted with the members of the American crew for a few minutes. He looked well but fine-drawn, and he told me he was a little tired. No wonder!

the Director of Military Operations, General Kennedy, recalled, recollecting also that Monty was wearing his

> desert kit . . . that is to say, his battle dress with a sweater sticking out a foot below his jacket, and of course, his usual beret bearing the Tank Corps as well as the General's badge. His official photographer took some photographs, and then we drove off, to the accompaniment of cheers from the men at the R.A.F. station, who were assembled to greet him. . . .
>
> I deposited him at Claridge's, where his rooms had been booked in the name of 'Colonel Lennox', since we did not want the Germans to know he was coming before he arrived.
>
> Next day, at his request, we assembled the senior officers of the Canadian division, which was to be sent by sea direct to Sicily, and he gave them an exposition of the 'Husky' plan. This he did in a most impressive way, explaining it all most clearly and with tremendous confidence. He repeated the important points many times – repetition had become a pronounced mannerism of his. His statement was immensely effective, and when it was completed, there could be no doubt in anybody's mind about what was to be done. . . . I got the impression that any officer who might have come to the conference with misgivings in his mind must have left it feeling that the operation could not possibly fail.[1]

There were meetings with the Canadian Army Commander, General McNaughton, the Divisional Commander, and with the heads of the various departments at the War Office where, among other things, the plans for cross-Channel attack were discussed. The object of Monty's visit to England had been to rest, but as he wrote to Phyllis Reynolds the day after his arrival, it did not look as though he would now get away from London until the weekend.

That afternoon (18 May) Monty had been invited to tea at Bucking-

---

[1] John Kennedy, *The Business of War*, London 1957. The 1st Canadian Division had been belatedly included in the invasion for political reasons, replacing Monty's old 3rd (Iron) Division.

ham Palace. He had ascertained, via the Military Secretary, that it was permissible for him to appear in his now famous desert dress; the King, Queen and Princesses Elizabeth and Margaret were there – 'a family party and quite delightful,' Monty appended to his letter to Phyllis Reynolds that night:

My dear Phyllis,
    I will be home on Friday (21st) about 12.30 or so. I cannot manage it earlier. It will be delightful to see you all again.
    Life here is very hectic. I went to a theatre tonight and got completely mobbed by the crowd.

The play *Arsenic and Old Lace* was performed to a packed house; at the end the audience stood and cheered not the cast, but General Montgomery in his box. Outside the theatre there were crowds ten deep, gathering to catch sight of him, even to touch him as he left. The same was repeated at his hotel, and he was relieved to reach the asylum of Amesbury on 21 May. There, for the first time since the previous year, he was able to have a complete rest, without responsibilities or engagements, and to drive over to Winchester to see David. He stayed at Amesbury for a week, which must have done much for his mental as well as physical health, for his letters thereafter had the same jaunty ring as his first letters from the Western Desert and were filled with what one can only call boastful self-irony over the sudden manifestations of fame. On 27 May he addressed at the War Office the senior officers of the three services who were to participate in the invasion of Sicily. Even General McNaughton was moved to write of the 'very fine impression' Monty had made, and how the Eighth Army Commander had 'earned the confidence of all present in his plans',[1] In the evenings Monty either dined quietly with colleagues, or attended another theatre 'show'. Indeed, restored to energetic good health, he now began to enjoy himself and the unexpected public adulation so much that Brooke was obliged to send him a peremptory summons to return to the field of war and attend the great council of war which Churchill, on his way back from Washington, had convened in Algiers.

Claridges, Brooke Street, W1
1 June

My dear Phyllis,
    I am off this morning. I had arranged various things for today, including the theatre tonight. But Winston is at the other end,

---

[1] Quoted in G. W. L. Nicholson, *The Canadians in Italy* (Official Canadian History), Ottawa 1956.

shouting for me!! So I have to cancel the theatre and go. . . .
Goodbye and thank you ever so much,
Monty

However, the next day he wrote again to say that bad weather had caused the postponement of his departure, thus enabling him after all to see *The Watch on the Rhine* at the theatre, which he considered 'first class'.

Meanwhile, to the consternation of his ADCs, when they now went to the cashier to settle their hotel bill, they found it had already been settled.

> When we came back to England before the Sicily landing we stayed at Claridge's

Johnny Henderson later recalled. He and the other ADC, John Poston,

> had everything we wanted in our bedroom – champagne sent up, theatre tickets, etc. – and we went down the day before we were to leave to tell the accounts department to send the bill to us, we wanted to pay for it. And they said, 'Oh no, the General has told us he is paying.'
>
> And we said, 'You can't do that – you simply can't! He'll see what we've been up to – you can't!'
>
> And the cashier said, 'Matter of fact, it's been paid, and you're leaving in the morning. It's all been paid.'
>
> We were shocked. 'Good Heavens!' And we decided the only thing was to say, 'Well, Sir, there's been a most awful mistake, and we're frightfully sorry, let us put this right.' So we did. And he said, 'No, no, I wanted you fellows to enjoy yourself. That's it, that's all.'
>
> Do you know, you couldn't even thank him! – if you tried to thank him, he just discarded it – it embarrassed him. . . .[1]

To Henderson, this was an illustration of the untrumpeted generosity that went in strangest tandem with Monty's boastful ego: a quality that would remain entirely unknown to outsiders. Yet even on the return journey to Algiers in the Flying Fortress Monty's consideration for others was in evidence, as the young Commander of the Desert Air Force discovered. The weather on the night of 1 June had seemed to preclude departure on 2 June, 'but I decided to go as far as Cornwall anyhow, and on getting there we found it was possible and started off,' Monty explained in a subsequent letter to Phyllis Reynolds. Air Marshal Broadhurst recalled:

[1] J. R. Henderson, interview of 13.8.81.

He [Monty] called me up about two o'clock in the morning. I was staying in a pub on the south coast and he said, 'We've got to be back for the conference tomorrow. I'm taking off at eight and if you like I'll give you a lift.' So I galloped off to the aerodrome, sat in the bomb bay and we took off at nought feet right across the Atlantic, and he sat there reading *The Times* newspaper as if nothing was happening. I was absolutely scared stiff.

Broadhurst's ADC followed him in the Hudson which the RAF provided. It never arrived.

I said, 'Signal England and find out what's happened.' Back came a message: my aeroplane shot down in the Bay of Biscay. Everybody killed.[1]

The Flying Fortress had proved to be far more than a status symbol. But at Algiers on the night of 2 June Monty walked quite innocently into a dressing-down from Brooke that must have reminded him of the day in France 1940 when Lord Gort was crying for his blood after the issuing of instructions about contraception, sexual hygiene and the avoidance of VD. The occasion is well described in Brooke's diary: 'Montgomery arrived last night and I had a long talk with him until PM sent for him. He requires a lot of educating to make him see the whole situation and the War as a whole outside the Eighth Army orbit. A difficult mixture to handle, brilliant commander in action and trainer of men, but liable to commit untold errors, due to lack of tact, lack of appreciation of other people's outlook. It is most distressing that the Americans do not like him, and it will always be a difficult matter to have him fighting in close proximity to them.'[2] In fact Brooke had got a garbled version of the Flying Fortress story which he muddled when, after the war, he wrote his *Notes on My Life*, but there was no mistaking the American ill-feeling towards Monty which Brooke encountered in Algiers, or the dressing-down he gave to the Eighth Army Commander. Some weeks later, writing from London, Brooke wrote to Monty:

It was a great joy seeing you again for a short time in Algiers. If I told you a few home truths I feel confident that you bear no ill will. You know well how fond of you I am and what an interest I have taken in ensuring that your fine qualities were realised and given their proper chance. It has not always been an easy job and I have had to fight several pretty tough battles for your benefit. That is the reason why I am so *very* anxious that you should not do things that

[1] Loc. cit.
[2] Brooke's diaries, in Sir Arthur Bryant, *The Turn of the Tide*, London 1957.

lay you open to criticism and seriously detract from your value as a higher commander. The higher the command the more difficult are the outside influences, quite distinct from 'winning battles on the battlefield', which make for success or failure in the long run.

That is why I felt it desirable to bring home to you the importance of your relations with allies and other Services, it is so easy to create impressions through which you may be misjudged and completely misappreciated.[1]

Monty may well have felt, as he would later in North-west Europe, that his very success as a British general on the battlefield doomed him to ill-will in the rivalry-ridden, hot-house atmosphere of Algiers. Certainly he had tried his hardest to keep on the best of terms with Eisenhower – had invited him to visit Eighth Army after the battle of Mareth, had called on him in Algiers to thank him for the Flying Fortress on 19 April, and on conclusion of the campaign had written a most loyal and well-intentioned letter. Eisenhower had, on 12 May, congratulated Monty not only for his 'sustained drive across the desert that in many respects stands unique in history', but also for driving the enemy forces in southern Tunisia 'back into his final bridgehead before he was completely ready for the move' and for reinforcing the final First Army thrust with 'exemplary' speed and 'cheerful cooperation'. Monty had replied on 15 May:

My dear General,
Thank you so very much for your letter of 12 May. I hardly know how to reply to your kind words. Throughout the campaign we have tried to do our duty. I myself, and my soldiers, have only one idea – to see this thing through to the end. It is the fighting man of America and Britain, together, that will have to do it.

I, and my Eighth Army, will always be at your disposal. And if ever I can do anything to help the American Army you have only to command – and it will be done.[2]

Evidently, in view of Brooke's experience in Casablanca and Algiers, nice words did not cancel out bad impressions. Jealousy was rife. But refreshed and invigorated by his trip home, Monty was determined at least that the Allied invasion of Sicily be a resounding success.

---

[1] Montgomery Papers. The letter took seven weeks to arrive. 'I have today got your letter of 22 June,' Monty replied on 14 August. 'Everything you said to me at Algiers was good. I can always take anything from you; my affection and admiration for you is 100%, and in my eyes you can do no wrong.'

[2] *The Papers of Dwight David Eisenhower*, op. cit.

CHAPTER FOUR

'The Stern Fight That Lies Ahead'

Once the initial shock had subsided, Patton's Western Task Force had quickly begun to perceive the benefits of Monty's new 'Husky' plan. Bradley, who was appointed to command the first American Corps to land, was unequivocal about the merits of Monty's plan over its predecessor. 'At one time thinking extended to a landing further west,' he later recounted. 'At one time they were even thinking of a landing on the north coast of Sicily, east of Palermo, and one on the south coast opposite that, around Licata. . . . Before we got into planning it, it was decided to make the landing on a continuous stretch of beach. I thought more of that plan. When you've so broad a front, you like to know there's someone on your right and left to prevent flankings. It's rather important. I liked the choice of landing spots for ourselves and the British. . . .'[1] Similarly, General Lucas, Eisenhower's 'eyes and ears' Deputy at Patton's headquarters, approved the change, and this confidence on the part of the senior American commanders was soon reflected by their staffs. As Patton's chief Intelligence officer noted in his unpublished memoirs, Patton's 'Task Force 343, instead of being spread over the western portion of Sicily, would make the assault as a unit, at one time, and relatively at one place, a great help. . . . It would now be a concerted effort on the part of the American troops, and the defence could be evaluated more in terms of a concerted defence as well, instead of an assumed reaction to piecemeal assaults around the perimeters.'[2]

The Allied armies had much to be grateful to Monty for. However Tedder and Cunningham, humiliated by Eisenhower's decision in favour of Monty's plan, now did everything in their power to sabotage direct support for the army. Tedder refused to permit Monty's Desert Air Force commander to take charge of air operations in the invasion and drove the American generals to distraction by his intransigence in this direction. Patton, Lucas and Bradley complained time after time to Alexander and even to Eisenhower about

---

[1] Bradley Commentaries, loc. cit.
[2] Colonel Oscar Koch, 'A One-way Ticket', MHI, Carlisle, Pennsylvania.

the failure of the Air Force to provide direct ground support – Patton even attempting to get Admiral Hewitt to import American naval aircraft into the theatre if the Air Force remained unwilling. The situation over air photographs was a similar scandal – taking some four weeks before army headquarters received prints of beaches, gradients, and so on. Worse, Cunningham refused to prepare his naval forces for the vital British and American airborne operations: parachute drops which had no hope of success if the navy fired on the troop carrier planes, as they did. At a conference convened after the tragedy Cunningham's representative remarked: 'Will you gentlemen please remember that up to the present any airship over our naval aircraft in the Mediterranean has been an enemy ship, and while the navy is now in the transition period, it was extremely difficult to impress upon all "light-fingered gentry" that there were such things as friendly planes flying over our craft.'[1] Yet Cunningham had been warned for six weeks before the invasion that the problem of air recognition must be sorted out if the Allied parachute troops were to stand a chance of reaching the dropping zones, and he had consistently declined to discuss the problem, let alone rehearse the operation. As Ridgway, the Commander of 82nd Airborne Division, lamented: 'We were informed that the Navy would give no assurance that fire would not be delivered upon aircraft approaching within range of its vessels at night. . . . In spite of this reply, the matter was repeatedly represented.' Only when on 23 June General Ridgway declared that 'unless satisfactory assurances were obtained from the Navy, I would recommend against the dispatch of airborne troop movements',[2] was Cunningham goaded into reaction. However, Tedder's intransigence meant that the Air Forces would give no satisfactory flight paths for the transport planes and, to General Lucas's consternation, a few nights before the invasion began the routes had still not been given. 'Places had been designated for dropping them,' Lucas recorded in his diary on 7 July, 'but the routes over which the planes were to fly had not been selected. It was important that this be done early. . . . I asked why this situation had been allowed to develop and was told by Patton that he had been trying to get this information from the Air Corps and from General Alexander since 3 July.'[3] Lucas had also been trying for over a month to get Tedder to organise and rehearse air support. As he noted in his diary on 9 June 1943: 'Told General Eisenhower that in my opinion the success of the operation was being jeopardised by the lack of fire

[1] In Chester B. Hansen Papers, MHI, Carlisle, Pennsylvania.
[2] Memorandum prepared by Maj-General Matthew B. Ridgway, 2.8.43, in Chester B. Hansen Papers, loc. cit.
[3] J. P. Lucas, 'From Anzio to Algiers', in MHI, Carlisle, Pennsylvania; and Admiral Hewitt's Action Report, quoted in S. E. Morison, *Sicily–Salerno–Anzio*, London 1954.

support. Artillery couldn't help in all cases. Air was an absolute necessity. He promised to reopen the matter for study. I heard he had directed Air Marshal Tedder [sic] to do so. The latter was not pleased.'[1] When a month later the 7th Army headquarters prepared to embark, the matter had still not been resolved and Tedder was asking for a minimum of twelve hours advance warning before close air support could be given. Eisenhower was so concerned at Patton's and Lucas's representations on the matter that he threatened to put 'the American Air Forces at least under ground command . . . unless the necessary results could be obtained.'[2]

Just how divorced the navy and air were becoming from the army at this time is well illustrated by the capture of the island of Pantelleria on 11 June 1943. Although its airfield had been rendered unserviceable by the Allies, it was resolved to make a 'laboratory experiment' by seeing whether the island's 11,000 Italian defenders could be bombed into submission. This unfortunate distraction involved no fewer than 5,258 sorties by Allied aircraft (apart from preliminary bombing), and the dropping of 4,656 tons of high explosive. Sixteen bombers and no less than fifty-seven Allied fighters (together with their crews) were sacrificed to this airman's fantasy of how the Axis enemy could be beaten by airpower alone. Moreover General Spaatz's papers reveal the near-incredible delusions of air grandeur to which the bombing of this strategically insignificant island gave rise:

The application of the air available to us can reduce to the point of surrender any first class nation now in existence, within 6 months from the time that pressure is applied,

he declared one week after the wholly Italian garrison surrendered on Pantelleria. He favoured 'bombing of Naples with offer to surrender while it is being destroyed, and then hitting Rome' as an alternative to concentrating upon the 'Husky' operation – an operation in which 'the same mistake is being made which was made in the Pantelleria assault – that of placing air as a secondary power to the ground forces and not giving them the top command, when air success is first in importance in making the operation a success'.[3]

The destruction of Pantelleria, the unwillingness of Navy and Air Forces to rehearse ground support for the invading troops, and the total failure of Cunningham and Tedder to consider the interdiction of the Messina Straits, either for German re-supply or later for evacuation, were sorry examples of the inter-service rivalry and lack

[1] J. P. Lucas, loc. cit.
[2] In Butcher Papers, loc. cit.
[3] Spaatz Papers, Library of Congress, Washington.

of effective co-operation which would prejudice the outcome of the Sicilian enterprise. Small wonder that Monty had required a period of recuperation in England, and was soon exhausted on his return. But the cardinal error, in Monty's eyes, was Eisenhower's failure to set up a combined headquarters of army, navy and air staffs for the 'Husky' operation, thus negating the lessons learned from the successful conquest of Tunisia, with the surrender of more than a quarter of a million Axis troops. Instead, with Tedder at Tunis, Cunningham at Malta and Eisenhower at Algiers, the seeds of chaotic Allied Mediterranean mismanagement were sown, resulting in due course in the Germans evacuating their entire surviving forces from Sicily, and the subsequent fiascos at Salerno and Anzio. 'I am afraid that it must be admitted that throughout the preliminary planning stage, and during the actual operations in SICILY 15 Army Group[1] has been completely and utterly ineffective,' Monty would note in his diary at the end of the Sicilian campaign. Moreover he was 'convinced that you cannot plan and conduct large scale operations in a theatre of war when the Commander-in-Chief and the heads of his three fighting services are all sitting in different places. . . .'

Monty's private reflections on the conduct of hostilities in the Mediterranean would indeed be scathing. For the moment however, in the absence of any 'firm grip' from Alexander, he himself sought to ensure that the invasion plans he had fought for would prove triumphantly successful. 'The Prime Minister cross-examined me a good deal about HUSKY,' Monty recorded of his visit to Algiers from 2 June to 4 June, 'and called on me at one of the conferences to give my views on the operation; I expressed confidence in the plan and in our ability to carry it out. It was, in fact, my plan!!'

Monty's concern was to make sure the remaining five weeks before the invasion were used to train and motivate the participating troops to the maximum extent. He returned to Eighth Army field headquarters after bidding goodbye to Brooke in Algiers on 4 June 'and continued to Cairo on 8 June to see my staff there'. The following day, as he had upon his arrival in the desert the previous August, he gathered all his staff officers and addressed them.

The year before Monty had addressed the headquarters of an army which had retreated from Libya and was defending the Egyptian capital. Now they were once again in that Egyptian capital, planning the first Allied seaborne invasion of an enemy-held territory. The object was the clearance of the Sicilian strait in order to open up the Mediterranean to Allied shipping, and, as Churchill had declared in Algiers, to use Sicily as the spring-board to an invasion of Italy in

---

[1] Alexander's 18th Army Group headquarters was retitled 15th Army Group for the Sicilian enterprise, a number obtained by adding the numerals of Patton's Seventh US Army and Monty's Eighth Army.

order to knock the latter out of the war. With Italy's capitulation, the way would be open to the launching of the long-awaited Second Front: the invasion of France across the English Channel.

The invasion of Sicily was therefore not only a prerequisite to the invasion of France, but also a rehearsal for it. Moreover as Eighth Army Commander Monty not only had command of the eastern assault force in Husky: Churchill had also charged him with responsibility for the follow-up in Italy. 'As a result of the Algiers talk I had decided to bring the Comd 10 Corps [Horrocks] in to the HUSKY planning. If the HUSKY operation was to be pushed hard, then it would be a good thing to get a footing on the mainland of ITALY as quickly as possible,' he recorded in his diary. 'The study of this problem was a task for a third Corps Commander. . . . The special task of 10 Corps was to study the operation of crossing the Straits of MESSINA, and to get a lodgement on the mainland of ITALY. There were three contingencies:

1. Resistance negligible. We could almost row over.
2. An opportunity presented for a quick move, with an ad hoc plan.
3. A proper set-piece operation. This would have to be mounted from North African ports, and probably could not be done before September.

'If the toe of ITALY was going to be strongly held then the obvious way to tackle the problem was to make landings behind the enemy positions and to go on doing so – like the Japanese did against us in MALAYA.'

From being a desert army, Eighth Army was rapidly turning into the main Allied amphibious army in the West. Though often criticised as overcautious and rigid, Monty now demonstrated how the energy, foresight and charisma of a great commander can infuse his men with the unbreakable will to succeed – whatever the task. He had determined, on his return from England, to visit every formation under his command, whether embarking from North Africa or Malta; but first he felt he must ensure that his own headquarters staff was given the picture: a picture in which all the essential elements of the operation were abstracted so that all officers would be clear about the undertaking and exude resolute confidence in administering the Eighth Army. Unfortunately no verbatim record exists of this address, but it was undoubtedly as historic, in its way, as that given on the Ruweisat Ridge the previous August; it was to be the direct forerunner of the great addresses Monty would give before the invasion of Normandy almost exactly one year later. Among his papers, happily, Monty kept his handwritten notes for the Cairo address, and from them it is possible to reconstruct the moment in

June 1943, as Monty prepared his victorious Eighth Army, like so many conquerors before him – Scipio, Caesar, Duke William of Normandy – to fight overseas. It would be the first major Allied assault landing against an enemy-held country since the ill-fated Dardanelles in 1915. But the way to see the assault, Monty determined, was in its Eighth Army context. For here was an army that had already successfully fought its way across two thousand miles of North Africa. It was a great instrument of war – 'the fighting machine as weapon' as Monty's first note for the conference ran: 'Eighth Army and W[estern] D[esert] Air Force.'

Now, however, the Allied navies would be added to that machine – 'Now got R. Navy added.' The machine was thus 'very powerful', but owing to the problem of seaborne communications it would be 'unable to develop its own power initially' until seaports were opened, and supplies could be got forward to the troops in battle. 'Therefore got to be careful,' Monty's notes ran: it was imperative not to barge across blindly, but to separate important objectives from the unimportant – and to plan accordingly. The strategic verdict at Algiers had been that Italy must now be knocked out of the war ('Decision at Algiers – knock Italy out of the war'). This would be accomplished by not exposing the Allied forces to the risk of failure by dispersion and romanticism, as in earlier planning, but by the ruthless adherence to those principles which had brought victory to Eighth Army at Alamein and ever since. 'How to fight the Axis commander,' Monty set down in his notes – 'Three rules.' These, one may infer, concerned the build-up to an all-out, blitz offensive at a selected point in the enemy defences; the relentless concentrated pursuit of the selected objective (the 'dog-fight'); and the ability to bring up reserves, particularly of armour, for the break-out which finally destroys the enemy line.

'Apply this to our case,' Monty continued. Seen this way, the problem was primarily one of artillery – 'Gun problem' – namely, how to bring sufficient concentrated firepower to ensure the passage of Eighth Army troops onto their selected objectives – 'How we want the battle to develop in Sicily, & quickly on to mainland.' The answer here was to ignore western Sicily, and to concentrate on racing for the vital eastern seaports of Syracuse, Augusta, Catania and finally Messina.

Everything depended, it was clear to Monty, on the speed and violence of the assault. But could surprise be guaranteed beyond the evening prior to the assault? 'Enemy will know by dusk where landing is coming, roughly,' Monty estimated. Moreover the enemy had some '500 fighters on island' – it would be all the RAF could do to protect the ships of the Task Force, and however much Eighth Army might like El Hamma-type air support, it was clearly not going to get it from an air force whose job it was to win the land battle. . . .

Certain things we must do for ourselves,' Monty warned. Without air support it was 'vital to think out and organize every form of supporting fire from the sea; M.G.'s from assault craft; fire from ships; etc.

We must get ashore.
Those who do must work outwards and help those who are in trouble.
Bombing of beaches, etc. on night D – 1/D; can be done; must be laid on. support landing craft, flak ships; gun boats.
Go for least expected part of beach.
Use of smoke to blind searchlights.

Monty was confident that, with no less than five divisions landing simultaneously in Eighth Army, the assault on Sicily would be successful if the divisions could be landed successfully. Eighth Army must get ashore: 'this is the really difficult thing; given success here, the other points are easy.'

It is as well perhaps to remember the magnitude of the undertaking. Patton, commanding the Western Task Force, was largely indifferent to the problem of landing, believing, as General Lucas noted in his diary, that 'little training is necessary for a landing operation because all the men had to learn was to move straight inland after being put ashore on the beach'. This attitude gave rise to 'something of an argument with Patton during dinner over amphibious training,' as Lucas recorded. 'There is no use barging in with your head down and depending upon a willingness to absorb punishment to gain you the victory. Joe Louis doesn't do that,' he remarked presciently, 'although he could win that way against a weak opponent.'[1]

Lucas's concern was well-founded. As the British Official Historians later wrote, the 'Torch' landings in North-west Africa, 'carried out as they were in face of an uncertain and short-lived opposition, had produced scenes of lamentable confusion. On the American beaches 34% of the assault craft had been lost, chiefly through mishandling. Under the guns of a resolute enemy such a performance could lead only to humiliating disaster.'[2]

Whatever Patton's attitude, Monty was determined that his men should not be let down by mismanagement. The 'managers' had been assembled: in their hands rested the lives of Eighth Army. 'Once ashore we must stop the counter-attack while we are building-up, best way to stop c/a is to be offensive ourselves,' Monty declared; 'must not let initiative pass to the enemy.'

[1] J. P. Lucas, loc. cit.
[2] I. S. O. Playfair and C. J. C. Malory, *The Mediterranean and the Middle East* Vol. IV, London 1966.

Once surprise is lost, and it is clear to enemy where we are going, we will begin to bomb the beaches and will continue all night until just before zero hour. Once ashore, and daylight comes, we must not let initiative pass to enemy. We must crack about, *and force battle to swing our way*.

Italian is not good at the counter-attack; seldom comes within 1000 yds. Good in defence, until you get behind him.

Best way to stop counter-attack is to be offensive ourselves.

The German, however, 'is very good at c/a,' Monty warned. 'Therefore must have a firm base; best firm base is A/Tk guns and tanks. Vital to get A/Tk guns and tanks ashore early; infantry can then be offensive without difficulty.'

Important points are:
    Bomb the beaches
    Get tanks ashore early + A/Tk guns
A/Tk guns better A/Tk weapon than the tank.
Value of tank for mopping up.
Must always mop up – never neglect this.
Value of high ground; a few tanks on the high ground with the infantry.
Use of armour working with infantry.

Finally there was the most important single objective of all. Airfields were significant prizes in that their capture would bring 'increased air support, and so everything becomes easier'. But the critical aim was to take Syracuse.

There must be no mistake here.
We have got to have the port on D Day.
30 Corps must be prepared to operate to the right, thus freeing 13 Corps for operations towards Syracuse. Risks must be taken to get the port; be defensive elsewhere if necessary.
If we do not get the port,

he warned,

we will have great admin problems.
Vital also for the Americans; more important than Ragusa.

Once again, the staff officers of Eighth Army Headquarters in Cairo rose. Those who went on, later, to plan the Normandy landings in 1944, the greatest seaborne invasion that will probably ever be undertaken, would remember this address as archetypal. The campaigns of Sicily and later of Normandy would involve setbacks reminiscent of Alamein itself; but both campaigns would be won, as was Alamein, essentially by the plan of initial assault: the 'break-in'. By fighting uncompromisingly for a proper plan for the break-in, Monty had guaranteed the lives of many thousands of his troops. Casualties during the landings on Sicily would, as in Normandy, be nominal, as the violence and weight of the assault carried the invaders to victory. It was time for the British defeats in France, Crete, Hong Kong and Singapore to be avenged.

By addressing his staff on the tactics and techniques by which he wished to transform Eighth Army into an amphibious 'machine', Monty now set the pattern for an historical development without parallel. It remained for him to address the troops themselves, the men upon whom rested, in the end, the responsibility for defeat or victory. On 19 June King George VI paid a four-day visit to Eighth Army at Tripoli,[1] giving Monty the public accolade of knighthood which he had earned at Alamein, after which Monty returned to Cairo 'and spent three days with 13 Corps,' as he recorded in his diary on the eve of the invasion.

> I visited every unit; saw, and was seen by, every man, and spoke to them; and addressed all officers at two big gatherings of about 1000 officers each. I also spoke separately to a gathering of all commanders in the Corps down to the Lt-Col level, and explained to them the HUSKY plan and the development of the operations. I then went across North Africa by air to TUNISIA and did exactly the same with 78 Div, which was at Hammamet, about 40 miles south of Tunis. 51 Div I shall do from MALTA; also the Airborne Division. I will then have seen every unit taking part in HUSKY, have been seen by all the men, and have addressed all the officers. My custom is to have each unit drawn up in three sides of a square, and make the men break ranks and gather round the car; I then talk to them and ask questions about them. The troops like this informal and friendly way of making contact with them and it has excellent results.

There were some, particularly in 78th Division which had previously belonged to First Army, who resented such attempts of the Army Commander to put himself 'across' to the men. But as General Horrocks had noted at Tripoli, troops are, by and large, mightily sceptical of 'brass', and it was an incredible sight to see the way the troops responded to this slight figure with his steel-blue eyes, his sharp cheek-bones, his pointed nose and black beret as, with demon-

---

[1] 'The King is to stay with me at my H.Q. and my cook is very excited' – letter of 16.6.43 to Phyllis Reynolds. In fact Monty himself was proud and delighted by this, the first visit paid by King George VI to an army commander in the field in World War II. The King was put up in Monty's personal caravan.

strative forefinger, he took the trouble to meet them: to explain his plan, and to encourage them to believe, as he did, that victory would be theirs. As General Sir Sidney Kirkman recalled:

> Just before Sicily we were at Suez, and Monty had one of his usual conferences of all the officers in my [50th] division, down to Lt-Colonel, in a cinema outside Suez, in the desert, and across the road there was a big NAAFI. . . . We arrived in our cars, Monty's flag and my divisional flag and he addressed them as you'd expect. . . . And when we came out there were fifty or sixty or a hundred soldiers waiting at the gates of this cinema to see Monty! He was a film star.
>
> That is a bigger growth of Monty than anything else I can tell you. It's like – in the Peninsula War a glimpse of Wellington's nose, and they knew all was well!
>
> And there they were, incredible to me – incredible to think about for me – there they were as I say, looking at a film star. Of course, Monty at once seized the opportunity, stood up in the jeep, and made a speech to them. Straight away.
>
> That is, as far as Monty was concerned, the art of command.
>
> And the next day he said he'd like to go round my division. He wanted them to be training in various areas, he'd visit the troops training. The technique was, we'd go to find a company – I knew where they all were of course – we reached the training area and he'd call out to the officer there who'd come and salute him. He'd say: Bring them all round here, bring them round my car. They'd all crowd round the car, Monty would stand up in the car and make a speech.
>
> What I didn't realise at the time, I realise it now, because he made the same speech to all the groups, one after the other. It would have gone down equally well, whoever they were. The same jokes came out! He was very skilful. At that time I hadn't the experience to know that you've got to make the same speech every time, you can't have a new one every time. But it was a boost to the troops. They were *delighted* to see him.
>
> I've never forgotten this crowd outside the cinema, waiting there purely to see Monty. And it's that sort of thing which people don't realize he achieved in the Eighth Army. He not only hadn't lost a battle, but he was the object of . . . he was the English film star if you like.[1]

'It involves a lot of continuous travelling and flying, but this is the battle-winning factor and must be done well,' Monty explained to Alexander in giving his reasons for staying in the Suez area in late

---

[1] General Sir Sidney Kirkman, interview of 16.4.80.

June. 'I must spend 3 days with them [13 Corps]; see the soldiers; address all officers of each division; and get the Eighth Army technique instilled and generally binge men up for the battle. Dempsey does not know about these things as he has not fought; so it is vital I should go.' On 28 June he planned to return to Eighth Army field headquarters at Tripoli, on 30 June/1 July 'with 78 Div doing the same as I did with 13 Corps, on 2 July return Tripoli,' and on 3 July 'go Malta – I shall do 51 Div in Malta'.[1] For a full week in Malta, Monty then addressed invasion units and went over the plans for the last time with his entire headquarters staff.

If Monty's insistence on a Flying Fortress had caused eyebrows to be raised in Algiers, his critics would have done well to study Monty's itinerary in the months of April, May and June 1943 as the Allies prepared for Operation 'Husky'.[2] Unlike any army commander in living memory Monty had gone all out to enthuse his men, and to gain their trust. By the eve of invasion Monty could note in his diary, 'My Army is in tremendous form, the soldiers are very enthusiastic, and are soberly confident of the issue. So am I myself,' he added with supreme confidence. 'But I am under no illusions as to the stern fight that lies ahead' – and in the privacy of his diary he recorded his misgivings, which were profound. Far from having achieved air supremacy over the invasion area, the Allied air forces had failed to force the Axis fighters into combat – 'they are holding back and not fighting, obviously according to orders. We are going to embark on the land battle *before* we have won the air battle,' Monty noted. Worse still, there were now estimated to be some 208,000 Axis troops on Sicily, including two German mobile divisions. 'There are two German Corps in ITALY itself, and the enemy can built up strength in SICILY, across the Straits of MESSINA quicker than we can.' Given Eisenhower's original reluctance to undertake the 'Husky' operation if Sicily were defended by more than a single German division, the situation was certainly far from promising. 'If we were working on the original plan, agreed to by Allied Force HQ and by Force 141, the result could only be complete failure. I knew that these overriding conditions [gaining air supremacy, no reinforcement of existing Sicilian garrison by German troops and overcoming the submarine menace] would not be complied with and for that reason I fought hard for the present plan – which can give success in any case.

The present plan – my plan – ensures concentrated effort.
In most battles you hope for average luck.

[1] Message of 20.6.43 in Alexander Papers (WO 214/21), PRO.
[2] 'I should be completely lost without my Fortress aircraft; it is the greatest blessing and saves me much fatigue' – letter to Sir Alan Brooke, 6.5.43.

As things stand at present I consider that if we are to succeed *we must have* average luck, and probably 60 or 70 per cent luck.

I consider it can be done.

But it will be a hard and very bloody fight, and we must expect heavy losses.

I consider that we shall require all our resources to capture SICILY, and that the further exploitation on to the mainland – with a view to knocking ITALY out of the war – is definitely unlikely to be possible,

he forecast in a mood of private pessimism.

CHAPTER FIVE

The Assault upon Sicily

That the Allies could have launched the largest seaborne invasion ever attempted without being detected was the major piece of the luck Monty needed. In fact the invasion force *was* detected, as early as 9 July, but until it struck on 10 July, the Axis high command simply ordered a general alert – and waited. As at Alamein, Monty thus achieved tactical surprise – the German radar operators being so incredulous at the number of 'blips' appearing on their screens on the night of 9 July that, refusing to believe their eyes, they waited until morning before reporting.

The assault went better than anyone could have predicted. Even without direct air support from Tedder, the two Allied armies touched down and made their way ashore with minimal opposition, many of the Italian coastal defenders being surprised in their beds. Thus, despite the relative failure of the airborne operations,[1] Monty's insistence on overwhelming concentration of force proved triumphantly successful. The German plan to defeat dispersed Allied landings in detail was shown to be hopelessly ill-conceived. Within a few hours of daylight on 10 July 1943 some eight Allied divisions were ashore – a veritable disaster for the German-Italian alliance. Not only was the German offensive in Russia suspended, but the very future of Italian coalition put in doubt.

Monty was beside himself. To his premonition of a 'hard and bloody fight' had been added a gale which arose on the afternoon of 9 July and caused him 'some anxiety'. 'But the convoys were going well and up to time, and we left things alone and trusted to the weather forecast which said the wind would moderate. This it did, and troops landed at the right beaches at the right time, some two hours before dawn on 10 July,' as he noted in his diary. 'The work of the Royal Navy throughout has been beyond all praise,' he added. 'The whole movement and transportation work, and all the organisation and plans for landing the expedition in SICILY, were quite first-class.' Indeed Monty was so proud and excited that at 10.30 that

[1] Both British 1st Airborne Division and the US 82nd Airborne Division suffered heavy casualties and disastrous dispersion owing to untrained pilots and fierce flak, both hostile and friendly.

morning he went to see Admiral Cunningham in Malta in person to 'express my great appreciation of the work of the Navy'. Moreover, although air supremacy had not been demonstrably established by the time of invasion, it very quickly became clear that the Allies were indeed masters of the skies. 'I was wrong. The Allied Air Forces had definitely won the air battle, and this was quite apparent from the first moment we stepped ashore in SICILY. The enemy air force was swept from the sky and was never allowed to inconvenience us, except for night bombing of the ports,' Monty recorded later in his diary. 'This was a remarkable achievement and I wrote to Air Chief Marshal Sir Arthur Tedder and expressed the great appreciation of the Eighth Army in the matter.'

Flushed by success and generously overlooking Cunningham's and Tedder's previous lack of co-operation, Monty was soon anxious to get ashore himself and 'grip the land battle'. Far from being the reluctant general beloved of American military caricaturists, Monty was now almost indecently concerned with making haste rather than consolidating the bridgehead. By the early evening of 10 July he was urging Leese by radio cypher to 'operate with great energy towards NOTO and AVOLA' from his 30 Corps Pachino peninsula landing beaches. 'Essential to free 13 Corps for operations against SYRACUSE as most of [air] landing brigade landed in sea and thus could not contribute towards the operation.' At the same time he signalled to Dempsey, 'Air recce shows no enemy movement closing in on you so far. Operate with great energy towards SYRACUSE. Have ordered OLIVER [Leese] to push North towards AVOLA with all speed. Delighted with your success so far.'[1]

Nor was this mere exhortation from the rear. Monty himself boarded the destroyer HMS *Antwerp* that night at Malta, and landed with Lord Mountbatten on the southern end of the Pachino peninsula at 7 a.m. on 11 July,[2] to find that Syracuse had been captured intact, and the whole of the Pachino peninsula was in British hands, complete with a thousand prisoners and a working air landing strip. 'The port of SYRACUSE was completely undamaged and all the cranes and quay facilities were in good order,' Monty recorded in his diary after reaching Syracuse on the afternoon of 11 July. 'We have

[1] RL 113 1850 hrs, Eighth Army HQ War Diary (WO 169/8494), PRO.
[2] 'About this time I received word that Monty himself was landing on "Amber" Beach, and I was to go and meet him. . . . They had, I imagine, landed by launch as they had apparently no land transport of any kind in which to get about. . . . It must be realised that, at this stage, no troop carrying transport was ashore' – unpublished memoirs of Maj-General D. N. Wimberley, communicated to author. Wimberley lent Monty his Dukw to tour 51st Highland Division's area and then to 'motor North to see how the landings had fared on the southern beaches of 13 Corps'. Only after Monty had left did Wimberley find his ADC had left their rations for the next five days aboard – including a bottle of whisky!

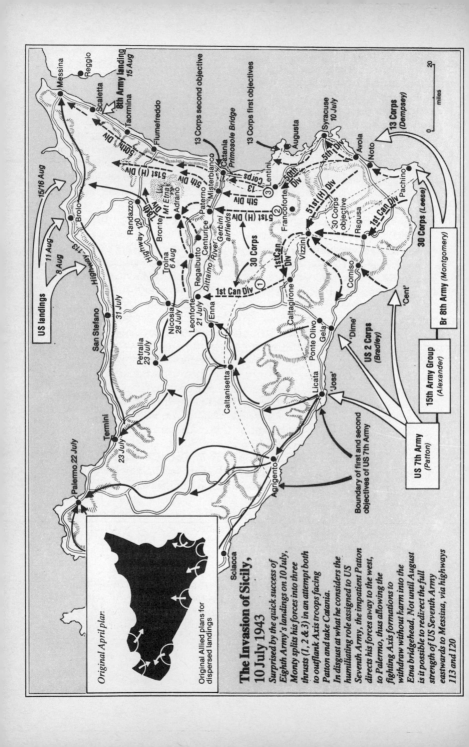

The Invasion of Sicily, 10 July 1943

Surprised by the quick success of Eighth Army's landings on 10 July, Monty splits his forces into three thrusts (1, 2 & 3) in an attempt both to outflank Axis troops facing Patton and take Catania.

In disgust at what he considers the humiliating role assigned to US Seventh Army, the impatient Patton directs his forces away to the west, to Palermo, thus allowing the fighting Axis formations to withdraw without harm into the Etna bridgehead. Not until August is it possible to redirect the full strength of US Seventh Army eastwards to Messina, via highways 113 and 120

Original April plan:

Original Allied plans for dispersed landings

US landings

US 7th Army (Patton)

15th Army Group (Alexander)

US 2 Corps (Bradley)

Br 8th Army (Montgomery)

'Joss'

'Dime'

'Cent'

30 Corps (Leese)

13 Corps (Dempsey)

Boundary of first and second objectives of US 7th Army

13 Corps first objectives

13 Corps second objective

Places:
Messina · Reggio · Scaletta · Taormina · Flumefreddo · Brolo · Milazzo · Randazzo · Bronte · Adrano · Centuripe · Regalbutto · Troina · Nicosia · Leonforte · Enna · Caltanissetta · Petralia · San Stefano · Termini · Palermo · Sciacca · Agrigento · Licata · Gela · Ponte Olivo · Caltagirone · Vizzini · Comiso · Ragusa · Francoforte · Lentini · Catania · Misterbianco · Primosole Bridge · Augusta · Syracuse · Avola · Noto · Pachino

Mt Etna · Dittaino River · Gerbini airfields

Highway 120 · Highway 113

8th Army landing 15 Aug

50th DIV · 51st (H) DIV · 5th DIV · 1st Can DIV

1st Can Div · 30 Corps

30 Corps objective

Dates/annotations:
15 Aug · 15/16 Aug · 11 Aug · 8 Aug · 31 July · 23 July · 22 July · 6 Aug · 21 July · 28 July · 23 July · 23 July · 10 July

miles 0 — 20

become so used to capturing *damaged* ports that it was quite refreshing to capture one like this. It can take 5 ships berthed alongside, and a further 8 personnel ships tied up end on; and a great
number of LST's can discharge onto the roadways.' If he could take
the port of Augusta, as well as striking inland to dominate the main
road network, then the conquest of Sicily seemed assured. 'The
battle in SICILY is a battle of key points,' he noted in his diary that
night. 'The country is mountainous and the roads poor. The few big
main roads are two-way and very good; these run North–South and
East–West, and once you hold the main centres of intercommunication you can put a stranglehold on enemy movement and
so dominate the operations. As we drive forward on the main axes so
the enemy tries to escape down the side lateral roads; but they cannot
actually get away, and are then rounded up in large numbers. On the
right flank – the sea flank – the Navy moves along keeping touch
with the land battle and bombards effectively towns and villages
where resistance is being offered. Fought in this way the battle is
simple and the enemy is being forced back by our relentless pressure.
On my left the American 7th Army is not making very great progress
at present; but as my left Corps pushes forward *that* will tend to
loosen resistance in front of the Americans.'

This somewhat condescending attitude to Patton's Western Task
Force was based partly on lack of information relayed by Alexander,
and partly on Monty's growing tendency, when excited, to exaggerate the prospects for his own victoriously advancing army. So far
very little German opposition had been met; together with the
surrender of Syracuse intact this undoubtedly led Monty into fatal
overconfidence – the more so since he had privately entertained
such grave private doubts about the campaign on the eve of
embarkation. With Syracuse falling so easily and 30 Corps racing
inland to take the Ragusa–Augusta highway, Monty became now
brazenly over-optimistic. To Alexander he signalled rudely on 11
July:

Everything going well here. I have sent my present situation and
future plans to Freddie [de Guingand]. No need for you to come
here unless you wish. Am very busy myself and am developing
operations intensively so as to retain initiative.
Have no repeat no news of American progress. If they can press
inland and secure Caltagirone and Canicatta and hold firm against
enemy action from the West I could then swing hard with my right
with an easier mind. If they draw enemy attacks on them my swing
north will cut off enemy completely.[1]

[1] Alexander Papers (WO 214/22), PRO.

This was to be the first of Monty's imperious 'suggestions' for the way Alexander should run the Sicilian campaign. Meekly, Alexander complied – and the stage was set for the historic rivalry between Patton and Montgomery that would become an almost manic obsession with Patton, as well as spawning books and films for decades after his death.

Whether Monty was aware of such rivalry at this time is doubtful. Because of King George's visit to Tripoli in June, Monty had been unable to attend Alexander's conference of commanders on 21 June. He thus never saw Patton during the later planning stages of Husky – and the likely development of the campaign was therefore never discussed between them.[1]

Patton, however, had other ideas than holding firm against enemy attack in order to allow Monty to swing north to 'cut off enemy completely'. Alexander failed to make clear Monty's suggested strategy, and when Bradley tried to slow down the American advance to consolidate his bridgehead, Patton overruled him – and later complained to Eisenhower that Bradley was insufficiently aggressive.

'One incident after landing made me angry,' Bradley narrated after the war.

On landing a gap developed between 1st Div on left and 45th on right, along a ravine leading up to airfield, astride Gela–Comiso road. I wanted to clear up the pocket and take the road before I moved on. They had the capability of building up here and to cut in behind 1st Div on beach. George came along and issued instructions directly to 1st Div ordering them to push on up the ridge [inland], leaving this German pocket behind them. I had given instructions that they were to hold with their leading elements, get some tank help and drive these people out before they proceeded. He countermanded my Corps order to the Div without consulting me in any way.

When I spoke to him about it George apologised and said he should not have done that. But George didn't like it. Ike told me afterwards George had complained to him that I was not aggressive enough.[2]

What was happening, in fact, was that two Army Commanders were already competing to make the running in Sicily, and Alexan-

---

[1] At the presentation of plans at Algiers on 21 June Patton had spoken for six minutes. He outlined his plan to fight his way ashore and establish a 'secure base line from which to undertake further operations for the complete subjugation of the island as directed' – *The Patton Papers*, op. cit.

[2] Bradley Commentaries, loc. cit.

der, rather than imposing himself as Army Group Commander, allowed himself to become the 'go-between' – or, as Bradley put it, 'Alexander provided for co-ordination between the two.'[1]

Patton was soon counter-attacked by German armoured elements. 'Had it been anyone else but the 1st [Division], the Germans might have got to the beaches,' Bradley reflected after the war;[2] but while the Americans fought for their very beachhead now, Monty attempted to seize the chance of 'cutting off the enemy completely'.

Like Patton, Monty was oblivious to the protocol whereby an Army Commander issues orders to divisional commanders only via his Corps Commander. It was important not to waste time, and by the evening of 12 July General Wimberley found that Monty had been giving orders direct to one of his Highland brigade commanders; General Kirkman, commanding 50th Division, also recalled the way Monty's sense of urgency overrode protocol at this time:

I only want to tell you a few things which affect Monty. I landed at a place called Robolla, and I didn't do much the first day. I lost all the transports, all the transport of 50 Div went to the bottom of the sea, bombed after we arrived. And then I was brought in to relieve part of 5 Div. 5 Div was to go up the coastal road towards Syracuse, I was to go on more inland, on the inland road. I won't go into my battle. I went on and we had a battle. And the next day, we had made a night advance, we went to a place called Sortino and I was up there at dawn to see what had happened. And the troops reckoned they'd done a good night's work and they were going to sit down and rest. And I said to the Brigadier, 'You're not going to sit down and rest. There's no one in front of you, the place is empty. You go on now until you drop if necessary – occupying this ground which you'll have to fight for tomorrow. Get 'em all on the move, go on, go on – now is the time to go on.'

I knew nothing whatever about the plans, I was merely horrified at the thought of sitting down when the Boche wasn't there. I said, 'Use your carriers as tanks, get on, get on. I don't care how tired the men are – walk.' And whilst I was there, having just said this, one went about with a wireless of course, I got a message, return at once to your headquarters, Army Commander wants to see you. So back I went, quite happy that I'd done the necessary gingering up in the forward area. And Monty then explained to me that he was going to drop parachutists that evening or the next night, and that I'd got to get forward as fast as possible to relieve them.

Now the point I want to make is this. It's Monty who gave these instructions to me, not Dempsey. Dempsey was the Corps Com-

[1] Ibid.
[2] Ibid.

297

mander. Dempsey was there, in the tent, but it was Monty who gave the instructions – 'Go on at all possible speed.' Fortunately I'd only just been up there and done the very thing, not knowing that Monty was going to land this operation in front of me.

And I went back and found that my Brigadier had gone on about ten miles, troops quite exhausted, and they were held up by a hill and we discussed the plan of attack the next morning. And eventually they reached the Primosole Bridge and the CO of the Regiment said to the parachutists: 'Sorry we're about four hours late.'

And the chap said: 'Oh, don't mention it! When I was with First Army they were two months late!'

And though we weren't there in time to occupy the bridge, we were just in time to stop the Boche blowing it up. I passed the other brigade through and we just got there before the Boche destroyed the Primosole Bridge. And we then had this frightful battle against the [German] para division.

But all I wanted to make clear was the point of Monty calling me back and personally giving me the order, which is very unusual. Usually in an army, the Army Commander would give the orders to the Corps Commander and he would summon the divisional commander.

Monty was determined to impress his personality on the chap who was going to do the job. That's the answer![1]

Monty was indeed determined to impress his personality. He was certain that, given the great luck the Allies had enjoyed in landing virtually unopposed, there was now a fleeting chance that the campaign could be won in a matter of days. If the Americans could hold the German counter-attack down near Gela, one Eighth Army Corps could cut behind them by driving inland towards Enna ('Harpoon Force' comprising 23rd Armoured Brigade, infantry of 51st Highland Division and on their left 1st Canadian Division), while the other Eighth Army Corps blitzed its way up the coast towards Catania and Messina. Thus already at 10 p.m. on 12 July Monty was signalling to Alexander: 'My battle situation very good. Have captured AUGUSTA and my line now runs through SORTINO –PALAZZOLO–RAGUSA–SCICLI. Intend now to operate on two axes. 13 Corps on CATANIA and northwards. 30 Corps on CALTA-GIRONE–ENNA–LEONFORTE. Suggest AMERICAN DIV at COMISO [45th US Division] might now move westwards to NEIS-CEMI and GELA. The maintenance and transport and road situation will not allow of two armies both carrying out extensive offensive operations. Suggest my army operate offensively northwards to cut

[1] Loc. cit.

the island in two and that the American Army hold defensively on line CALTANISETTA–CANICATTI–LICATA facing West. The available maintenance to be allocated accordingly. Once my left Corps reaches area LEONFORTE–ENNA the enemy opposing the Americans will never get away.'[1]

Tactically, Montgomery's suggestion made good sense. Had the American 2 Corps been put under Monty's command, as Monty had urged early in May 1943 ('Only one commander can run the battle in HORRIFIED in the new plan. It seems clear that Eighth Army HQ should command and control the whole operation, with 2 US Corps included in Eighth Army'), the plan might well have worked. But with Alexander attempting simply (as would Eisenhower later) to co-ordinate the offensive intentions of two prima donna army commanders, the cumbersome mechanics of a superior headquarters and the intricacies of coalition warfare made quick tactical manoeuvre impossible. The American 45th Division went on fighting up to the Vizzini–Enna highway and Monty became beside himself with frustration. 'It was now becoming clear that the battle in SICILY required to be gripped firmly from above,' he recorded in his diary for 12 July. 'I was fighting my own battle, and 7th American Army was fighting *its* battle; there was no co-ordination by 15 Army Group (ALEXANDER). Without such co-ordination the enemy might well escape; given a real grip on the battle I felt convinced we could inflict a disaster on the enemy and capture all his troops in SICILY.'

Alexander, loath to incur an inter-Allied furore by transferring all maintenance and reserves to Monty for his suggested 'end-run', did nothing. Without instruction or direction, Monty therefore made do with his existing maintenance (the vital D + 3 convoy only docked at Syracuse on 13 July), and attempted to carry out his plan unilaterally, without American co-operation. Pushing infantry of 51st Highland Division and 23rd Armoured Brigade up the Vizzini–Enna Highway, he attempted to outflank the enemy facing the Americans. Meanwhile he called in Browning, his airborne adviser, and prepared his plan for a combined air-sea-and-land assault on Catania:

I decided to make a great effort to break through into the plain of CATANIA from the LENTINI area on night 13/14 July, and to use one parachute brigade and one commando to help this operation; the parachute brigade to be dropped so as to secure the main road bridge over the SIMETO river, and a mobile force of tanks and armoured cars to be pushed towards CATANIA after dawn on 14 July.

I intended to make a great effort to reach CATANIA by nightfall

[1] Montgomery Papers.

on 14 July; given some luck I felt it could be done; but I must have the luck,

he wrote on 13 July.

In the event both Monty's efforts failed, and with their failure the Sicilian campaign became, for Eighth Army, a war of attrition.

Could it have been helped? Had Alexander reacted with greater alacrity and resolution, could sufficient forces have been given to Eighth Army to make the two thrusts successful?

The question is not easy to answer. However, the fateful few days after the initial Allied invasion of Sicily do demonstrate that Montgomery was very far from being the ponderous, cautious general beloved by his detractors. For here was a Montgomery bursting with an offensive eagerness that was, to be fair, beyond the capabilities of his troops. After all, until the arrival of the $D + 3$ convoy, these troops were only equipped at assault scale – i.e., with weapons and transport for a maximum of ten miles of fighting. Yet within forty-eight hours all four infantry divisions of Eighth Army had fought and marched some forty miles – and many as far as a hundred. 'Rapid progress was not possible as no MT was [yet] available for troop lifting and the infantry have to move entirely on foot, and also fight, in the hot Sicilian sun,' Monty had acknowledged in his diary on 12 July. 'This is exhausting. But they are very cheerful and respond splendidly to my calls on them; I am keeping up the tempo of the operation as if I "let-up" the enemy will seize the opportunity to pull himself together.' By the following evening he was noting that 'the fatigue of the infantry, and the enemy resistance in rather difficult country, slowed up the operations somewhat. The infantry had to move and fight on foot, and it was very hot; they had been going now for 4 days, i.e. since dawn on 10 July. . . . The Canadian Div had definitely to be rested; the men were not fit and they suffered severely from the hot sun and many got badly burnt; generally, officers and men are too fat and they want to get some flesh off and to harden themselves.'

Alexander's procrastination now led to the first fiasco of the land campaign. That Monty was on edge, knowing how brief a time he had before the enemy began cohesively to react to the invasion, is evidenced by his signals. Though he might write, on 13 July, to the Reynolds that 'all goes well with me; I am very well and am enjoying the battle . . . it has all been very successful; I am driving ahead and capturing a lot of Italians', he was furious with de Guingand, who had not made sure that the Army Commander's Tactical Headquarters was assault-loaded ready to put ashore within twenty-four hours of invasion. On 11 July he signalled 'Rule re visitors to be strictly observed and none repeat none are to come here. Am extremely angry about delay of Tac Army and in future it will always

300

be loaded before D-Day and held ready for instant move.' Not until 13 July was the headquarters – consisting of fourteen officers and sixty-seven other ranks, one Grant tank, four Stuart (light) tanks, two scout cars, three Bantams, fourteen 15-cwt trucks, four 3-ton trucks, and two motor-cycles – put ashore in Sicily, and at 10 a.m. on 14 July it moved northwards alongside Dempsey's 13 Corps headquarters. By then the situation was already deteriorating. An Eighth Army liaison officer had reported on the evening of 13 July that '45 American Div was advancing North between VIZZINI and CALTA-GIRONE and would strike 30 Corps in the left flank. The grip on the battle by 15 Army Group is not very good at present. If my telegram had been acted on, all this wasted effort would have been saved. I again wired ALEXANDER (on night 13 July) asking him to do something about it.' In his telegram Monty predicted a 'scene of intense military confusion' if the American 45th Division ran into the side of the Canadian Division as it sought to outflank the enemy. The following day Alexander responded, but the 45th Division's fight northwards had not only wasted a field division's effort, but it had forced the enemy back in front of the Canadians, who could not now outflank them and, without adequate transport, tanks or artillery, found their prospects of a quick move to Enna shattered by the resultant opposition. Moreover Bradley was naturally indignant at this belated Army Group order, for the outline plan before the invasion of Sicily had clearly marked the British-American boundary extending no further west than Vizzini. Had he been alerted to the change in boundary when Monty sent his original cable on 12 July, and been given Monty's reasons, Bradley would undoubtedly have understood the logic. Instead he was appalled, as he recalled afterwards:

> We had a boundary for II Corps which went through Ragusa to the north to Vizzini. We were supposed to hold the line from Vizzini through Caltagirone to Enna. It followed the ridge line there. Our intermediate objective was to hold that line until we were ready to break out.
>
> Just before we got there, we got order changing the boundary – switching us off to the north-west and giving that road as boundary to the British including the road. Here we were facing North, and we were within 1,000 yards of the road. We had to back off, come clear round to the beach in trucks and put them in on the left. I was very peeved, obeyed my orders, but often wondered if I received such orders now, would I really obey them? They were so obviously wrong and impractical. We should have been able to use that road, even if we would have shifted to the left – used it to move to the left.[1]

[1] Bradley Commentaries, loc. cit.

Many writers have since criticised Monty for his 'stolen road' in Sicily, without understanding that it was part of a tactical strategy to cut off the enemy facing the Americans, and that immediate response to Monty's original signal to Alexander would have averted the painful withdrawal and belated redirection of an entire American division.

Nevertheless the question remains whether, with hindsight, Monty did right in continuing to insist on this strategy, once the American 45th Division had merely driven back the enemy and thus missed an opportunity of surrounding him. For the Americans, equipped with 2½-ton four-wheel-drive trucks, were far more mobile than the Highlanders, particularly since most of the Highlanders had by then marched twice as far as the 45th American Division to reach Vizzini. Wimberley felt that Harpoon Force had 'done well . . . [it] had covered, that day, some forty miles from Noto to Vizzini.' However, 'the marching troops, particularly of 153rd Brigade, were by now getting tired. When we were planning at Djidjelli [in North Africa] it had always been assumed that we would not be called upon to operate north of the Tellare river until more transport had been landed behind us.'[1]

In fact, fifty miles north of the beaches upon which they had landed, 'Harpoon Force' had met its first serious opposition, opposition which could now have been outflanked by the American 45th Division if the latter had been permitted to take their rightful road.

There was at this time some difference of opinion with the Americans,

General Leese afterwards recalled,

as to the use of the Caltagirone–Enna road. This was reserved for use by the 8th Army and I often think now that it was an unfortunate decision not to hand it over to the Americans. Unknown at any rate to 30 Corps, they were making much quicker progress than ourselves, largely owing, I believe, to the fact that their vehicles all had four wheel drive. They were therefore far better equipped to compete quickly with the endless deviations with which we were confronted, as a result of the destruction of every bridge by the Germans. We were still inclined to remember the slow American progress in the early stages in Tunisia, and I for one certainly did not realize the immense development in experience and technique which they had made in the last weeks of the North African campaign. I have a feeling now that if they could

[1] Maj-General D. N. Wimberley, loc. cit.

have driven straight up this road, we might have had a chance to end this frustrating campaign sooner.[1]

Leese's honesty does him credit. Monty, however, loath to admit that he might be in error, refused to relent, and Alexander was too much in awe of him to take proper charge of the situation.

This was perhaps the deciding moment of the whole Sicilian campaign. Sensing the enemy's weakness, Monty had sought to exploit the hour by splitting Eighth Army into two major thrusts, inland and coastal. But the moment 'Harpoon Force' failed to drive through Vizzini the whole logic of his strategy fell apart. Owing to lack of transport he was too weak in infantry to get round Vizzini, which was held by the enemy for a vital forty-eight hours; he was, as it proved, also too weak in strength to reach his main Eighth Army objective on the coast, the port of Catania. For on the night of 12 July, as 'Harpoon Force' met its first German tanks on Highway 124, and Monty made plans for a parachute drop on the Primosole Bridge leading to Catania, the sky above the Catania plain filled with unexpected German transport planes. At last, three days after the invasion had begun, the Germans were reacting. The days of easy advance were over for Eighth Army: the 'hard and very bloody fight' was about to begin.

---

[1] General Sir Oliver Leese, loc. cit.

CHAPTER SIX

Monty's Gamble

There can be little doubt that, just as the invasion of Sicily was a forerunner of that larger cross-Channel invasion that was set to take place in the summer of 1944, so too the airborne operation to take the Primosole Bridge and seize Catania was the forerunner of the great battle for Arnhem – the 'bridge too far'.

As later in Belgium, so in the first few days after landing in Sicily, Monty seems to have been made heady by success. Far from cautiously building up stocks, troops and transport, he was determined to exploit the enemy's confusion by an audacious bid to reach Catania and the Gerbini airfields after daylight on 14 July. But when dawn broke that day, it was clear his luck had run out. 'On night 13/14 July a parachute brigade had been ordered to be dropped at the [Primosole] bridge, to hold it. But again the pilots of the aircraft failed us; 23 aircraft returned to Africa without dropping the paratroops, 16 aircraft were reporting missing [shot down by the Royal Navy in error], and 11 aircraft dropped the paratroops into the plain of CATANIA,' Monty recorded in his diary. 'But those dropped were very dispersed, all over the place, and the operation of getting a really firm hold on the bridge in this way was a failure.'

Monty himself spent the day trying to sort out his left thrust – ordering the Canadian Division now to by-pass the Vizzini hold-up and take the lead in the drive northwards towards Enna. 'I spent this day visiting every unit in the Canadian Division and talking to the men. They are a grand Division and when we get them tough and hard and some of the fat off them, they will be absolutely first class.' As with the New Zealanders in the desert, there was every prospect that a powerful 'left hook', like those at Agheila, Tripoli and Mareth, would over-stretch the enemy and permit the frontal coastal thrust to drive through.

The days of the desert were, however, over. Movement in the rocky, mountainous country with its high stone walls surrounding the olive groves was confined almost entirely to the roads, a fact which had initially favoured the Allies, but which now militated against them. Far from falling to the Eighth Army on 14 July, Catania would be held by the Germans for another month.

Nor was lack of bravery the fault. As General Bradley later re-marked, the British soldier was braver than his American counter-part, if bravery meant head-on assault. 'Our men may be a little more cautious, but that is not always a disadvantage. He lives to fight another day. Contrasted to our troops, British troop leaders are amateur tacticians. They have no school system, no courses to help their officers grow professionally. They believe their officers should lead and show their men how to die. We emphasise the ability to live – to press through and accomplish their objective. We teach our men to use fire and movement. You'll find fewer frontal assaults in the American Army than you will with the British.'[1]

In fact the fighting around the Primosole Bridge was to prove some of the most bitter and contested of the entire war. Crack German paratroops had been landed on the Gerbini airfields west of Catania as the Germans recognised their error in counter-attacking the American assault and now hurriedly sought to contain the two more dangerous British assaults. 'On 14 July the enemy began to re-act seriously to our thrusts. It must have been clear to him by now that our whole effort was in the South-East part of Sicily and that elsewhere we were merely making diversions. Very heavy fighting took place on both axes of advance,' Monty noted in his diary. The town of Vizzini 'changed hands several times', but this was as nothing compared with the saga of the Simeto Bridge. 'On night 14/15 July it was reported that we had secured the vital bridge over the SIMETO river; but later, about midnight, a second report said we had NOT secured the bridge,' Monty recorded on 15 July. 'At 0800 hours 15 July I received a report that the enemy had blown the bridge; this was bad news. At 1500 hours I received a further report that we had secured the bridge, and that it had NOT been blown, and that our troops were advancing Northwards beyond the bridge. This last report was later, at 1900 hours, reported to be NOT correct. The situation now was that our troops and the enemy faced each other across the bridge; the bridge was intact and neither side could now blow it; an attack was to be staged after dark to get across and secure a bridgehead.'

The failure of the airborne operation was really the death-knell to Monty's post-invasion strategy. Understandably, he was upset, sensing, as no one else could, that the chance of ending the campaign quickly was already passing. Moreover, having departed from the pre-invasion strategy by splitting his army into two widely separated Corps thrusts, he was now off-balance, with neither Corps sufficiently strong to make rapid progress. Like a cornered man he began to flail in different directions. In his diary he vowed not to use airborne troops again in the campaign.

[1] Bradley Commentaries, loc. cit. This was of course a fallacy; Bradley had never visited British Army training establishments.

I decided today that I would carry out no further operations with the Airborne Division.

I had now done two operations; both had failed because of the fact that the pilots of the aircraft were completely untrained in navigation, and were frightened off their job by flak. The operation of the Air Landing Bde on night 9/10 July failed badly.

The operation of the Parachute Bde also failed. If this parachute Bde had been dropped correctly in the right place on night 13/14 July, we would have got a firm grip on the bridge over the river, have burst through towards CATANIA on 14 July, and all our trouble on 15 July would not have taken place.

As it turned out the few parachute troops that *were* dropped at or near the bridge did magnificent work; they reached the bridge, removed the explosive charges, cut the leads, and held the bridge for a considerable time. This action prevented the enemy getting back, and large numbers were captured.

Eventually we ourselves (50 Div) got up to the bridge; the parachute troops had by that time been driven off it. But we were now facing the enemy across the bridge and it could not be destroyed. The parachute troops undoubtedly saved the bridge for us.

But the race to Catania was off. 'The big lesson about the employment of airborne troops is that we must not be dependent on American Transport aircraft, with pilots that are inexperienced in operational flying; our airborne troops are too good and too scarce to be wasted.'

Monty's vexation was not confined to his diary. When he heard that Browning, the airborne adviser to GHQ, was discussing future proposals with Leese and Dempsey before reporting to the Army Commander, Monty sent a furious signal to Alexander's Chief of Staff via Eighth Army Main Headquarters. 'Browning must discuss future employment of airborne troops with me and not with my Corps Commanders. The conduct of operations in Sicily is nothing to do with him and suggest you inform him accordingly.'[1]

Frustration with the setback at Vizzini and the Simeto Bridge now served to bring out stubbornness in Monty. De Guingand, monitoring the repulse of Monty's left thrust at Vizzini, signalled early on 14 July: 'If 51 Div is having difficulties General Alexander suggests American 45 Division whose leading elements are on general line about 5 miles north of the airfields might move Northwards and so threaten if NOT repeat NOT cut off enemy facing 51 Div advance. There is of course danger of shooting each other but on the other hand such movement might well accelerate our operations. C-in-C

[1] Message of 14.7.43, in Eighth Army HQ War Diary (WO 169/8494), PRO.

suggests that if you wish such action it should be arranged direct with 45 Div through liaison officer with 30 Corps.'[1] This was, in effect, a reversal of Monty's earlier offer to move 30 Corps inland in order to lessen resistance in front of the Americans, and 'cut them off completely', and Monty did not like it. Maintaining his prediction of a 'scene of intense military confusion', he insisted that the American division withdraw, to which Alexander meekly consented. 'I spoke to Patton to this effect yesterday and have since issued written instructions to this effect. You should have received these instructions by now,' he cabled back lamely.[2]

By then 30 Corps was indeed breaking out beyond Vizzini, with the Canadians leap-frogging through the Highlanders. But by splitting his army and refusing the help of Bradley's 2 US Corps Monty had unwittingly passed up the last chance he would have of a speedy conclusion to the campaign.

Strategically Monty was, of course, right when he said to Alexander – who visited him at 2.30 p.m. on 15 July – that the battle for Sicily, so triumphantly successful in its invasion stage, would be won in the eastern half of Sicily. But he was wrong in thinking that Eighth Army could win the battle on its own, particularly now that Monty had turned his back on the pre-invasion plans, had usurped the northward roads designated for the American Seventh Army, and split his own army in an attempt to decide the campaign single-handedly.

Monty's idea was to repeat his Mareth manoeuvre, so that if Dempsey's 13 Corps failed to reach Catania in its coastal thrust, Leese's 30 Corps would, by striking northwards and then turning east, come in on the enemy rear. To do this Monty asked that Patton's army should push northwards on Eighth Army's left flank 'through CALTANISETTA . . . to PETRALIA. It must then position one Division in the [triangular] area ENNA–CALTANISETTA–CATERINA and keep it there; the possession of this area puts a stranglehold on enemy operations from the West. With my rear secure, I would then turn 30 Corps to the East from the area LEONFORTE and would operate Eastwards towards ADRANO and Mt ETNA,' Monty recorded in his diary. 'General Alexander agreed to this general plan for the continuance of the battle. He does not take a very firm grip himself and I generally have to suggest things to him, but he always acts on my suggestions.'

Alexander's feeble grip was indeed a misfortune, for not only had Monty misread the difficulty of fulfilling his strategy against determined German opposition, but he clearly had little idea of American reaction to the notion of simply protecting Eighth Army's rear,

[1] Eighth Army HQ War Diary (WO 169/8494), PRO.
[2] Alexander Papers (WO 214/22), PRO.

particularly when Eighth Army was pinching virtually the only good road network leading north. Bradley was indignant when recalling Monty's suggestion that 'there was only room for one Army on the offensive in Sicily. . . . There was 2/3 of the island on the left to fight on. I thought it was one of the worst proposals Monty made.'[1]

General Leese was astute enough to recognise what Monty did not: that by treating the Seventh Army as a poor relation Monty might well irk the Americans into moving in the opposite direction – westwards – and thus lose the chance of the Americans even guarding Leese's flank.

> There was a moment when General Patton was very angry about the controversy over this road and I was led to believe that at one time he was threatening to advance towards Palermo instead of towards Messina if he wasn't allowed to use this road,

Leese recalled.

> General Montgomery and General Patton were not on all that good terms and General Alexander did not have a Tac Headquarters on the island so the situation was quite tricky; and one day Freddie de Guingand came to see me in order to ask if I could do anything to help, as I was then in close daily contact with General Bradley, with whom I was on excellent terms. That afternoon I went over to see General Bradley. I discussed the problem with him and he told me that General Patton was at his Army Headquarters at Agrigento and that the only prospect of success lay in my going to see him personally. It was well outside my Corps area but I felt it was the only sensible thing to do, so I went to Agrigento where I spent a most entertaining night with General Patton who eventually agreed to continue in the same direction as ourselves! Next morning I hastened back towards my Corps area as I had an appointment with the Army Commander, but I soon realised that I could not make it, so I signalled to him to that effect. I returned to my Headquarters where I bought a proper rocket in his return signal for going out of my Corps area. But Monty was very good about it and he never said a word to me about it afterwards; at any rate the two Armies continued to advance side by side![2]

But did they? Patton was polite to Leese, and outwardly willing to conform to the orders Alexander gave him; but Monty's signal about there only being room for one offensive army in Sicily had riled him incalculably. As later in France, the restless cavalry general had ideas

---

[1] Bradley Commentaries, loc. cit.
[2] Loc. cit.

of his own. 'If we wait for them [Eighth Army] to take this island while we twiddle our thumbs, we'll wait forever. There's plenty of room for both of us to fight,' he told Bradley;[1] and from Alexander he sought permission to extend his bridgehead westwards along the southern coast to Agrigento, which would obviate the necessity of bringing American stores through British lines from Syracuse.

Alexander, wary lest he sanction anything that might provoke fierce fighting on Monty's left flank just as Eighth Army was poised to strike north towards Catania and ultimately Messina, only agreed to 'a reconnaissance in force'.[2] Patton's Intelligence officer, Colonel Koch, was not fooled.

By D + 5 operations had gone so well that the restless General Patton sought authority to do more than form a firm operational base on the left of the British Eighth Army. He wanted to cut the island in half by moving straight to the north end . . . do an end run around the western portion to Palermo. After using all the influence to hand, including General Wedemayer who was returning to Algiers to report to General Eisenhower, a tongue-in-cheek authority was given with provisos. In order to start this end run Agrigento had to be taken. Patton sought authority specifically to attack it. Instead of getting a clear-cut answer his request was approved by the 15th Army [Group] with a caveat – the action is approved provided by so doing he did not bring on a major engagement.

'If I attack Agrigento will I bring on a major engagement?' General Patton asked [me].

'No, Sir,' was the answer – whereupon General Patton turned to his G3 Colonel Maddox and directed him to issue the order.[3]

Amazingly, Patton's disguised bid to capture Palermo was kept secret from Patton's own Corps commander, Omar Bradley, for to Bradley and the British there was simply no strategic value in capturing Palermo now that both Syracuse and Augusta ports had been taken intact. The vital strategic prize was Messina, the narrow funnel through which the enemy could reinforce or withdraw its Sicilian garrison. Even the American Official Historians of the campaign considered that Patton's 'preoccupation with Palermo amounted to an obsession', and failed to understand what possible purpose its priority could serve. Agrigento's harbour (Porto Empedocle) would provide all the extra maintenance facilities Seventh Army might need, so why Palermo too? they asked.

---

[1] Bradley Commentaries, loc. cit.
[2] *The Patton Papers*, op. cit.
[3] Oscar Koch, loc. cit.

'Perhaps [Patton] thought of a rapid, dramatic thrust to draw attention to the capabilities of US Arms.' Perhaps 'it was the only objective that could compensate partially for having been relegated to the mission of acting as Alexander's shield.' Palermo, General Truscott would write after the war, 'drew Patton like a lode star.'[1]

No serious historian can deny that Patton's 'obsession' with Palermo was a wild and unmilitary distraction from the main campaign in Sicily. Equally no fair-minded historian can exonerate Monty from having fuelled Patton's obsession by his arrogant assumption that Eighth Army could win the Sicilian campaign single-handed. In his diary, General Lucas puzzled over Alexander's unwillingness even to let the Americans tackle Agrigento:

It would seem that perhaps they do not want us to advance. The essence of the campaign is speed. I believe the Seventh Army could take Palermo in ten days. If it advanced in that direction the enemy would have to concentrate and fight – or lose it.

But Lucas was quite clear that Palermo was of no strategic significance compared with Messina.

It would be better to send the Americans against Messina, north of Mount Etna, and let the British, after taking Catania which they have not done yet, move on Messina through the corridor east of the mountains.[2]

Ironically this is what would have happened had not the success of the British landings given Monty such delusions about completing the Sicilian campaign alone.

Monty himself seems to have been oblivious to such murmurings in the American camp. For several crucial days he continued to think he would crack the German front without active American assistance. All day on 16 July Kirkman's 50th Division attempted to extend its penetration beyond the Primosole Bridge – 'the bridge was found to be intact and undamaged, and fit for heavy tanks and all traffic, which was a great thing. The depth of the bridgehead was only some 500 yards,' Monty noted in his diary, 'and the troops holding it were very tired; the enemy was trying to stop it from being deepened and we were opposed by very determined Germans. During the afternoon we strengthened our hold on the bridgehead, and after dark a strong attack was launched by 50 Div (D.L.I. Bde) which by dawn on 17 July had secured a good bridgehead over 1000 yds deep; tanks and

[1] A. N. Garland and H. M. Smyth, *United States Army in World War II: Sicily and the Surrender of Italy*, Washington 1965.

[2] J. P. Lucas, op. cit.

anti-tank guns were got over and the bridge was now I think secure; this bridgehead was vital to me. I gave orders that 13 Corps was to stage a strong attack from the bridgehead area towards CATANIA on night 17/18 July.'

To Leese, in a letter he sent by hand, Monty described Dempsey's forthcoming 13 Corps offensive: 'Tomorrow night, 17/18 July, 13 Corps will land two commandos and one Inf Bde behind, and in, CATANIA (which is in flames). At the same time, i.e. night 17/18, 13 Corps will launch a big attack from the bridgehead and astride the main road to CATANIA.' However he was under no illusions. 'The enemy is resisting strongly in the coastal plain south of CATANIA, and has determined Germans there opposing our bridgehead. . . . He is concentrating his main strength on his left against 13 Corps, and the task of 13 Corps will not be too easy.' Leese was thus to drive hard with 30 Corps north from Vizzini, using his 51st Division, and in a wide swing north and then eastwards across the lower slopes of Mount Etna with his Canadians: 'The road centre at ADRANO is a most important place, and if we secure *that* and also PATERNO the enemy could not stay in the plain of CATANIA – since 51 Div could if necessary work S.E. from PATERNO towards CATANIA.' Still he balked at involving the Americans, though: 'I will get the Americans to safeguard the left and rear of the Canadians.'[1]

The parallel with Mareth was, however, eerie. Monty was once again trying to break through the enemy's main defensive position on a one-brigade front, against fanatical resistance. Reflecting on Eighth Army's 'surprisingly slow' progress, General Lucas blamed, in his own diary on 15 July, the 'strong opposition' and the fact that 'Montgomery is notorious for the meticulous care with which he prepared for his operations. This virtue, like any other, can become an obsession that finally defeats its object. He will not move until every last ration and round of ammunition is ashore and in its proper place. This may have been what was needed in the desert against Rommel. Here in Sicily, speed would seem to be the part of wisdom. Destroy the enemy before he can be reinforced from the mainland.'[2] Lucas evidently had no idea that Eighth Army's failure, far from being the result of Montgomery's notorious meticulousness, stemmed directly from his rash and impetuous desire to finish off the campaign before the enemy had a chance to react cohesively. With a little more meticulousness, Monty might well have recognised his error, and ensured that the coastal thrust across the river Simeto was conducted, as had been visualised before the invasion, by the entire two-corps resources of Eighth Army.

As it was, the left wing of Monty's second Eighth Army corps was

[1] Handwritten letter in the possession of Mr Daniel Andrews.
[2] J. P. Lucas, op. cit.

fighting many miles away in the interior, doing a job which even Leese admitted would have been far better entrusted to the American Seventh Army. Yet the drive for speed, to drive on before the Germans could start ferrying further divisions over from Italy, and the fact that it was too late to rectify his mistake made Monty stick obstinately to his doomed strategy. The Canadians must redouble their efforts in the 'left hook' as at Mareth – seizing Leonforte and then swinging right towards Adrano, on the slopes of Mount Etna, above Catania; and in order to help them he would now unleash 51st Highland Division, which had been protecting the gap between the two Eighth Army thrusts, northwards across the Catanian plain in order to capture the Gerbini airfields and then Paterno. 'This would in itself greatly assist 13 Corps on the right in its operations towards CATANIA from the bridgehead over the SIMETO river. I issued orders accordingly on night 16/17 July.'

Monty had in fact now split Eighth Army into *three* thrusts: a left 'hook' through the mountains; a central thrust; and a right-hand coastal drive. In fact he was committing the self-same error which had dogged Anderson and then Alexander in Tunisia, the 'partridge-drive' he had himself mocked so contemptuously.

It was not a good spectacle, and as if to add insult to injury, he sent a further signal to Alexander instructing him what to do with the American Seventh Army, as he had promised Leese. Still refusing to enlist their direct help, he wanted the Americans to occupy the line northwards from Caltanisetta to Petralia 'so as to secure the left and rear of 30 Corps' as it swung right from Leonforte. 'I said that all indications pointed to the enemy being very stretched, and that we must hustle him without relaxing by the speed and strength of our thrusts.'

In reality it was Eighth Army which was stretched, and the speed and strength had gone from its mistakenly dispersed thrusts. The British Official Historian later obtusely blamed the two 'inexperienced' divisions of Dempsey's 13 Corps (5th and 50th),[1] but those who participated in the savage battles to push beyond the Simeto knew this was not true. For once Monty had let down his army by his overambitiousness and his lack of ruthless adherence to his own rule of concentration in strength.

Not unnaturally, Patton saw red when he received Alexander's dutifully passed-on message from Monty about protecting 30 Corps 'rear', and while Monty vainly wrestled with the problem of reaching Messina before Sicily could be reinforced, Patton now dropped even his pose of obedience to Alexander's wishes. 'Monty is trying to steal the show and with the assistance of Divine Destiny [Dwight D.

---

[1] C. J. C. Molony, op. cit.

Eisenhower] he may do so,' Patton had noted in his diary on 16 July;[1] now, on 17 July, Patton committed the same error as his Eighth Army rival: he split his army.

---

[1] *The Patton Papers*, op. cit.

CHAPTER SEVEN

Patton Absconds to Palermo

At nine minutes past one on the afternoon of 17 July 1943 Patton and
Wedemayer arrived in Tunis to protest about Alexander's latest
directive. Patton carried with him an alternative directive, to which
Alexander also now agreed. 'He explained that he had planned to do
just what I asked but that his chief of staff had failed to tell me when
issuing the order,' Patton recorded in his diary – an excuse Patton
did not believe for one moment.[1]

Patton's proposal was to create another US Corps in Sicily; to give
it Seventh Army's armour and mobile infantry, and to race not to
Messina now, but to Palermo. Alexander, daunted by Patton's
protest, meekly gave in, providing Patton promised to leave at least
the semblance of an American force to guard Monty's left flank. 'He
gave me permission to carry out my plan if I would assure him that
the road net near Caltanisetta would be held. . . . If I do what I am
going to do, there is no need of holding anything, but it's a mean man
who won't promise, so I did,' recorded Patton.[2] Leaving part of his
forces in the Caltanisetta area Patton now split off the rest to race in
the wrong direction. While the Axis commanders Guzzoni and Hube
had been withdrawing all German and the remaining fighting Italian
units back towards Mount Etna, Patton had wrested permission
from Alexander to split off the majority of his Seventh Army into a
drive in the contrary direction. General Maxwell Taylor later recalled:

I was a Brigadier-General, and Artillery Commander of 82nd US
Airborne Division. We took the north-west corner of Sicily [from
Agrigento] . . . it was a pleasure march, shaking hands with
Italians asking, 'How's my brother Joe in Brooklyn?' Nicest war
I've ever been in! Monty – he had a different problem – he was up
against Germans.[3]

General Truscott, commanding the reinforced 3rd US Division
(which became the main formation of Patton's Provisional Corps),

[1] Ibid.
[2] Ibid.
[3] General Maxwell Taylor, interview of 17.10.81.

was later asked by the American Official Historian why 'there was no attempt to try to cut off a part of the Germans' (who were known to be retreating eastwards rather than westwards); moreover, why was 'Seventh Army not directed in pursuit of the Germans towards the Catania plain?' Truscott blamed the slowness of Intelligence ('there was a lag of a day or two before the whole picture of the enemy could be assembled'), but primarily Patton's obsession with Palermo: 'I had offered to go on to take Caltanisetta, but Patton wanted to capture Palermo. . . . It is my belief that the glamor of the big city was the chief thing that attracted Gen. Patton.'[1]

Had Montgomery only enlisted full American partnership in his offensive, none of this need have happened. Apart from Alexander's absentee generalship from Tunis, Monty had no one to blame but himself, particularly since the commander of 2 US Corps, General Bradley, was well-disposed towards his neighbouring British Corps Commander, General Leese, and fully appreciated the strategic need to drive on Messina rather than Palermo.

But while Patton and Wedemayer put an end to any hopes of quick completion of the Sicilian campaign, Monty was living in a fool's paradise. Even on 17 July, three days after the failure of his first plan to rush Catania, Monty was still fantasising that Eighth Army could bring the campaign to a rapid conclusion on its own. 'Situation in bridgehead over SIMETO river now very good,' he informed Leese on 17 July; 'it is about 2000 yds deep and a whole Inf Bde and a lot of tanks are over the river. 50 Div attack goes in tonight up to within about 3 miles of CATANIA. 5 Div will come forward tomorrow. . . .' Indeed so sure was Monty that his offensive would be successful that he now wanted Leese to 'think ahead' on the lines of a 30 Corps left-hand wheel by the Canadians 'round the west and north of ETNA, so as to cut off any enemy who are east of ETNA and facing 13 Corps at CATANIA.'[2]

To be sure, events at that time did make it look as though the Axis front was cracking. Optimism about cutting off the enemy in the Catania area, however, soon rubbed off the following day (18 July), when Eighth Army's three separate thrusts ran into determined opposition. 'It was quite clear now that the enemy was going to fight with great determination to prevent me from getting possession of the CATANIA airfields. His troops opposing me were all German, and he kept dropping small parties of very stout-hearted parachute troops in order to stiffen up his weak places,' Monty acknowledged in his diary. Dempsey, despairing of breaking out beyond the Primosole bridgehead, was attempting to outflank the opposition

[1] Smyth interview of 19.4.51 in OCMH collection, MHI, Carlisle, Pennsylvania.
[2] Handwritten letter in the possession of Mr Daniel Andrews.

there by bringing up his other division (5th), and passing it round the west of Kirkman's 50th Division, aiming at Misterbianco, to the west of Catania. 'The attack of 50 Div last night from the bridgehead, due north astride the main road to CATANIA, met very strong opposition,' Monty informed Leese. 'So this thrust is not being persisted with. Instead, 5 Div was this morning put in on the left of 50 Div and will develop a strong thrust direct on MISTERBIANCO. . . . I do not think there is much enemy opposition in the area between 50 Div and 51 Div and it is through this area that 5 Div is now moving. . . . If all goes well 5 Div may well secure the high ground overlooking MISTERBIANCO from the south, by dawn tomorrow.' 5th Division's thrust would, he hoped, force the Germans to thin out in front of 50th Division at Catania, while Leese's two thrusts towards Paterno and Adrano would complete the 'discomfit of the enemy'.[1]

Far from being aware that it was Eighth Army that was being overstretched by such dispersion of effort, Monty still believed that he was on the brink of decisive victory:

> From my own angle I had now developed four strong Divisional thrusts. . . . These four strong thrusts were slowly but surely making progress. The river crossings were in our hands but the scrub country in the plain of CATANIA was good defensive country and the enemy had excellent observation behind on the foothills of Mt ETNA between MISTERBIANCO and PATERNO.
>
> The Canadian Division was really doing a big left hook moving on the outer circle on the left flank via ENNA-LEONFORTE against ADRANO. This was hilly country, and enemy demolitions made progress difficult. The nett result was a strong right flank pressing hard, with a strong left wheel done by the Canadians. The enemy is very stretched and I do not see how he can hold us off so long as we keep up the pressure.

Had Alexander insisted that Patton remain on Eighth Army's left flank, Monty's gamble might well have succeeded, for the Axis forces *were* stretched to breaking point, and with the introduction of American forces, already on the island and at full fighting establishment, into the Eighth Army line, Alexander could have won a great victory. But as resistance before Eighth Army stiffened, and as Monty belatedly began to cast his eye around for more troops to break open the enemy's stretched defences, he found that Seventh Army had departed in the opposite direction. Like a horse that has bolted – Alexander having meekly opened the stable door – Patton was racing westwards. So intent was Patton to have 'equal glory in the final stage of the campaign' – which he, like Montgomery,

[1] Ibid.

thought was about to end – that his staff resorted to deceit. When on 19 July Monty belatedly appealed to Alexander for American help in finishing off the campaign, Patton's Chief of Staff deliberately kept Alexander's directive from Patton!

Monty's signal to Alexander, at 6 p.m. on 19 July, outlined his four areas of advance: 'These four thrusts are very strong and the enemy will not be able to hold them all' – and his new idea of driving north on both sides of Mount Etna: 'If I can reach MISTERBIANCO and PATERNO tomorrow night and ADRANO by 21 July I will be well placed for extension of battle round either side of ETNA.' It was now that he suggested, for the first time, an offensive role for the Americans, even offering them the chance of taking Messina. 'Suggest that when Americans have cut coast road North of PETRALIA one American Division should develop a strong thrust Eastwards towards MESSINA so as to stretch the enemy who are all Germans and possibly repeat the BIZERTA manoeuvre.'

Alexander, embarrassed that he had given Patton permission to bolt in the opposite direction, now lamely offered to put the American division under Monty's direct command, explaining why he had given Patton permission to split off the major portion of his Seventh Army in its drive to Palermo: 'Would you like to have one American Div front under your command now for operating in your northern sector? Seventh Army should take advantage of Italian demoralisation to clear up the west of the island and at least seize Palermo, from which port they can be based, and if Germans are too strong for you Seventh Army can take over a sector in the north from St Stefano to Troina.'[1]

Had Monty been the glory-seeking British bigot of Patton's imaginings, he would undoubtedly have taken up Alexander's offer. Instead Monty insisted the American division stay under Patton's command, no doubt as a gage in ensuring, belatedly, that Seventh Army face eastwards and not westwards: 'Re American div. Would like one to operate eastwards on North coast road, but suggest it should remain under Patton,' he signalled back.[2]

Alexander had meanwhile sent a new directive to Patton that night (19 July), ordering him first to drive north from Petralia and cut the island in half; only then was he to drive on to Palermo. But when Patton's Chief of Staff received the signal, at 10.20 p.m. on 19 July, he seems deliberately to have kept it from Patton, passing on only that part which related to the way in which Palermo was to be taken: '[General] Gay saw to it that the message (after taking out the portion he planned to use) was a long time being decoded and then, saying the original message had been garbled, asked 15 Army Group for a

[1] Alexander Papers (WO 214/22), PRO.
[2] Ibid.

317

repeat. By the time this process was completed, the Seventh Army was on the outskirts of Palermo.'[1]

Bradley was dismayed. He had assumed that when Patton flew with Wedemayer to see Alexander on 17 July, the Seventh Army Commander was anxious to overturn Alexander's directive and get an offensive role for 2 Corps in the assault on *Messina*. But when early on 20 July, he received Seventh Army's latest orders regarding the seizure of *Palermo*, his heart sank. There was no mention of an American drive to 'repeat the Bizerta manoeuvre', and he assumed that, in addition to helping Patton take Palermo, he would have simply to station one division in the north to protect Eighth Army's flank again.

Gay's deceit, Patton's obsession with Palermo, and Monty's over-ambitiousness had now conspired to wreck the Allied offensive in Sicily. A note of realism began to creep into Monty's over-optimistic diary entries. Alexander, meeting Monty at Cassibile airfield, 'agreed to the suggestion made by me in my cable of 19 July and will order the Americans to operate Eastwards along the Northern coast road with one Division,' Monty noted on 20 July; but equally he acknowledged that, after ten days of fighting, the 'four Divisions I have over here are getting very tired and I must rest them in turn; continuous operations in this hot weather are very exhausting'. Instead of holding 78th Division ready for use in any immediate follow-up to the Sicilian campaign, he now ordered it to 'come over from SOUSSE at once' to reinforce Eighth Army. The following day he lamented: 'the attacks put in last night by 50 Div, 5 Div and 51 Div did not make any great progress. Very determined resistance was met. We have definitely won the battle for the plain of CATANIA and we are in possession of the whole plain; our advanced troops have got a footing in the foothills of ETNA. . . . But the enemy is securely positioned in CATANIA itself, which is a strong bastion or fortress, and he is firmly established in the foothills mentioned above. My troops are getting tired as the heat in the plain of Catania is very great.'

Without consulting Alexander, Monty now unilaterally decided to alter his strategy. The Germans were 'going to hold the CATANIA flank against me to the last,' he believed; therefore he would shift his main weight from the plain to the mountains. 'The proper answer to the problem is now to reorganise; to hold on my right while keeping up a good pressure; to continue the left hook with 30 Corps using the Canadian Division. I will give 78 Div to 30 Corps and go hard for ADRANO and then Northwards round the west side of Mt ETNA.'

At 10.30 a.m. on 21 July 1943 Monty therefore called in his two Corps Commanders and explained the new plan. Dempsey's offen-

[1] Garland and Smyth, op. cit.

318

sive would be closed down entirely. His front, including also 51st Highland Division's sector south of Paterno, was 'to be defensive; aggressive patrol activity and "jabbing tactics", so as to keep the enemy there;[1] meanwhile Leese was to propel the Canadians forward in the mountains, bringing in 78th Division as soon as it arrived from Sousse. If the Americans would drive eastwards along the north coast in conjunction with Leese's offensive, and if the 'full weight of all our power that can be made available from North Africa were turned on the enemy' hemmed into the north-eastern corner of Sicily, then Monty 'did not see how the enemy could get his army away from SICILY; it was doomed if we acted properly'.

'The left hook is now the thing,' Monty felt, 'with the Americans driving along the North coast towards MESSINA.'

These, however, were paper tactics. Most of Bradley's 2 US Corps was moving not eastwards to Messina, but westwards towards Palermo. Not until *four days* after Monty's request did American forces finally reach the north coast, missing the remaining Axis forces as they abandoned Palermo and made off eastwards to Messina. Only on 23 July, the day after the fall of Palermo, did 2 US Corps turn part of its forces eastwards, and by then a single divisional thrust was insufficient to break the enemy's defensive line.

The chance of cutting off the enemy by a repeat of the 'Bizerta manoeuvre' had been lost. 'It was clear to me that a definite plan of battle was now necessary,' Monty noted in his diary on 21 July. 'We had captured practically the whole island and the enemy was cornered in the North-East portion – a situation resembling the Cape Bon peninsula. It was now a case of re-grouping and of collecting ourselves for the final effort.'

On 12 July, having watched Patton's misguided drive westwards to Palermo, Monty sent a goodwill message: 'Many contratulations to you and your gallant soldiers on securing PALERMO and clearing up the western half of Sicily.' Now however he hoped Patton would address himself to the primary task in Sicily, defeating the enemy. 'Would be very honoured if you will come over and stay with me for a night and bring your Chief of Staff. We can then discuss the capture of Messina.'

Patton arrived only two days later, on 25 July, fearing the worst. But to his astonishment Monty greeted him with seemingly genuine cordiality at Syracuse aerodrome and took him straight to the bonnet of his car – where he had a map of north-eastern Sicily spread out.

It was their first meeting since Tripoli. Alexander had still not arrived. Now, instead of asking Patton to protect his rear while Eighth Army pinched all the best roads, Monty suggested the reverse. Patton should take Messina, not Eighth Army. To prove his

[1] Diary, Montgomery Papers.

seriousness Monty proposed that Seventh Army capture Messina by taking *both* major highways north of Etna – 113 and 120. Patton could not believe his ears. 'I felt something was wrong, but have not found it yet,' he recorded with disbelief in his own diary on 25 July.[1]

> After all this had been settled, Alex came. He looked a little mad and, for him, was quite brusque. He told Monty to explain his plan. Monty said he and I had already decided what we were going to do, so Alex got madder and told Monty to show him the plan. . . . The meeting then broke up. No one was offered any lunch and I thought that Monty was ill bred both to Alexander and me. Monty gave me a 5¢ lighter. Someone must have sent him a box of them,

Patton commented sarcastically.[2]

In fact Monty had completely revised his strategy. The erstwhile thrust eastwards by a single American division was now to become a full Seventh Army offensive using four divisions. 'On my left, I urged that 7 American Army should develop two strong thrusts,' Monty recorded in his own diary. 'a) With two Divisions on the axis NICOSIA–TROINA–RANDAZZO. b) With two Divisions on the axis of the North coast road towards MESSINA. This was all agreed.' Furthermore, not only did Monty now directly offer Patton the prize of Messina, he even asked him to push his right-hand thrust, if necessary, beyond Randazzo 'and down the coast at TAORMINA; we would then cut off the whole of two German divisions' facing Eighth Army.

Patton's surprised agreement masked an important fact, however. In overrunning the whole of western Sicily he now had to find forces to garrison it; and far from being able to put four divisions into the field for the Messina offensive, as he could have done straight away if he had not moved west on Palermo, he was hard-pressed to contribute two.

Patton left Syracuse astonished by Montgomery's almost contemptuous brusqueness to Alexander, and incredulous at his volte-face over Messina. Having initially refused to involve Seventh Army in the campaign in eastern Sicily, Monty was now offering Patton the major prize. Why?

The question has never been answered – indeed it has never been asked by historians. The American naval historian S. E. Morison thought Monty's change of plan 'had a vital effect on the entire campaign. It required shifting the pressure from a flat terrain, where he [Monty] could have used his tanks, to a rugged, tangled interior,

---

[1] *The Patton Papers*, op. cit.
[2] Ibid.

perfect for defense; from the seaboard where the Navy could have helped, to mountains that naval gunfire could not reach. It meant a static defense at the plain for almost two weeks while the Seventh and most of the Eighth Armies fought their way into new positions north of Mount Etna. . . . In retrospect, it would have been worth heavy ground casualties to have pushed the enemy out of Catania. If only he could then have been thrown off balance and pursued to Messina, his mobile forces would have been bottled up and compelled to surrender.'[1]

Morison's view reflects the romanticism of a naval historian in awe of big ship guns. The battle of Catania plain was, to many of the participants, the bitterest of the entire war. 'I can still smell the stench of decaying flesh on the banks of that [Simeto] river,' wrote one artillery officer decades after the war. He also remembered being visited by a naval lieutenant 'who said he had a "monitor" and could he help. I apologised for my ignorance and he explained it was a seaborne 15-in gun. I asked him his accuracy of ranging and he said "about a hundred yards". I declined his help!'[2]

Only if Monty had kept Eighth Army concentrated and attacked Catania with both Corps in the first few days of invasion could he conceivably have broken through. It is to Monty's credit that, having recognised his mistake, be belatedly brought Patton's Seventh Army into the picture and closed down his Catanian offensive. The reason for doing so was quite simple, for it mirrored his decision when, on 29 April 1943, recognising that he would not break through the Enfidaville position without excessive casualties and knowing that his divisions would be required for the forthcoming 'Husky' operation, Monty had suddenly closed down his Eighth Army offensive, transferred half of his force to First Army and recommended a concentrated assault from the First Army front. Similarly, almost three months later, when the truth finally dawned on him that he had failed to 'gate-crash' the Catanian defences, Monty took everyone by surprise by the suddenness with which he faced up to reality, handed over the climax of the campaign to Patton's Seventh Army, and began instead to plan the invasion of Italy.

[1] S. E. Morison, *Sicily-Salerno-Anzio*, op. cit.
[2] Quoted in S. W. C. Pack, *Operation 'Husky'*, London 1977.

CHAPTER EIGHT

The End of the Flying Fortress

Patton's bolt westwards and the inevitable delay while 78th Division was shipped to Sicily and up into the mountains south-west of Etna now dictated a lull in the Sicilian campaign, a lull during which Monty hoped to prepare the assault upon the Italian mainland. In his own mind he recognised that the bid for a quick conquest of Sicily had been lost, for in his diary he recorded warning Patton and Alexander at Syracuse that the campaign would probably take a further five weeks to complete: 'I gave it as my opinion that we ought to complete the occupation of SICILY by 1 September, but it would mean hard fighting and everyone must go all out.'

Monty's 'generosity' to Patton was predicated on Eighth Army being allowed to mount the mainland invasion of Italy, and already on 23 July, when closing down his Catanian thrust, Monty had put forward his claims to command this invasion:

Consider that whole operation of extension of war on to mainland must now be handled by Eighth Army as once SICILY is cleared of enemy a great deal of my resources can be put on to mainland,

he signalled to Alexander. By handing over the lion's share of the Sicilian campaign now to Patton, he would be able to rest his tired divisions on the Catania front, ready for the mainland assault, in cor.junction with Horrocks's reserve (10) Corps:

I will carry the war into ITALY on a front of two Corps,

Monty's 23 July signal continued, blithely confident that Alexander would do whatever Monty proposed. Dempsey's 13 Corps, having been rested in the Catanian plain, would strike at Reggio, across the narrow straits dividing Sicily from the mainland; 10 Corps would land at Gioja direct from North Africa – 'the whole being a normal Eighth Army operation. We should aim at earliest possible date which if 56 Div and 7 Armd Div sail from TRIPOLI could be about 21 August but C-in-C Med will presumably say what this date is to be.' Without waiting even for Alexander's approval Monty had 'told

Horrocks to carry on with above outline plan and to establish a small advanced HQ with me here at once. . . . Am certain we must get cracking on BUTTRESS [code name for the invasion of Italy] as early as possible after we have cleared up SICILY.'

All this was a far cry from the pachyderm-like attitude ascribed to Monty by certain writers ever since, including Eisenhower himself who would turn out to be the unfortunate architect of the chaotic mess which befell Allied planning with regard to the invasion of Italy.

For the moment, however, Monty assumed that in return for giving Patton the major role in Sicily, Eighth Army would conduct the operations in Italy. At Syracuse therefore he declared on 25 July 'that once we had cleaned up SICILY the Eighth Army could operate against ITALY as stated in my U 24 [signal] of 23 July'.

The GIOJA landing had the code name of BUTTRESS.
The REGGIO landing had the code name of BAYTOWN.
There were several factors to be worked out:
a) What would be the time-lag between the end of operations in SICILY and the launching of BUTTRESS?
b) Could BUTTRESS be launched before BAYTOWN?
c) Could the RAF support BUTTRESS and BAYTOWN at the same time?
I asked to be informed as to the whole policy of future operations on the mainland.

Alexander, as usual, had no idea about the policy. Nor had Eisenhower, and the following day both the Axis and the Allied camps were thrown into confusion by news of the fall of Mussolini. Would Italy now be 'knocked out of the war', the strategic reason for invading first Sicily and then the mainland? Mussolini, dismissed by King Victor Emmanuel and exiled to the Isle of Ponza, was succeeded as Premier by the ex-Chief of Staff, Marshal Badoglio, and a period of amazing treachery and double-dealing followed.

Monty was unimpressed. 'As far as we ourselves were concerned it seemed that it would make no difference to our immediate problem of turning the Germans out of SICILY. But it might have far-reaching political repercussions,' he noted in his diary on 26 July. Anxious lest the fickle C-in-Cs, Eisenhower and Alexander, become distracted by the Italian political machinations, Monty now determined to ensure that both Eighth Army and Seventh Army kept their eyes on the ball. That same day he went to see Leese to make a 'firm Army plan for the next operations' and sent a cable to Patton asking if he could pay a call on him in Palermo:

Would like to visit you on Wednesday 28 July. Would arrive

airfield 1200 hours in my FORTRESS. Query, is this convenient to you. Would bring my Chief of Staff.[1]

As Monty's ADC recalled, it was 'as if someone sent a telegram saying, Can I come to lunch in my Rolls-Royce?'[2] – particularly as Patton did not possess one. Piqued, Patton replied in the affirmative, though refusing to greet Monty in person at the airfield, and ignoring the question: was the airfield big enough for a Flying Fortress to land there?

Monty's obsession with his Flying Fortress was now about to be rudely ended. On 27 July he sent a further signal to Patton: 'Will you please notify all your anti-aircraft guns stations that I will be travelling in a FORTRESS round the South coast tomorrow and landing at PALERMO at 1200 hours.'[3] At noon the next day the coastal AA batteries on Sicily fell silent as General Montgomery's green giant took off the Syracuse runway and began to circle the island.

'I used to sit in the nose of this bloody machine,' recalled Monty's ADC, Johnny Henderson, almost four decades later.

The most frightening thing that ever happened to me was landing at Palermo in Sicily. . . . They hadn't cleared whether the runway was long enough. And we went down this runway and it absolutely ate it up. The hangars were at the end and it wasn't long enough. I remember I was sitting in the glass dome in which I always sat, and I saw the hangar coming up – and the pilot did the most amazing job. He swung the whole thing round and we landed on our side. I mean he put all the brakes on one side and revved one engine and swung the whole thing round – which wrote it off. That was the end of it. It collapsed on one side. We got out pretty shaken.[4]

Air Vice-Marshall Broadhurst, commanding the Desert Air Force, was also in the plane. 'The strip was too short,' he recalled with a laugh, 'and we only just got away with it – I thought we were going to turn over!'[5] 'I very nearly got killed in my Fortress the other day,' Monty wrote a fortnight later to Brooke, 'trying to land at Palermo to see Patton. He had said it was OK for a Fortress, but it was far too small.'[6]

It was probably the nearest Monty had come to death or serious injury in the war so far, but at least it put paid to his delusions of

[1] Eighth Army HQ War Diary (WO 169/8494), PRO.
[2] J. R. Henderson, interview of 13.8.81.
[3] Eighth Army HQ War Diary (WO 169/8494), PRO.
[4] Loc. cit.
[5] Loc. cit.
[6] Letter of 14.8.43.

grandeur with regard to big aeroplanes. Ever since the eve of 'Husky' Monty had fretted and fussed over the Flying Fortress, displaying a veritable neurosis about its whereabouts and return. In fact he pestered Tedder with more signals about the Flying Fortress than he did about operational matters. As Henderson later remarked, Monty 'did get certain things on his mind, in his head, and wouldn't drop them. Bees in his bonnet'[1] – and this was certainly true about his prize Fortress. He had left it in Cairo on 29 June to have new engines fitted: 'I have done so much travelling in the Fortress that it now needs 4 new engines,' he boasted to Phyllis Reynolds on 30 June. 'This will take some little time as the new engines will have to be flown over to Cairo from Algiers. So the RAF have given me a Hudson aircraft and I am using that till the Fortress is ready again. The Hudson is not so steady in the air as the "Fortress", and I was very very "air sick" yesterday flying back from Cairo.' A week later, on 9 July, Monty was chasing Tedder:

What is situation regarding FORTRESS and when can I expect it to join me. I would like it sent to me in MALTA.[2]

The following day, the day of the invasion of Sicily, he sent another signal:

How is FORTRESS and when can I expect it. Grateful you send it MALTA when ready.[3]

Tedder at length replied that the aeroplane was expected to be ready 'by Wednesday July 14 and will arrange to have it delivered MALTA'; thus on 14 July, as Eighth Army battled vainly for Catania, Monty signalled to Alexander's Chief of Staff in Tunis:

Hudson can return to Cairo. Get FORTRESS to MALTA and keep it there.[4]

This was a mistake, for four days later the Hudson was gone but there was still no sign of the Fortress.

Grateful if you will send me news of my FORTRESS and particularly when it will arrive MALTA,

Monty signalled impatiently to Tedder.[5] Two days passed, but there

---

[1] Loc. cit.
[2] Eighth Army HQ War Diary (WO 169/8494), PRO.
[3] Ibid.
[4] Ibid.
[5] Ibid.

was still no word of the aircraft's whereabouts, so Monty now appealed directly to Eisenhower's Chief of Staff, who had made the original bet:

Have lost my FORTRESS. It went to MALTA on 15 July and then disappeared over your way [Algiers]. May be at CASABLANCA or CHATEAUDUN. Can you find it for me and send it to MALTA fit for flying duties again. Hope you are well. Come and visit me if you can get away.[1]

This invitation, clearly related to the return of his 'Rolls Royce', must have astonished Monty's Tactical Headquarters staff when it was taken for enciphering, for Monty had up until then refused to allow any visitors, however eminent, to Eighth Army – had indeed provoked lasting umbrage by his refusal, in particular, to allow the GOC of the Canadian First Army to step ashore in Sicily only a few days before his signal to Bedell Smith. General McNaughton, anxious not only to see his men in battle, but to gather lessons that would be of value in planning further Canadian operations in Europe, was understandably livid. It seemed an act of callous chauvinism by Monty towards a Canadian general he had despised since his command of South Eastern Army in England in 1941. Monty had in fact asked the young commander of the 1st Canadian Division, Major-General Guy Simonds, if he wanted to be visited by McNaughton, but in such a way that Simonds was encouraged to say no. Not content with refusing McNaughton permission to land in Sicily, Monty added insult to injury by threatening to have him arrested if McNaughton disobeyed the injunction! Word very soon spread, and when Mountbatten wrote to Monty on 15 July he was veritably obsequious in his thanks:

From the earliest days of my job I noticed that you knew far more about Combined Operations than any other General & I was therefore not surprised at your success in Africa, but it is only since I had the privilege of landing in Sicily with you and seeing the way you handled the battle & the astonishing hold you have over your Army that I have definitely joined the ranks – in fact the front rank – of your Fans.

The PM has called you 'the man of destiny' & now I have formed exactly the same opinion. . . .

It was only when I saw Andy McNaughton & the Canadian C.G.S. kicking their heels here waiting for your permission to go to Sicily that I fully appreciated the great honour you had done me in letting me . . . come over.[2]

[1] Ibid.
[2] Letter of 15.6.43, Montgomery Papers.

McNaughton, though he was eventually permitted to land in Sicily once hostilities had ceased, never forgave Monty, as Sir Alan Brooke related to Monty in a letter of September 1943 from Canada:

> You fairly infuriated him for forbidding him access to his troops in Sicily!! He wasted an hour of my time on his return explaining to me how strained imperial relations must in future be owing to such treatment, the serious outlook of his Government, etc. etc.[1]

Such favouritism towards some and excessive hostility to others certainly struck Monty's staff as an embarrassing eccentricity of their 'Chief': a fantasia of unpredictable personal relations that would continue to astonish those closest to Monty throughout his life. 'I mean if he'd got it in for someone, he didn't change his mind easily,' Johnny Henderson later explained. 'I think that's a weakness. There are a lot of people who have the ability, because circumstances change, conditions, information, to change their mind. He didn't. He would never change it – and if he did he would never let you know.'[2] It became, Henderson soon learned, positively dangerous to speak badly of someone in Monty's hearing, for Monty's almost photographic memory seemed peculiarly attuned to storing the evil that related to people.

> If you said somebody was not to be trusted, he would take notice. And often afterwards he'd say: But you said that fellow was not to be trusted! And if you said that someone was good or frightfully nice or something, he took no notice. I mean that you never heard it repeated that he was a good fellow. But if you said the fellow was bad – well, one very soon learned not to disparage people. He *always* remembered if anyone said someone was bad, he would come out with it at some time.
>
> He never really gave real credit to anyone else.[3]

There was therefore distinct relief when the oversized and neurotically nurtured Flying Fortress met its end. The aeroplane had been located at Châteaudun by Tedder on 20 July – one of its new engines had failed – and it had been sent to Syracuse as soon as it was ready. Almost immediately it was 'written off' on Patton's Palermo runway. A sheepish Eighth Army Commander cabled to Bedell Smith after returning from Palermo in a borrowed B-25:

> Had difficulty with Fortress today at Palermo and consider should change it in view of small airfields on which we are now working.

[1] Letter of 29.9.43, Montgomery Papers.
[2] Loc. cit.
[3] Ibid.

Can you send me a C-47 with JEEP. Will you have long range tanks fitted. Grateful if you will sent it to CASSIBILE airfield near SYRACUSE.[1]

Bedell Smith responded immediately, and a grateful, chastened Montgomery thanked him four days later:

C-47 has arrived. Thank you very much. Am glad to have it as escaped a nasty accident in FORTRESS only by skill of pilot and might have been killed. Am sending C-47 to MAISON BLANCHE to be fitted with seats and have other minor adjustments made. Grateful if you will tell depot at MAISON BLANCHE to do this work.[2]

Meanwhile in Palermo on 28 July, having sent only his ADC to meet the shaken Eighth Army Commander and entourage at the airfield, Patton then put on an American extravaganza, a whole escort of scout cars and motorcycles to bring Montgomery to the Palace of Palermo where Patton had already established his headquarters for some five days. There was a guard of honour at the palace and a band. 'We had a great reception,' Monty recorded in his diary. 'The Americans are very easy to work with. I discussed plans for future operations with General Patton.'

Once again Monty went over his plan that the Americans take Messina, and the incredulous Patton listened while Monty 'kept repeating that the move of the 45th Division along the [Northern] coast was a most significant operation. I can't decide whether he's honest,' Patton noted suspiciously in his own diary.[3] Was Monty stressing the northern coastal route so as later to claim the parallel inland highway? 'On the other hand, he said that if we got to Taormina [on the eastern coast] first, we were to run south.' To Patton this volte-face, when 'previously he had insisted that we not come as far as the coast', was a mystery, and he was taking no chances. The moment Monty had left that afternoon he sent signals to Bradley and the 45th Division's Commander, General Middleton, to start pushing hard. 'This is a horse race, in which the prestige of the US Army is at stake. We must take Messina before the British,' he signalled to Middleton. 'Please use your best efforts to facilitate the success of our race.'[4]

Patton's patent disbelief in Monty's motives was the direct result of Monty's earlier dismissive attitude, and if Patton now made a

[1] Eighth Army HQ War Diary (WO 169/8494), PRO.
[2] Ibid.
[3] *The Patton Papers*, op. cit.
[4] Ibid.

great hue and cry about a 'race to Messina' after being offered all the routes to the port, Monty had only himself to blame. As Monty's Chief of Intelligence later acknowledged:

> I think the fact is that we behaved [in the early part of the campaign] very badly, by and large, because there was old Patton who really was cracking away and occasionally had to be halted to make room for Eighth Army to go through the door – he really got his whips out and made a monkey out of us, I reckon . . . had got the campaign sewn up while we were still, you know, clearing our throats!
> Monty I think was left standing by Patton's speed.[1]

Equally, Brigadier Williams was clear that there was no 'race' involved, once Patton had proved himself and Monty had altered his strategy: 'I don't think the sort of notion of race occurred.'[2] Monty's Chief of Staff, who flew with Monty to the fateful Palermo meeting, was more forthright. As far as General de Guingand was concerned there was neither race nor rivalry from Montgomery's point of view – 'no, none. It was all balls that, about who was going to get to Messina first. We were *delighted* when we heard that Patton had got to Messina first – and about the fictitious scene in the film *Patton*, de Guingand was even more acid: 'Absolute cock, in the film: Monty marching at the head of the Highlanders – all balls!'[3]

For de Guingand had been present at the Palermo conference, and knew the real truth: not only had Patton accepted Monty's plan for the Americans to take Messina via the northern axis, but Patton had even made wild predictions about how quickly he could do it. 'We had a very, very pleasant talk and discussion, and Patton agreed with Monty's plan – said he'd use the Navy to help him along the coast – but it didn't seem to work out so well.'[4]

Patton's 'race' therefore was inspired by distrust of Monty's intentions and the need to match his own wildly optimistic forecast about the time it would take him to reach Messina. The proof of this would be the unpopularity Patton now evoked as he belatedly turned his whole Seventh Army eastwards – and began to face the same sort of determined German resistance that had put paid to Monty's original ambitions in Sicily.

[1] Sir Edgar Williams, loc. cit.
[2] Ibid.
[3] Loc. cit.
[4] Ibid.

CHAPTER NINE

'The Americans Have Done Splendidly'

Omar Bradley, Commanding 2 US Corps, naturally found Patton's directive to turn first west to Palermo, then right towards Messina, a poor way to run a military campaign. With the 45th Division headed leftwards to Palermo and the 1st Division still anchoring Leese's 30 Corps around Enna, 'we were fighting enemy with back and front,' he later recalled. As regards Palermo, 'I wasn't too keen about it. Not interested. Our objective later the east. Nothing to be gained by going into Palermo.'[1] Moreover Palermo harbour was blocked by some forty-four ships, so that the erstwhile importance of the port was irrelevant. Bradley was thus all the more aggrieved when Patton met him on the road and listened to an explanation of 2 US Corps tactics – outflanking points of enemy resistance and bringing artillery well forward. 'Asked me how I was doing. Then in a grandiose fashion said I want you to get into Messina just as fast as you can. I don't want you to waste time on these manoeuvres, even if you've got to spend men to do it. I want you to beat Monty into Messina. I was very much shocked. I replied: "I will take every step I can to get there as soon as I can." To me the quickest way was through manoeuvre and that I continued to do.'[2]

To the thoughtful, bespectacled infantryman, Patton's cavalry histrionics were painful. 'Patton was developing as an unpopular guy,' Bradley later confided. 'He steamed about with great convoys of cars. Great squads of cameramen. Became unpopular with the troops.' With his commanders Patton was even less popular. 'To George, tactics was simply a process of bulling ahead. Never seemed to think out a campaign. Seldom made a careful estimate of the situation. I thought him a rather shallow commander,' Bradley declared.[3]

An example of Patton's shallowness was the way he ran his Army Headquarters – 'that great silence we call Army,' as Bradley's Corps Intelligence officer, Colonel Dickson, once remarked.[4] 'Seventh

---

[1] Bradley Commentaries, loc. cit.
[2] Ibid.
[3] Ibid.
[4] Ibid.

Army was usually disorganised. It seemed to be too busy trying to be an headquarters to worry much about its troops,' he later recalled.[1] 'We learned how not to behave from Patton's Seventh Army' – for when Bradley's Corps began to hit serious opposition near Troina, it was found that Seventh Army had no ammunition in its eastern dumps. As Bradley remembered, 'the supply position began to get critical when we reached [the northern coast] and turned east with two divisions – one on coast, one in middle. Just before Troina we immobilised the artillery and took all our trucks including Prime Movers and sent them back to the [southern] beach for ammo. Took one day back to beach, one back to position.' In the whole of Seventh Army's ammunition dump at Caltanisetta, Bradley recalled, there were only twenty-five rounds! 'We were always short on supply, largely because Seventh Army showed a complete lack of understanding of the fundamentals of supply,' Bradley summarised.[2]

Worse still was the situation over air support at Seventh Army, which was graphically illustrated when American bombers began bombing not only Bradley's ground forces, but even Leese's British troops and tanks. 'Now why in hell are you bombing us?' signalled Leese one day; and Bradley recorded: 'Map study showed that road net on his town was similar to that on Troina. We did not have proper method of co-ordinating ground and air – was not worked out until we got into Normandy.'[3]

Bradley's remarks were made after the war; but Monty's brief visit to Patton's headquarters in Palermo was enough to give him a pretty shrewd idea of its strengths and failings as an Army HQ. 'The two weak points I would say with the American Army are,' he noted in his diary on 28 July 1943:

a) Administration. Administration in the field is not understood by the Generals, and so it is not gripped on a high level.
b) Use of air. They do not realise the need for a combined army-air plan, and the airman is left out and hardly knows what is going on. What they really need is an Air Force; at present their air is part of their army.

Much specious comparison has been made over the years between Montgomery and Patton. Patton certainly got his subordinates to fight; he had a cavalryman's eye for terrain and had, as his Intelligence officer observed, an excellent 'intuition' about likely enemy moves – 'he could figure enemy reactions in simple formulas'.[4] Or as Bradley observed, 'he had a good feeling of what the enemy could or

[1] Ibid.
[2] Ibid.
[3] Ibid.
[4] Oscar Koch, loc. cit.

331

could not do – had this instinct developed to a higher degree than any commander I knew';[1] but beyond this, Patton's capabilities as an Army Commander did not go. As the Sicilian campaign progressed to its climax, Bradley was more and more outraged by Patton's childish histrionics, his back-seat driving, his fantasies of seaborne 'end-runs', his hopeless inability to run an efficient army headquarters and his failure to visit his commanders in the field, so much so that by the end of the campaign in Sicily, particularly after the 'slapping incidents', Bradley was glad to be ordered to leave Seventh Army and go to England.

'If it had been up to me in Sicily,' he later confessed,

I would have relieved him instantly and would have had nothing more to do with him. . . . He was colorful but he was impetuous, full of temper, bluster, inclined to treat the troops and subordinates as morons. His whole concept of command was opposite to mine. He was primarily a showman. The show always seemed to come first.[2]

There was of course a similarity here between Patton and Montgomery. 'Patton didn't particularly like Monty,' Bradley felt. 'Too cocky for him. Possibly too much like Patton himself.'[3]

Certainly the extent of Monty's showmanship has vexed historians ever since. One month before the Sicilian landings, Eisenhower had penned his 'opinions and impressions' concerning several senior officers, and had discussed this aspect of the Eighth Army Commander's personality.

General Montgomery is a very able, dynamic type of army commander. I personally think that the only thing he needs is a strong immediate commander. He loves the limelight; but in seeking it, it is possible that he does so only because of the effect upon his own soldiers, who are certainly devoted to him. I have great confidence in him as a combat commander. He is intelligent, a good talker, and has a flare for showmanship. Like all other senior British officers, he has been most loyal – personally and officially – and has shown no disposition whatsoever to overstep the bounds imposed by Allied unity of command.[4]

By contrast, Eisenhower considered Patton 'a shrewd soldier who believes in showmanship to such an extent that he is almost flamboyant. He talks too much and too quickly and sometimes

[1] Bradley Commentaries, loc. cit.
[2] Ibid.
[3] Ibid.
[4] The Eisenhower Diaries, ed. Robert H. Ferrell, New York 1981.

332

creates a very bad impression. Moreover, I feel that he is not always a good example to subordinates, who may be guided only by his surface actions without understanding the deep sense of duty, courage and service that makes up his real personality. He has done well as a combat corps commander, and I expect him to do well in all future operations.'[1]

Inevitably of course Eisenhower favoured quiet dependable men like Bradley, men who could be trusted to get on with the job without questioning directives from above, and forgetting that he, Eisenhower, owed his continued overall command of the Allied forces in the Mediterranean, especially after the disaster at Kasserine, to Montgomery and to Patton: field commanders who, whatever their failings, had the measure of their Axis opponents.

Patton and Montgomery were undoubtedly the best Allied combat generals of their time. Both were showmen; but whereas Patton's showmanship comprised outrageous bluster founded on profound military intuition, Monty's represented a strangely simple egoism that rested on unequalled professionalism. The power of the press, for instance, had only really begun to dawn on Monty when, as his Canadian ADC recalled, he took command of South-Eastern Army in England in 1941 – and had to put himself 'across' to some 50,000 Canadian subordinates.[2] Then in the desert, Geoffrey Keating's camera and cameramen had started to transform his sharp, unphotogenic profile into an identifiable image that could be matched against the rippling effects of his personality. There is, in the diary kept by Eisenhower's naval aide, an amusing account of Keating, who on 3 June 1943 successfully gate-crashed Churchill's top level conference of senior commanders at Eisenhower's villa in Algiers. Keating's pictures have gone into history with Churchill seated on the veranda over a map, flanked by his Allied army, air and naval chiefs.

Captain Keating and his photographers accepted my invitation for a highball after the distinguished personages had retired to the meeting-dining room. Keating disclosed that he is the personal press agent of General Montgomery. Said he eats in the General's mess, knows all the plans and personally supervises the photographic units. He was responsible, he said, for *Desert Victory*, the film that has created such a popular impression of Montgomery in America. He said England had no hero so he set out to make one and Montgomery was now 'it'.[3]

Captain Keating certainly had reason so to boast. Utterly fearless, he had indeed been responsible for the film footage of the battle of

[1] Ibid.
[2] Testimony of Lt-Colonel Trumbull Warren to author, 26.5.82.
[3] Diary of Harry C. Butcher, loc. cit.

Alamein that was the backbone of *Desert Victory*, and as Monty's
ADC Johnny Henderson recalled after Keating's death, Monty was
well aware of the debt he owed Keating:

> Geoffrey Keating was the fellow who built him up. And when
> Monty came back to England after Tunis he was the one fellow he
> wanted to bring – there was myself and John Poston *and* Geoffrey
> Keating – the *one* fellow he took.
>
> He took him as a sort of gratitude. . . . He *did* the PR whether he
> was paid or not – it just came automatically. He had the entrée in
> those days. I never even questioned his role! No, it was strange, he
> seemed to be under no one, he just swanned about, no one
> questioned what he was doing. But he was responsible for all the
> photographs, filming. . . .[1]

Keating's moment of glory was, however, almost over, for Monty
was a general who allowed great latitude in a subordinate's exercise
of his duties – as long as he did not overstep the mark. For Monty's
unique professionalism did not merely mean a deep knowledge of
the various arms of his army – it meant his amazing control over it.
Beneath his showmanship an indefatigable 'Inspector General'
watched over the intricate 'machine' that was Eighth Army, ensuring
that all felt answerable to him, personally, for the efficient and
professional performance of their departments – chaplains, medical
officers, supply troops. . . . Although he might form lasting personal
convictions about certain officers, his final concern was professional
performance, and not even his Corps Commanders were spared the
lash of his tongue if he felt they had failed in this respect, as Air
Vice-Marshal Broadhurst witnessed:

> Now another thing happened in Sicily which will show you
> something about Monty. 'Bimbo' Dempsey, who'd then got 13
> Corps, they were completely new . . . they'd given a bombline,
> asked for air support, close support, they were going to attack
> somewhere. And the Germans withdrew before we got there. So
> they advanced without bothering to tell us. And we attacked the
> place they said. And of course it was Dempsey's own troops [who
> were hit].
>
> So Dempsey was stinkingly rude. Freddie [de Guingand] rang
> me up and said. 'This is terrible, attacked our troops. I thought
> we'd grown out of that.' I said, 'Well, I'll go into it.' And of course
> Freddie signalled Monty.
>
> I went into it and found they'd advanced after they'd asked for
> air support and then forgotten to cancel it. So I rang up Freddie and
> said, 'It's your lot this time, boy.'

[1] Loc. cit.

Monty sent for Dempsey. I was there with him. And he lined Dempsey up and gave him the biggest strip I've ever seen a general get – don't know if that's in his diary. Made him apologise. . . .

You see, there was no bias at all. If the chap was wrong, that was it, he got a rocket. If I'd been wrong, he'd have been bloody rude to me![1]

Conversely, whatever reputation he might possess for the way he ruthlessly weeded out the 'dead wood' in his fighting formations, Monty was in fact much more circumspect about sacking people than is sometimes imagined. He had refused McNaughton permission to land in Sicily in order to 'protect' the young commander of 1st Canadian Division in his first battle. When Simonds sacked the commander of 1st Canadian Infantry Brigade, Monty wrote at once to Leese, the Corps Commander:

This is a great pity. Graham is an excellent fellow and much beloved in his Bde; I expect Simmonds [sic] lost his temper.

Simmonds is a young and very inexperienced Divisional general and has much to learn about command. He will upset his Division if he starts sacking the Brigadiers like this.

I will of course hear the story, but Simmonds would be well advised to consult his superiors before he takes violent action in which he may not be backed up.

I think I had better see Simmonds tomorrow.[2]

It was this professional pride in the performance, cohesion and morale of his Eighth Army that led Monty to believe it should undertake the assault of Italy. Thus while Patton drove himself to the point of hysteria in his distrust of Monty and his insistence on seeing the final phase of the Sicilian campaign as a 'horse race' with Eighth Army to Messina, Monty simply made sure that Leese co-operated with Bradley and meanwhile concentrated on Eighth Army's preparations for the extension of the war onto the Italian mainland. The day before flying to Palermo he had written a long letter to Brooke, his first since his return to the Mediterranean:

Sicily
27 July 1943

My dear Brookie,
All goes well here. We have now got the enemy pinned in the NE corner of the island, and are in a position to be able to set about

---

[1] Loc. cit.
[2] Letter of 16.7.43 in possession of Mr Daniel Andrews. Brigadier Graham was reinstated.

him. It will not be easy as he is in ideal defensive country, and his troops are all German, and very good and determined Germans too. Once we get the air stepped up we can give him a nasty time, but it takes time to get the communications necessary to operate a big air force. I do not believe myself that you can operate a tactical air force without a telephone lay-out; you miss all the good opportunities.

I am planning to develop a very heavy pressure about 2nd August directed towards ADRANO, and if the 7th American Army puts in a full-blooded effort on my left then I believe the end should be in sight. We have not done so badly; in two weeks we have got the whole island and pinned the Germans in the NE corner. I tremble to think what might have happened if we had launched this party on the original plan; I suppose a good deal of mud has been slung about, and chiefly directed at me, during the pre-Husky period; but we have won the battle and that is really what matters.

The fighting for possession of the plain of Catania has been quite some of the hardest we have ever had in my Army. Picked German parachute troops were used and they were really tough and fanatical Nazis. It was a very bloody killing match. I won the battle for the plain and now own the whole of it, with my troops up to the foothills of ETNA. I am making airfields on the South edge of the plain, and stepping up my air; I now have 10 Spitfire Sqns and Kittybomber Sqns working with me. But the Germans hold Catania itself and the foothills running round the South of Etna; they are very strongly posted.

Catania itself is of little value to me; I am getting 4,000 tons a day in through Syracuse, and some more through Augusta. But I want the foothills so that I can make full use of the plain for more airfields; at present he can shell me off airfields, except on the South edge of the plain, with his long range guns which can do up to 27,000 yards. I am therefore going 'to hold' on the Catania front and stage a blow about 2nd August on the thrust line ADRANO– BRONTE–RANDAZZO, working round the West and North of ETNA; this will cut off the enemy in the Catania area. If the Americans work along the North coast towards Messina, we should end the party.

But it will have to be an 'all-in' party, with everyone 100% out and especially the air. The Bosche will fight desperately and with great determination; I imagine he wants to gain time for preparing the defence of Italy, and hoping for early winter rains.

The Americans have done splendidly on our left and are very easy to work with.

The Canadians are going great guns; they are very willing to learn and they learn very fast; they will be one of the best Divisions I have in due course.

My casualties to date are 400 officers and 5400 other ranks. A marked feature is the high proportion of officers killed to other ranks killed – as high as 1 to 6 in some units; and averaging 1 to 9 in the whole army. It has never been more than 1 to 15 before.

Having filled Brooke in on the Sicilian campaign, Monty moved on to the next question: Italy.

I would be very interested to hear your views as to the political repercussions of the fall of Mussolini.

From our point of view here it seems to make no difference to our job, which is to turn the Germans out of SICILY. But can you persuade the Italians to help us turn the Germans out of ITALY?

Mussolini having gone, it seems that the Fascist party will now disintegrate, and that is bound to affect the fighting services and the civil population.

I am sure we must go on here, and put everything in to knocking ITALY out of the war this year. I believe it could be done.

I would like to take a strong force and sail into the Bay of NAPLES, land there, capture the city, and cut off all the Germans in the toe of ITALY. How about this? The effect in ITALY would be terrific.

Ironically, it was on this day that Eisenhower finally charged General Mark Clark with the possible assault on Salerno, the next bay south of Naples. Like Monty, Clark also favoured the Bay of Naples itself; but, as will be seen, the Air Force chiefs declared it was beyond fighter cover, and the Navy refused to countenance risking aircraft carriers without such cover.

Eisenhower chose Clark not in order to deprive Montgomery of command, but in the innocent hope of retaining flexibility. Mussolini had fallen, but the response of Hitler and the Italian fascist party was still indeterminate. Eisenhower thus intended to have three possible main assaults in hand: Clark's Anglo-American landing south of Naples ('Avalanche'), Horrocks's landing at Gioja ('Buttress') and Montgomery's simple crossing of the Messina Straits ('Baytown'). He seems never to have considered the various landings as related to one another, and thus the whole sorry seedbed of muddle, ambiguity and confusion was sown.

Monty's disappointment would be extreme. In the meantime, ignorant of Eisenhower's orders to Clark, he had assumed that Eighth Army, having granted Patton the major role in ending the Sicilian campaign, would be chosen to mount whichever Italian assault was decided upon. Monty was anxious about the future, however, as his letter to Brooke demonstrated:

I don't know if you have any plans to pull Alex home as Supreme Commander in England. If so, I think you would have to leave me here; there is quite definitely no one else out here who could command the land armies for Eisenhower,

he considered.

I have always regarded Alex and myself as a very good team; between us we have the qualities necessary to do the business.

But I have a very definite feeling that if you want Alex at home you would be wise to leave me here, so long as there is a war to be conducted in this theatre; we could join up again later if necessary when we have cleaned up here. I do not believe we ought both to leave this theatre at present.

But all this is of course none of my business,

he added, evidently unaware that Brooke himself coveted the post of Supreme Commander for the cross-Channel assault. 'The very best wishes to you. You must be having a terrific amount of work, and some anxious times. But I feel that things are going very well, and as you want; if we keep our feet firmly on the floor now, there should be no doubt about the final result.'

In Monty's eyes, however, the Allies did *not* now keep their feet firmly on the floor – in fact there seemed, over the ensuing days, a veritable conspiracy among the higher commanders to levitate, and to keep Monty in the dark about the Allies' real intentions. Thus on 27 July, the day Eisenhower charged Mark Clark with 'Avalanche', employing Horrocks's British 10 Corps as well as an American Corps, Monty received a signal from Alexander's headquarters putting Horrocks's 10 Corps 'under command 8th Army forthwith for planning and execution operation BUTTRESS'.[1] Overnight Horrocks thus became victim of a tug-of-war, both Clark and Monty determined to have, rather than share, his favours.

Small wonder that the Allied invasion of Italy was so marred by contradictory planning. Poor General Marshall has had to take much of the blame, since he emphatically refused to promise further American reinforcements to the Mediterranean theatre and insisted that Eisenhower make do with what he had. This Eisenhower failed competently to do, instead falling victim to conflicting Allied exigencies and opportunities. Instead of concentrating, as Monty had finally insisted in 'Husky', on one concerted plan that would give the constituent forces ample time to prepare and train for the assault, Eisenhower dithered in an ill-fated attempt to retain flexibility. The result was a chaotic shambles.

[1] Alexander Papers, loc. cit.

From Monty's point of view, the decision by Eisenhower to charge Mark Clark's untried Fifth Army Headquarters (still in North Africa) with the assault on Naples was particularly galling. Had Monty not bent over backwards to hand Messina to the Americans so that Eighth Army could conserve its assault divisions for the invasion of Italy? Furthermore, if Clark took Horrocks's 10 Corps, Monty would be left with only a single British Corps to command and the crossing of the Messina Straits as his only goal.

The situation began now to parallel that of 'Husky' – in reverse. Only Eisenhower, who was conducting the delicate and treacherous negotiations with Mussolini's successor, could really decide what further operations should be undertaken in Italy, and Eisenhower evidently did not agree that Montgomery should conduct them. Instead, Eighth Army was rapidly relegated to the same secondary role as Patton's Force 343 had been in the 'Husky' planning. Moreover, as in Sicily, the army charged with the secondary role would in time be called upon to carry out the more spectacular one.

Alexander, caught between Eisenhower and Montgomery, could give no clear idea which projected plan would be undertaken, and for three weeks, between 27 July and 16 August 1943, he did not dare take Horrocks's 10 Corps away from Monty's command. Yet by early August it was obvious to Eighth Army planners that 'Avalanche' was threatening not only to make Horrocks's 10 Corps landing at Gioja unnecessary, but also the crossing of the Messina Straits at Reggio (Operation 'Baytown'); for there would be little point in dispersing the Allied effort by landing two armies, over 250 miles apart, each requiring sea transport, supply and air protection from the now limited resources in the Mediterranean. 'If AVALANCHE is a success then we shall reinforce that front, for there is little point in laboriously fighting our way up southern Italy,' de Guingand would comment at one planning conference. Yet this, eventually, was what Eighth Army would have to do.[1]

Monty's disgust – not only at the tragi-comedy relating to the Allied plans for Italy, but also at the total failure of the Allies to stop the German evacuation of Sicily – was barely concealed.

[1] Eighth Army HQ War Diary, entry of 10.8.43 (WO 169/8495), PRO.

CHAPTER TEN

The Axis Evacuation of Sicily

Monty's plan for the final reduction of Sicily hinged on the capture of Adrano, the gateway not only to the north-west road round Mount Etna but also the lateral road running south of the mountain to Catania. On 31 July a German officer was shot 'who had with him an attaché case containing map, tracings, and orders giving the whole enemy defensive layout and his plans for withdrawal if unable to hold on. This was a most valuable capture, the best we have had,' Monty noted in his diary.

The German plans indicated a three-stage withdrawal to Messina, together with evacuation by ferry. By 2 August Monty expected to 'storm Adrano on night 5/6 August', and once that happened he was certain the 'enemy would be in a very difficult situation' and possibly begin evacuation, as he cabled Alexander. What Allied preparations had been made to meet this contingency?

Alexander rushed to Sicily to see Monty, spending the night of 3 August at Eighth Army Tac HQ. From Monty's headquarters he now sent the following signal – in which Monty's somewhat bitter irony is plain:

Personal for Admiral of the Fleet CUNNINGHAM and Air Marshal TEDDER from General ALEXANDER.
Indications suggest that Germans are making preparations for withdrawal to the mainland when this becomes necessary. It is quite possible he may start pulling out before front collapses. We must be in a position to take immediate advantage of such a situation by using full weight of Naval and Air power. You have no doubt co-ordinated plans to meet this contingency and I for my part will watch situation most carefully so as to let you know the right moment to strike and this may well come upon us sooner than we expect.[1]

There was, however, no answer. Eisenhower, the overall Commander-in-Chief, was too deeply engaged in dealing with the British

[1] Eighth Army HQ War Diary, entry of 3.8.43 (WO 169/8494), PRO.

and American Chiefs of Staff to take more than a sideline interest in the Sicilian campaign, and without his intercession Tedder and Cunningham did nothing. The addition of General Evelegh's 78th Division had given Leese's 30 Corps just the extra impetus it needed and one by one the towns leading to Adrano fell.

There were signs that the Germans recognised the vulnerability of their Catanian front, which could soon be attacked from the rear via Adrano. 'The enemy line was now in grave danger and he began to withdraw his positions South and South-West of CATANIA,' Monty noted on 3 August, and by 4 August Eighth Army was on the outskirts of Catania and Misterbianco, objectives they had once thought to capture on 14 July. The following day Catania, Misterbianco and Paterno all fell. On 6 August, as Monty had promised, Adrano was captured, and the German Etna line was finally broken. Yet still there was no news from Eisenhower, Tedder or Cunningham. On 7 August Monty sadly noted, after seeing the latest RAF reconnaissance reports:

There has been heavy traffic all day across the Straits of MESSINA, and the enemy is without doubt starting to get his stuff away.
I have tried hard to find out what the combined Navy-Air plan is in order to stop him getting away; I have been unable to find out.
I fear the truth of the matter is that there is NO plan,

he lamented.

I cannot stop it myself.
The trouble is that there is no high-up grip on this campaign.
CUNNINGHAM is in MALTA; TEDDER is at TUNIS; ALEXANDER is at SYRACUSE. It beats me how anyone thinks you can run a campaign in that way, with the three Commanders of the three Services about 600 miles from each other.
The enemy should never be allowed to get all his equipment out of SICILY, and we should round up the bulk of his fighting troops.
It would clearly be impossible to stop him getting his key personnel away. But the rest we should stop, but we will not do it without a very good combined plan and such a plan does not exist.

Eisenhower was juggling with too many balls in the air – with the inevitable result that all tumbled. Although he signalled to the Combined Chiefs of Staff on 5 August that the Etna line 'depends mainly on successful defence of Adrano' and that 'once we are through his main defensive line it is likely that progress will be rapid',[1] Eisenhower did not arrange a meeting of all his commanders

[1] In Alexander Papers (WO 214/22), PRO.

until 9 August – when it was too late to co-ordinate and mount a coherent interdiction of the German evacuation.

The miraculous Axis evacuation of Sicily thus went ahead unhindered, and the opportunity for another major Allied victory like the one at Tunis was lost. As far as Admiral Cunningham could later recall, 'the Commanders in Chief never discussed it';[1] while Tedder was too busy considering the attacking of the Rome marshalling yards with his heavy bombers to give the matter proper attention. Impotently Monty was forced to watch while the Germans and Italians ferried over 100,000 troops back to the mainland, together with guns, vehicles, stores and equipment. It was a sorry spectacle.

Monty's reaction was strange. From having been very much the 'prime mover' of Husky, from having seen his concentrated invasion of Sicily prove spectacularly successful, from having watched while his over-confident plans to capture the eastern coast of the island failed, from having gone back on his earlier condescension towards Patton and given him the major role in the final reduction of the island so that Eighth Army could prepare for the invasion of Italy, Monty seems for the first time to have resigned himself to the likelihood of a 'cock-up' by Eisenhower and the Commanders-in-Chief. Cunningham and Tedder had both bitterly opposed him over 'Husky'; Monty's view had in the end prevailed because without Eighth Army there could be no 'Husky'. Now the situation was different: the island would inevitably fall to the British and American armies within weeks if not days, but interdiction of the Axis evacuation was not within Monty's purview: he could only impotently protest to Alexander and urge Cunningham and Tedder to co-ordinate a plan.

In the meantime, therefore, Monty concentrated on the welfare of his army, and consoled himself with canaries. On 3 August 1943 he wrote to Phyllis Reynolds:

All goes well here. I am extremely fit and in spite of the doctors warning about Sicily being full of malaria, and mosquitos, I have had no fever. I keep my HQ always high up, above the plain country; it is cooler there, and there are less mosquitos. The present view from my caravan is quite wonderful. My HQ is right up on a mountain side and we look over a tangled mass of mountains, with Mt Etna towering above and dominating everything.

I have begun to collect birds, of which I have always been very fond. I now have some canaries, bought in LENTINI, and in one cage I have a pair with the hen sitting on 3 eggs. She built her nest, laid the eggs, and began to sit, all in my caravan. We moved the

---

[1] S. W. C. Pack, *Cunningham, the Commander*, London 1974.

HQ 30 miles yesterday, but she sat firmly on the eggs all the time. I also have a peacock, given me by a grateful Sicilian;[1] he is a very fine bird and struts round my caravan and the mess.

In the mess we have about 12 chickens and two turkeys; these are all very tame and walk about in the tent during meals and get fed by everyone. The turkeys now take food out of my hand. The hens lay very well; and we produced a family of 3 chicks, as we had a broody hen. So we are kept quite busy in our spare time.

Monty's menagerie was not entirely popular with the young ADCs, who thought the birds a 'bloody nuisance' and regularly plotted their demise; but to Monty they proved a strange solace. A week later he would be writing, 'Today's bad news is that the hen canary has got fed up with sitting on her eggs and has deserted them; she has been sitting for about two weeks and I suppose she couldn't be bothered with it.' Though some, like Harold Nicolson, considered Monty's canaries just another public relations exercise, the domestic antics of these birds undoubtedly helped Monty overcome, in part, his frustration.

The Mediterranean was not the only problem on Monty's mind. His trip to London in May 1943 had convinced him that the Allies would never succeed in a cross-Channel invasion unless they appointed a commander for the expedition who could infuse some realism into both planning and training. Already on 25 July Monty had written to Mountbatten, attempting to enlist his help, both on the Chiefs of Staff Committee and as a protégé of Churchill.

My own view is that someone must 'take hold' in England at once; and I believe Alex is the man,

Monty considered – as he also suggested to Brooke. It was essential that something be done to galvanise the cross-Channel 'show', and Mountbatten could be 'a most useful ally and your influence in high places will be able to keep the show on the rails. There are *so* many people at the top who do not really understand the matter; and there are *so* many vested interests. In order to win battles, and so carry out the policy of the Government, certain basic things are essential; if you don't have them, then you don't win the battle. Someone has to fight for these things, and whoever takes on this job is bound to make enemies and get a lot of mud slung at him. Ever since I went to Africa in August 1942 I have fought for these things – for first principles – to get the big thing right. And as a result I have won my battles. I do not in the least mind the mud that is slung about; I shall go on

---

[1] In fact the peacock was given by Major Hamilton-Russell after a memorable dinner at Monty's Tac HQ mess.

fighting for the things that matter. All I want to do is win the war. With your very great enthusiasm and sound practical common sense, and knowledge of what is wanted, you are exactly the man we want to help us.'

Monty obviously felt that only by transferring Alexander and himself to London could the cross-Channel assault be put on a sure footing. 'But I also feel that Alex and myself cannot *both* leave here if it is the intention to carry on against Italy and knock her out of the war. Someone will be required to command the field armies for Eisenhower i.e. 15 Army Group; we shall probably have three Armies, two American and one British.[1] It would be a biggish undertaking and the Army Group Commander would have to know his stuff 100%. If Alex and I *both* go home there is *no one* out here who could command the three armies and knock Italy out. So if Alex goes home, as I think he must, then I must stay here and take on his job – and knock Italy out. I could come home early next year, in the spring, to help Alex. That is how I see the matter.'

Others, however, saw it differently. Only Marshall had the necessary commitment to the cross-Channel attack to bring back a senior field commander at the end of the Sicilian campaign – General Bradley. Brooke, by contrast, ignored Monty's suggestion, and left both Alex and Monty in the Mediterranean. 'I think as things go at present it is probably right to leave the 1st XI out here,' Monty wrote with resignation to Mountbatten on 3 August. 'But they must remember the need in England; and if anything is contemplated then someone must "catch hold" at home. To delay after November would be very dangerous.' What Monty feared was a repetition of 'Husky', as he pointed out in a further letter to Mountbatten a week later:

I have just been reading Head's 'Notes on the Planning, Training and Execution of Operation "Husky"'. I think his report is excellent.

The two really big points which want to be very clearly understood are the following:

A. Force 141 was totally unfit to do the detailed planning for a large combined operation. It was a collection of staff officers gathered in from all over the place; it was completely theoretical and no one knew the battle end of the problem – either operationally or administratively.
The C.G.S. was quite unfit for his job; the problem was above his capacity; he was a second-rater, and cut no ice.
B. There was no experienced fighting commander who could give

[1] Patton's Seventh Army, Clark's Fifth Army, and Montgomery's Eighth Army.

344

his whole and undivided attention to the problem. Alexander was meant to be doing this. But he was really commanding First Army because Anderson was useless. I was fighting hard and commanding my own Army. It was not until the Tunisian campaign was nearly over that I could find time to go into the matter.

And so you see from the above how the thing was handled. . . .

What is past *is past*.

But do not let us make the same mistake again.

Let us learn from our mistakes.

Unfortunately I see no signs that we are doing so.

a) A big operation is envisaged in 1944. A planning staff in London is dealing with it, or, trying to do so; this staff is completely theoretical, there is no one on it who knows the battle end of the problem, war atmosphere is completely lacking.

Force 141 again.

b) There is no experienced fighting commander who is giving his whole and undivided attention to the problem.

Force 141 again.

Freddie Morgan[1] and his three Major-Generals are very decent chaps; but they know nothing whatever about the battle end of the problem and all their knowledge is purely theoretical. The orchestra is playing without a conductor, and is making very queer noises. And so you see history is repeating itself and the whole dismal affair will be gone through again. Finally someone will have to fight hard to get the show on the rails. You cannot get away from A and B of para. 1 above; and we are doing exactly the same again in England.

Possibly this is why it generally takes us some years to win our wars!!

Yours ever,
Monty[2]

Whether, in view of Alexander's failure to run Force 141, Monty really felt Alexander could be expected to 'catch hold' of the cross-Channel operation is a moot point. Consciously or unconsciously Monty hoped perhaps to get Alexander moved to England not simply to pave the way for his own eventual return, but precisely in order that he, Monty, could now take command of the impending

---

[1] Lt-General 'Freddie' Morgan was the Chief of Staff to the Supreme Allied Commander (as yet unappointed), and responsible for all cross-Channel assault planning in London.

[2] Letter of 12.8.43, copy in Montgomery Papers.

assault on Italy. 'You remember I told you I could write a book about the whole HUSKY affair, but it would be quite impossible to publish it,' he would write to Mountbatten in September. 'It is nothing to what I could write about what I was asked to do when we invaded the mainland of Europe. The trouble we had to get the thing on a good wicket is almost unbelievable. . . .'[1]

With Brooke's refusal to bring Alexander home (and let him usurp Brooke's own hoped-for role as commander of the cross-Channel assault), as well as Eisenhower's decision to put Clark's Fifth Army in charge of the main assault on Italy, Monty was left with nothing to do but concentrate on the conduct of operations in Sicily. Just as in the Canal zone in 1931–3, Monty was definitely beginning to out-grow his command. The suggestion of taking over 15th Army Group was in fact the first evidence that he now thought himself capable of elevation to Army Group Commander, and the military historian must needs consider whether he would not in fact have made a better commander than Alexander.

But if Monty had, after twelve months of campaigning, begun to outgrow command of a single Army, Eighth Army had not outgrown him. Neither the heavy casualties sustained in the bitter fighting first for Catania, then for the mountains west of Etna,[2] nor the alarming rise in sickness from dysentery and malaria, could douse the loyalty and admiration Monty inspired. When McNaughton reported un-favourably on Monty's refusal to let him set foot in Sicily, an attempt was made to clip Monty's wings by separating the Canadians from Eighth Army. 'There had been some trouble with the Canadian political authorities, who want to keep their troops independent,' Monty noted in his diary. To Alexander Monty signalled on 10 August:

It is definitely the wish of every officer and man in Canadian formations here that they should be a part of Eighth Army and be known as such. They definitely do NOT repeat NOT want to be nominally independent. They consider that the present method by which they are referred to as Canadian troops of the Eighth Army is quite satisfactory. This makes it clear that the Canadians are in the Eighth Army and they are very proud of this fact and do NOT repeat NOT want any other arrangement.

Nor was this unduly biased. The Canadians had taken up the mantle once held by the 9th Australian Division at Alamein, and their performance, as a virgin division under a new commander

[1] Letter of 22.9.43, copy in Montgomery Papers.
[2] Casualties in Eighth Army during the Sicilian campaign amounted to 4,706 dead or missing, with 7,137 wounded.

346

(General Guy Simonds) was exemplary – so much so that Monty was determined to use them in the follow-up assault on Italy. As one officer wrote, Monty might well have been hated for his punishing expectations and exercises in South-Eastern Army in England, but in the heat of battle in Sicily, this soon turned to boundless enthusiasm and respect:

In our minds [in 1942] he was an overbearing martinet – a proper bastard. He demanded that we undergo hardships. To toughen us, he broke many in the process. We thought his methods were madness. But his system of training prevailed, and when we eventually went into action we knew he was right. . . . When we ended our five weeks of warfare in Sicily successfully, we realised it was because we had been moulded into a hard, disciplined force by the hand of Montgomery, the *bête noire* of our days in Southern England.

The most remarkable thing about General B. L. Montgomery, as we Canadians knew him in our early days together, was his lack of remoteness. Six distinct levels of command existed between the man with the rifle and 'Monty'. These levels were platoon, company, battalion, brigade, division and corps. Yet, to the private soldier the Army Commander seemed to be his own personal commander, with no one else really in between. . . . It was this remarkable ability of Montgomery to project his personality over the heads of all his subordinate formation commanders, right down into the forward slit trench, that made him the soldiers' general.[1]

Neither Monty's disquiet over the planning for Italy, nor his frustration at the lack of inter-service planning for blocking the imminent Axis evacuation of Sicily, were allowed to interfere in the day-to-day command of Eighth Army. 'An Army Commmander has got to think in terms of Divisions. And he must think well ahead, so that his "grouping" and general lay-out of Divisions is always suitable for operations actually in progress, and will fit in easily for future operations that are being planned,' he wrote in his diary on 2 August 1943. This was the secret of his success with British or Commonwealth troops. As his Chief of Intelligence later observed, Monty did not really have the cavalryman's eye for terrain that Patton possessed, still less the legendary 'map-sense' of General Dempsey. His *coup d'oeil militaire*, as de Guingand called it, was not so much topographic as tactical – and human. Often, for instance, he was frankly surprised by the exploits of his own troops in

[1] Colonel Strome Galloway, *The General Who Never Was*, Belleville, Ontario 1981.

unimaginably difficult country, for what Monty dealt with were abstractions from a lifetime's soldiering: a mental chess game in which he sought to learn or intuit what was important to the enemy, and so to organise his own formations that he might take such positions with minimum casualties. The morale of his various formations and units was a vital factor in such an approach, morale he could only measure by personal visits to the men concerned and, where necessary, by giving inspiration and encouragement. Thus early morning and evening might be given over to reflection; but the major part of the day was spent visiting commanders and units in the field – 'getting the form'. Casualties, for instance, were carefully tabulated, and formed the basis for what could and could not be undertaken. When, for instance, at the end of July he saw the figures for each division – 50th Division having suffered 1500 casualties and 51st Division over a thousand, each involving over a hundred officers – he determined to 'rest 50 Div and 51 Div after we had cleared SICILY; these two divisions had been fighting hard for a year and must be given a rest; they would be kept in SICILY doing garrison duty, and resting and training,' as he wrote in his diary on 2 August. 'When the island of SICILY was cleared, I planned to cross to the mainland North of REGGIO with 13 Corps, using 5 Div and Canadian Div. 78 Div would be a follow-up Division.' But if 5th Division and Canadians were to be used, they too had to be rested before the assault: 'I therefore wanted 30 Corps to get the Canadian Div into reserve after ADRANO has been captured, and 13 Corps to get 5 Div into reserve. These two Divisions could then be rested, could consider and assimilate all the many lessons that had been learnt since they had first landed in SICILY on 10 July, and could check up on things and decide on a technique, and could plan the BAYTOWN operation with 13 Corps.' On 6 August, after the fall of Catania, Dempsey was thus told to pull 5th Division immediately into reserve, as Leese was with the Canadian Division the same day.

This careful nurturing of his troops was part of the professionalism which commanded such respect from Monty's Corps Commanders. He might make wrong individual decisions, as over the Vizzini-Enna highway; but in the long run his determination not to squander the lives of his troops, and to ensure operations were planned and conducted within the capacity of the respective formations, was salutary, and reflected his profound military realism. 'I have had some very heavy fighting, fiercer than any I have had since I commanded Eighth Army,' Monty had remarked in his letter to Mountbatten on 2 August. 'I am now operating in very mountainous country, somewhat like Switzerland – with Mt Etna towering above everything. It is ideal defensive country and the Bosche is fighting well and bravely, and with great determination. There is no doubt he is a very good soldier; he is far too good to be left "in being" as a menace to the world, and *must* be stamped on. He was thrown right off his balance by the speed and violence of our initial assault; but he recovered well on the Etna line and is now fighting a very skilful delaying battle.'

Monty's response had been to regroup, and only expend lives on the real pivot of the Etna line, at Adrano. Patton by contrast seems to have been obsessed by his 'horse race' to Messina, and having failed to put in an appearance on the eastern flank of Seventh Army since the beginning of the invasion, he now began to rant and rave not only at Bradley and the divisional commanders, but at his own GIs.

CHAPTER ELEVEN

The End of the Honeymoon

The story of Patton's brutal outburst of temper and his hysterical humiliation of American soldiers in two field hospitals is well known; but the context in which Patton lost his self-control is often not appreciated. He was certainly egged on by Eisenhower, who on 3 August, the day of the first slapping incident, signalled to Patton:

> The next few days will add immeasurably to the lustre of its [Seventh Army's] fame. I personally assure you that if we speedily finish off the Germans in Sicily you need have no fear of being left there in the backwater of the war.[1]

This was a reference to the choice of Mark Clark to command Fifth Army for 'Avalanche', rather than Patton. Knowing that Montgomery also intended to take Eighth Army to Italy, Patton was understandably anxious about his own future as an Army Commander. The BBC had broadcast a provocative report 'that the Seventh Army has been lucky to be in Western Sicily eating grapes,' as Eisenhower complained to Alexander;[2] and Patton, incensed, was pulling out every stop to reach Messina. When German resistance stiffened on the two highways leading to the Messina peninsula, Patton ordered a series of commando-style landings in the rear of the enemy. All were ill-advised and expensive in American lives. As Bradley later commented about Patton, his Seventh Army Commander: 'I disliked the way he worked. Upset tactical plans, interfered in my orders; his stubbornness on amphibious operations . . . sickened me and soured me on Patton.'[3]

The first amphibious operation, despite gaining complete surprise on 8 August, landed on the wrong beach and was too puny to do more than force the Germans 'to give up the San Fratello ridge a few hours earlier than intended' as the American Official Historian caustically remarked – and certainly failed in its intention of cutting

---

[1] *The Eisenhower Papers*, loc. cit.
[2] Signal of 5.8.43, Alexander Papers (WO 214/227), PRO.
[3] Bradley Commentaries, loc. cit.

off 29th Panzer Grenadier Division.[1] 'On second operation we were setting it up on a grander scale. Truscott [Commander of 3rd US Division] and I wanted to pull the amphibious operation one night later than George [Patton] did,' recalled Bradley. 'He couldn't wait, refused to hear us, went ahead and slammed in the operation. As a result we were unable to complete the [inland] outflanking operation. Result, we had to push a frontal assault to rescue the amphibious troops after their landing. . . . Cost all our artillery and tanks.'[2] The American Official Historian was similarly critical of the landing, made on 11 August, acknowledging that it 'accomplished little' and at considerable loss, largely because Patton's landing force 'was too small, and because continuous air and naval support was not available'.[3]

Patton's third attempt at an amphibious 'end run' took place four nights later, against Bradley's and Truscott's heated appeals not to pursue the landing. 'By that time we were moving rapidly down road,' Bradley recalled. 'I estimated we would be beyond landing point by the following morning. I urged him to call it off. . . . Patton was stubborn and refused to call it off. Insisted that it go all right. I said, "We'll meet them on the beaches to guide them in." We were well beyond the point and we did greet them when they came in.

'Again Patton wanted to be spectacular, whatever the sense to the men.'[4]

Patton's obsession with beating Montgomery to Messina, regardless of the advice of his Corps and divisional commanders, certainly caused Bradley to question Patton's generalship at that time. On 3 August, on his way to Bradley's headquarters, Patton inspected 15th Evacuation Hospital near Nicosia, where he flew into a rage over a young soldier who said he was not ill but 'couldn't take it' in the front line. Patton bawled out the man, slapped his face with his gloves, then grabbed him and threw him out of the tent. 'You coward, you get out of this tent. You can't stay in here with these brave, wounded Americans!' Patton yelled,[5] and that night dictated a memorandum to all senior commanders:

It has come to my attention that a very small number of soldiers are going to the hospital on the pretext that they are nervously incapable of combat. Such men are cowards, and bring discredit on the Army and disgrace to their comrades who they heartlessly leave to endure the danger of a battle which [sic] they themselves use the hospital as a means of escaping. . . .

[1] Garland and Smyth, op. cit.
[2] Bradley Commentaries, loc. cit.
[3] Garland and Smyth, op. cit.
[4] Bradley Commentaries, loc. cit.
[5] Garland and Smyth, op. cit.

Those who are not willing to fight will be tried by Court-Martial for cowardice in the face of the enemy.[1]

Six days later, the day after the first of his seaborne 'end runs', Patton again visited a Field Hospital while on his way to Bradley's headquarters, and repeated his behaviour on 3 August. 'Your nerves, Hell, you are just a goddammed coward, you yelling son of a bitch. . . . You ought to be lined up against a wall and shot,' Patton shouted this time. 'In fact I ought to shoot you myself right now, goddamn you!' Waving his pistol in the terrified soldier's face, Patton actually struck the man, and screamed, 'I won't have these other brave boys seeing such a bastard babied!'[2]

At Bradley's headquarters Patton then boasted about what he had done. 'He was pleased with what he had done, he was bragging about the incident. . . . Thought if he made the man mad he would be mad enough to go up into the front line to fight. Thought men were showing a yellow streak. He didn't agree with me that every man had a breaking point. Some are low, some are high. We call the low points cowards. To George anyone who did not want to fight all the time was a coward,' Bradley later remarked.[3]

By 10 August the surgeon in charge of the 93rd Evacuation Hospital had submitted a report of the incident to Bradley, who attempted to hush it up. 'I couldn't go over Patton's head,' Bradley explained,[4] so the report was put in a sealed envelope in Bradley's safe.

Inevitably, however, word reached Eisenhower. A journalist leaked the story in America, and soon Eisenhower's mail was flooded with enraged parents protesting at Patton's unbecoming behaviour to his own troops.

Patton's own instability was obviously triggered by those weaker than himself. Much of his bluster was an attempt to overcome his own shyness, and much of his 'bulling ahead' was a response to his own timidity. He freely confessed to being frightened by heavy shelling, and his appearances in or near the front line in Sicily were extremely rare for a commander who has gone down in American mythology as an aggressive, front-line commander in the image of Rommel. The cowardice he saw in his Field Hospital was the cowardice he himself had to conquer each time he approached the front, and he could not forgive the troops who failed to conquer it. Nor could he forgive Monty for humiliating him in the first few days of the campaign, when he wanted to 'bull ahead'. When, at the end of

[1] *The Patton Papers*, op. cit.
[2] Garland and Smyth, op. cit.
[3] Bradley Commentaries, loc. cit.
[4] Ibid.

the campaign, he was told by a civilian Intelligence aide of the widespread impression in America 'that American forces had knifed through token resistance while the British had faced the brunt of the fighting around Catania', Patton let loose about Montgomery. Montgomery didn't even know how to 'run around end', only knew how to 'make a frontal attack under the same barrage they used at Ypres'. As the aide departed from Sicily, however, Patton – who was already in trouble over the slapping incidents – took him aside: 'The other night I was somewhat critical about my distinguished opposite number in the British Army. I think I said he didn't know how to run around end and other things. Now I seem to be in a lot of hot water lately, and suppose we just forget the episode.'[1]

Whether Monty realised the extent to which Patton was irked and obsessed by him is doubtful. Monty's ADC could only remember Monty rarely mentioning Patton after the Flying Fortress crash and their visit to Palermo on 28 July,[2] and this is borne out by the lack of any reference to Patton in Monty's diary after that date. While Patton's eyes were preoccupied with Messina, Monty was concerned with the forthcoming invasion of Italy, and the question of the cross-Channel invasion being prepared in Britain. Yet, had he known of Patton's hysterical outbursts in the two American field hospitals, he would probably have had more sympathy with Patton than did Bradley, Eisenhower, or the American divisional commanders. Much more than Patton realised, Monty was impressed by American mobility, speed of manoeuvre, and sheer boldness. Indeed, as Bradley observed, there was much more in common, at a personal level, between Patton and Montgomery than Patton himself recognised. Like Patton, Monty enjoyed creating effect by disparaging the performance of others in public, as witness his remarks about Anderson, the 'good plain cook'. Monty too had to struggle continually with an ego which, under the pressure of battle and of war, threatened to take him at times beyond the conventional evident boundaries of sanity. Even in military terms there was a similarity between Patton and Montgomery which historians have largely overlooked. As Monty's Chief of Intelligence later remarked, 'Monty had saddled himself in the desert with a *Corps de Chasse* that wouldn't chasse.'[3] How enviously Monty watched Patton driving his armour across Sicily – armour that had not the all too frequent British fear of enemy 88s. Even in the matter of 'end runs' historians have failed to understand Montgomery's kinship with Patton. It was, after all, not Patton but Montgomery who used parachute troops to try and speed up the initial Sicilian campaign by seizing the

[1] Charles R. Codman, *Drive*, Boston 1957.
[2] J. R. Henderson, loc. cit.
[3] Sir Edgar Williams, loc. cit.

353

Primosole bridge from the air. Eighth Army's Planning HQ War Diary bristles with projected operations for further air- and seaborne landings along the eastern coast. The airborne operations Monty cancelled because, as he noted in his diary after there had been two abortive missions, it was unfair to use brave trained parachute troops until the pilots could be taught to face 'flak' and drop their men in the right place. Similarly, though he put all his Eighth Army commandos in a brigade under Brigadier 'Bob' Laycock, he refused to sanction small-time landings behind the enemy lines – landings which would have to be mounted against a much steeper coast than Patton's northern seaboard, and which could so easily be contained and crushed by the German forces there. Yet once the Etna line had been broken at Adrano and then Troina, he was all in favour of American landings in the north which could outflank not only the Germans facing Bradley, but possibly the Hermann Goering Division and parachute troops pinned down by the Eighth Army west and east of Etna. Far from running a campaign of 'Ypres barrages', Monty seemed almost pragmatic in the way he marshalled his thrusts. No sooner had the 30 Corps assault met stiffened resistance on the inland road around Mount Etna, towards Randazzo, than Monty again shifted his weight to Dempsey's coastal flank. 'If I could not get round the *West* of ETNA, I would get round the *East*,' he noted in his diary on 9 August – and even considered the possibility of a drive northwards up the coast to Messina that would cut off the Germans in the mountains opposing both Leese and Bradley. Combined with American seaborne landings on the northern coast, he felt there was at least a chance of trapping considerable numbers of enemy troops before they could evacuate. In order to rejuvenate his 13 Corps thrust north of Catania, he even put 5th Division back into battle, the very division he had taken out of line three days earlier to conserve it for the invasion of Italy.

To 15 Army Group 0.58 10 Aug [1800 hours]
Most Secret. For General ALEXANDER from General MONT-
GOMERY.
Enemy resistance North of BRONTE is stiffening and country very difficult for deployment off the road because of terraced vineyards and of lava belts. Am persisting strongly with thrust on RANDAZ-ZO but 30 Corps can employ only one Division. On right flank have put 5 Div back into battle and 13 Corps is pushing North-wards on front of two Divisions to secure area TAORMINA –FRANCAVILLA–LINGUAGLOSSA. Once this area is secured enemy will have to fall back Northwards towards MILAZZO or along East coast to MESSINA. He is more likely to go Northwards. A landing by Americans on North coast to seize the FURNARI area and hold it would cut off the enemy completely. Having secured

above area with 13 Corps I will advance on MESSINA along East coast route.

Alexander, having taken no effective control over the campaign since the invasion on 10 July, one month earlier, was hardly to be expected to take a firm grip now. The next day, at 10.55 a.m., he obtusely informed Monty that 'Patton is preparing a combined operation including sea and air landing [sic]. Am not certain of exact area of assault yet.'[1]

Patton's sea landing was in fact mounted at Brolo, some thirty miles short of Furnari, where it came to grief, as we have seen, losing all its tanks and artillery, and its American infantry escaping only by running into the hills with light weapons. Had Patton held his cards and put in a bigger assault at Furnari as Monty suggested, the German withdrawal route to Messina might well have been cut. Equally, at this stage in combined operations, it might have proved as disastrous as the Brolo landing; but whatever the case, Monty was very far from being the anti-end-runner whom Patton mocked.

However, even as Monty urged Alexander to grip the final phase of the campaign, his attention was diverted to the mainland once more. All day on 9 August the Allied Commanders-in-Chief had conferred in Tunis, and the following day de Guingand signalled urgently to his Army Commander:

Have news of conference decisions. Important I discuss with you earliest. If you are moving East tomorrow suggest we meet HQ 86 Area at any time you suggest.[2]

At this meeting de Guingand revealed that Eisenhower wished to launch both 'Baytown' (an Eighth Army crossing of the Messina Straits) *and* 'Avalanche' (Fifth Army's assault on Naples) on 7 September – just three weeks away. Anticipating this, Monty had already on 10 August told his GSO 1, Operations (Colonel Belchem) that he would replace 5th Division by 51st Highland Division on 13 August; in fact Dempsey's whole 13 Corps headquarters was to be withdrawn from the battle in order to prepare detailed 'Baytown' assault plans. General Leese, whose 78th Division was to allow itself to be edged out of the battle north of Etna by Bradley's 2 Corps, would then take over the Eighth Army front with his 30 Corps headquarters.[3]

Yet if, as de Guingand claimed, both 'Baytown' and 'Avalanche' were to be mounted, what of the assault north of Reggio in the Gulf

[1] Alexander Papers (WO 214/22), PRO.
[2] Eighth Army HQ War Diary (WO 169/8494), PRO.
[3] Ibid.

of Gioja – Operation 'Buttress' – which General Horrocks had been planning for his 10 Corps under Monty's command? Horrocks's 10 Corps constituted half of Mark Clark's potential Fifth Army for 'Avalanche'. If 'Avalanche' was on, was 'Buttress' therefore cancelled? In his diary Monty gave rein to a kind of priggish incredulity. 'I do not know what transpired at that meeting [of Commanders-in-Chief]. But on 11 August my staff was informed by the CGS 15 Army Group that operation BUTTRESS was "off", and in its place operation AVALANCHE was first priority.' But was it? 'General Alexander came to see me on 12 August and after cross-examination by me he said that BUTTRESS was "on" and was first priority, but that later it might be switched to AVALANCHE. We thus had two separate and distinct statements.'

Anyone who ever came under cross-examination by Montgomery can sympathise with poor Alexander. Monty's relentless logical mind tolerated no shades of doubt. Things were either one thing or another, and if he was to be honest, Alexander did not know which they were. Not wishing to disappoint or upset Monty in the critical last days of the Sicilian campaign, he therefore pretended that 'Buttress' still claimed first priority and stated that 10 Corps was to remain under Montgomery's command.

Behind Alexander's confusion was of course Eisenhower's vacillating personality, in so many ways similar to Alexander's own. Eisenhower had favoured an assault on Sardinia rather than Italy, until overruled first by Churchill, then by the Combined Chiefs of Staff. But the problem with Italy was the question of where the Allies might best land: and after Mussolini's fall this became doubly complicated. If the Germans, fearing an Italian sell-out, sent down large forces from Northern Italy, then the defection of Italy from the Axis partnership was of little consequence: the Allies would be up against first-class troops who could be reinforced more speedily than could the Allies. Eisenhower sought therefore to retain flexibility by planning various possible operations and only deciding at the last moment which one to select. Had he possessed unlimited troops, equipment and sea-transport this would no doubt have been sensible, but with Marshall's restriction against deflecting either Pacific or cross-Channel forces into the Mediterranean it was a grave mistake. Eisenhower's signal to Cunningham, Tedder and Alexander on 10 August, confirming their conference decisions, was a masterpiece of double-think. Every sentence was at variance with its predecessor, and from it Alexander could evidently make neither head nor tail.

1. a) All preparations for AVALANCHE with target date 7 September to proceed.
   b) Allocation of craft to X Corps and flexibility of X Corps to

enable BUTTRESS or AVALANCHE to be launched to remain unimpaired.

c) Every effort will be made to seize bridgehead in Calabria [BAYTOWN] with resources remaining after allocation of necessary landing craft to X Corps.

d) Actual dates of operations to depend on completion of Sicilian campaign.

2. Fifteenth Army Group will report urgently minimum number of craft necessary to enable BAYTOWN to be carried out with object of seizing and holding bridgehead in CALABRIA. Decision will then be made upon timing of AVALANCHE in relation to BAYTOWN.[1]

Such gobbledegook made it abundantly clear how little Eisenhower yet understood about Corps or Army command. Monty primly attempted to achieve clarity by sending Alexander a signal on the evening of 12 August recording Alexander's statement 'given by you to day which is as follows. First, BUTTRESS is on and is scheduled to take place. Second. If the going looks good you may switch BUTTRESS to AVALANCHE. Meanwhile my staff have been told by Richardson [CGS to Alexander] that 10 Corps is under command 5 American Army for planning of AVALANCHE. In view of your talk with me today consider it must be made clear that my demands on 10 Corps have priority.' In his diary Monty remarked:

I could not get any satisfactory answer to this telegram.

There are various influences at work and ALEXANDER does not know what he really wants and he cannot give a decision. I have heard whisperings from the staff at 15 Army Group that life is very difficult there owing to the inability of ALEXANDER to give a quick decision.

Monty's long honeymoon as Army Commander under Alexander was coming to an end. The misunderstandings over the planning and command of 'Avalanche', 'Baytown' and 'Buttress' were however only a foretaste of Alexander's – and Eisenhower's – further mistakes that autumn.

[1] *The Papers of Dwight David Eisenhower*, op. cit.

CHAPTER TWELVE

Reflections on Teams

Monty's concern with the conduct of operations and their command was not academic. Better than anyone Monty understood that in war simplicity and clarity are of paramount importance. It was only as a staff officer in the First World War that he had begun to recognise how blessed he was himself in this respect, and his objections to muddled Allied thinking were to be borne out in the days ahead as his staff battled to bring sanity to the plans for invading the mainland of Europe.

In the meantime the Sicilian campaign was approaching its climax. By 13 August the last lateral connecting the two Axis-held highways to Messina was broken by the capture of Randazzo and Fiumefreddo, and both Seventh and Eighth Armies began preparing seaborne landings to cut the two highways.

Patton, having been given the northern sector including Messina, was now desperate lest Monty abrogate their agreement and steal a march on him. He threatened to reduce both Bradley and General Truscott (commander of 3rd US Division) to the rank of colonel when they protested that their third amphibious landing would beach too late to be of any assistance to the advance, and the abortive landing thus took place on 16 August, twenty miles to the rear of Truscott's front line.

Monty's own amphibious operation, launched the same night as Patton's, did at least by-pass the minefields and demolitions holding up Leese's movement north of Taormina, though it trapped no Germans. With the Americans now in the Milazzo plain, fifteen miles from Messina, there was really no question but that the Seventh Army would reach Messina first. British naval gunfire had caused a landslide which required at least two days to clear, and shellfire from the Italian mainland helped the German rearguard stymie any attempt by Leese to push on with unsupported infantry.

General Kirkman, who commanded 50th Division, later remarked there was no question of a 'race'. He had no knowledge of the precise position of Truscott's 3rd US Division on the north coast: 'I did not even know where the Americans were. They got to Messina eight hours before I did, because when I reached Taormina the road was blown and we couldn't get any transport beyond it. I summoned boats, went round. It delayed us too much, otherwise we'd have arrived there just together. The Americans derived great prestige from the fact they got there first. In point of fact if you've got two armies pursuing a retreating enemy, the enemy normally dictates when you get there. You probably get there together, both in touch with the enemy. But I was defeated by the road at Taormina being completely blown away so that I couldn't get a single gun or transport through. It was no blow to me.'[1]

Typical of the problems caused by German demolitions and mines was the capture of Taormina itself, an old resort much loved before the war by English tourists. Here Monty was to move his headquarters, but the seizure of the town marked the beginning of the end of Geoffrey Keating's status as publicity power behind Monty's throne. As Keating remembered:

There's no doubt about it that Oliver Leese and his Corps were expected to make much quicker progress than they could possibly do, really. The bridges were all blown, the terrain was very difficult indeed. I had Edward Ardizzone [the war artist] with me. I can remember that one morning we'd been sleeping on a terrace of some old villa and I woke up in the morning very early, because it was light, and I could tell immediately that, as it seemed to me, the enemy had withdrawn. And I said to Edward Ardizzone, 'Look, it seems to me the enemy are no longer in front of us, don't you think we should just push along to Taormina which is a very fashionable international resort – and we might find a hotel functioning or something. Anyway it's a very interesting historical place.' And off we went.

We came to our forward positions, and Robin Hastings, he had been seconded to command a battalion of, I think, the DLI [Durham Light Infantry] – he was only about twenty-four, probably the youngest colonel commanding a regiment in Eighth Army – and they were lifting mines in the bed of a dried-up river. The bridge had been blown and it seemed to me we could easily get through the minefield – you could see the mines. So I said to Robin, 'We'd like to go on to Taormina, have you any objections?' He said, 'No, but be careful not to step on any mines – we've got to lift this minefield.'

So we went through the river bed, avoiding the mines, and got on the road, and we walked a few miles along to where the road curves up to Taormina, which is a mountain point. And as we walked up, it became painfully obvious that we were under observation from hostile forces. Shots were fired. In fact the enemy *hadn't* gone – there was a regiment at least of Bersagliere, I don't

[1] Loc. cit.

359

know if there were any Germans or not, the Germans had probably pulled out by then. But we pressed on, we couldn't obviously run away. So I was credited with capturing Taormina single-handed!

We went to a hotel and I sent for the [enemy] commanding officer and told all the troops to pile their arms in the square, which they did, and told them to march back to our lines, which they did. And towards evening some war correspondents arrived, found us in possession, having met the enemy formations marching back, disarmed. And this was transmitted back as a story – single-handed officer – nobody gave Ardizzone any credit for being there at all – and it was on the BBC that night.

And of course Monty was absolutely beside himself with rage. He sent for the Corps Commander, Oliver Leese and – this was all reported back to me later by Oliver Leese's ADCs, you see – and said, 'If Keating can get to Taormina, why can't your infantry?'

And this was so badly taken by Oliver Leese that he announced that he would never have me in his headquarters again.[1]

Keating was probably exaggerating Monty's anger. In his diary for 15 August 1943 Monty noted: 'The enemy has made very complete demolitions about TAORMINA, and probably elsewhere between that place and MESSINA. I expect that progress down the East coast road to MESSINA will be very slow. This is now the only axis of advance for Eighth Army.' Leaving only 50th Division to clear the road to Messina he therefore pulled the rest of Eighth Army's forces into reserve that day.

Far more important in Monty's eyes was the failure of the Allies to stop the Axis forces evacuating Sicily across the Messina Straits. Already on 11 August his Main Army HQ was recording in its War Diary:

The enemy's evacuation scheme was in full swing and reports enabled an idea of his method to be formed. Under cover of a fierce flak cone a fleet of landing craft, siebel ferries and 'F' lighters was plying back and forth. About 75 such craft were being used. Photo recce immediately SOUTH of CAPO PELLRO found 33 craft of which 26 were actually crossing the Straits, all the Eastbound ones being loaded and the Westbound ones empty.[2]

[1] Geoffrey Keating, interview of 30.11.79. 'What he [Keating] did, well he sent a message back that he was sitting in whichever one of those hotels it was. And so we told Monty that Taormina was taken, because Geoffrey was in the Something Hotel. And at that time a message came through to say there was heavy fighting south of Taormina and Monty got on to Oliver Leese and said, "But we've got a message that Geoffrey Keating's in a hotel there." Oliver Leese was absolutely furious with Geoffrey Keating – said he's never to enter my headquarters again' – J. R. Henderson, loc. cit.
[2] Eighth Army HQ War Diary (WO 169/8494), PRO.

Day and night the ferries operated – a veritable Dunkirk which, just as Goering had vainly boasted in 1940 the Luftwaffe could tackle on its own, Tedder now failed utterly to halt. The lack of a combined plan became hourly more evident, as tens of thousands of Axis troops, complete with weapons and even vehicles, made their way across the straits. Air Marshal Coningham had assured Tedder he could halt the flow with attack aircraft, just as he had promised after Alamein. But although many pilots braved the fierce flak, their results were negligible. With complete air superiority over the area the Allies managed to hit only five siebel ferries and a handful of barges and motor boats in seven days; the Allied navies under Admiral Cunningham made no attempt whatsoever at interdiction.[1]

Patton was unconcerned. At 10 p.m. on the night of 16 August 1943 the first American patrol entered Messina, and in the early hours of the next morning phone calls were made to the various American unit and formation commanders to tell them that Patton would take the formal surrender of the city at 10 a.m. on 17 August. General Truscott had been told to hold back all but a handful of his 3rd Division so that Patton could make a triumphal entry, and from Truscott's command post Patton's cavalcade set off shortly after 9 a.m. Bradley, the Corps Commander who had fought all the battles from Palermo to Messina, was conspicuous by his absence. 'Bradley not there – must have failed to get the message. This is a great disappointment to me, as I had telephoned him, and he certainly deserved the pleasure of entering the town,' Patton recorded in his diary.[2]

But Bradley *had* received the message. His absence was intentional, for in his shy and puritan way, he was 'sickened' by Patton's mania for publicity. In Bradley's later version he was uncompromisingly forthright. Patton 'had directed that I do not permit any units to enter Messina until he could make triumphal entry. I was furious. I had to hold our troops on the hills instead of pursuing the fleeing Germans in an effort to get in as many as we could. British claimed near beat him into Messina because of that.' Had it not been so far from his own headquarters he would have 'gone up there and gone into Messina to greet him [Patton] on a street corner when he arrived,' Bradley afterwards maintained. But 'that would have been playing George's game,' he acknowledged.[3]

Not only was Patton's triumphal entry unsoldierly, Bradley felt, but it was an unnecessary endangering of men's lives. The town was still under shellfire from the mainland, and all the occupants of the car travelling behind Patton were hit. Unperturbed, Patton went on

[1] Cf. S. E. Morison, op. cit.
[2] *The Patton Papers*, op. cit.
[3] Bradley Commentaries, loc. cit.

into the city where a short-lived parade took place, broken up by further shelling from the mainland which caused further casualties. In his diary General Lucas declared himself 'greatly relieved when he got the Army Commander back over the hill without mishap'.[1]

Patton, still recovering from sand-fly fever, was first elated, then depressed. He had an almost manic conviction that Eisenhower's headquarters was against him and would refuse to recommend promotion. 'I feel let down,' he noted in his diary, after returning to his command post. 'The reaction from intense mental and physical activity to a status of inertia is very difficult.' The next day he recorded, 'I feel awful today, all let down. I have no inkling what is going to happen to the Seventh Army.'[2] This foreboding was confirmed almost immediately by a letter from Eisenhower, who had got wind of the 'slapping incidents'. Eisenhower's letter, dated 17 August – the same day Patton had triumphally entered Messina – was a reproach that would have humbled even the most confident of men: 'I am well aware of the necessity for hardness and toughness on the battlefield. . . . But this does not excuse brutality, abuse of the sick, nor exhibition of uncontrollable temper in front of subordinates.'[3]

Patton was made to apologise to the two sick men, to the doctors and nurses, and to the two divisions from which the men came. 'When Patton spoke before the 1st Division in Sicily to apologise for his conduct in the campaign, he ended on a great inspirational note. The massed division remained stonily silent,' Bradley's Chief of Intelligence later recalled. 'Not a man applauded and the division was dismissed. It faded away in the silence to the great embarrassment of its commander and the total chagrin of Patton.'[4]

Monty's stock, by contrast, was still rising in Eighth Army. Almost 12,000 casualties had been sustained in the thirty-nine-day campaign; 140,000 prisoners had been taken. Monty's over ambitiousness after the successful first landing had cost the Allies the chance of a lightning victory, but thereafter Monty's generalship had shown a consideration for his troops which simply did not exist in Seventh Army. He had *not* submitted his Army to unnecessary casualties by 'broad front' attacks, but had regrouped and concentrated the fighting in those areas that were vital to the integrity of the enemy's defence line. Moreover he had spent part of every day of the campaign visiting units, in battle and out – a concern with the morale and welfare of his men that was judged by the men themselves to be, despite his quirky clothes, his high-pitched voice and

---

[1] 'From Algiers to Anzio', loc. cit.
[2] *The Patton Papers*, op. cit.
[3] *The Papers of Dwight David Eisenhower*, op. cit.
[4] Colonel Dickson, in Bradley Commentaries, loc. cit.

his beaky nose, fundamentally genuine.[1] In this the soldiers were not mistaken. The term 'family' might seem sentimental for a body of men fighting a very professional enemy which booby-trapped its dead and ditched its Italian allies whenever it suited it: but the word was not inappropriate. No other Army in the West would match Eighth Army in this respect. Patton, reduced to titular generalship after the slapping incidents, spent months concocting – as had Lord Gort after Dunkirk – a great history of the exploits of the Seventh Army; but the men of Monty's Eighth Army were content in the pride of belonging to an already legendary formation. As one Canadian officer recalled, by the end of the Sicilian campaign the 1st Canadian Division considered itself so much a part of the Eighth Army that it was 'as if the glory of El Alamein and the Mareth Line was already our own. At the end of the Sicilian campaign Monty had arrived one day in an open car to where our whole brigade was formed up awaiting him. He had us break ranks and gather round his vehicle. He then gave us permission to smoke and extolled the fighting virtues of Canadian troops and flattered us by telling us how much we had helped in the conquest of Sicily. He said, "I regard you now as one of the veteran divisions of my Army; just as good as any, if not better. I knew the Canadians on the Western front in the last war and there were no finer soldiers anywhere. I wonder what they would say to you now if they could speak to you? I think they would say something like this: 'Well done. We have handed you the sword and you have wielded it well and truly.' " We lapped it up.'[2]

Monty's jokes and catch-phrases might well be schoolboyish – but they established a rapport between Army Commander and his soldiers that had never before existed in the British Army. As the Canadian officer recalled: 'When talking to our troops none of us would have referred to our battalion commander as "Ralph" or "Dan", or spoken of the brigadier, the divisional commander or the corps commander by their Christian names. Yet, in bivouac or on the line of march, or going into the attack, I have heard company officers discussing the Army Commander with their men as "Monty". "Monty" has ordered this, "Monty" has planned this, "Monty" has

[1] 'Sicily was the time of the build-up with the soldiers. People sent out cigarettes from England, packets and packets and packets. Always when we went in the car there were fifty parcels of cigarettes, and he'd draw up at the side of the road and hand out these cigarettes. They were cigarettes sent to him *personally*. How it started I don't know, but they were sent to him personally, addressed to him. They arrived, thousands and thousands.

'This was also the time when, in Sicily, he started going to a battalion or a unit and getting them to gather round his car, and he'd speak to them. I mean he'd stand on top of the car and speak to them – it was in Sicily that that started' – J. R. Henderson, loc. cit.

[2] Colonel Strome Galloway, op. cit.

promised us this. I did it myself. We never employed the vague "they" which became the term for our unknown masters after Monty left the theatre and the Eighth Army lost its desert character.'[1] This rapport, moreover, was a two-way relationship – the loyalty and courage of the men reminding Monty of his responsibility for their lives. Indeed so close did this bond become that his informal addresses to his soldiers, as they gathered round his car or jeep, were unforgettable in the minds of those present. Speaking to a gathering of artillerymen who had fought in Greece, Crete, Syria, the Western Desert, Libya, Tunisia and the Sicilian campaign he assured them:

'You are the finest artillery group in the world. I'd like to take you with me wherever I go.
    This produces a wave of groans,

one gunner remembered.

A pause and then:
    'Ah! But I may be returning to England.'
    The groans are metamorphosed to cheers. We have been given a lesson in the psychology of leadership.
    I can remember the great roar that rose into the hot, sunny air when he made the reference to home,

the gunner recalled vividly, almost forty years later.[2]
    That Monty sincerely cared for the lives of his men is paradoxically most movingly demonstrated by Monty's response to the courageous German parachute troops who managed to thwart his assault on Catania, particularly those who landed behind British lines in plain clothes, as Warwick Charlton later recalled:

Monty published an order in Sicily – there was a group of German paratroops of a special order that were in civilian dress behind our lines. And this was very worrying because Eighth Army hadn't experienced that before. And Monty put out a proclamation that anyone captured behind our lines, German soldiers in civilian uniforms, would be treated as spies and shot.
    And they were captured – one of them was captured early on and Freddie de Guingand had him brought up to his headquarters, he was being interrogated. And he was rather a tough guy, young guy, spoke beautiful English and Freddie was making him dig his own grave.
    And I said to him, 'Wnat do you think of this?'

[1] Ibid.
[2] W. G. Holloway, letter to author, 1.7.81.

He said, 'Look, if you have been dropped as I have three times behind the lines in Russia, this is nothing!'

But Monty got to hear what was being done. And immediately sent an order round that they were to be treated from now on as prisoners of war, no more nonsense.

He had said they should be shot because they were spies (unless they gave themselves up). And he changed his mind because he'd seen the reality of what that meant. Everybody thought, Jolly good show, they should be bloody well shot, bastards. But here were these young guys, very very brave, who'd done what they'd been ordered to do, were captured, and that was it. But how do you shoot them in cold blood?

I thought that was – I was rather impressed with that.[1]

This strange compassion in a man so seemingly emotionally arid as Montgomery struck even those who found his bombast and vanity deplorable.

'Could I just say something about this business of vanity,' Charlton remarked later with feeling.

I get very fed up when I hear people talking about the vanity side of Monty. I served on the following staffs: Cunningham's, Ritchie's, Auchinleck's and Mountbatten's.

Now compared with Mountbatten, Monty was a shrinking violet! I mean, it really didn't start. . . . Every picture that went out, of Mountbatten, had to be seen. Had to be checked by him personally – not by a member of his staff – every one. He [Mountbatten] confiscated whole wodges of magazines that were going out in S.E. Asia, when there were more important things to do, because there was an article that was slightly angled wrongly towards himself and this myth he was building.

Now it seemed to me that Monty, once he made for example a decision that the camera was a weapon that could be used – that was it! There was no more discussion about it: forever afterwards, that was it – he would never interfere.

In the same way, when he was sold the idea of the printed word, that there were ways of communicating through the printed word to all the army, and bouncing back through the correspondence – that was it!

Obviously he had made the decision that it was a citizens' army, that it was that type of army, that it wasn't a regular army, that they were thinking people in it. Now that was all quite revolutionary. And to keep to it, and not to mess it around – to let it go, let it be, and take the risks with it. I thought that was pretty good.[2]

[1] Warwick Charlton, interview of 31.3.83.
[2] Ibid.

Not only had Monty given total licence to Eighth Army's news-papers in North Africa and in Sicily to publish what they wished, but he had defended this freedom against all manner of complaints from outside Eighth Army. In all the campaigning from Alamein to Messina, Charlton only remembered one occasion on which Monty complained about an article – an editorial Charlton had written about Patton!

It happened when we were in Catania. The news trickled through.
    There were of course great stories about Patton that sort of filtered through, you know, not very bad: there was this general that was an old toughie, this American general.
    And then this story started coming through from the correspon-dents – they used to come into the office – about slapping, a lot of rumours. So I talked to people who knew and I published a thing about a report that Patton was being investigated.
    And I got one of only two raps from Monty – that he was very upset – that he didn't think this was right, that Patton was a good man and although it was true that there was this report, that I should have checked back, because he had his responsibilities, and it reflected badly on him.[1]

Whatever he might feel about Patton's strategic judgment, Monty had been genuinely impressed by Seventh Army's mobility, speed, and on its eastern flank, rugged determination and professional-ism – and he would have nothing derogatory printed in Eighth Army's newspapers.
    Unlike Patton, Monty was indeed in the best of health and spirits. 'I have kept wonderfully fit and well. Active service campaigning seems to suit me, and I am never better than when we are fighting. Now I am enjoying the bathing,' he wrote to Phyllis Reynolds after the campaign was over. The crash of his Flying Fortress seemed to have done Monty much good – as had his menagerie of birds. He bathed 'every evening at 6.30', and drank 'gallons of fresh lemonade every day' from the ripe lemons in the Sicilian orchards. After the fall of Messina he moved his headquarters into a village in Taormina – 'a very delightful seaside resort,' as he informed the Reynolds; 'it is very beautiful scenery, and is famous as a resort for honeymoon couples, and so on. I am living in the villa of a millionaire, high up and overlooking the sea. The owner was here when I arrived and was very angry at being ordered to leave,' he went on. 'It is a superb villa, quite undamaged, and full of priceless pictures and very fine furni-ture. After living for a year in a caravan it is really rather nice to be in a house, and to have a proper bathroom; and we use all his china,

[1] Ibid.

glass, cutlery, table linen and so on!! The owner is a well-known member of the Fascist party.' When he found that Air Vice-Marshal Broadhurst's driver was the golfer Dai Rees, who had coached his son at Hindhead, he asked Mrs Reynolds to 'look in and see Mrs Rees, and tell her that I often talk to her husband out here and think very highly of him. She would appreciate that.'

With his 'face, arms and knees burnt almost black' by the Sicilian sun he confidently toured the units that would be going to Italy, and in the evening, after 'glorious' bathing, and a meal served at the fascist millionaire's table, he retired to read a novel from the millionaire's 'good library of English books . . . all rather old fashioned, and a good many by William Le Quex, detective stories, and so on' – and to write up his diary. The diary closed on 17 August 1943 when 'organised resistance in Sicily may be said to have ended'; but in a separate section, dated 22 August, Monty set down 'Some Reflections on the Campaign in Sicily – July/August 1943 – certain outstanding points' which, he felt, 'should be noted down for historical purposes'.

The reflections are too long to be quoted verbatim, but also too important to be passed over. In particular Monty's notes about Allied planning, outlined the month before in his letter to Lord Mountbatten, are crucial to an understanding of the authority and clear-cut leadership which he would impart to the planning of the Normandy invasion. Sicily was, in Monty's eyes, a rehearsal for the invasion of France, yet the bigger lessons seemed to be ignored. 'The Chiefs of Staff, and the War Cabinet, decide that a certain operation will be carried out; the matter is then handed over to the Joint Planners in London and they are asked to produce an outline plan. This outline plan is approved by the Chiefs of Staff, and it is then sent out to the theatre of war concerned. But this system is quite wrong,' Monty maintained. 'Once the Chiefs of Staff and the War Cabinet have decided that some operation is to be carried out, then a Commander must be appointed and *he* must produce the outline plan; when the outline plan has been approved, *then* detailed planning can commence. . . . I have discussed this problem with the CIGs, the VCIGS, members of the Army Council, the Secretary of State for War, and the DMO. Each one individually listens, and as far as I can gather they express their agreement in principle. But nothing happens.' The reason was beyond Monty's comprehension. 'There must be some big influences at the top, political or inter-Allied, which prevent us from doing the thing in a sensible manner. The whole thing is really so extremely simple; we make it as complicated as we can. And it would seem that we might at least learn from our past mistakes; but we make no attempt to do so.'

There was much truth in this, especially in so far as it related to the future invasion of France. 'The same mistake is being made in

England today. A cross-Channel operation is being envisaged; various planning staffs are at work; no outline has been produced by the Commander who is to take charge of the operation, *because no Commander has been appointed*. The staff of the Commander have been appointed and they are busily engaged in planning; but none of them have fought in this war and they know nothing about the battle end of the problem. . . . A further point is that the Commander, when appointed, has got to create his fighting machine and train his forces for the battle. This takes time, and it is not being done.

'There seems to be no one person in England who knows what is wanted, who says so quite clearly, and who has such prestige and fighting experience that everyone will accept his opinion and get on with it. Until such a person is appointed to "take hold" of the Army in England, we will do no good.

'At present there are too many people in England who think they know what is wanted; but they all disagree with each other; and they have got the basic set-up wrong; and they bellyache about non-essentials, they do not really know what *are* the essentials.'

At which Monty listed his 'axioms' of modern war – air superiority, good and simple army planning, seizing and retaining the tactical initiative, aiming for the vital hinges in the enemy's defensive layout and concentrating one's efforts upon them, re-grouping if necessary to do so; and, above all, ensuring that the men have 'commanders with terrific "drive" and energy'.

However logical, the flaw in Monty's argument was the simple fact that the Allies possessed very few higher commanders with sufficient experience and drive to undertake major operations such as the amphibious landings on Sicily, let alone the crucial cross-Channel operation. Monty had himself suggested to Mountbatten that Alexander should return to England to 'take hold' of the cross-Channel attack. But Monty can hardly have conceived Alexander to be the sort of commander appropriate to the task if one considers the judgments on Alexander contained in his diary. Of Alexander's headquarters – 15th Army Group – Monty remarked, 'I am afraid it has to be admitted that throughout the preliminary planning stage, and during the actual operations in SICILY, 15 Army Group has been completely and utterly ineffective.' Both Alexander's Chief of Staff and his Chief of Administration were 'out of their depth'; moreover Alexander's vast staff of 480 officers alone – excluding other ranks – was 'definitely a great waste, and in fact a scandal'.

'A further trouble is that Alexander cannot make a decision when faced with a difficult and complex problem. Therefore his staff have a very difficult time.

'He is so used to reaching agreement by compromise, and to finding a formula that will suit all parties, that he has lost the gift of quick decision – if he ever had it.'

This might seem a harsh commentary on a man 'whom we all love'; but it was the considered view of an Army Commander who had been serving under Alexander since August 1942. 'He will take action at once when the form is given him by me, or by someone else whose opinion he trusts,' Monty went on. 'If his staff would give him the proper line, he would be all right. But his staff is a very poor one, and his CGS and MGA are out of their depth. ALEXANDER requires a Chief of Staff who is the "cat's whiskers", and who will tell him what is wanted. Give this he would be excellent. But he has not got one.' In another section of the reflections Monty went even further:

15 Army Group in 1943
Alexander was Army Group Commander; he is not clever and requires a C.G.S. who knows the whole business and will get on with it. ALEXANDER in fact requires a really high-class C.G.S. who will tell him what to do, and the operational repercussions of any particular course of action, and who understands thoroughly the air aspect of battle. Given such a C.G.S. he is excellent. But without such a C.G.S. nothing happens. . . .

The whole set-up at 15 Army Group has been bad; the planning for operations, the grip on the battle and the conduct of the war generally, has been a complete failure.

Was this, then, the man to galvanise the Allied cross-Channel assault? Alexander's 'great asset is his charm, and if he lost that he would go right under,' Monty opined.

The answer, Monty felt, was not simply to look at individual commanders, but to look at 'teams': 'I have seen so many mistakes and disasters happen in this war that I feel I would like to put down my ideas on the whole question of "teams". . . . It is in the realm of "teams" on the higher level that we so often go wrong. I will give some examples:

a) *B.E.F. in France, 1939/40*
GORT was C-in-C and POWNALL was C.G.S.
GORT had never commanded anything higher than a Bde, and was quite unfit to be a C-in-C in the field. He should therefore have had a C.G.S. who had commanded a Division, who was clever and practical, and who thoroughly understood the whole business. POWNALL had never commanded anything above a battery as far as I know; he is completely theoretical and is unfit to command anything.
GORT and POWNALL together had not got the necessary knowledge or qualities.
Consequently the higher command in the B.E.F. was a ghastly failure.

b) *Middle East Command in 1942*
   AUCHINLECK was C-in-C and CORBETT C.G.S.
   AUCHINLECK suffers from an inferiority complex; he has spent his military life in the Indian Army and has no idea how to fight Germans. He has an active brain but cannot harness it to the job in hand. He relies on advisers and he chooses these badly; he is a bad judge of men. He required a really high class Chief of Staff. But he selected CORBETT. CORBETT was, and is, the stupidest officer in the Indian Army; he has no brains at all.
   There could be only one end to this party, i.e. complete failure, and this is what happened – both of them being removed.
c) *First Army in North Africa 1942/3*
   ANDERSON was Army Commander. When he took over, his B.G.S. was [A. A.] RICHARDSON, who would be quite good under a skilled or gifted commander.
   ANDERSON is not skilled or gifted; he is somewhat stupid, is tactless and rude, is small-minded and likes fiddling with details.
   He sacked RICHARDSON in the first week and took on McNAB.
   McNAB knew nothing about the business on that level; he was a somewhat dour Scotsman, rather like ANDERSON.
   The 'team' did not exist, and the whole North African party got in a fearful mess; it was saved from complete disaster by ALEXANDER. ANDERSON of course is quite unfit to command an Army in the field, so the team started badly.

   Alexander's 15th Army Group team in Tunisia had coped until May 1943; but then 'McCREERY left him after the Tunisian campaign was over. ALEXANDER then took on GAIRDNER as C.G.S.; GAIRDNER was completely out of his depth from the very start and the whole HUSKY planning got in a fearful mess. . . . So GAIRDNER was removed' – to be replaced by A. A. Richardson. 'It very soon became apparent that the job was far too big for RICHARDSON and he was completely out of his depth; I think myself he would have been adequate if he had been given a firm lead, and guidance, by ALEXANDER. But this does not happen; in the side of high command in war ALEXANDER is not too sure-footed, and he has got to be given a lead himself. So ALEXANDER and RICHARDSON were a failure too.'
   Meanwhile in England things were no better:

e) *Home Forces in England 1942 and 1943*
   PAGET was C-in-C and SWAYNE C.G.S.
   PAGET is definitely not a Commander; he does not understand training and he does not understand the operational repercussions of battle plans; he cannot plan operations.
   SWAYNE had not seen a shot fired in the last war (he was taken

prisoner in August 1914) or in this war. His military knowledge was pure theory.

Result: The team was a failure. SWAYNE then left and was given command of an Army – a truly amazing appointment for an officer who had not seen a shot fired during the whole of his service.

MORGAN became C.G.S.[1]; he had not got up-to-date operational experience and knew nothing about the air.

This team was also a failure.

I should say that it would be difficult to fix up PAGET with a good C.G.S.; he is too much a staff officer himself. His C.G.S. wants to be well versed in the command aspect in battle; PAGET would of course probably quarrel with such a C.G.S.

On the other hand there were teams which Monty *did* feel were good. He cited Churchill and Brooke, Eisenhower and Bedell Smith ('Eisenhower is a very "big" man who takes the large view and keeps clear of all detail; BEDELL SMITH implements all the big decisions and keeps the whole show on the rails') – and Alexander and himself.

ALEXANDER has great personal charm and a sterling character; so much so that he likes to reach agreement whatever may happen, quite regardless of whether that agreement will win the battle. He is therefore liked by everyone, as all find him easy to work with.

I think I can say that I do know the battle side of war; I think even my enemies will admit this. I can therefore help ALEXANDER a lot in that respect, and do, insisting that the right things are done.

In other ways I have not got those fine qualities that he possesses,

Monty acknowledged in a rare display of introspection;

and because I fight for the things that matter I make certain enemies. But I win the battle. Between us we have the knowledge and the qualities necessary for most jobs in war. And we are great friends. So we are a good team and I believe that each of us is necessary to the other. We ought to remain a team for the duration of this war.

Brooke evidently felt so too, as did Eisenhower. Thus Alexander was left commanding 15th Army Group, with Monty the Eighth Army Commander. But Brooke and Eisenhower both saw a problem which Monty missed: namely, that Alexander was not firm enough with his Eighth Army Commander. Alexander's conduct of the

---

[1] Lt-General F. ('Monkey') Morgan – not the COSSAC Chief of Staff.

Sicilian campaign had in fact been feeble from beginning to end. His planning of 'Husky' had been a virtual shambles, and his failure to take a grip on the campaign, once started, had led to the very Anglo-American rivalry he had been appointed to dispel. He had permitted Monty to usurp American highways and objectives in the first few days of operations, fatally splitting the strength of Eighth Army, and then permitted Patton to race off in the wrong direction. Apart from despatching a cable dictated by Monty regarding the need for a combined plan to defeat the Axis evacuation, he had done nothing to ensure that the withdrawal of almost 100,000 fighting enemy troops from the island, together with their equipment and vehicles, was stopped. Far from being the 'good team' which Monty felt it was, the Alexander-Montgomery duo was rapidly deteriorating into a very bad team. Instead of lasting the whole war, as Montgomery suggested it ought, the relationship would come unstuck within a matter of months, as Alexander repeated all the errors in Italy that had disgraced his command in Sicily: poor planning, and failure to impose a real grip on his two prima donna Army Commanders, Clark and Montgomery.

Monty's 'reflections' were completed on 22 August 1943, six days after the fall of Sicily. On 16 August Alexander had finally plucked up sufficient courage to tell him that Operation 'Buttress', employing 10 Corps under Eighth Army Command, was 'off'. 'The 10 Corps would be placed in 5th American Army, and that Army would carry out Operation AVALANCHE [the landing near Naples] about 10 September. Eighth Army was to carry out Operation BAYTOWN; this was to be on night 30/31 August, some 10 days before AVALANCHE, and I was asked if I could do this,' Monty recorded in his diary. 'Operation BAYTOWN is an invasion of the mainland of ITALY, so as to secure the "toe" and open up the Straits of MESSINA for the Navy. I said I would do the operation on night 30/31 August. It will not be too easy to do in the time, as the demolitions on the [Sicilian] roads are very extensive. But it will be done somehow.'

In fact Monty had been forced to send telegram after telegram to Alexander in order to be given an objective for 'Baytown', and in what he called 'a unique incident in the history of war' he had finally wrung from Alexander a directive, written on a half sheet of notepaper.

It was a sorry way, after completing the capture of Sicily, to begin the first Allied assault upon the European mainland.

PART FOUR

Italy

CHAPTER ONE

'A Unique Incident in the History of War'

In conquering Sicily the Allies had secured a stepping stone across the Mediterranean. The mainland of Italy, only a few miles across the Messina Straits, was now vulnerable to invasion anywhere along its Mediterranean or even Adriatic coast.

Instead of ensuring, as ultimately he had done in 'Husky', that the Allies invaded Italy in one place with overwhelming force, poor Eisenhower tried vainly to mediate between the conflicting theories and pressures of his advisers. The result was near disaster; indeed if proof were needed to vindicate Monty's intransigent insistence on an all-out single landing in 'Husky', the historian need look no further than the chaotic invasion of Italy.

Politically, Eisenhower coped remarkably well with the situation; using the threat of imminent and devastating Allied assault he was able to force the Italian High Command into a treacherous rupture of the Rome-Berlin alliance, involving a formal capitulation timed to coincide with Clark's intended seizure of Naples in the second week of September 1943. Militarily however his leadership was so lacking in professionalism that it is difficult, in retrospect, to understand how Eisenhower was subsequently chosen as Supreme Commander for the invasion of France. Not only did he fail to ensure concentration of effort, but he became the willing believer of all that his Intelligence staff, under Brigadier Strong, led him to believe concerning Italian assistance in fighting the Germans. The story of his planned seizure of Rome by Ridgway's 82nd Airborne Division is perhaps the most telling example of Eisenhower's military fantasy – an operation so wildly and vaguely conceived that it would have made Arnhem look respectable. The story of how the air landing was stopped, when the division's commander was already in the air, well illustrates the delusions and misconceptions that characterised Eisenhower's headquarters, and how near they came to destroying America's élite parachute formation.

On land fate was less kind, and the Naples operation, entrusted by Eisenhower to a commander who had not yet seen a shot fired in the war, resulted in a near-débâcle at Salerno.

Monty watched the antics of his colleagues and superiors with something approaching disbelief. It seemed to him that the experience and military expertise so laboriously gained by the Allies over the past year was now being sacrificed to fantastical schemes founded on woolly thinking and the most dangerous assumptions. Having lost Horrocks's 10 Corps to Clark's 'Avalanche' assault on 16 August, Monty found great difficulty in obtaining even an objective for his own 'Baytown' landing, let alone adequate provision of sea transport for Eighth Army. Was he to plan for 'strong resistance' in the toe of Italy, or was it 'going to be negligible'? 'Without such definite information,' he signalled Alexander on 19 August, 'I must plan for strong resistance as otherwise there might be a disaster;[1]

I have been given no clear object for the operation. . . . All that I could do with the present allotment of resources is to put across less than four b[attalio]ns with a very slow build-up. Therefore if I am to work on present allotment of resources I can only carry out a major raid across the Straits. . . . Request definite instructions as to the timing and object of any operation I am to carry out across the Straits.

The next day, 20 August, Alexander replied, saying only that Eighth Army's task was to establish a bridgehead across the Messina Straits and to engage enemy forces in the southern tip of Italy in order to draw Axis divisions away from 'Avalanche':

Most Secret
Headquarters
15th Army Group

Aug 20th 1943

Your task is to secure a bridgehead on the toe of Italy, to enable our naval forces to operate through the Straits of Messina.
In the event of the enemy withdrawing from the toe, you will follow him up with such force as you can make available, bearing in mind that the greater the extent to which you can engage enemy forces in the Southern tip of Italy, the more assistance you will be giving to Avalanche.

H.R. Alexander
Commander 15th Army Group.[2]

Monty was almost disbelieving, as his annotation to the letter, written thirty years later, showed:

---

[1] Diary entry, Montgomery Papers.
[2] Original in Montgomery Papers.

A unique incident in the history of War
On the 19th August 1943 I sent a cable to General Alexander saying that I had been ordered to invade the mainland of Europe with the Eighth Army – but had been given no object.
On the 20th August I received a half-sheet of note-paper – giving me an object.

Monty's disdain was not only that he had been forced to ask for an object, but that the object given was so daft.

It is not clear what BAYTOWN is meant to achieve,

his Chief of Staff General de Guingand had declared as early as 10 August; moreover de Guingand had voiced the opinion of all in Eighth Army headquarters when he stated:

If AVALANCHE is a success, then we should reinforce that front for there is little point in laboriously fighting our way up Southern ITALY. It is better to leave the enemy to decay there or let him have the trouble of moving himself up from the foot to where we are concentrated.[1]

Again, on behalf of the Eighth Army Commander, de Guingand had declared at a Planning Conference on 19 August that 'Baytown' ought to be cancelled and merely used as a threat, for if 'Baytown' was intended to be a genuine diversion to help 'Avalanche' by tying down enemy divisions in the toe of Italy, it could only work if mounted simultaneously, and for reasons of naval and air support, this was considered impossible.[2] During the week that would elapse between 'Baytown' and 'Avalanche', the Germans would have ample time to withdraw their divisions to the Naples area, using rearguards to delay Eighth Army.

Aware that there were divided feelings about Allied plans, Eisenhower convened a conference for 12 o'clock in Algiers on 23 August, to which Monty flew from Catania at 7 a.m. 'Baytown' *was* to go ahead, Eisenhower declared, and asked Monty to outline his plans for invasion. 'This I did,' Monty chronicled in his diary;

I brought out how the Naval delays now made it quite impossible for me to do the operation on night 30/31 August; I said that I had *now at last* got the necessary resources in craft and Naval personnel and could do the operation on night 2/3 September; the Navy,

[1] Eighth Army HQ War Diary, Minutes of Planning Conference (WO 169/8494), PRO.
[2] Ibid.

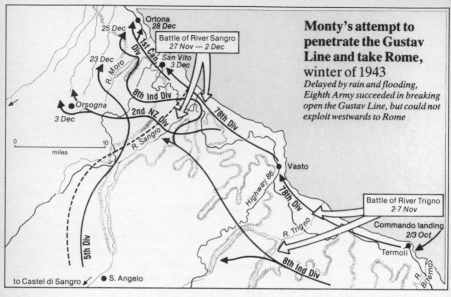

Monty's attempt to penetrate the Gustav Line and take Rome, winter of 1943

Delayed by rain and flooding, Eighth Army succeeded in breaking open the Gustav Line, but could not exploit westwards to Rome

Ortona 28 Dec

Battle of River Sangro 27 Nov — 2 Dec

San Vito 3 Dec

25 Dec

1st Can Div

R. Moro

23 Dec

8th Ind Div

Orsogna 3 Dec

2nd NZ Div

78th Div

R. Sangro

0   miles   10

Highway 86

78th Div

Vasto

Battle of River Trigno 2-7 Nov

Commando landing 2/3 Oct

5th Div

R. Trigno

Termoli

R. Biferno

8th Ind Div

to Castel di Sangro

S. Angelo

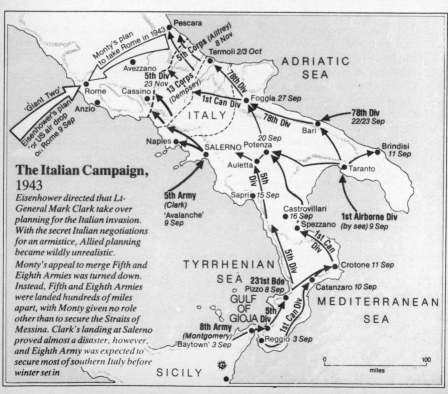

Pescara

Monty's plan to take Rome in 1943

5th Corps (Allfrey) 8 Nov

Termoli 2/3 Oct

ADRIATIC SEA

78th Div

Avezzano

5th Div 23 Nov

13 Corps (Dempsey)

1st Can Div

Foggia 27 Sep

'Giant Two' Eisenhower's plan for US air drop on Rome 9 Sep

Rome

Cassino

ITALY

78th Div

78th Div 22/23 Sep

Anzio

Naples

SALERNO

Potenza 20 Sep

Bari

Brindisi 11 Sep

The Italian Campaign, 1943

Eisenhower directed that Lt-General Mark Clark take over planning for the Italian invasion. With the secret Italian negotiations for an armistice, Allied planning became wildly unrealistic.

Monty's appeal to merge Fifth and Eighth Armies was turned down. Instead, Fifth and Eighth Armies were landed hundreds of miles apart, with Monty given no role other than to secure the Straits of Messina. Clark's landing at Salerno proved almost a disaster, however, and Eighth Army was expected to secure most of southern Italy before winter set in

5th Army (Clark) 'Avalanche' 9 Sep

Auletta

Sapri 15 Sep

5th Div

Taranto

1st Airborne Div (by sea) 9 Sep

Castrovillari 16 Sep

Spezzano

1st Can Div

TYRRHENIAN SEA

231st Bde Pizzo 8 Sep

GULF OF GIOJA

5th Div

1st Can Div

Crotone 11 Sep

Catanzaro 10 Sep

MEDITERRANEAN SEA

8th Army (Montgomery) 'Baytown' 3 Sep

Reggio 3 Sep

0   miles   100

SICILY

however, had told me that the earliest they could manage was the night 4/5 September.

Andrew CUNNINGHAM here intervened and said my statements were not true, and that this was the first he had heard of any Naval delays or any inability to do the operation by the time required by the Army.

This was without question the biggest bluff that I have ever seen put up by an Admiral-of-the-Fleet. I said I could prove my statements. EISENHOWER took my side and said I was only saying what the local Admiral in SICILY had told me: he then told Andrew CUNNINGHAM that he had better get into an aeroplane and go over to SICILY and sort the matter out, adding that we must aim at getting the operation launched on night 2/3 September.

Andrew CUNNINGHAM was very angry and left the room shortly afterwards en route for SICILY. I was told afterwards by ALEXANDER that EISENHOWER had (before the meeting) accused Andrew CUNNINGHAM of not co-operating properly; that CUNNINGHAM had said he would resign, and that he (CUNNINGHAM) would hardly speak to ALEXANDER.

CUNNINGHAM went to SICILY, saw Admiral McGRIGOR and DEMPSEY (Comd 13 Corps), and the Navy agreed to do BAYTOWN on night 2/3 September. DEMPSEY told me he had never seen such a change in any man; CUNNINGHAM was almost servile in his offers to do anything that the Army wanted.

So the whole thing has done a very great deal of good, and the Navy are all delighted we had the show-down with CUNNINGHAM. He is a very difficult person; I suppose no one would fight a big fleet action better: but he has not much brains, and is out of his depth when planning a big-scale operation; he does everything himself and does not understand how to work through a staff; everyone is frightened of him.

Unfortunately EISENHOWER thinks he is the cat's whiskers; he is very far from being so, and EISENHOWER would be far better served with a Naval C-in-C like Bertie RAMSAY who is quite first-class and has a very good and very clear brain.

Monty's stricture regarding Admiral Sir Andrew Cunningham was shared by Alexander who, at a dinner after the conference, made the same complaint to Eisenhower: 'Cunningham has carried the Mediterranean naval operations so completely in his head and is so adamant in his expressions and desires that all of his staff is afraid of him and will take no decisions without consultation with their Commander-in-Chief,' Alexander confided. 'Thus when the Admiral is absent from Malta where details of the amphibious operation are under closest observation . . . no staff decisions may be obtained.'[1]

Eisenhower, however, *did* consider Cunningham a paragon, as his naval aide, Commander Butcher, noted. 'The Admiral has always conducted his amphibious landings with skill and bravery and has unfailingly cooperated with AFHQ. In fact he has been the model.'[2] In such circumstances, with Eisenhower loath to criticise or cajole Cunningham, only Monty's insulting accusations could stir Cunningham into action – a further black mark in Monty's 'co-operation with AFHQ' book, but essential if the first Allied invasion of mainland Europe was to be properly executed, and without delay.

As for Eisenhower's main assault, however, Monty had profound misgivings, which were further reinforced by Eisenhower's latest report on armistice negotiations and Mark Clark's presentation of his 'Avalanche' plans. Given Eisenhower's latest news of Italian capitulation 'it did not now look as if the opposition could be very great' to Eighth Army's 'Baytown' landings at Reggio; at Naples, however, it would be a different story.

AVALANCHE was to take place on night 9/10 September,

Monty recorded in his diary.

The Germans had some 15 Divisions in ITALY and at least four could be concentrated fairly quickly against the 5 American Army. CLARKE [sic] expounded his plan at the conference and it seemed to me to be open to criticism; the Airborne Division was being landed a long way away from the main body of the Army and would be out of supporting distance; the build-up on the beaches was very slow.

Unfortunately Eisenhower's strategic thinking was the result of his secret surrender negotiations with emissaries from Badoglio – something which fatally affected the unrealistic, back-seat-driving atmosphere now pervading Allied Force Headquarters at Algiers. 'If the Italians changed sides, and began fighting the Germans, anything was possible' was the AFHQ approach – an attitude Monty refused to share:

I doubt if the Italians ever would really fight the Germans; they are quite useless and would be hit for six; the most we can hope for I feel is non-co-operation.

---

[1] Diary of Harry C. Butcher, in Papers of Dwight D. Eisenhower, 1652 series, Eisenhower Library, Abilene, Kansas.
[2] Ibid.

Instead of acceding to Monty's request to merge Eighth Army into an improved 'Avalanche', however, Eisenhower tolerated the same notions of dispersed landings which had characterised his original planning for 'Torch' and 'Husky', aided and abetted by both Cunningham and Tedder, who naïvely believed the Allied armies would have no problem in over-running Italy. Indeed even Clark's plan for an airborne drop to the north of Naples was cancelled, to be resurrected as an airborne assault on Rome – a city the Allies would not reach for almost a year.

It is in the context of this almost culpable carelessness concerning the lives of so many Allied soldiers – men who had fought across North Africa and through the plains and mountains of Sicily – that Monty's behaviour in the late summer of 1943 must be viewed. If he began to dig his heels in, to become almost pedantic in his insistence that the Allies approach the invasion of Italy with clearer notions of what they wished to achieve, it was a pedantry based on injured professionalism. He who had remoulded the Eighth Army at Alamein and had brought it so many thousands of miles, who had breached the Axis flank in Sicily and brought Italy to her knees, was now forced to watch a charade of high command, a wilful relapse into the same ignorant, opportunistic amateurism that had characterised, in his eyes, British and Allied leadership through the worst days of World War II: the blind foray into Hitler's trap in Belgium in 1940, the Norwegian débâcle that year, the desperate expedition to Greece the following year, and the endless bunglings in North Africa. The sanity he thought he had brought back into British military operations; the refusal to attack until he knew his blow would be decisive: was all this to be squandered once more on a campaign lacking any coherent objective, full of the wildest of plans predicated on the shakiest of assumptions?

Outwardly Monty attempted to put a brave face on his misgivings. On 29 August he invited Generals Eisenhower, Patton, Bradley, Gay (Patton's Chief of Staff), Keyes (Provisional Corps Commander) and Truscott to lunch at his Tactical Headquarters at Taormina. Patton was quiet, knowing his future lay in Eisenhower's hands;[1] Monty's lunch he interpreted humorously as 'trying to make up for not feeding me last time'. Using the millionaire-owner's silver, china and table-linen, Monty certainly went all out to be affable, prompting Eisenhower's naval aide to record of this private dinner: 'Monty

---

[1] *The Patton Papers*, ed. Martin Blumenson, Vol. II, Boston 1972. Patton did amuse the gathering by his earthy wit, however. 'They had a get-together, and the subject arose, whether the soldiers should be allowed to talk to the local civilians. And Georgie Patton came to the point about what it was really all about, you see, and said: "I say fornication ain't fraternisation! That is, if you keep your hat on and your weight on the elbows!" And Monty roared with laughter!' – J. R. Henderson, interview of 13.8.81.

showed he had the soul of a host and although he neither drinks nor smokes, he freely offered these inevitable tokens of hospitality . . . seeing Monty at close range I found I liked him.'[1] Eisenhower too was won over, dismissing Butcher's cynical explanation of the invitation (that Monty wished to show first-hand 'the extraordinary difficulty which confronted and slowed the 8th Army') and insisting that Monty 'because of his experience in the Sicilian campaign had decided to "join the family" '.[2]

To the whir of cameras, Eisenhower now formally pinned the Legion of Merit to the tunic of the famous Eighth Army Commander; and together they drove up to Messina where they 'stood at the water's edge and carefully surveyed the Italian mainland only two miles away.'[3]

The narrowness of the Straits, scarcely wider than the Mississippi, and the delay before Monty would commit himself to cross, irked Eisenhower. In his war memoirs, Eisenhower referred to Monty's 'Baytown' assault as taking place 'ten days later than I had hoped it could be done', and even blamed this delay for the near-catastrophe at Salerno. The proximity of the mainland tantalised him, as is clear from his interview with the American Official Historian in 1949:

> I was pressing for speed all along . . . I believe that there is a picture of Montgomery and me looking across the Strait from Messina. I believed that the Germans would withdraw, that we could make a landing practically unopposed. General Montgomery wished to have everything fully prepared and thought there would be considerable German opposition. Meanwhile there was General Patton moaning – asking that he be allowed to make the crossing. I told General Alexander I believed we could do it in a row-boat. We sat there in Messina from 17 August until 3 September.[4]

Since then, other writers have condemned Monty for his seeming dilatoriness, as well as his insistence on making 'Baytown' such a formal invasion, with so much massed artillery and air support. Yet the delay was not of Monty's making, as de Guingand's conference minutes all through the last weeks of August 1943 demonstrate; for without landing craft or naval co-operation General Dempsey, commanding the only Corps that could cross, simply refused to go ahead with the invasion – an invasion which no one in Eighth Army

[1] Diary of Harry C. Butcher, entry of 2.9.43, loc. cit.
[2] Ibid.
[3] Ibid.
[4] Interview of 16.2.49 by H. M. Smyth, in OCMH Collection, Military History Institute, Carlisle, Pennsylvania.

Headquarters[1] felt was necessary, least of all Monty. If the object had been simply to put across four British battalions and to secure the Straits for the Navy, Eisenhower's row-boat crossing could of course have been mounted immediately; but if Eighth Army – against its will and advice – was being asked to put across sufficient troops, equipment and bridging material to follow up a German withdrawal from Reggio to Naples – a distance of almost 300 miles – then it was idle to talk of row-boats.

Eisenhower, for all his political panache, utterly failed to see the absurdity of 'Baytown' – for to his inexperienced eye, frustrated by desk-soldiering, the mainland across the Straits of Messina simply *demanded* Allied occupation. Instead of keeping Eighth Army concentrated for landing further north and ordering the Messina Straits to be seized by small forces to ensure their safe use by the Allied navies, Eisenhower thus committed himself to one of the most senseless assaults of the war, and then blamed Monty for being slow.

Monty, amazed but determined not to lose his professional composure, insisted that if Eighth Army had to undertake the 'Baytown' invasion, then it would be undertaken as an Army – an Army not of muddled opportunists hoping for miraculous Italian help, but with the cohesion and professional soldierliness for which it was now renowned; an Army which, even if it had to 'crawl up the leg [of Italy] like a harvest bug' (in Churchill's vivid phrase)[2] would at least be a bug big enough to 'knock Italy out of the war' – the only clear object Monty could discern in all the Allied machinations over the invasion of Italy.

It is surely to Monty's credit that Eighth Army's 'Baytown' invasion achieved precisely this, five days after Eighth Army assaulted the mainland, and mercifully one day before Eisenhower's setback at Salerno. Moreover, what later writers chose to interpret as Monty's extreme inflexibility in the detailed mounting of Eighth Army's 'Baytown' assault was in fact an estimable determination not to endanger the lives of his men. Negotiations with senior members of the Italian High Command were in progress: but Italy and the Allies were still technically at war, and would be for a week *after* Eighth Army's invasion. No information about the intended Allied landings, obviously, could be given to the Italian negotiators. In the circumstances, therefore, Monty refused to take any risks. His diary records his attempt to discover the reception he was likely to face on the Italian mainland; but without solid evidence to go on, Monty insisted that Eighth Army adhere to its formal invasion plan:

[1] 'SALERNO was feasible, although improperly planned and mounted. None of us could understand BAYTOWN' – letter from General Sir Charles Richardson to author, 11.12.82.
[2] J. Ehrman, *Grand Strategy* Vol. V, London 1956.

26 August

Preparations for BAYTOWN continued. We have deployed in, and behind, MESSINA a good weight of artillery:

48 American heavy guns.

80 medium guns.

Three Divisional Artilleries (50 Div, 51 Div, 78 Div).

Tonight we are landing a small party on the mainland at BOVA MARINA, to get a prisoner and ascertain 'the form generally'.

27 August

The party sent to BOVA MARINA found the place deserted. They brought back an Italian railway worker who said the Italian civil population have left the villages and gone into the hills, anxiously awaiting our arrival. Also that Italian soldiers have changed into civilian clothes and have joined the civil population.

On this information five more parties were sent in with W/T sets with orders to establish themselves at:

BOVA MARINA

CAP SPARTIVENTO

BAGALADI

MELITO

Between MELITO and REGGIO

These parties went tonight 27/28 August.

Their orders were to get contact, report enemy movements, and remain there. They were self-contained for some days.

Unfortunately the landing parties failed to report back, as Monty noted in his diary the next day: 'No news from the parties on the mainland.'

If, however, the reports 'when made are favourable' Monty decided he would land further troops at Bova Marina or Melito, take Reggio from the Straits, and dispense with the whole 'Baytown' plan:

If this [the informal landing of further troops at Bova Marina] went well, we might not have to do BAYTOWN: we could ferry 5 Div across from Catania.

But when, after two days, there was *still* no news of the landing parties Monty decided to play safe and adhere to his original plan: 'Having had no further news from the parties, I decided that the planned operation of invading the mainland of ITALY would go ahead without any change.'

Yet even this was not possible, for, far from being dilatory as Eisenhower later implied, Monty now found that there were insufficient ferrying craft and bridging equipment to mount a full-scale invasion by Eighth Army. Instead of being followed by 30 Corps, 13

Corps would therefore have to land and conduct the campaign on the mainland alone, with two divisions. The area south of Reggio would be ignored and all bridging equipment sent north; 1st Canadian Division would immediately cross the mountains and work its way up the east coast; meanwhile 5th Division would drive up the west coast of the Calabrian toe, aided by outflanking Commando landings. 'By these tactics I hoped to be able to get a secure footing on the mainland very quickly, and to get possession of the main laterals between the North and South roads. I was prepared to develop "left hooks" to assist the progress of the 5th Division. For this purpose I had two Commandos ready in MESSINA, and I had 231 Bde Gp ready at RIPOSTO.'

Despite the lack of a clear-cut objective let alone coherent strategy from Alexander and Eisenhower, Monty was satisfied that Eighth Army would, by the professionalism of its operations, ensure that the Italian High Command did not renege on its intention to sue for peace, as well as securing, by the time Eisenhower's other invasion was launched, the whole of the toe of Italy – an area as great as that won by Eighth Army in the thirty-nine days of the Sicilian campaign. Given the fact that most of Eighth Army's ferrying craft were to be released for use in 'Avalanche', this two-divisional objective seemed as much as Monty could hope to achieve. 'Forward to Victory! Let us knock ITALY out of the war!' he exhorted in his now customary 'Personal Message to be read out to all Troops', adding that Eighth Army had been 'given the great honour of being the first troops of the Allied Armies to land on the mainland of the continent of Europe'. Without further news from the landing parties Monty insisted that the artillery bombardment take place, in order to minimise casualties from possible enemy rearguards and mines, and at 4.30 a.m. on 3 September 1943 – the fourth anniversary of the outbreak of the war – men of the Canadian and 5th British Divisions touched down on Fortress Europe. Three thousand prisoners were taken, the harbour at Reggio was reckoned to be operable within forty-eight hours, and Eighth Army's two divisions both began striking northwards. Monty himself landed north of Reggio during the morning and radiated optimism. To Brooke he wrote that evening:

3.9.43

My dear Brookie,

I attacked across the Straits of Messina this morning at 0430 hrs. And at 1030 hrs I stepped ashore myself on the mainland of Europe just North of REGGIO. It was a great thrill once more to set foot on the Continent from which we were pushed off three years ago, at Dunkirk!!

The opposition was slight. I landed between REGGIO and S.

GIOVANNI and took these places by encircling movements to the South and North respectively.

I now have my Tac H.Q. in Europe. It is a great day and it is the anniversary of the outbreak of the war, and the beginning of the fifth year of the war. I have enjoyed it all greatly.

The Germans evacuated REGGIO before we got into the town, so we had no opposition there from soldiers,

Monty explained;

but there is a zoo in the town and our shelling broke open some cages; a puma and a monkey escaped and attacked some men of the HQ 3rd Canadian Bde, and heavy fire was opened by the Canadians; the puma got away; it is believed the monkey was wounded but it escaped in the confusion!!!

he remarked with hilarity.

It is without doubt a curious war!

Yet behind the mark of confidence and good humour, Monty was deeply concerned about the conduct of the Mediterranean campaign. His two 'follow-up' divisions in Sicily particularly deserved to go home, he felt:

There is no doubt that some of my chaps are getting tired.

50 DIV are definitely so; so are 51 DIV. Both of these splendid divisions have been fighting almost continuously for over a year, and 50 DIV for much longer.

I have left them both out of this party, and they are resting in Sicily; they ought to be taken home to the UK; they will be grand to have for 'Overlord'.

Oliver Leese is also definitely tired and I have sent him off in my aeroplane to Syria for two weeks holiday.

Continuous and hard fighting is a great strain

he commented – though excluding himself.

The only person who does not get tired is myself. I have the feeling you think I am idle and ought not to go to bed after dinner and read a novel, or do some quiet thinking in bed. But I can assure you,

he pointed out,

that if I did not do this I could not possibly go on with the business at the present tempo and pace.

I expect you had a terrific time at Quebec. I shall be interested to hear the results. I think Dickie Mountbatten's appointment [as Supreme Commander, South-east Asia] is good; he will go down well with the Chinese and Americans, which is very important.

What Monty did not say was that he was tormented by private doubts about the invasion of Italy. To Charles Richardson, his erstwhile GSO1 (Ops), whom he had loaned as a British Deputy Chief of Staff to Mark Clark, he had already written on 1 September: 'You have been a member of our team for a very long time and you will be greatly missed. But when appealed to by the Americans we had to send our best; and you are very much wanted in that show. I do not altogether like the way things are shaping in your "party".'[1]

But it was not only Clark's inexperienced mounting of an opposed amphibious landing that worried Monty; it was, as has been seen, the foolhardiness of the Allied High Command and the incredible administrative bungling to which this patent lack of realism and clarity were leading. As he was to write to Brigadier Simpson at the War Office some three weeks later:

I told you I could write a very good book about the whole Husky affair. . . . It is nothing to the one I could write about the invasion of the mainland of Italy. You would think we would learn by our mistakes, but apparently not. Some of the things I was asked to do, and the way the whole party was stage-managed, is past all belief.[2]

[1] Communicated to author by General Sir Charles Richardson. Richardson found Fifth Army HQ embarrassingly (though understandably) 'green', as he did 6 US Corps Headquarters. The Fifth Army Chief of Operations Staff (G3) he considered 'useless' and the impression made by General C. J. Dawley, the 6 US Corps Commander, at the final pre-landing conference 'very poor' – letter to author of 11.12.82.

[2] Letter of 30.9.43, copy in Montgomery Papers.

CHAPTER TWO

'Giant Two' and Salerno

Despite lengthy negotiations, it was only after Montgomery's Eighth Army landed in Calabria on the morning of 3 September 1943 that Marshal Badoglio was finally persuaded to authorise an Italian armistice, which General Castellano signed at 5.15 that afternoon in a secret session with Eisenhower's Chief of Staff, General Bedell Smith, in Sicily. Formal capitulation was to be broadcast to the Italian nation on the eve of 'Avalanche', five days later.

The Allied High Command was carried away by this diplomatic coup, for as Bedell Smith later confirmed, 'there was a certain degree of bluff, we had only limited means for the invasion of Italy and we led Castellano to believe that our invasion would be in greater strength than actually was intended.'[1] By the use of only two Eighth Army divisions and the threat of a bigger landing further north, Eisenhower had 'knocked Italy out of the war'.

But who was bluffing whom? General Marshall had made it clear that America would not commit more than nine divisions to the Italian campaign, and these only while the Foggia airfields were secured for the Allied air forces; then the majority were to be shifted to Britain for the cross-Channel assault in 1944. Instead of downgrading his expectations accordingly, Eisenhower now began to fantasise that, with Italian help, the Allies could not only secure the Foggia airfields, but take over the greater part of Italy before his American divisions were pulled out. In spite of the obvious Italian fear of the Germans, Eisenhower encouraged the Italians to promise not only to lay down their arms, but to join the Allies in ousting the Germans. Thus instead of helping the inexperienced Clark to mount a more powerful 'Avalanche', Eisenhower now took away Clark's airborne troops – and in a single night laid plans for the seizure of Rome. General Lemnitzer, Alexander's American Chief of Staff, later recalled the 'all night session – so great was the haste to get the plan together – after working all night on the plan they saw the morning sunlight streaming into the tent where they worked.'[2]

[1] Smyth interview, 13.5.47, loc. cit.
[2] Smyth interview, 3.3.47, loc. cit.

The plan was 'Giant II' – in which elements of the élite 82nd Airborne Division would be dropped outside Rome and, together with the equivalent of four Italian divisions stationed there, would secure the Italian capital by *coup de main*. Bedell Smith believed, even after the war, that the plan had 'a better than even chance of success'.[1] It was Bedell Smith who urged General Alexander to use the 82nd Airborne, supported by Admiral Cunningham who, though he could not land Clark even as far north as Naples because of lack of Allied air cover, 'planned to land guns up at the first bridge on the Tiber'.[2] For Smith it was 'a matter of regret that the plan was called off . . . with an Italian General with guts the plan might have succeeded.'[3] Against these five Allied divisions (four of them Italian), Bedell Smith felt that the two and a half German divisions in the vicinity would have been powerless: 'It would have been a bold move, and it would have caught the Germans off balance.'[4] Courageously led, but completely lacking in air or sea support, the four Italian and lightly-equipped elements of one American division 'could have held Rome indefinitely. The population would have aided – dropping kettles, bricks, hot water on Germans in the streets of Rome – the worst possible place to fight. . . . It would have compelled Kesselring to retire immediately to the North – to the regions of the "Gothic Line". By holding Rome we would have the RR center and would have cut all communications and supply lines of the Germans along Western side of the Appenines. The RR and lines along the Eastern Appenines were inadequate to supply the German forces in Southern Italy. Caught by the surprise of the American airborne landing in Rome, and with his communications cut, Kesselring would have been compelled to retire to the North, and to abandon all southern and central Italy.'

This fantastical statement was made to the senior American Official War Historian, Dr H. M. Smyth, in 1948. Lest it be thought the ramblings of a sick veteran, it must be pointed out that Bedell Smith was speaking for the entire Allied High Command in Algiers. Eisenhower himself told Smyth:

> I wanted very much to make the air drop in Rome, and we were all ready to execute that plan of Giant II. . . . Certainly we were prepared – all ready to make the drop in Rome. I was anxious to get in there.[5]

[1] Smyth interview, 13.5.47, loc. cit.
[2] Ibid.
[3] Ibid.
[4] Ibid.
[5] Smyth interview, 16.2.49, loc. cit.

Eisenhower's Chief of Intelligence, Brigadier Strong, was similarly enthusiastic about 'Giant II':

My opinion is that the cancellation of Giant II was a great mistake. If the airborne division had been sent, the people – the Italians – would have welcomed us, and they would have held the [air] fields for us.[1]

An air of utter madness seems to have overtaken these men – none of whom had ever personally fought in battle. It was their culpable misreading of Italian intentions that doomed the Allies to failure in Italy; unhappily they afterwards invidiously and insidiously sought to blame the few men who resisted their crazy fantasies.

It was never to be a division,

General Maxwell Taylor pointed out in retrospect.

It would have been little more than a regiment [of 82nd Airborne Division] – because we didn't have the air lift. And what we were planning was in response to Castellano's insistence that we do this.
Yet when I got [secretly] into Rome, there had been no real communication with Castellano. Neither Badoglio nor Carboni, the Italian Corps Commander responsible for Rome, knew that the proposition was really pressing till I got there! . . . Castellano I'm afraid was more of a politician, although he was a military man. He was under great pressure from Beedle Smith – who said, 'Of course you can do it: You know you can!' I suspect that while there was no physical arm-twisting there was a lot of psychological arm-twisting. Castellano may well have been agreeing to things which in his heart he knew couldn't happen. . . . But Ridgway and I were so sceptical, we insisted we would not take our troops unless one of us went in to get at least a real 'fix' on what the situation was. And I was the one sent.[2]

General Ridgway, commander of the American Division which was to make the air drop, was pilloried for being 'quite skeptical about Giant Two from the start';[3] worse still, Maxwell Taylor, the divisional artillery chief who was slipped clandestinely into Rome and who doubted the Italian will to fight against the Germans, was branded before Smyth as a coward:

[1] Smyth interview, 29.10.47, loc. cit.
[2] General Maxwell Taylor, interview of 17.10.81.
[3] General L. Lemnitzer in Smyth interview, 3.3.47, loc. cit.

General Smith now considers that it was a mistake to send General
Taylor on the mission to Rome,

Smyth recorded.

This, he said, is a good example of the fact that it is a mistake to
send a *specialist* when what is needed is someone who can make a
decision and enforce it. Smith said that he himself could not have
been sent. But if someone had been – with authority – who would
have shocked Italian top leaders to their senses – 'See here – you
signed this agreement – and if you don't live up to it – you will all
be lined up against the wall and shot' – then the thing might still
have been pulled off.[1]

Brigadier Strong, by contrast, thought that Bedell Smith would
have been just the right man:
'Do not quote,' he cautioned Smyth:

I have the greatest respect for Maxwell Taylor who is a fine chap,
but in a sense it was a mistake to send him on that mission. . . .
Either General W.B. Smith should have gone on that mission, or
else I should have gone. It was a mistake that Giant II was called
off.[2]

Taylor's negative report from Rome was to become the scapegoat
for failure in Italy in the minds of these desk-soldiers. Taylor, soon to
become the distinguished commander of the 101st Airborne Division, never faltered then or later in his conviction that 'Giant II' was
madness.

The [Italian] Corps Commander just threw up his hands and said,
'Look, the Germans have control of our POL and our ammunition.
We have three divisions nearby, but they have about 24 hours of
gasoline and they couldn't fight for but a few days. And if you
come in you're gonna move a real battle into the Eternal City and
destroy Rome' – and for that they could think of no price they
would be willing to pay. Incidentally the real issue became quickly:
would Badoglio declare the armistice? And my problem became
not the Brigadier-General [of the 82nd Airborne Division] but
speaking for my Chief [Eisenhower] in the importance of the
armistice.[3]

[1] Smyth interview, 13.5.47, loc. cit.
[2] Smyth interview, 29.10.47, loc. cit.
[3] General Maxwell Taylor, loc. cit.

Using his one clandestine radio set, Taylor radioed the real situation, as distinct from Castellano's version, to Eisenhower. Because Eisenhower and Bedell Smith had invested such fantastical hopes in active Italian support, they later blamed others for their own stupidity. Not only was Taylor blackened for this – but Monty also. Brigadier Strong, who had believed that, with the Germans tied down at Salerno, Carboni's Italian Corps around Rome would have been freed to secure the city, indicted first Taylor, then the Eighth Army Commander:

My opinion is that the Italian campaign – that is with the capture of Rome – might have been won at any time up to about the 18th October. (Do not quote.) Gen Montgomery's caution was also in part responsible; he advanced too slowly and this gave the Germans their chance.[1]

Strong's indictment was, in almost conspiratorial fashion, echoed by Eisenhower and Bedell Smith. Eisenhower frankly confessed,

The situation was one which called for determination, a willingness to take some risks in a bold course –[2]

and blamed Montgomery for delaying Salerno by insisting on having 'everything prepared' for 'Baytown' – thus missing a unique opportunity, as Bedell Smith concurred:

General Smith went on to state that the things which spoiled our bold stroke were two, and which caused us to be bogged down in southern Italy: (1) The slowness of Montgomery's advance – 'with his tail dragging' and with nothing or practically nothing opposing his advance. . . . (2) The failure of the plan for Giant Two – and of the Italians to try to defend Rome.[3]

Even the dispassionate General Marshall was subsequently infected by this 'Algiers' view of Montgomery. As he told Smyth, he had been ' "strongly in favour of the Salerno operation" but had been irritated by the slowness with which this operation was mounted. The Logistical people were too cautious about what could be done, and the speed with which it could be done.'[4] In Marshall's view 'the British in the Middle East (8th Army) had committed about every mistake in the book'.[5] Far from applauding Montgomery's march

[1] Smyth interview, 29.10.47, loc. cit.
[2] Smyth interview, 16.2.49, loc. cit.
[3] Smyth interview, 13.5.47, loc. cit.
[4] Smyth interview, 25.7.49, loc. cit.
[5] Ibid.

across North Africa from Alamein to Tunis, Marshall considered it was 'no model campaign. The pursuit of Rommel across the Desert was slow. . . . Here Marshall formed an opinion: that Montgomery left something to be desired as a field commander.'[1]

More and more, after Sicily, Monty began to feel the rift between his own concept of the professional conduct of war, and the unrealistic fantasies of his superiors. Marshall might well scoff at El Alamein as being a battle 'blown up out of proportion to its importance',[2] but Monty himself knew how much the battle still meant in the hearts and minds of his soldiers. On the anniversary of the battle he had received messages from all over the world, but it was those of his headquarters staff, his commanders and men he most valued. The battle had not only begun an historic march of victories unknown in the British Army since the days of Wellington, it had demonstrated in its agonising course the bravery and professionalism of the German soldier: a lesson repeated again and again in the long crusade across North Africa, as it was in the plains and olive groves of Sicily. The German soldier was not to be underestimated: this was a cardinal lesson, but a lesson that seemed to dissipate and fade with every mile away from the battlefield. Eisenhower's wild hopes of what the Italians would do to help against such a foe, Monty considered incredible.

We have now got Italy out of the war,

Monty wrote to Phyllis Reynolds the day after the official broadcast of the armistice.[3]

I can tell you a good deal later about all the negotiations that went on. The armistice terms were actually signed by the Italians on 3rd Sept, the anniversary of the outbreak of the war and the day the Eighth Army landed in Italy. The story of how the Italians got rid of Mussolini is very interesting.

If you analyse the matter in cold blood there is no doubt that the Italians have carried out a really good double-cross; they change sides on one day!! I wouldn't trust them a yard, and in any case they are quite useless when it comes to fighting.

Monty's views about the Italians had already been set down in his diary on 23 August 1943; for Monty, the Italian offer to turn against their Axis partners if the Allies landed in Italy 'was probably the

[1] Ibid.
[2] Ibid.
[3] After tantalising hesitation, Badoglio finally made his armistice broadcast over Rome Radio at 7.45 p.m., 8 September 1943. Eisenhower had already announced the armistice over Radio Algiers at 6.30 p.m.

biggest double-cross in history. . . . The Italians are wonderful people, and obviously not to be trusted one yard. . . . I doubt if the Italians ever would really fight the Germans; they are quite useless and would be hit for six; the most we can hope for I feel is non-cooperation.'

These were the doubts of an experienced soldier; on 5 September, as Eighth Army began to encounter severe delays caused by German demolitions and rearguards, Monty had in fact become seriously alarmed. Alexander had flown over to Reggio and had told him of the Italian surrender, to be broadcast three days later, on 8 September. He also told Monty that three hours after the broadcast 'American airborne troops would land near ROME. At the same time the city would be seized by the Italian divisions near there.' The Italians were also 'to seize TARANTO, BRINDISI, BARI, NAPLES, etc'; meanwhile early the following morning (9 September) the Allies would land not only Clark's Fifth Army near Naples but also the British 5 Corps at Taranto. '5 Corps would come under Eighth Army later on, when I get within supporting distance of it,' Monty recorded in his diary. He was aghast.

ALEXANDER was very optimistic and was obviously prepared to think that the Italians would do all they said. I took him aside for a talk. I told him my opinion was that when the Germans found out what was going on, they would stamp on the Italians.

The Italian soldiers were quite useless and would never face up to the Germans.

I said that he should impress on all senior commanders that we must make our plans so that it would make no difference if the Italians failed us. I said the Italians *might possibly* do useful guerilla work, sabotage, and generally insure complete non-co-operation on the part of the entire population; but I did not see them fighting the Germans.

They were carrying out a colossal double-cross, and we must not trust them too much, or tell them our plans just at present.

The Germans were in great strength in ITALY and we were very weak. We must watch our step very carefully, do nothing foolish, and on no account must we risk a disaster. If we knock Italy out of the war, and contain 20 German divisions in Italy, and get the Italian fleet, we would have done very well.

I begged him to be careful; not to open up too many fronts and so dissipate our resources; and to be quite certain before we landed anywhere that we could build-up good strength in that place, sufficient to be quite safe in that area. I said that we knew the Germans were strong about ROME and NAPLES, and could concentrate against AVALANCHE quicker than we could build up; if there was any danger of a disaster to AVALANCHE we should cancel it, and put that effort in to TARANTO and so get a firm grip on Southern Italy.

Monty's warnings fell on deaf ears. General Alexander was only the land forces C-in-C, and not strong-minded enough to stand up to the combined recklessness that now prevailed in Algiers and in the naval and air force headquarters. Admiral Cunningham, who had in August been the first to suggest an assault on Rome, was wholeheartedly in favour of 'Giant II', 'Avalanche' *and* the landings at Taranto, regardless of the resultant dissipation of Allied strength. Tedder meanwhile had done his best to sabotage 'Avalanche', as Mark Clark ruefully explained to the American Official Historian.

Salerno was not specified in the initial plan for AVALANCHE. He [Clark] preferred the area north of Naples, the beaches along the mouth of the Volturno River, as the landing place. He did not like the Salerno area because of the mountains which hemmed in the coastal plain and were favourable to the defense. He explained that three commanders were appointed for the AVALANCHE operation, Air Marshal Tedder, Admiral Cunningham, and himself (Clark). Tedder had final say in planning about the air, Cunningham about the navy. Clark was anxious to have the Volturno beaches selected, and flew to discuss the problem with Tedder, but did not find Tedder in Algiers. There [in Algiers] the British air people were rather favorably inclined toward choice of the Volturno area, and believed it practicable to provide air cover there. The U.S. air people definitely supported the idea of striking at the Volturno beaches. General Clark's trip to Algiers was, he believes, 3 August, and he spent two days in a series of conferences. He finally reached Tedder by telephone, and Tedder stated that proper air support could not be given north of Naples. This veto determined selection of the Salerno area.[1]

The passage of time did nothing to dim General Clark's recollection:

I picked to land north of Salerno, because the beaches were better and I could rest my flank on the Volturno river. I could drop Ridgway's paratroops along there and hold those bridges – 'cause there were ten German divisions in the Rome area that I didn't want to come down on my neck. If we went in south of Naples – which eventually I did – we went into a bottleneck, there were mountains all around. But I was forced to go in there because the Airman says I won't support you north – I can't. The Navy says I

---

[1] Smyth interview, 5.8.48, loc. cit.

won't support you north because your transports are too unpro-
tected. . . . There was no one man to say, 'You'll do it!'[1]

Clark, without battle laurels, had not the standing to insist – as
Monty had been able to do over 'Husky'. Eisenhower, egged on by
Marshall who was 'strongly in favour of the operation',[2] and Churchill who was determined not to crawl up Italy like a harvest bug,
would brook no criticism. Not only did Eisenhower squash Clark's
objection to the switching of 82nd Airborne Division from the
Salerno operation to the 'Giant Two' Rome fantasy, but he misunderstood and later mocked Monty's soldierly reaction to the Salerno
plans. 'Montgomery at first opposed the Salerno operation as too
risky,' he misled Smyth after the war, and even went on to blame
Monty's delay in mounting 'Baytown' as the reason for failure at
Salerno. 'If we could have crossed the Strait earlier, we could have
done the Salerno operation earlier.'[3]

This travesty of Montgomery's position shocked the American
Official historians by its frankness: 'General Eisenhower's remarks
about General Montgomery revealed not the slightest ill will, but
only a difference of judgement, yet his remarks did not all convey the
impression of being guarded. He spoke rather rapidly.'[4] Yet
Eisenhower's rapidity of speech, defying interruption, belied his
shame at the fiasco his Supreme Command in the Mediterranean had
engendered, as well as his knowledge that Monty had warned him
again and again, directly and through Alexander, not to plan on
active co-operation from Italian fighting units, but to mount a
concentrated invasion that exploited Allied strength, not weakness.
Monty had opposed not the idea of the 'Avalanche' operation –
which was his own original suggestion to Brooke, in any case – but
the necessity for doing 'Baytown' as well – an operation which was
bound to dissipate the forces, administration, ferrying craft, naval
and air support required for a successful Avalanche. Subsequently,
noting German concentration in the areas of Rome and Naples,
Monty had recommended cancellation of the Salerno assault, switching the assault instead to Taranto, which would put the Allies within
easy reach of the Foggia airfields, the primary military objective in
invading Italy at all.

Alexander, though he may personally have credited Monty's
warnings, was quite unwilling to risk another 'Husky' argument
now. The 'Avalanche' convoy was already setting sail, and he was
not a man to rock the Allied boat. He thus did nothing, bar pass on to

[1] General Mark Clark, interview of 26.10.81.
[2] Ibid.
[3] Smyth interview, 16.2.49, loc. cit.
[4] Ibid.

Eisenhower Monty's views. Meanwhile Monty, noting that the Italians in the toe of Italy were all surrendering, whereas the two German divisions were fighting and mining most skilfully, grew more and more fearful about Eisenhower's and Alexander's crazy optimism and dispersion of effort. On 7 September

I went over to MESSINA and had a conference with my Chief of Staff and senior administrative staff officer.

After this conference I sent General ALEXANDER a message on the following lines:

a) The Germans have got 20 divisions in ITALY, including 5 armoured divisions.

b) At the moment we have 2 divisions in the toe of ITALY, and are to land 3 more South of NAPLES on 9 September.
Total: 5 divisions.
Owing to shortage of shipping and craft, my build-up is very slow: also I cannot get over to ITALY many units that I require for L. of C. work, port development, and so on.
The RAF has also got to be installed on the mainland, and that will take a very great deal of shipping.

c) ROMMEL is a good soldier and I know him better than most people. With 20 divisions, 5 of which are armoured divisions, he will have to be carefully watched. We must not have a disaster. Where we land we must be strong and able to fight; the build-up must be good, with reserves readily available.

d) We are so short of shipping that any troops we put ashore on the mainland must be really good and experienced troops, able to fight Germans. Divisions like 8 Ind Div from the Middle East are no use; this Div has never fought and would be useful only for dock labour etc. I am not in favour of using Indian troops in EUROPE in any case; the climate and damp is against them and it complicates the administrative machine.

e) The problems are so many and so intricate that I hoped a staff conference would assemble to discuss the whole matter before any firm decisions were taken.

f) We must be careful.
On no account must we have a disaster anywhere. We must not be carried away by having knocked ITALY out of the war; they are quite useless as fighting troops and will not fight the Germans. *We* shall have to fight the Germans in ITALY; they are in great strength and we are very weak; we must watch our step carefully.

g) The landings South of NAPLES may go against us, and we may be in for a long and hard fight. Before we embark on major operations on the mainland of ITALY we must have a good and sound plan; we must be quite clear as to how we propose to develop the operations; *and we must have no disasters*. We must NOT be 'carried away' and think it is all going to be easy.

It is all going to be very difficult, because the Italians are such an unknown factor: and our admin problems are going to be immense. Small detached forces all over the place are useless; where we propose to fight, there we must be strong.

h) Of course, if the Italians will help at all, then the whole picture could be altered. If, for instance, all trains ceased to run in ITALY, then the Germans would be in a most awkward situation and might have to pull out to the North. But the Italians won't really do anything.

It was the last, vain cry from the most experienced battlefield general in the Allied armies. Condemned to carry out a pointless, diversionary landing almost three hundred miles from the main Allied assault, Monty could only watch helplessly now as Eisenhower, Alexander, Bedell Smith, Cunningham and Tedder committed the greatest blunder since the dark days of 1941 and 1942. To Monty's chagrin all his worst fears were, one by one, confirmed. The next evening he received from Alexander confirmation of the Italian armistice, but it was soon followed by another message.

Personal for Generals CLARK and MONTGOMERY. Armistice was announced this evening by Allied C-in-C and by BADOGLIO. Italians have evidently been caught napping by speed of our operations and have NOT made detailed arrangements to receive us as planned. We have to postpone operations of 82 Airborne Div owing to lack of arrangements to meet them on airfields. But we hope this is only a postponement. If bodies of Italian troops under their own officers wish to help Allied cause you should take every advantage of their assistance.

Eisenhower's concern to speed up operations had produced the opposite effect. Not only had he been forced to postpone his air drop on Rome, but he had deprived Clark of his airborne arm in 'Avalanche'. How close the 82nd Airborne Division had come to disaster was only known, however, to one man – Brigadier-General Lemnitzer.

When the message came from General Taylor that Giant Two was cancelled,

Lemnitzer revealed to the American Official Historian,

General Lemnitzer flew immediately to cancel the order of the 82nd Airborne Division, flying from Africa and looking for Gela [in

Sicily] – but the pilot almost cracked up getting off the field, and then missed his way, hit wrong part of Sicilian coast and soon Mt Etna loomed up. The ['Avalanche'] convoys were on their way and General Lemnitzer knew better than ever to fly over a convoy. The pilot – who was a good night pilot – got confused in daylight. By the time General Lemnitzer got to the field there were already 62 planes in the air which had to be flagged down.[1]

Ridgway's élite paratroop division had been saved – but it was too late to stop the near-débâcle of Salerno. On 9 September Monty noted in his diary:

The Fifth American Army, with 10 Corps under command, landed in the gulf of SALERNO at 0430 hours this morning. I hope this goes well. The Germans could bring some four divisions to oppose it: but they may be occupied with dealing with the Italians; personally, I consider they will stamp on the Italians.

Monty's worst fears about Salerno were soon to be confirmed: Clark, thanks to Tedder's veto, had sailed straight into a trap. Meanwhile Monty, with half of his army still stranded in Sicily and all his ferrying craft diverted to Salerno, could do little to assist. 'Baytown' had never been conceived as a real adjunct to 'Avalanche' – it was a futile diversion whose only benefit had been that it secured the Messina Strait for shipping and, more importantly, forced Badoglio to sign the instrument of surrender. From a military point of view it was a complete misuse of limited resources, for it was apparent to all, even in August, that the Germans would leave no sizeable forces in the toe of Italy if the Allies landed further north.
Monty's two divisions, occupying now some four hundred square miles of territory in Calabria, had never been planned by Eisenhower, Alexander or Clark as a relieving force for 'Avalanche', hundreds of miles to the north; but so certain was Monty that 'Avalanche' would prove a disaster that he immediately decided, on 9 September, to start concentrating his units in case they were asked to help Clark, or worse still, to hold on in southern Italy, without reinforcement, if Clark was pushed back into the sea.

As far as my own troops were concerned, Divisions of 13 Corps had now marched and fought over a distance of about 100 miles in 7 days. They were strung out and the infantry were definitely tired.
   I decided they must be rested. Heads of Divisions will tomorrow [10 September] reach the line CATANZARO–NICASTRO. I gave

[1] Smyth interview, 3.3.47, loc. cit.

orders that they are to halt on this line and to 'wind-up' their tails; they will then rest for 2 days. . . .

I have 30 Corps, with three divisions, in SICILY, but cannot bring them over to ITALY as I have no craft or shipping for the purpose.

The following day, 10 September, he summoned the senior officers of his Main Headquarters. In three or four days' time he wanted Dempsey's two divisions to move north and rope off the neck of the Calabrian peninsula; this would secure the whole of the toe of Italy for the Allies, together with the important airfields at Crotone, in the event of German success further north. 'The neck would be blocked from the North. And the CROTONE area would be quite secure.' That evening, already, he received a second signal from Alexander informing him that things were not going according to AFHQ's ridiculously optimistic plans. 'It is beginning to look as if his previous optimism was not quite justified,' Monty noted with a certain degree of self-righteousness. The message read:

AVALANCHE landings were made successfully in spite of considerable confusion caused by sea mines and a certain amount of enemy resistance on the beaches. Progress has however been slow due to enemy counter attacks. I have NOT yet heard that the [Rome] aerodrome due to be ready for use today has been captured. I believe that the Germans are now in occupation of Rome and have set up some sort of Fascist administration there.[1]

Monty's prediction that the Germans would stamp on the Italians had come true. But if the troops of 'Giant II' had been spared, those of Clark's Fifth Army had not. Alexander's signal continued:

We are giving AVALANCHE full priority in craft to assist them in their build up but if the Germans have dealt successfully with the Italians in the NAPLES–ROME area I am anxious about their possible rate of concentration against 5th Army.

This frank admission of the precarious 'Avalanche' beachhead was not given simply to keep Monty in the picture. Having failed to give Monty a proper objective for 'Baytown' other than to secure the Messina Straits and divert German attention from 'Avalanche', Alexander was belatedly beginning to link the two operations:

I fully realise that you are short of shipping and that your rate of build up is consequently extremely slow. It would appear however

---

[1] Included in Personal Diary, Montgomery Papers.

that the Germans are withdrawing on your front to CASTROVIL-LARI. This may enable you to make use of the port of CROTONE and so shorten your L. of C. It is of the utmost importance that you maintain pressure upon the Germans so that they cannot remove forces from your front and concentrate them against AVALAN-CHE. I have sent Brit Airborne Div into TARANTO. This Div will have little or no transport as it is being moved by Naval ships. It should however have some 8,000 men ashore by 15 September. . . . When 5 Corps builds up and you arrive within supporting distance of them I shall place 5 Corps under your command. I am doing all I can to magnify the size of our landings in the German eyes. I feel certain that if the Italians play even a small part in assisting us the Germans will have to withdraw to a line North of NAPLES. The next few days are critical as they were in operation HUSKY.

Fortunately Monty had anticipated the need for Crotone; patrols of Eighth Army reached the area that evening, and by midday on 11 September the port, harbour and undamaged installations were in Monty's hands. But what of the future? Alexander's signal still made no reference to a link-up between Eighth and Fifth Armies, merely to the need to keep German forces from pulling out from Eighth Army's front. Moreover, instead of concentrating all Allied forces in Taranto as Monty had suggested, Alexander had now opened three separate fronts in a single week, all requiring organisation and administration, troops, reinforcements, sea supply and air cover. Monty's first act was to summon his own airman, Air Vice-Marshal Broadhurst:

The AOC (BROADHURST) flew to VIBO VALENTIA to see me.
    I arranged with him that we would fly the Desert Air Force in to CROTONE and COSENZA as soon as the airfields at those places could be got ready. . . .
    I discussed with Broadhurst the future. We were about to become involved in large scale operations on the mainland of Europe and there was no firm plan known to me as to how those operations were to be developed.

Monty's response was that of a soldier, unable quite to understand the wilful incompetence, even bungling, of his superiors. Although he sensed the urgency and anxiety in Alexander's signal he now deliberately decided to make Alexander pay for his mistakes. He would not undertake any further operations for the moment, merely sit and watch. Although he ordered Broadhurst to conduct air operations 'to help 5 Army', he was adamant that Eighth Army itself 'would not move beyond the CASTROVILLARI neck until the situation was clearer,' as he noted in his diary.

It was this digging-in of his heels, at the critical moment of the Italian invasion, that was to infuriate all those who, in the heady days before the assault, had considered the matter a foregone conclusion, and who now began to look anxiously to Monty for help.

To be sure Alexander's signal made no mention of an Eighth Army dash to the north – but with his irritatingly cool grasp of military realities, Monty was well aware that he might be asked soon to undertake such an operation. From experience he knew that the real test of the Salerno bridgehead would come now, as the Allied troops began to tire and the Germans assembled their armour and artillery. Yet instead of pushing Eighth Army north together with its Desert Air Force in order to help his sister army, Monty chose to wait. If the Salerno bridgehead had to be abandoned, he would be in a good position to meet a German thrust southwards – 'I could deal with anything the Germans tried to do,' he claimed confidently to the Reynolds several days later.[1] To Alexander he signalled that he would 'fly DAF in to CROTONE and COSENZA earliest possible. Am very stretched at present but will push on as soon as admin situation allows.'[2]

There can be no doubt that Monty likened the situation to that of the desert earlier that year, when the Germans had attacked at Kasserine and Alexander had asked Monty to push forward and draw the Germans on to Eighth Army's front, resulting in the great defensive victory at Medenine. Two days later, on 13 September 1943, Monty noted as much in his diary:

It was rather similar to the situation in North Africa in February, 1943, when Rommel attacked the Americans and I received a cry for help from Alexander; I was then South of the Mareth line, but I drew Rommel off and beat him at Medenin on 6 Mar.

From Intelligence sources Monty was aware that Rommel was once again in charge of German troops in the theatre. 'It was known from agents, and from the Italians that the Germans had twenty divisions in Italy, and that Rommel was in command in the north. I look forward to taking on my old opponent again,' he had recorded on 5 September. As long as he collected Eighth Army into a cohesive front, Monty felt he was in no danger.

Ironically Monty's caution was mirrored by that of Rommel in the north, for despite their vastly superior strength the Germans were too concerned with the possibility of Allied landings there to risk sending forces south. Thus, while Rommel and Montgomery watched cautiously from north and south, the true battle for Italy took

---

[1] Letter of 15.9.43, Montgomery Papers.
[2] Signal of 11.9.43, Diary, Montgomery Papers.

place in the gap between them. Rome and Naples were secured by the Germans; meanwhile the Allies fought a life and death struggle for their fragile beachhead in the bay of Salerno. Alexander's messages now began to urge Monty to drive north, while Hitler vainly urged Rommel to drive south. 'As my mother and I well remember,' Rommel's son later recalled,[1] 'Hitler discussed with my father the possibility of launching a counter-offensive to retake southern Italy and possibly Sicily. My father saw not the smallest chance of this.' In fact Rommel specifically refused to release the two Panzer divisions which Kesselring begged for.

To his great credit, General Mark Clark managed to stave off defeat at Salerno, but plans for evacuation *were* drawn up on 13/14 September[2] and until 16 September the situation was critical in the extreme. Clark had felt grave misgivings from the start, and was not surprised by the 'mess', as he later related:

The night before I was to get on the boat [to sail with the Salerno invasion force], I got a radiogram from Ike in Sicily – told me to fly to such and such an airport in Sicily immediately. It was in the late afternoon. And so I got in and flew off, was met, I was taken to a house where the Italians had come to surrender. . . . Ike said they will act on the surrender, drop out of the war, when your troops hit the beaches at Salerno. He said, 'I wanted you to have this [information] before you went. I'm sorry to bring you here at such

---

[1] *The Rommel Papers*, ed. B. Liddell Hart, London 1953.

[2] See Butcher Diary, 15.9.43: 'This morning Ike was bemoaning the fact that plans were being made by General Clark for evacuating Fifth Army Headquarters. He said headquarters should be moved last of all and the Commanding General should stay with his men to give them confidence. He should show the spirit of a naval captain and, if necessary, go down with his ship.' Though Clark later denied to the Official American Historian (Smyth interview, 5.8.48, loc. cit.) that at any time he had 'contemplated withdrawal', this was wishful post-hoc thinking, since Admiral Hewitt, the US Naval Commander, signalled the plans to Admiral Cunningham, who informed Eisenhower's headquarters. Indeed Eisenhower had himself prepared for such a possibility on 13 September: 'Considering for a moment the worst that could possibly develop, I would, in that event, merely announce that one of our landings had been repulsed – due to my error in misjudging the enemy at that place,' as he wrote to Marshall. On 16 September he commented to his naval aide 'that if the Salerno battle ended in disaster he [Eisenhower] would probably be out' – diary of Harry C. Butcher, loc. cit. Clark's British Deputy Chief of Staff later recalled the preparations made for withdrawal: 'We were certainly near disaster and I recall a midnight Conference, under German *mortar* fire, when it was decided to get the HQ ship brought back from PALERMO. I have never been clear in my mind what turned the scale: the airborne drop, the naval gunfire, or Mark Clark's gallantry when he went forward and rallied a battalion that was retreating in great disorder. I doubt whether 8th Army's action *at that critical time* had any effect on 5th Army's situation' – letter from General Sir Charles Richardson to author, 11.12.82.

a trying time. And that's about all,' he said, 'except: our governments have decided to drop an airborne division in the Rome area to protect the Italian government.'

And I said, 'Ike, where are you going to get your airborne division?'

He said, 'The 82nd.'

'That's mine!'

He said, 'It *was* yours!' He said, 'We're going to drop it!'

I said, 'Why that's my whole scheme of manoeuvre! You just can't do it!'

Ike said, 'What do you mean, can't?'

I said, 'Well, this is a helluva mess, really, for you to do this – because I've got up to ten divisions coming down on me; I've got Kesselring down there, already, anyhow' – the Germans knew the Italians were going to drop out of the war.

So Ike said, 'Well, Wayne' – always called me Wayne – 'don't get too excited! When it [82nd Airborne Division] drops, it passes to your command!'

And I said, 'Thanks, Ike, that's five hundred miles away! That's like a half-interest in the war! You got anything else? I got to get back!'

He said, 'That's all.'

So I flew back, at night, with great misgiving.

And that's how messed up that campaign was!

My thinking was: My God: I would tell my government, 'that's nuts!' They can't do it! You're putting your first American army on the continent of Europe, with the British 10th Corps under McCreery (you [British] had two battle-trained divisions; I didn't, I had a brand new outfit) – and if those were kicked out, and people have been kicked out before . . . I wanted to say: 'You just can't assume you're going to be successful. You may not be! Just think what a shattering blow to Allied morale!' I said that to myself, flying back; I said, I wish *I* were in a position to send the radiogram to the President!

I went on board ship the next day. As dusk came I was on the bridge. I could see the silhouettes of a hundred ships with my men in them. And I had never had such a forlorn feeling in all my life.

I felt: My God, I have no control over these men now, it's in the lap of the gods, and here I am going in there with my plan and my whole scheme of manoeuvre changed at the last minute.[1]

There was 'no time' to appeal to Alexander; indeed it was only after sending a radio message to Eisenhower that Clark discovered

[1] Loc. cit.

his 82nd Airborne Division was available once again, following postponement of the Rome drop.

We went in to Salerno, and we had a hard time. It was a touch and go situation, very much. And Monty was coming up, see, and the BBC – that's all we heard, lots of my men had little radios, all they could get was the BBC – and Monty was sending me messages: 'Hang on, we're coming!' And I'd send back: 'Hurry up – I'm not proud, come and get me!'
So it was really something. . . .
Ridgway was in Sicily when I sent a radiogram to Ike: 'Haven't heard from the 82nd, what happened?' I get a message back saying, 'It didn't drop – it passes to your command with this message.' I only found that out in response to my question.[1]

At first, on 11 September, Clark wished to use the airborne troops in an effort to smash his way forward to Naples;[2] but as the hours went by he began to realise that far from pushing on to Naples, he himself was in danger of being pushed back into the sea. Indeed in retrospect Clark frankly acknowledged that if Kesselring had acted properly, Salerno might well have been a disaster:

If Kesselring had massed his forces to make one grand drive, he might have driven us out – yes, American and British: for if one went, he'd get the next. . . . It was a touch and go situation. As Churchill said, it was a close-run thing.[3]

With Kesselring threatening to break through the American sector, where troops of the green 36th US Division unhappily began to retreat without authority, Clark now clutched at his last straw: the 82nd Airborne Division.

I said to Al Gruenther [Chief of Staff, 5th Army], we'd put some matting down there, I said, 'Get me one of those fighter pilots, a good one, get him up here to my headquarters' – hell, we had no headquarters, we were just out in the woods.
So I wrote a note. I said, 'I want you to take this to General Ridgway' – his airbase was near his headquarters in Sicily. 'I want you to get it to him personally as fast as you can – it's a question of very great importance.' And I wrote on a piece of pad:

[1] Ibid.
[2] The Papers of General Mark Clark, The Citadel, Charleston, South Carolina.
[3] Interview of 26.10.81. Churchill said of Salerno, in a letter to Clark dated 8.1.44, that it was a 'battle of which it might be said, as the Duke of Wellington in after life said of the battle of Waterloo: "It was a damned close run thing"' – communicated to author by General Clark.

Dear Matt [Ridgway],

I know it takes you at least a month to make up your mind where you'll drop that precious division of yours. But I direct, and I hope you will cooperate. . . . I want one combat team to drop tonight at 9 o'clock behind our lines ready to be taken to the front lines during the night. Tomorrow night I want the second Regimental Combat Team, and I want you to drop with it, because I want to put you in as Deputy Corps Commander, 6 US Corps; and the next night the third.

And I said – at Sicily, remember, our own ships shot 'em up [the transport planes carrying 82nd Airborne Division] – I said, 'Nobody'll shoot you up. I'll have one of my officers of my staff on every anti-aircraft site, ship or ground, and if the Germans come over and bomb us' – which they did – 'no gun'll answer.'

And so they came in, they came down. They dropped in the zone (we lit up flares). And by daylight I had a regiment of the 82nd, our best fighters, up in the front line. The next night I had another. It began to turn the tide.[1]

Clark's improvisation averted total disaster, though it is clear from the casualties that McCreery's British 10 Corps had taken the brunt of the real fighting, suffering more than twice as many losses in both killed and wounded.[2]

I knew that Dick McCreery was catching hell over there. I went over to see him whenever I could – I had to go over by boat. I remember the first day I went, he took me to where they were assembling their dead. It made a hell of an impression on me. I'd seen dead in World War I, but I hadn't since. And here I saw these fine young fellers dead – it really made a hell of an impression on me.[3]

The stubborn resistance by McCreery's 10 Corps, the arrival of the combat teams of 82nd Airborne Division, and the leadership of General Clark himself – who won the Distinguished Service Cross for gallantry – all helped turn imminent defeat into victory.

Monty's caution, over 150 miles away, did not meanwhile endear him to Clark, particularly as Monty not only waited to see the outcome of Fifth Army's death-struggle, but then claimed the credit for saving it. Only on 14 September, after dictating the terms under which he would begin an offensive (complete closing down of

[1] Ibid.
[2] Casualties were, on 16 September: British 10 Corps – 531 killed, 1,915 wounded, 1,561 missing; US 6 Corps – 225 killed, 853 wounded, 589 missing: figures in the Papers of General Mark Clark, loc. cit.
[3] Interview of 26.10.81.

offensive operations at Taranto and concentration of all support effort on Fifth and Eighth Armies) did Monty gingerly push forward his 5th Division, with a single brigade reaching Sapri on 16 September. By then Clark had won his spurs, but Monty behaved in his most offensive 'saviour' manner. At a meeting with Alexander's senior staff officers at Reggio on 15 September 'the attitude was that Eighth Army could have everything it wanted if it could pull the show out of the fire, and save AVALANCHE. We asked for everything we wanted, and got it. All this made a very great difference,' Monty noted blithely. 'I could now drive ahead hard, and by very energetic action I could save a possible disaster to the American Army on the SALERNO front. . . . I sent an ADC over in my launch to see General CLARK, taking with him the following letter.' The letter, pompously worded and condescending in tone ('It looks as if you may be having not too good a time, and I do hope that all will go well with you . . .'), gave no explanation of Eighth Army's three-day pause but merely promised that reconnaissance detachments would be pushed forward the following day, and the advance of 5th Division only on 17 September. Clark answered politely, but was understandably incredulous. 'As to the current battle at Salerno,' Eisenhower's naval aide recorded in his diary on 16 September,

Montgomery has a great chance to be a hero. Yesterday his Eighth Army made good mileage and is now sixty miles from the Fifth Army. . . . Ike wondered what the result would have been in the toe of Italy if Patton had been the commander instead of Montgomery. He felt certain Patton would have burned shoeleather as he did in Sicily. I told him I thought Montgomery would be inspired by the competition and the opportunity to 'out Patton' Patton by reaching Clark under heroic acclaim. My guess was that Monty will move as he has never moved before. He is the potential hero of a grand melodrama and he will be quick to grasp the possibility of adding further and perhaps more lasting luster to his name.[1]

Clark, driving his army out of the near-débâcle of Salerno, could have no idea what lay behind Montgomery's dilatory approach, and put it down to British slowness. But in truth both Rommel and Montgomery, the two most famous generals of the desert, had failed to intervene because they both found the respective strategies of their colleagues in central Italy to be utterly misguided.

On 17 September, after patrols of Eighth Army had met troops of Fifth Army, Monty's ADC brought back from Clark's headquarters an account of the Salerno battle, together with Clark's future plans.

[1] Diary of Harry C. Butcher, 16.9.43, loc. cit.

It seems that the critical night was night 13/14 September. The Germans had attacked the 36 American Division, an untried Div, with about one Bn and 20 to 30 tanks; the Div did not fight very well and the thrust got to within 3 miles of the beach and within two miles of Army HQ. The Army, Corps and Div staffs were completely untrained and there were chaotic scenes, with lack of news, little control over the air, less control over formations and units and so on.

The situation was saved by some American paratroops, who were dropped in the area and did very well.

It was clear that as my threat from the South began to develop the Germans began to pull out; on the afternoon of 16 September the pressure on the American front lessened.[1]

Though it is true that Kesselring and von Vietinghoff gave up any aggressive intentions after 16 September in view of Eighth Army's imminent arrival, the real battle for the beachhead had already been won by Clark, as even Alexander later admitted: 'the battle was won before they [Eighth Army] got up,' he told the American Official Historian, 'mainly as a result of the heavy naval gunfire brought up in support during the counter-attack, the air support and the sterling qualities of the troops.'[2]

The next question, however, was the development of the Allied campaign. About this Monty was quite clear; indeed, after dictating to Alexander's Chief of Staff the conditions on which he would step up his Eighth Army advance, Monty believed for a moment that he might run the campaign. On 16 September his staff gave him details of the time it would take to build up 5 Corps at Taranto – ferrying in a further three and a half divisions by the first week in October – and he felt quite confident that, after a near-disastrous beginning, a coherent tactical strategy could be imposed:

The general layout of the battle now became quite clear.
In the SALERNO area was 5 Army, as a firm pivot – to be hoped.
In the TARANTO area was a firm base, gradually growing in strength.
In between these two 'holding' areas I would advance with my Army, directing its thrust on to the area POTENZA-AULETTA.

Unfortunately, far from 'holding', and allowing Eighth Army to strike inland. Clark revealed to Monty's ADC that Fifth Army would almost immediately break out of its bridgehead and seize Naples.

[1] Diary, Montgomery Papers.
[2] George Howe interview, n.d. (possibly January 1948), Military History Institute, Carlisle, Pennsylvania.

My ADC brought me back the future intentions of General CLARK, 5 Army. He was very optimistic, and pleased about things, and he intended to advance on Naples on 20 September. This seemed to me very curious; his maintenance was still over open beaches, he had no port, his troops had suffered heavy casualties, and there was great disorganisation.

I thought he would have got SALERNO port, made his position secure, re-organised, and built up strength.

However,

Monty acknowledged regretfully,

it was no concern of mine. . . .

There is no doubt that the Americans do not understand the vital need to have your administration behind on a scale commensurate with what you want to achieve in front. It was a great mistake to be led off the path by seemingly great prizes like NAPLES and other cities. The real point was to have no more disasters. If 5 Army rushed off to NAPLES, and got into trouble again, I would not be able to help them.

I had already saved their bacon this time.

Once again Monty felt the Allies were drifting into battle, without clear objectives or strategy. To Alexander he signalled his disagreement with Clark's policy, and insisted there be, at least in Eighth Army's front, a pause while he transferred his lines of communication and maintenance from the 300-mile road from Reggio to the port of Taranto.

There was as yet no plan known to me for developing the war in ITALY,

Monty remarked with some sourness in his diary,

but I was quite used to that!

CHAPTER THREE

Haphazard and Untidy

The reason Monty was perplexed by Alexander's lack of a coherent plan was simple. There was none – for no one knew why the Allies were in Italy, apart from the need to 'knock Italy out of the war' and to take possession of the Foggia airfields. Now that Italy *had* been knocked out and the Foggia airfields were within easy reach of Eighth Army, there was a vacuum in the councils of Allied power. The United States of America had no wish to pursue an offensive campaign in Italy, whereas Churchill did. Moreover, to add to the confusion, there was now no real Italian government to deal with, only a septuagenarian king in Brindisi surrounded by generals who talked of waging war as a co-belligerent against the Germans, but whose forces would never fight.

Had Eisenhower insisted upon a proper directive from Roosevelt and Churchill, the Allies might have been spared the tragedy of the Italian campaign. Exploitation according to the circumstances had, however, been the policy determined at the Quebec Conference in July, and this pragmatism, in the hands of a military commander as conciliatory as Eisenhower, proved fatal, for in his concern to sort out the 'messy situation' from the political angle, Eisenhower necessarily delegated the fighting to Alexander, the C-in-C 15th Army Group; and without strong direction from above and with two chief staff officers he would have to sack within the next few months, Alexander was at sea. As in Sicily, his failure to exercise real command in the field meant that the local commanders put forward their own intentions for the campaign, with Alexander simply mediating between them.

Eisenhower, aware that his earlier hopes of seizing the major portion of Italy were dashed, blamed the shortage of landing craft, the paucity of bombers, and Monty for his slowness. As he wrote in pique to Marshall on 20 September: 'I think you should consider Patton for command of one of these Armies [for the cross-Channel invasion of France]. Many generals constantly think of battle in terms of, first concentration, supply maintenance, replacement, and, second, after all the above is arranged, a *conservative* advance. This type of person is necessary because he prevents one from courting disaster. But occasions arise when one has to remember that under particular conditions, boldness is ten times as important as numbers.'[1]

For the rest of the war, and after, Eisenhower would continue to blame the Allied lack of boldness for the mess in Italy – as, for instance, his belief that 'Giant Two', the airborne drop on Rome, ought to have been undertaken. Noting that 'the German is wily and tough and knows how, with little cost to himself, to make an advancing enemy pay for every foot it gets',[2] he felt that only great daring on the part of the Allies could avoid an expensive and laborious Allied campaign, and that the chances for this were now lost.

No doubt Eisenhower's judgement was influenced by his experience in North Africa, where with greater boldness in the first few weeks of 'Torch' he believed he could have secured the whole of Tunisia.

To Monty this romantic approach to war was anathema. His experience of fighting the Germans in the First World War and again since 1940 had convinced him that, against soldiers as professional and well-trained as the Germans, one must ensure that one was even more professional, even better trained and, above all, better led. Risks must by all means be taken, but they must be accepted within the overall framework of a battle plan that gave the Allies a reasonable assurance of success. The Allies held the initiative; the Germans were now on the defensive in Europe. If the Allies intended to deliver their major blow across the Channel, then they must not show their weakness in the Mediterranean, but must convince the Germans of their strength. From Allied Intelligence it was known that most senior German officers favoured a policy of withdrawing north of Rome. Now, with the chaotic Allied performance at Salerno, the Allies had merely served to demonstrate their weakness to the Germans. It was not therefore the lack of Allied speed which Monty felt was responsible, but the lack of realism and cool, clear judgement displayed by the Allied High Command. And instead of learning from this, the Allies were continuing to make unrealistic assumptions about future progress, without even the semblance of a coherent plan as to how this progress was to be achieved. Clark was planning to try and take Naples in an attack to commence only four days after Eighth Army had (as Monty believed) 'saved' him; and even Eisenhower was predicting to Marshall on 20 September that Naples would fall to Clark within a few days.

To be sure, Marshall was making Eisenhower's life hell. On 23

---

[1] *The Papers of Dwight David Eisenhower*, ed. Alfred Chandler, Vol. III, Baltimore 1970.
[2] Letter to Marshall in *The Papers of Dwight David Eisenhower*, op. cit.

September Marshall 'took the starch out of Ike'[1] in a message which casts some doubt about Marshall's legendary astuteness as American Chief of Staff of the Army. Not only did he castigate Eisenhower for giving in to Monty's insistence that Fifth and Eighth Armies build up supplies and reinforcements before beginning an Italian offensive, but chided Eisenhower for not mounting Salerno earlier. 'We are fearful that in a deliberate approach to the development of a secure position including the port of Naples, you will afford the other fellow so much time that he will be in a position to make things more difficult in the matter of an advance to Rome or in preparations for any attempts on his part to secure a prestige victory. With air and sea power on your side . . . have you considered the possibility of pausing in your Fifth and Eighth Army effort when you have Naples under the guns as it were and merely a matter of a week or two, and making a dash in the Rome area?' As regards Salerno, 'I might say that both [Field-Marshal] Dill and I feel that your AVALANCHE should have started earlier before operations in the toe. . . . At long range it would seem that you give the enemy too much time to prepare and eventually find yourself up against a very stiff resistance.'[2]

What this amounted to was victory on the cheap, since Marshall would commit no further American soldiers to the campaign, was insisting that certain divisions be withdrawn to England for the cross-Channel invasion, and demanded the return of no less than three bomber groups to Britain.

But the battle for Italy could not be won on the cheap, however much Eisenhower might fret about missed opportunities. He had been proved wrong in dispersing his landings instead of concentrating them, as in 'Husky'; but even a combined landing by Clark and Montgomery would not necessarily have achieved very much more, though it would have avoided the blow to Allied morale when Salerno almost gave the Germans a victory. There were some twenty German divisions in Italy – and no hare-brained dashes to Rome or outflanking landings by small forces could miraculously alter this fact. As Eisenhower replied to Marshall, 'If we landed a small force it would be quickly eliminated, while a force large enough to sustain itself cannot possibly be mounted for a very considerable period.' Yet still Eisenhower did not insist on a reconsideration of Allied war aims in Italy, but, having defended his record, assured Marshall that he could not 'see how any individual could possibly be devoting more thought and energy to speeding up operations or to attacking boldly and with admitted risk than I do.'[3]

[1] Diary of Harry C. Butcher, loc. cit.
[2] Signal from Marshall in Diary of Harry C. Butcher, loc. cit.
[3] Signal of 24.9.43 in *The Papers of Dwight David Eisenhower*, op. cit.

It was against this background that Monty, almost single-handedly, attempted to champion the cause of sanity and military reason. An immediate attack on Rome with Clark's exhausted army and the two tired divisions of Eighth Army – who had come almost 300 miles from Reggio – was sheer madness, whatever the dictates of speed. The Allies must only go for what they really wanted, and knew they could attain. He therefore proposed that Eighth Army's 13 Corps should anchor Clark at Salerno while Fifth Army built up its forces for its assault on Rome; meanwhile the forces at Taranto, once landed, should secure the Foggia airfields and then swing westwards to loosen enemy resistance around Naples if Fifth Army failed to take the city in its frontal advance. 'General Alexander visited me at Tac Army at SCALEA today, and I explained to him what I was doing,' Monty noted on 20 September. But in the privacy of his diary he added his own personal evaluation of the Italian campaign so far:

One cannot get away from the fact that I was ordered to invade the mainland of EUROPE without being given adequate resources, and without even being given any object. . . .

One has to admit that the High Command in the Mediterranean Theatre of War invaded ITALY, and thus embarked on a major campaign on the continent of EUROPE, without having any clear idea – or plan – as to how they would develop the operations and fight the land battle.

There was no object laid down. The whole affair was haphazard and untidy – in fact typically British.

The original idea was that my Army was not to operate beyond the CATANZARO neck. But in actual fact I had to operate some 200 miles beyond that neck, and go very quickly too, and if I had failed to do so the whole of 5 American Army would have been pushed into the sea.

As it turned out I just arrived in time to relieve the pressure, and make the Germans pull out.

Even the enemy admits this. . . .

The more one reflects on past events the more one is forced to the opinion that every operation teed-up by 15 Army Group heads straight for disaster and has to be pulled out of the fire by Eighth Army.

If the High Command in the Mediterranean Theatre had not got such a first class army to do the business for them, they would have had one long series of disasters; in fact we would still be fighting in AFRICA.

Monty was well aware that Eighth Army was considered by cynics to be slow and ponderous. But what had supposedly speedier armies achieved? O'Connor's Western Desert Force had performed bril-

413

liantly against Italians, and ignominiously against Germans, with O'Connor himself being captured. Auchinleck's original Eighth Army had thrust forward to Agheila and then been run back by Rommel to the gates of Cairo. Anderson's First Army, similarly, had attempted to seize Tunis by *coup de main*, and been condemned to an entire winter of stalemate, culminating in the American disaster at Kasserine. Even in Sicily, Seventh Army had attempted to show its dash and brio, and raced off in the wrong direction, thus forfeiting any chance of achieving a breakthrough by the combined weight of Allied forces. By contrast Eighth Army had, under Montgomery's command, won a seminal victory at Alamein; thereafter it had secured some two thousand miles of North African coast up to Enfidaville, as well as providing the Corps Commander and primary units for the Allied triumph at Tunis. Its landing in Sicily had forced the German and Italian High Command to concede inevitable defeat within four days, even though the campaign had lasted thirty-nine. Thereafter, with a mere two divisions in the field, it had secured the toe of Italy and helped to force the Germans to abandon further attempts at defeating the Allied bridgehead at Salerno. Though sometimes checked, Eighth Army had never once come near defeat by German forces or needed to be rescued by another Allied army, and if Monty was over-boastful on its behalf, it was a record of which its soldiers too were proud, as was to be demonstrated when 192 men of the 50th and 51st Divisions staged a mutiny at Salerno rather than serve in 10 Corps on Mark Clark's Fifth Army front.[1] Because 10 British Corps had once been a spearhead of Eighth Army Monty watched its fortunes with particular concern. The Reynolds' son, Tom, was serving in an infantry battalion at Salerno, and Monty asked his ADC/Liaison Officer to check up on him. 'I had one of my A.D.C.'s over on the SALERNO front yesterday,' he wrote on 22 September, 'and made him find out about your Tom. He got through on the telephone to his battalion and ascertained that Tom was perfectly all right and in very good form in all respects. I wanted to make certain about it as Tom's Division had a bad time in and about SALERNO and suffered nearly 3000 casualties. So that is all right.' But to the CIGS, Sir Alan Brooke, Monty was more forthright when he wrote some weeks later. Criticizing Clark's battlefield tactics he added:

Another factor is that 46 and 56 Divs have both had very severe casualties since 9 Sept – 10 Corps have had some 8,000 casualties, nearly all in 46 and 56 Divs.
   A Division that suffers such losses requires time to absorb its new drafts, to build up the broken teams, and so on. From what I

<hr>

[1] Cf. Alan Patient, 'Mutiny', published in the *Listener*, 25.2.82.

hear of 46 Div it requires a good period for rest and training. I doubt if Dick McCREERY [a Cavalryman and erstwhile Chief of Staff to Alexander] understands the Infantry Division.[1]

There can be no doubt that Monty's concern for the lives and conditions of his soldiers was genuine, indeed unparalleled in the Allied armies. Patton, marooned without an Army in the palace he had seized when capturing Palermo, was missed by no one save Eisenhower, whose failure at Salerno had brought him as close to losing his job as he had ever come. Anderson had also been denied further field command, and Clark, despite his personal drive and bravery,[2] was soon embarrassed by the frank refusal of British troops and commanders to accept the casualties inherent in his somewhat piecemeal, broad-front offensive tactics, similar to those employed by Anderson and later Alexander in Tunisia. Monty might well offend the jealous and the gentlemen by his exorbitant ego – 'I have made the Navy give me a fast Motor Launch (ML240); it does 20 knots and is well armed, and has a crew of 2 officers 15 ratings. I use it to cross over to Messina, or to nip round the coast. I find in this sort of business one has got to have good means of transport by sea, land and air,' he wrote with the same conceit that had once characterised his ownership of a Flying Fortress. 'So I now have: one aeroplane, one Motor Launch, five Motor cars. . . . I forgot to mention that amongst my means of transport is also one DUKW. This is a large lorry which can go on the road or on the sea. . . .'[3] The men of Eighth Army knew, however, their commander *cared*. Not only did he visit them; issue 'Personal Messages' to the soldiers and further 'Notes on the Conduct of War' to the officers, fight for proper medical back-up services ('a bad medical scandal was narrowly averted,' he reported later to Brooke, 'the reason was a useless DDMS at AFHQ, *and* Charles Miller [Alexander's Chief Administrative Officer]');[4] but he seemed to take a personal and almost paternal interest in their welfare. When Carol Mather, son of his wife Betty's Lancashire friends the Mathers, escaped from POW camp in Italy and reached Eighth Army lines, Monty had him put up at Eighth Army Head-quarters – as well as rushing a note to the Reynolds asking them to inform Carol's parents: 'Will you telephone the Mathers and let her know; I think it is Putney 4259. I have written to Loris Mather but *she* may get your message first if *he* is away.'[5] Equally he fretted about his stepson Dick, captured after Alamein, and was overjoyed when Dick

[1] Letter of 14.10.43, copy in Montgomery Papers.
[2] On 10.12.43, Clark was personally decorated by President Roosevelt with the DSC for bravery and leadership at Salerno.
[3] Letter to Phyllis Reynolds of 9.9.43, Montgomery Papers
[4] Letter of 14.10.43, loc. cit.
[5] Letter of 19.10.43, loc. cit.

too found his way back through Eighth Army lines: '5 Dec – Dick Carver has just come in. He is very well, but is thin and wants feeding up I should say. I shall send him home at once . . . it will be nice for him to be home for Christmas.'[1]

A family spirit pervaded Eighth Army, giving heart to troops who would otherwise have thought only of returning to Britain after so many months and even years of battle in the Middle East without home leave. Noel Coward, on a visit to an Eighth Army hospital in Sicily in the summer, had encountered the typical gritty determination and humour of 'Monty's men', as he recalled in his diary:

> One chipper little man who had been shot full of shrapnel and machine-gun bullets was very chatty. I asked him what he thought of Sicily and he said, 'The Germans were all right and the Eyties were all right but the mosquitoes were bloody awful!'[2]

Moreover the faith of such soldiers in their Army Commander was not misplaced. On their behalf Monty not only sought to ensure that the operations they were asked to conduct were conceived according to an overall strategy that guaranteed a reasonable chance of success, but he tried constantly too to draw lessons from the fighting that would benefit both of his own formations, and others at home and elsewhere. At the close of the Sicilian campaign he wrote to the VCIGS urging the War Office to reconsider the tactical grouping of British armoured units and, particularly, to improve the gunpower of Allied tanks. 'It is gun power that counts in the battle. . . . In pushing forward in search for good fire positions, tanks often have to expose themselves, and casualties follow rapidly. . . . We must produce a tank with a gun as primary armament which is superior to the present 88 mm of the enemy, and superior to anything he is likely to produce in the future. I suggest that in the past we have tried to fit the gun into the tank. Instead we should select the gun, and build the tank round it. . . . When I have discussed these questions with Senior Officers of the Army in ENGLAND, the answer has always been the same – viz: "Your experience is of the DESERT, and it is quite different in EUROPE." This answer is generally the same whatever the subject under discussion. But this mentality is no use, and will get us nowhere. I fashioned an Army in AFRICA that would be suitable for making war anywhere: and I evolved a set-up, and a technique, that enabled the weapon to be wielded to the best advantage. I have now brought that Army across the sea to EUROPE, and have fought a campaign in SICILY – not unsuccessfully – in

---

[1] Loc. cit.
[2] Noel Coward, *Middle East Diary*, New York 1944.

which we encountered all and every type of country. We fought in very close country; in the plain of CATANIA; in terraced vineyards; in rugged mountainous country where only donkey transport could be used; in lava belts; and up the slopes of a volcanic mountain. I employed the same organization, the same set-up, the same technique – modified where necessary to suit the problem. It proved successful; my method and technique have stood the test in a European setting. I hope therefore that one will no longer have flung at one the answer referred to in para 17.'[1]

In this, as in Monty's other letters to senior officers in the War Office, one can hear the authentic voice of the professional soldier, a general who did not simply delegate such duties to others but sought to give them his personal stamp of authority lest they be ignored or neglected.

Behind such concern with the technology of Allied armour, and the organisation of units and formations, was Monty's conviction that one day he would be recalled to England to command at least an army in the cross-Channel operation to be mounted in 1944. Even as Clark's army fought for its toehold at Salerno, Monty was writing to the VCIGS, on 11 September:

> I have recommended to Alex that Oliver Leese should go home to command 8 Corps. I am certain that for the good of the show as a whole we *must* get some good chaps back to you. I do NOT recommend Evelegh [Commander of 78th Division] for a Corps yet; he wants to mature a bit and get more balance and a bigger horizon. Bucknall has done well in battle with 5 DIV and I recommend that he gets 30 Corps. Templer was stepped down, like Bucknall, and has got no benefit from it, as he is doing nothing in Africa and his division may well be stripped of men. I recommend he comes to Italy and gets 5 DIV.
>
> In this way we shall be making the best use of 8th Army as a training ground for Corps Comds and DIV Comds. I do concentrate on teaching my generals, and I am certain one has got to do so.
>
> 30 Corps are doing nothing in Sicily and Oliver could go home to you at once.

To Brooke, some days later, Monty developed this idea still further:

> I would like to suggest to you that, for the good of this war as a whole, you ought to ship 30 Corps home to England. It at present consists of

[1] Letter to Lt-General Archibald Nye, 28.8.43, Montgomery Papers.

30 Corps HQ
30 Corps troops
50 DIV
51 DIV

The whole lot are in Sicily and I see no possibility of employing them in this campaign. In the Corps troops you have an A.G.R.A [Artillery Group, RA] that is probably unequalled anywhere for knowledge and experience; it is

7 Medium Regt
64 Medium Regt
4 Survey Regt

and these units have fought together for a year and are a great team. It seems to me that if you get home to the UK the Corps HQ and the Corps Artillery and the two Divisions of the Corps, and *you keep the whole party together in England as a Corps*, then you will have a Corps that has taken part in every type of fighting, which is a superb team, and which could be a model for the whole army in England to study. To break up such a weapon would be a thousand pities – such an experienced Corps would be worth untold gold when it comes to a cross-Channel venture. I am sure you will agree that it is not necessarily the 'big battalions' that give success in war; it is the best weapon, properly wielded, even if it is relatively small.

As Eisenhower considered Marshall his mentor so too Monty thought of Brooke:

I often feel I would like to spend a quiet week-end with you, free from all interruptions, when I can put my ideas clearly to you, get your views, and generally draw inspiration from you. Inspiration has got to come from somewhere, and generally from above. I try and do my stuff in this respect to my own Army, but sometimes feel the need to draw some in myself. Perhaps when the winter sets in and the tempo of the operations has to pipe down a bit, an opportunity may occur. Meanwhile I am glad to say I am in first class health and spirits, and am in the best of form generally. I have never been sick or sorry since you sent me out to Egypt in August 1942, except for two days fever in April last.

Poor Brooke, at the top of the pyramid, had to draw his own inspiration from Churchill and his sanity from bird-watching. Brooke had fought hard for a concerted Allied plan in the Mediterranean, but had been worsted by the American contingent attending the Allied council of war at Quebec, who feared that Italy would so drain the resources of the Allies that a cross-Channel attack even in 1944 would be impossible. 'Our Quebec meeting was as strenuous and more unpleasant than most. I can't stand many more of them!'

Brooke wrote to Monty on 29 September. 'It is child's play deciding what should be done as compared with getting it done. I have come to the conclusion that strategy is not one of the arts in which the anglo-saxon race shines! The number of individuals who can see beyond the end of their noses are few and far between, and the remainder have surprisingly short noses!'[1] Brooke's particular bug-bear was Mountbatten, whose chameleon-like ability to change his views according to his surroundings, made Brooke bristle. 'We have secured Dickie [Mountbatten] down onto a bit of concrete in the shape of [Lt-General] Pownall [as his Chief of Staff]. I hope this may ensure that the output of this dynamo is directed in proper channels and does not swing in new directions with every breeze it meets!' Brooke noted.[2]

Mountbatten, meanwhile, had already rushed off a letter from Canada to Monty, intimating the results of the Quebec Conference: the 'very staggering decision' that Mountbatten himself was to be the Supreme Commander in South-east Asia; and that the Supreme Commanders for the cross-Channel invasion and in the Mediterranean were to be, in all likelihood, an American and a Briton respectively. 'Please keep this to yourself for the present,' Mountbatten had written – adding that he had made, as one of his first requests to the CIGS, 'that he should release you as soon as you were available to come out [to S.E. Asia] to be Army Commander-in-Chief. He laughingly replied that that would not be until the war in Europe was over. . . . I am following your meteoric progress with great enthusiasm. If you ever have time to jot down some "Advice to very young Supreme Commanders" I should be grateful.'[3] This Monty now did, still incensed by the mess Eisenhower had made of the Italian campaign:

You remember I told you I could write a book about the whole HUSKY affair, but it would be quite impossible to publish it!! It is nothing to what I could write about what I was asked to do when we invaded the mainland of Europe. The trouble we had to get the thing on a good wicket is almost unbelievable, including a 1st Class row with 'the Old Man of the Sea';[4] he was seen off, and we got what was necessary and the whole thing was a success.

But my advice to you as a Supreme Commander is to get a good sound plan drawn up before you begin detailed planning; get an experienced fighting commander 'in' on it and make certain that what you want to do *is possible* and that you have *the necessary resources to do it.*

[1] Letter of 24.8.43, original in Montgomery Papers.
[2] Ibid.
[3] Original in Montgomery Papers.
[4] i.e. Admiral Sir Andrew Cunningham.

And do one or two things really properly; and don't try and do five or six things all of which are starved for lack of resources – and which will probably all produce no results.[1]

Phase One, as Monty called it, was now over in Italy; Phase Two was about to begin. Yet to Monty's consternation there was *still* no concerted plan. Did the Allies wish to reach Rome before the winter rains set in, or did they intend simply to occupy southern Italy, with possession of Naples and the Foggia airfields? Were all efforts to be put into the Italian campaign, or were there to be subsidiary efforts in the Mediterranean? Dutifully and loyally Monty continued to lead Eighth Army northwards, but his patience with Eisenhower and Alexander was getting very thin. If he was to drive on Rome by switching his whole Army to the Adriatic at Taranto, fighting up the Adriatic coast and then crossing the mountains, he would need great stocks of petrol, ammunition and supplies. It was on this principle that Eighth Army had campaigned so successfully in North Africa – the principle of not simply breaching the enemy defensive line, but having sufficient momentum and resources to continue in one bound to one's main objective. As Eighth Army had once pierced the Buerat line and continued all the way to Tripoli, so Monty now hoped for an Allied plan that would make possible a similar advance on Rome, if Rome was the Allied objective. But from Alexander he could neither wrest a strategy nor the sort of administrative support that would make such an object feasible. Ships arrived in Taranto and at Brindisi without anyone knowing what was inside them, and it was painfully clear that without adequate stocks of equipment – especially bridging – Eighth Army would not get far.

> The operation of switching my tail from Reggio and the Toe of Italy, round to the Taranto-Brindisi area and the Heel, was a very large undertaking. Taranto port was fully occupied with receiving incoming troops.
>
> I could not open Brindisi port until today, 27 September, and thus was not able to build up a reserve of stocks which could carry me right through to the ROME line.

For this Monty blamed, in his diary, Alexander's and Eisenhower's administrative officers Miller, Gale and Lewis.

> The immediate result of a thoroughly bad administrative set-up is that my offensive 'drive' up through FOGGIA and right on to the ROME line has got to be limited in scope because of lack of stores, petrol, and so on. When a ship comes in no one knows what is

<hr />

[1] Letter of 29.9.43, copy in Montgomery Papers.

inside the ship until the lid is taken off; thus any planning ahead is impossible. We ought to be allotted certain tonnage, this being loaded to our specification.

Those historians who later judged the wartime campaigns in terms solely of tactics have done a great disservice to military history. Eisenhower might, like Marshall, decry the rule of logistics and rue the lack of Allied boldness, but the bitter battle of attrition that Clark's Fifth Army fought in its premature bid for Naples is a testament to Montgomery's point.

'How has this come about?' Monty asked himself.

In my opinion it is due to the fact that we entered into a major war on the continent of EUROPE without a very clear plan as to how we would fight the campaign.

The administrative set-up is thoroughly unsound and as a result there was no administrative foresight; the switching of the 'tail' from REGGIO and the TOE, to TARANTO area was not foreseen early enough.

Monty's solution was to put his erstwhile Eighth Army administrative chief, Brian Robertson, in charge of all administration in Italy, answerable to AFHQ in Algiers. On the advice of Major-General Miller, Alexander had refused.

Alexander does not really understand the problem, and he is badly advised by MILLER.

I am certain that unless we get our set-up right *now*, we will have great troubles later on. . . .

As this campaign goes on the more clear it becomes that 15 Army Group is very ineffective. There is no grip of the battle.

In the end I decide what I want to do, and what is best. I then get CLARK (5 Army) to agree, and between us we fix up a plot, boundary and so on.

This, Monty felt, 'is not the proper way to make war'. It was not – and in disgust Monty sent Alexander a signal on 29 September insisting that, having taken the Foggia airfields and reached the Termoli line, Eighth Army must pause for about 10 to 14 days. 'I have no reserve stocks and the whole admin business in rear is in a bad way and must be tidied up.'[1]

Though Monty did not yet realise it, strategic muddle, incompetent army group command, and administrative failure had squandered any chance of the Allies reaching Rome in 1943.

[1] Copy of signal in Personal Diary, Montgomery Papers.

CHAPTER FOUR

'Do You Want to Drive the Germans from Italy?'

Monty's initial hope was that, once stocks were built up behind the Termoli line, he would 'get through to the ROME line in about 10 days', as he signalled to Alexander on 29 September.[1] But in the ensuing days Monty began to recognise that the situation was even worse than he imagined. Far from retreating behind a plethora of demolitions, the Germans were starting to counter-attack, almost driving Eighth Army out of Termoli on 5 October. It was the same story on Fifth Army's front, but there, in the aftermath of the Salerno crisis, vast stockpiles of petrol and spares had at least been brought in. In the first few days of October Eighth Army was down to twenty-one tons of petrol, whereas 10 Corps of Fifth Army alone possessed six thousand tons! Urgent vehicle spares were required; instead some fifteen hundred new motorcycles had been unloaded. Worse still, the Air Force was busily installing the Tactical Bomber Force in Italy, whereas 'the conditions of the problem are such that we can get no targets for the bombers and we can do all that is necessary with the Kittybombers. It is the Strategical Air Force that should come in first,' Monty reflected in his diary on 2 October.

The gist of the whole matter is this. We are installing a weapon in ITALY. No one has laid down what that weapon is to be, and so everyone is trying to get in at the same time; the maintenance situation will not stand this.

The old dictum that it is the 'big battalions' that win the battle, is not true today; it is the best weapon, properly wielded.

It is far better to have a small weapon with a good administrative organisation behind it, and which can thus develop its maximum power, than a large weapon, which is starved administratively, and which can never develop its full power.

In this connection it is not generally known that I drove ROMMEL and his army from ALAMEIN in EGYPT to the MARETH line in Tunisia, and I never used more than three divisions the whole

[1] Diary, Montgomery Papers.

time; I could not do so for reasons of administration; but those three divisions had a first class administration behind them.

ROMMEL had six divisions, but he could never get the best value from them as his administration was very precarious.

Having got a small and efficient weapon installed in Italy, and having got the administration on a really good wicket, then the size of the weapon can gradually be increased.

To Brooke a few days previously Monty had warned of the consequences of poor administration in a long drawn-out campaign:

The administrative set-up is faulty and we get tied up into dreadful difficulties; the new plan issued by AFHQ is a step in the right direction, but it is *not* the answer in order to put us on a really good wicket for the whole of this campaign. I tried to get Riddle-Webster to visit me, but he could not manage it; I then got Ronnie Weeks to come, but he could only stay for 3/4 of an hour and that is no use. I am convinced that if we do not get our administrative set-up on a really good and firm basis we shall always be struggling with adversity, and this is no good when we are embarking on a major campaign in Italy.[1]

By 7 October, when Alexander finally visited Monty in person, the administrative crisis had reached its climax. Fifth Army was now releasing petrol, but there was a great shortage of transport, with some '500 vehicles off the road waiting for new engines' – and broken-down vehicles being sent back to Egypt for repair. There were insufficient clearing stations for the sick and wounded, and rising unrest regarding those troops who would be selected to return to England:

We are playing with a very highly explosive material when dealing with the question of formations and personnel returning to U.K.

If 1 Armd Div go home and 7 Armd Div stay here, the resulting unrest would be serious.

50 and 51 Divs know they are going home to U.K., they have had their sick and wounded, when fit, sent to Divisions in 5 Army.

This may have been necessary as an emergency measure, but it is vital that these men be sent back to their Divisions at once – to avoid unrest.

Monty insisted that Eighth Army deal direct with 10 Corps, to which Alexander agreed; but it was too late to avoid the tragic mutiny on the beaches of Salerno – where out of fifteen hundred men, many

[1] Letter of 29.9.43, loc. cit.

of them returning from hospital, almost two hundred soldiers refused to join Clark's army and were subsequently court-martialled.

Monty's new plan for pausing and then taking Rome in a single bound was predicated upon the return of 10 Corps from Fifth Army. As in the desert, 10 Corps would be held in reserve behind the two Corps already in line, ready to be pushed through at the appropriate moment, as at the battle of Mareth and again at Wadi Akarit. At 9 a.m. on 8 October Monty therefore assembled his senior staff and field commanders for a conference, at which he laid down his intentions. 5 Corps would hold on the right, 13 Corps on the left; 10 Corps, 'to come over from American 5 Army as soon as it can be released', would be in reserve, consisting of '46 Div, 56 Div, 7 Armd Div, 23 Armd Bde'. To Monty's insistence, on 17 September, that Eighth Army be British with British administration, and Fifth Army be American with American administration, Alexander had agreed. But having fought his way out of the Salerno beachhead and been stopped from taking Naples by fierce German resistance throughout the latter part of September, Clark was ill-disposed to surrender a complete Corps – in effect half his army – and Alexander was too weak to order the transfer.

Once again the campaign began to founder, to Monty's chagrin. 'I much fear that in this phase, as in Phase 1, 15 Army Group has been ineffective and has failed to grip the show – operationally or administratively,' Monty recorded in his diary on 12 October. 'General Alexander is very badly served by his staff. He ought to choose better men.' Miller was sacked, new men were rushed from England, but the hours of autumn were ticking away and the whole Allied campaign in Italy was stymied. Though Eisenhower's prediction that Naples would fall by the end of September had come true – it was finally overrun on 30 September – Clark was still trying to cross the Volturno, fifteen miles beyond, in mid-October, and his 10 Corps Commander, General McCreery, was balking at the task. 'On my left the Fifth Army is attacking across the VOLTURNO river. I am not too happy myself about this attack and it may well be costly,' Monty warned Brooke. 'It has been launched with very hasty preparation and I don't think they know very much about the enemy in front of them. Five divisions are attacking on a front of 35 miles; in my view that is not the way to fight the Germans when you are definitely held. I believe the Fifth Army would have been well advised to pause, study the problem very carefully, re-group, and then launch a terrific and *concentrated blow* at the key area in the German layout. . . . I doubt very much if Fifth Army are administratively on a very firm wicket just at the moment, and you cannot launch big scale attacks if you are like that. However, all this is not my business. I am doing every possible thing I can to help CLARK and I hope very much that all will be well . . . he is very easy to work with, and we have a very close liaison. I should say he is clever, but lacks the practical knowledge of how to tee-up the various types of battle.'[1]

Clark *did* manage to break the Volturno line, but it would take Fifth Army four weeks to advance just twenty miles beyond it. Casualties were frightening and 10 Corps was thereby rendered useless as a battle-fit formation for the use of Eighth Army; and on 13 November Clark informed Alexander he would have to close down the offensive.

Sensing that Clark would have a difficult battle and that Eighth Army would probably meet equally determined resistance, Monty sought to make a last appeal for a strategic plan before the Allies committed themselves to heavy casualties:

The enemy is definitely stiffening up his front and it may well be that he will try to make a big effort to keep us from getting to ROME. . . . The country in front of us is good defensive country, and skilful demolitions would make the next advance very slow,

he warned Brooke.

If the enemy resistance is very stiff, our advance to PESCARA [Eighth Army's next objective 'as first bound'] and ANCONA would be very costly; it could be done, but we would need plenty of reinforcements to hand, especially infantry.
    It is not country where we can get any advantage from our great superiority in armour.
    What do you want to do?

he asked.

I presume you want the ROME airfields. Do you want ROME for political reasons, and to be able to put the King back on his throne?
    Do you want to establish the air forces in the Po Valley?
    Do you want to drive the Germans from Italy?
    Are you prepared to have heavy losses to get any, or all of the above?

Monty's own opinion was clear-cut.

My own view rather inclines to the idea that it is a mistake to drive the German armies from ITALY. I would keep them there, with a hostile population, and difficult communications which we bomb daily. But we must have as much of ITALY as we want for our own purposes. That is, enough to enable our air forces to be able to

[1] Letter of 14.10.43, loc. cit.

425

reach the Southern German cities and the Roumanian oil fields.

I would like to establish ourselves in the Valley of the Po. Once there we would drive the German air forces back to GERMANY. . . . This would be a great thing and would put us on a very good wicket – and the German on a very bad wicket.

We would also constitute a very serious threat to GERMANY in several directions: Eastwards into AUSTRIA, Northwards into South GERMANY, and Westwards into Southern FRANCE. We could play on this and keep the Germans guessing – and thus help OVERLORD [the cross-Channel invasion set for 1944].

Are my paras 10 and 11 more or less on the right lines as regards your ideas?[1]

Sadly they were not. By 1 November Brooke was lamenting in his diary that his Mediterranean strategy had fallen apart, thanks to American reluctance to treat it as a serious theatre of war. 'We should have had the whole Balkans ablaze by now, and the war might have been finished in 1943,' he noted,[2] adding, when he read over this period of his diary after the war: 'Reading between the lines I think I cannot have been far off a nervous breakdown.' He particularly bemoaned the fact that the Allies did not take Crete and Rhodes, and did not exploit the Italian campaign more fully: 'The enemy flanks therefore remained open to combined operations on both sides throughout the length of Italy. The main artery of rail communications consisted of one double line of railway open to air attack throughout its length. Conditions were therefore ideal for hitting the enemy hard and for enforcing on him the use of reserves in the defence of Italy.'[3]

To be sure, Brooke did not have his whole heart in the cross-Channel operation – as was the case with Churchill and Smuts. Not even the disasters at Cos and Leros in October, when the Germans retook the islands, could dampen their Mediterranean obsession. Monty's letter went unanswered. Like Fifth Army, Eighth Army had to prepare for an autumn campaign involving heavy casualties, and without any clear strategic objective agreed upon, either by the local Commanders-in-Chief or by the Combined Chiefs of Staff. 'All indications pointed to the enemy doing all he could to stop us from getting to ROME. On the left, Fifth Army was across the VOLTURNO, but resistance was stiffening,' Monty noted on 21 October. Four German divisions were barring the Eighth Army line of advance, in good delaying country. By 22 October Monty had learned that 'the Germans are moving Divisions into ITALY; there are 11 in the South, and a further 12 in the North; total 23 or 24'.

[1] Ibid.
[2] A. Bryant, *Triumph in the West*, London 1959.
[3] Ibid.

Given this number, were the Allies correct in 'bulling ahead' – especially now that winter was about to break? Monty was doubtful. He was confident he could storm the enemy's Trigno River line – but whether he could go on to cross the Sangro was less sure. 'Incoming [German] divisions will be brought into the SANGRO line,' he noted; 'the present forward divisions, which are tired and need resting, will pull back through that line.' Behind the Sangro line, furthermore, 'there are signs that he intends to pull into reserve the armoured divisions, and possibly the P.[anzer] G.[renadier] Divisions. . . . I do not anticipate any great difficulty in crossing the TRIGNO. . . . Bad weather is the only thing that would hamper us. We will then have to square up to the SANGRO position and the forcing of that line may be difficult.'

Was it worth accepting inevitable casualties and going ahead? Ironically the reason Alexander gave, on 21 October, was that, with the build-up in German divisions, Hitler might launch a counter-attack. The Allies must therefore keep the offensive initiative.[1]

Monty, noting the source of this view, pooh-poohed the idea:

15 Army Group consider that the enemy is planning an offensive, to re-capture NAPLES and the FOGGIA airfields. He has say 24 Divisions against our 14.

Provided we are not rash,

Monty retorted,

and are always well balanced, I do not consider any offensive on his part could succeed; it would merely play into our hands; I consider his policy is 100% defensive.

Ignoring Monty's strategic doubts about launching an offensive campaign so late in the year, Alexander was blithely reported on the BBC as having given, at a press conference on 23 October, his next objective as Rome, as well as acknowledging that casualties in Fifth Army had already exceeded fourteen thousand – as against Eighth Army's which were under a thousand. 'To give the enemy our objective and our casualties is quite monstrous,' Monty fumed; 'in any case, the casualties of Eighth Army have been 3,000, and NOT 1000.' By 27 October he was noting:

What we want in ITALY is a proper and firm plan for waging the campaign. At present it is haphazard and go-as-you-please.

I fight my way forward as I like; I stop and pause when I like; I choose my own objectives.

[1] J. Ehrman, op. cit.

CLARK (Fifth Army) does the same; I have very close touch with him and we see that our actions are so coordinated that all is well.

But we each do *what* we like, *when* we like; the total military power in the two Armies is not applied on one big plan. In other words, there is no grip or control by 15 Army Group.

As far as I know no high authority has ever said what is wanted. Do we want ROME and its airfields? Do we want the Po valley?

What *do* we want, and when?

Until some very clear directive is issued we shall continue to muddle on.

To Monty, this was scandalous.

We entered on a major campaign in ITALY this summer. The campaign began in SICILY on 10 July.

By the end of September we had captured SICILY, had knocked ITALY out of the war, had got the Italian fleet locked up in our own harbours, and had occupied half ITALY including the FOGGIA airfields.

These were spectacular results.

Then the tap is turned off (it was known it would be) and craft and shipping are removed to other theatres. Down goes the rate of build-up, and serious admin and medical scandals are narrowly averted.

Meanwhile the Germans bring more Divisions into ITALY; today he has 24 Divisions to our 14 Divisions. Therefore, spectacular results can no longer be expected, and in fact further progress Northwards up ITALY is bound to be slow and difficult.

The Allies have not got the resources in craft and shipping to fight two major campaigns at the same time. If ITALY is to be the main theatre, then turn the tap on there and leave it on till you have got what you want.

We turned the tap off before we got what we wanted.

If Western EUROPE is to be the main theatre, then turn the tap on there; in this case you must not expect spectacular results in ITALY.

I put all the above very plainly to ALEXANDER when he came to see me today. I said it was my opinion that we should have as our objective the ROME line; we should then halt for at least three months in order to bring up reserves in our depots and prepare for the spring campaign; in the spring we should launch an offensive into the PO valley.

If some simple plan as above was laid down, we could all plan ahead.

But nothing is laid down.

ALEXANDER agreed, and said he would order the above plan.

There is no doubt we conduct our wars in a most curious way; ALEXANDER is the nicest chap I have ever known, but he does not understand the conduct of war,

Monty stated sadly;

the indecision and lack of grip at 15 Army Group is bad – it is more than that, it is a scandal. I very much doubt if we shall now get the ROME line without great difficulty – and not before the middle of December.

This was prophetic, as Monty himself noted a few days later, when rain, mud and slush brought the right flank of Eighth Army's advance to a standstill. Rome was out of the question, now – 'the reason is that we are now paying for the lack of fixed policy, lack of planning, and lack of "grip", that has been noted in this diary all through the Italian campaign.' He had warned Alexander again and again in his signals, and in person on 7 October. 'I also put the whole thing very clearly to EISENHOWER when he visited me on 11 October.

But nothing was done.
An enormous Air Force is pouring in.
But the land armies remain unchanged, I have many units still in AFRICA. I have four infantry divisions. I cannot get to the ROME line with these.
I was told I was to have 10 Corps after NAPLES was captured, but now it seems 10 Corps cannot leave the NAPLES front; if I had got 10 Corps I would have had six infantry divisions, which is what I require and which is what I based my plans upon.
I have had to tell ALEXANDER that I must have one more infantry division, and unless I get it there will be a definite limit to the distance I can go. I have suggested 1 Div from NORTH AFRICA; but even if it started now it could not possibly be here before the end of November; the middle of December is far more likely.
Now another complication has arisen,

Monty went on, for Alexander, shamed by the slow progress of the campaign, had dreamed up another mad operation, on a par with 'Giant II' – a landing at Anzio.

ALEXANDER has now told the C.I.G.S. that he must be allowed to keep craft and shipping for one division, so that he can land this division up near ROME in an assault operation; he has said that if he cannot have the craft he cannot get to ROME.
In my opinion this is complete nonsense; the weather is too

429

uncertain now for assault landings; one division landed near ROME would find itself taken on by several enemy armoured Divisions, as the Germans are withdrawing their armoured Divisions to rest in the ROME area; there are very few beaches where such a landing could be made, and they will all be closely watched.[1]

If we are to get to ROME we shall have to fight our way forward by land,

Monty stated categorically.

If any craft can be secured they should be used for bringing over formations and units from NORTH AFRICA to reinforce my ARMY and FIFTH Army; I still have many units there, and 5 Corps HQ has much of its Corps tps still there.

To keep a division locked up in craft, waiting for an assault landing that may never come off because of adverse weather or of enemy concentrations, is monstrous,

he felt.

ALEXANDER is trying hard to find a way out of the mess. But he won't do it by landing a Division at ROME; he will merely make it worse and the Division may well be written off by the Germans,

Monty prophesied.

The answer is quite simple. If you want to wage successful war, you have got to have a commander who understands the business.

ALEXANDER is my great friend. But he does not understand the business, and he is not clever; he cannot grasp the essentials. The plain truth is that so far he has been 'carried', from inclusive ALAMEIN onwards, by the Eighth Army, and he has never failed to take its advice. This time he *has* failed to do so, and as a result, we are now having very great troubles.

I think we can very probably pull the thing out of the fire for him; but we have lost valuable time and the bad winter weather will soon be on us on the ADRIATIC side.

What happened, of course, was that in the discussions at AFHQ

[1] Clark's British Deputy Chief of Staff felt likewise: 'ANZIO was a complete nonsense from its inception. At an early date the Colonel G2 [Chief of Army Intelligence] discussed with me the estimate of the German build-up. . . . It was quite clear [from Ultra] that short of a miraculous panic by the Germans, the landing force would be bottled up very rapidly. . . . We put this point forward strongly and repeatedly' – letter from General Sir Charles Richardson to author, 11.12.82.

ALEXANDER was 'seen off' by the other C's-in-C; he did not really know what *he* wanted so the others got what *they* wanted. He is not a strong man and gives way too easily.

In any future set-up the Prime Minister wants to be very careful as to the job given to ALEXANDER; he has definite limitations, and he has not got that sure and certain hand on the helm which indicates the true professional.

CHAPTER FIVE

The Sangro: a Sea of Mud

A 'true professional' was how Monty saw himself, having devoted a lifetime to the study and exercise of command.

What took place now, in 'Phase Three' of the Italian campaign, was very discouraging, for although Alexander accepted all Monty's suggestions, temporarily abandoning the madcap Anzio plan, and attempting belatedly to get more infantry reinforcements, it was, as Monty had feared, too late in the season to break through to the Rome line. 'My operations have been badly held up by rain,' he wrote to Brooke on 4 November;

> and the mud was so bad that movement off the roads was not possible for vehicles. I see the BBC announced the great 8th Army offensive on 25 October; but nothing took place then except a small enlargement of my bridgehead over the TRIGNO. I was preparing to attack strongly on 28 Oct, but the rain came and I could not. So I then had to pull back a bit as I was too overlooked; the BBC announced this as a German counter-attack; but there was no counter-attack.
>
> I often wonder where the BBC gets it all from. However it is probably very confusing for the enemy!!
>
> Meanwhile I was waiting for 48 hours fine weather on the coast axis. This was very successful and I got S. SALVO very quickly and operations are now proceeding to clear up all the northern end of the big lateral VASTO–ISERNIA. The enemy doesn't like this and is reacting violently,

he commented, though it was only a week later, in a letter to Major-General Simpson, the new Director of Military Operations at the War Office, that Monty explained how he had to intervene personally in the battle:

> All day on 3 Nov the issue hung in the balance. H.Q. 5 Corps is somewhat amateur according to our standards and we had not seen them in battle before; there was a lack of grip. Finally I intervened myself, threw in an armoured brigade, put some life

into it, and forced the battle to swing our way. The Germans had brought up tanks to counter-attack, and had been seen off; after dark these went into leaguer behind S. SALVO, presumably with a view to further offensive action on 4 Nov. Our plan was to advance by night to secure the high ground between S. SALVO and VASTO. The leading Bn walked – unawares – straight into the German armoured leaguer; a scene of complete military confusion followed and it is difficult to say which side was most alarmed – and astonished!! However the 6th R. West Kents (78 Div and a very good Bn) recovered first, drew back slightly, and opened heavy fire. This was too much for the Germans; they pulled right out and went back the other side of VASTO; they were followed up rapidly at dawn on 4 Nov, and during the next few days were pushed right back across the SANGRO River.

I have no doubt that the decisive feature in the battle was the night operation on 3/4 Nov. A bad Bn might have lost all cohesion after the confusion resulting from bumping into the German armour in the dark. The 6th R. West Kents, by remaining calm and holding firm, turned the scale at a critical moment.

And so by the 6th Nov the TRIGNO battle was won. And by 8th Nov my leading troops were up on the SANGRO, with O.P.s established, and with patrols across the river and tapping in on the main German positions on the high ground to the North.[1]

But could Eighth Army penetrate further? On 9 November 'the weather broke and heavy rain set in'. Not only did Eighth Army lack the promised 10 Corps, still in Clark's Fifth Army, but General Allfrey's performance as 5 Corps Commander from Taranto onwards had filled Monty with foreboding. To Brooke in mid-October Monty already remarked that he now had 5 Corps 'fighting in the line. I have not had Charles ALLFREY under me in battle before; he is not yet up to the standard of my other Corps Commanders; he is inclined to fiddle about with details, is very slow, and is inclined to bellyache.'[2]

Monty's plan was to launch his attack across the Sangro on 20 November. The winter weather made a flank attack through the mountains impossible; equally a frontal attack, with the roads so bad, was unlikely to succeed. Monty therefore opted for a coastal drive, using 78th Division and 8th Indian Division *encadrés* – passing Freyberg's newly arrived New Zealanders through the hole. If this could be achieved Freyberg could dominate the Pescara–Rome lateral, cutting German communications 'and all Divisions facing Fifth Army would have to withdraw or be cut off.'[3]

---

[1] Letter of 10.11.43, Montgomery Papers.
[2] Letter of 14.10.43, loc. cit.
[3] Diary entry of 6.11.43, Montgomery Papers.

Given this possibility Alexander ought perhaps to have switched all available weight to Eighth Army's offensive. Fear of counter-attack on Fifth Army's front[1] and timidity in overruling Clark caused Alexander, however, to do nothing. There was not a single infantry officer replacement for Eighth Army in Italy, Monty complained, yet he was still expected to go ahead with the Sangro attack. The position in fact was lamentable, with 'no platoon in 78 Div commanded by an officer,' Monty noted in his diary on 7 November.

If Clark could mount diversionary attacks and keep the Germans from reinforcing their Adriatic front, Monty felt there was a chance that Eighth Army might however break through, if the weather favoured them. When Monty wrote to Simpson on 10 November he was still hopeful: '2 NZ Div (directly under my command) will advance on the left rear of 8 Ind Div. . . . It will then turn left handed and operate on the axis POPOLI–AVEZZANO, and get in behind the German divisions facing 5 Army. These German divisions will either have to come out of it and retire hurriedly, or be cut off. In any case I hope to accompany the N.Z. Divisions into ROME!! It is a very powerful Division; 20,000 men and 170 tanks; it will take a bit of stopping. . . . When we have captured ROME I shall want some leave. I shall probably write a book entitled "ALAMEIN to ROME" – I don't think!'[2] To Sir Oliver Leese, commanding 30 Corps in England now, he wrote in the same confident terms:

Bernard Freyberg is with me and his outfit takes over a sector on the front on the SANGRO tomorrow; he will be directly under me. I am loosing him in a right hook on ROME in my next battle; he is terribly excited about it and is neighing like a horse. He is just like a child; at one moment he says the Germans are pulling out of Italy and the war is practically over; the next moment he says the whole operation is hazardous! I remember having heard that word before!!

The great thing is that he has 170 Sherman tanks in his Division; and so long as he has plenty of tanks he will do anything.

If, and when, he reaches ROME he will have no tanks left; that is all according to form!!

I shall move Tac Army with the NZ Div and enter ROME with them.

I shall then be exhausted and will want some leave. I shall probably write a book 'Alamein to ROME'!!![3]

---

[1] It was estimated that five German divisions were in line facing Fifth Army, with two armoured divisions in reserve. 'This is pretty strong,' Monty acknowledged in his diary on 6 November. 'He has only three divisions facing me.'
[2] Loc. cit.
[3] Copy of letter communicated by Mrs Frances Denby.

This letter was written on 12 November. The next day Monty was less confident. Allfrey's 5 Corps artillery chief had been 'captured by the Germans on 10 November. He was reconnoitring for artillery areas and was too far forward; his GSO 2 was with him. He had marked maps and certain papers with him. The German news today, 13 November, reports his capture and says: "It is clear from maps and documents on him that General MONTGOMERY attaches great importance to the deployment of artillery in the coast sector." There is nothing to be done. One must just hope that the measures we have taken to get surprise will in fact deceive the enemy.'

This capture was however, a depressing omen. Not only were the Germans now prepared for a coastal thrust, but the heavy rain, day after day, bogged down all preparatory movement for the battle; worse still, the rivers Sangro and Trigno began to rise alarmingly as the mountain rain swirled seawards. By 17 November the attack had to be postponed by twenty-four hours; if it had to be postponed further, Eighth Army would lose the advantage of the full moon and have to attack at dawn – 'this would involve a different technique, especially as regards dealing with minefields'.

Though he was confident of breaking through the German defensive line, Monty's hopes of Eighth Army taking Rome were now dwindling. As long as he could outflank the Rome line by reaching the Pescara river, however, he felt sure the Germans would withdraw in front of Clark's Fifth Army. To Brooke he explained the situation on 18 November:

I am preparing to deal the Germans a heavy blow on the Adriatic side. All I want is good weather. I have gone all out for surprise; and have concentrated such strength on my right flank that given fine weather, and dry ground underfoot, I will hit the Bosche a crack that will be heard all over Italy. I have lined up three divisions on my right: 78 DIV, 8 Ind DIV, 2 NZ DIV, with 400 tanks and the whole of my air power. . . . I have now to wait for fine weather. All my chaps are in tremendous form. If I can then get Freyberg's party to POPOLI and on to AVEZZANO, then Rome should fall to the 5th Army.

However even this was predicated on 5th Army co-operation.

I fear however that 5th Army is absolutely whacked. So long as you fight an army in combat teams and the big idea is that every combat team should 'combat' somebody all the time, then you don't get very far. My own observations lead me to the conclusion that Clark would be only too delighted to be given quiet advice as to how to fight his army; I think he is a very decent chap and most co-operative. If he received good and clear guidance he would do very well.

The failure to give Clark 'quiet advice' Monty laid at Alexander's door, as Army Group Commander; yet Monty had himself encouraged Clark, on their very first meeting at Salerno, to ignore Alexander – much as he had done when first meeting Patton during the Sicily campaign. As Clark remembered:

He [Monty] sent me a message 'When may I come and see you?' And I said back, 'Maybe tomorrow, if it's convenient to you.' And so Monty did. He came by boat – I remember I went out to the beach. We shook hands and he said, 'Congratulations for hanging on, and here's my map. Here's where I am.'

Alex was there. We had lunch out in the field, at a table, and we talked. And after lunch, and this is really interesting, we were just chinning there and talking about things, and I said we were going to capture Naples now, the road's open – I'd put my Rangers up to Malfi Drive, up on the hill. And Monty said: 'May I have a talk with you?'

I said, 'Yes, Sir.' And he said, 'Where can we talk?' – Alex was sitting there!

And I said, in my little van (they'd gotten it ashore). And so we went in there and sat on the bunk. 'Well' he said. 'Do you mind if I call you Mark?'

I said I'd be very pleased.

In fact Clark 'turned it loose', flattering Monty by saying what a great honour it was to have the Eighth Army fighting alongside Fifth Army.

And I said, 'As you know, my only battle experience was in World War One, and I've never commanded anything – a Corps, but not in battle.' And I said, 'So there'll be times when I'll – if I need to call on you for advice, may I do so?'

He said, 'I'd be delighted – feel free at *any* time, any time you want me, to call me.'

And then he said: 'How well do you know Alex?'

And I said, 'Well just a few days, since this thing's been announced. But what I've seen of him I like him very much.'

'Well,' he said, 'he's our common commander. . . .'

whereupon Monty surprised Clark by saying that from time to time Alexander would issue instructions 'that were not right, and that I should not hesitate to protest, and so forth. That really shocked me . . .' Clark recalled, as the meaning for the tête-à-tête suddenly became clear.[1]

Monty's contempt for Alexander as a military commander and tactician was one thing; that he should have deliberately and uncouthly sought to denigrate Alexander from the moment he met Clark at Salerno on 24 October was another. Even de Guingand, who felt Alexander's military direction since North Africa to have been 'vague' and indecisive, was shocked by the way Monty rode rough-shod over Alexander during this period of the Italian campaign.

'Orders to 8th Army were very vague,' de Guingand told the American Official Historian after the war, pointing out that Eighth Army 'was never intended to get up to Salerno in time to support the American [sic] landings.' The subsequent mess was the result of a 'tactical plan so vague that administrative people had little basis for calculating needs'.[2] Thus when Alexander convened a 15th Army Group Conference on 8 November to decide on a new strategy for reaching Rome, Monty would brook no opposition to his planned Eighth Army out-flanking attack.

At meeting on 8 November, Alexander got up and gave his plan of how divisions should be shifted from 8th Army to support the attack of Fifth Army towards Rome. . . . Monty interrupted and said, 'Sit down; I'll show you how to do it.' Then he sketched plan of pushing up to Pescara then across to Avezzano where he could threaten Rome and, he added, take it if necessary. De G. says Alexander was a student at the Staff College where Monty was instructor and that he never got over that relationship. Always deferred to Monty's tactical judgement.[3]

De Guingand felt that 'there was no future' in the Adriatic drive, given the poor road network and the easily defensible river-lines; instead he felt Eighth Army 'should have given up forces to support Fifth Army',[4] as Monty had insisted in the final offensive in Tunisia.

Monty had, however, no confidence that Clark could engineer a frontal breakthrough on Fifth Army's front, even if reinforced by Eighth Army formations. As he pointed out to Brooke, Fifth Army was 'whacked'; amphibious outflanking assaults could not be mounted in sufficient strength to be worthwhile; therefore Eighth Army's Adriatic thrust was the only hope of breaching the German defensive line and securing Rome by the end of the year – if the weather allowed.

'Given fine weather, nothing can stop us,' Monty commented on

[1] General Mark Clark, loc. cit.
[2] Interview of 31.3.47 by G. A. Harrison, in OCMH Collection, loc. cit.
[3] Ibid.
[4] Ibid.

the situation in his diary. Two Eighth Army divisions were attacking a poorly defended sector held by only three German companies; behind these was a tired German Panzer Division with only 15 tanks.

I have in all 400 tanks.
I have a very powerful air effort.
All I want is fine weather.

Without fine weather, Monty acknowledged though, he was sunk. 'I *must have* fine weather. If it rains continuously I am done.' Though he prayed each night, it was to no avail:

18 November
Very wet night
19 November
Fine day.
20 November
Very heavy rain began at 0500 hours, and went on all the morning. This has thrown everything out of gear. I have put back 'D' day for operation 'ENCROACH' to 23 November.

Vainly he tried to modify his plan, to dispense with surprise and try to sneak enough light forces, under heavy artillery cover, to secure the high ground dominating the Sangro on the far side. This was already done on the night of 19 November, but despite Monty's insistence that Allfrey 'stiffen up the forward companies across the river', they were thrown back on the left flank the next day. 'I discovered that no gunner F[orward] O[bservation] O[fficer] was with his company, or with any of the other companies over the river. I spoke very severely to the Corps Commander on that subject; I am informed that this is now in hand and that gunner F.O.O.s are across the river,' he recorded in his diary. But on 21 November, with heavy rain suspending all activity from the Desert Air Force airfields, the right flank company of Evelegh's 78th Division was thrown back across the Sangro. 'On enquiring I ascertained that there was no gunner F.O.O. with this company. This made me very angry. I had been assured by the Corps Commander, BGS of the Corps, Div Commander, G1 [GSO 1] of 78 Div, that each coy had a F.O.O. . . . I sent for ALLFREY, GOC 5 Corps, and told him that his Corps was completely amateur according to Eighth Army standards; there was a lack of "grip" and "bite", and things must change at once.' Five battalions were to be put across the river that night, and three Bailey bridges to be constructed. Anti-tank guns were to be got over, as well as tanks, one by one, even in daylight. This was done, and by dawn on 22 November one Bailey bridge was ready, and the two others almost completed. 'A fine day,' Monty recorded hopefully. 'I believe we are at last in for a fine spell.' But he was wrong.

23 November
Heavy rain all day. The SANGRO valley is completely waterlogged, and for the moment offensive operations are at a standstill.

Already Monty had begun to revise his expectations. Instead of the New Zealanders racing up to the Pescara line, the high ground overlooking the Sangro would have to be secured and held while Eighth Army bridged the river properly and ensured that the forward units could be adequately maintained. 'A breakthrough attack by a complete Division, supported by 200 tanks, was clearly not possible unless we got dry weather; we do not seem to be able to get dry weather; therefore we must employ methods which can be used in wet conditions and which are independent of tanks.' Yard by yard the bridgehead across the Sangro was extended until it was a mile and a half deep and seven miles wide. Then on 27 November the New Zealand Division crossed, and the dog-fight for possession of the high ground began in earnest. 'Tomorrow (28 Nov) I am attacking from the bridgehead with 78 DIV, 8 Ind DIV, centre (5 Corps), 2 NZ DIV, left (under Army HQ).' The fight to gain the bridgehead had been arduous, he acknowledged in a letter to the VCIGS, General Nye:

> In spite of continuous rain and acres of mud I managed to get a good bridgehead over the SANGRO; the trouble was to get any tanks and supporting weapons over, as the river was in flood and low level bridges merely disappeared. I took a good few risks.
> Twice I was pushed back to the river – once on my right, and once on my left. But we came again and refused to admit it couldn't be done.
> The troops were quite magnificent, and in the most foul conditions you can ever imagine; the SANGRO, normally is about 80 feet wide, and it became swollen to 300 feet and rose feet; the water was icy cold as heavy snow fell in the mountains where the river rises. Many were drowned.
> Eventually we succeeded.[1]

Further success, however, was to be measured in yards. Within days Monty was acknowledging:

> I am fighting a hell of a battle here. The right wing of my Army on the Adriatic side consists of three divisions. I am opposed there by

[1] Letter of 27.11.43, loc. cit.

439

3½ divisions; this, combined with the mud, makes it not too easy.

I am now going to move troops over to my right, from my left – i.e. I am sending 5 DIV over.

I don't think we can get any spectacular results so long as it goes on raining; the whole country becomes a sea of mud and nothing on wheels or tracks can move off the roads. Given fine dry weather we could really get a move on.

My total casualties in the SANGRO battle were 113 officers, 1650 Other Ranks – which was quite light considering what was achieved.[1]

By dawn on 1 December Eighth Army had captured a thousand German prisoners, and in a desperate attempt to stop Eighth Army breaking out, the Germans began to throw in units of 90th Light Division, reconstituted after its surrender to the New Zealand Division in May that year. 'We now had to smash our way forward to the PESCARA before the enemy could recover,' Monty noted in his diary, elated that he had apparently broken open the German winter line: the so-called Gustav Line. His satisfaction was short lived, however; not only did the Germans fiercely contest further movement forward by 5 Corps, but on 4 December the heavy rain caused the Sangro to rise 8 feet, and by the morning of 5 December 'all bridges over the river were under water and most washed away. All communications across the SANGRO were cut. There was nothing to be done except to put all the R.E. on to the job, and to stop all movement. It rained in the mountains for 18 hours without a break.'

Operations came to a standstill, and when on 7 December the New Zealanders tried to take Orsogna, insufficient supporting weapons could be brought up – 'finally our troops were withdrawn clear of the village to save casualties'. Reinforcing 5 Corps with a division from his mountain flank, Monty attempted to rekindle his breakthrough to the Pescara river. But on 10 December the rain again brought operations to a standstill, and Eighth Army was fortunate to reach both Orsogna and Ortona, across the river Moro. Three further German divisions had been put into the line, one from Clark's front, one from Genoa and one from Venice, and it was unlikely that a British breakthrough was now attainable. Nor was one likely on Clark's Fifth Army front, as Monty quickly perceived when he flew over to see Clark on 8 December. Indeed both Army Commanders discounted each other's chances of offensive success, Clark because he found 10 Corps so unwilling to take further casualties and assumed Eighth Army was the same, and Monty because he felt

[1] Undated original (possibly 7.12.43) in Alanbrooke Papers (14/21), Liddell Hart Centre for Military Archives, King's College, London.

Clark's piecemeal fighting 'gave the Germans ample time to re-group between the Fifth Army attacks'.[1]

What was clear was that time had run out, and the Allies had failed in their bid to reach Rome. Already on 18 November Monty had written to Simpson:

I have been thinking a great deal about the whole Italian campaign. I consider that we (the Allies) made a great many mistakes and have made a sad mess of it; if our strategy, and the conduct of the campaign, had been kept on a good wicket we would have had ROME by now easily. . . . If you make mistakes in war it is not easy to recover.[2]

To Mountbatten, on 14 November, he had written the same:

I have travelled some way with the Eighth Army since you were with me in Sicily . . . It has been difficult to find out what is wanted, and even where we are supposed to be going to, or what is the policy. Given some clear and firm directive, followed by a firm hand on the tiller which guides the military effort in these parts, we would have been in Rome by now. As it is, I think we may make it by the middle of December. . . . I understand Caesar used to go into winter quarters about this time, when he commanded an Army in these parts!! And very wise too!![3]

By 23 November he had begun to doubt his chances of reaching Rome in December, and begged Simpson to give him some idea of current War Office strategic thinking:

The great point that seems to want a firm decision is: where will we make our major effort from now on?
A. *Will you continue here?*
You have got a firm lodgement; good bases for the air; and so on. You will get no spectacular results here in the winter – nor will you anywhere. But you have got already secured a firm base from which to conduct operations. . . .
B. *Will you open up a front in Western Europe?*
You have to start in and get your lodgement, and your base on the continent. All this takes time. In the case of 'A' you have it already. Eventually I believe you must cross the Channel.
C. *Can you do both A and B?*
Personally I would say 'No'.

[1] Diary entry of 8.12.43, Montgomery Papers.
[2] Montgomery Papers.
[3] Ibid.

D. *If it is to be 'B':*
Then I consider that you must *at once* begin to prepare the instrument or weapon, and get the plan properly shaped.
That means you must transfer from here some good chaps who really understand the business. . . .
So there you have it quite simply.[1]

As he explained to Simpson a few days later, Italy should be held as a dormant front for the rest of the winter, with a drive to secure the Po valley in the spring of 1944, thus drawing away German strength from France, and providing an alternative front to reinforce in the case that 'Overlord' proved less than one hundred per cent successful. But the state of the Army in England worried him still, as it had that summer:

We must get the Army in England in good shape, and tee-up the cross-Channel venture so that it could be launched when the moment is opportune.
I am not certain from what I hear that the Army in England *is* in good shape. Some fresh air seems to be needed. And a good deal of dead wood needs to be cut out, and the whole show made younger, and more virile. . . .
I have no doubt you will decide all these things in due course!![2]

In similar vein he wrote the next day to Leese:

To make it [the Second Front] a success, you want really good commanders and staffs at the top, and especially do you want a high class 'Q' set-up and a high class movement and S.D. [Staff Duties] branch, ferry control, and so on. I do not believe myself that 21 Army Group, or 2nd Army, know anything about it. Anderson [Commander of 2nd Army in England] is not high class. Every First Army formation [i.e. having fought under Anderson in Tunisia] that comes to me is amateur compared to our standards. Charles Allfrey and 5 Corps H.Q. are very amateur; they have never been properly taught and I have to watch over everything they do. 78 Div is good, in the 'frigging about' battle; but when you get down to a solid dog-fight like we are having now, then they are not so hot. It would be interesting to hear your private views of 21 Army Group, Second Army, and the set-up in England generally. Eventually we must go across the channel, and the 'weapon' in England wants to be prepared. Can the present chaps do this?[3]

[1] Ibid.
[2] Ibid., letter of 27.11.43.
[3] Letter copy communicated by Mrs Frances Denby.

The need for a more concerted Allied policy had meanwhile become apparent to Churchill in October, and after numerous exchanges of telegrams a summit meeting in Tehran had been agreed for late November, with a preliminary Anglo-American military conference in Cairo.

I am told that Mr BULLFINCH is frigging about in North Africa,

Monty had written to Simpson on 18 November, referring to the Prime Minister,

and is coming this way to Italy – possibly tomorrow. I understand he wants to see me. I have said I cannot have him up here; everyone is far too busy, and my Tac HQ is so far forward it would not be safe for him. If he wants to see me I shall have to go back by air to Army Group.

Churchill's 'indictment of our mismanagement of operations in the Mediterranean during the two months which had passed since our victory at Salerno',[1] penned during his voyage through the Mediterranean, owed much to Monty's private letters to him. Churchill regarded 'our combined operations from the beginning of the Battle of Alamein to the end of the battle of Naples . . . as an extremely well-managed and prosperous affair', on the whole. 'However since then there has been a change. We have been overtaken and in a sense outrun by our own successes. . . .'[2]

Like Monty, Churchill blamed the current failure in Italy on the fact that the 'tap' had been turned off too soon in the Mediterranean – vital troops and landing craft being withdrawn at Marshall's insistence before the Allies had secured the Rome line. 'Thus the whole campaign on land has flagged. There is no prospect of Rome being taken in 1943. . . .'[3]

It is easy to see how, far from taking the American view that the campaign had flagged owing to the inability of the Allies to seize boldly their chances of cheap victories – as in 'Giant II' – Churchill seemed to have accepted Monty's more professional version of events. Yet even this conjunction of views concealed a fundamental divide between the Prime Minister and his victorious Eighth Army Commander, for with his restless imagination Churchill still dreamed of 'making amphibious scoops along either coast' of Italy,[4] and made no reference in his Cairo conference indictment to his own disastrous failure over Cos and Leros – the kind of dispersal of effort

[1] W. S. Churchill, *Closing the Ring*, London 1952.
[2] Ibid.
[3] Ibid.
[4] Ibid.

and concentration that Monty, as a 'true professional', most abhorred. 'And then that frightful party in COS. Why we start frigging about in the Dodecanese, and dispersing our efforts, beats me,' Monty remarked to Simpson. 'I shall ask Mr BULLFINCH!!!'[1]

[1] Letter of 18.11.43, Montgomery Papers. 'It has puzzled me for a long time as to why we want to start "frigging about" in the Dodecanese. The party has ended in the only way it could end – complete failure' – letter to Sir Alan Brooke, 18.11.43. On 14 September 1943 British forces had been landed on Cos and Leros. Cos was retaken by the Germans on 4 October 1943 and Leros on 16 November 1943.

CHAPTER SIX

'Who will Command "Overlord"?'

The days went by, but Churchill did not appear in Italy. By 27 November Monty was writing: 'No "great ones" have appeared here. I fancy they have moved east. Exactly what they are discussing I don't know. But I imagine they are trying to push Turkey in to the war; and also trying to decide how to win the war. Both are difficult jobs!!'[1] On 4 December, having heard a little of the discussions at Cairo and Tehran, Monty commented to Simpson: 'The "great ones", having decided how they will win the war, will now presumably re-group the generals to get on with it. I suppose they know the real and true form; I often wonder if they really do; if they make mistakes, and get the generals in the wrong places, we will have endless trouble.'[2]

Ironically this was the matter which Stalin had raised, on 29 November, in Tehran – 'who will command "Overlord"?'[3] Churchill, stunned by such a direct question, faltered. Roosevelt explained there was no commander, and Churchill offered to hold a meeting of the *three* heads of Governments (i.e. Russians, Americans and British) to choose one, an idiocy Stalin promptly crushed by saying the Russians merely wished to know who the commander would be.

Like Stalin, Monty realised the urgency of appointing an 'Overlord' commander if it was seriously intended to mount 'Overlord', rather than allowing the preparations to drift on under the direction of a staff officer who had not properly fought in the war so far – Lt-General F. E. Morgan. Churchill promised Stalin that a commander would be appointed within a fortnight, and tension began to mount in the various Allied headquarters as to who would be chosen.

Already in early October, Eisenhower had heard from the American Secretary of the Navy that Marshall 'had been named supreme commander' and it was 'probable' that Ike would be recalled to

[1] Letter to General Simpson, loc. cit.
[2] Loc. cit.
[3] W. S. Churchill, op. cit.

Washington to succeed Marshall as Chief of Staff of the US Army[1] – for supreme command in the Mediterranean was, as a *quid pro quo* for the Overlord appointment, to be given to a British general. For weeks Eisenhower anxiously 'sweated it out', waiting for the return of Bedell Smith, whom he had sent to Washington partly to 'find the lay of the land'. Reluctant to see Alexander 'inherit his mantle', Eisenhower plotted to 'make Tedder the Allied Commander, thus promoting Spaatz to Air C-in-C and leave Alexander as the ground commander' in the Mediterranean. 'On the American side he would make General Wayne Clark the Theatre Commander and Deputy to Tedder. Patton would take over the 5th Army. . . .'[2] There was no mention of Montgomery.

Meanwhile in Washington, Roosevelt not only went cool on the idea of Marshall leaving for Europe, but was advised by incompetents that Allied bombing of Germany, added to the success of the Russians in the east, meant that the cross-Channel attack might never actually need to be mounted. 'Transfer of General Marshall from his present high position to this command might therefore be anti-climactic,' Bedell Smith reported on 21 October.[3]

Pressure for the appointment of the 'Overlord' commander had therefore waned, until stalemate in Italy and the looming conferences at Cairo and Tehran rekindled the fire. Roosevelt pressed for a dual Supreme Commander, responsible for both the cross-Channel invasion *and* the Mediterranean, but Churchill torpedoed this. Churchill had told Bedell Smith at Algiers that Marshall was still 'certain' to be Supreme Commander for 'Overlord' – if the Americans insisted upon a cross-Channel attack. For, according to Bedell Smith, 'the PM and the British are still unconvinced as to the wisdom of OVERLORD – the cross-Channel operation – and are persistent in their desire to pursue our advantages in the Mediterranean, especially through the Balkans.'[4]

American faith in 'Overlord', as well as Stalin's instinctive fear of a British-sponsored break-through in the Balkans, forced Churchill's hand, and once again the question of 'Overlord' command began to vex the various headquarters. When Eisenhower returned from Cairo on 1 December, it looked as though Marshall would be the Supreme Commander,[5] with Brooke as the Allied invasion commander. Eisenhower was slated to go to Washington to succeed Mar-

---

[1] Diary of Harry C. Butcher, 5.10.43, loc. cit.
[2] Ibid., entry of 19.10.43.
[3] Ibid., entry of 28.10.43.
[4] Ibid., entry of 17.11.43.
[5] On 6 December Eisenhower rephrased this: Marshall might be temporarily seconded to Europe as the Executive of the Combined Chiefs of Staff until the invasion was successful.

shall, and by 5 December he was 'practically resigned to his prospective assignment'.[1]

Although Eisenhower had only once visited his Eighth Army Commander during the entire Italian campaign, he still dreamed of himself as a field commander, and detested the idea of going to Washington. He was thus astonished and yet delighted when a cable from Marshall arrived on 10 December in Algiers, indicating that 'Ike is to be Supreme Commander of the Allied Expeditionary Force in England after all'. According to Roosevelt, who passed through Tunis later that day, 'Ike's battlefront knowledge' was the main reason for the appointment, as well as his 'demonstration of his grasp of the military situation' when summoned by Roosevelt to Cairo.[2]

Monty, commanding Eighth Army in the mud and rain in the mountains above the river Moro, tried to maintain a brave front. The glorious Mediterranean summer, when he could flit about in his armada of launches and DUKWs, had given way to cold nights necessitating 'six blankets'. 'This Adriatic coast is terribly cold and damp in the winter and sometimes I long for the warmth of the summer in the desert, or even in Sicily,' he had written to Phyllis Reynolds on 11 November. 'I have gone into thick winter vests, and a battledress, and have put away all my summer and hot weather kit. I have got an Indian tailor working in a tent outside, making alterations to my new battledress suits; he can speak no English and I have had to summon my Urdu to my help.' By 17 November he was describing his surroundings as 'a complete quagmire . . . I found that one of my caravans leaked very badly. . . . They are really meant for use in desert country. . . . This is the one I captured from Field-Marshal Messe, the Italian who surrendered to me in Tunisia. Curiously enough he is now back in Italy; he was released in England when Italy left the war against us, and has been sent back here as Minister of War in the Badoglio Government. It would be rather amusing if he asked for his caravan back. I must say he would *not* get it!!'[3]

As if to ward off his frustration at the lack of proper leadership displayed by his superiors Eisenhower and Alexander, Monty had increased his menagerie, to the annoyance of his personal staff who had to feed, clean and arrange transport for the fauna. No sooner had they conspired to rid themselves of Monty's peacock than 'Master' bought more budgerigars for his collection – 'I have had a large cage made and put all the canaries and love birds in to it; they all live together quite happily and there is no bickering. . . . The general

[1] Diary of Harry C. Butcher, loc. cit.
[2] Ibid., entry of 10.12.43.
[3] Letter to Phyllis Reynolds, loc. cit.

effect is very decorative.' To the pheasants which had survived the displeasure of the ADCs were added, in mid-November, a less decorative animal. 'We now have a young pig in our mess farmyard; it runs about the mess just like a dog,'[1] he remarked with amusement.

Birds and farmyard animals were not the only source of mirth; as in the desert Monty found the company of his young entourage at Tactical Headquarters both stimulating and a captive audience when, as an almost patriarchal figure, he wished to deliver judgement on some subject. Major 'Dick' Vernon had been in charge of Tactical Headquarters during the Sicilian campaign and the first months of the Italian campaign; when he asked to return to regimental duty Monty asked for Major 'Bill' Mather, who had also served with him in the desert:

We had this sort of Tactical Headquarters overlooking the Sangro and it was a very simple Tac headquarters – just tents and the two caravans and the ACV [Armoured Command Vehicle],

Sir William Mather later recalled.

And one day an Australian fighter pilot was shot down quite near us. Monty saw a parachute going down, so he said, 'Send somebody out, bring him back to lunch.' So the platoon commander was duly sent off in a Scout car to fetch this chap and bring him back to lunch.

Now Monty had decided to rewrite the Principles of War – at least to introduce his new principle of war, the first and great principle of war, which was: Win the air battle first. And he was very proud of this and kept telling everybody, 'You know the first principle of war? Win the air battle first!'

About halfway through lunch he turned to this Australian and said, 'Now, do you know what the first and greatest Principle of War is?'

'Well, I don't know much about principles of war, but I should say it's stop frigging about!'

Monty was absolutely speechless.[2]

What 'impressed me most about Monty', Mather reflected almost forty years later,

was that – I'm not pretending to be particularly intelligent or to have a particularly good memory, but when I was running his Tac

[1] Ibid.
[2] Sir William Mather, interview of 3.1.80.

448

Headquarters he would call me into the caravan before breakfast and tell me what he was going to do that day, what his orders were to Main Army, and then leave it to me to go and ring up Freddie de Guingand and tell him exactly what was required, whatever it happened to be. Normally speaking I'd have to take notes, jot it all down, worry about whether I was getting it all right. But with Monty I didn't bother to write notes, I could go and have my breakfast and ring them up afterwards. I'd know I'd have it absolutely pat, because he made it so clear!

And he had this complete confidence in you, in your getting it right, that he gave *you* confidence, so that you got it right too.[1]

Monty's letters to colleagues at the War Office, full of self-confidence, constructive suggestions and wry if somewhat school-boyish humour, were considered a tonic in the bleak corridors of military power. 'I wish I could visit you again soon,' the Secretary of State for War, Sir James Grigg, wrote in October. 'Much better the sirocco with the Eighth Army than the miasma of indecision in Whitehall.'[2] Indeed Monty's very jauntiness became infectious – as when, in response to Monty's request for 'a mackintosh suit – the sort of thing you get at Cording's: trousers and a short coat',[3] the VCIGS, General Nye, procured the articles, despatched them via the Bishop of Southwark, and sent a special signal to the Eighth Army commander 'to be read as verse':

We've despatched, pour la guerre
A mackintosh pair
Of trousers and jacket, express;
They are coming by air
And are sent to you care
Of the Bishop of Southwark, no less.

So wherever you go
From Pescara to Po,
Through mud and morasses and ditches,
You undoubtedly ought
To be braced by the thought
That the Church has laid hands on your breeches.

We think they'll suffice
(As they should at the price)
To cover your flanks in the mêlée,

[1] Ibid.
[2] Handwritten letter, Montgomery Papers.
[3] Letter to Sir Alan Brooke, 18.11.43, loc. cit.

And avert the malaise
(In the Premier's phrase)
Of a chill in the soft underbelly.

According to Moss
(The outfitting Bros.)
T'wont matter, so stout is their fibre,
If you happen to trip
And go arse over tip,
Like Horatius, into the Tiber.

And you'll find – so we hope
When you call on the Pope,
That his blessing's more readily given
On learning the news
That your mackintosh trews
Were brought down by a Bishop from Heaven.

Moreover Monty remained as watchful over the health and welfare of his men as ever. When Brooke recalled Leese to England at Monty's request, Monty remarked: 'Am sending Leese home on leave at once. It will be a good thing for him to have a rest before other matters develop. He has been fighting continuously since Alamein, except for the short interval between the end of the war in Africa and the beginning of HUSKY – and that interval was very hard work in planning HUSKY. He began to get irritable with his staff and difficult with them after Sicily was over and I sent him off for a few days holiday in Syria. You would not think it, but he is of a nervous disposition and temperament and there have been times when his staff have found him very difficult. This continuous fighting is a great strain for a Corps Commander who has of necessity to deal with certain things in considerable detail and thus to have a firm grip on the tactical battle. A good rest of 2 to 3 weeks will put him quite O.K. He is a very valuable officer and has done splendidly as a Corps Cmd in my Army – he is easily the best I have.'[1] 'My sick rate *throughout the whole army* is just over 2 per thousand per day, which is good,' he noted in a letter to Brooke on 4 November; after the battle for the Trigno, however, he insisted that 78th Division would need proper rest:

78 Div is very tired and must be rested. The Division has had 10,000 casualties since it landed in Tunisia in Nov 1942 – one year ago. It has had 2,000 casualties in Italy; it landed here and went into battle on the 1st October. Of these 2,000 casualties, over 700 (or about

[1] Postscript to letter to Brooke of 29.9.43, loc. cit.

450

40%) are 'missing'. This is a very high percentage, and far higher than I have ever known before; I fear it means that the division is weary and requires rest and training in order to build up the broken teams; bad leadership is causing undue prisoners.[1]

This concern with casualties and morale was relentless, as his erstwhile Canadian ADC, Major Warren, discovered while serving with the 1st Canadian Division in the bitter fighting in the Italian mountains across the river Moro in December:
'We were having a terrible time,' Warren recalled –

guys were just getting slaughtered. I was G[SO]2 of the division and Monty sent for me. After tea he asked me point-blank, 'What's going on up there?'
I said, 'Sir, you can't ask me that!'
He said, 'Well, look at the casualty lists – what's going on? What's your divisional commander doing?'
'Sir – you can't do that to me now!'
He apologised – but added, 'I'll find out.'[2]

But what of Monty's *own* health? Brooke, when he finally visited Monty on the way back from Cairo on 14 December, found Monty 'looking tired and definitely wants a rest and a change'.[3]
Was he to get it, though? Brooke returned to Tunis where Churchill was in bed with suspected pneumonia, and for some considerable time they discussed the new appointments, exchanging telegrams with the Deputy Prime Minister Clement Attlee and the War Cabinet in London.
Meanwhile Eisenhower had written on 17 December to Marshall that he would like a 'single ground force commander. If the British could give him to me, I would like to have Alexander. My conception of his job would be that his eventual assignment would be in command of the British Army Group but that until the time for employment of two complete army groups arrived, he would be my single ground commander. Under him a British Army and an American Army will carry out the direct assaults and will expand as rapidly as possible.'[4]
Before Brooke or Churchill had time to tell Eisenhower of their decision about who should be the 'single ground force commander', Eisenhower left for his second visit to Monty's Italian front in four long months.

[1] Letter to Lt-General Sir Archibald Nye, VCIGS, 18.11.43, loc. cit.
[2] Lt-Colonel Trumbull Warren, interview of 9.11.81.
[3] A. Bryant, op. cit.
[4] *The Papers of Dwight David Eisenhower*, op. cit.

21 December

General EISENHOWER and his Chief of Staff, Maj-Gen. BEDEL SMITH, visited me. He has been appointed Supreme Commander to the Western Europe Command. Further appointments consequent on this have not yet been decided. It seems that Jumbo WILSON, ALEXANDER, and myself, are the three who are in the pool for three appointments:

    (a) Supreme C-in-C Mediterranean Theatre
    (b) Army   C-in-C   ditto
    (c) Army   C-in-C Western Europe.

I hear privately that Jumbo WILSON's stock is rather high with the Prime Minister; possibly because between them they have a good deal to hide away about the COS and LEROS episodes!!

Monty noted in his diary.

I have an idea that Jumbo will get (a). What will be done about the other appointments is not known; Winston is in bed at TUNIS recovering from pneumonia and only he can decide the answer. Meanwhile vital time is passing.

Monty had definitely hoped that Eisenhower would put him out of his misery – 'we all thought we would hear the answer – but we didn't,' as de Guingand recalled.[1]

In this atmosphere of apprehension, Alex's chief personal aide, Bill Cunningham, decided to play a trick, as Monty's ADC Johnny Henderson laughingly remembered:

It was about ten days before Christmas that year, and Bill Cunningham and I were both saying, 'Well thank heaven, we'll go back to England' – sort of having a nice friendly sort of discussion about it. And after that, Bill Cunningham sent us a telegram, saying would we, would Monty like Alexander's caravans?

And so we swallowed this bait – hook, line and sinker! 'Bloody Hell – that means he's got the job and is going back', we said. 'Well, we'd better go in and ask Monty.'

So we said to Monty we'd had this telegram, asking would he like Alex's caravans. So he presumed that Alex was going back and he wasn't, like we did; and there was rather a sort of gloom in the camp. Two days went by and he'd heard nothing. And he said to Freddie [de Guingand]: 'I think you'd better go back to Alex and find out about taking over from him there.'

So Freddie got in an aeroplane, flew down to Alex's headquarters and said to Alex, 'Oh Monty wants to know, you know,

[1] F. W. de Guingand, *Operation Victory*, London 1947.

whether he's taking over from you here' – this was said to Alex!

And Alex said: 'I don't know anything about it, what are you talking about?'

And Freddie said: 'But you're going back, aren't you, to do the Normandy landing?'

Alex said, 'Not that I know of.' And so the telephone rang – well, when it was found out that it was just a joke, from Bill Cunningham to us, Alex absolutely split his sides! Thought it was so funny. And Monty was so relieved. . . ![1]

So anxious indeed was Monty to know the final decision that he had arranged a set of codes with 'Simbo' Simpson at the War Office – names of garden flowers each denoting a possible combination of appointments.

A year and four months had passed since the last round of musical chairs, when Churchill and Brooke sacked Auchinleck but chose the wrong man to take command of Eighth Army: Lt-General Gott. Would they once again mess up the crucial decision, Monty must have wondered.

On tenterhooks Monty concentrated on the task at hand, mopping up at Orsogna and Ortona after the bitter Sangro battle. 'Our casualties since the SANGRO battle began on 27/28 Nov have been as follows,' he noted in his diary, and entered the figures, amounting almost to 5,000 men. 8th Indian Division, in particular, had already lost so many troops and had so few reinforcements that it would have to be taken right out of line. There was no chance on earth of continuing to Rome before March at the earliest, he had told Brooke, but having gained the Sangro, Eighth Army must secure a strong defensive line through Orsogna and Ortona. If this could be done, operations could be closed down on Christmas Day, and thereafter for a full week. Eighth Army would then push on towards its next objective – Pescara.

But would Monty still be in command? 'Poppy' was the code-word for Alexander's departure as Army C-in-C to the Supreme Command in Western Europe; 'Daffodil' if Monty was chosen to command 21st Army Group in England, in the place of General Sir Bernard Paget.[2]

Before the telegram from Simpson could be despatched, however, a signal arrived from the CIGS, Sir Alan Brooke:

[1] J. R. Henderson, interview of 13.8.81.
[2] Under the COSSAC plan of 19 July 1943 the C-in-C 21st Army Group would be responsible for planning and mounting the cross-Channel invasion. Only on 30 November 1943 however did the War Office officially charge General Paget, Commander of 21st Army Group, as Joint Commander of the invasion, together with the C-in-C Allied Expeditionary Air Force, Air Marshal Leigh-Mallory. Their first formal meeting took place on 7 December, but rumour was rife and Paget knew in his heart that it was only a temporary appointment until Churchill, as Minister of Defence, made up his mind.

It has been decided you are to come back to U.K. to relieve PAGET in command 21 Army Group the date to be decided according military exigencies. This decision is subject however to governmental approval but there is NO reason to suppose this will NOT repeat NOT be forthcoming. This is for your personal information and is NOT repeat NOT to be disclosed to anyone else.

The date was 23 December 1943. The next day, Christmas Eve, confirmation was received. There was low cloud and heavy rain, making flying impossible. But Monty was over the moon.

'My dear Phyllis,' he wrote hurriedly to David's guardian,

I shall be home soon, as you may have guessed from the recent news. . . .
Do not write any more letters here, and cancel the sending of books from the Green Frog.
I am at present living in my caravans in a filthy wet and muddy field, and will be delighted to get back to England. . . .[1]

All that remained to do now was to decide who to take with him – and to say goodbye to the Army which had brought him such personal renown.

[1] 27.12.43, loc. cit.

CHAPTER SEVEN

Alexander: A Very Dear Person, but . . .

Eisenhower, when he heard the news of Monty's appointment, was chagrined. Why Monty? Eisenhower had never visited Monty at all during the Eighth Army campaign in Sicily, and only twice in all the months Monty had been fighting in Italy. He blamed Monty for the near-débâcle at Salerno, and felt Monty's reputation as a general in the field was much overrated. Alexander, by contrast, had served him loyally and uncritically, acting as a welcome buffer between Algiers and the bitter realities of the battlefield. Why then could he not take Alexander rather than Montgomery to Western Europe?

Monty's view was very different – indeed, given the mess in Italy, he had trembled at the thought of the catastrophe Eisenhower and Alexander might together make of 'Overlord'. Only hours before receiving Brooke's signal, Monty had written a letter to Mountbatten:

> I hope all goes well with you. You were I presume 'in' on the discussions at Cairo and Tehran. I presume the 'great ones' have now decided how to win the war, and I hope they will tell us what they want in clear and definite terms.
>
> Their next task will be to re-group the generals, admirals and air marshals, so that we can all get on with the business; but I see certain signs of hesitation here, and of lack of clear decision, which is a great pity as vital time is slipping away.
>
> The only firm thing is that Eisenhower is to be Supreme Commander in Western Europe. He will find a proper 'dog's breakfast' waiting for him in England,

Monty warned,

> and there will be a good deal of weeding out to be done; he and his party will not be popular and will be somewhat like a skunk at a kitten party!!
>
> We are on a very good wicket now and we have the winning of the war in our pocket – provided we play the cards properly. But if we

make mistakes, and don't put the right men in the right place, we shall merely prolong the whole business.

The Eisenhower-Alexander combination had been, in Monty's eyes, a complete failure.

I shall be interested in years to come to read the judgement of history on the campaign in Italy. We started brilliantly – after a very shaky planning period – and in three months we had:
(a) captured Sicily
(b) knocked Italy out of the war
(c) got the Italian fleet locked up in Malta
(d) captured the great port of Naples, the Foggia airfields, and one-third of Italy.
These were spectacular results.
My Army landed on the toe of Italy on 3 September and by 3 Dec we had fought our way over 700 miles of country.
It was vital to get the Rome line before the weather broke, and the winter rains set in; and it could easily have been done

he opined.

But to do so required a very firm grip of the campaign by 15 Army Group, and I fear it was lacking; there was no 'grip', no policy, no planning ahead; indecision, hesitation, ineffective command, led to a great waste of time, and we narrowly averted appalling administrative scandals.
An essential feature of high command is skilful grouping, and re-grouping as the situation changes; there was none of this. There was no imagination in the planning; the two armies just fought their way forward as they could. To do the job before the weather broke meant a firm grip, quick decision, and a clear directive; all this was conspicuous by its absence. The weather broke, and the winter rains descended on us.
Now we are faced with rain, low cloud, and mud. All this means that neither the Army nor the Air can operate properly; the whole tempo of offensive operations is cut down.
You cannot operate in Italy during the rains; the mud is quite frightful, and no vehicle – wheels or tracks – can move off the roads.
So there we are.
After a brilliant start, we rather fell off. And it could have been otherwise.
I have enjoyed the party myself, and am full of beans. I spoke my views in no uncertain voice at various times, but it was no use.
The lesson is obvious.
The high command entered on a major campaign in Europe

without a clear idea as to how they were going to fight the battle. There was no clear policy, or planning ahead; the whole thing was ad hoc. . . . So I am not terribly happy about the future. There will be a proper rough house in Overlord, and the military commander will have to know exactly what he is doing.

In such a rough house, Monty was certain that Eisenhower and Alexander would be utterly at sea. Though he had not mentioned Alexander by name in his letter to Mountbatten, and tried not to do so to Brooke or even Churchill (he had stopped sending copies of his private diary for this reason), he was quite clear where the fault in 15th Army Group lay. Already on 23 November, recognising that Rome was now out of the question as a 1943 objective, he had penned some 'Reflections on The Campaign in ITALY 1943'. In this he was brutally, cruelly frank.

'15 Army Group comes very badly out of the business,' he considered.

In my opinion 15 Army Group is a very bad and inefficient H.Q. I think the staff there works under great difficulties since they find it quite impossible to get any decision out of ALEXANDER, or any firm line of country on which to work. There is no proper planning or thinking ahead. ALEXANDER does not really know clearly what he wants; and he has very little idea as to how to operate the Armies in the field. When he has a conference of commanders, which is very seldom, it is a lamentable spectacle; he relies on ideas being produced which will give him a plan; he does not come to the conference with *his own* plan, and then give out clear orders. No one gets any orders, and we all do what we like.

The three people who are responsible for the conduct of the campaign are:

ALEXANDER – Army C-in-C
TEDDER   – Air C-in-C
CUNNINGHAM – Naval C-in-C

But these have, all the time, lived in separate places miles apart:

ALEXANDER in Sicily or ITALY
TEDDER in TUNIS
CUNNINGHAM in MALTA

When difficulties arise, and some quick decision is required, they start sending each other telegrams. The result is that we get no quick decision; and when a decision *is* finally given it is not one that will help in any way to win the battle – it is generally a compromise because no one will give way: they are all too far apart to discuss the problem and so reach a sensible answer.

One by one Monty went through Alexander's 'useless' staff officers, and the battle he had had to get 'Husky' launched properly.

'Luckily I did not lose my nerve and was able to maintain my balance and morale. My plan was carried out and we captured SICILY in 38 days. It was in fact a roaring success; but to this day I believe many people consider I behaved very badly over the whole thing; they little know the real trouble.

When ITALY was knocked out of the war everyone, including ALEXANDER, lost their heads. They all thought the Italians were going to be of great use to us; I told ALEXANDER at REGGIO on 5 September that the Italians were quite useless and must never be trusted to do anything that involved fighting. He did not really grasp it, and in the end we were badly let down.

Owing to lack of grip from above my invasion of the mainland of ITALY was delayed and did not begin till 3 September; it could have started on 30 Aug. This delay was to have serious repercussions later on. The sad point is that, if there had been firm handling from above, there need not have been delay at all. There was no attempt to co-ordinate my activities with those of the Fifth Army; in fact I was never intended to go further than the CATANZARO neck, and my resources were cut down accordingly. It was never intended that I should intervene in the SALERNO battle. What happened is now well known; the SALERNO landings very soon were in grave danger, and from our intelligence information it was always quite obvious that this was bound to be so.

I had to push on to try and help save a disaster; my resources were totally inadequate and I had grave administrative troubles in consequence. . . .

Small landings were suddenly made all over the HEEL by 15 Army Group. These got out of hand and I was begged to take them over at very short notice and get things sorted out. This increased my administrative troubles. . . .

A British Corps was put in an American Army on the NAPLES side (the 10th Corps). . . . The nett result of having 10 Corps in the Fifth US Army has been that proper grouping to meet a battle problem is not possible. The military effort available on the NAPLES side is very great; but it has never yet been properly applied – nor can it be.[1]

CLARK, commander of the The Fifth Army, is a very delightful person and very easy to work with. But he does not know a very great deal about commanding in the field; he has been a staff officer most of his service. He wants guidance and advice, and I am quite certain he would welcome this.

[1] General Clark appreciated this: 'The only thing we had in common was our language!' he later remarked. 'Different equipment, different customs – I didn't have the flexibility of moving even a battalion over here [denoting 6 US Corps area] – different ammunition, different food – different everything!' – loc. cit.

The Americans do not understand how to fight the Germans; they operate in regimental combat teams and the big idea is to have every combat team 'combatting'; you do not get very far this way. They do not understand the great principles of surprise and concentration.

The Army Group should take a firm grip of the operations of the Fifth Army, and get them on a proper basis. But then, ALEXANDER himself does not know much about how to operate an Army in the field.

Monty remarked.

After the SALERNO front had been saved, the two armies lined up side by side. We then moved North-West up ITALY; there was no co-ordination, no plan, no grip; I did what I liked, CLARK did what he liked. Finally we arrived at a situation on 17 Nov. when the Fifth Army was exhausted, and was incapable of further action.

I had to continue the battle alone, and this made it easier for the Germans.

15 Army Group definitely failed to grip the battle and to co-ordinate the action of the land armies.

It has always been untidy, and ad hoc. . . . The whole truth of the matter is that we entered on a major campaign in EUROPE without any clear plan as to how we would fight that campaign. Ad hoc plans were suddenly produced for various situations; there was no planning ahead, and no firm grip on the campaign after it had started.

ALEXANDER is a very great friend of mine, and I am very fond of him. But I am under no delusion whatsoever as to his ability to conduct large scale operations in the field; he knows nothing about it; he is not a strong commander and he is incapable of giving firm and clear decisions as to what he wants. In fact no one ever knows what he *does* want, least of all his own staff; in fact he does not know himself.

Was this unfair?

All through the Eighth Army campaign in AFRICA to TUNISIA

Monty went on,

ALEXANDER took no part whatever in making plans or deciding what was to be done. The whole thing was an Eighth Army affair and was handled by Eighth Army HQ.

Later, when the First and Eighth Armies joined up in TUNISIA, ALEXANDER had to handle the party. His first task was to restore

order out of the frightful mess which First Army had got into; he
should have sacked ANDERSON who was quite unfit to command
an Army in the field, but he got down to it himself and saved the
show.

It then became necessary to break through to TUNIS; his first
attempt to do this was quite dreadful and failed dismally. The next
and final plan was made in my caravan at Eighth Army HQ, and it
was carried out by an Eighth Army Corps Commander.

The whole truth of the matter is that ALEXANDER has got a
definitely limited brain and does not understand the business; the
use of air power in the land battle is a closed book to him.

Defensively he is good, and he will pull a bad situation out of the
fire,

Monty acknowledged. But was this the sort of man who should lead
the Allies in 'Overlord', an assault landing deemed so difficult by
Churchill, Brooke and the War Office that for a year and a half the
operation had been postponed, and still, in November 1943, had no
appointed commander?

He does not understand the offensive and mobile battle; he cannot
make up his mind and give quick decisions; he cannot snap out
clear and concise orders. He does not think and plan ahead; his
staff have a terrible time and can never get anything out of him.

He has never himself commanded an Army or a Corps in the
field. He loves battle schools and minor tactics. The higher art of
making war is beyond him.

And so ALEXANDER has acquired a false reputation as a great
commander in the field, and as a great strategist. This is very far
from the case; he is a very dear person, but he is definitely not a
commander in the field on a high level – nor does he understand
the higher conduct of war.[1]

Not even Alexander's biographer would dispute such a judgement
of Alexander as a military commander at this period. 'I found when
writing my book that I liked Alex more, but admired him less, when
I'd finished it,' Nigel Nicolson later reflected.

I started off with great admiration for his performance as a soldier.
And then as I went into it, particularly after the period when he
became C-in-C Middle East, from Alamein onwards, I found that
he, well that he lacked genius. . . .

He was associated with success. But I don't think his conduct of
the African campaign was more than an administrative job – it

[1] Montgomery Papers.

wasn't a true general's job. He was sort of quartermaster in a way, right up until the armies met in Tunis. . . .

I don't think the end in Tunisia was a very high performance – I mean a performance to go down in history as a great feat of generalship. And then Sicily was mucked up and I think that the early part of the Italian campaign was badly handled. . . .

I don't think he was a very clever man, Alex. I don't think he had great imagination. He had great courage but not much daring. You can never see in any of Alex's battles or campaigns something that makes you gasp with admiration. . . . You see how much he was, depended on advice and upon very, very brilliant subordinate generals who often disobeyed his orders, but brought it off! And Alex was wise enough not to reprimand them – I mean you can't reprimand a man for winning a battle, even though it wasn't a battle you'd planned! . . .

He was an English country gentleman, almost uneducated, who never read a book or had any interest in the arts at all, except for his painting – not other people's painting. But he had a particular charm and gift for making people like him; absolutely straight. And then added to that he had great courage – nobody could say Alex was a backstage general, a château general – he'd commanded everything there was to command and in the most desperate battles of the war, and he'd had Dunkirk, Burma, and this made people feel quite rightly, well this man's been through fire! And he knows what it's like to attack a crack German division and he's not going to make us do what he hasn't done himself.

All the same I don't think he was particularly compassionate. I asked John Harding, his Chief of Staff in Italy, about that. I said, 'Did Alex have compassion, did he mind his friends being killed, let alone his soldiers?'

And Harding said, 'No, not really. He'd say, oh, that's hard luck on so-and-so. And he thought of, you know, massacres of several thousand men in battle, he would think, well, now we've lost 6,000, how's that going to affect our next operation?'

He had no philosophy, you see. He had no politics. He wasn't interested in the causes of war, or the cause of that particular war in which he was fighting. He rather liked the Germans, rather admired the Germans. And therefore didn't feel we've got to win this war or this battle because we're fighting evil – which Winston kept saying. He said, we're going to win this battle because it's our job, and it'll be rather exciting if and when we succeed. We'll leap forward another ten miles and capture another famous city – he was very much affected by the drama of war. He did see it as very romantic.[1]

[1] Nigel Nicolson, interview of 22.1.81.

Churchill's admiration for Alexander Nicolson interpreted partly as genuine 'personal affection' and partly as a perception of Alexander's 'romanticism, his love of war, which Churchill shared'.

He was good in conversation, couldn't put it in writing but could talk well – and with this ineffable charm which everybody who ever came into contact with Alex felt – I did myself. . . . By no means a clever or brilliant man, he had this capacity to sway people to be able to trust him, like him. And Churchill was the victim of this himself – Churchill realised that in contrast to Monty Alex had a supreme gift for getting on with Allies which was becoming more and more important because we were getting more and more Allies! It was very important to have a diplomatist in that situation – not a Napoleonic figure. And Alex filled this role to perfection.[1]

It was not therefore surprising that Eisenhower had personally requested Alexander to command the 'Overlord' armies; nor that Churchill was initially undecided whether to choose Alexander or Monty – telegraphing the Deputy Prime Minister on 14 December that he had 'not made up my mind whether it will be Alexander or Montgomery but the CIGS is staying with Alexander now and when he rejoins me in a few days I shall be able to make a decision.'[2] Brooke, like Churchill, was initially in two minds. Time after time he had chronicled in his diary his misgivings about Alexander. 'Alexander, charming as he is, fills me with gloom,' he had noted on 18 November 1943. 'He cannot see big . . . he will never have either the personality or the vision to command three services.' Nevertheless he did not rule out Alexander as the appropriate field commander for 'Overlord', and on the eve of his visit to Italy, on 11 December, had noted that, as regarded the selection of Montgomery or Alexander, 'I don't mind much.'[3]

At this point the Secretary of State for War, Sir James Grigg, replied to Churchill's cable that the War Cabinet, alarmed by the choice of Eisenhower instead of the tough, no-nonsense Marshall, were 'disposed to think Montgomery would be a better choice than Alexander for "Overlord" '. Churchill's pneumonia had made him less wilful, and Brooke had little difficulty in finally proposing Monty for 'Overlord'. Monty, as has been seen, was immensely and righteously relieved. 'ALEXANDER is, actually, being passed over by Jumbo [Wilson],' he commented in his diary – for not only had Alexander been turned down for 'Overlord', but it was General Wilson who had

[1] Ibid.
[2] Prime Minister's Papers (PREM 3,336/1)PRO.
[3] Brooke Diary, Alanbrooke Papers, loc. cit.

been chosen to succeed Eisenhower as Supreme Commander in the Mediterranean and not Alexander, who remained simply C-in-C 15th Army Group.

But was Churchill's acquiescence over the choice of Montgomery for 'Overlord' an admission of Monty's greater military merit – or did Churchill, defeated by Stalin and Roosevelt at Tehran, secretly harbour visions concerning the development of the Italian campaign which Monty would stamp upon, but which Alexander could be relied upon to undertake? Brooke, having got agreement over the appointments, had departed on the night of 19/20 December to London. Churchill, by contrast, was to fly to Marrakesh to recuperate; but first, in the warm, dry winter sunshine in Tunis, as the men of the Fifth and Eighth Armies battled in the mud of rain-drenched Italy, Churchill resurrected his latest 'Dardanelles' scheme – a landing behind the German lines at Anzio: Operation 'Shingle'.

CHAPTER EIGHT

Leaving Eighth Army

If Churchill still dreamed of a great and metaphorical scoop upon the Italian coast, Monty himself was delighted to get away from such delusions. 'This is a very fine job,' he remarked of the new 'Overlord' appointment in his diary, 'and it will be about the biggest thing I have ever had to handle.' Indeed he was quite certain that 'Overlord' would be the deciding battle of the war – and exhilarated that he had been chosen to command it.

Ever since his trip to England in May 1943 Monty had fretted about the 'army at home' and the need to get it into shape for an eventual cross-Channel assault. The first thing he wished to make sure, then, was that everyone understood clearly that he, General Montgomery, was going to take sole command of the landings. There would be no infirmity of purpose, no absence of clear orders, no rudderless drifting as had been the case in Italy – he, Monty, would see to that.

On 27 December Monty arrived in Algiers to speak to Eisenhower. The idea of British and American army groups, currently the subject of much discussion between Eisenhower and Marshall, was scrapped. The next day Monty explained to Brooke both the decisions taken, and his own further suggestions:

secret & personal

23.12.43. Algiers

My dear Brookie
  I must thank you for promoting me to command the armies in England. It is a big job and I will do my best to prove worthy of your selection.
  There is a terrible lot to do and not too much time in which to do it. I have therefore asked you to let me have some of my team from 8th Army; this is a well-running show and there are plenty of very experienced chaps who can be stepped up.
  2. I am in Algiers discussing the problem with Eisenhower and Bedell Smith. Eisennower has told me that he wants me to be his head soldier and to take complete charge of the land battle.
      Initially there will be only one Allied GHQ and this HQ will conduct the war.

We will organise it in exactly the same way as we organise all our HQs in the field and we will use the same nomenclature.

Tac Allied HQ This will be my HQ from which I will fight the land battle. It will be small.

Main Allied H Eisenhower will be here with his Chief of Staff. This will be fairly large.

Rear Allied HQ may have to be thrown off later. There will initially be no army groups. From Tac HQ I will command the armies. Later, army groups may become necessary. The idea is that we should form this Allied GHQ from 21 Army Group and the American Army Group.

3. Bedell Smith takes this letter today. My Chief of Staff can get to London on 1st Jan.

They will have talks with Morgan and others and work out the organization. I have to go and spend a day with the P.M. I arrive at his place evening 31 Dec, stay there 1st Jan and shall be in England on 2 Jan. Eisenhower cannot get to England till about 10 or 12 Jan, but he has named me as his deputy and says I am to carry on till he comes. Immediately I arrive I will come and see you, and get your orders about taking over from Paget.

4. I suggest for your consideration that Second and Canadian Armies should be commanded by Leese and Dempsey respectively. The more I think of Harry Crerar the more I am convinced that he is quite unfit to command an army in the field at present. He has much to learn and he will have many shocks before he has learnt it properly. He has already (from Sicily) started to have rows with Canadian generals under me; he wants a lot of teaching; I taught him about training; Oliver Leese will now have to teach him the practical side of war.

From what I hear I believe the Canadians would gladly accept a British general whom they know and trust rather than have the troops mishandled by an inexperienced general of their own. Dempsey has served with them and they all know and like him. As soon as they can produce their own general, then he takes over at once; until that time, give the Canadian army to Dempsey.

5. I suggest that O'Connor[1] is the man to come out here and take over 8th Army. He had it before. He must have some leave, and then get up to date, and then come out here to relieve Oliver Leese.[2] Leese then returns to UK and takes the Second Army. What do you think of this?

6. If you do this, you get the two armies – Second British and

---

[1] General O'Connor had escaped to British lines in Italy in November 1943.

[2] Leese had, as a result of Monty's appointment, been appointed to succeed him as commander of Eighth Army in Italy.

465

First Canadian – led by two very experienced fighting generals who are completely up to date in every practical aspect of combined operations and you get a high class commander with 8th Army. Simonds should go to UK *now* to command the 2nd Canadian Corps. He is quite first class.

7. Replacements for all the officers I want to bring home can be produced quite easily. I have many excellent officers here who are well fitted for upgrading and who I have myself recommended. Alex agrees that everyone who is wanted from here for 'Overlord' must go at once.

8. I hope very much that the CAS will give us some simple air set-up which will fit in with the army set-up.

If there are no army groups, you do not want two tactical air forces.

Do you think you could ask Portal to bring Broadhurst home for the party; he has great knowledge of fighters and fighter-bombers and would be invaluable.

9. I believe 2 NZ Div under Freyberg would be better employed in Western Europe than Italy. It is a motorized division, highly trained in the mobile battle; its full capabilities cannot be properly exploited in Italy.

10. I hope you do not mind me putting forward the above. I feel it is best to write to you in advance my general ideas so you can think it out.

When I have handed over here I presume I should come home at once. I have had no orders re this; will you let me know. I could discuss the whole business further with you then.

Yrs ever
BLM

From Algiers Monty returned to his Tactical Headquarters in Italy on 28 December. He had already drawn up a list of officers he wished to take home with him, and had cabled it to the Military Secretary in London. On 30 December he convened all officers and men of his Main Eighth Army Headquarters in Vasto, together with Corps and divisional commanders, to say goodbye.

It was a moving occasion, and the tension was high. In August 1942 Monty had assembled, in the desert at Alamein, the headquarters staff of a beaten army – an army which had been run back seven hundred miles across North Africa and lost over 100,000 casualties in a bare six months. Now, eighteen months later, he was leaving an army that had victoriously traversed North Africa, conquered Sicily, and successfully secured southern Italy for the Allies, an army unbeaten in battle, an army whose reputation stood perhaps higher than any British army in the twentieth century, and the more remarkable in that it was, in December 1943, an army which contained only a single division that had served in the desert campaign.

Monty's quiet speech, outlining 'the things he considered important, and which guided his command', his appreciation of the current situation, his thanks for the support he had been given, and his appeal for similar support for General Leese who was to succeed him as Eighth Army Commander, was greeted by roaring applause. De Guingand wept and, watching Monty shake hands with his Corps and divisional commanders – Dempsey, Allfrey, Freyberg and others – thought of Napoleon and his marshals.

Was this an exaggerated comparison? Even the Official British Historian, not given to praise concerning Monty's battlefield tactics, considered that in gaining the loyalty and devotion of a largely citizen army, Monty had created a unique *persona* – military commander, father figure and representative – 'with an originality, insight, and skill that amounted to genius'. For Brigadier Molony, as for certain other historians, there was something essentially contrived about this persona. 'He studied intently his own appearance and bearing. His carefully unconventional uniform was designed to make a sharp visual impression of workmanlike plainness coupled with soldierly panache. . . .'[1]

Such historians could not understand that this persona had not been 'contrived', but had evolved, and in its eccentric, extraordinary way was real. Here *was* a military commander who thought ahead, who refused to commit his men to rash and ill-considered operations, who insisted on success not glory. Here *was* a father-figure, an infantry general who appreciated that his men were individuals, not numbers, and who sought to get them not only the best artillery, naval and air support he could, but to ensure that if wounded or sick or in need of spiritual comfort, they were well looked after. Here *was* their representative, a man prepared to fight for their welfare, for their right to return home after years of battle, and no other field commander so far produced by the Allies in the Second World War could match Montgomery in this. His casual dress had begun in the desert – where corduroy trousers, scarves and sweaters were *de rigueur* against the stinging sand and cold, dry nights. Like Stalin, he felt comfortable in such unofficial dress – and refused to modify it as his campaigns brought him nearer Europe. He was not, as Brigadier Molony claimed, skilful or even tactful with the press, who were handled by de Guingand and Keating. If he impressed war correspondents, it was by the very strangeness of the phenomenon; a general so simple, so boastful and yet at the same time utterly professional, not caring a fig for social class. His conceitedness irked even those most devoted to him, but was tolerated because, in a

[1] C. J. C. Molony, *The Mediterranean and the Middle East* Vol. V, London 1973.

world of muddle and confusion, his clarity of purpose and professional approach to the 'art of war' stood out like a beacon. So much so that when he left Eighth Army, as the commander of his Tac HQ put it, 'the whole atmosphere went flat – Oliver Leese who succeeded him felt it more than anyone else. He was furious – it was a calamitous situation.'[1]

Warwick Charlton, as Eighth Army's resident editor, also considered it a calamity. To him, Monty's uniqueness as a general had been the extraordinary freedom he had given his subordinates – a freedom which had led to questions being asked in the House of Commons, which had vexed outsiders, but which had led to a level of morale unmatched by any army in the world – morale based not only on professional military expertise, on 'killing ability', but on collective pride at belonging to an army in which the individual counted, and in which the principles of western democracy were reflected in the freedoms and concerns of the troops:

> I mean I remember when I went to join Mountbatten's staff the first thing, you know, Mountbatten produced my file, in the Botanical Gardens, and he said, 'I suppose, Charlton, you feel rather special, coming from Eighth Army?'
>
> I said, 'Yes, sir' – which I did.
>
> I must have been, truthfully, looking back – you *did* feel you were superior.
>
> Now that was a bad feeling, and you did get resentment. And Monty got the same resentment that we all got, down to the lowest soldier. That's what comes of achieving that type of morale.
>
> One of the things I felt, when I went back recently to look at the graves at Alamein, that was different about Monty as a general and as a human being, but particularly as a general, was that he really did see soldiers as individuals. You know, this thing about losing a battalion – it never occurred to him like that, he was always very conscious of casualties.
>
> And this thing about moving very slowly, being sure there were no setbacks. The individual was important, which was rare in a general because most generals can't afford that.
>
> What makes the great military leader – whether it's Alexander the Great, because his mother told him so, and people followed him because he transcended the natural, made things come right – but the great leaders have always managed to take what was happening at the time, the events, and to grasp men's minds and perhaps clarify their objectives. It's always been like that; and what Monty, who appears to be sometimes limited in his intellect and not very emotional – yet he did unleash all the things men really

[1] Sir William Mather, loc. cit.

wanted to do, to happen, to believe in and so forth. They would have followed him to any damned place! That is true, isn't it?

That's a rare thing, you know. It's not a rare thing to direct tanks or artillery or co-ordinate them or choose the right ground – there are good people who can do that. But to have this other quality, to my mind, is quite a rare phenomenon.[1]

Under Monty, Charlton had enjoyed 'this extraordinary protection, total protection, while he was there. And within a few weeks of his leaving it ceased.' The newspapers which had been furnished with Colonel Williams's Intelligence reports so that they would be completely 'in the know' in their battle reports, which had permitted free discussion of political issues, had printed the Beveridge Report on universal social security in Britain, debated openly the grievances of mining strikes at home, and begun to confront the issues of international political settlement at the end of the war as well as post-war reconstruction in Britain, were marshalled back into simple patriotic, non-contentious organs like *Stars and Stripes*.

It was Monty's unique achievement to harness the aspirations and talents of a largely citizen army, fighting on foreign shores, and imbue it with purpose, pride – and hope. And when, in his final Farewell Message to the men of Eighth Army, Monty declared that he was sad to leave, he was expressing no more than the truth:

It is difficult to express to you adequately what this parting means to me,

he wrote.

I am leaving officers and men who have been my comrades during months of hard and victorious fighting and whose courage and devotion to duty always filled me with admiration. I feel I have many friends among the soldiery of this great Army. I do not know if you will miss me; but I will miss you more than I can say, and especially will I miss the personal contacts, and the cheerful greetings we exchanged together when we passed each other on the road. . . . What can I say to you as I go away?

When the heart is full it is not easy to speak. But I would say this to you:

You have made this Army what it is. You have made its name a household word all over the world. Therefore you must uphold its good name and its traditions.[2]

[1] Warwick Charlton, interview of 31.3.83.
[2] Montgomery Papers. Full text in B. L. Montgomery, *Memoirs*, London 1958.

Even the sometimes sardonic BBC correspondent, Denis Johnston, was moved by Monty's farewell address at Vasto:

> And Monty – talking away on the stage, having the time of his life. He was sorry to go, he said, and to take with him so many experienced officers. But duty called, and he was leaving the Army in the charge of a good soldier – a fighting soldier, who would maintain the traditions of the past. But before he went, he would give them a few pointers – he would tell them how to win wars, so that they could continue to do their best, even without him.
>
> He did not put it quite like that, but it is what he meant; and as I listened to him, I thought to myself, what a headache, what a bore, what a bounder he must be to those on roughly the same level in the service. And at the same time what a great man he is as a leader of troops, and how right he is to wear funny hats so that the soldiers along the roads will know their general and answer his friendly wave. Maybe he is not as great as he thinks he is, but by God there's no getting away from the fact that he out-foxed Rommel, and turned the men of the Desert Army from the shoulder-shrugging cynics they used to be into the confident, self-advertising crowd they are now. . . .[1]

The 'dynamo' behind Eighth Army was departing, and General Leese was indeed the first to experience the effects. Although Leese flew out from England on Boxing Day, 1943, it took him no less than four days to reach his new headquarters. At Naples he was told that, owing to 'a little cloud showing over the mountains . . . nothing would be going over that day' to Eighth Army.[2]

It was now that Leese began to recognise the extent to which Monty had reversed the traditional edifice of British and Allied military protocol. Under Montgomery, it was the Eighth Army soldier who mattered, and who was the centre of attention throughout the world. Representing him, Monty had insisted on first-class supplies, medical service, padres, postal services. The only thing Monty had himself wanted was an aeroplane, so that if he wished to attend a conference or visit a commander, he could do so independently of the RAF transport service, which characteristically could not even fly Leese to his new Army command.

Thus Leese stood impotently on the runway at Naples on 30 December 1943, knowing that Monty would be leaving early the next morning to return to England via Marrakesh. Only in the evening did he find a young pilot willing to fly him to Foggia, where the same

---

[1] Denis Johnson, *Nine Rivers from Jordan*, London 1953.

[2] Sir Oliver Leese, unpublished memoirs, communicated to author by Ian Calvocoressi.

performance was repeated. In the end the young pilot who had brought Leese from Naples agreed to fly him to Eighth Army headquarters at Vasto. By the time Leese had motored from Vasto to Paglieto, Monty had finished his evening meal, which had already been delayed an hour, and was about to go to bed.

Eighth Army was about to sink back into the bureaucratic military pyramid, at the bottom − and the carelessness with which AFHQ in Algiers and Alexander's headquarters in Italy looked after Leese was symptomatic of the trend. Once again the comfort and convenience of staff officers in rear headquarters would come first, and the honour and pride of the fighting units of Eighth Army evaporated almost as if they had never existed.

For Monty things were different. 'In no uncertain terms' he had clarified the situation regarding command of 'Overlord'. Unlike Leese, he would wait upon no transport officer for help over his journey, and it was Eisenhower who was soon begging him to accept the offer of a bigger private aeroplane to take him back to England: 'I do not look with favor on risking your neck on a two engine transport. . . . I can arrange the very highest priority for you and whatever small staff may be accompanying you personally and I strongly urge that you allow me to do this.'[1]

Monty thus 'allowed' himself to be flown home in a giant C54. On the way he was to stay the night with Churchill at Marrakesh, and it was there, in a villa overlooking the Moroccan mountains, that Monty first began to study in detail the plans for 'Overlord'. The North African, Sicilian and Italian campaigns were over; Eighth Army was a thing of the past. Monty had outgrown single army command. From 1 January 1944 he would be commanding no fewer than four Allied armies in the greatest amphibious assault in human history.

[1] *The Papers of Dwight David Eisenhower*, op. cit.

PART FIVE

Preparations for D-Day

CHAPTER ONE

The Take-over of 'Overlord'

The manner in which Monty took command of 'Overlord' must rank, beside his take-over of Eighth Army in August 1942, as his greatest performance of the war. Sadly, Monty's lack of generosity towards Lt-General Morgan, the architect of the original plans for 'Overlord', and his neglect of Eisenhower's contribution have both rebounded and thus drawn attention and acknowledgement from the magnitude of this achievement.

There are remarkable similarities between the campaign in Egypt in the late summer of 1942 and that of 'Overlord' – for in both cases Monty took over a bewildered formation; built it into a mighty army, confident of victory; and despite many setbacks (which made ridiculous his later claim that *everything* went 'according to plan') ensured that victory was won.

That the COSSAC plan for a 3-divisional assault in 'Overlord' was a recipe for disaster now seems undeniable. Had Alexander been appointed to command the land forces in the invasion, would Morgan's COSSAC plan have been enacted? Monty was not alone in recognising its flaws, as will be seen, but he *was* alone in having the courage and conviction to see that it was thrown out and a better plan adopted. He had done so at Alam Halfa, he had done so again over 'Husky', and whatever mud was slung at him, he was determined that he would do so over 'Overlord'. For Morgan's 'Overlord' plan, the result of one and a half years of research and discussion, had no prospect of succeeding, as Morgan's planners themselves confessed.

Eisenhower, when he was shown the COSSAC plan for 'Overlord' in Algiers on 27/28 October 1943, was appalled. 'Commenting today on OVERLORD Ike said the planning seemed such a mess that he really doubted if he wanted a command there. Not enough wallop in the initial attack,' Lt-Commander Butcher recorded.[1] 'I had Beetle Smith come in with me during this examination,' Eisenhower him-

---

[1] Diary of Harry C. Butcher, Eisenhower Library, Abilene, Kansas.

self recalled a decade and a half later, 'and we decided off the cuff, that a five-division attack was far more desirable.'[1]

Eisenhower and Bedell Smith were not the only ones to pour scorn on Morgan's work. Indeed much of Churchill's and Brooke's shyness in pursuing the 'Overlord' operation after the Quebec conference of 1943 can be attributed to their lack of faith in Morgan's conception of the invasion.[2] General Paget, C-in-C Home Forces and then 21st Army Group – the British group of armies assigned for the operation – preferred the idea of an assault in the Pas de Calais area to the distant beaches of Normandy, the objective in Morgan's plan. Field Marshal Smuts also felt that Normandy was too far from the main enemy army. Brooke for his part hated the idea of the Normandy *bocage* through which he had evacuated the last Allied army in July 1940. Churchill favoured Normandy, but wanted wild and imaginative thrusts inland which were logistically impossible in a three-divisional assault landing as proposed by Morgan. General Devers, until Eisenhower's appointment the American Theater Commander in Britain, also wished an increase in the size of the assault. Morgan's plan was argued before Churchill, Roosevelt and a thousand senior generals, airmen and admirals; but until Monty returned home to England, no one acted.

'It won't work, but you must bloody well make it,'[3] Brooke had said when charging Morgan with the drawing up of formal plans for Overlord, and Morgan did not have the bravado to refuse, as he himself acknowledged after the war: 'On matter of decision to go through with plan, this was the background: we had worked like beavers for months. . . . I reckoned it was up to me to make a decision Yes or No. Question was, can this be done with these resources? What is right thing to do? Spent several sleepless nights. Finally said may as well be hung for a sheep as a lamb and said, Yes we will do it.'[4]

In the event, however, Morgan refused to be hung for his part in the unworkable COSSAC plan; he joined Eisenhower's staff at

[1] Letter to Lord Ismay, 3.12.60, in Presidential Papers, Eisenhower Library, Abilene, Kansas. See also Eisenhower's annotation written in 1966, in relation to his own letter of 5.1.44 to Bedell Smith, quoted in *The Papers of Dwight David Eisenhower, The War Years* Vol. III, Baltimore 1970: 'The big point I made was that the plan visualised a front that was too narrow. I thought it should be expanded above the planned 3 div. assault to 5–6.'
[2] The Combined Chiefs of Staff's directive to Morgan in April 1943 had in fact called for a five-divisional assault. See 'Draft Supplementary Directive to the Chief of Staff to the Supreme Commander' of 25.5.43, in 21 AGP/1061/1/C-in-C, Montgomery Papers.
[3] F. E. Morgan, *Overture to Overlord*, London 1950.
[4] Interview of 8.2.47 by F. C. Pogue, in OCMH Collection, Military History Institute, Carlisle, Pennsylvania.

Supreme Headquarters and thereafter pursued what seemed like a vendetta against Montgomery.[1]

The situation, then, resembled that of an armada setting sail without charts and without an admiral, and Monty was determined to see they got both. In Algiers Eisenhower and Bedell Smith had both indicated that the Morgan assault was too puny, but then they had been aware of this same fault at the time Clark presented his plans for 'Avalanche', and they had allowed Salerno to go ahead nevertheless. Indeed at Carthage on 25 December, three days before Monty's arrival in Algiers, Eisenhower had also agreed to Churchill's proposal for 'Shingle' – the unbelievably impotent assault at Anzio – and confirmed his approval at Marrakesh on 31 December 1943.

To those involved in the planning of 'Overlord', Monty's arrival thus came as a kind of miracle. However much they might abhor his arrogant manner, they knew in their hearts that this was the very thing that was needed: a battlefield commander with guts, experience, and the will to ensure that 'Overlord' succeeded.

Churchill was the first, after Eisenhower, to feel the confidence and enthusiasm that now radiated from Montgomery. Arriving at 6 o'clock on the evening of 31 December in Marrakesh, Monty found Churchill 'in bed reading a copy of OVERLORD' flown out specially in its latest edition from Morgan in London. Churchill was 'recovering from his recent illness and did not look very fit,' Monty noted in his diary.

> He said I was to read OVERLORD and give him my opinion about it. I replied that I was not his military adviser. He then said he was very anxious to have my first impressions of OVERLORD, which I had never yet seen. So I said I would read it through and would give him my 'first impressions' in the morning.

The next morning, sitting beside Churchill in his car on the two-hour drive that had been planned to the Atlas mountains, Monty went over the 'Overlord' plan with the Prime Minister, and declared it to be 'impracticable'. Not only was the size of the invasion force too small, but it committed the assaulting army to the same error that had doomed the Allies at Salerno, and would do so again, despite the approval of Eisenhower, Bedell Smith, Alexander, Clark, Wilson, Tedder and Admiral John Cunningham (who had succeeded Sir Andrew Cunningham as Naval C-in-C, Mediterranean) at Anzio: namely the confinement of the invasion to one easily contained

---

[1] See, for example, the Diary of Harry C. Butcher, loc. cit. See also Morgan's own *Peace and War*, London 1961. In his *Memoirs* of 1958 Monty remarked of Morgan: 'General Morgan had made the COSSAC plan. . . . He considered Eisenhower was a god; since I had discarded many of his plans, he placed me at the other end of the celestial ladder.'

beachhead. Worse still, in terms of subsequent build-up, was the attempt to land too many formations, both on D-Day and during the succeeding days, across the same beaches – beaches that would become fatally congested.

By D + 12 a total of 16 Divisions have been landed on the same beaches as were used in the initial landings. This would lead to the most appalling confusion on the beaches, and the smooth development of the land battle would be made extremely difficult – if not impossible,

he told Churchill. The answer, by contrast, was simple: to land on a broad enough front to ensure that each succeeding wave of reinforcing divisions was fed straight into their respective Corps which had landed on D-Day:

a) The initial landings must be made on the widest possible front.
b) Corps must be able to develop their operations from their own beaches, and other Corps must NOT land *through* those beaches.
c) British and American areas of landing must be kept separate.
d) After the initial landings, the operations must be developed in such a way that a good port is secured quickly for the British and for American forces. Each should have its own port or group of ports.[1]

Monty's idea was that 'if such a thing were possible there would be many advantages in putting [the] armies on shore in such a way that' the British should secure the whole Caen-Cherbourg coast, while the Americans took the west side of the Cherbourg peninsula, securing St Malo, St Nazaire and Brest. Above all, 'air battle must be won before the operation is launched. We must then aim at success in the land battle by the speed and violence of our operations.'[2]

Once again, as in the Egyptian desert, Churchill was won over by the clarity and authority of the new commander he had only reluctantly appointed. 'Evidently he was a firm believer in the operation,' Churchill recorded almost incredulously, 'and I was very pleased at this.'[3] When Churchill suggested they drive up to a favourite panoramic viewpoint in the mountains, Monty 'got out and walked straight up the hill "to keep himself in training" as he put it. I warned him not to waste his vigour, considering what was coming . . . that

[1] 'First Impression of Operation "OVERLORD"' made at the request of the Prime Minister by General MONTGOMERY', dated Marrakesh, 1.1.44, in Montgomery Papers.
[2] Ibid.
[3] W. S. Churchill, *Closing the Ring*, London 1952.

athletics are one thing and strategy another. These admonitions were in vain,' Churchill recalled with amusement. 'The General was in the highest spirits; he leaped about the rocks like an antelope, and I felt a strong reassurance that all would be well.'[1]

Churchill's 'admonitions' were reciprocated by Montgomery. Aware that the Morgan plan was hopeless, Monty was consumed by vexation at the way – as in 'Husky' and as in Italy – major military operations were planned on paper and handed over to their commanders too late for them to make the alterations that would ensure their success: 'I impressed on him the need to get experienced fighting commanders "in" on any future operational plans early: if left too late it might not always be possible to change the layout of the operation; in every operation which I have been brought into in this war, changes in plan have been necessary and there has been all too little time, e.g. HUSKY in May, 1943, and now OVERLORD did not look too good.'

That Monty would 'grip the show' was clear to Churchill, as it became, too, for a second time, to Eisenhower who stopped in Marrakesh briefly on his way back to Washington and had a secret meeting with Monty – a meeting he neglected to mention in his war memoirs.[2] Monty, however, remembered the occasion very well, as he recalled when reading Eisenhower's book in 1948: 'Montgomery met Eisenhower at Marrakesh quite by accident, and took the opportunity to explain to him the tactical faults in the COSSAC plan. On having these faults pointed out, Eisenhower asked Montgomery to examine the whole plan in England, and gave him the necessary authority to do so.'[3]

Churchill and Eisenhower might respond positively to Monty's 'grip'. Not all were happy about this, though – particularly those who, like Harold Nicolson, resented Monty's growing fame in Britain. 'Montgomery today is the second most popular figure in England,' Nicolson noted with distaste in his diary on 5 January 1944.[4]

Was Monty aware of this? He had felt a measure of his fame when visiting England 'incognito' in May 1943; since then much might have changed, and it fell to Lord Beaverbrook, the slightly sinister newspaper owner and confidant of Churchill to inform Monty of the facts. Churchill's doctor overheard the conversation.

'Of all the soldiers, sailors and airmen in this war, you,' Max said, addressing Monty, 'are the only one the public knows.'

[1] Ibid.

[2] D. D. Eisenhower, *Crusade in Europe*, New York 1948.

[3] 'Some Notes on Eisenhower's Book *Crusade in Europe*, 1948', dictated by Montgomery, in Montgomery Papers.

[4] H. Nicolson, *Diaries and Letters* Vol. II, London 1967.

Monty faintly demurred.

'Oh, yaas, I tell you, it is so,' Max went on. 'The only one. There's nobody else who counts. After the war you can have a great political future if you like. You will appeal to all parties. You have no political past, only the glory of your victories, which has taken your name into every cottage.'

Monty sipped the heady wine. He made a few rather feeble, deprecating interjections.

'Isn't it so, Charles?' Max appealed to me.[1]

Moran, if he is to be believed – for he doctored not only Churchill but his diaries – quoted the example of Cromwell; thereafter discussion froze.

Monty may well have been influenced by Beaverbrook's flattery. Lord Beaverbrook 'is commonly supposed to be an unpleasant person, but he seemed to me to be a very pleasant person and all out to win the war,' Monty recorded in his own diary – for something in Beaverbrook's courtier-like mouthings struck Monty: the accidental suggestion of a weapon he might now add to his 'Overlord' armoury, namely the power of public morale. He had seen the effect of good publicity for Eighth Army in the desert, in Sicily, and in Italy – men proud to fight, knowing that their achievements were reported and thus gave heart to their families at home. Now Monty would himself be 'at home', and the opportunity might come to use his popularity to good effect, raising public confidence in the cross-Channel enterprise and thus boosting the morale of the participating troops.

For the moment, however, such a consideration was secondary. The first priority was to cast a new plan for 'Overlord' – 'the more I examined it the more it became clear that the original plan was thoroughly bad,' he noted on 3 January, after his arrival in London. 'The front of the assault was too narrow; only one Corps HQ was being used to control the whole front; no landing was being made on the East side of the CHERBOURG peninsula though the early capture of the port of CHERBOURG was vital; the area of the landing would be very congested.'

Monty's Chief of Staff, de Guingand, his heads of administration, Intelligence, and armour had all preceded him. Given the suddenness of his appointment, however, there was nowhere for Monty to live. So, while waiting for a flat to be got ready in Latymer Court, opposite the headquarters of 21st Army Group in St Paul's School, Monty booked in temporarily at Claridge's Hotel,[2] and at 9 o'clock on

---

[1] Moran, *Winston Churchill: The Struggle for Survival*, London 1966.
[2] According to his ADC, Johnny Henderson, there were delays and Monty was forced to spend three or four weeks in Claridge's – 'the best Tac HQ accommodation we ever had' – interview of 5.5.83.

3 January, the morning after his arrival from Marrakesh,[1] he convened his first 'Overlord' conference in St Paul's School. Morgan and his planners had been summoned from Norfolk House to give a brief presentation of their COSSAC plan, after which Monty stood up, and took the floor. There would be a pause of twenty minutes, he declared, after which he would give his views.

The COSSAC plan had been presented by General West and Brigadier McLean, the senior officers of COSSAC's planning section. At great length they had enumerated the reasons why Normandy had been chosen as the site of the invasion, the limitations of landing craft and transport aircraft, and the consequent decision that, rather than landing in weakness on a broad front, the assault should concentrate on a single primary objection – Caen:

We could make sure of Caen, or try for Caen and the Cotentin [Cherbourg peninsula],

General West later recalled.

I told Monty he couldn't take Caen the first day. He [Monty] was very optimistic. After all it is nearly 12 miles from some of the beaches. It would take troops a day to move that far. Only large airborne forces could have taken [Caen].[2]

When Monty stood up, after the interval, it was to express his complete disagreement with the COSSAC concept. What was needed, Monty declared, was not a town so much as a bridgehead, and a port. It was no good attempting to drive inland with only a narrow corridor for reinforcements, entailing congestion and confusion. The whole scale of the operation needed to be re-thought, for on this landing depended the future course of the war.

The meeting broke up in some consternation, for the COSSAC planners were told to go away and re-examine the possibility of extending the invasion site as far west as Brittany and as far east as the fateful port of Dieppe.

21 Army Group churned OVERLORD around half-heartedly before Monty got there. Things dragged along. Monty arrived in

[1] Among those who accompanied Monty on the C-54 flight from Marrakesh had been a young Resistance leader who refused to swear allegiance to de Gaulle and therefore possessed no papers. 'The coast of England was in sight when Montgomery told me what was on his mind. As he did not know who I was, he apologised for not being able to drop me off in London, where security services had no sense of humour, and proposed letting me off the plane in Glasgow, which he did.' The Resistance leader was François Mitterrand, later President of France – F. Mitterrand, *The Wheat and the Chaff*, London 1982.

[2] Maj-General C. A. West, interview of 19.2.47 by F. C. Pogue, loc. cit.

481

January 1944 – couple of weeks before Ike. Then I had to explain OVERLORD to Monty and [Bedell] Smith,

Major-General McLean later recalled.

Went into great detail. There was a pause of 20 minutes and Monty gave his harangue on the narrow front. Spoke of going to Brittany and Dieppe. Was not convinced of my arguments. Thought that we could land more troops in the first assault from the craft we had.[1]

Morgan's American deputy, Major-General Ray Barker, recalled the conference: 'Monty took the floor. In grandiose style he said the plan was too restricted. Wanted to attack north side of Brittany Peninsula or at least as far south as Granville and St Malo. Wanted to broaden left flank, but realise[d] could [not] go too far because of shore batteries. Said he wanted the planners to study the situation and give him an answer the next day. It was quite clear that Monty was the ground commander. Entirely within his rights.'[2]

Monty had challenged the planners, who had laboured over a year on the COSSAC plan, head on. The following day they met for a second conference:

Next day Monty challenged all our figures. Quoted Sicily to us.[3]

However Monty did moderate his views after Admiral Ramsay explained why he could not 'guarantee landings on the west side of the Cotentin'.

He agreed that we could not go to Brittany, Dieppe, and West of the Cotentin.[4]

History, military history, was being made – in hours now, not months or years. 'On the second day's meeting,' Morgan's deputy recalled, 'Monty said if we can't go any further west, we must at least go to Utah Beach. This was fully accepted that day. It was decided that we would prepare an outline and develop a statement of requirements in craft.'[5]

On the third day we reduced his demands to extending to 'Sword' beach . . . and to the Cotentin. He decided not to use airborne for

[1] Maj-General K. G. McLean, interview of 13.3.47 by F. C. Pogue, loc. cit.
[2] Maj-General R. W. Barker, interview of 16.10.46 by F. C. Pogue, loc. cit.
[3] Maj-General K. G. McLean, loc. cit.
[4] Maj-General R. W. Barker, loc. cit.
[5] Ibid.

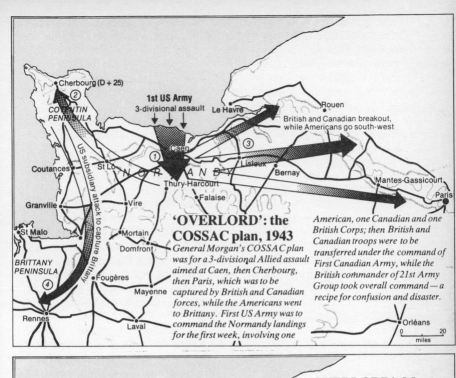

Cherbourg (D + 25)
②
COTENTIN PENINSULA
1st US Army
3-divisional assault
Le Havre
Rouen
British and Canadian breakout, while Americans go south-west
US subsidiary attack to capture Brittany
Coutances
St Lô
① Caen
③
Lisieux
Bernay
N O R M A N D Y
Mantes-Gassicourt
Paris
Granville
Vire
Thury-Harcourt
Falaise
St Malo
Mortain
Domfront
BRITTANY PENINSULA
Fougères
④
Mayenne
Rennes
Laval

'OVERLORD': the COSSAC plan, 1943

General Morgan's COSSAC plan was for a 3-divisional Allied assault aimed at Caen, then Cherbourg, then Paris, which was to be captured by British and Canadian forces, while the Americans went to Brittany. First US Army was to command the Normandy landings for the first week, involving one American, one Canadian and one British Corps; then British and Canadian troops were to be transferred under the command of First Canadian Army, while the British commander of 21st Army Group took overall command — a recipe for confusion and disaster.

Orléans
0   20
miles

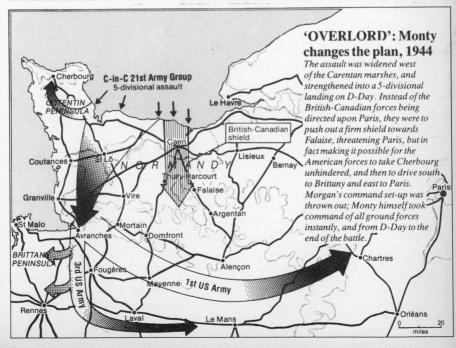

Cherbourg
C-in-C 21st Army Group
5-divisional assault
Le Havre
COTENTIN PENINSULA
Caen
British-Canadian shield
Coutances
St Lô
N O R M A N D Y
Lisieux
Bernay
Granville
Vire
Thury-Harcourt
Falaise
Argentan
Paris
St Malo
Mortain
Domfront
Avranches
BRITTANY PENINSULA
3rd US Army
Fougères
Alençon
Chartres
Mayenne
1st US Army
Rennes
Laval
Le Mans
Orléans
0   20
miles

'OVERLORD': Monty changes the plan, 1944

The assault was widened west of the Carentan marshes, and strengthened into a 5-divisional landing on D-Day. Instead of the British-Canadian forces being directed upon Paris, they were to push out a firm shield towards Falaise, threatening Paris, but in fact making it possible for the American forces to take Cherbourg unhindered, and then to drive south to Brittany and east to Paris. Morgan's command set-up was thrown out; Monty himself took command of all ground forces instantly, and from D-Day to the end of the battle.

Caen, but to land on the Vire and the neck of the Cotentin. He didn't believe in the Mulberry [floating concrete pontoon harbour]; stressed Cherbourg heavily, which we didn't. This is partially why he wanted the Cotentin. On the third day Monty took the line we must have more craft. He said it must be a five division front or no show. Give me this or get someone else. A wave of relief came over us.

[General] West was extremely insistent on the three division assault. He and [General] Bull made a last despairing visit to Monty at night. He chased them away. . . .

Monty's action was like a breath of fresh air.[1]

Even Ralph Ingersoll, later to be Montgomery's most vitriolic critic, recorded the relief felt by American planners involved in the COSSAC plan: 'Now that the great Montgomery was in command, I think we all experienced a kind of relief; at least we no longer carried our dreadful burden of responsibility.'[2] Or as the new Chief of Intelligence, 21st Army Group, recalled: 'I came back to England shortly before Monty. Various people had spoken of Utah landing [on Cherbourg peninsula]. However the difference which Monty's arrival made was the incredible decisiveness which followed his arrival.'[3]

In three days Montgomery had met the existing planners, explored alternative possibilities, and come to his conclusion. Henceforth there would be no 'bellyaching', for as Eisenhower's representative in London and as Land Forces Commander his authority was unimpeachable. The planners were told to draft a new 'Overlord' embodying a five-divisional assault, flanked by airborne landings, and stretching from the Orne to the east side of the Cherbourg peninsula: a fifty-mile-wide beachead.

Caen, the bitter thorn in the side of 21st Army Group from D-Day until August 1944, was thus surrendered as a guaranteed objective.[4]

[1] Maj-General K. G. McLean, loc. cit.

[2] R. Ingersoll, *Top Secret*, London 1946.

[3] Brigadier E. T. Williams, interview of 30/31.5.47 by F. C. Pogue, loc. cit.

[4] In fact Morgan's plan did not even guarantee Caen, which could only be attacked three days after D-Day, according to General Paget's 21st Army Group Staff in December 1943, and perhaps not even then. 'It may be considered that, compared with the COSSAC outline plan, this study presents an unduly pessimistic picture,' Paget's team considered in their first operational study – 'but given the small size of the Overlord landings [and] the Allies' numerical inferiority . . . the attack may have to be postponed until further forces have been built-up.' This accorded with Paget's private view, given to Brooke on 15 November 1943, just before the CIGS left for Tehran: 'An assault by three divisions in this sector will use the beaches and beach exits to maximum capacity and leave no margin for failure. . . . At most, we can expect to establish a covering position some three to five miles inland by the evening of D-Day, by which time,

War involves compromise, and the target date for the invasion – 1 May, 1944 – was less than twelve weeks away. The Allies needed not a town, Monty felt, but a plan by which they could get their armies safely ashore, as they had in Sicily, in such magnitude that the enemy would have no chance of driving them back. His new plan promised this, and from 6 January 1944 a spirit of tremendous optimism began to infect the once 'defeatist'[1] halls of the COSSAC organisation and 21st Army Group.

---

taking present dispositions, two panzer divisions might be in a position to stage a counter attack. We may be able to hold this attack, but hemmed in behind the shallow covering position, and with beaches within range of enemy field artillery, the landing and deployment of our follow-up formations is liable to be seriously hampered. Unless the scale of resistance is much lower than that envisaged in the OVERLORD plan, the operation will be very risky.' Paget suggested a small diversionary landing on the Cotentin peninsula to distract the enemy, as well as a preliminary invasion of southern France from the Mediterranean: 'OVERLORD, Early history and various Staff Studies' file, Montgomery Papers.

[1] 'Churchill called me defeatist . . . used to say, "Why can't I get someone who wants to fight?" ' – General Sir Bernard Paget, interview of 6.2.47 by F. C. Pogue, loc. cit. 'Paget and his staff were defensive minded' – Maj-General C. A. West, loc. cit. 'I was Chairman of the [COSSAC] planning group. . . . There were many cold feet on the operation. The head of the 'I' section thought it was impossible' – Maj-General K. G. McLean, loc. cit. 'He [Col Bonesteel] stressed the feeling he had that the COSSAC planners were not planning for an actual operation they believed would take place. . . . Tends to adopt the Ingersoll thesis about the defeatism of the COSSAC staff' – Colonel C. H. Bonesteel (US planner), interview of 18.6.47 by F. C. Pogue, loc. cit.

CHAPTER TWO

Preparing the Weapon

Few historians, after the Second World War, paid much attention to Montgomery's role in preparing the Allied armies for D-Day. By then, in retrospect, victory looked inevitable and, as in recounting the battle of Alamein, so in chronicling the battle of Normandy they concentrated on numbers before D-Day and tactics thereafter.[1]

Monty's contribution to the success of 'Overlord' cannot, however, be so easily dismissed. For millions of soldiers, their families and relatives, Monty came to symbolise the Allied commitment to victory in Europe in 1944, and this transformation in morale was not merely the result of clever publicity; rather, the publicity arose from one man's determination to forge a new weapon, as he had once recreated Eighth Army.

Again and again Monty had pointed out the mistake in letting planners be responsible for devising operations of war, rather than commanders. Now, as commander of the 'Overlord' armies, he had changed a plan which was as doomed to fail as Auchinleck's plan at Alam Halfa into something which, if the Naval and Air C-in-Cs could help to mount it, looked bound to succeed. Indeed so convinced was General Bradley, the commander of the First US Army, when he attended Monty's first meeting of the 'Overlord' Army Commanders on 7 January, that he not only accepted Monty's new plan as a *fait accompli*, but surrendered his right – enshrined in Morgan's COS-SAC plan – to command the actual D-Day landings. Morgan and Paget had laid down that First US Army carry out the 'assault phase', with one British Corps and two American Corps under command. Thereafter the First Canadian Army would be landed, and its commander would assume command of the British-Canadian troops, while the First US Army Commander reverted to command of American troops – 'the whole being under command of C-in-C, 21 Army Group.'[2]

---

[1] E.g. the British Official History (L. F. Ellis, *Victory in the West* Vol. I: *The Battle of Normandy*, London 1962) in which Montgomery's contribution receives a few lines in a book of 576 pages.

[2] Operation 'Overlord', 20.12.43 (21A Gp/00/74 Ops), Montgomery Papers.

Monty's new plan did away instantly with such gobbledegook. 'General Montgomery has been appointed to command all Allied forces to be employed in the land battle,' he announced as his credentials – as as Commander he had decided that the landings would be mounted by two Allied armies, assaulting simultaneously and alongside one another:

Two armies must be committed. The extended area will run from Varreville (E coast of the Cotentin) to Cabourg (west of the Orne). The American army will be on the right. . . . the task of the American army will be the capture of Cherbourg and the clearing of the Cherbourg Peninsula. They will subsequently develop operations to the south and west.

On the left of the beachhead would be not a Canadian but a British army:

The task of the British army 'will be to operate to the south to prevent any interference with the American army from the East.' He [Montgomery] hoped eventually to get a firm lodgement from Caen to Nantes with the British being built up through Cherbourg and the US through Brittany.[1]

This complete clarity of conception was much to Bradley's liking, after some four and a half months commanding an American army in England without any real faith in either Morgan or Paget. Moreover when Monty said he had not sufficient staff officers to form both a British Army Group Headquarters and an Allied HQ for 'Overlord', Bradley willingly surrendered most of the staff for his own eventual Army Group Headquarters, thus ensuring that Monty's 'Allied Army Group Headquarters' was a more effective Allied organisation.

Though later writers, both veterans and historians, would question Monty's strategy in the Normandy campaign, Bradley himself did not, for Bradley had known the COSSAC plan intimately since September 1943, and knew that Monty's objections were not simply to its size of assault-landings, but to its subsequent strategy too. Morgan's error was not merely the product of limited landing craft, as many later writers assumed: for Morgan's overambitiousness was inherent in his plan of campaign too. With only three divisions ashore on D-Day, Morgan intended that Caen be the first Allied objective, together with the airfields south-east of the city. The Allied

[1] 'Notes taken on Meeting of Army Commanders and their Chiefs of Staff at Headquarters, 21 Army Group, 7 January 1944,' in 'Various Conferences' file (21 A Gp/1065/2/C-in-C), Montgomery Papers.

forces would then swing westwards to capture Cherbourg and the Cherbourg peninsula. Thereafter, following an administrative build-up through Cherbourg, the British and Canadian armies were to fight their way eastwards to the Seine ports and Paris, and advance on the Somme. As the Germans fell back on Paris, the Americans would mount a 'much smaller operation' to capture the Brittany peninsula and its ports against 'second quality divisions', while the main body of the Allied forces reached the Seine.[1]

Neither Paget nor Bradley had considered this plan 'practicable with our existing resources' and against the current 'strength of enemy forces in North-West Europe'.[2] Monty's revised plan ensured that the Allies would land on a broader front in greater strength. Far from then attempting a fantastical British Canadian break-out to the Seine ports, Paris and the Somme, 21st Army Group would instead drive a deep defensive shield south of Caen, beyond which the Americans could secure both the Cherbourg and Brittany peninsulas – 'a firm lodgement from Caen to Nantes'. With reinforcements brought through Cherbourg and the Brittany ports, the Allies would only then turn east, stretching the German forces to breaking point.

So important was it to create the British-Canadian defensive shield to protect the American First Army against counter-attack that Monty declared his intention of landing five brigade groups in the British sector, allowing only three to be put ashore in the American sector. 'Commander FUSA [First United States Army] stressed it would be difficult to explain to the American public the small US part. To be discussed on the 12th,' Monty's MA recorded.[3]

Already, on the day Monty revealed his plan to Bradley, political and public-opinion considerations were rearing their heads – matters which would obscure and bedevil Monty's command in Normandy all through the summer. Nevertheless, though he asked Ramsay to increase the naval lift in order to put an equal number of Americans ashore, Monty held to his own military strategy, using the British army to create a protective wedge around Caen, thus shielding the Americans from the powerful German Panzer Army being held in the Pas de Calais:

'He considered the marshy area in conjunction with the river Orne would assist to protect the left flank of Second Army. The town of Caen is an important road centre and must be secured. The object of Second Army, therefore, is to seize Caen and the airfield area to

[1] 'Overlord – Summary of the COSSAC outline plan', 13.12.43 (21 A Gp/00/74 Ops) in 'OVERLORD, Early History and various Staff Studies' file, Montgomery Papers.
[2] Ibid.
[3] 'Notes taken on Meeting of Army Commanders . . . 7 January 1944', loc. cit.

the S.E., subsequently exploiting to the South to cover more effectively the flank of First (US) Army.

'In view of the urgency of securing the airfields and ensuring protection of the FUSA,' C in C considered that it would entail 5 British landing brigade groups, giving FUSA only three. . . .

'C in C pointed out that as he had been appointed Commander of the land battle, he must control the administration of both armies involved. C in C further pointed out that the administrative set-up was difficult to determine until it was known whether, when the development of operations necessitated an American Group Headquarters controlling two American armies operating from the Brittany Peninsula, General Eisenhower would assume control of the two Army Groups.' As Gen Eisenhower's views couldn't be obtained until his arrival, commander FUSA [General Bradley] said he agreed in principle to administrative control being under C in C. To be confirmed at meeting on 12 Jan. . . .[1]

Here, then, on 7 January 1944, the three most controversial issues of the subsequent Normandy campaign were aired – and later ignored by those writers determined, in the aftermath of victory, to discount Monty's achievement. The necessity of taking Caen, the strategy of the British army protecting the American flank, and the vexed question of whether Eisenhower truly intended to take over field command when once two separate army groups were operating, were all discussed – to be subsumed in the long, desperate struggles of the summer.

The same had been true of Alam Halfa and Alamein; indeed by October 1944 when the second anniversary of the battle was celebrated, Monty was aware that jealous tongues were already murmuring 'that I made certain mistakes at Alamein and that there are military secrets'.

I have made many mistakes in my military career and shall doubtless make many more,

Monty acknowledged – but he refused to believe the battle could have been won any more quickly; moreover he was quite clear that the real secret of Alamein lay in the days before the battle ever began:

The facts were that the Eighth Army was full of splendid fighting men of great battle experience; these men had more than once seen all their hopes frustrated and all their efforts brought to nought, and this through no fault of their own; they knew that man for man they were far better than the Germans and the Italians. It was a

[1] Ibid.

weary and dispirited Army, and it wanted proper equipment, a clear lead, and a simple doctrine.[1]

These were the things Monty had provided, and the story of Monty's assumption of command at 'Overlord' was to be very similar. Having decided on the point and strength of the invasion, Monty made clear his operational strategy to his Army Commanders and, leaving the details to be settled by his staff,[2] immediately set about spreading his 'simple doctrine' to the soldiers who would be fighting the battle of Normandy. From St Paul's he drove straight to Camberley, where he gave the first of his great doctrinal talks to the students of the Staff College, many of them destined to hold staff appointments in the coming conflict in North-west Europe.

'Address – Staff College 7 Jan 44',

he headed the pencil notes which he kept in a file marked 'The notes for addresses given by me when I returned to England in January 1944'. Like the notes of his address to Eighth Army Headquarters on the day of his arrival at Alamein on 13 August 1942, they are historic – for they reveal, better than the words of any historian, the mind of a great military commander during the prelude to one of the most decisive battles of modern history:

1. The Staff College. Why do you come to it?
   What do you want to learn?
   The study of war.
   Command aspect ⎱ The Human factor.
   Staff aspect ⎰
   All failures due basically to faulty command or bad staff work (or both) or neglect of the human factor.
   Soldiering a life study.
2. *Reasons for success*
   Adherence to the basic fundamental principles that really matter.
   What are these principles (of war)?
   Subject of a paper for the Staff College.
   Win the Air Battle.
   Admin.

[1] 'Speech made by Field Marshal Montgomery at The Alamein Dinner on 23 Oct 44' in 'Personal Messages to Troops and other Services' file (21 A Gp/1065/3/C-in-C), Montgomery Papers.

[2] Once Monty's staff got down to the detailed planning of the Normandy invasion it became apparent how much was owed to those planners who had preceded them, at Combined Operations Headquarters, COSSAC and 21st Army Group Headquarters. Without their preliminary work on beach data, the Mulberries and Gooseberries (artificial harbours), Pluto pipeline, manufacture of armaments, work on assembly areas, etc., the invasion could not have been mounted in the summer of 1944.

Decide what you want to do, and do it.

Haphazard methods useless.

Surprise.
Concentration.
Fighting spirit and morale.
Simplicity.

3. The stage-management of Battle – 6 points.
   (a) Surprise – tactical surprise always possible.
   (b) Enemy dance to your tune. Foresee your battle and decide how you will fight it; make the battle swing your way.
   (c) Balance and poise.
   (d) Initiative. Cannot win without it.
   (e) Essentials of plan known right down.
   (f) Confidence in plan.
   (g) Troops wild with enthusiasm. Spoken word that counts.

4. Battle a contest between two wills.
   Problem studied, plan made, machine set in motion.
   Running taken up by subordinates.
   Foundations of victory laid, and battle begins to take shape, long before battle is fought.
   Examples: Alamein
                Mareth
                Sicily
                Sangro.
   Personal command.

5. *German soldier*
   Generalship falling off.
   Soldiers have certain characteristics.
   (a) High standard of technical efficiency.
   (b) Good eye for country.
   (c) Obedience.
   Do not like concentrated fire and bombing.

6. *British soldier*
   Best in the world.
   Easy to lead – willing to be led – bad if not led.
   Importance of Corps of officers.

7. *Importance of morale*
   Medical factor; sick rates.

8. *Use of armour*
   One type of Armd Bde.
   All tanks work with infantry – need for Combined plan – not pillboxes . . .

9. The doctrine of the *Firm Base*

10. Fighting
        or
    Frigging about.

11. Evils of decentralization.
   Keep things on a Brigadier level in the planning stage.
   Examples: Tanks
              Artillery.
12. Consolidation: no – Reorganisation.

BLM.

Monty's second personal address was given four days later, on 11 January. This time it was given, as before Alamein, to his staff:

Address to Staff: 11 Jan
1. Taken over command; large HQ; must get to know each other; not easy in a large HQ.
2. *The new set-up*
   Eisenhower.
   Ramsay – Self – L.M.[1]
   I take full charge of the land battle with all American armies under me.
   21 Army Group to become Allied Army Group.
   An immense task.
   The assault on Europe.
3. *My system*
   Keep clear of all details; indeed I must.
   Great responsibilities.
   Have a chief of staff, with full powers; he gives all decisions on all staff matters once I have made my plan. Everyone is under him.
   I see no papers – no files.
   I send for senior staff officers; they must tell me their problems in 10 minutes.
   I do everything verbally.
4. I believe in personal command; I give all orders re battle operations, or anything else, verbally to my subordinate generals. Never confirmed in writing.
   Ex. Sangro battle.
   Within the general framework of my plan and instructions, commanders or staff officers carry on in their own way.
5. Admin staff.
   How I deal with it.
   No cheating.
6. No training instructions.
7. Dress. Holidays.

[1] Air Chief Marshal Sir Trafford Leigh-Mallory. From November 1942 Leigh-Mallory had commanded RAF Fighter Command in Britain. He was appointed C-in-C Allied Expeditionary Force on 15 November 1943.

8. No drastic changes.
    But must cut our HQ down.
    Tng reduced.
    I reduced
    Inf } abolished
    C.W. }

Again, two days later, Monty convened his army, Corps and Divisional commanders at St Paul's. Tirelessly he sought to put across his gospel:

Talk to Generals – 13 Jan 44
1. Reason for assembling the senior commanders and their staffs.
    Big things lie ahead.
    Explain the set up:

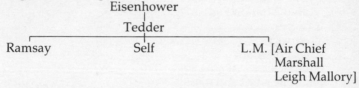

                          Eisenhower

                              Tedder

Ramsay   Self   L.M. [Air Chief
                                                         Marshall
                                                         Leigh Mallory]

Command of the land armies, all under me – great honour to command USA Army. Allied Army Group. We do not know each other well; much to be done; vital you should know my views on war, the fighting of battles, training, and so on.
Time is short and there is much to be done; I have got to prepare the weapon.
We must stop experimenting and prepare for battle. I will lay down the general form; everyone must accept it and act on it; all bellyaching will cease. You must give me your confidence. American doctrine their own affair and General Bradley will act as he thinks most suitable. The British and Canadian Armies will do as I say.

He explained his Chief of Staff system for details and 'personal command', based on verbal orders, uncluttered by bureaucracy, a system in which he expected 'everyone to act on my verbal orders, in battle or out of it'. Army Commanders were not to make formal approaches, they were to 'ring me on the telephone *direct*, or come to see me and discuss their problems, whichever they like'.

Don't let us make mistakes.
Have personal command and touch *backwards*, as well as for-wards.
Deal with Chief of Staff also.

When in doubt, ask verbally; do not write; previous discussion saves mistakes.

Must cut down all the mass of paper.

It was vital that the battle staffs be integrated – intelligence, operations and air support operating cheek by jowl. Administration must be on the basis of professional integrity, with commanders ensuring they did not 'beat the pistol or wangle up additional troops', a form of cheating which wrecked the administrative chain.

4. *Basic principles of War*

Start by giving my views on the general matter of making war.

First

The things that matter i.e. the basic fundamental principles on which everything is based.

The 7 principles of war:

Win the Air Battle (or aim at doing so).

Administration.

Co-operation.

Surprise.

Concentration.

Simplicity.

Fighting spirit and morale.

Every commander to be quite clear as to what are the things that matter on his own level.

Different things matter on different levels.

Difference between

Fighting

and

Frigging about (light forces).

5. *The stage management of the Battle*

The rules for winning battles:–

a) Surprise

b) Foresee your battle and make enemy dance to your tune (Ex: Mareth).

c) Balance and poise.

d) Initiative. 'Drive' required right down.

e) Plan communicated right down below.

f) Confidence established e.g. no failures.

g) Troops made wild with enthusiasm.

6. The technique of 'grouping'.

Cannot group till the problem has emerged.

Then group Divisions, the armour, in the best way to fit the problem.

Similarly within Corps and Divisions.

No fixed organisation for a Corps.

Divisions the only fixed organisation.

7. *The conduct of the Battle*

(a) The initial blow; carefully prepared; resources built up; great fire power; enemy hit a colossal crack.

Generally best to 'break in' at one or two carefully selected points; then to bring up fresh troops, pass through the gap, and attack remaining enemy positions from the flank and rear.

The 'schwerpunkt' and 'aufrollen'.

(b) As battle becomes more mobile, essential to thrust deep with armoured formations and seize important ground; *armoured pivots well ahead*; staggered dispositions and layout.

Need to swing the battle about, and make it difficult for the enemy to by-pass your pivots.

Thereafter Monty considered in turn the various facets of the 'weapon': the use of armour according to a combined infantry-armour plan, ensuring that tanks were withdrawn 'when the task is done . . . do not let them be used as pillboxes all over the place' – for the proper use of artillery made this unnecessary – the 'great battle-winning factor if properly used, and applied in concentrated form'. There was, too, the need for flexibility, regrouping at formation or even unit level to 'suit particular conditions', not War Office dictates – 'the only real test is – what will win the battle?' No longer would 21st Army Group be responsible for training, for the men of the Allied Armies were now serving individual commanders, men who would lead them in battle, and who must establish their own, direct authority – 'the first responsibility of a commander is to lay down a tactical doctrine and indicate how the battle will be fought. The organization of training to fit the conditions is then the task of DIV and lower commanders. . . . Do not cramp or break the chain of command, in the issue of training instructions.' Above all, all commanders must take the trouble 'to learn about the air'; to watch casualties, remembering that if a division lost too many of its leaders 'it will never recover quickly'. Medical efficiency was a vital ingredient in 'maintaining morale, and morale is the big thing in war'. All Commanders must 'take a keen interest in their medical services, and ensure they have what they need. . . . The soldiers all know that should they fall in battle they will have the best possible expectation of sound treatment and human consideration', and it was vital for commanders to 'take personal responsibility' for prompt air evacuation, good surgical teams, the availability of blood transfusion, and nurses well forward'.

These addresses by Montgomery were uniformly ignored by later chroniclers,[1] but they were a seminal part of Monty's almost miracu-

---

[1] No history of 'Overlord' or the Normandy campaign, nor any biography or biographical reference to Montgomery, has ever mentioned the addresses.

lous raising of morale and battle-confidence in the first days of January 1944, and they deserve to be recorded.

Monty's faith in himself was indeed remarkable. Admiral Ramsay and Air Marshal Leigh-Mallory had attempted from their first conference to question his authority, pointing out that under the revised COSSAC agreement, there was to be no Land Forces C-in-C in the same way as there was a Naval and Air C-in-C for 'Overlord', for the Supreme Commander was eventually to command the land armies.[1] Notwithstanding this jealous interruption Monty had waved his copy of the letter from Eisenhower designating him as his representative in England, and insisted there was no time to bicker over formalities.[2] As in Cairo in April 1943 he then unilaterally revised the 'Overlord' plan and told his planners to get on with the details, without waiting for Ramsay or Leigh-Mallory to confirm that the enlarged landings could be supported by sea and air, or getting the approval of Eisenhower as Supreme Commander. When Eisenhower received Monty's cable on 10 January, telling him that Monty wanted a five-divisional assault on D-Day and that this could easily be mounted if 'Anvil', the scheme for a simultaneous landing in the south of France, was cancelled, he procrastinated: 'I will go into the matters brought up by your W-9418 10 Jan on my arrival which will be very soon,' he replied after an interval of three days; and a further three days elapsed before his arrival in London.

As had been the case when he took premature command of Eighth Army, Monty refused to waste time, however, waiting for Eisenhower. With Ramsay and Leigh-Mallory's tentative support he had 'decided we must begin to plan, working on the assumption we would get what we wanted. . . . This was sufficient to allow our staffs to carry on with the work.'[3] The important thing was to get things moving, and to make himself scarce, having made this unilateral decision. Having addressed all the 'General Officers of the field armies in England, British and American, with their principal staff officers' on 13 January, therefore, he packed his bags and left London. It was time, he felt, to 'binge up' the troops.

[1] W. S. Chalmers, *Full Cycle: The biography of Admiral Sir Bertram Home Ramsay*, London 1959.
[2] Cf. Eisenhower's letter of 27.12.43 to General Morgan ('General Montgomery . . . is acquainted with my plans for initial organisation for combat control of the ground forces. Please look upon him as my representative in getting forward with these things as rapidly as may be practicable') in *The Papers of Dwight David Eisenhower*, ed. Alfred D. Chandler, Baltimore 1970.
[3] Diary entry of 12.1.44, Montgomery Papers.

CHAPTER THREE

Eisenhower: Buffeted by Winds from Every Side

On 14 January Monty 'left London on a 5-day tour of the First American Army. I was anxious to visit the American troops at once, and to talk to them, and so gain an impression of the quality of the American Divisions. It was also essential that they should see me, and that personal touch should be established between us,' he recorded in his diary.

> My immediate aim was to gain their confidence.
> I therefore set off in my special train[1] to visit the following troops of the first Army:
>
> | | |
> |---|---|
> | 5 *Corps* | 29 Div |
> | 7 *Corps* | 1 Div |
> | | 9 Div |
> | | 2 Armd Div |
> | | 3 Armd Div |
> | *Airborne Div* | 82 Airborne Div |
>
> I arranged that there would be about three parades of about 3,000 to 4,000 each in each Div area, and I would address the officers and men using a loud speaker. I would see them and talk to them; they would see me; in this way I hoped that mutual confidence would be established.
> I returned from the Tour on 20 January and there is no doubt it was a great success.

The tour, organised by Bradley's staff, was certainly a novelty, for no British field commander had ever gone out of his way to assemble and address large numbers of American troops on the eve of battle. Lt-Colonel Trumbull Warren, Monty's Canadian PA, travelled with Monty – and vividly remembered Monty's first address:

---

[1] The train, made up for Monty's predecessor at 21st Army Group, General Paget, comprised two 30 feet-long covered wagons for the C-in-C's cars, a luggage van and four coaches converted into a self-contained headquarters with kitchens, messrooms, sleeping accommodation and offices. It was called Rapier.

Before D-Day in England he went round, as he called it, to 'binge up' the people. As I would call it – sales talk, you know! And he did this in brigade groups of about 5,000 people. And he would commandeer a big common and he would have a jeep in the centre and he would get up on the hood – what you would call the bonnet: 'Now get gathered round here fellows – this is how we're going to knock the Germans all to hell,' and so on.

The first one he did with the Americans, he was very nervous. He didn't really know the Americans. And he got up there and he called them around and said: 'Now I don't know you people, but,' he said, 'I know General Eisenhower – Ike and I are good friends and we're going to do this business together. Now,' he said, 'I've never been to the States,' he said, 'but,' he said, 'Ike has asked me to come over after the war and I want to go over and visit your country. And,' he said, 'I hear so much about it and I don't know whether to start in the North or South.'

And some black soldier at the back said:

'What the hell are you trying to do? Start another war?!'[1]

Thereafter the subject was dropped from Monty's addresses. With his instinctive grasp of the psychology of the citizen soldier Monty had nevertheless touched the heart of the matter: the desire of the men to see the end of the war, and to return home. Around this perception Monty cast his simple spell: the responsibility carried by those about to launch the Second Front, the need to train well in order to carry out their task successfully, and return home to their wives and families proud men.

Some troops sniggered, some found Monty's English accent and swagger irritating, but the vast majority of troops were amazed that the Commander-in-Chief of armies totalling almost two million men should come to speak and be known to them, personally. One divisional commander, General Leroy Watson, was unhappy that 'every man of the [Third Armoured] division did not get to hear and see our new Allied ground commander. I am sure that all those who did see and hear him were instilled with a feeling of great confidence in our leader,' he stated in a General Order to be read to every man in the division on 18 January. 'I sincerely wish that everyone of you could have had the unusual experience that I had of being with General Montgomery and conversing with him throughout the day. I shall always consider it as one of the highlights of my military career. To know him is to understand his sincerity of purpose, complete confidence in himself and in his plans, whatever they may be, on the coming struggle.'[2]

---

[1] Interview of 9.11.81.
[2] Contained in Appendix to Diary, Montgomery Papers.

To Oliver Leese, who had succeeded him in command of Eighth Army, Monty wrote buoyantly of the way things were going:

My dear Oliver

Thank you for your letter of 8 January. I am sorry to hear about the storms and bad weather you had just after I left. I arrived in England on 1 Jan, having spent 24 hours with the P.M. in Morocco en route. On arrival in London I was plunged straight in to the problems of the invasion of Europe – the so-called 'Second Front'!! I considered that the plan was quite theoretical and un-practical, and was not in any way a sound operation of war. I said so in open court, and then gave my views on what form the plan should take. This led to great argument and discussion, during which I went round and saw the C.I.G.S., the First Sea Lord, the C.A.S., the Deputy Prime Minister, and other 'great ones' – and squared them and put my ideas to them. I then cabled to Ike, who was in USA, and he rushed over here at once. . . . I have assembled all the General Officers, British and American, in the field armies in England and have talked to them for a whole day on how to make war and to win battles, given my views on tactical doctrines, use of tanks and armour and so on.

This has, I think, done good.

I then set out on tour in my train and visited every American Division in England, and talked to the troops on big parades. This went down very well I gather.[1]

Eisenhower, meanwhile, landed in England on 15 January, but took a further six days to convene a conference to decide whether to accept Monty's new plan or revert to Morgan's COSSAC concept. Moreover, rather than standing by his original commitment, in Algiers, to make Monty, in effect, Land Forces C-in-C, he now 'wobbled', for on 19 January Bedell Smith pointed out 'that Ike again will be the target for those critics who say the British have cleverly accepted an American as Supremo Commander but have infiltrated British commanders for land, sea and air, even though a majority of the troops are American and the ratio of British to American planes in the U.K. is 4 to 7. This is something on which we shall be on the defensive and therefore Beetle was anxious for Ike ultimately to take over the ground operations, particularly after we have two army groups and he can get his advanced command post in France.'[2] At a

[1] Letter of 22.1.44, communicated by Mrs Frances Denby.
[2] Diary of Harry C. Butcher, entry of 20.1.44, loc. cit. In fact Bedell Smith's original idea had been that Eisenhower should command the assault itself. '[General] Handy and I agreed on the command for the assault. We wanted Eisenhower to control it from the first, and to go ashore the second day with a tactical Headquarters. We wanted to handle it like a river crossing' – General Bedell Smith, interview of 9.5.47 by F. C. Pogue, loc. cit.

press conference on 17 January Eisenhower had been asked point-blank if Monty was to be the ground Commander-in-Chief – and Eisenhower had failed to answer, cautioning the reporters not to 'go off on the end of a limb'.[1] Thus most journalists assumed that Monty was simply to be Bradley's 'opposite number', and when reports of Monty's first address to the US 29th Division came in, quoting Monty's statement about his command of American forces ('I came home the other day from Italy to take command of the British Army and the American Army of which General Eisenhower is the Supreme Commander and he has put one Army, the First American Army, under me for the battle'), the report was censored.[2]

However much Eisenhower's headquarters might seek to censor word of Monty's appointment as Ground Forces C-in-C, Eisenhower had, from a military point of view, no other option but to stand by his promise of 27 December 1943, and he did so eventually at his first Supreme Commander's Conference on Friday 21 January, three long weeks after leaving the Mediterranean theatre.

Tedder, Ramsay, Leigh-Mallory, Morgan, Smith, Bradley, Anderson [still GOC British Second Army], Spaatz, Bedell Smith, de Guingand, and senior staff officers of 21st Army Group gathered at Norfolk House as Brigadier McLean first of all outlined Morgan's original COSSAC plan, and Monty then stood up and demolished it.

For Morgan the occasion must have been excruciating. One by one Monty listed the flaws in the COSSAC plan – which were not simply those of size, but were also of strategic, tactical and administrative dimension.

COMMENTS BY GENERAL MONTGOMERY

General Montgomery considered that, in view of the enemy's strength and rate of build-up, it was essential that we should obtain a quick success, and that an assault by three Divisions, as at present planned, was not sufficient to achieve this object. According to the original plan, we should be attacking on a relatively narrow front; this would make it easier for the enemy to locate and hold us, and more difficult for us to emerge quickly and strike hard and deep. We should be limiting the area in which it was possible for us to discover a soft spot in the enemy's positions.

What then was the answer?

The early capture of a port was also important,

Monty pointed out,

[1] Ibid., entry of 25.1.44.
[2] Ibid.

500

in order that we should not remain totally dependent on 'MUL-BERRY'. If one considered the approaches to CHERBOURG, one found that the marshes and rivers at the neck of the COTENTIN PENINSULA provided a natural defensive barrier; we had ourselves taken advantage of this line in 1940 when we had succeeded in holding off the GERMANS with a force of only one brigade.

It followed that a plan to capture CHERBOURG quickly must provide for a landing on the near [i.e. Cherbourg] side of the defensive barrier. For these reasons it was desirable to extend the proposed area of assault so as to include an additional area on the Eastern side of the COTENTIN PENINSULA.

Under the existing plan, there would be a small original bridge-head through which all subsequent operations would have to develop, and this area would be likely to become very congested. It would be preferable to make the widest possible landing between the areas of heavy fire of the CHERBOURG guns on the right and the HAVRE guns on the left.

It should be the task of the US forces to capture CHERBOURG and then to make a drive for the LOIRE Ports and BREST, while in the meantime the BRITISH-CANADIAN forces would deal with the enemy main body approaching from the EAST and South-East.[1]

This strategic task for the two armies was so clearly defined that it is nothing short of amazing that Eisenhower, later, should have misrepresented it. Although the minutes of the meeting were denied to historians for almost forty years, the surviving witnesses of the conference clearly remembered the occasion after the war's end, and recalled it for the Official American Historian, Dr Pogue. In particular General Charles West, the Chief of the Operations staff at COSSAC, 'says it is true that at first Norfolk House conference with Monty he stressed the firm left flank, which would make Caen a hinge', something which West felt to be entirely logical, since even 'in our original plan we supposed the Germans would counter-attack at Caen. Germans couldn't afford to give way there. That had to be the hinge.'[2]

Time after time veterans and historical writers would accuse Monty of deceit in having claimed, in his *Memoirs* of 1958, that he adhered to his overall strategy of a British 'hinge' at Caen, yet the documents quite clearly support Monty's claim, as do the testimonials even of senior COSSAC planners such as General West who

[1] 'Minutes of Supreme Commanders Conference, 21 January 1944, Meeting No. 1', filed in the Diary of Harry C. Butcher, loc. cit.
[2] Loc. cit.

disliked Monty's arrogant take-over of 'Overlord' planning, and Brigadier McLean who was 'never pro-Monty'.[1]

Monty's tactical aim, then, was to hold off the German counter-blow with his British-Canadian armies (21st Army Group), while Bradley secured Cherbourg and then 'made a drive' for the Brittany ports. To achieve this British-Canadian shield, Monty intended, as at Alamein, to break into the vital sector of the German defences, push out his British armour, and force the Germans to counter-attack on ground of British choosing: 'In the initial stages, we should concentrate on gaining control quickly of the main centres of road communications. We should then deeply push our armoured formations between and beyond these centres and deploy them on suitable ground. In this way it would be difficult for the enemy to bring up his reserves and get them past these armoured formations.'

Monty went on to explain how he had scrapped the COSSAC idea that Bradley command a hotch-potch of assault forces. 'The expedition should be organized on a front of two armies, each of which would be on a front of two corps. The area from inclusive BAYEUX Eastwards should be BRITISH, and the area from exclusive BAYEUX should be AMERICAN. The airborne division should be employed in the COTENTIN Peninsula, so as to assist in the rapid capture of CHERBOURG.'

In Monty's view, 'as at present planned, he did not consider that "OVERLORD" was a sound Operation of War. He had throughout been considering how he wanted to fight the land battle; and it remained to be seen whether the Navy and the Air would be able to meet his requirements. . . . As for the timing of the Operation, in order that we should be in a position to achieve our "quick success" it was desirable that we should leave ourselves the maximum number of months of good campaigning weather. From the point of view of the army, therefore, the Operation should if possible begin early in May.'

Monty's presentation was decisive. To Morgan's embarrassment the COSSAC plan was now officially thrown out, and Monty's plan, treating Cherbourg as the Allies' first and major priority, was accepted by Eisenhower:

> The Supreme Commander agreed with General MONTGOMERY that it was desirable that the assault should be strengthened and that CHERBOURG should rapidly be captured,[2]

the minutes of the Conference recorded. Moreover, to confirm his faith in Monty, Eisenhower

---

[1] Loc. cit.
[2] 'Minutes of Supreme Commanders Conference, 21 January 1944', loc. cit.

proposed that General MONTGOMERY should be left in sole charge of the ground battle.[1]

After the war, however, personal and political considerations dictated that a new version of events be manufactured. The minutes of the conference were suppressed, while Eisenhower's naval aide, Captain Butcher, was encouraged to invent a false diary entry for 21 January 1944. 'Ike Changes the Plan,' Butcher called it – and pretended that the changes to the COSSAC plan were conceived by Eisenhower. Even his published account of the changes was erroneous.[2]

Butcher hoped, along with many others, that a new legend could be created about Eisenhower after the war – a legend in which Eisenhower would be seen as the architect of victory in Normandy from the very beginning. It is a legend which gained much credence but which, sadly, does not accord with the truth. Although Eisenhower had always demurred over the puny size of the D-Day assault in the COSSAC plan, his objection was based purely on a vague, intuitive anxiety about size, not on tactical reasons. Morgan too would have liked a bigger-sized landing, but had made do with a three-divisional assault on D-Day because, with rapid build-up in the days thereafter, Morgan felt the Normandy campaign could be won.

Monty's objection to Morgan's plan was of a different order entirely. It was an 'unsound Operation of War' because it would *not* enable the ground force commander to win the subsequent campaign. Congestion on the beaches and in the narrow corridor to Caen and the long delay before the armies could turn and fight their way to Cherbourg (estimated to be at least a month[3]), meant that the Allies would be entirely dependent on the artificial 'Mulberry' harbour that was to be created. Moreover, Morgan planned, once Cherbourg was taken, to break out of the British eastern sector towards the Seine and

[1] Ibid.

[2] In Butcher's fake entry, published in H. C. Butcher, *Three Years with Eisenhower*, London 1946, Butcher claimed that 'Leigh-Mallory felt that it would be wrong to use the airborne on the Cotentin Peninsula and that losses will be seventy-five to eighty percent'. In fact the minutes of the meeting state quite clearly: 'As for the employment of airborne forces, he [Leigh Mallory] had never cared for the CAEN proposal, and greatly preferred General MONTGOMERY's recent proposal for their employment in the CONTENTIN Peninsula' – 'Minutes of Supreme Commanders Conference, Room 126, Norfolk House, 1030 hrs, 21 January 1944, Meeting No. 1', filed with entry of 2.2.44, the Diary of Harry C. Butcher, loc. cit. Monty's own notes from the conference were filed as an Appendix to his Personal Diary, Montgomery Papers.

[3] 'Under the COSSAC plan without a Contentin landing they could not have taken Cherbourg before D plus 30 and might never have gotten it' – Colonel C. H. Bonesteel (US planner at First US Army Group Headquarters in 1943), interview of 18.6.47 by F. C. Pogue, loc. cit.

Paris. Far better, Monty felt, to go for Cherbourg and the Brittany ports and to ensure such an overwhelming build-up of men and *matériel* that the German armies in France could be brought to battle and defeated.

Whether Eisenhower really understood Monty's strategy is difficult to assess. Behind the seemingly chequered career which had led to his appointment as Supreme Commander lay a trail of military mismanagement redeemed only by his warm personality and shining determination to obtain Allied rather than American success. The 'Torch' landings over which he had presided had committed the Allies to a costly winter stalemate in Tunisia, climaxed by the American disaster at Kasserine, and caused him to beg Alexander to take field command of his armies; the original 'Husky' planning for the invasion of Sicily had demonstrated all the disadvantages of desk planners, as well as Eisenhower's own fluctuating views; and the muddle over the invasion of Italy – the mad 'Giant Two' venture, the ill-conceived Salerno landings, the failure to give Eighth Army a strategic objective – all demonstrated profound failures of generalship which made commanders such as Patton incredulous of his advancement. Ironically, the day after the Norfolk House meeting of 21 January, Operation 'Shingle' was launched in Anzio. Commander Butcher noted the excitement in Eisenhower's headquarters in London that 'Shingle has started well'. It was a 'brilliant maneuver' of which Eisenhower was the true progenitor, whatever the British press might say:

> Under Ike's direction SHINGLE was already well advanced. . . . Thus another [i.e. Alexander] gets credit for a long-layed plan which developed under Ike. But the truth eventually 'will out'.[1]

The truth never did out. Within a week 'Shingle' was acknowledged to be a disaster, 'a stranded whale' in Churchill's vivid phrase,[2] without any hope this time of a miraculous Eighth Army rescue. As with the minutes of the Norfolk House conference, Butcher deliberately excised this passage from his published official diary, and it was only declassified by the American government in the 1970s.

Swayed by Monty's convincing argument, meanwhile, Eisenhower agreed to the change of plan for 'Overlord', a change already being worked upon by the army commanders. 'We had a meeting of Cs-in-C (Self, Ramsey, Leigh-Mallory) under the chairmanship of Ike, and my revised plan has now been accepted in all its details,' Monty informed Leese in Italy.

---

[1] Diary of Harry C. Butcher, entry of 23.1.44, loc. cit.
[2] W. S. Churchill, op. cit.

This will have repercussions in other theatres of war, and so we have now got to get the Allied Chiefs of Staff to agree.

It is all very exhausting work. And it is curious how history repeats itself and we never seem to learn from our mistakes; it is 'Husky' all over again with all the frightful troubles in the planning stage. But this time it is very serious as if Overlord were to fail, or to be only a partial success, it would put the war back months and months.[1]

Yet even now, Monty was being over-optimistic in assuming he had won his fight for a sound 'Overlord' plan. The day he wrote to Leese, planners of Morgan's COSSAC headquarters put forward a revised COSSAC plan, keeping Morgan's single assault on the Caen beaches, but increasing the naval lift to accommodate *four* divisions on D-Day – and begged Bedell Smith to include it in Eisenhower's signal to the Combined Chiefs of Staff as an alternative, asking them to decide. Monty stamped on this renewed attempt to 'pass the buck'; he reiterated that the Morgan plan, while hopefully aiming at early seizure of Caen, was too narrow in concept to allow the tremendous build-up which the Allies must achieve if they were to face and defeat a determined German counter-attack. Caen in itself was not important: the object should be so to land and position the Allied forces on the left (around Caen) that no German counter-attack could interfere with the American advance to Cherbourg and subsequently Brittany on the right or western flank. At last, late on Sunday 23 January – two days after Eisenhower's supposed 'acceptance' of Monty's plan, Bedell Smith gave way. 'Sunday evening Beetle dropped in at Hayes Lodge to report on his meeting with General Montgomery and planners. As a result, agreement has been reached, subject to Ike's approval, and along lines desired by both Monty and Ike in a large assault over a wide bridgehead,' Eisenhower's naval aide recorded in his diary. 'A message was ordered by Ike to be dispatched to the Combined Chiefs. . . .'[2] In the meantime Eisenhower informed Marshall:

After detailed examination of the tactical plan I clearly understand Montgomery's original objection to the narrowness of the assault. Beaches are too few and too restricted to depend upon them as avenues through which all our original build-up would have to flow. We must broaden out to gain quick initial success, secure more beaches for build-up and particularly to get a force at once into the Cherbourg Peninsula behind the natural defensive barrier separating that feature from the mainland. In this way there would

[1] Letter of 22.1.44, loc. cit.
[2] Diary of Harry C. Butcher, entry of 23.1.44, loc. cit.

be a reasonable hope of gaining the port in short order. We must have this.[1]

This, at last, seemed a firm and final decision by the Supreme Commander. But was it? The 'repercussions' which Monty anticipated in his letter to Leese referred primarily to the American Combined Chiefs' desire to start up a third front in southern France – a suggestion put forward by Roosevelt, without prior consultation with Churchill, at Tehran: Operation 'Anvil'. Anxious lest the Allies become involved in a thrust towards central Europe and Russia through the Balkans, Stalin had applauded the scheme, and Marshall had subsequently ordered Eisenhower to include it in his strategic planning.

From the moment he heard of 'Anvil', Monty was against it.[2] Once again, as at Salerno, Eisenhower was failing to concentrate on his primary objective, which must be 'Overlord'. If 'Anvil' was cancelled, and merely mounted as a threat (in the same way as 'Fortitude', the operation which was currently being organised under Colonel Johnny Bevan to deceive the Germans into thinking the Allies would land in the Pas de Calais area), then the 'Anvil' landing craft, naval and air support, troops and maintenance could be concentrated instead on 'Overlord', thus guaranteeing that it could be mounted in May.

Eisenhower, aware that his master and mentor, General Marshall, favoured 'Anvil', turned down Monty's plea.

> We must remember that the Russians had been led to expect that Operation ['Anvil'] would take place. . . . We had to make recommendations to the Combined Chiefs of Staff not later than 1st February as to the future of 'ANVIL' . . . We must consider whether we could not manage a successful 'OVERLORD' without damaging 'ANVIL'.[3]

That afternoon (21 January) another meeting was held at Norfolk House – this time with only the main participants present. Monty's new plan was to be encapsulated as a telegram to the CCOS, together with a ' "bill" . . . listing requirements . . . This cable-gram was to include a strong statement to the effect that the success of the

---

[1] *The Papers of Dwight David Eisenhower*, op. cit.

[2] 'While I was in Washington received the first analysis made by Montgomery and Smith. That estimate agreed with my own views, except that their immediate answer was to abandon ANVIL but adhere to a target date of the first of May' – Eisenhower cable to General Marshall of 8.2.44, in *The Papers of Dwight David Eisenhower*, op. cit.

[3] 'Comments by Supreme Commander' at Norfolk House Meeting No. 1, 21.1.44, filed with entry of 2.2.44 in the Diary of Harry C. Butcher, loc. cit.

OVERLORD operation was the crisis of the European war both for the U.S. Government and the British Government; that it must not fail but must be a complete success.'[1]

Monty had thus succeeded. Or had he? The minutes of the meeting went on to give Eisenhower's infuriating rider:

The Supreme Commander desired that this cablegram not minimise ANVIL as he felt that ANVIL would have a great political and psychological effect upon the European war.[2]

Nothing Monty could say could dissuade Eisenhower.

In Monty's eyes, 'Anvil' was not only an evil distraction, it was, as Eisenhower admitted in a personal cable to Marshall the following day, bound to 'cost us a month of good campaigning weather'.[3]

Monty was not alone in his aversion to 'Anvil'. Churchill did not favour the operation, and in an official comment on the Supreme Commander's cable to the CCOS, the British Chiefs of Staff – Field-Marshal Brooke, Air-Marshal Portal and Admiral Cunningham – wondered whether it would be 'better to continue to maintain the largest practicable amphibious threat in the Mediterranean and concentrate our Mediterranean effort on maintaining and increasing our offensive in Italy.'[4]

Marshall would give no decision. The 2 February deadline came and went, and only on 8 February did Marshall send an interim American reply, pointing out the irony whereby the British, at one time so Mediterranean-oriented, were now all for 'Overlord' at the expense of the Mediterranean, whereas the Americans, once so chary of committing themselves to further operations in the Mediterranean theatre, were now all in favour of 'Anvil'. Three days later, on 11 February, the American Chiefs of Staff took the unprecedented and amazing decision: they decided to 'pass the buck' and leave the decision up to Eisenhower.[5]

Meanwhile Monty visited Churchill and, while waiting for the American Joint Chiefs of Staff to make up their minds, set forth on the second of his 'binge-up' tours.

Churchill he found 'in very good form and seemed to have made a good recovery from his illness,' as Monty noted after lunching at Chequers on 23 January. 'It is terribly important that he should keep fit and well; we shall need his strong support and backing in the

[1] Ibid.: Minutes of Meeting No. 2.

[2] Minutes of Meeting No. 2, 21.1.44, loc. cit.

[3] *The Papers of Dwight David Eisenhower*, op. cit.

[4] Cable of 26.1.44, included with entry of 27.1.44, in the Diary of Harry C. Butcher, loc. cit.

[5] *The Papers of Dwight David Eisenhower*, op. cit.

preparations for the second front, and during the initial days of fighting.

'I explained to him the revised plan which I had recommended to EISENHOWER for the operation "OVERLORD". I also explained how I proposed to develop the operations after the initial landing, and my plan for securing quickly important road centres, for pushing armoured and mobile forces forward quickly, and generally how I proposed to swing the battle about.

'He was delighted with the revised plan, and with the new aspect of the land battle on the continent.'

Leaving an encouraged Churchill, Monty boarded his train and in ten days spoke to the troops of seven different divisions in three British Corps. 'I had parades of about 5,000 men each, walked through the ranks, and then got up on a jeep and got the men round and addressed them. My general theme was – the war has gone on long enough; together we will see it through and finish it off; it can be done, and we will do it,' Monty recorded in his diary. 'The tour was a great success.'

So successful was the series of visits that it soon became front-page news in the British press, to the chagrin of Eisenhower's naval and PR aide, Commander Butcher: Feb 3, 1944: Monty has hit the front pages again with a speech to soldiers in southern England saying he is fed up with the war and hopes therefore, to get it finished this year. Using the pronoun "I" in customary fashion, he said he never takes an army into battle until he is certain of victory.[1]

Despite the suspicion of some Americans, Monty was not trying to blow a single trumpet. He persuaded Eisenhower that he too must play his part as Supreme Commander in this critical phase of the war by 'going to meet the men who were to do battle' – and a week after Monty left on his second tour, Eisenhower too began a series of visits to fighting units which were to participate in 'Overlord', using a special train.

However much certain historians might mock Monty's visitations, there was an additional reason why they were vital to the coming campaign – namely, the equivalent visitations of Rommel.

Since 15 January 1944 Rommel had been given tactical command of all Axis troops in Europe facing invasion from Britain. For Monty this was of special interest, since he was the only Allied commander to have defeated Rommel in battle. As his diary had indicated, Monty had looked forward to a renewed military contest in Italy – a contest Hitler had thwarted by removing Rommel from command in Italy in October 1943.

Now the contest was to be revived, on the beaches of North-west Europe. Tirelessly Rommel toured the German defences and

[1] Diary of Harry C. Butcher, loc. cit.

although he misjudged the real site of invasion (he felt it was bound to come in the Pas de Calais area, or at least north of the Somme) his energy and ingenuity were such that even the less well-defended Normandy and Brittany coasts received the full blast of his endeavours. He too became headline news in the German press – a popularity he encouraged because it undoubtedly raised the morale of the soldiers defending the coast.

That he could defeat Rommel, Monty had no doubt whatsoever. At Alamein Rommel had laid hundreds of thousands of mines and inspected every inch of the front, but although it had led to a much 'rougher house' than many had expected, it was always clear to Monty that, if the British could just make the decisive break-in, then by sheer guts and dogged determination they must eventually prise open Rommel's defensive line. For Monty, the battle of Normandy presented itself in an almost identical way. The Allies could not conceal their intention of mounting an offensive; but where the blow would fall, and when, were matters they *could* disguise: forcing Rommel to spread his forces and subjecting the defenders to a war of nerves.

About his own Allied superiors Monty was less sure. Churchill, he felt, was in his pocket; Brooke too was solidly behind him; but Eisenhower's desire to have his cake and eat it, by mounting both 'Anvil' and 'Overlord', as well as continuing the offensive campaign in Italy, reminded him uncomfortably of Eisenhower throughout 1943: a man without battle knowledge and lacking a clear sense of priorities; a man buffeted by winds from every side and fatally anxious to satisfy all expectations. Worst of all, perhaps, was Eisenhower's fear of being thought over-cautious, as so many desk soldiers considered Montgomery – a fear that haunted Eisenhower's conversation with his personal staff as well as his diary. 'Giant Two'; the disaster at Salerno; Eisenhower's planning for Operation 'Shingle': all were, at heart, motivated by his fear of being thought slow or unimaginative. On 7 February, as the debate over 'Anvil' 'boiled',[1] Eisenhower pencilled a memorandum for the diary which gives a good insight into his neurotic fear of being excluded from the pantheon of bold heroes:

Much discussion has taken place concerning our command set-up, including newspaper evaluations of personalities and abilities. Generally speaking the British columnists (not the C.S. [Marshall] or the P.M. [Churchill]) try to show that *my* contributions in the Mediterranean were administrative accomplishments and 'friend-

[1] 'Ike and Beetle had been in a sweat because of questions relating to OVER-LORD . . . were boiling and Beetle had advised Ike against leaving London at this time' – Diary of Harry C. Butcher, entry of 7.2.44, loc. cit.

liness in welding an Allied team'. They dislike to believe that I had anything particular to do with campaigns. They don't use the words 'initiative' and 'boldness' in talking of me – but often do in speaking of Alex and Monty,[1]

he protested. Moreover as his aide's diary shows, Eisenhower could not understand why his Anzio project had failed[2] – indeed without any first-hand knowledge he attempted to excuse it in a long cable to Marshall a few days later, wagering 'that bad weather in the early days of the landing made it impossible to give the necessary mobility to strong armoured detachments that could have safely pushed forward across the Appian Way and secured the high ground to the east thereof.'[3] When Marshall spurned Monty's suggestion that 'Anvil' be cancelled (save as a threat) and accused Eisenhower, as Supreme Commander of 'Overlord', of 'localitis', Eisenhower was mortified. In his diary memorandum he recognised that, 'with SHINGLE stalemated', the resources for 'Anvil' would have to go into Italy to retrieve it. 'It looks as if ANVIL is doomed,' he went on. 'I hate this – in spite of my recognition of the fact that Italian fighting will be some compensation for a strong ANVIL.'[4] Thus when the American Joint Chiefs of Staff 'passed the buck' to Eisenhower, Eisenhower was too torn by fear of being thought unimaginative actually to cancel 'Anvil', despite his recognition that it was doomed. He had already decided that 'Overlord' should be postponed by a month in the hope that increased production of landing craft would make both assaults possible[5] – and could not now bring himself to concentrate solely on the critical campaign.

Such procrastination irked Monty no end. 'On return to London,' he noted in his own diary, 'I found that telegrams were still going on between London and Washington as to the whole question of "ANVIL", and the five-div lift for OVERLORD. The Combined Chiefs of Staff had been invited to come to London to discuss the matter but had declined to come; instead they had given EISENHOWER full power to act for them. But EISENHOWER seemed to be trying to please both parties and did not come down

---

[1] Ibid.; and *The Eisenhower Diaries*, ed. R. H. Ferrell, New York 1981.
[2] 'Ike commented at lunch that he wondered what was causing the slowness' – Diary of Harry C. Butcher, entry of 29.1.44, loc. cit.
[3] Cable to Marshall of 9.2.44, in *The Papers of Dwight David Eisenhower*, op. cit.
[4] Memorandum of 7.2.44, loc. and op. cit.
[5] To Marshall on 8.2.44 Eisenhower summarised: 'I felt so strongly that ANVIL should be preserved while we were achieving the necessary strength for OVER-LORD that I replied [to Montgomery's plea that 'Anvil' be cancelled, and that the 1st May target date be kept] we would accept a date of 31st of May in order to get an additional month's production of every kind of landing craft' – Diary of Harry C. Butcher, loc. cit.

hard on the side of OVERLORD; he still wanted an 'ANVIL'.[1]

That evening Monty went again to see Churchill. 'I told him that we were fighting hard in ITALY, and would have to fight hard in OVERLORD; to open up a third front in Southern FRANCE was quite absurd. I also said that a successful OVERLORD required a five-divisional assault with a good build-up behind it, and to cut this down in any way would be to risk failure. The Prime Minister agreed.'[2]

It was in this unfortunate atmosphere that Monty convened his second conference of army commanders for 'Overlord' on 11 February at St Paul's. Attempting to ignore the hiatus over 'Anvil' he radiated a professional confidence in his plan that impressed all who attended. He had ensured that General Anderson, the Commander of the British Second Army, be relieved of his command by late January,[3] and had replaced him by General Dempsey. It had been decided, with Monty's approval, that Patton should command the Third US Army – against Bradley's wishes. 'Had it been left up to me,' Bradley later confessed, 'frankly I would not have chosen Patton. I had so many misgivings about George. I had seen so many things he had done in Sicily . . . that I disapproved heartily of him. I was soured on him. I didn't think he was too good an Army Commander.'[4]

If Monty knew of Bradley's misgivings about Patton, he did not show it. Patton's presence in England was to be kept secret – for he was destined only to command the Third US Army when Bradley's First US Army had captured Cherbourg and was ready to drive south towards Brittany. Despite his disappointment that he would not be used in the assault phase, Patton was complimentary about Monty in his diary: 'Monty – who is an actor but not a fool', as he described the Allied Ground Forces Commander after the meeting.[5]

Monty's concern at this conference was not to discuss the strategy of the Normandy campaign once the beaches were secured; it was to lay down a tactical approach to the landings themselves. There were so many theories circulating at that time – based on Pacific, Sicilian and Italian experience – that Monty was anxious to define a common doctrine and thus be able to move on to the next problem – the development of the land battle. 'I emphasised the need for simplicity,' he noted in his diary. 'Complicated fire-support methods' were to be cancelled. 'Go for *utmost simplicity* in all things,' he exhorted. Given the propensity for things to go wrong in war it was essential,

[1] Diary entry of 10.2.44, Montgomery Papers.
[2] Ibid.
[3] General Anderson was given a Home Forces command, Eastern Command.
[4] 'Bradley Commentaries on World War II', Military History Institute, Carlisle, Pennsylvania.
[5] *The Patton Papers*, ed. Martin Blumenson, Boston 1974.

he felt, to get all five divisions ashore on the first tide – with supporting weapons and with tanks. 'Tank best initial supporting weapon,' he stated. In contrast to the original COSSAC plan for a 'silent' assault, he wanted 'heavy air bombing before, and at, H hour [1½ hours after nautical twilight between daybreak and sunrise]. The maximum number of special tanks were to be put ashore with the first troops – DD-tanks, Arks, Flails, Plough and Snakes – 'so as to develop the land battle quickly.'[1]

Bradley and Dempsey left the meeting to ensure that this would be done, but would the Allied navies furnish the necessary craft to ensure such a policy? Two days later Monty left on his third tour of participating forces, speaking to the men of some four further divisions as well as Corps troops in five days. However, when he returned to London on 17 February he found the situation regarding shipping was not only no better, with Eisenhower still refusing to cancel 'Anvil', but actually worse.

> During my absence on tour the question of the craft and shipping necessary for OVERLORD made little headway. Actually, matters got worse as two delegates were sent over from WASHINGTON with a plan for cutting down our demands and giving more craft to ANVIL. Their proposals were put to me and I refused to accept them.[2]

In a terse message dated 17 February Monty had dismissed Eisenhower's attempt at a compromise situation. 'I consider that in planning OVERLORD we must ensure initial success, and must have such a good build-up that the initial success can be rapidly exploited and maintained,' he began, and declared that Eisenhower's proposals 'compromise tactical flexibility, introduce added complications, bring additional hazards into the operations, and thus generally tend to endanger success'. Eisenhower had in fact proposed on behalf of the Washington planners that some seven LST (Landing Ship Tanks)

---

[1] Diary entry of 10.2.44, Montgomery Papers.

[2] Diary entry of 17.2.44, loc. cit. Cf. also Brigadier K. G. McLean's recollection in 1947: 'Abe Lincoln and Osborne sent by War Dept to argue with us. We called them the "American Gestapo" as they challenged our statistics and went about measuring things' – loc. cit. Also Bedell Smith: 'We were always accused of localitis by the War Department during this period. We had all sorts of missions which came over and gave us advice. The people were our friends but we accused them of being desk soldiers . . . we had to tell them the facts of life. We told them to look at the beaches and not theoretical capacities.' Ironically Bedell Smith agreed with Monty over 'Anvil' – while de Guingand agreed with Eisenhower. As Bedell Smith remarked: 'The division of opinion on ANVIL was not American-British. I agreed with Churchill and supported Brooke's view, while [Admiral Andrew] Cunningham supported Eisenhower's view. It was not a national issue' – interview by F. C. Pogue, loc. cit., and de Guingand, interview of 9.5.78.

and thirty LCI (Landing Craft Infantry) vessels be axed from the Normandy programme to help 'Anvil'. 'From an Army point of view the proposals put forward are not acceptable,' Monty concluded. 'I recommend, definitely, that the proposals be turned down, and that the craft and shipping essential for OVERLORD be made available.'[1]

Eisenhower was unmoved, and begged Monty on 18 February to agree to a compromise, and to consider whether he could not in fact mount 'Overlord' without the thirty-seven LSTs and LCIs. De Guingand and Bedell Smith were sucked into the argument and rather than risk an Allied 'row' when all his main demands for the new 'Overlord' plan had been met, Monty surprisingly gave in. That evening he dined with Brooke, who was horrified that 'Overlord' was being compromised by an operational undertaking in the South of France which, given the tough state of affairs in Italy (Alexander had secretly signalled on 16 February that the Anzio commander ought to be relieved and a 'thruster like George Patton' put in his place, might never be mounted. 'Luckily I had discovered last night from Monty that he and Bertie Ramsay had agreed to curtail the cross-Channel operation to provide for a South of France operation. They should have realised that the situation in Italy now made such an operation impossible. They had agreed to please Eisenhower, who was pressing for it to please Marshall!' Brooke noted with virtual disbelief in his diary.[2]

Armed with Brooke's views on the likely cancellation of 'Anvil', Monty visited his friend Major-General Simpson, now Director of Military Operations at the War Office. 'I am told by the Operations Directorate at the War Office that the Divisions in ITALY have had a lot of casualties, are tired, and generally are not too well situated for getting on to ROME and beyond,' Monty now wrote to Eisenhower. 'They require re-grouping, resting, and so on. Also the battle has to be continued so as to keep drawing GERMAN divisions down that way – all of which is very good.

'Under these circumstances, I do not see how the withdrawal of Divisions from ITALY for ANVIL is possible,' he went on. 'If this is the case I hope that we shall get the full number of craft that we would really like for OVERLORD, there is no point in cutting ourselves down and accepting a compromise solution for OVER-LORD, if ANVIL can never come off; it would be better to have a really good OVERLORD, with a good choice of craft, a good reserve of craft, a good margin all round, and so on. I suggest that this aspect should be cleared up.'[3]

In effect Monty had rescinded his compromise agreement. Hear-

---

[1] Appendix to Diary, Montgomery Papers.
[2] A. Bryant, *Triumph in the West*, London 1959.
[3] Letter of 19.2.44 in Appendix to Diary, Montgomery Papers.

ing no answer, he wrote again to Eisenhower on 21 February, employing heavier artillery now:

My dear General,

I was asked out to Chequers yesterday (Sunday) to have lunch with the Prime Minister. He gave me a great deal of information about the Italian front which was news to me. It seems quite clear that we are now engaged in Italy in a major war; it is not just a battle for ROME. We are suffering heavy casualties; but so is the enemy, and all this will help OVERLORD far more than would a reduced ANVIL.

As a result of what he told me about the situation in Italy it is my definite opinion that all resources in the Mediterranean theatre should be put into the campaign in Italy. I further consider that we should now make a definite decision to cancel ANVIL; this will enable the commanders in the Mediterranean theatre to devote their whole attention to fighting the Germans in Italy – at present they have to keep ANVIL in their minds, and plan for it, and this must detract from the success of the present battle in Italy.

If para 2 above is agreed, then all the craft now being kept for ANVIL can be released at once for OVERLORD. The effect of this on OVERLORD will be tremendous.

To sum up.

I recommend very strongly that we now throw the whole weight of our opinion into the scales against ANVIL. Let us have two really good major campaigns – one in Italy and one in OVER-LORD.

Yrs ever
B. L. Montgomery.[1]

Eisenhower, trying to retain an acrobat's balance between his position of protégé of Marshall and his responsibility as Supreme Allied Commander of 'Overlord', refused to back down. That the Allied soldiers in Italy needed relieving was something which he, as a desk-soldier, could not conceive, just as he had failed to see it during the long winter in Tunisia in 1942/3. Holding Monty to his compromise agreement, he insisted that Monty had said he could carry out 'Overlord' with the available shipping, thus leaving the powers that be free 'to preserve flexibility in strategic plans for as long as we can without hurting our own planning'.[2]

Monty protested that, although his initial assault was not greatly affected, the rapid build-up thereafter, particularly on the fourth and fifth tides, *was* at risk – 'when speed is most vital. It is essential

---

[1] Also in Appendix, loc. cit.
[2] Letter of 21.2.44, *The Papers of Dwight David Eisenhower*, op. cit.

therefore that we should know without delay whether the additional craft are likely to be available,' he finished. 'If the decision is postponed, it will be impossible to make the best use of the additional craft, and moreover, the last moment alteration in the plan may lead to hasty and inadequate preparations with consequent risk of confusion.'[2]

Eisenhower, touched by the presentation by Admiral Cunningham and Air Marshal Tedder of a silver salver to commemorate the brilliant conduct of his command of the Mediterranean, stonewalled, and on 26 February the Combined Chiefs of Staff ordered that twenty LSTs and twenty-one LCI(L)s be 're-allocated to ANVIL from OVERLORD'. Monty had lost.

[1] Letter to Eisenhower of 23.2.44, in Appendix to Diary, Montgomery Papers.

CHAPTER FOUR

Cracking Along on the Revised Plan

If Monty could not dictate high strategy, though, he was convinced he was right over 'Anvil'. In fact, it was this sort of self-righteous conviction that made him most enemies: the officers he had sacked on arrival at 21st Army Group in order to make way for men with 'sand in their shoes'; General Anderson, the Commander of Second Army; General Morgan, the former Chief of Staff to the Supreme Allied Commander (Designate); displaced COSSAC planners; men in the War Office who had established comfortable 'empires' and resented the incursions of a subordinate commander; Americans who envied the popular appeal of a Britisher rather than an American. All conspired to create a distinct groundswell of hostility. 'Here in England I found everything and everyone was just drifting along,' Monty summed up in a letter to Mountbatten. 'Rather pathetic really.

'The plan for OVERLORD was definitely quite impractical and could never have succeeded. It all had to be changed. I myself, of course, again became the bad man – just like HUSKY.

'However I don't mind; it is put on a sound basis now and everyone is cracking along on the revised plan.'[1]

Not only had he changed the plan for 'Overlord' however, he had also been ruthless in cutting the staff of 21st Army Group,[2] and

---

[1] Letter of 24.2.44, copy in Montgomery Papers.

[2] It seems that in asking Bradley on 7 January 1944 to provide American officers for 'HQ Allied Army Group' Monty hoped to face Eisenhower, on his return from the USA, with a command set-up that would preclude Eisenhower from reneging on his agreement to allow Montgomery command of the land forces for 'Overlord'. Though he succeeded, Eisenhower refused to permit the title 'HQ Allied Army Group', lest it inhibit him from ultimately taking command of the land forces when two American army headquarters were introduced into France, and American soldiers out-numbered British and Canadian. 'Monty wanted to establish an Allied Headquarters,' Bedell Smith recalled after the war. 'Not sure whether he was told to do so by Eisenhower or not. . . . Thinks he probably told Morgan that he had such an authority' – loc. cit. After Eisenhower's arrival in England Monty dropped the name Allied Army Group, and reverted to 21st Army Group.

replacing the 'duds' who remained. As he informed Leese in January already: 'I am busy trying to reduce my staff here. I have already made the following reductions:

Infantry Directorate	Abolished
(Utterson – Kelso's party)	
C.W. [Chemical warfare] Directorate	Abolished
Training	Cut 50%
Intelligence	Cut 50%
Operations	Cut 25%

'A very large number of major-generals and other senior officers who were in this party have gone to their homes to await other jobs; they were mostly quite useless.'[1]

One of the few survivors was Brigadier Otway Herbert – who was astonished that Monty kept him on at all:

I don't know how it was that I was taken on at all. Everybody else was sacked – of any consequence. . . .

21st Army Group Headquarters was already set up and had been going for about a year I should think – the HQ was in London, St Paul's. There was a completely set-up headquarters. With Paget as Commander.

Then it became increasingly obvious that Paget, who had no war experience in this war (except going to Norway where of course he didn't have a chance), wasn't going to be a suitable person to command the invasion of Europe. Everybody, including Paget himself, began to realize that in fact he wasn't going to fill the bill. And it was decided to bring Monty home.

Freddie Morgan's COSSAC set-up was a planning set-up, pure and simple. He had no boss, no control – it was far too small a planning staff to be able to compete with us and nobody really paid very much attention to what he said – Freddie Morgan. I'd known him for years. He never really did much detailed planning at all. And he felt rather bitter about it.

The other Freddie – 'Monkey' Morgan, the Chief of Staff, 21st Army Group – had a much bigger staff. And his headquarters was Paget's, which could take decisions, was a going concern. And we who were working there began to get a bit concerned that one of these chaps [Monty or Alexander] was going to come back and take the whole thing over. Now this was a bit alarming for us, to put it mildly, because a vast amount of planning had already been done – huge quantities, sheafs, books of photographs, detail all being worked out. And in point of fact it wouldn't have been

[1] Letter of 22.1.44, loc. cit.

possible for anyone who didn't hurry up to intervene in proceedings because it had reached the stage where it was almost impossible.

When Paget's 21st Army Group Staff heard the news that Monty was to take command, some senior officers departed even without being sacked.

For example, Willoughby Norrie, who had been a Corps Commander in the desert – he and Monty didn't hit it off, so I remember him coming in to me, to my office: 'Well I'm off, anyhow – that's absolutely certain', the moment he heard Monty was coming! And off he went!

I don't think anybody expected to be kept on. 'Monkey' Morgan – he was already a lieutenant-general, Chief of Staff – I think he was a bit upset about being outed. But he expected it!

The BGS Intelligence was no good at all – he should have been out before – so that he was a certainty to go. . . .

The major-general Administration – he was a bit of a dud too. . . .

And the BGS Operations – that was a shambles. Charles Lewin, a Canadian, a funny chap, very capable, had done the main planning – most of the original planning was done by him, for the whole of the operation. But while I was away sick he had a hell of a dust up with the Chief of the General Staff 'Monkey' Morgan and was sacked. By the time I came back Charles Lewin had gone and [another] chap . . . came in his place. Well he was hopeless – honestly, that was a frightful disaster. . . . He was I consider a pretty poor number altogether. I'd known him for years – a perfect misery, didn't grasp the thing at all.[1]

However cruel, Monty's axe had been wielded, in Herbert's view, only just in time. The 'miracle', as even Paget called it,[2] of 21st Army Group's preparations for D-Day had begun. De Guingand took over as Chief of Staff, Richards took over as head of Armour, Williams as head of Intelligence, Graham as head of Administration. Belchem was summoned from Eighth Army to become BGS Operations, and Charles Richardson, still on loan as Deputy Chief of Staff to Clark, was even brought back from Fifth Army to be head of Plans.

Already by 1 February 1944, barely four weeks after arrival, the new staff at 21st Army Group had drawn up a revised plan for 'Overlord' – a triumph of integrated staff work. As before, it was the

[1] General Sir Otway Herbert, interview of 8.1.80.
[2] 'Miracle of war was what was done in the six months after Ike and Monty arrived' – General Sir Bernard Paget, interview of 6.2.47 by F. C. Pogue, loc. cit.

particular genius of de Guingand who, responding to Monty's clear leadership, transformed the 'shambles' of 21st Army Group into the most professional and successful Allied Army Group Headquarters of the war. As Brigadier Williams put it: 'Monty commanded the Armies under him, and . . . de Guingand commanded 21 Army Group.'[1]

That Dempsey, Bradley and Patton and the Canadians[2] would do as they were told, Monty had little doubt. Yet in his restless desire to ensure the success of 'Overlord', Monty would not now stop at armies. A kind of messianic fervour seems to have gripped him. He was certain that 'Overlord' was to be the supreme test of his life, the critical battle of the war, and he was determined, especially after the failure of 'Shingle', that there should be no weak links in the Allied chain of preparations. Anzio had proved, like Salerno, that it was not enough to achieve surprise and to get ashore. With their superiority in numbers and available equipment, the Germans could, if well commanded, seal off the beachhead and stalemate the assault, if not push the invader back into the sea. As at Alamein, there could be no rapid Allied advance, for Hitler could not simply watch while his 'Atlantic Wall' was breached and the Allies massed for a western offensive as mortal as that threatening in the east. Within four days, Williams had estimated in an assessment of 'possible build-up of enemy reinforcements' in the 'Overlord' area that within four days of D-Day the Germans would have at least three Panzer divisions and four infantry divisions counter-attacking the beachhead; within six, if they were unsuccessful in defeating the invasion, they would be able to bring upwards of a million soldiers in France and the Low Countries to contain it.[3]

Such a likelihood had driven Paget and the COSSAC/21st Army Group planners of 1943 to frank defeatism, just as Churchill, Roosevelt and Marshall had once feared that Eighth Army could not smash its way through the Axis defences at Alamein. No one recognised the problem better than Monty; however, no good would be served by such doubts, he felt. It was vital to 'binge up' his staff, his army commanders, and the troops themselves. Moreover, as he had recognised in the long march across North Africa, it was important that the soldiers feel that the public was behind them in their endeavour. Publicity was therefore vital in giving the men in the field

---

[1] Brigadier E. T. Williams, loc. cit.

[2] First Canadian Army Headquarters was intended to command its own Canadian Corps and British 12 Corps in the build-up after D-Day. Lt-General Harry Crerar was recalled from Italy against Monty's advice, and assumed command of First Canadian Army on 20 March 1944.

[3] 'Possible Build-up of Enemy Reinforcements in the "Neptune" Area', dated 1.2.44, in 'Neptune – Initial Joint Plan' file (21 A Gp/1061/3/C-in-C), Montgomery Papers.

the sense that what they did *mattered*. Few commanders in history have recognised to such an extent the part played by the friends, relatives, wife and children of a soldier in battle. 'Overlord', Monty was certain, would be the greatest western battle of the war; but it would only be won by men who felt their country was behind them. Like Morgan before him, Monty was aware that it would take the Allies a mimimum of two and a half months of battle to reach the Seine, perhaps three and a half months. Beside the twelve days of Alamein this was an undertaking that would require the utmost fortitude. The soldiers must not feel that their relatives at home were disheartened when swift victory was not won – it would be, like Alamein, a long, hard slogging match, a test of will as much as of armour and ammunition. To mobilise the courage and perseverance of the soldier was not enough, then; he must go out and mobilise the will of the nation itself.

It is doubtful whether Eisenhower, tortured by his need to satisfy expectations that he act imaginatively and boldly, understood any of this. When he heard Monty speak of 'quick success' in the initial landings his mind pictured Patton's race in the wrong direction, against nominal opposition, to Palermo, not Bradley's laborious struggle through the mountains and stone-walled olive groves to Messina. The unpublished version of Commander Butcher's diary reveals the sheer amateurism of Eisenhower's expectations – from the 'Torch' landings, to Sicily, Italy, and finally to Normandy. Not until Air Vice-Marshal Broadhurst flew him over the battlefield of Mareth in April 1943 had Eisenhower ever seen a dead body[1] – and yet, less than a year later, this man was the Supreme Commander for the greatest operation by the Western Allies of the war so far, and one who intended to take command of the Allied army groups in the field when once the invasion had succeeded. Like Tedder and Cunningham – whom he considered in his memorandum of 7 February 1944 were the only 'bold British Commanders in the Med' – Eisenhower lacked the true soldier's view, based on bitter battle experience, of what was possible and impossible against German opposition. Men like Tedder lived physically and metaphorically in the clouds; indeed Tedder's Chief of Staff in the Mediterranean, Air Commodore Wigglesworth, later claimed to the American Official historian that he, Wigglesworth, could have easily won the battle of Alamein himself – and certainly captured Rommel's army in the aftermath.[2] Admiral Cunningham had been the first to press for a Salerno landing, despite the obviously inappropriate terrain, and the first to recommend the amphibious assault at Anzio. The

[1] Air Chief Marshal Sir Harry Broadhurst, interview of 21.12.79.
[2] Air Marshal Sir Philip Wigglesworth, interview of 1.4.47 by F. C. Pogue, loc. cit.

surrender of 11,000 terrified Italians on Pantelleria after massive and wasteful bombing had miraculously convinced both Tedder and Cunningham that even stout-hearted German troops could be so cajoled into surrender – that the Allies need only act more boldly and the fruits of the Mediterranean were theirs for the taking. And because Eisenhower had never had an opportunity to learn the dirty, uncomfortable truths of battlefield command – the truths of what soldiers can and cannot be asked or expected to do – Eisenhower also lived in the clouds and entertained airmen's fantasies about the winning of battles. So, to be fair, did his mentor, General Marshall. As late as 13 February 1944 Marshall was begging Eisenhower to consider dropping an Allied airborne division on Evreux, 45 miles from Paris: 'This plan appeals to me,' he badgered poor Eisenhower, 'because I feel that it is a true vertical envelopment and would create such a strategic threat to the Germans that it would call for a major revision of their defensive plans. It should be a complete surprise, an invaluable asset of any such plan. It would directly threaten the crossings of the Seine as well as the city of Paris. It should serve as a rallying point for considerable elements of the French underground. In effect, we would be opening another front in France and your build-up would be tremendously increased in rapidity.'[1]

The plan, as mad as 'Giant Two' and as criminal in its indifference to the lives of the brave paratroops committed to such a wild scheme, was, after a week of analysis, shot down by Eisenhower's advisers, including Monty. But the effect was constantly to goad poor Eisenhower into realms of fantasy, and to distract him from the hard, tough fight ahead. This search for panaceas had bedevilled his operations in the Mediterranean for more than a year and would sadly lead to great bitterness and misunderstanding in Normandy.

Monty, meanwhile, entertained no such delusions, and in the first of his evangelical attempts to raise the morale of the English nation he addressed, by arrangement with the Ministry of Transport, some five hundred leaders of the railway trade unions at Euston Station in London. In his diary Monty was quite unembarrassed about staging what would inevitably be construed by jealous minds as 'politicking'.

I would say that the great mass of the people are getting war weary,

he considered.

Enthusiasm is lacking.
    The miners, the factory workers, the dockers, the railwaymen,

---

[1] Quoted in *The Papers of Dwight David Eisenhower*, op. cit.

the housewives – all have been working at high pressure and the tempo has been great. They cannot get away for holidays; so holidays have to be spent at home. The blackout lends a dismal tone.

I consider it is very important to try and win the war in EUROPE early next year. I consider also that it could be done – providing we make no mistakes.

But to do so requires a great effort on the part of everyone, and the nation must be roused to make the effort. And above all, there must be great enthusiasm.

It is easy, decades later, to scoff at such self-appointed evangelism, for there is indeed something naïve and arrogant in the picture of an English battlefield general deliberately taking the time to address railway workers and their leaders. To men like Churchill's doctor, Monty's self-projection represented the distasteful side of democracy – epitomised in Monty's caravans and his tank commander's beret.

Yet the men who gathered to hear Monty address them at Euston Station were neither embarrassed nor dismissive. A British battlefield general, charged with command of the entire Allied armies in Britain for the invasion of Europe, had *bothered* to come to speak to them. Moreover it was no perfunctory, goodwill address. General Montgomery's speech lasted almost an hour and a half, and with its simple phraseology, his radiating conviction touched their hearts.

Talk to Railway men: Euston
22-2-44
1. Glad of chance to speak to the Railwaymen. Without your help we could achieve no results on any front; *you* handle the stuff *we* want; the better you do *your* work, the better we can do *our* work; if we do *our* work well it helps *you*.
2. The great principle of co-operation.
   The best co-operation is born of confidence.
   Cannot have confidence each in the other unless we know each other.
   Your co-operation is vital to me.
3. Would like to tell you something of the Army, and my methods. I want to interest you in what we are doing, and I will tell you how I fight my battles and what influences everything I do.
4. *The human factor*
   The big thing in war. It is the man that matters and not the machine; the men in the tank and not the tank itself.
   It is the same in every profession, and in every concern.
   Study the human factor.
   The team – tank and crew.

5. *The German General*
   Apply this to the German commander.
   He is good so long as he is allowed to dictate the battle.
   Therefore he must be made to dance to your tune. How is this done? Decide how you will fight the battle before you start it, and force it to swing your way.
   Examples
      Alamein
      Mareth
6. *No failures*
   How is this done?
   Limit the scope to that which can be done successfully. Tell the soldiers what you are going to do. Then do it. Every man knows that when the army gets on the move it is going to win. Having won, he then has great confidence. And *that* is a pearl of very great price. The British soldier is a wonderful person – and never fails you.
7. *The sick and wounded*
   Sick always about 6 times the wounded.
   Obvious importance of a healthy army.
   The 4 things that save many lives:
      Surgical teams.
      Blood tranfusion.
      Air Evacuation.
      Nursing sisters well forward.
8. *The German soldier* His three main characteristics.
      Technical ability.
      Eye for country.
      Obedience.
   Very good soldier.
   But well trained British soldier is better.
9. *The Italian soldier*
   Stories of:
      5 divisions in my Army.
      Rizzio wanting to command me!
10. *The war*
   The black days of 1940, and after.
   Change since 1942.
   The future outlook.
11. *The Second front*
   Has begun.
12. The war has gone on long enough.
   The women bear the real burden.
   Let us all rally to the task and finish off this war; it can be done; and together, you and I, we will see this thing through – to the end.

Monty's 'politicking' did indeed win him enemies, as well as admirers. There was already a rumpus brewing in the War Office owing to Monty's peremptory alterations in rules and regulations regarding size, grouping, equipment of divisions – and even dress! Whole months were spent by War Office bureaucrats trying to stop units wearing coloured berets, for example, for, having administered the forces in Britain since war began, War Office officials hated to see a successful battle commander come home and dictate on matters which they regarded as their prerogative. There was a stand-up row between Monty and the Secretary of State for War, Sir James Grigg. Monty's MA, Lt-Colonel Dawnay, recalled Monty's attitude at this time:

> His view on all these things – when he hit a problem, whatever it was, he would always tackle it head-on, and come to a quick conclusion: 'There's only one answer and it's this – and everybody else will support me and get this through.' Which P.J. [Grigg] pointed out once or twice wasn't always administratively or politically possible. I think in the end he came to understand that – but it didn't prevent his going on at times asking for the moon![1]

The row between Monty and Grigg did both men good. Grigg needed to be reminded that the greatest battle of the war in the West was about to be fought, the winning of which would require an army backed one hundred per cent by the War Office; Monty needed to be reminded that riding rough-shod over everyone whose views differed from his own would result in lasting resentments, thus harming the overall war effort. 'I shall want wisdom, understanding, and a sound judgement to see the thing through,' Monty acknowledged in his diary on 20 February) 'also divine guidance.'

Indeed, as Eisenhower was dogged by desk-soldiers, Intelligence staff, naval and air advisers into a more and more unrealistic appreciation of battlefield command, so Monty too was driven by pen-pushers and malcontents into an almost messianic view of his own part in 'Overlord'. Eisenhower, himself without experience of battlefield command, was surrounded by men who urged that he assume immediate command of the assault armies, yet were not noted for their own bravery. Of Bedell Smith's insistence that Eisenhower move his headquarters out of London and in the opposite direction to the vital Air communications centre at Stanmore, Commander Butcher noted: 'Beetle is mortally afraid of the rocket bombs which he thinks will be released on London in the near future.'[2] Brigadier Strong, Eisenhower's Intelligence chief was, in

---

[1] Lt-Colonel C. P. Dawnay, interview of 1.2.83.
[2] Diary of Harry C. Butcher, entry of 23.1.44, loc. cit.

the words of one senior Intelligence officer in the field, 'a faceless wonder. Coward. Wouldn't go near the front if he could help it.'[1] These men, reinforced by the defunct COSSAC officers whom Eisenhower had not the heart to sack, contributed to a dangerously unrealistic air around the Supreme Commander while Monty, for all his battlefield experience, became the object of increasing jealousy and suspicion, as he himself noted in his dairy:

> The public, and the Army, are firmly behind me and would support me to the end. But not so the Generals; my own Generals in the field armies are my firm supporters, but outside the field armies is much jealousy.

Monty's answer was to fight even harder for the things which he knew mattered, because 'I am bound to make enemies whatever I do. I shall go on doing my duty, come what may.'[2] But there can be little doubt that, as in the desert when Eighth Army captured Tripoli and commenced its final triumphant drive into Tunisia to 'rescue' First Army after the débâcle at Kasserine, the pressure upon him began to tell, in as yet small but biographically significant ways: ways that may be seen to prefigure the somewhat isolated, bitter Army Group Commander who would later refuse to confer personally with the Supreme Commander and would bring the warring Allied alliance in Western Europe to the very brink of collapse.

As in the desert, such manifestations of pressure told first in Monty's relations with his kith and kin. He had already forbidden David to go to Jocelyn Carver during the Christmas and New Year's holidays; he now began to 'freeze' other members of the family in a way which his own ADCs and military assistants found difficult to credit.

'We were on one of these tours,' Colonel Warren later recalled,

> and when we were standing there a policeman came up – a civilian policeman – and said, 'General, your sister is up on the hill, by the car, about a quarter of a mile away.'
>
> Monty said, 'Thank you very much.'
>
> As we were walking up to the car I said, 'Sir, your sister's there.'
>
> He said, 'Thank you very much.'
>
> We got up to the car – it took a bit of time because he stopped and spoke to several people on the way. Then he got into the car.
>
> I thought he had forgotten about her. So I put my head in through the window and said, 'Sir, your sister –'

---

[1] Testimony to Dr F. C. Pogue, Pogue interviews, loc. cit.
[2] Personal Diary, Montgomery Papers.

He said, 'I heard you the first time! Get in and drive off!' Just as cold-blooded as that.[1]

Monty's stepson, Dick Carver, witnessed an almost identical occasion when accompanying Monty on a tour near Guildford, the home of Monty's sister Una. Monty refused to see his mother and even erstwhile friends were cold-shouldered – like Liddell Hart, towards whom he had shown an exaggerated respect throughout the inter-war years. In 1942, before going out to the desert, Monty had begged Liddell Hart to call on him at South-Eastern Command, an invitation which Liddell Hart had unwisely spurned. Now, in January 1944, Liddell Hart wrote to ask if he might take up the offer, and Montgomery replied coldly that he had 'no time to see you now; possibly later on I might be able to manage it and if so I will let you know'. He never did; in fact not until the 1950s did he, after considerable correspondence, agree to meet Liddell Hart in person: a humiliation Liddell Hart found difficult to swallow.[2] Curiously, in May 1946, Monty wrote again to decline a meeting ('I fear I am too busy at present to meet you for a talk') – but in a postscript added: 'I have come to realise in the last few years that the way to fame is a hard one. You must suffer, and be the butt of jealousy and ill-informed criticism; it is a lonely matter. One just has to go on doing what you think is right, and doing your duty: whatever others may say or think; and that is what I try to do:'[3] Liddell Hart, in a scribbled note he penned on receiving this letter, remarked, 'what a pathetic self-defensive note is sounded in the long postscript. Very small-boyish – rather touching, yet hardly worthy of a man who has reached such eminence. . . . A curious psychological case!'[4]

Liddell Hart's tag of 'small-boyish' was well aimed, for Montgomery never did rise to the heights of maturity and magnanimity which so marked Eisenhower's greatness as soldier and statesman. But then, it was Eisenhower who had so continually foisted onto Monty the responsibility for his own failings as a field commander – a tab which Monty had always done his best to pick up. 'Ike stepped in only to sort out disagreements,' General West later recalled.[5] 'Ike never really commanded. He was an arbiter or tribunal between services,' Colonel Bonesteel acknowledged.[6] As such, Eisenhower's

[1] Lt-Colonel Trumbull Warren, interview of 9.11.81.
[2] 'The offhand note of your Jan 1944 reply to me . . .' Liddell Hart drafted for a letter to Montgomery more than two years later – see draft letter of 17.5.46, Liddell Hart Papers, King's College, London.
[3] Loc. cit.
[4] Ibid.
[5] Maj-General C. A. West (senior COSSAC and SHAEF operations staff officer), loc. cit.
[6] Colonel C. H. Bonesteel (First United States Army Group planner), loc. cit.

contribution to the successful mounting of 'Overlord' as a truly Allied undertaking was incalculable and has rightly been lauded by subsequent historians; but it also served to obscure the role and performance of Monty. It was Monty who held the military reins of 'Overlord', and who considered it his historic task to ensure the 'mighty endeavour' was properly 'stage-managed', despite the seemingly endless red herrings propagated by Eisenhower, Marshall, Tedder and others – the chief of which, in Monty's mind, was 'Anvil'.

CHAPTER FIVE

The 'Things that Really Matter'

On 23 February Monty, accompanied this time by Eisenhower, Tedder and Bradley, made his third tour, inspecting the 2nd and 3rd US Armoured Divisions as well as the 51st Highland Division, whose massed pipes and drums played two new airs: 'El Alamein' and 'Wadi Akarit'. Despite his later bitterness towards Monty after the American catastrophe in the Ardennes, Bradley was unequivocal in his praise for Monty at this vital period before invasion:

> Monty's incomparable talent for the 'set' battle – the meticulously planned offensive – made him invaluable in the OVERLORD assault. For the Channel crossing was patterned to a rigid plan; nothing was left to chance or improvisation in command. Until we gained the beachhead we were to put our faith in The Plan. . . .
>
> Psychologically the choice of Montgomery as British commander for the OVERLORD assaults came as a stimulant to us all. For the thin, ascetic face that stared from an unmilitary turtle-neck sweater had, in little over a year, become a symbol of victory in the eyes of the Allied world. Nothing becomes a general more than success in battle, and Montgomery wore success with such chipper faith in the arms of Britain that he was cherished by a British people wearied of valorous set-backs.
>
> But nowhere did the slight erect figure of Montgomery in his baggy and unpressed corduroys excite greater assurance than among the British soldiers themselves. Even Eisenhower with all his engaging ease could never stir American troops to the rapture with which Monty was welcomed by his. Among those men the legend of Montgomery had become an imperishable fact.[1]

Monty was fully aware of this. 'I have been travelling round a great deal recently, visiting the troops, and getting their tails up,' he wrote on 27 February to Phyllis Reynolds. 'In each case I speak to them by means of a loudspeaker, the audiences varying from 3000 to 6000 . . . wherever I go the enthusiasm of the local population is a very marked feature of the day's programme.'

[1] Omar N. Bradley, *A Soldier's Story*, London 1951.

Not even the King of England could now prevail against this tide of popular support for Monty, although King George made a vain effort when giving an audience to Monty at Buckingham Palace at 5.30 p.m. on 1 February. Monty was not unprepared, having 'privately heard that the King objected to his wearing a black Royal Armoured Corps beret,' as Monty's Military Assistant later recorded. 'At this audience therefore General Montgomery spoke to the King about the value of high morale throughout the Army, and of how it could be achieved. As one of his methods in building up a high morale, he instanced his wearing of a black beret, by which all the soldiers now knew him. He claimed that this beret was worth at least an Army Corps, and that, while the war lasted, it was vital that he should continue to wear it. . . . No further objections were raised to his wearing it.'[1]

The King, the Prime Minister, the Secretary of State for War, the CIGS, General Bradley – all seemed to be behind Monty in his great undertaking, yet Eisenhower still faltered, fearful of offending Marshall. On 26 February Eisenhower convened another top conference on 'Anvil', attended by Ramsay, Leigh-Mallory, Montgomery, Bedell Smith, Morgan, Gale, Butler, Creasy, de Guingand, Whitely, Bull and Strafford. Ramsay declared he must have a final decision immediately, since his imminent Navy plan for 'Overlord' would be rendered 'useless if additional craft from a cancelled ANVIL were to become available'. With additional craft he could land all the follow-up troops, currently scheduled for D + 1 or 2, some twenty-four hours earlier. Taking this up, Monty stated that 'the proper course of action now was to plan for a lift to mount what he termed a real and proper OVERLORD. He felt there no longer could be any compromise between OVERLORD and ANVIL, other than leaving in the Mediterranean lift sufficient for one division.'[2]

Eisenhower was on the brink of agreeing, as Commander Butcher noted some days later: 'Ike was almost at the point at a meeting at Norfolk House Saturday to say "Abandon ANVIL" but he and his Commanders decided to "saw wood" for a while longer.'[3]

To the Ground Forces Commander, as to the Naval Commander, Eisenhower's continued hesitation was galling – for what Eisenhower did was to put off for another *month* any decision on 'Anvil': 'General EISENHOWER gave as the reason for postponing final study on the ANVIL problem until March 20 that the U.S. Chiefs of Staff desire to hold off as long as practicable for a possible change in the situation in Italy.' In fact Eisenhower did offer to 'send a telegram to General MARSHALL stating it was his view that ANVIL

[1] 'Notes on planning the campaign in North-western Europe, January to June 1944', in Personal Diary of C-in-C, Montgomery Papers.

[2] Ibid.

[3] Diary of Harry C. Butcher, entry of 29.2.44, loc. cit.

was impossible' – but this personal concession to Monty was soon scotched by Bedell Smith, who 'felt that there was little necessity for sending this message, and feared that it would give the impression of changing our minds too quickly'.[1]

Bedell Smith's loyalty to Eisenhower's likely image in the US Army Chief of Staff's eyes did him proud, but it was poor generalship in the larger sense. The lives of tens of thousands of British and American troops were at stake, and the sands of time were running out.

Monty had seen both Churchill and Brooke before Eisenhower's meeting, and hated to admit defeat. In his diary he tried to put the best face upon it:

On 20 March a decision is to be taken as to whether ANVIL is possible; if it is found to be NOT possible, then all the craft wanted for OVERLORD are to be sent to England – so as to make a really good OVERLORD.

The President has agreed to this plan.

This is, at last, a firm statement. There has been a great deal of passing the ball backwards and forwards between London and Washington. EISENHOWER has had great pressure from WASHINGTON, where opinion is very much in favour of ANVIL. But the tactical picture in WASHINGTON as to what is going on in ITALY is not so clear as it is in LONDON, as the British Commanders in the MEDITERRANEAN communicate direct with the P.M. and the C.I.G.S. The British Chiefs of Staff in London 'get at' EISENHOWER and he is accused by Washington of being influenced by the British.

So it is very necessary that we should all try and save EISENHOWER from reproaches from WASHINGTON, and save his face when he wants to come down hard on the side of what we want to do.[2]

This recognition of Eisenhower's 'piggy-in-the-middle' position does demonstrate the extent to which Monty understood Eisenhower's critical role in 'Overlord', as a chairman capable of commanding the loyalties of all nationalities. In Monty's Military Assistant's summary of the pre-D-Day planning, Eisenhower's contribution was somewhat condescendingly given as one of approval: 'General Eisenhower accepted the amended plan, which he realised neither he nor his staff had the operational experience to have produced themselves.'[3] Yet this approval was vital in harnessing the energies of different national contingents, as well as air and naval support,

[1] 'Minutes of 6th SCAEF Meeting, 26 February 1944' (21 A Gp/1062/1/C-in-C), Montgomery Papers.
[2] Entry of 26.2.44.
[3] 'Notes on planning the campaign in North-western Europe', loc. cit.

and although Eisenhower's procrastination throughout January, February and March over 'Anvil' had painful repercussions on the men charged with mounting 'Overlord', his very vulnerability to the pressures of Washington and Downing Street reflected his tolerance and sincere desire not to offend national sentiment. Like Alexander in the Mediterranean he exasperated Monty by his inability to see clearly the priorities and realities of the battlefield, but like Alexander he commanded from the ascetic, ruthlessly professional Montgomery a strange personal loyalty which went far beyond military obedience. In fact as the Italian campaign receded further into the distance, much of Monty's erstwhile affection for the charming but to him ineffectual Alexander now shifted to the grinning, personable American who had been charged with supreme command of 'Overlord'. The news from Italy was epitomised in a message Alexander sent on 26 February to Clark and Leese 'to be communicated to all commanders down to British Brigades and US Regiments', blaming the comparative success of the Germans in Italy on 'slow and cumbersome' methods of the Allies in combat, a document Monty felt was ridiculous.

In Monty's eyes it was useless to blame the soldiers in Italy, or even the field commanders, for it was Alexander himself who ought to take the blame. 'The Italian campaign has now become a major war,' he remarked in his diary. 'We have had 16,000 casualties in the [Anzio] bridgehead since 23 January; any further offensive action on our part is not possible for the present; we will have to re-group and assemble fresh forces for an offensive later on. It is not good, and, in my opinion, ALEXANDER has failed to "grip" the war in ITALY. See my comments in my diaries.'[1] Moreover when Leese wrote to the War Office asking if he could sack General Allfrey, the Commander of Eighth Army's 5 Corps, Monty felt Leese was wrong. As he wrote on 22 February to Brooke:

When Allfrey came to Eighth Army in September 1943 I found he was below the standard of the experienced Corps Commanders in my army i.e. Leese, Horrocks, Dempsey. It seemed to me he had never been properly taught by his former Army Commander. He began rather shakily and was not too good. I accordingly moved my Tac H.Q. near his Corps H.Q., and watched over his operations carefully, and taught him his trade.

I had found exactly the same thing previously with Leese, and with Horrocks, and with Dempsey; all required help initially and had to be taught. . . .

I consider that one of the first duties of a commander is to teach his subordinates, and in accordance with his teaching so he will get

[1] Entry of 26.2.44

531

results, provided the subordinate has character and is teachable. Allfrey is very teachable, and is very willing to learn, and is very grateful for help given. I consider that Leese must teach Allfrey, and bring him on; he is very well qualified to do so and he will get good results.[1]

This willingness to tolerate the inexperience and failings of others was a facet of Monty's character which, in the legend of the ruthless 'Chief', has often gone unrecorded. Time was short, experienced commanders were in small supply, and though his clear-out of 'dead wood' in the staff of 21st Army Group was necessarily wholesale, Monty was remarkably careful never to recommend dismissal of a field commander unless he had a better man at hand to replace him by. General Sir Sidney Kirkman, commanding the 50th Division which had returned from Sicily for 'Overlord', later recorded:

I attended the first meeting at St Paul's School, and I can remember what he said there was:
'We must be more careful about sacking people! The stage of the war has been reached when we just can't afford to get rid of experienced brigadiers and colonels. I don't want to have a whole lot more of these adverse reports.'

As Kirkman commented,

This is a complete change! For in the early days of the war it was, 'Let's get rid of this chap. If it's a heart attack, well and good, he's out of the way!!' And this was [in early 1944] a complete change. He's now going to cross-post a lot of senior officers. He said to me at the meeting, publicly: 'I'm going to take C— C— who was my brigadier – I'm going to take him away from you and post him to some other division so that there's someone experienced to help them.'[2]

'Kit' Dawnay, as Monty's divisional Intelligence officer in 1940 and now his MA, witnessed this change at a more intimate level. It was the same Monty, he considered, but a Monty whose 'wings were expanding all the time. . . . Even before the invasion of Normandy he was beginning to realise that there were too few good people to go round; he was finding that certain people were not up to the job they were doing, but equally there was probably no better chap to do it.' Moreover Monty was attempting, for the first time since the happier

[1] In 'Miscellaneous Correspondence' file (21 A Gp/1065/C-in-C), Montgomery Papers.
[2] General Sir Sidney Kirkman, interview of 16.4.80.

days of his marriage to Betty Carver, to take an active interest in spheres beyond the army. Once or twice a week he would ask Dawnay to 'furnish' an 'interesting visitor' for lunch or to dine at his Mess in Latymer Court:

I don't know if it was to broaden his horizons, but he was fascinated by the fact that he was becoming a very public figure, that he was meeting, as Invasion Commander, some extremely interesting people, which he enjoyed and which he thought he could benefit from, not politically or in terms of power, but simply by learning more. He was avid to learn more about the way the world runs, the way this or that happens. These visitors opened wholly new horizons to Monty – he hadn't been used to being with such people, since possibly his father's day, the bishop's day.

Latymer Court – he had his dinners in his own Mess there – it was the same small Tac Mess, I mean Johnny [Henderson], Noel [Chavasse] and myself and Trum Warren, and that was all to start with. It was his own small personal Mess – Freddie de Guingand had *his* own Mess elsewhere. But Monty's mess was very small, very intimate, and continually I was being told to get so-and-so to lunch, to hear about something. He was very good at provoking arguments and getting people to argue the toss. . . . What was frightfully dangerous – what he was frightfully dangerous and bad at doing was that he used to have two or three of these arguments, generally or quite often with different people on the same subject. And then he'd suddenly say, 'Well I see the answer to that is *that*.' And then he was almost immovable, from then onwards – he'd say, 'Well the answer to that question is *that*' – and there could be no other answer.

But is was quite often the wrong answer. I mean I remember one of these arguments in Germany, I can't remember what it was about, finance, or educating the Germans, and he had three or four meetings with different groups of people – two or three at a time – and he would throw the ball in and make them argue about the right course of action on this or that subject and then at the end of these arguments he'd say, 'Well the answer is *that*' – became absolutely *fixed* on it, which was very dangerous. Because great soldier as he was I don't think he was a great civil governor or any of those other things. . . .[1]

Prior to the Normandy landings, however, Monty simply flirted with the 'wider' world beyond the army. The effect he made on non-military personalities is epitomised in the story of the portrait he commissioned of himself in February 1943. Recognising, perhaps,

[1] Loc. cit.

533

the historic role he was about to play, Monty asked Dawnay to find him a good portrait painter, to match the portrait done by Neville Lewis in the North African desert.

I was told that Augustus John was the best portrait painter in the country at the time, and that he might be willing to undertake the commission,

Dawnay recalled.

Monty was getting a bit vain, there is no doubt about it. 'Kit – get the best portrait painter in England,' he said.
Well I went to Augustus John, and he agreed to paint the picture. I explained that the General was not a wealthy man, and John agreed to take a very modest fee.

The first sitting was to take place in John's studio in Tite Street. Monty went alone.

It was immediately obvious that the sitting had gone extremely badly,

Dawnay remembered,

for when Monty came back he said, shaking his head: 'Kit – I don't know where you found that chap. He's dirty, he drinks – and there are women in the background!'

Dawnay acknowledged that this might be so, but that John was reputed to be the best portrait painter in the country.
For the second sitting, Monty insisted that Dawnay accompany him – to John's displeasure.

I was made to sit facing the wall!

Dawnay laughed.

Between Monty and Augustus John there was an instant antipathy, mutual dislike.

When Augustus John mentioned his portraits of Bernard Shaw, however, Monty expressed a wish to meet the writer; and at a further sitting Shaw was fetched. To Dawnay's amazement the famous general and the famous writer now 'hit it off' to an electric degree.

It was the complete opposite to the relationship between Monty and Augustus John – the complete opposite! They agreed on *everything*. I can remember Monty talking about command, which fascinated Shaw. Monty claimed that only two per cent of the population are fitted to make good leaders. Inevitably one had to sack a lot. 'Who do you use then?' Shaw asked. 'The only thing is to reach deeper into the barrel,' Monty answered – 'take them younger. In war you have to. But of course if you do that and they don't succeed, you break the young ones for all time – they can never come back again.'

Shaw was enthralled. I mean the invasion was only months, weeks away. Another thing Monty said was:

'You have to learn to make quick decisions, as a Commander – quick decisions. Doesn't matter if you're right or wrong – but you must be able to give quick decisions. As long as fifty-one per cent of your decisions are right, you'll succeed. . . .'

When, some weeks later, the portrait was finished, neither Monty nor Dawnay liked it. In fact both were horrified. 'I don't like it – and I won't pay for it!' Monty announced. Dawnay agreed.

It was a cruel picture. It was Don Quixote, not Monty – tilting at windmills, not the enemy. There was no *attempt* to define the man, the general, on the verge of decisive military achievement. So eventually I went back to Augustus John. I said, 'General Montgomery doesn't like it.' John was delighted.

'Good!' he clapped his hands. 'Now I can sell it to someone else' – and his eyes grew larger – 'for *much* more.'

And he did so.[1]

Shaw's response was mirrored by that of the troops – and the public. On 28 February Monty set off on his fourth tour, this time inspecting formations and units of the Canadian Army, followed, on

[1] Ibid. Shaw also objected to the portrait, which he considered a self-portrait, not one of General Montgomery. 'Your portrait reminded me of yourself in the Leicester Gallery.' Shaw suggested that John start again. 'Paint him at full length . . . leaning forward with his knees bent back gripping the edge of his camp stool, and his expression one of piercing scrutiny, the eyes unforgettable. . . . The present sketch isn't honestly worth more than the price of your keep while you were painting it. You really weren't interested in the man. . . . What a nose! And what eyes! . . . Fancy a soldier intelligent enough to want to be painted by you and to talk to me!' – letter in possession of Lt-Colonel Dawnay. The following day Shaw suggested that if Monty was too busy to give another series of sittings for a new portrait, John should 'steal a drawing or two made from the chair in which I sat . . . and then paint the picture for yourself.' Augustus John did the drawing, which was also hung in the Royal Academy's summer exhibition in May 1944. It was purchased by Mr J. E. B. Hill.

his return to London, by an address to some 16,000 dockers, steve-dores, and lightermen in the London docks. The response was extraordinary, and emboldened by this, Monty paid a visit in the afternoon to Eisenhower. He wanted a final decision by the Supreme Commander on the closing of the south coast to visitors, in the interests of security; and he wanted Eisenhower to drop 'Anvil' without waiting a further three weeks.

We really could not go on any more in this indecisive way,

he noted with exasperation.

We could not possibly do:
   The ANZIO battle
   The ANVIL operation
   The OVERLORD operation
The first and the last were obviously essential. Therefore ANVIL must be cancelled. It should be cancelled NOW; we could not wait till 20 March.[1]

According to the Washington emissary in London, all American battleships except one had been directed to the Mediterranean; meanwhile Alexander had refused, on 28 February, to release for 'Overlord' some thirteen LSTs which were desperately needed to supply the Anzio beachhead.

'I obtained the complete agreement of EISENHOWER and Bedel SMITH on these two points,' Monty recorded in his diary, and in fact Eisenhower did tell the meeting of the British Chiefs of Staff that day (3 March) that 'he believed the time had come to abandon ANVIL' in its present conception 'as a two-division assault'. Not until the eve of the meeting planned for 20 March did he finally recommend une-quivocally that ANVIL be cancelled, three months after Monty had first pleaded with him to 'hurl' himself 'into the contest'[2] over 'Anvil'. Even at this conference of Commanders-in-Chief on 20 March there were, according to Monty's diary, 'signs of wavering at the meeting as American opinion very definitely favours an ANVIL; but at long last they now see it is quite impossible; however much they would like it, the troops for it are not available.'

Eisenhower's decision went, on 22 March, to the British Chiefs of Staff, who accepted it and to the American Joint Chiefs – who accepted it only as a temporary postponement, however, to be resurrected after 'Overlord'.

Monty shook his head. Throughout the long argument over

[1] Diary entry of 3.3.44.
[2] Signal of 10.1.44, in Appendix to Diary, Montgomery Papers.

'Anvil' the desk soldiers of Washington had toyed with shipping figures rather than the realities of battle, as Monty saw it. In this sense the debate over 'Anvil' adumbrated the agonising disagreements that were to take place later that summer, indeed throughout the autumn and winter of 1944/45. To the American strategists, the opening of as many fronts as possible, leading to a broad-front approach to war, accorded with the unconscious assumption of men who lived in a vast nation, untouched by war and with massive industrial and manpower potential. Yet, however imperiously Churchill might sweep his hand over the map of Europe and the Mediterranean, few British planners believed this expansive attitude to war to be realistic. One by one Britain had been worsted by the Germans and Japanese of her outlying territories, and when she had sought to spread her limited resources in the defence of others – from Norway to the Greek islands – she had been miserably defeated.

Opinion in Whitehall, then, tended to favour Montgomery's view, despite all the distaste felt for his dictatorial methods at 21st Army Group. Disquiet was already being voiced as to whether Britain could successfully replace the inevitable casualties if 'Overlord' proved to be – as was likely – contested to the death by the Germans. 'Anvil', as another new front to supply, reinforce, and support, was therefore anathema to most soldiers in Whitehall, who applauded Monty's determination to see the project buried.[1]

Monty's own negative response to 'Anvil' went much deeper, though. For him it was not simply a matter of craft, aircraft, men, materials – of numbers. Battle was, he felt, a test of wills – and the Allies would not survive this test unless they fixed their entire will on winning 'Overlord'. To Monty 'Anvil' was not merely an unwelcome numerical distraction, it threatened the very determination of the Allies to prosecute 'Overlord' to its final bitter end. How many people had counselled him to alter his plan for Alamein, to attempt inland hooks, amphibious landings in the rear . . . anything but the terrible test of battle. For the price of 13,500 casualties Monty had however insisted on an all-out, decisive clash with the enemy – a victory which had ensured that the enemy, fearing a repetition of Alamein, never again seriously stood to fight for almost 2,000 miles. The battle for Normandy would, Monty felt, be the same – and history would prove him right.

On the same day, 20 March, that he finally forced Eisenhower formally to come down against 'Anvil', Monty addressed the generals and senior commanders of his British Second Army, under their

---

[1] Already on 26 February casualties on Clark's Fifth Army front totalled a staggering 56,000, with a further 22,000 sustained on the Anzio beachhead (reported in Diary of Harry C. Butcher, entry of 28.2.44, loc. cit.).

new Commander, General Dempsey. In its way this address, like the talks he gave before Alamein, was historic. On foolscap War Office paper Monty had pencilled the points he wished to put over:

HQ Second Army: 20-3-44
1. We are going to be associated in great events. Must know each other. Very important you should know my views on things.
2. In the business of war, very clear thinking is required. You have to sort out those things that *really* matter; certain other things will matter too, but not so much. The really vital points must be your beacon lights through all your soldiering.
   We British have had many disasters in this war; they have been due to neglect to define clearly these matters, and to give clear guidance on them.
3. What are the things that *really* matter when you go fighting?

he asked – and listed the eight imperatives he had enumerated in his first addresses in January: winning air superiority above the battle-field; ensuring an administrative back-up commensurate with one's objectives; seizing and retaining the initiative by having always the overall framework of a plan, known to the commanders; attempting always to achieve at least tactical surprise, by good deception plans and a professional attitude to security; concentrating one's efforts rather than combating all along the line; assuring professional co-operation between arms – tanks, artillery and infantry – as well as services – army, air and navy; maintaining clarity on the battlefield by insisting on simplicity; and last, but most important of all, creating a real offensive fighting spirit or morale, powerful enough to see the soldiers through prolonged exposure in battle.

4. Many other points matter in a less degree. These sort themselves out in battle, and you get your sense of values.
   You get a dividend in accordance with your training i.e. ability to teach your officers and N.C.O.'s, who are the leaders.
   Battle cunning can be learnt only in battle.
5. Among these other points I suggest you have a good line of approach if you use the following questions:
   a) Can you launch your troops properly into battle i.e. can you tee-up the various types of battle that occur.
   b) Do you realise that, having done this, the issue then passes to the regimental officers and men. Their training is there-fore vital.
   c) Do you understand that the human factor is the big thing in war.
   d) Do you understand the requirements of a good plan for command and control.

e) Do you understand battle admin.
6. We have many troops as yet untried in battle. Vital to see they have a good show in their first battle.
7. *The Human Factor*
   The man and not the machine.
   Inspiration for the armies.
   Carry the doctrine into everything.
   Divisions are all different.
   Generals are all different.
   You want the right man in the right place at the right time.
   It is all a great study of human nature; you have certain human material at your disposal and what you can make of it will depend on yourself
   Battle a contest between two wills.

In the aftermath of D-Day and the Normandy campaign all this would be forgotten and a thousand historians would dither over a thousand particulars – Mulberries, Ultra Intelligence and the like – losing sight of the 'things that really matter.' It is to Monty's credit that, however much fame turned his head and inflated an already insufferable ego, he retained his grip and grasp of the essential factors that would determine, he felt, the coming battle. Before presenting plans, counting warships, support bombers and the minutiae of the impending operations he wanted first to clear the air: to apply that relentless logic which had characterised his command of Eighth Army before Alamein, and was now to be associated with the commanders of Second Army in 'great events'.

CHAPTER SIX

Exercise 'Thunderclap'

The day after settling the 'Anvil' question – as he thought – Monty left on his sixth tour, this time inspecting the docks at Portsmouth and speaking to the men at the Nuffield factories in Birmingham and Coventry.[1] On 24 March he returned to London to help launch the 'Salute the Soldier' campaign on behalf of the National Savings Committee. His speech at the Mansion House, Guildhall, was fully reported in *The Times* the following day, a speech in which Monty publicly predicted the war would last a further year.[2]

In the meantime Eisenhower's headquarters had been reconsidering plans for Operation 'Rankin', a contingency plan in case Germany suddenly collapsed, as in October/November 1918; Air Marshal Harris, chief of RAF Bomber Command, was refusing to co-operate with the Air Commander-in-Chief of 'Overlord', Sir Trafford Leigh-Mallory, on the grounds that, given good weather, he could bomb Germany into submission by June 1944 – a claim supported by the American bomber chief, General Spaatz, Pyrrhic victor of Pantelleria. The mood at Supreme Headquarters and in the corridors of air power was becoming dangerously fantastical.

'I can see trouble ahead in AIR matters,' Monty had noted in his diary on 7 March. 'HARRIS (Bomber Command) and SPAATZ (American Heavy Bombers) will not take orders from LEIGH-MALLORY. I am not surprised. L.M. is a very nice chap indeed and is easy to work with; but he is definitely above his ceiling in his present job and is not good enough for the job we are on.' The answer would have been to put Tedder in charge of all Allied air

---

[1] The factories selected for Monty's visits were not random ones, but those where, in the opinion of the Ministry of Supply, labour problems were leading to bottlenecks in the production of critical war items. The Director of Supply at the War Office had written as early as 2.2.44 to ask if 'in the course of your visits to the troops, you could, in isolated cases, go to some of the Works, where the bottleneck items are being manufactured' (21 A Gp/1065/1/C-in-C, Montgomery Papers). Monty agreed and on 14.3.44 wrote to Phyllis Reynolds, 'I am in my train on my way back to London; it has been a very good tour, and I think my visit to Birmingham and the factories there will pay a good dividend' (Montgomery Papers).

[2] The speech is given in full in B. L. Montgomery, *Memoirs*, op. cit.

operations, as Eisenhower had originally wished when considering commanders for 'Overlord'. Tedder however had coveted the post of Deputy Supreme Commander, Churchill had naturally wanted a British deputy to Eisenhower, and Eisenhower was too diplomatic to insist.

Monty himself was under no illusions about the fantasies of such airmen. It was the British Army which had failed at Dunkirk, in Norway, in the Mediterranean and the Far East in the public mind. The Royal Navy and the Royal Air Force were still considered the services of victory – the Navy for having brought the BEF off the beaches of Dunkirk and for safeguarding the convoys to Britain; the Air Force for winning the Battle of Britain and then taking the war over the very heart of Germany. Monty was thus filled with evangelical fervour on behalf of the Army, without which, he felt, the war could not be won. 'I would like to plead for the help of the whole nation in the task of inspiring the soldiers of our land at this momentous time,' he begged – and referred in Crusader terms to the Sword of State: 'the task now in hand is the use of His Majesty's consecrated sword; "with this sword do justice, stop the growth of iniquity."'

Monty's speech at the Mansion House, peppered with a kind of Old Testament religiosity ('Let God arise and let His enemies be scattered. . . . And The Lord mighty in battle will go forth with our Armies and His special providence will assist our battle') was, strange to say, only the tip of the iceberg. Among Monty's papers there exists, from this time, an extended correspondence he conducted with the Archbishop of Canterbury – all centring on the 'hallowing' of the Sword which he had made the symbol of the 'newborn national vigour' in his Mansion House speech. Bursting with missionary zeal for 'Overlord', Monty even drew up a two-page outline service, to be held in Westminster Abbey, complete with prayers, hymns, professions, submissions, sermon, lessons, benediction and blessing all compiled at the request of the Land Forces C-in-C of the coming Second Front. The service was to be held in coronation regalia, not only 'to consecrate the Nation's Strength; but also so that:

a. The whole people think more of the battle to be fought than of the good time coming.
b. The whole people faces afresh the true function of the Sword.
c. The whole people see this so clearly that they will not again hand back the Sword to gangsters, or leave armed force to the evildoer.

Archbishop Temple, balked by Churchill from holding a National Day of Prayer, replied that he was impressed by Monty's suggestion.

541

There was the danger, of course, 'that people will interpret these arrangements as designed in order to win God, so to speak, for our support rather than pledging ourselves to this service'; but it was a danger worth facing, and the 'outline service which you sent me is, I think, quite amazingly successful in giving the right, and avoiding the wrong suggestion, and its dramatic quality would strike the imagination. I think the notion of connecting it up with the elements in the Coronation Service which are really a dedication of the King and his Realm is a brilliant inspiration, and I hope that it may be welcomed by the King and Prime Minister, whose full agreement would of course be essential.' Here, however, the Archbishop 'passed the buck' – 'I think it much best that you should make the proposal to them' – and delicately wriggled off the hook.[1] Though Monty wrote to the Secretary of State, there was consternation in Government quarters. 'I am sorry for the decision you report,' Temple wrote in solace. 'I have indeed been extremely disappointed by the line taken in official quarters on this whole subject. I have not heard their reasons, and of course it may be that I should be persuaded by them if I did. Meanwhile it seems to me that an opportunity of great value is being missed.'[2]

Grigg, who had a decisive intelligence, had stamped on the idea, feeling that Monty ought to concentrate on leading the armies, not the nation. Many of those who heard of the scheme must have wondered as to Monty's sanity; certainly there was a feeling that Monty was getting 'too big for his boots' at this time.

Monty's 'Public Hallowing of the Armed Services of the Crown' *was* eccentric for a soldier charged with a military mission; yet however risible to the irreligious and the cynical, there can be no doubt that the idea stemmed from a genuine belief in the *moral* importance of the Second Front, and this moral concern was not something that could be shelved until Armistice Day or Victory Day. So often in World War I the soldiers had been confused, after the early excitement of hostilities had worn off, as to why they were fighting. It was vital, Monty felt, for the leaders of the country to give leadership, morally as well as professionally – and to give it now 'when our men *go forth to battle on this great endeavour*', not afterwards.

In this connection there exists, among Monty's papers of this period, another little-known facet of Monty's genuine concern for others, and his compassion. Although guilty of malice, and mean feeling in particular cases – as with his family – he had, too, what his Canadian PA called 'a heart as big as a church'. When he heard of the court-martial of men of his erstwhile Eighth Army for refusing to

[1] Letter of 8.4.44, in 'Miscellaneous Correspondence' file (21 A Gp 1065/1/C-in-C), Montgomery Papers.
[2] Letter of 26.4.44, loc. cit.

serve at Salerno in Fifth Army, he wrote immediately to Sir Ronald Adam, the Adjutant-General:

10th April 1944

My dear Bill,

I think you should know certain facts about the Courts-Martial that took place over the refusal of men of 50 Div and 51 Div to serve in other Divisions in Italy. Of these, the case of Pte J. T. Pettitt has been represented officially from here.

2. As far as I know the basic features of the case are as follows:

(a) Reinforcements were urgently required for British Divisions in the Fifth Army on the Naples front.

(b) Charles Miller [Alexander's Administrative Chief] could not find enough men from their own reinforcements, so he ordered up certain men of the Eighth Army from my depots in Tripoli.

(c) Before taking action as in (b) he did not consult me, nor did he consult Alexander.
If I had known what was to be done, I would have said 'No'. Alexander would also have said 'No'; I am sure of this as we discussed it together afterwards.

3. You know well what happened. The men refused to go into battle, which is of course quite inexcusable – and cannot be condoned.

4. But when soldiers get into trouble it is nearly always the fault of some officer who failed in his duty. The real culprit in this case is Charles Miller, now M.G.A. [Major-General, Administration], Southern Command.

5. I know Charles well; he was a dismal failure in Africa and in Italy, and in my opnion is unfit to be a Major-General i/c Administration. He is quite unable to face up to a big problem; he tries to bypass it, and leaves it unsolved; in the end, the resulting confusion is appalling, and was so in Italy. However, all this is not my business, but I thought you might like to know my views.

Yrs ever
B.L.M.[1]

If this was 'interfering in things that had nothing to do with him',[2] as General Sir Sidney Kirkman aptly phrased Monty's habit, then it says much for his humanity as a general. His constant reference to 'the human factor in war' was not simply rhetoric, it was the seminal feature in the generalship of a man whose popularity, in Britain, was

---

[1] In 'Miscellaneous Correspondence' file (21 A Gp/1065/C-in-C), Montgomery Papers.
[2] Loc. cit.

now second only to Churchill, as Harold Nicolson had noted in his diary in January. Unfriendly historians might later try to deprecate this popularity, marshalling every possible conceit to belittle it: but the loyalty Monty inspired was, as Bradley acknowledged, unique among Allied generals, American or British; moreover it was a trust inspired not merely by 'stardom', but by the conviction that, in Monty, the soldiers had found a leader who cared deeply about them: their welfare, their casualties, and their families.

That Monty managed to summon and radiate such confident energy in the mounting of 'Overlord' was extraordinary. Since August 1942 he had had but one brief vacation, and after the frustration and disappointments of the Italian campaign it would have been entirely understandable had he shown signs of weariness. Yet it seemed as though a new dynamo was now driving him, akin to that of desert days. Insufferable he might be to some, but to most he was, as Bradley put it, 'a tonic' of immeasurable value: a feat, ironically, only paralleled across the Channel on the coast of France by Field-Marshal Rommel, who was driving his staff and subordinate commanders to distraction by the frantic fervour with which he was preparing for Montgomery's invasion.

Buoyed up by a growing sense that the 'nation' was behind him, Monty now glanced at his colleagues and masters. The end of March was near, leaving a bare two months before D-Day, which had now been put back to 5 June. On 29 March he had dinner alone with Churchill, and found him 'very tired. He had been having a bad time in the House of Commons over the Education Bill, and should not be bothered with those sort of things now. He told me that STALIN was being very difficult – about the Polish question I understand. It is a tragedy the P.M. is so tired,' Monty reflected. 'His broadcast to the nation on Sunday night 26 March was not very good. We want him in his full vigour just at present; no one else could take his place.'

At the end of the first week in April Monty had arranged for the first presentation of tactical plans for 'Overlord', a two-day exercise in which not only the planning but the machinery of command would be tested. Realising how important it was that he should not, like Churchill, disappoint his generals, Monty decided to go down to Amesbury for a few days. There, in the seclusion of the Reynolds' school, he cast his mind over the events and personalities with which and with whom he had been associated over the past three months. 'I have a lot of thinking to do and notes to make, and I would like to sit quietly alone on Saturday, and most of Sunday too,' he warned Mrs Reynolds.[1] In his diary he wrote:

[1] Letter of 28.3.44, loc. cit.

General Comments

(1) This seems a good time at which to close this section of the diary. I arrived in England from Italy on 2 January and it is now 2 April; the past three months have been hard work, and things have not been too easy.

(2) The original plan for 'OVERLORD' was wrong; there was little fighting experience in the Army in England; HQ 21 Army Group was very theoretical and many of the more senior staff officers were definitely not good enough for their jobs; many changes had to be made, and quickly.

All this has drawn a good deal of adverse comment, and much mud has been slung at me; I have always had enemies and now probably have many more.

But the job has been done; 'Overlord' is now properly 'teed up' and the plan is good; I have got my H.Q. well organised, and have brought in the experienced officers I required. . . .

(3) Operation 'OVERLORD' is now in good shape.

We have got ANVIL relegated to a back seat and got agreement that we must have what we want for 'OVERLORD'.

He considered that Churchill, Grigg, Brooke, Portal, Cunningham, Eisenhower, Ramsay, Tedder and Leigh-Mallory were at least on his side: 'I think I have their trust and confidence. For my enemies I care little. The public and the Army are firmly behind me and my earnest prayer is that I may not let them down.' He was fortunate, he recognised, in having de Guingand as his Chief of Staff, and Graham as his administrative chief: 'We are an Allied H.Q. and they work in very well with the Americans.' But about the 'mess' in Italy and the Mediterranean he was scathing:

(6) The campaign in ITALY has definitely got into a real good mess.

Jumbo WILSON is, of course, no good; I told the C.I.G.S. so when he visited me in ITALY in December last.

ALEXANDER is not fit to conduct large scale operations in the field; his reputation as a great commander is quite false, and it will be a great shock to many people when that bubble is pricked – it definitely should not be pricked during this war, and he must be bolstered up somehow.

The reasons for the mess in Italy were the same, in Monty's view, as those he had identified when fighting there – to which he added now his opinion of the Anzio battle:

There was no proper plan for the ANZIO landing; the whole operation was haphazard and patchy, and was not properly

545

thought out and carefully planned. CLARK (5 American Army) is a good man; but he needs help. He got no help from ALEXANDER and 15 Army Group exercised no proper 'grip' on the operation – until it had failed.

'It will be interesting,' Monty continued, 'to see when the Prime Minister, and the Statesmen generally, realise that ALEXANDER is NOT fit to conduct large scale operations in the field. He wants someone to tell him what to do; I used to do this, and he always took my advice except once – that time he neglected it and failed, and has got into a worse mess since. He is a terribly nice chap and my very great friend; but he knows nothing about high command in the field.'

If Monty's judgement seems harsh, it can scarcely be contested. The Italian campaign had fizzled out into the very drain of Allied man-power and resources which Marshall in particular had so dreaded. Only when Brooke sent out a new Chief of Staff to Alexander, a soldier schooled and trained by Monty (Lt-General John Harding, erstwhile Commander of 7th Armoured Division who had been severely wounded in Eighth Army's fight for Tripoli), did Alexander's 'grip' improve. But by then it was too late, and Clark for one had ceased to regard Alexander as more than a charming Allied figurehead.

More important than the aptness of Monty's judgement was, however, its place in his own thinking. Like Gort's inept perform-ance in command of the BEF before Dunkirk, it was Alexander's performance in Italy which served now to needle Monty into his most outstanding display of 'grip' and great generalship, on the eve of the greatest land battle in the West of the war. He permitted no 'bellyaching' – when, for instance, General Sosnkowski, the C-in-C of the Polish Army, refused to bring the Polish Armoured Division up to full strength, with reserves, Monty crushed him simply by saying he would not take the Polish Armoured Division to Nor-mandy. Sosnkowski gave in instantly: 'I have given orders to com-plete the Division at the expense of other Polish units in Scotland.'[1] Yet if he was hard, Monty mixed a certain amount of sugar in his pills. To Sosnkowski he complimented the men of the Polish Armoured Division which he had inspected in March – 'I met quite a number of men that had fought *against me* in the Afrika Corps under Rommel [sic]; I now know why the Africa Corps was so good!!'[2]

The point was, Monty complained to Major-General Simpson, that 'to be dictated to by nations who have been under the heel of Germany as to how their forces should be used is, to my way of thinking, quite wrong. We have got a difficult problem ahead, and to

[1] Letter of 19.4.44, in 'Miscellaneous Correspondence' file, loc. cit.
[2] Letter of 14.3.44, loc. cit.

employ the forces of these Allies circumscribed by various restrictions is militarily unsound, and appears to me politically unwise. Some of these countries who did very little to help us against the enemy, e.g. France, now appear to be laying down conditions because they see the end in sight. I consider that nations who have been under the heel of Germany *must do as we tell them* until the war is over and Germany is defeated. They will probably have to do as we tell them even after that. My view is, if I am to be saddled with Allied troops tied down by various restrictions, I would rather not have them at all. . . . .'[1]

Having taken a few days' rest at Amesbury over the weekend, Monty felt ready for the final run-in to the invasion. Moreover he had not spent the weekend merely contemplating the past: it was the future which concerned him. 'By the end of March everything was 'set' for OVERLORD and the Armies were mostly on the move to concentration areas. These moves were to take some time and had to begin early; they would seriously test the transportation and railway services,' he noted in his diary. 'The whole of April was to be taken up with exercises, culminating in a very large "grand rehearsal" by all assault forces between 3rd and 5th May.'

While the troops began these unit and formation exercises, Monty summoned the entire general officers of the field armies to St Paul's for Exercise 'Thunderclap'. 'My object was to put all senior officers and their staffs completely into the whole OVERLORD picture – as affecting the general plan, the naval problem, and the air action. This was done on the first day, 7 April.'

Based on the system of exercises and conferences he had been developing since the First World War, Exercise 'Thunderclap' was Monty's answer to General Morgan and his COSSAC team. Staged entirely by his own 21st Army Group Headquarters, it was an amazing demonstration of the manner in which, within twelve weeks, Monty had transformed a contentious (though deeply researched) proposal in which few commanders had any faith into a clear, simple plan, the presentation of which stunned all. Here was Montgomery at his most professional – opening the conference himself with a one-and-a-half-hour address.

'Monty led off with a talk of an hour and a half, broken by a ten-minute interval in the middle,' General Kennedy, the Assistant CIGS (Operations), noted; 'he went over the Army plan with great lucidity.'[2]

Brooke, Portal, Cunningham, Eisenhower, Grigg and the entire complement of participating commanders and their staffs were there to hear the presentation. It was 'a wonderful day that Monty ran,'

[1] Letter of 20.3.44 (21 A Gp/1012/C-in-C), Montgomery Papers.
[2] J. Kennedy, *The Business of War*, London 1957.

Brooke recorded in his diary on 7 April, the highlight of which was Monty's 'opening remarks'.[1] In the unheated lecture room, in front of two huge maps of Normandy, Monty outlined for the first time his intended Normandy strategy – a battle which, he estimated, would last no less than three months.[2]

The most striking feature of his conception is the deliberate nature of his proposed operations,

Kennedy noted.

He means to expand the bridgehead gradually, get ports, and eventually arrive, in about three months, on the line of the Seine –Paris (exclusive) – Brittany ports. Of course, if an opportunity offered for a quick advance towards Germany, he would take it. But the main idea is to get established in great strength.[3]

It was precisely this aspect which most worried the romantics present: Churchill and Patton. Churchill had seen his own pet operation at Anzio turn out as calamitously as his Dardanelles venture in the First World War; both he and Patton as will be seen, blamed the Corps Commander General Lucas for timidity in not breaking out, rather than the conception and planning of the operation.

Fortunately Monty preserved, in his diary, the address he gave at Exercise 'Thunderclap' – and from it one can reconstruct the aura of quiet, professional confidence he radiated.

To help illustrate his presentation Monty had asked his MA, Lt-Colonel Dawnay, to ink coloured phase lines onto the maps – as Dawnay later remembered:

I had the maps prepared and drew on them the D-Day targets for the troops along the invasion front. And the dropping zones of the paratroopers. And then after consulting with Monty I drew the D plus 90 line – showing where he felt we should get by D plus 90 – which included Paris and a line back along the Loire.

And I asked Monty how I should draw the lines in between. And he said, 'Well it doesn't matter Kit, draw them as you like.' So I said, 'Shall I draw them equally, sir?' and he said, 'Yes, that'll do.' In his opinion it was not of any importance where he would be

[1] A. Bryant, op. cit.

[2] 'Montgomery radiated entire confidence and the very strong feeling that nothing had been forgotten or left to chance. . . . What sticks most in my memory is a large wall map showing where Montgomery expected to be at the end of three months' – P. J. Grigg, *Prejudice and Judgement*, London 1948.

[3] Op. cit.

548

groundwise between D plus 1 and D plus 90, because he felt sure he could capture the line D plus 90 by the end of 3 months, and he was not going to capture ground, he was going to destroy enemy forces.[1]

Using Monty's presentation notes, Dawnay drew in the arbitrary lines, never dreaming that they would be used in evidence against Monty when the campaign did not go 'according to plan'. Bradley made it known he did not like such phase lines, but those involved in administration and in airfield construction were pleased, as the BGS (Plans) Brigadier Richardson, afterwards recalled:

My view was that they were convenient forecasts, nothing more. The main purpose was to help Admin planners who had to plan a hell of a long time ahead, and the Air Force planners, who wanted to know where their future airfields were going to be.[2]

Monty's actual address, never published before, makes it quite clear that, with the exception of ports, the battle for Normandy would not be conducted with the object of capturing towns, but of step by step building up of men and resources until the moment when the Americans would be strong enough to drive south into Brittany and to the Loire. It was a strategy which Monty unfolded with absolute conviction, two months before the new date set for the invasion: the first full moon in June. As in his address to senior officers before Alamein the calm authority with which Monty outlined his plan, the likely enemy response, and the phases through which the battle would go, was almost incredible to those present who did not already know Montgomery. By personalising the enemy as 'Rommel', he was able to clarify and simplify the scenario – alerting all to the sense of contest between opposing wills:

[1] Lt-Colonel C. P. Dawnay, interview of 24.8.78.
[2] General Sir Charles Richardson, interview of 20.11.79. Bradley objected to the phase-line *date* forecasts on the maps. 'When General Bradley and I arrived at St Paul's School we found that on the profile map they had displayed on the floor, here were these phase lines. Bradley and I insisted that they be removed from the American sector because we had not agreed on any specific dates for any phase lines. Monty was a bit put out by that – that was the first indication I ever saw of a little tiff between Monty and Brad. But Monty finally removed the phase-lines on the American side' – General J. L. Collins, interview of 21.10.81. It is quite clear from Bradley's testimony that he was not opposed to phase lines as a conceptual method of imparting the 'masterplan' to subordinate commanders, but was concerned only by the dates given, as these had not been agreed by him. In his summary of the early stage of the Normandy campaign to his ADC after the war, Bradley declared that there was 'no change in general plan, the general plan of invasion. . . . We were carrying out orders from England to reach initial phase lines' – 'Bradley Commentaries', loc. cit.

Since ROMMEL toured the 'Atlantic Wall' the enemy has been stiffening up his coastal crust, generally strengthening his defences, and re-distributing his armoured reserve.

The present general trend of movement of his mobile reserves is SOUTH – i.e. away from the NEPTUNE area; this shows that our target is not yet known to the enemy.

ROMMEL is likely to hold his mobile Divisions back from the coast until he is certain where our main effort is being made. He will then concentrate them quickly and strike a hard blow; his static Divisions will endeavour to hold on defensively to important ground and act as pivots to the counter-attacks.

Those who were surprised by Monty's certainty about Rommel assumed he must have an excellent Intelligence staff, and it is true that much of Monty's appreciation of Rommel's likely tactics owed its origin to the work of his brilliant Intelligence chief, Brigadier Williams. Williams had, however, not previously served in Home Forces, and it was undoubtedly in the period after Dunkirk, when Monty held command first of a division, then a Corps, and finally an army on the southern coast, that Monty's real insight into likely German response to invasion derived. For Rommel's response was a projection of his own in 1940 and 1941 when he developed his 'Plan to Defeat Invasion'. As Williams himself acknowledged, when in doubt as to how the enemy might react to Allied moves, it was often helpful to ask Monty how *he* would react.[1]

Rommel's defensive strategy has often been misrepresented as one of attempting to defeat the Allies on the beaches. Because Rommel went to such inordinate lengths to improve beach and coastal defences, this did not signify that Rommel believed in static defence. He would, Monty was certain, hold his mobile divisions *away* from the coast, committing them only when certain of the area of main enemy assault:

By dusk on D − 1 day the enemy will be certain that the NEPTUNE [or 'Overlord'] area is to be assaulted in strength. By the evening of D day he will know the width of our frontage and the approximate number of our assaulting Divisions; it will be quite evident that ours is a major assault. The enemy is likely that night to summon his two nearest Panzer Divisions to assist.

By D + 5 the enemy can have brought in 6 Panzer Type Divisions. If he has decided to go the whole NEPTUNE hog, he will continue his efforts to push us into the sea.

Monty did not think Rommel would succeed:

---

[1] Brigadier Sir Edgar Williams, interview of 20.12.79.

We ourselves will have 15 divisions on shore by then. After about D + 8 I think the enemy will have to begin to consider a 'roping-off' policy i.e., trying to stop our expansion from the lodgement area.

Nevertheless he acknowledged that Rommel was a tough foe: 'Some of us here know ROMMEL well. He is a determined commander and likes to hurl his armour into the battle,' Monty acknowledged, remembering the fierce armoured engagements during Alamein. 'But according to what we know of the chain of command the armoured divisions are being kept directly under RUNDSTEDT, and delay may be caused before they are released to ROMMEL. This fact may help us, and quarrels may arise between the two of them.' This, and the hopefully savage effect of Allied air superiority, ought to give the Allies a period of perhaps four days' grace in which to face the real test: 'The enemy build-up can become *considerable* from D + 4 onwards; obviously therefore we must put all our energies into the fight and get such a good situation in the first few days that the enemy can do nothing against us.'

There then followed an outline of Monty's strategic and tactical plans for developing the Normandy battle, once the initial Allied bridgehead, comprising Second British and First US Armies, was established. While the British army pivoted on Caen and struck south to form a great inland shield, Bradley's American army would seize Cherbourg, cut off the Cherbourg peninsula and break out behind the British shield, capturing the Brittany ports and wheeling eastwards for a final offensive towards Paris.

The tasks given to the armies are as follows:
First US Army
(a) To assault astride the CARENTAN estuary
(b) To capture CHERBOURG as quickly as possible
(c) East of CARENTAN, to develop operations southwards towards St LO in conformity with the advance of Second British Army.
    After the area CHERBOURG – CAUMONT – VIRE – AVRANCHES has been captured, the Army will be directed southwards with the object of capturing RENNES and then establishing our flank on the R. LOIRE and capturing QUIBERON BAY.

Patton's Third Army was to push through First US Army's Front, 'clearing the BRITTANY peninsula and capturing the BRITTANY ports'; then, having seized St Nazaire and Nantes on the Loire, it was to cover 'the south flank of the lodgement area while the First US Army is directed N.E. with a view to operations towards PARIS'.

The task of Dempsey's Second British Army was less dramatic, but equally vital. It was 'to assault to the west of the R. ORNE and to develop operations to the south and south-east, in order to secure airfield sites and to protect the eastern flank of First US Army while the latter is capturing CHERBOURG. In its subsequent operations the ARMY will pivot on its left [CAEN] and offer a strong front against enemy movement towards the lodgement area from the east'. In this it would be reinforced, after sufficient formations had been landed, by the headquarters of First Canadian Army, which would take over Dempsey's left or northern Corps in the Caen area and whose ultimate task would be the capture of Le Havre.

To illustrate his plan, Monty pointed to a large-scale map of northern France. There would be, he prophesied, four phases: phase 1, covering the first 20 days – 'this gives us a good base for subsequent operations. I estimate we may have this area by D + 20, and we will fight continuously till we get it. There may then have to be a pause to see how we stand administratively; if not, so much the better.' The line ran south from Cabourg to Falaise, then westwards towards Avranches, at the eastern base of the Cherbourg peninsula. Phase 2 would then see the British Second Army pushing marginally forward on its left flank to the line of the river Touques, maintaining its shielding position in the centre, but swinging out its right flank, hitherto anchored on Falaise, to Argentan, near the rise of the Orne. Behind Second Army's shield, First US Army would break out 'southwards towards the LOIRE and QUIBERON Bay . . . I estimate that, if all goes well, we may have the area up to the Yellow [phase 2] line by D + 35 to D + 40' – though the actual clearing up of the Brittany peninsula, by the newly introduced Third Army under Patton, was 'not possible to estimate with any likelihood of accuracy; it may be up to D + 60'.

Phase 3, the final phase of the battle, would take the Allies to the Seine: the Canadians responsible for the front from Rouen northwards to Le Havre and the Channel; British Second Army the front between Rouen and Paris; and First US Army would 'be directed on PARIS, and the SEINE above the city. It will be prepared to cross the river and operate to the N.E.,' with Patton's Third Army given a role 'to protect its right or southern flank' in the drive towards the Ruhr and Berlin – currently identified by Eisenhower's long-term planners as the subsequent strategic objectives.[1] 'We might reach the black [Phase 3] line by D + 90,' Monty suggested.

[1] 'An appreciation of the German defence of the West after the establishment of an Allied lodgement or beachhead in France, has been submitted to the Supreme Commander by General Whiteley, the G2,' Commander Butcher recorded in his diary on 6.4.44. 'It says that once the Ruhr Valley is taken by the Allies, Germany will lose 65% of her productive capacity for crude steel, and 56% of her total coal production . . .' – loc. cit. See also Brigadier K. G. McLean, loc. cit.: 'In April we worked up a paper on the advance into Germany. . . .'

In the subsequent bickering in rear headquarters, the failure of Monty's armies to conform precisely to this outline plan would cause deep and lasting resentments, the more so since Monty would not afterwards admit that the battle of Normandy had not gone 'according to plan'. Ought he therefore to have kept quiet, in the days before D-Day, about his intended stategy? However, the task of a general is not to please historians. It is to mount and conduct his operations so that they have the best possible chance of success; and by presenting such a clearly defined strategic plan for the battle there can be no doubt that Monty brought to his Allied land, sea and air forces a unity of purpose and conception that was remarkable – and often confused later with Eisenhower's role as Supreme Commander. Against a background of uncertainty over Allied strategic and tactical bombing policy,[1] of continued naval concern over the possible resurrection of 'Anvil',[2] Monty presented an army plan that gave all those present a surge of confidence. Even more remarkable was the fact that at the climax of the battle Monty hoped to have in the field some thirty-five divisions, still by no means a preponderant force when in France alone Hitler could dispose of upwards of sixty.

Monty's address was followed by brief presentations by Ramsay, Leigh-Mallory, Bradley and his two Corps Commanders, then Dempsey and the two British Corps Commanders.

'All this constituted a heavy dose for absorption in one day,' General Kennedy noted. 'But it was well worth while to hear it in this way.'[3]

Churchill now appeared. Up to this point Monty had permitted no smoking; but hearing that the Prime Minister would be attending the exercise after tea, Monty relaxed his rule: 'As the Prime Minister would undoubtedly arrive with a large cigar, smoking would be allowed after tea. He made the announcement in such a puckish way that there was a great roar of laughter,' Kennedy recalled.[4] As he dismissed us for a ten-minute break late that afternoon,' Bradley also remembered, 'he sniffed the air of the room and grinned. "When we re-assemble, gentlemen," he said, "you may smoke if you wish." There was a ripple of laughter in the audience, for both the Prime Minister and Eisenhower were to join us.'[5]

---

[1] In his Memorandum of 22.3.44, Eisenhower declared his intention of resigning unless the air command situation and air preparatory plans were settled 'at once' – *The Eisenhower Diaries*, op. cit.

[2] Within days of the 'final' decision on 'Anvil', the American Chiefs of Staff were calling for a renunciation of the Allied offensive towards Rome, and resurrection of 'Anvil', with a target date of 10 July 1944 – see the Diary of Harry C. Butcher, entry of 27.3.44, loc. cit.

[3] Op. cit.

[4] Ibid.

[5] Omar N. Bradley, *A Soldier's Story*, op. cit.

Winston duly arrived. He looked puffy and dejected and his eyes were red. When he had taken his seat, Montgomery spoke again for ten minutes, as he said, to emphasise three main points. The first was that he himself had the most complete confidence in the plan. This confidence must be imparted all the way down the chain of command – he had no room for any doubters. He said that, in effect, the assault was by two armies against two German battalions, which was all they had on the coastal sector at that moment.[1]

Monty's second point made Churchill prick up his ears. At a conference of Army Commanders on 20 March, a fortnight earlier, Monty had issued a paper concerning 'Some Army Problems' that he wished to discuss. In this he had considered the problem of getting ashore, the best tactical layout of breaching parties (including the 'menu' of special tanks and equipment) and command and control; however the primary matter was that of penetration inland: 'As we penetrate inland we may expect to find important areas, such as high ground or centres of communication, held by static and immobile Divisions. . . . We must not let these areas hold up our rapid penetration inland. We have to gain the tactical advantage quickly, and to push ahead and seize our own pivots – using armoured and mobile forces.' He insisted too that the capture of airfields was vital – 'as we secure airfields, and good areas for making airfields, so we get increased air support, and so everything becomes easier. It is very important that the area to the S.E. of CAEN should be secured as early as Second Army can manage.'[2] He mentioned, too, the need for gaining depth in the bridgehead ('we must have space in which we can develop our administrative lay-out') – but in the consequent discussion with Dempsey, Bradley and Crerar, Monty 'particularly . . . stressed the very great importance of a speedy penetration inland.'[3]

It was this theme which, before Churchill and the assembled officers in St Paul's, Monty now re-iterated:

His second point was to emphasise the need for boldness and enterprise in pushing forward mobile forces – even a few armoured cars 20 miles inside the German lines would create confusion and delay,

[1] J. Kennedy, op. cit.
[2] In C-in-C's Directives (21 A Gp/1062/2/C-in-C), Montgomery Papers.
[3] 'Minutes of C-in-C's Conference with Army Commanders, 20 March 1944', in 'Various conferences' file (21 AGP/1065/2/C-in-C), Montgomery Papers.

Kennedy recorded.[1] It was a point which the American planner, Colonel Bonesteel, also vividly remembered, according to the Official Historian who interviewed him in 1947:

> Remembers first day at St Paul's when he counted more than 70 admirals, generals and air marshals and wondered at the effect of one bomb. Remembers that Monty and Dempsey planned to get a pivot of manoeuvre by sending tanks down beyond Caen in the first 36 hours. Impossible business in the bocage. Thinks Monty wanted something which would sound good and that he said it with his tongue in his cheek. Sounded big beside Bradley's plan for slower advance.[2]

There was much truth in this, for although Monty had a deep instinctive feel for important tactical terrain, it was not so much a feeling for the ground in question, rather a profoundly professional grasp of what was crucial to the enemy. In wishing Dempsey to 'penetrate inland' he was seeking to disrupt Rommel's inevitable counter-attacks until the Allies were firmly established on ground of their own choosing, just as he had sought to drive out his armour at Alamein. As at Alamein, however, such tactical boldness could only succeed if the terrain and the dispositions of the enemy favoured such thrusts. At Alamein they did not, nor would they in the small fields and thick hedges of the Normandy *bocage*.

Churchill, however, was delighted by such talk. Monty's third and final point was the need to take airfields – but Churchill had ears only for the armoured thrusts with which he was obsessed. Mounting the platform Churchill gave what he intended to be one of his finer military orations. 'He was in a short black jacket and had a big cigar as usual. He said he had not been convinced in 1942, or in 1943, that this operation was feasible. He was not expressing an opinion on its feasibility now. But, if he were qualified to do so, and if he were one of us, he would have the greatest confidence from all he had heard of the plans.'[3] As Eisenhower later recalled: 'Gripping his lapels firmly in his hands, he said, "Gentlemen, I am *now* hardening to this enterprise." '[4]

This was a phrase Churchill had first used the month before in a signal to General Marshall,[5] but it shocked Eisenhower: 'I then realised for the first time that Mr Churchill hadn't believed in it all

[1] Op. cit.
[2] Loc. cit.
[3] J. Kennedy, op. cit.
[4] Interview of 3.6.46 by S. L. A. Marshall, Military History Institute, Carlisle, Pennsylvania (Eisenhower's memory served him badly: he believed the date of the presentation had been 26 May 44).
[5] Signal of 11.3.44, in W. S. Churchill, op. cit.

along and had had no faith that it would succeed. It was quite a shocking discovery.'[1]

Churchill, struggling to hold the attentions of a tiring audience, declared 'that the time was now *ripe*' for 'Overlord': 'We had experienced commanders, a great Allied army, a great air force. Our equipment had improved. All the preparations, strategical and tactical, had been made with the greatest skill and care. We were now going to write a glorious page in the history, not of one country or of two, but of the world.'[2]

From glory Churchill passed to tactics. 'He felt very strongly that this should not be an operation designed to dig in on a bridgehead. At Anzio we had lost a great opportunity – *there* was a lesson for all to study.'[3]

Patton, sitting in the audience, was delighted. ' "Remember that this is an invasion, not a creation of a fortified beachhead," ' he quoted Churchill in his diary.[4]

'The object,' Churchill concluded his remarks,[5] 'must be to fight a battle. We needed a battle to break the will of the Germans to fight. Therefore he was glad to hear what had been said about pushing forward armoured spearheads, and *unarmoured* spearheads. He ended by wishing good luck to all those engaged in the operation.'

In inviting Churchill, Monty had hoped the Prime Minister would round off the day on an inspiring note. 'He looks tired and worn out, and I fear did not create the inspiring influence I had wanted,' Monty recorded in his diary that night. 'I cannot feel happy about the P.M.; if he cracks up now we shall be in a bad way; it is vital he should keep fit and well; his personality and drive are essential for what we have to do.' Brooke was equally disappointed: 'He [Churchill] was looking old and lacking a great deal of his usual vitality,'[6] he noted – as did Kennedy:

He spoke without vigour. He did not look up much while he spoke. There was the usual wonderful flow of fine phrases, but no fire in the delivery. . . . But I heard afterwards that members of the audience who saw him on that day for the first time were tremendously impressed and inspired.[7]

Patton certainly was: 'The Prime Minister made the last talk and the best.' Of Monty's careful exposition, involving a three-month-

[1] Interview by S. L. A. Marshall, loc. cit.
[2] J. Kennedy, op. cit.
[3] Ibid.
[4] *The Patton Papers*, op. cit.
[5] J. Kennedy, op. cit.
[6] A. Bryant, op. cit.
[7] J. Kennedy, op. cit.

long battle, Patton recorded nothing save that, in discussing the roles of the four army commanders under Monty's command, he, Patton, 'was the only one . . . to be mentioned by name. The other three he mentioned by number [of the Army].'[1] Patton was all for bravado, and Monty's whole strategy for 'Overlord' he felt to be cautious and pedantic. The fact that he, Patton, might not be called into the fighting until the final break-out into Brittany taxed his patience to breaking point – and within weeks he was compromising his very appointment to command Third US Army by an outspoken speech at his first public engagement in England: the 'Knutsford Incident'.[2]

[1] *The Patton Papers*, op. cit.
[2] Patton's ill-advised speech was given at Knutsford on 25 April 1944. Marshall recommended Patton's relief, and Eisenhower was on the point of giving General Hodges, Bradley's Deputy Commander, command of Patton's army when the true ridiculousness of the incident – which Churchill regarded as a storm in a teacup – finally dawned on him. On 3 May Eisenhower cabled Patton: 'Go ahead and train your army' – *The Patton Papers*, op. cit.

CHAPTER SEVEN

The Problem of Manpower

Since August 1943 Patton had, as a result of the 'slapping incident', been denied combat. His impatience was becoming volcanic – to the point where he lived and dreamed break-out.[1]

Monty's task, however, was to prepare the seedbed for the American strike into Brittany, and although he talked, in front of Churchill, of 'armoured spearheads' thrusting deep into the German lines it was, as Colonel Bonesteel perceived, said almost tongue-in-cheek: for what was vital was that the British should form an unbreakable shield against the enemy's armour, not risk a broken lance. As his Chief of Staff, General de Guingand, later reiterated: 'Monty was absolutely against taking any risks of loosening his hold on the left – he wanted to hold on absolutely firmly. . . . He said Ike never appreciated the importance of holding on the left – and that's true!'[2] De Guingand could not, afterwards, understand Eisenhower's misunderstanding of Monty's Normandy strategy: 'Why was Ike unclear? He shouldn't have been! He shouldn't have been – I had talks with him, talked to him every day practically and made it quite clear to him that we were going to hold on and take no risks.'[3]

What seems clear today, four decades after 'Overlord', is that Monty, in stressing the need for aggression from the moment the troops landed, involuntarily gave rise to an expectation in the minds of Eisenhower, Churchill and Patton that British forces would be mounting a major thrust eastwards and south-eastwards – in contrast to Anzio, where Lucas had deliberately refrained from striking into the Alban hills. This impression, created at the presentation of

---

[1] Despite Monty's enlargement of the assault area, Patton still thought the invasion front too narrow. 'There should be three separate attacks on at least a 90 mile front. I have said this for nearly a year,' he recorded on 1 May 1944. He claimed that Eisenhower had agreed 'that this attack is badly planned and on too narrow a front and may well result in an Anzio, especially if I am not there' (*The Patton Papers*, op. cit.) – but despite his obsession with 'Anvil' it is unlikely that Eisenhower believed any such thing. The guns of Le Havre and Cherbourg determined the maximum width of the assault, and Monty refused ever to countenance separate landings which could be defeated in detail.

[2] Interview of 9.5.78.

[3] Ibid.

plans at St Paul's on 7 April 1944, was further compounded when, a week later, Monty put the matter into print by issuing another memorandum to Dempsey and Bradley, copies of which were sent this time to Eisenhower and Churchill. 'In operation OVERLORD,' Monty remarked, 'an uncertain factor is the speed at which the enemy will be able to concentrate his mobile and armoured Divisions against us for counter-attack. On our part we must watch the situation carefully, and must not get our main bodies so stretched that they would be unable to hold against determined counter-attack; on the other hand, having seized the initiative by our initial landings we must ensure that we keep it.' Monty's tactical proposition, therefore, was to 'interfere with the enemy concentrations and counter-measures' by pushing out 'fairly powerful armoured force thrusts on the afternoon of D-Day. If two such forces, each consisting of an armoured Bde Group, were pushed forward on each Army front to carefully chosen areas, it would be very difficult for the enemy to interfere with our build-up. . . . I am prepared to accept almost any risk in order to carry out these tactics. I would risk even the total loss of the armoured brigade groups which in any event is not really possible; the delay they would cause to the enemy before they could be destroyed would be quite enough to give us time to get our main bodies well ashore and re-organised for strong offensive action.'[1]

As will be seen, Dempsey's attempt to do this failed, while Bradley only followed the directive on paper: 'Monty . . . urged me to explore the possibility of a similar tank knockabout behind Omaha Beach. Although knowing there was scant chance of carrying it through, I nevertheless devised such a mission. As I anticipated, we never even tried it. In contrast to Monty, I had foreseen a hard enemy crust on the Normandy coast.'[2]

Churchill, however, was excited by the directive. 'For what my opinion is worth, it seems to be exactly the spirit in which the execution should proceed, and I only wish that a similar course had been attempted when the forces landed at Anzio,' he wrote back.[3]

Did Churchill confuse this limited manoeuvre, designed to help the establishment of the bridgehead behind, with the idea of a break-out from what might otherwise become a 'fortified beachhead' as at Anzio?[4] Politicians make inspiring leaders, but ignorant com-

[1] Quoted in B. L. Montgomery, *Memoirs*, London 1958. Original in Montgomery Papers.
[2] Omar N. Bradley, op. cit.
[3] B. L. Montgomery, *Memoirs*, op. cit. Original in Montgomery Papers.
[4] Churchill's cycle of elation and anxiety led to alarming contradictions. He was all for immediate break-out from the bridgehead – yet, as Eisenhower recalled after the war, Churchill never believed the Allied armies would get beyond the Seine before 1945. – see interview by S. L. A. Marshall, loc. cit. Moreover,

manders – and Churchhill was no exception. Like Monty he was, to all intents and purposes, a democratic dictator; like Monty his restless energy led him to interfere in matters not strictly his concern; and like Monty he was forgiven by those whom he wearied and upset because he was so palpably greater, as a leader, than any other Britain seemed able to produce. Nevertheless this misunderstanding over Montgomery's strategy (it must be remembered that Churchill did not attend Monty's 1½-hour presentation on the morning of 7 April) was to have serious repercussions that summer – as would Eisenhower's.

Meanwhile on the day after Monty's presentation at St Paul's, the 'Overlord' plans were 'second-guessed'. A list of questions had been prepared by Monty's staff and was shot, in turn, to the commanders of each section of the assault. A huge scale model of Normandy had been made – in the same manner as Monty's amphibious invasion exercise in Studland Bay in 1937 – and, resting on the floor, was tilted to give a better view from the tiered auditorium – 'a relief map of Normandy the width of a city street,' over which Monty strode 'like a giant through Lilliputian France', in Bradley's words.[1] When the turn of the American commander of 7 US Corps came, he was asked what would happen if his command ship were sunk on the run-in to 'Utah' beach. 'Sir, if my ship sinks, you'll find me swimming like hell for the shore!' answered the brave general.[2]

The question put to General 'Lightning Joe' Collins had been intended to discern his command arrangements (if any) in the eventuality that his own vessel was sunk. More searching was the question fired at General Bradley. Colonel Bonesteel, seconded by Bradley to Monty's Allied headquarters, 21st Army Group, later remembered it well: 'On the second day, the 21 A Gp war gamed Bradley and Dempsey. Threw situations at them. Tested plans with unlikely situations. One of the questions to Bradley was "what would Bradley do if just before D-day he had to change the airborne plan".'[3]

This was a salutary question, for seven weeks later newly discovered German dispositions in the Cotentin *did* force Bradley to make a vital last-minute change in his airborne plan. It was a change he was able to make instantly, thanks to the day of 'second-guessing' at St Paul's on 8 April.

As the invasion approached, meanwhile, Monty cast his eye

Morgan's COSSAC plan for a British-Canadian break-out eastwards towards the Seine may have confused Churchill, who did not attend the full 'Thunderclap' exercise.

[1] Omar N. Bradley, op. cit.
[2] R. F. K. Belchem, *All in the Day's March*, London 1978.
[3] Loc. cit.

anxiously over the reinforcement situation. The battle for Rome in 1943 had been lost, in his view, because the Allied High Command had failed to conceive its operations in line with what was administratively possible, and he was adamant there should be no repetition of that. Almost immediately, however, he ran up against Churchill. Churchill had served briefly with a battalion of the Grenadier Guards in 1915; the battalion of Royal Scots Fusiliers which he commanded early in 1916 had been quickly cannibalised and merged with another battalion, depriving him of command. When Monty therefore suggested that, in view of the worsening manpower outlook, a certain cannibalisation should take place immediately in the Brigade of Guards, Churchill put his foot down. Wishing to emulate the Russians and the Germans, he insisted that the Guards obtain reinforcements by reducing their strict standards of intake, and that Monty's plan to 'melt down' the Guards Tank Brigade, to provide Guards reinforcements, be quashed.[1] Monty reacted as he had over the Poles: he informed the Director of Staff Duties at the War Office that he was dropping the 6th Guards Tank Brigade from his 'Overlord' team:

You cannot suddenly take Line reinforcements and draft them into Guards units – 'just like that'; the two types of discipline are quite different and it does not work. . . . Meanwhile I have got to do something very quickly. The action I have taken is as follows:
a) I have withdrawn 6 Gds Tank Bde into Army Group reserve. This means it is not in the build-up for OVERLORD, and will not be called over to France for a long time.
b) I have replaced it in Second Army by 31 Armd Bde, which was in Army Group reserve. One of the Regts of this Bde is a flame thrower Regt; so it suits me very well. . . .
I suppose the Prime Minister is within his rights to disregard the considered advice of the Secretary of State and the CIGS. But I cannot 'mess up' my operations,

Monty stated categorically,

and I must have a tidy set-up; I know so well what happens when the set-up is not tidy and is unbalanced; I shall therefore not take 6 Gds Tank Bde to the war.

It is easy to see why Churchill preferred the compliant Alexander, despite all his failings as a field commander, to the dictator now running the 'Overlord' armies.

[1] Personal Minute from Churchill to Montgomery of 9.4.44, in 'Miscellaneous Correspondence' file (21 A Gp/1065/C-in-C), Montgomery Papers.

Monty's concern with the need to 'melt down' formations was, however, no isolated necessity, for the more Monty pondered the problem, the more alarming seemed the state of British army manpower. The tortuous question of the Guards had arisen from a recognition by the War Office in late March that 'if our estimates of casualties in OVERLORD (based on our recent experience in Italy) turn out to be correct', there would be a 'total deficiency in units in the field . . . of the order of 60,000, of which 40,000 will be infantry'.[1] At least one division would have to be cannibalised during the Normandy fighting, it was estimated, and by July 'there will be no British operational formations left in the UK except 52 Division which is trained in mountain warfare and earmarked for Norway'.[2] Even the non-operational, static defence forces in Britain would by then be reduced to cadres.

The outlook for Britain, with major offensive campaigns to be conducted also in Italy and the Far East, was grim, and should be borne in mind when assessing Monty's alleged cautiousness as senior British commander in 'Overlord', and thereafter.

Though Monty undoubtedly worried about the manpower problem, he refused to let his doubts show to his men. Throughout the rest of April he tirelessly visited Allied units on rehearsal exercises for 'Overlord', as well as further factories where bottlenecks were reported in the production of critical components and arms. His pattern of addresses, from the bonnet of his jeep, was repeated again and again. Academic historians would pass over such things, but to the soldiers involved, Monty's visits were of the same inspirational quality as Churchill's in the dark days of 1940. Two days after his headquarters exercise at St Paul's, Monty was once more on tour. He attended 3rd Canadian Division's exercise at Slapton, inspected establishments and ships of the Royal Navy's Plymouth Command, visited 4th US Division in the Exeter area, followed by 30th US Division near Oxford. Breaking in London for a single day on 16 April, he set off to attend a 50th Division exercise assault at Studland, followed by a journey to Scotland to visit certain factories in Glasgow and inspect airborne troops of the SAS Brigade. After three days at his headquarters in London he left again on 26 April to attend an air bombing exercise at Studland, followed by an assault landing exercise by 4th US Division at Slapton, during which German 'E' boats penetrated the British naval screen and sank two LSTs. On this day more than six hundred men lost their lives – more fatal casualties, as Bradley later noted, than would be suffered by the whole 7th US Corps on D-Day itself. 'April has been a busy month, with exercises,

[1] 'Manpower' Memorandum from Secretary of State for War to Prime Minister, 25.3.44.
[2] Ibid.

visits to factories, and much travelling,' Monty recorded in his diary. 'I began to feel somewhat tired by the end of the month.' He planned to take a week's holiday in May, but first he had to attend the final dress-rehearsal by all assault divisions on 4 May.

CHAPTER EIGHT

'I Send you a Salmon'

Preparations for D-Day were not confined to the field armies. Major Paul Odgers, who had been brought back from Eighth Army Headquarters in Italy, later recalled the creation of Monty's Tac Headquarters for Normandy.

> I came back at the end of March. David Belchem said I could have a week's leave. So I did that and it must have been the 7th or 8th April they said, we'd like you to do Monty's Tactical Headquarters – we'd like you to form it.
>
> Right, a Tactical Headquarters. Well fortunately I knew roughly the size of Tac at Eighth Army – I knew it had got to be a bit bigger than that. But I also knew it's got to be a small outfit and so – it was very interesting, it was a most extraordinary experience, which I still look back on because, for once, I had unlimited resources. You only had to ask, and it would be provided. I could have asked for the world and it would have arrived.
>
> Of course you had to limit yourself, be bloody careful what you *did* have, but it was a most extraordinary situation, and I mean, not in a week's time, it would be there today. It was most remarkable really.
>
> So I did that. I designed this thing and with careful consultations with everybody, technical requirements and so on, and got the various officers who were appointed – they were all appointed at this time. I saw the chap who was going to be Quartermaster, etcetera – all these people were instructed to go off and order various things and get it in the pipeline, I remember.
>
> I took as given the immediate requirements of Monty's personal staff – that was given to me. It was the Ops business, the supporting signals and administrative stuff, defence stuff and all that – it all had to be thought of and done. I had a very free hand.
>
> That was all done in about 10 days. It was worked at at such great speed. I then issued orders for the thing to assemble at Southwick Park in that quadrilateral – a group of large, shady trees for concealment in a corner of Southwick Park, just outside Portsmouth.

I then went off and got married, and had three or four days honeymoon. And I came back, drove down to Southwick Park, and there it was!

'I'd recce'd the thing, and so on – but there it was. The whole outfit was in tents, the entire thing was tented down there, with a marquee for Monty's dining room. He himself was living in Broomfield House, and didn't come to the headquarters except to meet the officers – we had a dinner party. We had a B mess – there was A and B Mess – A was his, B was us.

I remember I'd first seen Monty in Malta, and it was the most awe-inspiring sight, I remember at the time almost shaking in my shoes. Only two people have ever made me shake in my shoes – Monty, and a very great headmaster at Rugby where I was at school.

However what did occur is that you went through what was in a sense a period of fire, you were aware that if you made the slightest balls of it you'd be in the deepest trouble and you'd be out. But if you survived and you came through, you realised you were 'inside', that Monty would stand behind you! He would look after you – and did. And that gave you a great feeling of security, of feeling that of course you mustn't make a balls of it, but that you could get on with the job with great confidence. That was one of the things I do remember – how *confident we all were*.[1]

De Guingand, as Monty's Chief of Staff, looked upon the creation of this new Tactical Headquarters with understandable misgiving. It would enable Monty, as in the desert, in Sicily and Italy, to impose a 'grip' on the battle well forward; but with the likelihood that Main Headquarters of 21st Army Group would be kept back in England co-ordinating air, navy, administration and reinforcements, there was the danger that the two headquarters might become divorced from one another. De Guingand therefore asked Monty to accept, as Tac HQ Commander, a senior colonel from 21st Army Group Operations staff: Colonel Leo Russell.

Without question this was a grave mistake of de Guingand's. Russell had no experience of running a Tac headquarters, and, with his somewhat abrasive manner, was an 'unknown quantity' in terms of how he would go down with Monty.

We had this officer appointed to command the outfit, Colonel Russell, who was a very nice fellow – I liked him very much,

Odgers recalled;

[1] P. R. Odgers, interview of 18.1.83.

his trouble was, he had no field experience – he really hadn't. I think he was probably a very good staff officer, very bright. . . . So it wasn't really any help when he came.

Odgers himself prepared the headquarters for its future role, in 'proper' Eighth Army fashion, by rehearsing the art of movement until it became almost second nature:

I did the training – I am very glad the thing was postponed – there was talk of an earlier date – I am very glad we were given the extra month. There really was no time because, again, these chaps were admirable who arrived, all very well versed in handling their stuff, but they didn't have experience of moving – how you packed up headquarters, what you did. One thing you have to do, if you're doing this, is you've got to be prepared to move very fast – the notice you'd be given would be very limited and you can't just dream up something on the day, you've got to have a plan, you have to have a drill. Everyone's got to know, and all these things had to be practised.

So I was very glad to have the chance to do that – and a great deal of our time was spent making these people pack and unpack themselves and go off. I'd been away [overseas] a long time, I enjoyed it very much, the Sussex countryside, 30 or 40 miles – making them pack, go off, pack again. Eventually having done these exercises, eventually I suddenly realised it was clicking, and these chaps would be capable of moving in an orderly way.[1]

Monty was similarly satisfied when he attended the dress-rehearsal for the D-Day assault, on 4 May. 'The results were good and I am satisfied that all the British Divisions have reached a high standard of efficiency, and that the Naval Task Forces are well integrated with the Army formations,' Monty noted in his dairy. 'Also for American Divisions.'

The invasion was now four weeks away. On 5 May Monty left for Scotland, first to pay a series of visits to the Home Fleet, then, on 9 May, to take a few days' holiday walking and fishing in the highlands. 'I garaged my special train (Rapier) at DALWHINNIE, and walked on the mountains and fished. I had begun to feel the need of a rest, and it did me good,' he remarked in his diary. His military assistant, 'Kit' Dawnay, recalled that Monty was becoming 'extremely tired', despite his regime of early nights. Sleeping each night on the Rapier at Dalwhinnie, Monty would religiously set off each day to fish. 'He failed to catch one!' Dawnay recalled with a laugh.[2]

[1] Ibid.
[2] Lt-Colonel C. P. Dawnay, interview of 24.8.78.

Monty's stepson, Dick Carver, commanding a field company destined for Normandy, also accompanied Monty on the trip to Scotland, and remembered how at Dalwhinnie they were joined by de Guingand, who also 'deserved a rest' as Monty had told him.

I went on this trip before D-Day on Rapier, when we had rather a holiday in Scotland. He was visiting the Fleet up there – that was the excuse for going up!

He went fishing, yes. The train was parked at Dalwhinnie, which is the very highest point on the line, I think, near Inverness, and we went off in parties, fishing – fishing for salmon. De Guingand of course was a fisherman, but Monty wasn't at all! And of course he wasn't very successful. He was lent a rod, the thing was laid on by the local admiral. And we got back to the train one night, and Monty laid bets with de Guingand that he had caught the biggest salmon. And of course Monty was bluffing because he hadn't caught one at all![1]

There was a more serious side to Monty's Scottish holiday though, for while Monty attempted vainly to master the secrets of salmon fishing in the waters of the river Spey, he was being watched by an actor due to impersonate him in North Africa as part of a deception plan designed to draw German attention to possible landings in southern France.[2]

Lieutenant M. E. Clifton James was mesmerised by the dress worn by Monty's staff on the train:

All the cars with their drivers were drawn up beside the train with the General's Rolls in front. . . . Ever since I had held a commission I had been under the shadow of strict discipline regarding dress and I imagined that on H.Q. Staff of the discipline would be even stricter. Yet here were officers wearing battledress blouses, suede shoes and corduroy slacks of many colours. . . .

When Monty appeared on the count of twelve I understood why his Staff wore coloured corduroys. Their Chief was similarly dressed with a grey roll-top sweater and of course the black beret. He gave us all a quick smile, chatted about the arrangements and got into his car. We all got in too. The engines started up, but instead of moving off the procession remained immobile.

I saw Monty glance up at the windows of the two cottages by the station, and presently several small children and some women

---

[1] Colonel R. O. H. Carver, interview of 17.2.78.

[2] M. E. Clifton James arrived in Gibraltar on 26 May 1944, and in Algiers the following day. Unfortunately, flushed with success, he then became drunk and operation 'Copperhead' had to be abruptly terminated – see J. Haswell, *The Intelligence and Deception of the D-Day Landings*, London 1979.

appeared up above to cheer and wave small Union Jacks. Monty at once waved back at them with a gay smile, and gave the word to move off.

Some people might have taken this for an act of a showman, of a man who loved publicity, but it did not seem like this to me. Monty is genuinely fond of children and he did not wish to disappoint the little Scottish boys and girls who cheered so shrilly from the windows. He knew they wanted to see him go, and so he waited until *they* were ready.[1]

In this, Clifton James saw the 'charming gesture' of a 'great soldier'. He watched too while Monty broke his car journey to the Spey at an isolated stone building standing by the road. It was a Highland village school. Without prior arrangement Monty marched in – and gave the children a short talk.

It was certainly a strange situation, this line of cars drawn up by a remote school in the Highlands, with officers and men sitting in silence while their General gave an impromptu address to a classroom of bairns. All the more so as the world imagined him working day and night in preparation for the greatest invasion in history. He had that power of detaching himself completely from his worries and enjoying the passing moment. . . .

The next few days I tailed Monty, except when I was forbidden to, watching his every movement and trying to catch his fleeting expressions; and I began to realise that he had himself under control in a way that I have never seen paralleled.

The whole nation was on tenterhooks about the coming invasion which might easily be a blood-bath, and even a shattering defeat. And one of the exceptions to this general nervousness was the man who had most cause to worry, the man who was in charge of it.

Clifton James was finally summoned, after dinner one night, to Monty's room aboard the train.

The General was sitting at his desk writing his daily diary. . . . He stood up with a smile.

As we stood facing each other it was rather like facing myself in a mirror. . . .

As he talked he stood up again so that I had a close view of him from every angle. I was also trying to record in my mind the rather high-pitched, incisive tone of his voice and the way he chose his words. He never used high-flown phrases; some people have even described his speech as dry and arid.

[1] M. E. Clifton James, *I was Monty's Double*, London 1954.

568

When it was time for James to leave, Monty asked him squarely: 'You have a great responsibility, you know. Do you feel confident?' And when James faltered, Monty answered for him. 'I'm sure everything will be all right. Don't worry about it.'

And in that moment not only did my qualms vanish, but I saw how Monty had only to tell an army that it could do the impossible and it just went and did it.

We shook hands and I went out.

Walking back to my hotel I thought of that slight figure sitting in his bare, unfurnished room completely alone with his burdens and I wondered how I should feel if I were in his shoes.[1]

Monty's consideration did not stop there. His vanity was tickled by the thought of an actor detailed to impersonate him in front of thousands of onlookers in Gibraltar and North Africa – but he was alive, too, to the risk of assassination, as well as the obvious repercussions if James's impersonation failed. He therefore personally insisted that James be awarded general's pay during the period of his impersonation. The War Office protested, but Monty was adamant. James received a full General's pay.[2]

Finally, on Sunday 14 May 1944, Monty returned to London. He had failed utterly as a highland angler, but he did not come back empty-handed. In almost biblical fashion he sent a gift to the Reynolds: 'I have just got back from Scotland and I send you a salmon – a magnificent fish of some 18lbs. I hope it will feed the whole school.'[3] But the true fruit of his time in the Highlands he reserved for a more critical audience: the King, the Prime Minister, the Chiefs of Staff and the generals who assembled at his headquarters in St Paul's on Monday 15 May 1944 for the 'Final Presentation of Plans'.

[1] Ibid.
[2] Ibid.
[3] Letter of 14.5.44, loc. cit.

CHAPTER NINE

The Final Presentation at St Paul's

As Eisenhower remarked at the end of proceedings on 15 May, 'in half an hour Hitler will have missed his one and only chance of destroying with a single well-aimed bomb the entire high command of the Allied forces'.[1]

In the 'ordinary' panelled lecture room of the public school Monty had himself attended without distinction from 1902 to 1906, Operation 'Overlord' was recited. The King, Churchill, Smuts and the British Chiefs of Staff sat in chairs placed as a front row; the generals sat behind on hard wooden benches. Eisenhower opened the meeting with an exhortation to be honest: 'I consider it to be the duty of anyone who sees a flaw in the plan not to hesitate to say so.'[2] 'Throughout the day EISENHOWER was quite excellent,' Monty noted in his diary; 'he spoke very little, but what he said was good and on a high level.'

To begin the actual presentation of plans Eisenhower asked Monty, as Land Forces Commander, to come forward. Strangely, Monty's address has never been published, while every word Eisenhower put to paper at this time has been exhaustively located and put into print, giving rise to a false impression that Eisenhower himself was the directing mind. However, no one either involved in the planning of 'Overlord' or present at the presentation of plans had any doubt that Montgomery, not Eisenhower, was the driving force behind the invasion. As Brooke noted in his diary: 'The main impression I gathered was that Eisenhower was no real director of thought, plans, energy or direction. Just a co-ordinator, a good mixer, a champion of inter-Allied co-operation, and in those respects few can hold a candle to him. But is that enough? Or can we not find all the qualities of a commander in one man?'[3] As co-ordinator, Eisenhower certainly displayed statesmanlike qualities that contributed immeasurably to the success of 'Overlord'; but a co-ordinator is not a commander, and it was Monty's sheer display of command

[1] 'Impressions of the meeting at St Paul's School on 15 May 1944 by Air Chief Marshal Sir Trafford Leigh-Mallory', in AEAF Record (AIR 37/784), PRO.
[2] Ibid.
[3] A. Bryant, op. cit.

which impressed all. Churchill's Military Secretary, General Ismay, likened Monty to Henry V before Agincourt – yet as Leigh-Mallory recorded, Monty's demeanour was 'very quiet and deliberate'. He was 'wearing a very well cut battle-dress with a knife-like edge to the trouser creases. He looked trim and businesslike. He spoke for ten minutes in a tone of quiet emphasis, making use of what is evidently a verbal trick of his, to repeat the most important word or phrase in a sentence more than once.'

Monty's address was to stand out like a beacon. Ramsay, exhausted by the detail of the naval operation, seemed 'indifferent and overwhelmed by all his own difficulties,' as Brooke recorded.[1] Air Marshall Harris 'told us how he might have won the war if it had not been for the handicap imposed by the existence of the two other Services'; Spaatz did not trust himself to speak from notes only and 'read every word'[2] of his address; Leigh-Mallory was clear but not inspiring.

Although Monty's address was not taken down verbatim, his notes have survived and, given their historic importance, ought now to be published. As Lt-Colonel Dawnay, who kept them, recalled, these handwritten notes were quintessential 'Monty', not the product of his staff:

Oh no, he would go into his office and he would write it very slowly himself and then get one of his staff to type it. He would write it almost always in longhand. He was very insistent on doing this – entirely personally. Mark you, having written it he would discuss it with Freddie [de Guingand] before he put it over, and Freddie would comment, get him to alter things, anything he thought was wrong.[3]

De Guingand, in this case, had no alterations to make, and the typed version is, almost word for word, identical to the original.[4]

First, Monty gave the object of 'Overlord'. Then he passed directly to his own role:

General Eisenhower has charged me with the preparation and conduct of the land battle.
My HQ is an Allied HQ, exercising operational command and control over the land forces of the Allies.

[1] Ibid.
[2] Ibid.
[3] Loc. cit.
[4] Original communicated to author by Lt-Colonel C. P. Dawnay, typescript in Montgomery Papers.

There are 4 armies under my command:

First American ⎫
Second British ⎬ Assault armies
Third American ⎫
First Canadian ⎬ Follow up

Next he outlined 'the intention':

To assault simultaneously
(a) immediately north of the Carentan estuary
(b) between the Carentan estuary and the R. ORNE with the
object of securing, as a base for further operations, a lodgement area which will include airfield sites and the port of
Cherbourg.

A port is essential for our administration; initially we want Cherbourg and later HAVRE.

As in his presentation the month before, Monty decided to perso-
nalise the impending contest. He therefore began by outlining
Rommel's plans for defence in France.

The Enemy
Last Feb. Rommel took command from Holland to the Loire. It is
now clear that his intention is to deny any penetration; *Overlord is
to be defeated on the beaches.*

To this end Rommel has:
(a) thickened up the coastal crust.
(b) Increased the number of infantry DIVS not committed to beach
defence, and allotted them in a layback role to seal off any
break in the coastal crust.
(c) Redistributed his armoured reserve.

The German situation was, in fact, formidable, as Monty made
clear.

There are now 60 enemy DIVS in France, of which 10 are Panzer
type.
12 are field infantry, mobile.
There are 4 Pz DIVS in or near the Neptune area:

21 Pz – Caen
12 SS – Lisieux
17 SS – Rennes
Lehr DIV – Tours.

Given such forces, what reception could the Allies expect on
D-Day?

572

The immediate situation is 5 divisions opposing us initially:
    Two coastal – one opposite each Army
    One field Inf – St Lo
    One field Inf – Coutances
    One Pz – Caen (21)

Within hours of the Allied touch down a further enemy division could be expected:

By 1200 hrs D Day
The Pz DIV from LISIEUX could be on the scene (12 SS)
Total 6

By the evening of D-Day there could be yet another enemy division on the scene:

By dusk on D day
The Pz DIV from RENNES could be appearing (17 SS)

In order to clarify the likely progression of the battle Monty now began to chart the opposing tallies of forces: the Allies on the left of a projected blackboard, the Germans on the right:

Ourselves ⎫ We should be fighting hard against 6 divisions, with
    $7^2/_3$ ⎭ one more Pz DIV from RENNES approaching – to be
              effective on D + 1
By dusk on D + 1
Ourselves ⎫ Two more Pz divisions can arrive:
    $10^1/_3$ ⎭   One Pz – TOURS (Lehr)
                    One Pz – MANTES (116)
              Total 9, of which 5 are PZ
By D + 2
Ourselves ⎫ Same number.
    12   ⎭

At this stage Monty foresaw danger:

But by now Overlord will have become an overriding menace requiring the concentration of all available formations that can be spared.
13 divisions may begin moving to the Neptune area:
    5 Pz (from Amiens, Toulouse, Bordeaux, Sedan, Belgium)
    8 Inf (from W. Brittany and Pas de Calais)

Thus within five days of the invasion a frightening array of enemy forces could be in the process of being assembled:

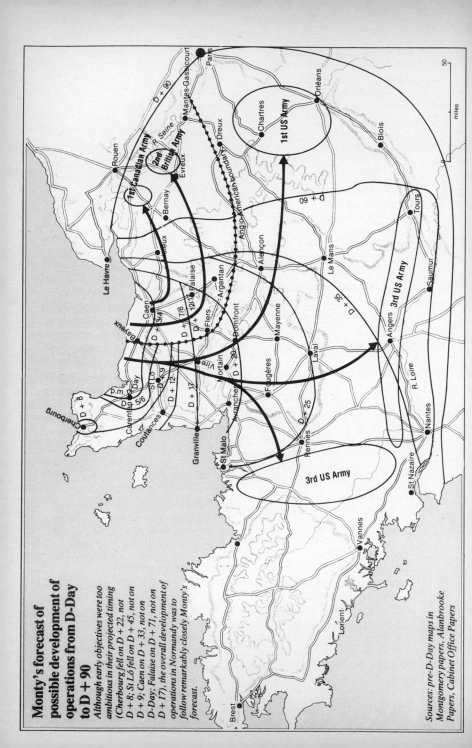

Monty's forecast of possible development of operations from D-Day to D + 90

Although early objectives were too ambitious in their projected timing (Cherbourg fell on D + 22, not D + 8; St Lô fell on D + 45, not on D + 9; Caen on D + 33, not on D-Day; Falaise on D + 71, not on D + 17), the overall development of operations in Normandy was to follow remarkably closely Monty's forecast.

1st Canadian Army

2nd British Army

1st US Army

3rd US Army

3rd US Army

R. Seine

Anglo-American boundary

R. Loire

D + 90
D + 60
D + 35
D + 25
D + 20
D + 17
D + 12
D + 9
D + 8
D + 7/8
D + 12/17
D + 3/4
D Day p.m.
D-Day 5/6

Paris
Orléans
Blois
Chartres
Dreux
Évreux
Rouen
Le Havre
Bernay
Lisieux
Mantes-Gassicourt
Tours
Saumur
Angers
Nantes
St Nazaire
Vannes
Lorient
Brest
Le Mans
Laval
Mayenne
Alençon
Argentan
Falaise
Flers
Domfront
Mortain
Vire
Fougères
Rennes
St Malo
Granville
Avranches
Coutances
St Lô
Caen
Bayeux
Carentan
Cherbourg

50
miles

Sources: pre-D-Day maps in Montgomery papers, Alanbrooke Papers, Cabinet Office Papers

By D + 5
Ourselves ⎱ The 13 divisions mentioned in para 8 may not yet all
15 ⎰ have arrived. But the enemy is beginning to have the
necessary ingredients for a full scale counter-attack
after proper recce and deployment – with infantry
holding essential ground and 10 Pz divisions available for the blow.
The full blooded counter-attack is likely at any time
after D + 6.

Monty's voice betrayed no emotion as he relentlessly painted the
picture to the assembled audience, a picture in which the Allies were
now outnumbered:

By D + 8
Ourselves ⎱ The total number of enemy divisions can now be up
18 ⎰ to 24 – of which 10 are Pz. The majority will be
securing the vital ground forward of the lateral
which links his front and which controls the essential
routes and nodal centres.
The Pz divisions will have the mobile role to push us
back into the sea.

After long discussions with Brigadier Williams, his Chief of Intelligence, Monty was however convinced, particularly in view of the
alarming number of new obstacles appearing on the Normandy
beaches, that Rommel would not in fact wait until D + 8 before
counter-attacking: and it was vital that all assault commanders
should understand this.

Rommel is an energetic and determined commander; he has made
a world of difference since he took over. He is best at the spoiling
attack; his forte is disruption; he is too impulsive for the set-piece
battle.
He will do his level best to 'Dunkirk' us – not to fight the armoured
battle on ground of his own choosing, but to avoid it altogether by
preventing our tanks landing by using his own tanks well forward.
On D day he will try to:
(a) Force us from the beaches.
(b) Secure:
            Caen
            Bayeux
            Carentan
In relation to Neptune [the choice of beaches for 'Overlord'] his
obsession is likely to be Bayeux; this important nodal point splits our
frontal landings in half.

If he can hold firm in the above three nodal points, we would be awkwardly placed.

The Allies would, Monty felt confident, seize and hold fast these three key towns, or nodal points. This being so, Williams had predicted that Rommel would revert to his Alamein tactics – an attempt to 'rope off' the Allied salient – at least until further Panzer divisions could be brought in:

> Thereafter he will continue his counter-attacks. But as time goes on he will combine them with a roping-off policy, and he must then hold firm on the important ground which dominates and controls the road axes in the 'bocage' country.
> The areas in question are:
> (a) the high ground east of the R. DIVES
> (b) the high ground between FALAISE and St LO, between the rivers ORNE and VIRE
> (c) the high ground west of the R. VIRE

Several hundred generals and their senior staff officers craned forwards as Monty's Chief of Operations, Brigadier Belchem, tapped the high ground on the huge model in front of them. No one could but be aware of the magnitude of the Allied undertaking.

The Problem
The enemy is in position, with reserves available.
There are obstacles and minefields on the beaches; we cannot gain contact with the obstacles and recce them.
There are many unknown hazards.
After a sea voyage, and a landing on a strange coast, there is always some loss of cohesion.
We must time our assault so as to make things as easy as possible for the leading troops. Therefore we shall touch-down so that all obstacles are dry, and so that we have 30 minutes in which to deal with them before the incoming tide reaches them.

As regards the wider problem – winning the 'Overlord' battle – Monty now gave his own answer:

The Solution
We have the initiative.
We must then rely on:
> (a) the violence of our assault.
> (b) our great weight of supporting fire, from the sea and air.
> (c) simplicity.
> (d) robust mentality.

We must blast our way on shore and get a good lodgement before the enemy can bring sufficient reserves up to turn us out.

Armoured columns must penetrate deep inland, and quickly, on D day; this will upset the enemy plans and tend to hold him off while we build up strength.

We must gain space rapidly, and peg out claims well inland.

And while we are engaged in doing this the air must hold the ring, and must hinder and make very difficult the movement of enemy reserves by train or road towards the lodgement area. The land battle will be a terrific party and we will require the full support of the air all the time, and laid on quickly.

Once we can get control of the main enemy lateral Grandville–Vire–Argentan–Falaise–Caen, and the area enclosed in it is firmly in our possession, then we will have the lodgement area we want and can begin to expand.

As in April, Monty ran through the tasks of the four armies, as well as those of the commandos and airborne troops. Turning to the wall maps he gave his strategic intentions for 'the development of Operations up to D + 90', outlining again the manner in which the British and Canadians would 'contain the maximum enemy forces facing the eastern flank of the bridgehead' while the American forces, 'once through the difficult *bocage* country' were to 'thrust rapidly towards Rennes', seal off the Brittany peninsula, and wheel round towards Paris and the Seine, pivoting on the right flank of the British Second Army. As Bradley recalled, 'the British and Canadian armies were to decoy the enemy reserves and draw them to their front on the extreme eastern edge of the Allied beachhead. Thus while Monty taunted the enemy at Caen, we were to make our break on the long roundabout road toward Paris. When reckoned in terms of national pride, this British decoy mission became a sacrificial one, for while we tramped around the outside flank, the British were to sit in place and pin down Germans. Yet strategically it fitted into a logical division of labors, for it was toward Caen that the enemy reserves would race once the alarm was sounded.'[1]

This strategic vision of the Normandy campaign filled the assembled audience with a sense of pride and anticipation, as it had Monty's own Chief of Intelligence when Monty first laid down his post-D-Day strategy soon after changing the COSSAC plan. As the American Official Historian noted after an interview with Brigadier Williams in 1947:

Thinks as early as January or February 1944 there is this idea of a swing from the American side towards the Seine. Remembers a

[1] Omar N. Bradley, op. cit.

map showing line out from Caen running South East and a line up the Cotentin and two lines direct down south of the Cotentin and one down and around the corner and one straight down to cut the neck of the Brittany Peninsula and one straight line down inside the Loire. 'After Cherbourg Peninsula (Monty never said Cotentin) cleaned up we shall be formed up the same way. I [Williams] plotted this on my own map. Felt an immense thrill.'[1]

Looked at on the larger map of France, there was indeed something majestic in this, as though a giant boxer was holding off his opponent with his left hand, only to swing his right and deliver a blow to the enemy's solar plexus that would send him reeling against the ropes – the river Seine.

Morale
We shall have to send the soldiers in to this party 'seeing red',

Monty concluded his address.

We must get them completely on their toes; having absolute faith in the plan; and embued with infectious optimism and offensive eagerness.
Nothing must stop them.
If we sent them in to battle in this way – then we shall succeed.

Monty stepped down. 'It went off superbly, I thought, on that occasion,' his Military Assistant, Colonel Dawnay, later recalled. 'Monty was at his best. He was a supremely confident man – it was astonishing how confident he was.'[2]
The invasion was now three weeks away.

[1] Loc. cit.
[2] Loc. cit. In a letter of 16.5.44 the American Deputy Theater Commander, General John Lee, wrote: 'Your clear and convincing estimate of the situation at St Paul's yesterday would merit in West Point language "a cold max"' – original in Montgomery Papers.

CHAPTER TEN

Showdown with Churchill

Monty's air of confidence was not a mask. His genius had been the taking of an unsound operation and its transformation into a simple, clear-cut plan in which the participants could have, at last, complete faith.

Those on the sidelines, however, were a different matter. King George VI, inspired by Monty's presentation, sprang up at St Paul's to give a surprise speech: 'absolutely first-class, quite short, and exactly right,' Monty noted in his diary. Field-Marshal Smuts, on the other hand, dwelled in his address rather gloomily on the prospect of an all-out fight in France with an enemy which had overrun the entire country in 1940 with a ruthlessness the Allies could reasonably expect to meet again in Normandy. At a private lunch in Knightsbridge Smuts then gave Monty a depressing picture of post-war Europe unless Britain took a firm hand in ensuring security and peace, and asked Monty 'when the war was nearly over' to 'speak out and say these things; he said I must give the lead in the matter. . . . He said that I had made a great name, and would make a greater one still. I could say practically what I liked; my position with the public in ENGLAND was secure and they would "swallow" whatever I said.'[1]

Monty was 'startled', but his bristling self-confidence was further flattered by Smuts's attention. This was to be the seed of something to which, in the years after 1948, Monty would devote the rest of his career – but to soldier-statesmen like Brooke, such encouragement was dangerous. Ten days after the presentation of plans Brooke dined with Monty at the latter's new headquarters mess at Broomfield House, Portsmouth. 'I had to tell him off and ask him not to meddle himself in everybody else's affairs. Such as wanting to advise Alex on his battle or War Office as to how to obtain reinforcements,' Brooke noted in his diary.[2]

Certainly Monty tolerated no such meddling in his own affairs – and the worst meddler, in Monty's opinion, was Churchill. 'Today

[1] Diary entry of 17.5.44, Montgomery Papers.
[2] A. Bryant, op. cit.

he was quite a different person and was full of life,' he recorded on 15 May after Churchill had given a rousing speech to end the presentation of plans. But all through Monty's own address Churchill had, in his characteristic pugnacious way, seen fit to interrupt Monty, asking questions 'which seemed designed to show his knowledge of strategy and tactics'.[1] When Monty's chief administrative officer recounted the magnitude of the supply problem, Churchill scowled. Two days later he was bombarding Monty with his wrath:

> The Prime Minister has asked me to tell you that he was much concerned by some of the statements made at last Monday's Conference on the subject of administrative arrangements for OVERLORD,

Churchill's Military Assistant, General Ismay, wrote.

> He was told, for example, that 2,000 officers and clerks were to be taken over to keep records, and he was given a statement (copy attached) which shows that at D plus 20 there will be one vehicle to every 4.84 men.
>
> The Prime Minister would like to have a discussion with you and your staff on the whole question of the British tail, and he wonders whether it would be convenient to you to have this before dinner at your Headquarters next Friday, 19th March.[2]

Churchill duly came, but he never penetrated beyond Montgomery to address the staff of 21st Army Group. Steering Churchill instead into his office, Monty asked the Prime Minister to be seated. Before Churchill had time to speak, Monty pre-empted him. 'I understand, sir, that you want to discuss with my staff the proportion of soldiers to vehicles landing on the beaches in the first flights,' he began. 'I cannot allow you to do so. My staff advise me and I give the final decision; they then do what I tell them.' In this case he had already given the final decision, and there could be no going back on his word. The staff had done a 'terrific job preparing the invasion; that work is now almost completed, and all over England the troops are beginning to move towards the assembly areas, prior to embarkation.'[3] To make a change now would cause tremendous disruption, and shake their confidence in their C-in-C who took sole responsibility for such decisions.

One by one Monty ran through the battles he had won in the past two years: Alamein, Tripoli, Mareth, Wadi Akarit, the assault upon

[1] Air Chief Marshal Leigh-Mallory, 'Impressions', loc. cit.
[2] Original in 'Miscellaneous Correspondence' file (21 A Gp/1065/1/C-in-C), Montgomery Papers.
[3] B. L. Montgomery, *Memoirs*, op. cit.

Sicily, the invasion of the Italian mainland – all under the overall leadership of the Prime Minister. The invasion of Normandy was all set; the men were confident they would succeed. Did the Prime Minister wish to shake that confidence, to come between a general and his men, his own staff in fact? 'I could never allow it – never,' Monty pronounced. 'If you think that is wrong, that can only mean you have lost confidence in me.'[1]

In later years it would be one of Monty's favourite stories. Before Alamein, Churchill had harassed Monty (usually via Alexander) with message after message, warning, cajoling, urging: during the battle itself, and continually during the subsequent campaigns in Africa, Sicily and Italy. Yet this harassment had always been by signal, combated equally by signal. Now the two men were alone, closeted together, in the office of the Commander-in-Chief of armies that would soon total some two million men. Monty's steel-blue eyes stared into those of the Prime Minister, and there was silence.

What could Churchill possibly say? Behind the office desk sat a general who, for all his eccentricity of dress, of behaviour and of mind, had become associated, if not positively identified, with the renascence of British military performance in battle. In the coming conflict he would be commanding not only a British army, but a Canadian one, as well as two American armies.

That Churchill was moved there can be no doubt, though he threatened to sue Alan Moorehead in 1946 if he dared print the episode. Moorehead was aggrieved because in relating the incident in his biography of Montgomery,[2] 'he didn't tell in the book about Churchill breaking down and weeping, which was true,' as Dr Pogue, the American Official Historian, noted after an interview with Moorehead.[3]

In threatening to sue Moorehead, the by then ex-Prime Minister of Great Britain was anxious lest he seem to have weakened at this still critical stage of the war. But to Monty Churchill's weeping was not a sign of weakness, nor did he ever cause it to appear so when recalling the incident. For Monty, Churchill's tears were identical to those of his other master – Alan Brooke. Brooke's tears, when handing over command of 2 Corps on the beaches of Dunkirk in 1940, had demonstrated the humanity of an otherwise austere commander – tears which sealed a bond of trust and mutual esteem which, in the cold years after Betty's death, Monty could share with only a few. Possibly Brooke and Churchill answered the aching longing Monty had experienced for parental approbation – and love. Certainly the sight of Churchill giving way to tears in his office remained one of the

[1] Related to author by Field-Marshal Montgomery, 1962; and see B. L. Montgomery, *Memoirs*, op. cit.
[2] A. Moorehead, *Montgomery*, London 1946.
[3] Interview of 21.1.47 by F. C. Pogue, loc. cit.

most striking memories Monty retained of the war. Two tireless and egotistical tyrants had confronted one another – and Monty had won. Yet in winning he had touched the heart of a man he revered, like Brooke. Not in triumph therefore but in humility Monty quietly suggested they go next door, where he would like to present his staff to the Prime Minister. 'Everyone there sensed there had been a crisis. Most of them guessed what had taken place in the study,' Moorehead narrated.[1]

Having been introduced to the officers, Churchill cleared his throat. 'I'm not allowed to talk to you, gentlemen,' he pronounced. 'The scene was all his,' Moorehead remarked.[2] Then they went in to dinner – 'one of those unforgettable occasions,' de Guingand later recalled. 'He was in great form, and prepared to talk – we let him. The Commander-in-Chief's betting book was brought out, and several wagers were laid on diverse subjects. The date by which the war in the West or in the East would end. The type of Government we would elect after the war. . . . Monty never *laid* a bet himself, but he was always prepared to *accept* one.'[3]

Not only did Churchill lay bets; he also added a new 'chapter' to the autograph book which Monty kept: 'Chapter V'. Monty had 'expressed to him my confidence in the successful outcome of our operations', and had shown him 'a copy of the final talk I am giving to the senior officers of all Armies; he was very taken with it and said he would circulate it as a Cabinet paper,' Monty recorded in his diary. In the autograph book Churchill searched for a way in which he could compliment Monty, and yet record his anxiety about the administrative 'tail' of 21st Army Group:

Chapter V

On the verge of the greatest Adventure
with which these pages have dealt
I record my confidence that
all will be well
& that
the organisations and equipment of the army
will be worthy of the valour
of the soldier
& the genius of their chief

Winston S. Churchill

19.v.44[4]

[1] A. Moorehead, op. cit.
[2] Ibid.
[3] F. W. de Guingand, *Operation Victory*, London 1947.
[4] B. L. Montgomery, *Ten Chapters*, London 1945.

CHAPTER ELEVEN

Dinner with Monty

Three nights after Churchill's visit it was the turn of King George VI to come to dinner; he too was given a copy of Monty's intended final sermon to senior officers, as well as Monty's latest edition of 'Notes on High Command in War'. These 'Notes' Monty had sent to leaders and commanders all over the world – to Wavell, Auchinleck, Marshall, Mountbatten, Smuts, Fraser, Mackenzie King – often with a photograph of himself, and a request for a photograph also of the recipient. Though all thanked Monty kindly and reciprocated, many found this form of self-advertisement embarrassing, if not distasteful. The Reynolds' house at Amesbury was now filled to overflowing with paintings, trophies and photographs of Montgomery, so much so that the Reynolds' son Tom found himself treated almost as an outcast when he returned home from Italy.[1] Such flourishing vanity would certainly have seemed ridiculous, indeed almost Napoleonic, had not the historical moment been so critical. The Allies had, as Monty admitted in his address to senior officers, 'worked themselves into a position where they cannot lose'; no longer were Britain and the Commonwealth under threat – it was Germany now that was fighting for her life. But the Allies had by no means won the war, and in his address Monty was careful not to minimise the difficulties in mounting a successful Second Front. The Germans were in prepared positions, with powerful reserves, and only 'offensive eagerness' would ensure the Allies were successful.

Once on land we must be offensive, and more offensive, and ever more offensive as the hours go by. We must call on the soldiers for an all out effort.

Every officer and man must have only one idea, and that is to peg out claims inland, and to penetrate quickly and deeply into enemy territory. After a long sea voyage and a landing followed by fighting, a reaction sets in and officers and men are often inclined to let up and relax. This is fatal; senior officers must prevent it at all costs on D-Day and on the following days. The first few days will

[1] Major Thomas Reynolds, interview of 19.3.78.

be the vital ones; it is in those days that the battle will be won, and in those days that it could well be lost.

Great energy and 'drive' will be required from all senior officers and commanders.

I consider that once the beaches are in our possession, success will depend largely on our ability to be able to concentrate our armour and push fairly strongly armoured columns rapidly inland to secure important ground or communications centres. Such columns will form *firm bases in enemy territory* from which to develop offensive action in all directions. Such action will tend to throw the enemy off his balance, and will enable our build-up through the beaches to proceed undisturbed; it will cut the ground from under the armoured counter-attack. . . .

Inaction, and a defensive mentality, are criminal in any officer – however senior.[1]

For a week Monty toured his assault armies, visiting every Corps and divisional area and addressing, as before Alamein, all senior and even junior officers. The response was, even among American forces, tumultuous. 'Confidence in the high command is absolutely without parallel', one American officer later reported to Eisenhower's Chief of Staff – 'and unanimously what appealed to them [the assault troops] was the story . . . that the General visited every one of us outfits before going over.'[2]

No general in history had done as much as Monty in this respect. It was, as Bedell Smith wrote to Monty after D-Day, a 'triumph of leadership',[3] yet one which, in the bitter Anglo-American wrangles thereafter, was often forgotten. That Monty had transformed a recipe for defeat into a guarantee of victory; had conceived, clarified and rehearsed a tactical strategy for the campaign, from D-Day to the seizure of the Seine some three months ahead; had not only ensured professional planning and administrative arrangements of the very highest order for British, Canadian and American armies, but had taken it upon himself to spread his military gospel to men and officers of those armies in person, in a matter of five months – was something his own subordinates would never forget. If his vanity had been, in Brigadier Williams's phrase, the 'dynamo of Eighth Army', then it was now the dynamo of the largest amphibious army ever assembled in human history. It is inconceivable that any other Allied field commander could have matched Monty in this; indeed judging from 'Torch', from 'Husky', from 'Avalanche' and 'Shingle'

---

[1] Quoted in B. L. Montgomery, *Memoirs*, op. cit., original in Montgomery Papers.

[2] Letter of 22.6.44 from Bedell Smith to Montgomery, in Appendix to Personal Diary, Montgomery Papers.

[3] Ibid.

Monty takes the King round units of Eighth Army. It was King George VI's first visit and, like Churchill's in January, it remained one of the most inspiring memories of the war for him. (*Imperial War Museum*)

At Algiers Monty talks to Churchill and General Marshall, US Army Chief of Staff, whom he met for the first time. (*Imperial War Museum*)

Arriving in Malta on 3 July 1943 Monty spent the final week before the invasion of Sicily teeing up plans with his Desert Air Force Commander, AVM Broadhurst, and Naval Task Force Commander, Vice-Admiral Ramsay. (*Imperial War Museum*)

Ammunition being passed ashore by hand on D-Day, 10 July 1943. (*Imperial War Museum*)

Patton flew to meet Monty on 25 July 1943. Monty's eyes were now on Italy, of whose invasion he hoped to be given command. (*Imperial War Museum*)

For Monty the lesson of Sicily was that American co-operation was essential, and he went all out to improve relations. At his Tac HQ in the villa of a Fascist millionaire at Taormina Monty invited Eisenhower and all the American generals who had participated in the Sicilian campaign on 29 August. (*Imperial War Musuem*)

Monty salutes troops in Reggio. (*Imperial War Museum*)

Monty receives a delegation of military observers from Russia on 10 December 1943, after Eighth Army's crossing of the Sangro. (*Imperial War Museum*)

'Who is to command Overlord?' At the Allied summit meeting in Tehran on 29 November 1943, Stalin's simple question floored both Churchill and Roosevelt. Eisenhower was then appointed Supreme Commander for the cross-Channel assault, Monty to command the armies. (*Imperial War Museum*)

Monty's successor in Italy was General Sir Oliver Leese, seen arriving at Algiers *en route* for Eighth Army headquarters. (*Imperial War Museum*)

The new Commander of the Allied invasion armies drives down a street in Birmingham named after him. (*Imperial War Museum*)

The only drawing of Monty before D-Day, by Augustus John. Monty rejected the oil portrait he had commissioned John to paint, but never saw this fine crayon sketch — perhaps the only portrait ever to capture the ascetic missionary behind the soldier's mask. (*Collection of J. E. B. Hill*)

'Overlord' As in Sicily, the landings were more successful than could have been hoped. Rehearsals on 5 May were an important part in achieving victory.
(*Imperial War Museum*)

Monty gives his first press conference in Normandy at his Tactical Headquarters at Creully on 11 June 1944 as Dempsey's Second Army seeks to envelop Caen.
(*Imperial War Museum*)

In January 1944 Field-Marshal Rommel was formally charged by Hitler with the coastal defence of 'Fortress Europe'. Here, with Vice-Admiral Ruge and others, he surveys the Normandy coastline. (*Imperial War Museum*)

The Prime Minister arrives at Monty's Tac Headquarters at Broomfield House, Portsmouth to complain about the administrative 'tail' of the armies. (*Imperial War Museum*)

General Charles de Gaulle is received at Monty's Tac HQ at Creully on 14 June 1944 – the French leader's first steps on the soil of the French mainland since 1940. (*Imperial War Museum*)

Monty was intimately aware of the human cost to the Allies of a long drawn-out battle in Normandy. Here he watches an operation to remove a bullet from a soldier's spine at No 84 General Hospital. (*Imperial War Museum*)

Monty takes Churchill to see the terrible destruction in Caen, 22 July 1944. (*Imperial War Museum*)

it is all too likely that without Monty's force of personality and battle experience the invasion of Normandy would – as Mountbatten predicted – have failed. As Churchill had once personified the indomitable British spirit in 1940, so now in Britain, America and occupied Europe the double-badged black beret of Montgomery personified the Allied will to achieve offensive victory.

The days and the hours before the invasion began were slipping away. New Intelligence forced Bradley to re-direct the drop of 82nd Airborne Division, and in spite of Leigh-Mallory's prophecies of doom, Monty stood up for his American army commander. Leigh-Mallory was urging Monty to use the 82nd Airborne Division on Caen; but Bradley, in view of the three new enemy divisions facing his Utah sector, had threatened to cancel his entire landing there if the 82nd Airborne were not re-allocated to protect it.

How much difference an extra airborne division would have made in the seizure of Caen, which was the bugbear of the great battle for Normandy. Yet Monty did not hesitate for a moment, nor did he regret his decision in all the subsequent years of American – and British – criticism for his failure to capture early enough the Caen area and its airfields. To Monty, the professional soldier, the words of General James Wolfe were as true in May 1944 as they had been two hundred years before: 'war is an option of difficulties'. His entire Normandy strategy, unlike that of the original COSSAC planners, was predicated on the early capture of Cherbourg and the subsequent build-up of American forces in the Cherbourg peninsula, prior to the great break-out into Brittany, to the Loire, and thence eastwards to Paris.

If Bradley insisted upon going ahead with the direction of 82nd Airborne onto Ste Mère Eglise in the Cherbourg peninsula, Leigh-Mallory warned, 'he will have to accept full responsibility for the operation', adding, 'I don't believe it will work.' Bradley, irritated as much by Leigh-Mallory's pompous Englishness as much as his pessimism, answered, 'That's perfectly agreeable to me. I'm in the habit of accepting responsibility for my operations.' However it was Monty who put an end to the discussion.

'Montgomery rapped quietly on the table,' Bradley afterwards recalled. 'That is not at all necessary gentlemen,' he said, 'I shall assume full responsibility for the plan.'[1]

Perhaps no other decision, in the months leading up to D-Day, would better illustrate Monty's efforts to be a truly Allied commander, not merely a British general. Though he expected Bradley to take complete charge of the training of his forces, he tried hard, though vainly, to get him to accept more of General Hobart's 'funnies' – the special tanks and vehicles being produced by 79th Armoured Divi-

[1] Omar N. Bradley, op. cit.

sion, designed to overcome the most difficult obstacles that would be confronted by the assault forces. Moreover he insisted, vainly too, that Bradley and Patton, and Crerar the Canadian Army Commander, pay more attention to air co-operation in the coming battle. To his chagrin, First US Army would go into battle with only the vaguest notion of how to use the tremendous air weapon available to it. 'As a result of our inability to get together with air in England, we went into France almost totally untrained in air-ground co-operation,' Bradley later confessed, and blamed the Ninth US Air Force Commander, General Brereton:

> Not sincere, nor energetic, nor co-operative. . . . Did not seem interested in air-ground team. Was a purist in air effort. Difficult for him to realise full use that could be made of air effort in assistance to ground operations. Brereton lacked enthusiasm.[1]

The problem was not only one of Air Force Commanders, however – as General 'Pete' Quesada, commanding the American direct air-support squadrons, freely confessed:

> Co-ordination? Not really did I realise it before the invasion; as a matter of fact, and I don't like to admit this but it's true, there was an attitude that went all through the Air Force, that I adopted, my juniors adopted and my seniors adopted, that this was not our mission. It was not our mission to participate that close in battle.[2]

It was not for want of trying on Monty's behalf. Tedder might dislike Monty, Coningham (the Commander-in-Chief of the Tactical Air Forces) even 'loathe'[3] him, but they and all other senior British airmen acknowledged that Monty towered above any other Allied field general in his practical appreciation of the 'air weapon'. As even Coningham confessed,[4] Monty had been the first soldier to accept the principle of 'air flexibility', the notion that a commander in the field cannot simply 'howl' for his own air support as he would for Corps artillery. Only an airman could decide the priorities of air strikes, and Monty had pioneered a closeness of co-operation between army and air staffs which became the model for the Allied

[1] 'Bradley Commentaries', loc. cit. Noting Bradley's recollections, his ADC Major Hansen remarked: 'In England Bradley and Brereton seldom got together, though Bradley went out several times to Brereton's headquarters' – ibid.
[2] Lt-General P. Quesada, oral interview of 1975, Military History Institute, Carlisle, Pennsylvania.
[3] General Alexander in George Howe interview, Military History Institute, Carlisle, Pennsylvania.
[4] Air Marshal Sir Arthur Coningham, interview of 14.2.47 by F. C. Pogue, loc. cit.

world. In May 1944, however, he lamented in a special letter sent to Bradley, Dempsey, Crerar, Patton, Coningham, Broadhurst and Bedell Smith, that this intimate co-operation no longer existed:

> During the last four months, i.e. since I got back from Italy, it has gradually been brought home to me that there is a definite gulf in England between the Armies and their supporting air forces. Of course I naturally compare the situation in England with that which obtained in the Allied Armies overseas. There the Army concerned and its Air Force were welded into one entity; the two HQ were always adjacent; and the spirit of unity went right down to the individual soldier and airman. These fine results were achieved only by a great deal of 'give and take' on both sides; gradually mutual confidence and trust grew up, and the Army and its supporting Air Force became one fighting machine.

The problem, Monty felt, was that until the Normandy landings started, the air forces simply failed to see what practical help they could give the army, and neglected to practise, in advance, the sort of operations, control and command arrangements which battle in France would necessitate. Army commanders must not fall into this trap, however unwilling were the air forces to rehearse in advance. Under no circumstances, Monty ordered, was an Army HQ ever to be set up anywhere save directly alongside the Air HQ. In fact the very location of an Army HQ would probably be dictated by its telephone communications with airfields – 'the deciding factor in the location of Main Army will be whether it will suit Air HQ' – and this concern must spill over into almost every action taken by an Army: 'Before the Army staff initiates or takes any action the first question must always be: "How will this affect the air." ' Not only was this so in terms of operations, but also of administration, and the pooling of Intelligence.

The problem went far deeper than the intimacy of headquarters staffs, however. Air Vice-Marshall Broadhurst had, after the departure of Coningham from Eighth Army in the desert, pioneered the effective use of the 'taxi-cab rank' method of direct air support, a system that would play a vital part in Normandy:

> On the air side, every pilot in air forces allotted specifically for the support of an Army, must realise that his sole job is to help win the land battle; sometimes this involves fighting in the sky; at other times it involves *coming right down* and participation in the land battle by shooting up ground targets. . . .
>
> I feel very strongly on the whole matter, and I know that we can achieve no real success unless each Army and its accompanying Air Force can weld itself into one entity. . . . The two HQ have got

to set themselves down side by side, and work together as one team; that is the only way.

I wish Army Commanders to give this matter their personal attention. There is much to be done and not much time in which to do it. We must not merely pay lip service to a principle; we must put into practice the actual methods that will achieve success.[1]

Since January Monty had done his best to spread this gospel, lecturing at the RAF Staff College and visiting air force headquarters and squadrons. He had insisted that in field rehearsals in April and May, the technique of air support be specially studied, and right up until June he kept reiterating the critical importance of air operations in the field; indeed it was to the headquarters of Fighter Command that he went after completing his tour of the assault armies in late May. His address (too long to be quoted in full) demonstrates Monty's profound grasp of the air weapon. Monty stressed that only by developing a combined army/air plan could the armies hope to win the battle, but warned – prophetically – that although the army might strive to gain space for airfields to accommodate the air weapon, it took time. To fight successfully against an enemy as tough as the German, the Allies would have to group their ground forces skilfully: 'skilful grouping is one of the basic factors for success'. The battle for airfields would not be won overnight: 'Time to get established, especially as regards communications – if you want to fight,' he wrote in his notes for the address. Each must understand the other, techniques of army/air recognition must be developed and rehearsed until all were 'experts'. Nor did air support stop there, for the vital role of the Recce Wing must be understood by both soldiers and airmen. If the Recce Wing was bad it would be 'like having one hand tied behind your back,' Monty noted – and insisted that the 'amount of aerial recce required', particularly in operations in France, had 'greatly increased. Present establishment cannot produce all that is required,' he remarked, and urged an expansion of the Recce Wing. The Army Chief of Staff and the senior air staff officer (SASO) must 'be personal friends,' he exhorted; headquarters must be adjacent to one another, Intelligence shared, and operational conferences must be combined.[2]

On 31 May Monty addressed all the officers and men of his Tac HQ, and on 2 June all officers of Main and Rear HQ, again stressing the need for intimate co-operation between army and air. Meanwhile he asked Bradley, Dempsey, Crerar and Patton to a 'final conference' at 7 p.m. on 1 June, and to stay for dinner. In his diary Patton

[1] Dated May 1944, in 'C-in-C's Directives' file, loc. cit.
[2] Handwritten notes for 'Address at Fighter Command, Friday 28 May 44', Montgomery Papers.

recorded: 'Bradley and I left at 1530 and flew to Portsmouth to see General Montgomery who lives at Southwick. Montgomery, Bradley, and I had tea, and then we went to his office, and without the aid of any staff officers, went over the plans.'[1]

Since 26 April Monty's Tac HQ had been set up in Southwick Park, comprising some twenty officers and two hundred men; nearby was the Main Headquarters of 21st Army Group, also in tents and caravans. In this way the layout and conditions of life of a headquarters in the field could be rehearsed. Visitors were put up in either a tent or caravan; only Monty, de Guingand and their personal aides messed and slept in Broomfield House.

Bradley, despite his later remarks about being less confident than Monty in breaking through the 'crust' of German opposition, had told Patton at a briefing the day before that First US Army would perform the break-out. 'If everything moves as planned there will be nothing left for me to do,' Patton noted with disappointment. Monty, however, reassured Patton that there would be a great deal for Third Army to do. Patton had rehearsed the hopeful role of Third Army with his staff on 29 May in the presence of the Ninth US Army Commander, General Simpson, 'so I was very fluent,' he maintained, in reciting his proposed operations to Monty, prompting Monty to say twice to Bradley 'Patton should take over for the Brittany, and possibly the Rennes operation'.[2]

Bradley was less sure, for relations between the two American commanders were far from the intimate, friendly ones assumed by later writers and public. 'General Patton, of course, is extremely unpopular in this Headquarters,' Bradley's aide, Chester Hansen, recorded in his diary on 2 June. 'Most of our officers have carried with them the punctured legend from Sicily. When I told the Captain of the MPs to provide a motorcycle escort for Patton's arrival, he grinned and asked, "Shall we have them wear boxing gloves?" He was referring, of course, to the slapping incident.'[3]

Bradley, shy, diffident, a soldier's soldier, abhorred the braggardly bearing of his erstwhile Seventh Army Commander, and hoped, understandably, that First Army's progress in Normandy would render Patton's Third Army headquarters unnecessary, have as an adjunct. Patton, keenly aware that Bradley, once his junior as a Corps Commander in Sicily, would become his senior, as First Army Group Commander, the moment that Third Army was introduced into the Normandy fighting, attempted to keep his injured pride in check. Dempsey and Crerar then arrived, neither of whom impress-

---

[1] *The Patton Papers*, op. cit.
[2] Ibid.
[3] Diary of Chester B. Hansen, Military History Institute, Carlisle, Pennsylvania.

ed Patton. 'I take him to be a yes-man,' he noted of Dempsey – the Corps Commander who 'failed to take Catania' in the early days of the Sicilian campaign. 'The Canadian is better – but not impressive,' he remarked of Crerar.[1]

The dinner, however, was convivial. Monty toasted his four Army Commanders, and Patton, 'as the oldest Army commander present', replied by toasting 'the health of General Montgomery' and declaring 'our satisfaction in serving under him'. 'The lightning did not strike me,' Patton noted in his diary – for his satisfaction was, to his tortured, impatient soul, a lie. Nevertheless he acknowledged that 'I have a better impression of Monty than I had'.[2]

'They all stayed to dinner and we had a very cheery evening,' Monty noted in his own diary, oblivious to the undercurrents of jealousy, pride and ambition. Besides, Monty had his own opinions on those present. Patton he regarded as a sabre-rattler, wilfully ignorant of battle in its administrative dimension, and of army/air co-operation, but still the most aggressive 'thruster' in the Allied camp; Bradley he considered dull, conscientious, dependable and loyal (Bradley would continue to call Monty 'sir' until September 1944); Dempsey, though he lacked the Guardsman's ruthlessness and drive of Leese, was cleverer, and he possessed a legendary eye for terrain, ran a high-calibre headquarters and was, behind his quiet manner, completely imperturbable. Only Crerar really worried Monty, having known the Canadian ever since Crerar accepted demotion in order to command a division and subsequently the Canadian Corps in Monty's South-eastern Army Command in 1942. Though undoubtedly an efficient headquarters managers, Monty felt grave doubts about Crerar as a battlefield leader, doubts which were to be unhappily confirmed in the months ahead.

It was not, therefore, the most spectacular team of Army Commanders to be leading the largest invasion in history. Indeed, of the four Army Commanders, only Patton had actually commanded an Army in battle before – a campaign which had ended in dishonour and near dismissal. Yet Monty seems to have had no doubts about the victorious outcome of impending operations: he would be in sole command, and he was absolutely convinced he could beat Rommel in a 'ding-dong' battle. As at Alamein, he wanted only luck enough to help achieve the break-in, the landings themselves. Once ashore luck was not necessary, only nerves. As at Alamein, Rommel would fight like a tiger, but as long as he kept his head, Monty knew he had the measure of his opponent.

What Monty was less sure about were his superiors, the desk soldiers and politicians. Like children, all were now clamouring for a

---

[1] *The Patton Papers*, op. cit.
[2] Ibid.

ringside seat to witness the historic occasion – Grigg, Churchill, Ismay, Smuts, King George VI. Only Eisenhower seemed to Monty to have grown in stature in this testing period, and that because Eisenhower had given Monty a free rein to plan, prepare and rehearse the invasion without hindrance. Indeed except for the distraction over 'Anvil', Eisenhower had supported Monty over operational matters with a firmness that surprised even Monty. On 2 June the two men dined together at Monty's Tactical Headquarters. 'I do like him tremendously,' Monty noted in his diary; 'he is so very genuine and sincere.' Together the two men then 'went up to Southwick House and had a conference with the Met experts on the weather' at 9.30 p.m. The sea forecast was good, the air forecast poor – 'making the airborne operations difficult, and especially the landing of gliders'. 5 June was still the target date for D-Day. 'It was decided to lay on the whole operation,' Monty recorded, with the proviso that they meet the next evening at the same time to review the weather forecast.

Grigg had already proposed in May that he should accompany the invasion forces, as Secretary of State for War, a 'request' Monty had instantly turned down, as diplomatically as he could: 'I fully appreciate your wish to come with us, and it is a great thing to know we have a War Minister with such a spirit. It is difficult for me to refuse you anything as you have been so good to me throughout; but your presence could not fail to be an embarrassment to some commanders, however incognito you may wish to remain. The operation is so difficult, and so full of hazards, that my object throughout has been to make everything as simple as possible; every commander must be free to devote his sole and undivided attention to the battle, and this could hardly be possible if you were present. . . .'[1]

Thereafter Monty was deluged with requests, culminating on the evening Monty entertained his Army Commanders to dinner. As Patton recorded in his diary, during the meal a phone call came from General Ismay, saying that Churchill wished to visit the Portsmouth area over the weekend. Monty's reaction was negative, to say the least: 'If Winnie comes, he'll not only be a great bore, but also may well attract undue attention here. Why in hell doesn't he go and smoke his cigar at Dover Castle and be seen with the Lord Mayor? It would fix the Germans' attention to Calais.'[2]

In vain Monty appealed to Eisenhower and even Brooke to stop him:

[1] Letter of 14.5.44 in 'Correspondence with Secretary of State' file, Montgomery Papers.
[2] *The Patton Papers*, op. cit.

The Prime Minister decided to spend the week-end in the Portsmouth area, on his train, and to spend the time visiting everything he could.

I immediately got on to Supreme HQ and asked them to try and stop him coming; I also spoke to the C.I.G.S.

The real point is that at this last stage we do all want to be left alone, and no one has any time to devote to organising tours for Prime Ministers,

Monty recorded in his diary.

Furthermore, there is the danger of drawing attention to this area; the cover plan is that we are going across the Straits of DOVER to the Pas de CALAIS, and the best place for the P.M. would be DOVER – if he cannot stay quietly at CHEQUERS or in LONDON.

He *also* wants to go to sea in a cruiser and see the assault and the bombardment on D day; wherever he is he must be an embarrassment and a liability, and might compromise success in that area; I hope the Cabinet will not allow him to go.

Quite apart from everything else, he is too valuable and should not take such risks; if anything were to happen to him we should be in a bad position. His own good sense and judgement may prevail over his great fighting spirit, but I doubt it!!

Monty's doubt was well founded, for on Friday 2 June Churchill appeared.

The Prime Minister arrived yesterday in his train; all attempts to stop him were quite useless. He must know that it was I who tried to stop him, and I shall not be popular!!

Churchill later claimed that his interest in watching the embarkation and landings of the Allied armies was in antidote to the complete ignorance of conditions on the Western Front displayed by political and military leaders in World War I.[1] Few believed him, and none saw clearer than Brooke who, noting Churchill's growing excitement, began to sense forthcoming difficulties – exactly as had transpired during the battle of Alamein: 'Winston returned on Sunday evening in a very highly-strung condition. . . . I found him over-optimistic as regards prospects of the cross-Channel operation and tried to dampen him down a bit.'[2]

The weather was worsening by the hour, and the last thing responsible commanders wished was to have to impress and enter-

[1] W. S. Churchill, op. cit.
[2] A. Bryant, op. cit.

tain an itinerant Prime Minister with his necessary but demanding retinue – Smuts, Bevin, Ismay, security officers and aides. By Saturday 3 June Monty was aware that a crisis was brewing, in which cast-iron nerves would be required. Some would probably caution cancellation until the next appropriate tides, a fortnight later. His own view was unshakeable:

> The weather forecast is not so good. The depression over ICELAND is spreading to the south and the high pressure system which was coming up this way from the AZORES is now being pushed back. So the chance of a good belt of high pressure over the Channel area is now receding.
>
> All this is awkward, and some very big decisions may be necessary. My own view is that if the sea is calm enough for the Navy to take us there, then we must go; the air has had very good weather for all its preparatory operations, and we must accept that it may not be able to do so well on D day.

Monty had determined the plan, prepared the armies. It was now up to Eisenhower to say whether those armies should go. Like Lord Gort in May 1940, it was Eisenhower's moment of trial – and he responded with what can only be called greatness.

CHAPTER TWELVE

To Go or not to Go

If D-Day was to be, as intended, 5 June 1944, then the decision of whether to go must be made twenty-four hours before, earlier if possible, since a large proportion of the four thousand vessels would already be at sea, prior to their passage across the Channel.

As the weather deteriorated on Saturday 3 June, Eisenhower's meteorologist became more pessimistic – 'the nadir of strain and despondency,' as Group Captain Stagg later recalled.[1] The Azores anticyclone, bearing warm air from Bermuda, had vanished; the depression off Iceland loomed larger, and was approaching Scotland.

To complicate matters, Spaatz's meteorological team was still optimistic, though even they were beginning to frown. At the 9.30 p.m. conference at Southwick House on 3 June, therefore, Group Captain Stagg presented a gloomy picture: 'the extension of the Azores anticyclone towards our south-west shores, which some of us thought might protect the Channel from the worst effects of the Atlantic depressions, is now giving way. It can no longer be expected to act as a bumper to push the depression northwards . . . from tomorrow winds will be . . . force 4 to 5, maybe 6 at times, on the English side of the Channel. . . . They will continue fresh, even strong at times, till Wednesday (June 7).'[2]

Eisenhower asked if the Force 5 winds would continue on Monday and Tuesday. Stagg replied in the affirmative. Leigh-Mallory asked about cloud, which was expected to be thick and low – as low as five hundred feet on both sides of the Channel.

Stagg then left the room, and the debate amongst the commanders began. It was an hour or more before Stagg was recalled, to be told that no decision had been made. The first ships would set sail; at 4.30 the next morning (4 June) the situation would be reviewed and thereafter a final decision given.

We are now on the eve of the Second Front. The weather forecast does not look too good, and tomorrow, 4 June, will be an interest-

---

[1] J. M. Stagg, *Forecast for Overlord*, London 1971.
[2] Ibid.

ing day; at 0800 hours tomorrow the final decision must be taken,

Monty noted in his diary,

and once taken must be stuck to; everything will be at sea, and if it is to be turned back, it must be turned back then. Strong and resolute characters will be very necessary.

In the meantime, while Eisenhower read Westerns, Monty set down on paper a review of the last few months and current situation. 'The last five months have been a strenuous and very difficult time; few really know how difficult it has been, and one hopes that it will never be known. Initially I had some friction with the War Office as they did not understand the tempo at which I and my staff are accustomed to work; the robust methods of the Eighth Army were not popular in Whitehall, where indecision generally rules.' Yet now, on the eve of 'the great adventure', Monty recognised that, for all its initial obstructionism, the War Office had achieved miracles in getting Monty's armies the tools and men they needed. 'It is clear to me that the War Office has been quite first-class in doing what we wanted. . . . The War Office itself had its own troubles and difficulties with other Governments, and I do not think we always realized that. The great lesson I have learned is that the War Office, and the C-in-C and his staff, are together a team; they must all pull together, and work in closely with each other.' Already he had written a letter of gratitude to Grigg, and felt better for it. 'At this stage of the war,' he went on, however, 'when great events are impending, it is interesting to record my own views about the chief actors.' He began with the Combined Chiefs of Staff.

I know only MARSHALL and DILL. I have the highest opinion of DILL and I believe he is doing sterling work in WASHINGTON, is much liked by Americans, and is really first-class.
I have met MARSHALL only once [at Algiers in June 1943]', but I took to him very much and would say that he is a man of great integrity and of high principles; he seemed just the man for his present job,

Monty remarked – well aware that, had Roosevelt not determined otherwise, Marshall would have been Monty's Supreme Commander. As for the British Chiefs of Staff, Monty was equally laudatory. Brooke 'is, in my opinion, the best soldier we have ever produced in England; he is brilliant and I am absolutely devoted to him; he has been very good to me and very tolerant of my faults – which are many,' Monty confessed in the penitent vein that had, for the moment, overcome him. Even the hopelessly ignorant Cunningham could be forgiven in such a mood – 'a first-class fighting sailor; he will do anything to win the war and I like him very much'. For Portal he reserved special praise, for only Portal really understood the need for army/air co-operation and was not deluded by the fantasies of Harris and Spaatz: 'he is splendid; he is all out for close touch between the Army and the R.A.F., and I think he has confidence in me as a soldier and as a friend of the R.A.F.'

Eisenhower, too, merited full marks: 'Eisenhower is just the man for the job; he is a really "big" man and is in every way an Allied Commander – holding the balance between Allied contingents.' That Eisenhower managed to do this not by harping on his authority but by the effect of his personality was all the more remarkable – 'I like him immensely; he has a generous and lovable character and I would trust him to the last gasp'.

Here, however, Monty's hyperbole ended. The Supreme Commander in the Mediterranean, General Sir Maitland Wilson, 'may have been good once, but he is past it now. In my opinion he is now unfit to be a Supreme Commander.' Alexander, by contrast, had never reached it. 'He is a most delightful person and I love him dearly; I would do anything for him. But I have served under him for a long time and have suffered greatly; he has a military reputation that is quite false. He knows what he wants in a vague way, but he has no idea how to implement it; he gives his staff no guidance, he cannot make up his mind, and he never gives firm decisions. He is not clever and has a slow brain.' His forces in Italy, six months late, had finally reached Rome – but as Monty had pointed out to Brooke when Brooke chafed and complained about Alexander's new Chief of Staff, General Harding: 'the trouble is that ALEXANDER is quite unfit to hold high command and has to have a very good Chief of Staff who will run the show for him; it seems [pace Brooke] that HARDING is not good enough and things are not going well. I gave it as my opinion that the trouble is not HARDING – who is quite first-class. The trouble is ALEXANDER – who is very definitely third-class as a high commander.'[1]

Ironically, as Monty knew, Alexander had been heavily tipped for command of the armies in 'Overlord', and unless he had miraculously found a brilliant Chief of Staff and Army commanders the result would have been a shambles: 'I would say he might be compared to HINDENBERG [sic] in the Great War; he must have a LUDENDORF [sic] to do the business for him. If he has a good Chief of Staff, then all is well. He also wants a good Army Commander under him who will fight the battle for him; he himself has no grip of the battle, and lets things slide and take their own course.

[1] Diary entry of 15.5.44, Montgomery Papers.

'He has himself never commanded an Army in battle and he does not know how to tee-up the battle. He will, I hope, go down in history as a great British General, and will become, I hope, a Field-Marshal; I will do anything I can to prevent the bubble being pricked so as not to cause a loss of confidence in the public.'

If this seems harsh, it must be remembered that Monty had served as Eighth Army Commander under Alexander for eighteen critical months of the war. No one knew better Alexander's qualities of leadership and soldierly imperturbability. It was Monty himself who had persuaded Lord Gort to promote Alexander, not Barker, to command of 1 Corps for the final evacuation of Dunkirk in 1940; but since then there had been much to set against the reputation of Alexander as a higher commander. He had become embroiled too closely with the failings of First Army in Tunisia, thus failing to concert the efforts of First and Eighth Armies and allowing the planning of 'Husky' to degenerate into a farrago; as C-in-C in Sicily he had failed to take a grip on the operations of the two Army Commanders, Patton and Montgomery; moreover he had failed to ensure a combined plan to prevent Axis evacuation of the island. In Italy he had approved Eisenhower's Salerno plan, given Monty's 'Baytown' landings no proper stategic objective, authorised the catastrophic 'Giant Two' plan, and allowed administration to deteriorate to the point where Eighth Army was without petrol, medical supplies or reinforcements. English soldiers had mutinied as a result of his administrative chief's incompetence at Salerno, and the operations of the two Armies, Clark's Fifth and Montgomery's Eighth, had been allowed to develop in the same unharnessed way as in Sicily. Moreover the Anzio landing, which Monty had squashed in November, Alexander had resurrected and authorised in January – with dire results. Only the introduction of a new Chief of Staff and the growing battle experience of General Clark, together with Leese at the helm of Eighth Army, had rescued Alexander from stalemate in Italy; and even so the Germans had only been forced to withdraw to a position they had been expected to occupy the previous autumn. 'He has many great qualities,' Monty concluded, 'but in actual fact he is not a high class soldier.'

About Mountbatten, Monty was even more scathing. 'Dickie MOUNTBATTEN is, of course, quite unfit to be a Supreme Commander. He is a delightful person, has a quick and alert brain, and has many good ideas. But his knowledge of how to make war is really NIL; this is not to be wondered at, as his highest command before was a Captain of Destroyers in the NAVY. His Army C-in-C is GIFFARD;[1] he is a very pleasant person and a very great gentleman, but he is not really any good.'

[1] General G. J. Giffard was in fact given notice in May 1944 and relieved in November of that year.

CONCLUSION

The nett result is that we have a good team only in Western EUROPE. In ITALY the form is poor; but the problem is not difficult, in fact it is easy, so it does not matter.

In S.E. ASIA the form is very poor indeed; but again I do not think it matters overmuch; all we want to do there for the moment is to have no disasters.

It is the large scale air and land operations of the Second Front from ENGLAND that are going to be the deciding factor – in conjunction with the Russian effort – in the winning of the war.

The Russians, still facing the Germans on a line bisecting Russia from Leningrad to the Crimea, could not be expected to push back the German armies in the east more than a thousand kilometres to the German border without an equivalent Allied offensive in the West. Stalin's question, 'Who will command Overlord?' was not academic. All else, to the Russians, was secondary, and the response to his question must have confirmed all Stalin's deepest suspicions about the Western Allies.

Six months later the situation was transformed. Churchill, who had once depicted his fears of the English Channel running red with the blood of Allied troops, was now desperately 'frigging about' Southampton and diminishing Eisenhower's stock of whisky,[1] vainly hoping to see battle-painted troops embarking and dreaming of a place upon the bridge of HMS *Belfast*. 'He is a tower of strength,' Monty acknowledged in his diary. 'But there is no doubt he is getting very tired. He finds difficulty in giving a quick decision and he is too easily led off on small details.' This was an understatement. Yet 'he is a wonderful man and we could not do without him,' Monty added. 'I trust he will keep going till we have won the war against Germany. He has been very good to me,' he also acknowledged – not realising, perhaps, the extent to which Eisenhower had borne the brunt of the Prime Minister's endless harassment.

Regarding his own 21st Army Group 'team', Monty was well pleased. 'I can say definitely,' he recorded, 'that if I had not brought my own team of senior officers back with me from ITALY, I could never have done the business and got ready for the OVERLORD operation. It was essential to have practical knowledge of the job,

---

[1] 'They are on a special train parked at Southampton from which they set out to see troops loading on Friday, but had bad luck hitting the right loading places at the wrong time, and vice versa, so the P.M. didn't do so well. . . . As [Eisenhower and staff] returned to camp last night, the P.M.'s caravan of cars and dashing cyclists swirled in behind unexpectedly. Filled their gas tanks and diminished our small supply of Scotch like the devil, there being some ten or more parched mouths to moisten' – entry of 4.6.44, Diary of Harry C. Butcher, loc. cit.

with officers who knew the battle end of the business; those that PAGET had collected round him in England were pure theorists, and were mostly useless anyhow. I like PAGET very much, and he is a very old friend; but he is not,' as Monty had remarked of Auchinleck almost two years before, 'a good judge as to what constitutes a high-class soldier.'

This entry, dated 3 June 1944, was the last in Monty's diary before D-Day. In the early morning of 4 June he made his way to Southwick House to hear Stagg's latest weather forecast. It was no better than the night before, but this time there was open dissension among the forecasters, with Spaatz's American team at Widewing predicting a favourable upturn, a fact which had become known to the assembled commanders via Ramsay's naval meteorologist at Southwick, next door to Monty.

'The tension in the room was palpable,' Stagg later recalled. He was not asked to leave the room after his forecast, and thus witnessed the dilemma. Ramsay felt Stagg was being defeatist. 'The sky outside at the moment is practically clear and there is no wind: when do you expect the cloud and wind of your forecast to appear here?' Ramsay asked. Stagg answered, 'In another four or five hours from now, sir.'

Ramsay counselled Eisenhower that the invasion should commence. Eisenhower turned to Leigh-Mallory. Leigh-Mallory was against, saying the air forces would not be able to carry out their programme. Eisenhower asked Monty.

Monty had foreseen such indecision. Some of Leigh-Mallory's programme would probably have to be cancelled, but the majority of it, he was sure, could go ahead. It was a moment for resolution, for the sort of courage Monty had quoted in his message to be read out to the troops as they set sail: 'O God of battles, steel my soldiers' hearts. . . .'

'We must go,' Monty recommended. Every hour's delay diminished the ability of the troops to face their ordeal, and complicated the entire mounting procedures.

It was now the turn of Eisenhower's deputy, Tedder – an airman. Tedder disagreed with Monty, in fact he later referred to Monty's 'amazingly asserted willingness'[1] to undertake the operation with reduced air support.

To go, or not to go. . . .

Eisenhower stood up. 'In that case, gentlemen, it looks to me as if we must confirm the provisional decision we took at the last meeting [i.e. to postpone the invasion pending better weather]. Compared with the enemy's forces ours are not overwhelmingly strong: we need every help our air superiority can give us. If the air cannot

[1] Tedder, *With Prejudice*, London 1966.

operate we must postpone. Are there any dissentient voices?'[1]

Monty was chagrined. The early morning sky was clear outside, yet the entire 'Overlord' operation was being postponed because of a weather forecast which was itself the subject of dissenting opinions. The recall of so many vessels would be a tremendous operation, increasing the chance of German air or naval craft spotting the armada. On the other hand he had himself decreed, as his Number One maxim on the prosecution of battle, air supremacy.

Leigh-Mallory had opposed Monty over the drop of 82nd US Airborne Division, but on that occasion Tedder had upheld Monty's decision, in the name of Eisenhower. Now both Leigh-Mallory and Tedder were against launching 'Overlord' on 5 June.

Eisenhower's question hung in the air. Monty did not speak.

'Now we must call off the sailing of the last forces S and J, and take steps to recall the forces that have already sailed,' Eisenhower ordered. The meeting was adjourned until nine-thirty that evening – when the forecast for 6 June would be reviewed.

Ironically a 'beautiful dawn glow' was lighting the north-eastern horizon as the Allied Commanders filed out of Southwick House to their cars, and instead of the low cloud that had made Tedder and Leigh-Mallory oppose launching the invasion, the skies remained clear all day. Poor Stagg feared, if not for his life, at least for his Group Captain's rank. By one o'clock on the afternoon of Sunday 4 June, however, a stiff breeze was blowing, evidence of the expected cold front. But the prognosis was now reversing itself: the skies would be clear enough of cloud for the air forces to operate, but the sea itself might be too rough to guarantee naval success.

In the midst of this meteorological confusion, a new hope began to appear. The depression in the mid-Atlantic had intensified to the point where it must slow down, giving a breathing space of possibly a full day on Tuesday 6 June: 'a heaven sent break,' as Stagg recalled.[2] Excitedly Stagg attended a conference of forecasters at 4.30 p.m. – but instead of being 'short and happy' about the possible break, the session turned into 'the most heatedly argumentative and most prolonged of the whole series: it lasted well over two hours'.[3]

If the forecasters could not agree, how could the Commanders responsible for the invasion? When, at 9.30 that evening, Eisenhower asked what the weather would be like after 6 June in the Channel and over the French coast, Stagg 'hesitated . . . for two dramatic minutes and finally said, conscientiously and soberly, "To answer that question would make me a guesser, not a meteorologist."'[4] Nevertheless Stagg's forecast for 6 June itself was good – little

[1] J. M. Stagg, op. cit.
[2] Ibid.
[3] Ibid.
[4] Tedder to Butcher, in Diary of Harry C. Butcher, loc. cit.

cloud, and quieter seas than at present or on Monday. Creasy, Leigh-Mallory and de Guingand cross-examined Stagg. Ramsay seemed moderately content; Leigh-Mallory still worried about the effectiveness of his heavy bombers in such conditions; Tedder supported him. Finally Eisenhower turned to Monty.

'Do you see any reason why we should not go on Tuesday?'

According to Stagg, Montgomery's reply was immediate and emphatic.

'No. I would say – *Go*.'[1]

After further discussion of the air ramifications of a decision to go, Eisenhower sided with Monty. The convoys that had been ordered to return were now to be told to put to sea again. A final irrevocable decision would be made at 4.30 the next morning, 5 June.

By now, the depression Stagg had forecast the night before had arrived, bringing driving rain and high winds. Yet most of the forecasters now agreed that Tuesday 6 June would see fair weather. Only the forecast thereafter was in doubt.

In the early hours of 5 June the senior commanders of 'Overlord' met again at Southwick House. 'All were in battle-dress uniform except General Montgomery,' Stagg recalled. 'Conspicuous in his customary front seat he was dressed in a high-necked fawn coloured pullover and light corduroy trousers.' Facing the Commanders 'General Eisenhower seemed as spruce and immaculate as ever. At the earlier meetings the Cs-in-C and their staff chiefs exchanged pleasantries among themselves as they settled into their easy chairs and sofas: but at this meeting, as at the last, the atmosphere was sombre. Faces were grave and the room was quiet.'[2]

Stagg's forecast was hopeful. 'Immediately after I had finished tension seemed to evaporate and the Supreme Commander and his colleagues became as new men. Winds along the assault coasts would not exceed force 3 generally, cloud would be high enough to permit both bombing and naval spotting. The further outlook was variable, but with sunny intervals.'[3]

Eisenhower confirmed his decision of the previous night. D-Day the sixth of June was 'on'.

Weather in the Channel was still so bad that even Monty later admitted that 'if we had persisted with the original D-Day of 5th June, we might have had a disaster'. By delaying a day, Eisenhower had been able to turn to his advantage one of the luckiest weather breaks of the war.

Nevertheless the issue was not over. Amidst rancorous bickering about who had been proved right or wrong, Stagg returned to face

[1] J. M. Stagg, op. cit.
[2] Ibid.
[3] Ibid.

601

his forecasting teams; in London, by the Thames, it had been 'blowing half a gale' on 4 June; now, on Monday 5 June, there seemed little improvement when Monty telephoned General Kennedy, the ACIGS to say 'the weather forecast indicated that the sky would be clear and therefore good for aircraft on the 6th'.[1]

That evening Monty drove up to Hindhead to see the Reynolds, and to make 'final arrangements' regarding David. 'I had not seen him recently and did not want to indicate the nearness of D-Day to all the boys at Winchester by going there to say goodbye to him,' Monty recorded in his *Memoirs*. As before his voyage to North Africa in August 1942, however, it seems more likely that Monty wished to avoid any 'emotional scenes'. He certainly said nothing to the Reynolds; but he could not fool Phyllis. 'Mrs Reynolds told me afterwards that she knew it was the eve of D-Day – not from anything I said or from the way I behaved, but because I had taken my plain clothes and had put them away in a wardrobe,' Monty recorded.[2]

In a matter of hours his armies would be in battle. Already some 500 warships of all kinds and 3,000 landing craft were at sea. Aircraft fitters throughout Britain were checking the planes that would participate in an aerial armada even greater than that at sea. Monty's Tactical Headquarters was – as a consequence of the mix-up in the invasion of Sicily – already loaded on board three tank landing craft, together with Dempsey's vehicles and personnel.

The great adventure was beginning, and Monty had reason to be proud of his achievement in getting ready the armies of Britain and America. His Personal Message, as before Alamein, had been printed and distributed 'to be read out to all troops' once embarked:

The time has come to deal the enemy a terrific blow in Western Europe.

The blow will be struck by the combined sea, land and air forces of the Allies – together constituting one great Allied team, under the supreme command of General Eisenhower.

On the eve of this great adventure I send my best wishes to every soldier in the Allied team.

To us is given the honour of striking a blow for freedom which will live in history; and in the better days that lie ahead men will speak with pride of our doings.

Let us pray that 'The Lord Mighty in Battle' will go forth with our armies, and that His special providence will aid us in the struggle.

I want every soldier to know that I have complete confidence in the successful outcome of the operations that we are now to begin.

[1] J. Kennedy, op. cit.
[2] B. L. Montgomery, op. cit.

With stout hearts, and with enthusiasm for the contest, let us go forward to victory.

And as we enter battle, let us recall the words of a famous soldier spoken many years ago:–

'He either fears his fate too much,
   Or his deserts are small,
Who dare not put it to the touch
   To win or lose it all.'

Good luck to each one of you. And good hunting on the mainland.

Thereafter officers broke open the seals on their specific instructions. As the boats dipped and swayed in the sea that had once kept Hitler from invading Britain, the secret of the past five months was at last revealed to the 130,000 men of the two armies whose task it was to breach the Atlantic wall, across the beaches of St Laurent, Varreville, Ouistreham, Courseulles and Asnelles.

As before Alamein, Monty retired to bed at his usual hour, in Broomfield House. He was, as Dawnay remembered, 'supremely confident' of the outcome.[1] In the past five months he had proved himself as the outstanding commander of armies in the ranks of the Allied nations. Two million men had looked to him for inspiration, and a plan that would give them a proper chance of success. He had provided both.

Yet his methods had not passed without comment or criticism, and only battle itself would determine whether he had been right. At his Main 21st Army Group Headquarters there was an air of great expectancy and excitement. De Guingand drove down to Southsea to watch the ships set sail. 'As I gazed at this great array of ships heading south, I asked myself whether it was really possible that at long last our months of planning in stuffy offices had reached fruition.'[2] Brigadier Williams, however, pored over the latest Intelligence reports, aware that there were distinct gaps in Allied knowledge about enemy dispositions: 'the chief gaps . . . are the strength and location of 21 Panzer Division, [and] the location of 352 Division,' he had begun his final weekly Intelligence summary, which Monty saw fit to keep in a separate file. 'Nothing more has come to light about 21 Panzer Division; but there is slowly growing evidence in photographs of tank tracks North of the Caen-Bayeux lateral.' The evidence about 352nd Division was 'flimsy', but worried Williams as the divisions previously allotted a layback role had begun to 'nose forward' towards the 'Neptune' beaches.

Nor was Williams the only uneasy spirit at 21st Army Group

[1] Loc. cit.
[1] F. W. de Guingand, op. cit.

Headquarters, Britain had been at war since 1939 – some five years. Many of the British troops were, inevitably, tired. By bringing home divisions such as the famous 'Desert Rats', the Highland Division, and the Geordies of 50th Division, Monty had hoped to leaven the otherwise green formations of Dempsey's Second Army. But was this wise? Tirelessly Monty had sought to 'binge up' the troops – but was he asking too much of men who had risked their lives and lived with death for too many months and years to relish the 'great adventure'? Brigadier Herbert later acknowledged what a powerful effect Monty had had on the troops, but recalled that he was not entirely happy:

I mean the troops were not altogether all right. For example we were – Monty's headquarters were at Southwick, the hinterland of Portsmouth. The armour which was going to embark at Fareham area was running along the road that went past Southwick, more or less. Well, that included at least one regiment from the 7th Armoured Division [the 'Desert Rats']. Now two or three people came up to me and said: 'Do you realise that these people are out of hand?' They were responsible, senior fighting soldiers, and they were really very worried about it [the indiscipline]. And I went out and had a look, and I agreed. They were not under control – they were forcing people off the road, assing about generally – *in a way that experienced troops going into battle would not behave*. I mean they were the Desert Rats, the most famous division in the British Army, and they were fed up and irresponsible. So that there was some reason to be uncertain as to whether everything was all right or whether it wasn't.[1]

Only the trial of battle would tell.

---

[1] General Sir Otway Herbert, loc. cit.

PART SIX

Normandy

CHAPTER ONE

Last-minute Interference

In the disused annexe behind a house on Prinsengracht, Amsterdam, a girl in hiding had been anxiously awaiting news of the invasion. 'It's no exaggeration to say that all Amsterdam, all Holland, yes the whole west coast of Europe, right down to Spain, talks about the invasion day and night, debates about it, and makes bets on it and – hopes.'

Anne Frank's life depended on the Allied invasion, and when at 10 a.m. on 6 June 1944 she heard the BBC broadcast in Dutch she was beside herself. 'Oh, Kitty, the best part of the invasion is that I have the feeling that friends are approaching. We have been oppressed by those terrible Germans for so long, they have had their knives so at our throats, that the thought of friends and delivery fills me with confidence!' she recorded in her diary. 'Now it doesn't concern the Jews any more; no, it concerns Holland and all occupied Europe. Perhaps, Margot says, I may yet be able to go back to school in September or October.'[1] She was still only fourteen and had been in hiding almost two years.

Much has been written about D-Day and the Allied invasion of Normandy; it is important, however, to recall the context in which the landings took place, for like Alamein, the invasion of Normandy signified far more than a battle. Upon its outcome rested the hopes and anxieties of millions, giving the battle a moral significance which, as at Alamein, went far beyond military statistics. If indeed the battle for Normandy mirrored in many ways its desert counterpart, this had much to do with the 'directing staff'. As Monty noted in his own diary, life at 21st Army Group Headquarters was very much like being at Eighth Army Headquarters at Alamein: de Guingand, Williams, Richardson, Belchem, Richards, Graham. . . . As at Alamein, Monty had not only decided on a clear and simple plan of battle, but had personally addressed all field officers down to Lt-Colonel, as well as the troops of both assault armies. Deception too, as at Alamein, had played an important part in the battle plan, helping to achieve tactical surprise. And, as at Alamein, the air plan

---

[1] *The Diary of Anne Frank*, London 1953.

formed a vital counterpoint to the land battle, a plan in which the Allied air forces fought not only for air supremacy but direct air interdiction of the enemy's supply and movement routes.

It was in the realm of air operations, however, that Monty was to encounter his worst tribulations – tribulations that began already on 3 June 1944 when the Deputy Supreme Commander, Air Marshal Tedder, attempted to dismantle the entire operation of air support to the assaulting armies.

Here was the antithesis to Eighth Army's experience in the desert, as Brigadier Williams later recalled:

> In the desert they'd got this doctrine that was carried over [to 21st Army Group]: that 'we ask and they provide. We don't tell them how to do it.' Freddie [de Guingand] had worked out with chaps like Harry Broadhurst a quite interesting technique of talking it over with them. . . .
>
> But when we came back that rapport didn't exist. There was no real co-operation . . . no one was commanding the Air Force so to speak, and Tedder had to try and command because Leigh-Mallory was – well he'd got the job of being the Expeditionary Air Force Commander because it was alleged he was one of those airmen who understood the army. And he didn't, I don't think – he didn't have any control over Bert Harris [commanding RAF Bomber Command] at all, anyway. Leigh-Mallory didn't have any 'guts' – therefore Tedder provided the 'guts'.
>
> I remember going to those ghastly conferences at Norfolk House – you had a sort of role, you were brought in to give views on how you disrupt railways. I remember one splendid Trade Unionist saying afterwards [in North country accent], 'Well, Air Marshal, if you'll take my advice, you'll bomb the junctions!'
>
> The Americans were liable to get into intellectual arguments: 'because you've said something, I've got to say I disagree' – it was all rather childish, but dangerously childish because the great thing was to get all these airmen to agree on *something*. One of the biggest difficulties when Monty came back to England was that the RAF, Bomber Command in particular, were the men 'in possession' and we had been playing 'away matches'. They didn't even really believe in Normandy, they really thought then they could bomb the hell out of the Germans and that would be enough. And then send a few soldiers over – that sort of attitude.
>
> The result was, and it's significant I think, that this awful phrase grew up: 'selling a target'. And that's what you had to do, you see, if you wanted the Air Force to do something.[1]

[1] Sir Edgar Williams, interview of 7.9.78.

This lack of whole-hearted co-operation was memorably summed up by one of the American planners at 21st Army Group, Colonel Bonesteel: 'The U.S. Air Corps-RAF was a house divided. The air side stank beyond belief.'[1]

Ironically Tedder is best remembered for having backed Monty's and Leigh-Mallory's call for a proper Air Force interdiction plan in February and March 1944 – a plan which forced Harris to use his heavy bomber effort on military targets rather than cities. Yet when, on 2 and 3 June 1944, Leigh-Mallory attempted to lay down the military targets to be bombed *on* and *after* D-Day, Tedder opposed him. 'Tedder told the Air C-in-C [Leigh-Mallory] that he could not approve of the bombing of French towns and villages, which would cause high civilian casualties and might be of very little use. He said that they had undertaken to the Prime Minister not to bomb anything after D-Day but batteries and Radar targets.'[2]

How Tedder can have believed that Montgomery's armies should assault the mainland of North-west Europe – the long-awaited Second Front – without direct air support remains one of the least known and least comprehensible of Tedder's 'contributions' to 'Overlord'. He had, of course, attempted to do the same in 'Husky', the invasion of Sicily, insisting then that it was the primary task of the Allied Air Forces to defeat their Luftwaffe counterparts, not to help the armies. Leigh-Mallory was justly furious.

> The Air C-in-C said that he didn't know of any such undertaking made to the Prime Minister, and that once the battle was joined, strategic considerations must be paramount. They would have at all costs to prevent the Allied armies from being pushed back into the sea. There would no doubt be civilian casualties, but they would perhaps not be higher than our own military casualties.[3]

It is almost incredible to think that, less than forty-eight hours before the intended mounting of D-Day, the Allies were unable to agree on an air plan to support their armies. Yet this is the case – concealed by decades of historiographical wool:

> At the conference at H.Q. A.E.A.F. on June 3rd at which the Air C-in-C was in the chair, A.C.M. Tedder reiterated his criticism of the communications bombing plan, speaking in support of Gen. Spaatz and Gen. Doolittle who advocated direct attacks on German airfields as the proper task of the Strategical Air Forces on D-Day and after.

[1] Interview of 18.6.47 by F. C. Pogue, OCMH Collection, Military History Institute, Carlisle, Pennsylvania.
[2] AEAF Record, June 1944 (AIR 37/1057), PRO.
[3] Ibid.

On this occasion, Tedder said nothing of the civilian casualties, according to the Air Force historian, but repeated the same objections as in Sicily, insisting that road-blocking would be 'ineffective' and that 'in concentrating all our bomber effort on assisting the Army we were ignoring the danger from the German Air Force to both Army and Air Forces.'[1]

It was in this atmosphere that Monty, who heard personally from Leigh-Mallory of Tedder's attempts to cancel bomber support, went to war in June 1944. That he was anxious is indicated by the AEAF historian's record of his phone call to Leigh-Mallory soon after the 3 June meeting of Allied Air Commanders:

> At 15.00 hours on 3rd June, General Montgomery, who had heard from his L.O. that argument on the bombing plan had been reopened at H.Q. A.E.A.F., telephoned the Air C-in-C to find if any modification had been made. The Air C-in-C assured him that he stood by the plan absolutely, and would resign rather than abandon it.[2]

This threat of resignation by the Air C-in-C on the eve of the Normandy invasion was a sad reflection of Tedder's interference. Unfortunately it was the first of several such performances, although the alarums over the deteriorating weather forecast prevented the issue from reaching the Supreme Commander's morning or evening conferences at Southwick House thereafter.

So vital did Monty consider the air programme in 'Overlord' that he had transferred Brigadier Richardson, his Chief Plans Officer at 21st Army Group, to Leigh-Mallory as a personal Liaison Officer, and finally, at 10.30 a.m. the morning before D-Day, agreement was reached on the bombing of 'choke-points on main routes into the lodgement area'[3] on D-Day, but with leaflets being dropped at least an hour before bombing as a concession to Tedder. 'The weapon on which we were relying – the weapon of air superiority in order to delay the rate of German build-up' had been unsheathed. D-Day, as a concerted effort 'by the combined sea, land, and air forces of the Allies – together constituting one great Allied team',[4] was on – just.

[1] Ibid.
[2] Ibid.
[3] Ibid. Also testimony of General Sir Charles Richardson: 'Leigh-Mallory was not a big enough man. You needed to have a very big man to put pressure on these autonomous air forces. Leigh-Mallory seemed to be a complete cypher – the final D-Day plan we only settled literally within hours of the setting off of the forces' – interview of 20.11.79.
[4] Personal message from the C-in-C, 21st Army Group.

CHAPTER TWO

The D-Day Landings

In many respects the D-Day landings resembled those of 'Husky', the invasion of Sicily in 1943. Two allied armies landed abreast – with the American landing very soon in trouble. Bradley had declined to use Hobart's 'funnies', German opposition was fierce and the Omaha Beach landing looked so precarious that by the evening of 6 June Monty was signalling to Dempsey to ask if he could receive 5 US Corps on one of the British beaches – a secret signal that was afterwards 'hushed up': 'It is not usually known that Monty wired me on the night of D-Day asking, "Can you take V Corps?"' Dempsey related to the American Official Historian. 'I said, "No, unless you want to leave our people out, because it is too crowded to go in together."'[1]

Omaha lay between the American right flank (Utah) and the British Gold, Juno and Sword beaches. Without successful landings at Omaha, Monty's entire concept of 'Overlord' – an assault broad enough for the American army to break out quickly and take Cherbourg – seemed doomed, since Rommel could then keep the two Allied armies separated, and defeat each in turn before they could be built up.

Monty's inner anxiety, therefore, was in direct contrast to the mood of triumph which pervaded much of the Allied camp on the evening of D-Day.[2] Apart from Omaha, the D-Day landings were indeed a triumph, with more than 156,000 Allied soldiers landed by nightfall. As in Sicily the extent of tactical surprise astonished even Monty – who felt sure the Germans *must* learn of the seaborne assault at the latest by the eve of the invasion. In this respect the deception plan ('Fortitude') and the inclement weather had given the Allies the luck they needed. Rommel was so certain that no invasion could take place in such conditions that, as at the commencement of the battle of Alamein, he was not even at his post, having decided on 4 June to drive to Germany to his home in Herrlingen for a brief

[1] Interview of 12/13.3.47 by F. C. Pogue, loc. cit.
[2] 'Ike was ready to go a visitin', to Monty's post [outside Portsmouth], where the sweatered one was wearing the countenance of the day and pleased about it' – Diary of Harry C. Butcher, Eisenhower Library, Abilene, Kansas.

vacation. The sea had been considered too rough to station even a single German patrol boat offshore, and the German Seventh Army in Normandy was not even on alert. Only at 10 p.m. on the night of 6 June did Rommel finally get back to his headquarters.

Getting ashore was, as in the break-in at Alamein, one thing; creating an impenetrable lodgement area another. Dempsey and Bradley were necessarily pre-occupied with the movements of their own contingents; only Monty himself could judge the vital importance of linking the two Allied armies before the Germans began to react with their Panzer divisions. Monty therefore decided to leave his Portsmouth headquarters on the night of D-Day, and to go over to France by destroyer. 'If things were not going well, he said, he would put them right; if they were going well, he would make them go better,' a phone call to the ACIGS, General Kennedy at the War Office, made clear.[1] At 9.30 p.m. HMS *Faulknor* set sail, and soon afterwards Monty was asleep.

'We went onto the boat,' Monty's ADC, Major Johnny Henderson, later recalled with a grin,

and he said he was going 'straight to bed'. I was the only fellow with him [Tactical Headquarters was already being shipped over in LSTs to France] and he said, 'Now come and tell me news of the battle at 6 o'clock.' We had wireless contact back with Main [Headquarters] on shore, at Portsmouth.

The next morning at half-past five I went up on the bridge and said, 'Well, where are we?'

The captain, a fellow called Churchill, said, 'I wish to hell I knew! We lost the swept channel two hours ago and we've heaved to – we're waiting for daylight to see if we can see where we are.'

I said, 'Good heavens! Sounds rather awkward. I think I'd better go and tell the Army Commander.'

And he said 'Oh, please don't do that, there's still time!'

We waited a little until it started to get light, at about six o'clock, and still we couldn't tell where we were, so I said, 'I must tell the C-in-C, I must – I can't wait, there's too much at stake.'

So I went and told him, at half-past six.

And he seemed very unperturbed. Got dressed, came up on the bridge. And said, 'Oh, I hear we're lost!'

Angry? No, not at all. And as it started to get lighter, you know, there was suddenly a cry from wherever, that a battleship was in sight. And so there was 'Action Stations!', everyone at their guns. And it transpired it was an American battleship, we had floated down right off Cherbourg peninsula! And jolly lucky with the minefields. . . .

[1] John Kennedy, *The Business of War*, London 1957.

So we turned round and steamed up there [towards the assault beaches].

Very unperturbed. You know never at any time did he seem to appear to wake up early or turn the light on, or anything. . . .[1]

Compared with the question of linking the two Allied armies into a cohesive bridgehead before Rommel could counter-attack, the temporary disorientation of his destroyer was of little consequence to Monty. Within a very short time Captain Churchill was able to locate Bradley's command ship, the *Aurora*, and Bradley came aboard the *Faulknor*. 'Bradley was concerned about the operational situation on Omaha, his eastern beach. We discussed his problem and agreed on how it could be solved,' Montgomery recorded in his *Memoirs*. To the participants at the time, however, the 'problem' seemed far more dramatic than Monty's later recollection, as the diary kept by Bradley's aide, Major Hansen, confirms:

Kean [Chief of Staff to Bradley] was afraid first day that he [the enemy] might kick us off . . . situation on the Omaha beach is critical. We've got to get our stuff ashore, get V corps in across the lateral road and establish themselves on the high ground before he gets ready to hit us.[2]

Having ascertained the previous night that the follow-up forces in General Gerow's 5 US Corps could not be accommodated via the British beaches, Monty felt there was only one answer: to delay the American dash for Cherbourg and turn Collins's 7 US Corps inland, and eastwards instead of westwards from the Utah beaches. Meanwhile Dempsey's western flank was to be pushed as far inland as possible to relieve the pressure on Gerow. While this would inevitably delay the attacks upon the Allied target – Cherbourg – it would at least stop Rommel from exploiting the separation of the Allied lodgement areas.

'Monty told us we gotta join up – before pushing west or north,' Hansen recorded Bradley's message to Collins's 7 US Corps headquarters. 'Brit may have to pull us out on Omaha. When they take Bayeux and get farther inland that should relieve the pressure on us.'[3] Later in the morning Eisenhower's minelayer, HMS *Apollo*, arrived off the British beaches, and Monty informed the Supreme Commander of his decision. 'On the whole US Army front the immediate tactical plan has been altered with the purpose of both

[1] J. R. Henderson, interview of 13.8.81.
[2] Diary of Chester B. Hansen, Military History Institute, Carlisle, Pennsylvania.
[3] Ibid.

Corps making an early drive to Carentan to join up, after which the original conceptions will be pursued,' Eisenhower signalled to the Combined Chiefs of Staff in Washington the following day.[1]

Eisenhower, condemned to watch rather than command the invasion of Normandy, had fretted since waking on D-Day. 'It's Tuesday afternoon, Ike and Jim [Gault, British MA][2] have trudged off to the war room to see what's being done about G and his V Corps, this news having bothered Ike so much. I could see from his questions he wished he were running the 21st Army Group so he could do something about it himself,' Commander Butcher had recorded in his diary, 'but from where he sits he can't just step in. . . .'[3] By 8 June when he had to address war correspondents at Southwick 'he seemed tired and almost listless,' Butcher considered. 'He said the operation was still "hazardous". . . . He wanted them to report faithfully but not paint a false picture of optimism; indeed the situation is somewhat critical and we are now in the inevitable race for build-up.'[4]

To Monty it was a sign of bad generalship ever to show such anxiety. In Butcher's words, when 'General Montgomery came aboard from a destroyer' on 7 June, 'Monty was happy. He was establishing the tactical headquarters ashore.'[5] To de Guingand, having spoken first to Bradley, then to Dempsey, Monty signalled at eleven-thirty that morning:

Utah landings good and 4 [US] Div lodgement area about 5 miles deep with 82 and 101 [US Airborne] Divs further to West and South, Omaha not so good and lodgement area about 2 miles deep.

Nevertheless he did 'not want US troops brought in through Second Army beaches', but had 'given orders' as follows:

Bradley to secure his D-Day objective and in particular to capture Carentan and Isigny so as to link up his two lodgement areas. Then to thrust towards La Haye du Puits and thus cut off the Cherbourg peninsula.

The British and Canadian landings, meanwhile, had gone excellently. 50th Division had already been attacking Bayeux 'yesterday', and 3rd Division was in possession of Ouistreham and Bieville 'and advancing on Caen today'. Already the 6th British Airborne Division

---

[1] *The Papers of Dwight David Eisenhower*, ed. Alfred D. Chandler, *The War Years* Vol. III, Baltimore 1970.
[2] Later Brigadier Sir James Gault.
[3] Loc. cit.
[4] Ibid.
[5] Ibid.

was across the Orne, to the north-east of Caen, and threatening Cabourg, on the coast. Since it appeared 'likely 21 Pz Div intends to hold Caen', Monty had agreed with Dempsey that it would be better to capture the city by envelopment: 'Dempsey to proceed relentlessly with the original plan. He will hold a flank on the River Dives and capture Caen and Bayeux. He will then pivot on Caen and swing his right forward. Likely that 51 Div will cut in behind Caen moving east of the River Orne.'

As in the first days after the Sicilian landings, Monty radiated confidence. That Second Army had failed to take Caen on D-Day did not at this stage alarm him, for with an energetic drive on Second Army's eastern flank, he was confident Caen must fall by envelopment. At 8 p.m. he signalled the latest news to Eisenhower: 'General situation very good and am well satisfied with results of today's fighting. 7 US Corps has a lodgement area nearly 8 miles deep . . . 5 Corps has made a grand recovery from a difficult situation and I have asked Bradley to congratulate the Corps from me. Have ordered Bradley to join up his two lodgement areas and to thrust towards La Haye du Puits. Dempsey has captured Port en Bessin and Bayeux and is on the general line of the railway between Bayeux and Caen. Caen,' he added, 'still held by enemy. Will pursue vigorously plans outlined to you today.'

Most of Monty's Tactical Headquarters was still at sea in two LSTs, off Juno Beach, waiting vainly for Rhino ferries. Like Bradley, therefore, Monty had to spend the night at sea again, on board the destroyer HMS *Faulknor*. 'We anchored off the British beaches at about 8.30 p.m. and I asked Captain Churchill if he could put me on shore at 7 a.m. the next morning, the 8th June,' Monty recalled.[1] From his destroyer there had been little sign that 'a battle was being fought which was deciding the fate of Europe';[2] the Allies seemed to have complete air superiority, and it was difficult to imagine the traumas that lay ahead. Admiral Vian, however, had told Monty that, owing to the rough sea, unloading of stores and vehicles was well behind schedule, and that he had ordered LSTs to run aground on the beaches in an effort to speed up the operation. In his diary Dempsey noted that 'unless the wind drops and the sea moderates, the build-up is going to be very difficult'.[3] Although he was reasonably pleased with the progress of his two Corps, Dempsey was anxious about the lack of clear information regarding his forces to the north and north-east of Caen: 'The situation of 3 Div North of Caen and 6 Airborne East of the two rivers is still rather obscure,' he noted at 6 p.m.[4]

[1] B. L. Montgomery, *Memoirs*, London 1958.
[2] Ibid.
[3] Diary of M. C. Dempsey (WO 285/9), PRO.
[4] Ibid.

Meanwhile at the headquarters of the AEAF at Stanmore, Leigh-Mallory was puzzled by the lack of German air response to the invasion. He saw his historical task as a dual one: the establishment of air superiority and the dislocation of the German army from the air. 'In general, I am satisfied with my preparations,' he had remarked on 5 June. 'My main task has been to delay the movements of the German army in order to prevent it from carrying out that oldest maxim of war – it is the General who concentrates the largest number of men in the shortest possible time at the vital point who wins the battle. I believe,' he added, 'that our progress across the beaches will be necessarily slow and I look to the Air Forces to redress the balance which is against us, in so far as the problem of building up is concerned.' To his chagrin the six-tenths cloud over Normandy at 2,000 feet had made 'effective bombing by the American heavies impossible' on D-Day.[1] The result was that all the carefully laid plans for the delay of German movements by creating 'choke-points in towns on the roads could not be executed.'[2]

Cloud on 7 June was even worse – 'cloud was in many places 10/10th at 1500–3000 ft. The result has been another serious interference in the bombing programme, which has allowed the Germans by the end of the day to have moved their nearer reserves into the battle area,' the Headquarters Historian recorded.[3] By evening Leigh-Mallory was a worried man: 'The weather has interfered with my air programme all day and is seriously upsetting me. The German army is being reinforced and I cannot bomb the reinforcements in daylight . . . I have a feeling we are losing precious time at a moment when the main movements of the enemy are beginning. . . . Generally speaking, Allied Air Forces are not doing as well against the German army as I had hoped. No effective day bombing has yet taken place, and this is most unfortunate.' The relative inactivity of the Luftwaffe did not mean that air superiority had been won – 'it may be that the Hun is trying to lull us into a false sense of security. We shall soon know.'[4]

Hitler had indeed remarked on 5 June, after the Allies had seized Rome, that 'the invasion this year is going to result in an annihilating defeat for the enemy at the one place where it really counts'; and once the seriousness of the Normandy invasion became plain, Hitler was 'confident' in anticipating a German Panzer attack on 8 June that would drive the Allies back into the sea.[5]

Knowing from Intelligence that the German Panzer reserves were moving up for an attack, Monty was doubly anxious to be ashore on 8

[1] Diary of Sir Trafford Leigh-Mallory (AIR 37/784), PRO.
[2] AEAF Record, loc. cit.
[3] Ibid.
[4] Diary of Sir Trafford Leigh-Mallory, loc. cit.
[5] D. Irving, *Hitler's War*, London 1977.

June. That the British had sufficient artillery and anti-tank weapons to meet such an attack he was confident, for they were so far inland that advantage could now be taken of the close, hedge-ridden *bocage*. About the American bridgehead he was less sure. The Omaha beachhead was connected neither on its left nor its right with the adjacent Allied forces, and the lack of ammunition and equipment was worrying Bradley. If the British could hold on to their lodgement area between Caen and Bayeux, it might even be advisable to send the follow-up British forces in on Omaha beach in order to bolster the front there. One thing was vital in fighting Rommel, however: not to allow him to assume the tactical initiative. With the Allied Air Forces unable to stop the movement of Rommel's reserves, it would be necessary for Dempsey to attack so aggressively that Rommel would not be able to keep his own Panzer assault concentrated, but must, as at Alamein, be forced to act as local firefighter, reducing the concentration of the German attacks.

At 9.30 p.m. on 7 June, therefore, Monty retired to his bunk. The next days would require unfaltering leadership – and he proposed to give it.

CHAPTER THREE

A Chance to Checkmate the Enemy

Immediately after breakfast, at 6.30 a.m. on 8 June 1944, HMS *Faulknor* 'began to move in towards the beach on which I had asked to be landed,' Monty recorded in his *Memoirs*. 'It was low water and, as I had asked we should get in as close as possible, the captain began sounding with hand leads and started the echo sounder. All beach-marks were obliterated by smoke-screens. The next thing that happened was that a slight shudder went through the ship; we were aground aft on some outlying sandbank or boulders. I was on the quarter deck with an ADC, and I sent him up to the bridge to ask if we were going to get any closer to the shore. This was not well received by the captain.'

Monty's first landing on French soil since the evacuation at Dunkirk began, then, on an inauspicious note. Poor Captain Churchill, after having lost his way on the voyage out from England, must have feared for his command; but Monty, undaunted, was concerned only with getting ashore. 'Splendid,' he announced to the First Lieutenant, on being informed that they were aground. 'Then the captain has got in as close as he possibly can. Now, what about a boat to put me on shore?'[1]

Eventually Monty was fetched by his Tac HQ staff in one of their landing craft; Colonel Russell had landed the previous night and thereafter set up Monty's field headquarters at Ste Croix-sur-Mer, in 'a series of fields interspersed with German trenches', selected off the map, and under enemy artillery fire. Monty took one look at this 'exceedingly moderate location' as its chronicler, Major Odgers, delicately described it,[2] and ordered it to be moved. His Canadian PA, Lt-Colonel Warren, had fortunately stumbled on a better location at Creully, a village two miles further inland. There, in the grounds of the local château, Monty set up his field headquarters for the next fortnight – missing only a chamber pot in his caravan, as he recorded in his *Memoirs*. Owing to British shyness the owner was

---

[1] *Memoirs*, op. cit.
[2] P. R. Odgers, 'A Tac Chronicle' (1945), communicated by Lt-Colonel C. P. Dawnay.

asked merely to supply a vase, and only when she had paraded the château's entire collection of flower vases did Madame de Druval realise what it was that General Montgomery required.

That morning the German attack by 1 SS Panzer Corps began – but it made little headway and lacked cohesion. By evening over half of 21st Panzer Division's tanks had been lost, and Rommel made perhaps his greatest error since resuming his post on the night of D-Day. Sensing that the Allies were now too strong for a German breakthrough to the sea north of Caen, he split off half of 21st Panzer and 12th SS Panzer divisions and sent them north-west in a fruitless and too-late attempt to recapture Bayeux, over twelve miles further west. 'Thus the fist was unclenched just as it was ready to strike,' the Commander of Panzer Group West, General Geyr von Schweppenburg, later wistfully remarked.[1]

Monty, by contrast, was delighted, for although the enlarged bridgehead was proving problematic in terms of linking up the beachheads, it was obvious that its very breadth had confused Rommel, who was, as Monty had predicted, caught between three stools: defending Caen, recapturing Bayeux, and retaining Carentan. At 2.30 p.m. Monty saw Dempsey at the latter's headquarters. Dempsey felt that the Canadian and British 3rd Divisions north of Caen were 'a bit messy' and needed to get their armour and artillery under better control; once this was done Dempsey wanted General Crocker, the Corps Commander, 'to be prepared to operate offensively' from the 6th Airborne Division's bridgehead 'with a view to capturing CAEN from the EAST in two or three day's time'.[2]

Monty did not agree. As he explained in a letter that evening to Major-General Simpson at the War Office, Caen was only a name; he did not want to waste British and Canadian lives à la Stalingrad:

The Germans are doing everything they can to hold on to CAEN. I have decided not to have a lot of casualties by butting up against the place; so I have ordered Second Army to keep up a good pressure at CAEN, and to *make its main effort*[3] towards VILLERS BOCAGE and EVRECY and thence S.E. towards FALAISE.

This was in accordance with Monty's promise to Leigh-Mallory, in developing his 'Overlord' concept, that he would take the airfields south-east of Caen. Once established in this area, the British Second Army would present an offensive shield, behind which the Amer-

[1] D. Irving, *The Trail of the Fox*, London 1977.
[2] Diary of M. C. Dempsey, loc. cit. De Guingand, in a conversation with Leigh-Mallory in England, at 3.10 p.m., presumed the same thing, 'that General Montgomery was hoping to attack, and possibly outflank CAEN from the EAST' – noted in AEAF Record, loc. cit.
[3] Author's italics.

icans could build up their lodgement area, cut off the Cherbourg peninsula, and gradually swing south, pivoting on the Falaise-Argentan ridge before striking east to Paris.

All day Monty toured the British sector, which was still abounding in German snipers left behind by the speed of the assault. 'Our initial landings were on a wide front,' he explained to Simpson, 'and there were gaps between landings. The impetus of the assault carried us some way inland and many defended localities were by-passed; these proved very troublesome later. In one case a complete German B[attalio]n, with artillery, was found inside 50 Div area; it gave some trouble but was eventually collected in (about 500 men). There is still one holding out – the radar station west of DOUVRES; it is very strong and is held by stout hearted Germans.' The Germans were 'fighting well', he remarked, though 'the Russians, Poles, Japanese, and Turks, run away, and, if unable to do so, surrender'. The sniping, however, was a serious problem. Two infantry brigade commanders had been wounded, and a 'good many C.O.'s killed', including Lt-Colonel Herdon, commanding the 2nd Battalion of his old regiment, the Royal Warwicks. 'Sniping in back areas has been very troublesome. . . . The roads have been far from safe and we have lost several good officers. I have been all right myself, though I have toured the area all day,' he assured Simpson – unaware that a German soldier was hiding under a stone seat in the grounds of his field headquarters at that very moment.[1]

Bradley too was vexed by the problem of snipers in the rear areas, he confessed to his ADC, who commented: 'Talk of sniping and Brad says he will not take action against anyone that decides to treat snipers a little more roughly than they are being treated at present. Sniper cannot sit around and shoot and then capture when you close in on him. That's not the way to play the game.'[2]

The most perplexing problem was, however, that of supply. The Americans were 'two tides behind now',[3] as Bradley knew. Though the British had held all the German Panzer attacks so far, the failure of the Americans to join up their bridgeheads and lock onto the British right flank would inevitably give Rommel a chance to exploit the gaps. Monty therefore sent a message to Bradley, convening a conference for the next morning. In the meantime, at 4.30 on the afternoon of 8 June, Dempsey received news that Port-en-Bessin had been captured and that the Anglo-American armies had joined

---

[1] 'The discovery of an exceedingly frightened Boche under a stone seat in the château grounds brought the realisation that one defence platoon was hardly sufficient' – P. R. Odgers, loc. cit. Some extra commandos and tanks were thereafter deployed.

[2] Diary of Chester B. Hansen, entry of 8.6.44, loc. cit.

[3] Ibid.

hands there, 'which is most satisfactory,' he noted with relief.[1] 'The two armies have now joined hands west of BAYEUX,' Monty informed Simpson, equally pleased. To Eisenhower he signalled at 8 p.m.: 'Today has been spent in repelling attacks in the CAEN sector and in cleaning up centres of resistance still existing inside our lodgement area. . . . In the centre the two armies have now joined hands. On the right progress has been made towards ISIGNY and CARENTAN. . . . Am organizing strong thrust south towards VILLERS BOCAGE and EVRECY. Am very satisfied with the situation.'

The 'strong thrust' by Second Army was to kick off in earnest early the next morning. Already at 5 p.m. on 8 June Dempsey had gone to see the Corps Commander, General Bucknall, at his headquarters at Ryes. '8 Armd Bde coln [column] has started its advance SOUTH on the axis TILLY-VILLERS BOCAGE. Progress so far has been slow. He is giving it strong artillery support at 1900 hrs. I told him that we would try to keep 7 Armd Div out of the battle until the day after tomorrow. I will then probably tell him to get VILLERS-BOCAGE and to swing EAST on the axis TILLY-NOYERS so as to come in on the flank and rear of the divisions attacking 1 Corps [north of Caen].'[2]

Whether Dempsey or Montgomery realised how difficult it would be to make quick progress through the bocage countryside in the face of a Corps of enemy Panzer divisions is difficult to assess. 'We are strong in tanks in this sector,' de Guingand had explained to Leigh-Mallory,[3] and, given the 24-hour delay in the US build-up schedule, it was imperative that the British keep Rommel's attention to the east. Indeed so worried was Leigh-Mallory by the failure of the Americans to join up their two bridgeheads at the base of the Cotentin peninsula at Carentan, that he – the Air Forces C-in-C who had once bitterly opposed a second airborne division drop north of Carentan – now offered to drop 1st British Airborne Division in the area.[4] Far from being optimistic, Leigh-Mallory was dejected by his inability to help Montgomery by using his heavy bombers. 'The situation is evolving,' he dictated to his diarist that day, 'but it is a terrible thing to me to feel all these [German] troop movements going on while I am not able to stop them because of bad weather and low cloud.'[5] What he did not say was that at the 11 a.m. Allied Air Commanders' Conference that day, 'there was a resurgence of the old controversy between the Air C-in-C and the US Strategic Air Force Commanders over the use of strategic bombers for attacking rail communications in support of the Army, instead of for direct

[1] Diary of M. C. Dempsey, loc. cit.
[2] Ibid.
[3] AEAF Record, loc. cit.
[4] Conversation with de Guingand, AEAF Record, loc. cit.
[5] Diary of Sir Trafford Leigh-Mallory, loc. cit.

offensive against the German Air Force. The Air C-in-C admitted that the time might come (perhaps very soon) when the G.A.F. [German Air Force] would constitute a major threat, but it had not come yet; whereas the threat to our Armies from the quick build-up of German reserves was a very real threat.'[1]

That evening (8 June), with the sky still overcast, Leigh-Mallory was in a sombre mood. 'The weather is still lousy, however; it depresses me, though the met people say it will clear tomorrow. I doubt this myself. There is another depression in the Atlantic, they tell me, eight hours away . . . at the moment I repeat the weather, from the point of view of air operations, is not at all good.'[2] 'Weather was still poor, and deteriorating,' the AEAF headquarters diarist recorded. 'Visual bombing by day had not been possible, and prospects for the following day were not good.'[3]

Nevertheless, as in Sicily, Monty seems to have been made heady by the very magnitude of his achievement. 'There is no doubt that the Germans were surprised, and we got on shore before they had recovered. The speed, power, and violence of the assault carried all before it,' he boasted to Simpson, with justification. Contrary to some later accounts, he was the very reverse of cautious. The slowness of the American build-up ('First US Army had a very sticky party at OMAHA, and its progress at UTAH has not been rapid') still bothered him, but with regard to the British sector he was, as in Sicily, so excited by the way things seemed to be going that he began to imagine he was on the threshold, already, of a great and perhaps decisive victory. For if the Germans continued to fight north of Caen with their Panzer Corps – comprising almost their entire armour in the immediate Normandy area – then there was a chance that he could, by vigorous offensive tactics, actually entrap if there. The following day, therefore, as 30 Corps began to drive south from its flank, Monty bristled with confidence. Leigh-Mallory had failed, owing to the poor weather, to stop the German Panzer divisions from moving into the area and from counter-attacking; but in allowing them to come forward, there was a completely unexpected chance of achieving quick victory. When he wrote again to Simpson at 9 a.m. on 9 June he was filled with a kind of astonishment that things had gone so well:

> The country here is very nice; green fields; very good crops; plenty of vegetables; cows & cattle; chickens, ducks, etc.
> The few civilians there are appear well fed; the children look healthy; the people have good boots and clothing.

[1] AEAF Record, loc. cit.
[2] Diary of Sir Trafford Leigh-Mallory, loc. cit.
[3] AEAF Record, loc. cit.

The locals did not believe the British would ever invade France or come over the Channel; they say that the German officers and men thought this also – which may account for the tactical surprise we got.

At 10 a.m. Dempsey arrived, and for an hour and a half the two generals went over Second Army's plans for the thrust south to Falaise and Argentan. It was now that the first mention was made of a British airborne operation to assist in the trapping of the German Panzer Corps. Dempsey stressed that he would want the American 5 Corps to join with him in the thrust – 'I asked him to impress on 5 American Corps the importance of their driving SOUTH, to get, firstly, DODIGNY and then CAUMONT. I gave him my future intentions with 7 Armd Div, 51 Div and – possibly – 1 Airborne Div.'[1] Indeed when Dempsey went on to Courseulles to see General Crocker, commanding 1 Corps north of Caen, Dempsey made clear that the operations starting that day might lead to a victory of incalculable significance: 'I gave him my intention regarding 7 Armd Div who will start operating tomorrow morning – and the probability that I will get him to employ 51 Div EAST of the two rivers in order to isolate CAEN from the EAST and SOUTH-EAST. He is to be prepared to carry out this operation on 11 June.'[2] Dempsey would thus be side-stepping 51st Highland Division surreptitiously eastwards along the coast, passing it through 6th Airborne Division's Orne bridgehead, and encircling Caen from east and – by virtue of 7th Armoured Division's thrust – west. 'If the attacks of 7 Armd Div and 51 Div went well, the landing of 1 Airborne Div to the SOUTH of CAEN might well be decisive,' Dempsey recorded in his diary, and by 1 p.m. he was consulting with the British Airborne Corps Commander, General 'Boy' Browning, on the 'possibility of employing 1 Airborne Div SOUTH of CAEN on the evening of 11 June or later. He [Browning] set in motion the machinery for planning and carrying it out.'[3]

Monty, meanwhile, moved westwards to see Bradley and emphasise personally the importance of linking up now with the American right flank. General Collins, commanding 7 US Corps, was 'exuding great gusts of optimism over the situation. He is anxious to drive through to Cherbourg,' Bradley's aide noted when Bradley visited Collins and gave him Monty's 'verbal order . . . suggesting that main effort be fixed first in joining the corps and thereafter in cutting over the peninsula to cut off the German'.[4] Collins, made in the same

[1] Diary of M. C. Dempsey, loc. cit.
[2] Ibid.
[3] Ibid.
[4] Diary of Chester B. Hansen, loc. cit.

mould as the swashbuckling Patton and a veteran of Guadalcanal, was disappointed and asked Bradley for greater latitude. 'Collins is independent, vigorous, heady, capable and full of vinegar. Needs a check rein if anything,' Hansen recorded, reflecting Bradley's feelings. Bradley, however, was adamant that Monty's orders be obeyed. There was no prospect of the Germans being able to reinforce the Cherbourg peninsula quickly; Cherbourg would therefore fall in good time to Collins. What was important now was to ensure that the last gap in the Allied bridgehead be sealed. 'Want the corps connected up as quickly as possible,' Bradley therefore ordered. 'Use the air. Dump 500 or 1,000 tons of air [i.e. bombs] on it [Carentan] and take it apart. Then rush it fast and take it. We've got the Navy here and they can help you with fire.'[1]

Monty was confident that Bradley would close this gap 'by tomorrow', as he wrote to de Guingand during the afternoon of 9 June.[2] In Monty's view Rommel had now clearly divided his counter-attack into two main efforts – 21st Panzer and two infantry divisions (711 and 346) east of Caen, and two Panzer divisions, 12th and Lehr, west of Caen around Bretteville. In both sectors Monty was quite certain of holding the attacks, while hatching his own master-stroke. The American 5 Corps would attack southwards towards Caumont; alongside it Dempsey would unleash 7th Armoured Division, the famous Desert Rats, through 8th Armoured Brigade's bridgehead at Tilly on the Seulles river. The Desert Rats were to be 'launched tomorrow southwards through BAYEUX to secure VILLERS-BOCAGE and NOYERS and then EVRECY; then to exploit to the S.E.'. Meanwhile, through the Orne bridgehead, east of Caen, he would 'pass 51 Div across R. ORNE, through 6 Airborne DIV, to attack southwards east of CAEN towards CAGNY'. To complete the encirclement of the German forces he would drop 1st Airborne Division in the gap created by his pincers – 'to put down 1 Airborne Div somewhere south of CAEN as a big air hook, and to link up with it from EVRECY and CAGNY. This is being worked out now; I would want the whole Division, which should get ready to load now.'[3] Thus Monty welcomed the very German counter-attacks which were so worrying Leigh-Mallory. 'If the Germans wish to be offensive and drive in our lodgement area between CAEN and BAYEUX, the best way to defeat them is to be offensive ourselves,' he remarked, 'and the plan given [above] will checkmate the enemy completely if we can pull it off.'[4]

[1] Ibid.
[2] Demi-official Correspondence of C-in-C, 21st Army Group (WO 205/5D), PRO.
[3] Ibid.
[4] Ibid.

This was hardly the ultra-cautious general, beloved by certain writers. 'Tell Eisenhower my plans,' he ordered de Guingand, as well as sending his own personal cable at 7.30 p.m. to Eisenhower, outlining the operations towards Evrecy and Villers Bocage.

De Guingand, as ordered, went straight to the Supreme Commander's headquarters to show Monty's letter: 'On Friday evening, nearly midnight, de Guingand had come over to our war room and given Ike the "picture",' Butcher recorded in his diary. But Monty's personal signal, though it reached Eisenhower's British ADC, Lt-Colonel Gault, that night, was ignored – Gault 'having deferred handling it until he got up at eight', Butcher chronicled. It was then found to be – naturally enough – in Most Secret cypher, and by the time a signals officer had been found to decode it, Eisenhower had left his headquarters in a rage. 'He had awakened in a snit . . . no information from Monty, who had agreed to cable every night his latest impression of the way of the battle.'[1]

Eisenhower, itching to become at long last a field commander and feeling no doubt lonely and isolated now that the Allied assault armies had departed from England, was a frustrated man. Legends would grow up after the war that Monty had not kept him, as Supreme Commander, fully abreast of his plans and strategy in Normandy and that because of this Eisenhower had failed to understand the logic of his Ground Force Commander's operations. But this is without foundation, as de Guingand angrily attested when the point was raised.[2] De Guingand saw or spoke on the telephone to Eisenhower almost every day of the campaign, as he had done in the build-up to 'Overlord'; and if Eisenhower 'failed' to understand the logic of Monty's generalship in Normandy, it was because he *knew* what Monty was attempting to achieve – and was excited by the ambitiousness of Monty's battlefield intentions. The chance that Monty might surround the whole of Rommel's immediate Panzer force in Normandy filled Eisenhower with nervous anticipation; and when finally his idle ADC brought him Monty's decoded signal 'its contents buoyed Ike,' as Butcher noted.[3]

All day on 10 June, then, Eisenhower waited for further news, unable to accept the fact that it took so long for planned operations to be executed in the field of battle. Meanwhile Monty, Bradley and Dempsey all met at 11 a.m. at Port-en-Bessin – the junction between the Allied armies – to go over the plans. 7th Armoured Division was already advancing through the 8th Armoured Brigade's shield on the high ground east of Tilly. It was directed south-eastwards on Evrecy, with its southern flank to be established at Villers Bocage, and

<hr>

[1] Diary of Harry C. Butcher, entry of 11.6.44, loc. cit.
[2] Interview of 7.5.78.
[3] Loc. cit.

Bradley, whose Omaha beachhead was still only two miles deep, did not see how he could do much to help it until 12 or 13 June, when he hoped to send one division through to Caumont, about six miles west of Villers Bocage. In fact so shallow was the Omaha beachhead that Bradley was still commanding First US Army from the USS *Augusta*:

> Monty had called a meeting that morning at the fishing village of Port-en-Bessin to coordinate First Army movements with those of the British Second Army

Bradley recalled.[1] It took place in a 'field on the right, next to an ordinary Fr.[ench] stucco house, fixed with many gables and a curious Fr. maid that peered through the open window with several moppets in her arms,' Bradley's aide described in his diary. Below the maid the two Allied assault Army Commanders conferred with their Commander-in-Chief. 'Monty was in an old loose-fitting grey gabardine hunting jacket with bellows pockets that seemed to accentuate its flappiness,' the astonished American recorded, 'a grey sweater, corduroy trousers and the well known beret with its double insignia – one of them nicely fixed in gold embroidery. Map case spread on hood of his open tonneau and he lounged easily behind his sharp beaklike nose, the small grey eyes that dart about quickly like rabbits in a Thurber cartoon. Gen Dempsey next to him in a camouflage coat of paratroop length, flat hat and regulation insignia. Monty wore none although his car carried the Brit flag and carried the four stars of an Amerk commander with the 21 Group flash. Brad shook hands (dressed in OD's with combat jacket, helmet – GI), broad grin. "Glad to see you here, sir". . . . Proceeded to go over their plans.'[2]

As Bradley recalled:

> Dempsey had plotted an attack south of the unspoiled town of Bayeux, partly to extend his bridgehead and partly to envelop Caen from the west. . . . Two Panzer divisions were dug in before Caen and Dempsey and his staff sought to outflank them in his attack from Bayeux. We were to parallel this British attack and drive south in the direction of Caumont. There Gerow was to establish a strong defensive outpost for V Corps. An attack on this end of the lodgement, we estimated, might also help divert enemy reinforcements from Collins' attack towards Cherbourg.[3]

[1] Omar N. Bradley, *A Soldier's Story*, London 1951.
[2] Diary of Chester B. Hansen, loc. cit.
[3] Omar N. Bradley, op. cit.

With American build-up still twenty-four hours behind schedule, and with the pressing need still to link up his two American corps beachheads, Bradley could not promise Dempsey any immediate assistance. The Desert Rats would have to go it alone. 'The bad weather is a great nuisance as what we want is to take quick advantage of our good position by striking deep before the enemy can build up strength against us,' Monty had lamented in a second letter to de Guingand the night before. 'However we are not doing too badly.'[1] He accepted Bradley's delayed undertaking, and sought to ensure that, if Dempsey could get no American support, he would at least get Allied air and airborne help. At Leigh-Mallory's head-quarters at Stanmore Brigadier Richardson outlined, also at 11 a.m., Monty's plans to envelop Caen, despite German counter-attacks which had been so fierce that 6th Airborne Division had been forced to give ground. 'The plan for the capture of CAEN was by an outflanking movement employing the 51st Highland Division on the left, and the 7th Armoured Division on the right, with the possibility of dropping the 1st Airborne Division between the two,' Richardson explained.[2] Casualties were estimated at 4,000 in the British sector, 3,000 in the American.

In his diary the night before, Leigh-Mallory had recorded yet another day without proper air assistance to the armies. 'It is depressing to think that I have, as the P.M. said, more than 11,000 aircraft and cannot make full use of them, and I confess to experiencing a certain sense of frustration. . . . I repeat that it is very annoying, when we have reached a stage on land where the army has got enough elbow room to do a proper build-up, not to be able to mount a decent air attack on the enemy's ground forces. I believe that if I had been able to carry out intensive air operations today I could have delayed them at least twenty-four hours and thus increased our own chance of making a successful attack on land. Today seems to me a very crucial day and very little has been done in the air. This is, indeed, the first critical moment.'[3]

Because of the impossibility of giving full bomber support, therefore, Leigh-Mallory was – in contrast to Eisenhower – ambivalent about Monty's chances of a quick victory around Caen. 'There is a possibility that we may get through them with a rush though I am not counting on it,' he recorded that night – followed by the remark: 'I cannot but be optimistic today, however, and think that if we break the crust there may not be an awful lot the other side.'[4]

All afternoon on 10 June Dempsey deliberated about where best to

[1] Demi-official Correspondence of C-in-C, 21st Army Group (WO 205/5D), PRO.

[2] AEAF Record, loc. cit.

[3] Diary of Sir Trafford Leigh-Mallory, loc. cit.

[4] Ibid.

drop the paratroops – whether to tie them in with 51st Division's attack from the east, or with 7th Armoured Division's in the west. Monty meanwhile, having ascertained that the American 5 and 7 Corps had at last joined hands, gave the green light for Collins to race for Cherbourg and to cut the peninsula. 'Am very pleased with today's operation,' he signalled to Eisenhower, for although he was keen to envelop Caen and, if possible, trap the Panzer divisions there, he was, as the hours went by, concerned at the growing enemy resistance in the Second Army sector and the rising British casualties. He had thought for a while on 8 June that he could, by seizing the enemy's Queen – his armour – checkmate him; but by 11 June he was becoming more realistic. The troops were tiring and the ideal defensive country, though it gave security to the Allied bridge-head now that it was homogenously established, also favoured the German defenders. The Allies had put ashore sixteen divisions, but casualties – now around 15,000 – had blunted their impetus, faced by fourteen enemy divisions *in situ*; and heavier casualties were expected. The drive to encircle Caen might or might not be success-ful, he felt, but as he reminded Brooke at 9 a.m. that morning: 'my general policy is to pull the enemy on to Second Army so as to make it easier for First Army to expand and extend the quicker' – the original strategy he had laid down for operations after D-Day. To de Guing-and and Eisenhower he signalled the same: 'My general object is to pull the Germans on to Second Army so that First Army can extend and expand' – and later that day Eisenhower replied: 'Thanks for your messages. They are very helpful. Please pass my congratula-tions on to your commanders.'[1]

American veterans and writers would later ignore this aspect of Monty's generalship, and all too often seek to present the Allied success in Normandy as an exclusively American achievement. The truth about Normandy cannot however be tarnished: namely that there, on the beaches and in the closely-hedged fields and woods of the erstwhile Norman dukes, the first great Allied battle of the war was fought in which there was parity between British and American armies, and in which the overall Commander sought not simply to 'bull ahead' on all fronts, but to orchestrate the various Allied efforts within an overall strategy that would result in German defeat, not simply territorial gain. That Monty's strategy began, very quickly, to succeed in Normandy is best demonstrated by its effect on the German commanders. Unable to push the British back into the sea with his Panzer Corps, Rommel decided on 11 June that his only hope of defeating the invasion was to switch his whole counter-attacking effort onto the thinner and more vulnerable American

---

[1] 'Monty' file, Papers of Dwight D. Eisenhower, Eisenhower Library, Abilene, Kansas.

sector. He wished to 'replace the armoured formations now in the line [facing the British Second Army] as soon as possible by infantry, so that the armour can be used to form mobile reserves again behind the front', as he explained in an appreciation he wished to be personally shown to Hitler. He felt that Montgomery had two options or intentions: to build up a bridgehead in the east 'for a powerful attack later into the interior of France, probably towards Paris,' and secondly, to 'cut off the Cotentin peninsula and gain possession of Cherbourg' in order to gain a major port. Rommel now wanted to shift his Panzer strength to the American sector, therefore, to cripple the threat to Cherbourg, and then return to stifle the British threat to Paris. 'The Army Group also intends to shift the gravity of its operations into the Carentan-Montebourg area during the next few days, in order to destroy the enemy in that sector and divert the danger from Cherbourg. Not until then can any attack be made against the enemy between the Orne and the Vire.'[1]

Such was Rommel's request to OKW and to Hitler. But Rommel added a rider. There were indications that Montgomery might drop his Cherbourg thrust and concentrate solely on breaking through to Paris – 'there seems also to be a possibility, as things are developing, that the enemy will dispense with the Cotentin peninsula if the battle is too fierce, and make an early thrust with all his available means, into the interior of France.'[2]

This latter possibility had gained credence throughout 10 June, as Dempsey's armour pushed out towards Villers Bocage. Hitler was alarmed, and decided to overrule Rommel. Rommel was not to switch his counter-offensive to the American front; he was to put everything he possessed into stopping the British break-out. 'Hitler vetoed Rommel's plan to move against the American bridgehead in the Caen-Montebourg area,' General Bayerlein later recorded, 'and gave orders instead for Army Group B to mount an attack against the British bridgehead from the Caen area, using the reinforcements with which it had been supplied.'[3]

For General Collins on the right flank of the American bridgehead, this was a crucial reprieve. But for Dempsey, planning the envelopment of Caen and the German Panzer divisions, it was a decision which effectively ruled out the possibility of spectacular success. By 11 a.m. on 11 June Dempsey was noting that 'it appeared from various indications during the morning that the enemy was preparing an attack North-West from CAEN'.[4] Could he then risk sending

[1] Appreciation of the situation on 11.6.44, in German Army documents dealing with the war on the Western front, from June 1944 to October 1944 (Templehoff papers), Montgomery Papers.
[2] Ibid.
[3] *The Rommel Papers*, ed. B. H. Liddell Hart, London 1953.
[4] Diary of M. C. Dempsey, loc. cit.

the tanks he had intended to support 51st Highland Division's thrust through the Orne bridgehead? An hour and a half later he met Crocker at 1 Corps headquarters and cancelled the plan for 4th Armoured Brigade to participate in the encircling attack – 'told him to retain 4 Armed Bde in the COLOMBY area today'.[1] The Desert Rats, meanwhile, were 'still meeting considerable resistance'[2] in the other pincer of the intended attack towards Villers Bocage, and by the following day both Dempsey and Monty were seriously alarmed. More Panzer divisions were on their way to Normandy; there was thus little time left if Second Army was to profit from Hitler's mistake. An Ultra decrypt on 12 June showed that 2nd Panzer Division was on the move to reinforce Panzer Lehr in the Villers Bocage area;[3] it was imperative, then, that 7th Armoured Division move faster. All morning on 12 June Dempsey conferred with General Erskine, the commander of the Desert Rats, at the latter's headquarters. 'Their advance is going very slowly against stiffening opposition, and the country is very close and difficult,' he lamented.[4] However at 11.45 a.m. Dempsey met Bucknall, the 30 Corps Commander, at Bayeux railway station. Bucknall told him that the 11th Hussars, on the extreme western flank of Second Army, were 'in contact with American 5 Corps' and 'were making good progress SOUTH of the road from BAYEUX to CAUMONT'. By sidestepping 7th Armoured Division onto this easier axis Dempsey hoped he could increase the tempo of his thrust – 'I told him to switch 7 Armd DIV from their front immediately, to push them through behind 11 H[ussars] and endeavour to get VILLERS BOCAGE that way. Provided this is carried out with real drive and speed, there is a chance that we will get through before the front congeals.'[5] Driving to Monty's headquarters, Dempsey outlined his latest plan, which looked increasingly promising as units of both First and Second Armies reached Caumont that evening. 'Advance of 7 Armd DIV met strong opposition just WEST of TILLY from PZ LEHR DIV,' Monty signalled to de Guingand. 'Thrust line was switched quickly further to WEST and DIV moved south through LA BELLE EPINE and leading troops reached BRICQUESSARD at 1900 hrs and will move on VILLERS BOCAGE and NOYERS tomorrow. Joint patrols of First and Second Armies are in CAUMONT. All this is very good and PZ LEHR may be in grave danger tomorrow. Inform EISENHOWER and DMO at War Office.' As he would write to the CIGS, this was, once the assault troops had established contiguous beachheads, the 'turn-

[1] Ibid.
[2] Ibid.
[3] R. Bennett, *Ultra in the West*, London 1979.
[4] Diary of M. C. Dempsey, loc. cit.
[5] Ibid.

ing point of the battle'.[1] It was also the day on which, to add to Monty's cares, Churchill, Smuts and Brooke arrived on a visit from England, and Leigh-Mallory, refusing to transport 1st Airborne Division to help 7th Armoured Division's thrust, was denounced by Monty as 'a gutless bugger'.

[1] Letter to Brooke (M501), Montgomery Papers.

CHAPTER FOUR

Serious Opposition

Churchill, denied a place aboard a battleship on D-Day, had naturally been anxious to 'set foot' in France. On D plus 3, therefore, he
signalled to Monty his intention of visiting the British bridgehead on
12 June. Eisenhower decided to take General Marshall, Admiral
King, and General Arnold (the American Air Chief) on a simultaneous visit to Bradley, but failed to inform Bradley until the night
before. Thus the conference Monty had ordered with Bradley at
10 a.m. on 12 June had to be cancelled, while the two senior American and British field commanders received their distinguished
guests.

Bradley's headquarters had only been established ashore for a day,
and the American Chiefs of Staff had thus to lunch on 'C rations and
hard tack biscuits'.[1] Monty's welcome, in the grounds of the château
of Creully which he had occupied since 8 June, was more lavish,
though the visit was equally distracting.

Montgomery, smiling and confident, met me at the beach as we
scrambled out of our landing-craft. His army had already penetrated seven or eight miles inland. . . . Montgomery's headquarters, about five miles inland, were in a château with lawns and
lakes around it. We lunched in a tent looking towards the enemy.
The General was in the highest spirits. I asked him how far away
was the actual front. He said about three miles. I asked him if he
had a continuous line. He said, 'No.' 'What is there then to prevent
an incursion of German armour breaking up our luncheon?' He
said he did not think they would come.[2]

Churchill's presence was an honour, but his indefatigable curiosity was a trial to Monty, who had prefaced luncheon, as in the desert
before the battle of Alam Halfa, with an 'explanation on the map of
his dispositions and plans. All, as usual, wonderfully clear and
concise,' Brooke noted in his diary, reflecting on the wondrous

[1] Diary of Chester B. Hansen, loc. cit.
[2] W. S. Churchill, *Triumph and Tragedy*, London 1954.

change in fortunes since the same day in June 1940 when he awaited the German onslaught that would sweep the last British forces from France. 'I knew then that it would not be long before I was kicked out of France . . . but if anybody had told me then that in four years I should return with Winston and Smuts to lunch with Monty commanding a new invasion force, I should have found it hard to believe.'[1]

On the great map of Normandy in his newly-built operations caravan Monty outlined his strategy: the drawing of main German forces onto the British east flank so that the Americans could 'expand' behind; indeed now that the beachheads were all conjoined, he had given Bradley the green light to cut off the Cotentin peninsula and go for Cherbourg. Within this overall strategy, Monty pointed out, the Allies would seize every opportunity to exploit German mistakes. The Germans had, for instance, concentrated their Panzer strength in a bid to hold Caen and to smash what they considered to be the Allied thrust towards Paris. Second Army thus had an excellent chance of encircling the Panzer Corps, and on the coloured wall map he pointed to the two pincers Dempsey was trying to create. As Churchill excitedly informed Stalin on his return, 'we hope to encircle Caen, and perhaps to make a capture there of prisoners'.[2]

At no point in this military lecture to Brooke, Churchill and Smuts, did Monty ever suggest that Dempsey was to do more than bring the German forces to battle around Caen, however – and when, after the war, Eisenhower wrote that 'in the east we had been unable to break out towards the Seine',[3] Monty was furious, for this was a complete travesty of the facts. To Churchill Monty had made it quite clear that there was no question of wild break-outs. How could there be when the Allies had only fourteen divisions ashore, many of which, particularly the parachute and first assault divisions, were inevitably running out of steam? As Churchill pointed out to Stalin, the battle for Normandy would be a slow and deliberate one: 'I should think it quite likely that we should work up to a battle of about a million a side, lasting through June and July. We plan to have about two million there by mid-August.'[4]

Eisenhower's unfortunate obfuscation has coloured military accounts ever since, polarising chroniclers into nationalistic camps. This was, Monty felt, a tragedy in view of the fact that the battle for Normandy was, at all stages, an *Allied* battle, in which Allied soldiers gave their lives conforming to an Allied plan to defeat the German

[1] A. Bryant, *Triumph in the West*, London 1959.

[2] W. S. Churchill, op. cit.

[3] D. D. Eisenhower, *Eisenhower's Own Story of the War* (Despatch by the Supreme Commander, N.W. Europe), New York 1946.

[4] W. S. Churchill, op. cit.

armies in the West – not to 'break out towards the Seine' in some mythical Lancelot charge.

Eisenhower's Despatch was the product, however, of an idle Supreme Headquarters at the end of the war; at the time in question Eisenhower was fully 'in the picture', as were Marshall and the American Chiefs of Staff after their visit. Some days later Eisenhower cabled to Washington: 'The plan of battle of that [British] flank remains almost identical with that explained to you when you were here. I am very hopeful it will actually break up the German formations on that front.'[1]

Dempsey's brief, then, was not to 'break out towards the Seine', but to play his part in a truly Allied undertaking, bringing to battle the mobile German forces that would otherwise – as Rommel wished – destroy the American assault on Cherbourg. Having packed off his distinguished visitors after a tour of the bridgehead, Monty meanwhile was able to redirect his attention to the battle. The weather was fine and sunny, the Air Forces could at last put in their heavy bombers to support the land armies, yet it was at this crucial moment that Leigh-Mallory chose to thwart Monty's operations. At a special meeting the previous night, Leigh-Mallory had considered Monty's proposal for an air drop at Evrecy, and refused to carry it out.

> The Air C-in-C said that he had called this meeting to consider a plan that he had just received from the Army for the employment of the 1st Airborne Division,

the minutes ran.

> The plan was to drop this division early on the 13th June in an area South-West of CAEN behind the German line in order to assist in the encirclement of the German Panzer troops in the CAEN area.[2]

Leigh-Mallory had been forced to eat humble pie once the revised American air drop near Utah beach had proved triumphantly successful in facilitating Collins's 7 US Corps assault. This time, however, he stuck his heels in, using the same arguments as before D-Day:

> He thought this would be a very expensive operation and that the Army should realise that if it were undertaken it might prejudice the planning of future airborne operations for three months to come.[3]

[1] Cable of 19.6.44 in *The Papers of Dwight David Eisenhower*, ed. Alfred D. Chandler, *The War Years* Vol. III, Baltimore 1972.
[2] AEAF Record, loc. cit.
[3] Ibid.

Leigh-Mallory's opposition was implacable. General Urquhart, the 1st Airborne Division's commander, wished to land in daylight, but Air Vice-Marshal Hollinghurst, commanding the air group responsible, felt that this was 'impossible' over such a heavily defended area, and insisted the operation be conducted at night. But Leigh-Mallory would not let the aircraft fly over the Channel at night lest the Navy shoot at the transport craft, and when he telephoned Admiral Creasy, the Chief of Staff at Naval Headquarters, Creasy stated 'he was perfectly certain' the Navy would 'give no such guarantee' that it would hold its fire during the air passage.[1]

De Guingand signalled all this to Monty, who was understandably irate. At 7 p.m., only minutes after receiving de Guingand's doleful message, he cabled:

Do not understand refusal of LM to carry out airborne operation. I am working to create such favourable conditions as would make the dropping of one airborne DIV in EVRECY area a good operation or war and one which if successful would pay a good dividend.

In fact, he informed de Guingand, he did not want the drop to take place on 13 June, since the sidestepping of 7th Armoured Division had altered the likely schedule.

Conditions have not yet been created but may well be created by 14 June. LM should come over and see me and ascertain the true form before he refuses to carry out an operation. He could get here by air in 30 minutes. Meanwhile I want planning to go ahead so that when conditions are favourable the operation can be laid on quickly. Am sending BROWNING to see you tomorrow leaving here by air at 1000 hrs. Inform LM as above.

Monty's signal did nothing to alter Leigh-Mallory's refusal, and the following afternoon Monty was writing to de Guingand:

12.6.44

My dear Freddie,

Had the P.M. C.I.G.S. and Smuts here today; all in very good form; the PM very obedient and I pushed him away at 1500 hours and would not let him go beyond my H.Q.

I sent you a wire last night re LM and his refusal to drop 1 Airborne DIV. The favourable conditions I am working up to are that the DZ [Dropping Zone] would be within range of the artillery of 7 Armd DIV in the VILLERS–BOCAGE area; if we then drop the

[1] Ibid.

Airborne DIV in EVRECY area we would be very well placed and might get a big 'scoop'.

The real point is that LM sitting in his office cannot possibly know the local battle form over here; and therefore he must not refuse my demands unless he first comes over to see me; he could fly here in a Mosquito in ½ hour, talk for an hour, and be back in England in ½ hour. Obviously he is a gutless bugger, who refuses to take a chance and plays for safety on all occasions. I have no use for him.[1]

Without such an airborne drop, Dempsey would be hard pressed to surround three Panzer divisions – with a fourth identified by Ultra Intelligence as on its way. Even Dempsey's left-hand pincer, from the Orne bridgehead east of Caen, had had to be cut down in scope, since the concentration of German armour north-west of Caen precluded the move of 4th Armoured Brigade in support of the Highlanders.[2] As the fighting continued throughout 12 June, Monty cursed Leigh-Mallory and, once the visitors from England had departed, attempted to give heart to his commanders. He sent a cheery note – his first from Normandy – to Phyllis Reynolds, and wondered whether, given the tribulations that surely lay ahead, the French people really wished to be freed from the Nazi yoke:

> The French civilians in Normandy do not look in the least depressed; there is plenty of food, plenty of vegetables, cows, milk, cheeses, and very good crops,

he observed.

> I often wonder if they want to be liberated!!

To de Guingand he signalled the latest moves in the attempt to checkmate the enemy; but only the following day did he learn not only that Dempsey's thrust had hit more serious opposition than he had bargained for on the eastern Allied flank, but that there was trouble too in the American western sector where, according to reports received at 5 p.m., the Germans had recaptured Carentan, the vital junction between 5 and 7 US Corps. For the moment this did not deter him, and he wrote to Brooke reiterating his overall strategy, and outlining the latest progress of operations. 7th Armoured Division had reached Villers Bocage that morning (13 June) and was 'now

[1] Demi-official Correspondence file (WO 205/5B), PRO.
[2] 'Until 33 Armd Bde is landed and is available to relieve them on this commanding ground [at Colomby], they cannot be moved in view of the strong enemy threat North-West of Caen' – Diary of M. C. Dempsey, entry at 1530 hrs, 12.6.44, loc. cit.

in a good position to get right in behind Pz LEHR DIV'; behind it 'the right wing of Second Army was to swing forward; this meant 50 DIV and 49 DIV (now about to enter the battle) pivoting on TILLY and sweeping round in a south-easterly movement. Pz LEHR DIV are somewhere in the middle and we want to stop them from getting away. We may get some of them; it is too early to say yet; I expect they will pull out tonight,' he predicted. Unfortunately the left-hand pincer, without armour, was unlikely to entrap the other two German Panzer divisions, who could now be expected to escape:

> Away to the east, 51 Div is developing operations to the east of the R. ORNE, north-east of CAEN. The division is moving southwards with its right flank on the ORNE; this movement is slow as just at present it cannot be given any tanks.
>
> So my pincer movement to get CAEN is taking good shape, and there are distinct possibilities that the enemy Divisions may not find it too easy to escape; especially Pz LEHR. 21 Pz and 12 S.S. could escape easily, but would have to pull out soon – unless they can hold up the western half of the pincers i.e. 30 Corps swing.
>
> At the present moment,

he countered,

> the Armd Recce Regt of 7 Armd DIV (8H) is moving on NOYERS; there are a lot of enemy, including some TIGER tanks, milling about in the triangle HOTTOT–NOYERS–VILLERS BOCAGE. The situation will clarify later!!

Meanwhile, having supported Dempsey's right-wing pincer movement by taking Caumont, Bradley was dangerously stretched. The weather had deteriorated, and it was important that with only limited numbers of tanks ashore, Bradley should preserve the integrity of his front – 'Bradley's left Corps, 5 US Corps, is getting rather stretched and he has had to send some armour over from 2 Armd DIV to lend a hand at CARANTAN' – thus making Gerow's Caumont salient vulnerable to Panzer attack. 'So I have told him to hang on firmly to CAUMONT . . . and not to push the right of the Corps forward to St LO until he feels he can safely do so. 30 DIV will be coming in through the beaches tomorrow and then the Corps will be able to move on again.'

As he was writing these words, the Germans penetrated back into Carentan. 'This is a nuisance,' Monty remarked, but he had made quite clear to Bradley that the linking sector at Carentan was to take priority over Gerow's Caumont sector, which the British armour could help defend if necessary, and he was sure Bradley would throw the Germans out. 'It is important we should not lose it and I have told Bradley that he must concentrate all available resources on holding it. There is a strong naval force that is giving good covering fire from the sea, but it is bad weather for good air support.'

Despite the growing German resistance, Monty still felt sanguine about the development of his master-plan, therefore; and once again he set out his strategy. Far from actually bursting out towards the Seine, Dempsey's task was simply 'to capture CAEN and establish a strong eastern flank astride the R. ORNE from the sea as far south as THURY-HARCOURT'. This flank would be 'gradually' pushed eastwards, allowing 8 Corps to be introduced southwards into the line in such a way as to secure all the ground south of Caen which Monty had promised the RAF for their airfields. It would also present the firm shield behind which Bradley could spread his American net. The plan upon which the Americans were to uncurl and deliver their great thrust southwards towards Brittany and the Loire was set out before Brooke and General Simpson (the DMO, to whom a copy was sent), in simple, clear English, a month and half before it was enacted. 'The First US Army,' Monty declared under the heading: 'Para 14. Future Intentions', was:

e) To hold on firmly to CAUMONT; to recapture CARENTAN and to hold it firmly.
f) To capture ST LO and then COUTANCE.
g) To thrust southwards from CAUMONT towards VIRE and MORTAIN; and from ST LO towards VILLEDIEU and AVRANCHES.
h) All the time to exert pressure towards LA HAYE DU PUITS and VOLOGNES, and to capture CHERBOURG.[1]

A glance at the map will show that this was, *town for town, the layout of Operation 'Cobra'* – the great American offensive that paved the way for Patton to be unleashed into Brittany and the Loire in August 1944. As Monty saw it, the operation could be conducted while Collins made his 7 US Corps attack towards La Haye du Puits, cutting off the Cherbourg peninsula, and subsequently advancing on the port of Cherbourg itself.

On 13 June, when Monty wrote this appreciation of his intentions, the two key pivots in these operations – Caen for the British, St Lô for the Americans – still seemed within imminent grasp. Indeed earlier that day, in writing to de Guingand, Monty had asked his Chief of Staff to 'lay on a very strong air (other things being equal) to assist' Bradley both in holding 'CARENTAN against counter-attack' and 'left Corps of Bradley to capture St LO' (an order he had had to amend when the indifferent weather precluded heavy air assistance,

[1] Letter to CIGS of 13.6.44 (M501), Montgomery Papers.

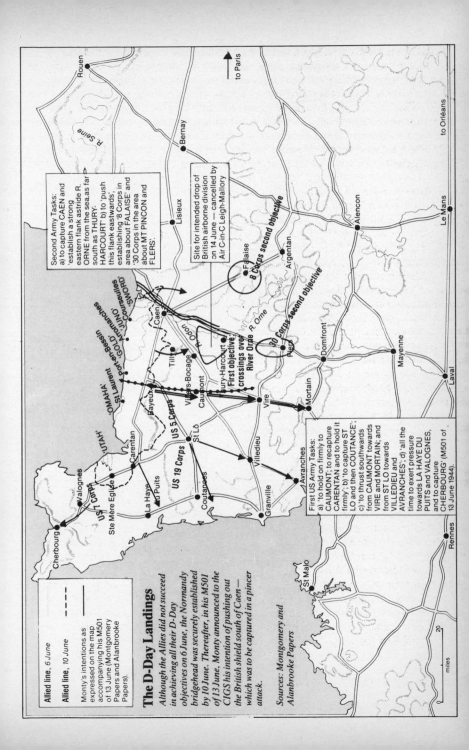

The D-Day Landings

to Paris

to Orléans

to Mans

Le Mans

Alençon

Argentan

8 Corps second objective

Falaise

Site for intended drop of British airborne division on 14 June — cancelled by Air C-in-C Leigh-Mallory.

Second Army Tasks: a) to capture CAEN and 'establish a strong eastern flank astride R. ORNE from the sea, as far south as THURY-HARCOURT b) to 'push this flank eastwards, establishing 8 Corps in area about FALAISE' and '30 Corps in the area about MT PINCON and FLERS'.

Rouen

R. Seine

Bernay

Lisieux

Caen

'SWORD'

Courseulles

'JUNO'

Arromanches

'GOLD'

Port-en-Bessin

St Laurent

'OMAHA'

Bayeux

Tilly

R. Odon

Villers-Bocage

Thury-Harcourt

First objective crossings over River Orne

R. Orne

Caumont

20 Corps second objective

Flers

Domfront

Mayenne

Laval

Rennes

St Malo

Avranches

Mortain

Vire

Villedieu

Coutances

Granville

St Lô

US 5 Corps

US 19 Corps

Carentan

La Haye du Puits

Ste Mère Eglise

'UTAH'

US 7 Corps

Valognes

Cherbourg

First US Army Tasks: a) 'to hold on firmly to CAUMONT; to recapture CARENTAN and to hold it firmly'; b) 'to capture ST LO and then COUTANCE'; c) 'to thrust southwards from CAUMONT towards VIRE and MORTAIN; and from ST LO towards VILLEDIEU and AVRANCHES'; d) 'all the time to exert pressure towards LA HAYE DU PUITS and VALOGNES, and to capture CHERBOURG' (M501 of 13 June 1944).

Allied line, 6 June

Allied line, 10 June

Monty's intentions as expressed on the map accompanying his M501 of 13 June (Montgomery Papers and Alanbrooke Papers).

The D-Day Landings

Although the Allies did not succeed in achieving all their D-Day objectives on 6 June, the Normandy bridgehead was securely established by 10 June. Thereafter, in his M501 of 13 June, Monty announced to the CIGS his intention of pushing out the British shield south of Caen—which was to be captured in a pincer attack.

Sources: Montgomery and Alanbrooke Papers

miles

20

and Bradley had to switch his tanks from the projected attack on St Lô to the vital Carentan defence).

Monty's strategy, then, was unmistakably clear; only the timing would require altering. He was, as he wrote to de Guingand, 'enjoying life greatly and it is great fun fighting battles again after five months in England'.[1] He was in his element, his headquarters three miles from the largest concentration of Panzer forces he had faced in the war, and with a crystal-clear idea of how he intended to win the battle.

[1] Postscript to letter of 12/13.6.44, in Demi-official Correspondence file (WO 205/5B), PRO.

CHAPTER FIVE

A State of Crisis

'Once we get CAEN, and can establish a strong flank astride the ORNE from the sea to THURY-HARCOURT, we will be very well placed to develop the operations as originally planned – and as outlined in para 14,' Monty wrote on 13 June. 19 US Corps was 'in the process of coming in now. It is probably *that* Corps which will thrust south towards VILLEDIEU and AVRANCHES vide para 14(g).'[1]

Alas, both the British attempt to envelop Caen and the American attempt to encircle St Lô were to fail. Ignorant observers would later scorn the Allied method of advance in Normandy, when heavy bombers were used to blast a way forward for the troops – a method which Tedder and senior American airmen felt was a misuse of the air arm. Their legitimate objections have unfortunately served to obscure the truth about the battle for Normandy, which was that, in the early stages after D-Day, both Monty and Bradley sought to take their objectives by envelopment, rather than by staged frontal assaults with heavy bomber support, and neither succeeded. 'Don't give a damn about St Lo if I can get the ground to the east and west of it. If I can take it, fine, but I don't want to spend a lot of soldiers just to take it. And I don't want another Cassino,' Bradley cautioned Gerow.[2] Like Caen, St Lô was to be taken in a pincer movement – if the enemy allowed.

Meanwhile, although Dempsey had sidestepped 7th Armoured Division through the American salient at Caumont in his attempt to outflank the Panzer Lehr division, his action was to no avail. The chance of British encirclement depended, as Monty predicted in his letter to de Guingand, on the Germans continuing their attempt to break the vital British lateral between Caen and Bayeux. 'We are VERY strong now astride the road CAEN–BAYEUX about junction of 3 Div and 3 Canadian DIV, and if the enemy attacks he should be seen off; I have 400 tanks there. Any such attack here would be good, so long as we see it off and the right flank of Second Army swings round to NOYERS and EVRECY.'[3]

[1] Letter to CIGS (M501), loc. cit.
[2] Diary of Chester B. Hansen, loc. cit.
[3] Demi-official Correspondence file, letter of 12.6.44, loc. cit.

Rommel, with his keen sixth sense based on years of battlefield fighting, sent in the newly arrived 2nd Panzer Division not to reinforce the three Panzer Divisions already in line north of Caen, but westwards towards the American sector – in defiance of Hitler's order. This division now smashed into 7th Armoured Division's thrust, with consequences that were to affect the whole fabric of the Normandy operations. 'Late last evening (13 June) 2 Pz DIV came into the battle,' Monty informed Brooke; 'it counterattacked 7 Armd DIV in the VILLERS–BOCAGE area and we took some prisoners. A real good dogfight went on all the evening. The village itself is in low ground and finally 7 Armd DIV withdrew and occupied firmly the high ground immediately to the west – which dominates the village.' Thus at 9 a.m. on 14 June 'the situation in that area is still a bit confused'.[1]

In fact the heavy artillery of the American 1st Division at Caumont had had to be summoned to halt the German counter-attack, and it was plain to Monty that, without more armour or the air drop which Leigh-Mallory was vetoing, Dempsey's right-hand pincer was stalled, leaving the Americans extremely anxious about the vulnerable Allied salient at Caumont. If 7th Armoured Division remained on the defensive, on high ground, Monty had no fear that the salient could be pinched off by Rommel; but the chance of successfully delivering the pincer attack had now gone: there would be no surprise, the Germans were installed in depth on the upper Odon, and a costly failure would risk putting Bradley 'in the soup' now that his American armour was enmeshed in the fight to hold Carentan, further west. As at Alamein, when his 'crumbling' efforts ran into heavy opposition, Monty thus decided to re-group in order to deliver a heavier blow. Eisenhower was appalled. 'Last night Ike was concerned that Monty couldn't attack until Saturday,' Butcher recorded in his diary the following day (15 June). 'Ike was anxious that the Germans be kept off balance and that our drive never stop. But apparently Monty wants to tidy up his "administrative tail" and get plenty of supplies on hand before he makes a general attack. Ike also said that yesterday we had made no gains, which he didn't like.'[2]

Eisenhower's response does him no credit as a would-be field commander: an approach to tactics in the field – constantly bulling ahead in an effort to 'make gains' and 'unbalance the enemy' – that revealed his lack of battle experience. Montgomery's attitude towards Eisenhower would later be portrayed by American writers as competitive, nationalistic and glory-seeking; but the true story of Monty's campaigns from North Africa to North-west Europe proves

---

[1] Addendum of 14.6.44 to letter to CIGS (M501), loc. cit.
[2] Loc. cit.

that this was not so. Monty's objection to Eisenhower 'descending from his lofty perch' as Supreme Commander, in order to assume field command of the Allied armies, would be strictly that of a battle soldier. 'In the higher sphere of Supreme Command,' he would write, Eisenhower's qualities 'stood him in good stead. But a Supreme Commander sits on a very lofty perch; he exercises command in a great strategical sphere and he cannot exercise tactical command at the same time, and he should never attempt to do so. . . . He [Eisenhower] is not a battle commander and had had no previous experience in the field'; in fact, he did not 'understand how to command *in the field*'. Eisenhower's version of the campaigns – *Crusade in Europe* – Monty would consider 'a very mediocre work, and in fifty years' time it will be completely unreadable. In the long run the only reputation it will damage will be Eisenhower's own, for it shows clearly that, whatever else he may have been, he wasn't a great soldier [i.e. battlefield commander]; had he kept silence' in the tradition of Auchinleck, Wavell and others, Monty felt, 'he might, through other men's silence have passed for one.'[1]

Eisenhower, having delegated all responsibility for Air Force and airborne operations to Tedder and Leigh-Mallory, was, like Patton, understandably frustrated at having to watch the battle for Normandy from the far side of the English Channel, a 'lofty perch' which seemed all the loftier when he had to accompany the American Chiefs of Staff to Bradley's bridgehead on 12 June. According to Bradley's aide, Eisenhower was silent throughout the visit – 'saying almost nothing'.[2] Like every active minded soldier he dreamed of being 'in the fray', directing field operations. A few days later, tumbling gratefully into an air raid shelter beside his SHAEF headquarters, he would be heard to say: 'At least they can't put another goddam piece of paper in front of me here to sign!' Desk soldiering drove him to distraction, for all the time he yearned for the simple, manly life of the battlefield, and failed to see that his very talent for Supreme Command – a brilliantly sensitive, honest and open mind – ruled him out as a battlefield commander. At one level he recognised the need to delegate field command to qualified field commanders; but in the words of Sir Edgar Williams, 'he always had the afterthought, perhaps reinforced by his courtiers, that he must be prepared to intervene. And choosing between these two requirements put a very great strain on him – the more so because, as a regular soldier, he had the natural desire to be involved in the battle, and disliked the office side of soldiering.'[3]

[1] 'Some Notes on Eisenhower's Book *Crusade in Europe*', in Annexe 354, Montgomery Diaries 1948/49, Montgomery Papers.

[2] Diary of Chester B. Hansen, loc. cit.

[3] Sir Edgar Williams, interview of 28.1.83.

It was not quite true that Eisenhower, as Monty later claimed,[2] failed to understand the strategy Monty was applying in Normandy; the trouble was, rather, that Eisenhower's imaginative and sensitive brain would not be content – as were Brooke and the senior desk generals at the War Office – with Monty's strategic and tactical appreciations of the battle. Those voices which had urged him in Algiers to undertake bold moves, to counsel neither his fears nor even, in Marshall's view, logistics, had come to haunt him again. He *understood* Monty's overall strategy excellently; on the surface he even accepted it. But in his heart Eisenhower revolted at such careful, ruthlessly professional generalship. That the Allies had conquered North Africa, taken Sicily and the main Mediterranean portion of Italy was a source of satisfaction to him; but his very openness of mind permitted him to take seriously the criticism that he had failed to act boldly *enough*, had failed to push Anderson harder and seize Tunis in December 1943; had failed to mount 'Husky' earlier, after the conquest of North-west Africa; had failed to entrap German forces in Sicily by more ambitious amphibious landings; had failed to take Rome by an ambitious airborne *coup de main*. . . . In all these cases, he accepted, he had permitted slowness of operations and caution in planning to give the enemy time to build up his defences. Therefore *time* was the critical factor in Allied operations, he believed.

Only a soldier unversed in battle technique could hold such an unrealistic view, in Monty's opinion. The failures of the Allies before Alamein could not simply be ascribed to lack of speed; nor could the failures thereafter, such as Kasserine. There were many factors that contributed to success or failure in war; but paramount among them was the human factor. Men were not machines, though they might fight *in* machines. Only a man who had spent his entire career behind a desk could believe that a likely three-month battle in Normandy could be won by ordering men to 'bull ahead' night and day on all fronts. Operations, Monty considered, should be conducted within an overall framework or 'master-plan' – but they must be operations *within the capabilities of the men who were asked to conduct them*. Pushing American forces forward at Kasserine was the typical blunder of a military novice, as were the abortive plans for dispersed landings in 'Husky', the madcap scheme for the air drop on Rome ('Giant Two'), the near-fiasco at Salerno, and the overambitious winter fantasy at Anzio.

When writing to Brooke Monty explained the real reasons why he had to suspend offensive operations for forty-eight hours in Normandy early on 14 June:

[1] 'This . . . is a clear indication that Eisenhower failed to comprehend the basic plan to which he had himself cheerfully agreed' – *Memoirs*, op. cit.

The arrival of 1 Pz DIV at this place [Villers Bocage, Caumont area] puts a different complexion on the problem.

I have got to be very certain of my position, step by step; I must at all costs remain well balanced and able to handle easily any situation that may develop as the enemy reserves come into battle.

I am now very strong defensively on the left of Second Army, in the CAEN sector; I would be stronger still if I had CAEN itself, but I am quite well positioned as things are at present.

I have not yet sufficient strength to be *offensive* on both flanks of Second Army,

he warned.

I have therefore decided to be *defensive in the CAEN sector* on the front of 1 Corps, but aggressively so. I am going to put all my offensive power, ammunition and so on, into the offensive by 30 Corps on the right of Second Army. That is – 30 Corps will operate offensively in the VILLERS–BOCAGE area with:

7 Armd DIV ⎫
50 DIV ⎪   33 Armd Bde will be ready on shore by
49 DIV ⎬   evening 15 June and will join this party.
8 Armd Bde ⎭

The general idea will be to establish ourselves very firmly in the VILLERS–BOCAGE area, and swing towards the area EVRECY –THURY HARCOURT–AUNAY SUR ODON, keeping close touch with the left of First US Army all the time.

In other words, the eastern pincer of Dempsey's two-pronged attempt to encircle Caen was to be closed down, with all effort now being placed in the Caumont salient. 'The offensive movement of 51 DIV vide para 6 ["north-east of CAEN"] will now be piped down.'

Such was the immediate tactical plan. The general strategy, however, remained the same: 'to pull the Germans on to Second British Army, and fight them there, so that First US Army can carry out its task the easier,' he reiterated to Brooke.

To sum up, he added, 'I shall hold strongly, and fight offensively, in the general area CAUMONT–VILLERS BOCAGE, i.e. at the junction of the two armies.' It would not be easy, however. 'Enemy reserves look like coming in here – in fact where we broke in. It is here that 2 Pz DIV has come in, and it attacked the Americans at CAUMONT last evening as well as 7 Armd DIV at VILLERS BOC-AGE.' There were thus four Panzer divisions in line, side by side, facing the British front – and '2 SS Pz (ex TOULOUSE) may appear soon.'[1]

[1] Addendum of 14.6.44 to letter to CIGS (M501), loc. cit.

Having penned the letter at 9 a.m. Monty spoke by telephone to Bradley. 'He is quite happy about CARENTAN and is strongly positioned now, some 2000 and 3000 yards to the west and south of the town.'[1] However Gerow was so anxious about the German tanks facing Caumont that Bradley was unable to fulfil Monty's intention of lining up the incoming 19 US Corps, under General Corlett, for the break-out southwards towards Brittany via Avranches. 'His left Corps (5 Corps under GEROW) is getting rather stretched,' Monty related to Brooke at 10 a.m. 'So he is putting in 19 Corps (CORLETT) at 1200 hrs today to take over the sector between ST LO and CARENTAN.'[2]

In effect this meant the postponement not only of Dempsey's pincer attack to entrap the Panzer divisions, but also the postponement now of Bradley's break-out, which Monty had hoped to launch simultaneously with Collins's attack on Cherbourg. The delay was galling to Eisenhower in his hope of 'making gains' which he could report from England to General Marshall in Washington; but in Normandy there could not have been greater trust and agreement between Bradley and Montgomery on the necessity. As Bradley's aide observed, Bradley's manner towards Monty was as respectful as it was to Marshall – 'Brad's greeting to Marshall quite simple: "I'm very glad to see you, sir" – completely respectful. Similar manner to Montgomery. . . .'[3] Bradley's respect and professionalism made a deep impression on Monty, who would come to see him, in the weeks ahead, as by far and away the finest all-round field commander produced by the US Army. General Collins also impressed Monty – like 'hot mustard' as Bradley's aide noted – but in the quiet, assured manner with which Bradley allocated his resources and priorities within First Army, Monty recognised a fellow professional: an admiration that went so deep and which was so sincere that in August Monty would offer to serve in turn *under* Bradley – whose American forces by then outnumbered the British and Canadian forces almost two fold. 'Bradley is strongly positioned at CAUMONT. He beat off the attack of 2 Pz DIV there last night, and will hold the area firmly,' Monty assured Brooke with complete confidence[4] – a confidence which Bradley reciprocated. That evening, 14 June, General Gerow came to Bradley's headquarters to say he was 'worried. I wanted to show it to you and see if it looks the same to you that it does to me. He [the enemy] may come in through here,' Gerow warned, pointing to the Caumont salient, 'pinch off that stuff and sweep me up. I've got nothing in depth, nothing to

[1] Ibid.
[2] Ibid.
[3] Diary of Chester B. Hansen, loc. cit.
[4] Addendum of 14.6.44 to letter to CIGS (M501), loc. cit.

stop him with.' Gerow begged for the tanks of 2nd US Armoured Division – but knowing how much effort Monty was packing into the left British pincer at Caumont, Bradley refused to be panicked. 'Yes, I know,' he answered. 'I'm worried about that too. But I just had to send Rose and the CC"A" of the 2nd Armoured to Carentan until that situation clears up. They've hit tanks there. He [the enemy] might try to hit us in the center [i.e. the junction between US 5 and 7 Corps], break through and destroy the flexibility we now have. We can't risk that, Gee.'[1]

Whatever Eisenhower might feel about Monty's postponement of offensive operations while he brought up more forces, Bradley was as anxious as Monty not to prejudice the eventual outcome of the battle by trying to do too much too soon. Like Monty he was watching carefully his supply position: 'worried now on beach situation especially with regard to the unloading of ammo. Short on art[iller]y – 155 [millimetre shell size] which is loaded on bottoms of the coasters. Had to limit 19 Corps to 25 rds per gun per day. 1st [Division] shoots 200 rds per day. Corlett [19 US Corps Commander] objects. Gen [Bradley]: "Pete, I hate to do it as much as you – but hell we've got no choice. It's either that or we simply shoot what we've got, pack up and go back home." '[2]

It was therefore becoming increasingly clear to Bradley that Monty's intention of breaking-out towards Brittany while Collins attacked Cherbourg was not feasible, and that First US Army would have to tackle the two objectives in turn, not simultaneously as Monty had hoped. 'Brad, looking at the map with a line marked "Final Objective": "Erase that word 'final' – there is no final objective until we get to Germany or Tokyo . . ." B. [Bradley] went up to G.3 [Operations] tent to give them his new limited objective line. Fear of overextending himself on the Omaha beachhead. "I don't want to involve myself in the V Corps – may hamper my freedom of movement in the VII [Corps] drive on Cherbourg." '[3]

The Normandy battle was now taking shape, with both the British and American armies having to adjust their ambitions. If Eisenhower appreciated the logic, which he must have done since he was in continual telephone contact with de Guingand at Main HQ, 21st Army Group as well as with Bradley ('Eisenhower called on ammo sit. Nasty,' Bradley's aide recorded on 14 June)[4] – he nevertheless allowed his desire for 'gains' to loom larger than his military realism, infecting all those around him with the misconception that the British were flagging while the Americans were bulling ahead.

[1] Diary of Chester B. Hansen, loc. cit.
[2] Ibid.
[3] Ibid.
[4] Ibid.

Although Eisenhower cannot be held liable for the misunderstandings and later scurrilous misrepresentations by his entourage, from his driver Kay Summersby to Commander Butcher, it was unfortunate that he failed to support his commander in the field by crushing irresponsible criticism by his aides. Collins's thrust towards Cherbourg was now being facilitated by a British army that had drawn the entire Panzer divisions onto the Caen–Caumont sector and two American corps, 5 and 19 US Corps, who had had to defer their own Brittany break-out until the supply situation permitted its resumption. Yet nowhere did Eisenhower make this clear to his colleagues, in London, Washington or elsewhere, thus opening history to the subsequent claim that it was the failure of the British forces in the east which had prompted Eisenhower, Bradley, Patton and the Americans to dream up alternative plans to secure victory in Normandy.

The truth, as Bradley knew, was the reverse. As he told his Assistant Chief of Staff on 14 June, 'the corps commanders are all filled with piss and vinegar. They want to go like hell. I've got to stop them, get them solid and dug in. He [the enemy] is going to hit us hard and I don't want a [German] breakthrough.'[1]

The two men, Bradley and Montgomery, met the following day (15 June) at Bradley's Command Post. With 2nd Panzer Division edging westwards towards the main American front,[2] Monty was determined to keep the main Panzer force in the east, so that Collins could take the vital Cherbourg port without delay or attack upon his rear. Whether Monty quite realised what doubts were being sown in England we do not know, for he had little time for what the 'rats at home' might be up to. On the morning of 13 June he had signalled to de Guingand that, given Leigh-Mallory's refusal to drop the airborne division at Evrecy, the 'airborne plan was abandoned, and a visit to Montgomery's Headquarters [by Leigh-Mallory] would not be necessary' – the 'gutless bugger' could stay where he was. In fact, as Browning [commanding the British Airborne Corps] explained to Leigh-Mallory that night, the 'plan to encircle Caen from East and West had broken down in both sectors, and the assistance of the Airborne Division was therefore not at the moment required'.[3]

The failure of 7th Armoured Division's thrust towards Evrecy had however produced pandemonium at Stanmore, and on 14 June, while Monty and Bradley recast their tactical intentions in the light of German resistance and the Allied supply problems, a conference took place under Leigh-Mallory's chairmanship at 11 a.m. that was

[1] Ibid.
[2] 'I think the next on the scene will be 2 SS Pz DIV; it will be interesting to see where that comes in!!' – letter to Brooke of 14.6.44, loc. cit.
[3] AEAF Record, loc. cit.

'remarkable for a very great divergence of opinion between the Army Liaison Officers and some of the Air Force Commanders in their appreciation of the military situation before Caen, and it was later alleged that the AEAF War Room had invented a state of crisis for the Army,' as the AEAF Record for 14 June ran. Completely disregarding Bradley's real situation and revised intentions regarding the Brittany breakout via St Lô and Coutances, the Air Force Commanders did indeed invent a state of crisis. The German attack at Carentan was magnified into a crisis, with Brigadier Richardson insisting that the town was held by the Americans, the Air Force claiming that it was 'now probably in the hands of the enemy'.[1] However it was concerning the junction between British and American sectors that the worst mischief was made, kindled by Air Marshal Coningham, who held command of all the tactical fighter and fighter–bomber forces for 'Overlord'. 'In Air Marshal Coningham's view there was the element of a crisis in the central sector, the Allied position being worsened by the fact that no fresh Allied formations were due to land today or tomorrow, and those now engaged had been fighting almost continuously for a week and were getting tired.' Coningham was supported by Tedder who, like Coningham and Leigh-Mallory, had not yet set foot in France. 'Air Chief Marshal Tedder said that the present military situation had the makings of a dangerous crisis.'[2] In his later memoirs, Tedder repeated the same Eisenhower allegation that would so infuriate Monty: 'When a week had passed since D-Day without the capture of Caen, it became clear to us at SHAEF that the hopes of a rapid breakthrough on the left were now remote.'[3] Yet Monty had *never* suggested or intended a *break-through* on the left: only a battle around Caen that would permit him to establish and extend the shield behind which Bradley could take Cherbourg and break out via St Lô and Avranches to Brittany.

Some of the misunderstanding was undoubtedly caused by Monty himself, as his MA, Lt-Colonel Dawnay, later recognised:

I think he had given the RAF a totally false impression, at St Paul's and elsewhere, as to when he was going to get those airfields, south of Caen – a totally false impression. Because when we got there [to Normandy] we realised quite clearly that he didn't care a damn about those airfields, as long as he could draw all the German armour on to that [eastern] side and give a chance for his right swing to break out![4]

[1] Ibid.
[2] Ibid.
[3] Tedder, *With Prejudice*, London 1966.
[4] Lt-Colonel C. P. Dawnay, interview of 1.2.83.

In Dawnay's view Monty later did himself an injustice by insisting after the war that the battle in Normandy had gone 'exactly' according to plan. That he retained the overall framework of the strategy he had laid down as early as January 1944 was indisputable, Dawnay felt, but in suggesting that the battle ran true to his *detailed* conception Monty was doing his own generalship a discredit. It was the sheer acuity and speed with which he realised Rommel was playing into his hands by disputing possession of Caen that impressed Dawnay, as it did Brigadier Williams, Monty's Chief of Intelligence.

He was always trying to 'job backwards' and say it was always planned,

Dawnay explained.

Well, you could always pick him up on something which showed it *wasn't* planned in point of fact. The general *principle* of the thing was planned, but the detail was *never* planned, and he always tried to make out in his writings afterwards that all the detail had been planned from the word go. Which was totally untrue! And thereby belittling himself in his generalship.[1]

To Sir Edgar Williams the manner in which Monty revised his intention to get Caen and the airfields south of the city – a primary feature of the St Paul's presentation of plans – was reminiscent of the way Monty had revised his plan at Mareth, as soon as he saw the German strength being committed on one flank:

As at Mareth it would seem to me that his rapidity of adjustment was his generalship [in Normandy], and to pretend in after years that everything went according to plan was nonsense, and he [Monty] thereby underestimates, as at Mareth, his own contribution, by his agility to get into the main framework of the design when things *didn't* go according to plan.[2]

Williams was intimately aware of Monty's adjustment, for Williams had himself briefed the Allied codebreakers at Bletchley Park before D-Day on the plan:

I went down a few days before D-Day to Bletchley to brief them on what we hoped would happen, because it was frightfully important from their point of view – for they were full of enormous

[1] Ibid.
[2] Loc. cit.

knowledge of the enemy, but no knowledge of what *we* were trying to do.

And the two things I remember stressing there were first of all that Caen must be taken on the first day or as soon as possible, as part of the original plan; and secondly there was this notion of armoured brigades, which one recognised as possibly expendable, getting deep inland. It was the point that Winston Churchill seized on at St Paul's, because it was a rhetorical thing that fitted into his way of looking at things!

Now neither of these things happened. We didn't take Caen on the first day and we didn't therefore get the subsequent airfields which had been 'promised' to the Air Force, and we didn't in fact – because of the slowness of our proceedings and the nature of the country and the rapidity of enemy reaction – get the expendable armoured brigades out, making deep drives – 'staking out claims'. So both those things, which were certainly in the original plan, were not in fact carried out.

But the speed with which he adjusted to that, and his recognition that, as long as he represented a *threat*, a real threat to Caen – as long as he kept that threat, then the enemy armour became magnetised to it, shall we say – and that he must keep that going in order to get Bradley going. . . .

I think that the post-hoc, post-war business of pretending that everything went according to plan – I think he did thereby underestimate, looking back on it, his own shrewd, adjusting capacity – as at Alamein. Because Alamein didn't go precisely according to plan, as you know.[1]

Rommel's reaction had suited Monty admirably, Williams felt, because it accorded with Monty's overall framework for the development of Allied operations in Normandy. However it was a framework which, in the inevitable presentations and preparations in England, had gathered 'a number of labels that people pin on. And one was Caen, and the other was the airfields at Carpiquet. And these were of course seized on by the people who didn't do land battle fighting, people who saw things from the sky – these were the things he failed to deliver, from *their* point of view, their impatience to be on with things.'[2]

So worried was Leigh-Mallory by the atmosphere of crisis in the Air Force War Room, then, that he elected now to fly over to France for the first time. Perhaps, too, he felt guilty at having resolutely opposed the new airborne operation; certainly, like Tedder, he seems to have temporarily lost sight of the strategy which Monty had

[1] Ibid.
[2] Ibid.

651

prescribed alongside him at St Paul's in April and again in May, for in his diary for 13 June he noted: 'The weather has been damnable. The army position is improving but they will not be able to do anything until they can clear up Caen, then they may go forward.'[1] This notion of the Allied army's task in Normandy as that, simply, of 'a general attack launched all along the line'[2] is illustrative of the almost incredible ignorance of ground fighting that pervaded both the RAF and the USAAF at this time. Yet Leigh-Mallory was by no means an enemy of the army. In fact, in comparison with the 'Bomber Barons' Harris, Spaatz, Doolittle and Vandenberg, he was a positive friend, and at the 'crisis' meeting at Stanmore on the morning of 14 June he indicated his willingness to help the army by an historic offer of heavy bomber support: 'He suggested that if the Allied attack were to take place on a narrow front the entire force of medium bombers might be able to blast an area about 1000 yards ahead of our troops.'[3] However at this novel suggestion Coningham baulked, fearing Air Force casualties – and now reversed his earlier view about the military crisis. 'Air Marshal Coningham said that he did not regard the situation as critical, and that our troops still held the initiative'![4] This was back-pedalling indeed – and Leigh-Mallory's flight to see Monty at his Tac Headquarters in France on the afternoon of 14 June was designed, above all, to clarify the truth of the matter. Tedder had said, as Deputy Supreme Commander, that 'though he did not want to panic, the situation in the Eastern Sector was such that it might become critical at any moment, and he felt that they ought to hold the Air Force in readiness to give all out assistance, as and where necessary. Later in the day he refused to sanction the programme of the 8th Air Force for a heavy attack on Berlin for the 15th, and ruled that they should be held ready for employment in the battle area.'[5] The question of heavy bomber assistance was thus left in abeyance.

When Leigh-Mallory arrived at 4 p.m. on 14 June at Monty's headquarters, however, Monty was nonplussed. Early that morning he had, as he had written to Brooke after breakfast, received news that Carentan was back in American hands. He was not in the least worried by the situation, as his note at 11.30 a.m. to Major-General Simpson at the War Office demonstrates:

[1] Diary of Sir Trafford Leigh-Mallory, loc. cit.
[2] Ibid., entry of 28.7.44.
[3] AEAF Record, loc. cit.
[4] Ibid.
[5] Ibid.

Tac Headquarters
21 Army Group
14-6-44
1130 hrs

My dear Simbo

All quite O.K. and I am very happy about the situation. I had to think again when 2 Pz DIV suddenly appeared last night. I think it had been intended for offensive action against 1 Corps [i.e. north of Caen]. But it had to be used to plug the hole through which we had broken in the area CAUMONT–VILLERS BOCAGE.

So long as Rommel uses his strategic reserves to plug holes – that is good.

Yrs ever
B. L. Montgomery.

In the aeroplane, having picked up de Guingand at Thorney Island aerodrome on the way from Northolt to France, Leigh-Mallory discussed the situation with Monty's Chief of Staff. Opinion at Main Headquarters of 21st Army Group (still at Portsmouth) was that, given the growing opposition to Dempsey's forces, it might be better if the whole Anglo-American front went over to the defensive while Collins made his way up to Cherbourg. 'On the way across General de Guingand had suggested to the Air C-in-C that it might be sounder for the Army to concentrate on the Cotentin Peninsula and Cherbourg as their first objective, and to hold along the rest of the line.'[1]

Monty would have no truck with this idea. To him, as he would put it a day or two later, 'Caen is the key to Cherbourg'. Rommel *must* be made to believe that the British *were* attempting to break out in the eastern sector, so that the enemy would not dare release the four Panzer divisions which had now been put in 'to plug holes' there. For the Allies to go on the defensive would in fact give Rommel the initiative, and imperil the American thrust to Cherbourg. Thus when Leigh-Mallory entered Monty's headquarters at the end of a long day – de Gaulle had just lunched with him on this, the French leader's first, historic return to French soil and then threatened a political crisis by visiting Bayeux[2] – Monty did not at first take Leigh-Mallory's presence as more than yet another polite ritual. 'I am

[1] AEAF Record, loc. cit.
[2] According to Johnny Henderson, Monty's ADC, de Gaulle arrived virtually unannounced for lunch on 14 June. He was late, having been unable to find the Tac HQ. In the afternoon de Gaulle went off to Bayeux – his first visit to a liberated French town. During his 'walkabout' there, he brought all military traffic to a standstill. When news of the traffic jam reached Tac HQ, Monty was indignant. An order was given that de Gaulle be escorted immediately back to England, under arrest if necessary. For this de Gaulle never forgave Monty.

being bombarded with visitors,' he wrote that day to Phyllis Reynolds – 'the Prime Minister on 12th, De Gaulle today, the King on 16 June, Secretary of State for War on 18th. All very nice for them, but it does take up a great deal of time. I am well installed in my caravans in the very pleasant Normandy country; and I am delighted to be leading the open life again. I can wear again my battle clothes – corduroy trousers and grey sweater; you will see photos of them I expect,' he remarked, thinking of the posse of photographers who had accompanied the elect. Leigh-Mallory's failure to come over sooner, when Monty had first been plotting the pincer movement on Caen, was, in Monty's mental book, a black mark and he was less than civil to the C-in-C, Allied Air Forces – as Leigh-Mallory recorded:

> I saw Monty this afternoon and he was not in a good temper for I had sent him a signal shooting down an airborne operation which he wanted mounted. When I met him, therefore, he was not very kindly disposed.[1]

Monty's satisfaction with the military situation struck Leigh-Mallory as disingenuous, as did the reports filed by journalists at the front. 'The great thing to realise, my dear St George,' he dictated in his somewhat pompous manner to his official diarist, Hilary St George Saunders (later Official Air Force Historian), 'is that the well-worn platitude, "Don't believe a word of what you see in the papers", is perfectly true. The press takes the biscuit, and the situation as given by them, particularly in the evening papers, bears no resemblance to reality. As far as I can see the whole show on land is bogged up. The Hun has kicked us out of Villers Bocage and there is no sign of any big forward movement,' he remarked, 'or a chance of it.'[2]

This statement was made after Monty's exhaustive recapitulation of the military situation and strategy in his operations caravan. There, on the great wall map of Normandy, Monty had – as Leigh-Mallory reported to the Allied Air Commanders the following day – explained his current plans. 'General Montgomery did not regard the situation in the Eastern Sector as in any way a critical one, but shortage of artillery ammunition had led to something like a stalemate round Caen, and he felt compelled to keep a strong holding force north of the town to meet any attempt of the enemy's armour to break through to the sea which was very close.'[3]

Monty's satisfaction was not complacent, but rested on the firm

[1] Diary of Sir Trafford Leigh-Mallory, loc. cit.
[2] Ibid.
[3] AEAF Record, loc. cit.

conviction, as he had written to Brooke the previous evening, that Rommel had missed his only chance of defeating the Allies. 'The first vital moment in the battle was, I think, on the afternoon and evening of D day when the left American Corps had a beachhead of only 100 yds after fighting all day. Other parts of the lodgement area were not linked up, and we were liable to defeat in detail.' 21st Panzer Division had in fact sent an armoured column right through the centre of the British eastern flank, reaching the sea, showing how straightforward such defeat could be. Rommel, however, had been on holiday, and the Allies had not given him a second chance. 'The answer to invasion from across the sea is a strong counterattack on the afternoon of D day, when the invading force has no proper communications and has lost certain cohesion. That was Rommel's chance. It was not taken, and we were given time to recover – thank goodness. If you saw OMAHA beach,' he remarked in admiration, 'you would wonder how the Americans ever got ashore.'[1] This was very much in line with Bradley's 'someday I'll tell Gen. Eisenhower just how close it was,' as he confided to his ADC.[2]

Rommel's failure had given the Allied armies time to join up and to get 'our teeth well into the Germans', as Monty wrote to Brooke; 'and if we don't let go, and avoid mistakes, we ought to be in a very good position in another week or two,' enabling them to 'develop operations as originally planned – and as outlined in para 14'.[3]

Thus when Leigh-Mallory offered that, in order to ' "unfreeze" the situation, an air bombardment might be launched by medium and heavy bombers on a front of say 5,000 yards, behind which the army might advance,' Monty changed his tune: '. . . he brisked up a bit when I offered him, in exchange for the operation I was not prepared to carry out [the airborne drop at Evrecy], a much more attractive proposal.' In fact Monty's whole demeanour changed. 'When I made it he just swallowed it up, though even now I am not sure that he will choose the right area,' Leigh-Mallory commented condescendingly. 'We shall see.'[4]

For Monty, who was acutely aware of the discussion among the senior Air Force Commanders on the proper use, particularly, of medium and heavy bombers, Leigh-Mallory's sudden offer of medium *and* heavy bomber support came like a bolt out of the blue. Could he believe it? To make certain he asked if Leigh-Mallory could send over some of his planning staff the next day 'to discuss aiming points for such a bombardment'[5] with Dempsey and the staff of 30 Corps.

[1] Letter of 13.6.44 to CIGS (M501), loc. cit.
[2] Diary of Chester B. Hansen, entry of 11.6.44, loc. cit.
[3] Letter of 13.6.44 to CIGS (M501), loc. cit.
[4] Diary of Sir Trafford Leigh-Mallory, loc. cit.
[5] Ibid.

The two men parted on much improved terms. But if Monty frankly disbelieved Leigh-Mallory's authority to mount such an air bombardment, Leigh-Mallory disbelieved Monty's ability to use it to decisive advantage. 'As an airman I look at the battle from a totally different point of view,' he explained to his diarist on his return that night. 'I have never waited to be told by the army what to do in the air, and my view is not bounded, as seems to be the case with the army, by the nearest hedge or stream. I said as much, though in different words, to Monty and tried to describe the wider aspects of this battle as I see them, particularly stressing the number of Divisions which he might have had to fight had they not been prevented from appearing on the scene by air action. He was profoundly uninterested. The fact of the matter is, however, that we have reduced the enemy's opposition considerably and the efficiency of their troops and armour even more so. In spite of this, the army just won't get on. It looks to me,' he opined from his comfortable armchair at home near Stanmore, 'as though if they catch a prisoner or see a tank belonging to a particular enemy Division they at once assume that the whole of that Division is intact and moving against them. I may be doing them an injustice, but they don't appear to me to realise that, due to our action, that Division has certainly been disorganised and is probably very much below strength.

'So we have a bog, but I hope my scheme will unstick things. Nevertheless, the fact remains that the great advantage originally gained by the achievement of surprise in the attack is now lost,' he lamented. 'I hope my scheme will loosen things up, but I can't be sure.'[1]

Had Monty known of Leigh-Mallory's armchair criticisms of his Allied troops, he might well have suggested that Leigh-Mallory go nearer to the front and learn at first hand what the troops were up against. Doubtless there was a temptation, as there will always be amongst 'civilian' troops of democratic countries, to magnify the strength and scale of the opposition. These men, however, were not machines, and Monty was adamant that their lives should not be flung away needlessly and heedlessly. As long as Dempsey *threatened* to break out on the eastern flank, Collins would be free to advance on Cherbourg, and Leigh-Mallory's medium and heavy bombers promised both to accentuate the threat in German eyes, as well as blasting a path that would help Dempsey close up to the Orne.[2]

At his meeting with Bradley on 15 June, therefore, Monty radiated

[1] Ibid.
[2] 'I have decided to use my main offensive strength at the junction of the two armies, and to fight offensively in the area VILLERS BOCAGE–EVRECY–AUNAY; eventually I hope to force the enemy back to the Orne' – letter to Brooke of 14.6.44, loc. cit.

good humour. 'Good morning Brad, how's your nose? Last time I saw it I thought you got it from drinking!' he joked – referring to a recent boil on Bradley's nose. 'If I did it might have been worthwhile!' Bradley retorted, and they both laughed.[1] Monty was so confident about the situation in Dempsey's British sector that he had arranged to tour the American sector all morning. Travelling in the front seat of his Humber, with Bradley in a jeep behind and American Military Police outriders, the Ground Force C-in-C and his American Army Commander set off in a small cavalcade at 11 a.m. 'Monty waved to troops as we go along. They recognise him and normally salute the car,' Bradley's aide jotted in his diary. 'Many of them recognize Brad and smile.'[2] If it seemed strange that American troops should more frequently recognise Monty than their own Army Commander, Bradley was not one to take umbrage. A great Allied battle was in progress, and whatever others might make of Monty, he was deeply conscious that Monty was fighting an Allied fight, regardless of nationalities. With the 'Brit 7th [Armoured] on the left flank there in good condition' Bradley was satisfied he had done the right thing in sending his main armour to Carentan – indeed to his aide's surprise Bradley did not even 'raise issue of salient on 1st Div sector'[3] that had so worried Gerow. Thanks to the British Bradley was free to concentrate on Cherbourg.

In the afternoon, having visited Isigny and a large portion of the American sector, Monty returned to his headquarters. He was delighted by all he had seen. But waiting for him was another surprise. The day before he had received a sudden visit by Leigh-Mallory. Now, sitting in his tent at his Tactical Headquarters he was visited by no less personages than the Supreme Commander and Deputy Supreme Commander, come also, as Tedder later put it, 'to see whether there really was a crisis'.[4]

[1] Diary of Chester B. Hansen, loc. cit.
[2] Ibid.
[3] Ibid.
[4] Tedder, op. cit.

The Class is Dismissed

At their meeting at 10 a.m. on 15 June, Monty asked if Bradley could take St Lô – 'Monty desirous that we take St Lô,' Bradley's aide recorded in his diary.[1] However, like Dempsey in regard to Caen, Bradley was reluctant to bleed his American strength 'to take a place name', and Monty accepted this. Both he and Bradley were agreed that Cherbourg was the top priority. 'Nobody's going anywhere until Joe [Collins] gets Cherbourg,' Bradley told Gerow and Corlett.[2] The American sector from Caumont to the neck of the Cherbourg peninsula thus became a holding one, with the British threatening to encircle Rommel's Panzers in the east, while Collins drove on Cherbourg in the west.

Had Eisenhower and Tedder attended this conference they might well have gained greater insight into the nature of Allied land warfare. However, they only left England around 9 a.m. and, accompanied by no less than thirteen P-47 Thunderbolts, their Flying Fortress arrived too late to catch Monty, who had gone to meet Bradley.

Eisenhower had taken along his recently commissioned son, John, who was innocent of the true purpose of the mission. 'Dad noted with some amusement that when we reached General Montgomery's Headquarters we went through a gate inside of which was a small turn-about with a sign saying "Keep to the left". General Montgomery's Headquarters was in a group of tents. . . . Dad had missed General Montgomery at his Headquarters, as the latter had gone to visit General Bradley. Our plans were changed in order to meet General Montgomery at 4 o'clock, necessitating our being about one hour later than we had planned in making the trip back.'[3]

Eisenhower blamed himself, but Tedder's pride was injured by this snub on his first touchdown on French soil. In Monty's absence the group motored over to Dempsey's Second Army Headquarters nearby – where Dempsey was busy planning the first use of heavy

---

[1] Diary of Chester B. Hansen, loc. cit.
[2] Omar N. Bradley, op. cit.
[3] Lieut. John Eisenhower, in Diary of Harry C. Butcher, loc. cit.

bombers in direct support of a land attack. Dempsey had met Leigh-Mallory the previous afternoon at Monty's Tac HQ. 'He can give me Bomber Command, 8 USAAF and all the mediums for tactical support of an infantry attack. He can do this at first light on 17 June. I said that, if I could have them, I would attack with the LEFT of 1 Corps and take Caen,' Dempsey had noted gratefully in his diary; and at 6.30 p.m. he had gone to see General Crocker at his headquarters 'and gave him the outline plan for the taking of CAEN on 17 June. RAF representatives will fly over from the UK tomorrow to settle details.'[1]

Dempsey had thus reverted to the original plan, out-flanking Caen from west *and* east. As 30 Corps brought up more formations and artillery for its thrust from the Caumont sector, Crocker would meanwhile push infantry and armour behind the bomber barrage to envelop Caen from the east. But at 10.30 a.m. on 15 June, when Eisenhower, Tedder and Coningham arrived at his headquarters, Dempsey was told that the plan was off. 'Upon reaching General Dempsey's Headquarters, Dad was told of a plan for an attack which had been made but which had not been discussed with the airmen,' John Eisenhower innocently recorded.[2] Dempsey was more blunt. '1030 – Discussion with General Eisenhower, Tedder and Coningham disclosed that Leigh-Mallory had not told anyone else of his project for supporting an infantry attack with Bomber Command and 8 USAAF. Both Tedder and Coningham are sure that it cannot be done effectively. For the present we will drop it,' Dempsey noted with resignation.[3]

Leigh-Mallory was in fact simultaneously in session with the remaining Air Force Commanders at Stanmore, attempting to convince them of the merits of such a plan – having sent, as he had promised, a team of staff officers to work out the arrangements with Dempsey. It was this group of Air Force officers which Tedder now chased out of Second Army Headquarters and sent home. 'On arrival at General Dempsey's Second Army headquarters I found in session a joint Army/Air conference. The purpose was to consider the tactical use of heavy bombers on the lines that Leigh-Mallory had agreed. Neither Spaatz nor Coningham was represented. I was much disturbed at these developments, and found Coningham, who happened to be in Normandy that day, incensed.'[4]

Tedder's account, published in 1966, was deceitful; for Coningham did not 'happen' to be in Normandy that day. Leigh-Mallory had spoken to Coningham on the telephone on the night of 14

---

[1] Diary of M. C. Dempsey, loc. cit.
[2] Loc. cit.
[3] Loc. cit.
[4] Tedder, op. cit.

June – a call which stirred Coningham to phone Tedder secretly and arrange to meet him not at the Air Force Headquarters meeting at Stanmore the next morning, but in France. In other words Tedder and Coningham had conspired to overturn Leigh-Mallory's scheme by disrupting it not at Leigh-Mallory's headquarters in England, but at the vital Army-Air conference in the field of battle. As Solly Zuckerman, the scientific expert on the effects of heavy bombing – who was attending the conference on behalf of Leigh-Mallory – later observed, 'the class, as it were, [was] dismissed.'[1]

Monty, when he heard the news at 4 p.m., was alarmed – and blamed Dempsey, to some extent, for his lack of expertise regarding air co-operation – the very topic which had so worried Monty in May, before the invasion. For the moment, however, he treated the Supreme Commander and his Deputy to a military appreciation such as he had given Churchill, Brooke, Smuts, de Gaulle and Leigh-Mallory in the past days, so that even Tedder was forced to admit: 'As for the military crisis, it was apparent to Eisenhower and to me that it was over-emphasised.'[2] Leigh-Mallory made the same point to the Air Force Commanders in England: 'The Air C-in-C said that he had seen General Montgomery in France yesterday and he believed that the appreciation of the military situation given at yesterday's conference by Brigadier Richardson was a truer picture than the more alarming appreciation given by Air Marshal Coningham.'[3]

To Eisenhower Monty outlined the administrative and supply problems hampering the Allied effort – and dutifully, like General Alexander in the desert, Eisenhower made notes to take back to Supreme Headquarters with him. Top priority, Monty felt, should be given to speeding up the ferrying of ammunition, as well as the movement to France of fresh fighting divisions, for units that had been fighting continuously since D-Day could not now be expected to undertake offensive operations with the same gusto and willingness to suffer casualties as before.

Eisenhower duly ordered his vast headquarters to look into the matter, but his disappointment with the lack of 'gains' can best be judged by the alacrity with which he now shifted his restless attention to an alternative operation – 'Anvil'. There is no evidence that he made any attempt to see Leigh-Mallory, or took any interest in what had promised to be the first major integration of army offensive operations and heavy Allied air attack. Instead, restless and impatient, he switched his attention back to the old American demand for 'Anvil', a further Allied landing in France. The favoured target area for forces to be embarked in the Mediterranean was Marseilles, but in

[1] S. Zuckerman, *From Apes to War Lords*, London 1978.
[2] Op. cit.
[3] AEAF Record, loc. cit.

his anxiety to avoid stalemate in Normandy, Eisenhower now wanted them to land at Bordeaux, thus hopefully drawing German reserves away from Normandy to meet them.

To Monty this resurrection of a scheme which had delayed planning in 'Overlord' month upon month between January and March 1944 was absurd. Worse, it threatened to produce another Anzio, since the Atlantic seaboard at Bordeaux would be difficult to supply or cover by air. Once again it promised only *distraction*, whereas what was wanted was to bang a few heads together and to *force* the Allied Air Force commanders to use their great weapons in intimate co-operation with the ground forces, not to secure Pyrrhic gains, but to help the armies execute the plans presented at St Paul's in April and May – and unanimously approved at that time. There were sixteen German divisions in line in Normandy: it was a battle of build-up as much as of fighting now, and every effort should be made, Monty felt, to win *this* battle, not embark on subsidiary ventures.

That Monty's Normandy strategy was succeeding was proved, ironically, by Rommel's response. Thus while Coningham strode into the Allied Commander's meeting at Stanmore on 16 June and declared that 'the Army plan had failed'[1] (or, as the AEAF Record saw it: 'AM Coningham asked for a greater sense of urgency from the Army, and a frank admission that their operations were not running according to plan'[2]), Rommel and von Rundstedt were begging Hitler for an urgent conference in France, before it was too late. On 15 June, while Tedder sabotaged Leigh-Mallory's bombing plan, Rommel had written to his wife: 'Was up forward again yesterday, the situation does not improve. We must be prepared for grave events. The troops, SS and Army alike, are fighting with the utmost courage, but the balance of strength tips more heavily against us every day. . . . You can no doubt imagine what difficult decisions we will soon be faced with, and will remember our conversation in November 1942.'[3] In this conversation, shortly after Alamein, Rommel had told his wife that the war was lost and that the Axis should best sue for peace. Now, once again, Rommel was faced by his former foe from the desert, and knew in his heart that he was doomed. As at Alamein, Montgomery would relentlessly press his advantage till the German cordon snapped, and nothing would stop him. Hitler, sensing that Rommel's nerve was failing him, flew to France and met his two Field Marshals at his reserve headquarters at Soissons. According to some accounts Rommel openly asked Hitler to make peace: but Hitler knew that the time was not yet ripe for negotiation. To secure success in international politics one must argue from

[1] Tedder, op. cit.
[2] Loc. cit.
[3] *The Rommel Papers*, op. cit.

661

strength; to sue for peace now would be tantamount to an admission of defeat in Normandy. For years he had boasted of 'secret weapons' that would bring any enemy to his knees: now the time had come, and from 13 June London began to be bombarded by V1 rocket bombs in an onslaught that recalled the height of the Blitz. If Rommel could contain the enemy in Normandy long enough for German reinforcements to move into line, and if the expected main enemy landing in the Pas de Calais could be defeated on the beaches, as it had been at Dieppe in 1942, then the German position would be totally different.

Rommel left the meeting utterly convinced – leading Ruge, Rommel's naval aide, to shake his head in disbelief at Hitler's 'sheer magnetism'[1] over Rommel. It was too late to save the Cherbourg peninsula, as even Hitler now conceded: a fighting withdrawal into the Fortress – which was instructed to hold out until mid-July – was authorised; meanwhile Rommel was to regroup his Panzer divisions for a counter-attack upon the British sector. The lull while Dempsey built up his forces for a renewed pincer attack on Caen, without heavy bomber support, caused Rommel to regain his confidence. 'A quick enemy break-through to Paris is now hardly a possibility,' he wrote to his wife on 18 June. 'We've got lots of stuff coming up.' He admitted that in many places the battle had been 'going badly', but felt that 'much of this has now sorted itself out and I am looking forward to the future with less anxiety than I did a week ago.'[2]

His confidence was short-lived. To regroup his Panzer divisions he needed to pull them out of line, but until reinforcements arrived this was simply not possible, given the British pressure around Caen. It was, then, a race – but a race which Eisenhower was ignoring, preferring to concentrate instead on 'Anvil'.

On 16 June King George VI visited Monty at Creully: 'the King was here on Friday; but you saw that in the papers I have no doubt,' Monty wrote to Phyllis Reynolds. 'I told the King that I did not think the people of Normandy had any wish to be liberated,' he went on in a note of irony. 'When you read in the paper that another town has been "liberated" it really means that very heavy fighting has taken place around it and that it has been destroyed – that not one house is left standing – and that a good many of the inhabitants have been killed. Such is the price,' he remarked, 'the French are now paying. When you chucked their hand in in 1940 they thought they could avoid all this – but they cannot.'

Monty himself was in good heart. Lt-Colonel Dawnay had brought over the remaining portion of his Tac Headquarters – 'including two Rolls Royce cars!!' and Monty conferred closely with Dempsey over

[1] D. Irving, op. cit.
[2] *The Rommel Papers*, op. cit.

the revised plan for offensive operations to take Caen and the ground south of Caen down to Falaise. This called for a demonstration on the British right flank near Caumont, aimed by 30 Corps across the upper Odon towards Aunay, Mont Pinçon and Thury Harcourt, fifteen miles south-west of Caen. Meanwhile from the Orne bridgehead Dempsey would unleash the newly arrived 8 Corps in a blitz attack to try to envelop Caen from the north-east: Operation 'Epsom'. 30 Corps would start immediately, with 8 Corps putting in its surprise attack just when the other thrust was reaching its climax, and in the hope of getting Rommel looking the wrong way. 'It is not an easy operation to stage owing to the lack of depth in the 1 Corps [staging] sector, the bottleneck of the bridges over R. ORNE, and the limited space available in the bridgehead itself,' Dempsey noted on the afternoon of 17 June. Bad weather and supply difficulties had already delayed operations by 48 hours and 'although I very much want 8 Corps to start their attack on 22 June, it is clearly going to be difficult to get it as early as this.'[1] Viewing Collins's drive on Cherbourg, Bradley was equally realistic about his American effort. 'As you know the enemy has built up a much stronger force in the peninsula than we had anticipated. This has made our progress slow,' he explained to Eisenhower. He had already made arrangements for an extra division to be given to Collins when it arrived on 20 June, but meanwhile he had conferred with Monty about the feasibility of bringing a further three divisions in through the Omaha beachhead to 'give Gerow and Corlett each an extra infantry division and hold the other infantry division in army reserve,' as he requested to Eisenhower.[2]

It was important, Monty now began to feel, that there be no misunderstandings about the Allied ground situation in Normandy, nor the logic of his strategy. He therefore decided to set down in writing, at the risk of seeming pedantic, his appreciation of the current position and his concept of how the battle would now develop – a document which could go to Eisenhower, the British Chiefs of Staff, the War Office and Washington. 'My own view,' he wrote in a covering letter to Simpson, 'is that we have got the Germans in a very awkward situation, and if we rub in our advantage heavily in the next two weeks, we shall be very well placed.'

1. Today is D plus 12, and we have now been fighting since 6 June,

the document (M502, dated 18 June) began.

[1] Loc. cit.
[2] Bradley file, Papers of Dwight D. Eisenhower, 1652 series, Eisenhower Library, Abilene, Kansas.

During this time we have been working on the original directive issued by me in England, and we have:
   a) gained a good lodgement area in Normandy
   b) linked up all our different thrusts to form one whole area, and made the area we hold quite secure
   c) kept the initiative, forced the enemy to use his reserves to plug holes, and beaten off all his counter-attacks
   d) replaced our casualties in personnel and tanks, etc, so that Divisions and armoured units are up to strength again
   e) placed ourselves in a sound position administratively.
2. After the very great intensity of the initial few days we had to slow down the tempo of the operations so as to:
   a) ensure we could meet the enemy counter-attacks without difficulty
   b) build up our strength behind the original assault divisions.
And while doing this we had to continue our offensive operations in order to get well positioned for the next moves, and also to ensure that we kept the initiative.
3. All this is good. But we are now ready to pass on to other things, and to reap the harvest.

Describing the 'general situation', Monty noted that, even though Rommel could call on reserves from Brittany and elsewhere 'he still lacks good infantry to release his Panzer divisions so that the latter can be grouped for a full-blooded counter-attack.' In the Cherbourg peninsula his infantry forces were doomed, and he would have to 'make a decision as to whether he will continue to fight for Cherbourg.' Though Rommel had 'never had the initiative' he had nevertheless 'been in sufficient strength to stage local counter attacks and these have delayed the full expansion of our plans,' Monty acknowledged. However 'once we can snap the enemy "roping off" policy, he is going to find it very difficult to gather the stuff to stabilise again. The old policy of "stretch", which beat him in SICILY, then begins to emerge.' At the moment 'our own armies are facing in different directions. Once we can capture CAEN and CHERBOURG, and all face in the same direction, the enemy problem becomes enormous. . . . It is then that we have a mighty chance,' he predicted, 'to make the German army come to our threat, and to defeat it between the SEINE and the LOIRE.'
   The immediate imperative, then, was to complete the captures of Caen and Cherbourg and line up the two armies facing the same way – 'the first step in the full development of our plans. CAEN is really the key to CHERBOURG,' he pronounced; 'its capture will release forces which are now locked up in ensuring that our left flank holds secure.'
   When General Collins heard this phrase, he is reputed to have said

to Bradley: 'Brad, let's wire him to send us the key!'[1] – for the fiery Corps commander foresaw a tough fight for the vital Cherbourg port, and could frankly not see any relationship between the two towns.

Collins, brash, brave and every inch a fighter, was not in a position to appreciate the subtlety or the logic behind Monty's relentless strategy.[2] The fight around Caen had enabled Collins to cut off the Cherbourg peninsula – which he did on the day Monty issued his new directive. The fight for Caen, magnetising Rommel's armoured forces, *had* been the key to Cherbourg; now the task was to secure Cherbourg port and the town of Caen, enabling the Allied lodgement area to swell in size and become the staging area for the next phase in Allied operations: the fight to smash the German armies between the Seine and the Loire.

The capture of Caen promised 'to provide a strong eastern flank for the Army Group' in the east. 'The operations against CAEN will be developed by means of a pincer movement from both flanks.' 8 Corps, 'strong in armour', would mount the left pincer, its eastern flank on the river Dives, and circling southwards along the Bourguébus ridge; meanwhile 'the right flank of the [British] Army, forming the western half of the pincer movement against CAEN' would make for the bridges over the Orne around Thury Harcourt. 'The above operations will be begun on 18 June, and will work up to a crescendo on 22 June – on which date 8 Corps will pass through the bridgehead east of the R. ORNE on its task,' Monty laid down in his directive.

Later that day, however, Monty agreed with Dempsey that the narrow coastal salient east of Caen would ill favour the assembling of a complete armoured and infantry Corps without time-consuming local operations to elbow more room for it: '1830 – Saw C-in-C at my Headquarters. I told him that I had come to the conclusion that an attack by 8 Corps from the bridgehead EAST of the two rivers is too risky. The bridgehead is too small to form up satisfactorily; there is no room to deploy artillery EAST of the rivers; the L of C would be dependent on the bridges, and there is always the risk that the enemy, who is very active in this sector, might upset our arrangements just before the start of the attack. The staff had been into the matter very carefully during the morning.' Dempsey's answer was to launch 8 Corps through his *western* flank, thus reinforcing the 30 Corps attack on the Caumont side of Caen.

Ought Monty to have resisted Dempsey's suggestion and given

---

[1] J. Lawton Collins, *Lightning Joe*, Baton Rouge 1979.
[2] 'Collins had a greater aggressiveness than any other Corps Commander we had. But Collins had limitations. Cocky and sure of himself, sometimes inclined to take a one-sided view of the situation' – 'Bradley Commentaries on the Second World War', Military History Institute, Carlisle, Pennsylvania.

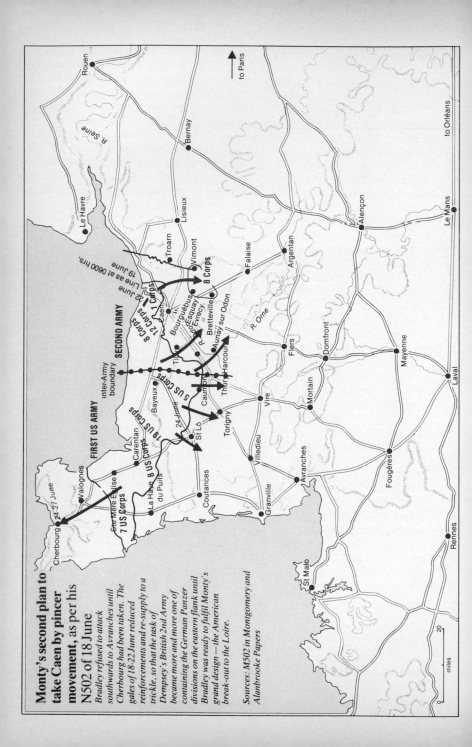

Monty's second plan to take Caen by pincer movement, as per his N502 of 18 June

Bradley refused to attack southwards to Avranches until Cherbourg had been taken. The gales of 18-22 June reduced reinforcements and re-supply to a trickle, so that the task of Dempsey's British 2nd Army became more and more one of containing the German Panzer divisions on the eastern flank until Bradley was ready to fulfil Monty's grand design — the American break-out to the Loire.

Sources: M502 in Montgomery and Alanbrooke Papers

to Paris

to Orléans

Rouen

R. Seine

Le Havre

Bernay

Lisieux

Le Mans

Alençon

Troarn

Vimont

Falaise

Argentan

SECOND ARMY

Line as at 0600 hrs, 19 June

22 June

1 Corps

8 Corps

12 Corps

8 Corps

Caen

Bourguébus

Esquay

Evrecy

Bretteville

Aunay sur Odon

R. Orne

Flers

Domfront

Mayenne

Ti—

Thury-Harcourt

Inter-Army boundary

FIRST US ARMY

5 US Corps

Caumont

Torigny

Vire

Villedieu

Mortain

Laval

Bayeux

19 US Corps

24 June

St Lô

Coutances

Avranches

Granville

Fougères

Carentan

La Haye du Puits

8 US Corps

Ste Mère Eglise

7 US Corps

Valognes

Cherbourg

24-27 June

St Malo

Rennes

0   20
miles

him instead more time in mounting the left pincer rather than transferring all his eggs into one basket? It is easy to think so in retrospect, knowing that Dempsey's revised plan failed utterly, and that Caen was ultimately to fall only when a left pincer *did* envelop it from the east, a whole month later. Moreover there is evidence that Monty, still flushed by the success of 'Overlord' to date, did not sufficiently weigh the problems of fighting in the bocage terrain of Normandy. When he wrote, on 19 June, to tell General Simpson at the War Office of the change of plan he was still thinking in terms of the desert: 'It will be a blitz attack supported by all available air power – on the lines of EL HAMMA.' At El Hamma, Monty had successfully switched 10 Corps over to the inland pincer, with triumphant results. Normandy, however, was a far cry from the open desert, and even Monty recognised that Dempsey could not match the unique army-air relationship that had made El Hamma such a success. 'The trouble in Second Army is that there is no one at Army HQ who knows anything about the practical side of air co-operation in the land battle; so I am lending Charles Richardson to Dempsey as a BGS (Air) to teach them all. I fear that Chilton is not really fit to be Chief of Staff to a large Army; however, we will try and teach him.'

In his directive of 18 June, Monty had accepted that Bradley's southern flank between Caumont and the Cherbourg peninsula should remain defensive; but soon after issuing the directive, news came in that Collins had cut off the peninsula. With 700 tanks at his disposal Bradley need not wait for the capture of Cherbourg before beginning his break-out towards Brittany, Monty now felt; the bulk of Rommel's armour was tied down at Caen, and he wanted Bradley therefore to start pushing southwards now, while the time was ripe: 'It is important that the [First US] Army should not wait till CHER-BOURG is actually captured before extending its operations to the south-west. As soon as they can be organised, operations will be developed against LA HAYE DU PUITS and against COUTANCE. Later, as more troops become available, these operations will be extended towards GRANVILLE, AVRANCHES and VIRE.' He was even considering landing an airborne division on St Malo so that Patton's Third US Army could be brought into Brittany straight through St Malo – 'enabling the whole tempo of the operation to be speeded up, since Third Army would be in close touch with First Army and everything would thus be more simple.'

It was at this juncture that luck, which had hitherto so favoured the Allies, began to run out. While Hitler's 'secret weapon' rained upon London, a gale blew up, wrecking the American artificial 'Mulberry' harbour just as it was nearing completion, and paralysing all move-ment of supplies and reinforcements into Normandy.

CHAPTER SEVEN

'This Weather is the very Devil'

'Yesterday (Monday) was a frightful day, wet and cold, and a high wind, and we could get nothing landed on the beaches,' Monty wrote to Phyllis Reynolds on the morning of 20 June. 'The pilotless aircraft seem to be creating rather a sensation in London and to be causing certain casualties. The great point is that people should not panic; they must remain calm and stick it out somehow.'

The people didn't panic; but the evidence shows that, as Hitler hoped, the politicians and rear headquarters staffs did. Night after night Eisenhower spent in a cramped air-raid shelter; and when he saw Monty's offensive plans in Normandy being postponed again and again, he became a prey to doubt. At the request of the Combined Chiefs of Staff he had since 14 June been reconsidering the launching of 'Anvil'. On 20 June he insisted, in a letter to Marshall, that General Wilson, the Supreme Commander in the Mediterranean theatre, be ordered to start 'Anvil'[1] – though there was no hope of landings being mounted before mid-August.

Monty meanwhile watched with growing despondency as the weather played havoc with his carefully laid plans. 'This weather is the very devil,' he wrote to Simpson at the War Office on 20 June. 'A gale all day yesterday; the same today; nothing can be unloaded. Lying in ships off the beaches is everything I need to resume the offensive with a bang; in particular I must have 43 DIV complete, and more artillery ammunition; if I can unload these by tomorrow night, then I am O.K.; if I cannot do so I shall have to postpone the attack – which would be a great nuisance as every day's delay helps the enemy.

'I am now 5 days behind in my estimated build-up; all due to bad weather. We cannot, in this weather, complete the "mulberries". However,' he added with resignation, 'one cannot have everything;

---

[1] 'In spite of any local success achieved in northern France, Operation OVER-LORD will be in urgent need of any assistance possible from elsewhere for some time to come . . . I think that Wilson should be directed to undertake Operation ANVIL at the earliest possible date' – *The Papers of Dwight David Eisenhower*, op. cit.

the movement on Cherbourg is going very well and that port in our hands will help greatly.

'The real point is that the delay imposed on us by the weather is just what the enemy needs i.e. time to get more Divisions over here, and we know some more are on the move. It is all a very great nuisance.'

To de Guingand Monty signalled that evening that Dempsey's 'blitz attack' of 8 Corps could not now take place until 25 June, and 'each further day of bad weather will mean a further postponement of a day. Inform Eisenhower and D.M.O. at War Office for C.I.G.S.' By the time Eisenhower met General 'Jumbo' Wilson's Chief of Staff from the Mediterranean on 22 June, Eisenhower was in a state: 'He said he wanted ANVIL and he wanted it quick,' General Gammell signalled to Wilson[1] – despite the fact that it would break up the whole Allied offensive in Italy, and provide no instant relief to Montgomery – whom Eisenhower declined to consult, even though he insisted on 'Anvil' as part of the overall 'Overlord' strategy.

Bradley was as chagrined by the weather in Normandy as was Monty. 'We've got him [the enemy] on the run and we can't afford to let him stop,' he remarked on 19 June as the storm washed away his American 'Mulberry'; 'we have the initiative and now we must keep it.'[2]

If the Germans were on the run, however, they showed little sign of being out of breath. While the Allies cut down heavy artillery fire to 25 rounds per gun or less, the Germans began to increase their shelling of both British and American sectors. Hitherto Monty had refused to sleep anywhere but in his accustomed caravan, under the portrait of Rommel; now even he was forced to spend the night in a blanket in a slit trench.[3]

Eisenhower had planned to visit Bradley on 20 June, but the appalling weather prevented this too;[4] and without ammunition or reinforcement supply Bradley now cancelled Monty's instruction regarding the simultaneous thrust southwards to Coutances and Brittany. 'Corlett tells of results of 19th corps attack which extended front for 29th [Division] at cost of casualties. "We took them heavily," he [Corlett] said. Brad, who didn't particularly want attack said, "Yes, you greatly improved position and gains were worth what you paid. But now let's stick where we are, dig in and hold until we can clean up this [Cherbourg] peninsula." Urgent that we do so and

[1] *The Papers of Dwight David Eisenhower*, op. cit.
[2] Diary of Chester B. Hansen, entry of 20.6.44, loc. cit.
[3] J. R. Henderson, loc. cit.
[4] In fact Eisenhower failed to arrive, despite signalled intentions to do so, for the next four days. 'Ike . . . due again and didn't show up. Four days in a row without a show and things are exasperating' – Diary of Chester B. Hansen, entry of 23.6.44, loc. cit.

quickly – get the stuff in from States, directly without transhipment through England.[1]

'Corps commanders are eager beavers, always anxious to bust through and attack new objectives,' Bradley's aide remarked. 'Gen. reluctant to demonstrate on this front.' The following day Hansen recorded: 'Gen looks tired tonight, worried by situation – not actively but over supply crisis which today brought [General] Lee here for discussions.' Each day the staff looked anxiously at the barometer; by 23 June ammunition was having to be flown into the American sector and coasters beached rather than wait another day while they bobbed at anchor offshore. 'Old man looks morose today,' Hansen noted yet again in his diary.[2]

Monty, meanwhile, was anxious that his subordinate generals not lose heart; thus on the evening of 22 June, as the weather began to moderate slightly, he summoned all the corps and divisional commanders in Second Army to a conference at his Tactical Headquarters at Creully. There he addressed them, as he had done in England before D-Day, to review the past and to reiterate the overall framework of his strategy in Normandy. The first two phases of the Normandy battle were, he declared, already won – the D-Day assault and the subsequent fight for a contiguous lodgement area. They were now about to begin the third phase, to 'snap the enemy "roping off" policy and write off as many of his holding troops' – the 'crumbling' operations he had made the hallmark of the battle of Alamein. But 'we are 5 days late,' he confessed, 'owing to rough weather on the beaches, which prevented all unloading. This has been a tragedy, and was exactly what the enemy needed as it has given him TIME to collect reserves.'

It was important, as Second Army moved into this third phase, not to lose sight of the overall pattern – 'the four great principles on which I have worked,' as Monty put it in his notes:

A. To retain the initiative.
   Done successfully; so well in fact that the enemy has had to use his reserves to plug holes.
B. To increase and improve our own build up.
   We have failed here; the weather has been against us and we are 5 days behind now – possibly 6.
C. To delay and hamper the enemy build up against us.
   Done successfully by air action and the operations of SAS units.
D. To pull the enemy reserves on to the British Second Army so that the First US Army could carry out its task the easier.

[1] Ibid.
[2] Ibid.

670

Few commanders in history have conducted their operations with such openness, both before the battle and during its execution. That his strategy would eventually become misrepresented deeply distressed Monty, as will be seen, for he had at all times striven to maintain clarity of purpose during the battle, both in his communications and meetings with his superiors, from Eisenhower to the Chiefs of Staff in London and Washington, and with his officers, the leaders whose task was to fight the battle. 'We have been successful in pulling the German reserves to the CAEN, or eastern, sector of our lodgement area,' he went on. 'This has relieved pressure in the American sector, and as a result we now own the whole of the Cherbourg peninsula except the port of Cherbourg itself.' His strategy remained the same as it had been when he addressed them all at St Paul's:

It will be obvious that we must gain possession of the Cherbourg and Brittany peninsulas, to form the main framework of our lodgement area in France, as we need the ports that are in them. We have practically got Cherbourg.
Next we will deal with Brittany. The Americans,

he predicted confidently,

will do all that quite easily so long as the Second British Army will pull the Germans on to *it*, and will fight them over this side.

It was, then, an *Allied* battle, and every British life given was given in an Allied operation, in order to put the American army into Brittany. Once this was done, Monty predicted, the 'enemy would then have to make a big decision:

A. To bring the German Army to the south and west of the SEINE and have a big battle there,
      or
B. To sit back behind the SEINE.

Personally Monty believed, as he had always done, that Hitler would never permit a withdrawal to the Seine. He would order his troops to fight tooth and nail in the field, as he had done at Alamein, in Tunisia, in Italy, and in the east at Stalingrad. Phase 3 would not therefore 'be so easy', Monty warned: 'The bad weather has put us 5 to 6 days behind and this has given the enemy time to build up against us – and to get three divisions into reserve.' East of Caen he now had three divisions in line; from there to Caumont stretched the four Panzer divisions: '21, 12, Lehr, 2 Pz'; while in line against the Americans the enemy only had 'an odd collection of Divisions and bits of pieces', with no less than four infantry divisions doomed in the Cherbourg peninsula. Unfortunately the Allied supply crisis had given Rommel the chance to bring 'three Divisions in reserve:

1 S.S. Pz SW of EVRECY
2 S.S. Pz South of ST LO
353 Inf About Periers

'He obviously means to hold us in the CAEN sector,' Monty prophesied; 'and he will pivot on ST LO and COUTANCE as he is forced southwards by the American thrust towards GRANVILLE and AVRANCHES. . . .

'We have now reached the "show down" stage,' Monty announced. 'The first rush, inland to secure a good lodgement area, is over. The enemy is "firming up" and trying to hem us in. He will bring up Army artillery, mines and so on. He has been helped by the bad weather which has put back our build-up by 5 to 6 days; this has enabled him to bring in more troops and to get three divisions in reserve.'

The Allies now had twenty-three divisions ashore; the Germans had nineteen divisions in Normandy, of which seven were élite Panzer or Panzer Grenadier divisions. If Hitler chose to milk all his other sectors along the Atlantic Wall, he could build up a total of 63 divisions against the Allies; he would not of course dare do so, given the threat of Allied amphibious assaults elsewhere: but it was a measure of what the Allies were up against. If the Allies could continue to draw the German armies in the West into piecemeal battle in Normandy where they could be destroyed on the ground and from the air, then the outcome of the war was in no doubt; but it would be a tough and demanding struggle. 'We have thus reached a stage where carefully prepared operations are essential,' Monty exhorted. 'We must have no set-backs. What we take we must hold. I want to impress on commanders the following points:

a) the close co-operation of air forces in the land battle. This is the work of Army HQ.
b) infantry and tanks must keep right up to the barrage. The weight of gunfire is useless unless you take immediate advantage of it.
c) attacks must be in sufficient depth to ensure adequate mopping up.
d) tanks and supporting weapons must be got forward quickly to compete with counter-attacks.
e) method of command, staff control, and conduct of the battle. Troops may fight magnificently, but lack of coordination and control from above will ruin the battle.

f) throughout the battle there must be aircraft up all day. They attack all movement seen; and in particular enemy guns – especially those that cannot be reached by our own guns.

The establishment of First Canadian Army was to be phased back until mid-July, when Second Army would be able to give it room. This it would achieve by enveloping Caen and taking the high ground to the south, the shield behind which Bradley could strike towards Brittany. 'The main feature,' he summarised Dempsey's forthcoming 'Epsom' operation, 'is a strong attack by 8 Corps, delivered through the right Bde front of 3 Canadian DIV. The front is becoming "glued up' and care must be used to ensure success by great fire power from the ground and air. The attack must not go in till 8 Corps is assembled complete: i.e. 15 DIV, 43 DIV, 11 Armd DIV, 4 Armd Bde, 31 Armd Bde. Then the *whole Army front* must flare up and the enemy be fought to a standstill.'

The generals rose and replaced their caps. Sadly it was Second Army, not the enemy, which would be fought to a standstill.

CHAPTER EIGHT

Planning the Break-out

Although the Allies would go on to win the battle for Normandy, it was clear to Monty that all hopes of a quick victory were now busted by the gale. By forcing Rommel to keep his Panzer divisions around Caen, Monty had created the ideal conditions for the strategy he had laid down before the battle: an American break-out to Brittany that would stretch Rommel's rope until the German cordon broke and the Allies could swing triumphantly to the Seine. But the wreck of the American 'Mulberry' and the lack of supplies and reinforcements had convinced Bradley that First US Army must go on the defensive save in its drive on Cherbourg, and even then Bradley needed time to switch his offensive. Thus Monty informed Simpson on 23 June:

> I am just back from touring the Cherbourg front. 7 US Corps is doing well and I think they will be in the town very soon; the Germans there are fighting very well. . . .
> I have ordered First US Army as follows:
> a) to capture (or liberate!!) Cherbourg with all speed
> b) to re-group so that it can operate strongly on the axis:
>   LA HAYE DU PUITS
>   LESSAY
>   COUTANCE
>   GRANVILLE-VILLEDIEU
> This thrust to begin as early as possible.
> Bradley does not think it can begin till 4 days after Cherbourg is captured (or liberated!!).
> The enemy has had a great stroke of luck in the bad weather. It has saved him.

That Bradley could not start his offensive towards Brittany for a further ten days or fortnight was a grave disappointment to Monty, who felt that Second Army had done well to contain the four German Panzer divisions on its front for the first seventeen days of the battle – longer than Alamein, in fact. That it would have to go on doing so for a further two weeks before Bradley could begin his breakout was a considerable task for Dempsey, but one which Monty accepted on behalf of his overall Allied plan of battle, and in spite of his own Chief of Staff's preference for closing down the British offensive, as Bradley was closing down his southern flank, until Cherbourg port was captured and working. In Rommel's shoes Monty knew that this would be the very respite the Germans needed: that Rommel would thus be enabled to withdraw his Panzer divisions, replacing them with artillery-backed infantry, and might then stop Bradley from *ever* breaking out southwards to Brittany. 'The Americans are doing awfully well,' he wrote the next day to his successor at Eighth Army, Sir Oliver Leese. 'Bradley is first class as an Army Cmd and is very willing to learn; the same with Bimbo [Dempsey]. Both are very inexperienced, especially on the air side, but both are anxious to learn and are doing so. I have grave fears that Harry Crerar [commanding 1st Canadian Army] will not be too good; however I am keeping him out of the party as long as I can. Georgie Patton may be a bit of a problem when he comes into it!!' he predicted.[1]

> I tried very hard to get First U.S. Army to develop its thrust southwards, towards COUTANCE, at the same time as it was completing the capture of Cherbourg,

he explained to the CIGS, Sir Alan Brooke.

> I have no doubt myself that it could have been started in a small way, and gradually developed. But Bradley didn't want to take the risk; there was no risk really; quick and skilful re-grouping was all that was required.
>   I have to take the Americans along quietly and give them time to get ready; once they are formed up, then they go like hell. I have got to like them very much indeed, and once you get their confidence they will do anything for you. In the end it will work out all right,

he was confident; for once the Second Army attack was launched, it promised to

> pull some more stuff over to the CAEN sector from the St LO area, and then First U.S. Army will have an easier party when its attack southwards is begun.[2]

The only dangerous moment had been on D-Day, as he described to Leese:

---

[1] Letter copy communicated to author by Mrs Frances Denby.
[2] Loc. cit.

I have had only one really anxious moment.

After fighting all day on D day we had a bridgehead of only 100 yards on the beaches of 5 American Corps. Very awkward.

However they pulled it through somehow and the Bosche cracked. The American soldier is without doubt a very brave chap; the more I see of him the more I like him.[1]

In fact casualties had been 'less than half what we had thought was likely', with 2,000 British troops killed so far, and 3,000 Americans. Given that some 750,000 Allied soldiers had been put ashore *over the beaches* in under three weeks – not a bad effort,' Monty remarked. 'Our total will go up to two million!!'

As regards the British divisions, Monty was pleased with the performance of 50th Division under Major-General Graham, though added that 'they have had a lot of casualties'. The Highlanders of 51st Division had performed less well: '51 DIV have not been so good under Bullen-Smith; but I have no doubt the Division will be all right when it settles down, and when Bullen is more in the saddle. 3 Canadian DIV started well, but then became rather jumpy; the Bosche snipers in our own back areas rather upset them.'

To Monty every division had its strengths and foibles, and he treated each one like a conscientious father still, despite his exalted role as Allied Ground Forces Commander. To outsiders this often smacked of interference in the proper affairs of the individual Army Commander; an instance of this was Monty's address to the corps and divisional commanders of Second Army on 23 June. Yet both Leese and Dempsey accepted such 'interference' because, whatever protocol might be and whatever jealous tongues might say, it was such palpable evidence of Monty's 'grip': his desire to see that his intentions were understood by every subordinate under his command.

One unexpected result of the Allied success in 'Overlord', Monty explained to Leese, was that 'once we were firmly on shore, everyone in England wanted to come to Normandy. In one week I had:

The PM ⎫
C.I.G.S. ⎬   all the same day
Smuts ⎭
De Gaulle
The King
Secretary of State for War

'I finally said I would not have it and got Eisenhower to forbid any more visitors to come.

[1] Loc. cit.

'In any case it was not safe, as all HQ are within range of long range guns – and the odd Bosche plane nips over frequently,' he excused the prohibition, adding that it was the King's visit which had just forced him to move his Tac Headquarters:

The Press that came with the King gave away the area of my HQ; I was in the gardens and grounds of a chateau. A nearby chateau was destroyed by bombing two nights later; and heavy gun fire was opened on my HQ two days after that, and I had one killed & two wounded. I then decided to move my HQ, and am having no more visitors!!![1]

The next evening, on 25 June, as the British offensive began, Monty signalled to Eisenhower that 'blitz attack of 8 Corps goes in tomorrow at 0730 hrs and once it starts I will continue the battle on the eastern flank till one of us cracks and it will NOT be us. If we can pull the enemy on to Second Army it will make it easier for First Army when it attacks southwards,' he reminded Eisenhower of the overall purpose.

That Eisenhower understood, at the time, is proved by his letter to Bradley that evening: 'I most earnestly hope that you get Cherbourg tomorrow [26 June]. As quickly as you have done so we must rush the preparations for the attack to the southward with all speed. The enemy is building up and we must not allow him to seal us up in the northern half of the Peninsula. The Second Army attack this morning and enemy reinforcements should be attracted in that direction. This gives us an opportunity on the West that may not obtain very long,' he warned. 'I know that you already have General Montgomery's directive on these matters; all I am saying is that I thoroughly agree with him and know that you will carry out your part of the task with resolution and boldness.'[2] To Monty Eisenhower wrote with equal comprehension: 'I am hopeful that Bradley can quickly clean up the Cherbourg mess and turn around to attack southward while you have got the enemy by the throat on the east.'[3]

Late on 26 June Monty jubilantly reported to Eisenhower: 'it can be accepted that CHERBOURG is now in First Army hands and the enemy commander has been captured.' Despite 'very bad' weather with such low cloud that little air support could be given, Dempsey's blitz attack had meanwhile begun. 'Fighting will go on all day and all night and I am prepared to have a show down with the enemy on my eastern flank for as long as he likes.' On 27 June, after a meeting with Bradley 'on the tactics or strategy to be employed from this point,'[4]

[1] Ibid.
[2] *The Papers of Dwight David Eisenhower*, op. cit.
[3] Ibid.
[4] Diary of Chester B. Hansen, entry of 27.6.44, loc. cit.

he sent his MA, Lt-Colonel Dawnay, to England with a personal letter to Brooke, in which he re-stated his overall strategy:

My dear C.I.G.S.

I was glad to hear from you. Do fly over and have a talk some day; I would love it. It is quite easy for me if you fly over, have a good talk and then fly back to U.K. But it is NOT easy when large parties come, who want to go about and see things; we will be fighting very hard now for some weeks, and all commanders will be very busy.

It is a pity the weather went bad on us just when we wanted it to be fine. I had planned to get Second Army offensive launched on 20th June, and given fine weather we could have done it – and the Germans would not have had the extra time *they have now had* to bring up more stuff.

We got it launched yesterday (Monday); it was a bad day, with rain and low cloud, and our air was grounded; the air plays a big part in the plan and there were attempts to postpone the operation; but the troops were all ready formed up and I ordered it to go, air or no air; and it went – successfully. I cannot give Rommel any more time to get himself organised,

Monty explained. This brought him to the overall master-plan:

I think my general broad plan is maturing quite reasonably well. All the decent enemy stuff, and his Pz and Pz S.S. Divisions are coming in on the Second Army front – according to plan. That has made it much easier for the First U.S. Army to do its task; and once that Army had collected itself after the initial dogfights, then it very quickly 'roped off' the peninsula and advanced to Cherbourg.

Bradley's reluctance to strike south simultaneously with the attack on Cherbourg was a pity, but Monty was sure that 'in the end it will work out all right; Second Army attack, now launched, may pull some more stuff over to the CAEN sector from the St LO area, and then First U.S. Army will have an easier party when its attack southwards is begun.' What worried Monty much more than the somewhat cautious approach of General Bradley was the Allied air force problem:

My main anxiety these days is the possibility that we should not get the full value from our great air power because of jealousies and friction among the air 'barons'. The real 'nigger in the woodpile' is Mary Coningham; I know him well and he is a bad man, not genuine and terribly jealous. There is constant friction between him and L-M [Leigh-Mallory]. L-M does not know much about it;

678

but he is a very genuine chap and will do anything he can to help win the war; he has not got a good staff and he fiddles about himself with a lot of detail he ought to leave alone; but he does play the game.

Mary [Coningham] spends his time in trying to get L-M to 'trip-up' and putting spokes in his wheel; he would prefer to do this rather than winning the war quickly; he *does* know his stuff, but he is a most dangerous chap. The man who ought to keep the whole show on the rails is Tedder; but he is weak and does nothing about it; actually he and Mary are in the same camp, and *both of them* combine against L-M.

So L-M is fighting hard to hold his own. I myself am determined to keep right clear of the whole dirty business; but I am also determined not to lose the battle; and the chap who will do anything to help in that respect, and who does not spend his time trying to 'trip-up' other people, is L-M.

We manage all right so far. But several hours a day are wasted in argument with the opposing camps, and in ensuring that the 'air jealousies' do not lose us the battle.

It is a curious world is it not? But I expect you could add very considerably to the above story, as I am sure similar happenings are of daily occurrence in your circles!!!

With or without Allied air support Monty was determined to adhere to his overall design. 'The battle is going very well,' he continued.

a) Cherbourg is now definitely captured; the enemy commander was collected yesterday afternoon (26 June) and that ended organised resistance.

b) On Second Army front the 8 Corps has broke[n] through the enemy position on a 400 yard front. . . .

   On the first day (26 June) it reached the line GRAINVILLE –MOUEN, on the railway line from VILLERS-BOCAGE to CAEN.

   Today (27 June) 15 DIV is moving forward to the ODON valley, and I hope to see 11 Armd DIV at ESQUAY tomorrow (28 June). . . .

d) It is again very bad weather, with low clouds – today is also bad.

Since the primary object of Dempsey's attack was to force Rommel to commit his main strength – particularly armour – on the eastern flank, Monty was 'keeping my eyes very firmly directed to the suspected enemy concentration of three S.S. Pz divisions in the area ALENCON–EVREUX. That may mean dirty work ahead, in the shape of a full-blooded counter stroke. However, we will see. I have got my British strength well built up now, and am prepared to go on fighting on my eastern flank for as long as the Germans like.' With Rommel committed on the eastern sector, Bradley could begin his belated thrust southwards, having now captured Cherbourg:

On my western flank . . . I am also very strong. First U.S. Army will get cracking southwards on 1st July,

he announced.

So the whole situation is now becoming most interesting. It requires all my time and attention, and a close grip on the battle, to ensure that the battle swings the way I want.

The object was to magnetise the main German strength on the eastern sector, and to achieve this Dempsey had to keep up his offensive operations. At the same time, however, Dempsey must be careful not to so unbalance himself that he could not deal with a full-scale Panzer counter-attack. 'At the moment my tender spot is the bridgehead east of the R. ORNE [east of Caen], containing 51 DIV and 6 Airborne DIV.' As soon as 8 Corps reached its objective, therefore, Monty intended to close down this thrust and concentrate on improving the 1 Corps bridgehead east of Caen: 'As soon as 8 Corps has got to the ORNE via EVRECY and ESQUAY, then we will get busy on 1 Corps front and push eastwards to the [defensive line of] R[iver] DIVES.'

That night he signalled to Brooke that 8 Corps had reached the river Odon, and, hopefully, Dempsey would put 11th Armoured Division onto the 'Esquay feature' next day – the high, defensive ground between the Odon and the river Orne (Hill 112). He certainly showed not the least disappointment or vexation at Dempsey's limited progress – for Rommel seemed to be reacting exactly as intended. 'I am trying to procure locally (a) a dog, (b) some canaries,' he wrote contentedly to Phyllis Reynolds. 'I think pets are a good thing when living a caravan life in the fields as we do.' His MA, who was taking over the long letter to Brooke, would tell Mrs Reynolds 'all about our life in Normandy. We get any amount of fresh milk, and butter, and cheese; this is a rich dairy farming area. But they will not sell their poultry,' he noted.

Fierce fighting resumed on 28 June and, having secured the northern part of the Esquay 'feature', 8 Corps that evening went over to the defensive. By midday the following day Monty was convinced that his strategy was succeeding, for by then Rommel had thrown in 1st SS *and* 2nd SS Panzer Divisions in an effort to throw back the British eastern offensive: 'since offensive began on eastern flank on

26 June we have pulled two extra Panzer Divisions in to that flank,' Monty reported. 'Have now six Panzer Divisions involved in trying to hold my advance west and south-west of CAEN. Have since D day worked on the general policy of getting enemy heavily involved on eastern flank so that my affairs on the western flank could proceed the easier. So am well satisfied with present situation.'[1]

To the world at large this might seem a strange satisfaction considering the relative lack of 'gains' in the blitz attack by the British 8 Corps, but the world at large tended to see Monty as the British commander and all too often failed to recognise his position as overall Allied Ground Forces C-in-C. That his strategy was working was not only demonstrated by the Panzer divisions committed piecemeal to plug holes in the eastern sector, but by Rommel's reports to OKW. By 26 June Rommel recorded that whereas there had been a 'slackening of the enemy's fighting activities' on the American front (excluding Cherbourg), the British had 'attacked on both sides of TILLY SUR SEULLES after intense bombardment and corresponding preparation in the air, along a front of 7km in width and managed to break through to a depth of 5km. In this fighting the enemy again sustained high and serious losses, as he himself concedes, and since the 6.6 has lost 750 armoured vehicles. Our own losses are, however, also exceedingly great.'

The Germans had, in fact, suffered 43,070 casualties – including 6 generals, 63 commanders and 4 General Staff officers – equalling those of the Allies, despite being in prepared positions of defence. Rommel and his Chief of Staff, General Speidel, were certain that, from the distribution of forces and from Intelligence sources, all signs 'point to a thrust from the area to the North and North-West of CAEN in the direction of PARIS' – a threat which, combined with the possibility of further Allied amphibious landings between Le Havre and the Somme, completely outweighed the other threat: that, once the Cherbourg area was cleaned up, the enemy might 'regroup his forces to the south and advance between CARENTAN and PORT BAIL for the thrust south, in order to obtain possession first of all of the St. LO–COUTANCES line,' and then with 'the possibility of a thrust being made from the area S.E. of CARENTAN to the S.W. with known target [i.e. Brittany].'[2]

This was indeed Monty's aim, though any hope of a quick American break-out was dashed when, on 29 June, Bradley regretfully reported to Monty that he would have to postpone the thrust:

The storm in the UK has delayed the sailing of VIII Corps troops so that we will be lucky if we have them available by Monday [3 July],

---

[1] Signal sent at 1 p.m., 29.6.44 (M33).
[2] Army Group B, Weekly Report, 26.6.44 (Templehoff Papers), loc. cit.

he informed Monty.

> I hope to have enough by that time to jump off. In addition, it has taken longer to clean up the Cherbourg peninsula than I had hoped . . . I am very sorry to have to make this postponement but I feel that we must be set for this next attack so that when we once break his present defensive lines we will give him no chance to get set but can keep right on pushing until we get at least to the base of the peninsula. In fact, I would like to keep right on to the [Brittany] corner. I feel that this is entirely feasible due to the fact that he has placed so much of his strength in front of Dempsey,

Bradley acknowledged.[1] But could Dempsey, whose troops had now been fighting hard since 25 June against the toughest German opposition, keep up the tempo of their operations until Bradley 'kicked off' on 3 July? By 29 June Dempsey was aware that a *further* two Panzer Divisions were entering the fray on his front – 9th and 10th SS Panzer Divisions, making no less than 'eight PANZER Divisions located between CAEN and CAUMONT,' as Monty signalled to Churchill and Brooke. This was a frightening tally – the largest concentration of German Panzer strength assembled in battle in the West since Dunkirk.

On 30 June, therefore, Monty gathered his Army Commanders at his new headquarters above the village at Bray, in the American sector, beyond the Cerisy forest. For the first time Monty now had a resident 'Ultra'-reading Intelligence officer, Colonel Ewart, and a greatly improved 'Y' and 'Phantom' service (an updated version of the 'J' service in the desert), listening in to both German and Allied radio transmissions throughout the front. Together with the reports of his team of specially selected young Liaison Officers, Monty had an almost unique grip on the battle for an Army Group Commander.

The conference took place at 4 p.m., after the first abortive counterattacks by the newly arrived Panzer divisions had started. 'They were all seen off,' Dempsey recorded confidently. It was agreed that, given the German strength now opposing the British, Bradley would take over some of the British sector around Caumont,[2] thus enabling Dempsey to bring 7 Armoured Division into reserve at Bayeux, just in case a German break-through did succeed. 'Second Army task remains the same,' Dempsey noted after the conference: 'to attract to

---

[1] Bradley Papers, West Point, Virginia.

[2] Monty had first asked for an American armoured division; but Bradley declined. 'I may be a bad horse trader, but I got us out for half,' Bradley told his staff afterwards. 'Agreed to take over a portion of the Brit. sector . . .' – Diary of Chester B. Hansen, entry of 30.6.44, loc. cit.

itself (and to defeat) all the German armour and, when opportunity offers, to take Caen.'[1]

It says much for Dempsey that he performed his role so selflessly, and took upon himself, together with Monty, much of the criticism that the British had 'failed' at Caen, and it was a selflessness that Bradley deeply admired, even if lesser American commanders scorned it. One distinguished American historian would even blame the failure of the Allies to finish the war in 1944 on the decision to place Dempsey on the Allied left flank, with Bradley on the west; yet it is frankly inconceivable that the 'piss and vinegar' American generals would have accepted a role so self-effacing and lacking in 'glory gains' as that which Dempsey unhesitatingly took on, under Montgomery. Dempsey afterwards declined to write the memoirs which would explain his thankless role in Normandy, and received insults and decades of self-perpetuating American mythology with quiet equanimity, and even ordered that his diaries be burned rather than that they be used to stir up inter-Allied bickering. Only in a brief personal interview with the American Official Historian Dr Pogue in 1947 did he try to set the record straight.[2] Dempsey's modesty and his loyal post-war silence in the interests of Anglo-American unity are testaments to the strength of character and self-abnegation of a great Allied general.

Had Monty possessed the same virtues of stoicism and reticence he too might be classed as a greater man in the American book of heroes. As will be seen, he tried, refusing to pen his memoirs until a full decade after Eisenhower, Bradley and other American generals had 'had their say'. Then, however, he retorted, with the result that neither Eisenhower nor Bradley would ever speak to him again.

For by then Monty was adamant that, once and for all time, the truth should be told, as he had known it – a truth not designed to serve a British cause, but to remind the world of the *Allied* nature of the Normandy battle, in which so many British lives had been laid down to serve an *Allied* purpose.

Meanwhile, although disappointed by Bradley's delayed southern offensive, Monty refused to lose his nerve or stampede Bradley into premature operations that might result in failure. 'My broad policy, once we had secured a firm lodgement area, has always been to draw the main enemy forces in to the battle on our eastern flank,' he summarised at the conference.

---

[1] Diary of M. C. Dempsey, loc. cit.

[2] 'General Dempsey declares that he and Monty and Brad worked out together the main points of the assault and the build-up. He affirms Montgomery's claim to have planned the attack as it developed until 1 September' – interview 12/13.3.47 by F. C. Pogue, loc. cit.

We have been very successful in this policy. Cherbourg has fallen without any interference from enemy reserves brought in from other areas; the First US Army is proceeding with its re-organisation and re-grouping, undisturbed by the enemy; the Western flank is quiet. All this is good; it is on the western flank that territorial gains are essential at this stage, as we require space on that side for the development of our administration.

By forcing the enemy to place the bulk of his strength in front of the Second Army, we have made easier the acquisition of territory on the western flank.

Our policy has been so successful that the Second Army is now opposed by a formidable army of German Panzer divisions – eight definitely identified, and possibly more to come. . . .

It is not yet clear whether Hitler proposes to concentrate great strength in NW Europe so as to annihilate the Allied forces in Normandy. He may decide that this is a good proposition; and in order to achieve success he may be quite prepared to give ground gradually on the Russian front, and to accept reverses in that theatre.

His policy in this respect will emerge in due course,

Monty remarked.

For the present it is quite clear that he has reinforced the Normandy front strongly, and that a full-blooded counter-attack seems imminent,

he stated, having just received an Ultra signal relating to 9th SS Panzer Division's intended attack on Cheux, at the centre of the British offensive. 'We welcome such action,' Monty added. 'Our tactics must remain unchanged,' he laid down: not only to ensure that Bradley, Dempsey and Crerar be quite clear, but because his written directive (M505) was to be shown also to Brooke, Simpson, Eisenhower and de Guingand as well:[1]

a) *To retain the initiative*
   We shall do this only by offensive action. On no account must we remain inactive. Without the initiative we cannot win.
b) *To have no set-backs*
   This is very important on the eastern flank; the enemy has concentrated great strength here and he must not be allowed to use it successfully. Any setback on the eastern flank might have direct repercussions on the quick development of our plans for the western flank.

[1] ACKS, Distribution Lists (21 A Gp/1064/9/C-in-C), Montgomery Papers.

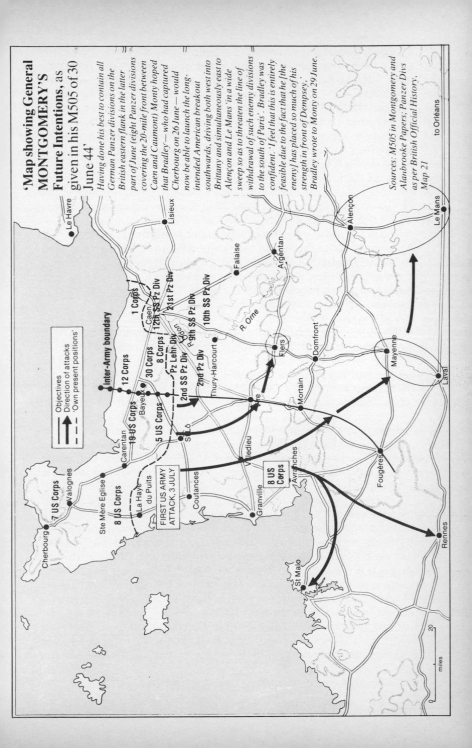

'Map showing General MONTGOMERY'S Future Intentions, as given in his M505 of 30 June 44'

Having done his best to contain all German Panzer divisions on the British eastern flank in the latter part of June (eight Panzer divisions covering the 20-mile front between Caen and Caumont) Monty hoped that Bradley — who had captured Cherbourg on 26 June — would now be able to launch the long-intended American breakout southwards, driving both west into Brittany and simultaneously east to Alençon and Le Mans 'in a wide sweep so as to threaten the line of withdrawal of such enemy divisions to the south of Paris'. Bradley was confident. 'I feel that this is entirely feasible due to the fact that he [the enemy] has placed so much of his strength in front of Dempsey,' Bradley wrote to Monty on 29 June.

Sources: M505 in Montgomery and Alanbrooke Papers; Panzer Divs as per British Official History. Map 21

Le Havre

Cherbourg

Valognes

7 US Corps

Ste Mère Eglise

8 US Corps

Carentan

La Haye du Puits

Coutances

Granville

St Lô

Tedieu

FIRST US ARMY ATTACK, 3 JULY

8 US Corps

Avranches

St Malo

Fougères

Rennes

Lisieux

Falaise

Argentan

R. Orme

Flers

Domfront

Mortain

Mayenne

Laval

Alençon

Le Mans

to Orléans

Bayeux

Inter-Army boundary

12 Corps

30 Corps

8 Corps

1 Corps

Caen

12th SS Pz Div

21st Pz Div

Pz Lehr Div

2nd SS Pz Div

9th SS Pz Div

10th SS Pz Div

Thury-Harcourt

19 US Corps

5 US Corps

Objectives

Direction of attacks

'Own present positions'

20

miles

c) *To proceed relentlessly with our plans*
These will be based on the broad policy indicated in para 1 above [drawing 'the main enemy forces in to the battle on the eastern flank, and to fight them there, so that our affairs on the western flank could proceed the easier'].
We must retain such balance and poise in our dispositions that there is never any need to re-act to enemy moves or thrusts; the enemy can do what he likes; *we* will proceed with *our* plans.

PLAN IN OUTLINE
To hold the maximum number of enemy divisions on our eastern flank between CAEN and VILLERS BOCAGE, and to swing the [American] western or right flank of the Army Group southwards and eastwards in a wide sweep so as to threaten the line of withdrawal of such enemy divisions to the south of PARIS.
The bridges over the SEINE between PARIS and the sea have been destroyed by the Allied air forces, and will be kept out of action; a strong Allied force established in the area LE MANS–ALENCON would threaten seriously the enemy concentration in the CAEN area and its 'get-away' south of PARIS.

Later historians, particularly the American Official Historian Dr Martin Blumenson, would try to appropriate the credit for this plan for their heroes General Patton and, to a lesser extent, General Bradley. In his edition of Patton's papers, Dr Blumenson quoted Patton's diary entry of 2 July 1944, in which Patton noted his own new 'Schlieffen' plan for a 'rear attack on the Germans confronting the First U.S. Army, and then driving on to the line Alencon –Argentan, and thereafter on Evreux or Chartres, depending on circumstances, we will really pull a coup'. Commenting, Blumenson remarked on Patton's 'remarkable' intuition and stated that some weeks later 'Bradley would come up with an interesting idea' for such a coup, 'an operation called Cobra'.

That 'Cobra' was in fact the plan given out by Montgomery at his headquarters on 30 June 1944 was to become a fact which some American historians hated to credit, preferring to take at face value Patton's misrepresentation, penned in frustration in his English headquarters, that the Allies were merely pursuing 'phase lines' and that 'we will die of old age before we finish'.[1] However unpalatable to such writers, the fact remains that Bradley, Dempsey and Crerar all attended Monty's conference on 30 June, all concurred in Monty's strategy, and that Eisenhower, Brooke, the War Office and Main Headquarters of 21st Army Group at Portsmouth all had copies of Monty's plan. Nor was it some vague notion, for Monty laid down at the conference how he wished the plan to be executed in the coming

[1] *The Patton Papers*, ed. Martin Blumenson, Boston 1974.

weeks. Originally, in England before D-Day, he had intended to push the British Second Army south of Caen to secure space for airfields and provide the shield he needed for Bradley's southern thrust to Brittany. Rommel's fierce reaction at Caen had, however, made this unnecessary. Indeed a British thrust too far from its present sector would open Second Army to a German counter-thrust by extending the front to be defended, whereas although it was greatly congested, the British front was currently almost impregnable. Dempsey's task as Second Army Commander was therefore:

a) To hold the enemy main forces in the area between CAEN and VILLERS BOCAGE
b) To have no set-backs
c) To develop operations for the capture of CAEN as opportunity offers – and the sooner the better.

A full-blooded enemy counter-attack seems likely, put in somewhere between CAEN and VILLERS BOCAGE; the main axis of such an attack is not yet apparent. In order to provide a mobile reserve in the hands of the Army Commander, the 7 Armd DIV, now holding the right divisional sector, will be relieved tomorrow by First Army and that divisional sector will be included in First Army area.

Meanwhile, as Dempsey continued to act in his flypaper role, Bradley was to uncoil his American spring. With over a thousand tanks and an army of more than 350,000 American troops,[1] he was to start his southern offensive on 3 July. His first thrust was to be launched from the right flank, furthest from the Panzer base, on that day. Dempsey, in mortal combat with the Panzer divisions at Caen, would not be able to provide the deep inland shield that had been planned in England; therefore the American thrust would have to hinge on the Caumont salient – 'the Army to pivot on its left in the CAUMONT area, and to swing southwards and eastwards on to the general line CAUMONT–VIRE–MORTAIN–FOUGÈRES.' From this an attack was to be mounted eastwards towards 'the important intercommunication centre of FLERS.' This thrust would, like the British attack at Caen, preoccupy the enemy and, it was to be hoped, draw to it any incoming reserves. Behind it Bradley was to sneak down his westernmost forces: 'On reaching the base of the peninsula at AVRANCHES, the right hand Corps (8 Corps) to be turned westwards into BRITTANY and directed on RENNES and ST MALO.' This Corps was to 'consist of three infantry divisions and

[1] 21st Army Group Headquarters estimated that, in the first week of July, Dempsey's efforts on the eastern flank had so denuded the enemy's forces on the western flank that the Americans enjoyed a superiority there of 3 to 1 in infantry and 8 to 1 in tanks – 'Review of the situation at D + 30' (WO 205/644), PRO.

one armoured division'. However this was not all; for Monty wanted Bradley to start planning for a third thrust, employing the remainder of his army, in a wide encircling movement eastwards towards Paris:

Plans will be made to direct a strong right wing in a wide sweep, south of the bocage country, towards successive objectives as follows:
a) LAVAL–MAYENNE
b) LE MANS–ALENCON

The tactical strategy that would defeat the German armies in the West had been given out. Although it entailed Bradley mounting his own shield between Caumont and Fougères, Bradley accepted the plan for no one could have done more to contain the main German fighting strength than Dempsey: a role Dempsey was committed to keeping up. The army commanders therefore returned to their headquarters with something of the same excitement they experienced when, in England, the master-plan had first been given out. Only now it was no longer a scheme predicated on successful landings and a successful build-up. More than could ever have been dreamed possible in England, Rommel had concentrated his strength against the British eastern sector. Cherbourg, the key priority in Monty's revised 'Overlord' plan, had been captured and the way seemed open to fulfil what had, only weeks before, appeared to many but a dream – if all went well.

CHAPTER NINE

The Fear of Stalemate

July 1944 was to be a month of tremendous strain for Monty, the equivalent, in its way, to the last days in October 1942 when, after days and nights of continuous battle at Alamein without decisive result, even the staunchest of hearts began to weaken, tongues to wag, and fingers of suspicion be pointed at the Eighth Army commander. In 1942 it had been Anthony Eden who began to orchestrate a campaign of rumour that turned even the Prime Minister against his appointee in the field; in July 1944 the culprits were to be found in Washington, Whitehall and at Supreme Headquarters itself.

The campaign of rumour began in 1 July when Monty's new directive to his Army Commanders reached Eisenhower's headquarters at Widewing. For days Eisenhower had been locked in paper combat over 'Anvil', and after threatening Churchill with an American shift of priority to the Pacific, Eisenhower had forced the British Chiefs of Staff to capitulate, as Major-General Simpson, the Director of Military Operations at the War Office, recalled:

> I don't think it was entirely Ike's fault. I think the Americans in the US were very keen on doing that particular operation, and Ike was a loyal subordinate of his Chiefs-of-Staff. . . .
>
> But there is no doubt that in a telegram sent by Eisenhower on June 26 to the Combined Chiefs-of-Staff – his masters in Washington – he mentioned that General Wilson, then Supreme Commander in the Mediterranean, was prepared to carry out 'Anvil' providing he received in time certain assault ships and craft. Eisenhower added: 'I attach such importance to the early launching of "Anvil" that I am prepared to do my utmost to ensure its success. Admiral Ramsey and General Montgomery share my conviction with regards to the importance of "Anvil".'
>
> Now that was completely untrue.[1]

Monty's dislike of 'Anvil' was known in all quarters, and had been consistent since Churchill first asked his opinion on the operation at

[1] Recollections of General Sir Frank Simpson, recorded by Eugene Wason for Sir Denis Hamilton, 1978.

Marrakesh in December 1943 – as Churchill ruefully pointed out to Roosevelt after capitulating: 'I was impressed with General Montgomery's arguments when he came to Marrakesh. After he had been nominated to the "Overlord" command he explained that it would take 90 days for a force landed at Anvil to influence the "Overlord" operation.'[1] To Churchill it seemed unlikely that Monty had now changed his mind, and when Monty heard of the allegation he was furious:

> Understand from DAWNAY that EISENHOWER has stated that I support his views regarding ANVIL

he signalled to Brooke on the evening of 1 July.

> Want to make it quite clear that I have had no discussion with him about ANVIL and do NOT know what his views are.

Monty had not in fact seen Eisenhower since the latter's visit, with his son, on 15 June – a full fortnight past. However Eisenhower was now known to be on his way over for a visit to Normandy and would be coming to Monty's headquarters on 2 July. 'Do you consider I should discuss the matter with EISENHOWER who is coming this way tomorrow Sunday?' Monty asked. Brooke, aware that Churchill had given in already to the American demand for 'Anvil' in a telephone conversation with Eisenhower that day, counselled Monty not to mention the subject – 'I note what you say but consider you should NOT discuss matter with EISENHOWER. That may do more harm than good at this stage.'[2]

In fact it was impossible not to mention the matter, since it was uppermost in Eisenhower's mind when on 2 July he duly arrived at Monty's headquarters, at 10.30 a.m.:

> It was a typical Sunday morning as the sun was shining and General Montgomery and his officers were just returning from church,

Eisenhower's British MA recorded.

> It was indeed a peaceful scene as General Montgomery's two puppies were playing in the grass and the only sign of war was a Panther and a Tiger tank which arrived the day before.
> Major-General Richards, R.A.C., 21 Army Group, gave a most interesting lecture on the Panther and Tiger tanks. The main

---

[1] W. S. Churchill, *Triumph and Tragedy*, op. cit.
[2] 'Correspondence with CIGS and DMO, 1944' file, Montgomery papers.

discussion after his lecture was on the best method of dealing with the Panther. . . .

The General [Eisenhower] and General Montgomery then went into conference.[1]

Bradley had escorted Eisenhower; Bradley's ADC was equally distracted by the German Panzers, as well as the almost Cromwellian piety and tidiness of the headquarters:

Got to Monty's as spoonily clad guards officers were returning from chapel with prayer books and bibles in their hands. Very proper. Attitude of ease and comfort in their headquarters. It was Sunday. Nothing in our [Bradley's First Army headquarters] to suggest it.

[Monty's] CP [Command Post] was remarkable. All the vans and caravans . . . Monty not there originally, arrives downy, corduroys and sweater with black beret . . .

Two new puppies playing around his van; one a rugged little terrier named Snoops, picked up by correspondents near the Douve river and the other a spaniel named Rommel. . . . Trees green in the valley, tiny church visible on opposite hill to the west and we could hear the ringing of bells mingled with the thunder of cannon down on 1st Div front. Monty's CP is in V [US] Corps sector, at Bray.

Took us out to show us Panther and Tiger tanks which he had in CP. Covered with laminated plastic to prevent stick bomb or magnetic bomb used by Russians from sticking. Huge tank. Panther had been hit by 75 which simply glanced off it. Tankers are concerned about it. Need a heavier gun. . . .

They retired to van.[2]

Inside his map lorry Monty explained his current tactical strategy, for his directive had not arrived at Supreme Headquarters when Eisenhower left the previous day. One of Eisenhower's purposes in making a five-day visit to France was – as Churchill had attempted to do in the desert in 1942 – to speed up operations; and like Churchill in the desert Eisenhower was totally won over by Monty in the latter's presence, but almost immediately a prey to other views and exigencies when out of it. Thus he accepted Monty's revised strategy whereby Bradley was to provide his own shield as far as Vire and Flers, but when, in the days ahead, Bradley ran into the same problems as the British of slow progress in the bocage countryside, Eisenhower's frustration knew no bounds.

[1] Lt-Colonel J. Gault, in Diary of Harry C. Butcher, loc. cit.
[2] Diary of Chester B. Hansen, loc. cit.

Meanwhile at Bray, having discussed Bradley's forthcoming attack, Eisenhower brought up the question of 'Anvil'. Aware that Brooke would not forgive him if he weighed in against the landings in southern France, Monty capitulated much as Churchill and Brooke had done. In Monty's subsequent opinion it was 'one of the great strategic mistakes of the war. Eisenhower had a tremendous argument about it with the Prime Minister at the end of [June] and early in [July]. He thought it would help him with the Prime Minister if he could say that I agreed with him that ANVIL must be launched in August as planned. . . . I wish now – as I have often wished – that I hadn't half-heartedly concurred that early [July]day. But I wanted to show willing to Ike; I had been showing unwilling in other matters, and I sensed then that there were more of these "other matters" to come.'[1] That evening, 2 July 1944, Monty signalled to Simpson: 'Saw EISENHOWER today and he opened the subject of operations in Mediterranean theatre and asked me for my views. Gave him my personal views as follows. First. We should continue the battle in ITALY so long as we get a good dividend and can destroy German divisions. Second. When we no longer get a dividend in Italy then an ANVIL would help us here. Third. It seemed to me that we would not do much good operating over and beyond the ALPS in winter but my opinion of this matter was not of much value as I did not know the various pros and cons.'

Monty's willingness to give way over 'Anvil' was in fact a trade, for with the prospect of the American forces breaking out into Brittany and swinging east to the Seine, it was necessary, Monty felt, to consider the command angle. Eisenhower had declined to make Monty his Land Forces C-in-C and deputy as he had done with Alexander in the Mediterranean: he had merely given Monty temporary command of the Allied armies until such time as there would be two American armies operating in Normandy. At that juncture Bradley would be promoted to Army Group Commander, commanding the two American armies, while Monty would revert to command of the British and Canadian forces – the two Army Group Commanders being under Eisenhower's field command.

Plainly this would not be feasible, as Monty pointed out to Eisenhower. He had broached the subject with Bradley the day before issuing his 30 June directive, but Bradley would not commit himself on such a sensitive matter, and rumours soon began to fly in Bradley's camp 'that Montgomery now favors securing control of the British and American Armies as well as his Canadian buco [administration and supply] to lead an assault east to the Pas de Calais area in an effort to crack the defenses surrounding the pilotless aircraft sites and knock them out permanently. Political considerations are ob-

[1] *Memoirs*, op. cit. The dates have been corrected.

vious. . . . If the Amerk first army reverts to Monty's control after group comes ashore, it will violate all our original plans. We would continue with administration control while British would retain tactical control. Violates our principle of American command for American troops, a fundamental thesis of the general. . . .'[1] Such nationalistic fears were perhaps inevitable amongst young and patriotic aides, and Monty had quickly dropped the question until he could talk to Eisenhower. A few days after the conference with Eisenhower Monty reported the gist of the matter to Brooke:

SYSTEM OF COMMAND IN FRANCE
There is great pressure at SHAEF to get the U.S. Army Group in operation, commanding the two U.S. armies; the pressure comes chiefly from the younger element.

I am keeping right clear of all discussion on this subject.

But I have explained very clearly to Eisenhower that the direction and control of the land battle in France is a whole-time job for one man; the battle can very easily become untidy and the armies unbalanced; it takes me all my time to keep the battle swinging our way, to ensure that we retain the initiative, and to ensure there is no possibility of a set-back; we are up against a skilful and desperate enemy and we must not give him any opportunity to deal us a blow which might unsettle us.

I have then explained that if he forms a US Army Group, and SHAEF wants to take direct charge of the battle, he himself must come over here *and devote his whole and undivided attention to the battle*. Any idea that he could run the land battle from England, or could do it in his spare time, would be playing with fire.

Eisenhower himself has, I fancy, no delusions on the subject,

Monty considered. Eisenhower, in the wake of the ding-dong paper battles over 'Anvil' fought between Washington, London and the Mediterranean, certainly accepted that the time had not *yet* come for him to take field command:

He has now decided to form the U.S. Army Group, with Bradley in command, and to put it under me,

Monty informed Brooke therefore.

I will then command:
    First US Army Group.

[1] Diary of Chester B. Hansen, entry of 29.6.44, loc. cit. Hansen did not accompany Bradley to the meeting with Monty when the matter was discussed; he was merely reporting hearsay.

Second British Army.

First Canadian Army.

And I see no difficulty in this.

I do not think very much of Hodges who will take over First U.S. Army from Bradley. But I shall deal with Bradley; we know each other well now, and he is most co-operative.[1]

This was written on 7 July; but in the intervening few days the anti-British and anti-Monty pressure had been mounting at Eisenhower's headquarters – a rear headquarters far removed from the battlefield.

Eisenhower's naval aide and PR chief, Commander Butcher, for instance still did not know on 22 June which American Corps General Collins was commanding in the critical assault on Cherbourg; meanwhile, he confessed in his diary that, as a result of the V1 bombs, Supreme Headquarters was to be scattered to the four winds: 'Dispersal of Headquarters staff to the Advanced C.P. [at Portsmouth] and elsewhere, leaving only the absolute essential personnel at SHAEF headquarters is now seriously considered and probably will take place within a week. Our defensive measures against the flying bombs and attacks against the site have failed to stop the nuisance. . . . The total number of casualties [in Britain] for the week is about 500 dead and nearly 1500 seriously wounded . . . . there is considerable uneasiness approaching jitters.'[2] By 1 July the extra camp had been set up at Portsmouth, though Eisenhower himself was embarrassed by the undignified flight: 'Ike said that there was considerable reluctance amongst officers, both British and American, to leave Main Headquarters under conditions which must appear that we are running away from the flying bombs.'[3] The roof over the corridor between Eisenhower and his Chief of Staff's office had been sucked away by one bomb blast, and when Eisenhower arrived at Bradley's headquarters that night, Major Hansen recorded: 'Talked of the flying bombs on London. . . . They are a dreadful nuisance. Ike now living underground as is everyone else. . . . Will not win the war for the Germans but it will cause great political pressure to be brought upon the govt to clean them out.'[4]

[1] Bradley was both too modest and too good a soldier to take umbrage at this extension of Monty's time-limit as C-in-C Allied Ground Forces. 'Monty was in operational control of both army groups until September 1st, even though I took over [US] Army Group on August 1st. Ike had not yet moved headquarters over to France. Until SHAEF did come in I was to be under operational control of Monty. Ike did not want to handle campaign from so great a distance' – 'Bradley Commentaries', loc. cit.

[2] Diary of Harry C. Butcher, loc. cit.

[3] Ibid.

[4] Loc. cit.

Disturbed by the flying bombs, Eisenhower was glad to leave London and go to France. Apart from 'Anvil' he had been studying the plan to put Patton's Third Army straight into Brittany if one of the Brittany ports – St Malo, Brest, Nantes, Rennes 'or even Bordeaux' – could be seized: 'The whole point is that we must get planning fully coordinated, and drive ahead just as hard as we possibly can,' he wrote to Bedell Smith.[1]

Driving ahead as hard as possible was, as in the Mediterranean, becoming an obsession with Eisenhower, and when Monty's projected pincer attack on Caen was delayed by the bad weather Eisenhower became sulky and morose. 'Monty's attack started on Sunday morning, the 25th but so far we have had little concrete information about it,' Butcher recorded on 27 June. 'He waited so long that at least two additional Panzer divisions faced him.'[2] To Butcher, who had not even visited the front, this was a matter for contempt, but he took his cue too from the Supreme Commander who was 'considerably less exuberant these days. He didn't even seem to get a kick out of the fall of Cherbourg.'[3] In fact Eisenhower blamed Collins for accepting General von Schlieben's personal surrender instead of insisting first that von Schlieben order all Germans in the Fortress to surrender too. 'The pool correspondents have been in to see me and I told them that if I were writing a story on Ike's activity of the past two weeks I would emphasise his concern in the weather and the fact that he may be looking at one battle but he is thinking ahead weeks and months. . . . Just now he is concerned about slowness of Monty's attack, the build-up and Bradley's attack to the south.'[4] To Bradley Eisenhower wrote – imagining the American thrust was to start on schedule on Friday 30 June – 'I feel sure that a strong attack on your side will go with a bang once it gets started.'[5] Butcher, on his first visit to France on 1 July, found that 'some of the people I talked to venture that Monty has been too slow to attack and thus permitted the Germans to get set in fixed positions and to bring up reserves'[6] – so that Butcher, like Eisenhower, was chagrined to learn that Bradley too had been forced to delay his American offensive, and could only kick off on 3 July, and even more chagrined when Bradley's offensive failed to make the great 'gains' which he had anticipated. A vast posse of reporters and cameramen had been despatched to cover Eisenhower's stay in France – and no less than 'fifty photographers, newsreel men and reporters'[7] had

---

[1] Memo to Chief of Staff, SHAEF, 23.6.44, in Diary of Harry C. Butcher, loc. cit.
[2] Diary of Harry C. Butcher, loc. cit.
[3] Ibid.
[4] Ibid.
[5] *The Papers of Dwight David Eisenhower*, op. cit.
[6] Diary of Harry C. Butcher, loc. cit.
[7] Diary of Harry C. Butcher, entry of 7.7.44, loc. cit.

greeted Eisenhower when he made a short aeroplane flight with General Quesada – making later allegations that all would have been well if Monty had not been such a 'publicity hound' in Normandy seem ridiculously exaggerated.[1]

Bradley's slow progress and heavy casualties were a bitter blow to such onlookers who, since North Africa, had become used to measuring military success solely by gains in territory. Thus when Monty's directive of 30 June finally filtered through to Eisenhower's loyal aides, they were doubly vexed, not only because they failed to comprehend the military strategy at issue, but wanted a scapegoat for the lack of American 'gains'. 'First reports indicate satisfactory gains,' Butcher recorded on 4 July.

> Monty has issued another directive now saying it is his policy to 'contain' German armor around Caen on the left front of the beachhead so that the Americans on the right would not be bothered in taking Cherbourg. Now he wants Bradley to expend [sic] his holdings in the peninsula to give room for 'administration'. In Monty's previous directive he seemed to be all out to capture Caen which he still doesn't have. For purposes of illustration of nimbleness of mind I am incorporating this directive in the diary,[2]

Butcher noted insolently, for the diary was officially the Desk Diary of the Supreme Commander, and regularly checked by Eisenhower. By 7 July, however, British difficulties at Caen were being matched by American problems in the southern advance, despite a three-to-one superiority in infantry and eight-to-one in tanks. Tanks were, however, of limited value in the jungle-like *bocage* country, as General Collins, commanding 7 US Corps, later recalled:

> The bocage was not a surprise, but it was tougher than we first anticipated. You see none of the – I had combat experience in the South Pacific, fighting through jungle country – real jungle country. Now the bocage was tough, but it was not real jungle. But the problems were essentially the same.
>
> I was the only senior commander that had had that experience in fighting against the Japs out in the jungle. And I don't think any of the Britishers that were in Normandy had had much experience in jungle country either so that the difficulties of – particularly of moving tanks over bocage-type country were unknown. Neither we nor the British were familiar with what real obstacles these growths of trees and dividing lines between small bits of property

[1] Leonard Mosley, *Marshall*, London 1982.
[2] Loc. cit.

in France were – they were real obstacles! They gave wonderful cover and frequently they were double. In other words there was one row of trees between one piece of property marking the boundary, then a little space, and then another row of trees immediately back of them, but with a space in between which could be used just like a communications trench, and also as a place to put mortars. And very difficult to determine which one of these combinations held the mortars – which were very effective, those German mortars.[1]

Collins could remember no restrictions on casualties such as that which, understandably, made the British more cautious – 'I can readily see how the British commanders were more cautious – after all, Britain had been in the war for two or three years before we were even in it, and you had all taken very heavy casualties in North Africa and other places, whereas our casualties were relatively light.'[2] Nevertheless, even without such a restriction, the fighting in the bocage was a gallingly slow process for the fiery Collins. 'We began attacking southward with the VIII Corps on the 3rd [July] and the VII Corps joined in with one division on July 4th,' Eisenhower informed Marshall. 'I was particularly anxious to visit these Corps and their Divisions during actual operations. The going is extremely tough, with three main causes responsible. The first of these, as always, is the fighting quality of the German soldier. The second is the nature of the country. Our whole attack has to fight its way out of very narrow bottlenecks flanked by marshes and against an enemy who had a double hedgerow and an intervening ditch almost every fifty yards as ready made strongpoints. The third cause is the weather. . . .'[3]

Neither Monty nor Bradley had expected rapid progress in the First Army offensive; both were confident that they were working to a carefully conceived strategy that would bring eventual victory as long as the commanders and the troops kept their nerve. There is evidence, sadly, that Eisenhower did not – and now blamed the British for Bradley's lack of 'gains':

Monty's confident and eloquent directives which are embodied in the diary,

Butcher remarked with sarcasm,

and which first called for an all-out slash on the British front to take Caen and in the second said that this was merely a holding

[1] General J. L. Collins, interview of 21.10.81.
[2] Ibid.
[3] *The Papers of Dwight David Eisenhower*, op. cit.

operation to contain the German army while Americans took Cherbourg and resumed their push southward has left me at least, cold.

Nor was Butcher merely speaking for himself.

Ike has been smouldering and today burst out with a letter to Monty which in effect tells him to get busy to avoid having our forces sealed into the bridgehead, take the offensive and Ike would support him in every way, as if it were necessary. Actually Monty is following his characteristic, which is super-cautiousness.[1]

Eisenhower should not be damned for the crass stupidity of his naval and PR aide, and the letter he wrote to Monty was far more comprehending and profound than ever the Butchers of this world could understand. Yet at a SHAEF headquarters which had dispersed in order to escape the V1 attacks, it did reflect the frustration of those officers anxious to go to France, and imbued with the same fear that had alarmed rear headquarter staffs and overseas onlookers at the height of the battle of Alamein: the fear of stalemate.

[1] Diary of Harry C. Butcher, loc. cit.

CHAPTER TEN

'What is Vital and What is Not'

To be sure, Eisenhower was not alone in his 'smouldering' disposition; nor would it be true to claim that all was as well in Normandy as Monty wished his superiors to believe. However satisfactorily Second Army had performed Monty's flypaper role on the left flank of the Allied lodgement area, the fact remained that despite its superiority in tank numbers,[1] the British sector had failed to expand, causing administrative congestion and leading to a lowering of morale in some divisions. Rommel's Panzer counter-thrust was successfully repulsed around Rauray in the Odon salient,[2] but by 3/4 July Intelligence began to point to the relief of some of the German Panzer divisions by infantry – an ominous sign. The Canadian attack on Carpiquet airfield failed ('the operation was not well handled,' Dempsey noted in his diary[3]), and a mood of recrimination, which had been latent for some time, set in. Already on 25 June Monty had had to close down the extensive network of officers at Corps and Divisional level who had been instructed to send in 'Immediate Reports' about the battle, with their views on operations, equipment, and so on. 'I have had to stamp very heavily on reports that began to be circulated about the inadequate quality of our tanks, equipment, etc., as compared with the Germans. . . . I enclose a copy of the letter I have sent out on the subject of alarmist reports,' he wrote to Brooke.[4] 'At this early stage such reports can be of little value,' Monty explained in his directive; 'they are bound to be influenced by local conditions, and are unlikely to be the carefully considered views of those whose opinions are of real value.

'In cases where adverse comment is made on British equipment such reports are likely to cause a lowering of morale, and a lack of confidence among the troops,' he warned.

[1] 21st Army Group Headquarters calculated that, overall, Dempsey's Second Army had a superiority of two-to-one in infantry (not sufficient for offensive success), but four-to-one in tanks – 'Review of the situation at D + 30', loc. cit.

[2] '9 SS Pz Div and, to a lesser extent, 10 SS Pz Div attacked throughout the day. By nightfall, however, our line was intact and the enemy had suffered a considerable defeat' – Diary of M. C. Dempsey, entry of 1.7.44, loc. cit.

[3] Loc. cit.

[4] Letter of 27.6.44, copy in Montgomery Papers.

'It will generally be found that when the equipment at our disposal is used properly, and the tactics are good, we have no difficulty in defeating the Germans.

'I have therefore decided that GSO 1's Liaison will write no more reports for the present. You will issue orders at once that further reports are forbidden,' he instructed Dempsey, 'until I give permission.

'At a time like this,' he added, 'with large forces employed with great issues at stake, we must be very careful that morale and confidence are maintained at the highest level. Alarmist reports, written by officers with no responsibility and little battle experience, could do a great deal of harm.'[1]

But if Monty thought that such a directive, which went also to General Crerar who was soon to command First Canadian Army, would keep the lid on the simmering pot, he was mistaken. Success, as General Wimberley later observed,[2] was at the very heart of Monty's leadership, and since the heady first days when the British and Canadian forces stormed ashore in Normandy, there had not been sufficient success to preserve morale at its peak. The battle, after all, had raged for a month; casualties, particularly from artillery shelling and mortars, were steadily rising and the phrase 'we are holding the ring while the Americans expand their sector' began to sound hollow when repeated day after day, week after week. When the Canadians failed to take Carpiquet on 4 July Monty could not avoid friction. It came in the form of a letter from the 1 Corps Commander, General Crocker, to General Dempsey, who passed it on to Monty. If it is singled out here it is not because it was unique, but because the story of the Canadian 3rd Division was in fact the story of the British Second Army in the thankless role to which it had been committed:

The Div. as a whole carried out its D-Day tasks with great enthusiasm and considerable success,

Crocker acknowledged.

Once the excitement of the initial phase passed, however, the Div lapsed into a very nervy state. . . . Exaggerated reports of enemy activity and of their own difficulties were rife; everyone was far too quick on the trigger, and a general attitude of despondency prevailed. Everyone was naturally tired and a bit shaken by the first impact of real war and there was a quite understandable reaction after the pent-up excitement of the assault. It was just here and

[1] 'C-in-C's Directives' file, Montgomery Papers.
[2] Letter to author.

now that the steadying hand of the Commander was required. It was totally lacking, indeed the state of the Div was a reflection of the state of its Commander. He was obviously not standing up to the strain and showed signs of fatigue and nervousness (one might almost say fright) which were patent for all to see.

Although it had subsequently regained a little 'poise', the offensive operation at Carpiquet had once more revealed the rot:

In this last Day or two 3 Cdn Div has started active operations again. . . . The limited success of this operation I am afraid can only attribute to a lack of control and leadership from the top. When things started to go not quite right all the signs of lack of calm, balanced judgement and firm command became evident again.[1]

Dempsey, in his covering letter to Monty, 'entirely agreed'[2] with Crocker's criticisms, and recommended the removal of the Division's Commander. Monty passed the two letters on to Crerar, saying 'I have little to add to these letters. I definitely agree with them.' The Commander 'has certain qualities which are assets,' Monty acknowledged. 'But taken all round I consider he is not good enough to command a Canadian division; the Canadian soldier is such a magnificent chap that he deserves, and should be given, really good generals.'

The Canadians may have felt that their division was being made a scapegoat, but other performances like that of the veteran 51st Highland Division, also came under Monty's withering scrutiny. Monty had himself decided to replace the beloved commander, General Wimberley, who had led the recreated formation from Alamein to the end in Sicily, by one of Monty's protégés from the days of 1939–1941, Charles Bullen-Smith, a hugely built Lowland Scot. A week after the reports on 3rd Canadian Division Monty was signalling secretly to Brooke:

Regret to report that it is the considered opinion of CROCKER DEMPSEY and myself that 51 Div is at present NOT repeat NOT battleworthy. It does not fight with determination and has failed in every operation it has been given to do. It cannot fight the Germans successfully. I consider the Divisional Commander is to blame and I am removing him from command. BULLEN-SMITH has many fine qualities but he has failed to lead the Highland

[1] 'Correspondence on M.S. Appointments etc.' file, Montgomery Papers.
[2] Ibid., 8.7.44.

Division and I cannot therefore recommend him to command any other Division. . . .[1]

It is understandable how, in his impatience to see the Allied armies on the move, Eisenhower dreaded the notion of stalemate. 'I am familiar with your plan for generally holding firm with your left, attracting thereto all of the enemy armor, while your right pushes down the Peninsula and threatens the rear and flank of the forces facing the Second British Army,' he wrote on 7 July, after news of Bradley's slow progress, the failure at Carpiquet and the new Intelligence regarding the relief of Rommel's Panzer divisions. 'However the [American] advance on the right has been slow and laborious, due not only to the nature of the country and the impossibility of employing air and artillery with maximum effectiveness, but to the arrival on that front of reinforcements, I believe the 353rd Div. In the meantime, I understand from G-2 [Intelligence] that some infantry has arrived on the front opposite the British Army allowing the enemy to withdraw certain Panzer elements for re-grouping and establishing of a reserve.

'It appears to me that we must use all possible energy in a determined effort to prevent a stalemate or of facing the necessity of fighting a major defensive battle with the slight depth we now have in the bridgehead.'[2]

Eisenhower's letter amounted to a plea to Monty to drop his Normandy strategy, which Eisenhower, with superficial justice, felt was not working. Moreover any hope that Bradley's thrust could be accelerated by using the Allied airborne divisions was now dashed by Eisenhower's decision on 'Anvil'. 'Because of the transfers that we have to make to the Mediterranean to help out in ANVIL, I think we cannot put on a full-scale three or four division [airborne] attack before early September.' Eisenhower's answer was either to overrule the planners and mount an amphibious operation at St Malo (with all the attendant risks of another Anzio), or for Monty to try to break out in the east:

We have not yet attempted a major full-dress attack on the left flank supported by everything we could bring to bear. To do so would require some good weather, so that our air could give maximum assistance. . . .[3]

By the time Monty received Eisenhower's letter the next day, Dempsey was in the outskirts of Caen. Eisenhower's fear of stale-

[1] Ibid., 15.7.44.
[2] *The Papers of Dwight David Eisenhower*, op. cit.
[3] Ibid.

mate Monty accepted as a legitimate anxiety; Eisenhower's proposal that Monty abandon his Normandy strategy by attempting to break out in the east did not, however, impress him. The day before he had written confidently but with soldierly realism to Brooke, saying, 'I am working quietly on the general plan contained in my Directive M505 dated 30 June. We must keep the initiative and not let the enemy "dig in".

'The American offensive on my western flank is gathering momentum slowly. When it began on 3 July,' he remarked with sympathy, 'the weather was too awful; driving rain, mist, low cloud, no visibility; and since then we have had fine periods only, and no continued spell of good weather. The country over that side is most difficult,' he acknowledged; 'it is very thick and approximates to jungle fighting. However the Americans are gaining ground gradually, and will shortly go much quicker I think. At the time of writing this they have got past LA HAYE DU PUITS, and are pushing on southwards.

'In order to help the *western* flank I am going to set things alight on my *eastern* flank, beginning tomorrow,' Monty explained; 'the enemy is very sensitive to thrusts eastwards in the CAEN sector, and I shall make use of that fact.'

By 10 July Monty hoped to have Caen, or 'that part of CAEN which lies north of the river, and I think it might be got by Monday [10 July]'. Thereafter he would mount operations 'to get that part of CAEN which lies south of the ORNE, and to organise operations to push S.E. on that axis'. As this further south-eastern arm was pushed out from Caen, the gap between it and Caumont would be filled by simultaneous attacks up the Orne. In this way he hoped at last to get the airfield area he had originally promised Leigh-Mallory; though his primary task was still, as he reminded Brooke, to 'draw attention away from my western flank'. By pushing an 'armoured force out into the good going to the S.E. of the town' he was confident he could once again magnetise the German Panzer divisions, as well as giving the British lodgement area greater security in the event of a German counter-offensive employing all eight Panzer formations: 'Also, we cannot be 100% happy on the eastern flank until we have got CAEN. We have pulled such weight of enemy on to our eastern flank that I want to be 100% happy there!!' he added.

That Monty refused to share the doubts and fears of Eisenhower and others is evidenced both by his staff and by his letters and signals of this period. On 7 July he wrote also to Phyllis Reynolds, without trace of impatience. As in Sicily and Italy he had armed himself against the strains and stresses of an extended battle by reviving a small menagerie:

My dear Phyllis,
    All goes well here – except the weather which is completely

foul; it seems to be quite impossible to get a whole fine day –
actually today *has* been fine. I have been collecting livestock.
I now have 6 canaries, 1 love bird, 2 dogs.
The dogs are puppies, about 10 weeks old. One is a fox terrier,
given me by the BBC men in France; I have named him Hitler. The
other is a golden cocker spaniel, brought back by Col Dawnay –
who bought it from some girl in a girl's school!! I have named him
Rommel – as his coat is the colour of golden sand from the desert.
Hitler and Rommel both get beaten when necessary,

he remarked with irony;

they are both 'coming to heel' well.
They are delightful dogs and when this war is over I shall bring
them back to England – doing the 6 months quarantine.

Monty's vanity was not to everyone's liking, neither his gifts of
signed photographs of himself, nor his strangely cruel humour that
delighted in embarrassing or even humiliating those not in a position
to answer back. When Bradley stayed for tea at Monty's Tac Headquarters on 30 June Monty had asked Bradley's aide (knowing quite
well the answer) what his insignia denoted. When Hansen replied
that he was a major, Monty taunted Bradley:

I say now, do you have a major for an ADC? Simply a dog's body,
you know, a whipping boy. I would not have an ADC who is more
than a captain.[1]

Bradley chewed on this a moment, then asked in that case why
Monty seemed surrounded by so many Lt-Colonels – his PA, MA,
his 'personal cabinet. . . .'
Those like Bradley who could meet such humour were not
offended, but the young Hansen (who would later help ghost
Bradley's memoirs) was. 'Monty is beginning to believe in the Monty
legend, that he is a great man of history, fully convincing himself of
his godlike role,' he remarked sourly in his diary.
Malicious though Monty could be – a carry-over from his bullying
manner as a schoolboy and cadet – it was not intended to be more
than conversational, provocative jest: to coax Hansen into standing
up for himself, as Monty's own ADCs did. However much he might
taunt or provoke them, they knew his devotion to them was paternal
and inviolate. Their loyalty to him and their acceptance of his quirky,
schoolmasterly character he rewarded with both affection and, at
times, fierce protectiveness. Thus when Colonel Russell, the senior

---

[1] Diary of Chester B. Hansen, loc. cit.

officer in charge of Tactical Headquarters, arrested two of the seven Tac HQ Liaison Officers for 'looting' a pig and then complained directly to the War Office, Monty had the hapless colonel flown straight back to England. He, Monty, might taunt his personal staff in public or insult their pride, but woe betide anyone else who attempted to do so.

This 'family' loyalty – all the more strange considering his negative attitude towards the members of his real family or relatives – harked back to desert days, as did his decision to call the gold-haired puppy 'Rommel' – for there, in the nomadic tent and caravan existence of North Africa, a new Monty had been born. Side by side with growing vanity as his name became household and his mailbag required first one, then two, and finally three ADCs to help, there had developed the 'Monty "team" '. No longer was he the austere, faintly ridiculous, eccentric general, the lonely widower with revenge – first for his wife Betty's death, then for Dunkirk – written across his heart. The baggy corduroy trousers, the simple grey sweater with the single medal ribbon of the American Legion of Merit, and the well-worn black beret were symptomatic of an outsider who had made his way at last inside. If he was not the barking 'driver' of men that Patton certainly was, it was because he did not despise the men who were fighting for him, something which, as long as Patton's paranoid ambition remained unsatisfied, could not be said for the Pasadena cavalryman. Monty's mushrooming fame had been predicated on the courage of troops who fought and died in his campaigns – a bravery, often on the part of 'civilian' soldiers, that Monty did not take for granted. And, because command of Eighth Army had restored in Monty a sense of 'belonging', Eighth Army had become 'his' army in the way that perhaps no other army in English history has been personalised by its commander. When Phyllis Reynolds wrote to tell him that a boy named Blake had won the 'Montgomery Cup' at Amesbury School, Monty replied: 'Congratulate Blake from me . . . I am only sorry I could not present it in person, and as I could not I would like to give him the enclosed photograph. Please give it to Blake from me; he is a jolly good lad, whose father was killed while serving under me.'[1]

'Serving under Monty' – now that Monty held command of the Allied Armies in Normandy even American troops and officers used the phrase. Even the fiery Collins[2] and the proud, patriotic Ridgway[3] recognised the gift of leadership and haunting professionalism that lay behind the popular, boastful image of the man. Aides like Hansen were irritated by the very mention of Monty's command

---

[1] Letter of 7.7.44, Montgomery Papers.
[2] Interview of 21.10.81.
[3] Letter to author of October 1981.

over American battle troops ('Letters from Monty and Dempsey both congratulating Bradley on the job he did [in taking Cherbourg]. Monty uses phrase "I am proud to have them in my command" and Bill Sylvan [ADC to General Hodges] objects violently to the obvious statement which he thinks unnecessary,' Hansen recorded on 27 June[1]); but the commanders and troops themselves were, for the most part, profoundly impressed by the generalship he displayed.

When Eisenhower's anxious letter arrived on 8 July 1944, therefore, Monty was in no mood to discard the whole strategy on which his Normandy battle was being fought. Bulling ahead on all fronts in the hope that the enemy would crack somewhere had proved the most expensive military theory in history when applied on the Western Front in the First World War. Eisenhower's 'major full dress attack on the left flank' may well have reminded him of the fatuous slaughter on the Somme, in which Monty had participated. Whatever the political pressures for a swift advance towards the Pas de Calais area in order to capture the V1 rocket launching sites, Monty was certain there was no way through the German defences on the eastern flank; and that, however painfully slow, it was the strategy of swinging Bradley to the south that would ultimately defeat the German armies opposing the Allied bridgehead in Normandy. He therefore sat down and wrote as calm a rebuff as he could:

My dear Ike,
    Thank you for your letter of 7 July.
    I am, myself, quite happy with the situation. I have been working throughout on a very definite plan, and I now begin to see daylight. . . . I think we must be quite clear as to what is vital and what is not; if we get our sense of values wrong we may go astray,

he warned. There was no question of the British breaking out eastwards; what was wanted was that the Americans should break out from the back of the scrum and overwhelm as much of the enemy's field as possible. Brittany was the next objective after the fall of Cherbourg; and despite the bad weather and appalling terrain, Bradley would get there. To help him, Monty had decided to 'set my eastern flank alight, and to put the wind up the enemy by seizing CAEN and getting bridgeheads over the ORNE; this action would, indirectly, help the business going on over on the western flank. These operations by Second Army on the eastern flank began today; they are going very well; they aim at securing CAEN and at getting our eastern flank on the ORNE river – with bridgeheads over it.' However successful Dempsey might or might not be, there was no question of a British break-out to the east; his job was to help

[1] Loc. cit.

706

Bradley's army, not to gain glory, and it could best do this by establishing the shield, running southwards from Caen, that could help protect Bradley's southward thrust from German flank attack; Dempsey would be ordered either to drive south up the banks of the Orne, or towards Falaise, as originally conceived in the St Paul's plans. If this proved impossible against fierce Panzer resistance, 'it may be best for Second Army to take over all the CAUMONT area – and to the west of it – and thus release some of Bradley's divisions for the southward 'drive' on the western flank. Day to day events in the next few days will show which is best.'

Whatever happened, Monty was certain, it was silly to imagine that the battle was more than beginning; he did not expect Bradley's 8 US Corps to reach the Brittany coast at Avranches for another four weeks: 'sometime about the first week in August, when I hope 8 U.S. Corps will have turned the corner and be heading for [the Brittany ports] RENNES and ST MALO.' He therefore declined Eisenhower's offer of American armour on the British flank:

I do not need an American armoured division for use on my eastern flank; we really have all the armour we need. The great thing now is to get First and Third U.S. Armies up to a good strength, and to get them cracking on the southward thrust on the western flank, and then turn Patton westwards into the Brittany peninsula.

To sum up.

I think the battle is going very well.

Later that evening, as British and Canadian troops fought in the outskirts of Caen, Monty informed Brooke that he would opt not for Falaise, but for a shield running from the Orne at Thury Harcourt back to the American sector at Caumont: 'Have decided on this line of advance for Second Army as being the best way to help First US Army forward.'[1]

With almost a million troops ashore in Normandy in a bare month, Monty had cause to be satisfied; even Stalin had said to Averell Harriman that the crossing of the Channel and landings in Normandy were ' "an unheard of achievement", the magnitude of which has never been undertaken in military history' and spoke of 'the remarkable achievement of landing so many men so rapidly, etc.'[2]

Eisenhower, however, was still dubious. When he met Churchill on 9 July Monty's letter of 8 July had still not arrived. 'He [Churchill] had lots of questions,' Eisenhower reported, 'most of which I answered by saying we were going to the offensive all along the line

---

[1] M45, 2215 hours, 8.7.44, Montgomery Papers.
[2] Letter of 24.6.44, in Diary of Harry C. Butcher, entry of 8.7.44, loc. cit.

and would gain room and kill Germans. I didn't have your letter at the time. . . .'[1]

This travesty of Monty's intentions was unfortunate, and would be the main reason why both Brooke and Monty lost confidence in Eisenhower as a field general. Though he affected to understand tactical strategy when it was outlined to him, Eisenhower quickly forgot its framework when beset, as Supreme Commander, by the myriad problems – administrative, political and personal – of his office. In this he was very similar to Churchill, and both men, despite the endless briefings and military appreciations, clung to obsessive notions of military progress. Although, in thanking Monty for his letter and signal of 8 and 9 July, Eisenhower was grateful 'for the clear exposition of your ideas which I am bound to say seem to me perfectly sound and practicable', he burned with impatience to announce and applaud tangible victory. 'As soon as I get confirmed information that CAEN is definitely ours, I want to send you a message for Dempsey and his army,' he added in a postscript[2] – just as Churchill was doing. By the evening of 8 July the city of Caen, save for the southern suburb of Vaucelles, was in British and Canadian hands, and both Eisenhower and Churchill were free to send their telegrams. But at his headquarters at Bray, Monty was not concerned with capture celebrations (the battle for Caen had been bloody and, like the earlier towns 'liberated' by the Americans, more reminiscent of Ypres in the First World War than the popular image of liberation) but rather with the overall unfolding of his strategy. He therefore assembled all four Army Commanders, Bradley, Dempsey, Crerar and Patton, and reiterated 'what is vital and what is not'. Patton, who had landed in France on 6 July and lunched with Montgomery on the 7th, could barely contain his impatience to get fighting, and was little interested in the mechanics of victory à la Monty. 'Montgomery went to great length explaining why the British had done nothing,' he recorded obtusely in his diary on 7 July;[3] moreover he hated the idea of waiting until August before smashing into Brittany with his Third Army, and saw Monty's concern not to make Third Army operational until the First US Army reached the Brittany corner at Avranches as an insult. Yet even Patton, for all his pathological distrust of Monty, could not fail to be excited by the grander aspect of Monty's Normandy strategy, and his own role as Third Army Commander. As soon as the green light was given by Montgomery he was to send one corps of three divisions to clean up the Brest Peninsula and gain the 'administrative' space the Allies would need for a thrust into Germany; meanwhile with the remaining ten

[1] *The Papers of Dwight David Eisenhower*, op. cit.
[2] Op. cit.
[3] *The Patton Papers*, op. cit.

divisions of Third Army he was to wheel eastwards on the outer (R. Loire) flank of Bradley's Army Group and help roll up the German armies facing Dempsey's Second Army. 'When I do start, I will, if current plans hold, have a swell chance,' he reported to his wife on 8 July.[1]

At his conference on 10 July Monty shielded both Bradley and Dempsey from the Supreme Commander's impatience. As Dempsey recalled, 'the American break-out attack was launched on 3rd July, but made small and slow progress, contrary to expectation. At a conference in Monty's caravan on 10 July Bradley frankly said that he had failed in this effort to break-out.'

Monty was, as Dempsey related, singularly understanding:

Monty quietly replied: 'Never mind. Take all the time you need, Brad.' Then he went on tactfully to say: 'If I were you I think I should concentrate my forces a little more' – putting two fingers together on the map in his characteristic way.

Then Monty turned to me and said: 'Go on hitting: drawing the German strength, especially some of the armour, onto yourself – so as to ease the way for Brad.'[2]

After the conference Dempsey even offered, in private, to mount the break-out on the eastern flank if Bradley's thrust remained blunted – 'but Monty did not favour such a change of aim,' Dempsey remarked. In his new M510 Directive to the four army commanders Monty summarised the position now that Caen had fallen. 'My broad policy remains unchanged. It is to draw the main enemy forces in the battle on our eastern flank, and to fight them there, so that our affairs on the western flank may proceed the easier,' he began. Copies of this directive (M510) would go not only to the four Allied Army commanders but also to Eisenhower, de Guingand, Leigh-Mallory, Coningham, Brooke, Simpson and General Graham, responsible for administration in Normandy; he wanted no misunderstanding, and was prepared to repeat his strategy *ad nauseam* rather than risk confusion in the higher echelons of Allied command – confusion that could so quickly spread to lower levels in the weeks of hard fighting still ahead. Bradley's news of his southern thrust was, however, disappointing, and in order to help him, Monty accepted that Second Army must not allow Rommel to withdraw further Panzer divisions from the British front:

The enemy has been able to bring reinforcements to oppose the advance of the First Army. It is important to speed up our advance

[1] Ibid.
[2] Notes of 18.3.52, in Dempsey file, Liddell Hart Correspondence, Liddell Hart Centre for Military Archives, King's College, London.

on the western flank; the operations of the Second Army must therefore be so staged that they will have a direct influence on the operations of First Army, as well as holding enemy forces on the eastern flank.

To achieve this, Dempsey was to withdraw his armour from the battle, grouping it into a Corps of three armoured divisions; meanwhile he was to push infantry southwards towards Thury Harcourt and Le Bény Bocage, securing bridgeheads across the Orne. Rommel would not be able to ignore the threat of a British armoured breakout employing the massed tanks of three British armoured divisions: he would thus be forced into a do-or-die defence of the sector. Meanwhile, pivoting behind Dempsey's southward thrust to Le Bény Bocage, Bradley would continue to drive south to break out of the bocage; once through, 8 US Corps would turn into Brittany while the remaining American forces were to wheel eastwards:

Plans will be made to direct a strong right wing in a wide sweep, south of the bocage country towards successive objectives as follows:
   a) LAVAL–MAYENNE
   b) LE MANS–ALENCON.

In the following days Dempsey duly drew up his plans for Second Army's role in the scheme, with 17 July fixed as the target date for the start of the operation, code-named 'Goodwood'.

The primary consideration in the 'Goodwood' plan was necessity of hitting hard; attracting the enemy's armour to the eastern flank; and wearing down his strength there – so as to weaken his capacity to resist a renewed break-out effort on the western flank,

Dempsey later recalled.

But another consideration was the need to expand the bridgehead, which was becoming overcrowded as reinforcements and supplies were pouring in all the time. To gain more room it was necessary to capture [the rest of] Caen, which blocked our expansion and was an awkward wedge in our flank. Its capture would loosen the enemy's hinge, and provide us with a firm hinge. . . . There was also an increasing need for new airfields, and the best area for these was around Caen – particularly on the Bourguébus plateau. To gain that airfield area had been a feature of our planning before D-day.[1]

---

[1] Ibid.

710

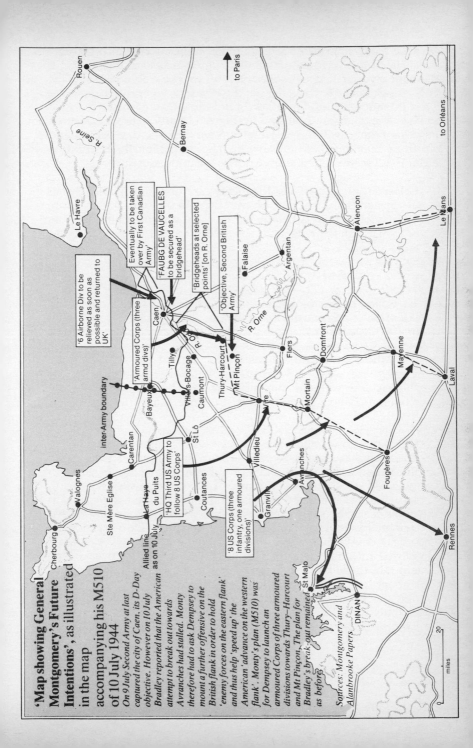

'Map showing General Montgomery's Future Intentions', as illustrated in the map accompanying his M510 of 10 July 1944

On 9 July Second Army at last captured the city of Caen, its D-Day objective. However on 10 July Bradley reported that the American attempt to break out towards Avranches had stalled. Monty therefore had to ask Dempsey to mount a further offensive on the British flank in order to hold 'enemy forces on the eastern flank' and thus help 'speed up' the American 'advance on the western flank'. Monty's plan (M510) was for Dempsey to launch an armoured Corps of three armoured divisions towards Thury–Harcourt and Mt Pinçon. The plan for Bradley's break-out remained as before

Sources: Montgomery and Alanbrooke Papers

to Paris

Rouen

R. Seine

Le Havre

Bernay

to Orléans

Le Mans

Alençon

'Eventually to be taken over by First Canadian Army'

'FAUBG DE VAUCELLES to be secured as a bridgehead'

Falaise

Argentan

'Bridgeheads at selected points' [on R. Orne]

'6 Airborne Div to be relieved as soon as possible and returned to UK'

Caen

'Objective, Second British Army'

R. Orne

'Armoured Corps (three armd divs)'

R. O——

Tilly

Thury–Harcourt

Mt Pinçon

Flers

Domfront

Mayenne

Bayeux

Villers-Bocage

Caumont

inter-Army boundary

St Lô

——e

Mortain

Laval

Allied line as on 10 July

Carentan

Villedieu

Fougères

Ste Mère Eglise

Valognes

La Haye du Puits

Coutances

Avranches

Granville

Rennes

'HQ Third US Army to follow 8 US Corps'

Cherbourg

'8 US Corps (three infantry, one armoured divisions)'

St Malo

DINAN

20

miles

Aware that this British offensive might not only convince Rommel that the British were about to break out towards Paris but Churchill too, Monty signalled to Brooke on 12 July that he would send over his MA, Lt-Colonel Dawnay, to brief the War Office in private about the real intention behind the attack.[1] On 14 July Dawnay duly reported to General Simpson, bearing a letter from Monty to Brooke, written after another meeting of Army Commanders the day before, and with instructions that he, Dawnay, should personally ensure that Monty's 'Goodwood' offensive not be misunderstood:

General Montgomery has to be very careful as to what he does in his Eastern flank because on that flank is the only British Army there is left in this part of the world. On the security and firmness of the Eastern flank depends the security of the whole lodgement area,

Dawnay emphasised.

Therefore, having broken out in country S.E. of CAEN, he has no intention of rushing madly Eastwards, and getting Second Army on the Eastern flank so extended that that flank might cease to be secure.
  All the activities on the Eastern flank are designed to help the force in the West, while ensuring that a firm bastion is kept in the East. At the same time all is ready to take advantage of any situation which gives reason to think that the enemy is disintegrating.[2]

Dawnay's explanation, on top of Monty's seven-page letter to Brooke, was as clear as crystal. Rarely in military annals can a commander, engaged in a decisive battle being fought over an anticipated period of three months, have gone to such lengths to ensure that his superiors, political and military, were kept 'fully in the picture'. In his diary even Commander Butcher was now excited by the prospects: 'I have gotten started inserting in the diary Monty's epistles to his Commanders,' he had noted on 11 July. 'Perhaps it is because I am attracted by the simplicity of Monty's directives. In any event I think the large-scale operations in which our ground troops are about to engage – operations which may be spectacularly deci-sive – should be backgrounded by at least this order from Monty dated July 10th.'
To support Dempsey's Second Army attack Monty had personally

[1] M50, 2140 hours, 12.7.44, Montgomery Papers.
[2] 'Notes given verbally by Lt-Col Dawnay to DMO on 14 July' – Simpson Papers; copy deposited with Montgomery Papers by General Sir Frank Simpson.

requested Eisenhower to put pressure on Air Marshal Harris to provide heavy bomber assistance.[1] This Eisenhower did, but in order to 'sell the target' Eisenhower seems, in his enthusiasm, to have forgotten the underlying strategy yet again. Thus on 14 July, as Dawnay relentlessly reiterated Monty's real purpose, Eisenhower was signalling to Monty: 'All senior airmen are in full accord because this operation will be a brilliant stroke which will knock loose our present shackles. Every plane available will be ready for such a purpose.'[2] To Bedell Smith Eisenhower had remarked that if Bomber Command could saturate an area 'half a mile in diameter . . . at night, the infantry in a quick attack could then practically walk through'.[3]

To disabuse Eisenhower of any ideas that 'decisiveness' meant a British break-out from the eastern sector, Monty sent de Guingand to brief Eisenhower personally on 14 July, in the same way as Dawnay was doing at the War Office. The 'plan if successful promises to be decisive,' Monty signalled Eisenhower, but it would be decisive in that it would write off the German ability to marshal Panzers and reserves and stop Bradley's southern sweep. 'The real object is to muck up and write off enemy troops,' Dawnay explained; in mounting Dempsey's attack Monty was 'aiming at doing the greatest damage to enemy armour'. Far from bursting out eastwards, however, 'if the proposed plan can be completed, next moves would be *westwards* in order to ring round and eliminate troops in the VILLERS BOCAGE–EVRECY area', thus smashing Rommel's ability to hit Bradley's flank. Far from trying to shift the field of battle further east, Monty wanted to win it where the Allies were strongest, with the enemy retained as far as possible from his supply, reserves and air support – in Normandy. 'It does not matter much whether enemy troops are eliminated in NORMANDY or near PARIS. NORMANDY is better,' Dawnay made clear. Certainly there was no prospect of a British advance directly eastwards, either to take the Le Havre and Rouen ports or to make for the Pas de Calais rocket sites:

General Montgomery does not think the capture of HAVRE and ROUEN will be so easy as was originally thought [before D-Day]. His present idea is that the Germans will do all they can to prevent

[1] 'Grateful if you will issue orders that the whole weight of the air power is to be available . . . to support my land battle' – M49, 12.7.44, Montgomery Papers.

[2] *The Papers of Dwight David Eisenhower*, op. cit. Dempsey later cautioned the American Official Historian, Dr Pogue: 'Do not be misled by Coningham. . . . It is as well to know the air people were almost guilty of disloyalty. One reason why there has been a misunderstanding concerning our intentions at Caen stems from the fact that in order to get proper air support for the attack, de Guingand had to exaggerate the importance of the attack' – Pogue interview, loc. cit.

[3] Diary of Harry C. Butcher, loc. cit.

him from crossing the SEINE and getting up to the PAS DE CALAIS area, because they rely on the latter area for flying bomb and/or rocket activities against ENGLAND. They will want to keep these activities going until the last day of the war in order to hope for better terms. General Montgomery therefore thinks that the decisive battles in the West may be fought South of the SEINE and that HAVRE and ROUEN may not be captured before the war is over. If this view is correct, it would have certain repercussions on his administrative lay-out and plans. He would therefore be very glad to know the War Office view on the subject.[1]

It was partly for this reason that Brittany seemed such an important 'administrative' prize to Monty. Cherbourg was still uncleared for the unloading of ships, and once the early autumn gales began, beach supply would be unreliable. The port of Cherbourg should therefore become a British supply port, he felt, while the Brittany ports supplied the Americans. If his armour could get out south of Caen on the Caen-Falaise road, he could do the utmost destruction, 'and the air would have an absolute field day,' he wrote to Brooke: a terrific blow 'designed to "write off" and eliminate the bulk of his [the enemy's] holding troops'; meanwhile he hoped that Bradley, taking immediate advantage of this, would launch his own, American blow.

The First [US] Army has been battling its way since 3 July through very difficult country, thickly wooded and very marshy, and with canalised avenues of approach to enemy positions. The Americans have had very heavy casualties; but they have stuck it well and have killed a great many Germans, and have severely mauled the enemy divisions facing them. The First Army is nearly through this country. Once it can get a footing on the road PERIERS–ST LO, it will be able to launch a real 'blitz' attack with fresh troops. This attack would break in on a narrow front with great air support, and fresh divisions would pass through the gap. I have discussed the problem with Bradley and this operation will be launched on 19 or 20 July.

With first Dempsey frightening the life out of the Germans south of Caen, then Bradley smashing out of the bocage to Avranches, the enemy would be unable, Monty felt, to 'collect more troops to rope us off again *in the west* [opposite Bradley], and it is in the west that I want territory, i.e. I want Brittany.'

The layout and plans for the two attacks were then described to Brooke, as de Guingand was describing them to Eisenhower. 'I shall

---

[1] 'Notes given verbally by Lt-Col Dawnay', loc. cit.

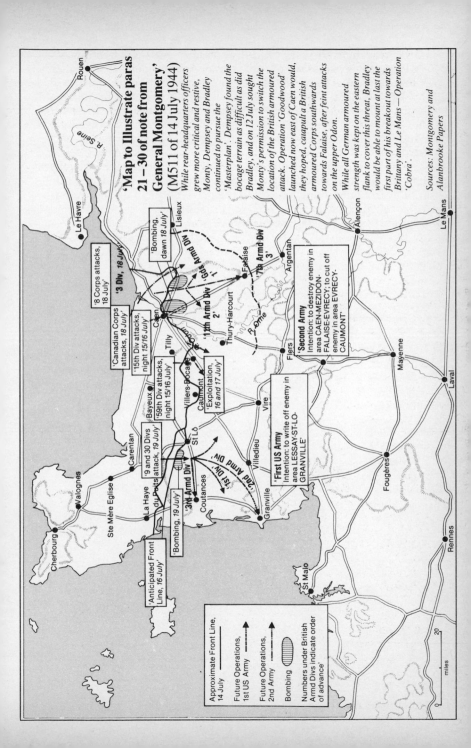

'Map to Illustrate paras 21 – 30 of note from General Montgomery' (M511 of 14 July 1944)

While rear-headquarters officers grew more critical and restive, Monty, Dempsey and Bradley continued to pursue the 'Masterplan'. Dempsey found the bocage terrain as difficult as did Bradley, and on 12 July sought Monty's permission to switch the location of the British armoured attack. Operation 'Goodwood' launched now east of Caen would, they hoped, catapult a British armoured Corps southwards towards Falaise, after feint attacks on the upper Odon.

While all German armoured strength was kept on the eastern flank to cover this threat, Bradley would be able to mount at last the first part of his breakout towards Brittany and Le Mans — Operation 'Cobra'.

Sources: Montgomery and Alanbrooke Papers

'Second Army'
Intention: to destroy enemy in area CAEN-MEZIDON-FALAISE-EVRECY; to cut off enemy in area EVRECY-CAUMONT'

'First US Army'
Intention: to write off enemy in area LESSAY-ST-LO-GRANVILLE'

Approximate Front Line, 14 July

Future Operations, 1st US Army

Future Operations, 2nd Army

Bombing

Numbers under British Armd Divs indicate order of advance'

'Anticipated Front Line, 16 July'

'Bombing, 19 July'

'9 and 30 Divs attack, 19 July'

'59th Div attacks, night 15/16 July'

'Exploitation, 16 and 17 July'

'15th Div attacks, night 15/16 July'

'Canadian Corps attacks, 18 July'

'8 Corps attacks, 18 July'

'Bombing, dawn 18 July'

'3 Div, 18 July'

'Guards Armd Div 1'

'11th Armd Div 2'

'7th Armd Div 3'

'1st Div'

'2nd Armd Div'

'3rd Armd Div'

miles 0   20

Rouen

R Seine

Le Havre

Lisieux

Falaise

Argentan

Alençon

Le Mans

Caen

Thury-Harcourt

R Orne

Flers

Mayenne

Laval

Tilly

Villers-Bocage

Caumont

Vire

Villedieu

Bayeux

St Lô

Coutances

Granville

Fougères

St Malo

Rennes

Carentan

La Haye

Ste Mère Eglise

Valognes

Cherbourg

R Odon

watch over the battle very carefully,' Monty emphasised in reviewing Dempsey's plans; 'we must be certain that we neglect no chance of inflicting a real heavy defeat on the enemy . . . the general aim in this battle will be to destroy all possible enemy troops in the area CAEN–MEZIDON–FALAISE–EVRECY, and to see if we can cut off those in the general area between EVRECY and CAUMONT. Whether we can do all this remains to be seen; but we will have a good try.'[1]

As in his hopes of surrounding Rommel's three Panzer divisions after D-Day, it was not to be. Moreover bad weather would preclude Bradley from mounting his part in the plan. Within days Monty was to be, in his own parlance, 'dicky on the perch', as rumour and counter-rumour swept the corridors of power.

---

[1] Letter of 14.7.44 (M511).

CHAPTER ELEVEN

The 'Plot' to Sack Monty

Meanwhile Tedder's and Coningham's obstructiveness was driving Leigh-Mallory to the point of resignation. Air supremacy, despite the failure of the army to 'deliver' the promised airfields south of Caen, had been achieved. As the Air Force C-in-C for 'Overlord', Leigh-Mallory felt it his duty to give the army all possible air support. By 8 July Leigh-Mallory was recording in his diary:

> The policy of [Tedder's and Coningham's] double-dealing, the effect of which has been to deny the Army what it wanted in the field, has failed. Monty wishes to deal in future direct with me, and we have told Eisenhower so. . . . If he [Coningham] does not like the situation, he will have to clear out. If Tedder does not like it, then he or I will go. My mind is now fully made up. Either I am to be allowed to direct, if necessary, the whole Air Forces available to the full and immediate support of the Army, or I shall resign on that issue.[1]

Tedder did not yet dare invoke Leigh-Mallory's resignation. Despite Coningham's overt hindrance, Leigh-Mallory now pledged himself to put the entire Allied air forces at Monty's disposal:

> My relations with Monty have always been cordial. . . . Now I hope we shall have an opportunity of even closer collaboration. In fact I'm sure we shall have, for I am determined on it. Let this be my last word. I shall give the Army all the support for which it asks,

he noted on 8–10 July.[2]

With Tedder and Coningham working silently against him, however, Leigh-Mallory had neither the power nor the personality to dictate to the Air Force what they were to do. Tedder's obstructionism rapidly turned into behind-the-scenes pressure amounting

---

[1] Diary of Sir Trafford Leigh-Mallory, loc. cit.
[2] Ibid.

almost to conspiracy. It was Tedder who had drafted Eisenhower's letter of 7 July to Monty; on 8 July he plotted with Air Marshal Portal, together with General Morgan (the defunct COSSAC chief and now British Deputy Chief of Staff to Eisenhower) and General Gale, in charge of administration at Supreme Headquarters. Dempsey's eastern flank fighting was dismissed as 'company exercises', and Morgan murmured that the Prime Minister was 'alive to the danger' of stalemate unless new ports were captured.[1] 'Unless we seized our opportunity at once, Germany would recover,'[2] Tedder broadcast his fear and, in the manner of a medieval baron, began to spread as much alarm as possible, in the hope of putting a new king on the Normandy throne when the opportunity occurred. He did not have long to wait.

It was Tedder who now urged Eisenhower to see on Monty's flank the real chance to break out towards the Seine, despite Gale's insistence that ports, not the Seine, were the vital necessity. 'It seemed clear to me that Montgomery did not attach sufficient importance to the pressing time factor. Few weeks of summer remained. Our urgent need was to get across the Seine.'[3] Like so many airmen, Tedder, who had left the army in 1915, lacked the concept of defeating an enemy army in land battle. As in the desert he was contemptuous of the Allied armies' difficulties and believed that, in some miraculous fashion, an Allied advance to the Seine would signify enemy defeat. He thus encouraged Eisenhower to read into Monty's new eastern sector offensive, code-named 'Goodwood', the very aim which de Guingand and Dawnay were taking such pains to dispel. 'I told Eisenhower on 11 July that in my view Montgomery's directive [of 10 July] was most unsatisfactory. It seemed to be a repetition of the "Company Exercises" to which I had objected a day or two before.'[4]

Monty and Dempsey were now forced into a difficult situation. Sir Ronald Adam, the Adjutant-General at the War Office, had come out to Normandy 'and in a talk in my caravan he warned me that if our *infantry* casualties continued at the recent rate it would be impossible to replace them, and we should have to "cannibalise" – to break up some divisions in order to maintain the rest,' Dempsey later recorded. 'For we had put almost all our available man-power into Normandy in the first few weeks.'[5]

Dempsey's answer was to use his armour, of which there was a surplus in the British sector. This would have the added advantage that the enemy would be 'bound to react – and move their reserves

---

[1] Tedder, op. cit.
[2] Ibid.
[3] Ibid.
[4] Ibid.
[5] Notes of 18.3.52 in Dempsey file, loc. cit.

to meet it. They could not run the risk of a breakthrough by massed armour.'

Armour alone could not break into the heavily-defended German lines. However the shortage of 25-pdr ammunition meant that artillery support would be restricted. It was imperative, therefore, to get full bomber support. Though Leigh-Mallory was willing, Tedder, Coningham, Harris, Vandenburg and Spaatz were against it.

So it became necessary to depend on large-scale bomber support,

Dempsey chronicled.

To obtain this from the Air Staff and Bomber Command, who disliked being diverted to aid ground operations, Monty felt it was necessary to over-state the aims of the operation.[1]

Operation 'Goodwood', after preliminary attacks to obtain better overall positions, was to begin on 18 July, but Bradley's simultaneous attack to the south, Operation 'Cobra', had to be postponed – first from 18 to 20 July, then to 21 July. Ideally Monty would have liked to delay 'Goodwood' in tandem, but knowing that Rommel was attempting to withdraw his Panzer divisions and regroup them as a mobile reserve, Monty dared not delay 'Goodwood'. Accordingly the great British armoured attack began on 18 July, preceded by heavy bombing by both British and American air forces. Disliking the bocage country south-west of Caen, Dempsey had decided to launch his armoured corps from his coastal salient, east of Caen. He hoped to strike south-west, rolling up the German front line in the southern outskirts of Caen, seizing the high ground at Bourguébus, and striking on in the same south-westerly direction parallel to the Orne, a reverse of his original Odon pincer in June. Countered by four Panzer divisions, with two further Panzer divisions echeloned behind them, the British armoured attack soon ran into trouble. The spearhead reached the Caen railway line without difficulty; but thereafter the fighting became 'sticky'. The Bourguébus ridge was in British hands by lunchtime, but as at Alamein it proved impossible to stir the tank commanders into further losses. 'There is a maximum of 50 enemy tanks around BOURGUEBUS,' Dempsey lamented at 4.45 p.m. 'I told BGS 8 Corps not to let the enemy build up a gun line against us';[2] they were ordered to drive on before the Germans could cordon off the assault.

As at Alamein, such exhortations were futile, and by the following evening (19 July) Dempsey reported to Monty that the armoured part

[1] Ibid.
[2] Diary of M. C. Dempsey, loc. cit.

of the offensive was spent. Monty, who had watched the battle most carefully, ordered him to rush infantry into the area captured, and to pull out the armour, which was to be re-grouped and refitted ready to renew the fight following the real 'Cobra' break-out on 21 July, when Bradley would begin his wheel into the interior of northern France. 'Once it was evident that the armour were not going to break out, the operation became an infantry battle – and it was no part of the "Goodwood" plan to get drawn into a costly struggle of that kind. So I really lost interest in the operation by evening,' Dempsey later recalled, 'and was ready to call it off – except for trying to get onto the initial objectives, which were necessary if we were to obtain a satisfactory tactical position.'[1]

Monty's alacrity in accepting the disappointing results of 'Goodwood' caused consternation at Eisenhower's headquarters – and particularly among the air force commanders. 'In order to get proper air support for the attack, de Guingand had to exaggerate the importance of the attack,' Dempsey later explained in an effort to make clear the real purpose of 'Goodwood' to the American Official Historian. 'He kept telling the air people this attack is absolutely essential to the war and will be the turning point. Because of this statement, it has been difficult to convince people that we had not intended to do more than strengthen our line. Monty realised that this attack was open to exaggeration and for this reason gave me one of the first written orders I ever received, in which the limited nature of the attack was made clear.'[2]

That Monty's Chief of Staff had to deceive his own air force colleagues in order to get full air support was a remarkable reflection on the state of affairs. In an attempt to retain their reluctant support Monty signalled at 7.40 p.m. on 18 July: 'The weight of air power used was very great and its effect was decisive. Second Army has three armoured divisions now operating in the open country to the south and S.E. of CAEN and regts of armoured cars supported by tanks are being directed to the crossings over the DIVES between MEZIDON and FALAISE. First Army has made much better progress today with 7 and 19 Corps and I hope to get their big attack launched on Friday 21 July.'

[1] Notes of 18.3.52 in Dempsey file, loc. cit. Dempsey had put his Tac Headquarters alongside 8 Corps HQ, just in case the German line *did* crack. 'It was always possible that the enemy's resistance might break down, and it was therefore necessary to foresee such a situation arising and be *mentally* prepared for it.' He planned, in this instance, to 'seize all the crossings of the Orne from Caen to Argentan' – not with a view of breaking out towards Paris, but with the idea of 'shutting off the enemy's main force, which lay west of the Orne. . . . The idea of such an exploitation was in my mind, but I did not disclose it to, or discuss it with, my subordintaes' – ibid.
[2] Pogue interview, loc. cit.

Not only had Monty to deceive the reluctant barons of the Allied air forces; it was essential that the Germans be made to believe that 'Goodwood' was serious, and that unless all reserves were committed to the eastern flank, a British break-out towards Paris would result. 'Both Bradley and I agreed we could not possibly tell the Press the true strategy which formed the basis of all our plans,' Monty recalled; he therefore gave a press conference, in the midst of the 'Goodwood' battle, to give the impression that the decisive moment in the Normandy campaign had come. As Chester Wilmot, the BBC correspondent, noted in his diary after the *true* break-out in the west 'the military offensive did not fail, but propaganda offensive did'[1] – for the war correspondents were as chagrined by the apparent failure of the 'Goodwood' break-out as were the Air Force barons:

> The Press interpreted the battle as a deliberate attempt to break-out, and one that had failed. Their misappreciation followed the view taken in various higher quarters, R.A.F. and American,

Dempsey later recalled.

> Maurice Chilton, my Chief of Staff, was very upset about it and urged me to take steps to check such a 'slander'. I told him: 'Don't worry – it will aid our purpose, and act as the best possible cover-plan.' For I could see that such criticism would tend to convince the enemy that we were trying to break-out in the Caen area, and would help to keep him fixed there while Bradley was mounting his fresh break-out attack ['Cobra'].[2]

To the enemy, the sight of armoured cars pushing through towards the Dives crossings, had been intended to 'spread alarm and despondency', particularly if the preliminary attacks by 12 and Canadian Corps were successful in their effort to 'make the Germans think we are going to break out across the ORNE between CAEN and AMAYE'. Yet the whole concept behind 'Goodwood' was not to break out, but to force the Germans into all-out battle on the eastern

---

[1] Notebook IV, Wilmot Collection in Liddell Hart Papers (15/15/62–93), loc. cit. Sir Edgar Williams also felt Monty's press conference to have been a mistake: 'In his attempt to keep that magnetic attraction of Caen going, he [Monty] laid on operations and made the mistake, I think, looking back, of getting the press involved. At that press conference during 'Goodwood' he talked about break-out or break-through or whatever, and the press took this up and in fact we hadn't made any such progress at all. They felt they had been let down. I can remember this press conference so well – I can see Alan Moorehead's face, sitting looking up at Monty. They were crouching on the ground. I think it was a great mistake' – interview of 28.1.83.

[2] Notes of 18.3.52 in Dempsey file, loc. cit.

flank, 'to engage the German Armour in battle and "write it down" to such an extent that it is of no further value to the Germans as a basis of the battle,' as Monty set out in his secret order to Dempsey. Geographically, all that was wanted was 'to gain a good bridgehead over the ORNE through CAEN and thus to improve our positions on the eastern flank': an essential preliminary to 'a possible wide exploitation of success' when once 'Cobra' was launched. For behind the 'effect of this operation on Allied policy' lay the cardinal aim of 'Cobra', as Monty reiterated:

We require the whole of Cherbourg and Brittany peninsulas.
A victory on the eastern flank will help us to gain what we want on the western flank.

By victory Monty understood 'generally to destroy German equipment and personnel' – he did not intend Dempsey to risk anything that would prejudice the security of the eastern 'shield':

The eastern flank is a bastion on which the whole future of the campaign in NW Europe depends; it must remain a firm bastion; if it becomes unstable the operations on the western flank would cease.
Therefore, while taking advantage of every opportunity to destroy the enemy, we must be careful to maintain our own balance and ensure a firm base.[1]

It followed that the moment Dempsey informed Monty that his 8 Corps thrust had run out of steam, Monty withdrew his armour so that it could be kept concentrated, out of line, ready to be relaunched at the opportune moment, as soon as 'Cobra' was under way.

The relationship between Dempsey's offensive and Bradley's thrust was, however, ignored by SHAEF and the Allied air commanders, the endless reiterations of Monty's overall Allied strategy having been subsumed in wild hopes of a British offensive victory that would 'knock loose the shackles' roping off the Allied bridgehead.

With the closing down of 'Goodwood' on 19 July, the roof began to fall about Monty's ears, and all the more noisily as, day by day, Bradley's 'Cobra' breakout was tragically postponed owing to bad weather. For a full week, until 'Cobra' was finally launched, Monty was now forced to bat for his life, not against the enemy, but against his own superiors.

[1] 'Notes on Second Army Operations, 16 July–18 July' of 15.7.44. The copy in Alanbrooke Files, Liddell Hart Centre for Military Archives, bears a postscript by Montgomery: 'Above given to General Dempsey on 15 July. He gave a copy to General O'Connor, 8 Corps. [Signed] B. L. Montgomery, General, 15.7.44.'

Tedder's campaign to get Monty sacked began, according to Commander Butcher, on the night of 19 July: 'The Air people are disgusted with Monty, Tedder telling Ike last night, "I told you so," the Air Marshall always having burned inside, and not always succeeding in suppressing this to the air and navy'.[1]

By the next day, Eisenhower's British and American aides were openly discussing 'who would succeed Monty':

> While waiting, Jim and I have been talking about who would succeed Monty, if sacked. I thought his chances now are 60–40, in his favor,

Butcher considered – though they would be a great deal less, he was sure, once Eisenhower crossed the Channel, as he was planning to do, and found that Monty had deliberately halted his successful advance 'until the customary counter-attack of the Germans had been met', at which time Butcher expected Monty to resume the advance, 'the worst being over'.[2]

That Butcher, having included in the Supreme Commander's desk diary all Monty's directives and signals of the preceding weeks, could have so misread Monty's strategy at this stage of the battle says little for his intelligence; that it was paralleled by an Air Marshal of Tedder's intellect and experience says a great deal less for Tedder, for on the night of 19 July at 9 p.m. Tedder had phoned Eisenhower 'and said that the British Chiefs of Staff would support any recommendation that Ike might care to make, meaning that if Ike wanted to sack Monty for not succeeding in going places with his big three armored division push, he would have no trouble, officially'.[3]

Butcher assumed that Tedder had learned this from a talk with Brooke, who had visited Monty on the afternoon of 19 July, in Normandy. Butcher was, however, wrong – for Brooke, as is evident from his diary, found Monty 'in grand form and delighted with his success east of Caen'[4] and had scant cause to be disappointed, knowing from Monty's letter of 14 July and Dawnay's visit the true rationale behind Dempsey's attack. Tedder could only have been speaking for Portal, the Chief of Air Staff – in the hope that Churchill, briefed by Eisenhower's Deputy Chief of Staff Morgan, would support them. With Montgomery's sacking, Tedder would relieve Leigh-Mallory and take the latter's place.

'On 20 July, I spoke to Portal about the Army's failure,' Tedder later confessed.

[1] Loc. cit.
[2] Ibid.
[3] Ibid.
[4] A. Bryant, op. cit.

We are agreed in regarding Montgomery as the cause. We also talked about the control of the Strategic Air Forces. Portal felt that the time was drawing near when their control could revert to the Combined Chiefs of Staff exercised through him. Second, and more immediate, was the problem of Leigh-Mallory's flirtation with Montgomery at Coningham's expense. I said: 'In these circumstances, Leigh-Mallory has no time for the direction of the Strategic Air Forces, and I, at SHAEF, will have to do that.'[1]

If Monty's exposition of his plans at St Paul's had reminded onlookers of Henry V before Agincourt, Tedder's conspiracy now conjured up *Macbeth* – or *Julius Caesar*. Tedder's intrigue, as Deputy Supreme Commander of the Allied Expeditionary Force, must rank as one of the most reprehensible performances by a senior Allied commander in modern battle history. Day after day Tedder wove his web, attempting to enlist Portal, Eisenhower, Bedell Smith and Churchill. On 25 July, before Eisenhower left on another visit to Normandy, Tedder telephoned him yet again, even as Allied bombers flew across the Channel to open Bradley's delayed 'Cobra' break-out: 'Tedder called Ike this morning . . . and was coming down this afternoon to pursue his current favorite subject, the sacking of Monty,' Butcher chronicled.[2] That Eisenhower and Bedell Smith were parties to the 'plot' was revealed, shortly before his death, by de Guingand:

There was no doubt that feelings were mounting about Monty, and suggestions that possibly he'd had enough and they ought to appoint someone else. I was aware of it, and so was he [Monty]! I think Monty heard about it through a letter Tedder sent to the Air Chief of Staff Portal, where Tedder definitely suggested Ike wouldn't mind a change and neither would he.[3]

Consideration of an alternative field commander is the rightful prerogative of a Supreme Commander, de Guingand felt. What astonished him after the war was to learn of Eisenhower's incredible naïveté in contemplating a successor to Monty:

After the war Bedell Smith told me, we were talking about that phase, the failure [of 'Goodwood'], and the agitation against Monty. He said, 'Do you know, at one point we were discussing successors, and your name was suggested?'
I said, 'Good Christ! Thank God *that* never happened!' I couldn't

[1] Tedder, op. cit.
[2] Loc. cit.
[3] Major-General Sir Francis de Guingand, interview of 7.5.78.

have done it. There is all the difference in the world being a Chief of Staff and a commander – tremendous difference.[1]

Fortunately, as in 1939, Brooke was one step ahead of the mischief-makers. Knowing how much was at stake, Brooke had counselled Monty on 19 July to discard his current ban on visitors and ensure that by personal meetings Monty kept his masters sweet. In the C-in-C's own caravan Brooke made Monty write a personal invitation to Churchill; that night (19 July) Monty also sent a secret signal to Eisenhower, inviting him to visit him the next day – 'alone – meaning don't bring Tedder or other top airmen'.[2] Thus to the astonishment of his own ADCs Monty proceeded to cut out the venom from Tedder's snake-in-the-grass conspiracy. Captain Henderson, for instance, watched with disbelief as the august visitors arrived, looking grim-faced and sullen, and emerged an hour later from Monty's operations caravan looking radiant with confidence.[3]

Eisenhower's blood-pressure had risen, he was listless and suffered from ringing in his ears. 'Ike hasn't been feeling so hot these last few days,' Butcher had noted on 19 July, as Eisenhower lay in bed the entire day. 'The slowness of the battle, the desire to be more active in it himself, his inward but generally unspoken criticism of Monty for being so cautious: all these pump up his system. It ain't good. He'll have to take care of himself, but his troubles are not from physical exertion, they are from mental strain and worry.'[4] Yet after his visit to Monty's headquarters on the afternoon of 20 July Eisenhower became a changed man: he went fishing, piloted a liaison plane, threw away the 'slow-down potion' given him for his high blood pressure, and told Butcher to telephone Bedell Smith and 'caution him against even hinting at the subject we have been discussing'[5] – in other words, the sacking of Monty.

This 'shot-in-the-arm' was repeated when Churchill visited Monty the following day. In Henderson's recollection it was 'common knowledge at Tac that Churchill had come to sack Monty. I mean we all knew it. He came in his blue coat with a blue cap, and in his pocket he had the order, dismissing Monty. There was quite an "atmosphere". However Monty showed not the least nervousness. He shook hands, took him into the Operations caravan – and when they came out Churchill was beaming. I've no idea what happened to that piece of paper – but we all knew how near "Master" had come to

---

[1] Ibid.
[2] Diary of Harry C. Butcher, loc. cit.
[3] J. R. Henderson, loc. cit.
[4] Diary of Harry C. Butcher, loc. cit.
[5] Ibid.

being sacked. I remember it quite clearly, near the Cerisy forest. . . .'[1]

It is unlikely that Churchill really had such an order in his pocket, but the rumour that he did illustrates the frighteningly black moment among the Allied counsels of power – a moment that stretched from 20 to 24 July as Bradley's 'Cobra' attack was postponed owing to bad weather for the vital heavy bombers, first from 21 to 22 July, then to the 23rd and again to the 24th. Moreover when finally 'Cobra' did 'kick-off', the American bombers, by tragic misplanning, followed the wrong flight path and began to bomb American troops. The attack was put off a further day, to 25 July, and once again American troops were bombed. This time, however, Collins decided to continue the attack. With agonising slowness the infantry smashed their way across the fields and hedgerows. 'The first U.S. Army attack began very stickily; their bombing killed a good many chaps in their own units, including one very high ranking General from the United States who should NOT have been up near the front line. However it is going better now,' Monty wrote to Brooke on 26 July; and by 27 July, as the American movement began to gather momentum against minimal opposition, Bradley put in his armour. Dempsey had indeed fulfilled his mission, and with their main Panzer forces locked in line against the British Second Army sector, the Germans could do little to stop the gathering flood.

As at Alamein, it had been a test of nerve and patience, of fortitude and restraint on Monty's part. But when his liaison officers gathered on the evening of 27 July 1944 and told him how well Bradley's advance was going a great weight was lifted from him. His perch was, he felt, secure: for the harvest of his Normandy strategy was about to be reaped.

---

[1] J. R. Henderson, loc. cit.

CHAPTER TWELVE

At the Bottom of the Celestial Ladder

The most irksome aspect of Tedder's conspiracy was that, while he schemed Monty's downfall, the enemy was behaving in precisely the way Monty intended. By the end of June both von Rundstedt and Geyr von Schweppenberg had protested that the battle was lost – and both were relieved of their commands. Hitler was determined not to yield an inch. Though the Germans appreciated the danger of an American break-out towards Brittany they simply could not withdraw their Panzer divisions from a British front that threatened to break open and thus outflank their forces facing Bradley. Until 'Cobra', the American sector was thus for the Germans a matter of 'local holding operations',[1] as the British and Canadians smashed their way into Caen:

> Plans of the MONTGOMERY Army Group [Second Army] correspond, according to indications and data, with what has hitherto been anticipated,

Rommel's HQ Weekly Report summarised after the fall of Caen.

> After taking possession of the entire CAEN area and sufficient bridgeheads over the ORNE, the enemy intends to launch the thrust against PARIS, in the course of which, as before, we shall have to reckon with large scale landing of the 1 American Army Group [Patton] in the 15 Army Zone for strategic cooperating with the MONTGOMERY Army Group and for the elimination of the long range weapon.[2]

'Fortitude', the deception threat of an Allied landing in the Pas de Calais area, was thus still playing an important part in the Normandy battle in mid-July, while Patton foamed about the delay in making his Army operational, and Eisenhower eventually overruled Monty, permitting American units and formations to be identified by journalists in the field for 'home publicity'.

---

[1] Weekly report, Army Group B, 10.7.44 (Templehoff Papers), loc. cit.
[2] Ibid.

That Patton would be launched not on the Pas de Calais coast, but through Bradley's Brittany thrust, was not considered a possibility by the German High Command, even though, after the British capture of Caen, Bradley's pressure at St Lô began to build up also into a break-through threat. By the eve of 'Goodwood' Rommel's headquarters still considered that 'the well-known operational intentions of Montgomery's Army Group still appear to exist. The British 2nd Army is clearly concentrated in the area of Caen and the south-west, and will carry out the thrust across the Orne towards Paris. . . . There are no fresh indications for estimating the aims of the American 1st Army Group.'[1] Worse still, the policy of withdrawing the Panzer divisions and replacing them with infantry was simply not possible in view of Montgomery's pressure at Caen: 'The replacement of armoured formations by infantry formations has not yet succeeded . . . the reserve groups of the armoured formations had, to a large extent, to be put back in the field.'[2]

Rommel's road injury on 17 July, after an aircraft attack, did not alter any of this, for on 18 July the British armoured corps almost breached the Panzer cordon at Caen: and even the two Panzer divisions defending the Caumont area were now recalled. Rommel had warned on 15 July that 'the position on the front in Normandy is becoming more difficult daily and is approaching a serious crisis', for his Panzer divisions and their reserves were 'tied down by the fighting on the front of the Panzergroup West [facing Dempsey]' and there were 'no mobile reserves to defend against a breakthrough. . . . The force is fighting heroically everywhere, but the unequal combat is nearing its end. It is in my opinion necessary to draw the appropriate conclusion from this situation.'[3]

These words, so reminiscent of Rommel's message to Hitler in the final days of the battle of Alamein, leave little doubt that, had he not been wounded, Rommel would have been relieved of his command of Army Group B, just as von Rundstedt had been sacked from command of Army Group A. Yet von Rundstedt's successor, von Kluge – who also took temporary command of Army Group B – agreed with everything Rommel said, particularly after the British armoured offensive on 18/19 July. 'The views of the Feld-marschall are unfortunately right,' he reported to Hitler on 21 July. 'My discussion yesterday with the commanders of the formations near Caen, held immediately after the recent heavy fighting, has, particularly, afforded regrettable evidence that . . . there is no way by which, in the face of the enemy air force's complete command, we can find a strategy which will counter-balance its actually annihilat-

[1] Ibid.
[2] Ibid.
[3] *The Rommel Papers*, op. cit.

ing effect without giving up the field of battle.'[1] Tedder had done his best to sabotage heavy bomber support for the troops, believing that Dempsey's army must fight its own way out of Normandy, yet von Kluge's appeal to Hitler is ample proof that Monty's insistence on using the full weight of the Allied air forces was justified. 'I came here with the fixed determination of making effective your order to stand fast *at any price*. But when one sees by experience that this price must be paid by the slow but sure annihilation of the force . . . anxiety about the immediate future of this front is only too well justified.'[2]

By this time, however, dissatisfaction with Hitler's conduct of the war had reached a pitch – and von Stauffenberg's bomb in Rastenburg on 20 July was its passionate expression, followed by an intended *putsch* by the army.

Early on 21 July Ultra signals alerted Monty's Chief of Intelligence, Brigadier Williams, to the coup:

I went and saw Monty very early. I said, 'Something has happened in Germany, it looks like real big stuff. The generals are involved, and so on and so forth.'

And Monty said: 'Well, the Prime Minister's coming in about five minutes, so let's do this:

'You tell him about the enemy in front of us and then I will tell him how I'm going to defeat them; and then we'll turn to him and I shall say: "But we understand something's going on in the great wide world beyond, and perhaps you know about it? . . ."'

That was the plan. I can remember the 'monster' arriving, so to speak, and Winston came in – I remember him sitting on the only stool there was in the caravan, the map caravan.[3]

Churchill had spent the night on board the cruiser *Enterprise*, swanning about the bridgehead and out of touch with the latest information save that which came by secret cypher telegram. Monty's contrived scenario therefore worked perfectly. 'The Commander-in-Chief was in the best of spirits on the eve of his largest operation, which he explained to me in detail,' Churchill later recorded.[4] Churchill, however, had not had time to be briefed on the latest situation, having come accompanied only by a naval aide. When Monty asked about the German *putsch*, Churchill drew out a long gold key chain from his waistcoat and like a magician, opened the two red boxes he had brought with him. Williams was utterly amazed:

[1] Templehoff Papers, loc. cit.
[2] Ibid.
[3] Brigadier Sir Edgar Williams, interview of 7.9.78.
[4] W. S. Churchill, op. cit.

He had two red boxes with him and I remember him unlocking them with a key on a sort of long gold chain. And he handed one box to me and one to Monty! Now these were, you know, the *most* secret stuff that had come in. But it was all muddled up – Ultra and so on.

And Monty and I lay on the floor like two schoolboys saying, 'My God, I've got a good one here! Have you seen *this*?' And I remember looking up and saying to the Prime Minister: 'Oh, so Witzleben *was* involved!'[1]

Churchill, it seemed, had no idea of the fabric of the German conspiracy and listened intently while Williams explained how a German parachute deserter in Italy, when asked who the German Badoglio would be, had replied, 'Oh, Witzleben!' Witzleben was to be the titular head of the revolution, General Fromm, the Home Army Commander, was to control the signals network of the uprising.

What appalled me was that: a) Winston hadn't read the stuff and b) was getting Ultra 'naked' – which I hadn't realised. There were just bits of green handwriting on it.

Whether Monty got the better box I can't remember. But it was an example that horrified me: the Intelligence arriving without any context – and when you thought what an alarming chap Winston was: if I hadn't given him the context, he might very well have made a speech out of this fragmentary material – muddled up and everything – have gone off at an angle, painting a tremendous rhetorical panorama in no time at all. . . .[2]

Churchill, having been given the background, was soon packed off with a bottle of whisky to 'play' in Air Vice-Marshal Broadhurst's captured Storch aeroplane, much as Eisenhower had done when General Quesada took him over the German lines two weeks previously. Meanwhile at Tactical Headquarters Monty issued another directive, M512, to his four army commanders on the lines of the military appreciation he had just given Churchill. If he was satisfied with what others believed to have been a disappointing display by the British armoured corps in 'Goodwood', it was not, as Eisenhower's aides whispered, an attempt to 'make virtue of necessity', or a cover up for the 'ebbing manpower' that made 'the commanders feel the blood of the British Empire, and hence its future, is too precious to dash in battle.'[3] At Alamein Monty had shown that, if he

[1] Loc. cit.
[2] Ibid.
[3] Diary of Harry C. Butcher, entry of 25.7.44, loc. cit.

felt a certain thrust was critical to the development of his tactical strategy, he would press and reinforce it relentlessly until it succeeded. If it was *not* critical, as at Mareth and in Sicily, he had shown instant resolution in closing it down rather than accept heavy casualties. Tedder might stalk the corridors of SHAEF headquarters complaining that Monty had deliberately and rigidly 'restricted' Dempsey's break-out; and that SHAEF had been 'had for suckers. I do not believe there was the slightest intention to make a clean breakthrough [at Caen]';[1] moreover he might fantasise that Bradley, 'now that it was clear there was going to be no breakthrough on the British Front' had therefore been 'urging Eisenhower . . . to plan a breakout on the western flank';[2] but the truth was otherwise. Bradley's break-out via Brittany had originally been conceived in England before D-Day, and throughout the long bitter weeks of fighting in June and July, Dempsey had been instructed to lock in combat the main enemy formations. Six thousand British and Canadian soldiers had fallen, even before 'Goodwood', to make possible the expansion of the American sector behind them, first to Cherbourg, and now towards Brittany. Ten thousand Americans had fallen in fulfilling their part of Monty's strategy – a just balance considering the vast and growing preponderance of American troops in the lodgement area. Far from being dreamed up because of British 'failure', as Tedder maintained, the American break-out had originally been intended as a simultaneous operation to take place on the same day that Dempsey set the eastern flank aflame.[3] Initial difficulties in capturing an advantageous jumping-off point, then bad weather delayed 'Cobra', day after day: but Monty's M512 directive of 21 July was the culmination of those weeks of Allied co-operation in the field, and Monty's satisfaction with the situation and the outlook, despite the delay in mounting 'Cobra', was genuine and as utterly convincing to Churchill as it was to the army commanders. By taking the southern outskirts of Caen, across the Orne, Second Army was in a strong position to 'take quick advantage of any situation that may suddenly develop', he declared, particularly any collapse resulting from the German *putsch*.

It is now vital that the western flank should swing southwards and eastwards, and that we should gain possession of the whole of CHERBOURG and BRITTANY peninsulas. The whole weight of the [21] Army Group will therefore be directed to this task,

[1] Tedder, op. cit. 'Around evening Tedder called Ike and said Monty had in effect stopped his armor from going further. Ike was mad' – Diary of Harry C. Butcher, 19.7.44, loc. cit.

[2] Tedder, op. cit.

[3] 'The main reason it was a failure, "Goodwood", was that "Cobra" couldn't take its proper part in the battle' – Maj-General Sir Francis de Guingand, loc. cit.

he made clear. To help Bradley get full value from the delayed 'Cobra' operation it was important that Dempsey continue to hold the German Panzer divisions in the east. First Canadian Army was to be inserted, therefore, on the left of the British flank, taking command of the four infantry divisions in line between the Caen railway and the coast; this would release Dempsey for the mounting of a new feint, launched from the remaining British sector: 'The enemy must be made to believe that we contemplate a major advance towards FALAISE and ARGENTAN, and he must be induced to build up his main strength to the east of the R. ORNE so that our affairs on the western flank can proceed with greater speed.'[1] In doing so Dempsey was to take over some of Bradley's eastern boundary in order to give Bradley extra weight in 'Cobra'. Bradley, meanwhile, was to head for Avranches, and while sending a corps to take the Brittany ports of Rennes and St Malo, to swing the main bulk of his forces southwards and eastwards: 'a strong right wing in a wide sweep, south of the bocage country, towards successive objectives as follows: a) LAVAL-MAYENNE; b) LE MANS-ALENCON.'

Had Tedder bothered to consult de Guingand, or to look at the copy of this directive sent to Eisenhower and to Bedell Smith, he would have seen that this was still the *same* strategy outlined in so many of Monty's directives of the preceding weeks – M502, M504, M505, and M510. Yet Tedder now broadcast the legend that Eisenhower, not Monty, was responsible for this 'new shift' in strategy – misleading not only his colleagues at SHAEF,[2] but many subsequent historians as well. The best complexion that can be put on such misrepresentation is that it was intended to honour a Supreme Commander whom all admired. As Monty pithily remarked in his *Memoirs*, men like General Morgan 'considered Eisenhower was a god . . . he placed me at the other end of the celestial ladder'.[3] Morgan's original COSSAC plan had envisaged a primary British-Canadian break-out to the Seine from the Caen lodgement area, and this may have added fuel to his vision of Allied failure, for which Monty was to be the scapegoat.

Eisenhower's performance in keeping together the Western Allies in this, the final year of the war, was indeed a prodigious feat. Moreover, it is unjust to consider him solely as a political figurehead, devoid of soldierly knowledge or insight – for Eisenhower had been his life long a superlative military staff officer, with a penetrating intellect and a remarkable grasp of logistics. Had he been encouraged to recognise his great virtues and rest content with them – as did,

[1] Copies of M512 went to Bradley, Dempsey, Patton, Crerar, Eisenhower, Bedell Smith, de Guingand, Bradley's Chief of Staff, Leigh-Mallory, Coningham, Brooke, Simpson, Graham and Churchill.

[2] C. F. Pogue interviews, OCMH Collection, MHI, Carlisle, Pennsylvania.

[3] *Memoirs*, op. cit.

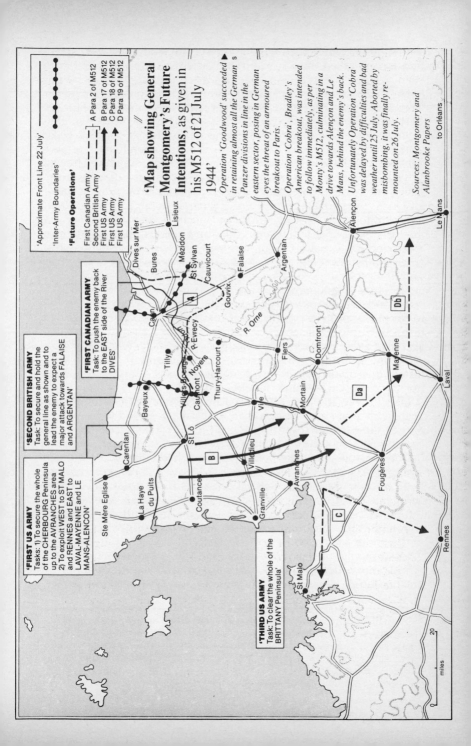

Map showing General Montgomery's Future Intentions, as given in his M512 of 21 July 1944'

Operation 'Goodwood' succeeded in retaining almost all the German Panzer divisions in line in the eastern sector, posing in German eyes the threat of an armoured breakout to Paris.

Operation 'Cobra', Bradley's American breakout, was intended to follow immediately, as per Monty's M512, culminating in a drive towards Alençon and Le Mans, behind the enemy's back.

Unfortunately Operation 'Cobra' was delayed by difficulties and bad weather until 25 July. Aborted by misbombing, it was finally re-mounted on 26 July.

Sources: Montgomery and Alanbrooke Papers

Legend:

'Approximate Front Line 22 July'

'Inter-Army Boundaries'

'Future Operations'
First Canadian Army
Second British Army
First US Army
First US Army
First US Army

A Para 2 of M512
B Para 17 of M512
C Para 18 of M512
D Para 19 of M512

'FIRST US ARMY
Tasks: 1) To secure the whole of the CHERBOURG Peninsula up to the AVRANCHES area 2) To exploit WEST to ST MALO and RENNES and EAST to LAVAL-MAYENNE and LE MANS-ALENCON'

'SECOND BRITISH ARMY
Task: To secure and hold the general line as shown and to lead the enemy to expect a major attack towards FALAISE and ARGENTAN'

'FIRST CANADIAN ARMY
Task: To push the enemy back to the EAST side of the River DIVES'

'THIRD US ARMY
Task: To clear the whole of the BRITTANY Peninsula'

say, Marshall and Brooke – then much of the wrangling and conflict that accompanied the campaign in North-west Europe might have been avoided. Despite Alexander's severe limitations as a Ground Force Commander in the Mediterranean, Eisenhower had never sought to usurp Alexander's role; yet from the moment in January 1944 when Bedell Smith insisted that Monty drop the designation 'Allied Army C-in-C' and only temporarily act as Ground Force Commander, Eisenhower was propelled to envision himself as field general. This he was not, and could not now become, never having served in the field, save in the disastrous few days leading up to the American fiasco at Kasserine – and his experience of running Allied HQ in Algiers for the rest of 1943, followed by SHAEF in London, hardly fitted him to lead armies on the field of battle. Yet like a medieval king urged on by ambitious and jealous noblemen to take command in the field, Eisenhower was subjected to insidious pressure on all sides to become something he was not, and to dispense with the commander in charge. The name of Alexander was circulated at his headquarters as a possible replacement of Monty in command of 21st Army Group, while Eisenhower was himself urged to take overall field command. 'Chief Big Wind', as SHAEF had dubbed Monty, could then 'be made a peer and sit in the House of Lords, or even given a Governorship, such as Malta, whose governor is leaving to take over racially-conscious Palestine,'[1] Eisenhower's British MA opined on 20 July after Eisenhower's return from Normandy. Monty was thus to follow Lord Gort.

Eisenhower, however, bolstered by Monty's promise of a great victory once his true strategy had unfolded, resorted to his role of harrier.[2] In a letter to Monty on 21 July he now blamed Dempsey for the slowness of Bradley's southward offensive, saying that Dempsey had been too defensively minded and had allowed too much strength to oppose Bradley, and insisted that Monty keep his eastern flank aflame. 'As Bradley's attack starts Dempsey's should be intensified. . . . In First Army *the whole front* comes quickly into action to pin down local reserves and to support the main attack. Dempsey should do the same . . . we must go forward shoulder to shoulder, with honours and sacrifices equally shared.'[3]

Many would say that it was *because* the whole American front came quickly into action that the Americans achieved so little after the fall of Cherbourg – certainly Patton believed, on 2 July that 'one or two

[1] Diary of Harry C. Butcher, loc. cit.
[2] 'Bedell Smith once summed it up pretty well when he said, speaking of this period, "General Eisenhower was up and down the line like a football coach, urging everyone to the greatest possible aggression"' – Chester Wilmot in BBC Radio Third Programme, 5.2.49 (Wilmot Papers, Liddell Hart Collection, King's College, London).
[3] Original in Montgomery Papers. Eisenhower's italics.

armoured divisions abreast and going straight down the road, covering the leading elements with air bursts' could split open the German defences.[1] At the time when Monty wanted Bradley to strike south as well as assaulting Cherbourg, First US Army had not been opposed by a single German armoured division on its southern flank, and even a month later it was faced by only two, while no less than seven Panzer divisions and two SS Werfer brigades were facing Dempsey.

Monty himself never criticised Bradley or showed any impatience with the slowness of the American expansion while Dempsey held the ring. The terrain did not favour a quick American advance, and although Dempsey was fulfilling his task by containing the bulk of the German armour on the British front, Bradley was faced by a formidable array of German infantry battalions, dug in behind hedgerows that made every 50 yards' advance an expensive business – hence the high rate of American wounded compared with Second Army (the number of killed remained comparable). Whatever legends were later concocted, there can be no doubt that Monty was, at this time, a most patient and understanding 'boss' to Bradley, allowing the Americans time to learn their battlefield lessons without the eternal chivvying and criticism which Monty, as overall C-in-C, had to bear; for as long as Bradley performed his role in the 'masterplan', Monty was convinced all would be well.

The same service was performed in turn by Brooke for Monty. When, on 6 July, Churchill began to abuse Monty in front of a meeting of Ministers and Chiefs of Staff, Field-Marshal Brooke exploded: 'I lost my temper and started one of the heaviest thunderstorms that we had. He [Churchill] was infuriated . . . [and had] begun to abuse Monty because operations were not going faster, and apparently Eisenhower had said that he was over-cautious. I flared up and asked him if he could not trust his generals for five minutes instead of belittling them.'[2]

Given the endless backbiting and back-seat driving during July, it is a miracle that Monty himself remained, at this time, so confident and patient. While Churchill was taken up in Broadhurst's captured Storch aeroplane to inspect the bridgehead, Monty wrote a little note on 22 July to Phyllis Reynolds. Churchill was due to lunch with Monty at Tac HQ, after which Monty had promised to take him to Caen:

22.7.44

My dear Phyllis,
    This goes to England by the Prime Minister who will post it to you. The weather all day yesterday was quite foul; tropical rain the

[1] *The Patton Papers*, op. cit.
[2] A. Bryant, op. cit.

whole day. Luckily I had a day in as I had a lot of stuff to clear up; the P.M. looked in during the morning and we had a good talk. He is coming to lunch today, and I am then going to take him to see CAEN; I don't like doing it as the place is very often shelled, but it will please the old chap and he likes to go to dangerous places.

I suppose you are getting ready to disperse for the holidays.
Give my best wishes to all the boys. . . .

Yrs ever
Monty

To Eisenhower's harrying letter he replied by cable that night: 'Have received your letter dated 21 July. There is not and never has been any intention of stopping offensive operations on the eastern flank.' He explained how, as in the M512 directive he had sent to Eisenhower the day before, he was bringing in First Canadian Army to take charge of the sector facing east, while Dempsey concentrated on a thrust southwards towards Falaise, in order to keep German attention away from Bradley's delayed 'Cobra' operation. 'Does that assure you that we see eye to eye on the main military problem? If not do please let me know,' Monty ended.

Tedder was still pressing hard for Monty's removal, and was trying to discredit Leigh-Mallory as an accomplice of Monty. Thus when Eisenhower spoke by phone to Churchill on the latter's return from Normandy, Eisenhower was still in two minds about the battle. To Monty he had signalled 'we are apparently in complete agreement'[1] – but when Churchill telephoned on the night of 24 July on his return from Normandy, Eisenhower kept his options open. Perhaps Churchill too felt Monty should go. 'What do your people think about the slowness of the situation over there?' was Eisenhower's first question: 'meaning, was the P.M. also after Monty's scalp, as Tedder obviously is,' Commander Butcher noted in his diary.[2]

Butcher had gone back to bed after Eisenhower began talking to Churchill. He was therefore surprised when, the following morning, Eisenhower 'said he had talked more than a half hour to the P.M. and that during the P.M.'s recent trip Monty obviously had sold Winston "a bill of goods". The P.M. was supremely happy with the situation.'[3]

With Churchill's new support for Monty, the wind went out of

[1] *The Papers of Dwight David Eisenhower*, op. cit.

[2] Diary of Harry C. Butcher, entry of 25.7.44, loc. cit.

[3] Ibid. In a handwritten letter to Monty from HMS *Enterprise* on 23 July, Churchill thanked Monty for his hospitality: 'I enjoyed my day with you enormously and only hope that fruitful results will come from my more intimate impressions of the war scene, and from another opportunity of having a good talk with you' – Montgomery Papers.

Tedder's sails. Within days his judgement over the battle in Normandy would be proved misguided, and his attempt to get Monty replaced mischievous at the very least; his brief moment as potential king-maker past, he would fade into the background. Indeed by the end of the year his own scalp would be demanded, on the grounds of his poor performance as Deputy Supreme Commander of the Allied Forces in Europe.

Monty, meanwhile, hearing from colleagues how near he had come to dismissal in the preceding days, determined to make quite sure that Eisenhower was now kept fully abreast of proceedings. Hitherto he had relied on cables, copies of his directives to the Army Commanders, and personal liaison through de Guingand. On the eve of the yet again postponed 'Cobra' operation, he wrote directly to Eisenhower to ensure his support against Tedder:

24-7-44

My dear Ike
The weather here has been quite frightful; we have not seen the blue sky for days on end; there is 10/10ths cloud, and air operations have been practically closed down. The heavy mud turned the area S.E. of CAEN into a complete sea of mud, and everything came to a stop.

With weather conditions making air support impossible it was indeed fortunate that Monty had instantly closed down the 'Goodwood' offensive when the chances of 'exploitation' were shown to be false. 'Today it is still cloudy and misty, and we could not get Brad's attack launched,' Monty went on. Lest Eisenhower be disappointed, however, Monty went to great pains to reiterate the essential features of the coming engagement – 'I sent you M.512, which gives my broad plan. The following paragraphs will show you in more detail how it will work out.'

In many ways Operation 'Cobra' was reminiscent of Alamein. A force of three infantry divisions was to start the attack – but using the crushing impact of American heavy bombers to stun the defenders, instead of artillery. Hard upon this barrage the infantry would establish a break-in area, and through it would be passed the armour. As at Alamein the enemy had been made to expect the main Allied attack elsewhere. 'It is a large scale operation and, once we can get it launched,' Monty declared, 'I am sure it will go well; it has great possibilities and Collins is a grand leader. The opening gambit is an attack by three divisions west of ST LO, under a great air bombardment. The objective of this "break-in" is the general line MARIGNY –ST GILLES. Three more divisions then pass through, turn right handed, and make for COUTANCE and GRANVILLE.'

It was, in fact, the first full-scale *concentrated* attack mounted by the

Americans in the Second World War. Once again, Dempsey's task was to act as decoy:

> It is very necessary that, while Third U.S. Army is swinging southwards and eastwards on the *western flank*, Second Army should fight hard on the *eastern flank* so as to draw the enemy attention and strength over to that side – keep the enemy pinned down in the CAEN sector – and constitute the definite and continuous threat of an advance on FALAISE and ARGENTAN. See para 13 of M512.

Dempsey's decoy attack was to be mounted in four consecutive phases, so that the Germans could not possibly withdraw divisions in line or even reserves to oppose Bradley. First the Canadians would attack east of the Orne, on the same day as 'Cobra', hopefully, kicked off: 25 July. Then on 28 July 12 Corps would assault west of the Orne, aimed upon Evrecy. This would be followed, on 30 July, by an armoured Corps attack through the Canadian bridgehead east of the Orne, down the Falaise road, drawing the main attention of the enemy while the Canadian corps seized the Forêt de Cinglais. The climax was then to be an armoured drive 'by possibly three or four armoured divisions, which I want to launch towards FALAISE. See para 14 of M512. The object would be to create complete chaos in the FALAISE area, and generally to put the wind up the enemy.' If this succeeded it would 'bring about a major enemy withdrawal from in front of Brad'; at the very least it would stop reinforcements moving west to oppose Bradley's break-out. 'If the general form was not too good, we can always withdraw into our own lines of the Canadian Corps' firm base, and repeat the operation a few days later.' This fourth attack was intended to jump off 'about 3 or 4 August'. What it amounted to, Monty wrote in his summary, was a 'really hard fight' on 'both flanks simultaneously'. But while the enemy *must* counter the eastern offensive, since it threatened a direct route to Paris and the Seine, Bradley's southern attack was the real Allied priority, and would succeed because the Germans could not possibly transfer sufficient forces to stop Bradley in time:

> The really big victory is wanted on the western flank, and everything will be subordinated to trying to make it so.

There was always a chance that, by a series of 'left-right-left' blows on Dempsey's and Crerar's front, a British break-through might occur, but it would be incidental to the grander strategy, not a pre-requisite.

With the spectacular success of 'Cobra' and the ensuing launch of Patton's Third Army into Brittany Monty's months of patient nurtur-

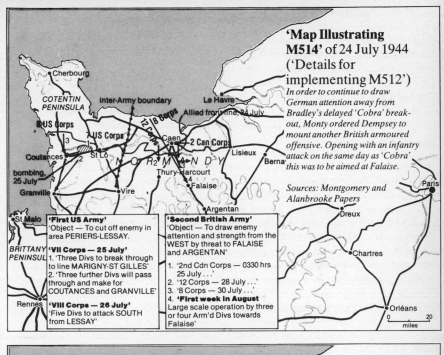

'Map Illustrating M514' of 24 July 1944 ('Details for implementing M512')

In order to continue to draw German attention away from Bradley's delayed 'Cobra' break-out, Monty ordered Dempsey to mount another British armoured offensive. Opening with an infantry attack on the same day as 'Cobra' this was to be aimed at Falaise.

Sources: Montgomery and Alanbrooke Papers

'First US Army'
'Object — To cut off enemy in area PERIERS-LESSAY.'

'VII Corps — 25 July'
1. 'Three Divs to break through to line MARIGNY-ST GILLES'
2. 'Three further Divs will pass through and make for COUTANCES and GRANVILLE'

'VIII Corps — 26 July'
'Five Divs to attack SOUTH from LESSAY'

'Second British Army'
'Object — To draw enemy attention and strength from the WEST by threat to FALAISE and ARGENTAN'

1. '2nd Cdn Corps — 0330 hrs 25 July . . .'
2. '12 Corps — 28 July . . .'
3. '8 Corps — 30 July . . .'
4. **'First week in August'** Large scale operation by three or four Arm'd Divs towards Falaise'

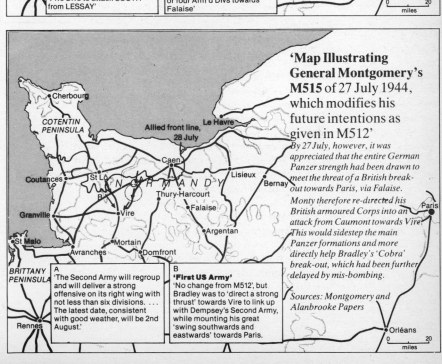

'Map Illustrating General Montgomery's M515 of 27 July 1944, which modifies his future intentions as given in M512'

By 27 July, however, it was appreciated that the entire German Panzer strength had been drawn to meet the threat of a British break-out towards Paris, via Falaise.

Monty therefore re-directed his British armoured Corps into an attack from Caumont towards Vire. This would sidestep the main Panzer formations and more directly help Bradley's 'Cobra' break-out, which had been further delayed by mis-bombing.

Sources: Montgomery and Alanbrooke Papers

A
'The Second Army will regroup and will deliver a strong offensive on its right wing with not less than six divisions. . . . The latest date, consistent with good weather, will be 2nd August.'

B 'First US Army'
'No change from M512', but Bradley was to 'direct a strong thrust' towards Vire to link up with Dempsey's Second Army, while mounting his great 'swing southwards and eastwards' towards Paris.

ing of his master-plan would be forgotten. Generations of young Americans would be brought up to believe, from the accounts of certain American journalists, writers and even Official Historians, that victory in Normandy had been achieved by American guts and genius, while the British 'sat on their butts'.

How sad this was. Those like Lt-Colonel Dawnay who had been Montgomery's aide during the long weeks while the master-plan unfolded, were distressed but, like Dempsey, disinclined later to protest publicly. Following the Second World War, America became the superpower of the West; the presence of its troops and its military capability would be crucial to combat the Russian menace in Europe. No good would be served therefore by reminding Americans that their stunning successes in France in 1944 were predicated on the selfless role of British and Canadian troops in Monty's great design. Yet how unfortunate – for of all the Western battles of the war, the battle for Normandy was the greatest, the most decisive and the most *Allied* in its conception and relentless, painstaking execution.

CHAPTER THIRTEEN

Eisenhower Scents Victory

Poor Dempsey's selfless dedication to the Allied cause in Normandy is well illustrated by his diary for 25 July, the day 'Cobra' was launched. The previous day he had discussed with Generals O'Connor and Ritchie two armoured attacks he wished to set up in the ensuing days; but at 5.30 p.m. on 25 July, when he flew to Monty's Tactical headquarters, he was told to scrap such ideas:

> 1730 – Flew to Headquarters 21 Army Group and saw C-in-C. In order to give even more help to the First Army operation, he wishes Second Army to carry out an operation at the beginning of August, either EAST or WEST of R. ORNE. It will have no geographical objective, but will be a continuation of the policy which has held good the whole time – that Second Army shall deal with the main enemy force while First Army swings forward with its right.[1]

It was, in Dempsey's view, a thankless task, for it meant another attack in the difficult bocage terrain instead of the easier ground around Caen. 'I want heavy air support for this operation, which will be in difficult country and will not have very heavy artillery support.'[2] Dempsey lamented the next day, though loyally carrying out Monty's orders.

When Tedder phoned Eisenhower on the morning of 25 July, meanwhile, it was to hear that Eisenhower 'had talked to the P.M. and the P.M. was satisfied and Tedder rather ugh-ughed, being not at all satisfied, and implying the P.M. must have sold Ike a bill of goods, as well.'[3]

The move to replace Monty appeared to have collapsed. That morning Monty's detailed letter to Eisenhower arrived, and de Guingand telephoned to make sure there was no misunderstanding. Yet still Eisenhower hesitated to give his Commander-in-Chief in the

---

[1] Diary of M. C. Dempsey, loc. cit.
[2] Ibid.
[3] Diary of Harry C. Butcher, loc. cit.

field his full support; and when American bombers aimed short, hitting their own troops, Eisenhower, who had flown to Normandy to witness the 'Cobra' kick-off, returned 'glum' and full of foreboding. By early afternoon the Americans had only advanced a few thousand yards, and fearing another stalemate Eisenhower gave in to his worst fears. To his guide at First Army, Eisenhower remarked that he 'does not believe in tactical use of heavies', Bradley's ADC recorded. ' "I look upon heavies as an instrument for stategic attack on rear installations," ' he now declared, reflecting Tedder's view. ' "I don't believe they can be used in support of ground troops. That's a job for artillery. I gave them the green light on this show but this is the last one" ' – forgetting that shortage of ammunition was so critical in the American sector that Bradley was rationing its use. When Churchill phoned late that night, Eisenhower thus said that, though he now saw 'eye to eye' with Montgomery, the battle was 'touch and go, with hard fighting under way and much more in prospect'.[1] The following day, after Tedder had again put his oar in, Eisenhower went to lunch with Churchill, accompanied by Bedell Smith. Commander Butcher's diary went silent for several days, but Brooke kept up his own, and was irritated by Eisenhower's fickle performance in front of Churchill, as the Americans strove to undermine Monty. After the war Bedell Smith would go on record, in a conversation with the American Official Historian, as saying that he did not 'see how it would be possible to give a correct portrayal of Montgomery without showing him to be a SOB. . . . Monty's trouble was that he never rose to Army Group Commander level. He was a Corps commander or an Army commander. He liked to go off by himself and fight the Corps or the Army himself. That is, he did that in his own area. He tended to let Bradley alone.'[2]

Given such misrepresentation of the facts it is small wonder that American historians have in turn misrepresented history. In the first two months of the Normandy campaign there is only one record of Bedell Smith visiting the Normandy beachhead, and not until 23 August, after the battle of Normandy was won, did Bedell Smith visit Monty in the field. Yet on 26 July Eisenhower and Bedell Smith so decried Montgomery that Churchill summoned Brooke after lunch: 'Eisenhower had been lunching with him and had again run down Montgomery and described his stickiness and the reaction in the American papers.' Churchill's response was to ask Eisenhower and Bedell Smith to repeat their criticisms the following evening at dinner with Brooke present. Thus, at the very moment when Monty's Normandy strategy was paying off (for after a further bombing mishap on 25 July Collins had driven his 7 Corps through the

[1] Ibid.
[2] Pogue interview of 8.5.47, loc. cit.

southern breach), Eisenhower and Bedell Smith were deriding Monty before the British Army Chief of Staff.

> It began to look as if the policy we have been working on for so many weeks is now going to pay a dividend,

Monty signalled to Brooke during the evening of 27 July.[1]

> When the American attack went in west of St LO at 1100 hrs on 25 July the main enemy armoured strength of six panzer and SS divisions was deployed on the eastern flank opposite Second British Army. That was a good dividend. The Americans are going well and I think things will now begin to move towards the plan outlined in M512.

He informed Brooke too that he was not now going to attack towards Falaise 'as enemy is very strong in that sector'. Instead he was ordering Dempsey to mount a 'big attack with six divisions from CAUMONT towards VIRE and hope to get it launched not later than 2 August'. In a new directive (M515) to Bradley, Patton, Dempsey and Crerar that day, Monty had outlined the plan. Intelligence showed that all six enemy Panzer and SS divisions were in line east of Noyers. To assault there would be futile: 'any large scale operations by us in that area are definitely unlikely to succeed; if we attempt them we would merely play into the enemy's hands, and we would not be helping on our operations on the western flank.'

It was this western offensive that was, however, the primary factor in the Allied plan: 'On the western flank the First U.S. Army has delivered the main blow of the whole Allied plan, and it is making excellent progress. Anything we do elsewhere must have the underlying object of furthering the operations of the American forces to the west of ST LO, and speeding up the capture of the whole of the Cherbourg and Brittany peninsulas; it is ports that we require, and quickly.'

Dempsey was to sidestep his armoured divisions and strike hard through the bocage country around Caumont, which was currently denuded of Panzer or SS Divisions. Dempsey's object was to drive south-westwards towards Vire; if Bradley meanwhile attacked with his left wing towards Torigny-sur-Vire, then this would become the new hinge for the great American wheel into Brittany and then eastwards towards Paris. 'The main blow of the whole Allied plan has now been struck on the western flank; that blow is the foundation of all our operations, and it has been well and truly struck,' Monty concluded his directive. 'The armies on the eastern flank must

[1] M67, Montgomery Papers.

now keep up the pressure in the CAEN area; and Second British Army must hurl itself into the fight in the CAUMONT area so as to make easier the task of the American armies fighting on the western flank.

'I have got to fight very hard on the eastern flank while the Americans are battling on the Western flank,' he wrote in a special letter to Brooke, accompanying his new directive to the Army commanders. 'From one or two things Ike said yesterday when he was here, there is no doubt that public opinion in America is asking why the American casualties are higher than the British – and why they have captured so many more prisoners,' he also acknowledged.

It was clearly impossible to make a public statement, outlining the whole strategy of the battle to the public at home – and consequently the enemy. The Germans still had no idea of Patton's presence in Normandy, nor of the full weight of American infantry and armour in the western sector compared with that of the east, where the Germans still believed the primary threat to lie. Yet this cavilling and miscomprehension worried Monty, as it threatened to undermine the morale of his British and Canadian troops in their thankless role. He complained to Brooke:

> It is not good for the morale of British troops in Normandy to see headlines in the English Newspapers:
> Set-back in Normandy
> etc
> etc
> I wonder if Grigg could have lunch with some leading editors and get this across to them.
> From the beginning it has been my policy to try and pull the main enemy strength, and especially his main armoured strength, on to the British Second Army on the eastern flank so that our affairs on the western flank could proceed more easily. After a great deal of hard fighting we got the main enemy armoured strength deployed on the eastern flank when the big American blow was struck in the west on 25 July at 1100 hrs. This was not a bad achievement. Very heavy fighting took place south of CAEN on 25 and 26 July and on the front of 2 Cdn DIV, *which was fighting its first battle in Normandy*, we were forced back 1000 yds in two places, i.e. at MAY and at TILLY.
> I would give 5 miles on the eastern flank if I could thereby get the whole of the Cherbourg and Brittany peninsulas!!

No more telling phrase could illustrate Monty's strategy; that night he sent a similar message to Churchill, rejecting any sensational notion of a reverse. 'I know of no "serious set-back". The enemy has massed great strength in area South of CAEN to oppose our advance in that quarter,' he explained. 'Very heavy fighting took place yesterday and the day before and as a result the troops of Canadian Corps were forced back 1,000 yards from the furthest position they had reached.' This was no 'set-back' since 'my policy since the beginning has been to draw the main enemy armoured strength on to my Eastern flank and to fight it there so that our affairs on Western flank could proceed the easier. In this policy I have succeeded; the main enemy armoured strength is repeat is now deployed on my eastern flank to East of the river ODON, and my affairs in the West are repeat are proceeding the easier and the Americans are going great guns.'

Sir Edgar Williams later cautioned against 'blaming' such miscreants in the Press, in the Air Force, in SHAEF and at home:

I think it is important not to suppose that everybody who didn't back Monty to the hilt or who got in the way or who interfered or who didn't understand, was necessarily ill-motivated. From Monty's point of view of course they were a lot of, you know, chaps who got in the way – from Monty's point of view it was sabotage – but in fact they were only trying to win the war like the rest of us! They were . . . according to *their* lights, they weren't being disloyal.[1]

The whole structure of Air Force command militated against close co-operation with the armies, a fact aggravated by the very personalities of the barons and the independent bureaucracies of their 'fiefs' in England. Men like Air Vice-Marshal Broadhurst and General 'Pete' Quesada – responsible for direct fighter-bomber support in the field – quickly adjusted to the limited airfield space in Normandy:

Harry Broadhurst was a sensible chap who got on with it, because he'd got a job to do,

Williams recalled.

But people higher up – the higher they go . . . you have to understand that they had a different sort of view, because there were too *many* senior Air Force commanders, Tedder, Leigh-Mallory, Coningham, all in a sense treading on each other's heels: they can't get into the main battle physically until they can set up their headquarters in Normandy, and so on – and for that they need those airfields.[2]

[1] Brigadier Sir Edgar Williams, interview of 28.1.83.
[2] Ibid.

Leigh-Mallory had very little knowledge of heavy bombing, having served as C-in-C of Fighter Command before his appointment to 'Overlord'; conversely Harris, who had Churchill's ear, was loth to place Bomber Command under Leigh-Mallory's jurisdiction; while Coningham, who had become more and more jealous of Monty since Alamein, was the first to connive with Tedder against Monty.

Tedder wasn't a fool. He was a thin-skinned, awkward, nervy individual, but he was far from being a fool,

Sir Edgar Williams pointed out.

He was a pretty shrewd chap, in fact. Monty's arguments didn't convince Tedder and he began to feel that if you were going to get any real results, from his point of view, then you'd got to be prepared to get rid of Monty. He didn't seem to me to measure the extraordinary blow to morale that would have resulted had Montgomery been removed. I think there would have been a *hell* of a political storm. . . .
   Tedder was exasperated again and again by Monty, couldn't stand his bombast, because in a way Tedder's own pride was exhibited by the opposite, a slightly bogus diffidence. The two men were antipathetic as human beings, quite apart from being from different arms of the services. . . . Monty's vocabulary, his strutting – everything that Tedder wouldn't do. Tedder's quizzical, pipe-sucking . . . sort of bogus amateurism (because he was a highly professional chap). It was a temperamental antipathy, quite apart from a doctrinal one.[1]

In Williams's view Monty had played into the hands of such men by his actions – like the ill-fated 'Goodwood' press conference, 'utilising the press by giving them misleading information'.[2] But in the end, he felt, Monty's problem was an insoluble one. Monty *had* to show unflagging confidence:

he'd got to be overconfident all the time in order to get people to be willing to be killed [on the Caen flank]. It was this overconfidence, I think, that misled those people who began to be impatient for results and therefore impatient with Montgomery because he wasn't producing results for them. If, when you go to see him, you're always told everything's fine, and so on, you do set up a barrier, do you see. . . . It becomes a problem of credibility.[3]

[1] Ibid.
[2] Ibid.
[3] Ibid.

It was this problem of Monty's credibility which had led to the 'whole atmosphere' becoming 'charged' in July, Williams considered. Men like Lt-Colonel Dawnay and Major Odgers, who saw the battle of Normandy from the vantage point of Monty's Tactical Headquarters, agreed.

Oh I think there's no doubt about it, he knew actually that there was considerable questioning of his way of fighting the battle,

Dawnay acknowledged.

And people were saying he had failed. I think Brookie made that perfectly clear to him the day he came over [19 July]. And Monty did then make a tremendous effort to convince the others – Ike, Marshall and the PM and so on. But I think he was very well aware that they were gunning for him. . . .

We were *all* worried, in July; people didn't understand what was going on, the hinge, all the weight there and giving time for the Americans to break out: we thought the Americans were being very slow, and the fact that they were twice bombed by their own bombers didn't help.

But we were all very worried, not worried about the outcome of the battle, we were worried about the effect on other people it was having. We all felt that given time Monty's strategy would succeed. But it *had* to be given time.[1]

Major Odgers, not being privy to Monty's more secret M signals or letters, well remembered 'that long July', and the hopes that were quite naturally pinned on 'Goodwood'. Retrospectively he acknowledged that:

you couldn't conceivably have had an operation spelt out, what the troops were going to do, saying, 'Your objective is to hold the firm hinge of Caen; subject yourselves to increasingly massive opposition, while Bradley is left free to get on with the breakout.' You couldn't possibly, because apart from anything else what made Monty's position/problem so difficult was that the role of Dempsey could only be discharged by the most intensely aggressive, severe fighting. You *had* to have the troops, when launched on Operation 'Goodwood' or whatever it was, aiming to go through to the Carpiquet airfields and beyond them, the thought being, 'we're going to go through, to punch through'; and that *had* to be the objective given to the troops because otherwise if you didn't give them that objective, if you come to think of it. . . .

[1] Lt-Colonel C. P. Dawnay, loc. cit.

747

Nothing is more destructive of morale than being put into a 'holding' position – so they have *got* to be thrusting. And indeed, I'm sure in the back of Monty's mind, and it certainly was in the back of mine when I used to read these things in our Ops room, was the possibility that you *might* in fact get through, it [the enemy front] might give way, and if so, then Monty would have *had* to in fact rather revise the thing: if the Caen hinge burst open. . . . There were moments, I can remember them, when it looked as if their front *was* beginning to shake and go. But it never did.

What I'm saying is that I think at that time . . . there was by definition an almost insuperable problem, because you could not be totally frank with people about what was going on – because you couldn't; if you *had* been, they would have said – a lot of people, 'I'm not bloody well going to do that.'

By the same token I think it was very difficult for people at home, although they heard the plan from Monty. I think when they were actually confronted with what was actually going on, day to day, I think it was very difficult for them to say, 'Okay, it's all right, boys, it'll be all right on the night' sort of thing. I think the problems were both on the ground and back home. There was a real problem of Monty's credibility which we – or I was – very conscious of in that long July. I began to think, 'This is very worrying' – as it was![1]

The miracle, in retrospect, was that Monty never lost his 'grip' on the battle, or on the hearts and minds of his soldiers. To Odgers this was a tribute to the way Monty operated in the field, from his Tactical Headquarters. As he had in the desert, in Sicily and Italy, Monty spent much of the day visiting formations and units in the field; what was different now was Monty's deliberate use of a carefully chosen team of young personal Liaison Officers, his 'eyes and ears':

They were a particular and characteristic method of Monty's – this liaison business. And it could only have been done by youngish men, because the strain of it was so great, you had to have the stamina to do it. It was no good having somebody who would take it more leisurely because he couldn't do it. Time was the essence of the thing – I mean he [Monty] wanted to know, if he could, what the situation was two hours ago in a certain Corps headquarters. And that could very often be achieved.[2]

If Monty could not dictate what was being said in rear headquarters, he was in total command of all that went on in the field. No visitor who ever set foot in his Tactical Headquarters in Normandy

[1] Major Paul Odgers, interview of 18.1.83.
[2] Ibid.

could doubt the unique aura of authority and informed military grip. The special map lorry which he had had built prior to D-Day contained a vast wall map of Normandy, constantly updated by the latest information from the Tac HQ Operations room:

There was a duty ADC always on. They would come to us for the information, we'd either send it or phone it across to them at once.

The master map was in a way ours. We were putting on stuff in very considerable detail – a great big wall, if you can picture the scene. We had a caravan which had a central passage with two sorts of tables, either side, well-lit, and the sides of it, which were solid, would lift up and supports would come down, and you then had two lean-tos.

And in one of the lean-tos on the whole wall of it was a great big map covered in talc. The other one we used just as a place where people could come and sit – I mean LOs and people could come and put their stuff down.

The LOs would come in and – depending entirely on the urgency of the thing I used to favour their coming to me first and collecting themselves and giving us a report, they'd dictate straight out. This typewriter, in a big operation, was going all the day, like a ticker tape! And copies were held back for historical purposes for Main 21 Army Group, and always a copy went off to the ADC in Monty's caravan. And then, their minds to a degree ordered, they would go in and talk to Monty. And I never allowed the poor chaps to go into a meal or anything until they'd unburdened themselves and we'd got this thing straight from the horse's mouth.[1]

Two of the Liaison Officers died in the course of their duties, two were wounded; all were decorated for personal bravery. Subordinate commanders might well have felt vexed by such young and relatively junior officers (all were majors) reporting back to the Commander-in-Chief not only the latest military situation as seen in their headquarters, but also the state of morale. Yet few commanders took this unique system amiss, partly because the officers chosen by Monty were sincere, loyal and courageous, and partly because their presence was tangible evidence of Monty's relentless desire to keep in closest touch with his fighting commanders – to feel continuously, like a caring doctor, the pulse of his men.

Did we ever feel in doubt about the way the battle was shaping? I think one must say – I don't think we ever did,

Odgers reflected.

[1] Ibid.

Because you see we had this vast confidence in Monty at the time. I mean, let's face it, it was too plain to us that we were not actually breaking-through [at 'Goodwood']. Second Army was butting its nose against the most formidable opposition the whole time. In 'Goodwood' yes, certainly, we were hoping; and we *were* disappointed when in fact they came to a halt – because, initially, there were signs that they were going places. And indeed I remember one afternoon when we had a report that they had taken a certain crossroads south of Caen, I remember Monty being most excited about it, that they'd got it. In fact, sadly, they hadn't: one of those occasions where these things get . . . where they are in fact 1/4 mile short of it – that sort of thing. So that one, yes, one did [feel disappointed] because the operation was presented – that there is to be an attack which is going through, as it were. But no, I think I can say to you, I really think this is true: I never remember being in a state of great despondency, though I think one felt it was dragging one. One did feel 'hope we can do it', but I didn't feel that something was dreadfully wrong, no. But I do remember this long July wait. And realizing the strains that were being created.[1]

That Monty managed to maintain the faith of his commanders and men in the field throughout the long and arduous development of his overall master-plan was perhaps the most telling illustration of his leadership. That command of such a prolonged battle was, as he pointed out to Eisenhower, a 'whole-time job for one man' was evidenced by the unique and unyielding 'grip' Monty had had to apply since taking that command. No battle in the West had equalled the struggle for Normandy. The battle of France, up to the Anglo-French evacuation at Dunkirk in 1940, had taken barely three weeks. The battle of Alamein in 1942 only twelve days, and even then hearts had failed. The entire assault and campaign to take Sicily had taken only thirty-eight days. Yet, as in Sicily, the astonishing success of the D-Day landings had given rise to hopes of a quick victory in Normandy thereafter, and it had required all Monty's patient guidance to keep his forces working towards the master-plan. 'Monty's plan never changed – his design from the start was to break-out from the Western (American) flank of the bridgehead,' Dempsey reiterated later to the English Historian Basil Liddell Hart;[2] in the field, on 6 August 1944, Monty's Chief of Staff would say the same to the BBC Correspondent, Chester Wilmot: 'Monty stuck to his original plan and didn't try altering it to any marked degree, despite everyone's

[1] Ibid.
[2] Notes of 18.3.52 in Dempsey file, loc. cit.

natural impatience.'[1] Recalling Eisenhower's impatient letter of 7 July, prior to 'Goodwood', Monty told Wilmot in 1946:

> Yes, I did get a letter like that. The trouble was that Ike began to lose his nerve. He didn't understand the battle and there was no one at Shaef who did. In this letter Ike said that he feared that we would be roped off in the bridgehead, and that a stalemate might result. He had evidently talked to Winston on these lines, for Winston came to see me. I explained to him what my plan was, and he understood at once, and assured Ike that he was certain that Ike's fears were groundless. Much the same situation arose in the battle of Alamein, when the people in London thought I wasn't getting anywhere.[2]

Churchill's understanding had served to smash Tedder's conspiracy, but with Eisenhower still fretting, Churchill's faith began again to waver on 27 July. If Churchill thus failed to stand up for Monty's strategy consistently, Brooke at least continued to battle hard for his protégé. To Brooke, Monty's Normandy strategy was so clear that he could not understand Eisenhower's apparent obsession with side issues, such as accusations in the American press that the British were leaving all the fighting up to the Americans:

> The strategy of the Normandy landing is quite straight-forward. The British (on left) must hold and draw Germans on to themselves off the western flank whilst Americans swing up to open Brest peninsula,

Brooke noted in his diary.

> But now comes the trouble; the Press chip in and we hear that the British are doing nothing and suffering no casualties whilst the Americans are bearing all the brunt of the war.
> There is no doubt that Ike is all out to do all he can to maintain the best relations between British and Americans. But it is equally clear

[1] Notebook IV, Wilmot Papers (15/15/62–93), loc. cit. De Guingand never wavered in his admiration for Monty's patient generalship in Normandy – 'he was determined to hold fast there and not give an inch on the left.' Whatever impatience there might be, 'I don't think there was much that could have been done. You see, all the German armour was concentrated against us, and Monty wasn't going to risk having his armoured forces wiped out' – as might have happened 'if Patton had been there'. The 'plot' at SHAEF he was disposed to forgive: 'I think you must look at it like this – that in all wars and big battles there are always these sorts of occasions, and you just have to get on with it. Which we did' – Major-General Sir Francis de Guingand, loc. cit.

[2] Notes on conversations with Monty, 18.5.46, Wilmot Papers (LH 1/230), loc. cit.

that Ike knows nothing about strategy. Bedell Smith, on the other hand, has brains but no military education in its true sense. He is certainly one of the best American officers, but still falls far short when it comes to strategic outlook. With that Supreme Command set-up it is no wonder that Monty's real high ability is not always realised. Especially so when 'national' spectacles pervert the perspective of the strategic landscape.[1]

If Eisenhower had criticisms of the way his Ground Forces Commander was directing the battle, Brooke therefore stated, he should go to Normandy and put them to Monty, not cavil behind his back. The suggestion was even made that Brooke accompany Eisenhower; but as General Simpson later recalled, the notion 'was a little worrying to Ike. He knew jolly well that if he went to Monty, Monty would run circles round him with a clear exposition of his strategy and tactics.'[2] No visit was thus arranged.

Brooke, however, was worried that he had not completely stopped the rot, and the next morning penned a long letter to Monty warning him of Eisenhower's 'mischief-making':

My dear Monty
The trouble between you and the P.M. has been satisfactorily settled for the present, but the other trouble I spoke to you about is looming large still and wants watching very carefully.

Ike lunched with P.M. again this week and as a result I was sent for by P.M. and told that Ike was worried at the outlook taken by the American Press that the British were not taking their share of the fighting and of the casualties. There seemed to be more in it than that and Ike himself seemed to consider that the British Army could and should be more offensive. The P.M. asked me to meet Ike at dinner with him which I did last night, Bedel was there also.

It is quite clear that Ike considers that Dempsey should be doing more than he does; it is equally clear that Ike has the very vaguest conception of war!

I drew attention to what your basic strategy had been, i.e. to hold with your left and draw Germans onto the flank while you pushed with your right. I explained how in my mind this conception was being carried out, that the bulk of the Armour had continuously been kept against the British.

He could not refute these arguments, and then asked whether I did not consider that we were in a position to launch major offensives on each Army front simultaneously. I told him that in view of the fact that the German density in Normandy is 2½ times

[1] A. Bryant, op. cit.
[2] Recollections of General Sir Frank Simpson, loc. cit.

that on the Russian front, whilst our superiority in strength was only in the nature of some 25% as compared to 300% Russian superiority on Eastern front, I did not consider that we were in a position to launch an all out offensive along the whole front. Such a procedure would definitely not fit in with our strategy of opening up Brest by swinging forward Western flank.

Evidently he has some conception of attack on the whole front which must be an American doctrine judging by Mark Clark with 5th Army in Italy!

However, unfortunately this same policy of attacking (or 'engaging the enemy') along the whole front is one that appeals to the P.M. – Ike may therefore obtain some support in this direction.

I told Ike that if he had any feeling that you were not running operations as he wished he should most certainly tell you, and express his views. That it was far better for him to put all his cards on the table and that he should tell you exactly what he thought.

He is evidently a little shy of doing so, I suggested that if I could help him in any way by telling you for him I should be delighted. He said that he might perhaps ask me to accompany him on a visit to you! So if you see me turn up with him you will know what it is all about.

Nevertheless, in order to allay American resentment, Brooke did urge Monty to ensure that Dempsey launch his attack 'at the earliest possible moment on a large scale. We must now allow German forces to move from his front to Bradley's front or we shall give more cause for criticism.'[1]

While Eisenhower was fretting in England, there were, thankfully, no such machinations in the field. On the second day of 'Cobra', Major Hanson recorded in his diary: 'Meanwhile the British effort east of CAEN continues with attacks from their positions south and east of Caen. Hoped that German would accept our preliminary Cobra [i.e. the previous day's abortive bombing] simply as diversionary attack for the Caen operation and thrust his weight over there while we got off on the real business in our sector.' That afternoon Monty arrived 'from his hqs to discuss progress of the attack, plan the employment of FUSAG [First US Army Group] when we reached our objective calling for the employment of both [American] armies. Monty dressed in same peculiar uniform and he sauntered up, greeted cordially by Brad who unfailingly hangs on the sir term of address.'[2]

By the 27 July, as Bradley pushed through his armoured divisions, the German front began to disintegrate. Patton came to Bradley's

---

[1] Handwritten original in Montgomery Papers.
[2] Diary of Chester B. Hansen, loc. cit.

headquarters 'worried for fear the war may end here before he gets in. . . . Patton admits to Bradley that he is anxious to get in [the American armour]: 'I must get in and do something spectacularly successful,' he says, 'if I am to make good.'[1]

Thus while Eisenhower still worried, the battle of Normandy was reaching its long-awaited climax. On 28 July Monty brought Dempsey to Bradley's headquarters to discuss the next Allied moves. 'Brad's welcome to them was warm and refreshing, came out of his truck, wrung their hands and said he was glad to see them. . . . Dempsey is planning to jump off his 30th corps on the left of the V [US] Corps and protect our flank on that side as we move out.'[2]

With the success of 'Cobra' now becoming apparent even to SHAEF, Eisenhower suddenly changed his tune. A cable from Monty reached him on the evening of 28 July, bearing out all that Brooke had predicted. 'On west flank the battle is going splendidly and Bradley's troops are in COUTANCE. It begins to look as if the general plan on which we have been working so long is at last going to pay a dividend,' Monty informed him. To ensure that nothing leaked from the German Caen sector to Bradley's salient he had also ordered Dempsey that afternoon to advance the date of the British attack from Caumont: 'I have ordered DEMPSEY to throw all caution overboard and to take any risks he likes and to accept any casualties and to step on the gas for VIRE.'[3] This was followed by a message from Monty early the next morning, thanking Eisenhower for his cable sent on the evening of 28 July – 'which arrived here late last night.' In this Eisenhower had at last complimented Monty: 'Am delighted that your basic plan has begun brilliantly to unfold with Bradley's initial success' – and begging Monty to speed up Dempsey's Caumont attack, which Monty had already put forward to July 30. Such constant *post factum* harrying was a trial to Monty, but in view of Brooke's warning he answered:

Expect you have got my M68 saying that attack from CAUMONT area goes in tomorrow Sunday. Two divisions can reach that area by then and others will be thrown in to the battle as they arrive. BRADLEY DEMPSEY and myself met together yesterday afternoon and drew up agreed plans to complete the dislocation of enemy and on eastern flank CRERAR will play his part. Have great hopes we shall win a great victory and achieve our basic object.

Later that day, elated by the news of events, Eisenhower boarded his B-25 and flew to Normandy to see Bradley and Monty, taking his

[1] Ibid.
[2] Ibid.
[3] This order was given to Dempsey on the morning of 28 July; Brooke's letter arrived that evening at 6.30 p.m. – see signal M69, Montgomery Papers.

driver Kay Summersby on her first trip to France – a fact that had not stopped her, like Tedder and Bedell Smith, from joining the chorus of those accusing Monty of over-cautiousness and 'reluctance to attack until he had a force as powerful as that at El Alamein', as she wrote after the war in her book *Eisenhower Was My Boss*.[1]

In Normandy Eisenhower recognised at first hand that victory was indeed in sight. Back in England the following day, as Bradley pushed further south and Dempsey's Caumont attack kicked off, Eisenhower belatedly attempted to make up for his lack of wholehearted support of Monty during the preceding weeks. Addressing a telegram to the American military censor, General Surles, he took to task those writers who in America had expressed 'sharp criticism' of Montgomery – criticism which he took upon his own shoulders: he was, he now claimed, himself responsible 'for strategy and major activity' in Normandy;[2] therefore criticism of Montgomery was criticism of him, the Supreme Commander. Considering that less than forty-eight hours previously Eisenhower had been levelling these same criticisms against Monty in the presence of Churchill and Brooke, this was a trifle hypocritical. But now that he had seen for himself in Normandy that Monty's long-drawn out strategy was about to produce victory, he could at last with sincerity stand up for his 'principal subordinate'.

[1] Kay Summersby, London 1949. 'This book should never have been written,' Monty would later note in his diary; 'it can do no good to General Eisenhower. If American generals were in the habit of dealing with women drivers and secretaries as Eisenhower and others appear to have done if this book is true, then their characters must slump in the eyes of the world. This book makes it clear that Eisenhower discussed with Kay Summersby, his *woman car driver*, his views on Generals under him and also disclosed to her the most secret matters; all this is now given to the public in her book. Her views on the leading war figures are enlightening, since they are obviously Eisenhower's views; the British come out badly, the Americans always win' – Montgomery Papers.

[2] *The Papers of Dwight David Eisenhower*, op. cit.

The Falaise Gap

A few days later Brooke was writing to Monty:

> I am delighted that our operations are going so successfully and conforming so closely to your plans.
>
> For the present all the 'mischief making tongues' are keeping quiet; I have no doubt they will start wagging again and am watching them.[1]

The sudden ripening of Monty's Normandy strategy had transformed the moment. At last the doubters, the belly-achers, grumblers and men of faint heart were silenced, and those armchair strategists who wanted 'gains' could mark up their atlases once more. Von Kluge was mesmerised, and in his weekly report on 31 July believed that the Canadian diversionary attacks from the area of Caen had been the primary Allied break-out attempt. 'After hard fighting and counter-attacks, 1st SS armoured corps gained a complete defensive victory,' he claimed.[2] Not only had Monty thus succeeded in keeping the German 'Armoured Group West' away from the American breakout, but he had kept it east of Noyers. When on 30 July Dempsey launched the start of his full-scale armoured attack from Caumont, von Kluge was therefore doubly mispositioned. He was still certain that Monty would make directly for Paris, expecting Montgomery first to enlarge the bridgehead and then to 'make the thrust towards Paris' from the British sector.

Like Rommel, von Kluge was playing straight into Montgomery's hands. Within hours of the 30 July kick-off, Dempsey had a British armoured division nearing Le Bény Bocage, thus shielding the left flank of Bradley's new salient – which in turn had reached Avranches, at the base of the Cherbourg peninsula. 'On west flank right Corps of First US Army is now fighting in AVRANCHES and I hope to turn it westwards into BRITTANY tomorrow or Wednesday,' Monty signalled Brooke on the evening of 31 July.

Patton was now to become operational, though in order to conceal

[1] Letter of 4.8.44, original in Montgomery Papers.
[2] Templehoff Papers, loc. cit.

the importance of the American break-out, it was decided (much to Patton's chagrin) not to release his name as Commander of Third US Army publicly.

'I must throw everything into the present battle,' Monty wrote in high spirits on 1 August to Simpson at the War Office:

> The American armies *on the right*, and the Second British Army *in the centre*, are now in process of carrying out the big wheel that will I hope clear Brittany – push the Germans back behind the ORNE – and swing the right flank of the wheel up towards PARIS (possibly).
>
> If the Second Army can progress steadily now, we have the German 'roping off' force cut in two. Once we get to VIRE and CONDE, it will be awkward for the Germans – and I am working to that.
>
> *On the left*, Canadian Army must hold, while the force pivots on that flank. I must take everything I can from the left and put it into the right swing. . . .
>
> Everything is going very well. The full plan, which I have been working to all the time, is now slowly working out as planned. I hope to turn the right Corps of 12 Army Group westwards into Brittany tomorrow.

There *was* something moving about this long-awaited moment. Had the June storms not forced Bradley to close down his southern offensive at the time of the advance on Cherbourg, a month might have been saved – a month in which Dempsey had had to keep up his costly feint on the esaetern flank, and Bradley to take the heavy casualties necessitated by a belated St Lô offensive. Yet these were the fortunes of war. Despite the 'real tragedy in delaying build up and deployment of your forces' as Brooke had called it in June,[1] Monty had nevertheless stuck relentlessly to his strategy, a strategy which was now paying off in the most spectacular way. Thus at one moment Eisenhower's headquarters was openly discussing the dismissal of Monty; hours later Eisenhower was agreeing to give tactical command of the two new Army Groups – 12th US Army Group[2] and 21st British Army Group – to Montgomery. At twelve noon on 1 August, despite the original agreement that Eisenhower would assume field command of Allied ground forces now that two Army Groups were becoming operational in Normandy, not Eisenhower

[1] Letter of 23.6.44, original in Montgomery Papers.
[2] The title was changed from the intended First US Army Group partly in order to avoid confusion with First US Army (to be commanded by General Courtney Hodges once Bradley took command of the Group of US armies), but primarily so that the Allied deception plan for a landing in the Pas de Calais by the supposed First US Army Group could be maintained.

but Monty controlled the climax of the battle. By the following evening Monty was writing to Simpson:

The battle goes well and completely according to plan. RENNES is now ours – and ST MALO.

I doubt if there are many Germans in the whole of Brittany, except base wallahs, etc. George Patton should be in BREST in a day or two.

The broad plan remains unchanged.

I shall swing the right flank round, and up towards PARIS. And while this is going on I shall try to hold the enemy to his ground in the CAEN area. Then I hope to put down a large airborne force, including 52 [British] Div, somewhere in the CHARTRES area and cut off the enemy escape through the gap between PARIS and ORLEANS.

The big idea would be to push the enemy up against the Seine – and get a 'cop'.

However these things don't always work out quite as planned!!

he remarked presciently.

'The present operations are absolutely as planned,' Monty claimed. But were they? Time and again Monty had hoped that Second Army would achieve *more* than just the overall execution of the Normandy master-plan; had hoped that Dempsey might in fact achieve a local envelopment that would do *more* than merely retain the enemy on the British flank. So when Major-General 'Pip' Roberts smashed his 11th Armoured Division some twelve miles through the German front at Caumont in less than thirty-six hours, there arose the chance that, if Dempsey could keep up the momentum towards Vire, a whole pocket of German troops facing Bradley's left flank could be rolled up. To do this, Dempsey must push out enough armour on Roberts's left flank to allow him to swing east without hindrance towards Flers, cutting off the Germans in Vire.

To Dempsey's disappointment such exploitation proved impossible, partly because 7th Armoured Division simply failed to push out its flanking shield in time. By midday on 2 August Dempsey was aware that it was too late, that by then no less than three German Panzer divisions – 21st, 10th SS, and 9th SS Panzer Divisions – were shifting westwards to counter the threat. As Monty lamented that evening to Simpson, 'I fear I shall have to remove Erskine from 7 Armd DIV. He will not fight his division and take risks. It was very easy in the desert to get a "bloody nose", and a good many people did get one. The old desert divisions are apt to look over their shoulder, and wonder if all is OK behind, or if the flanks are secure, and so on. 7 Armd Div is like that. They want a new General, who will drive them headlong into, and through, gaps torn in the enemy defence – not worrying about flanks or anything.' Some 90,000 Germans had surrendered already since D-Day – 'the big mass of German soldiery want an opportunity to surrender, and they must be given it; this does not apply to the S.S. troops,' he remarked. 'Great vistas are opening up ahead, and we want Generals now who will put their heads down and go like hell.'

Such a man was, of course, Patton, and in the ensuing weeks Patton was to give perhaps the finest performance of 'headlong' mobile operations ever seen in military history – certainly on a par with the German armoured break-through to Boulogne and Calais in 1940. Disregarding his flanks Patton set about surprising the enemy by sheer speed rather than by fighting, with stunning results. At 10.30 a.m. on 1 August Monty had given orders to Bradley that, when Third Army 'takes up the reins at midday' it was to 'pass one Corps through AVRANCHES straight into the BRITTANY Peninsula. Its other two Corps will be directed on LAVAL and ANGERS' on the Loire. Though Bradley and Patton both faltered before committing so large a part of Third Army to the wheel eastwards, the lack of German resistance did not prejudice such indecision as it had on Dempsey's front, and over the ensuing days Patton would belatedly make the sweep on Paris which Monty wanted.

Patton's giant eastward wheel, however, would only succeed if Crerar, Dempsey and Bradley kept von Kluge's main attention between Caen and Mortain; it was vital to ensure that the Germans formed no new defensive line behind which they could withdraw mobile forces to deal with Patton. By smashing the main enemy pivots, Monty felt, the Germans must accept all-out battle on the whole Fifth Panzer Army/Seventh Army front, for fear of it disintegrating. Meanwhile General Hodges – who with the elevation of Bradley to 12th US Army Group had taken command of First US Army – and General Patton could wheel eastwards towards Paris. Hodges was to swing around Dempsey's right flank, and make for Argentan, while Patton would send two corps racing round in a deep envelopment towards Paris, pivoting on the Mayenne at Laval. 'The broad strategy of the Allied Armies is to swing the right flank round towards PARIS, and to force the enemy back against the SEINE – over which river all the bridges have been destroyed between Paris and the sea,' Monty's M516 directive of 4 August to the Allied armies stated.

The day before, at 10 a.m., Monty had visited Dempsey at his headquarters. With the three Panzer divisions contesting his advance at Le Bény Bocage and further forces fighting hard to deny American access into Vire, Monty began to see a new shape forming: the possibility of cutting off the Germans facing Dempsey and Hodges in what would become known as the 'Falaise gap'. For if Crerar could also be made to strike southwards towards Falaise, von

Kluge's forces would be pinched off, and surrounded if Hodges and Patton could envelope their southern flank. Thus on the evening of 3 August Monty gave telephone instructions for Crerar to 'launch a heavy attack from the CAEN sector in the direction of Falaise',[1] which he confirmed in writing the following day:

Object of the Operation
To break through the enemy positions to the south and south-east of CAEN, and to gain such ground in the direction of FALAISE as will cut off the enemy forces now facing Second Army and render their withdrawing eastwards difficult – if not impossible. . . .
The attack to be launched *as early as possible* and in any case not later than 8 August – dependent on good weather for air support. Every day counts, and speed in preparing and launching the attack is very necessary.

This was Operation 'Totalize', and since Crerar and Simonds had been considering for some days how a possible break-through might be affected from the Caen 'hinge', it proved possible to mount it already on the night of 7 August, using new techniques of night bombing by flare markers and specially cut-down American 'Priest' guns to form armoured infantry carriers.

This was possibly the most exciting moment of the war – and Monty was in his element. 'My dogs, rabbits, and birds, are all in good health. We are acquiring large areas of France at a rapid rate,' he boasted on 6 August to Phyllis Reynolds. He had moved his Tac HQ near to 21st Army Group's Main Headquarters which had at last come over from England and was established at Le Tronquay. Having drawn up a new directive for his armies – M517 – he sent a copy to Brooke with a grateful covering letter:

Tac Headquarters
21 Army Group
6-8-44

My dear CIGS
I am sending Dawnay over with my directive for the advance to the SEINE, and he will take this letter.
All goes well. In fact everything is working out so much according to plan that one wonders, sometimes, whether it isn't a bit too good.
On the other hand we have been through our difficult days, as you know. And if we had faltered in those days we might well not be where we are now.
I would like to thank you for your firm support at all times. It

---

[1] C. P. Stacey, *The Victory Campaign*, Ottawa 1960.

makes a great difference to me to know that you stand like a firm rock behind us, and your faith in what we are trying to achieve is constant.

In this new directive Monty was still unsure whether von Kluge was perhaps pulling back to 'some new defensive line; but there is no evidence yet to show exactly what that line is;' he certainly did not expect von Kluge to put his main Panzer strength into the Allied noose. If the Canadians were successful in reaching Falaise, then all von Kluge's forces west of Falaise were in danger of being cut off; if von Kluge withdrew eastwards in front of the Canadians, then Patton could cut them off by moving behind: 'if he [the enemy] holds strongly in the north as he may well do, that is the chance for our right flank to swing round and thus cut off his escape. But whatever the enemy may want to do will make no difference to us,' Monty declared in his directive. 'We will proceed relentlessly, and rapidly, with our own plans for his destruction.' No more troops were to be used for the clearing of Brittany 'than are necessary, as the main business lies to the east', he went on. 'Plans will be made for the right flank to swing rapidly eastwards, and then north-eastwards towards PARIS; speed in this movement is the basis of the whole plan of operations.' By dropping two airborne divisions at Chartres, the Germans retreating south-west of Paris would be blocked; while the absence of bridges to the north of Paris would enable the Germans to be squeezed against the Seine if they retreated that way. If this aim was achieved, Monty stated, 'we shall have hastened the end of the war.'

That night however, the shift of von Kluge to a 'new defensive line' was revealed to be a shift to an *offensive* line – a secret counter-attack by four Panzer divisions ordered by Hitler to take place on 7 August, with the object of splitting the Allied army groups at Avranches. Although Ultra Intelligence did not reveal the German Panzer attack in advance, the rapid decrypting of ancillary orders for air support and the like enabled both Monty and Bradley to assess the scale of the offensive almost immediately. Thus, when Monty reported by signal to Brooke on the evening of 7 August, shortly before the Canadian night-attack towards Falaise began, he was delighted by the way things were going:

Enemy attack in MORTAIN area has been well held by the Americans and all positions intact. . . . When the attack developed three American divs were moving southwards between MORTAIN and AVRANCHES and these were halted this morning to provide additional security in this gap. I have no fears whatever for the security of this part of the front and am proceeding with my offensive plans elsewhere without change.

761

Forty-five minutes later he was signalling:

> My L.O. has just returned from the LAVAL front and reports that the leading troops of 15 US Corps have reached LOUE which is only about 15 miles from LE MANS. This is very good news and it is quite possible that this Corps will reach LE MANS tomorrow. . . . If only the Germans will go on attacking at MORTAIN for a few more days it seems that they might not be able to get away.

Monty still favoured a wide envelopment that would permit Patton to shut off the Orléans escape-route and then swing north to the Seine and the Channel. Such a deep envelopment would ensure the least opposition, since the bulk of the German fighting units were inextricably bound up in the fighting from Falaise to Mortain. Bradley, however, favoured a shorter hook, and was supported by Monty's own senior staff officers, de Guingand and Williams:

> Monty was sold on the wide outflanking move – blocking the Orléans Gap with paratroops etc and switching the armour Northwards along the left bank of Seine to form a big pocket,

Brigadier Williams confessed to Chester Wilmot after the battle.

> Did not change this till *after* Mortain began – and then only on urging of Freddie, Bradley and Bill [Williams].[1]

'Bill now thinks Monty's original plan was right,' Wilmot noted, after the shorter envelopment at Falaise had failed to bottle up as many German forces as was hoped; Monty himself seems however never to have rued his decision. In war a commander must be prepared to take quick decisions, Monty claimed; and by 8 August American patrols on Hodge's front at Mortain suggested that von Kluge was withdrawing from his abortive Panzer attack. If Patton moved immediately *north* from Le Mans, as well as continuing with the planned wider envelopment of the enemy at Chartres and up to Paris, then there was a chance of bottling up von Kluge's armies between Mortain and Falaise. 'A strong force of four divisions will operate tomorrow northwards from the LE MANS area towards ALENCON. . . . I am trying to get FALAISE and ALENCON as the first step to closing the ring behind the enemy,' Monty signalled to Brooke on the evening of 8 August.

Just as Monty sought to encircle the enemy – 'to surround and destroy the German army west of the SEINE', as Patton put it in his new orders to 15 US Corps – there arose complications of a haun-

[1] Notebook XIX, Wilmot Papers (15/15/62–93), loc. cit.

tingly familiar kind. Churchill had flown across the Channel the previous day (7 August) and had tried to enlist Monty's support in cancelling 'Anvil', due to take place on the Mediterranean coast of France on 15 August. Like Churchill Monty thought the operation was a grave irrelevance, particularly if the 'Anvil' forces could be re-routed and brought in through the Brittany ports once they began to fall. On the other hand it was vital not to delay the main victory at Falaise by having to concentrate Patton's Third Army on the reduction of these Brittany ports, as Monty explained to Churchill: 'I told him as follows', he reported to Brooke:

a) I was not in touch with the strategical and political issues involved;

b) the date for DRAGOON [the new name for 'Anvil'] was 15 Aug and that is only 7 days off;

c) we have not yet captured the ports in Brittany in which the ships would come. The ports may all be mined, as was Cherbourg;

d) from the purely military aspect it seemed to me to be too late to make a switch;

e) from other aspects, it would probably mean a quarrel with the Americans, and would do us no good;

f) taken all round, I was in favour of deciding *well ahead* what we wanted to do – and then doing it. You cannot make big changes at the last moment.

The P.M. struck me as looking old and tired; he seemed to find it difficult to concentrate on a subject for more than a few moments; he seemed restless and unable to make up his mind about anything.[1]

It was important to decide on one's priorities – and stick to them, Monty felt. As he cabled to Brooke on the night of 9 August:

Heavy fighting is going on in outskirts of ST MALO, BREST and LORIENT. There is considerable pressure from outside sources that more troops should be sent into the peninsula to get the ports cleaned up quickly. I do not agree with this myself and consider that the main business lies to the east.

In this all the field commanders as well as Eisenhower himself – who set up a Command Post in Normandy on 7 August – were agreed, though Patton, it was reported, did not like the idea of a short envelopment at Falaise, preferring Monty's original policy of a Third Army drive eastwards towards the Orléans gap. There is, in

---

[1] Letter of 9.8.44, Montgomery Papers.

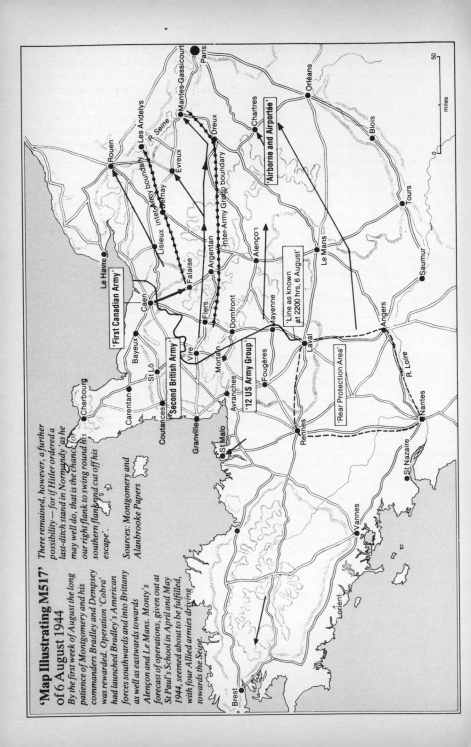

'Map Illustrating M517' of 6 August 1944

By the first week of August the long patience of Montgomery and his commanders Bradley and Dempsey was rewarded. Operation 'Cobra' had launched Bradley's American forces southwards and into Brittany as well as eastwards towards Alençon and Le Mans. Monty's forecast of operations, given out at St Paul's School in April and May 1944, seemed about to be fulfilled, with four Allied armies driving towards the Seine.

There remained, however, a further possibility — for if Hitler ordered a last-ditch stand in Normandy 'as he may well do, that is the chance to our right flank to swing round his southern flank and cut off his escape'.

Sources: Montgomery and Alanbrooke Papers

Le Havre

Rouen · Les Andelys

R. Seine

inter-Army boundary

Lisieux Bernay

Evreux

Dreux

Mantes-Gassicourt

Paris

Orléans

Blois

Tours

Chartres

'Airborne and Airportée'

Falaise

Argentan

Alençon

Le Mans

inter-Army Group boundary

Caen

'First Canadian Army'

Flers

Domfront

Mayenne

Angers

Saumur

Bayeux

St Lô

Vire

Mortain

Fougères

Laval

'Line as known at 2200 hrs, 6 August'

'Second British Army'

Coutances

Avranches

'12 US Army Group'

Rennes

Nantes

R. Loire

'Rear Protection Area'

Cherbourg

Carentan

Granville

St Malo

St Nazaire

Brest

Lorient

Vannes

50 miles 0

fact, evidence that Monty was in two minds himself about the short envelopment at Falaise. 'There are great possibilities in the present situation,' he signalled to Brooke on 9 August. 'If we can get to ALENCON ARGENTAN and FALAISE fairly quickly we have a good chance of closing the ring round the main German forces and I am making all plans to drop an airborne division at GACE about 15 miles east of ARGENTAN in order to complete the block.' But would it work in the confined bocage countryside which so favoured defence? By 12 August Bradley's ADC, Major Hansen, was recording: 'There is some discussion now concerning an alleged disagreement in strategy between Brad and Monty concerning the timing of this northward movement [of Patton's Third Army]. I am told that Monty is anxious that the continued movement toward Paris in seizure of more terrain while Brad is equally insistent that we turn north now at Le Mans and trap the German army containing the hinge of the 1st Army and those elements facing the 30th and 12th Corps in the 2nd British Army.'[1]

Certainly Monty seems to have been unsure whether the German pocket could be successfully closed, for at the end of his 9 August signal he added: 'Should the Germans escape us here I shall proceed quickly with the plan outlined in M517' – the wider envelopment. The outlook was promising, either way – as he wrote to Brooke that day:

9-8-44

My dear CIGS

Simbo takes this and will give you our news.

The enemy attack at MORTAIN was just what we wanted. It was held without difficulty; I put the 2nd T.A.F. [Tactical Air Force] on to it, as well as the [9th] Air Force, and all the pilots all had a great day. They claimed 120 'flamers'; but I doubt that.

On the left the Canadian attack is aimed at FALAISE. I have ordered them to hold that place securely, and from it to operate southwards towards ARGENTAN and westwards towards CONDE.

8 Corps, the right wing of Second Army, is moving on TINCHEBRAY today, but I do not expect this advance to progress far. Its main task is to hold the enemy to his ground.

The right wing of 12 Army Group, 15 U.S. Corps, is at LE MANS, where it will secure a bridgehead. I have ordered it then to operate northwards to ALENCON; this is a very important thrust.

I am aiming at closing in behind the Germans. The Canadians should be able to fight their way to FALAISE,

<hr>

[1] Diary of Chester B. Hansen, loc. cit.

he felt – but warned Brooke not to expect spectacular results;

they will not have the easy time they fancied, but they should get there; at present their forward movement is not making rapid progress.

The Germans will fight hard for FALAISE I think. I don't think the Americans will have any difficulty in getting to ALENCON, as there is nothing there to oppose them.

If we can get to FALAISE, and can also hold ALENCON strongly, we should then be able to close the gap in between – and that would be very excellent.

But the Germans will fight hard; it is good defensive country and we must not expect things to go too rapidly.

So far the Poles have not displayed that dash we expected, and have been sticky.

Crerar had not impressed Monty as Commander of 1st Canadian Army. At the critical moment on 23 July when Crerar's Army headquarters became operational, Crerar had had a stand-up row with his Corps Commander, Lt-General Crocker, whom Crerar attempted immediately to sack.[1] Now Crerar was 'fighting his first battle and it is the first appearance in history of a Canadian Army H.Q. He is desperately anxious that it should succeed. He is so anxious that he worries himself all day!!

I go and see him a lot and calm him down.

He will be much better when he realises that battles seldom go completely as planned, that you keep at it until the other chap cracks, and that if you worry you will eventually go mad!!

He seemed to have gained the idea that all you want is a good initial fire plan, and then the Germans all run away!!

Crerar's naïveté about battle was something Monty felt he could cure; the 'mischief-making tongues' at Eisenhower's headquarters were, however, something he could not, and when the true story of the recent attempts to unsaddle him was narrated to him, he was justifiably annoyed.

[1] 'Harry Crerar has started off his career as an Army Comd. by thoroughly upsetting everyone,' Monty had written to Brooke on 26 July, after sorting out the affair; 'he [Crerar] had a row with Crocker the first day and asked me to remove Crocker. I have spent two days trying to restore peace, investigating the quarrel and so on. As always there are faults on both sides, but the basic cause was Harry; I fear he thinks he is a great soldier, and he was determined to show it the moment he took over command at 1200 hrs on 23 July. He made his first mistake at 1205 hrs; and his second after lunch. . . . I have had each of them to see me . . . and I now hope I can get on with fighting the Germans – instead of stopping the generals fighting amongst themselves!!'

Rumours keep reaching me of bad influences at work at SHAEF,

he began. To his surprise Bedell Smith, who had still not visited him *since D-Day*, was quoted as one of these, something Monty felt hard to credit, for he had regarded Smith as a tough and sensible Chief of Staff to Eisenhower ever since Algiers:

> My own feeling is that Bedel Smith is all right and not bad in that way. He is intensely 'national'; but I would say he is a good member of the Allied team.
>
> His intense national pride may be at work to try and make it appear that the war in Normandy is being fought by two separate parties – a British party and an American party, with no connection between the two.
>
> If this were so, we would NOT be where we are today,

Monty pointed out emphatically. 'It is of course one party, working on one plan, and controlled by one H.Q. IKE is quite clear on this aspect of the matter.' It distressed him that British officers like Generals Gale and Morgan should have shown such little loyalty to the self-sacrificing efforts of the British forces throughout the battle, preferring to curry favour with Eisenhower and Bedell Smith by conspiring against the British commander in the field, and helping to polarise SHAEF and the War Office: 'the senior British officers at SHAEF must realise that, in addition to being good Allied chaps, they have definite loyalties to their own side of the house; and, in our side of the house, we must all pull together.'

For the moment Monty hoped that the looming Allied victory would serve to keep the critics at SHAEF silent – for it was vital to ensure Allied co-ordination if the enemy was to be decisively defeated west of the Seine. Would the Germans go on fighting to the bitter end in Normandy – or would the mobile divisions attempt to flee, like the Afrika Korps at Alamein, leaving the infantry to its fate? Certainly if Bradley turned north to Argentan too early, he risked missing the wider envelopment on the line of the Seine. 'There are certain indications that he [the enemy] intends a big attack tomorrow between DOMFRONT and MORTAIN. I do not really know what is likely to happen on that front tomorrow or in the future,' he informed Brooke on 10 August. The Canadians were held short of Falaise;[1] he had ordered Dempsey to shift his weight over to his left

---

[1] 'P.S. Latest reports are that 4 Canadian Armd DIV is well on. The Poles are still on their start line & thus exposing the eastern flank of the Canadian spearhead,' Monty added below his letter to Brooke of 9 August. 'I have told Harry to give the Poles a kick up the fork.'

flank[1] and attack towards Falaise also, with the Canadian Army pushing armour 'towards TRUN and ARGENTAN' instead of a paratroop drop.

As the hours and days passed it seemed unbelievable that the Germans would risk sacrificing their entire Panzer Army Group in the Mortain salient. 'The German is either crazy or he doesn't know what's going on,' Bradley remarked with incredulity to his ADC on 10 August. 'I think he is too smart to do what he is doing. He can't know what's going on in our sector. Surely the professional soldier must know the jig is up.'[2] That day Ultra Intelligence decrypted von Kluge's suicidal order for a renewed German attack at Mortain – and given the fanatical way in which many of the German units were fighting, neither Monty nor Bradley really expected the Germans to surrender. On 11 August Monty therefore issued another directive, M518, in which he congratulated Bradley's Army Group for the way it had blunted the German armoured bid for Avranches, and considered what would now happen. It was obvious that the enemy, in danger of being surrounded, would attempt to escape. But how?

> The bulk of the enemy forces are west of the general line LE MANS–CAEN.
>
> All their supplies, petrol, etc. must come from the east. But the gap through which this must all come is narrowing; in the north we are approaching FALAISE and in the south we are approaching ALENCON.
>
> Obviously, if we can close the gap completely we shall have put the enemy in the most awkward predicament.
>
> a) As the gap narrows the enemy is certain to re-act.
>
> b) He will possibly bring in additional divisions from the east.
>
> c) His armoured and mobile forces in the MORTAIN area are likely to operate to break out eastwards, as it is in that direction they will find petrol and supplies. Should this happen, I consider they are more likely to operate in the general area DOMFRONT–ARGENTAN–ALENCON, so as to have the benefit of the difficult 'bocage' country. Their object would be to hold off the right wing of 12 Army Group, and generally to facilitate the withdrawal of their forces on the FALAISE–VIRE front.

[1] Monty met Dempsey at General Ritchie's 12 Corps Headquarters at 4.15 p.m. on 10 August to ensure the vital nature of the shift was understood – cf. entry of 10.8.44, diary of M. C. Dempsey, loc. cit. The conference was repeated at the same time the following day: 'Flew to Headquarters 12 Corps and there met C-in-C and Commander First Cdn Army. Cdn Army is now definitely held up four or five miles NORTH of FALAISE. The capture of FALAISE is of great importance and C-in-C wishes me to thrust strongly with 12 Corps so as to assist Cdn Army in their task' – ibid., 11.8.44.

[2] Diary of Chester B. Hansen, loc. cit.

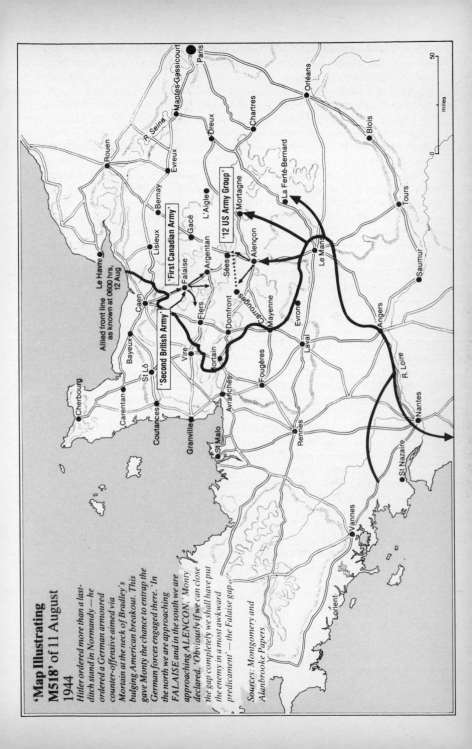

'Map Illustrating M518' of 11 August 1944

Hitler ordered more than a last-ditch stand in Normandy — he ordered a German armoured counter-offensive aimed via Mortain at the neck of Bradley's bulging American breakout. This gave Monty the chance to entrap the German forces engaged there. 'In the north we are approaching FALAISE and in the south we are approaching ALENCON', Monty declared. 'Obviously if we can close the gap completely we shall have put the enemy in a most awkward predicament' — the Falaise gap.

Sources: Montgomery and Alanbrooke Papers

Allied front line as known at 0600 hrs, 12 Aug

'First Canadian Army'

'12 US Army Group'

'Second British Army'

Paris

Mantes-Gassicourt

Orléans

Rouen

R. Seine

Dreux

Chartres

Blois

Evreux

L'Aigle

La Ferté-Bernard

Tours

Bernay

Lisieux

Gacé

Mortagne

Le Havre

Falaise

Argentan

Sees

Alençon

Le Mans

Caen

Flers

Domfront

Carrouges

Mayenne

Evron

Angers

Saumur

Bayeux

Vire

Mortain

Fougères

Laval

St Lô

Avranches

Rennes

R. Loire

Coutances

Granville

St Malo

Nantes

Carentan

Cherbourg

St Nazaire

Vannes

Lorient

50

miles

0

In Monty's directive the Canadians were instructed to pivot on Falaise, and close the German escape route by pushing a phalanx of armour down to Argentan; meanwhile Bradley would swing forces up from Le Mans to Alençon and then to a line between Carrouges and Sées, about twenty kilometres south of Argentan, thus depriving the Germans of any roads out of the pocket. In a final rider Monty warned, however, 'we must be ready to put into execution the full plan given in M517 [for full envelopment] should it appear likely that the enemy may escape us here. 12 Army Group will therefore continue to plan the airborne operation against the CHARTRES area as referred to in para 17 of M517; this may have to be put into execution at short notice, and it must be on very simple lines.' In his evening telegram to Brooke he added: 'I have instructed BRADLEY to collect a fresh Army Corps of three divisions in the LE MANS area and to hold it ready to push quickly through towards CHARTRES if and when we suddenly put M517 into operation.'

To capture Falaise, Monty predicted, would take forty-eight hours, but the speed of Patton's manoeuvre now surprised Monty as much as it did the Germans who, according to Ultra decrypts the next day, were indeed planning the southern armoured shield against 12th Army Group which Monty had considered their most likely plan for extricating the forces tied down by the British and Canadians. At 10 p.m. on 11 August Patton had not even reached Alençon; by the same time the following evening, when Monty drafted his signal to Brooke, American forces were in Argentan, with reconnaissance elements in the Carrouges-Sées area. 'It was this situation that this evening caused Gen. Patton in a moment of lightheartedness to call Brad and ask, "We now have elements in Argentain [sic] – shall we continue and drive the British into the sea for another Dunkirk?"' Hansen noted in his diary.[1]

So far, of course, Patton had missed all the shooting, as Bradley had remarked when having to issue direct orders to one of Patton's Corps commanders for a better 'hinge' between First and Third Armies: 'We can't risk a loose hinge . . . German hit us with three divisions there and it'll make us look very foolish. It would be embarrassing to George. George is used to attacks from a single division. He's buttoned up well enough for that, But he's not used to having three or four German divisions hit him. He doesn't know what it means yet.'[2]

But with Patton's 15 US Corps already at Argentan on the evening of 12 August it was time to ensure proper coordination of the Allied army and air effort – and Monty asked Bradley to fly to his headquar-

---

[1] Diary of Chester B. Hansen, loc. cit. Some writers – e.g. M. Blumenson, op. cit. – consider Hansen's diary untrustworthy in its dating, believing that Patton's remark was only made on 16 August.
[2] Ibid.

ters for lunch the next day. 'Our great object will be to see that whatever part of the enemy forces escapes us here does not get back over the SEINE without being so mangled that it is incapable of further action for many days to come,' Monty assured Brooke. 'The whole weight of the AEAF is being used tonight, tomorrow and every day and every night in the task of destroying the enemy forces.'

These were laudable sentiments, but the entrapping and annihilation (or enforced surrender) of an entire enemy army group within a matter of days was, Monty knew full well, no easy matter. Von Paulus's Sixth Army had been actually surrounded at Stalingrad on 23 November 1942; it took a month before the Russians mounted their final artillery and armoured attack, on Christmas Day – and only on 30 January 1943, some five weeks later, did von Paulus finally surrender the 94,000 surviving troops. At Falaise not even the passionate valour of the Poles had enabled the Canadian 'Totalize' operation to reach its objective at Falaise, for after the brilliant initial Canadian break-out, American bombers of Spaatz's 8th US Air Force had run amuck, bombing their own Allied troops and causing more casualties than on the first day of 'Cobra', when Collins had had to close down the offensive and start again the following day. However much Monty might exhort Crerar to take Falaise, it was clearly impossible to do so without mounting a second 'Totalize'-type operation, complete with heavy bomber support – and Patton's alleged jest about driving the Canadians back into the sea was in bad taste, considering the awful casualties suffered by the Canadians in their attempt to get Falaise. With Panzers, Tigers and 88mm guns the 12th SS 'Hitler-jugend' Panzer Division wrought havoc with Poles and Canadians alike, one armoured regiment of the Canadians being so entirely annihilated that for years afterwards the 'riddled hulls of the regiment's tanks'[1] could be seen like an involuntary memorial in the fields near Estrées village, eight miles from Falaise.

Both Crerar and Simonds were clear that only a second, full-scale assault on the lines of 'Totalize' could propel the Canadian First Army through the German SS forces screening Falaise, and Monty accepted their judgement. Thus when, at 12.15 on 13 August 1944 at his headquarters, Monty met Dempsey and Bradley, it was to ensure that the proposed encirclement was properly conducted, and that Patton, for instance, was prepared for a sort of fighting he had so far merely by-passed.

Many erroneous tales would be told in subsequent years about this fateful day – indeed there is now an industry in books concerning the Allied failure completely to cut off the German retreat through

[1] C. P. Stacey, *The Victory Campaign* (Vol. III of the Official History of the Canadian Army in the Second World War), op. cit.

the Falaise gap and re-enact Stalingrad – an industry which has sadly assumed nationalistic lines in explaining the decisions made that day. Yet the truth remains that the decisions made by the senior field commanders that day were Allied decisions in an Allied cause, and that national sentiment played no part. The plan agreed between Monty, Bradley and Dempsey was that First Canadian Army should deliver its concentrated attack, supported by heavy bombers, within twenty-four hours, a feat which Crerar considered possible. To help Crerar, Dempsey would, under cover of the Canadian assault, seize Falaise itself and thus allow the Canadians to keep up their momentum towards Trun and Argentan. Hodges was to do the same on the southern flank by pushing Collins's 7 US Corps eastwards towards Argentan, thus permitting Patton to bring up another corps to act as 'long-stop', east of the German salient's neck, at L'Aigle:

> 1215 – Flew to 21 Army Group and there met C-in-C and General Bradley. We discussed future operations – particularly as regards Army Group and Army boundaries; and the bringing up by Third Army of another Corps directed on LAIGLE.
> So long as the Northward move of Third Army meets little opposition, the two leading Corps will disregard inter-Army boundaries,

Dempsey recorded in his diary.

> The whole aim is to establish forces across the enemy's lines of communication so as to impede – if not prevent entirely – his withdrawal.[1]

Such was Dempsey's understanding of Monty's decision – yet by that evening Bradley's ADC was noting that the 'British [sic] were still short of their objective, apparently unable to drive farther though I know not why. . . . It is suggested in G-3 that we were ordered to hold at Argentan rather than to continue the drive to Falaise since our capture of that objective would infringe on the prestige of forces driving south and prevent them from securing prestige value in closing the trap'.[2]

Whatever jingoistic rumours junior personal staff officers might spread, however, there was no misunderstanding between Monty, Bradley, Dempsey and Crerar. National prestige was simply not involved; it was a matter of military efficiency, and of men's lives. With a carefully planned attack by the Canadians, involving both medium and heavy bomber support, Bradley was unwilling to allow Third Army units to run unnecessary risks in pushing north from Alençon; nor was he anxious for Patton's still comparatively virgin 15

[1] Diary of M. C. Dempsey, loc. cit.
[2] Diary of Chester B. Hansen, loc. cit.

US Corps under General Haislip to be smashed and fragmented by the German Panzer divisions as they stampeded out of the pocket. Therefore when Patton had phoned him shortly before midnight on 12 August to ask if he might continue towards Falaise, Bradley had responded without hesitation: 'Nothing doing. You're not to go beyond Argentan. Just stop where you are and build up on that shoulder. Sibert [Bradley's Chief of Intelligence] tells me the German is beginning to pull out. You'd better button up and get ready for him.'[1] Patton had meanwhile told Haislip to continue cautiously until he contacted 'our Allies' at Falaise[2] – evidently oblivious to the weight of German armour and artillery moving out through the neck. He did not immediately rescind his order, but at 4 a.m. on the morning of 13 August Patton gave Haislip new orders telling him that 'elements of your command, which may be in the vicinity of FALAISE or to the north of ARGENTAN, who are not fighting, should be gradually withdrawn to the ARGENTAN area'.[3] Haislip was meanwhile to 'assemble your forces in that vicinity and to the east preparatory for further movement as will be directed', but this was not an order to disengage if in fact he had hit the enemy: 'Nothing in this order affects any battle you are now engaged in.'[4]

Patton later sought to blame Monty for the decision not to push Haislip north of Argentan: 'I believe that the order . . . emanated from the 21st Army Group, and was due to jealousy of the Americans or to utter ignorance of the situation or to a combination of the two. It is very regrettable that XV Corps was ordered to halt, because it could have gone on to Falaise and made contact with the Canadians northwest of that point and definitely and positively closed the escape gap.'[5] However this was jotted down days later, when the situation was considerably clearer. On the evidence in front of him – air reconnaissance, Ultra, Phantom and operational reports – Bradley had had no hesitation in stopping Haislip's corps from over-extending itself: 'I much preferred a solid shoulder at Argentan to the possibility of a broken [American] neck at Falaise,' he afterwards mused.[6]

In fact Patton's new order to halt Haislip only reached the 15 US Corps Commander at 11 a.m.; he had not actually captured Argentan and, with a thirty-kilometre gap between himself and First US Army on his left, cohesion was at this moment vital. To suggest that

[1] Omar N. Bradley, op. cit.
[2] 3rd US Army Headquarters Diary, kept by General Gay, Military History Institute, Carlisle, Pennsylvania.
[3] Ibid.
[4] Ibid.
[5] The Patton Papers, op. cit.
[6] Omar N. Bradley, op. cit.

Monty was to blame was silly. Bradley willingly shouldered responsibility for the decision: 'In halting Patton at Argentan, however, I did not consult with Montgomery. The decision to stop Patton was mine alone.'[1]

In fact Patton never even took Argentan (which was to elude the Americans for another seven critical days), let alone strike north to Falaise. To say therefore that, without the interdiction of Bradley or Montgomery, Patton would simply have bottled up the Falaise pocket on 13 August is ridiculous – for if his forces could not even secure Argentan, which was *within* their allotted sector, or the next village eastwards, Gacé, for a further week, the protestations of conspiracy to deprive American troops of prestige or glory ring very thin. When Patton phoned Bradley at Eisenhower's new headquarters during the morning, Bradley repeated that he wanted a firm shoulder built at Argentan rather than strung-out patrols getting cut off at Falaise; and Dempsey's diary record of his meeting with Monty and Bradley proves that there was certainly no plot to deny Patton glory, since Dempsey specifically recorded: 'So long as the Northward move of Third Army meets little opposition, the two leading Corps will disregard inter-Army boundaries.' That night Monty signalled to Brooke, in the mistaken impression, based on exaggerated Third Army reports, that Patton was actually in possession of Argentan:

The ring is gradually being drawn tighter round the German forces. Two Armoured Divisions of 15 US Corps are now firmly established at ARGENTAN. 7 US Corps of four divisions is moving northeast from MAYENNE and its leading division has reached CARROUGES.

Tomorrow at 1200 hours Canadian Army launches a strong attack with powerful air support towards FALAISE and I am fairly confident that they will reach that place tomorrow night. There has been considerable enemy movement by day going on but my view is that only administrative echelons have so far passed eastwards through the gap FALAISE–ARGENTAN and it is doubtful if they can move out of the ring owing to shortage of petrol. The tactical air forces have today been operating intensively with excellent results.

I am continuing operations on the assumption that the bulk of the enemy forces are still inside the ring as stated by my Intelligence staff.

But in order to head off any who get through the gap 20 US Corps is being directed east of 15 US Corps towards LAIGLE and

---

[1] Ibid. Monty could, however, have overruled Bradley, as he was urged to do by de Guingand and others.

12 US Corps is being assembled at LE MANS ready for any action that may be necessary in an easterly or northeasterly direction.

Allied tactical policy on 13 August was clear and undivided. It was only on the following day, on 14 August 1944, that doubts began to arise over which portion of the German armies *was* still entrapped in the pocket – and the accusations began.

CHAPTER FIFTEEN

A Fateful Week

Aug 13/44

My dear Monty,

I am sorry not to have answered your letter sooner, but have had a bad week with the P.M. – we had 14 hours in two days with him trying to get a decision on the Pacific Strategy!!! We got one of a sort at last, but you would have been surprised if you had listened in to some of his arguments.

Your telegrams are of great value & help to keep me in the situation which is not easy as Shaef are usually very badly informed.

I have been watching your battle with enormous interest. There are wonderful possibilities and I do hope that fortune may favour us, and that you succeed in dealing him a crippling blow S.W. of the Seine.

You can go on relying on my firm support, my dear old Monty. We have now been working together for a long time, and in some unpleasant places, where we have been able to appreciate each other properly. If I do talk plainly to you at times it is because I know that I can help you by doing so. There are people who don't understand you and I have had some pretty stiff battles on your behalf at times. I know therefore the types of action that are calculated to raise the criticism that must be countered and prevented.

You can go on relying on me to the utmost to watch your rear for you. I have complete confidence in your ability to beat the Bosch. Unfortunately there are a lot of jealous, critical, narrow minded individuals in this world. They can succeed in making the easiest things difficult, & in perverting the truth in a marvellous way. Waging war may well be difficult, but waging war under political control becomes at times almost impossible!!

I am off to Italy for a few days on Friday, but may have a chance of looking you up bef. starting.

Very best of luck to you in your great task

Yours ever

Brookie.[1]

---

[1] Original in Montgomery Papers.

To receive such a letter in the field from his military chief was, to Montgomery, a moving example of Brooke's faith and confidence. 'I am very occupied with the battle,' Monty wrote on the morning of 14 August to Phyllis Reynolds. 'I have the bulk of the German army in N.W. Europe nearly surrounded; this present week will undoubtedly be a fateful week, and if he escapes me here he can only be driven back on to the Seine – over which river there are now no bridges below Paris, as we have destroyed them all. We will see what happens.'

To Brooke Monty wrote with relief:

Things really do seem to be going very well. We have a ring round the enemy forces and the only way out is now between FALAISE and ARGENTAN. What actually is inside the ring one cannot tell. How much has so far got away eastwards, one cannot tell. But I very much doubt if he dare 'firm up' again this side of the Seine.

I had a conference yesterday with Bradley, Dempsey, and Crerar, and we have our plans well tied up – for any eventuality. . . .

The present week may well see great happenings.

About Eisenhower, who had shown such impatience with his strategy as it unfolded, but was now as excited as a child over the prospect of a great victory, Monty was scathing:

Ike is apt to get very excited and to talk wildly – at the top of his voice!!! He is now over here [in Normandy], which is a very great pity. His ignorance as to how to run a war is absolute and complete; he has all the popular cries, but nothing else.

Lest this sound too harsh a judgement on his own Supreme Commander, Monty added the rider:

He is such a decent chap that it is difficult to be angry with him for long. One thing I am firm about; he is never allowed to attend a meeting between me and my Army Commanders and Bradley!

It was vital, Monty felt, to keep a 'grip' on the battle – and not allow over-excitement to masquerade as military judgment. If the gap could not be closed fully between Falaise and Argentan, the Allies must not miss the wider envelopment on the Seine. At 12 noon on 14 August the second Canadian offensive towards Falaise began – but again large numbers of bombs were dumped upon Allied troops, this time by RAF Bomber Command. Moreover Intelligence reports began to suggest that the real bulk of the German armies was already out of the pocket – prompting Monty to send an urgent message by Liaison Officer to Bradley:

14-8-44

My dear Brad

It is difficult to say what enemy are inside the ring, and what have got out to the east. A good deal may have escaped. I think your movement of 20 Corps should be N.E. towards DREUX.

Also any further stuff you can move round to LE MANS, should go N.E.

We want to head off the Germans, and stop them breaking out to the S.E.

I will get Bimbo [Dempsey] here at 1100 hrs tomorrow and we will all meet and discuss the situation.[1]

That night Monty signalled to Brooke, recording the heavy fighting 'against determined resistance' in the pocket, but pleased that Collins had now reached the main road east of Argentan and that there was therefore no Mayenne gap left on the southern flank. 'In the North First Canadian Army attacked at 1200 hours today and the last reports were that leading troops had reached ERNES, SASSY and OLENDON and were pushing on towards FALAISE. Considerable chaos was caused to the attack when about twenty per cent of heavy bombers dropped their bombs well inside our lines on attacking divisions. There is no doubt that a good many enemy have managed to escape eastwards out of the ring. I have ordered 12 Army Group to direct 20 US Corps on the axis LE FERTE BARNARD [sic] through NOGENT LE ROTROU on DREUX as it is important to stop the enemy from turning south-east. We want those who have escaped us here to be pushed up against the Seine.'

In fact Bradley did not transmit the order for 20 US Corps to advance on Dreux, allowing Patton instead to split his 15 US Corps near Argentan into two, half remaining at Argentan, half being directed on Dreux. This permitted Patton meanwhile to swing the whole of his 20 Corps not on Dreux but on Chartres; moreover the nascent 12 Corps (once it picked up its armoured division from Brittany) was directed on Orléans, negating the whole thrust of Monty's wider envelopment north eastwards to the Seine. Thus by evening on 15 August, after a morning conference with Bradley and Dempsey, Monty was lamenting to Brooke: 'The general picture in this part of the front [Third Army] is that PATTON is heading straight for PARIS and is determined to get there and will probably do so.' It was Palermo all over again – for, in order to cut off those Germans who had escaped the pocket, it was vital that Patton swing northwards.

[1] Bradley Papers, Military History Institute, Carlisle, Pennsylvania.

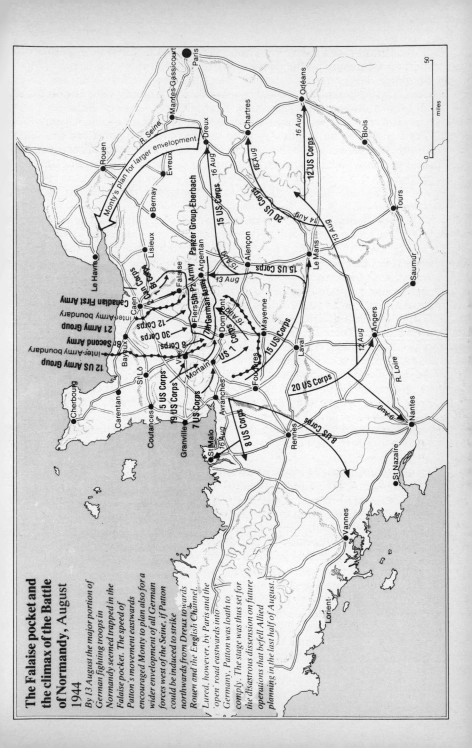

The Falaise pocket and the climax of the Battle of Normandy, August 1944

By 13 August the major portion of German fighting troops in Normandy seemed trapped in the Falaise pocket. The speed of Patton's movement eastwards encouraged Monty to plan also for a wider envelopment of all German forces west of the Seine, if Patton could be induced to strike northwards from Dreux towards Rouen and the English Channel. Lured, however, by Paris and the 'open' road eastwards into Germany, Patton was loath to comply. The stage was thus set for the disastrous dissension on future operations that befell Allied planning in the last half of August.

As Patton raced eastwards, however, he left 'a scene of intense military confusion' in the pocket. 'We discussed future operations – in particular as regards closing the gap between FALAISE and ARGENTAN, neither of which we hold yet,' Dempsey noted in his diary of the morning conference.[1] Yet with only a virgin infantry division and one French armoured division left in the Argentan area, Bradley was in no position now to offer to close the gap from the south; so the task was handed over to Crerar and Dempsey, Falaise being given to Crerar, and Argentan to Dempsey. 'The general picture in this area is of a full scale withdrawal by the enemy to get eastwards out of the pocket,' Monty described the situation to Brooke.

The problem was now one of pressure. It was believed that over 100,000 Germans were still in the pocket. The bag must therefore be kept sealed, and the neck tied; meanwhile Patton must be forced to complete the Allied envelopment by pushing at least some formations east and north: something which Bradley now tried belatedly to make him do. Bradley phoned Patton on the evening of 16 August and asked him to form a new corps out of the remnants left near Argentan, and to drive it north-eastwards towards Trun, where he would meet Poles and Canadians advancing from the direction of Falaise. With the British 30 Corps aimed on Argentan, and 5 US Corps thrusting north to Trun, the jaws of the Allied trap would fold behind each other and shut.

Meanwhile Patton's racing movement towards Paris was not lost on General Leclerc, commander of the 2nd French Armoured Division near Argentan. Reluctant to risk heavy casualties Leclerc now refused to carry out the Trun attack, desiring instead to be first into Paris.

General Gaffey [Temporary Commander 5 US Corps] outlined in general the plan of attack proposed for the 17th August on TRUN, with the main effort on the right, 90th Division leading with two Combat Teams; the 2nd French Armored Division to follow through when the 90th Division had seized a bridgehead over the DIVES RIVER; the 80th Division to assemble generally in the area south of ARGENTAN in Corps reserve.

In the discussion of the plan, General LeClerc said he would not carry out the plan and he wished that General Patton would be so informed, because he did not think it was a suitable plan, making him split his Division the way it was split, to be defeated piecemeal. General Gaffey told him that he, General Gaffey, was ordered to attack and that if he issued the order to his Division Commanders, he expected it carried out. He asked General Le-

[1] Diary of M. C. Dempsey, loc. cit.

Clerc if it was true that if he, General Gaffey, issued the order to attack in the morning, General LeClerc would not carry it out. This was taken down by stenographer, and General LeClerc edged out by saying he would attack, but the attack was impossible; his Division would be ruined.[1]

How it can be claimed that Patton was stopped from closing the Falaise gap and would easily have done so if allowed to, thus stretches credulity. The 90th US Infantry Division had yet to receive its baptism by fire – but when Patton telephoned with a message for Gaffey – who was replaced by General Gerow on Bradley's strict orders – it was to order 5 US Corps to cut right across the neck of the pocket to 'another Dunkirk'.

Gen Patton:
'Start attack. Initial objective [Chambois] four miles southeast of present assigned objective. When initial objective is taken, continue to original objective [Trun], thence on.'
Gen Gay [Patton's Chief of Staff]:
'What is meant by "thence" on?'
Gen Patton:
'Another Dunkirk. Do you understand?'
Gen Gay:
'Yes sir, I understand.'
Gen Patton:
'Issue orders. I will be home soon.'[2]

Far from leading to another Dunkirk, Patton's 5 US Corps attack came to an abrupt stop; when a Liaison Officer arrived from Crerar's headquarters to ensure proper liaison between Canadians and Americans, Patton sent the officer away, insisting that he must have written authorisation by Bradley himself before Third Army would allow him back. 'He was told that unfortunately the Army Commander could not accept Liaison Officers from the Canadian Army, but that the liaison between the two would have to be through the Commanding General, Twelfth U.S. Army Group.'[3]

Wilful obstructionism and an atmosphere of near-anarchy per-

---

[1] 3rd US Army Headquarters Diary, loc. cit. In Bradley's recollection, soon after the war, Leclerc did actually send some of his division towards Paris before being stopped: 'While Leclerc was still engaged in the Falaise pocket, to avoid being scooped on the liberation of Paris he secretly despatched his reconnaissance battalion in the direction of that city. Gerow, the Corps Commander, learned of Leclerc's action and immediately ordered Leclerc's troops to "get the hell back where they belonged".' – 'Bradley Commentaries', loc. cit.
[2] Ibid.
[3] Ibid.

vaded Third Army's activities, so that Bradley soon determined to give the operations to close the Falaise gap to Hodges' First US Army – which he did on 17 August.

To Monty this sort of haphazard approach to battle was anathema, bearing out his earlier fears about the launching of Patton. Apart from infantry he was sure on 16 August 'that six panzer and SS divisions are still inside the pocket and elements of five of these divisions are trying to break out eastwards between ARGENTAN and SEES', but as at Mortain, Bradley's imperturbable reaction gave him confidence that the Germans would not succeed: 'I think the Americans are strong enough in the ARGENTAN area to hold this attack.' Between them, Monty was sure that Crerar, Dempsey and Hodges would finish off the pocket; his attention was meanwhile shifting to the next step in the campaign, beyond the Seine. Leigh-Mallory also assumed that that battle was over; indeed so certain was Leigh-Mallory that the battle of Normandy was won, that he now closed down his battle diary, a full twenty days before the projected 'D + 90' term had expired.

15th August 1944 – D + 70
Air Chief Marshall Sir Trafford Leigh-Mallory decided today to discontinue his personal day-to-day notes on the battle, which he dictated to me. His reason for so doing was that he regarded the campaign in France and Western Europe (as far as the air was concerned) as won and his eyes were turning in the direction of the Far East whither he was shortly to proceed [as Allied Air C-in-C, Far East].[1]

In his penultimate entry, Leigh-Mallory predicted that it might take a week or ten days to capture or annihilate the remaining German forces in the pocket. 'They are almost surrounded. When that army in the pocket has gone, what can the Hun do? He will, I suppose, try to hold the Seine for a short time but he has no more troops, or certainly none of any value, and with the large forces at our disposal, we shall be able continuously to outflank him.'[2]

While Leigh-Mallory lost interest in the campaign, Monty was left to consider the future. He had already, on 16 August, ordered Crerar to start a simultaneous eastward thrust towards Lisieux while his right flank pinched off the pocket at Trun; on the southern flank he had got Bradley to swing 'detachments from 20 US Corps from DREUX up on to the Seine between VERNON and MANTES,' he hoped – vainly as it happened. Overall he was pleased with progress; remembering the confusion at the climax of the battle of

[1] Diary of Sir Trafford Leigh-Mallory, loc. cit.
[2] Ibid.

Alamein it seemed inevitable that there would be similar confusion and questioning of priorities. That the battle of Normandy was on the same scale as Stalingrad, however, he was quite clear; prisoners already on 16 August totalled some 140,000 and there were a great many more to be counted. 'Here everything goes well,' he wrote again to Phyllis Reynolds on 17 August. 'I now have troops in ORLEANS, CHARTRES and DREUX. And I have some 100,000 Germans almost surrounded in the pocket. The whole prospect of what may lie ahead is fascinating.' With discernible excitement he signalled to Brooke that night:

The best news I can give you tonight is that the gap has now been closed and the Polish Armoured Division has reached TRUN and is pushing on to CHAMBOIS.

On the SEINE all barges and ferries have been openly moved in daylight to the south bank and are waiting at points where the roads lead to the river. This has never been done before and seems to be a sure sign that the Germans are going to attempt a major breakout tonight.

It is really impossible to say exactly what is inside the ring and what has escaped so far to the east. It seems quite clear that the best part of five Panzer divisions are still west of the road FALAISE –ARGENTAN together with a good mass of immobile infantry. We now sit astride the main roads leading east but have not had time to organise definite blocks on every avenue of exit. If a major breakout is attempted during tonight it is quite possible that elements will get through and we shall not know what the situation is until later tomorrow.

The First U.S. Army is now facing north between BRIOUZE and LAIGLE.

The Third U.S. Army is facing east between DREUX and ORLEANS. We hold DREUX, CHARTRES and ORLEANS and recce elements have been pushed eastwards from DREUX and CHARTRES some fifteen miles towards PARIS. The role of the Third Army has been to stop the enemy escaping through the PARIS–ORLEANS gap and the intention now is to wheel the northern flank of this army up to the SEINE about VERNON. But the Corps at DREUX and the one at CHARTRES are in a very difficult administrative situation and it is doubtful at the moment whether they can move very far until the situation improves.

It was on the same day, 17 August, that Hitler relieved von Kluge of his command, replacing him by General Hausser in the Falaise pocket and by Field-Marshal Model outside. Though Model had orders to form a new defensive line forward of the Seine–Yonne line, not only the battle of Normandy but the battle for France was now lost. Von Kluge died two days later, ostensibly of a heart attack but actually from potassium cyanide, his pride as a Field-Marshal shattered alongside his armies. For with the closing of the Falaise gap by the Canadians and Poles the carnage within became a holocaust. 'I should doubt if ever before in the history of this war air forces have had such opportunities or taken such advantage of them,' Monty signalled to Brooke. 'The whole area is covered with burning tanks and MT. One column of 3,000 plus was caught head to tail and almost totally destroyed. I would say that any German formations or units that escape eastwards over the SEINE will be quite unfit to fight for months to come.'

The question in Monty's mind was the direction in which the Allied armies should now thrust. When he first broached the subject, on 17 August, after flying to see Bradley, Bradley appeared to agree that the Allies should aim straight for the Ruhr. The previous night Monty had cabled to Brooke that he had 'directed 12 Army Group to thrust northwards from DREUX through EVREUX to LOUVIERS', and it seemed entirely appropriate that the two Allied Army Groups should both cross the Seine north-west of Paris and take the most direct route to the German industrial heartland, the Ruhr – dealing with the V1 rocket sites in the Pas de Calais as they went.

M99. TOPSEC [RET]. Personal for CIGS from General Montgomery –

Have been thinking ahead about future plans but have NOT yet discussed subject with IKE. My views as follows.

After crossing SEINE 12 and 21 Army Groups should keep together as a solid mass of some 40 divisions which would be so strong that it need fear nothing. The force should move northwards.

21 Army Group should be on the western flank and should clear the Channel coast and PAS DE CALAIS and WEST FLANDERS and secure ANTWERP.

The American armies should move with right flank on the ARDENNES directed on BRUSSELS, AACHEN and COLOGNE. The movement of the American armies would cut the communications of enemy forces on the Channel coast and thus facilitate the task of the British Army Group.

The initial objects of the movement would be to destroy the German forces on the coast and to establish a powerful air force in BELGIUM. A further object would be to get the enemy out of V1 or V2 range of England.

BRADLEY agrees entirely with above conception. Would be glad to know if you agree generally. When I have got your reply will discuss matter with IKE.

The telegram was sent at 8.30 on the morning of 18 August. This was unfortunate, since Brooke had planned to leave the following day for Italy and the Mediterranean, entailing his absence from the war office. The ACIGS, General Kennedy, was already a sick man, and the Director of Military Operations, General Simpson, had departed on a fortnight's leave. Churchill was in Italy, having desired to watch the 'Anvil' invasion of Southern France (renamed 'Dragoon') on 15 August from a battleship: a privilege denied him in 'Overlord'. All this was tragic, for as Brooke was often to say to Simpson: 'Monty is my tactical master. You will notice that I never criticise any of his tactics. He is probably the finest tactical general we have had since Wellington. 'But,' he added, 'on some of his strategy, and especially on his relations with the Americans, he is almost a disaster.'[1]

Given Brooke's insight into Monty's failings it is all the more surprising that Brooke did not recognise that one of the critical decisions of the war in the West was emerging, and must be dealt with immediately, before local decisions on the battlefield prejudiced future strategy. Brooke scribbled a brief, cryptic acknowledgement before he left – 'I entirely agree with your plan contained in M99 of 18 August' – but only the following morning, at 11 a.m. on 19 August, did Monty receive a reply to suggest more than cursory War Office interest:

TOP SECRET. PERSONAL FOR GENERAL MONTGOMERY FROM VCIGS [Lt-General Nye].
CIGS is away and before leaving told me to come over to see you to discuss certain secret and urgent operational matters. Propose coming 22nd [August] arriving approximately 1500 hours and returning that evening.

For Nye to delay his visit for three days was (unwittingly) to fiddle while Rome burned, for although Bradley had stopped Patton in the Orléans–Châteaudun area for a forty-eight-hour administrative pause, and had agreed with Hodges and Patton a strategy of First US Army squeezing the pocket while Third US Army drove north to Mantes–Gassicourt, there was Eisenhower to be considered. Monty had perhaps taken Bradley's agreement for granted, for according to Bradley's ADC, Bradley now favoured a strike *eastwards* into Germany. Thus when Eisenhower arrived at Bradley's headquarters on the morning of 18 August to 'talk turkey' the true divergence between the two strategies was made clear to Eisenhower:

Ike arrived with Jim Gaunt and Kay Summersby this morning for a conference with Brad on the strategy from this point onwards.

---

[1] Recollections of General Sir Frank Simpson, loc. cit.

Believe he favors the Brad plan of driving eastward to Germany rather than diverting too much strength up over the northern route to the Lowlands and into Germany from that direction. . . .

Ike feeling lighthearted and gay and he is taking active part in determining the strategy – allocating missions to Bradley and Monty. . . .

Busy on maps, General had several other callers in and tomorrow Monty and the army commanders will be in.[1]

The following day, 19 August, Bradley in fact went to Monty's headquarters at 10 a.m. 'for conference on plan after the Seine'.[2] Patton was burning to drive east and Bradley, far from agreeing with Monty's northern thrust, was lured by the seeming absence of opposition in front of Patton. Hearing this, Monty insisted that whatever the plan of battle *beyond* the Seine, it was vital at least to cut off the Germans escaping from the Falaise pocket. Bradley therefore agreed to furnish two corps, which would come under Hodges' command, and which would drive immediately northwards towards the mouth of the Seine, cutting off all Germans fleeing towards the river, and also seeking to establish Allied bridgeheads across it. Hodges was apparently quite satisfied with this, as his ADC recorded:

The General flew up . . . this morning to make rendezvous with General Bradley in the vicinity of Vire. Both were early for their appointment with General Montgomery, and so they cruised about, following each other through the blue, until it was time to land.

The conference with General Montgomery was successful in every way. General Hodges' map, with plan, was approved without change. First Army, with its XIX Corps, is to strike north, by-passing Dreux, to Gouches, Evreux, and then on further north to Elbeuf and Le Neubourg. . . . The attack is to capture Elbeuf and prevent escape of the enemy across the Seine.[3]

Patton however was disappointed:

Bradley has just returned from a visit to Monty and Ike,

he recorded in his diary.

He now has a new plan. He thinks there are still Germans east of Argentan and in order to check up on this pocket, he wants me to

[1] Diary of Chester B. Hansen, loc. cit.
[2] Ibid.
[3] Diary of William Sylvan, Military History Institute, Carlisle, Pennsylvania.

move the 5th Armoured Division of the XV Corps north along the west bank of the Seine to Louviers, while the XIX Corps of the First [US] Army comes up on its left.[1]

Bradley had in fact suggested that Dempsey bring round two divisions through the American sector and execute this, the long envelopment, himself; not unnaturally Dempsey felt it would waste time, be difficult administratively, and lack punch, for at the heart of Monty's northern-thrust concept was the distressing manpower problem in 21st Army Group, a problem that had grown steadily worse over the preceding weeks as casualties in the British sector rose. Without reinforcing divisions such as the Americans could call upon, the British Army was now wasting so fast that whole divisions were having to be broken up as reinforcements for other divisions. Yet if Bradley agreed to furnish the forces for the Seine envelopment, he still remained, according to his ADC, anxious that the long-term American thrust be mounted eastwards:

He is desirous of pursuing a direct route to Metz and the German border. Monty in deference to the political angle involved in the effort is, of course, desirous of taking the rocket coast and relieving London of the terrific burden there. Bradley agrees that reduction of the coast will deprive Germany of one of his primary secondary weapons now bolstering the German people in the belief of retaliation.

Ike likewise favours Bradley's desire to drive eastward and violate the German border as quickly as possible. There is evidence that little remains to stop us on the far side of the Seine. It is now clear that the German intend[ed] to make the war an issue in the Normandy front and had not planned for our current extension and a crossing of the Seine. He has been thrown into a complete tailspin and is confounded by the current turn of events.[2]

Bradley was already making tentative plans for an American 'army of occupation of Germany', but aware that his British manpower resources were dwindling Monty strove desperately to keep the Allied armies together in one 'solid mass of some 40 divisions'. That night he prepared, as one of his last directives as C-in-C of the Allied land armies in France, a document setting out the situation – sending a copy with a covering letter to Brooke the following day:

I must impress on all commanders the need for speed in getting on with the business.

[1] *The Patton Papers*, op. cit.
[2] Diary of Chester B. Hansen, loc. cit.

The Allied victory in N.W. Europe will have immense repercussions, it will lead to the end of the German military domination of France; it is the beginning of the end of the war.

In its way, the directive was reminiscent of Haig's great message to his commanders in the autumn of 1918: 'risks which a month ago would have been criminal to incur, ought now to be incurred as a duty'. Until Bradley's break-out could be effected, the task of 21st Army Group had been to hold the main enemy forces in combat on the eastern sector. With the imminent destruction of the remaining enemy forces in the Falaise pocket it was vital that neither fatigue nor complacency set in.

If these great events are to be brought about, we must hurl ourselves on the enemy while he is still reeling from the blow; we must deal him more blows and ever more blows; he must be allowed no time to recover.

This is no time to relax, or to sit and congratulate ourselves. I call on all commanders for a great effort. Let us finish off the business in record time.

But how best to finish off the business? Haig, despite his rhetoric, had failed to do more than push back the enemy's defensive line; had the German commanders not panicked in the autumn of 1918 and asked for an armistice, they could well have held the Allies to another winter stalemate, for the Allies merely attacked all along the line. Recognising that this had to be a decision made by the Supreme Commander, Monty contented himself with orders concerning the 'destruction or capture' of the enemy still 'inside the Normandy "bottle"', and the wider envelopment on the Seine by the two appointed American corps under Bradley.

General Policy for Forward Movement
As the situation develops, the Supreme Allied Commander will be issuing orders regarding the general movement of the land armies,

he went on, loyally.

Meanwhile, we must be so disposed that we can very quickly develop operations in any way he [Eisenhower] requires, and to meet any situations that may suddenly arise.
As a first step we have got to cross the SEINE, and to get so disposed beyond it – tactically and administratively – that we can carry out quickly the orders of the Supreme Allied Commander.

788

Second Army was to be prepared to drive north-east across the Seine, via Beauvais into Belgium, with Antwerp as its target and boundary. Whether 12th Army group would accompany it, taking Brussels and then swing eastwards into Germany at Aachen, was still a matter for the Supreme Commander to decide. For the moment it would 'advance on the general area ORLEANS–TROYES–CHALONS–REIMS–LAON–AMIENS'. In this way 'it will be so disposed in this general area that it retains the ability to operate north-eastwards towards BRUSSELS and AACHEN, while simultaneously a portion of the Army Group operates eastwards towards the SAAR'.

Already this was a concession to the American unwillingness to countenance the entire weight of all forty Allied divisions being directed north; but Monty still hoped that Eisenhower would see reason: 'Alternatively the whole [12 U.S.] Army Group may be required to move to the N.E., on the right flank of 21 Army Group.'

Monty, without guidance from Churchill, Brooke, Kennedy or Simpson, was now in the most difficult of positions. Hour by hour came ever more horrifying reports of the carnage in the Falaise pocket. Even on 20 August his Intelligence staff estimated 'that the best part of sixteen German divisions are still west of a north and south line through ORBEC', and by 21 August it was estimated that 160,000 German prisoners had been taken in the eleven weeks of battle since D-Day, with many more expected. Not even Stalingrad could match the strategic scale of the German defeat in Normandy, and some of the scenes within the Falaise pocket exceeded in death and destruction the worst memories of the Western Front in World War I. As Monty wrote on 21 August to General Sir Oliver Leese, commanding Eighth Army in Italy:

The campaign in Normandy has been of very great interest. The real gist of the matter is that the German armies in N.W. Europe have had a most terrific hammering, and they have ceased to exist as effective fighting formations. We could capture Paris any time we like; I am holding back from that commitment just at the moment, as the very large population of that city is short of food and fuel.

At the time of writing this we have some four to five SS divisions locked up in the 'pocket'; they cannot possibly escape; we are right round the southern flank and I have two corps moving north from the line MANTES–DREUX–VERNEUIL, with their right on the Seine.

The prisoners total 160,000 so far. . . .

My next move is to cross the Seine; clear the Pas de Calais and West Flanders and secure Antwerp; establish a powerful air force in Belgium; and invade the Ruhr – via Aachen and Cologne.

I do not see what there is to oppose us; and provided I can persuade the Americans to put everything into this movement, then it would end the war – and quickly.

But many political cross-currents are now likely to arise; and if these are to be allowed to influence what we do, then the quick end of the German war may be endangered.[1]

Casualties in the four Allied armies had reached 194,000, and this – particularly with regard to the British reinforcement situation – militated against attempting to do too much in too many directions at once: a failing as endemic in Eisenhower as it was in the Far East Supreme Commander, Lord Mountbatten:

Dickie Mountbatten came to see me the other day. He is a most delightful person but I fear his knowledge of how to make war is not very great!! You ought to go out there as his Army C-in-C, and keep him on the rails![2]

From a professional soldier's point of view the lack of reinforcements was bad enough: 'I have had to break up one complete division, one independent Inf Bde, and two armoured Bdes; our casualties have necessitated this'; but there were casualties too in the quality of performance:

I have had to get rid of a few people you know. Bucknall could not manage a Corps once the battle became mobile, and I have Jorrocks [General Horrocks] in his place in 30 Corps.

Bullen-Smith could do nothing with 51 DIV so had to go; Thomas Rennie is there now and the Division is quite different under him.

7 Armd DIV went right down and failed badly; so I removed Bobbie [Erskine] who had become very sticky, and put in Verney of the Gds Tank Bde. I also had to remove Loony Hinde; I have put Mackeson to 23 Armd Bde.[1]

To suggest, as later writers have done, that Monty wished to strike north for political and nationalistic reasons is absurd. To his fingertips Monty was a professional soldier, and quite uninterested in making 'gains' or taking the surrenders of cities, whether Cherbourg or Paris. Despite all his responsibilities as Commander-in-Chief of the greatest offensive land battle so far waged by the Allies in the West, his finger had constantly remained on the pulse of his British

[1] Letter of 21.8.44, copy communicated by Mrs Frances Denby.
[2] Ibid.
[3] Ibid.

and Canadian forces in 21st Army Group, and every beat of that pulse called for a concentration of the Allied thrust beyond the Seine if it was to succeed in penetrating into Germany and ending the war. In all the critical planning issues of the war in the West since 1942, Monty had argued against dispersion of effort, and in his own eyes had been proved right: in the thrust on Tunis, in the landings in Sicily, in his vain attempt to get concentration of effort in Italy, and then successfully in 'Overlord'. Day after day the figures of enemy troops captured rose – 25,000 alone on 20/21 August – representing the cream of the German armies in the West. If Monty grew short-tempered and not a little bitter now, it was perhaps understandable. He had seen victory in the Mediterranean fall short of what it should have been; he had since demonstrated how battle *should* be conducted on the grandest scale, involving two million troops in the field; and he would *not* watch silently while Eisenhower failed to gather the fruits of his achievement – an achievement made at the expense of so many Allied lives.

CHAPTER SIXTEEN

A Lost Cause

Much has been written concerning the 'Single Thrust versus Broad Front' dilemma; it is surprising therefore that no historian has managed to give the true chronology of how this fateful decision was taken.

Only on 19 August, at his conference with Dempsey, Bradley, Crerar and Hodges, did Monty learn that 'Ike wants to split the force and send half of it eastward to Nancy'. As Monty wrote to the ACIGS, General Kennedy, on 20 August he would throw all his 'weight and influence' into the plan for a concerted Allied effort of forty divisions. Bradley had accepted the need for 15 and 19 US Corps swinging north to envelop the German forces withdrawing towards the Seine, but according to Hansen Bradley had acceded 'although he is more particularly desirous of driving eastward to Germany and taking a force into that country for the tremendous psychological effect it would have on the people,' as he noted on 20 August.

Why Bradley was so concerned with the dubious 'psychological effect' at this time remains a mystery – though it must have been a strongly-held conviction, for on the evening of 21 August he addressed a meeting of war correspondents at his headquarters in which he spoke of 'the psychological effect of the capture of Paris' and the 'psychological effect of a violation on the German border' as two of the five main considerations in 'planning for future operations' – considerations so important that, he told the correspondents, the British would now thrust north to take out the V-bomb sites 'while we go into Germany'.[1]

The twenty-first of August was, in fact, a critical day in the growing rift between the Allies. Monty had argued his case for a

---

[1] Bradley always recognised the need for the Allies to drive north. 'There was never any question in anyone's mind but that you had to do that thing to the north,' he told his ADC after the war. But he felt this was a task Monty could tackle on his own with 21st Army Group, with only one American corps to help. 'I wanted to go due east with all American troops except one corps. I wanted to give Monty one corps to drive to the north. Then take First and Third Armies due east' – 'Bradley Commentaries', loc. cit.

concentrated Allied drive via his Chief of Staff, de Guingand, who had meetings with Eisenhower on the evening of 20 August and again on 21 August.

On 21 August Eisenhower held a meeting of his staff at his Advanced HQ in Normandy to discuss plans for the future conduct of the war,

Monty related to the VCIGS in a summary of the 'discussions that have been going on regarding future operations' a few days later.[1]

It was not a conference at which the Supreme Commander gave out his orders; it was a meeting to collect ideas.

At the meeting certain decisions were reached, briefly these were:
a) to change the system of command on 1st Sept
b) Eisenhower to take personal command of the two Army Groups himself
c) 12 Army Group to be employed towards METZ and the SAAR.

A cable was then drafted to be sent to the Combined Chiefs of Staff, and a Directive to be sent to me.

My chief of staff suggested that it might be as well to consult me in the matter before any action was taken. This was agreed, and my Chief of Staff brought the draft telegram up to my Tac HQ that night.

I did not agree with the decisions that had been reached. I sent my Chief of Staff back to see Eisenhower on the morning of 22 August, and I gave him some 'Notes on Future Operations' to take with him; he was to inform Eisenhower that these notes represented my views and that Bradley had expressed to me his agreement with them.

Monty's 'Notes on Future Operations' were a model of clarity. 'The quickest way to win this war,' he began, 'is for the great mass of the Allied armies to advance northwards, clear the coast as far as Antwerp, establish a powerful air force in Belgium, and advance into the Ruhr.' As in the invasion of Normandy, the enemy would have to guard against numerous possible Allied thrusts; by putting their whole effort into one thrust the Allies would ensure both full offensive power and, as in Normandy, invulnerability to counter-attack. 'The force must operate as one whole, with great cohesion and so strong that it can do the job quickly,' he went on. The ultimate

[1] Letter of 26.8.44 (M521), Montgomery Papers.

triumph in Normandy had been the result of a single directing mind, employing an Allied strategy in which national considerations were subordinated to the good of the cause. 'Single control and direction of the land operations is vital for success. This is a *whole time* job for one man. The great victory in N.W. France has been won by personal command. Only in this way will future victories be won. . . . To change the system of command now, after having won a great victory, would be to prolong the war.'

The force of Monty's argument is undeniable – indeed most senior German commanders considered it to be the strategy the Allies ought to have employed; and even Patton, as will be seen, was won over by the military logic of such a plan. Eisenhower, however, demurred. 'I knew I was arguing a lost cause,' de Guingand later confessed. 'I remember a long conversation we had in an apple orchard. And at the end of it he [Eisenhower] said, "Would you like to see me present a medal to the American Naval Commander?" . . . I couldn't get him to budge.'[1]

My Chief of Staff spent two hours on 22nd August trying to persuade Eisenhower on certain basic points of principle,

Monty chronicled;

he reported to me the result of this talk.[2]

The result was procrastination. Eisenhower insisted that he must take field command of the armies as soon as he could establish a proper headquarters on the Continent; he agreed that Monty must clear the Pas de Calais and make for Antwerp; and he left the question of whether Bradley join Monty in a northern thrust or a strike east to be decided by circumstances. This was embodied in a signal sent to the Combined Chiefs of Staff at 4.55 p.m., and in a covering letter Eisenhower indicated that he did not want Monty to plan on using American ground forces in his northern thrust: 'You may or may not see a need for any U.S. ground units, after the crossings of the Seine have once been secured. . . . Initial estimates of such additional forces should be kept to a minimum, not only because of increased difficulties in maintenance if U.S. lines of communications are stretched too far, but because of the desirability of thrusting quickly eastward and severing almost all of the hostile communications in the major portion of France.' The most he was prepared to offer was American assistance if the British ran into trouble: 'as indicated in the attached message, you can always be

[1] Maj-General Sir Francis de Guingand, loc. cit.
[2] Letter to Nye of 26.8.44 (M521), loc. cit.

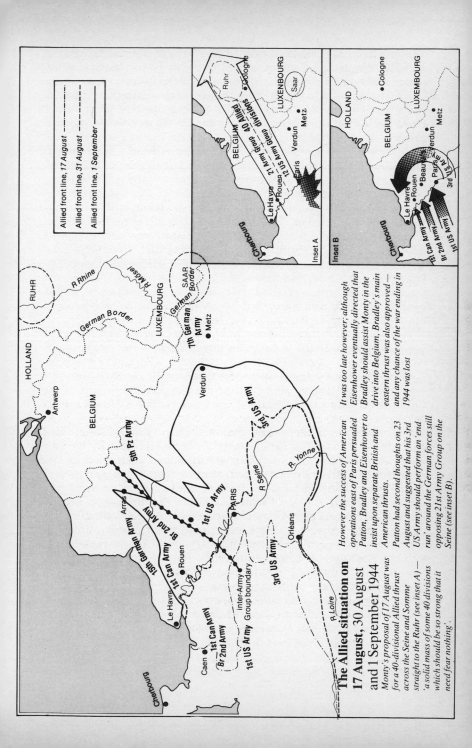

Allied front line, 17 August ––––––
Allied front line, 31 August – – – –
Allied front line, 1 September ————

The Allied situation on 17 August, 30 August and 1 September 1944

Monty's proposal of 17 August was for a 40-divisional Allied thrust across the Seine and Somme straight to the Ruhr (see inset A) — 'a solid mass of some 40 divisions which should be so strong that it need fear nothing'.

However the success of American operations east of Paris persuaded Patton, Bradley and Eisenhower to insist upon separate British and American thrusts.

Patton had second thoughts on 23 August and suggested that his 3rd US Army should perform an 'end run' around the German forces still opposing 21st Army Group on the Seine (see inset B).

It was too late however; although Eisenhower eventually directed that Bradley should assist Monty in the drive into Belgium, Bradley's main eastern thrust was also approved and any chance of the war ending in 1944 was lost

Map labels

HOLLAND
Antwerp
BELGIUM
RUHR
R Rhine
R Mosel
German Border
LUXEMBOURG
German Border
SAAR Border
Metz
7th German Army
Verdun
5th Pz Army
15th German Army
Arras
Rouen
Le Havre
Caen
1st Can Army
Br 2nd Army
1st US Army
PARIS
R Seine
R Yonne
3rd US Army
Orléans
R Loire
inter-Army Group boundary
Cherbourg
Br 2nd Army
1st US Army

Inset A
Cherbourg
Le Havre
Rouen
Paris
21 Army Group
40 Allied
divisions
12 US Army Group
BELGIUM
Ruhr
Cologne
LUXEMBOURG
Saar
Verdun
Metz

Inset B
Cherbourg
Le Havre
Rouen
Beauv
Paris
1st Can Army
Br 2nd Army
1st US Army
3rd US A
HOLLAND
BELGIUM
Cologne
LUXEMBOURG
Verdun
Metz

reinforced quickly in case of need, either from positions east or west of Paris'. Bradley, as Commander of an 'Army Group of the Center' was to position his American forces east of Paris in such a way that it could either assist Monty, the Commander of the 'Army Group of the North' or 'if the enemy strength in that region is not now greater than I now believe, it can alternatively strike directly eastward, passing south of the Ardennes'.

General Nye was present at Montgomery's headquarters while Eisenhower went ahead with this cable to the Combined Chiefs of Staff. Realising that one of the critical decisions of the Allied alliance was being made he sought, on Brooke's behalf, an assurance that Monty would not precipitate an Allied crisis while both Churchill and Brooke were absent. 'Montgomery told me his attitude would be that he would make it abundantly clear that he strongly disagreed with any plan which split the Allied forces and would give his reasons in full' to Eisenhower, whom he now arranged to meet the following day, 23 August. 'He would say that if, after having heard these views, Eisenhower still decided to adhere to his plan, he would loyally accept it and carry out whatever orders were issued to him.'

The alliance, Nye pointed out to Monty, *must* come before logical military strategy. Back in England Nye discussed the subject with both Grigg, the Secretary of State for War, and General Ismay, Churchill's Military Assistant and Secretary of the Defence Committee, 'and we feel it preferable not to send a telegram to Prime Minister but to leave it to your judgement to give information to him whenever you think best,' he cabled to the CIGS.[1]

It seems almost unbelievable that the British Prime Minister (also still acting as Minister of Defence) should have been kept in the dark about this, perhaps the most momentous Allied decision since the commitment to mount 'Overlord'. Undoubtedly Nye, Grigg and Ismay feared that Churchill would make the same protest as he had done over 'Anvil', a protest which could not alter a decision already made by the Americans, but which merely encouraged Washington to see in the British attitude special pleading of a political nature while they, the American Chiefs of Staff, were willing to support the views of the Supreme Commander in the field.

This was ironic – for as Monty soon found out, the Supreme Commander was not concerned with military logic, but only with the political ramifications of his decisions back in America.

Eisenhower was due to meet Monty at Monty's headquarters at midday on 23 August. Leaving early Monty now attempted to get Bradley to support him over the northern thrust:

[1] Alanbrooke Papers, Liddell Hart Centre for Military Archives, King's College, London.

Early on 23 August I flew to LAVAL to see Bradley; I wanted to check up with him again before I saw Eisenhower. I found, to my amazement, that Bradley had changed his views completely; on 17 Aug. he had agreed with me; on 23 August he was a whole-hearted advocate of the total American effort going eastward towards the SAAR. He had obviously been 'got-at' in the interim period,

Monty considered.

I know Bradley well; my own opinion is that he is not voicing his own views when he advocates the SAAR venture.[1]

In this Monty was mistaken – for with each passing day after the closing of the Falaise pocket, Bradley had become less willing to operate under Monty's command. With Allied victory in Normandy the American army had finally come of age, effacing their failures at Kasserine, Salerno and Anzio. They had carried out their part in Monty's master-plan with tenacity and growing confidence, and it was easy to forget what sacrifices the British had made to keep the real weight of the enemy on the eastern sector. Decades later a distinguished American military historian would attribute the failure of the Allies to win the war in Europe in 1944 not to Eisenhower's broad-front strategy, but to the original decision to place the American armies on the right of the British on D-Day – arguing that with their flair for mobility they would have taken Caen earlier and broken out on the eastern flank. Whether the American armies could, at that stage of the war, have done so is unlikely, for as the captured ADC to General Bayerlein, Commander of the only Panzer division to 'leak' into the American sector during the period, related to Bradley's staff when interrogated:

He said our [American] infantry was poor, but tanks and artillery was excellent. British infantry superior to ours. . . .[2]

The captain had served 'with distinction' in North Africa, Hungary, Russia and finally Normandy, and was not afraid to tell the truth. Lines of communication from America and bases in Western Britain had in fact dictated the positioning of the respective armies for D-Day; but even if Bradley's armies *had* been positioned on the eastern flank it is unlikely that, faced by the combined weight of Rommel's Panzer and SS Panzer divisions, they would have achieved as much as Dempsey – and they might possibly have provided a less solid flank, as would be the case in the Ardennes. By

[1] Letter to Nye of 26.8.44 (M521), loc. cit.
[2] Diary of Chester B. Hansen, loc. cit.

containing the bulk of the enemy armour and best infantry opposite Dempsey, and giving Bradley time and space to bring the greater numerical strength of the American divisions into battle on the western flank, Monty had out-generalled von Rundstedt, Rommel, Hausser and von Kluge who, limited by the edicts of Hitler, had insufficient strength to defend British, American and Pas de Calais sectors in equal strength. Compared with Hitler's conduct, the impatience of Eisenhower, Tedder and Churchill had proved merely tiresome to the Ground Forces Commander, and had not affected the course of the battle. Montgomery's victory was, without doubt in even Hitler's mind, the decisive battle of the war: 'the worst day of my life,' as Hitler remarked on 15 August 1944 as the true dimensions of the catastrophe in Normandy became apparent.

By giving the role of break-out to the American armies in the less well-defended western sector, Monty had capitalised on American speed and bravura, for just as it is unlikely that Bradley could have matched the British performance on the eastern flank, so it is unlikely that the British could have matched the American performance in mounting first 'Cobra', then launching Patton on his rocket-like manoeuvre into Brittany and then eastwards to encircle the enemy. Relying on speed and daring, Patton had simply moved faster than the Germans could react, tied down as they were by the fierce fighting on Hodges', Dempsey's and Crerar's fronts; and, if Bradley had wished, he could then have swung Patton right up to the English Channel, along the banks of the Seine, to cut off the survivors of Falaise and put Patton on a course towards the Ruhr. Indeed Patton *himself* drew up such a plan, as will be seen, only to be overruled by Bradley.

That the Allies might now throw away their greatest victory in a vain attempt to do all things at once was not in itself a surprise to Monty. It was the story of Italy all over again, of 'Giant Two', of separated landings at Reggio and Salerno, and the forfeited chance of reaching the Rome line in 1943. Yet it saddened Monty that Bradley, whom he had so patiently 'brought on' as an Army and then Army Group Commander, should now be lured by the same fantasies of Eisenhower and Patton at their worst – for instance, the belief that, if an area was relatively undefended by the enemy, it was good strategy to rush in, like fools, and seize it. Patton had demonstrated the fatuousness of this in Sicily when thrusting westwards to Palermo instead of eastwards to Messina; Eisenhower had similarly insisted that Eighth Army cross the Straits of Messina and establish itself in the toe of Italy, merely because it was visible across the water from Messina, regardless of strategic logic, and his insistence on 'Anvil' had issued from the same desire to 'bull ahead' wherever possible – never to face up to the reality of actual battle.

Bradley, flushed with pride at having given a 'magnificent' press conference on 21 August, was therefore in no mood to climb down when Monty pressed him on the morning of 23 August.

> Meeting of war correspondents that evening at Eagle Forward [Bradley's Tac HQ] attended by entire corps of 1st Army correspondents, including Red Knickerbocker, Charles Wertenbach, Don Whitehead, Jack Thompson, Bob Cabba, Clark Lee, Al Dinny, Bert Bryant,

Bradley's ADC recorded.

> Knickerbocker suggested 'Bradley for President Club' and Lee called Bradley the military Lincoln. All fantastically pleased with the conference which resulted in several offhand jibes at the BBC to which the BBC representative objected but the innuendo nevertheless stuck. . . .
> The General was buoyant after last night and he conducted himself magnificently. . . .

The next day Bradley had been 'off early' to see Eisenhower, 'campaigning now on the drive to Germany which everyone now thinks may go quickly with the Bosche falling apart in front of us and still fleeing with small rearguard movements which hamper our progress but do not delay it sufficiently for them. . . . Everyone is confident he will take care of our interests and even Col Conrad says, "Brad'll look out for us." Interests himself particularly in the American picture and he is certainly our spokesman here. . . . This may be the turning point and if we do not quickly follow up our advantage to slam through into Germany and end the war on his ground, we may be forced into a longer fight in the lowlands where the terrain is better suited for defense and where he will have time to make a stand and prepare a line. If he does not defend here, he has no intention of defending anywhere.'[1]

With the belated discovery that Bradley was now won over to the Patton cause of racing into Germany via Metz, Monty returned by air to his Headquarters to face Eisenhower. Suddenly the outlook appeared grim. Moreover when he reached his Tactical Headquarters, he found Eisenhower arriving with his Chief of Staff, Bedell Smith, and General Gale, Chief of Administration.

> I returned to my Tac HQ by 1200 hrs on 23 August to meet Eisenhower. He had sent to England for Bedel Smith and Gale to come with him, and they all three arrived together.

[1] Diary of Chester B. Hansen, loc. cit.

This was the first time I had seen Bedel Smith since I left Portsmouth for Normandy on D day, 6th June,

Monty said pointedly.

I told Eisenhower that I must see him alone, and get his decision on certain big points of principle; we must do that ourselves, and the staff must not be present.
  He agreed, and we talked alone for one hour.
  I put to him my views as outlined in M99 –

the plan for the Allies to move north in a 'solid mass of some 40 divisions which should be so strong that it need fear nothing', the British moving along the coast to Antwerp, the Americans to Brussels, Aachen and Cologne.

I also said that he, as Supreme Comd., could not descend into the land battle and become a ground C-in-C; the Supreme Comd. has to sit on a very lofty perch and be able to take a detached view of the whole intricate problem – which involves land, sea, air, civil control, political problems, etc., etc., etc. Someone must run the land battle for him; we had won a great victory in Normandy *because* of unified land control and *NOT in spite of it*. I said this point was so important that, if public opinion in America was involved, he should let Bradley control the battle and put me under Bradley – this suggestion produced an immediate denial of his intention to do anything of the sort!!!

Ought Monty to have insisted? The notion was not unthinkable, for Patton, erstwhile superior of Bradley in Sicily, was now serving beneath Bradley – with distinction. The problem was not, as so many historians have made out, that Eisenhower was thinking already in terms of a broad front and did not therefore wish to concentrate his armies under one commander; his cable to the Combined Chiefs of Staff on 22 August demonstrated that, although he favoured two separate thrusts, one north and one east, he was still undecided whether the eastern one should be launched, or kept ready to assist in the event of the Pas de Calais proving a struggle to seize.[1] No, what was at issue now was the idea that the American armies *must be separated from the British*, as Monty quickly discovered.

[1] The Army Group of the Center [11 and 3 US Armies] will advance, under General Bradley, to the east and northeast of Paris, from which area it can either strike northeastward, thus assisting in the fall of the Calais area and later advance through the Low Countries, or, if the enemy strength in that region is not greater than I now believe, it can alternatively strike directly eastward' – *The Papers of Dwight David Eisenhower*, op. cit.

The American armies in the west had come of age on the beaches and in the bitter bocage fighting in Normandy. They had acquitted themselves with growing confidence and distinction – and in the nature of coalition warfare could no longer be expected to tolerate further tutelage under a Briton or even the rigorous subservience to a master-plan as in Normandy. They had passed the test both of battle and of command under General Bradley's 12th US Army Group; they must now be given their own distinct objective and sector, quite separate from those of the British and Canadian forces: the breaching of the Siegfried Line and entry into Germany via the eastern route.

> After some talk, Eisenhower agreed that 21 Army Group was not strong enough to carry out the tasks on the northern thrust, alone and unaided,

Monty recorded. It followed then that Eisenhower's letter of 22 August, in which he asked Monty to keep 'estimates of such additional forces . . . to the minimum', was unrealistic.

> He agreed that whatever American assistance was necessary must be provided.

If this was so, who was to command the thrust?

> He agreed that the task of coordination and general operational direction on the northern thrust must be exercised by one commander; he said he would give that task to me.

Now, however, came the knotty part of the problem. 21st Army Group could provide fourteen divisions for the Army Group of the North, and there was also available the Allied Airborne Army. Ideally Monty wanted a force of forty divisions; if this was out of the question, how many American divisions would be needed to help carry out the essential tasks – seizing the Pas de Calais area with its ports, capturing Antwerp, establishing the Allied Air Force in Belgium, and providing sufficient forces to mount, eventually, a thrust towards the Ruhr?

> I said I wanted an American army of at least twelve divisions to advance on the right flank of 21 Army Group.

Eisenhower was stunned.

> He said that if this were done then 12 Army Group would have only one Army in it, and public opinion in the States would object.

This Monty did not believe.

I asked him why public opinion should make him want to take military decisions which are definitely unsound. He said that I must understand that it was election year in America; he could take no action which was calculated to sway public opinion against the President and possibly lose him the election.

That because of this he must now separate the two Army Groups, take command himself of the ground forces, and send the two Army Groups in such different directions that there could be no question of the American Army Group being under the operational control of a British General.[1]

This is really the guts of the whole matter.

Monty did not credit Eisenhower's excuse of American public opinion; still less did he consider Eisenhower was concerned not to unseat the President – since this was no concern of a soldier. What Monty saw was the whole panopoly of SHAEF – of frustrated, rear headquarters soldiers: men who had conspired against him during the long, bitter weeks of battle before the master-plan came to fruition – and who could not now bear the idea of another relentless master-plan, with similar demands of patience and professionalism.

I believe that Eisenhower in his heart of hearts knows he is wrong; I believe he is being pushed into his present decision by Bedel Smith and certain others at SHAEF. I do NOT believe that things in America are really as he says they are.[2]

The result was an unholy compromise. The northern thrust became the Allies' first priority; 21st Army Group could not achieve its objectives without American reinforcement; however, this reinforcement could not be put under a British general. With growing preponderance of men and arms, American armies must remain under the tactical command of American generals. Bradley would be ordered to send whatever he could spare to shield 21st Army Group's right flank – but under the aegis of 12th US Army Group. The concept of Army Groups of the North, and of the Center, and of the South, so neatly laid before the Combined Chiefs of Staff the day before, was redundant. From now on, in effect, there would be British and American Army Groups, to satisfy the 'national' aspirations of SHAEF Americans. Monty would be empowered to exercise 'operational coordination between 21 Army Group and the left wing

[1] Letter to Nye of 26.8.44 (M521), loc. cit.
[2] Ibid.

of 12 Army Group', that was all – and even this was so vaguely defined that Monty wondered what it would amount to.

A great snag is likely to be this. In our talk, Eisenhower agreed that I should have the task of 'coordination and general operational direction' of the northern thrust –

but would Eisenhower stand by his word? 'They have now both [i.e. Eisenhower and Bedell Smith] gone off to draft a directive as a result of our conversation,' Monty reported in a cable to Brooke that evening. 'The draft is to be shown to me before it is issued. It has been a very exhausting day.'

Eisenhower and Bedell Smith duly drew up the directive – it took them six days to do so – but the true tragedy of the decision would never be made known to Monty in his lifetime. It was simply this: that when Patton began to think over Monty's preference for a northern thrust he quickly saw its merit, just as he had understood, in England, the logic of Monty's hinge at Caen, early in July, better than Eisenhower. Thus while Bradley travelled to SHAEF advanced headquarters on 23 August to wait for Eisenhower's decision, Patton began to work out a new tactical strategy for Third Army, as part of Monty's northern thrust. 'Mark this August 23rd,' he declared to his chief of operations, Colonel Muller. 'I've just thought up the best strategical idea I've ever had. This may be a momentous day.'[1]

Patton flew straight to Bradley's headquarters to tell him, outlining the Third Army plan to the 12th US Army Group Chief of Staff in great excitement: a plan in which Third Army would cross the Seine at Mélun and the Yonne at Sens (south-east of Paris) and swivel northwards across the Marne and Oise in a Schlieffen-type operation to cut off the forces fleeing before Dempsey and Hodges at Beauvais. General Allen took it down in writing and apparently said: 'Seems fine to me, General.' 'Tell it to Brad when he comes back,' Patton urged. 'I'm going back to my CP to have my staff put both plans in writing – the one I told you yesterday about going straight east, and this one going north. If Bradley approves the attack to the north he has only to wire me "Plan A" by 1000 tomorrow [24 August]. If I don't hear from you fellows by that time, I'll then move east as per my plan "B".'[2]

Eisenhower's decision, when Bradley relayed it on his return from Eisenhower's headquarters where he stayed the night, was to rule out 'the best strategical idea' Patton had ever had. 'At 1200 hours,' Patton's Chief of Staff recorded on 24 August, 'instructions went out

---

[1] L. Farago, *Patton: Ordeal and Triumph*, New York 1963.
[2] Ibid, and *The Patton Papers*, op. cit. Cf. also entry of 23.8.44 in General Gay's Third Army Headquarters War Diary, loc. cit.

to the XII and XX Corps to execute Plan "B" – the thrust east to the SAAR.

Thus the chance of a full-blooded Allied drive, combining the Canadian, British and American First and Third Armies, had been squandered. Each protagonist would blame the other, for the resultant stalemate was as inevitable as when Eisenhower had split his efforts in Italy. After the war Monty would be pilloried for having wanted to hog the limelight, glory, headlines, etc. Yet he had argued his case as a soldier, and just as 7 December 1941 would go down in history as a day of infamy, so in his book would 23 August 1944: the day Eisenhower lost the chance of an early end to the war in the West. When finally Monty said so in print, a full decade after Eisenhower, Bradley and Patton had published their own versions, Eisenhower broke off their friendship – for the rest of their lives. Eisenhower went to his grave protesting his innocence, and ridiculing Monty's 'pencil-like' thrust;[1] only Monty knew that this was not the truth, that he had proposed that all *four* Allied armies drive north to the Ruhr – Patton included – in a 40-divisional thrust that no German counter-attack could ever dent; and only Bradley and Patton knew that, on the fateful day when Eisenhower turned down Monty's proposal, Patton himself had suddenly supported it, with Patton's Third Army repeating its epic 'end-run' at the climax of the Battle of Normandy.

[1] Dwight D. Eisenhower, *Crusade in Europe*, New York 1948.

CHAPTER SEVENTEEN

Triumph, and Tragedy

That Monty was uninterested in the American idea of glory is best illustrated by his attitude towards the seizure and ceremonial liberation of Paris. He was far more concerned with the establishment of Allied crossings across the Seine below Paris – rendered bridgeless by the Allied air forces:

> The American bridgehead at MANTES is at present somewhat insecure and First US Army is anxious to expand it and make it quite secure before handing it over in a day or two,

he signalled to Brooke on 24 August.

> The Americans are having heavy fighting in the ELBOEUF area south of ROUEN where the Germans are trying desperately to stop our approach to the river as it is one of his main ferry crossings. . . .
> I do not know what the situation is in PARIS. The order to send troops in to that city was given by Eisenhower direct to Bradley and I was merely informed that it was to be done at the request of General Koenig. I am out of touch by telephone with Bradley at present and it is difficult to find out exactly what is going on. From all reports it looks as if the action taken was premature and may prove an embarrassment[1] and detract from our main business.

The 'main business' was the Allied thrust *beyond* the Seine – and an hour later Monty was signalling to General Nye, the VCIGS, the sad news. In the light of his manpower problems Eisenhower's decision tormented him. Monty had signalled earlier in the day that he was 'investigating the desirability of breaking up the CDL orga-

---

[1] On 21 August Bradley's ADC recorded similar unwillingness: 'The General's reluctance to enter Paris quickly lies in the fact that after the city is taken, we must feed the inhabitants, which will require a daily shipment of about 6,000 tons. . . .' The next day Hansen recorded: 'Gen agreed with Ike on necessity for taking city immediately to prevent hard feelings etc.' – loc. cit.

nisation for manpower reasons'[1] and had promised to send home 6th Airborne Division immediately.

> Ike has now decided on his line of action. His directive to me is about all that I think I can get him to do at present. He has agreed that we must occupy the Pas de Calais and get possession of the Belgian Airfields and then prepare to move eastwards into the Ruhr and he has given this mission to 21 Army Group.

But would the 21st Army Group be strong enough to achieve this?

> He has ordered 12 Army Group to thrust forward its left with what it can spare to assist 21 Army Group in carrying out its tasks and for this some six to eight U.S. Divisions will possibly be available.

This was a far cry from the great 40-divisional phalanx that Monty had proposed, and commanded so well in Normandy.

> The remainder of the 12 Army Group is to clear up Brittany and then to assemble east of Paris. Eventually the whole of 12 Army Group is to move eastwards from Paris towards METZ and the SAAR.
> Ike is taking command himself of 12 and 21 Army Groups on 1 September. He has given me the power to coordinate the action of the forces being used for the northward drive to the Pas de Calais and Belgium including those divisions of 12 Army Group which take part in this movement.

To Monty this was distressingly feeble:

> You will see that instead of moving the combined might of the two Army Groups [1st Canadian Army, Second British Army, 1st US Army and 3rd US Army] northwards into Belgium and then eastwards into Germany via the Ruhr Ike proposes to split the force and to move the American portion eastwards from Paris and into Germany via the Saar,
> I do not myself agree with what he proposes to do and have said so quite plainly.

Eisenhower, however, was the Supreme Commander – and like Bradley, Monty accepted that in the interests of Allied unity he must obey Eisenhower's decision.

---

[1] M110, 24.8.44, Montgomery Papers.

I consider that the directive which is being issued by Ike is the best that I can do myself in the matter and I do no[t] propose to continue the argument with Ike. The great thing is that I have been given power to coordinate and control the movement of the left wing northwards towards Antwerp and Belgium.

Even this was wishful thinking – as would emerge in the days ahead. Had Eisenhower only summoned a conference of Army commanders at this juncture, many subsequent misunderstandings might have been avoided; instead, each Army Group Commander and Army Commander understood something different from the other, since Eisenhower's draft directive was both vague, and not officially issued until 29 August. Thus the day after Monty's fateful conference with Eisenhower, at a time when Monty understood he would only receive the help of what Bradley could 'spare', i.e. 'six to eight US Divisions', General Hodges at First Army understood the opposite:

General Bradley had many interesting things to announce:
1 – General Eisenhower will assume command on September 1st.
2 – First Army's mission, as it is contemplated now, will be to advance northeast from Mantes to Beauvais to Albert to Antwerp. The British will be responsible from there to the sea. . . .

Far from being what could be 'spared' from the drive towards the Saar, Hodges understood this to be a full-blooded First US Army thrust to Antwerp, employing *at least* nine Divisions, subsequently more:

3 – It is contemplated that First Army will be composed in this drive of nine divisions: 1, 4, 9, 28, 30, 79, 2nd, 3rd and 5th Armoured, and that in addition we will get one or two of the divisions which are now completing the mopping up of the Brittany peninsula.[1]

Bradley even ordered that the 4th US Division cross the Seine on the north side of Paris, instead of the south. The following day Hodges's ADC noted:

We are to strike northeast with the British taking care of the Crossbow [V-bomb] sites and we are to have temporary XV Corps troops but not the Corps itself. This is not the most direct route to Germany and not a route which General Hodges wished to take,

---

[1] Diary of William Sylvan, entry of 25.8.44, loc. cit.

but at the time at least apparently there was nothing else politically to do.[1]

Hodges thus believed that he was being deflected from the direct Metz route to Germany by political pressure from the British, in view of the V-bomb menace. Patton believed it was not the V-bomb menace but Monty who was the root cause, and that if he, Bradley and Hodges all 'offered to resign unless we went east, Ike would have to yield'.[2] If allowed to drive east Patton felt that he could 'cause the end of the war in a very few days', and that the decision to let Hodges support Monty 'is a terrible mistake, and when it comes out' in the after years 'it will cause much argument'.[3]

This was no exaggeration, although it was written on 30 August, when the matter of northern versus eastern priority had become a national football, kicked between teams who did not meet. From 23 August Monty was out of telephone communication with his own subordinate American Army Group Commander – and he thus witnessed the saga of Leclerc's liberation of Paris with a sort of distant cynicism:

When the French Armoured Division entered the outskirts of PARIS on 23 August they received such a tumultuous welcome from the population that most of the men became very drunk and nothing happened for the rest of the day,

Monty cabled to Brooke on 25 August.

The Germans had retired to the north side of the city but when no armed forces appeared they came back and seized the bridges again.

When the French Armoured Division became sober they went forward into PARIS on 24 August and the Division is now on the left bank of the SEINE in the centre of the city. Fighting is going on for the bridges and desultory fighting continues in the streets. The Americans have had to send 4 US Division into the city to lend a hand.

The net result is that the report that PARIS has been liberated was premature. I suggest that no celebrations are held in LONDON until I can officially report to you the occupation of the whole city,

Monty's faintly spinsterish response to the liberation of Paris gives a good illustration of his state of mind at this critical juncture in the

[1] Ibid.
[2] *The Patton Papers*, op. cit.
[3] Ibid.

war. Having won one of the greatest battles in military history he could not bring himself to accept the distraction of Paris or consider Eisenhower's imminent assumption of field command as anything other than catastrophe. Thus on 26 August he cabled to announce that 'all resistance in PARIS has ceased and it can now be said that we have occupied and liberated the city', but when that evening Eisenhower signalled from Bradley's headquarters and asked Monty, who was still the Allied Ground Forces Commander, to accompany him into the city in the morning, Monty's reply was terse.

Eisenhower: 'If you should like to accompany me will wait until flying conditions permit you to arrive Bradley's headquarters. Request prompt reply to Bradley.'
Montgomery: 'Regret unable to go with you tomorrow. Thank you for asking me.'[1]

This stand-offishness – he spoke to Eisenhower for only a few minutes when Eisenhower passed through his headquarters on 26 August, directing Eisenhower, as he might a tourist, to 'the best place to see the results of the battle' at Falaise – was unfortunate, for it played straight into the hands of those intent on weakening Allied solidarity. Moreover if Monty did not understand Eisenhower's 'political' approach to a military problem, Monty was himself largely to blame. Ever since the triumph at Alamein he had been a law unto himself, deliberately distancing himself not only from the distracting detail of his Main Headquarters, but also progressively disaccustoming himself to discussion of the wider issues among senior staff officers at Main HQ.

Monty's ambition had been the perfection of the art of field command, and the great Allied victory in Normandy was his crowning achievement. Yet the more Monty commanded from his Tactical Headquarters, the less constructive use he made of his Main Headquarters, which became increasingly a rear headquarters, used for historical purposes rather than being intimately involved in the day-to-day fortunes of the battle. As the BGS (Plans), Charles Richardson, later reflected, this was a conscious decision on Monty's part, designed to avoid the pitfalls of command-by-headquarters-committee, as for instance practised by the Americans:

The American technique – and I saw a lot of this in Italy [as Deputy Chief of Staff to General Mark Clark] is that the staff beaver away; then boil up these plans and they take them along to the General – who often seemed to be rather old and stupid! – and the General said, 'God, that's a good plan,' and would adopt it.

[1] Diary of Harry C. Butcher, loc. cit.

Whereas Monty did all his own immediate planning – I was left to do the long-distance planning, such as the crossing of the Seine and Rhine, that sort of thing. That was Monty's method, and it was absolutely right. You could say what we [at Main headquarters, 21 Army Group] were doing was long-stopping, further elaborating, seeing whether there were any snags that hadn't been thought of, co-ordinating with the logistics side, which was very much left – I mean Monty never got involved in that. He realised its importance the whole time, but he left that entirely to Freddie [de Guingand] and Miles Graham; and the Air side, which needed a lot of discussion. But the actual tactical business was *entirely* controlled by Monty.[1]

One senior American staff officer, having served at 21st Army Group prior to the creation of 12th US Army Group, felt that Monty thus wasted a priceless asset:

'Let me say here,' Colonel Bonesteel remarked after the war to the American Official Historian,

that 21 Army Group was the best I saw in the war from a mechanical standpoint. But Monty sailed off across the Channel and didn't use it. Most unfortunate. Bad hiatus between him and staff.[2]

Bonesteel, who became Bradley's deputy G3 in charge of Operations, represented the typical American staff officer who believed in taking plans to his General, as Bonesteel's testimony to Dr Pogue demonstrates. Sir Charles Richardson, Bonesteel's senior officer at 21st Army Group, felt that, despite his great intelligence, Bonesteel was wrong – that this form of command was precisely what had produced General Auchinleck's failures in North Africa before Monty's arrival at Alamein. The Commander must command, Richardson felt, and even Mark Clark had recognised, from the moment his white-haired 6 Corps Commander broke down on the beaches at Salerno, that a modern battle-commander must be prepared to command at the front.

Well they [the Americans] had this extraordinary tradition – I suppose it was a method – in which they expected subordinate commanders to go back. And this is one of the things which Monty abhorred – I mean he taught his Commanders, 'Go forward when you want to confer.' And Monty flatly refused to go back to SHAEF, and therefore Freddie had to go back in his place.[3]

[1] General Sir Charles Richardson, interview of 27.1.83.
[2] Interview of 18.6.47 by F. C. Pogue, loc. cit.
[3] General Sir Charles Richardson, loc. cit.

It was in this respect that Monty's system of command failed, if at all, for if SHAEF refused to go forward (and Bedell Smith, Eisenhower's Chief of Staff, never *once* went to visit Monty during the entire struggle for Normandy), and Monty refused to go back, problems of communication and understanding were bound to arise. De Guingand was a brilliant staff officer, as well as a conciliator of great talent; but in the evolution of Monty's method of battlefield command, de Guingand was no longer the watchful *alter ego* he had been in desert days. Fearing this, de Guingand had deliberately appointed a senior Operations officer from Main 21st Army Group to take charge of Monty's Tactical Headquarters – for in this way he would ensure an intimate link between Main and Tac. When Colonel Russell was dismissed over the 'pig-looting' episode, Monty had not replaced him, and de Guingand was left without an experienced senior officer to represent him, or to report back to Main Headquarters the way the Commander-in-Chief's mind was working.

While Main Headquarters, 21st Army Group remained at Portsmouth there was a telephone link between Monty and de Guingand, Monty's MA Lt-Colonel Dawnay recalled.

And then when Main came overseas he had more personal contact, but he wasn't closely enough in touch with Freddie, to my mind, and Freddie quite often was not entirely clear about all facts of the position. And although we thought he was clear, and Monty had regular telephone contact, daily, with Freddie, it's not the same as a man-to-man contact.

And I think Freddie did get increasingly out of touch fully with the nuances of the situation as they were arising. He saw SHAEF and the SHAEF people much more often than he saw Monty. And so he got really quite often a different picture of the situation than he would have got if he had had more regular touch with Monty.

In Dawnay's view this separation between Tac and Main Headquarters was quite deliberate from Monty's point of view, since Monty deliberately wished to be relieved of the day-to-day clutter of a main, administrative headquarters:

Oh absolutely, absolutely deliberate! And planned from his experiences of the desert, planned for Europe – with his LOs, his 'eyes and ears', and who sometimes transmitted his orders which Freddie only got to hear about afterwards, so to speak. Freddie used to get very cross about Monty and his LOs on a number of occasions, because he didn't know what was happening, almost. It was very hard because Monty was giving direct orders right down sometimes to divisions and below!

To some extent Main HQ was considered only a record for things that had happened,

Dawnay considered – a policy that backfired when SHAEF refused to go forward to Monty, and de Guingand became mediator.

Of course Freddie initially had Leo Russell in command of Tac Headquarters – until the incident of the pig stopped that! He was a senior officer, a Brigadier at least, I think, and he was in command of Tac Headquarters, and that was that. And Freddie then could hear direct from his fellow up there exactly what was happening all the time.

Well, Leo was a very abrasive character. He was difficult to get on with, and then came the incident of the pig – and Monty kicked him out! Which was an unfortunate thing, for he wouldn't have anyone in his place. Freddie suggested several other people he could send out in Russell's place – and Monty wouldn't have it.

So Freddie was cut off from that source of information. Paul Odgers, I mean he was only GSO 2 and a Major then – I was 33, that sort of thing – we weren't *any* of us proper [i.e. Regular] soldiers, and it was very difficult for Freddie. I did my best to keep Freddie in the picture as far as I could, but then very often *I* didn't know what was happening! I mean Monty went out, he went out every day somewhere, wherever the battle was hottest, and he sent his LOs to other places to report back to him wherever he might be, forward, what was happening in this section of the front, in that section, and so on, and it was only when Monty got back in the evening that I could gather up a bit of information and find out what had happened myself! And then Monty had these meetings with the LOs in the caravan, when they marked up the map and told him the whole thing. And then Monty would talk to Freddie on the telephone. But they got further and further apart as time went on. And it was very unfortunate really. Twice when they were flying up to see him the weather closed in, they couldn't get down and had to go back – never saw him!

It was a great pity, that. Freddie, needless to say, was rather jealous that he wasn't in the picture, wasn't put in the picture properly by Monty – particularly when he was then expected to argue on Monty's behalf. He wasn't sufficiently in Monty's mind to be able to argue those things – especially with high-powered Americans who'd also got their own point of view and their own political point of view, strategic point of view, which Monty didn't appreciate. I mean there is no doubt about it, he thought winning the war was the only thing that mattered and he could do it best – and why couldn't people come to him and understand that!

If only de Guingand had been closer to Monty at this time, Dawnay later felt, much misunderstanding could have been avoided. The press conference over 'Goodwood' was a prime example:

Again, if only Freddie had been with him, he could have guided him much better than any of us very young ones *could* guide him on that sort of thing. It wasn't my business to guide him on that sort of thing, and anyhow I was very young – Freddie was the only person who could say, 'Really, sir, you can't – it's very unwise.'

It was a terrible pity that Freddie and he were not closer together more often during that whole campaign.

And of course, once we *did* break out the thing went so fast that we were moving Monty's headquarters about every second or third day – we were always on the move,

Dawnay recalled – a situation that made communication between headquarters even more difficult.

Therefore we were off the air from say eight or nine in the morning till five o'clock in the evening, when you'd got everything set up again, lines through and you could talk on the telephone again. And it was very hard to keep people informed for that reason. It went tremendously fast. Tremendously exciting too!

It was astonishing, the control he kept of his troops during that period.

This was indeed the nub. If Monty was able to demonstrate, in contrast to Lord Gort's ineptness in 1940, how a modern battle commander *should* exercise command in the field, it was a demonstration that carried incontrovertible penalties.

His conception of the battle, and the way he fought it, were exceptionally clear in his *own* mind,

Dawnay reflected.

But there were doubts in a lot of other people's minds whom he hadn't seen enough or talked to enough to explain exactly what he was doing. And I think Freddie and people under Freddie were at times considerably unclear what the situation was. I mean this was the great danger of having this split headquarters. And it became even worse when we got further forward.

He never wrote to Freddie – I can't remember a single letter going to Freddie. He must have written, but I personally can't remember any letters. He was in touch with Freddie admittedly on the telephone every day, sometimes more often than once a day.

But he never wrote to Freddie and I do think Freddie was put in a very difficult position at times. Of not knowing what Monty was up to and what Monty's feeling was, what was his *feel* of the battle. And I think by being as far forward as he was, he achieved a very great deal in getting enthusiasm in the troops, and getting a move on, and that sort of thing; but it did have, without any doubt, a loss of cohesion, a loss of contact with Main and Rear headquarters and a feeling that they didn't really know what was up – which I think was true!

And there ought to have been somebody considerably senior to me, representing Freddie at Tac Headquarters. If only there had been, not Leo because he was so abrasive, but some other individual who could have found out what was going on and really kept Freddie fully in the picture, it would have been a good thing – no doubt about that.

Monty looked at it *solely* through military eyes. There's no doubt that he never paid any attention to the political or other, national concerns at all. He said: 'I've proved myself militarily, I have shown them that their doubts in Normandy, that if you fight it my way, you – the results of winning a battle like that are tremendous . . . and surely by now they must understand that if we want to win the war quickly, this is the only way to do it.'

But of course it's a matter of national pride as well as what is militarily best! And Monty could not have been given command of the Americans *at that stage*, there's no question about it – it was not possible with the Americans, because they were supplying three-quarters of the soldiers! And the Air too![1]

Indeed it was now, if at any time during the war, that Monty's grave defects of character prevented him from showing a greatness of spirit that would match his generalship. His letters to Phyllis Reynolds, who had increasingly become a form of surrogate wife and mother, betray the strains and limitations to which he became prey. Once again the gremlin that urged him to reject his family resurfaced; once again it centred on possession of his son David. 'The idea that David should come out to see me here is quite ridiculous,' he had snapped on 17 August, 'and I cannot think who started such an idea. I quite agree with you; he needs to be kept quiet and to mature gradually; he should not see too much of Jocelyn; the more time he spends quietly at home, the better.' Once again Jocelyn Carver was made – largely through Phyllis Reynolds's manoeuvrings – the butt of Monty's almost manic suspicions. By 1 September Monty was writing: 'I always said that he [David] should never be allowed to go to Jocelyn, or any of her friends; and I still say so' – and he supported

[1] Lt-Colonel C. P. Dawnay, interview of 1.2.83.

Phyllis Reynolds's embargo on visits by David to his half-brother's home.

To say that Monty thereby demeaned himself is not the point, for his consideration for the lives and welfare of his men never weakened. When General Horrocks, only recently returned to command of 30 Corps, fell sick with fever, Horrocks tried to hide himself and his disability. 'I told [my ADC] to send a message to ask [Monty] to postpone his visit as I would be very busy away from my headquarters during the next few days. A couple of hours later the caravan door opened again and to my horror in came Monty. 'Ah, Jorrocks,' he said. 'I thought that something odd was happening so I came up to see for myself.' Monty immediately had Horrocks's caravan placed alongside his own at Tac HQ, and the best medical specialists in the army to see him. 'Each day Monty paid me a visit, and these talks proved more than usually interesting because this was the time when the big argument about the future conduct of the war was going on between Monty and Eisenhower.'[1]

What *was* at issue was in fact the Grand Alliance, something which nobody at Monty's Main or Tactical Headquarters seemed able to convey to 'Master'. The days when Britain was the preponderant power, in numbers of men, in arms, in naval and in air strength, were over. The great muscle of the United States was being flexed – and instead of visiting Bradley, his imminent 'opposite number', Monty talked to his ailing British Corps Commander. 'I have no news today from the American front,' he signalled to Brooke on the night of 27 August – and there is no record that between 22 August and 3 September Monty made any attempt to see Bradley. Not only was this a mistake in terms of Allied unity, but it was self-defeating, for in Monty's personal absence Bradley began to take a more and more 'American' line, egged on particularly by the jingoistic Patton. Thus Eisenhower's agreement that Monty assume operational control and co-ordination of the Allied armies in the north was frankly rejected by Bradley on 25 August: 'Brad renegs strenuously. "I get along with Monty fine enough," he said. "But we've got to make it clear to the American public that we are no longer under any control of Monty's." People back home are needling Marshall on this issue now.'[2] In this way Monty lost even the chance of operational control of Hodges's First US Army[3] which Eisenhower was initially disposed to grant him – and all because Monty remained in his ivory tower, scorning the chance to share with Bradley, Patton and Hodges the celebrations in Paris, and trying to bend Eisenhower to his will,

[1] B. Horrocks, *A Full Life*, London 1960.
[2] Diary of Chester B. Hansen, loc. cit.
[3] 'It now seems as if this will be cut down to "co-ordination" only,' Monty wrote resignedly to General Nye on 26.8.44.

without even allowing Bedell Smith to be present at their discussions.

On 29 August Brooke at last arrived at Monty's headquarters, shortly after his return from the Mediterranean. At a Chiefs of Staff meeting in London on 28 August, Eisenhower's proposals for the continuation of the war in North-west Europe had been discussed: 'this plan is likely to add another three to six months to the war,' Brooke noted with resignation in his diary. Eisenhower 'straight away wants to split his force, sending an American contingent towards Nancy, whilst the British Army Group moves along the coast. If the Germans were not as beat as they are this would be a fatal move; as it is, it may not do too much harm. In any case I am off to France tomorrow to see Monty and to discuss the situation with him. . . . The Germans cannot last very much longer.'[1]

Monty disagreed, in the same way as he had done when, the year before, he had cautioned Alexander not to assume that the Italian surrender would mean automatic victory for the Allies invading Italy. It was vital, Monty felt, to act immediately and in unison:

The enemy has now been driven north of the SEINE except in a few places,

he had declared in his M520 directive to 21st Army Group on 26 August,

and our troops have entered PARIS. The enemy forces are very stretched and disorganised; they are in no fit condition to stand and fight us.
This, then, is our opportunity to achieve our further objects quickly, and to deal the enemy further blows which will cripple his power to continue in the war.
The tasks now confronting 21 Army Group are:
  a) to operate northwards and to destroy the enemy forces in N.E. France and Belgium.
  b) to secure the PAS DE CALAIS area and the airfields in Belgium.
  c) to secure ANTWERP as a base.
Having completed these tasks, the eventual mission of the Army Group will be to advance eastwards on the RUHR.
Speed of action and of movement is now vital. I cannot emphasise this too strongly; what we have to do must be done quickly. Every officer and man must understand that by a stupendous effort now we shall not only hasten the end of the war; we shall also bring quick relief to our families and friends in England by over-running

[1] A. Bryant, op. cit.

the flying bomb launching sites in the PAS DE CALAIS. . . .

The enemy has not the troops to hold any strong position.

The proper tactics now are for armoured and mobile columns to by-pass enemy centres of resistance and to push boldly ahead, creating alarm and despondency in enemy rear areas.

Enemy centres of resistance thus by-passed should be dealt with by infantry columns coming on later.

I rely on commanders of every rank and grade to 'drive' ahead with the utmost energy; any tendency to be 'sticky' or cautious must be stamped on ruthlessly.

But could 21st Army Group achieve all this with First US Army only having as 'its principal offensive mission' the guarding of Dempsey's right flank between Paris and Brussels? Brooke was unconvinced: 'it remains to be seen what political pressure is put on Eisenhower to move Americans on separate axis from the British,' he noted in his diary after leaving Monty.[1]

By the next day British armoured columns were beyond Beauvais[2] and moving so fast that the projected airborne operations in the Pas de Calais area were dropped in favour of another at Tournai, thus securing the Escaut riverline – so familiar to Monty from his retreat in 1940. However Brooke's worst fears seemed well on the way towards being realised – as Monty cabled that night:

I have every hope that we shall have a strong armoured force astride the SOMME at AMIENS tomorrow [31 August]. The right hand corps of First US Army has reached LAON.

Third US Army has been told to go to FRANKFURT and the leading troops of 20 US Corps are now half-way between RHEIMS and VERDUN.

I am not at all happy about this eastward thrust into the SAAR and over the RHINE. The northward thrust is now proceeding very fast and we are going to be strained administratively and will require all available resources.

It is my opinion that administratively we cannot develop two strong thrusts simultaneously and all resources should be allotted to the northern thrust as being the really important one.

This is an example of how we may get into difficulties by not having a C-in-C for the land armies. . . .

Monty also reported that 'for the first time in this campaign I can now report that the total prisoners captured by the Allied Armies

[1] Ibid.
[2] Even Patton was surprised by the speed of Dempsey's advance, for Beauvais had been the target of Patton's Plan A.

817

exceed the total casualties suffered. The prisoners since D day now amount to 210,000 and our casualties are less than that by some thousands'. This was more than twice the number of prisoners taken by the Russians at Stalingrad, and all were German. The following day Horrocks's 30 Corps alone captured 5,000 men – including 'the complete Tac HQ of German 7th Army with the Army Commander of German 15th Army who presumably had been sent up to take command of 7th Army. The whole HQ was surprised while having breakfast and was captured complete with all documents, maps and so on.'

It was Monty's last day as C-in-C of all Allied armies in the field in Northern France, and it was a fitting end to the great battle which had begun at dawn on 6 June. Brigadier Williams had cautioned him in July not to invite captured German commanders to dine with him, even before the plot against Hitler:

I had already said to him several weeks before that, whereas it had been very jolly in the desert where we happened by luck to take von Thoma prisoner and Monty had him as his guest . . . [the situation was now different]. I was saying, 'If a German general appears now, for God's sake don't be cordial! Because he may be an SS chap. It's all very well, but you didn't have a very good press in England for gossiping with von Thoma, but that was a desert battle and it was in the days when the gentlemen were still batting and the players were in the field. Now with *these* people, if you have anything to do with German generals – which was very tempting to do because they were a very interesting lot – you probably want to ask them all sorts of questions – well, don't touch them because the whole political situation is fraught with danger.'[1]

This time, then, Monty did not dine with his captive, General Eberbach. Events were outpacing even the wildest imaginings of a month before. Dieppe fell to the Canadians almost intact, and St Valéry to the 51st Highland Division. Within days Monty expected to be 'visiting our former battle haunts at LOUVAIN. . . . You will remember,' he signalled to Brooke, 'that it was at that place that I offered to place myself and my division under Belgian command. But I trust the necessity for this will not occur again.' The signal was sent at 2225 hours on 1 September 1944 marked 'Personal for CIGS from Field Marshal Montgomery.'

Having won the greatest battle of the war in the west, General Montgomery had been promoted Field-Marshal by a Prime Minister now glorying in victory. 'In recognition of his responsibility for the

[1] Brigadier Sir Edgar Williams, interview of 7.9.78.

direction of the campaign in FRANCE, which had achieved the decisive defeat of the German Armies in Normandy, General Montgomery was on the 1st September made a Field-Marshal,' Monty's MA recorded.[1]

'The Field-Marshal business is rather amazing,' Monty wrote to Phyllis Reynolds, remembering the day, barely two years before, when he had left his son David in her care and travelled out to Egypt an almost unknown Lieutenant-General. Since then he had led a triumphant Eighth Army across two thousand miles of North Africa, had with Seventh US Army conquered Sicily, and had led Eighth Army from across the Straits of Messina to beyond the line of the Sangro. Charged with command of the Allied cross-Channel invasion, he had transformed morale and planning in England; and his subsequent defeat of the German armies in Normandy and Northern France had confounded his critics and given pride and hope to millions in both free and occupied countries of the world. German casualties up to 31 August alone amounted to 450,000 men.[2] Overnight the war seemed won.

Field-Marshal Sir Alan Brooke was the first to write to congratulate his protégé. Yet even in this moment of acclaim, Brooke's iron gaze peered into the future. For days the Russians had halted outside Warsaw, watching the Germans crush the Polish uprising and refusing Allied aircraft leave to land; the storms of alliance promised to be an even greater test than the resistance of the enemy.

Sept 1st/44

My dear Monty,

I cannot tell you what joy it gives me writing to congratulate you on becoming a Field Marshal – never has this distinction been better earned.

I knew your value and merits were bound to be recognised and have fought many battles for you with some who had not got sufficient vision to appreciate your true value. I personally have never had any doubt of it ever since we went through the difficult days from Louvain to Dunkirk!

[1] 'Notes on the Campaign in North Western Europe, Part III', War Diary of C-in-C, 21st Army Group, Montgomery Papers.
[2] 'Notes on the Campaign in Western Europe, Enemy losses: Battle of Normandy, June–August 1944', loc. cit. Enemy prisoners were given as 210,000; enemy dead as 40,000, and enemy wounded as 200,000; total 450,000. General Bradley's 12th US Army Group calculations were considerably higher: prisoners captured and counted in the American sector, up to the crossing of the Seine, amounted to 207,153, in the British sector 215,611 (up to 7 September). Estimated enemy killed in the American sector amounted to 32,437 (13,379 buried by the Americans). The total of enemy killed, captured and wounded therefore far exceeded half a million – Bradley Papers, loc. cit.

You may perhaps have thought during the last 5 years that I was occasionally unnecessarily rude to you. If I was I can assure you that it was only because I wanted to guard you against the effect of some of your actions which are incorrectly judged by others & lead to criticism which might affect your progress, a matter which has been of *great* concern to me.

I should like at this moment of your triumph to offer you one more word of advice. Don't let success go to your head & remember the value of humility.

'If you can meet with triumph & disaster and treat both those imposters just the same. . . .

'Yours is the world and everything that's in it, and what's more you will be a man my son.'

I have found the above lines from Kipling a great help during this war.

Well, God bless you Monty old boy, few things have given me more pleasure than to-day's recognition of the great work you have done for your country.

Your old friend
Brookie[1]

In his diary that night Brooke noted that Churchill, having suddenly realised that Alexander was still only a general, wished to know if 'Alexander could re-assume his senior position to Monty when he is made a Field-Marshal at a later date'.[2] The irony of war had perked up again, and Brooke must have shaken his tired head at the 'repeated telephone calls from Winston' all that day.

In the secret apartment on the Prinsengracht in Amsterdam there was neither jubilation nor irony. The diary of young Anne Frank had stopped a month before, on 1 August 1944. 'People dislike you and all because you won't listen to the advice given you by your own better half,' she had written. 'I can't keep that up: if I'm watched to that extent, I start by getting snappy, then unhappy, and finally I twist my heart round again, so that the bad is on the outside and the good is on the inside, and keep on trying to find a way of becoming what I would so like to be, and what I could be, if . . . there weren't any other people living in the world.'[3]

Anne Frank's attempt to come to terms with her difficult nature came to an end there, for on 4 August the apartment was raided, her family separated and a month later sent to different concentration

[1] Original in Montgomery Papers.
[2] A. Bryant, op. cit.
[3] *The Diary of Anne Frank*, op. cit.

camps in Germany, where all but her father would die. For Anne Frank, like so many millions of Jews, political opponents and ordinary people too weak to stand up for themselves against the grotesque tyranny of the Nazis, the Allies had simply arrived too late.

Sources and Bibliography

The Montgomery Papers

On 7 July 1982 the Montgomery Papers, together with additional collections of letters and documents relating to Montgomery, were formally donated to the Imperial War Museum, Lambeth, by Sir Denis Hamilton, on behalf of the Thomson Organisation. A committee, chaired by Marshal of the Royal Air Force Sir John Grundy, Chairman of the Trustees of the Imperial War Museum, was simultaneously established under the aegis of the Imperial War Museum to help administer and if possible extend the Montgomery Collections (which include the Field-Marshal's caravans, and numerous other Montgomery holdings). It is hoped that, as the nucleus of Field-Marshal Montgomery's records and relics, the Collections will grow over the years to form a complete and comprehensive record and repository relating to Monty's life and military career. Once catalogued, the Montgomery Papers will be made available to historians, though copyright remains reserved by the Thomson Organisation at the personal discretion of Sir Denis Hamilton. Copyright in all Field-Marshal Montgomery's writings *outside* the Montgomery Papers rests with the present Viscount Montgomery of Alamein, CBE.

Further unpublished sources

Although this volume is based primarily on the unpublished Private Papers of Field-Marshal Montgomery, I have been privileged to be given access to many other private and public collections of unpublished documents. Copyright in anything written by Field-Marshal Montgomery in such collections remains, as noted above, with the present Viscount Montgomery. Permission to see the material rests naturally with the respective owners, to whom I am most grateful.

The private collections I have used are as follows: The papers of Lt-Colonel C. P. ('Kit') Dawnay (Montgomery correspondence and notes for addresses); the papers of the late Major-General Sir Francis de Guingand (Montgomery correspondence now deposited with the Montgomery Papers in the Imperial War Museum); of Lt-General Sir Ian Jacob (the diary of his journey to Tripoli in 1943 with Mr Churchill); the private papers of General Sir Oliver Leese in the possession of Mrs Frances

Denby (Montgomery–Leese correspondence); of Major-General M. St J. Oswald (including his diary of the Desert Campaign 1942–3); of the late Major Tom Reynolds (Montgomery correspondence with Major Tom and Mrs Phyllis Reynolds, now deposited with the Montgomery Papers in the Imperial War Museum); of General Sir Frank Simpson (Montgomery–Simpson correspondence); of Brigadier H. R. W. Vernon (Alamein diary); of Major-General Douglas Wimberley (unpublished account of his campaigns when commanding 51st Highland Division, and account of his personal association with Montgomery).

The institutional collections I have used are:
    The Imperial War Museum, Lambeth: German War Diaries.
    The Public Record Office: Formation and Unit War Diaries, Cabinet Papers, Prime Minister's Papers, Alexander Papers, Dempsey Papers.
    Liddell Hart Centre for Military Archives, King's College, London: Liddell Hart Correspondence, Chester Wilmot Collection, Alanbrooke Papers.
    The National Archives, Washington: Formation War Diaries and War Department Files.
    Military History Institute, Carlisle, Pennsylvania: OCMH Collections, Bradley Papers, Chester B. Hansen Papers, Gay Papers, Lucas Papers, Sylvan Papers, Ridgway Papers, Bull Papers and papers of other WWII figures.
    Eisenhower Library, Abilene, Kansas: Eisenhower's correspondence with Montgomery and with other major WWII figures; Bedell Smith Papers; the Diary of Harry C. Butcher.
    The Citadel, Charleston, South Carolina: Mark Clark Papers.

Published sources

ALEXANDER, H., *The Alexander Memoirs* (London 1962)
AMBROSE, S. E., *The Supreme Commander* (New York 1970)
ARGYLE, C., *Chronology of World War II* (London 1980)

BALDWIN, H., *Battles Lost and Won* (New York 1966)
— *Great Mistakes of the War* (London 1950)
BARNETT, C., *The Desert Generals* (rev. edn London 1983)
BELCHEM, R. F. K., *All in the Day's March* (London 1978)
— *Victory in Normandy* (London 1981)
BELFIELD, E. AND ESSAME, H., *The Battle for Normandy* (London 1965)
BENNETT, R., *Ultra in the West* (London 1979)
BERNARD, H., *Guerre Totale et Guerre Révolutionnaire* (Brepols, Belgium 1966)
BIDWELL, S., *Gunners at War* (London 1970)
BLAIR, C. AND BRADLEY, O. N., *A General's Life* (New York 1983)
BLUMENSON, M., *Breakout and Pursuit* (Washington 1961)
BLUMENSON, M. (ED), *The Patton Papers* (Boston 1974)
— *The Duel for France* (Boston 1963)

BLUMENTRITT, G., *Von Runstedt* (London 1952)
BRADLEY, O. N., *A Soldier's Story* (New York 1951)
BRERETON, L. H., *The Brereton Diaries* (New York 1946)
BRYANT, A., *The Turn of the Tide* (London 1957)
— *Triumph in the West* (London 1959)
BUCKLEY, C., *Road to Rome* (London 1945)

CALVOCORESSI, P., *Top Secret Ultra* (London 1980)
CARELL, P., *Invasion – They're Coming* (London 1962)
CARVER, M., *Harding of Petherton* (London 1978)
— *The War Lords* (London 1976)
— *El Alamein* (London 1962)
CHALFONT, A., *Montgomery of Alamein* (London 1976)
CHANDLER, A. D. (ED) *The Papers of Dwight David Eisenhower – The War Years* (Baltimore 1970)
CHURCHILL, W. S., *The Hinge of Fate* (London 1951)
— *Closing the Ring* (London 1952)
— *Triumph and Tragedy* (London 1954)
CLARK, M., *Calculated Risk* (London 1951)
CODMAN, C. R., *Drive* (Boston 1957)
COLLINS, J. L., *Lightning Joe* (Baton Rouge, 1979)
COLVILLE, J., *The Churchillians* (London 1981)
COWARD, N., *Middle East Diary* (New York 1944)
CRUICKSHANK, C., *Deception in World War II* (London 1979)

D'ARCY-DAWSON, J., *Tunisian Battle* (London 1943)
— *European Victory* (London 1945)
DE GUINGAND, F., *Operation Victory* (London 1947)
— *Generals at War* (London 1964)
— *From Brass Hat to Bowler Hat* (London 1979)
DOUGLAS, K., *Alamein to Zem Zem* (London 1946)
DOVER, V., *The Sky Generals* (London 1981)
DUNCAN, N. W., *79th Armoured Division: Hobo's Funnies* (London 1972)

EHRMAN, J., *Grand Strategy*, Vol V (London 1956)
EISENHOWER FOUNDATION(ED), *D-Day* (Kansas 1971)
EISENHOWER, D. D., *Crusade in Europe* (New York 1948)
— *At Ease* (New York 1967)
— *Letters to Mamie* (New York 1978)
ELLIS, L. F., *Victory in the West*, Vol I (London 1962)
ENSER, A. G. S., *A Subject Bibliography of the Second World War Books in English 1939–1974* (London 1977)
ESSAME, H., *Patton the Commander* (London 1964)

FALLS, C., *The Second World War* (London 1948)
FARAGO, L., *Patton: Ordeal and Triumph* (New York 1963)
FERREL, R. H., *The Eisenhower Diaries* (New York 1981)
FLORENTIN, E., *The Battle of the Falaise Gap* (New York 1967)

FRANKEL, N., *Patton's Best* (New York 1978)
FRASER, D., *And We Shall Shock Them* (London 1983)
— *Alanbrooke* (London 1982)
FREIDIN, S. (ED), *The Fatal Decisions* (New York 1956)
FULLER, J. F. C., *The Second World War* (London 1948)
— *The Decisive Battles of the Western World* (London 1956)

GALE, R., *Call to Arms* (London 1968)
— *With the 6th Airborne Division in Normandy* (London 1948)
GARLAND, A. N. AND SMYTH, H. M., *Sicily and the Surrender of Italy* (Washington 1965)
GAVIN, J. M., *On to Berlin* (New York 1978)
GILBERT, F. (ED), *Hitler Directs His War* (New York 1950)
GOODENOUGH, S., *War Maps* (London 1982)
GORALSKI, R., *World War II Almanac* (London 1981)
GRANT, R., *The 51st Highland Division at War* (London 1977)
GREENFIELD, K. R., *American Strategy in World War II* (Baltimore 1963)
GRIGG, J., *1943 – The Victory that Never Was* (London 1980)
GRIGG, P. J., *Prejudice and Judgment* (London 1948)
GUDERIAN, H., *Panzer Leader* (London 1952)
GUNTHER, J., *D Day (Sicily)* (London 1944)

HARRISON, G. A., *Cross-Channel Attack* (Washington 1951)
HARVEY, J. (ED), *The War Diaries of Oliver Harvey 1941–1945* (London 1978)
HASWELL, J., *The Intelligence and Deception of the D-Day Landings* (London 1979)
HATCH, A., *General Eisenhower* (London 1946)
— *George Patton* (New York 1950)
HIGGINS, T., *Soft Underbelly* (New York 1968)
HINSLEY, F. H., *British Intelligence in the Second World War*, Vol II (London 1981)
HOBBS, J. P., *Dear General: Eisenhower's Wartime Letters to Marshall* (Baltimore 1971)
HORROCKS, B., *A Full Life* (London 1960)
— *Corps Commander* (London 1977)
HOUGH, R., *Mountbatten: Hero of Our Time* (London 1980)
HOWARD, M., *Grand Strategy*, Vol IV (London 1972)
HOWARTH, D., *Dawn of D-Day* (London 1959)
HOWE, G. F., *North-West Africa: Seizing the Initiative* (Washington 1957)
HUNT, D., *A Don at War* (London 1966)

INGERSOLL, R., *Top Secret* (London 1946)
IRVING, D., *The Trail of the Fox* (London 1977)
— *The War Between the Generals* (London 1981)
— *Hitler's War* (London 1977)
ISMAY, H. L., *Memoirs* (London 1960)

JACKSON, W. G. F., *'Overlord'* (London 1978)

— *The Battle for North Africa* (London 1975)
— *The Battle for Italy* (London 1967)
— *Alexander of Tunis as Military Commander* (London 1971)
JACOBSEN, H. A. AND ROWHER, J., *Decisive Battles of World War II: the German view* (London 1965)
JAMES, M. E. C., *I was Monty's Double* (London 1954)
JEWELL, D. (ED), *Alamein and the Desert War* (London 1967)
JOHNSON, G. AND DUNPHIE, C., *Brightly Shone the Dawn* (London 1980)
JOHNSTON, D., *Nine Rivers from Jordan* (London 1953)
JOLY, C., *Take These Men* (London 1955)

KEEGAN, J. (ED), *Encyclopaedia of World War II* (London 1977)
— *Six Armies in Normandy* (London 1982)
KENNEDY, J., *The Business of War* (London 1957)
KERSHAW, A. AND CLOSE, I. (EDS), *The Desert War* (London 1975)
KESSELRING, *The Memoirs of Field-Marshall Kesselring* (London 1953)
KIPPENBERGER, H., *Infantry Brigadier* (London 1949)
KREIPE, W. and others, *The Fatal Decisions* (London 1956)

LEASOR, J., *War at the Top* (London 1959)
LEWIN, R., *Montgomery as Military Commander* (London 1971)
— *The Life and Death of the Afrika Korps* (London 1977)
— *Ultra goes to War* (London 1978)
LEWIS, N., *Studio Encounters* (Cape Town 1963)
LIDDELL HART, B. (ED), *The Rommel Papers* (London 1953)
— *The other Side of the Hill* (London 1951)
— *The Tanks*, Vol II (London 1959)
— *History of the Second World War* (London 1970)
LOVAT, *March Past* (London 1978)

MACKSEY, K., *Kesselring* (New York 1978)
— *Armoured Crusader: Major-General Sir Percy Hobart* (London 1967)
MACMILLAN, H., *The Blast of War 1939–1945* (London 1967)
MALONE, R. S., *Missing from the Record* (London 1946)
MASON, D., *Who's Who in World War II* (London 1978)
MCKEE, A., *Caen: Anvil of Victory* (London 1964)
MCNISH, R., *Iron Division* (London 1978)
MELLENTHIN, W., *Panzer Battles 1939–1945* (London 1955)
MOLONY, C. J. C., *The Mediterranean and the Middle East*, Vol V (London 1973)
MONTGOMERY, B., *A Field Marshal in the Family* (London 1973)
MONTGOMERY, B. L., *Memoirs* (London 1958)
— *El Alamein to the River Sangro* (London 1948)
— *Normandy to the Baltic* (London 1947)
MOOREHEAD, A., *Montgomery* (London 1946)
MORAN, *Winston Churchill: The Struggle for Survival* (London 1966)
MORGAN, F. E., *Peace and War* (London 1961)
— *Overture to Overlord* (London 1950)

Morison, S. E., *Sicily–Salerno–Anzio* (London 1954)
Mosley, L., *Marshall* (London 1982)
Musgrave, V., *Montgomery in Pictures* (London 1947)

Nicholson, G. W. L., *The Canadians in Italy* (Ottawa 1956)
Nicolson, N., *Alex* (London 1973)
North, J., *North-West Europe 1944–5* (London 1953)

Owen, R., *The Desert Air Force* (London 1948)

Pack, S. W. C., *Operation 'Husky'* (London 1977)
Patton, G. S., *War as I Knew It* (Boston 1947)
Pawle, G., *The War and Colonel Warden* [Churchill] (London 1963)
Peniakoff, V., *Private Army* (London 1950)
Playfair, I. S. O. and Molony, C. J. C., *The Mediterranean and the Middle East*, Vol IV (London 1966)
Pogue, F. C., *George C. Marshall: Organizer of Victory* (London 1973)
— *The Supreme Command* (Washington 1954)
Pond, H., *Sicily* (London 1962)
Public record office, *The Second World War: A Guide to Documents in the Public Record Office* (London 1972)
Pyman, H., *Call to Arms* (London 1971)

Ridgway, M. B., *Soldier* (New York 1956)
Rohmer, R., *Patton's Gap* (London 1981)
Ruge, F., *Rommel in Normandy* (London 1979)
Ryan, V., *The Longest Day* (London 1960)

Saunders, H. St. G., *The Red Beret* (London 1950)
Schoenfeld, M. P., *The War Ministry of Winston Churchill* (Ames, Iowa 1972)
Sears, S. W., *Desert War in North Africa* (New York 1967)
Shepperd, G. A., *The Italian Campaign* (London 1968)
Sherwood, H. L., *The White House Papers*, Vol II (London 1949)
Shulman, M., *Defeat in the West* (London 1947)
Simonds, P., *Maple Leaf Up, Maple Leaf Down* (New York 1946)
Sixsmith, E. K. G., *British Generalship in the Twentieth Century* (London 1970)
— *Eisenhower as Military Commander* (London 1973)
Slessor, J., *The Central Blue* (London 1956)
Smith, W. B., *Eisenhower's Six Great Decisions* (London 1956)
Smyth, J., *Bolo Whistler* (London 1967)
— *In This Sign We Conquer* (London 1968)
Speidel, H., *We Defended Normandy* (London 1951)
Stacey, C. P., *Six Years of War* (Ottawa 1955)
— *The Victory Campaign* (Ottawa 1960)
Stagg, J. M., *Forecast for Overlord* (London 1971)
Stevens, W. G., *Bardia to Enfidaville* (Wellington, New Zealand 1962)

STRONG, K., *Intelligence at the Top* (London 1968)
SUMMERSBY, K., *Eisenhower was my Boss* (London 1949)
SUMMERSBY MORGAN, K., *My Love Affair with Dwight D. Eisenhower* (London 1977)
SWEET, J. J. T., *Mounting the Threat: July 1944* (San Rafael, California 1977)

TAYLOR, A. J. P., *English History* (London 1965)
— *The Second World War* (London 1975)
TEDDER, *With Prejudice* (London 1966)
TERRAINE, J., *The Life and Times of Lord Mountbatten* (London 1968)
THOMPSON, R. W., *The Montgomery Legend* (London 1967)
—*The Price of Victory* (London 1960)
TREGASKIS, R., *Invasion Diary* (New York 1944)
TUKER, F., *Approach to Battle* (London 1963)

WALKER, R., *Alam Halfa and Alamein* (Wellington, NZ 1967)
WARNER, P., *The D Day Landings* (London 1980)
WEDEMEYER, A. C., *Wedemeyer Reports* (New York 1958)
WEIGLEY, R. F., *Eisenhower's Lieutenants* (New York 1981)
WESTPHAL, S., *The German Army in the West* (London 1951)
WHEELER-BENNETT, J. (ED), *Action this Day* (London 1969)
WILLIAMS, E. T. AND NICHOLLS, C. S. (ED), *The Dictionary of National Biography 1961–1970* (London 1981)
WILMOT, C., *The Struggle for Europe* (London 1952)
WINTERBOTHAM, F. W., *The Ultra Secret* (London 1974)

YOUNG, D., *Rommel* (London 1950)
YOUNG, P., *Decisive Battles of the Second World War* (London 1967)

List of Abbreviations

AA	Assistant Adjutant
ADC	Aide-de-Camp
AEAF	Allied Expeditionary Air Force
AFV	Armoured Fighting Vehicle
ALG	Advanced Landing Ground
AOC	Air Officer Commanding
A & Q	Adjutant-General's (personnel, discipline) and Quartermaster-General's (supplies) Branch
ASC	Air Support Control
AT	Anti-Tank
ATS	Auxiliary Territorial Service
Bde	Brigade
BEF	British Expeditionary Force
BGS	Brigadier General Staff
BM	Brigade-Major
BRA	Brigadier, Royal Artillery
CB	Companion of the Order of the Bath
CCOS	Combined Chiefs of Staff
CCRA	Commander Corps Royal Artillery
CDL	Canal Defence Light (searchlight team)
CE	Chief Engineer
CGS	Chief of the General Staff
CIGS	Chief of the Imperial General Staff
C-in-C	Commander-in-Chief
CO	Commanding Officer
COS	Chiefs-of-Staff
CRA	Commander Royal Artillery
CRASC	Commander, Royal Army Service Corps
CRE	Commander, Royal Engineers
CSO	Chief Signals Officer
DAQMG	Deputy Adjutant & Quartermaster-General
DAK	Deutsche Afrika Korps
DCGS	Deputy Chief of the General Staff
DCOS	Deputy Chief-of-Staff

DDST	Deputy Director Staff & Training
DF	Direction Finding
DFM	Distinguished Flying Medal
DMI	Director of Military Intelligence
DMO	Director of Military Operations
DR	Despatch Rider
DSO	Distinguished Service Order
DUKW	amphibious landing vehicle
FDL	Forward Defence Locality
FOO	Forward Observation Officer
GHO	General Headquarters
GOC	General Officer Commanding
GOC-in-C	General Officer Commanding-in-Chief
GS	General Staff
GSO 1, *etc.*	General Staff Officer, First Grade, *etc.*
HE	High Explosive
I	Intelligence
i/c	in command
KCMG	Knight Commander of St Michael and St George
KOSB	King's Own Scottish Borderers
LCI	Landing Craft Infantry
LG	Lewis Gun
LRDG	Long Range Desert Group
LST	Landing Ship Tank
MA	Military Attaché
MC	Military Cross
MG	Machine-Gun
MMG	Medium Machine-Gun
MS	Military Secretary
MT (*also* MET)	Motor Transport
MTB	Motor Torpedo Boat
Mx	Middlesex
NCO	Non-Commissioned Officer
OC	Officer Commanding
OKW	Oberkommando der Wehrmacht (German Armed Forces High Command)
OP	Observation Post
OR	Other Rank
OTC	Officers' Training Corps

POL	Petrol, Oil and Lubricant
QMG	Quartermaster-General
RA	Royal Artillery
RAC	Royal Armoured Corps
RAF	Royal Air Force
RAMC	Royal Army Medical Corps
RAP	Regimental Aid Post
RASC	Royal Army Service Corps
RE	Royal Engineers
RFC	Royal Flying Corps
RHA	Royal Horse Artillery
RMA	Royal Military Academy
RSM	Regimental Sergeant-Major
R/T	Radio Telephony
RTC	Royal Tank Corps
SA	South African *or* Small Arms
SAS	Special Air Service
SASO	Senior Air Staff Officer
SCAEF	Supreme Commander Allied Expeditionary Force
SHAEF	Supreme Headquarters Allied Expeditionary Force
SO	Signals Officer
SOS	Emergency Call for Help
TA	Territorial Army
USAAF	United States Army Air Force
VC	Victoria Cross
VCIGS	Vice Chief of the Imperial General Staff
VTM	Vehicles per Mile
WO	War Office; *also* Warrant Officer
W/T	Wireless Telegraphy
Y service	Monitoring of Enemy Radio Signals

Index

AEAF, *see* Allied Expeditionary Air
  Force
Aachen, 784, 789, 800
Adam, General Sir Ronald Forbes,
  Adjutant-General: Salerno
  meeting, 543; Normandy
  casualties, 718
Adem, 26
Adrana (Aderno), assault on, 307,
  311, 312, 316, 317, 318, 336, 341,
  349, 354
Aerial bombing, use of: N. Africa,
  54–55, 67–68, 85, 125; Italy, 73;
  Bône, 162; Hamma, 199; Tunis,
  229; Pantelleria, 282; OVERLORD
  operation, 540, 553, 608, 609, 616;
  Normandy, 621–622, 628, 634,
  641, 651–652, 655–656, 658;
  GOODWOOD operation, 713,
  719, 728; COBRA operation, 726,
  737; Falaise, 777, 778
Afrika Korps, *see* German Army
Agedabia, 57, 60, 61, 89
Agheila, 55–57, 61, 65, 67, 68, 74; Axis
  retreat to, 10, 57–62, 68; defence
  of, 75; battle of, 85–94, 112, 123,
  125, 141, 184
Agrigento, Patton's HQ, 308, 309, 314
Air attacks: Tripoli, 95; Hamma, 196
Air borne operations: Sicily, 281, 282,
  293, 306; Naples, 381; Rome,
  389, 390 (*see also* GIANT II);
  Evreux, 521; Normandy, 623,
  624, 627, 631, 643; Orne River,
  614–616, 619, 623, 624, 627;
  Evrecy, 624, 634–636, 641, 648;
  Gacé, 765; Calais, 817; Tournai,
  817
Airfields: Sicily, 243; Normandy, 549,
  552, 554, 555, 572, 587, 619, 638,
  649, 699, 700, 702, 703, 710, 745;
  Belgium, 784, 793, 801, 806
Airfields 13 and 101, 31

Alamein, 105; occupied by 13 Corps,
  27
Alamein, battle of: media reports,
  3–10 *passim*; POWs, 3; casualties,
  38n, 114, 537; decisive battle, 12,
  37, 43, 123; Tac HQ, 13;
  aftermath, 13–15, 62, 118,
  119–120, 122, 161; tactics, 14,
  188–189, 197; lessons of, 44–51,
  103, 124, 141, 150, 161, 188–189,
  206, 288, 489, 750
Alamein Dinner, 490
Alam Halfa, battle of, 5, 37, 45, 117,
  121, 123, 126, 156, 158, 161, 475,
  489
Alam Halfa and Alamein (Ronald
  Walker), 42n, 43
Alanbrooke, Field Marshal Viscount,
  CIGS: letters from Montgomery,
  44–47, 63, 64, 69–72, 90, 96, 102,
  103–104, 140, 211, 244–245, 253,
  263–264, 385–387, 414–415,
  417–418, 435, 464–466, 631,
  675–676, 678–679, 744, 777, 783,
  817; theories on Second Front, 70,
  71, 426; BEF, 70; and
  Montgomery, 113n, 131, 132,
  278, 327, 545, 547–548, 725, 735,
  747, 751, 752–753, 756, 776, 816,
  819–820; Victory Parade, Tripoli,
  138; and Alexander, 140, 462,
  820; Montgomery's Flying
  Fortress incident, 221–222, 278;
  Casablanca, 279; Algiers, 278; and
  Churchill, 371, 418, 556, 742;
  letters/signals to Montgomery,
  419, 455, 752–753, 776, 819–820;
  Mediterranean strategy, 426
  OVERLORD operation: comd, 446,
    453–454, 455, 462–463; plan, 476,
    512–513; final plans, 570–578
  ANVIL operation, 506, 512–513, 692
  THUNDERCLAP exercise: 548–552;

Alanbrooke – *cont*.
    and Eisenhower, 708, 742, 743,
    752–753; Montgomery's plan,
    708, 709, 714; and
    GOODWOOD plan, 712; and
    Tedder re Montgomery, 723;
    and Montgomery's ban on
    visitors, 725; and Montgomery's
    directive, 731, 732, 743–744;
    Montgomery's promotion to
    FM, 818, 819; Alexander to FM,
    820
Alanbrooke (Sir David Fraser), 113n
Alençon, 762–766, 768, 770, 772
Alençon-Evreux line, 679
Alexander, Field Marshal Earl: Comd
    1st Corps (1940), 597;
    characteristics, 455–463 *passim*,
    545, 597; Alamein, 3; C-in-C
    Middle East, 24, 63, 139, 140,
    460–461; report of Eighth Army
    LO, 39; and Montgomery, 67, 74,
    136, 138, 139, 161–162, 208–209,
    210, 230–231, 246, 252, 261–265,
    307, 317–318, 320, 457–463, 596,
    597; portrait, 76, 83; Victory
    Parade, Tripoli, 138; and Turkish
    President, 139; Deputy C-in-C
    Allied Force HQ (dep to
    Eisenhower), 140, 143, 208, 214,
    216, 218, 220, 368–369, 370, 410,
    504; Comd 18th Army Gp, 148,
    370; 'cry for help', 148, 151, 153,
    155, 158–159; letters to
    Montgomery, 166, 209, 210, 213,
    214; opinion of US troops, 166,
    209, 210; letter from
    Montgomery, 194; and Patton,
    202–205; and Leese, 213; and
    Anderson, 213, 230–231
    VULCAN operation, 232, 233, 235,
    243, 245; Tunis: final offensive,
    227–238 *passim*
    HUSKY operation: planning, 223,
    225, 227, 238, 241, 243, 245, 250,
    253, 262, 372; letters to
    Montgomery, 234, 235, 246, 249;
    conference with Eisenhower and
    Montgomery, 247, 250; conference
    at Allied Force HQ, 255–257; and
    Eisenhower, 262; comd operation
    HUSKY, 264, 288–303, 306–313,
    314–321, 597; and Anderson,
    265; and Patton, 296, 312, 314,
    316–317, 318, 320, 597; and
    Montgomery, 320–321, 339,
    396–397, 423–424, 597

BUTTRESS operation: invasion of
    Italy, 322, 323, 356, 357; and
    Eisenhower, 338–339, 356, 379,
    530-531; and Cunningham, 340,
    341; and Tedder, 340, 341; as
    C-in-C Normandy invasion,
    343, 344, 368, 369, 371, 475, 597
AVALANCHE operation, 376, 396,
    398, 400–401; Italian armistice,
    394; lack of plans, 410, 427–428,
    429; and Montgomery, 424,
    425–429, 457–460, 531, 545; and
    admin staff, 424; advance to
    Rome, 427, 437; Anzio landing,
    429; timidity, 434; C-in-C 15th
    Army Gp, 463, 531, 545, 546;
    inability, 545, 546; as Field
    Marshal, 820
Alexander the Great, 227, 468
Alexandria, 57, 123
Algeria: TORCH landings, 5, 66
Algiers: landings, 10, 64; Allied HQ,
    143, 263, 264, 266–268, 274, 279
Allfrey, Lt-General C. W., Comd 5
    Corps, 143, 237, 438, 531; and
    Montgomery, 433, 438, 442, 531,
    532
Allied Air Forces: Alamein, 8; Sicily,
    293; Normandy, 608, 609, 610, 616,
    617; GOODWOOD operation,
    710, 712, 718–721; Belgium, 801 (*see
    also* Allied Expeditionary Air
    Force)
Allied Expeditionary Air Force, 492,
    609, 610, 616, 627, 634, 649, 652,
    653, 659, 661, 771
Allied Forces: Allied Force HQ,
    262–263, 264, 266–269, 274, 279,
    380, 400, 421, 423, 430, 471, 488,
    545; casualties, 790; separate
    commands, 800–802 (*see also*
    British Army, French Army,
    Polish Army, US Army, *etc.*)
Army Groups:
    15th Army Gp, Comd Alexander,
        Sicilian campaign, 283n, 293–303,
        304–313, 344; attack on
        Agrigento, 309–310; comd by
        Montgomery, 346; Italian
        invasion, 357, 410, 458, 459;
        Alexander as commander,
        368–369, 370, 427–428, 437, 457,
        463; enemy plans, 427;
        indecision, 429, 456; conference,
        437
    18th Army Gp, Comd Alexander,
        148, 231; HUSKY operation plan,

244, 259; becomes 15th Army Gp, 283n; and Salerno, 546

All in the Day's March (R. F. K. Belchem), 560n

Ambrose, Stephen E., *The Supreme Commander*, 71

American news media, 4, 77

Amesbury School, Hindhead, 133, 134, 172, 271, 276, 544, 547, 583, 602; 'Montgomery Cup', 705

Amiens, 817

Ammunition supplies, 14, 89, 90, 104, 106, 107, 114, 115, 148, 160, 161, 228, 229, 232, 331, 391; Normandy, 647, 648, 654, 660, 668–670, 719, 742

Amphibious operations: 7th US Army, 350, 351, 355, 358; 8th Army, 358 (*see also* Combined operations)

Ancona, 425

Anderson, Lt-General K. A. N., Comd 1st Army, 66, 133, 139, 143, 144, 162, 165, 246, 370, 414; advance to Tunisia, 66, 226; and Eisenhower, 161, 165; and Montgomery, 230, 244, 370, 460; and Horrocks, 236, 237; Comd 2nd Army, 500, 511; relieved, 511, 516; OVERLORD operation plan, 500

Angers, 759

Antelat, 61

Anti-personnel mines, 86, 87

Anti-tank weapons, use of, 5, 109, 111, 117, 155, 160, 168, 169, 205, 438, 617

Antwerp, 784, 789, 793, 794, 800, 801, 807, 816

Antwerp, HMS, 293

ANVIL operation, 496, 506, 507, 509–514, 527, 529, 530, 536–537, 553, 558n; Eisenhower reconsiders, 660–662, 668, 669, 689, 692, 693, 695, 702; US influence, 689; and Churchill, 507, 514, 690, 763, 785

Anzio: landing at, 249, 250, 283, 432, 463, 477, 504, 510, 519, 545, 559, 597, 797; Alexander's plan, 429–430, 597; casualties, 531 (*see also* SHINGLE operation)

Apollo, HMS: landed Eisenhower, 613

Approach to Battle (Francis Tuker), 142

Arco dei Fileni, *see* 'Marble Arch'

Ardennes, 784, 797

Ardizzone, Edward, artist, 178, 359, 360

Argentan, 732, 738, 759, 765–768, 770, 772–774, 777, 778, 780, 782

Armour, use of: Alamein, 10, 85, 188–189; operation GRAPESHOT, 14–15, 18, 19; advance on Fuka, 32, 35; advance on Matruh, 53, 54; pursuit of German army, 54–55, 58; advance on Tripoli, 104, 106, 109, 111–113, 117; Army Study Week, 141; tactical theory, 150, 155, 495; PUGILIST operation, 154–156; CAPRI operation, 167; Medenine, 159, 160, 167, 170; Mareth Gap, 184, 188–189; Axis armour, 196; Tunis final offensive, 230, 233, 234; Italy, 435, 438, 439; Normandy, 555, 707; GOODWOOD operation, 718–720; COBRA operation, 737–738; 21st Army advance, 817

Armoured Command Vehicle, Montgomery's HQ, 12, 21, 97, 448

Army/Air/Navy co-operation, 41, 50, 141, 150, 195–197, 199–201, 207, 285, 495, 538, 553, 586–588, 596, 607–610, 672; non-co-operation, 281, 282–283, 585–586, 587, 609, 651–652, 678

Army Group of the Center, Comd Bradley, 796, 802

Army Group of the North, Comd Montgomery, 796, 801, 802

Army Group of the South, 802

Army Study Week, Tripoli, 141–145, 172, 198; Bedell Smith attends, 151

Arnhem, battle of: cf Primosole, 304; cf Rome, 375

Arnim, Colonel General Jürgen von, 152, 164, 231; C-in-C Axis Army Gp, 205; Wadi Akarit, 216

Arnold, Lt-General H. H., Comd US Army Air Forces, Normandy, 632

Arsenic and Old Lace (play), attended by Montgomery, 276

Artillery, use of, 4, 5; Alamein, 11–12, 47, 188; Agheila, 86; Buerat, 112, 117; tactical use, 150, 151, 155; Medenine, 160–161, 169; Mareth, 195, 199; Tunis, final offensive, 229; invasion of Italy, 384, 385; Sangro River, 438; OVERLORD plan, 495; Normandy, 617, 669, 718

Asnelles, 603

Atlantic Wall, 519, 550, 672
Attlee, Clement, Deputy Prime
  Minister UK, 451
Auchinleck, Field Marshal Sir Claude,
  3, 79, 137, 246, 249, 453; and
  Montgomery, 49, 131, 370, 643;
  operations of 1941, 57, 414, 810
Augusta, HUSKY operation, 243, 257,
  285, 295, 298
Augusta, USS, 626
Aunay-sur-Odon, 645, 656, 663
Aurora, USS, 613
Australian Army: 9th Division, Comd
  Morshead, 26; to Australia, 75;
  at Alamein, 188, 346
AVALANCHE operation: assault on
  Naples, 337, 338–339, 355–357,
  385, 477; Comd Clark, 350, 376,
  380, 381; by 5th US Army, 372,
  376, 381, 388, 394–409 *passim*; and
  Montgomery, 395–396, 398, 407,
  584–585; and Marshall, 412
Avezzano, 437
Avola ('Acid'), British landing,
  250–251; advance to, 293
Avranches, 638, 641, 667, 672, 687,
  707, 708, 714, 732, 756, 759, 761,
  768
Aziz, 26, 39
Azizia, 108
Azizia-Sorman position, 116

BBC, *see* British Broadcasting
  Corporation
BEF, *see* British Expeditionary Force
Badoglio, Marshal Pietro, 323, 380,
  388, 390, 391, 398, 399
Bagaladi, 384
Baggush, 32
Bailey bridges, 438–439
Baldwin, Hanson, 210
Balkans, the, 426, 446, 506
Bardia to Enfidaville (W. G. Stevens),
  89n, 117n
Bari, 394
Barker, Major-General R. W., 482
Barnett, Correlli, *The Desert Generals*,
  175n
Bastico, Marshal Ettore, 63, 68, 74,
  103, 105, 122
Battle of Britain, 541
Battle Schools, 176, 231
Battle stress, 137, 701, 703
Bayerlein, Major-General Fritz, COS,
  Afrika Korps, 54, 168, 629
Bayeux: OVERLORD operation, 502,
  575, 613; German defence, 575

BAYTOWN operation: assault on
  Reggio, 322, 323, 335, 337, 348,
  355–357, 372, 376, 377, 382–384,
  392, 396, 399, 400, 597
Beak, Brigadier, VC: Comd 1st
  Brigade, 187; incompetence at
  Mareth, 194; dismissal, 212
Beamish, Air Commodore G. R., COS
  to Coningham, 198
Beauvais, 817
Beaverbrook, Lord, 480
Beda Fomm, 59, 92
Belchem, Major-General R. F. K.: HQ
  Eighth Army, 262, 272, 355;
  BGS, Ops, 21st Army Gp, 518,
  564, 576, 607; author of *All in the
  Day's March*, 560n
Belfast, HMS, 598
Belgium, 126
Ben Gardan, 160
Ben Ulid, 108
Benghazi, 56, 57, 61, 64, 65; Panzer
  Army retreat to, 50, 56–60; RAF
  supplies, 68; development, 76,
  95, 104, 106–107; 8th Army
  supplies, 106, 115
Bennett, R., *Ultra in the West*, 630n
Berlin radio, 4
Bevan, Colonel Johnny, 506
Beveridge Report, 469
Bir Khalda, 31
Bizerta, 66, 161
'Blitz' attacks, 196, 197, 200, 207, 234
Blumenson, Martin, ed. *The Patton
  Papers*, 142n, 264, 296, 312, 381n,
  511n, 557n, 558n, 589; 590, 686,
  708, 773
Bocage country, 555, 577, 617, 621,
  628, 667, 691, 696–697, 719, 741,
  743, 765, 801
'Bolo' Whistler (John Smyth), 168
Bône, 162
Bonesteel, Colonel C. H., 485n; FUSA
  Gp HQ, 526, 555, 558, 560, 609, 810
Bou Ficha, 232
Bourguébus, 710, 719
Bova Marina, 384
Bradley, General Omar N., 131; faulty
  censorship, 220; on Patton, 248,
  330–332; Comd 2 US Corps, 280,
  330; professionalism, 646, 697–698;
  and Tedder, 280; and Patton, 296,
  309–310, 350–352, 358, 361, 511,
  589, 590, 798; and British soldiers,
  305; and Leese, 308, 315; and
  Eisenhower, 333, 643, 647, 655,
  785, 798; plans for Normandy

invasion, 344, 486–488, 500, 549, 551, 552; lunch with Montgomery, *etc.*, 381; Comd 1st US Army, 511, 519, 551, 552; and Montgomery, 528, 544, 623, 624, 626, 627, 632, 637, 641, 646–648, 656–657, 682, 683–688, 690–691, 778, 786, 798, 800; exercise THUNDERCLAP, 547–553; Montgomery's plans, 559, 560; change of airborne plan, 585; and Brereton, 586; final plan, 589; Omaha Beach, 611–617 *passim*; visitors, 632; US Army operations, battle of Normandy, 624–631 *passim*, 632–640 *passim*, 641–657 *passim*, 668–673, 674–688, 689–755, 756–791, 792–804; visit from Eisenhower, 643; Cherbourg, 658, 677; Brittany, 667, 669, 670; conference at Tac HQ, 690, 691, 708, 709, 792, 798–799; Army Gp Comd, 692; US Army Gp Comd, 693; break-out, 706, 707, 731; Montgomery's plan, 708, 709, 754; Montgomery's directive, 731, 732, 743, 754, 759; battle experience, 735; Comd 12th US Army Gp, 757, 759, 770; battle tactics, 762, 767–768, 770, 772, 785–786, 792; and Patton, 770, 774, 780, 784, 799, 815; Falaise Gap, 756–765 *passim*; and Leclerc, 781; advance to Germany, 785–786, 787, 789, 792; Eisenhower's plans, 785–786, 788; and Hodges, 786; Comd Army Group of the Center, 796; tactical theories, 797, 798; war correspondents, 799; Paris, 805; author of *A Soldier's Story*, 528n, 553, 626

Brereton, Major General L. H., Comd 9th US Air Force, 586

Brest, capture, 758, 763

Briggs, Major-General R., Comd 1st Armoured Division, 26, 30, 31, 36, 37, 53

Brindisi, 394, 420

Briouze, 783

British Army:
  Army Groups: 21st Army Group: 442; Comd, 453; dismissals, 517, 518; comd Paget, 517, 518; comd Montgomery, 464–471, 475–485, 486–496, 497–515 *passim*, 516, 518, 791

Tac HQ, 465, 564–566, 588–589, 602, 612, 615, 618, 652, 658, 662, 670, 677, 682, 690, 730, 735, 747, 748–749, 760, 793, 799, 809, 811, 814

Main HQ, 465, 565, 571, 588–589, 603, 607, 612, 647, 653, 749, 760, 809, 811, 814

Rear HQ, 465, 588

London HQ: St Paul's School: 480, 481, 517, 545–547, 570–578

OVERLORD operation, plans: 500, 515, 570–578, 579–604, 607–631; de Guingand, COS, 545

THUNDERCLAP exercise: 547, 548; Final Presentation of Plans, 570–578; air support, 586–588, 596, 607–610, 615, 616, 627; casualties, 627, 628; conference on break-out, 686–688; visit of Eisenhower, 690, 691; Axis strength, 699; attack on Cherbourg and Brittany, 731; morale, 744; Falaise Gap (q.v.), 773, 788; Seine crossing plans, 784; to Antwerp, 784, 789, 793, 794, 800, 801, 807, 816; reinforcements, 787, 790, 801; northern thrust, 802, 816, 817; advance to Ruhr, 806

Armies:
  First Army: Comd, 140, 144, 247, 370; HQ, 144; withdrawal from Gafsa, 146–147, 148, 149; final offensive in Tunisia, 209, 228–238 *passim*; VULCAN offensive, 232–235; and Montgomery, 442

  Second Army: comd Anderson, 442; comd Leese, 465; comd Dempsey, 511, 538; and Montgomery, 537–538, 572, 676; advance to R. Orne, 552, 615, 621, 630; advance to Rouen/ Paris, 552; advance to Falaise, 623; Caumont, 630; visit by Eisenhower, 658; Normandy, 641–673 *passim*, 674–688 *passim*, 699, 709–710, 714, 731; to R. Orne, 707, 710, 719, 721; GOODWOOD operation, 710ff, 750; enemy strength, 735; Falaise Gap, 736, 738, 743, 758, 767; decoy for US Army, 738 (*see also* Caen); air support, 731; to Belgium, 806

British Army – *cont.*

Eighth Army: El Alamein, 3–10, 103, 414; Tac HQ, 11–14, 25, 42, 82, 97, 101, 108, 114, 156, 179, 191, 194, 261, 300, 326, 381, 386, 413, 442, 448, 466; Main HQ, 39, 42, 53, 96, 108; re-grouping, 26, 456, 460; strategic re-planning, 29–37, 63–73; POWs, 34, 50; advance to Fuka, 16–37; advance to Mersa Matruh, 39–43, 53; *Personal Message from the Army Commander*, 50–51, 166, 167, 180, 269–270, 385, 415; logistics, 56–58, 64, 69, 72, 74, 122; pursuit to Mersa Brega/ Agheila line, 55–62; advance on Tripoli, 66–73, 95, 96, 103, 105–120; casualties, 173, 466; Buerat position, 75, 105; battle of Agheila, 85–93, 103; communications, 97; morale, 77, 78, 80–82, 92, 166–167, 169–170, 219, 225, 250, 261, 289–290, 467–468; study week, 127, 140–145, 164, 176; address by Churchill, 132; Victory Parade, Tripoli, 132–133, 137, 138; plans for Tunisian campaign, 139, 145; to Rome, 146; attack on Mareth line, 151, 180–181, 206; battle of Medenine, 152–171; clearance of Egypt, Libya, *etc.*, 181, 422

PUGILIST operation, 183–193; battle of El Hamma, 194–207; battle of Wadi Akarit, 208–218; Eisenhower's opinion, 208, 209; meeting with US Army, 208; capture of Sfax, 225; capture of Sousse, 225; final offensive, Tunis, 225–238 *passim*, 263, 269, 414

HUSKY operation: 145, 228, 229–230, 304–313, 414, 457–458; Main HQ to Tripoli, 242, 257, 272, 273; planning staff to Cairo, 247; Comd, 262, 263, 265, 266; Comd 2 US Corps, 262–264, 265–266; assault, 304–313; casualties, 346n, 348, 362

BUTTRESS and BAYTOWN operations: invasion of Italy, 322–323, 335, 350, 354–357, 456,

458, 459; Comd 10 Corps for BUTTRESS: 358; BAYTOWN operation, 372–387, 388, 392, 396, 399, 413; BUTTRESS cancelled, 372

AVALANCHE operation, 407, 414, 437; transfer, 381; Marshall's opinion, 392; and the 5th US Army, 407, 413; future plans, 408, 420–421; Termoli line, 422; advance to Sangro River, 427, 438–441; casualties, 427; Pescara, 453; comd O'Connor, 465; comd Leese, 465n, 467, 468; Farewell Message from Montgomery, 469

Corps:

1 Corps: comd Crocker, 623; Caen, 645

5 Corps: *Exercise No. 3*, 13; comd Allfrey, in 1st Army, 233–234, 237; Taranto, 394, 401, 408; advance to Rome, 424; and Montgomery, 432, 433, 438, 439, 440, 442; Sangro River battle, 432–440; dismissal of Allfrey, 531–532

8 Corps: Normandy, 663; assault on Caen, 664–666; 'blitz' attack postponed, 669; EPSOM operation, 663, 673, 677, 679, 680; GOODWOOD operation, 720; Falaise Gap, 765

9 Corps: Tunisia, 218, 229, 233; comd Freyberg, 235; comd Horrocks, 236

10 Corps: N. Africa: HQ, 11; advance to Fuka, 18–28, 32; re-grouping, 26; advance to Mersa Matruh, 40; re-organization, 57; advance to Benghazi, 58; comd Horrocks, 68, 146n; Agheila, 89; transport ferrying, 107, 108, 115, 160; Benghazi, 159; Hamma, 195; comd McCreery, 214; attack on Enfidaville, 231, 232

Italy (BUTTRESS operation): invasion of Italy, 322, 323, 359–360, 372, 376; operation BUTTRESS/AVALANCHE, 357; under comd 5th US Army, 404, 406, 433, 458; Salerno casualties, 406n, 414, 440; Salerno mutiny, 414, 423, 424; petrol supplies, 422; return

to 8th Army, 424, 429; advance
to Rome, 424; attack on Volturno
River, 425
12 Corps: advance on Evrecy,
738
13 Corps: SUPERCHARGE
operation, 14; re-grouping,
26; occupy Alamein, 27, 39;
comd Dempsey, 146
HUSKY operation: comd
Dempsey, 226, 242; visit by
Montgomery, 288, 290; Sicily,
293–303, 307–312, 315, 354
BAYTOWN operation:
invasion of Italy, 322, 323,
348, 355, 384–385, 392, 396, 399,
400; Salerno, 413; advance to
Rome, 424
30 Corps: N. Africa: HQ, 11;
comd Leese, 18, 68, 107;
advance to Fuka, 22–37;
re-grouping, 26; grounded,
39; battle for Agheila, 68–93
passim; assault on Tripoli, 107,
109–120; visit by Churchill, 132;
preparation for PUGILIST
operation, 155; PUGILIST
operation, 184–193, 195;
advance to Gabes, 206; Wadi
Akarit, 215–218; HUSKY
operation: comd Leese, 215,
242; planning, 228; Sicily,
293–303, 304–313, 315–321, 330,
400; advance to Adrano, 341,
354; assault on Italy, 384–385;
return to UK, 417–418
Normandy, 621, 622, 645, 663,
665; Falaise, 780; comd Horrocks,
790; POWs, 817–818
Divisions:
Airborne Divisions:
1st Airborne Division: Sicily,
287–288, 292; Taranto, Italy,
401; Normandy, 623, 624, 627,
631, 634, 635
6th Airborne Division:
Normandy, Orne River,
614–615, 619, 623, 624, 627, 680;
to UK, 806
Armoured Divisions:
1st Armoured Division:
advance to Fuka, 24, 25–26,
29, 34; comd Briggs, 26, 27, 30,
36, 37; advance to Mersa
Matruh, 39–40, 42, 43; pursuit
of German army, 58–60; tank
re-inforcements, 160; Hamma,

195, 199, 200, 205, 207; Wadi
Akarit, 215; at Sfax, 229; to 1st
Army, 229, 230; to UK, 423
6th Armoured Division, 218,
229
7th Armoured Division
('Desert Rats'): advance to Fuka,
19, 23, 25–26, 29–30, 32, 34, 36;
comd Harding, 26, 27, 30, 112;
advance to Mersa Matruh, 40,
42, 43; advance to El Adem, 44,
57; advance to Tobruk, 57, 58;
Agedabia, 68; battle of Agheila,
85–87; advance to Buerat, 111,
117; battle of Medenine, 152,
159, 167–168; battle of Mareth,
189, 191; Wadi Akarit, 215;
transfer to 1st Army, 235; comd
Erskine, 238, 630; advance to
Rome, 424; Normandy: D-Day,
604; battle of, 623, 624, 625,
627, 630, 631, 636, 641, 642, 645,
648, 657, 758; Reserve, 682, 687;
dismissal of Erskine, 758, 790
8th Armoured Division:
operation GRAPESHOT, 14,
16
10th Armoured Division:
advance on Daba, 23; under
comd 30 Corps, 25–26; comd
Gatehouse, 25–26, 27; advance
on Fuka, 32, 34; advance on
Mersa Matruh, 40
11th Armoured Division: comd
Roberts. EPSOM operation,
673, 679, 680; Caumont, 758
79th Armoured Division (tank
'funnies'): comd Hobart,
585–586, 611
Infantry Divisions:
3rd Division, 37, 131; D-Day,
Ouistreham, 614, 615; north of
Caen, 619; Caen-Bayeux line,
641
5th Division: assault on Sicily,
297, 318, 354; Simeto, 315;
Misterbianco, 316; assault on
Italy, 348, 355, 384, 385;
advance on Sapri, 407; Sangro,
440
15th (Scottish) Division: comd
MacMillan, EPSOM
operation, 673, 679
43rd (Wessex) Division: comd
Thomas, 668; EPSOM
operation, 673
44th Division: comd Hughes,

British Army – *cont.*
26, 167
46th Division: Italy: casualties,
414; advance on Rome, 424
49th Division: Normandy, 637,
645
50th (Tyne and Tees) Division:
comd Nichols, 26; attack on
Buerat, 115; PUGILIST
operation, 184–194; comd
Kirkman, 212; Wadi Akarit,
215; HUSKY operation: reserve
division, 243; visit by
Montgomery at Suez, 289;
assault on Sicily, 297, 306, 310,
315, 318; Simeto, 315;
casualties, 348; Messina, 360;
rest, 386; Salerno mutiny, 410,
423–424, 543; return to UK, 418,
423, 532; assault exercise, 562;
D-Day, 604, 614; Normandy,
620, 637, 645; and Montgomery,
676
51st (Highland) Division: comd
Wimberley, 26; attack on
Agheila, 68, 85–87; attack on
Tripoli, 109, 111–118; Victory
Parade, 132; battle of
Medenine, 152, 155, 156, 159,
167; PUGILIST operation,
184–193; Wadi Akarit, 215–218;
casualties, 216, 348; Sfax, 230;
visit by Montgomery on Malta,
288, 290; assault on Sicily, 298,
299, 307–312, 318, 319; assault
on Italy, 355; rest, 386; Salerno
mutiny, 414, 423, 543; to UK,
418, 423; visit by Montgomery,
528; D-Day, 604; advance to
Orne River, 615, 623, 624;
attack on Caen, 627, 630, 637,
645, 680; comd Bullen-Smith,
676, 701; and Montgomery, 676,
701; comd Rennie, 790; capture
of St Valéry, 818
52nd (Lowland) Division:
reserve, 562; advance on
Paris, 758
56th Division: Tunisia, 234,
235; Italy: casualties, 414;
advance on Rome, 424
78th Division: visit by
Montgomery, 288–290; Sicilian
campaign, 318, 322; under 30
Corps, 318, 341; assault on Italy,
348; advance on Sangro River,
433–435, 438, 439; and

Montgomery, 442; sickness,
450; casualties, 450, 451
Brigades:
Armoured Brigades:
2nd Armoured Brigade, 19, 36,
60
4th Light Armoured Brigade:
SUPERCHARGE operation, 14;
under comd New Zealand
Army, 18, 19, 25, 26, 30, 34,
35–36, 43; advance to Matruh,
42; advance to Martuba, 58;
Agheila, 85–89; advance to
Garian, 111; advance to Tripoli,
117
4th Armoured Brigade:
EPSOM operation, 673
6th (Guards Tank) Brigade:
disbanded, 561; comd
Verney, 790
8th Armoured Brigade, 24, 40,
141, 160; Agheila, 85;
Normandy, 621, 624, 625, 645
9th Armoured Brigade, 18n, 42,
57
22nd Armoured Brigade, 37,
60, 109, 111–115, 152, 160 (*see
also* Roberts, Major General G.
P. B. ('Pip'))
23rd Armoured Brigade, 160;
'Harpoon Force', 298, 299, 302,
303; advance to Rome, 424;
comd Mackeson, Normandy,
790
31st Armoured Brigade:
transfer to 2nd Army, 561;
EPSOM operation, 673
33rd Armoured Brigade: 645
Infantry Brigades:
69th Brigade, 26
151st Brigade: PUGILIST
operation, 187, 189, 191, 194;
casualties, 194
152nd Brigade: Buerat, 115, 116
153rd Highland Brigade:
Agheila, 87
201st Guards Brigade:
PUGILIST operation, 184, 185,
187; Tunisia final offensive,
235; transfer to 1st Army, 235
231st Brigade, 385
Special Service Brigade: SAS,
visit by Montgomery, 562
Regiments:
Cavalry (Armoured) Regiments:
King's Dragoon Guards, 229,
230

842

8th Hussars, 637
9th Lancers, 36
10th Hussars, 36, 60
11th Hussars, 118, 630
12th Lancers, 113
Royal Artillery: Alamein, 10;
    Eighth Army gunners, 364;
    Corps troops, 418
Royal Engineers: Agheila, 94;
    mine-clearing, 107; bridging,
    440
Infantry:
    Grenadier Guards, 185, 561
    Coldstream Guards, 185
    Black Watch, 116
    Durham Light Infantry, 359
    Gordon Highlanders, 119
    Royal Scots Fusiliers, 561
    Royal Warwickshire Regiment,
        620
    Royal West Kent Regiment (6th
        Bn), 433
    Seaforth Highlanders, 116, 191
    Derbyshire Yeomanry, 12, 13
    Gurkha Regiments, 232
British Army: characteristics of
    soldiers, 70, 81, 177, 178, 270,
    305
British Broadcasting Corporation
    (BBC): Alamein, 3; Agheila, 93;
    Tunisia, 273; Sicily, 350, 360;
    Salerno, 405; Rome, 427; 8th
    Army offensive, 432;
    Montgomery's Farewell Speech,
    470; D-Day, 607; and
    Eisenhower, 734n; and Bradley,
    799
British Expeditionary Force (WWII),
    6, 70, 126, 142, 266, 369, 541,
    546
*British Intelligence in the Second World
    War* (F. H. Hinsley), 18n, 59n,
    105, 154n
Brittany: US Army break-out, 674–688
    passim, 692, 695, 706, 757; 3rd US
    Army, 708, 710; capture, 722,
    743; 21st Army Gp assault,
    731–732, 743, 744
Broadhurst, Air Marshal Harry:
    succeeds Coningham, 55, 198,
    200; policy, 198; tactical
    theories, 198; Comd Desert Air
    Force, 196, 200, 201; at
    Enfidaville, 235–236; HUSKY
    operation planning, 252,
    254–255; and Montgomery,
    259–260, 277–278, 334–335,

401; Montgomery's Flying
    Fortress, 324; his driver, 367;
    use of Crotone, 401; to N.W.
    Europe, 466, 587; and
    Eisenhower, 520; air support,
    608, 745; and Churchill, 730,
    735
Brolo, 355
Brooke, Alan F., *see* Alanbrooke, Field
    Marshal Viscount
Broomfield House, 565, 579, 589, 603
Browning, Lt-General Sir Frederick A.
    M. ('Boy'), 306, 623, 648
Brussels, 784, 789, 800
Bryant, Sir Arthur: *Triumph in the
    West*, 426n, 633n; *The Turn of
    the Tide*, 132n, 138n, 278n
Buckley, Christopher, 8–9, 118
Bucknall, Lt-General G. C., Comd 5th
    Division, 417; Comd 30 Corps,
    621, 630; dismissal, 790
Buelowius, Major-General Karl: and
    Rommel, 153; Medenine, 156
Buerat, 63, 74, 75, 85, 87; battle of, 95,
    105–120, 122, 123, 125, 141, 181,
    184
Bull, Major-General Harold R.: ANVIL
    conference, 529
Bullen-Smith, Major-General D. C.,
    Comd 51 Division, 676, 701;
    relieved, 701–702, 790
Burg-el-Arab, 39
Burma, 461
Business of War, The (General Sir John
    Kennedy), 275n, 547, 612n
Butcher, Lt-Commander Harry C.
    (naval aide to Eisenhower),
    162–164, 264, 273, 274, 380,
    403n, 412n, 508, 510n, 552n, 642,
    694–696; false diary entry, 503;
    criticism of Montgomery,
    697–698, 712, 713, 722–725,
    730–731nn, 734n, 736, 742;
    and Tedder, 741n; author of
    Three Years with Eisenhower,
    503n
BUTTRESS operation: assault on
    Gioja, 322, 323, 335, 337–338,
    356, 357; cancelled, 372

CE (Chief Engineer), 102
COSSAC (Chief of Staff, Supreme
    Allied Commander), *see*
    Morgan, General Sir Frederick
    E.
CSO (Chief Signals Officer), 102

843

Caen: plan of capture, 481, 484, 487–489, 501, 503, 585, 626–627, 628, 641–657, 658–667, 695, 697, 710; the pivot, 501, 505, 551, 552, 554, 555, 577, 614, 633, 634, 638, 641–657 *passim*, 671, 675, 678, 696, 697, 712, 744, 748, 753; German Defence, 575, 633, 636, 672, 744, 759; advance by 3rd Division, 614, 615, 617, 621, 636; hold enemy, 686, 687; advance by 2nd Army, 702, 703, 706–709, 716, 721, 723; Rommel's reaction, 727; capture of, 727, 728, 731, 738

Cagny, 624

Cairo. GHQ, 105, 109

Cairo radio, 93, 118

Caltagirone, 295, 301

Caltanisetta, 307, 312, 314, 315, 331

Calvocoressi, Ian, 86n, 142n

Canadian Army:
  Army: 1st Army: comd Crerar; assault on NW Europe, 465, 519, 552, 572, 673; visit by Montgomery, 535; advance to Le Havre, 552; Caumont, 630; alarmist reports, 700, 701; Caen front, 732, 736; Orne attack, 738, 757; morale, 744; Falaise Gap, 761, 763, 765–766, 767, 774, 777, 778; TOTALIZE operation, 759–760, 771–772; to Lisieux, 782; advance to Belgium, 806
  Corps: 2 Corps: comd Simonds, 466; Normandy, 744
  Divisions: 1st Division: operation HUSKY, 275; assault on Sicily, 298, 300, 304, 307, 312, 366; advance on Adrano, 316; comd Simonds, 326, 335; under 8th Army, 346, 363–364; assault on Italy, 348, 385, 451; comd in NW Europe by Dempsey, 465; north of Caen, 619
  3rd Division: Comd Keller: visit by Montgomery, 562; Caen-Bayeux line, 641; and Montgomery, 676; report on, 700–701
  4th Armoured Division, 767n
  Brigade: 1st Infantry Brigade, 336

Canicatta, 295

Cap Spartivento, 384

Cape Bon, Tunisia, 231, 273

CAPRI operation (battle of Medenine), 152, 167

Caravans: Montgomery's, 99, 100, 131, 236, 448; received Messe's caravan, 270, 447; Alexander's, 452; in Normandy, 131, 654, 691, 725, 729

Carboni, 390, 392

Carentan: German defence of, 575; advance by US Army, 614, 621, 624, 638, 642, 646, 647; counter attack, 636; re-taken, 652, 657

Carpiquet, 651; airfield, 699, 700, 702

Carrouges, 770, 774

Carver, Mrs. Jocelyn (*née* Tweedie), and Bernard Montgomery: re David, 134–136, 172, 186, 187, 525, 814; and Betty Montgomery, 134

Carver, Colonel John, 134, 169

Carver, Colonel R. O. H. (Dick): capture at Mersa Matruh, 39, 41, 44; escape, 415–416; with Montgomery in UK, 526, 567

Carver, Field Marshal Lord: on Gott, 6

Casablanca: landings, 10; conference, 121, 139, 143, 273, 279

Castel Benito, 118, 131, 132

Castellano, General, 388, 390

Castrovillari, 401

Catania: HUSKY operation, 243, 285; assault on, 298, 303–305, 309, 311, 312, 315–321 *passim*, 336, 341; combined arms assault, 299–300, 306

Catanzaro-Nicastro line, 399, 458

Caumont, 623, 624, 626, 630, 637, 638, 641, 642, 645–647, 653, 687, 707, 716, 743, 744, 754, 755

Cavallero, Marshal Ugo, 38, 58, 63, 68, 91, 103, 116, 117, 122

Chalmers, W. S., *Full Cycle: the biography of Admiral Sir Bertram Home Ramsay*, 496n

Chamberlain, Neville, 131

Chambois, 783

'Charing Cross', 22, 25–27, 31–36, 39–41

Charlton, Warwick: editor of *Eighth Army News* and *Crusader*, 77–81, 178, 366; Victory Parade, Tripoli, 136; and Robertson, 178–179; 8th Army, 219; Axis paratroops, 364, 365; and Mountbatten, 365; and

Montgomery's personality, 365, 468–469; and Patton, 366

Chartres, 758, 761, 762, 770, 778, 783

Chavasse, Noel, ADC to Montgomery, 533

Cherbourg, 480, 481, 484, 487, 501, 502, 505, 551, 552, 572, 578, 585, 623–624, 626–629, 638, 648, 658, 664, 665, 671, 674, 677, 679, 682, 684, 695, 714, 722, 743, 744, 790

Cheux, 684

Chief of Staff system, 493

Chilton, Maurice: COS to Dempsey, 721

Chott, 205, 207

Churchill, Captain, Comd HMS *Faulknor*, 612, 613, 615, 618

Churchill, Sir Winston S.: served WWI, 561; character, 559, 560, 581, 582; on Alamein, 5, 7, 101; letter to Alexander, 66; on N. African operations, 67, 126, 127; on Montgomery, 121; visit to N. Africa, 131, 132, 138; Victory Parade, Tripoli, 132, 133, 138, 177; and David Montgomery, 133, 135; Casablanca conference, 139; and Turkish President, 139; and Alexander, 140, 561; and Stalin, 171–172; and Montgomery, 175, 194, 283, 443–445, 477, 478, 507, 508, 514, 544, 545, 560, 580–582, 735, 736, 742, 751; invasion of Sicily, 225, 283; and Eisenhower, 257, 707, 742; Algiers Council, 276, 283; and Alanbrooke, 742; Salerno, 405; pursuit plan, Italy, 410, 443; Tehran summit, 443, 445, 446, 463, 506; OVERLORD operation, command, 446, 476–478; illness, 451, 452; anti-ANVIL operation, 507, 514, 690, 692, 763; NW Europe invasion plan, 548, 554–556, 559; OVERLORD plans, 570–578; present at, 591, 592; to Normandy, 632, 729–731; and Eisenhower, 707–708, 742, 796; invitation from Montgomery, 725; dismissal of Montgomery, 725, 726, 736, 737, 742; Montgomery's directive, 731, 732; to Italy, 785; author of *Closing the Ring*, 443n, 478n; *Hinge of Fate*, 66n, 171n; Triumph and Tragedy, 632n, 690n

Churchill: the Struggle for Survival (Lord Moran), 131n, 480

Clark, General Mark: Comd 5th US Army, 350, 458; entry into Rome, 146; plans for AVALANCHE operation, 337, 338, 339, 350, 380, 381, 387, 395, 396, 398; attack on Salerno, 337, 399, 400, 403–407, 435, 546; future plans, 406–407; Italian armistice, 398; and Eisenhower, 403n, 404–405, 407; awarded DCM, 406; advance to Naples, 408–409, 411; awarded DSC, 415n; advance to Volturno, 424, 425, 428; and Montgomery, 435–436, 437, 458, 459; and Alexander, 436, 437, 531, 546; as commander, 810

Clark, General Wayne: dep to Tedder, 446

Closing the Ring (W. S. Churchill), 443n, 478n

COBRA operation, 638, 686, 719–722, 724, 726, 727, 731, 732, 736, 737, 738–742, 753, 754, 771, 798

Codman, Charles R., *Drive*, 353n

Collins, Major-General J. L., Comd 7 US Corps, 560, 613, 623, 629, 648, 664–665, 695–697, 771, 778; author of *Lightning Joe*, 665n

Cologne, 784, 789, 800

Combined arms operation: Catania, 299–300 (*see also* Amphibious operations)

Comiso airfield, 243, 252, 298

Commando operations: Catania, 299; Calabria, 385

Condé, 757, 765

'Conduct of Battle, The' (B. L. Montgomery), 45, 123

Coningham, Air Marshal Sir Arthur, 25, 30, 55; AOC, Allied Tac AF, 197, 361; and Montgomery, 197, 200, 661, 678–679, 746; and Patton, 198n; theories, 198, 361, 649, 652, 661; to Normandy, 659, 660, 745, 746; Montgomery's plan, 708, 709; non-co-operation, 717; GOODWOOD operation, 719; Montgomery's directive, 731, 732n; and Tedder, 746

COPPERHEAD operation, 567n

Corbett, Lt-General T., 370

Corlett, Major-General Charles H., Comd 19 US Corps, 646, 663

Corps de Chasse, 15, 22, 29, 35–37, 40, 42, 52, 150, 188, 353

Corrandini, 111, 116, 117

Corsica, 70
Cos, 443–444, 452
Cosenza, 401, 402
Cotentin Peninsula, *see* Cherbourg
Courseulles, 603
Coutances, 638, 649, 667, 672, 737, 754
Coward, Noël, *Middle East Diary*, 416
Creasy, Rear-Admiral G. E.: COS,
    ANVIL conference, 529;
    OVERLORD operation, 601, 635
Crerar, General Henry: CGS
    Canadian Army, 150, 176, 465,
    588, 675, 700; Montgomery's
    plan, 708, 792; Montgomery's
    directive, 732n, 743, 744, 754, 759;
    Falaise Gap, 760, 761, 771–772;
    Montgomery's doubts, 766; and
    Crocker, 766
Crete, 7, 70, 426
Creully, Tac HQ, 618, 632, 677;
    conference, 670–673
Crocker, Lt-General J. T.: Comd 1
    Corps, 623; wounded, 235;
    Normandy, 619, 630, 659; letter
    to Dempsey, 700–701; vs Crerar,
    766
Cross, Air Commodore K. B. B., 236
Crotone airfield and port, 400–402
Crusade in Europe (Dwight D.
    Eisenhower), 479n, 643, 804n
Crusader (8th Army newspaper, ed.
    Charlton), 77, 178
Crusader tanks, 5, 58, 60
Cunningham, General Sir Alan, 79
Cunningham, Admiral of the Fleet Sir
    Andrew, 66, 521; and
    Montgomery, 246, 252, 254–257,
    280, 293, 379, 419, 545, 547;
    non-co-operation, 281, 282–283,
    293, 342; communications from
    Alexander, 340, 341; Axis
    withdrawal from Sicily,
    340–342, 361; Eisenhower plans
    for Italian invasion, 356, 381, 389,
    395; AVALANCHE operation,
    398; OVERLORD operation,
    Naval C-in-C, 457; ANVIL
    operation, 507; THUNDERCLAP
    exercise, 547–553
Cunningham, 'Bill', ADC to
    Alexander, 452, 453
Cunningham, Admiral John, Naval
    C-in-C, Mediterranean, 477
Cunningham the Commander (S. W. C.
    Pack), 342n
Custance, Brigadier E. C. N., Comd
    8th Armoured Brigade, 40, 41

Cyrenaica: evacuation by Axis forces,
    53, 55, 56, 91; RAF in, 67, 75

Daba, 14, 18, 22–25, 29–31, 39, 57
Daily Express: Alamein, 3, 4, 8;
    Tunisia, 10
Daily Telegraph: Alamein, 3, 8; Tripoli,
    118, 119
Dardanelles, the (1915), 285
Dawley, C. J., Comd 6 US Corps, 387n
Dawnay, Lt-Colonel Christopher P.,
    MA to Montgomery, 172, 524, 533,
    534, 535, 548, 566, 571, 578, 603,
    649, 662, 678, 690, 712, 713, 718,
    740, 747, 760, 811–814
D-Day, 6 June 1944, 7; forecast, 69–70;
    lessons of operation HUSKY,
    227, 367, 611; preparation,
    475–485, 486–496, 518, 539–604;
    Axis defence, 519, 520; final
    decision, 590, 592–603; landings,
    611–617
Deceptive measures, Allied, 121, 122,
    125; Agheila, 86; Medenine, 159;
    Pas de Calais, 506, 509, 592, 757n;
    Montgomery's double, 567, 568,
    569; Normandy, 607; Axis, 92,
    105, 156, 158, 165
de Druval, Mme, 619
de Gaulle, Général Charles: to
    Normandy, 653–654, 653n
de Guingand, Major-General Sir
    Francis: COS, 8th Army, 11–25
    passim, 34, 64, 80, 183, 196, 197,
    334–335, 449, 467; tactical
    theories, 15, 30, 192; BGS
    conference, 61; in hospital, 76, 84,
    101, 102; and Montgomery, 113,
    179, 192, 271–272, 300, 347, 355,
    558, 571, 582; PUGILIST
    operation, 200; promotion to
    Major-General, 244, 247
HUSKY operation: Montgomery's
    rep in Cairo, 244, 247; planning,
    247–248, 251–254, 261; plane
    crash, 252; plan approved, 262;
    assault on Sicily, 295, 300, 306,
    329; and Leese, 308; and Patton,
    329; and operation BAYTOWN,
    377, 382; and Alexander, 437;
    advance to Sangro River, 437; and
    operation ANVIL, 512n, 529
OVERLORD operation: plan, 500;
    final plans, 570–578; COS 21st
    Army Gp, 518–19, 545, 558, 601,
    603, 607, 630, 647–648, 713, 737,
    810–813; tactical operations, 558,

762; to Normandy, 653;
Montgomery's plan, 708, 709,
714, 751n
GOODWOOD operation, 714, 718,
720, 731n, 813; dismissal of
Montgomery plot, 724–725, 737
COBRA operation, 731n
Montgomery's directives, 731, 732;
Falaise Gap, 762; future plans,
792–794; and Montgomery's
Liaison Officers, 811, 812; and
Montgomery, 811, 812, 813
Author of *Generals at War*, 43n, 76n,
84n; *From Brass Hat to Bowler Hat*,
58n; *Operation Victory*, 452n, 582n
Dempsey, General Sir Miles, Comd 13
Corps, 146, 225
  HUSKY operation: Comd 13 Corps:
  226, 241, 243, 290; planning, 251;
  and Montgomery, 249, 334, 335,
  588; assault on Sicily, 293, 297–298,
  311, 315, 318–319; and Browning,
  306
  BAYTOWN operation: invasion of
  Italy, 322, 379, 382; Comd
  Canadian Army, N.W. Europe,
  465
  OVERLORD operation: Comd
  Second Army, 519; character,
  683, 738, 741; exercise
  THUNDERCLAP, 547–553;
  Montgomery's plans, 559, 588,
  708, 709; D-Day, 611; advance on
  Caen, 615, 626–627, 629–630, 633,
  636–640, 641–657, 658–667, 695,
  702, 703, 706–709, 714, 716;
  meeting with Montgomery,
  625–627, 708, 709, 792
  Normandy operations, 641–657
  passim, 658–673 *passim*, 674–688,
  706–707, 709, 710, 714, 716, 731,
  756–791; army/air conference,
  659, 660
  GOODWOOD operation: plans,
  710, 712–713, 718, 719, 720, 731;
  casualties, 718; Montgomery's
  directives, 731, 732, 743, 744,
  754–755, 759; Falaise Gap,
  756–775
Denby, Mrs Frances, 434n, 442n, 499,
789–790
Dennis, Colonel Mead, CCRA, 30
Corps, 47
Derna, 26, 27, 56–58
Desert Air Force, *see* Royal Air Force,
N. Africa
Desert Air Force Commander, Air

Vice-Marshal Harry Broadhurst,
196
Desert Generals, The (Correlli Barnett),
175n
'Desert Rats', *see* British Army, 7th
Armoured Division
Desert Victory (film), 171, 333, 334
Desert War, The (Alan Moorehead),
120n
de Stefanis, General Giuseppe, Comd
20 Corps, 63
Devers, General, 476
Diamond T transporters, 14, 16
Dickson, Colonel, 330
Dieppe, raid on, 70; capture, 818
Dill, Field Marshal Sir John, 173, 412,
595
Dives, River, 720, 721
Djebel Tebaga, *see* Tebaga
Djeida, 66
Dodecanese, the, 70–71
Domfront, Axis attack on, 767, 768
Don at War, A (Sir David Hunt), 105n
Doolittle, Lt-General James H., Comd
US 8th Air Force: bombing policy,
609, 652
Dorman-Smith, Major-General Eric
E., 137
Douglas, Air Chief Marshal Sir
William Sholto, AO C-in-C,
Middle East Air Command, 255
Douvres, 620
DRAGOON (ex ANVIL) operation,
763, 785
Dreux, 778, 782, 783, 784, 789
Drive (Charles R. Codman), 353n
DUKW, 415, 417
Dunkirk, 7, 9, 44, 126, 145, 385, 461,
541, 546, 597, 750, 819

Eastern front (WWII), 10, 72–73,
683–684
Eastern Task Force (ETF), Sicily, 242, 243,
251, 283–284, 304–13 *passim*,
314–321 *passim*
Eberbach, General H., POW, 818
E-boats, 562
Eden, Anthony, 689
Egypt: evacuation by Afrika Korps,
42–43, 44, 53, 54–55; battle of, 50,
90, 141
Ehrman, J., *Grand Strategy*, Vol. V,
383n, 427n
Eighth Army News, 77
Eisenhower, General Dwight D.:
C-in-C, N. Africa, 10, 63, 65, 66,
71, 139, 144, 164–165, 166, 274,

Eisenhower – *cont.*
275; Tunisian campaign, 103, 143,
273; lack of co-ordination, 148,
226; and Kasserine, 153, 170; diary,
162, 164; doubts on French
troops, 163–164, 165; promotion to
General, 164; US troop losses,
162, 164–165; and Churchill, 165,
555–556; and Montgomery, 170,
208, 209, 279; and Eighth Army,
208; letters to Marshall, 208, 209,
211; Montgomery's Flying
Fortress incident, 219–224
HUSKY operation:
letters to Marshall, 226, 227;
planning, 226, 241, 242, 244, 251,
254–255, 282; conference with
Alexander and Montgomery,
247, 250; conference at Allied
Force HQ, 255–256; final plan, 257;
approval, 281; and Marshall, 266,
274; unknown in US, 273; and
Bradley, 333; and Patton, 352,
362; Italy, invasion of, plans, 323,
342, 354, 356–357, 375–387, 412,
798; and Badoglio, 323, 380;
indecisiveness, 356, 410;
professionalism, 375, 509, 520,
732; and Bedell Smith, 371;
break-up of Axis Alliance, 375,
380
Italy, invasion of, 375–387; Algiers
conference, 377; and Tedder,
520; and Cunningham, 379, 520;
lunch with Montgomery, *etc.*, 381
BAYTOWN operation, 383
Italian armistice, 388, 391, 392,
403–404
AVALANCHE operation, 394, 398,
404, 405, 415; and Montgomery,
410, 411, 447, 451–452; letters to
Marshall, 410–412, 451; war
theories, 411, 451
OVERLORD operation:
and Marshall, 412, 445–446, 506,
514, 521, 529, 530; as COS, US
Army, 445–446; and Alexander,
446, 451, 455; planning theories,
451, 475, 476, 479, 509, 530–531,
754, 755; letters to Marshall, 451,
505–506; and Montgomery,
451–452, 455, 464, 475–485 *passim*,
499, 500, 502, 503, 528, 531, 545,
547, 559, 648, 734, 767
ANVIL operation, 506, 507, 509,
512, 531, 660–662; transfer of ships
for, 512–513, 514–515, 536;

conference, 529, 530;
abandonment of ANVIL,
536–537; visit to troops, 508;
character and professionalism,
509, 520, 524, 526, 642, 643, 725,
734, 751, 752
THUNDERCLAP exercise, 547–553
OVERLORD final plans, 570–578;
D-Day decision, 593–603;
landing in Normandy, 614; battle
of, 607–631 *passim*, 632–640,
641–657 *passim*, 658–667, 668–673,
674–688, 689–698, 699–716,
717–726, 727–740, 741–755; and/
vs Montgomery, 625, 630, 642, 644,
648, 657, 658, 677, 690, 691, 695,
698, 699, 702, 703, 706, 707,
708–709, 713–714, 716, 724,
741–743, 747, 751, 752, 754, 755,
767, 796, 804; visitors, 632; to
Bradley, 643; and Bradley, 647,
695; ANVIL reconsidered,
660–662, 668, 688, 692, 695, 702,
763, 798; doubts, 707; dismissal of
Montgomery plot, 717, 725, 736,
737, 742, 743; invitation from
Montgomery, 725; unwell, 725;
Montgomery's directive, 731,
732, 743, 754; battle strategy, 734,
735; to Normandy, 754–755;
future tactical plans, 786–787,
792–794, 803, 806–807; comd
Army Gps, 793, 794, 806;
political implications, 796, 801,
802, 806, 809, 817; capture of
Paris, 805, 808, 809; author of
Crusade in Europe, 479n, 643,
804n
Eisenhower, Lieutenant John, 658,
659
Eisenhower was my Boss (K.
Summersby), 755
El Hamma, *see* Hamma
Elbeuf, 805
Elizabeth II, Queen (as Princess), 276
Ellis, L. F., *Victory in the West*, Vol. I,
486n
ENCROACH operation, 438
Enfidaville, advance to, 137, 181, 218,
228–231, 233, 269
Enna, 298, 301, 304, 316, 330
Enterprise, HMS,729, 736n
EPSOM operation, 663, 673
Ernes, 778
Erskine, Major General 'Bobby' C. W.
E. J.: BGS, 75; Comd 7th Armoured
Div, 238, 630; dismissal, 758, 790

Escaut River, 817
Etna, Mt, 307, 311, 312, 314–318, 320, 321, 341, 342, 354, 399
Euston Station, 521–523
Evacuation Hospitals, *see* Hospitals
Evelegh, Major General V., Comd 78 Div, 341, 417, 438
Evrecy, 619, 621, 624–625, 634–636, 641, 645, 648, 655, 656n, 713, 716, 738
Evreux, 784
Ewart, Colonel J., 154, 682

FOOs (Forward Observation Officers), RA, 438
FUSA (1st United States Army), *see* US Army, 1st Army
Falaise, attack on, 619, 623, 707, 716, 720, 732, 738, 743, 763, 765, 783–784
Falaise Gap, 756–774, 777, 780–791, 809
Faulknor, HMS, 612, 613, 615, 618
Fehn, General Gustav, 74
Fighter Command, 588
FIRE-EATER operation, 106, 107–119
Fiumefreddo, 358
Flers, advance to, 687, 691, 758
Flying Fortress, Montgomery's, 137, 151, 219–224, 273, 290; crash landing, 324–328, 366
Foggia airfields, 388, 396, 410, 413, 421, 427, 470
Fondouk, 218
Force 141: 242, 243, 263–264, 268, 272, 290, 344, 345
Force 343: 242, 280
Force 545: 242, 244, 269
Forecast for Overlord (J. M. Stagg), 594
Forêt de Cinglais, 738
FORTITUDE operation: Pas de Calais deception plan, 506, 611, 727
Francavilla, 354
France, 7; defence of, 70; invasion of, 622–623; battle of, 819; *see also* ANVIL operation
Frank, Anne, *Diary* (Alanbrooke), 113n
Fraser, Sir David (*Alanbrooke*), 113n
Fredendall, Major General, Comd 2 US Corps, 163, 164
French Army: comd, 140; 2nd Armoured Division, comd Leclerc, 780; Free French Brigade, 26; 'L' Force, comd Leclerc, 182, 183; Vichy forces, 64, 241

Freyberg, General Sir Bernard: Comd 2nd New Zealand Div, 15, 18, 19, 22–26, 29–32, 35, 42, 43, 53, 195; under Lumsden, 25, 32, 42; at Halfaya, 55; attack on Agheila, 68, 86–89, 141; visit by Churchill, 132; on generals, 137; operation PUGILIST, 184; attack on Hamma, 195, 197; proposed Comd 30 Corps, 213, 226; Comd 9 Corps, 235; surrender of Messe, 270; Italy, 433, 434; to NW Europe, 466
From Algiers to Anzio (John P. Lucas), 362
From Apes to War Lords (S. Zuckerman), 660n
From Brass Hat to Bowler Hat (F. W. de Guingand), 58n
Fromm, Colonel-General F., German Home Army Commander, 730
Fuka, 29, 30, 37, 190; advance to, 16–28
Full Cycle: the biography of Admiral Sir Bertram Home Ramsay (W. S. Chalmers), 496n
Full Life, A (B. G. Horrocks), 177n, 195, 815
Furnari, 354–355

Gabes, 91, 105, 108, 145, 146, 149, 151, 161, 180, 181, 183, 187, 188, 193, 199, 202, 205–207, 210, 215
Gacé, 765, 774
Gaffey, General Hugh J., Comd 5 US Corps, 780, 781
Gafsa, 1st Army withdrawal, 146, 148; Allied threat, 152, 202; Montgomery's plan, 202, 204
Gairdner, General Sir Charles: Comd 8th Armoured Division, 14–16; HUSKY operation, 227, 242, 243, 250, 264; dismissal, 272; CGS to Alexander, 370
Gale, General Sir Humfrey: ANVIL conference, 529; officer in charge admin Supreme HQ, 718, 799; vs Montgomery, 767, 799
Gallantry, feats of, 170
Galloway, Colonel Strome, *The General Who Never Was*, 347, 363, 364
Gammell, Lt-General J. H., COS to Wilson, 669
Garci, 232
Garian, 108, 111

Garland, A. N. and Smyth, H. M., *United States Army in World War II: Sicily and the Surrender of Italy*, 310, 318n, 351, 352

Gatehouse, Major-General A. H.: Comd 10th Armoured Division, 23–26, 29, 32, 36, 40, 53; under Leese, 26, 34; under Lumsden, 29–37; advance to Mersa Matruh, 40–43; and Montgomery, 41, 137

Gault, Brigadier Sir James, MA to Eisenhower, 614, 625, 690, 691n, 785

Gay, Brigadier-General Hobart R., 317–318, 773n, 781

Gazala, 62, 125n

Gala airfield, 243, 249, 252, 255, 257, 298, 398

Gela, Gulf of, 249

General Who Never Was, The (Strome Galloway), 347, 363, 364

Generals at War (F. W. de Guingand), 43n, 76n, 84n

Generals, qualities of, 410, 411

George VI, King, 276; to Tripoli, 288; and Montgomery, 529, 583; OVERLORD plans, 570, 579, 591; visits Montgomery, 662, 676, 677

Gerbini airfields, 304, 305, 312

German Air Force, 24, 54, 68, 69, 616, 622

German Army:
at Alamein, 3–10; professionalism, 7, 393, 411, 697, 728; OKW, 91, 629, 681; strength, 106; strategic theories (Italy), 411; re-inforcements,426, 684, 709; NW Europe, strength in, 572, 682, 684; GOODWOOD operation, 720–722; Boulogne/Calais (1940), 759

Armies:
Army Group A: comd von Rundstedt: dismissed, 727, 728; relieved by von Kluge, 728
Army Group B: comd Rommel: response to Allied plans, 727
6th Army, 771
7th Army, 612, 818
Armoured Group West, 756

Corps:
Afrika Korps, 7, 15, 22–24, 29, 31–32, 37, 38, 42–44, 123, 150; retreat to Sidi Rezegh, 54; retreat to Mersa Brega/ Agheila line, 57–62, 85–94; casualties, 62n; evacuation of N. Africa, 63; withdrawal to Tunisian border, 140; evacuation of Sicily, 340–342, 360, 361

1 Panzer, 619
1 SS Panzer Armoured Corps, 756

Divisions:
Hermann Goering Panzer Division, 354
Lehr Panzer Division: Tours, 572, 573; Bretteville, 624; Villers Bocage, 630, 636–637, 641; Caen, 671
1st SS Panzer Division: Evrecy, 672; Esquay, 680–681
1st Panzer Division, 645
2nd SS Panzer Division: St. Lô, 672; Esquay, 680–681
2nd Panzer Division: Villers Bocage, 630, 645–648, 653; Caen, 671
9th SS Panzer Division: Normandy, 682, 684, 699n, 758
10th SS Panzer Division: Normandy, 682, 699n, 758
10th Panzer Division: attack on Medenine, 156, 158, 196; Gafsa, 202, 204–205; Wadi Akarit, 216; Kairouan, 218
12th SS Panzer Division: Lisieux, 572, 573; Bayeux, 619; Bretteville, 624, 637; Caen, 671; Falaise, 771
15th Panzer Division, 23, 31, 31n, 50; withdrawal to Sidi Barrani, 41; withdrawal to Matruh, 53, 54; defence of Capuzzo, 54; attack on Medenine, 156; defence of Mareth, 184, 189, 205; defence of Hamma, 196, 197, 205; Gafsa, 202; Enfidaville, 232
17th SS Panzer Division: Rennes, 572, 573
21st SS Panzer Division: 31, 34, 36, 50, 108, 109, 156, 170, 184, 189, 193, 202, 205, 215; Caen, 572, 603, 615, 624, 637, 655, 671; Bayeux, 619; Caumont, 758
90th Light Division, 19, 22, 38, 41, 50; evacuation of Tobruk, 54; evacuation of Homs, 116; attack on Medenine, 156, 167; defence of Mareth, 184, 189, 191, 205, 206; Enfidaville, 232; Sangro River, 440

116th Panzer Division, 573
164th Light Division, 38, 50, 112, 156, 167, 184, 205, 232
346th Division: Caen, east, 624
352nd Division, 603
353rd Infantry Division: Périers, 672; reinforcements, 702
711th Division: Caen, east, 624
Brigades:
Ramcke (Parachute) Brigade, 112, 191
Regiments:
Panzer Grenadier Regiment Afrika, 38, 189, 191
29th Panzer Grenadier Regiment, 351
Airborne troops: Gerbini, 305
German-Italian Panzer Army, 4, 13, 104, 119; Rommel (C-in-C) dismissed, 117, 122–123; comd Messe, 152
German news media, 4
Gerow, Major-General Leonard T., Comd 5 US Corps, 613, 626, 641, 646–647, 663, 781
Ghazal Station, 16, 23, 26, 29
Gheddahia, 109
GIANT II operation, 389–400, 405, 411, 443, 504, 509, 597, 798
Giffard, General Sir George, C-in-C to Mountbatten, 597
Gioja, 322, 355
Giraud, Général d'Armée H., C-in-C, French N. African forces, 211
Glaister, Private Geoffrey, 260
Godwin-Austen, Major-General A. R., 137
Goebbels, Dr. J. P., 119
Goering, Marshal of the Reich Hermann, 354, 361
GOODWOOD operation: plans, 710, 712, 718–719; Tedder's objections, 718ff; battle, 719–724, 728, 737; Montgomery's justification, 730, 731, 746, 747, 750; press conference, 813
Gort, Field Marshal Viscount, VC, 131; Field Marshal, 133; comd BEF, 142, 266, 363, 546, 593, 813; temperament, 245; and Montgomery, 278, 369, 813
'Gothic Line', 389
Gott, Lt-General W. H. E., 5–6, 137, 453
Graham, Major-General D. A. H., Comd 50th Division, 676
Graham, Major-General Sir Miles: HQ

Eighth Army, 262; Admin Chief, 21st Army Group, 518, 545, 607, 810; Montgomery's plan, 708, 709; Montgomery's directive, 732n
Grand Strategy (J. Ehrman), 383n, 427n
Grand Strategy (Michael Howard), 66n, 225n
Grant tanks, 16, 55, 60, 61, 160
Granville, 667, 672, 737
GRAPESHOT operation, 14, 15, 26
Graziani, General Rodolfo, 10, 57
Greece, 7; defence of, 70, 537
Greek Army: 1st Greek Brigade, 26
Grigg, Sir James, Sec of State for War, 449, 462, 524, 542, 545, 547, 591, 595, 744, 796; THUNDERCLAP exercise, 547–552; author of *Prejudice and Judgement*, 548n
Gruenther, General Alfred M., COS 5th Army, 405
Guettar, 203, 209, 215
Gustav Line, 440
Guzzoni, General Alfredo, 314

Haig, Field Marshal Sir Douglas: World War I failure, 192; message, 788
Haislip, Major-General Wade H., Comd 15 US Corps, 773
Halfaya Pass, 26, 39, 42–44, 54, 55
Haluf, 186
Hamilton, J. A. I. Agar, 6n
Hamilton-Russell, Major J., 343n
Hamma (the 'Plum'), battle of, 187, 193–207, 667
Hammamet, 232, 288
Hand-to-hand fighting, 192
Hansen, Major Chester B., ADC to Bradley, 586n, 589, 613, 620, 624, 626, 641, 643, 646, 647, 648, 655, 657, 658, 669n, 670, 693, 704n, 705–706, 753, 765, 770, 772, 785, 792, 797n, 799n
Harding, Field Marshal Lord: Comd 7th Armoured Div, 19, 24, 26, 30, 35, 53, 68, 112; and Lumsden, 24; tactical theories, 52, 54; Agheila, 87, 89; wounded, 112, 114; and Alexander, 461; COS to Alexander, 546, 596
Harris, Air Marshal Sir Arthur, RAF Bomber Command: OVERLORD operation, 540, 571, 596, 608, 609; Normandy, 652, 746; GOODWOOD operation, 713, 719

Harrison, G. A., 437n
Hart, Sir Basil H. Liddell: Alamein
follow-up, 15, 150; and
Montgomery, 526;
Montgomery's plan, 750; author of
the Second World War, 15n; *The
Other Side of the Hill*, 181n
Harwood, Admiral Sir Henry, 107
Hastings, Lt-Colonel Robin, Comd
DLI, 359
Haswell, J., *The Intelligence and
Deception of the D-Day Landings*,
567n
Hausser, SS General P.: Comd 7th
Army, 783; and Montgomery, 798
Henderson, Captain John, ADC to
Montgomery, 82, 83, 158n, 192,
222n, 277, 324, 327, 334, 360n,
363n, 381n, 452, 453n, 533, 653n,
669n, 725
Henson, Leslie, 177
Herbert, General Sir Otway, 517–518,
604
Herdon, Lt-Colonel, Comd 2nd Royal
Warwickshire Regiment, 620
Hewitt, Admiral Henry Kent, US
Navy, 281
Hey, Dr Richard, 85n, 101n
Hill 112: 680
Hill 369: 215
Hindenburg, Field Marshal Paul von,
596
Hinge of Fate (Sir Winston Churchill),
66n, 171n
Hinsley, F. H., *British Intelligence in the
Second World War*, 18n, 59n, 105,
154n
Hitler, Adolf: and Rommel, 38, 59, 63,
70, 73, 154, 403, 661, 662;
instructions from, 56, 798;
invasion of Spain, 65; in
defence, 70; re Tunisia, 71; and
Alamein, 103; and Sicilian
invasion, 254; and military
defeats, 269; and Italian
campaign, 426; and Normandy
invasion, 616, 617, 629; and
Normandy campaign, 661, 662,
671, 684, 727, 728, 761
Hitler's War (David Irving), 116n
Hobart, Major-General Sir Percy C.
S., Comd 79th Armd Division
(tank 'funnies'), 585, 611
Hodges, Lt-General C. H.: Comd 1st
US Army, 694, 759; Falaise Gap,
759, 772, 785; advance to Seine,
786; conference with

Montgomery, 792; tactical plans,
807
Holderness, Mrs Winsome (*née*
Montgomery; later Lady
Michelmore), 271
Hollinghurst, Air Vice-Marshal L. N.,
635
Holloway, W. G., 364n
Home Forces in England, 1942 and
1943 (C-in-C Paget), 370–371
Homs, 111, 112, 113–114, 116, 117
Homs-Tarhuna line, *see*
Tarhuna-Homs line
Horrocks, Lt-General Sir Brian, 43n;
Comd 13 Corps, 26, 27;
Montgomery's opinion, 45, 236;
Comd 10 Corps, 68, 146n, 195, 231,
and troops' entertainment, 177
PUGILIST operation, 193; Hamma,
195, 197, 199–200; Corps
Commander in NW Europe, 213,
214; attack on Enfidaville, 231;
Tunis final offensive, 236–238;
Comd 9 Corps, 236; operation
STRIKE, 237; and Montgomery,
288
HUSKY operation: Comd 10 Corps,
243, 284, 322; Messina Straits,
284
BUTTRESS operation: invasion of
Italy, 322–323, 356, 376; Comd 30
Corps, Normandy, 790; sickness,
815
Author of *A Full Life*, 177n, 195, 815
Horseshoe Hill, 184, 187
Horster, Professor, 136
Hospitals: 15th Evacuation, 351; Field,
352; 93rd Evacuation, 352
Hottot, 637
Howard, Michael, *Grand Strategy*,
66n, 225n
Howe, George F., *North-west Africa:
Seizing the Initiative*: 216n
Hube, General Hans-Valentin, 314
Hudson aircraft, Montgomery's, 325
Hughes, Major-General, Comd 44th
Div, 26
Hughes, Rev F. W., 173–174
Hunt, Sir David, *A Don at War*, 105n
Hurricane fighters, 200
HUSKY operation: planning, 137, 145,
223–228, 229–230, 238, 241–258,
259–268, 269, 280, 290, 372, 381,
475, 479, 504, 584, 750;
importance, 265; command, 266,
269; assault, 292, 303; airborne
operations, 292; 8th Army,

292–303, 304–313, 314–349 *passim*;
7th US Army, 295, 299, 307–313;
advance to Palermo, 315–321;
casualties, 337; completion, 367

I Was Monty's Double (M. E. Clifton
James), 568n
Indian Army:
Divisions:
4th Division, 35; PUGILIST
operation, 184, 185, 191; Wadi
Akarit, 215–218; casualties, 216;
Enfidaville, 231, 232, 235; enemy
casualties, 232; transfer to 1st
Army, 235
8th Division: advance to Sangro
River, 433–435; attack from
Sangro Bridgehead, 439;
casualties, 453
Infantry Officer with the 8th Army, An
(H. P. Samwell), 170n
Infantry, use of: Alamein, 10, 85;
Agheila, 68–87 *passim*; advance to
Tripoli, 109–118 *passim*; tactical
use, 150, 151, 155; at Medenine,
169–170; on Sicily, 300; COBRA
operation, 738
Ingersoll, Ralph, *Top Secret*, 484n
*Intelligence and Deception of the D-Day
Landings, The* (J. Haswell), 567n
International News Service, 4
In This Sign We Conquer (John Smyth),
174n
Irving, David, *Hitler's War*, 116n; *The
Trail of the Fox*, 58n, 62n, 123n, 153,
159n, 619n
Isigny, advance by US Army, 614, 621,
657
Ismay, General Lord, MA to
Churchill, 571, 580, 591, 796
Italian Army: Alamein, 8; Commando
Supremo, 38, 105; High
Command, 91
Corps:
10 Corps, 50
20 Mobile Corps, 24, 38, 50, 61
21 Corps, 50
Divisions:
Ariete Armoured Division, 19,
50, 87
Bologna Division, 50
Brescia Division, 50
Folgore Division, 50
Littorio Armoured Division, 50
Pavia Division, 50
Trento Division, 50
Trieste Division, 50

Regiment:
Bersaglieri, 359
Italian news media, 4
Italo-Turkish War (1911), 118
Italy: invasion of, 69, 72, 73, 253,
283–284, 337, 372, 375–387,
388–409, 410–419; Phase 2,
420–431; Phase 3, 432–441,
513–514, 531, 545; plans for
invasion, 322, 333, 461; defence of,
70–71; US non-offensive, 410; UK
offensive plan, 410; Italian
attitude, 410

Jacob, Alaric, 8
Jacob, Lt-General Sir Ian, 138–140
James, Lieutenant M. E. Clifton
(Montgomery's double),
567–569; author of *I Was Monty's
Double*, 568n
John, Augustus: painting of
Montgomery, 534–535
Johnston, Denis, *Nine Rivers from
Jordan*, 470
Juno Beach, 1 Corps, Tac HQ, 615

Kairouan, 218, 229
Kesserine, battle of, 140, 143, 144,
151–154, 159, 164, 173, 182, 402,
414, 504, 525, 797; casualties, 127,
166
Keating, Captain Geoffrey, Army
Film & Photographic Unit, 77,
79, 81, 82, 178–179, 218, 221, 275,
333–334, 359–360, 467
Keller, Major-General R. F. H., Comd
3rd Canadian Division, criticism
of, 700–701
Kennedy, Major General Sir John,
DMO, 275n; ACIGS (Operations),
547, 553–556, 602, 612n, 785; letter
from Montgomery, 792; author of
The Business of War, 275n, 547n,
612n
Kesselring, Field Marshal Albert: and
Rommel, 63, 74, 91, 105, 122,
152, 159, 403; war council, 68; and
Alamein, 103; planning
conference, Tripolitania, 105; and
Medenine, 168; El Hamma, 201;
withdrawal from Mareth, 201,
205, 215; withdrawal from Rome,
389; Salerno, 404, 405, 408; author
of *The Memoirs of Field Marshal
Kesselring*, 91n, 159n
Keyes, Major-General Geoffrey T., 381
Khalda, 36

Khamza, 26

King, Admiral E. J., C-in-C US Fleet, Normandy, 632

Kipling, Rudyard, 820

Kippenberger, Major-General Sir Howard, Comd 5th New Zealand Brigade, 43

Kirkman, General Sir Sidney, CRA, 12, 34, 40–41; on air forces, 55; transfer to 1st Army, 212; Comd 50th Division, 212, 213, 289, 358–359; and Montgomery, 289, 297–298, 532, 543

Kittyhawk fighter-bomber squadrons, 196, 199, 336, 422

Kluge, Field Marshal G. von: Comd Army Group B, 728, 756, 759; Falaise Gap, 759–762, 768; dismissed, 783; death, 783–784; and Montgomery, 798

Koch, Colonel Oscar, *A One Way Ticket*, 280, 309

Koenig, General, C-in-C of FFI, Paris, 805

LCI (Landing Craft, Infantry), 513, 515

LST (Landing Ship, Tanks), 513, 515, 536, 562, 612, 615

La Ferté Bernard, 778

L'Aigle, 772, 774, 783

Laval, 759, 762

Laycock, Brigadier R. G., Comd Special Service Brigade, 354

Le Bény Bocage, 710, 756, 759

Leclerc, Général de Division, Comd 'L' Force, 182, 183; Falaise, 780; to Paris, 780, 781, 808

Lee, General John, 578n

Leese, Lt-General Sir Oliver, 13; Comd 30 Corps, 18, 22, 23, 26–29, 120, 195; in UK, 434, 450; Montgomery's opinion, 45, 450; at Agheila, 68, 86, 88, 89, 90; FIRE–EATER operation, 107, 108, 111, 112, 114, 115, 117; diary, 109; Tripoli, 120, 121; visit by Churchill, 132; Army Study Week, 141; operation PUGILIST, 155, 184–193 *passim*; Medenine, 158, 159, 167–170; Hamma, 195; transfer to 1st Army, 213, 214, 226, 246; operation HUSKY: Comd 30 Corps, 226, 293, 355; planning, 248, 252, 262; assault on Sicily, 302, 303, 308, 311, 316, 319, 359; and Browning, 306; and Bradley, 308, 315; and

Montgomery, 308, 323, 360, 442; and Patton, 308–309; assault on Italy, 323; leave, 386; Comd 8 Corps NW Europe, 417; Comd 2nd Army NW Europe, 465; Comd 8th Army, Italy, 465n, 467, 468, 470, 597; letters from Montgomery, 499, 675, 676, 789, 790; and Alexander, 531; dismissal of Allfrey, 531

Le Havre, 713–714

Leigh-Mallory, Air Marshal Sir Trafford, 453n; C-in-C Allied Expeditionary Force, 492n, 717; and Montgomery, 496, 545, 634, 648–649, 651–654, 655–656, 679, 717, 723; operation OVERLORD, plan, 500, 540, 570–578; ANVIL conference, 529; exercise THUNDERCLAP, 547–553; pessimism, 585; D-Day, 594, 599–601; Normandy, 608, 609, 610, 616, 621, 622, 624, 627, 631, 643, 651–652, 653, 717, 745, 782; air drop refusal, 600, 631, 634, 635, 636, 642, 648, 649, 651–652; bombing, 659, 660, 746; and Coningham, 678, 679, 717; and Tedder, 679, 717, 724, 736; Montgomery's plan, 708–709; GOODWOOD operation, 719; Montgomery's directive, 731, 732n

Le Mans, 762, 768, 770, 778

Lemnitzer, General L., COS (US) to Alexander, 388, 390n, 398–399

'Lennox', Colonel (*pseud*. B. L. Montgomery), 275

Lentini, 299

Leonforte, 307, 312, 316

Leros, 443, 452

Le Tronquay, 760

Lewin, Brigadier Charles, BGS Ops, 518

Lewin, Ronald, *Montgomery as Military Commander*, 249n

Lewis, Neville, 76, 77, 83, 84, 98, 99, 100, 133, 134, 534; author of *Studio Encounters*, 77n

Liaison Officers, 682, 705, 726, 748, 749, 762, 778, 781, 811, 812

Libya, 10, 51

Lightning Joe (J. L. Collins), 665n

Lines of Communication: Allied forces, 97, 122, 125, 148, 163, 397, 401, 665, 794, 797; Axis forces, 122, 125, 180, 214, 772

854

Linguaglossa, 354
Loire River, 551–552, 578, 580, 664–665, 709
Long Range Desert Group, 103; to Agedabia, 56; Agheila, 87
Lorient, 763
Louvain, 818, 819
Louviers, 784
Lucas, Major General John P., Comd 6 US Corps: operation HUSKY, 280–282, 286, 310, 311; and Tedder, 280; and Patton, 286, 362, 548; and Montgomery, 311; OVERLORD operation, 548; author of *From Algiers to Anzio*, 362
Ludendorff, General Erich von, 596
Luftwaffe, *see* German Air Force
Lumsden, Lt-General Sir Herbert, Comd 10 Corps: advance to Fuka, 18, 20–28, 29–30 *passim*; and Montgomery, 20–24, 30, 31, 32, 34, 39, 42, 45, 59–60; and New Zealand forces, 25, 26, 29, 30–37, 42; attack on Matruh, 31, 32, 39, 42; advance to Benghazi, 58–61; Agedabia, 61; return to UK, 68, 261; knighted, 68n; Corps comd, NW Europe, 213, 214

Maaten Giofer, 87
MacArthur, General Douglas, 211
McCreery, General Sir David: COS to Alexander, 186n, 197, 230, 245, 370; Comd 10 Corps, 214, 404, 406, 415, 424; visit to Montgomery, 238; Volturno, 424
McGrigor, Rear-Admiral R. R., 379
McLean, Brigadier K. G., 481, 482, 484n, 485n, 500, 502, 512n, 552n
MacMillan, Major-General J. H. A., Comd 15th (Scottish) Division: EPSOM operation, 673
McNab, Brigadier, 144, 214, 370
McNaughton, General the Hon. A. G. L., Canadian Army Commander, 275, 276, 326, 327, 335, 346
'Main Lessons of the Battle' (Alamein) (B. L. Montgomery), 48–49
Mainwaring, Brigadier Hugh: capture of Mersa Matruh, 39, 41, 183n
Maknassy, 196, 203, 205, 209, 215
Malta, 27, 64, 124; relief convoys, 5, 39, 56, 57, 124; 8th Army HQ for HUSKY, 283; visit by Montgomery, 288, 290
Mantes-Gassicourt, 785, 805

Maps: OVERLORD phase lines, 548, 552
Marada, 122
'Marble Arch', 68, 85, 88
Mareth, 124; battle of, 137, 148–149, 180, 182–193, 206, 207; preparations for, 152, 154, 159, 166, 180–181; operation PUGILIST, 154, 155, 161, 180, 183–193, 199, 201, 209; Axis tanks, 196
Marigny-St Gilles line, 737
Marinella: US landing, 242
Marrakesh, 471, 479, 481
Marshall, General George, COS US Army: letters from Eisenhower, 208, 209, 211, 410, 451, 505, 506, 697; complaints re reporters, 220; pressure on Eisenhower, 257, 266, 274, 411–412, 514, 529; plan for assault on Italy, 338, 388; assault on Normandy, 344, 388, 410; blame on Montgomery, 392, 510; and Mediterranean campaign, 443, 507; Supreme Commander, OVERLORD, 445–447, 510; ANVIL vs OVERLORD, 507, 510, 514; experience, 521; and Montgomery, 595, 747, 815; to Normandy, 632
Marshall, S. L. A., 555n, 559n
Martuba airfields, 5, 26, 39, 56–58, 124
Mather, Carol, POW, 415
Mather, Major Sir William, 20–21, 448–449, 468n
Matmata, 197
Matruh, 26–27, 31, 36; pursuit to, 39–44 (*see also* Mersa Matruh)
Matthews, Sidney, 257n
Mayenne, 774, 778
Mechili (Martuba airfield area), 26, 56
Medenine, 105; battle of, 152–170, 171, 180, 182, 202, 402; casualties, 169–170
Medical services, 415, 495
Mediterranean and the Middle East, The: Vol IV (I. S. O. Playfair and C. J. C. Molony), 142n
   Vol V (C. J. C. Molony), 245n, 273n, 467
Medjez el Bab, 237
Melito, 384
Mélun, 803
Memoirs of Field Marshal Kesselring, The, 91n, 159n
Mersa Brega, 55, 56, 61; battle of, *see* Agheila, battle of
Mersa Brega/El Agheila defence line,

Mersa Brega/El Agheila – *cont.*
  55, 61, 85, 87, 90, 122, 125
Mersa Matruh, 16, 22, 25–27, 30–31,
  34, 37; pursuit to, 38–43, 53, 54
  (*see also* Matruh)
Messe, General Giovanni: Comd
  German-Italian Panzer Army,
  152, 183–184, 189, 196, 202, 205,
  206, 214; and Rommel, 152;
  Wadi Akarit, 215, 216;
  Enfidaville, 231; surrender to
  Freyberg, 270; Minister of War, 447
Messina: objective, 249, 309, 310, 312,
  315, 317–320, 358; assault on,
  298, 328, 330, 349, 350, 354–355;
  capture of, 361, 362, 366; as a
  base, 384, 397
Messina Straits, 282, 284, 372; HUSKY
  operation, 285; Axis
  reinforcement, 290; Axis
  withdrawal, 340, 341, 342,
  360–361; operation BAYTOWN,
  376, 382, q.v.
Metz, 793, 799
Mézidon, 716, 720
Middle East Command (1942), 370
Middle East Diary (Noël Coward), 416
Middleton, Major-General Troy H.:
  Comd 45th US Division, 328;
  Comd 8 US Corps, 681
Milazzo, 354, 358
Miller, Major-General Charles H.:
  Admin Officer, 15th Army Gp,
  420, 543; Supplies Officer, 18th
  Army Gp, 228; dismissed, 424
Mines and minefields:
  Alamein, 10, 18, 37, 509
  advance to Fuka, 25, 30, 34, 35
  advance to Agheila, 86, 87, 93–94,
  122
  defence of Buerat, 105, 106, 109, 117
  Army Study Week, 141
  defence of Mareth, 156, 207
  recognition, 174–175
  operation PUGILIST, 183, 185, 187,
  189, 193
  Sicily, 359
  Sangro River, 435
  Normandy beaches, 576, 613
Misheifa landing ground, 42
Misterbianco, 316, 317, 341
Mitterand, François, President of
  France, 481n; author of *The Wheat
  and the Chaff*, 481n
Mockler-Ferryman, 144
Model, Field Marshal W., Comd
  Army Group B, 783

Molony, Brigadier C. J. C., *The
  Mediterranean and the Middle East*:
  Vol. IV (with I. S. O. Playfair),
  142n; Vol V, 245n, 273n, 309, 467
Moltke, General Helmuth von, 6
Mont Pinçon, 663
Montgomery, Bernard Law, Field
  Marshal the Viscount
  Montgomery of Alamein
  (1887-1975).
  Home and Family:
    and David, 49, 98, 100, 133–136,
    169, 271, 814; and John Carver,
    134; and Jocelyn Carver,
    134–136, 172, 186, 187, 525–526,
    814; and Lady Maud
    Montgomery, 133, 134, 136, 271,
    526; and Betty, 77, 101, 581,
    705; at St Paul's School, 260;
    and Mrs Holderness, 271; and
    theatre, 276, 277; letters to
    Reynolds, 44, 49, 76, 96, 98,
    100, 134–136, 166, 169, 172,
    175, 186–187, 253, 271, 276–277,
    300, 325, 342, 343, 366–367, 393,
    402, 447, 454, 528, 540n, 636,
    654, 668, 680, 703–704, 735, 760,
    777, 814, 819
  Personal characteristics and
  qualities:
    ruthlessness, 6, 9, 12, 137, 532;
    professionalism, 45, 46, 97,
    101–102, 126, 131, 165, 168, 193,
    250, 332, 334, 348, 363, 381,
    411, 416, 417, 432, 467, 643, 705,
    790–791; training, 7, 141, 145,
    150, 176, 266, 347, 495, 538, 539;
    reputation, 46, 175, 363; as
    commander, 46, 101, 113, 137,
    173, 195, 250, 260, 265–266,
    272, 278, 332, 347, 362–363, 432,
    467, 528, 650, 651, 705, 706,
    751, 809–811; morale, 77,
    78–81, 260, 346, 451, 480,
    495–496; character, 83, 101,
    136, 137, 140, 260, 261, 298, 449,
    467, 814; publicity, 78–80, 178,
    179, 467–468, 479, 508, 519–520,
    521–524, 527; vanity, 101, 136,
    171–173, 207, 208, 213, 219,
    365, 583, 704, 705, 820; egoism,
    171, 213, 539, 704; messing
    arrangements, 96, 132, 533;
    human factor, 539, 581, 582,
    644, 705; leadership, 176, 254,
    284, 543–544, 750–751;
    concern for troops, 177, 259,

260, 362, 365, 415, 416,
450–451, 467, 468, 520, 747–748,
749, 815; firmness, 196; relations
with US Army, 259, 265, 278,
331, 657, 683; as Allied
Commander, 261–264, 266,
683; dress, 79, 98, 99, 171, 175,
275, 447, 449, 467, 470, 524, 626,
654, 691, 705; pets, 342–343, 366,
447–448, 680, 690, 691, 704, 760;
psychological pressures, 519,
689; entertaining visitors, 533,
657, 676, 677, 725; and smoking,
553; and Clifton James (his
double), 567–569; answer to
US critics, 683; Axis generals as
POWs, 7–10, 13, 18, 47, 818;
career, 819
Strategical and Tactical Theories:
war theories, 5, 123, 125, 126, 233,
267, 287, 288, 367ff, 416, 456,
490–495, 511–512, 538, 791;
exercise TIGER, 5; N. Africa,
vs Axis commanders, 285; US
Army, 331; Sicilian campaign,
358, 456; invasion of Italy,
358–372, 420, 421, 456; lessons
of, 367–369; 'teams', 369–372;
on Italian army, 393, 394;
Principles of War, 448,
490–495, 538–539; operational
theory (OVERLORD), 475–485,
486–496, 497–575 passim,
548–549, 550, 583, 584; lecture
at Staff College, 490–492;
lecture to HQ staff, 492–495
World War II, NorthWest Europe,
1939 – D-Day:
BEF, 6, 7, 44, 126, 142, 550
World War II, North Africa:
Advance to Tripoli:
Alamein, 3–10, 122, 125;
'meat-safe' incident, 131; HQ
8th Army, 12, 53; advance to
Fuka, 16–37; doubts on armour
efficiency, 27; strategical
theories and plans, 29–37, 52,
56–63, 67–68, 103, 123–127;
publicity, 44, 77–81; letters to
Alanbrooke, 44–47, 63, 64,
69–72, 90, 96, 102, 103–104, 126,
176; knighted, 49, 288;
promotion to General, 49;
'Personal Message from the
Army Commander', 50–51,
166–167, 180, 269–270, 385, 415;
farewell message, 469–470

Advance to Tobruk, 54–62:
diary, 56, 57, 75, 85, 90, 109,
111, 120, 125, 186, 189–190;
plans: capture of Tripoli, 63,
69–73, 95, 96, 105–120; letters to
Alexander, 64, 65; advance to
Agheila, 74, 75; portrait, 76,
77, 98, 99, 136, 172; morale,
77–82, 92; hats, 79, 98, 99, 171,
175, 470; battle of Agheila,
85–94, 173; dress, 98, 99, 175
Tripolitania:
FIRE-EATER operation, 106,
107–120; capture of Tripoli,
118–121; aftermath, 122–127;
Army Study Week, 127,
140–145, 164, 176; Victory
Parade, 132, 133, 137, 138
Tunisian campaign:
visit by Churchill, 131–133, 138,
175; caravan accommodation,
131, 270; letter to Simpson, 133,
171, 180; letter to Lady Maud
Montgomery, 133;
Montgomery's Flying Fortress,
137, 151, 219–224, 271, 278, 290,
415; warning to Alanbrooke,
140; letters to Alanbrooke,
143–145, 148, 149–151, 161,
162–163, 169–170, 176–177, 180,
192, 193, 211, 221; doubts on
1st Army, 143; strategical
theories, 149–151, 160–161, 193;
organization theories, 149–151,
422
Medenine, battle of, 152–170:
letters to Alexander, 155, 186,
194, 196, 200, 202, 210; opinion
of French troops, 162, 182;
opinion of US troops, 170,
176, 201, 202, 204; and padres,
173–174; and women, 174;
attitude to press, 178; Mareth
cf. Alamein, 189, 192; planning
of operation PUGILIST, 190,
191, 202; operation
PUGILIST, 154–170, 182–193;
and Churchill, 194
El Hamma:
Corps Commanders'
conference, 195; battle of, 187,
193, 195–207; Gafsa/Gabes
road, 202, 204; advance to
Maknassy, 203, 205
Wadi Akarit:
visit from Eisenhower, 208;
battle of, 208–218; visit from

Montgomery, Bernard Law – *cont.*
  Giraud, 211; Flying Fortress
    incident, 219–223; visit to
    Eisenhower, 223, 247
  Tunis:
    final offensive, 225–238, 525;
    letters to Alexander, 228–230,
    235; diary, 230–231; letters to
    Alanbrooke, 232–235; tactical
    theories, 232–233; regrouping
    of armies, 235, 263; visit of
    Alexander, 235, 236, 238;
    conference at Enfidaville, 236;
    and Messe, 270; and von
    Thoma, 7–10, 13, 18, 47; and
    Freyberg, 18, 19, 24; and
    Lumsden, 20–23, 25–26, 32,
    34, 39, 42, 45, 59–60, 213–214;
    and Gatehouse, 23–24, 41;
    and Auchinleck, 49, 131; and
    Alexander, 66, 209, 212,
    230–231; and Alanbrooke, 71;
    and Roberts, 102–103; and de
    Guingard, 80, 84, 101, 102; and
    Wimberley, 114–116; and
    Rommel, 126; and Anderson,
    133, 176, 213, 230; and
    Eisenhower, 170, 176, 208, 211,
    212; and chief padre, 173, 174;
    and Paget, 176; and Crerar,
    176; and Charlton, 178–179;
    and Leese, 213
  World War II, Sicily and Italy:
    Operation HUSKY, q.v. (Sicily):
      command British Task Force,
      225, 227–228, 242, 250–251,
      457–458; planning, 137, 224,
      229–230, 246, 247–248, 249–268,
      280, 290–291; letters to
      Alanbrooke, 225, 242, 244,
      245–250, 253, 263–264, 279,
      335–338, 415; Montgomery/
      Alexander plans, 145, 226, 227,
      238, 241, 242, 246, 251–252,
      264–265, 320–321, 338; letters/
      signals to Alexander, 226,
      241–243, 250–251, 257, 262, 295,
      298, 301, 302, 307, 312, 317, 354,
      357, 376, 377, 397, 400–403, 409,
      421, 422, 458; as Alexander
      the Great, 227, 468; Eastern
      Task Force, 242, 243; operational
      plans, 247, 285, 286;
      conference: Alexander and
      Eisenhower, 247, 250;
      objections by Cunningham
      and Tedder, 251–252, 254–257,

      280, 281, 282–283, 293; and
      Alexander, 252–253, 262–265,
      307, 318, 320, 457–462; letters to
      Simpson, 253; letters to
      Reynolds, 253, 271, 276, 277,
      300, 325, 342–343, 393;
      conference at Allied Force
      HQ, 256, 265, 296; Comd US
      Corps, 259, 262–263, 269; plan
      accepted, 262, 269, 280; comd
      structure, 262, 265–266;
      training for, 283, 286; tactical
      theories and operations,
      287–288, 299, 307, 318, 319, 340,
      413, 422; diary, 288, 290, 293,
      295, 299, 300, 305, 310, 315, 318,
      319, 331, 340, 354, 357, 367,
      376–379, 400, 401–402, 408, 413,
      422–423, 433, 434, 452; assault,
      292–303, 304–313, 314–321,
      322–349; suggestions to
      Alexander, 296, 307, 458;
      Patton rivalry, 296, 308,
      309–310, 316–317, 319, 320, 353,
      407, 597; and Browning, 306; cf.
      Patton, 331–333, 366; assault on
      Adrano, 340; capture of Axis
      plans, 340; Axis withdrawal at
      Messina, 340–341; pet birds,
      342–343, 366, 447, 448; and
      Leese, 360; Taormina,
      366–367
    Operations BUTTRESS and
    BAYTOWN, q.v. (Italy):
      Phase 1: invasion plans, 322, 323,
      338–339, 355–357, 372, 376, 381,
      383, 392, 410, 413; visit to
      Patton, 324, 353; visit by
      Mountbatten, 326; visit by
      McNaughton, 327, 346; and
      Mark Clark, 339; Comd 15th
      Army Gp, 346; Eisenhower's
      Algiers conference, 377; lunch
      at Tac HQ, 381; US Legion of
      Merit, 382; Personal Message
      . . . 385; letter to Alanbrooke,
      385–387, 414, 417–418, 423; 8th
      Army landing in Calabria,
      388, 413; and Italian armistice,
      392, 394, 398; blame, 392, 410;
      and Eisenhower, 396, 410, 429;
      reaction to Salerno plan, 396,
      413; and operation
      AVALANCHE (q.v.), 396, 405,
      407, 413; Rommel comd Axis
      force, 402; future plans for 8th
      Army, 408, 413; and lack of

plan, 410, 421; personal transport, 415; letter to Nye, 417; letter from Alanbrooke, 419; C-in-C to Mountbatten, 419
Phase 2: 420–431
Allied plans, 420–421, 424; admin failure, 420–422; Termoli line, 422–424; visit from Alexander, 423; advance to Rome plan, 424, 437; tactical plans, 425–429, 437, 441; and Alexander, 424, 426–431, 437, 457–460, 597; and Anzio landing, 429–430
Phase 3: 432–441
letters to Simpson, 432, 441–443, 445; letters to Alanbrooke, 435–444n; and 5th US Army, 437; plans for advance to Sangro, 438; advance to Sangro River, 432–440; battle for Sangro River, 439–441, 447, 453; casualties, 453; and 5 Corps, 432, 433, 438, 439, 442; letter to Nye, 439; letter to Mountbatten, 441; and 1st Army, 442; and Churchill, 443–445; visit from Eisenhower and Bedell Smith, 452; reflections on Sicilian and Italian campaigns, 457–460; and Alexander, 231, 289, 371–372, 436, 455–463; and Alanbrooke, 278–279, 327; and de Guingand, 271–272; and Rommel, 397; and Anderson, 345, 442; and Eisenhower, 211–212, 279, 393; and Marshall, 392–393; and Clark, 428, 435–436, 437, 458; and Allfrey, 433, 438

World War II, North West Europe: preparations for D-Day: comd, 266, 452, 454; Eisenhower as Supreme Commander, 455; Alexander as C-in-C, 343, 344, 368–369, 455, 457–460, 545, 596–597; letters to Mountbatten re Normandy invasion, 344–346, 367, 368–369, 441, 455–457, 516; advice to Mountbatten, 419–420; letters to Leese, 442, 499, 504–505, 517; and OVERLORD operation, 445, 455–457, 464, 471, 475, 687, 796, 797;

Eisenhower/Alexander combination, 456, 457, 462, 531; diary, 496, 507–508, 529, 530, 545, 548, 556, 599; letters to Simpson re OVERLORD appts, 453; visit to Simpson, 513; Comd 21st Army Gp, 454, 464, 488, 489, 493, 494–495, 500, 516–527, 528–539, 540–578, 590–604 passim, 607–631; comd ground battle, 503; dismissals, 517; and Eisenhower, 446, 464, 499, 500, 502–504, 509, 510, 512–513, 514, 527, 530, 545, 547, 558, 591, 596; and Churchill, 477, 478–479, 507–509, 511, 514, 544, 545; letters/signals to Alanbrooke, 464–466; OVERLORD plans, 477–485, 486–496, 497–515, 516–527, 687; COSSAC's plan demolished, 500, 501, 503; planning conference, 481–482, 511–512, 529; visits to troops, 497, 498, 507, 508, 512, 528, 535–536, 540, 562; anti-ANVIL operation, 506, 507, 510–511, 512, 573–574, 516, 536, 537, 546–547, 660–661; ANVIL conference, 529; and Alanbrooke, 509, 513, 545, 548, 595; transfer of ships for ANVIL, 512–513, 514, 530; de Guingand as COS, 518–519, 545, 558; and King George VI, 529, 579, 591; portrait, 534, 535; Mansion House speech, 541; 'Public Hallowing of the Armed Services of the Crown' in Westminster Abbey, 541, 542; and Grigg, 524, 542, 545, 547; and Portal, 545, 547, 596; and Cunningham, 545, 547, 596; and Ramsay, 482, 496, 545; and Tedder, 528, 545; and Leigh-Mallory, 496, 545; and Wilson, 545, 596; exercise THUNDERCLAP, 547–553; and Patton, 548, 590
OVERLORD operation: strategy, 548–555, 558, 559, 628, 629, 633, 687; final plans, 570–578, 595; and Rommel, 549–550, 551, 555, 572, 575, 576, 590; reinforcements, 560–562; and Smuts, 579; and Churchill, 579–582, 598; and

Montgomery, Bernard Law – *cont.*
  Dempsey, 249, 334, 335, 588;
  and Bradley, 528, 544, 588–589;
  and Mountbatten, 597; D-Day
  decision, 591–603; Personal
  Message to All Troops, 602,
  603; and Auchinleck, 599; and
  Alexander, 545, 546; and
  Rommel, 508, 509; and
  Eisenhower, 502–503, 545;
  and Paget, 599; and Crerar,
  588; and Charlton, 366; and
  Leese, 597; and Marshall, 595;
  and Allfrey, 531–532; and Trade
  Unions, 521–524, 536, 540,
  562–563; and Liddell Hart, 526;
  and Augustus John, 534, 535;
  and G. B. Shaw, 535; and Dill,
  595

World War II, North West
Europe:
Battle of Normandy:
  diary, 607; letters to Simpson,
  619–622, 653, 663, 667, 668, 674,
  692, 757, 758; air operations,
  608–610, 614–616, 619, 623, 624,
  627, 631, 634–638, 641–657, 717,
  741, 758, 761, 765, 770, 817;
  Caen, 614–615 (*see also* Caen):
  Bayeux, 613–615; landing in
  Normandy, 618; Normandy
  operations, 618–631, 632–640,
  641–657, 658–667, 668–673,
  674–688, 689–698, 699–716,
  717–726, 727, 740, 754–755, 756,
  774–775, 776–791; pivotal plan,
  633, 634, 638, 644–645, 649–651,
  652–653, 671; letters to de
  Guingand, 624, 625, 641, 647;
  and/vs Eisenhower, 625, 627,
  633, 644, 657, 659, 660, 677, 688,
  690, 691, 693, 706, 707–708, 713,
  717–718, 737, 742, 743, 750–753,
  754–755, 777, 794, 796, 797,
  799–802, 804, 806–807, 815;
  meeting with Bradley and
  Dempsey, 626, 771, 774, 777,
  778; visit from Alanbrooke,
  631–635; and/vs Leigh-Mallory,
  631, 634–636, 654, 655–656,
  678–679, 717; and Churchill,
  631–633, 635, 729, 735–736,
  744–745, 763; visit from Smuts,
  631–633, 635; battle strategy,
  611–617, 618–631, 632–640,
  641–657, 661–662, 663–664,
  666–667, 670, 671, 674–688, 691,
  709, 720, 727–740, 741–755,
  756–775, 784–785, 792–794,
  796–798; and Alanbrooke,
  644–645, 655, 675, 678–679, 690,
  693, 708, 709, 714, 742, 743, 744,
  747, 756, 760, 763–766, 776, 777,
  783–785, 803, 805, 817,
  819–820; and Bradley, 614, 615,
  623, 624, 625–626, 627, 632,
  637, 641, 646, 647, 648, 649,
  656–657, 658, 683–688, 694,
  708, 709, 731, 732, 771–772,
  785–786, 793, 796, 797, 800, 815;
  visit from Tedder, 659, 660;
  reinforcements, 660, 787, 790;
  conference at Tac HQ, 670–673,
  682–684, 686–688, 708–709, 792,
  798–800; letters to Leese,
  675–676, 789–790; and Patton,
  675, 686, 705, 708, 772–773, 781,
  798; break-out, 674–688,
  706–709, 710–726; plan,
  684–688; and Coningham,
  661, 678–680; and Tedder, 657,
  658, 679, 717, 723–724, 727, 746;
  rumours on Montgomery's
  ability, 689, 716, 723, 724,
  766–767; dismissal plot,
  717–726, 727, 736–737; ANVIL
  operation revival, 689–702
  passim; GOODWOOD
  operation, 710–722, 724, 728,
  730, 731, 737, 746, 747, 750;
  Land Forces C-in-C, 692;
  Comd, 693, 694n; report from
  Crocker, 700–701; visit from
  Adam (Adjt-Gen), 718;
  cancellation of visitors' ban,
  725; invitation to Churchill and
  Eisenhower, 725, 729, 752;
  anticipation of enemy's action,
  727, 743; directive to
  commanders, 731, 732, 737, 743,
  744, 754, 760, 761, 787–788;
  Falaise Gap, 756–775, 789; future
  plans, 784–786, 788, 789, 800,
  816; letter to Kennedy, 792;
  Comd Army Group of the
  North, 796, 801; and German
  generals, 798; published
  justification, 804; liberation of
  Paris, 808–809; promotion to
  Field Marshal, 818, 819; and von
  Thoma, 818; and Rommel, 650,
  798; and Crerar, 675; and de
  Gaulle, 653, 653n; and Wilmot,
  751

Author of:
  Memoirs, 15, 115, 121, 124, 559n,
    580n, 581n, 584n, 613, 615n,
    618n, 732n
  'Conduct of Battle', 45, 123
  'Main Lessons of the Battle'
    (Alamein), 48–49
  'Eighth Army Personal Message
    from the Army Commander',
    50–51, 166–167, 415
  'Notes for the Conduct of Battle
    for Senior Officers', 69, 415
  'Some Reflections on the
    Campaign in Sicily – July/
    August 1943', 367
  'Reflections on the Campaign in
    Italy, 1943', 457, 458–460
  'Plan to Defeat Invasion', 550
  'Some Army Problems', 554
  Ten Chapters, 582
  'Notes on High Command in
    War', 583
  'Notes on Second Army
    Operations', 722n
  'Notes on Future Operations',
    793
  'Notes on the Campaign in North
    Western Europe, Part III',
    819n
Montgomery, Mrs. Betty (*née* Hobart;
  wife of Bernard), 77, 101, 581,
  705
Montgomery, David (son of Bernard;
  guardian – Reynolds): letters to,
  44, 49, 96, 98, 100, 134, 135, 136,
  271, 602; portrait to, 133; and
  Maud Montgomery, 134; and
  Jocelyn Carver, 134–136, 172,
  186, 187
Montgomery, Harold R., 171
Montgomery, Bishop Henry
  Hutchinson (1847–1932; father of
  Bernard), 47
Montgomery, Lady Maud (*née* Farrar;
  wife of Bishop Henry; mother of
  Bernard): letter from Bernard,
  133; and Bernard, 134, 136, 271,
  526
Montgomery, Una (1889–1963), 526
Montgomery (Alan Moorehead), 581,
  582
'Montgomery and His Staff' (Sir
  Charles Richardson; film script),
  97, 98
Montgomery as Military Commander
  (Ronald Lewin), 249n
Montgomery Legend, The (R. W.

Thompson), 41n, 222n
'Montgomery Cup', 705
Moorehead, Alan: *The Desert War*,
  120n; *Montgomery*, 581, 582
Morale: Allied, 77–82, 92–93, 96, 133,
  146, 166, 170, 468; Axis, 78, 91
Moran, Lord, 131n, 132; author of
  *Churchill: The Struggle for
  Survival*, 131n, 480
Morgan, Lt-General F. ('Monkey'),
  371; COS 21st Army Group, 517,
  518
Morgan, General Sir Frederick E.:
  COSSAC, 267, 345, 445, 465,
  475, 487, 502, 512, 517, 519;
  dismissed, 516; OVERLORD
  plan, 477–485, 487ff, 499–503;
  revised, 505; demolished by
  Montgomery, 500, 502, 503;
  ANVIL conference, 529;
  anti-Montgomery, 718, 732, 767;
  author of *Overture to Overlord*,
  476n
Morison, S. E., *Sicily-Salerno-Anzio*,
  281n, 320, 361n
Moro River, 440, 447
Morocco: TORCH landings, 5
Morshead, Lt-General Sir L. J., Comd
  9th Australian Division, 26
Mortain, 759, 762; Axis attack on, 761,
  765, 767, 768, 782
Motorized infantry: Allied, 141, 168;
  Axis, 57, 58–59, 169–170
Mountbatten, Earl: Chief of Staff
  meeting, 70; raid at Dieppe, 70;
  landing on Sicily, 293, 326; and
  Montgomery, 326, 343, 344, 790;
  communications from
  Montgomery, 343–345, 348, 367,
  441–442, 455–457; Supreme
  Comd, SE Asia, 387, 597, 790;
  and Alanbrooke, 419
Msus, 61, 68
'Mulberry' harbour, 501, 503, 539,
  667–669, 674
Munday, William, 119
Murphy, Colonel, 102
Murray, Brigadier G., Comd 152nd
  Brigade, 116
Mussolini, Benito, 10, 43, 52, 58, 70,
  103, 116, 119, 122; dismissed, 323,
  337, 356, 393
Mutiny at Salerno, 414, 423, 424, 543,
  597

NLO, 14
Nancy, 792, 816

Naples, attack on, 337, 375, 389, 394, 403, 405, 408–409, 411, 412, 458; fall of, 424; Axis plans for recapture, 427
Naval attacks, Tripoli, 95
Neiscemi, 298
Nelson, Admiral Lord: and Montgomery, 175; and Rommel, 175
NEPTUNE operation (naval phase of OVERLORD), 550, 566, 575, 576
New York Times, 210
New Zealand Army, 18, 20, 27
Divisions:
2nd New Zealand Division, 23–25, 26–27; comd Freyberg, 26, 30, 32; advance to Mersa Matruh, 40, 42, 43, 57; Halfaya, 55; Bardia, 57, 58; attack on Agheila, 85–90, 103, 304; at Buerat, 111, 117; aftermath of Tripoli, 121, 159, 160; visit by Churchill, 132; PUGILIST operation, 184, 193; advance to Hamma, 195, 197, 205, 207; Wadi Akarit, 215; return to Egypt, 230; attack on Enfidaville, 231; occupation of Pescara-Rome line, 433, 434, 435, 439; attack from Sangro bridgehead, 439, 440; to NW Europe, 466
Brigades:
5th Infantry Brigade, 32, 43, 88
6th Infantry Brigade, 88
News Chronicle, 118, 119
News media reports: Alamein, 3–10 *passim*; Tunis, 187, 210; and Montgomery, 273, 468, 721, 744; and Eisenhower, 510, 696, 727; GOODWOOD operation, 721, 813; Normandy battle, 744, 751, 752
Nichols, Major-General J. S.: Comd 50th Div, 26, 190, 191; dismissal, 212
Nicholson, Cam, 214
Nicolson, Harold, 7n, 43n, 101, 214, 343, 479, 544; author of *Diaries and Letters*, 7n, 43n, 479
Nicolson, Nigel, 460–462
Night movement, 31, 53
Nine Rivers from Jordan (Denis Johnston), 470
Nofilia, 90, 93
Nogent le Rotrou, 778
Normandy: invasion plans, 475–604

passim; revised, 518–527; operations, 553; French opinion, 622–623; Churchill's queries, 580, 581; liberation, 662, 663
Normandy, battle of, 7, 73, 229, 304, 539; enemy defence, 519, 520, 550, 551, 572; enemy counter-attacks, 559, 575, 576, 616–617, 624, 628–629; preparations, 574–604; D-Day, 607–617; air superiority, 615, 616; advance through, 618–630, 632–640, 641–657, 658–667, 668–673, 674–688, 689–698, 699–716, 717–726, 727–740, 741–755; Montgomery's strategy, 663, 664, 666, 667, 670, 671, 684–688, 691, 709, 731–740, 741–755, 756–791; break-out, 674–688, 754, 755; prisoners of war, 818; casualties, Allied, 676, 731, 818; casualties, Axis, 681, 819; forces strength, 707
Norrie, Lt-General Willoughby, 518
North African campaign: battle of Alamein, 3–10; POWs, 3; aftermath of Alamein, 11–15, 103; advance to Fuka, 16–37; battle of Egypt, 50; POWs, 50; logistics, 57, 64, 69; advance to Agheila, 52–62; plans for advance on Tripoli, 63–73, 75; battle of Agheila, 85–94; command problems, 96; battle of Medenine, 152–171; 8th Army advance, 202; battle of Mareth, 180–193; battle of Hamma, 194–207; battle for Tunis, 202–238; defeat of Axis forces, 269; and Marshall, 392
North West Africa: landings, 10, 43, 64
North-west Africa: Seizing the Initiative (George F. Howe), 216n
North West Europe: invasion theories, 70, 72, 146, 288, 343, 346, 367–369; Eisenhower as Supreme Commander, 375; after Normandy: Montgomery's theories, 425–426, 442, 784, 786, 788, 789, 800, 804; Eisenhower's theories, 786, 787, 792–794, 802, 803; Patton's theories, 799, 803, 804; Bradley's theories, 797–799, 803, 804
Norway, 7, 537, 541
'Notes on the Conduct of Battle for

Senior Officers' (B. L. Montgomery), 69

'Notes on Future Operations' (B. L. Montgomery), 583

'Notes on High Command in War' (B. L. Montgomery), 583

'Notes on Second Army Operations' (B. L. Montgomery), 722n

'Notes on the Campaign in North Western Europe' (B. L. Montgomery), Part III, Enemy losses, 819n

Noto, advance to, 293, 302

Noyers, 743, 756

Nuffield factories, visit by Montgomery, 540

Nye, Lt-General Sir Archibald, VCIGS, 273, 416, 439, 449, 785, 796, 802, 805

O'Connor, General Sir Richard, 10, 57, 92, 118, 137, 413–414, 465

Odgers, Major Paul, 564–566, 618, 620, 747–750, 812

Odon River, 642, 680, 699

Olendon, 778

Omaha Beach, 5 US Corps, 611, 612, 614, 622, 626, 647, 655

One Way Ticket, A (Oscar Koch), 280, 309

Operation 'Husky' (S. W. C. Pack), 321n

Operation Victory (F. W. de Guingand), 452n, 582n

Oran landings, 10

Orléans, 778, 783, 785

Orne River, advance to, 615, 624, 641, 680, 706, 707, 710, 719, 721, 731, 732, 738, 757; Axis defence, 629, 680

Orsogna, 440, 453

Ortona, 440, 453

Oswald, Major General M. St J., 11–13, 19, 63; Montgomery and Lumsden, 21, 22, 108; Tac HQ, 97, 108, 111, 113, 179; Army Study Week, 141; attack on Mareth, 156, 191; attack on Hamma, 195, 196, 207; Flying Fortress incident, 219–224; surrender of Messe, 270

Other Side of the Hill, The (Sir Basil H. Liddell Hart), 181n

Ouistreham, 603, 614

Overture to Overlord (F. E. Morgan), 476n

OVERLORD operation (see also NEPTUNE operation): lessons of HUSKY, 227; 50th and 51st Divs earmarked, 386; Montgomery's plans, 442, 457, 499ff, 544, 547–548, 549, 550, 559; his comd, 445, 446, 453, 541; Alexander as C-in-C, 343, 344, 368–370, 426–429, 457, 459–460, 462; comd by Montgomery, 463, 464, 471, 475; plans, 475–485, 499–575; planning conference, 481, 482, 511, 512, 529; revised plans, 518–527, 529, 530, 548–563 passim; and Eisenhower, 451, 475, 476, 479, 509–510, 529–530; exercise THUNDERCLAP, 547, 548, 549–552; enemy reactions, 550, 552n; and Churchill, 555–556, 559, 561; reinforcements, 561, 562; estimated casualties, 562; final presentation of plans, 575–578; D-Day decision, 593–603; air programme, 610

PLUTO (Pipe Line Under The Ocean), 490n

Pachino airfield, 243, 293

Pachino peninsula ('Bark'), British landing, 250, 257, 292, 293

Pack, S. W. C., Cunningham the Commander, 342n; Operation 'Husky', 321n

Paget, General Sir Bernard, C-in-C Home Forces, 150, 172, 176, 246, 370, 453, 465, 476, 484n, 485, 486–488, 517

Palermo, 242; US landings, 257; Patton's theories, 309; Patton's attack on, 310, 314–321, 330, 520; capture of, 319

Pantelleria, capture of, 282; POWs, 521

Panther tanks, 690–691

Parachute troops, use of, 297, 299, 300, 303, 304, 306, 353–354; behind enemy lines, 365

Paris, 488, 521, 585, 620; advance to, 686, 688, 712, 727, 728, 738, 743, 762; Patton's advance to, 756–759, 761, 762; capture, 789, 790, 792; liberation, 805, 805n, 808, 815–816

Pas de Calais, 476, 488, 509, 592, 662, 692, 706, 713, 784, 798; deception plans, 506, 757n; advance to, 787; airborne attack, 817; clearance of, 789, 800, 801, 806, 816, 817

Paterno, 311, 312, 316, 317, 341

Patton, General George S., 123, 137;

Patton, General George S. – *cont.*
   hospital incident, 136, 350–353,
      362, 366, 558; Montgomery's
      Study Week, 140, 142, 143, 145;
      Comd 2 US Corps, 175–223
      passim; character, 332, 333;
      discipline, 175; and Coningham,
      197; and Montgomery, 201, 296,
      308, 319–320, 328, 329, 331–333,
      353, 354, 407, 548, 590, 798;
      advance to Maknassy, 204–209;
      and Alexander, 210, 264; Wadi
      Akarit, 216; failure to break out,
      222; relieved of command, 223;
      and Bradley, 248, 332, 361, 589, 590
   HUSKY operation:
      landings, 254, 255; 7th US Army
      (Western Task Force), 254–257,
      280, 286, 295, 308–313, 314–321;
      and Tedder, 265, 280; and
      Marshall, 266, 410; and
      Eisenhower, 274, 350, 362, 504;
      and Leese, 308; tactical theories,
      309, 557, 558n
   Palermo, advance to, 308–313,
      314–321, 329, 798; and Alexander,
      312, 314, 316–317, 318, 320;
      Provisional Corps, 314; Messina,
      advance to, 315–320, 328, 330,
      349, 361, 362; visit by
      Montgomery, 324, 328; future
      plans, 328; amphibious
      operations, 350, 351, 355; entry
      into Messina, 361–362; lunch with
      Montgomery, *etc.*, 381
   Comd European invasion army,
      410, 446, 548
   Comd 3rd US Army, NW Europe,
      415, 519, 551, 556–557, 812;
      exercise THUNDERCLAP, 548,
      552; tactical theories, 557, 558; and
      Churchill, 556–557; Knutsford
      incident, 557; final conference,
      588–589; and Dempsey, 588; and
      Crerar, 588; Montgomery's plan,
      708–709, 803, 804; and
      Montgomery, 675, 686, 705–709,
      794, 798, 803, 808; Montgomery's
      directive, 730–732n, 743, 744;
      Normandy battles, 753–754;
      break-out, 756–775, 778, 780,
      786–787, 799; Falaise Gap, 759,
      770, 773, 780; and Bradley, 770,
      774, 781, 786, 799, 803; Paris, 778,
      780; and Leclerc, 781; tactical
      plans, 803, 807–808; Plans A and
      B, 803

Patton Papers, The, see Martin
   Blumenson
Patton's Ordeal and Triumph (Ladislas
   Farago), 204n, 205, 215, 803
Patton's Provisional Corps, 314
Paulus, Field Marshal Friedrich von,
   269, 771
Périers, 714
Pescara, 425, 435, 437, 439, 440, 453
Petralia, 307, 312, 317
Petrol supplies, 14, 32, 34, 36, 39, 44,
   53, 56, 57, 58–61, 72, 74, 75, 85, 86,
   87–91, 95, 104, 106, 107, 114, 146,
   148, 160, 161, 202, 203, 228, 391,
   597, 768, 774
Pettitt, Private J. T., 543
'Phantom', service, 682, 773
Pichon, attack on, 164
Pienaar, Major-General, Comd S.
   Africa Div, 26
'Plan To Defeat Invasion' (B. L.
   Montgomery), 550
Playfair, I. S. O. and Molony, C. J. C.,
   *The Mediterranean and the Middle
   East*, Vol IV, 142n
'Plum' gap, 195, 205 (*see also* Hamma
   – the Plum: Tebaga)
Plumer, Field Marshal Viscount, 141
Po Valley, 426, 428, 442
Pogue, Dr F. C., 476n, 482n, 484n,
   485n, 499n, 500n, 501, 512n, 525n,
   581, 611n, 683, 713n, 720n, 742n,
   810
Poland, 7
Polish Army, 766, 767n, 771, 783; 1st
   Armoured Division, 546
Ponza, Isle of, Mussolini's exile, 323
Popoli-Avezzano axis, 434, 435
Port-en-Bessin, 615, 620, 625
Portal, Air Chief Marshal Sir Charles:
   Chief of Air Staff, 254, 466, 507;
   and Montgomery, 545, 547;
   exercise THUNDERCLAP, 548,
   553; and Tedder, 718, 723–724
Poston, Major John, ADC to
   Montgomery, 79, 99, 100, 277, 334
Potenza-Auletta, 408
Pownall, Lt-General Sir Henry, 369,
   419
Prejudice and Judgement (Sir James
   Grigg), 548n
Press, *see* News media reports
Primosole Bridge, 298; parachute
   drop, 303, 304, 354; cf Arnhem,
   304; battle of, 305–312 *passim*, 315
'Principles of War', Montgomery's,
   448, 490–495, 538–539

Prisoners of War: Alamein, 3; Mersa
    Matruh, 39, 41, 44; N. African
    campaign, 34, 50, 218, 269;
    Kasserine, 145, 159; Medenine,
    170; Mareth, 187, 190, 193;
    Hamma, 206; Wadi Akarit, 215;
    Tunis, 238; Stalingrad, 269;
    Pantelleria, 521; Pachino, 293;
    Sicily, 362; Reggio, 385; Sangro
    River, 440; Normandy, 620, 783,
    789, 790, 791, 817–818; Stalingrad,
    818
Public Relations Officers, 79
Pudney, John (poet), 101
PUGILIST operation (attack on
    Mareth line): attack on Mareth,
    154, 161, 180, 183–193; plan, 183

Quasaba, landing ground, 32, 40
Quebec, (Allied) Conference (1943),
    410, 418–419
Quesada, Lt-General Pete, 586, 696,
    745

RAF, see Royal Air Force
RAF Staff College, 588
Radar, 292, 620; bombing targets, 609
Ragusa, 301
Rahman track, 118
Ramsay, Admiral Sir Bertram:
    HUSKY operation, 241, 248,
    251–252, 255, 262; and
    Montgomery, 283, 482, 496, 545;
    OVERLORD operation, 482, 488,
    500; final plans, 571; ANVIL
    conference, 529; exercise
    THUNDERCLAP, 547–553;
    D-Day decision, 599, 601; and
    ANVIL, 689
Ramsden, Lt-General W. H., 137
Randazzo, 320, 354, 358
'Rankin' operation, 540
Rapier (Montgomery's train), 497,
    499, 508, 540n, 566, 567
Rauray, 699
Recce Wing (Air Force), 588
Rees, Dai (golfer), driver to
    Broadhurst, 367
'Reflections on the Campaign in Italy
    1943' (B. L. Montgomery),
    457–460
Reggio, 322, 348, 384–386, 409, 798
Rennes, capture of, 551, 577, 687, 707,
    732, 758
Rennie, Major-General T. G., Comd
    51st Division, 790
Renton, Major-General 'Callum', 137

Resach, Corporal William, 119
Reynolds, Tom and Phyllis: letters to
    and from Montgomery, 44, 49,
    76, 96, 98, 100, 134–136, 166, 169,
    172, 175, 186–187, 253, 271,
    276–277, 300, 325, 342–343,
    366–367, 393, 402, 447, 454, 528,
    540n, 544, 602, 636, 654, 668, 680,
    703–704, 735, 760, 771, 814, 819
Reynolds, Major Thomas (son of Tom
    and Phyllis): Salerno, 414; in UK,
    583
Rheims, 817
Rhine River, 817
Rhino ferries, 615
Rhodes, 426
Richards, Morley, 3
Richards, Major-General, RAC, 21st
    Army Gp, 518, 690
Richardson, Major-General A. A.,
    CGS, 1st Army, 370
Richardson, General Sir Charles:
    GRAPESHOT operation, 16; on
    Montgomery at Buerat, 113; on
    Leclerc, 182, 183; on Montgomery
    at Mareth, 194, 195; Desert Air
    Force, 199n, 200
    HUSKY operation: planning, 253,
    256, 262
    AVALANCHE operation, 383n,
    387, 403n; Anzio landings, 430n
    OVERLORD operation: Head of
    Plans, 21st Army Gp, 518, 549, 607,
    610, 627, 649; Normandy battle,
    660–667; on Montgomery as
    commander, 809, 810; American
    method of command, 809, 810
    Author of 'Montgomery and His
    Staff' (film script), 97–98
Ridgway, Major-General Matthew B.,
    Comd 82nd US Airborne Division:
    Sicily, 281; Rome, 375, 390;
    Salerno, 395, 399, 405
Ritchie, General Sir Neil, 79, 137;
    Comd 12 Corps, Falaise Gap,
    768n
Roberts, Major-General G. P. B.
    ('Pip'): Comd 22nd Armoured
    Brigade, 19–20, 60; tactical
    theories, 52, 53; to UK, 102–103;
    Comd 7th Armoured Division,
    112; transfer to 1st Army, 212;
    Comd 11th Armoured Division
    on EPSOM operation, 673, 679,
    680; Caumont, 758; see also
    GOODWOOD operation
Robertson, General Sir Brian, 60, 72;

Robertson, General Sir Brian – *cont.*
 GOC, Tripoli, 178–179; admin
 officer, 421
Robolla, 297
Rolls Royce, 662
Rome: entry by Montgomery, 146,
 434; entry by Clark, 146; seizure
 of, 388–392, 394, 403, 427, 616;
 advance to, 412, 421, 424, 428, 429,
 430, 432, 441, 513, 553; defence
 of, 425, 426; Alexander on, 427,
 437; objective, 457, 596; battle
 lost, 560
Rome Radio, 4
Rommel, Field Marshal Erwin:
 Panzer Army A:
 Alam Halfa, 117; Alamein, 5–10, 13,
 47, 52, 74, 103, 117, 123;
 withdrawal after Alamein, 18–27,
 53; 'escape', 27, 90; Fuka, 30–32,
 36; and Hitler, 38, 63, 71, 73, 74,
 91–93, 154, 215, 629, 642, 661,
 662, 728; stand at Matruh, 38–43;
 withdrawal to Mersa Brega/
 Agheila line, 52–62; stand at
 Agheila, 58–59; strategical
 theories and plans, 63, 74, 756;
 withdrawal to Tripoli, 63–73, 75,
 95, 122, 152; withdrawal to
 Tunisia, 73, 107; publicity, 77,
 93; battle of Agheila, 85–94;
 evacuation of Agheila, 86, 91,
 93; casualties, 90; and Mussolini,
 10, 43, 52, 63, 91, 103, 116–117, 125;
 stand at Buerat, 105–120;
 dismissed as C-in-C
 German-Italian Panzer Army,
 117, 122, 136; over-estimated
 enemy, 117; withdrawal from
 Tripoli, 117, 119, 121, 124, 125;
 surrender of Tripoli, 121, 122; as
 commander, 137, 143; Kasserine
 battle, 144, 166; C-in-C Army
 Group, N. Africa, 152, 170;
 battle of Medenine (operation
 CAPRI), 152–170; final
 departure from N. Africa, 170,
 254; Comd German forces, Italy,
 403; Comd German forces,
 France, 508–509, 544, 550, 603;
 defence strategy, 550, 575, 576,
 617, 624, 628–629; counter-attacks,
 555, 575, 576, 617, 624, 628–629
 Normandy:
 D-Day, on leave, 611–612; battle
 tactics, 642ff, 650, 655, 661, 664,
 681, 727, 756; Allied advance to

 Paris, 712, 728; road injury (17 July
 1944), 728; and Montgomery, 126,
 397, 508, 550, 551, 555, 572, 575,
 576, 590, 650, 798
 Author of *The Rommel Papers*, 38n,
 39, 42, 44, 54, 58, 62, 69, 104–106,
 112, 116, 136, 137, 403, 629
Roosevelt, Franklin D., President of
 USA, 5, 10, 121, 139, 220; invasion
 of Sicily, 225; OVERLORD
 operation, 445–447; Tehran
 summit, 463, 506
Rouen, 713–714, 805
Royal Air Force:
 Battle of Britain, 541
 N. Africa, 7, 23, 24–25, 30, 37, 50,
 55–57, 67, 68, 95, 96, 124, 125,
 156, 209; supplies, 67–68;
 build-up, 75; visit by Churchill,
 132; co-operation at Hamma, 196,
 197, 201, 285; ground/air support,
 198–201, 207; taxi-cabrank
 system, 201, 587
 Sicily: securing of airfields, 255, 257;
 Tedder's non-cooperation, 280,
 281; protection of Task force, 285;
 Axis withdrawal from Sicily,
 340, 341
 Italy: 397, 429; Sangro River, 438
 Normandy: OVERLORD
 operation, 540, 551, 560, 577,
 586, 587, 588, 649; Army
 co-operation, 586–588, 596,
 608–610, 745; Bomber Command,
 608, 609, 659, 777;
 GOODWOOD operation: views
 on, 710, 712, 718–721; Falaise
 Gap, 777; operation from
 Belgium, 784, 793, 801, 806
 (*See also* Allied Air Forces)
Royal Navy, 107, 541; assault on
 Sicily, 292; Axis withdrawal from
 Sicily, 340; BAYTOWN
 operation, 377; NEPTUNE
 operation, 550, 566
Ruge, Admiral, 662
Ruhr Valley, 784, 789, 793, 801, 806,
 816
Rundstedt, Field Marshal Gerd von,
 551, 661, 727, 728, 798
Russell, Colonel Leo, Comd Tac HQ,
 565–566, 704–705, 811, 812
Russian Front, 598
Ruweisat Ridge, 131, 250, 284

SHAEF, 693, 698, 802, 803; ignorance
 of Montgomery's plans, 722, 731;

and Tedder, 731, 732;
Eisenhower's decision to
Montgomery, 803; and de
Guingand, 811, 812
Saar, advance to, 789, 793, 797, 804,
817
St Laurent, 603
St Lô, advance to, 551, 637, 638, 640,
646, 649, 658, 737, 743; the pivot,
638, 641, 672, 675, 678, 714, 728
St Malo, advance to, 687, 707, 732,
763; capture, 758
St Paul's School, 260; HQ 21st Army
Group, 480, 481, 490, 493–495,
511–512, 560; exercise
THUNDERCLAP, 547, 548–552,
554, 559; Final Presentation of
plans, 570–578, 579, 650, 652,
661, 671
St Stefano, 317
St Valéry, capture, 818
Ste Mère Eglise, 82nd Airborne
Division, 585
Salerno, landing at, 249, 250, 283, 375,
392, 395, 396, 399, 402, 403,
408–409, 412, 415, 458, 459, 477,
504, 509, 519, 520, 597, 797, 798;
mutiny, 414, 423–424, 543, 597
'Salute the Soldier' campaign, 540
Samwell, H. P., An Infantry Officer with
the 8th Army, 170n
San Fratello, 350
San Salvo, 432, 433
Sangro River, 427, 435, 440; Axis
retreat to, 433; battle of, 439–441;
casualties, 440
Sardinia, invasion of, 66, 71; defence
of, 70
Sassy, 778
Saunders, Hilary St George, 654
Sbeitla, 165
Scalea, 413
Schlieben, General von: surrender of
Cherbourg, 695
Schlieffen-type operation: Patton, 803
Schweppenburg, General Geyr von,
Comd Panzer Gp West, 619;
dismissed, 727
Sciacca, US Army landing at, 242
Scoglitti, proposed landing at, 249
Scorpion tanks, 90
'Scottish Soldier' (D. N. Wimberley),
168n
Searl, Gp Captain F. H. L., 200
Second Front, Europe, 70–73, 284,
498, 583, 598; planning, 267 (see
also OVERLORD operation);

Westminster Abbey service, 541
542; bombing policy, 609
Second World War, The (Sir Basil H.
Liddell Hart), 15n
Sedada, 108, 109
Sées, 770, 782
Seine River, advance to, 552, 577, 578,
664, 762, 778; Axis withdrawal
to, 671, 771, 777, 782, 783, 784,
792; crossing of, 784, 788–789,
803, 805
Sfax, 66, 151, 161, 180, 181, 183, 193,
216, 219, 221–222, 227, 234, 242
Shaw, George Bernard: and
Montgomery, 534, 535
Sherman tanks, 5, 16, 36, 53, 60, 61,
176, 189, 191, 434
SHINGLE operation, 463, 464, 477,
504, 509, 510, 519, 584 (see also
Anzio)
Sicily: Allied objective, 66, 69, 71, 165,
193, 241, 253; defence of, 70; Axis
troops, 290; invasion of, see
HUSKY operation; cf
Normandy, battle of, 304; terrain,
304; capture, 367
Sicily-Salerno-Anzio (S. E. Morison),
281n, 320, 361n
Sickness rate, 450
Sidi Azeiz landing ground, 42
Sidi Barrani, 26, 39, 41
Sidi Bou Zid, 164
Sidi Haneish, 22, 30, 31, 32, 36, 40
Sidi Ibeid, 18n
Siegfried Line, 801
Simeto Bridge, 305, 306, 311–312, 313
Simonds, Major-General Guy: Comd
1st Canadian Division, 326, 335,
347; Comd 2 Canadian Corps,
466; Falaise, 771
Simpson, General Sir Frank, DMO:
63, 67, 133, 158, 159–160, 161, 253,
387, 432, 434, 441–443, 445n, 453,
546, 619–622, 638, 652–653, 663,
667, 668, 674, 692, 757, 758; visit
by Montgomery, 513;
Eisenhower on ANVIL, 689, 692;
Montgomery's plan, 708, 709, 785;
GOODWOOD operation, 712;
Montgomery's directive, 731–732
Simpson, Lt-General W. H., Comd
9th US Army, 589
Sirte, 96
Siwa, 6, 36
Smith, General Walter Bedell: COS to
Eisenhower, 148, 211, 371, 530;
and Montgomery, 151, 219,

Smith, General Walter Bedell – *cont.*
222–223, 263, 326–328, 584, 742,
767, 799; operation HUSKY
planning, 254, 256–257, 263, 264,
266; Italian armistice, 388;
operation GIANT II, 389, 390, 391,
392; operation AVALANCHE,
398; and operation OVERLORD,
446, 465, 476, 499, 500, 742; to
Normandy, 742; revised plan, 505;
and ANVIL, 512n, 529, 530;
sacking of Montgomery, 724, 725,
742
Smuts, Field Marshal Jan, 66, 77, 476,
570, 579, 591
Smyth, Dr H. M., 318n, 382–393,
395n, 396n, 399, 437; *see also*
Garland, A. N.
Smyth, Brigadier Sir John: 'Bolo'
Whistler, 168n, 168; *In This Sign
We Conquer*, 174
Sniping, 620, 676
Soldier's Story, A (Omar N. Bradley),
528n, 553, 626
Sollum, 26, 38, 39, 41, 52, 60, 62
Solodovnik, Lt-Colonel, 218
'Some Army Problems' (B. L.
Montgomery), 554
'Some Reflections on the Campaign in
Sicily July/August 1943' (B. L.
Montgomery), 367, 369
Somme, 817
Sortino, 297
Sosnkowski, General, C-in-C Polish
forces, 546
Sousse, 180, 181, 183, 193, 223, 242
South African Army: SA Division,
comd Pienaar, 26, 34; SA
Armoured Car Regiment, 23, 26,
34
Southwick House, Tac HQ, 564–566,
588–589, 591, 592, 599–601, 604,
610, 614
Spaatz, Major-General Carl, Comd
NW Africa Air Force, 221; delivery
of Montgomery's plane, 223;
bombing, 282, 659; Air C-in-C,
operation OVERLORD, 446, 500;
OVERLORD operation, 540,
571, 594, 596, 599, 609;
Normandy, 652, 659, 719, 771
Spain, landings in, 65
Speidel, Lt-General H., COS to
Rommel, 681
Spitfire fighters, 196, 199–201, 336
Stacey, C. P., *The Victory Campaign*,
760, 771

Staff College, Camberley: Lumsden as
student, 20, 22; Tuker as student,
142; Dempsey as student, 146n;
Alexander as Montgomery's
student, 238, 437; lecture, 490,
492
Stagg, Gp-Captain J. M., 594, 599,
600–601; author of *Forecast for
Overlord*, 594n
Stalin, Joseph: re *Desert Victory*, 171;
Tehran summit, 445, 463, 506; re
Poland, 544; OVERLORD, 598,
633, 707; Stalingrad, 10, 171,
771, 783, 789, 818
Stars and Stripes, 469
Stauffenberg, Colonel C. von: attempt
on Hitler's life, 729
Steele, Major-General James, Dep
COS to Alexander, 212
Stevens, Ed: war correspondent, 120n
Stevens, W. G., *Bardia to Enfidaville*,
89n, 117n
Strafford, Wing Commander C. H.:
at ANVIL conference, 529
Strategical Air Force, Italy, 422
STRIKE operation, 237, 238, 263
Strong, Brigadier K. W. D., 375,
390–392, 524–525
Studio Encounters (Neville Lewis), 77n
Summersby, Kay, 648, 755, 785;
author of *Eisenhower was my Boss*,
755
SUPERCHARGE operation
(Alamein), 14–19, 197
SUPERCHARGE operation (Hamma),
197, 198, 206
Supreme Commander, The (Stephen E.
Ambrose), 71
Surles, General: US censor, 755
Swayne, Lt-General Sir John, CGS,
Home Forces, 370–371
Sword Beach, plan, 482
Sylvan, William: diary of, 807n
Syracuse: HUSKY operation, 243, 257,
285; assault on Sicily, 292, 293, 295

Tac Army, *see* British Army: Eighth
Army Tac HQ
Tactical Air Force: 1st, 201; 2nd, 765
Tactical Bomber Force, Italy, 422
Tactical theory, 792–794, 816
Tadjera Khir, 158, 167, 169
Takrouna, 232
Tank tactics, *see* Armour, use of
Tanks, special: DD, Ark, Flail,
Plough, Snake, 512
Taormina, 320, 328, 354, 358–360, 366

Taranto, 394–396, 401, 407–408, 413
Tarhuna, 108, 111–114
Tarhuna-Castel Benito road, 112
Tarhuna-Homs line, 105, 107, 109, 112, 115–116, 122, 126, 153, 181
Taylor, General Maxwell, 314, 390–392
Tebaga, Djebel, 195, 197, 205
Tebessa, 209
Tedder, Air Marshal Lord:
  bombing policy, 55, 521; advice to Montgomery, 58, 67, 265; and/ vs Montgomery, 246, 252, 254–256, 280, 293, 528, 545, 586
  HUSKY operation: planning, 251–252, 254–255, 281, 282; non-cooperation, 281–283, 293; airfields on Sicily, 243, 248; conference at Allied Force HQ, 256, 257; and Patton, 265; HUSKY operation assault, 292, 293; Montgomery's Flying Fortress, 325; communications with Alexander, 340, 341; Axis withdrawal from Sicily, 340–342, 361
  AVALANCHE operation, 398; Eisenhower's plan, Italian invasion, 356, 381, 395
  OVERLORD operation: Allied Comd, 446; Air C-in-C, 457; plans, 500; air operations, 540–541, 608–610; D-Day decision, 599–600; Normandy, battle of, 641, 643, 659, 745; and/vs Montgomery, 657, 658, 679, 717–718, 751; and Coningham, 661, 679; ANVIL operation, 660, 661; non-cooperation, 718; and Portal, 718, 723–724; tactical theories, 718; GOODWOOD operation, 719, 729, 731; dismissal of Montgomery, 717, 723, 724, 727, 736, 737, 746, 751; succeeds Leigh-Mallory, 723–724; Montgomery's directive, 732; dismissal as Deputy Supreme Commander, 737; author of *With Prejudice*, 252, 599, 649, 718
Tehran summit, 443, 445, 446, 455, 463, 506
Teller mines, 87
Temple, William, Archbishop of Canterbury, 541, 542
Templer, Field Marshal G. W. R., Comd 56th Division, 417
Ten Chapters (B. L. Montgomery), 582n

Termoli line, 421
Thoma, General Ritter von: capture at Alamein, 7–9, 13, 18; re Rommel, 47; re organization, 181
Thomas, Major-General G. I., Comd 43rd (Wessex) Division, 668
Thompson, C. V. R., 4
Thompson, R. W., *The Montgomery Legend*, 41n, 222
Three Years with Eisenhower (H. C. Butler), 503n
THUNDERCLAP exercise, 547, 548–553, 559n
Thury Harcourt, 641, 645, 663, 707, 710
TIGER exercise, 5
Tiger tanks, 637, 690–691
Tilly, advance to, 621
Tilly-sur-Seulles, attack on, 681
Times, The: Alamein, 3, 7; Tripoli, 119; Montgomery's speech, 540
Tmimi, 56
Tobruk, 14, 26, 39, 43, 54, 59, 62, 121, 125n; British occupation of, 54–56, 58, 61; RAF supplies, 68; railhead, 75, 115
Top Secret (Ralph Ingersoll), 484n
TORCH operation, 5, 64, 71, 161, 226, 241, 286, 381, 504, 584
TOTALIZE operation, 760, 771
Toujane-Hallouf hills, 156
Tournai, 817
Trail of the Fox, The (David Irving), 58, 62, 123, 153, 159, 619
Training of troops: artillery, 47
Trigno River line, 427, 432, 433, 435
Tripoli, 10; Axis retreat to, 63; Allied plans for capture of, 63–73, 75, 95–96, 104, 105, 184; operation FIRE-EATER, 106-120; capture of, 118–122, 124–126, 141, 149; Victory Parade, 132; port, 140, 161; Army Study week, 141, 145
Tripoli Times, 178, 179
Tripolitania, evacuation of Axis forces, 91, 95; stand at, 105
Triumph and Tragedy (Sir Winston Churchill), 632, 690
Triumph in the West (Sir Arthur Bryant), 426, 633
Troina, 317, 331, 354
Trun, 768, 772, 780, 783
Truscott, General Lucian K.: Comd 3rd US Division, 310, 314, 315, 351, 358, 361; and Patton, 348, 361; lunch with Montgomery, 381

Tuker, Major General Francis, Comd
4th Indian Division, 35, 215; Army
Study week, 142; author of
Approach to Battle, 142
Tunis, 66, 161–162, 193; capture of,
180
Tunisia:
TORCH landings, 5, 64, 504;
German retreat, 10, 91, 55; Allied
occupation, 63, 65; Axis
reinforcements, 66, 71; campaign
in, 103, 104, 133, 148, 149, 504;
plans for conquest, 214; battle
for, 202–238
Turn of the Tide, The (Sir Arthur
Bryant), 132, 138, 278

Ultra:
North Africa, 18, 30, 43, 56, 59–60,
86, 91, 92, 105, 107, 124, 143,
144, 153–156, 165, 186; Italy, 430n;
NW Europe, 539, 630, 636, 682,
684, 729, 730, 761, 768, 770, 773
Ultra-reading Intelligence Officer, 682
Ultra in the West (R. Bennett), 630n
United Nations, 119
United States Air Force, 281, 771; *see
also* Allied Air Force
United States Army:
system of command, 693, 809;
concentrated attack, 737;
doctrine, 753; N. Africa, 10,
140; Tunisia, 148; casualties,
164; meeting with 8th Army,
199; Sicilian campaign:
Marinella, 242; Sciacca, 242;
Palermo, 242; Normandy:
strength, 687; OVERLORD
strategy, 797; advance to
Ardennes, 784, 797
Army Groups:
12th US Army Group: comd
Bradley, 757, 759, 765, 768, 770,
778, 784, 801; Seine crossing,
784; to Brussels, 789; to Metz
and Saar, 793, 806; support for
21st Army Group, 802, 803,
806
Armies:
1st Army: Gafsa, 148; comd
Bradley, 512, 519; assault on NW
Europe, 486, 488, 489, 500, 551,
552, 589, 647; advance to Paris,
551, 552; Cherbourg, 674, 678,
679; Brittany, 678, 707; comd
Hodges, 694; break-out,
706–709, 714, 731, 735, 737;

COBRA co-operation, 638, 686,
719–722, 724, 726, 727, 731,
732, 736–742, 756, 771, 798;
Avranches, 756; Falaise, 782,
783, 784; to Elbeuf, 786;
advance to Channel, 787;
Seine crossing, 805; to
Belgium, 806, 807, 817; at
Laon, 817
3rd Army: comd Patton: advance
to R. Loire, 551; drive to Berlin,
552; operation OVERLORD,
572, 589; Brittany, 667, 695, 707,
738; break-out, 707–709, 738,
757, 763, 765, 782; and
Leclerc, 780–781; Falaise, 782,
783, 785; tactical plans, 803; to
Belgium, 806; to Frankfurt, 817
5th Army: comd Clark: operation
AVALANCHE, 338, 339, 355,
372, 380, 394–409, 413, 458–459;
after Salerno, 422, 440; advance
to Volturno River, 424, 425;
casualties, 427, 537
7th Army (Western Task Force):
comd Patton: HQ, 282; assault
on Sicily, 295, 299, 307–313,
331, 363, 414; advance to
Palermo, 314–321
9th Army: comd Simpson, 589
Corps:
2 Corps: comd Fredendall, 163,
164; comd Patton, 175, 196; and
Montgomery, 202–204,
214–215; attack on Gafsa and
Maknassy, 202–207, 218, 220;
Patton relieved, 223; operation
HUSKY plan, 262; under comd
8th Army, 262–264, 299;
assault on Sicily, 304–313,
314–321; comd Bradley, 307,
330; advance to Palermo,
314–321, 330
5 Corps: comd Gerow, 613, 781;
visit by Montgomery, 497;
Omaha beach, 611–614, 676;
advance south, 623, 624, 637,
648; Falaise, 780; comd Gaffey,
780, 781
6 Corps: comd Dawley, 387;
deputy Ridgway, 406
7 Corps: comd Collins: visit by
Montgomery, 497; Utah
beach, 560, 613, 615; advance
to Cherbourg, 647, 674;
advance south, 697, 720, 742;
Falaise, 774

8 Corps: comd Middleton, 681, 687, 697, 707, 710
12 Corps: 775, 778, 804
15 Corps: comd Haislip, 762, 765, 770, 772–774, 778, 787, 792
19 Corps: comd Corlett, 641, 646, 648, 669, 720, 786, 787, 792
20 Corps: comd Walker, 774, 778, 782, 804, 817
Divisions:
Airborne Divisions:
82nd Airborne Division, 281; assault on Sicily, 292, 314; assault on Rome, 375; operation AVALANCHE, 380, 396, 398, 405, 406; operation GIANT II, 389, 390, 396, 404–405; visit by Montgomery (UK), 497; change of plan, 585, 600; Normandy, 614
101st Airborne Division: comd Taylor, 391; Normandy, 614
Armoured Divisions:
1st Armoured Division: Maknassy, 204
2nd Armoured Division: visit by Montgomery, 497, 528; Normandy, 647; Belgium, 807
3rd Armoured Division: comd Leroy Watson: visit by Montgomery, 497, 498, 528; Belgium, 807
5th Armoured Division, 787; Belgium, 807
Infantry Divisions:
1st Infantry Division: assault on Sicily, 296, 297, 330; and Patton, 362; visit by Montgomery, 497; Normandy, 642; Belgium, 807
3rd Division: comd Truscott, 314–315
4th Division: visit by Montgomery, 562; attack by E-boats, 562; Belgium, 807
9th Division: visit by Montgomery, 497; Belgium, 807
29th Division: visit by Montgomery, 497, 500; Normandy, 669
30th Division: visit by Montgomery, 562; Belgium, 807
34th Division, 216
36th Division, 405, 408
45th Division: assault on Sicily,

298, 299, 301, 302, 306, 330; comd Middleton, 328
79th Division, Belgium, 807
80th Division, 780
90th Division, 780, 781
United States Army in World War II: Sicily and the surrender of Italy (A. N. Garland and H. M. Smyth), 310, 318, 351, 352
Urquhart, Major-General R. E., Comd 1st Airborne Div, 635
Utah Beach, plan, 482, 484; 7 US Corps, 4th US Div, 614, 622

V1 flying bombs, 662, 667, 668, 692–695, 698, 706, 714, 784, 792, 808, 817; casualties, 694
Valentine tanks, 16, 113, 119, 160, 189, 192
Vandenberg, Major-General Hoyt S., USAAF Air C-in-C, 652; GOODWOOD operation, 719
Varreville, 603
Vasto, 8th Army Main HQ, 466
Vasto-Isernia, 432, 433
Verney, Brigadier G. L., Comd Guards Tank Brigade, 790
Vernon, Brigadier H. R. W., 14–16, 21, 448
Vernon, 20 US Corps advance to, 782
Vian, Rear-Admiral Sir Philip, 615
Victor Emmanuel, King of Italy, 323
Victory Campaign, The (C. P. Stacey), 760, 771
Victory in the West, Vol I (L. F. Ellis), 486
Vietinghoff, Colonel-General Heinrich-Gottfried von, 408
Villers Bocage, 619, 621, 624–626, 629–630, 635–637, 642, 645, 653, 654, 656, 686, 687, 713
Vire River, 629, 638, 667, 691, 743, 754, 757, 758, 759
Vizzini, 301–306, 311
Vizzini-Enna highway, 299, 348
Volturno, River, 395, 424, 426
VULCAN offensive, 232, 233, 235, 243, 273

WTF, *see* Western Task Force
Wadi Akarit, 206, 207; battle of, 208, 215–216, 217, 222, 231, 242
Wadi El Hatema, 61
Wadi Zemzem, 107
Wadi Zessar, 155, 168
Wadi Zeuss, 155
Wadi Zigzaou, 155, 185, 187, 189–192

Walker, Ronald, *Alam Halfa and Alamein*, 42, 43
War correspondents, Allied, 13, 792, 799
War diaries: 8th Army, 29n, 31n, 34n, 109, 153, 293, 306, 307, 323, 325, 328, 339, 354, 355, 360, 377; 10 Corps, 58, 61; 7th Armoured Division, 117–118; NZ Division, 32n-34n; 15th Panzer Division, 31n, 53–54; 90th Light Division, 167
War Office, 595, 612
Warren, Lt-Colonel Trumbull, Canadian ADC, 333, 451, 497, 525–526, 533, 618
Wason, Eugene, 689n
Watch on the Rhine (play), attended by Montgomery, 277
Waterloo, battle of (1815), 405n
Wathen, Mark, 45
Watson, General Leroy, Comd 3rd US Armd Division, 498
Wavell, Field Marshal Earl, 137, 249, 643
Weapons, 416, 417
Weather conditions: N. Africa, 15, 36–37, 40, 61, 106; Benghazi, 106–107, 115; Hamma, 199; Sicily, 292; Italy, 432; Sangro River, 433–435, 437–440, 447, 456; Anzio, 510; D-Day, 593, 594, 599–602, 610, 611, 616; Normandy, 621, 622, 627, 637, 638, 652, 667–670, 674, 678, 679, 681, 695, 703, 706, 726, 731, 735, 737
Wedemayer, General H. C., 309, 314, 315, 318
Weeks, Ronnie, 423
West, Major-General C. A., 481, 484, 485, 501–502, 526
Western Desert Force, comd O'Connor, 413
Western Task Force (WTF): Sicily, 254–257, 280, 286, 295; (US 7th Army), 308–313, 314–321
Westphal, Major-General Siegfried, 168
Wheat and the Chaff, The (F. Mitterand), 481n
Whistler, Major-General L., 168
Whiteley, General Sir John F. M., 144, 552n

Wigglesworth, Air Marshal Sir Philip, COS to Tedder, 520
Wilder's Gap, 186
Williams, Brigadier Sir Edgar T. ('Bill'), 21, 30, 59–60, 91–93, 154, 172, 194, 218, 219, 245, 259–261, 270, 274, 329, 353, 469, 484, 584; Chief of Int 21st Army Gp, 518, 519, 550, 575, 577–578, 603, 607, 608, 643, 650, 651, 729, 730, 745, 746, 747, 818; Falaise Gap, 762
Willkie, Wendell, 4
Wilmot, Chester, BBC correspondent: GOODWOOD operation, 721; on Eisenhower, 734n; and Montgomery, 750–751; Falaise Gap, 762
Wilson, General Sir Henry Maitland, C-in-C, Middle East Land Forces, 245, 452; Supreme Commander, Mediterranean, 462–463, 545, 596; and ANVIL operation, 668, 689
Wimberley, Major-General D. N.: Comd 51st (Highland) Div, 26, 141; Agheila, 85–87; Buerat, 109, 111–116; and Montgomery, 113–116, 168, 297; Medenine, 167; operation PUGILIST, 185–193 *passim*; Wadi Akarit, 215–217; assault on Sicily, 293n; Normandy, 700; replaced, 701; author of 'Scottish Soldier', 168n
With Prejudice (Air Marshal Lord Tedder), 252, 599, 649, 718
Witzleben, Field Marshal E. von, 730
Wolfe, General James, 585
World War I: Western Front battles, 124; Somme, 192
World War II: Allied command problems, 265–266; NW Europe 1939 – D-Day Allied Armies, 260; Far East campaign, 246

Y radio intercepts, 18, 24, 682
Ypres-Comines canal, 146n

Zarat, 189, 192, 194, 199
Zliten, 114, 115, 117
Zuara, 121
Zuckerman, Solly, *From Apes to War Lords*, 660